LET'S GO

EUROPE

Director of Publishing
Abdurezak Shemsu

Editorial Director
Shaun Gohel

Production Manager
Michael Goncalves

Researcher-Writers
Ana Chaves
Emily Corrigan
Tim Doner
Tiffani Driscoll
Andy Duehren
Ryan Furey
Zeb Goodman
Laura Hatt
Miles Hewitt
Noel Lee
Will Holub-Moorman
Claire McLaughlin
Petey Menz
Claire Rivkin
Mike Skerrett

EUROPE OVERVIEW

NORWAY

North Sea

DENMARK

IRELAND

GREAT BRITAIN

THE NETHERLANDS

GERMANY

Rhine

BELGIUM

LUX.

Atlantic

Ocean

Seine

Mosel

Danube

LICHTÉNSTEIN

Loire

SWITZER-LAND

Po

Dordogne

Bay of Biscay

FRANCE

Rhône

MONACO

Duero

ANDORRA

Corsica

PORTUGAL

SPAIN

Menorca

Ibiza

Mallorca

Sardinia

Guadalquivir

GIBRALTAR (U.K.)

CEUTA (SPAIN)

MELILLA (SPAIN)

MOROCCO

ALGERIA

TUNISIA

SWEDEN

FINLAND

ESTONIA

RUSSIA

LATVIA

LITHUANIA

RUSSIA

BELARUS

POLAND

Vistula

Elbe

Oder

UKRAINE

CZECH
REPUBLIC

SLOVAKIA

MOLDOVA

AUSTRIA

HUNGARY

ROMANIA

SLOVENIA

Black
Sea

CROATIA

Danube

BOSNIA
&
HERZ.

SERBIA

BULGARIA

SAN
MARINO

MONT.

KOS.

Adriatic
Sea

ALBANIA

MACEDONIA

ITALY

Aegean

TURKEY

Tyrrhenian
Sea

GREECE

Sea

Ionian
Sea

Rhodes

Sicily

Crete

MALTA

Mediterranean
Sea

0   200 kilometers

0   200 miles

CONTENTS

RESEARCHER-WRITERS

ANA CHAVES: Ana took her sass and humor from Prague to Warsaw this summer. Sipping coffee with the locals, trying to fall in love with Gothic architecture, and researching multi-story clubs were all in a day's work. When Ana wasn't getting caffeinated, she committed herself to writing up hilarious copy.

EMILY CORRIGAN: Traveling in search of the Holy Grail, Emily survived bloodthirsty rabbits, flesh wounds, and the Knights Who Say Ni. Or is that Monty Python? Well, she did survive an encounter with the infamous Athens Park Flasher, the loss of both her personal belongings and dignity in Mykonos, and third-degree sunburn on the Amalfi Coast. She is (and will always be) grateful that fried cheese is a legitimate Greek dish.

TIM DONER: Hopping from Oslo to Stockholm to Copenhagen, Tim traversed Scandinavia this summer. He reveled in all things Viking while munching on reindeer meat and enjoying a ridiculously high standard of living. Being a budget traveller in some of the most expensive destinations was never easy, but Tim always managed to turn in kick-ass copy.

TIFFANI DRISCOLL: Tiffani roamed the UK and Ireland this summer to further delay figuring out what she wants to do with her life. She got lost in the rolling green hills of Ireland, the majestic Highlands of Scotland, and the bustling cities of England (mainly because she's really bad with directions). When she's not having an early mid-life crisis, Tiffani spends her time reading, napping, and watching hydraulic press videos on Youtube.

ANDY DUEHREN: Andy Duehren hails from the mystical land of suburban Massachusetts. He traveled through Belgium and France this summer, so expect lots of vomit-inducing Hemingway references and vomit-covered hostel toilets. A news writer for *The Harvard Crimson* on campus, Andy had no trouble adjusting to the creative freedoms of travel writing and the hygienic freedoms of the French.

RYAN FUREY: The globetrotting Ryan took a break to call Germany his home for two months this summer. He sampled every beer he could get his hands on, waited long hours to get into Berlin's prestigious clubs, and still had time to go surfing on the side. When he wasn't taking killer shots for his Instagram, Ryan always made time for his one true love: currywurst.

ZEB GOODMAN: Zeb spent the better part of two months wandering around the southern coast of France, offending locals everywhere with his American accent and claiming he was Canadian in an poor attempt to avoid propagating American stereotypes. In the name of "research" and "journalism," Zeb train-hopped and hitchhiked his way to every beach and vineyard from Nice to Biarritz, narrowly escaping homelessness and all the while reassuring his editors and parents that he was visiting museums and living a healthy lifestyle.

LAURA HATT: "Pack light," said Laura's mom. "Mix and match neutrals," said Laura's roommate. "Just turn it inside out," said Laura's sixth grade camp friend. Grungy, obedient, and wary of checked luggage, Laura spent the summer traveling southern France and embracing the multipurpose: her gray tank top worked for day and night; her towel doubled as a pillow. She did not, however, purchase 2-in-1 shampoo & conditioner. That stuff is the worst.

MILES HEWITT: Miles took his poetry and flair to London and Amsterdam where he battled his verses against the Bard himself and spent more time than he'd like to admit rummaging around record shops. As Let's Go's official cool-cat-in-residence, Miles brought hipster charm and literary wit to everything he did across the pond.

NOEL LEE: From poetic Venetian alleys to clumps of stinging foliage in the Black Forest, Noel tramped, trekked, and tripped her way through Northern Italy and Switzerland. When not composing (hopefully) endearingly alliterative copy, she quavered before deadpan bouncers, stared pensively out train windows, and learned how to operate her universal-travel-charger-adapter-plug-gizmo-thing.

WILL HOLUB-MOORMAN: In search of relief from American election coverage, Will traveled to Vienna, Budapest, and Western Germany this summer. He braved WiFi wastelands, pulse-pounding prices, and oodles and oodles of strudel(s).

CLAIRE MCLAUGHLIN: After devoting her college years to Let's Go in the office, our beloved former Director of Publishing decided to give up corporate meetings for a life roughing it on the road in Italy. From experiencing majestic sunsets over the Tiber to eating delicious paninis in Florence, Claire did it all while sending in hilarious copy and great Instagram photos all summer long.

PETEY MENZ: This year, Petey gave up Scottish lochs for pristine beaches and scalding temperatures as he traveled through Slovenia and Croatia. Petey always went above and beyond for his job whether he was dressing up as a gladiator, discovering the alleged hometown of Marco Polo, or turning in killer copy every week.

CLAIRE RIVKIN: Claire Rivkin couldn't—and still can't—decide whether she's from Chicago or Washington D.C., but she dealt with her identity crisis with poise and grace and ham. Claire braved free sangria nights and multiple hills to bring you the best of Portugal and central Spain. In total, she has traveled to over 45 countries and would like to give special thanks to all the hostels that provided privacy curtains and air conditioning.

MIKE SKERRETT: Mike Skerrett is from Boston. This summer he traveled through Morocco and Spain and captured the whole thing with his new Smilewide SelfieStik (TM). Mike loves comedy and writing and the simple convenience of folding his Smilewide SelfieStik (TM) into the size of a standard pen! For questions, concerns, and vague criticisms, Mike can be reached at smilewide. com/selfiestik/shills/mike1.

DISCOVER

EUROPE

Everyone you know—parents, friends, and especially random old men in parks—probably has a few stories that start, "When I was in Europe..." For all the shenanigans that ensue, these tales might as well begin with, "Once upon a time..." Still, for the most part, they're true stories. A kindly matriarch will cook you dinner and insist on setting you up with one of her children; a shop owner will convince you to buy mooncakes before you figure out what's really in them; you'll spend all night trying to dodge a neighborhood's worth of stray cats who seem to think you're their king; you'll meet a princess disguised as a pixie-haired commoner and fall in love over Vespa rides and one hilarious prank at the Bocca della Verità. Wait, that last one was *Roman Holiday*—but you get the point.

The unifying theme of this guide is adventure. Not geography, not sights, not history. Europe has been the stomping ground of students for generations, precisely because of the opportunities for escapes and escapades it provides. It has the whole gamut of architectural periods and incredible renovations, brogues and rolling r's, and residents who drink alcohol like water. And you're always in the good company of fellow travelers, both young and old, out on adventures like you. Give Europe a chance, think outside of the box, and you can make your trip something worth bragging about. Who knows? Maybe *Roman Holiday* was based on a true story.

when to go

Summer is the busiest time to travel in Europe. The season's many festivals can jack up prices, but it might be worth it to catch Madrid's bullfighting festival or London's Proms. Late spring and early autumn bring fewer tourists and cheaper airfares—meaning they're good times to go, if you can get the days off. Winter travel is great for those looking to hit the ski ranges around the mountains, but not the best time to take a walking tour through Prague. Plus, you'll find that some hotels, restaurants, and sights have limited hours or are on vacation—from you.

what to do

FOOD FOR THOUGHT

From French *patisseries* to Italian *pizzerie*, the sheer wealth of cuisine options across Europe could keep your palate entertained for several lifetimes. It's a miracle that all travelers don't return home 50lb. heavier and desperately in need of a larger pant size.

- **RESTAURANTE BADILA (MADRID, SPAIN):** If reading *The Sun Also Rises* made you think, "Gee, I'd like to eat that suckling pig Hemingway mentioned," you're weird. You should also go to this restaurant that's a favorite among the locals. (p. 656)

- **LE COCHON BLEU (AVIGNON, FRANCE):** You're sitting in the south of France, eating the most quintessential, delicious French meal you can imagine. You're probably at Le Cochon Bleu. (p. 192)

- **MATHALLEN (OSLO, NORWAY):** A collection of pop-up restaurants right below a culinary school. Prepare your tastebuds. (p. 577)

- **PIEMINISTER (LONDON, GREAT BRITAIN):** You've likely heard not-too-great things about British food. These pies will certainly change your mind. (p. 315)

- **FRICI PAPA KIFOZDÉJE (BUDAPEST, HUNGARY):** For a meat-and-potatoes meal that you'll leave with both your stomach and your wallet full, this cafe can't be beat. (p. 384)

THE GREAT INDOORS

Let's get real: you didn't come to Europe for the trees—except the ones in the background of the *Mona Lisa*. These museums could keep you distracted for a lifetime or four.

- **THE LOUVRE (PARIS, FRANCE):** We promise it was famous before *The Da Vinci Code*. (p. 141)

- **THE BRITISH MUSEUM, THE NATIONAL GALLERY, THE TATE MODERN, AND THE VICTORIA AND ALBERT MUSEUM (LONDON, UK):** We couldn't pick just one—nor should you, because they're all free! (p. 300)

- **UFFIZI GALLERY (FLORENCE, ITALY):** Venus's flowing locks, a swan-like depiction of Mary with Jesus, and 43 other rooms full of art are waiting for you (and thousands of other sightseers) to appreciate their magnificence. (p. 507)

- **MOSTEIRO DOS JERÓNIMOS (LISBON, PORTUGAL):** Okay, so it's more of a church than a museum. But it's remained in near-perfect condition for over 500 years, so if you want to party (maybe pray is more appropriate) like it's 1502, this is the place. (p. 613)

- **VAN GOGH MUSEUM (AMSTERDAM, THE NETHERLANDS):** Come see a museum dedicated to everyone's favorite bad boy painter. Let's van Gogh. (p. 562)

- **KUNSTHISTORISCHES (VIENNA, AUSTRIA):** Say that three times fast. Now can you say Vermeer? How about Caravaggio? Honestly, this museum will probably leave you speechless. (p. 14)

- **WORST MUSEUM TO VISIT WITH YOUR FAMILY (ESPECIALLY CREEPY UNCLE NICK):** The Amsterdam Sex Museum (p. 564).

- **MOST NOSTALGIC:** Visit the fantastic home of **Hans Christian Andersen** in Odense, Denmark (p. 128). Become a swan and never need to fly Ryanair again. Dreams do come true.

- **BEST PLACE TO TURN LEAD INTO GOLD: Alchemia** (p. 604), a triple threat restaurant-pub-music venue in Kraków, Poland.

- **TOP PLACE TO FEEL BETTER ABOUT YOUR ARTISTIC SKILLS:** After roaming Europe and feeling bad that you can't draw a straight line with a ruler, the **Croatian Museum of Naïve Art** in Zagreb (p. 60) may boost your mood.

- **MOST AVANT-GARDE: Cabaret Voltaire** (p. 778), the Zurich nightclub where Hugo Ball donned his construction paper costume, chanted "blago bung blago bung," and birthed the Dada movement.

- **WEIRDEST COMBO OF HEAVEN AND HELL:** Museum of **Igreja de São Francisco** (p. 622) in Porto, Portugal. First check out the macabre chapel made entirely of human bones, then spend the rest of your day with the foremost collection of creepy amateur nativity sculptures.

- **DOX (PRAGUE, CZECH REPUBLIC):** If you're in Europe for more than 10min., you're bound to see something from (a) Antiquity or (b) the Renaissance. DOX and its constantly rotating contemporary art exhibits are a welcome and insightful reprieve. (p. 96)

- **FUNDACIÓ MIRÓ (BARCELONA, SPAIN):** Do you like bright colors, abstract shapes, and staring slightly puzzled to fully understand a piece of art? You'll love Joan Miró and this collection of his works and others inspired by him. (p. 682)

DON'T BE A SQUARE

Just hang around in one. While strolling along winding avenues and exploring tiny alleyways is certainly necessary, European life shines in its open spaces: Italy's *piazze*, Spain's *plazas*, and even Hungary's *tere* are not only beautiful to look at, but they are home to festivals, outdoor (free!) art, and even bustling nightlife. You might cut through on your way to a world-famous museum, but be sure to stop and appreciate what these outdoor spaces have to offer.

- **LA GRAND PLACE (BRUSSELS, BELGIUM):** Take your requisite giggle-worthy Instagram post at Le Mannekin Pis, then gorge yourself on fries as you take in the Gothic architecture. (p. 36)

- **MONASTIRAKI (ATHENS, GREECE):** Descend from the Acropolis to discover an expanse of cheap souvlaki, street dancers, and the famous Athens flea market. (p. 361)

- **PIAZZA DELLA SIGNORIA (FLORENCE, ITALY):** Disclaimer: there are a lot of *piazze* in Florence—and across Italy, for that matter. But this one, just outside the famed Uffizi Gallery, houses a portico of statues that rivals the museum itself. (p. 507)

- **WENCESLAS SQUARE (PRAGUE, CZECH REPUBLIC):** The square features a sprawling green, cobblestone streets lined with department stores, and the National Museum. But if you happen to be visiting in December, you're in for a treat: the annual Christmas Market, which lights up the city and features holiday food, drink, and (of course) merriment. (p. 85)

- **PLAZA MAYOR (MADRID, SPAIN):** As with Italy's *piazze*, Spain (and, specifically, Madrid) is full of *plazas*. But Plaza Mayor—the "main square"—is the king of them all. (p. 654)

1. POMPEII, ITALY: Ancient brothels, geological miracles, and plenty of opportunities to loudly repeat high school history factoids to your tour group makes Pompeii the perfect playground for any gung-ho nerd. (p. 537)

2. CAMBRIDGE UNIVERSITY (CAMBRIDGE, UK): Want to walk through the hallway where the speed of sound was measured? Or drink at the pub where the discovery of DNA structure was first announced? Or just really appreciate historic buildings and the sensation of so much college life happening around you? Cambridge University, and its 31 colleges, should give you more than enough exposure on where the smart people in the world go to learn stuff good. (p. 327)

3. REAL ALCAZAR (SEVILLA, SPAIN): History and television nerds both welcome: either you can freak out about the centuries of Moorish and Christian construction or just get a bit too excited that the fictional Prince Doran of House Martell "lives" here. (p. 717)

4. TRINITY COLLEGE (DUBLIN, IRELAN): Often considered the best college in Ireland, this is where the literary geeks can shine as they walk the same halls as such masters as Bram Stoker and Oscar Wilde. (p. 396)

discover

suggested itineraries

THE GRAND TOUR

Brace yourself. This is one serious trip, but it's absolutely worth it. We recommend you tackle it with the help of budget airlines or a railpass.

- **LONDON (4 DAYS):** Load up on history, tweed, and tea. Make every attempt to serendipitously run into William, Kate, and baby George. (p. 295)

- **COPENHAGEN (2 DAYS):** Experience the city where Nordic tradition combines with a budding culinary scene and charming atmosphere. (p. 116)

- **AMSTERDAM (3 DAYS):** Amsterdam has it all: imperial history, artistic pedigree, great music. Plus, coffeeshops and legalized prostitution! You might not want to write home to mom about this leg of the trip. (p. 558)

- **PARIS (4 DAYS):** The quintessential European city will have you singing of *la vie en rose* in no time. (p. 135)

- **BARCELONA (3 DAYS):** Stroll through the medieval streets of Barri Gòtic in search of damsels to rescue and dragons to slay. (p. 666)

- **LISBON (2 DAYS):** Sip *vinho do porto* while gazing at the sunset over the Rio Tejo. (p. 613)

- **MADRID (2 DAYS):** Eat dinner at midnight, go out until dawn, and explore the city between siestas. (p. 648)

- **ROME (4 DAYS):** Get the best of the old—the Colosseum owes a lot to facelifts—and the new—bars in the Centro Storico and clubs in Testaccio—in the Eternal City. (p. 420)

- **FLORENCE (3 DAYS):** Throw yourself into the Renaissance, which seems to live on in every Florentine building. (p. 502)

- **PRAGUE (3 DAYS):** During the day, the Charles Bridge is overrun with tourists and vendors, but there's nothing quite so magical at night. (p. 78)

- **MUNICH (2 DAYS):** Oktoberfest will leave you wishing for some January- through December-fests. (p. 282)

- **BERLIN (3 DAYS):** Look out for horn-rimmed glasses and cardigans among Friedrichshain's nightclubs, which are housed in former DDR buildings. (p. 220)

- **ATHENS (2 DAYS):** By now you've seen much of Western Europe—now see the city where modern civilization all began. (p. 360)

- **SPLIT (2 DAYS):** Explore the palm tree-lined waterfront and the remains of Diocletian's palace before raging the night away at one of Split's many night clubs. (p. 70)

ISLAND HOPPING

No, you haven't accidentally picked up a copy of *Let's Go Caribbean*. While much of Europe is landlocked, there are still plenty of opportunities to be surrounded by water. And we're not just talking the UK and Greece—the British and Greek Isles aren't the only way to get off the mainland. You'll be exchanging a boat ride to a palm-tree lined oasis for quick ferries and walks over bridges, but it's still a slice of "island life."

- **PARIS, FRANCE:** The city's neighborhoods spiral outward from the Seine, in the middle of which are two islands: Île de la Cité and Île St-Louis. Here you'll find one of Paris's most famous landmarks, the Notre Dame Cathedral. (p. 135)

- **BERLIN, GERMANY:** There's almost no way to avoid a trip to Museumsinsel (Museum Island), home of the Neue Gallery, the Berlin Dom, and—most notably—the Pergamon Museum. (p. 233)

- **PALERMO, ITALY:** Discover a whole other Italy once you ferry over to Sicily. See the influence of Byzantine, Norman, and Spanish conquests of the island as you wander through ancient churches and taste unique Sicilian flavors. (p. 539)

- **IBIZA, SPAIN:** It almost doesn't need mention: it's the destination for constant partying, and a trip to Spain wouldn't be complete without this island getaway. (p. 706)

STOP AND SMELL THE ROSES

In case you didn't know: you're going to spend a lot of time in Europe inside (with good reason—see "The Great Indoors" a few pages back). But that doesn't mean you shouldn't get a little fresh air, since Europe is packed with as many parks and gardens as it is with museums and cathedrals.

- **VIENNA, AUSTRIA:** Roam the gardens of the Hapsburgs at the **Belvedere** (p. 14) and pretend for an afternoon that you'll ever live in such lavish opulence.

- **LONDON, UK:** Sometimes flowers and trees aren't just for aesthetic beauty. Visit the **Royal Botanic Gardens** (p. 311) a scientific plant experience.

- **LJUBLJANA, SLOVENIA:** The ultimate outdoors experience awaits travelers at **Park Tivoli** (p. 636). A stroll in the garden? A walk around the pond? A few games of tennis? The choice is yours. (And if you're sick of being outside by now—or it's, you know, raining—Tivoli Castle offers an indoor respite from the elements.)

- **MONTPELLIER, FRANCE:** The **Promenade de Peyrou** (p. 187) is most spectacularly enjoyed at night, when the setting sun creates brilliant views in every direction.

- **HAMBURG, GERMANY:** Why would you not want to stroll through a park called **Planten un Blomen** (p. 259), which does mean exactly what it sounds like.

THE ULTIMATE PUB CRAWL

Partying is as legitimate a reason to go to Europe as any other. Drinking customs say a lot about a city's culture, and... who are we kidding? It's fun. Don't be ashamed!

- **DUBLIN, IRELAND:** Perhaps, more aptly, Publin? (p. 403)

- **AMSTERDAM, THE NETHERLANDS:** We recommend the GLBT nightlife. Other activities are yours to choose. (p. 568)

- **BRUSSELS, BELGIUM:** Home to a bar with 3000+ beers. Need we say more? (p. 38)

- **DÜSSELDORF, GERMANY:** Grab an Altbier and enjoy the non-stop party. (p. 272)

- **BUDAPEST, HUNGARY.** Down pálinka in one (or many) of the city's many ruin pubs. (p. 385)

- **PRAGUE, CZECH REPUBLIC:** The beer is cheaper than water! (p. 107)

- **MUNICH, GERMANY:** This is the birthplace of Oktoberfest and the beer garden. (p. 287)

- **BORDEAUX, FRANCE:** We get it, too much beer. Welcome to wine country! (p. 178)

- **ROME, ITALY.** Casually sip wine on the Spanish Steps. Classic. (p. 446)

- **BARCELONA, SPAIN:** Every good night ends with a beautiful sunrise. Well done. (p. 691)

- **SANTORINI, GREECE:** Mud baths by day; bar crawl by night. (p. 368)

- **STOCKHOLM, SWEDEN:** Probably not your first thought for the ultimate nightlife scene, but trust us: there are some places here that know how to have a good time. (p. 762)

discover

how to use this book

CHAPTERS

Conquering the great continent of Europe is no easy task. Many have tried—from Julius Caesar to Napoleon—and all have failed. That's why you've come to us. We've been criss-crossing the continent for 55 years, smelling out the sightliest sights and the homiest hostels, and now, dear reader, we will pass on all of our knowledge to you. Let's get this show on the road with the travel coverage chapters—the meat of any *Let's Go* book.

We'll start off with Austria, where you can embark on your own Alpine adventure, à la *The Sound of Music*. From there, we trek on over to feast on *frites* in Belgium, enjoy Adriatic views in Croatia, and take in the old-world magic of the Czech Republic. Get a little closer to *The Little Mermaid* and its author, Hans Christian Anderson, in Denmark. Trek to France to explore fine art and finer dining, and meet Beethoven and Berliners in Germany. We cross the Channel to get our fill of Beefeaters and double-decker buses in Britain, make a pit stop at the Parthenon in Greece, and head north to Hungary's thermal baths before returning to the Emerald Isle to drink Guinness over Joyce. Get the lowdown on Italy's artistic treatures. Learn how to navigate canals in the Netherlands. Become a viking (well, at least try to) in Norway. Give props to *pierogies* in Poland. We'll show you where to find Portugal's finest port and take a cruise on Slovenia's Lake Bled. Then, complete your grand tour on the sun-drenched beaches of Spain, the Baltic coast of Sweden, and the Alps of Switzerland.

But that's not all, folks. We also have a few extra chapters for you to peruse:

CHAPTER	DESCRIPTION
Discover Europe	Discover tells you what to do, when to do it, and where to go for it. The absolute coolest things about any destination get highlighted in this chapter at the front of all *Let's Go* books.
Essentials	Essentials contains the practical info you need before, during, and after your trip—visas, regional transportation, health and safety, phrasebooks, and more.

ACCOMMODATIONS

In this book, we've listed our favorite hostels, hotels, B&Bs, and guest houses, along with helpful information about navigating the accommodations market, in the "Accommodations" sections and "Get a Room!" boxes. Our full list of reviews—along with our hotel and hostel booking engine powered by ⚅**Hostelworld**—can be found at **www.letsgo.com**.

LISTINGS

Listings—a.k.a. reviews of individual establishments—constitute a majority of *Let's Go* coverage. Our Researcher-Writers list establishments in order from **best to worst value**—not necessarily quality. (Obviously a five-star hotel is nicer than a hostel, but it would probably be ranked lower because it's not as good a value.) Listings pack in a lot of information, but it's easy to digest if you know how they're constructed:

ESTABLISHMENT NAME TYPE OF ESTABLISHMENT $-$$$$
Address ☎phone number website
Editorial review goes here.
i Directions to the establishment. Other practical information about the establishment, like age restrictions at a club or whether breakfast is included at a hostel. Prices for goods or services. Hours or schedules.

ICONS

First things first: places and things that we absolutely love, sappily cherish, generally obsess over, and wholeheartedly endorse are denoted by the all-empowering ✍**Let's Go thumbs-up.** In addition, there are a couple more symbols you should be aware of:

✍	*Let's Go* recommends	☎	Phone numbers	*i*	Other hard information

PRICE DIVERSITY

A final set of icons corresponds to what we call our "price diversity" scale, which approximates how much money you can expect to spend at a given establishment. For **accommodations,** we base our range on the cheapest price for which a single traveler can stay for one night. For **food,** we estimate the average amount one traveler will spend in one sitting. The table below tells you what you'll *typically* find in Europe at the corresponding price range, but keep in mind that no scale can allow for the quirks of all individual establishments.

ACCOMMODATIONS	WHAT YOU'RE LIKELY TO FIND
$	Campgrounds and dorm rooms, both in hostels and actual universities, as well as some convents in Italy. Expect bunk beds and a communal bath. You may have to provide or rent towels and sheets.
$$	Upper-end hostels and lower-end hotels. You may have a private bathroom, or a sink in your room with a communal shower in the hall.
$$$	A small room with a private bath. Should have some amenities, such as phone and TV. Breakfast may be included.
$$$$	Large hotels, chains, and fancy boutiques. If it doesn't have the perks you want (and more), you've paid too much.
FOOD	WHAT YOU'RE LIKELY TO FIND
$	Street food, fast-food joints, university cafeterias, and bakeries (yum). Usually takeout, but you may have the option of sitting down.
$$	Sandwiches, pizza, low-priced entrees, ethnic eateries, and bar grub. Either takeout or sit-down service with slightly classier decor.
$$$	A somewhat fancy restaurant. Entrees tend to be heartier or more elaborate, but you're really paying for decor and ambience. Few restaurants in this range have a dress code, but some may look down on T-shirts and sandals.
$$$$	Your meal might cost more than your room, but there's a reason—it's something fabulous, famous, or both. Slacks and dress shirts may be expected.

discover

AUSTRIA

The Seine has its lovers' trysts. The Thames has its bridges. The Tiber has Romulus and Remus. The Danube has—well, put on the Blue Danube and lace up your waltzing shoes, traveler, because this river will have you dancing. For joy, that is. This area has been inspiring troubled writers, wacky musicians, and singing families for centuries, but it's still hard to pinpoint exactly what is special about Austria and its iconic waterway. Maybe it's that Austria has maintained much of the charming 17th- and 18th-century architecture built along the river, resulting in a picturesque scene whether you stay in Vienna or venture into von Trapp territory in Salzburg. Or you can experience Austria's second-largest but often overlooked city, Graz, whose local university makes it a haven for students. Or maybe it's that the Viennese really do dance the waltz en masse on New Year's Eve. We haven't found one, all-encompassing answer yet (though not for lack of trying). We challenge you to find it, one cup of Viennese coffee and Danube backdrop at a time.

greatest hits

- **CAPTAIN KIRCHE.** While Vienna boasts a number of churches—what European capital doesn't?—the most impressive of all is **St. Stephen's Cathedral** in the first district. (p. 14)

- **HOLY SCHNITZEL.** Test the limits of your appetite at **Schnitzelwirt** (p. 18). Based on the name, you know what you'll be eating; what you don't know is how you're going to finish the massive portions.

- **THE HILLS ARE ALIVE.** Let your inner Von Trapp child sing as you stroll through **Salzburg**, where you can see nearly endless renditions of the musical. (p. 24)

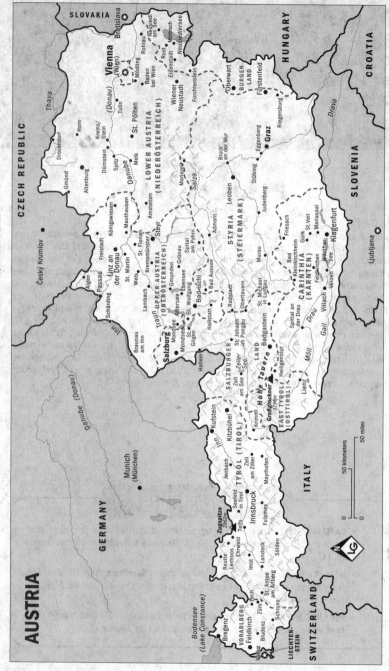

AUSTRIA

vienna

Austria's capital city is an ancient maze of breathtaking old buildings rooted in a rich history of rising and falling empires. Wandering down the stone city streets, you'll often find yourself at the steps of an opulent palace or a magnificent church. The spirits of Mozart, Beethoven, Schubert, and other famous composers still linger in Vienna, from the city's famous opera to the countless citizens who work to preserve its rich musical heritage. While Vienna can feel conservative, devoted to classics and tradition, newer generations of Viennese are bringing a modern edge to the historical city. Contemporary art is on the up and up, and its cool presence stands out even more clearly when juxtaposed with the Old World. The pace of Vienna, however, remains sleepy and relaxed. Here, loitering for hours in coffeeshops and parks is a God-given right. Yet among the loiterers, you'll find some of the most talented philosophers, artists, and musicians in the world, making Vienna the magical place it is today.

ACCOMMODATIONS

The Viennese are famous for their love of walking, but if long strolls aren't your thing, pay attention to the location of any potential hostels with respect to the city center (map it to the Opera House to get a good sense). Many of Vienna's best-known hostels lie a half-hour's walk or more from its central sights—and while there's always the city's excellent public transportation system, the cost of several rides a day can add up.

🏨 HOSTEL RUTHENSTEINER $

Robert-Hamerling-Gasse 24 ☎01 893 42 02

Ruthensteiner is such a good hostel that it's almost a bad thing. It's way too easy to spend hours at a time lounging in its comfortable living room, courtyard garden, or bar, enjoying its offbeat playlists and sipping on the free homemade lemonade it offers at reception—instead of actually making the 20min. walk into Vienna's city center, the reason you're staying at Ruthensteiner in the first place! Beds are comfortable and clean, with two power outlets within cable's reach of each. Another plus for the techy traveler is industrial-strength Wi-Fi throughout the whole complex. Just try to browse Vienna along with Facebook.

i Breakfast buffet €4; includes coffee, cereal, deli meats and cheese, fresh bread, and fruit. Dorms €20-25. Reception 24hr.

🏨 MYMOJOVIE HOSTEL $$

Kaiserstrasse 77, Apt. 8 ☎0676 551 11 55 www.mymojovie.at

In order to book a room at this beautiful converted apartment, you have to plan far in advance—don't rely on doing the classic student traveler move of booking the night before. While the hostel may be a decent walk from the city center, it is very close to a metro station that'll get you to Vienna's first district in a flash. But honestly, with all the free hostel food and great amenities, you might find yourself staying in more often than you'd think. For your comfort, the hostel offers a full bath (that's right, even a tub!), towels, comfortable beds, a TV and cozy living room, and a laptop for use in each room.

i Dorms €28-35. Reception 24hr.

HOSTEL HÜTTELDORF $

Schlossberggasse 8 ☎01 877 02 63

If you don't mind a decent trek to Vienna's main sights, Hostel Hütteldorf is one of the best values in town—beds in its 20-person dorms usually run just €15-20 a night. Plus, breakfast is free, which is rare in Vienna. In most other respects, Hütteldorf's amenities are on the sparse side: an abysmal outlet-to-person ratio

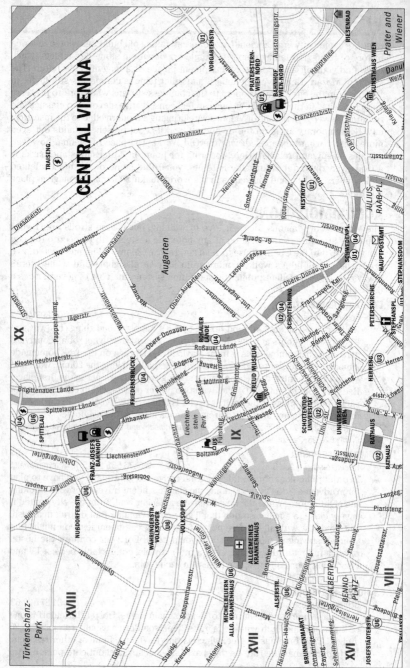

CENTRAL VIENNA

austria

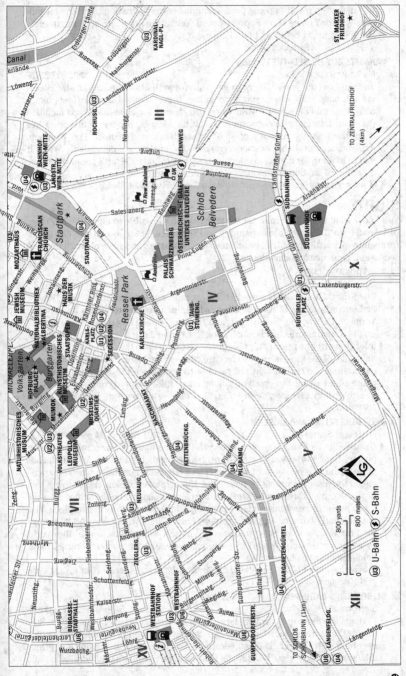

vienna

will definitely result in some perilous phone-battery situations, and the cleanliness wouldn't make Mary Poppins proud. Taking the price into account, though, Hütteldorf might be basic, but it isn't basic.

i Dorms €15-20. Reception 24hr.

WOMBATS CITY HOSTEL—THE LOUNGE $

Mariahilfer Strasse 137 ☎01 897 23 36

The only people you're likely to get to know well at this industrial-size hostel are the ones with whom you share a tiny bunk. Located in what feels like a converted middle school, Wombats scores points for cleanliness and facilities (kitchen, basement bar, enormous security lockers, private bathrooms) but lacks the friendly intimacy of smaller, youth-oriented hostels. The Wombats experience is probably best encapsulated by its slow yet dependable Wi-Fi: if you're looking for a place to sleep anonymously and safely, it's great, but those in search of anything more exciting should look elsewhere.

i Down the street from the Westbanhof train station. Dorms €20-26. Reception 24hr.

SIGHTS

You know what the fellow said: art for art's sake. It's possible to enjoy the offerings of Vienna even if you don't love painting and sculpture, but if you do, the city transforms into an earthly paradise, populated by Old Masters and new, chiaroscuro and secession, opulence and decadence.

▨ KUNSTHISTORISCHES

Maria-Theresien-Platz ☎01 52 52 40

The Kunsthistorisches is a world-class art museum, on par with the Met, Prado, or Louvre in terms of its collection, which includes masterpieces by Bruegel, Vermeer, Caravaggio, Rembrandt, and Raphael. Unlike those museums, however, the Kunsthistorisches is small enough to conquer in a few hours and has an interior worth the price of admission alone. Climb up to the third floor for a stunning view of the museum's bustling cafe, nestled among black marble and stucco decorations. You still might not be able to pronounce the Kunsthistorisches's name after leaving, but you'll be talking about it for years to come.

i €15, students €11, under 18 free. Free Wi-Fi. Open Tu-W 10am-6pm, Th 10am-9pm, F-Su 10am-6pm.

▨ BELVEDERE PALACE AND MUSEUM

Prinz Eugen-Strasse ☎01 79 55 71 34 www.belvedere.at

Gustav Klimt's *The Kiss*—you know, the source material for a million grainy posters hung portentously over dorm beds—lies behind inches of bulletproof glass in the central room of the Belvedere Museum. For those who've experienced the disappointment of seeing the *Mona Lisa* in person, don't worry: this time, the crowds are smaller, the painting (much) bigger, and the selfies are shut down by the dispassionate guards flanking Klimt's shimmering masterpiece. The magnificently baroque Upper Belvedere Palace, built in the early 18th century for Prince Eugene of Savoy, houses the largest Klimt collection in the world as well as eye-catching works by the painter's Austrian contemporaries Egon Schiele and Oskar Kokoschka.

i Upper Belvedere €14.50, students €11.50. Combined Upper and Lower Belvedere €20/17. Open daily 10am-6pm.

▨ ST. STEPHEN'S CATHEDRAL

Stephansplatz 3 ☎01 515 52 30 54 www.stephanskirche.at

Perhaps the most monstrously large thing ever to possess a pet name, St. Stephen's Cathedral (which the Viennese call "Steffl") stands looming in Vienna's ever-busy first district. The cathedral's history is as deep as the dirt and grime that give the once-white building its black tint. St. Stephen's Cathedral was built

tales from the vienna woods

Travelers only in Vienna for a few days might be aghast at the suggestion of leaving the sprawling, cultured metropolis. But after a few minutes on City Hiking Path 1 (Stadtwanderwege 1), which winds through the woods north of Vienna, it's easy to understand why so many locals decide to skip town for an afternoon. The mostly paved path runs through many of Vienna's famous vineyards, many of which operate wine taverns where you can sample their latest offerings. It also features a 500m climb up Kahlenberg hill, often crowded with people enjoying the panoramic view of Vienna it provides. To get to the hiking path, take Tram D north to the end of the line (in Nussdorf). Download a map of the 10K trail onto your phone before you go; the trail is mostly marked, but there are a few tricky spots. And wear temperature-appropriate clothing! Even in summer, the Vienna Woods are lovely, dark, and deep.

atop the ruins of two churches in 1106, but its expansion lasted into the 16th century. While you can get a glimpse into the beautifully Baroque interior of the cathedral without handing over any cash, this is only the tip of iceberg. If you decide to stop being cheap and are willing to cough up €4.50, you'll find yourself immersed in the cathedral's history (and potentially dust), as the giant limestone church holds many treasures (and a lot of old tombs). Guided tours of the cathedral catacombs and historical artifacts are given regularly, making sure you won't miss out on a single famous dead guy.

i €4.50. Open M-Sa 6am-10pm, Su 7am-10pm. Guided tours M-Sa 10:30am, 3pm, Su 3pm.

▨ LEOPOLD MUSEUM

Museumsplatz 1   ☎01 52 57 00 www.leopoldmuseum.org

The James Dean of painting in early-20th-century Vienna was Egon Schiele, a protégé of Gustav Klimt known for his striking (and often disturbing) self-portraits and landscapes. Schiele died at the age of 28 but left behind a substantial catalogue of drawings and paintings, the largest collection of which was bought up by art connoisseur Rudolf Leopold. Leopold used that collection as the centerpiece of his namesake museum (opened in 2001), which offers a detailed, chronological look at the life and oeuvre of Schiele and includes masterpieces such as his *Dead Mother* (1910) and *Self-Portrait with Chinese Lantern and Fruits* (1912). Don't miss the superb video commentary by Rudolf's widow, Elisabeth Leopold, at the end of the Schiele exhibit.

i €13, students €9. Open M-W 10am-6pm, Th 10am-8pm, F-Su 10am-6pm.

WIENER RIESENRAD

Prater amusement park   www.wienerriesenrad.com

Talk about reinventing the wheel. Built in 1897, this enormous Ferris wheel that overlooks Vienna's Leopoldstadt district was nearly destroyed during World War II, after which it was restored to its status as the tallest wheel in the world (an honor the Riesenrad held until 1985). The Riesenrad sits at the entrance to Vienna's Prater amusement park, where it is surrounded by overpriced rides (€4-7 per go) and eateries. Still, a spin around in one of the wheel's 15 gondolas provides a great view of Vienna and allows you to live one of the most famous scenes in the history of film, which occurs toward the end of *The Third Man*.

i €9.50. Open daily 9am-11:45pm.

SCHÖNBRUNN PALACE AND GARDENS

Schönbrunner Schlossstrasse 47

☎01 81 11 32 39

www.imperial-austria.at/schoenbrunn-palace.html

Clocking in as Vienna's most popular tourist destination, Schönbrunn Palace and its adjoining gardens draw truly Versailles-esque crowds during the high season. This can make the audio-guided walk through the lavishly decorated interior of the massive, 1441-room building feel more than a little claustrophobic. For those still keen on a look inside Maria Theresa and Franz Joseph's former residence, *Let's Go* recommends springing for the extra chinoiserie-decorated rooms included in the "Grand Tour," which give a beautiful (if problematic) look at European royalty's penchant for cultural appropriation. The palace's sprawling grounds and gardens house the world's oldest zoo (see below) and are overlooked by a selfie-spawning gloriette from its perch atop a hill. To save hours in line, buy your tickets online ahead of time or skip the queue at the very front of the palace and find the less populated ticket kiosk near the garden to the palace's left.

i Grand Tour €16.40, students €13. Classic pass (includes access to a variety of activities around the grounds, excluding the zoo) €21.60/18. Open daily 8:30am-5:30pm.

TIERGARTEN SCHÖNBRUNN

Maxingstrasse 13b

☎01 87 79 29 40 www.zoovienna.at

Even though the Tiergarten Schönbrunn is the oldest zoo in the world, don't think it's out of date. Constructed in 1752 by Emperor Franz I as the Hapsburg royal menagerie, the Tiergarten features a number of modern marvels, including a simulated rainforest, an Arctic region, and an oft-mating pair of pandas, Yang Yang and Long Hui. Make sure to head to the zoo well before its 6:30pm closing time (earlier in the winter), as many of the animals start falling asleep and hiding around 5:30pm.

i €18.50. Open daily Apr-Sept 9am-6:30pm; Oct 9am-5:30pm; Nov-Jan 9am-4:30pm; Feb 9am-5pm; Mar 9am-5:30pm.

THIRD MAN MUSEUM

Pressgasse 25

☎01 586 48 72 www.3mpc.net

If you don't know what the name of this museum is referring to, stop reading. Stop reading right now. OK, if you're still reading, go watch Carol Reed's classic 1949 film *The Third Man*, a thriller set in post-war Vienna—and then decide whether you want to know literally everything there is to know about the movie. The information-dense and rarely open Third Man Museum, opened in 1997 by two devoted—and we mean devoted—fans of *The Third Man*, is packed with memorabilia, photographs, and posters that outline the film's origins, historical context, production, and cultural impact. While the museum more resembles the work of hoarders than curators, it's an absolute must for fans of the film.

i €9, students €7. Open Sa 2-6pm.

ALBERTINA MUSEUM

Albertinaplatz 1

☎01 534 83 www.albertina.at

In pretty much any other city, the Albertina would be a must-visit, but it faces some tough competition from Vienna's many other wonderful art museums. Whether it rises to the level of that competition pretty much comes down to its temporary exhibitions—the permanent "Monet to Picasso" collection and the prints housed in the building's formerly Imperial apartments are great but nothing to write home about. Check out the museum's website before going, and if what's new is for you, great! If not, there are other (artistic) fish in the Danube.

i €12.50, students €8.50. Open M-Tu 10am-6pm, W 10am-9pm, Th-Su 10am-6pm.

there are no bored walks

More than almost any other European city, Vienna's key areas are dominated by green spaces: the sprawling Stadtpark, home to memorials to famous composers associated with the city (Schubert, Strauss, Bruckner); the pristine rows of roses housed at the central Volksgarten; and the former royal kickback spots: the huge Belvederegarten and the even huger Schönbrunner Schlosspark. On hot summer days (yeah, it gets hot in Vienna), youths and would-be-youths crowd onto the city's grassy expanses, bringing blankets, guitars, and more than a few chilled bottles of Vienna's famous Riesling.

FOOD

Eating in Vienna can be a stressful, expensive experience—but it doesn't have to be. Make your way outside the city center and (mostly) sacrifice English menus for far lower prices than you'd pay next to the famous sights.

◪ SCHNITZELWIRT $$

Neubaugasse 52 ☎01 523 37 71 www.schnitzelwirt.co.at

As Sarah Palin once tweeted, "English is a living language. Shakespeare liked to coin new words too. Gotta celebrate it!" We'd have to coin a few new adjectives to truly convey the size of the wienerschnitzel at this hole in the wall in Vienna's Neubau—"enormous," "colossal," and even "gargantuan" don't seem up to the task. You'll have to be seriously hungry, masochistic, or both to finish the two plate-size pieces of crispy pork cutlet (€7, more for add-ons) that comprise Schnitzelwirt's signature dish. Be sure to get it with a side of traditional potato salad—French fries are for interlopers.

i Beer €3-4. Cash only. No Wi-Fi. Open M-Sa 11am-9:30pm.

◪ HEINDL'S SCHMARREN & PALATSCHINKENKUCHL $$

Grashofgasse 4 ☎01 513 82 18

Dessert is deadly serious in Vienna. It's not tough to imagine bakers placing levels on top of slices of their picture-perfect *Sachertortes* before sliding them into protective plastic lining. Fortunately, a goofy side of the Viennese sweet tooth exists in the city's famed *Kaiserschmarrn*. Translating to the "Emperor's Shredded Pancake" (a reference to Franz Joseph I's uncontrollable feening for the stuff), *Kaiserschmarrn* generally consists of a ripped and fried pancake served with raisins, powdered sugar, and a cold fruit compote (traditionally made of plums). Heindl's is the place to go in Vienna for a picture-perfect *schmarrn*, served hot in a pan in two sizes: small (enormous, easily enough for two people; €10.50) and large (vast, enough for three or four people; €12.50). Heindl's also serves normal food, but nobody will give you an odd look if you, like Rihanna, say all you want is that (pan)cake cake cake cake cake cake.

i Schmarrn €10-13. Entrees €10-20. No Wi-Fi. Cash only. Open daily 10am-midnight.

◪ DR. FALAFEL $

Stand 560, Naschmarkt ☎01 585 00 90

Spanning several consecutive stands in Vienna's famous Naschmarkt, Dr. Falafel seems willing to serve dishes from any culinary tradition as long as they're (a) cheap and (b) delicious: enormous bowls of stir-fried noodles, sushi, döner kebab, and its namesake fried chickpea-fritter sandwiches, all for €3-6. Dr. Falafel's seating area has a decidedly state-fair feel, but it's probably better anyway to eat while wandering the rest of the Naschmarkt.

i Dishes €3-6. Cash only. Open M-Sa 8am-6pm.

austria

■ HARVEST CAFÉ BISTROT $$
Karmeliterplatz 1   ☎0676 492 77 90 www.harvest-bistrot.at

Set down the schnitzel, wave away the wurst—vegan refuge Harvest proves that
Austrian cuisine doesn't need meat to be tasty. Serving up small yet filling snacks
like vegetable ghee with roasted apple on nutty bread (€4.80) as well as substantial stews and soy dishes (€9-11) and a daily lunch buffet, Harvest offers up truly
guilt-free value. The schnitzel's always down the street when you want it.

*i Appetizers €4-6. Entrees €9-11. Cash only. Open M-Tu 11am-11pm, Th-F 11am-11pm, Sa-Su
10am-6pm.*

■ CAFÉ DRECHSLER $$
Linke Wienzeile 22   ☎01 581 20 44

Lying alongside the bustle of the Naschmarkt, Café Drechsler represents a modern take on Vienna's famous coffee culture. The elegantly decorated interior and
downbeat jazz convince Drechsler's mostly local patrons to linger at their tables
for hours at a time, enjoying a *mélange* (Vienna's take on cappuccino; €3.10) or a
multi-course lunch (€10-15). Drechsler may not be the most opulent (or oldest)
of Vienna's cafes, but it's among the best.

*i Coffee €2-4. Wine and beer €2-5. Cocktails €7.50. Meals €10-20. Free Wi-Fi. Cash only. Open
M-Th 8am-midnight, F-Sa 8am-2am, Su 8am-midnight.*

■ AM NORDPOL 3 $$
Nordwestbahnstrasse 17   ☎01 333 58 54 www.amnordpol3.at

Locals crowd onto the terrace of this decidedly off-the-beaten-path restaurant,
which focuses on serving traditional dishes with fresh ingredients and mixing
(enormous) homemade lemonades. While Am Nordpol 3 definitely doesn't cater
to tourists, it has an English menu, which saves you the embarrassment of bun-
gling 15-letter German words in front of Vienna's famously impatient servers.
Plus, the lack of sightseers keeps the prices low in comparison to the city center.

*i Appetizers €3-6. Entrees €7-12. Lemonade and beer €3-6. Open M-F 5-11pm, Sa-Su
noon-midnight.*

NIGHTLIFE

Vienna's cafe culture has heavily influenced its club culture, with many bars attempting to continue the laid-back vibe favored by the city's daytime haunts. In fact, many
of those daytime haunts transform into after-hours spots at which to grab a cocktail
with friends. Vienna doesn't have anything to rival Budapest's enormous clubs, but
that doesn't mean dancing is foreign to the city—ever heard of the waltz?

■ PICKWICK'S INTERNATIONAL CAFE
Marc-Aurel-Strasse 10-12   ☎01 533 01 82 www.pickwicks.at

"Happy hour" is a mostly foreign concept in Vienna, but it revels in its foreign-
ness at Pickwick's, an English-language bookstore/bar near the Donaukanal.
Every day between 6-9pm, the top-notch bartenders serve up heavily discounted
(but still strong) cocktails (€5.20, normally €7-8.50). Although it's open until 2am
on Fridays and Saturdays, Pickwick's isn't a turn-up spot; instead, it's an ideal
place to read or chat with a friend or two. Charles Dickens would be proud.

*i Beer €2-4. Cocktails €5-9. Cash only. Open M-Th 11am-midnight, F-Sa 11am-2am, Su
11am-midnight.*

■ POLKADOT
Albertgasse 12   ☎01 407 41 25 www.polkadot.at

Polkadot takes its music seriously. This recently opened "alternative music bar"
operates in the former lodgings of Josefstadt's infamous dive bar Narrenkast'l,
but the resemblance ends there. An always-changing blend of punk, indie, jazz,
and folk blasts through Polkadot's living room-esque seating area, which gives

it a house party vibe. If you don't like the current song, wait a few minutes—or distract yourself with a few sips from one of Polkadot's many excellent beers.

i *Beer €3-4. Cocktails €5-7. Open M-Th 7pm-2am, F-Sa 8pm-4am, Su 7pm-2am.*

⬛ IF DOGS RUN FREE
Gumpendorfer Strasse 1   ☎01 913 21 32 www.ifdogsrunfree.com

While it's named after an old Bob Dylan song, this bar, located on Vienna's all-too-hip Gumpendorfer Strasse, also lends its name out to some pretty entertaining drinking games. Vienna isn't lacking in chic, minimalist joints like If Dogs Run Free, but the bar stands apart from its crunchy peers due to its high level of execution. Everything, from the interior—red geometric sculptures hang over a cool gray bar—to the unique cocktails, is spot on. If you're looking to get the basic cocktails, If Dogs Run Free is not your place. But then again, if you're looking to get the basic cocktails, maybe you aren't offbeat enough for If Dogs Run Free in the first place.

i *Cocktails €9-10. Open M-Th 6pm-2am, F-Sa 6pm-4am.*

FLEX
Augartenbrucke 1   ☎01 533 75 25 www.flex.at

Are you into guys with gauges, chicks with shaved heads, or jumping around like no one is watching? If you answered yes to any of the above, Flex just might be the club for you. If you answered yes to all of the above, this small club along the side of the Danube was practically made for you. Although a popular club in Vienna, Flex maintains an offbeat vibe. Its crowd is young, casual, and generally grungy. You probably won't be hearing any of your favorite top 40 jams, but rather a mix of electronic, house, and reggae. The unassuming, unpretentious vibe of Flex allows for great dancing, which really means horrible dancing that is a tremendous amount of fun.

i *Cover depends on event, usually €5-10. Drinks €5-12. Open daily 8pm-6am.*

ESSENTIALS
Practicalities

- **TOURIST OFFICES:** The **City Information Centre** at Vienna's City Hall has brochures and pamphlets about Vienna's many attractions as well as on-site staff to answer any of your questions regarding the city. (Friedrich-Schmidt-Platz. Open daily M-F 8am-6pm.)

- **GLBT RESOURCES:** Austria is considered a conservative country. While same-sex partnerships are legal, the country's strong Catholicism has stood in the way of complete equality. Check out the Facebook page "Gayfriendly Vienna" for information about upcoming events.

- **INTERNET:** Wi-Fi (generally referred to as WLAN) is widely available in cafes and restaurants in Vienna—generally, you just need to ask the cashier for the password or connect to the common cafe WLAN provider Freewave.

- **POST OFFICES:** Most of Vienna's post offices are open daily 8am-6pm. Two post offices with extended hours are Post Office 1010 Wien (Fleischmarkt 19. Open M-F 7am-10pm, Sa-Su 9am-10pm) and Post Office at the West Train Station. (Open M-F 7am-7pm, Sa 9am-6pm, Su 9am-2pm.)

Emergency

- **EMERGENCY NUMBERS:** General emergencies ☎112. Fire ☎122. Police ☎133.

- **PHARMACIES:** Pharmacies in Vienna are called *apothekes*. Medicine can only be bought at pharmacies and not drugstores. *Apothekes* take turns operating at nights and on weekends, so you must check online at www.apotheker.or.at to see which pharmacy is open if you need to purchase something past 6pm or on a weekend.

- **MEDICAL SERVICES:** Vienna's hospitals are internationally renowned. The biggest is **General Hospital AKH.** (Währinger Gürtel 18-20. ☎01 40 40 00.) This hospital has English speakers, although you may also contact Vienna Medical Society Service Bureau for Foreign Patients at ☎01 50 15 12 53 with inquiries for English-speaking doctors and hospitals. For 24hr. medical assistance, call ☎01 513 95 95.

Getting There
By Plane
Vienna International Airport is about 16km east of the city in Schwechat. There are many public transportation options to quickly and easily get into the city:

The City Airport Train (CAT) operates daily between 5:30am-11:30pm every 30min. and takes about 16min. to get from the airport to Vienna. It costs €11 for a one-way ticket, which can be bought from ticket machines and tourists offices at the airport as well as at www.cityairporttrain.com.

Airport buses stop at City Centre, Westbahnof Station, and Kaisermühlen Vienna International Centre VIC. Buses run every 30min. from around 5am-11:30pm, depending on the bus. Tickets are €8 and may be purchased from ticket machines and tourists offices at the airport. Check www.postbus.at/en/Airportbus/Vienna_AirportLines for specific route and time details.

Getting Around
By Public Transportation
Getting around Vienna on public transportation is easy with the city's buses, trams, trains, and new metro lines. The U-Bahn is Vienna's subway. Tickets for public transportation are a uniform €1.70 , but you can purchase the Vienna card for €19, which allows unlimited use of public transportation in 72hr. increments. These are sold at information, tourist, and public transportation offices, as well as over the phone at ☎01 798 44 00148. For more information about transportation in Vienna, call Vienna Public Transport Information Center at ☎01 790 9100.

By Taxi
Taxis in Vienna have a basic, regulated fare of €2.50, plus €1.20 per kilometer.

graz

Con-Graz. If you've made your way to Austria's second-largest city, long overlooked by travelers in favor of Vienna and Salzburg, you've found the best of both those cities in one. Graz has arts and culture to compete with Vienna's but lacks the capital's long-cultured snobbery; its hilly setting matches the sublimity of Salzburg, but with a tenth of the tourists. Graz is a mix of lively college town and perfectly preserved old city, all wrapped in its distinctive Styrian culture.

get a room!

Graz doesn't find its way onto many Eurotrips, which means that its hostel scene is almost nonexistent. The city's only hostel **(A&O Graz Hauptbahnhof)** is essentially a cheap hotel, and not an especially good (or centrally located with respect to the Old Town) one at that. Exploring homestay or short-term rental options online is, for now, the best—and often cheapest—option for lodging in Graz.

austria

SIGHTS

While the highlights of Graz's Old Town can easily be seen in an afternoon, doing the city properly—which means a tour of Schloss Eggenberg—takes at least a full day.

◾ SCHLOSSBERG

Along with Russia and the 6 ft. mark, the fortress atop this hill overlooking Graz was one of the only things Napoleon never succeeded in conquering. Now a public park, the Schlossberg also houses the city's iconic clock tower (the Uhrturm), an off-kilter and stumpy medieval masterpiece that looks ripe for inclusion in a Tim Burton movie. The hike up is short (15-20min.) and ends with panoramic views of Graz's old town and the surrounding hills.

i Free.

◾ EGGENBERG PALACE

Eggenberger Allee 90   ☎0316 80 17 95 32 www.museum-joanneum.at

One of Europe's most intimate and best-preserved palaces, Eggenberg is also one of its strangest: designed by an Italian Renaissance architect, constructed around an older Gothic home built by the founder of the Eggenberg dynasty, and later redecorated haphazardly in Baroque and Rococo fashion. Eggenberg Palace often comes across like the product of a bored, wealthy family who impulsively added whatever they wanted to the place without ever taking anything away—and it's endlessly interesting, especially if you take the guided tour through the state rooms (€2.50), which happen on the hour. Eggenberg, as part of Graz's Universalmuseum Joanneum, also contains the Alte Galerie, a pleasant if uninspiring collection of medieval and Baroque paintings by people you've never heard of. We recommend buying the 24hr. "Joanneum Ticket," which provides you with access to all Universalmuseum Joanneum institutions in Graz for a day (including the state rooms, the Alte Galerie, and the Museum im Palais, the Styrian Armory, and the Neue Galerie).

i Joanneum Ticket €13, students €4.50. Open Tu-Su 10am-5pm.

FOOD

GLÖCKL BRÄU $

Glockenspielplatz 2-3 ☎0316 81 47 81

Styrian food: it's like Viennese food, but with a slightly unhealthy devotion to all things pumpkin. Far from a gimmick, though, it's a tasty way of switching up tried-and-true Austrian classics—and Glöckl Bräu pulls it off with panache. Although it occupies an enormous terrace and indoor seating area, this restaurant/brewery is nearly always full with locals, especially during lunch hours, when it offers a three-course menu for under €10.

i Beer €3-4. Entrees €8-15. Open daily 10:30am-midnight.

DELIKATESSEN-FRANKOWITSCH $$

Stempfergasse 2 ☎0316 82 22 12 www.frankowitsch.at

Frankowitsch might be overhyped, but unlike Public Enemy, we're not going to tell you not to believe all of it. The long-standing Graz bakery and restaurant is famous for its open-faced, tapa-size "sandwiches," served cold from behind the counter (€1-2.50). Offerings change daily and make for a tasty, if a little unwieldy, afternoon snack.

i Sandwiches €1-2.50. Beer €3-4. Wine €3-5. Open M-F 7:30am-7pm, Sa 8:30am-5pm.

NIGHTLIFE

STERN

Sporgasse 38 ☎0316 81 84 00 www.stern-bar.at

There's nothing stern about the laid-back vibe at Stern, a cocktail bar in the heart of Graz's Old Town. How could there be? Happy hour is, in the immortal words of the Miami Heat, not one, not two, not three—well, it actually is three, three glorious hours (5-8pm) of €5 mojitos, tequila sunrises, and whatever else cocks your tail. Shaking your tail at this decidedly non-dance environment, however, would likely result in a Stern talking-to.

i Cocktails €7.50-8; during happy hour €5-5.50. Cash only. Open M-Tu 4pm-1am, W-Th 4pm-2am, F-Sa 4pm-3am, Su 4pm-1am.

POSTGARAGE

Dreihackengasse 42 www.postgarage.at

After the party is the hotel lobby, but what's post-garage? Not a niche genre of indie rock, oddly enough—instead, it's Graz's top destination for students who want to party away from the top 40 scene. Regularly hosting electronica DJs to spin for its two dance floors, Postgarage also has a tasty vegetarian cafe to take care of those drunchies in the healthiest way possible.

i Drinks €4-7. Cash only. Hours vary depending on event.

ESSENTIALS

Practicalities

- **TOURIST OFFICES:** The tourist office has brochures and pamphlets about Graz's many attractions as well as on-site staff to answer any of your questions regarding the city. (Herrengasse 16. Open daily 10am-6pm.)

- **INTERNET:** Wi-Fi (generally referred to as WLAN) is widely available in cafes and restaurants in Graz—generally, you just need to ask the cashier for the password or connect to the common cafe WLAN provider Freewave.

Emergency

- **EMERGENCY NUMBERS:** General emergencies ☎112. Fire ☎122. Police ☎133.

- **PHARMACIES:** Pharmacies in Austria are called *apothekes*. Medicine can only be bought at pharmacies and not drugstores. *Apothekes* take turns operating at nights and on weekends, so you must check online at www.apotheker.or.at to see which pharmacy is open if you need to purchase something past 6pm or on a weekend.

- **MEDICAL SERVICES:** The biggest hospital in Graz is **LKH-Univ. Klinikum Graz.** It has English speakers. (Auenbruggerplatz 1. ☎0316 3850.) For 24hr. medical assistance, call ☎01 513 95 95.

salzburg

Salzburg has gone soft. What used to be the site of pillaging and burning, churches falling into piles of divine rubble, and Mozart clawing around the edges of truth sonata by sonata is now perfectly content to orient most of its typical tourist experience around an admittedly well-shot but absurdly plotted movie starring Julie Andrews and Christopher Plummer. Alas, all cities cannot retain their crusading kickassery, and it's probably a good thing for Salzburg's architecture, considering everything in the city has been destroyed and rebuilt multiple times. But then again, you would be remiss to define Salzburg solely by mountain-twirling and wistful singing about edelweiss. For one thing, the definitive symbol of Salzburg is a fortress (Festung Hohensalzburg) that has never once been conquered. If you fancy yourself an ascetic or devotee more than a war buff, Salzburg boasts a dozen famous cathedrals (the Dom), abbeys (Nonnberg Abbey), churches (Franziskaner Kirche), and monasteries (the Augustinian Monastery)—and then there's the shopping. Getreidsgasse is the Diagon Alley of Europe; its hundreds of stores are packed along the street, each with a classy metal banner hanging outside the front.

SIGHTS

In general, city "tourist cards" tend to be a break-even proposition at best and a scam at worst, but Salzburg's is a gem for those interested in seeing even only a few of the city's sights. The 48hr. card (€30-36, depending on season) provides enough time to hit all of Salzburg's key sights for free (and free public transportation, to boot), paying for itself at least twice over in the process.

▧ UNTERSBERG MOUNTAIN

You don't have to "climb ev'ry mountain" when in Salzburg—just the mile-high peak featured in the inescapable *Sound of Music*. In fact, you don't even have to climb it. The Salzburg Card gives you a free round trip on the vertigo-inducing cable car up to the summit, easily accessible via bus. Once at the summit, enjoy the stunning panoramic Alpine views and hike around the surrounding hills—just be sure to note the time of the cable car's final descent. Sturdy shoes and warm clothing are highly recommended, unless hypothermia, sore feet, and sprained ankles are a few of your favorite things. Remember to pack your own lunch, or be subjected to the mercy of the cafes atop the summit.

i Take bus #25 in the direction of Untersberg; the line ends directly next to the cable car. The same line runs past Schloss Hellbrunn (see below) on the way; as both are somewhat out of town, we recommend combining them into an afternoon. Cable car lift tickets €23, students €18, free with Salzburg Card.

SCHLOSS HELLBRUNN

It's no wonder this place starts with "Hell," as the devil surely lives in the trick fountains that dot this massive palatial complex. Built in the 1610s, Hellbrunn was the brainchild of the city's Prince Archbishop Markus Sittikus (talk about separation of church and state). The palace's excellent audio tour, folklore museum, and opulent gardens will satisfy those less willing to get wet.

i Bus #25 to Schloss Hellbrunn. Park free. Palace €12.50, students €8, free with Salzburg Card. Open daily Mar-Apr 9am-4:30pm; May-June 9am-5:30pm; July-Aug 9am-9pm; Sept 9am-5:30pm; Oct 9am-4:30pm.

FESTUNG HOHENSALZBURG

Mönchsberg 34   ☎0662 84 24 30 11 www.salzburg-burgen.at

The only army that has ever invaded this millennium-old fortress is tourists streaming from either the funicular that runs up the mountain or the perilous footpath (by which you literally have to pass through *die Höllenpforte*—"The Gates of Hell"). Overlooking the rest of the city, the castle provides the requisite beautiful view along with a series of eccentric attractions, such as a torture chamber and a truly bizarre marionette museum. (We know that, somewhere, Chuckie is proud.) Arrive before 10am for free access to the one-of-a-kind Gothic imperial apartments.

i €11.50, free with Salzburg Card. Open daily May-Sept 9am-7pm; Oct-Apr 9:30am-5pm.

MEININGER HOTEL SALZBURG CITY CENTER $

Fürbergstrasse 18-20 ☎0720 88 34 14

We'd like to think that the inclusion of "City Center" in the name of this enormous hostel/hotel in East Salzburg is something of a joke, because nothing worth doing or eating is closer than a 15min. walk. The facilities at Meininger, however, aren't a joke: top-notch Wi-Fi and power outlets, free soap, and TVs in every room. The hotel-y layout of Meininger doesn't lend itself to a student-hangout vibe, but it's a clean, hassle-free place to spend a couple nights.

i Dorms €25-30. Reception 24hr.

YOHO INTERNATIONAL YOUTH HOSTEL $

Paracelsusstrasse 9 ☎0662 87 96 49 www.yoho.at

If you're the sort of traveler who doesn't sweat the small stuff, mark your X at this spot, because Salzburg's YoHo might be a treasure. For the more easily annoyed, YoHo can feel like a potentially excellent hostel—good location, comfy beds, friendly student-age travelers—buried under an avalanche of neglected details. After encountering definite flaws such as lockers that beep when operated (so the whole dorm knows you're secure at 2am!) and inaccessible gaps between beds and walls that provide top-bunkers with a constant fear of losing their stuff, it's easy to wonder whether YoHo's operators have ever stayed in a hostel themselves. On the plus side, the hostel bar runs two excellent happy hours (beer €2; cocktails €3.50), so there's an easy way to forget those annoyances.

i Breakfast buffet available. All-you-can-drink coffee €1. Dorms €20-25.

MOZART'S BIRTHPLACE

Getreidegasse 9 ☎0662 84 43 13 www.mozarteum.at

While Vienna tries to emphasize that it's the city where Mozart actually wanted to live, Salzburg is indeed where the prodigious story began. This museum, which occupies two floors of the house where Lil' Wolfgang was born, is a study in romanticizing Mozart's life—even if the Romantic Period came a little later. While the collection includes a number of artifacts associated with Mozart—his kid-size violin, ebullient letters he wrote to his sister, etc.—it's more fun to view it as a monument to the original Tiger Dad, Leopold Mozart, who had Wolfgang performing in front of royal audiences by the age of six.

i €10.50, free with Salzburg Card. Open daily 9am-5:30pm.

ST. PETER'S ABBEY

St. Peter Bezirk 1/2 ☎0662 84 45 76 www.erzabtei.at

If you happen to be the sibling of a famous German-speaking musician, you're probably buried in St. Peter's Friedhof along with Mozart's sister, Haydn's brother, and a litany of other notables-by-connection. The monastery and church date back to the eighth century, making the complex the oldest monastery in the German-speaking world. The cool and somewhat creepy icing on the abbey's cake is the catacombs, which you can climb through in Hunchback of Notre Dame fashion for a small fee.

i Catacombs €1.50, students €1, free with Salzburg Card. Church open daily 8am-noon and 2:30-6:30pm. Cemetery open daily 6:30am-dusk. Catacombs open May-Sept Tu-Su 10:30am-5pm; Oct-Apr W-Th 10:30am-3:30pm, F-Sa 10:30am-4pm.

austria

FOOD

▨ DIE WEISSE $$

Rupertgasse 10   ☎0662 87 22 46 www.dieweisse.at

Believe it or not, brewing wheat beer used to be illegal in Salzburg—but that didn't stop the founder of Die Weisse back in 1901. Locals begin filling up Die Weisse's massive beer garden early (we're talking am, not pm). This can make it difficult to snag a table around dinnertime, when enormous platters of dumplings and sauerkraut, as well as the restaurant's signature fried chicken salad, start to emerge from the kitchen. Still, there's nothing quite like sipping on a pint of a once-illegal beer to tide you over while you wait.

i *Beer €4. Food €7-12. Free Wi-Fi. Open M-Sa 10am-midnight.*

▨ ZUM ZIRKELWIRT $$

Pfeifergasse 14   ☎0662 84 27 96 www.zumzirkelwirt.at

We suspect Zirkelwirt didn't have student specials when it opened in 1647, but flashing a college ID nowadays will score you homemade *spätzle*, dumplings, and a beer for under €10. Unlike many Austrian restaurants of a certain age, Zirkelwirt doesn't feel like it's older than George Washington's mom and isn't overrun by tourists—chalk the latter up to the fact that it's located a short walk away from the heart of the Old Town in West Salzburg. Instead, fresh ingredients and traditional recipes (don't miss the spinach dumplings) run the show at Zirkelwirt, ensuring it'll stick around for another century or two.

i *Entrees €10-15. Beer €3.50-4. No Wi-Fi. Open daily 11am-midnight.*

▨ AUGUSTINER BRAUSTUBL $

Lindhofstrasse 7   ☎0662 43 12 46 www.augustinerbier.at

Wandering around the non-touristy areas of Salzburg, it's easy to wonder where all of the people are. That's easy: they're all at Augustiner Braustubl, a massive beer pub overlooking the Salzach that could probably fit the entire permanent population of the city in a pinch. If you show up before opening in the warm months, there'll be a line, but it moves quickly. Both the beer garden and interior halls are self-service; pay the cashier up front, grab a stein, rinse it, and show your receipt to the bartender to get it filled with your one choice of beer, a refreshing recipe brewed by a local monastery since 1621 that still follows the Purity Law of 1516. Outside food is allowed, but sampling the various restaurant and bakery stalls that line the interior of Augustiner Braustubl is a fairly cheap way to fill up on roasted chicken, pork knuckles, strudel, and even pickled radishes, for which there's an entire stall.

i *Beer €3.10 per 0.5L. Food €7-10. Cash only. No Wi-Fi. Open M-F 3-11pm, Sa-Su 2:30-11pm.*

▨ CAFÉ SHAKESPEARE $$

Hubert-Sattler-Gasse 3   ☎0650 773 53 57

Who knew the Bard hated the States so much? This cafe/bar combo is decked out with a healthy dose of anti-American art, including a distressed bald eagle and a choice four-letter word to describe patriotism. Still, the outdoor terrace has clear views of nearby Mirabell Palace, and the ever-smoking youth indoors won't give you too much trouble if your Yankeeness is exposed. The food is conservative yet tasteful—the Hausgemachtes toast especially is a small step in your pursuit of happiness.

i *Entrees €9-13. Open daily 9am-2am.*

NIGHTLIFE

▨ STIEGL-BRAUWEL

Bräuhausstrasse 9   ☎050 14 92 14 92 www.stiegl.at

We could've slotted this bar/restaurant/museum at the headquarters of Salzburg's utterly inescapable Stiegl brewery into any number of categories—but considering that getting tipsy is a likely side effect of a visit, we'll put it here. Entry includes admission to a massive exhibit exploring the 500-year-old history of Stiegl, a beer tasting at the bar, and a free small stein at the gift shop. Do like the locals do and linger for hours in the beer garden, sampling Stiegl's many fantastic beers until closing time.

i €11, free with Salzburg Card. Beer €3-4. Open daily 10am-midnight.

▨ PEPE COCKTAIL BAR

Steingasse 3   ☎0662 87 36 62 www.pepe-cocktailbar.at

In the world of Austrian nightlife, it's occasionally nice to escape from the sight of a few varieties of beer being served to an increasingly rowdy crowd. Enter Pepe, which caters to its Zara-clad crowd as they throw back cocktail after cocktail amid remarkably chic surroundings. While most of the drinks are tropical-themed—daiquiris abound—we recommend the Schwermatrose (rum, kahlua, lime, and lemon) for a fresh beginning to a pub crawl along Steingasse.

i Cocktails €7-10. Open Tu-Sa 7pm-3am.

SODA CLUB

Gstättengasse 17   ☎0650 311 77 61

What better place to lose yourself in electronic beats and dubstep drops than a bar built into the side of a mountain (even if it once was filled with monks)? Exposed cave walls put exposed brick to shame as a decor option, and the drinks are surprisingly cheap given the upscale vibe.

i Beer €4-5. Cocktails €7-10. Open Tu 9pm-4am, W-Sa 9pm-5am.

ESSENTIALS

Practicalities

- **SALZBURG TOURIST OFFICE:** The main office is at Mozartplatz 5. (☎0662 88 98 73 30 www.salzburg.info. Open daily June-Aug 9am-7pm; Sept-May 9am-6pm.) Other tourist offices located at the airport (Innsbrucker Buddesstrasse 95) and the train station (Südtiroler Platz 1).

- **GLBT RESOURCES:** Austria is considered a conservative country. While same-sex partnerships have been recently legalized, the country's strong Catholicism has stood in the way of complete equality. HOSI (Homosexual Initiative) provides a list of GLBT-friendly establishments in Salzburg. (Gabelsbergerstrasse 26. ☎0662 43 59 27 www.hosi.or.at. Open M-W 10am-5pm, F 10am-5pm.)

- **INTERNET:** Salzburg has recently begun a free Wi-Fi program in the city, with coverage around the Salzach River daily 5am-midnight. Coverage includes Mozartplatz, Volksgarten, Mirabell Palace, and Max-Reinhardt-Platz.

Emergency

- **EMERGENCY NUMBERS:** General emergencies ☎112. Police ☎133. Fire ☎144.

- **MEDICAL SERVICES:** For doctors on call, dial ☎0662 87 13 27. For dentists on call, dial ☎0662 87 34 66.

Getting There

To **fly** into Salzburg, travelers pass through the W.A. Mozart International Airport. (Innsbrucker Bundesstrasse 95 ☎662 85 80 79 11.) Many airlines fly directly from other European cities to Salzburg, but those who are traveling from overseas might find it easier to fly into Flughafen München in southern Germany and take the airport shuttle to Ostbahnhof, then a DB or ÖBB train to Salzburg Hauptbahnhof (€24). To get to the city center from the Salzburg airport, take bus #2 (every 10-20min. M-F 5:30am-10:30pm, Sa 6am-11pm, Su 6:30am-11pm) to the Hauptbahnhof train station, from which you can take a number of buses to various locations in the city.

The Salzburg Hauptbahnhof receives a large number of international **trains**, including those to and from Zürich (€51; 6hr.), Munich (€25; 2hr.), Budapest (€44; 5½hr.), and Frankfurt (€107; 5hr.) as well as trains to and from Vienna (€50; 3hr.) and Innsbruck (€41; 2hr.). There is reduced coverage on Sundays, so check the ÖBB website at www.oebb.at, where you can reserve your tickets ahead of time. If traveling within Austria, simply buy a ticket at the offices in each major train station.

Getting Around

By Bike

If you're planning to spend an extended period of time in Salzburg, renting or buying a bike will probably be your best bet. Because the public transportation system relies on buses, traffic can build up around the Old Town. For shorter stays, **TopBike** provides bike rentals. (Staatsbrücke, Franz-Josef-Kai www.topbike.at. €7 per hour, €20 per day. Open daily Apr-June 10am-5pm, July-Aug 9am-7pm, Sept-Oct 10am-5pm.)

By Car

If you consider yourself the outdoorsy sort, then a car might come in handy to explore the surrounding Bavarian Alps and other mountaineering options. The downside is that many rental companies have a 3-day minimum rental period; nevertheless try **AutoEurope** if you're interested. (12 Gniglerstrasse ☎1 866 16 51 From €150 for 3 days.)

By Bus

Bus fares cost €2.10 per trip, €5 for a 24hr. pass, and €13.10 for a week-long pass. If you purchase the **Salzburg Card**, you have access to all public transportation (including the funicular to the top of Festungs Hohensalzburg and the Mönchsberg Elevator) for free. (Mozartpl. 5 ☎3662 88 98 70 www.salzburg.info. Includes admission to all sights in Vienna and use of public transportation network. 24hr. card €25, under 15 €12.50; 48hr. €34/17; 72hr. card €40/20.)

innsbruck

A winter sports mecca with millennia of history, Innsbruck feels like an Alpine village gone big. Students and skiers dominate the Tyrolian capital's vibe and nightlife for most of the year, until they're replaced by an older, outdoorsy crowd of tourists during the summer. Depending on when you visit, Innsbruck can feel like two entirely different cities—and we wouldn't miss either one.

SIGHTS

▨ HOFKIRCHE

Universitätsstrasse 2   ☎0512 58 43 02

Talk about carrying a torch for someone: Innsbruck's Hofkirche houses a magnificent tomb for the Holy Roman Emperor Maximilian I, who resided in the city during the 1490s but definitely isn't buried in its massive Gothic church. Larger-than-life bronze statues of famous European rulers (King Arthur and the like)

🏠 YOUTH HOSTEL FRITZ PRIOR SCHWEDENHAUS $

Rennweg 17b   ☎0512 58 58 14

June backpackers, you're out of luck: this small, centrally located hostel is only open in the summer during July and August. In fact, restrictive opening times are a recurring feature of what's otherwise a perfect place to stay—check-out is at the brutal hour of 9am, and check-in inconveniently doesn't begin until 5pm. However, in Innsbruck's underpopulated hostel scene, €20 for a clean, comfortable bed within a stone's throw of the main sights represents something of a steal.

i Dorms €20.

DOUG'S MOUNTAIN GETAWAY $$

Mühlwiese 12, Fulpmes   ☎0650 968 68 65

Someone thought of turning a youth hostel into an Alpine resort, and his name is… Doug. This isn't your standard bunk-and-cheap breakfast deal: staying at Doug's includes free access to a hot tub, sauna, pool tables, and video-game consoles. The downsides are the price and the distance from Innsbruck's city center, which is a 30min. bus ride away (€5). For a place to relax, though, Doug's can't be beat.

i Dorms €30-35.

flank Maximilian's empty tomb, which dominates the center of the Hofkirche. We don't expect Maximilian to be coming back to Innsbruck any time soon, but if he does, there's a holy place for him to crash. For discounted admission, consider combining your visit to the Hofkirche with the Tyrolean Museum of Popular Art and the Ferdinandeum Gallery, both of which are worth strolling through for half an hour.

i €7, students €5, under 19 free. Open M-Sa 9am-5pm, Su 12:30-7pm.

NORDKETTE

It's impossible to go 5min. in Innsbruck without catching a glimpse of the mile-high mountain that overlooks the city—but seeing Innsbruck from the Alpine heights of the Nordkette is anything but an everyday experience. While it's possible (with good boots) to hike up to the Hafelekar peak in a few hours during non-winter months, most opt for the Hungerburg funicular (up to €24 round-trip, depending on how far you take it; free with Innsbruck Card), which was designed by the late, great architect Zaha Hadid with her typically futuristic panache.

i Hours vary depending on season.

GOLDEN ROOF

Herzog-Friedrich-Strasse 15   ☎0512 53 60 14 41

First of all, the roof isn't actually gold—it's bronze, a fact you can announce to the hordes of tourists surrounding this Old Town landmark. Alloy or not, this early-16th-century home of Emperor Maximilian I (he built it for his bae) makes for an impressive photo, but feel free to skip the underwhelming museum that it houses.

i €5. Museum open daily 10am-5pm.

austria

FOOD

GASTHAUS ANICH $
Anichstrasse 15   ☎0512 57 04 50

Tyrolean cuisine is heavy on the potatoes and stingy with the flavors, a culinary trend that reflects the region's historical status as one of Austria's poorest. It's not worth splurging to have typical "rustic" dishes like *göstl* (fried potatoes and ham, topped with a fried egg) in an upscale setting, so if you're keen on getting a taste of Innsbruck, Gasthaus Anich makes for an excellent and affordable option. Many locals crowd in around lunchtime for Anich's daily menu (€7-9) and cheap beer (€3 per 0.5L). Be warned: If you order a la carte, the portion sizes at Anich are truly mountain-esque.

i *Entrees €8-15. Cash only. Open M-Sa 9am-midnight.*

STRUDEL-CAFÉ KRÖLL $
Hofgasse 6   ☎0512 57 43 47 www.strudel-cafe.at

Kröll is well-aware that it's catering to tourists, but it isn't afraid to experiment with dozens of unique flavors for the strudels stacked in its Old Town window. Although the savory strudels we sampled were on the dry and bland side, the sweet varieties were perfect, especially when warmed up. No, it's not how grandma made it (unless you go for the apple strudel). Unless you have an Austrian grandma, though, we're guessing you won't care.

i *Sweet strudels €4, Savory strudels €5. Cash only. Open daily 6am-9pm.*

NIGHTLIFE

When Innsbruck's students flee in the summer, many of the city's hippest bars and clubs shut down and weather the storm of older tourists. The ones listed below, however, are open year-round.

⬛ GOSSER'S
Adolf-Pichler-Platz 3   ☎0512 57 26 29 www.goessers.at

There was U2, and Blondie, and music still on MTV when the owners of Gosser's made their playlists, but the students and locals who frequent this lively bar don't mind being preoccupied with 1985 for a night. Home-brewed beer and cocktails (€4-8) flow freely, especially on Fridays, when a live DJ spins until 2am. If you find yourself drunkenly wondering when Mötley Crüe became classic rock as you stumble out of Gosser's, you've spent a night there just right.

i *Drinks €4-8. Open M-Th 9am-1am, F-Sa 9am-2am.*

WEEKENDER
Tschamlerstrasse 3   ☎0512 57 05 70 www.weekender.at

If you've ever wanted to pee into Mick Jagger's mouth, Weekender is the place to fulfill that desire. The men's restroom at this all-too-hip cafe/club is just one example of its relentless dedication to rock, but when live bands aren't playing, DJs spin electronica and indie for Weekender's mostly student and student-at-heart crowd. Drinks are a little more expensive than average, but no one ever said the rock and roll lifestyle came cheap.

i *Check website for concert dates; covers range depending on bands.*

ESSENTIALS
Practicalities

- **TOURIST OFFICES:** Burggraben 3. (Open daily 9am-6pm.)

- **INTERNET:** Wi-Fi (generally referred to as WLAN) is widely available in cafes and restaurants in Innsbruck—generally, you just need to ask the cashier for the password or connect to the common cafe WLAN provider Freewave.

- **POST OFFICES:** Most of Innsbruck's post offices are open daily 8am-6pm.

Emergency

- **EMERGENCY NUMBERS:** General emergencies ☎112. Fire ☎122. Police ☎133.

- **PHARMACY:** Pharmacies in Innsbruck are called *apothekes*. Medicine can only be bought at pharmacies and not drugstores. *Apothekes* take turns operating at nights and on weekends, so you must check online at www.apotheker.or.at to see which pharmacy is open if you need to purchase something past 6pm or on a weekend.

- **MEDICAL SERVICES:** The biggest hospital is **Tirol Kliniken.** (Anichstrasse 35. ☎050 50 40 www.tirol-kliniken.at.) For 24hr. medical assistance, call ☎01 513 95 95.

austria essentials

MONEY

Tipping and Bargaining

Service staff is paid by the hour, but a service charge is not usually included in an item's unit price. Cheap customers typically just round up to the nearest whole euro, but it's customary and polite to tip 10-15% if you are satisfied with the service. If the service was poor, you don't have to tip at all. To tip, tell the waiter the total of the bill with the tip included. Do not leave the tip on the table; hand it directly to the server. It is standard to tip a taxi driver at least €1, housekeepers €1-2 per day, and public toilet attendants around €0.50.

Taxes

Most goods in Austria are subject to a value added tax (VAT) of 20% (a reduced tax of 10% is applied to accommodations, certain foods, and some passenger transportation). Non-EU visitors who are taking these goods home unused may be refunded this tax for purchases totaling over €75 per store. When making purchases, request a VAT form and present it at a Tax Free Shopping Office, found at most airports, road borders, and ferry stations, or by mail. Refunds must be claimed within six months.

SAFETY AND HEALTH

Local Laws and Police

Certain regulations might seem harsh and unusual (e.g. jaywalking is a €5 fine), but abide by all local laws while in Austria; your embassy will not necessarily get you off the hook. Always be sure to carry a valid passport, as police have the right to ask for identification.

Drugs and Alcohol

The drinking age in Austria is 16 for beer and wine and 18 for spirits. The maximum blood alcohol content level for drivers is 0.05%. Avoid public drunkenness; it can jeopardize your safety and earn the disdain of locals. While possession of marijuana or hashish is illegal, possession of small quantities for personal consumption is decriminalized in Austria. Each region has interpreted "small quantities" differently (anywhere from 5 to 30g). Carrying drugs across an international border—considered to be drug trafficking—is a serious offense that could land you in prison.

BELGIUM

Belgium may not rank near the top of most people's lists of must-see European vacation spots. Next to the Netherlands or Greece, Belgium doesn't scream party central, and it doesn't have famous sights like you can find in Italy and France. But many people spend a whole Eurotrip searching for, and failing to find, the kind of small-town charm that is this entire country's specialty. Shift your vacation into a different gear and indulge in Belgium's own version of whimsy. Plus, Belgian cuisine revolves around fries, waffles, chocolate, and beer. It's basically the best Sunday brunch you've ever had, and it never ends.

If you have a penchant for public urination, you'll probably enjoy yourself in Brussels. Peeing statues aplenty await you; it's hard to turn the corner without seeing something taking a leak. It's cute when you're made out of bronze, but Let's Go doesn't recommend trying it yourself—indecent exposure charges don't make good souvenirs. While you're avoiding criminal charges, you might want to swing by the European Quarter, where you'll find more ambassadors and Eurocrats than you can shake a roll of red tape at. Brussels is also home to dozens of museums, art galleries, and theaters for the cultural traveler in you. And don't forget Bruges, one of Europe's most charmingly preserved medieval cities. It's not just small-town charm you'll find in Belgium; this is the place for small-country charm.

greatest hits

- **THE DEVIL'S IN THE DETAILS.** Part bar, part art gallery, all a bit of a mystery. But Bruges's **Lucifernum** (p. 45) is certainly not to be missed.

- **GHENT YOUR EXERCISE ON.** Work off the chocolate/waffle/chocolate-covered-waffle calories by climbing to the top of the **Belfort** (p. 54).

- **DRINK THE NIGHT AWAY.** We'll cut to the chase: we know you came to Belgium for the beer. Check out some of our top picks for brews—and even (gasp!) a cocktail bar—in Brussels (p. 38).

North Sea

Zeebrugge Knokke-Heist
Blankenberge
Ostend
Bruges
Roeselare
Ypres
Kortrijk/Contrai
Lille

NETHERLANDS
Turnhout
Antwerp
Ghent Mechelen Bree
Deinze Leuven Hasselt Maastricht
Brussels Aachen
Geraardsbergen Waterloo Liège
Tournai Namur Verviers
Mons Meuse R.
BELGIUM Charleroi
TO PARIS Dinant Rochefort
(200km) Chimay Han-sur-Lesse
FRANCE Lesse R.
Neufchâteau LUXEMBOURG
Meuse R. Arlon Luxembourg City

GERMANY

N
LG

0   50 kilometers
0   50 miles

brussels

It's hard to put your finger on Brussels. Home to both European bureaucracy and french fries doused in mayonnaise, the city plays the part of large, historical capital even as it dances to a more hoppy, greasy tune. Cobblestoned quaintness sits side-by-side with serious towers (many guarded by armed soldiers, as of late) that determine so much more than whether chocolate should be on that waffle. But debt relief (Mom, my credit card maxed out!) and nationalist violence (I am a Canadian, I swear!) will hopefully not be concerns of yours as you take on the Belgian capital. Mainly a good pair of walking shoes, a couple of loose notches on that belt, and an eye for subtleties will serve you well as you tour.

Brussels might not be Berlin, Paris, or Amsterdam, the larger neighboring cities that conquered and controlled Belgium for centuries. But even if it doesn't have the biggest art collections or loudest clubs, Brussels's waffles, urban comic strips, and friendly locals create an easygoing charm that will permeate your visit. Small enough to walk through but big enough to keep you engaged, Brussels is the center of Europe and it provides many of the continent's signature pleasures—historical buildings, fine art, delicious cuisine in iconic cafes, some nightclubs—without many of the hassles.

SIGHTS

Most of the tourist attractions in Brussels fall into a pentagonal slot between five streets in the city's very center, making it perfect for some solid, but not strenuous, day walking. (Don't worry too much about public transportation.) From La Grand Place, most of what you'll want to see slopes up to the west. This gentle topographical climb is a status one, too: starting with the old market places and restaurants around La Grand Place, a walk west will bring you by Mont des Arts, then Musées Royaux des Beaux-Arts, until you flatten out around Palais Royale and Parc de Bruxelles. Ambitious walkers (day-hikers, really) will continue all the way through le Parc de Bruxelles to Parc du Cinquantenaire for even larger lawns and a towering Arc.

get a room!

2GO4 QUALITY HOSTEL—DE BRUCKÈRES $

Blvd. Emilie Jaquman 99   ☎02 219 30 19 www.2go4.be/qualityhostel/brouckere.asp

2GO4 Quality hostel, a 10min. walk from La Grand Place and many of Brussel's primary tourist attractions, goes to great lengths to create a Belgian feel, even if it does verge on cutesy. Free Wi-Fi, a nearby laundromat, and a twice-daily free walking tour make 2GO4 one of the more charming and convenient places to stay in the city. The policy against large groups seems to attract more solo travellers like yourself, so making friends will be all the more straightforward. The reception desk closes everyday at 11pm and won't open again until 7:30am, so if you'll be coming in late or leaving early, it might be easier to stay elsewhere, or at least call ahead.

i Go to the left at the fork at place de Bouchère; it will be on your right. Wi-Fi included. Mixed dorm €18-20. Reception 7:30am-11pm. Communal kitchen and common room on the premises.

MEININGER HOTEL BRUSSELS CITY CENTER $

Quai du Hainut 33   ☎02 588 14 74 www.meininger-hotels.com/en/hotels/brussels/

While Meininger's canal-side location is less scenic than you might hope (gray-green sludge replaces the imagined *eau beau*), this hostel has just about everything else you would want in a place to stay. With Wi-Fi included, a 24hr. reception, daily clean linens, a kitchen, a small bar, collegial common space, and planned outings, Meininger gives you the bang for your buck. (But don't pay for the breakfast—it's not very good.) If the 20min. walk to Le Grand Place is too much for you, a metro stop that will connect you to the rest of Brussels is only a couple of blocks away.

i From le Compte de Flandre, walk toward the canal and turn right. Meininger will be about ¼mi. down, on your right. Wi-Fi. 6- and 10- bed dorms €15. Doubles €60.

YOUTH HOSTEL VAN GOGH $$

Rue Traversière 8   ☎02 217 01 58 www.chab.be/

Purportedly the one-time home of Vincent Van Gogh, Youth Hostel Van Gogh will not (we hope) inspire self mutilation or a revolutionary Impressionist period. Not that it's not a good place to stay for a couple of nights, plus, there's a small bar in the common room. A short walk from the city center, La Grand Place, and all that jazz, Van Gogh has free Wi-Fi and linens, and a laundry room for all those ear-blood-covered rags.

i From Boutanique, take a left onto Rue Royale. After walking a block, take another right onto Rue Traverseries; it will be on your right. Wi-Fi. Dorms €19-22. Bar on the premises.

SLEEP WELL YOUTH HOSTEL $$

Rue du Damier 23   ☎02 218 50 50 http://sleepwell.be

When you've spent most of the day climbing up the city of Brussels to see the Parc du Cinquantenaire (or sipping on Trappist beers), sleeping well probably won't end up being too much of an ask. Luckily, Sleep Well Youth Hostel offers more than just a comfy place to rest your head. Look out, though: at €24, Sleep Well is a few euro more than many hostels in the city, but you will enjoy a slightly nicer 6-person dorm (as opposed to the typical 10-12-person ones) for the premium.

i Head right at Place de Bouchère—take a right onto Rue de Malines and then a left onto Rue du Damier after a block; it will be on your right. Wi-Fi. 6-bed dorm €24. Bar on the premises.

brussels

LA GRAND PLACE

The historic center of the city of Brussels, it's hard to miss La Grand Place on any visit. Gothic, gold-plated spires stretch into the clouds, defining the Brussels skyline and encircling this cobblestoned square, which serves as the effective center of all things touristy in Brussels. Not to knock it, though: the buildings are beautiful and its central location makes stops to other nearby tourist favorites—like Le Manneken Pis (yep, the peeing boy) or Cathédrale de Saints Michel et Gudule—make it an essential stop on just about any trip to the Belgian capital.

A host of *friteries* (fry stands) and restaurants proper fall into Le Grand Place's gravitational pull, so a bit of discernment and deliberation will go a long way to separate the tourist traps from the tourist triumphs. Once you've had your fill and snapped enough selfies with the big, bad buildings (which are even prettier at night), Le Grand Place is also home to Maison du Roi—the museum of the city of Brussels—for you history buffs. A good way to get a sense of the city for not too steep a price, this museum will let you check off the I-looked-at-some-culture-today-Mom-I-swear box without having to wander too far from the city's central sights.

i From De Bouchére, take a right down Ave. D'Anspach. Take a left onto Rue de La Bourse, a quick right onto Rue du Midi, and then a quick left onto Rue au Buerre. Maison du Roi student admission €4.

PARC DU CINQUANTENAIRE

It's easy to feel like Belgium—historically a geographic trophy for larger kingdoms like the Netherlands, Austria, Germany, and France—largely enjoys a borrowed, if not entirely independent, national identity and culture. Is it to France what Canada is to the United States? Or a French-speaking Holland? Parc du Cinquantenaire, unfortunately, does not do too much to combat this sense. Its Arcade du Cinquantenaire feels like the less-famous, less-handsome cousin of Paris's well-known Arc du Triomphe and the main museum nearby—Musée Royal de l'Armée et d'Histoire Militaire—tells the tale of Dutch, French, Austrian, and German aggression in Belgium.

Still, giving this park and at least some its nearby attractions a visit is well worth your time on a trip to the city that is, after all, the capital (and de facto mixing place) of the European continent. Flowing fountains sprinkle vast, verdant lawns rolling out from the park's center. Locals flock here on sunny weekends to enjoy the lush tree cover, and the city even sets up some small markets and shops on Sundays. While Belgium may not boast the same enormous imperial and cultural heritage as its neighbors, the military museum merits a visit, even if it's only to climb to the top of the Arc and enjoy a splendid look at the city (the view felt worth it). Once you're back down, you can also swing by Autoworld, a museum that features a myriad of Belgian cars from the time before Germany became the most famous car producer in Europe. (At least give them some claim to fame besides waffles—France took the damn fries.) Alternatively, just rest your feet and enjoy one of the park's benches. Or, if you want to learn more about this European Union business, the European Parliament is only a short walk away.

i From Arts-loi, walk down Rue de la Loi toward the big arch. Musée Royal de l'Armée et d'Histoire Militaire admission students €4.

MAGRITTE MUSEUM: ROYAL MUSEUM OF FINE ARTS OF BELGIUM

Rue de la Régence 3   ☎02 508 32 11 www.musee-magritte-museum.be/

If you happen to be questioning the objectivity of your own reality, you might want to visit the Magritte Museum, dedicated to the famous Surrealist painter René Magritte (straight outta Brussels), and take some notes. While it's not home to many of Magritte's most famous works, it chronicles much of his life and work over the course of a three-floor exhibit, giving a visitor enough working knowledge of Surrealist art to really be "that guy" at your next family dinner. Not that the absence of pipes and bowler hats will leave you wanting for some head-scratching. Plus, leaves that look like, and then turn into, birds are always fun. It's also one of the cheapest museums in the city.

Once you're done with Surrealism and slowly ease back into reality, the Magritte Museum adjoins several other (including Musée Fin-de-Siècle), that are very accessible if you buy a cheap combo ticket.

Or head back outside (How can you really know it's outside? Does the word "outside" mean the same thing as not being inside a building?) to check out Mont des Arts, Parc de Bruxelles, or Le Palais Royal.

i From Gare Centrale, take a right onto Cantersteen. Then take a left up le Mont des Arts and continue straight on Coudenberg. The entrance to the Magritte Museum will be on your right. €8, under 26 €2. Open Tu-F 10am-5pm, Sa-Su 11am-6pm.

FOOD

▨ LA BOUSSOLE $$
Quai au Bois à Brûler—61 (Marché au Poisson)   ☎02 218 58 77 www.laboussole-be.com

Finding somewhere to eat *Moules-frites*—one of Belgium's iconic dishes—in Brussels shouldn't pose too much of a challenge for most tourists. Finding savory mussels with crispy fries at a place that doesn't make you feel like you just bought the equivalent of an "I <3 Brussels" T-shirt, on the other hand, can be more challenging. Luckily, there's La Boussole. Just a short walk from Le Grand Place and the more kitschy, touristy restaurants, La Boussole just might have you feeling like a real Belgian. Not only are the *Moule-frites* delicious (the rest of the menu boasts mostly seafood dishes), but also many of your *confrères* there will be French-or-Dutch-speaking, cigarette-smoking locals. You might even witness a couple of elderly Belgian ladies quibble with the chef. Granted, this authenticity comes at a bit of a price; the *Moules-frites* run up to €19 and beer is a couple of euros more expensive than at bars even a few blocks away. But if you're looking for a warm, eminently quaint place to enjoy a Belgian classic, it's hard to beat La Boussole.

i From Place St. Catherine, walk along the Quai au Bois—it will be on your right. Moules Frites €19. Entrées €13-30. Open M-Sa noon-3pm, 6pm-11:30pm.

PEK 47 $
Rue Marché aux Poulets 47   ☎02 513 02 87 www.facebook.com/peckbxl

Gird your loins here, kids. That evil, gentrified hipsterism you so desperately tried to leave behind in the United States knows a new name: delicious Belgian brunch and lunch. Pek 47, with its cutesy posters promising food "made with love" and drinks served in Mason jars with green- and white-striped straws feels more Brooklyn than Brussels. The poached eggs served on crispy waffles, maybe topped with smoked salmon or Belgian-style bacon, on the other hand, will make you glad that you crossed the Atlantic Ocean. Don't be afraid to pair the brunch with a mimosa or Bloody Mary for some hair-of-the-dog goodness. Beyond the all-day brunch offerings (up to €12), Pek 47 is also home to solid sandwich and salad options for reasonable prices.

i From la Bourse, walk left down Boulevard Anspach. Take a right on Marché aux Poulets—it will be on your right. Sandwiches €8-11. Brunch €11-13. Open M-Th 7:30am-9pm, F 7:30am-10pm, Sa 9am-10pm, Su 9am-9pm.

FRITERIE TABORA $
Rue de Tabora 2   ☎02 514 92 14

It's a common misconception that french fries are, in fact, French. While it's a historical toss-up for the origins of this mystical meal (think Indiana Jones,

brussels

but more deep friers), fries have become a way of life in Belgium. These home-grown heroes are everywhere in Brussels; *friteries* cover the streets like the mayonnaise slathered over your fries at Friterie Tabora, one of central Brussels' best. Humbler in size and stature than some of the neighborhood's more gaudy and greasy joints, Tabora combines the speed and ease of fried food with the flavor and care of a local speciality. Only €3 for a mound of fries cradled in a convenient cone, topped with your choice of sauce (mayonnaise, not ketchup, is the Belgian way) makes for a savory snack or, for the starving artists (read: backpackers) out there, a quick lunch or light dinner.

i *From la Bourse, walk left down Boulevard Anspach. Take a right onto Marché aux Poulets—it will be on your right. Fries with sauce €3. Open M-Sa 11am-6am, Su 11am-midnight.*

MOKAFÉ $

Galerie du Roi 9 ☎02 511 78 70

Wandering for waffles? Maybe something a little more refined than the dime-a-dozen and suspiciously quick-to-order ones that line Brussels's city streets? Tucked in the Galérie Royal, Mokafé provides all of that high-class Belgian charm for only a portion of the price. Oh, and the waffles—layered with fresh fruits and powdered sugar—are killer. Mokafé is clean and crisp in both food offerings and architectural design, making it easy to enjoy a cheap brunch (waffle €4) and the famous shopping arcade it calls home. Don't expect too much chocolate sauce here, though, as Mokafé will have you feeling more like an early 20th-century Zeppelin air traveller than a humble backpacker.

i *Right in the heart of Galérie Royal. Open Tu-Su 9am-11pm.*

DE PISTOLEI $

Rue de la Madeleine 5 ☎02 502 95 02 http://depistolei.be/fr

Need a break from the seemingly endless mounds of waffles and fries that define Belgian cuisine? Need protein to fuel your adventures? De Pistolei, with fresh bread and a host of cheap sandwich options (With meat! Made from real dead animals! With protein!), makes for a good lunchtime stop. Options range from pressed sandwiches and omelettes, to baguettes laden with luscious Italian meats. (Did we mention they have meat? For cheap!) Not a far stroll from La Grand Place or Le Manneken Pis, De Pistolei is also lucky enough to call several *frites* and waffle shops its neighbors. If you're missing home and want to let your inner American loose, you can easily combo that scrumptious meat-'n-bread mix with some fried potatoes.

i *From Le Grand Place, head onto Rue de Colline and take a right. Hug marché aux herbes until you come near Place d'Espagne—de Pistolei will be on your right. Lunchtime sandwich €5. Open daily 7am-7pm.*

NIGHTLIFE

DÉLIRIUM CAFÉ

Impasse de la Fidelitié 4 ☎02 514 44 34 www.deliriumcafe.be/

Délirium Café's name is both entirely misleading and completely accurate. First, it is in no way a "cafe." A three-story, multi-building complex wedged into the center of Brussels, Délirium is more like a European frat house—vomiting 20 year-olds and all—than a *petit café* out of a Hemingway novel. As goes without saying, Délirium can be, well, delirious. It boasts more than 3000 beers on its menu (the café earned a spot in the *2004 Guiness Book of World Records* for its enormous selection). The sprawling, fluid setup gives it a lively, if rowdy, feel. Travellers from all over Europe (not to mention whole classes of displaced fraternity brothers) fill this place right on up on weekend nights. It can take a bit of haggling, yelling, and waiting to put in an order. Boisterous beer bartering has its upsides, though. You'll hear plenty of other Americans yelling

how belgians drink beer

Beer in Brussels, and Belgium at large, is a big Flemish deal. You might know as much from that Stella Artois you swiped at your last formal. But even a Stella Artois—as refreshing as it is compared to gargling down Keystone Light through a raggedy, key-cut hole at the bottom of the can—cannot compare to the beer you'll spend time (and money, maybe too much) drinking in Brussels.

There are so many different Belgian beers that even if you were to try a new one with every drink, you'd only be sipping the head of the country's selection. Almost all of these beers are brewed locally, making the micro-brew movement in the United States the equivalent of what Belgian brewing was in, say, the 17th century. This is serious, historical business.

Consider *Trappiste* (Trappist) beers. Six different brands of beer that range from blondes to ambers to darks earn their common name from a once-practical, now-awesome historical fact: monks brewing beers in their monasteries. They did this both to make money to support themselves and to give the poor Belgians something reliable (and clean) to drink. Jesus didn't turn water into beer, so Belgian monks did it for him. Any Trappist beer you order in Brussels is straight from one of the country's six official beer monasteries, where monks (yes, beer monks) brew these highly alcoholic beverages. People who consider themselves servants of the Almighty spend their days brewing these beers. Think about it.

Then there are the glasses. Like Guinness at most bars you've been to, every beer in Belgium comes with its own branded, individual glass. Again, this is serious business; most Belgians will hesitate to drink a beer that doesn't come in the brewery's official glass. From wide tulips, to long flutes, to odd orbs, these are smaller than pints and serve a few purposes. First, they look damn cool. Their smaller size and thicker glass also helps the beer stay cold against the heat of your hand because everyone, and especially Belgians, hate warm beer. Sometimes, the long winding or really wide-set glasses help some sort of mysterious chemical, aerating process occur in the beer, but this isn't high-school chemistry class.

Even with the dozens of different glasses and god-brews, drinking beer in Brussels doesn't always have to be something out of an episode of Anthony Bourdain. Cheap beers like Maes and Jupilers are very drinkable and cheap. But if you're going to be a beer snob somewhere, best do it in Brussels. You'll practically be performing one of the sacraments.

brussels

for their beer, and, before you know it, you'll be buying each other rounds as you wade through Délirum's bars within the bar. Délirium is a good place to start, finish, or forget about a night out in Brussels.

i From Place de Bouchere, take a left down Rue L'Ecuyer. Take a right onto Rue de la Fourche and then a left onto Rue de Bouchers. Beer prices vary widely but start at €3. Open M-Sa 10am-4am, Su 10am-2am.

COASTER

Rue des Riches Claires, 28   ☎048 559 06 65 www.facebook.com/CoasterBrussels/

A hybrid between a cocktail bar and a club, Coaster offers a great, if slightly more pricey, selection of cocktails and mixed drinks—a comparative rarity in a country where people's idea of hard alcohol is, well, to keep strengthening the beer. Live and local DJs will also set up shop not too far from the bar in

top 5 beers to try in brussels

Beer is a big deal in Brussels. Don't know a Stella from a Chimay? We didn't either. Here are a few beers to try as you dive into Belgium's famed breweries.

LEFFE BLONDE. Didn't think beer could taste sweet after all of that PBR? Think again. One of Belgium's many "blonde" beers, Leffe will leave you with a sugary aftertaste, believe it or not.

DUVEL. One of the most common "amber" beers you'll find around the city, Duvel packs a bit of a punch, boasting roughly double the amount of alcohol you're used to in American beers. Still, this is a very drinkable—and a very Belgian—beer to enjoy as you begin your stay in the city.

KRIEK CHERRY. This one's a "lambic" beer, meaning it comes from B-town itself. It tastes more like wine than any brew you've ever come across. This one's almost worth it just for the cool red tint, not to mention the smooth, fruity feel.

KWAK. Served in an cone-shaped glass that descends into an orb, Kwak requires a wooden stand for proper consumption. Another "amber," you'll barely notice you drank your Kwak before it's gone.

ROCHEFORT 8. One of Belgium's Trappist beers, Rochefort 8 (huit!) is almost a religious experience. Strong and smooth, a few of these will do you for the night.

Coaster, so it's a great spot for that mid-night sway (or flail, or spasm) as you sip a gin and tonic. Between the DJ, dancing, and drinking, though, Coaster can get a bit crowded. But a few 2-in-1 specials, pounding music, and awkward dance moves make Coaster well worth the visit.

i From the front of La Bourse, take a right down Boulevard Anspach. Walk two blocks and then turn right onto Rue de Riches Claires. Coaster will be on your right. M-W 5:30pm-1:30am, Th 5:30pm-2:30am, F-Sa 5:30pm-3:30am.

GOUPIL LE FOL
Rue de la Violette 22 ☎02 511 13 96 www.goupillefol.com/

Looking for a low-key break from some of Brussels's more garrulous and grain-heavy night offerings? Swing by Goupil Le Fol for cheap, fruity wine (glass €1), soothing French music, and an underground ambiance that's a blend between the break-up scene from the last B-list rom-com you saw and the opium den where you spent most of your spring-break trip in Thailand. Vinyl records and posters from 20th-century French and Belgian concerts adorn the walls, lit solely by red candles placed on every table. Wine, soaring French couplets, and spacious leather seats are well-known aphrodisiacs, so you may catch a couple making out in the corner of this haunt. (Cool it with the tongue there, buddy.) Still, the cavernous, convivial vibe here and the tasty wine offerings are enough to earn Goupil Le Fol a spot on any night tour of Brussels.

i From Le Mannekin Pis, take a left down Rue de l'Etuve. Walk two blocks and then take a right onto Rue de la Violette; it will be on your right. Open M 4pm-2am, Tu-Sa 4pm-3am; Su 4pm-2am.

CAFÉ LE COQ
Rue Auguste Orts 14 ☎02 514 24 14 www.facebook.com/CafeLeCoq

Roosted only a couple of blocks away from Le Grand Place, Le Coq is just the place if you're looking for a more low-key, inexpensive way to sample some of Belgium's famed brews. Locals and tourists alike spill into this small bar with a beer selection and Dutch-language menu that give it that Flanders feel. Le Coq may not be the spot if you're looking to go crazy on a Saturday night; still, it's

belgium

relatively cheap beer, warm ambiance, and Wi-Fi included make it a great bar to start off a more lively night on the town or cap off a pleasant dinner at one of the area's myriad restaurants.

i From Le Grand Place, walk down Rue de Pierres, take a right onto Boulevard Anspach, and then a left onto Rue August Orts; it is right in front of La Bourse. Beer €2-5. Open M-Th noon-2am; F-Sa noon-4am, Su 4pm-2am.

ESSENTIALS
Practicalities

- **TOURIST OFFICES: Brussel's main office** sits right in La Grand Place. Multilingual guides there provide maps, offer wisdom, and sell the Brussels Card, a pass that gives you free or discounted access to a host of the city's museums, public transport, and restaurants. (24hr. card €2. 48hr. card €30. 72hr. card €38. Open daily 9am-6pm.) Also check out the USE-IT map and office, which are geared toward student travellers and beat out even the most knowledgeable hostel owner for tips.

- **CURRENCY EXCHANGE: DME Change**. (2 locations near la Bourse: Boulevard Adolphe Max 11 and Rue Marché aux Herbes 23. www.dmechange.be)

- **INTERNET:** Most restaurants and cafes in the center of Brussels offer Wi-Fi. You're guaranteed to find it at McDonald's and Quick Burger.

- **POST OFFICES:** (1 Boulevard Anspach. Open M-F 8:30am-6pm, Su 10am-6pm.)

- **POSTAL CODE:** 1000

Emergency

- **EMERGENCY:** ☎100 for an ambulance; ☎101 for police.

- **LATE-NIGHT PHARMACIES:** Small green crosses demarcate most pharmacies in the city; visit www.servicedegarde.be to find the nearest open one.

- **POLICE: Headquarters**. (Rue du Marché Chabon 30 ☎02 279 79 79)

- **HOSPITALS/MEDICAL SERVICES:** The Saint-Pierre University Hospital has two locations. **Saint-Pierre University Hospital–Site César de Paepe** is a 10min. walk from the Grand Place. (11 rue des Alexiens ☎02 506 71 11. www.stpierre-bru.be. M: Bourges. From the Grand Place, exit through the southernmost corner of the square and turn left onto rue des Alexiens.) **Saint-Pierre University Hospital (International Patients Service)** is to the south. (322 rue Haute ☎02 535 33 17 www.stpierre-bru.be. Tram #3, 4, 33, or 51 to M: Porte de Hal. Head south on rue Haute. Open 24hr.)

Getting There
By Plane

The **Brussels airport** (BRU ☎090 07 00 00 www.brusselsairport.be) is 14km from the city center. Trains run between the airport and Gare du Midi every 20min. (€6-7 max; 5am-midnight). STIB bus #12 runs until 8pm, later on weekends and public holidays; bus #21 runs every 30min. (5am-11pm, until midnight during the summer). **Brussels South Charleroi Airport** (CRL ☎090 20 24 90 www.charleroi-airport.com) is a budget airline hub 45km south of Brussels. A shuttle runs from the airport to Gare du Midi. (€13, round-trip €22. Every 30min.)

By Train

Brussels has three main train stations: **Gare du Midi, Gare Centrale,** and **Gare du Nord.** All international trains stop at Gare du Midi, and most stop at Gare Centrale and Gare du Nord as well. Gare Centrale is the closest to the center and the Grand Place. Gare du Nord is in the north just past Botanique. Gare du Midi is in the southwest on bd du Midi. Brussels can be reached from Bruges (€12. 30min.), Amsterdam (€43. 3hr.), and Paris (€55-86. 1hr. from M: Midi); trains also run from London (www. eurostar.com €60-240. 2hr.). There are also normal commuter trains that run between Amsterdam and Brussels that you can board without advance booking, but you can (and probably should) book in advance.

Getting Around

Getting around Brussels is cheap and simple on foot, especially in Lower Town. With skinny, winding streets that change names often (and often have two names to begin with), it's easy to get lost. Luckily, it's also easy to get found: look for tall signposts around Lower Town and the major museum districts of Upper Town. These will point you in the direction of major attractions and metro stations and will even suggest whether to walk or take the metro based on how far your destination may be. Cars rule the roads in Brussels, so bikes are only advisable for the truly brave. If you want to bike around Brussels, there are **villo** (bike rental) points located at key locations throughout the city; the first 30min. is free, but you pay incrementally for each 30min. thereafter (www.villo.be).

By Public Transportation

The metro system rings the city, with a main **tram** running vertically through the middle and two other lines running east to west. There are 18 trams in total. The **bus** and tram system connects the various quarters of the city, and night buses service major stops on Friday and Saturday nights every 30min. until 3am. All public transport in Brussels is run by the **Société des Transports Intercommunaux Bruxellois (STIB)**. (☎07 023 20 00 www.stib.be System operates daily 5am-midnight.) The **metro**, tram, and bus all use the same tickets. (€2, purchased inside vehicle €2.50; round-trip €3.50; day pass €6; 10-trip ticket €13.) It's a good idea to pick up a copy of the metro map, which also contains information about transfers and night buses. The map is free and available at ticket counters and at the Gare du Midi.

By Taxi

After the metro stops running, you can call **Taxi Bleus** (☎02 268 00 00), **Taxi Verts** (☎02 349 49 49), **Taxis Oranges** (☎02 349 43 43), **Autolux** (☎02 411 41 42), or **CNTU** (☎02 374 20 20). Official taxi signs are yellow and black. Taxi prices are calculated by distance (€1.66-2.70 per km), plus a fixed base charge (€2.40, at night €4.40). **Collecto** is a shared taxi system that has 200 pickup points in Brussels (☎02 800 36 36 www. collecto.org. €6. 11pm-6am. Call 20min. or more in advance).

bruges

Ah, Bruges. Home to narrow, winding cobblestoned streets; world-renowned, wonderfully preserved medieval buildings; glistening, flowing canals; and neo-noir British crime-comedy films that revolve around characters consuming cocaine and murdering their Irish countrymen under historic lights. Sounds like a tourist destination.

More a spot for the retired couples on that second (or third, or fourth) honeymoon with that second (or third, or fourth) spouse than a hot-spot for the young, Bruges nevertheless provides more than enough quiet, relaxing magic for a traveller of any age. A moat-esque canal circumscribes Bruges's city center, home to only about 25,000 people, making any kind of public transportation unnecessary. Tie up those shoelaces and get ready for just the right amount of walking.

In all its quaint, historic charm, a small city like Bruges can quickly lose the authentic Bruges-ness that first put it on the map. You will probably roll your eyes

get a room!

ST. CHRISTOPHER'S BAUHAU $

Langestraat 133-137 ☎050 34 10 93 www.st-christophers.co.uk/bruges-hostels

While perhaps not as saintly as its chain name suggests, a stay at St. Christopher's in Bruges is pretty damn good. It's a bit outside of the city center and main attractions, but walk five minutes and you're seeing everything Bruges has to offer. Or play it cool and stay at the hostel to enjoy a full-service bar and, for €5, a personal pizza. There will be plenty of people there to join you. Walking tours (including nighttime) and beer tastings are associated with the hostel, one of the two largest in Bruges. This popularity and the general touristy appeals of the city come with some downsides, though. There will be a bit of distance from your dorm to the less-than-clean bathroom. That bar? Yes, there will be drunk Scots yelling from it until 4am every night. Your bed? It will be right above said yelling Scotsman. Still, Wi-Fi included, breakfast, and a clean bed to sleep in usually make for a winning combo.

i From the Koeleweimolen, follow the river along Kruisvest and turn right onto Bapaumestraat. Take a slight right onto Langestraat, and it will be on the right. Wifi. Continental breakfast included. €16-22. Beer bar on the premises.

LYBEER $$

Korte Vuldersstraat 31 ☎050 33 43 55 www.hostellybeer.com/

One of the more activity-based hostels you'll come across in Bruges, Lybeer boasts pub crawls, walking tours, night walking tours, and everything in between. Count on expected and unexpected conveniences, ranging from free coffee to Wi-Fi and laundry. This is Bruges: you'll have an easy time meeting other young people and hanging out in this very clean, pleasant hostel.

i From St. Salvador's Cathedral, walk on Sint-Salvatorskerkhof and continue onto Korte Vuldersstraat; the hostel will be on the left. 8-bed dorms €25; singles €40. Walking tours included. Communal kitchen and common room with beer bar on the premises.

bruges

more than once at the over-the-top horse-drawn carriages, the overpriced waffles, and the long, long lines that make you think more of Barcelona than Belgium.

But it's hard to pollute a sense of place, no matter how many bovine tourists you pack into a city square. Climb the Belfort and the city's sprawling, main plaza, find some peace and quiet in the historic Beguinage, and sample morbid Medieval musings at the Groeningemuseum. When you've just about had it, stroll no more than five minutes from the most touristy of destinations. The same winding, Medieval streets quickly empty into a solitary serenity. (You may even find some windmills! Or sheep!) You'll be thankful you made your way to Bruges.

Easily conquered on a day trip, Bruges also makes for a restful overnight if you want to savor those waffles, sample that chocolate, and sip that Belgian beer.

SIGHTS

⬛ BELFRY

Markt 7 ☎050 44 87 43 http://bezoekers.brugge.be/en/belfort-belfry

In the movie *In Bruges* (which might be this city's biggest contemporary claim to fame, since it's hard to out-fame Colin Farrell), one of the main characters jumps off of the Belfry to his death. If that's not enough seamy intrigue to establish this Medieval guard tower as a must-see, we don't know what would be.

Suffer the slings and arrows of a pretty long line, an €8 ticket, and a 366-step climb to behold the undiscovered country—one of the best views in Belgium. At the top, watch as Bruges's buildings and canals alike ripple out from the city center before lulling into rolling, pastoral fields, and, on a high-visibility day, the North Sea. Enjoy a beautiful view and some of that I-am-just-like-Indiana-Jones-climbing-this-really-old-thing satisfaction but be ready for a potentially tiring ascent and annoying wait.

i *It's an 83-meter tower—just look out from the Markt. €10, under 26 €8. Open daily 9:30am-6pm.*

GROENINGEMUSEUM

Dijfer 12 ☎050 44 87 11 http://bezoekers.brugge.be/nl/groeningemuseum

You probably wouldn't do well during the second coming of Jesus Christ. Seriously: If you have followed half of our advice for the summer, you've engaged in enough hedonistic debauchery in Europe to land you in at least the fifth ring of the inferno. But don't worry: you're not alone. At the Groeningemuseum, you'll have plenty of opportunities to mentally prepare yourself for the torture and despair of the afterlife—and maybe even meet some of your future cellmates. In a collection that is largely Medieval, the Groeningemuseum hosts a series of paintings that will inspire the morbidly curious in just about anyone. (See that little goblin-devil biting that guy's skin off?) That's not all, though; at this museum, a collection of modern Flemish art also adorns the walls in the later exhibits. But the guys getting themselves chopped up remain the highlight, so look forward to that.

i *From the Markt, head southeast and continue onto Wollestraat. Turn right onto Dijver; the museum is on the left. €8, under 26 €6. Open daily 9:30am-5pm.*

FOOD

▨ BOCCA $

Dweersstraat 13 ☎050 61 61 75 www.bocca.be

Seriously, what doesn't get better when you put it in a little portable box? Pizza, Chinese take-out, and, for you Lonely Island fans, even more, can be best enjoyed that way. At Bocca, a cheap lunch stop near the center of Bruges, they've added another item to this list: penne pasta. Bocca serves up small, medium, or large boxes of it layered with tomato, cheese, or any number of sauces. Be ready for a bit of a wait, though: the Bruges locals (yes, we found them!) swarm this place at lunch time, and you might have to walk to a bench with your carb cube.

i *From St. Salvador's Cathedral, walk on Sint-Salvatorskerkhof and then turn left onto Zuidzandstraat. Turn right onto Dweersstraat; it will be on your right. Pasta €4-6. Open M-F 11:30am-8pm, Sa 11:30am-7pm.*

LE LION BELGE $$

Langestraat 123 ☎049 621 02 44 www.lionbelge.eu

At Le Lion Belge, understated is an understatement. Away from the kitsch and crowds in the center of town, the Belgian Lion, one of the up-and-coming lunch and dinner spots in Bruges, doesn't even have a formal menu to its name. You'll have to check the chalkboard and ask your waiter for a translation from the Dutch. A clean, well-lit ambience featuring smooth hardwood floors and bare white walls compliment the low-key vibe. But don't conflate understated with underwhelming: The Flemish food does not disappoint. For about €15, enjoy potatoes, beef, salmon and, of course, some fries in all of your favorite Belgian combinations. Head in early as locals line up for a meal here, leaving the unsuspecting backpacker alone at the bar.

i *From the Koeleweimolen, follow the river along Kruisvest and turn right onto Bapaumestraat. Take a slight right onto Langestraat; it will be on the right. Most entrees €15-20. Open W-Su 11:30am-11pm.*

is that waffle shop a tourist trap?

Let's get something out of the way: waffles in Belgium are probably going to be delicious no matter what. However, if you want to save a few euro and enjoy this classic treat like the locals do, look out for these signs before get ready to dig in.

- **THE WAFFLES COST €6.** While just about every waffle place across Belgium will veer toward a tourist trap, some places take this to a new level. Waffles should be €1-4, depending on the toppings you add. Even €4 for a waffle is pushing the boundaries of sanity and good manners. If you're paying anything more, you're probably being scammed.

- **THEY STICK A LITTLE BELGIAN FLAG IN IT.** Belgian waffles are one of Bruges's main tourist attractions. For many people, this small Medieval city will be the one place in Belgium they bother to visit in their entire lives—so they better get one of those waffles, right? Many money-minded locals understand this, branding their overpriced and underwhelming waffles as a piece of national heritage. Many less-informed tourists will literally eat this up—but you'll know better. If there's a flag in it, it's most likely a trap.

- **THEY WANT YOU TO PUT ICE CREAM, CHOCOLATE, OR FRUIT ON YOUR WAFFLE.** We admit: these toppings do seem delicious to enjoy with a Belgian waffle. But they're also a globalized bastardization of the way a Belgian waffle should be enjoyed: with a little bit of powdered sugar or maybe (just maybe) some whipped cream. Doing otherwise is like putting ketchup on your T-bone steak in Texas or avocado on your sushi roll in Tokyo. Any waffle shop that brags about its smorgasbord of toppings is just pandering to the same Americans who love frappuccinos from Starbucks. Don't play yourself and keep the waffles simple. They're sweet, succulent, and crisp as is.

bruges

OYYA WAFFLES $

Noordzandstraat 1   ☎050 33 32 13 www.oyya.be

When you're in Bruges, you're going to want to get a waffle. But so will every other tourist on the planet, creating a waffle market not unsimilar to the US sub-prime mortgage market circa 2007. You might get ripped off. And that whipped cream? It's a bubble (of air) waiting to burst. Be a responsible waffle buyer and go to Oyya. Instead of the €6 some places have you paying for a less-than-succulent waffle, Oyya will set you up with a crisp helping for €2, which would make any Belgian and prudent financial expert proud. You'll have to pay a bit more for chocolate or cream, but don't worry too much about kickstarting a worldwide financial crisis. Worry instead about whether you want this waffle for breakfast, a snack, or dessert.

i From the Markt, head north on Markt and turn left onto Geldmuntstraat. Continue onto Noordzandstraat; it will be on the left. Waffles and ice cream €2-4. Open daily 11am-10pm.

NIGHTLIFE

▨ LUCIFERNUM

Twijnstraat 6-8   ☎047 635 06 51 www.lucifernum.be/

Freemasonry is weird—that pretty much goes without saying. Freemasonry mixed with a haunted house, mixed with an art gallery, mixed with a Sunday-evening-only bar is, well, really weird. And really, really worth seeing. On Sunday nights, the Lucifernum opens its doors for drinks and an almost-art tour that makes for one hell of a vibe. That is, if its eclectic, charming host Retsin lets you inside. He's known to be a bit picky about who he accepts for the €10 cover.

This spot's got texture, verve, and ambiance that you may not find anywhere else on your European trip, let alone in Bruges.

i From Stadhuis, walk along Burg and onto Hoogstraat. Turn left onto Kelkstraat and then right onto Twijnstraat; it will be on your right. Cover €10. Open Sun 8-11pm.

ROSE RED

Cordoeaniersstraat 16   ☎050 33 90 51 www.cordoeanier.be/en/rosered.php

If you're going to Bruges, odds are that finding that special someone—and getting, eh hem, closer to them—is somewhere on your mind. Odds are that you're going to want to drink excellent Belgian beers under the guidance of an experienced Belgian bartender. And odds are you're going to want to drink this excellent Belgian beer in a classy (but not fancy) deep blue, candlelit ambiance that strikes the balance between romantic and homey. Whether you're with a date, looking for a maybe-date, or just want to sit in a great bar and shoot the shit with a totally (totally) platonic buddy for a few hours, Rose Red has you covered. Try a wine, drink a beer, and snack on some tapas. But don't expect any intense dancing—save that for later.

i From the Markt, continue onto Vlamingstraat and turn right onto Sint-Jansstraat. Turn right onto Sint-Jansplein and right again onto Cordoeaniersstraat; it will be on your left. Tapas €3.50. 4-beer flight €10. Open Tu-Su 11am-midnight.

ESSENTIALS
Practicalities

- **TOURIST OFFICES: The Bruges tourist office** is right in the Markt, near the Historium. (1 Markt. Open daily 10am-5pm.) They also have an installation in the train station. Pick up one of the USE-IT maps for useful tips.

- **CURRENCY EXCHANGE:** There are several exchange offices near the Markt.

- **INTERNET: St. Christopher's Bauhaus** is most reliable for free Wi-Fi. There is also free Wi-Fi in many parts of the city, but don't count on it.

- **POST OFFICES: The Post Office** is in the Markt. (Markt 5. Open M-Sa 9am-6pm).

- **POSTAL CODE:** 8000

Emergency

- **EMERGENCY:** ☎100 for ambulance; ☎101 for police.

- **POLICE:** General telephone number: ☎050 44 88 44.

- **LATE-NIGHT PHARMACIES:** To find which pharmacists are on duty, call: ☎040 61 62.

- **HOSPITALS/MEDICAL SERVICES:** Bruges has three different hospitals; **St.-Jan:** ☎050 45 21 11 **A.Z. St.-Lucas:** ☎050 36 91 11 **St.-Franciscus Xavieruskliniek:** ☎050 47 04 70.

antwerp

Pulling into Antwerp's Central Station gives a pretty decent, if subtle, primer on the city. Right off the train, you enter the boarding area, housed under a sleek, stylish red-steel-glass latticework that arches over in the late 19th-century Art Nouveau style. Sleek turns to slick as you descend down one of the elevators toward the main terminal and tour the impeccably modern, high-functioning parts of the station added in the early 21st century. Entering the main hall, the modern moves to majestic: marble pillars tower up in the style of an Italian palace, an architectural thrust of power from 19th-century merchants who prospered from Antwerp's massive port.

Fashionable, modern, historical, international, and rich in a typically European jumble of historical moments, Antwerp may play second Belgian flute these days to Brussel's international importance. But for all things fun, multicultural, artistic, and, above all, hip, Antwerp is one the most attractive cities on the continent.

Its port-side location has long made Antwerp one of the economic hearts of Europe, pushing Antwerp to become a decidedly multicultural and international city. There are large Turkish, Asian, and Hassidic Jewish populations here, making a tasting tour of Antwerp a small window into the world. They could film most of a James Bond movie here: scenic European setting, then a diamond theft (maybe paired with a boat chase on the river) followed up by a clandestine mission at a glitzy fashion show. Then, exploding trains in one very, very cool train station.

Come to Antwerp and feel the pulse of European culture and art as it melds with the world and its own past. Hit the too-cool-for-you nightlife, laze around by the river, pump yourself up for (and eventually chicken out of) the red light district, sample different cuisines, or pretend to know something about wearing nice clothing.

SIGHTS

Most of what you'll want to see in the city hugs the Schelde. The city center with all of its historical, touristy goodness, as well as many of the best art exhibits, concert venues, and restaurants are only a few blocks up from the river in the northern part of the city. Wandering away from the water will bring you past the Central Station, several of the city's ethnic neighborhoods, and even the Diamond District—one street here accounts for more than 5% of Belgium's entire GDP. Nelly didn't record the music video for his smash hit "Ride Wit Me" in Antwerp, but he very well could have.

MAS—MUSEUM AAN DE STROOM

Hanzestedenplaats 1   ☎03 338 44 00 www.mas.be/en

Towering over Antwerp's city center and the river Schedle like some sort of new-age firehouse, the Museum Aan de Stroom combines quality and quirk as it traces Antwerp's seafaring story and explores pseudo-profundities. (One exhibition is simply titled "Life and Death." Don't ask us). The museum seems to float in the middle of one of the city's docking areas; expect yachts and barges to line your walk up to the entrance. Existential considerations aside, the real reason you should visit is the panorama on the Museum's top floor. Totally free of charge if you don't want to see the museum's actual exhibits, the open-air deck on the top floor gives you a full 360-view of the city's cathedrals, ports, and red-tiled apartments. The museum also offers free coffee, study desks, and massages (and this isn't even the red light district!) to students on one of the top floors. So next time you're studying for finals you can, again, gripe about how the Europeans do everything better. It's also not too far from The Steen if you're in the mood for a Medieval-war fortress. Escalators take you to the top, so ready your sea legs and climb the crow's nest, ye be in Antwerp now!

i From the Steen, take a left onto Jordaenskaai. Take a right onto Sint-Aldegondiskaai when you see water on your right. MAS is the big red building with windows. €10, under 27 €8. Open Tu-Su 10am-5pm. Panorama open Tu-Su 9:30am-10pm.

DE KATHEDRAAL

Groenplaats 21   ☎03 213 99 51 www.dekathedraal.be/en/

Thanks be to God, Antwerp has this dope cathedral with a cool gold clock on it! Alleluia! Technically a work in progress since the 16th century ("we'll get around to that second tower sometime soon"), this spired place of workshop boasts both Gothic good looks and a collection of Baroque art. While just watching the sunlight hit the gray facade from Groenplaats will inspire the fear of some-thing-or-other in you, the inside may also merit a pilgrimage, even if it is €4. Some of Peter Paul Rubens's best work hangs here and the cool, cavernous cathedral is the perfect way to prepare your state of mind for some almighty moves on the dance floor. Just take King David's word for it. You'll also be right next to just about every restaurant, bar, and tourist site in the city if you swing by here—be sure to walk a block over to the Stadhuis for the fountain and flags.

i Right in front of you at Groenplaats—walk toward the big church tower. €6, students €4. Open M-F 10am-5pm, Sa 10am-3pm, Su 1-4pm.

get a room!

ANTWERP STUDENT HOSTEL $$

Italiëlei 237-239 ☎03 500 88 17 www.antwerpstudenthostel.com/

While just about every Antwerp hostel lacks a creative or sophisticated name, they get the job done. Antwerp Student Hostel is no exception. Students come here to enjoy a clean, well-prepared stay. Not that it doesn't make attempts at spunk and flare. There's a small garden area, plus you can count on Wi-Fi included, breakfast, laundry, and the rest. That said, this won't be the cheapest place you can find in Antwerp; it's about €28 euro for a night.

i From Centraal Station, take a left onto Gemeentestraat. Continue for a few blocks until you take a right onto Italiëlei; the hostel will be on your right. Wi-Fi. Breakfast included. Dorms €28. Laundry on the premises.

ANTWERP CENTRAL YOUTH HOSTEL $$

Bogaardestraat 1 ☎03 234 03 14

Probably the best-located hostel in the city, Antwerp Central Youth Hostel sits just a few blocks away from Groeenplaats, the Schelde, and many of Antwerp's largest tourist attractions. Concrete floors and black seating give this rather large hostel a very modern, pseudo-fashionable feel that fits right into the rest of Antwerp. You'll enjoy many of the expected amenities: Wi-Fi and breakfast included, an in-house bar, etc. But all of this comes at a bit of an elevated price. Be ready to pay about €10 more for a night here than you would at other locations in the city.

i From Groenplaats, walk down Nationalestraat. After several blocks, take a left onto Sint-Antoniusstraat; it will be on the square on your right. Wi-Fi. Breakfast included. €28.

ANTWERP BACKPACKERS HOSTEL $

Kattenberg 110 ☎047 357 01 66 www.abhostel.com/

Getting to this spot is a bit of a hike, even for "backpackers." At about a 20min. walk from the Central Station and a 40min. walk from many of the main tourist attractions, you should probably try renting a bike during your stay here. Only a few good restaurants call this hostel its neighbor, and you didn't come to Antwerp to eat in residential areas. That said, it is one of the cheapest places to stay in the city (less than €20 per night), and it has everything you would want in a hostel: Wi-Fi and breakfast included, as well as laundry facilities. Plus, the staff is more cool than corporate. You might just hear awesome war stories or develop a star-crossed romantic tryst with one of the young employees (we seemed to have witnessed this).

i From Sint-Willibrordus church, turn onto Lammekenstraat. Continue down this street and then snake onto Laar. Continue onto Kattenberg; the hostel will be on your right after a couple of blocks. Wi-Fi. Breakfast included. €20. Laundry facilities on the premises.

SINT-ANNATUNNEL AND DE ZWARTE PANTER CONTEMPORARY ART GALLERY

You shall not pass. Well, actually, you can go. Descend down under the Schelde through the Sint-Anna tunnell and discover that—surprise!—there's something on that other side. A relic of World War II, this fluorescently-lit, white-panelled tunnel that's home to bikers and pedestrians will let you live out most of your *Star Wars* dreams. Once you've escaped the Death Star, you'll enjoy comfortable rolling green lawns, a delicious fries stand, and a beautiful view of the city. It's a great place for a nap or a picnic. Once you head back to the other side of the river, check out De Zwarte Panter, a free contemporary art gallery that's tucked just beyond the entrance to the tunnel, back on the Antwerp side of the river.

i From Groenplaats, walk down Nationalestraat and take a right onto Steenhouwersvest. Entrance to the tunnel will be in front of you after 3 blocks—De Zwarte Panter will be to your right.

FOOD

DE ARME DUIVEL $$

Armedduivelstraat 1   ☎03 232 28 98 www.armeduivel.be/

Stitched right into the center of high fashion in Antwerp, De Arme Duivel offers delicious Belgian cuisine (we swear it exists) for the price of, like, a pair of socks at one of the neighboring retail shops. Crisp white-and-black design adorns the restaurant's interior and sleek black chairs populate the outdoor terrace, giving it that chic look that you'll see regularly around these parts. While your sweaty T-shirt and banged-up sneakers might mark you as the odd one out among the oh-so-fashionable crowd here, the €15 *stoofvleees* (beef stew) with fries is delicious. After you've mopped up that last bit of savory stew with a thick-cut potato slice, check out Rubens House or window shop and remind yourself of just how pointless fashion is. You smell great, trust us.

i From Centraal Station, walk down De Kyserlei, continue onto Leystraat and then Meir. Take a left onto Wapper and then a right onto Hopland; it will be on your right. Most entrees €15-20. Open M-Sa noon-10pm.

GRINGO'S CANTINA $

Ernest van Dijckkaai 24   ☎03 232 63 84

Yes, we know. You didn't come to Belgium to eat Mexican food. But Antwerp being Antwerp, with all its international flare, and Belgium being Belgium, with its sparse cuisine (fries and waffles only get you so far), Gringo's Cantina is well worth the stop. Nestled along the Schelde, Gringo's serves up delicious quesadillas and tacos that taste better than most Mexican food you'll eat back home, even if you are several thousand more miles away from Mexico itself. Locals melt together with tourists in the fairly small space to give Gringo's that it's-a-Tuesday-and-I-really-need-a-taco feel you know so well. Don't expect many of Belgium's best beers here, though. Corona and Desperados run to €4 a piece, which can add up when the quesadilla plates cost around €15. Or, pair that cheesy goodness with one of the Cantina's margaritas for €6-8.

i From the Steen, walk south along Enrest van Dijckkaii; it will be on your right. Tacos €8-11. Quesadilla plates €15. Beer €4. Margaritas €6-8. Open W-Su 6-11pm.

CAFÉ CAMINO $

Vrijdagmarkt 5   ☎03 289 91 97 www.cafecamino.be/

Again, Antwerp, home to one of the largest ports in Europe, is an international, multicultural city, and its cuisine offerings reflect just that. Watch as traditional European cuisine mashes and melds with the world's flavors. At Café Camino, sample savory, even sweet Vietnamese pork-belly spread over rice bowls and banh mi sandwiches as you gaze across a cobblestoned, postcard-perfect Belgian square. Outdoor seating might be competitive to snag, as some of the city's most well-dressed young professionals flock here for the relatively cheap and enormously delicious lunch. (Why does everyone wear so much black? Is this a Rolling Stones music video?) If you have to, take it to go and sit on one of the square's many benches, enjoy your sandwich, and shed a few tears that the nearby printing museum, which traces the history of Antwerp's printing industry since the 16th century, is closed for the summer.

i From Groenplaats, take a right onto Reydnerstraat and a left onto Leuwenstraat after a block. It will be in the square on your right. Sandwiches start at €9. Rice bowl €14. Open Tu-Su noon-6pm.

BELMONDO $

Zwaluwstraat 69   ☎049 782 00 62 www.facebook.com/belmondo.antwerpen

You are honor-bound not to go to Starbucks while you seek personal transcendence in Europe. That said, you may still want good coffee and comfortable leather chairs. Why not throw in tasty, affordable lunch sandwiches not too far from the heart of Antwerp? Check out Belmondo. The food runs to around €10, and you can enjoy a pretty large selection of both alcoholic and caffeinated beverages for a few euro more. Plus, there are books everywhere. Books are supposed to be good for you, right?

i From Groenplaats, walk down Zwaluwstraat. It will be on your right. Sandwiches €8-10. Open Tu-W 8am-7pm, Th-Sa 8am-10pm, Su 8am-7pm.

NIGHTLIFE

CARGO ZOMERBAR
Viaduct-Dam 64-80   http://cargozomerbar.be/

Hips tired from all those attempts at dancing? Head to Cargo Zomerbar (where there are not, unfortunately, any zombies) for lawn chairs and drinks in the north of Antwerp. Sure, you might trade in a bit of that heart-of-Antwerpian adventure when you ride your city bike all the way up here, but some good beer and a lush lawn are worth it. If you come by early enough, food will still be on the menu. Once again, pizza, beer, and grass are hard to beat. Maybe you'll finally be able to charm a local with your deep knowledge of European geopolitics. How about that whole Greece thing? Crazy, right?

i From Museum aan de Stroom, continue right onto Godefriduskaii, away from the Schelde. Take a left onto Entrepotkaai. Snake along that until you take a right onto Londenstraat. You'll open up into the park and Cargo Zomerbar. Pizza €10. Tapas €6. Beer €3. Open daily 10am-midnight.

CAFÉ D'ANVERS
Verversrui 15   ☎03 226 38 70 www.cafedanvers.com

If you do want to seek out a totally insane (and we mean it) Antwerpian adventure, Café D'Anvers is the place. One of the most talked about, if not attended, clubs in the city, Café D'Anvers is about as lively as nightlife will get here, which is probably for the best. DJs from across Europe visit the club throughout the year (not that you'll recognize many of them, unless you are one of those "music people"), though you'll have the choice between the main room and the balcony every night. Thursdays are free for students, so expect a bunch of 16-year-olds. Not that they'll show up early—this place doesn't really get started until 1 or 2am—and not that they sour an otherwise very good time. Rest assured: it's 18 and over on Fridays and Saturdays.

i From Museum aan de Stroom, walk down Van Schoonbekeplein. Fork left onto Falconplein and then take a right onto Vervesrui. It will be on your right. Open Th 11pm-6am, Fri-Sa 11pm-7:30am. Prices depend on DJ; check website.

DE MUZE
Melkmarkt 15   ☎03 226 01 26 http://jazzmuze.be/

With "JAZZCAFÉ" stamped across its green awning, De Muze is about as transparent as the Nixon administration was opaque during the Watergate scandal. Come here for live jazz music and—you guessed it—drinks! Antwerp is supposed to be a hip city, what with all of this clothing nonsense, but that hipness can sometimes teeter on the edge of stuffy, reserved, or even unwelcoming, especially to the average American backpacker. De Muze takes the best of the cultured chic and rips off the proverbial leather jacket, creating a chill, interesting, and jazzy vibe that goes right along with some smooth Belgian beer. Social but not quite sexy, De Muze is a good spot for a night on the town without all of that sweat and leather.

i *From Stadhuis, walk through the Grote Mark. Continue onto Kassrui and take a right onto Korte Koepoortstraat. It will be on your right. Open M-F 11am-1am, Sa-Su 11am-3am.*

ESSENTIALS

Practicalities

- **TOURIST OFFICES: The Antwerp City Tourist Office** should easily be one of your first stops to the city. Tucked right near Stadhuis and De Kathedraal, it's a convenient place to check-in on your first day. Expect free maps and helpful, multilingual guides. Make sure to grab one of the free USE-IT maps; locals gear them toward the young, hip traveller, so you'll fit right in. (Grote Markt 13. Open M-Sa 9am-4:45pm.)

- **CURRENCY EXCHANGE: Travelex** will be just on your left as you come out of Centraal station. (Koningin Astridplein 29 ☎03 226 29 53. Open 6am-10:30pm.)

- **INTERNET:** Most restaurants and coffee shops have free Wi-Fi. A guarantee is **Belhuis Atlas** (Huikstraat 3. Open M 8am-1pm, W-Su 8am-1pm.)

- **POST OFFICES:** You're most convenient bet will be **BPost Postkantoor Centraal**, also right near Centraal station. (Quellinstraat 6, 2018 Antwerpen. Open M-F 9am-6pm, Sa 9am-12:30pm.)

- **POSTAL CODE:** 2000

Emergency

- **EMERGENCY:** ☎100 for ambulance; ☎101 for police.

- **POLICE: Lokale Politie Antwerpen.** (Oudaan 5 ☎03 338 57 11. Open 24hr.)

- **LATE-NIGHT PHARMACIES:** These stay open late on a rotating business; check www.service-degarde.be/ or call ☎09 001 05 00 to find the nearest late-night offering.

- **HOSPITALS/MEDICAL SERVICES: ZNA St. Elisabeth** has got you covered, if you unfortunately need it It's right near the city center. (Leopoldstraat 26, ☎03 234 41 11)

Getting Around

Bike

Biking around Antwerp using a **Velo Antwerpen** bike is one of the cheapest and most fun ways to get around the city. The bike racks are basically everywhere. If you return your bike within 30min., you don't have to pay any extra; you'll rack up additional fees for longer rides. (Day pass €3.80. Week pass €9.00.)

Public Transportation

Antwerp is home to both a **tram** and **bus** system, but it's quite expensive. You can buy tickets on the **train** or at Centraal station for one of the longer-term passes. (60min. pass €3. Day pass €5.)

antwerp

ghent

Part college town, part Medieval dreamland, Ghent is a blend of young and old in more ways than one. In this small city in West Flanders, college kids commingle with gray-haired octogenarians on narrow cobblestoned streets, across winding waterways, and amid a millennium of history. Climb the heights of one the city's many stone towers, plumb the depths of its Medieval fortifications, and flirt with the youngsters all in just a few hours. The traveller crowd seems to be more middle-aged-to-elderly history buffs rather than ruffian ramblers. Still, the college part of town, away from the cozy city center, could make just about anyone feel young again. Stretched north to south along its canals, with many of the main tourist attractions and eateries banked along the water, Ghent is more charm than glamour—except, maybe, when the sun goes down and the city's award-winning light scheme illuminates the Gothic surroundings.

SIGHTS

BELFORT

Sint-Baafsplain ☎09 233 39 54 www.belfortgent.be/engels/homeen.html

Medieval towers are to Ghent what drunk Snapchats are to your special someone back home: They are so essential to its character that sometimes you wonder if you should be looking for something more. But unlike those inebriated attempts at suave selfies, these towers are actually worth looking at more closely. The largest of these towers, the Belfort, once served as Ghent's watchtower against invaders. Its call of duty these days is much less grandiose—to be something on which tourists can climb and take pictures for only a few euro. The panorama is high enough that you'll be able to snap a few shots from the top but not so high that you'll feel like you are a looking at a Google Maps printout. In short, it's affordable, it's beautiful, and it's good exercise.

i Look for the 91m bell tower in between Sint-Niklaaskerk and Sint-Baafskathedral. €8, age 19-25 €2.70. Open daily 10am-6pm.

GRAVENSTEEN

Sint-Veerleplein 11 ☎09 225 93 06 http://gravensteen.stad.gent/en

Castles are objectively cool. They're big, authoritative, very old, and home to dungeons. You won't have seen Flanders (and Medieval Flanders, at that) unless you enter at least one dark place of torture. For the real Flanders deal, head to Gravensteen, one of Ghent's more well-known and grandiose claims to fame. Snake through Medieval chambers and thank your lucky stars you weren't born in the Middle Ages: the spikes on that choker are no fashion statement. Be wary, though. Like the taxes the Flemish royalty who lived in this castle used to charge on the area's peasants, a visit to this castle can be a little expensive. But cool-ass castles, especially with dungeons, aren't a dime a dozen.

i It's a huge, moated castle where the Lieve and Leie rivers converge. €10, age 19-26 €6. Open daily summer 10am-6pm; winter 9am-5pm.

STAM

Godshuizenlaan 2 ☎09 267 14 00 www.stamgent.be/en/visit/info

It might be hard to avoid learning about just how old and Medieval this city is. But that doesn't mean your education has to be as somniferous as the content it covers. And so we have STAM, Ghent's city museum. In an exhibit that tours through modern, multimedia map layouts and abbeys from the Middle Ages, STAM manages to strike just the right pace as it traces centuries of (occasionally less-than-thrilling) history. The museum focuses almost exclusively on the Middle Ages. Given that the most a museum dedicated to the city of Ghent can say about the 19th century is that "industrialization was a big deal," that's probably for the best.

i *From the Vooruit, walk along Bagattenstraat and turn left onto Nederkouter. Take a quick right onto Verlorenkost and then a left onto Albert Baertsoenkaai. Keep walking until you get to God-shuizenlaan/R40; take a right and the museum is on the right. €8, age 19-25 €2. Open Tu-Su 10am-6pm.*

FOOD

◪ GOK II $

Sleepstraat 65/A   ☎ 09 223 38 98 www.gok2.be

You've probably seen a lot of Turkish food—probably in the form of kebap shops—around Ghent and, for that matter, Belgium. While that penchant for meaty, greasy goodness has had you munching on some pitas more than a few times (especially after a certain hour of night), Turkish food in Ghent merits a more serious and savory examination. Check out Gok II, located right in the heart of Ghent's largely Turkish neighborhood, for a more substantive sampling. Turkish pizzas layered with Mediterranean-style meats abound here, and for a modest price. Expect to spend about €10 for a full platter of pizza. Just when you are beginning to forget on which line of longitude you stand, a full Belgian beer selection reminds you that the pleasure of beer and pizza are, after all, universal.

i *From the Gravensteen, take a left onto Geldmunt and then a right onto Lange Steenstraat. Keep going straight onto Grauwpoort, then Sleepstraat; the restaurant will be on your left. Piz-za, barbecued meats, Turkish specialties €10. Open Tu-F 11:30am-2:30pm and 5-11pm, Sa-Su 11:30am-midnight.*

DE LIEVE $$

Sint-Margrietstraat 1   ☎09 223 29 47 www.eetkaffee-delieve.be

Chances are, you don't have a Belgian grandmother. Even if you did, and even if she had an army of Belgian grandmothers behind her, her home-cooked national specialties still wouldn't best those of De Lieve. Packed away into Ghent's Me-dieval, cobblestoned corners, this spot boasts a menu of Belgian classics. Prices run €15-20. Try making a reservation or showing up early, though; locals crowd this place and will have you sitting at the bar alone. Be the proverbial Little Red Riding Hood and hustle along to grandma's—kind of.

i *From the Gravensteen, turn left onto Geldmunt and continue onto Sint-Margrietstraat; the restaurant will be on your left. Stews, seafood, other Flemish fare €15-20. Open daily 11am-3pm and 5:30-10 pm.*

NIGHTLIFE

◪ HOT CLUB DE GANDE

Groentenmarkt 15b   ☎09 223 29 47 www.hotclub.gent

Sure, self-professed "hot clubs" merit a certain amount of skepticism. It's hard to believe that anything making so blatant a claim for itself can actually deliver. But this is Belgium, and Hot Club de Gande certainly does. This is because Hot Club de Gande is neither a club nor particularly hot. Instead, it's an enormously pleasant, lively, and harmonious jazz club that boasts live performances five times a week. Forget your shots of vodka; Hotel de Gande will have you stroking your almost-beard and thinking about which flannel you should buy when you get back stateside. More funky than fratty, this is a mature, laid-back break from some of the more high-energy student haunts of the city.

i *From the Gravensteen, turn left onto Geldmunt and continue onto Kleine Vismarkt. Keep going until you get to Groentenmarkt; the club will be on the left. Drinks €8. Open M-Sa 3pm-3am, Su 3pm-midnight.*

get a room!

BACKSTAY HOSTEL $$

Sint-Pietersnieuwstraat 128 ☎09 395 96 60 www.backstayhostels.com

Backstay may be a bit outside of Ghent's be-towered center, but worry not: you're that much closer to Overpoortstrat and giving Ghent the Old College Try. With more convenient offerings than your typical hostel, including a full restaurant and bar, Backstay is well worth an overnight. Sleek, modern decor is the name of the game here for a modest price.

i *From the Capitole Gent, head north on Graaf van Vlaanderenplein and turn left onto Woodrow Wilsonplein. Continue onto Lammerstraat and turn left onto Sint-Pietersnieuwstraat; the hostel will be on the right. Wi-Fi. Breakfast included. Mixed dorm €20-26.*

UPPELINK HOSTEL ST. MICHEL $

Sint-Michielshelling 21 ☎09 279 44 77 www.hosteluppelink.com/en/Home/Location

We g(h)e(n)t it: Ghent is an old place. Just about every building in town likes to remind you of this with a date stamp—in stone, mind you—of its creation. And Hostel Uppelink, while it caters to a much younger crowd, is no exception, flaunting its 17th-century inception with a stamp on its front facade. It makes sense, too. This hostel is so close to Medieval Ghent that one expects it has to be a part of it. The historic charm, including high-arched ceiling and a homey wood-panelled common room, doesn't distract or detract from this hostel's modern and practical appeal. For about €20 a night, count on free Wi-Fi, laundry services, a kitchen, free walking tours, a bar, and even kayak rentals.

i *From the City Pavilion, head west onto Poeljemarkt and continue onto Goudenleeuw-plein and then Klein Turkije. Turn left onto Korenmarkt and right onto Sint-Michielshelling; the hostel will be on your right. Wi-Fi. Mixed dorm €16-20. Kitchen and a bar on the premises.*

OVERPOORTSTRAAT

Frat row may seem like an exclusively American phenomenon, and, to a certain extent, it is. Where else can you find entire streets dedicated to the social group iconography of 20-year-olds? In Ghent, it appears. Home to tens of thousands of college students, the city has taken a page out of the American quarantine-the-partying-young-people-into-one-place playbook. Which gives us Overpoortstraat, a few-block stretch replete with student bars, clubs, a bowling alley/bar combo, and a dozen kebap shops. So relive your glory days; you'll easily spend your night on just this one street cavorting with Belgian frat boys (these actually do exist). Because it's a student area, these places can only charge so much—textbooks are expensive everywhere, right?

i *Runs from Normaalschoolstraat in the north to St. Peter's Square in the south. Bars and clubs vary, but many have happy hour specials.*

ESSENTIALS
Practicalities

- **TOURIST OFFICES:** The **tourist office** is right near the Gravensteen. (Sint-Veerleplein 5. Open daily 9:30am-6:30pm.)

- **CURRENCY EXCHANGE: Goffin Change.** (Henegouwenstraat 27. Open M-F 9:15am-5:45pm, Sa 10am-4:30pm.)

- **INTERNET:** There are plenty of places all over the city where you should be able to catch some Wi-Fi, but if you want a more standard internet cafe experience, head to **OutPost Gamecenter Gent.** (Ottergemsesteenweg 13. Open daily 11:30am-3am.)
- **POST OFFICES: Postkantoor Gent Centrum** (Lange Kruisstraat 55 ☎022 01 23 45. Open M-F 9am-6pm, Sa 9am-3pm.)
- **POSTAL CODE:** 1000

Emergency

- **EMERGENCY:** ☎100 for ambulance; ☎101 for police.
- **POLICE:** ☎09 266 61 11 www.lokalepolitie.be/5415
- **LATE-NIGHT PHARMACIES:** Small green crosses mark pharmacies; for information about late night services (which rotate between place), check www.apotheek.be/index.cfm?-cat_id=4&lang=nl
- **HOSPITALS/MEDICAL SERVICES: Ghent University Hosptial**—one of the biggest hospitals in Belgium, we're told. A bit outside the city. ((De Pintelaan 185 ☎09 332 21 11)

Getting Around

Buses and trams are the name of the game in Ghent—fairly straightforward to navigate. Look for Linjwinkels at the main bus terminals and railway stations to buy bus and tram tickets. Still, you can walk to just about everything you'll want to see.

belgium essentials

MONEY

Tipping

In Belgium, service charges are included in the bill at restaurants. Waiters do not depend on tips for their livelihood, so there is no need to feel guilty about not leaving a tip. Still, leaving 5-10% extra will certainly be appreciated. Higher than that is just showing off. Tips in bars are very unusual; cab drivers are normally tipped about 10%.

Taxes

The quoted price of goods in Belgium includes value added tax (VAT). This tax on goods is generally levied at 21% in Belgium, although some goods are subject to lower rates. Non-EU visitors who are taking these goods home unused may be refunded this tax for purchases totaling over €125 per store. When making purchases, request a VAT form and present it at a Tax Free Shopping Office, found at most airports, road borders, and ferry stations, or by mail. Refunds must be claimed within six months.

SAFETY AND HEALTH

Drugs and Alcohol

Belgium has fairly liberal attitudes regarding alcohol, with no legal drinking age. You have to be 16 to buy your own alcohol (18 for spirits), but it's perfectly legal for someone else to buy alcohol and pass it to someone under 16. Public drunkenness, however, is frowned upon.

Belgium's attitude toward even soft drugs is traditional and conservative. Marijuana is illegal and not tolerated. Coffeeshops in Belgium are just that.

CROATIA

With attractions ranging from sun-drenched beaches and cliffs around Dubrovnik to dense forests around Plitvice, Croatia's wonders and natural beauty never cease to amaze. With a history full of political divides and conflict, Croatia has a few skeletons in its closet. After the devastating 1991-1995 ethnic war, however, Croatia finally achieved full independence for the first time in 800 years. Nowadays, the major threat comes from the hordes of tourists who make their way to the Adriatic coast to check out Roman ruins or dance all night at summer music festivals like Ultra Europe. Despite the crowds and the rising prices, this friendly and upbeat country demands to be seen at any cost.

greatest hits

- **COLLECTOR'S EDITION:** One man's treasure is a painting enthusiast's dream at the **Muzej Mimara** (p. 58) home to pieces by some of the most famous names in the book.

- **THE WALL:** Stunning views of the Adriatic, the city, people's backyards; you'll get it all on your walk along Dubrovnik's **City Walls** (p. 64).

- **MY PRECIOUS:** One does simply walk into **Tolkien's House** (p. 62) in Zagreb, a world-class beer bar with a *Lord of the Rings* obsession. Prepare for walls decked out with swords and chainmail.

zagreb

About a million of Croatia's 4.3 million residents live in the Zagreb metropolitan area, so it's no surprise that this very, very old city (Romans founded a town nearby in the first century; more recognizable settlements followed around 1094) boasts a fair bit of activity. Though no sea coasts are to be found—even the river Sava lies outside the main urban area—Zagreb's museums, eclectic architecture, and gorgeous urban parks mean there's no shortage of things to do. At night, enjoy a glass of Croatian wine in a quiet bar, or take a bus out to Lake Jarun to rage at one of the city's infamous clubs. Or, given that most of these clubs are open until 6am, you could do both.

SIGHTS

◪ MUZEJ MIMARA

Rooseveltov Trg 5   www.mimara.hr

The Strossmayer Gallery of Old Masters may have the words "old masters" in its name, but make no mistake: the Muzej Mimara is Zagreb's strongest collection of classic art. Botticelli? Check. Caravaggio? Check. Rubens, Degas, Manet? Check, check, and check. All the more impressive is that the museum's treasures were once the private collection of one man, Ante Topić Mimara, for whom the museum is named. Think of it as Zagreb's version of the Frick Collection, complete with a portrait of Sir Thomas More by Hans Holbein—now that's a weird coincidence. Painting is the museum's strong suit, although there are more than a few fascinating pieces in the sculpture and design collections. After working your way through the museum's three large floors, treat yourself to a drink in the improbably well-stocked in-house bar, Café Gymnasium.

i *40 kn, students 30 kn. 20 kn for special exhibitions. Open July-Sept Tu-F 10am-7pm, Sa 10am-5pm, Su 10am-2pm; Oct-June Tu-W 10am-5pm, Th 10am-7pm, F-Sa 10am-5pm, Su 10am-2pm. Closed Mondays.*

MUSEUM OF BROKEN RELATIONSHIPS

Ćirilometodska 2   ☎01 485 10 21 www.brokenships.com

If you're traveling without your significant other, this museum will make you give him or her a call immediately, roaming services be damned. If you've just gotten out of a relationship, this museum will make you cry. If you're not sure about whether or not to start a relationship, this museum may cause you to join the church. This is the Museum of Broken Relationships, one of Zagreb's smallest and strangest institutions. People from all over the world have sent in mementos of their failed relationships, along with brief explanations or summaries: they range from poetically cryptic to way-too-much-information. The museum can only show a small segment of its total collection, but there's always tons of variety: anything from Magic 8 Balls to heroin tests can pop up. Bring a date—you never know what can happen.

i *25 kn, students 20 kn. Open daily June-Sept 9am-10:30pm; Oct-May 9am-9pm.*

MODERNA GALERIJA

Andrije Hebranga 1   ☎01 241 68 00 www.moderna-galerija.hr

Don't know the first thing about Croatian art? Well, Moderna Galerija might not be the best place to start; there's very little wall text, so you can't learn that much about the various movements that shaped Croatian art in the 19th and 20th centuries. On the other hand, that lets the art speak for itself—you might know nothing about Croatian art going into the Moderna Galerija, but you also might love it when you come out. The German artist Joseph Beuys, who collaborated with a Croatian artist on one work, is likely the only recognizable name here—still, that work hardly compares to the massive canvases

MY WAY HOSTEL $

Trpimirova 4   ☎95 462 22 60 www.mywayhostel.com

No, it's not affiliated with Burger King, nor does it allow you to redesign your rooms to your liking (wouldn't that really make it your way?). But My Way Hostel does provide comfortable accommodation, clean bathrooms, and extensive common space, all within a short walk from the train and bus stations. Though none of the doors to the dorms have locks, each resident is provided with a large storage locker. This may be all too secure—in the event you lose your key, the staff may have to break the lock open to retrieve your things. But so long as you don't lose your key, your stay at My Way Hostel is sure to be a comfortable one.

i Doubles 330 kn. Dorms 70-90 kn. Reception 24hr.

HOSTEL SWANKY MINT $$

Ilica Ulica 50   ☎01 400 42 48 www.swanky-hostel.com

There can't be many contenders in the "post-industrial loft-style hostel" category, but Swanky Mint would be top of the heap no matter what. This hostel, organized around a courtyard just off Ilica Ulica, is housed in a former textile factory, but there's nothing gritty about its sleek, modern bedrooms and bathrooms. Certain dorms open directly onto the courtyard, making it feel like you have your very own studio apartment (that you share with three to seven roommates, of course). If you don't feel like leaving the confines of the hostel, you still won't lack for nightlife; Swanky Mint has a large bar located within the hostel itself.

i Singles 350 kn. Dorms 140-160 kn. Reception 24hr.

HOSTEL CHIC $

Pavla Hatza 10   ☎01 779 37 60 www.hostel-chic.com

Despite the name, Hostel Chic is not located in a particularly chic area (although it is only a few blocks from the train station), nor are its purple and green rooms particularly, shall we say, fashionable. But if you're not looking for a trend-setting place to rest your head at night, Hostel Chic will certainly do the job. Free Wi-Fi? Check. Community kitchen? Check. Reading lights, laundry facilities, safety deposit box? Check, check, check. With a friendly staff and cheap prices, this is a solid choice for your stay in Zagreb.

i Dorms 98 kn. Reception 24hr.

on display by the Croats, which range from the romantic to the aggressively primitive.

i 40 kn, students 20 kn. Open Tu-F 11am-7pm, Sa-Su 11am-2pm. Closed Mondays.

MUSEUM OF CONTEMPORARY ART

Avenija Dubrovnik 17   ☎01 605 27 00 www.msu.hr

The Museum of Contemporary Art is not near anything else you will visit in Zagreb. It is also not like anything else you will visit in Zagreb. Sure, there are other modern art museums, but none of them have a giant metal slide that spans three stories. And yes, you're allowed to slide down it—just not head-first. Though Croatian artists are well represented, the Museum of Contemporary Art has a truly international scope; there's everyone from California conceptualist John Baldessari to Belgian provocateur Jan Fabre. Highlights include the mind-bending collection of op art (you may leave with your eyes

zagreb

crossed), early graphic works made with a computer, and the transplanted studio of sculptor Ivan Kozarić.

i *30 kn, students 15 kn. Free for toddlers and the unemployed. Free every first Wednesday of the month. Open Tu-F 11am-6pm, Sa 11am-8pm, Su 11am-6pm.*

CROATIAN MUSEUM OF NAÏVE ART

Cirilometodska 3   ☎01 485 21 25

Thought the Museum of Contemporary Art was weird? All that avant-garde posturing is nothing compared to what's on display in the Croatian Museum of Naïve Art, which features work made by untrained Croatians. Marvel at surreal depictions of peasant landscapes, gory crucifixions, and women with huge goiters. Consider the numerous portraits of cross-eyed people. Peruse the obsessive renderings of cathedrals in Vienna and Milan. And stop short in front of Guiana '78, a large work depicting a crowd of passed-out junkies sticking hypodermic needles into each other. There are also some very nice and placid landscapes, just to balance everything out.

i *20 kn, students 10 kn. Open Tu-F 10am-6pm, Sa-Su 10am-1pm. Closed Mondays.*

FOOD

✎ BISTROTEKA $

Ulice Nikola Tesle 14   ☎01 483 77 11

Sleek black furniture, exposed white brick walls, a well-stocked bar alongside an appealing breakfast menu—yep, Bistroteka is the place to go if you want to look cool while you're scarfing down a meal. If you sit outside, you don't even need to take your sunglasses off. Surprisingly enough, that sense of chic is coupled with refreshingly low prices; full-sized sandwiches only cost about 30 kn. With all your savings, maybe you can even buy another pair of sunglasses.

i *Sandwiches 30 kn. Meals 40-50 kn. Open M-Th 8:30am-midnight, F-Sa 8:30am-1am.*

STARI FIJAKER $

Mesnička Ulica 6

Stari Fijaker is located just off Ilica Ulica, one of Zagreb's busiest and most modern streets. But the vibe inside this massive restaurant is pure old world. Start out with some hearty tomato soup, then move onto deer medallions. Have a glass of Croatian wine. Marvel at the photos of Old Zagreb. Despite the strong sense of tradition, Stari Fijaker is highly accessible to those who don't speak fluent Croatian (the extensive menu is available in English) as well as to vegetarians (there are quite a few alternatives to those deer medallions). Be warned, though, that if you order the fish, it'll probably arrive with its head. We told you—this place is old school.

i *Starters 20 kn. Entrees 50-70 kn. Open M-Sa 11am-11pm, Su 11am-10pm.*

ROUGEMARIN $$

Ulica Frana Folnegovića 10   ☎01 618 77 76 www.rougemarin.hr

It's out of the way, even if you're headed to the Museum of Contemporary Art, but the oft-crowded tables at RougeMarin are a clear sign it's worth the trip. With a menu that rotates monthly, RougeMarin is committed to exciting ingredients and novel combinations: one recent item combined lamb, chickpeas, and blueberries. Despite this variety, RougeMarin has its staples: namely, the hamburgers that are always on the menu. Simple as they may be, these burgers are made with the same devotion as the more eclectic menu items—and the homemade fries are to die for. Wash it all down with some pomegranate juice, or choose from one of their carefully selected wines or beers. Then start on the long walk home—you'll need it after ingesting all these calories.

i *Starters 30 kn. Burgers 48 kn. Entrees 60-70 kn. Open M-Th 11am-11pm, F 11am-3pm.*

croatia

... NISHTA $

Masarykova Ulica 11   ☎01 889 74 44 www.nishtarestaurant.com

Croatian cuisine is known for meat and seafood, but vegans and vegetarians
need not worry; Zagreb has a number of excellent meatless restaurants, chief
among them being the interestingly punctuated ...Nishta. We suggest saying it
with a pause. The menu's almost as eclectic as the decor (check out the Bar-
bie and Ken dolls on the doors of the bathrooms), with Mexican and Indian
touches. Highlights include the burritos and the banana curry, both of which
will satisfy your stomach without a hint of animal byproducts. And every dish
is worthy of being posted to your Instagram—did we mention they've got free
Wi-Fi? The homey interior—check out the yellow and purple walls—might
also be worth a quick snapshot.

i Starters 30 kn. Entrees 50-60 kn. Open Tu-Su noon-11pm.

MUNDOAKA STREETFOOD $$

Petrinjska 2   ☎01 788 87 77

Mundoaka Streetfood doesn't make a lot of sense. Why do they serve their
food on imposing slabs of wood instead of plates? Why do they serve beer
from a Catalan brewery that's impossible to find elsewhere? And, most
importantly, why is this one of Zagreb's best restaurants? Yes, you heard us
right. This tiny joint (they've got a mirror on one wall to make it look bigger),
complete with a name that screams "straight outta Greenpoint!", is one of the
best places to grab a bite in Croatia's capital. And Croatia's yuppies know it;
you'll likely have to wait for a table, even if you arrive before 6pm. But once
you get a seat, the food will convince you it was worth the wait. The menu is
heavy on seafood and meats with Asian touches; order the massive pizza for
two if you really want to chow down.

i Entrees 70-90 kn. Open M-Th 9am-midnight, F-Sa 9am-1am.

FINI ZALOGAJ $

Radićeva Ulica 8   www.fini-zalogaj.hr

Want a fast bite that's more authentic than McDonald's? Look no further than
Fini Zalogaj, a self-described "fine food bar" on Radićeva Ulica. Its stock in
trade? Hearty sandwiches filled with huge hunks of meat (as an added plus, you
can have them wrapped in bacon or sprinkled with sesame seeds!). Though the
sandwiches are not always structurally sound (we recommend not unwrapping
the paper container you'll be given), they are always delicious.

i Sandwiches 25 kn. Open daily 8am-4pm.

ROCKET BURGER $

Tkalčićeva Ulica 44   ☎01 557 91 75

Here's the deal: burger restaurants are a legitimate trend in Zagreb now. You
can weep about globalization and how American culture devours all, or you can
shut up and enjoy a great meal at Rocket Burger, one of the best products of
this trend. Located near the many bars of Tkalčićeva Ulica, Rocket Burger is the
perfect thing to chow down on after a few pints of Ožujsko—or you could enjoy
a pint of craft beer from local brewers Nova Runda, available on tap at Rocket
Burger.

i Burgers 40 kn. Open M-Th 11am-11pm, F 11am-midnight, Sa 10am-midnight, Su 10am-10pm.

PIZZERIA ZERO ZERO $

Vlaška Ulica 35   ☎01 889 70 00

Pizza doesn't have the same cachet in Zagreb that it has along other regions of
Croatia, like the Istrian Coast. But that doesn't mean the capital city totally lacks
for good 'za; for proof of that, just swing by Pizzeria Zero Zero, which is not
code for how many calories are in its pizzas. Choose from a variety of toppings,

zagreb

including a strong selection of white pies (read: no tomato sauce); if you're not too hungry, best to opt for a salad, as it only serves one size of pizza.

i Pizzas 50-60 kn. Open M-Th 10:30am-11pm, F-Sa 10:30am-midnight, Su noon-11pm.

NIGHTLIFE

◙ TOLKIEN'S HOUSE
Opatovina 49 ☎01 485 20 50

Some of the bars on Tkalčićeva Ulica can feel a little juvenile—did you really come all the way to Croatia to watch American tourists chug cheap beer (even if it's cheap Croatian beer)? If the shots and EDM get to be too much for you, fear not; Tkalčićeva's cool older sibling, Opatovina, is just a few steps away. And there's nothing that sums Opatovina up quite like Tolkien's House. Featuring walls decked out with swords, chain mail, and giant clubs, Tolkien's House is a world-class beer bar with an inexplicable Lord of the Rings obsession. But even if you can't tell an elf from an orc, this cozy space will still hold some appeal—just have a pint of pale ale from Zmajska Pivovara, some of the first craft brewers in Croatia.

i Beers from 20-30 kn. Open M-F 7am-midnight, Sa 8am-midnight, Su 9am-11pm.

◙ RAKHIA BAR
Tkalčićeva 45

Rakija, for all intents and purposes, is Balkan schnapps—fruit-flavored liqueur, flavored with everything from plums to wild berries. They say the best rakija is made at home. But in case you don't feel like following a stranger home to try their homemade spirits, just find yourself a seat at Rakhia Bar. With over 30 types of rakija in its vaults, Rakhia lets you sample to your heart's content; with most of them priced between 10 and 16 kn, your wallet won't be complaining either. The vibe inside is low-key, with lots of exposed brick—though it's located on Tkalčićeva Ulica, its upstairs location means it's a bit removed from that street's excesses.

i Shots of every liquor you can imagine from 10-16 kn. Open M-Th 8am-midnight, F-Sa 8am-2am, Su 8am-midnight.

PINTA ZAGREB
Radićeva Ulica 3a ☎01 483 08 89 www.pinta.hr

There are no frills to Pinta Zagreb—the inside's smoky, the draft selection is small (Tomislav and two Ožujsko taps), and there's minimal decor. It's a dive bar in the heart of Zagreb (right next to a backpackers' inn, no less), but that doesn't stop the locals from streaming to it. The perfect antidote to some of the flashier bars that have opened up recently, as the city adds hostels and gains tourists. Chill out with the eclectic soundtrack (Sex Pistols, Bob Marley, etc) and enjoy a nice creamy pint of Tomislav.

i Beers 15 kn. Wine and cocktails 20 kn. Open daily 8am-11pm.

PIVNICA MALI MEDO
Tkalčićeva 34-36-38-42 ☎01 492 96 13 www.pivnica-medvedgrad.hr

The cheapest beer in Zagreb is, by some miracle, not synonymous with the worst beer in Zagreb. That's because the cheapest pints to be had are at this brewpub, and it makes beer that's a lot better than Ožujsko and Staropramen. If you can't decide which of the five regular and one rotating taps to choose from, order a taster of all six—only 20 kn! Evidently it's a business model that works—this is less of a bar and more of an empire, with its address stretching across nearly an entire block of Tkalčićeva Ulica. Even with all that real estate, the bar still manages to be packed on a regular basis—those prices, after all, are pretty darn low.

i Beers 10-15 kn. Taster of every beer available for 20 kn. Open M-W 10am-midnight, Th-Sa 10am-1am, Su noon-midnight.

croatia

SAVSKA 14

Savska Cesta 14

This large bar lacks a name, but it does have an address—and after all, which one is more important? Be sure you know that address, as there's no signage to indicate exactly where the bar is; look for a big hedge and listen for a fair bit of noise. In short, this is where you should go if you want to feel like a local—a cool local, even! At most hours of the night, you'll find big crowds excitedly talking and downing bottles of Staropramen and Karlovačko. The large tables, inside and out, will soon be filled with empties. One element of the sparse decor is a large painting of a girl puking into a toilet. Make sure you bring a friend to walk you home.

i Beers 10-15 kn. Open daily 8pm-2am.

VINTAGE INDUSTRIAL BAR

Savska Cesta 160   ☎01 619 17 15 www.vintageindustrial-bar.com

No, this is not a place where they play Skinny Puppy and Nine Inch Nails on loop. Located in what looks like a former auto body shop, Vintage Industrial Bar is not for the faint of heart. With a gritty rock-and-roll soundtrack and restored cars out front, VIB is a spot where alternative types throw down. Given its massive space and slightly removed location, it's no surprise that it has hosted bands and after-parties for concerts. If there are no events going on, however, the vibe is likely more reservedly cool than loud and raucous—though, of course, all that can change by the time the bar closes at 5am.

i Beers 15-20 kn. Cocktails 20 kn. Shots of rakija 10 kn. Open Tu-Th 10pm-2am, F-Sa 10pm-5am, Su 10am-1am.

AQUARIUS

Aleja Matije Ljubeka   ☎01 3640 231 www.aquarius.hr

Looking to party in Zagreb? No, not drinking a few glasses of wine with friends, not having a few pints and singing along to the jukebox, not discussing the finer points of a certain blend of rakija—partying. The kind with dry ice, strobe lights, glow sticks, and a cover charge. If this is the sort of party you are looking for, then you absolutely must go to Aquarius. Located on Lake Jarun, Aquarius boasts two floors, cutting-edge electronic music, and a lot of alcohol. Unfortunately, it also has a lot of cigarettes—sometimes it's hard to tell if the smoke on the dance floor is coming from dry ice or Pall Malls. Still, when it comes to clubbing in Zagreb, Aquarius is the best game in town.

i Cover 20 kn. Shows often require tickets. Beers and cocktails 20-30 kn. Café open daily 9am-9pm, club open 11pm-6am.

ESSENTIALS

Practicalities

- **MONEY:** ATMs are located throughout the city. An exchange office is located at the bus station. Most ATMs will disperse money in 200 and 100 kn bills, which may earn some annoyance from locals.

- **POST OFFICE:** There is a large post office located just to the left of the train station, on Ulica Kneza Branimira. It is open daily 7am-midnight.

- **TOURIST INFO CENTER:** Tourist Information Centre, Trg Bana J. Jelačića 11 ☎01 481 40 51. Open M-F 8:30am-9pm, Sa-Su 9am-6pm.

Emergency

- **GENERAL EMERGENCY NUMBER:** ☎112. The American Embassy in Croatia also maintains an emergency number for American citizens: ☎01 661 2400.

- **POLICE:** ☎192

- **PHARMACIES:** Gradska Ljekarna Zagreb, Trg Petra Svačića 17 ☎01 485 65 45. Open M-F 7am-8pm, Sa-Su 7:30am-3pm.

Getting Around

Zagreb is well served by a tram system; major hubs are located in Ban Jelačić Square and by the train station, at Kralja Tomislava Square. Tickets are 10 kn during the day and can be purchased on the tram; they are valid for 90 minutes. At the city outskirts, buses take over.

If you don't want to walk to the Upper Town (the site of St. Mark's Church, the Croatian Museum of Naïve Art, and the Museum of Broken Relationships, among other attractions), take the funicular, which costs 4 kn. With a length of only 66 meters, it's the shortest inclined railway in the world.

dubrovnik

Dubrovnik is commonly known as the Pearl of the Adriatic, but we prefer to call it the tourist trap of Dalmatia. That doesn't mean it's not fun to visit, though. Come for the striking city walls, the rocky beaches, and the unparalleled wine bars; stay because you ran out of money for a bus ticket and need your mom to wire some cash. Kidding—kind of.

SIGHTS

🏛 DUBROVNIK CITY WALLS

Let's be honest. The walls are why you came to Dubrovnik. Without these bad boys, it's just another random Croatian port town. So are they worth the journey? And once you get there, is walking around on them worth the 100 kn entrance fee? Yes and yes. Stunning views of the Adriatic, the city, people's backyards—you'll get it all on your walk along the city walls. And despite Dubrovnik's reputation as a city-turned-tourist-trap, the walls are so big and so well organized (traffic can only proceed one way) that it's possible to enjoy a smooth, largely crowd-free experience. Be sure to keep your ticket on you, as there are several checkpoints along the way. Street vendors provide water and other amenities inside, though you may want to bring your own supplies to save money. Make sure your camera is all charged up, as you'll be snapping pictures every step of the way.

i There are three entrance points, but the most prominent is directly next to Pile Gate. 100 kn. Open daily 9am-7:30pm.

FRANCISCAN MONASTERY AND PHARMACY MUSEUM

Placa 2 ☎020 321 410

You know that old pharmacy in your neighborhood that seems like it's been around forever, and you always wonder how they stay in business? Well, think of how the people in Dubrovnik must feel; within the walls of the Franciscan Monastery is a pharmacy that's been operating since 1317. Though the one that's used today (don't worry, you don't need to pay the 30 kn admission fee to enter) doesn't use the same shelves and ceramic jars that are lovingly preserved in the museum, the monastery is still worth a visit. The art collection is decent (it includes what may be the world's worst Rubens), but the old pharmacy collections are fascinating to look at, and the church still bears some historically intriguing scars from the Siege of Dubrovnik. Visited by Jackie Kennedy, Dick Cheney, and possibly you!

i 30 kn. Open daily 9am-6pm.

DUBROVNIK AQUARIUM AND MARITIME MUSEUM

Ulica Kneza Damjana Jude 2 ☎021 427 937

In general, you're best off exploring Adriatic ocean life in Croatia's restaurants rather than in its (generally lackluster) aquariums. The Dubrovnik Aquarium and Maritime Museum is a happy exception. Here, you'll see everything from sea turtles to locust lobsters in large tanks or giant pools of water. Housed in St. John's Fortress, a medieval structure with cavernous stone chambers, the aquarium has a quiet, serene feel. The English wall text is fairly comprehensive and includes information on how every fish is caught. We can't guarantee you won't work up an appetite here.

i 60 kn. Open daily 9am-10pm.

RECTOR'S PALACE

Pred Dvorom 1 ☎020 321 422

The Rector's Palace is sort of a one-stop shop for museum-going in Dubrovnik. Want to see some art? Some historical interiors and centuries-old jail cells? Vintage weaponry and silverware? Contemporary war photography? The Rector's Palace has it all, and with the large space set aside for rotating exhibitions, it's a safe bet you'll find something of interest. Highlights include the two large bronze figures that struck Dubrovnik's town bells for centuries, a painting showing the

get a room!

HOSTEL VILLA ANGELINA OLD TOWN $$$

Plovani Skalini 17a ☎091 893 9089

One of three hostels actually located within Dubrovnik's Old Town, Hostel Villa Angelina is a low-key delight. If Dubrovnik's nightlife doesn't impress you, you can always curl up in the large beds, each of which is equipped with a reading light, or you can watch TV in the common room. But if getting into the city is all you want to do, Villa Angelina's awesome location makes it as easy as stepping out the door. Bathrooms are well kept, and free towels are provided.

i Dorms 290 kn. Reception 24hr.

HOSTEL MARKER $$

Svetog Djurdja 6 ☎091 739 75 45

A fantastic location near the Old Town and Pile Bay (where you can rent a kayak and explore Dubrovnik from the sea) distinguishes Hostel Marker. Though it lacks a large common area, the dorms and other rooms are decently furnished, and the hostel is clean and well maintained on the whole. Let's be honest—you're paying for the location. Free towels, blankets, and Wi-Fi provided.

i Dorms 230 kn. Latest check-in at 12:30am. No curfew.

HOSTEL CITY CENTRAL $

Ulica U Pilama 7 ☎092 150 70 46

Located a few minutes from the Old Town, Hostel City Central is a solid choice for housing during your stay in Dubrovnik; you'll be able to get to the Old Town in minutes, and its close proximity to the Pile Gate bus stop means you can catch a bus going anywhere (not that there are tons of places worth visiting besides the Old Town). It's also noticeably cheaper than many other hostels in the Old Town; with prices like these, you'll think you're staying out in Dubrovnik's suburbs.

i Dorms from 200 kn. Latest check-in 10pm. No curfew.

dubrovnik

seals of every noble family in Dubrovnik, and the well-preserved dragon cells, tiny prison chambers that housed especially tough criminals. In the gift shop, you'll find scarves inspired by the collections, posters of past exhibits, replicas of small sculptures, and much more.

i 100 kn, students 25 kn for the Dubrovnik Museums ticket (includes admission to Maritime Museum, Ethnographic Museum Rupe, Revelin Fortress Archaeological Collections, House of Marin Držić, Dubrovnik Art Gallery, Natural History Museum, Museum of Modern Art, and Rector's Palace). Open daily 9am-6pm.

FORT LOVRIJENAC
Općina Dubrovnik

The one problem with Dubrovnik's city walls is that it's hard to get a really good look at them. Sure, you can marvel at them from up close, whether you're walking along them or just staring from Pile Gate, but does that really give a sense of just how impressive these babies are? Short of renting a helicopter, your best bet is to make the quick hike up to Fort Lovrijenac, an old military fortress-cum-tourist attraction and concert venue. You may not learn too much about Dubrovnik's history as a fortified city state, but the views of the city and the Adriatic are the best you'll find. As a plus, the shady walk to the top won't leave you drenched in sweat.

i 30 kn. Open daily 8am-5pm.

MUSEUM OF MODERN ART
Frana Supila 23   ☎020 426 590

There's a lot of cool stuff outside Dubrovnik's city walls, like bottles of water that don't cost 15 kn. On a more cultural note, there's Dubrovnik's Museum of Modern Art, a charming collection distinguished by its outdoor sculpture garden. Here, you'll find bronze figures that range from the geometrically stylized to the grotesquely bizarre; even if you don't like them, you'll have to appreciate the view from the giant balcony they stand on. Elsewhere in the museum, you'll find a brief overview of modern art in Croatia (yes, there are sculptures by Ivan Meštrović), along with a vast space for special exhibitions.

i Individual ticket free for students. 100 kn, students 25 kn for the Dubrovnik Museums ticket (includes admission to Maritime Museum, Ethnographic Museum Rupe, Revelin Fortress Archaeological Collections, House of Marin Držić, Dubrovnik Art Gallery, Natural History Museum, Museum of Modern Art, and Rector's Palace). Open Tu-Su 9am-8pm.

LOKRUM ISLAND
                                                                  ☎020 323 554

If you ended up booking a hostel or hotel outside of the whole town, you'll be doing a lot of hiking on your trip to Dubrovnik. Odds are, however, that hiking alongside strip malls and suburban homes isn't exactly what you had in mind. For a more "scenic height," take a short ferry to Lokrum Island, a.k.a. that large

game of thrones

Dubrovnik may be familiar to you even if you've never been to Croatia. That's because this coastal city stood in for the fictional city of "King's Landing" on popular fantasy show/masturbation fodder *Game of Thrones*. That means that if you visit Dubrovnik today, you'll find street performers dressed up like characters and run into tours where people say stuff like "in season 5, Cersei walks down this flight of stairs." Thrilling stuff. If you're a fan, be sure to check out Fort Lovrijenac, Pile Gate, Lokrum Island, and of course, those famous city walls, all of which have made appearances on the show.

land mass just off the coast of Dubrovnik. Here, you'll find miles of trails, a botanical garden that was nearly destroyed in the 1990s war, and a restaurant and a cafe-bar to stave off your hiking-induced hunger. We particularly recommend going to the top of Fort Royal, which provides great views of Dubrovnik.

i Ferries leave every half hour from the Old Harbor. 80 kn for a round-trip ticket. The island closes at 8pm when the last ferry leaves.

KUPARI

Some 8km southeast of Dubrovnik's Old Town lies one of the clearest signs that 20-some years ago, Croatia was indeed in the midst of a bloody war for independence. This is Kupari Beach, once a military resort filled with thriving hotels. They're still there, but they've been bombed out and deserted; balconies and staircases have collapsed, while windowpanes lie shattered on the ground. There are still tons of people on the largely untouched beaches, but only squatters live in the hotel now.

i Free.

FOOD

⚑ TAJ MAHAL $$
Ulica Nikole Gučetića 2 ☎020 323 221

"Hungry?" asks the first page of Taj Mahal's menu. You better be. This Bosnian restaurant is not for the faint of heart or the vegetarian of diet. If you want big hunks of meat on a skewer, potatoes stuffed with Bosnian cream cheese, and a rich cup of Turkish coffee—sorry, Bosnian coffee—to wash it all down with, this place is for you. Unlike most of Dubrovnik's restaurants, there are no seafood options, but if you need some protein to propel you around the city walls, there's no better place. Enjoy a nice chunk of baklava afterward.

i Entrees 70-150 kn. Open daily 10am-2pm.

... NISHTA $
Corner of Palmotićeva Ulica and Prijeko Ulica ☎020 322 088

Are you a vegetarian in Croatia who's sick of asking the waitress if you can have the octopus salad without the octopus? Are you sick of having the same tomato sauce and pasta entree that every restaurant seems to offer? Did you skip dinner last night and just eat the six bananas you bought at Konzum? Then steer yourself to ...Nishta, a small vegetarian restaurant in the heart of Dubrovnik's Old Town. Seitan burgers, tempeh burritos, and, yes, pasta with tomato sauce are all available for your consumption. Homemade juices, health food shots, and a selection of organic beers and wines round out the menu. Just try not to get a headache from the hot pink bathrooms.

i Entrees 60-80 kn. Open M-Sa 11:30am-11pm.

PIZZERIA OLIVA $
Lučarica Ulica 5 ☎020 324 594 www.olivadubrovnik.com

Yes, Pizzeria Oliva's pizzas cost a good 10 kn more than pizzas anywhere else in Croatia. But Dubrovnik is expensive enough to make this one of the cheaper meals in the city. Besides, the varied toppings—arugula with pesto, prosciutto, and the mushroom-ham-peppers combination are all worth exploring—make it some of the best food you're likely to find in the city. Inside, whirring fans keep it cool; outside, you'll find comfortable if not spacious seating.

i Pizzas 60-80 kn. Open daily noon-midnight.

BARBA $
Boškovićeva 5 ☎091 205 34 88

Barba is perhaps the only fast food joint in the world where you can get oysters. Surprisingly enough, they're really good too, whether you get them fresh or fried. This small restaurant (you can eat the food there or get it to go) is maybe the only place in Croatia to serve truly affordable seafood. Surprisingly enough, it's located in Dubrovnik, possibly the most expensive city on Croatia's Adriatic coast. Try the octopus burger or salad if you're looking for something especially hearty; otherwise, just grab some fried fish or a fish sandwich. And, of course, a few oysters.

i Sandwiches 30-40 kn. Burgers 40-50 kn. Fish entrees 39-54 kn. Oysters 12 kn each. Open daily 10am-2am.

POKLISAR $$
Ribarnica Ulica 1 ☎020 322 176 www.poklisar.com

Dubrovnik's Above 5 restaurant may have a flashier vantage point, but it's hard to beat the views of the Old Harbor that Poklisar provides. Whether you're chowing down on a full meal or just enjoying cocktails and ice cream, Poklisar is a great option for food in Dubrovnik. The menu focuses on Dalmatian cuisine, though it's a little more offbeat than your standard *konoba*; dig the shrimp skewers with blue cheese, or the beef tournedos with black truffle sauce.

i Entrees 90-180 kn. Open daily 9am-midnight.

SEGRETO PASTA AND GRILL $$
Cvijete Zuzorić 5 ☎020 323 392 www.segretodubrovnik.com

Sometimes Croatia feels a lot closer to Italy than other former Yugoslav countries, and this delicious Italian joint is a perfect example of that. The entrees can get a little pricey, so if you're trying to save, either go for lunch (meals are a good 10-20 kn cheaper) or order something off the pasta menu, which is also generally cheaper. Vegetarians will be enthused by the hearty eggplant parm, while meat eaters can pig out on the steak and seafood entrees. Be sure to wash it all down with a glass of Birra del Borgo beer, made by a cult-favorite Italian brewery.

i Pasta dishes 70-90 kn. Entrees 90-160 kn. Open daily 11:30am-midnight.

AZUR $
Pobijana 10 ☎020 324 806 www.azurvision.com

If you tire of Dubrovnik's many Dalmatian restaurants (pork medallions, prawns, octopus salads; we get it!), head to Azur, an Asian-Mediterranean fusion restaurant located in an Old Town back street. The curries and sauces are certainly less spicy than you'll find in India or China (or, to be honest, in any American Chinatown or Indian restaurant), but the varied menu is still packed with flavor. The wine list is on the pricier side, but most of the entrees are affordably priced. Bring a group and order one of the sharing plates—salmon tacos, anyone?

i Entrees 70-150 kn. Sharing plates 50-90 kn. Open daily 12:30pm-11pm.

DOLCE VITA $
Ulica Nalješkovićeva 1a ☎098 944 9951

Avoid the ice cream shops on Stradun; they're generic, overpriced, and overflowing with customers. Instead, turn onto Ulica Nalještovićeva and grab a cone at Dolce Vita, Dubrovnik's finest purveyor of frozen treats. Flavors range from the super sweet Dolce Vita to the Earl Grey-like bitter orange, but you're likely to pick a winner no matter what you choose. Crepes and cakes are also available if you're trying to avoid a brain freeze, though that might not be a bad thing in the middle of a Dubrovnik summer.

i 8 kn for one scoop, 17 kn for two scoops. Open daily 9am-midnight.

NIGHTLIFE

▨ D'VINO
Palmotićeva Ulica 4a ☎02 032 11 30 www.dvino.net

Dubrovnik's best wine bar is also one of its most accessible. If you know nothing about wine, order one of its helpful tasting flights: everything from an overview of the wines of Croatia to a comparison of several wines made with Plavac Mali grapes. If you know everything about wine and have tons of money to burn, ask about its vintage collection. No matter your wine knowledge, you'll enjoy this funky wine bar's comfortable leather seats, comprehensive snacks menu, and hipper-than-thou soundtrack.

i *Glass of wine 40-60 kn. Open daily noon-2am.*

BUZA

Crijevićeva Ulica 9 ☎098 361 934

Outside Buza, which is located on some rocks jutting out from the city walls, you'll see a sign that reads "Cold Drinks and the Most Beautiful View." Notice they didn't say anything about good drinks. By most standards, Buza is not a great bar—the menu is limited, they make you drink out of plastic cups, and there are way too many alternatives available—but the view is indeed tremendous. Sit down, enjoy a beer or a mini-bottle of wine, and gaze out at the Adriatic. Then buy a commemorative postcard, hat, or T-shirt. Yes, these are actually available for purchase.

i *Beer 40 kn. Open 9am-2am.*

ONOFRIO ICE BAR

Poljana Paska Miličeva 3 ☎091 152 0257

You've walked along the walls of Dubrovnik, you've hiked on Lokrum Island, and you carried your bags from the bus station all the way to the Old Town. One thing's certain: you're a sweaty mess. But there's a bar in Dubrovnik that can correct all that. A bar made of ice that, for reasons unknown, shares space with a Korean restaurant. This is Onofrio Ice Bar, perhaps the only place in Dubrovnik where you'll feel you're not wearing enough layers. The 75 kn cover charge includes a free drink, perhaps the only one you will have in Dubrovnik without feeling that it got a little too warm while you were drinking it. No windows and, in general, very little that would suggest you are not just partying in a meat locker, but the temperature is low enough to assuage any and all complaints.

i *75 kn cover, includes free drink. Open daily 7pm-2am.*

CAFFE BAR NONENINA

Pred Dvorom 4 ☎098 825 844 www.nonenina.com

If you're looking for a place to sip sophisticated cocktails and relax, you can't do too much better than Caffe Bar Nonenina. Located just across from the Rector's Palace and next to the cathedral, Nonenina will provide you with some serious eye candy while you sink into one of their large wicker chairs. The cocktail list is no slouch, whether you're looking for a classy aperitif or want to get seriously messed up; in the latter event, order an XXL cocktail, for three to six patrons.

i *Cocktails 60-90 kn. XXL cocktails 185-205 kn. Open daily 9am-2am.*

BUZZ BAR

Prijeko Ulica 21 ☎020 321 025. www.thebuzzbar.wix.com

As cafe-bars go, Buzz Bar is clean, has a slightly more expansive beer and liquor list, and has a helpful staff. There are quotes from Ernest Hemingway and Frank Sinatra on the menu (we get it, they drank alcohol), but the menu also has prices that are far better than most nightlife joints in Dubrovnik. Order a San Servolo or a medica (a sweet, honey-based liquor) and enjoy the free Wi-Fi.

i *Beers 20-40 kn. Liquors 12-20 kn. Open daily 8am-2am.*

RAZONADA

Od Puča 1 ☎020 326 222 www.thepucicpalace.com

A hotel wine bar sounds like a recipe for a very large bill, but Razonada, a clean, well-lit joint in Dubrovnik's Old Town, manages to keep prices fairly reasonable—unless you go for champagne or one of the cigars in its walk-in humidor. More to the point, the wine list is large and varied, making room for such oddities as orange wine, made by leaving the grape skins with the fermenting juice. The rest of the menu is similarly offbeat: check out the cold-brew coffee that comes in a wine glass or the flavorful olive-leaf tea. Atmosphere is friendly and low-key.

i *Wines 30-60 kn by the glass. Open daily 11am-midnight.*

ESSENTIALS

Practicalities

- **MONEY:** There are numerous ATMs and exchange offices up and down Stradun, the main street in the Old Town.
- **POST OFFICE:** Central Post Office, Vukovarska 16 ☎020 362 068. Open M-F 7am-8pm, Sa 8am-3pm. Closed Sunday. In addition, there are numerous post office boxes on Stradun.
- **TOURIST INFORMATION CENTER:** Brsalje 5 ☎020 312 011. Open daily 8am-8pm.

Emergency

- **EMERGENCY NUMBER:** ☎112
- **HOSPITALS:** Dr. Roka Mišetića 2, Dubrovnik ☎020 431 777.
- **PHARMACY:** Ljekarna Kod Zvonika, Placa 2 ☎020 321 133. Open M-F 7am-8pm, Sa 7:30am-3pm. Closed Sunday.

Getting Around

Dubrovnik's Old Town is small and easily navigable by foot. You will most likely not be staying in the Old Town, but 99% of what's interesting in Dubrovnik is located in it. Buses regularly connect the various parts of Dubrovnik to the Old Town; if you exit from the Pile Gate, you'll find a major hub for buses. Pro tip: if you're staying outside the city, walk to the Old Town and take a bus home (otherwise, you'll likely be walking uphill).

split

Zagreb may be Croatia's official capital, but let's be frank: the action is here in Split. Located on a peninsula jutting into the Adriatic, Split is the gateway to Hvar, Brač, Korčula, and other famed Croatian islands. Here, you'll find world-class restaurants, beautiful beaches (some with actual sand!), and an old town built into a former Roman palace. Walk along the palm-tree-lined waterfront or explore the remains of Diocletian's Palace before jetting off to one of the many beaches for a swim. At night, take it easy at a wine bar or rage at one of the many clubs, which cater to tastes from techno to karaoke.

SIGHTS

GALERIJA MEŠTROVIĆ

Šetalište Ivana Meštrovića 46 ☎02 134 08 00

One visit to Galerija Meštrović, and you'll know that sculptor Ivan Meštrović was no starving artist. Though he fled to the US in the 1940s (he was no fan of Marshal Josip Broz Tito), he intended this palatial villa to be his place of retirement. Today, it stands as a museum devoted to his idiosyncratic work. Meštrović was deeply concerned with religious themes, a fact that's very much evident in his striking sculptures of Jesus Christ, St. John, Moses, and a host of other biblical figures. Further proof can be found in a renovated chapel down the road (your admission ticket can be used here), which houses a series of Meštrović's wooden reliefs depicting the life of Christ. If the art isn't your cup of tea, just revel in the splendor of the estate. In terms of retirement homes, it's no palace of Diocletian, but it's still pretty darn nice.

i *Admission 40 kn; also buys admission to the Crikvine-Kaštele. Open May-Sept Tu-Su 9am-7pm; Oct-Apr Tu-Sa 9am-4pm, Su 10am-3pm.*

CATHEDRAL OF SAINT DOMNIUS
Near Peristil

The oddest thing about Split's cathedral is just how hard it is to take in. This is a monumental building, but the narrow streets of Split (it's located within the framework of Diocletian's Palace) make it difficult to really see; dig all the camera-happy tourists desperately trying to fit it into their frames. Of course, there's an easy solution: just go inside. From the relics in the treasury to the stunning heights of the bell tower, Split Cathedral is a dazzling monument that reminds you that, yes, things happened here post-Diocletian. You'll see the bones of saints, a very mildewy crypt, and some wood purportedly from the cross Christ was crucified on. Climb up to the bell tower for the best view of Split; not even the top of Marjan can beat this.

i *15 kn for admission to the cathedral, crypt, and nearby Jupiter's Temple. 45 kn for all that jazz plus the bell tower and the treasury. Open M-Sa 8am-7pm, Su 12:30-6pm.*

FROGGYLAND
Ulica Kralja Tomislava 5 ☎098 264 373 www.froggyland.net

Do cathedrals make you yawn? Do Roman ruins leave you unmoved? Are art galleries your cure for insomnia? Then proceed with haste to Split's weirdest attraction, a museum unlike any other in Croatia (and possibly the world). This is Froggyland, a century-old collection of stuffed frogs created by taxidermist Ferenc Mere. Yet this is no ordinary collection of stuffed frogs (if such a thing exists): these frogs, 507 of them in total, are posed in a variety of comic scenes that mimic human life. We see frogs getting shaved at the barber, going to school, cheating at cards. This is not a museum of students of biology, but for students of humanity. Our foibles, our fears, our frailties are captured in these frogs.

i *Admission 35 kn. Open daily 10am-10pm.*

GALLERY OF FINE ARTS
Ulica Kralja Tomislava 15 ☎02 135 01 12 www.galum.hr

Due to its stunning location on the coast, the Galerija Meštrović is undoubtedly the flashiest art museum in Split. But visitors to the city's Gallery of Fine Arts won't be disappointed; this is one of the best institutions in Split. The collection focuses on Croatian artists, though there are a few foreign heavyweights—including Albrecht Dürer, represented by a print of Melencolia I. The museum is organized chronologically, though the 1400 to 1900 section is tiny. Aside from a few highlights, like the Dürer and a striking stone relief of Saint Jerome, you can speed through this section quickly and head over to the selection of modern, high modern, and postmodern works. These range from naïve oil and glass paintings to satirical sketches of Croatian cultural bigwigs (including Ivan Meštrović himself) to vibrantly colored abstract works from the 1960s.

i *20 kn. Open Tu-Sa 10am-9pm.*

SPLIT CITY MUSEUM (MUZEJ GRADA SPLITA)
Papalićeva Ulica 1 ☎02 136 01 71 www.mgst.net

With daily opening hours from 9am to 9pm, Muzej Grada Splita is the city museum that never sleeps. That gives you all the time you'll need to explore these varied, intriguing collections, which cover just about every aspect of Split's history. We recommend going after a few days in the city, which'll give you a new perspective on now-familiar sights. Here's an example: that black sphinx by the

HOSTEL SPLIT BACKPACKERS (1 AND 2) $

Kralja Zvonimira 17; Poljišanska 18   ☎02 178 24 83 www.splitbackpackers.com

A hostel so nice they made it twice, Hostel Split Backpackers has two locations in Split. Both are great places to crash. The beds are roomy and large, with personal outlets, lights, and curtains for added privacy. Each also comes with a locker for extra security. Showers and common spaces are well maintained in both locations. The atmosphere is a little more low-key than some of Split's party hostels, but you'll still be able to find a crew of tourists ready to rage. Even better is the late checkout: sleeping until 11am never felt so good.

i Dorms 170 kn. Reception 24hr.

KISS HOSTEL $

Stari Pazar 2   ☎095 838 4437

This is the rare hostel where top bunks are preferable to those on the bottom, the reason being the exceptionally small space between the two. That unfortunate fact aside, Kiss Hostel is a solid choice for accommodation in Split. Located in the heart of the city (it's just steps from the Peristyle and the cathedral), Kiss Hostel offers comfortable beds, air conditioning, and well-kept showers. Common areas are small, but that encourages bonding.

i Dorms 140 kn in the summer, 100 kn during the off season. Reception 24hr.

HOSTEL SPLIT WINE GARDEN $

Poljana Tina Ujevica 3/3   ☎09 848 08 55

Don't let the name put you off (or entice you beyond reason). Hostel Split Wine Garden is not a boozer's paradise, but rather a perfectly nice hostel with a terrace partially covered by a grapevine. Located just behind the national theater (dangerously close to the best ice cream shop in town, Luka Ice Cream and Cakes), Hostel Split Wine Garden offers comfortable rooms and a tranquil terrace to relax on—you'll need it after hiking up and down Marjan, which is also nearby. Lockers and air conditioning provided.

i Dorms from 160 kn. Reception 24hr.

croatia

cathedral? Farmers used to cover their eyes as they walked past, for fear that they would be cursed by the pagan evil eye.

The museum is not organized chronologically, but you'll get a sense of Split's rollicking history (it was ruled by Venetians at one point, and some wanted it to join with Italy rather than a unified Croatian state) while marveling over swords, vintage photographs, and original sculptural decorations from the cathedral's bell tower.

i 20 kn, students 10 kn. Open daily 9am-9pm.

FOOD

BUFFET ŠPERUN $$

Sperun 3   ☎02 134 69 9

Hearty Dalmatian cuisine is the order of the day at Buffet Šperun, a small, appealingly rustic restaurant just steps from Split's waterfront. The cozy interiors and painted wooden walls give it a sort of country inn feel, even though you can easily walk here from Split's urban center. Seafood and meat dominate the menu, though pasta dishes pop up here and there. Check out the specials menu, which is usually very affordable. If you're not impressed by Split's flashier restaurants, set up shop here. You'll leave full, and so will your wallet.

i Appetizers 50-70 kn. Entrees 60-130 kn. Open daily 9am-11pm.

KOBAJE $

Vukovarska 35a   ☎02 153 70 09

Beer and sausages. That's what Kobaje offers—their slogan is "craft beer and street food"—and how can you argue with that? Not only is their selection of beer among the best in Split (certain bars specialize in Croatian craft beer, but nowhere else has the international selection), their meat-heavy menu is one of the cheapest. Most sausages can be had for under 20 kn, while the sandwiches and burgers fall between 30 and 60 kn. The crisp house lager is only 15 kn for half a liter—again, a better deal than you'll find anywhere else in town. Aside from a few poorly named menu items ("Afternoon Quickie," "Ménage à Trois," and "One Night in BangCock" all make appearances), Kobaje is a home run.

i Sausages 20 kn. Entrees 30-60 kn. Open M-F 10am-midnight, Sa-Su 5pm-midnight.

MAKROVEGA $

Leština Ulica 2   ☎02 139 44 40 www.makrovega.hr

If you're a vegetarian, you're probably used to having your meals at restaurants dictated for you. The one salad on the menu? Yeah, that's what you're having. Makrovega, despite being a vegetarian/vegan restaurant, won't buck that trend: they have a daily menu available for 60 kn, and that's what you're going to get. Lack of choice aside, the folks at Makrovega know how to put on a fantastic meal: Dalmatian classics like gnocchi happily rub shoulders with seitan and tofu. Just make sure you have Makrovega's address written down before going out—you'll never find it otherwise.

i Daily menu 60 kn. Open M-F 9am-9pm, Sa 9am-5pm. Closed Sunday.

ADRIATIC SUSHI AND OYSTER BAR SPLIT $$

Carrarina Poljana 4   ☎02 161 06 44

Do you love fish but hate Croatian cuisine? Just head over to Adriatic Sushi and Oyster Bar, where you can savor fresh fish in a wholly different manner. The prices may be a little steep—expect to pay between 40 and 60 kn for four sushi rolls—but it's still one of the best places to indulge in seafood. At 14 kn, however, the oysters are reasonably priced—and given the fact that *Condé Nast Traveler* named "eating oysters in Croatia" as one of the essential things to do in Europe before you die, there's no reason not to indulge. To accompany all this, we recommend a glass of Pošip.

i Sushi rolls 40 and 60 kn. Oysters 14 kn. Open daily 1-11pm.

KITCHEN 5 $$

Ulica Kraj Sv. Marije 1   ☎02 155 33 77

Spend a little time in Split and you'll realize one thing: these restaurants are big on tradition. For a fresher take on Dalmatian cuisine, check out Kitchen 5, a hip new spot just steps from Narodni Trg. Menu highlights include the very filling salads (if the tuna salad is on the specials list, be sure to order that) and the charmingly small hamburger. Sit at a high table inside or in the small outdoor terrace.

i Salads 40 kn, entrees 80-100 kn. Open M-F 8am-midnight, Sa-Su 8am-1am.

VEGE $

Off Poljana kneza Trpimira   ☎095 896 51 86

Split can get expensive, and one of the easiest ways to cut costs is by avoiding sit-down restaurants. If you want to stay healthy while sticking to fast food stands, then head directly to Vege, a vegan fast food joint located near Split's port. Enjoy a soy burger, fried seitan, or just a healthy helping of basmati rice with rich tomato sauce. Once your meal is served, you get free rein with a variety of spices and sauces, letting you add all the savory delight you need to a vegetarian meal.

i Meals 40-50 kn. Open daily 9am-11pm.

DIOCLETIAN'S WINE HOUSE $$

Julija Nepota 4 ☎099 564 71 11 diocletianswinehouse.com

If you can't enjoy any meal without the accompaniment of fermented grape juice, we have just the restaurant for you. Diocletian's Wine House, located on a narrow street in the former palace area, offers tasty chicken, beef, and fish dishes, all of which taste much better with a glass of Pošip, Malvazija, Crljenak Kaštelanski, or whatever unpronounceable wine you choose from the extensive menu. Sit outside on the quiet street, or relax in the air-conditioned interior. Despite the restaurants name, the decor is more Restoration Hardware than Roman Empire.

i Entrees 70-140 kn. Open daily 8am-1am.

NIGHTLIFE

PARADOX WINE & CHEESE BAR

Utica Poljana Tina Ujevica 2 ☎02 139 58 54

Despite the name, there's nothing difficult to understand about Paradox Wine & Cheese Bar: it's simply the best place to get a glass of wine in Split. The selection of Croatian grapes is unparalleled, and since you likely haven't heard of any of them, you'll be delighted to learn that the menu is organized by taste and strength. Of course, some of these are far more familiar than you think—if you get a glass made from Crljenak grapes, know that you're ordering Croatian Zinfandel. Be sure to supplement your boozing with a cheese plate, most of which come with Croatian jam as well.

i Wines by the glass 20-35 kn. Cheese plates served M-Sa 11am-11pm, Su 3-11pm. Open M-Sa 9am-midnight, Su 3pm-midnight.

LEOPOLD'S DELICATESSEN BAR

Ujevićeva Poljana 3 ☎095 538 5129

You've probably guessed that a "delicatessen bar" isn't exactly the liveliest place in Split, but it's hard to argue with a place where you can down a great beer, then make your own sandwich. Leopold's is devoted to Croatian craft beer—their lengthy menu includes tasting notes for each brew—and the low-key atmosphere makes it a perfect place to really savor your glass of Nova Runda pale ale. The seating is almost exclusively outdoors, which is perfect for the warm Croatian summers. For the adventurous, the bar offers donkey sausage.

i Beers 13-40 kn. Open M-Th 8am-1am, F-Sa 8am-2am, Su 8am-1am.

TO JE TO

Ulica Tome Nigerova www.facebook.com/ToJeToCaffe

You don't like techno or flashing lights, so the bigger clubs are out of the question, but you also want a night that's a little less sedate than chilling at a wine bar. It's a dilemma, but the solution is simple: go to To Je To. This small bar, located near Marmontova Ulica, is well worth a visit for its cheap prices, selection of Croatian craft beers, and appealingly rowdy atmosphere. Trivia nights, live music, and karaoke are all part of the weekly schedule. The last of these occurs every Friday, and its low-rent energy makes it absolutely essential for any vacationer in Split. Best deal beyond beer: a Croatian rakija taster for 50 kn.

i Beers 16-20 kn. Open M-Th 8am-1am, F-Sa 8am-2am, Su 9am-midnight.

croatia

FIGA

Ulica Andrije Buvine 1 ☎02 127 44 91

Figa bills itself as a cocktail party in the street, and that's impossible to dispute. Located on a stepped street just off of Maruliceva Ulica, a thoroughfare connecting Narodni Trg and Figa, this bar puts out cushions and small tables for its customers to chill out on. Walk by and you'll feel like you've crashed a party—so why not sit down and join it? The cocktail list stretches ever so slightly more than the usual fare, while beers from Istrian craft brewery San Servolo liven up the menu. If you need something to slow down your alcohol consumption, grab a tasty fruit smoothie.

i Beers 20-25 kn. Cocktails 40-60 kn. Open M-Th 8am-1am, F-Sa 8am-2am.

CAFFÉ GALERIJA

Ulica Kralja Tomislava 15 ☎02 135 01 12 www.galum.hr

Why is Split's best cafe-bar located in the city's Gallery of Fine Arts? We have no clue, but the combination of solid drinks, live music, and a garden courtyard turns out to be damn near irresistible and far more unique than the other cafe-bars in the city. Enjoy piano music as you sip a local liquor (try borovnica, based on blueberries, for an exceptionally sweet drinking experience), or take advantage of the long list of teas.

i Liquors 10-18 kn. Beers and wines 20-30 kn. Open Tu-Su 10am-9pm.

RIVA BARS

Riva

It's difficult to recommend any particular bar on the Riva, but it's also impossible to ignore them. This is one of the nicest streets in Split; even after dark, the view of the port is magnificent, and the energy is palpable. The bad news, of course, is that most of these bars are fairly generic. They all serve more or less the same cocktails (mojitos, check; Long Island iced teas, check) and shooters (you can gauge how "classy" a particular establishment is by whether they offer BSOs or Bloody Screamin' Orgasms). They all have approximately the same prices (that is, slightly too high). Here are a few distinguishing characteristics: Caffé Gentile offers a martini endorsed by Dolce & Gabbana. Twins and St. Riva both offer two slightly different varieties of Long Island iced tea. Ćakula has a better than average beer selection: Brooklyn Lager, anyone?

ESSENTIALS

Practicalities

- **MONEY:** ATMs are located throughout the town; there are several Splitska Banka ATMs located on the Riva, for instance.

- **POST OFFICE:** Papandopulova Ulica 1 ☎02 134 80 74. Open M-F 7am-8pm, Sa 7am-1pm. Closed Sunday.

- **TOURIST INFORMATION CENTER:** Peristil ☎02 134 56 06. Open M-Sa 8am-9pm, Su 8am-8pm.

Emergency

- **EMERGENCY NUMBER:** ☎112

- **HOSPITALS:** Klinički Bolnički Centar Split, Spinčićeva 1 ☎02 155 61 11.

- **PHARMACIES:** Gundulićeva 52 ☎02 134 07 10. Open M-F 7am-8pm, Sa 7:30am-3pm. Closed Sunday.

Getting Around

The attractions in Split's old town are easily walkable; in fact, the narrow nature of many of these streets makes car or rail transport impossible. Public buses connect the Split city center with the suburbs, as well as neighboring cities like Omis (bus number 60) and Trogir (bus number 37). Tickets can be purchased at Tisak kiosks or on the bus.

croatia essentials

VISAS

Croatia is a member of the EU. Citizens of Australia, Canada, New Zealand, the US, and many other non-EU countries do not need a visa for stays of up to 90 days. Citizens of other EU countries may enter Croatia with only their national identity cards. Passports are required for everyone else. Despite being part of the EU, Croatia is not in the Schengen area, however holders of a Schengen visa are allowed to visit Croatia for up to 90 days without the need of an additional visa.

MONEY

Despite being a member of the EU, Croatia is not in the Eurozone and uses the Croatian kuna (HRK or kn) as its currency.

Tipping is not always expected, but often appreciated in Croatia. For bars and cafes, tips are not expected, but it is common to round up the bill. So if the bill comes to 18 kn, leave 20 kn. Tipping in restaurants is much more common, and you should tip your server about 10%, or 15% for really exceptional service. Taxi drivers also do not expect tips, but customers generally round up the bill.

ATMs in Croatia are common and convenient. They are often located in airports and major thoroughfares. Just look for a sign that says "Bankomat." The two major international money networks are MasterCard/Maestro/Cirrus and Visa/PLUS. To find out what out-of-network or international fees you may be subject to by using ATMs, call your bank.

DRUGS AND ALCOHOL

The minimum age to purchase alcohol in Croatia is 18, though technically there is no minimum age to drink alcohol (cheers!). Remember to drink responsibly and to never drink and drive. The legal blood alcohol content (BAC) for driving in Croatia is under 0.05%, significantly lower than the US limit of 0.08%.

croatia

CZECH REPUBLIC

Throughout the Czech Republic, the vestiges of Bohemian glory and communist rule can be found on the same block. More recently, the'90s sparked the transformation of this country into an alternative, electrifying country. Döner kebabs, bockwurst, and Czech cheeses are peddled side by side. Freewheeling youth and a relentless drive toward the modern mean endless streets of hip hangouts and vehemently chill attitudes, making Czech cities, especially Prague, some of the best student destinations in Europe. And even though the locals might be too cool for school they do appreciate a tenacity to learn, evident from all the Czechs who cheer your blatantly wrong attempts at their language. Whether they're dishing heapings of local cuisine onto your plate, sharing beers with you at a low-key Prague pub, or inviting you to a local party, the citizens will open their arms to you.

greatest hits

- **ART NOUVEAU'S POSTER BOY.** Get the full picture of the artist at the **Alfons Mucha Museum** (p. 84), which features original posters as well as other designs.

- **VITUS IS VITAL.** A trip to the Czech capital would not be complete without a visit to Prague Castle, in particular **St. Vitus Cathedral** (p. 94).

- **DRINK DRINK.** In case you had doubts, they named it twice: **Bar Bar** (p. 102) is one of the best spots in the city for nighttime drinks and international cuisine. Yum yum.

prague

Prague is the idyllic European city that European inflation hasn't yet found. In Prague, century-old tradition collides with Jewish history and modernization to bring you a city with a royal castle, the oldest operating synagogue in Europe, and quaint minimalist cafes. A true definition of Prague, however, would be: Gothic churches on Gothic churches. In Prague, you'll find all the Gothic churches you never knew you needed. If your visit is limited to the areas by the river—Old Town and the castle district—you'll hit the major sights, but will miss out on much of the city's charm. Tourists own the areas by the Vltava (you'll get really good at Segway-dodging), but the locals prefer neighborhoods like Vinohrady and Žižkov. Farther neighborhoods hold a reputation of a lively and interesting cafe and pub culture; Vinohrady is particularly well-known for catering to the LGBTQ+ community.

Orienting yourself in Prague is made easy by the presence of the Vltava River, splitting the city in two. The most famous pedestrian bridge is the Charles Bridge, named after Prague's beloved Charles IV. Prague had more kings than just him, but you wouldn't know it by looking at its history. Besides the Charles Bridge, the castle in Hradčany, the astronomer's clock in Staré Město, and Letná Park in Holesovice are must-sees. As you cover the city on foot, consider seeing it from above at Letná Park (home to a giant metronome that replaced a Stalin statue), at the top of the clock tower, or at Vyšehrad (an old fortress). Prague's characteristic red rooftops and cobbled streets, somehow, look even more beautiful from on high.

ORIENTATION

The Vltava River runs through Prague, separating the city in two and making navigation infinitely easier. The more touristy areas hug the edges of the river—Josefov, Staré Město (Old Town), and Nové Město (New Town) can be found along the Vltava on the right bank from top to bottom, and Hradčany and Malá Strana on the left bank. On the left bank, farther from the center, you'll find Holesovice above Hradčany, and Smíchov below Malá Strana. On the right bank, farther out, you'll find Žižkov to the right of Staré Město, and Vinohrady to the right of Nové Město. Each neighborhood has its own reputation, though in general, the closer to Staré Město, the more touristy the establishments. On the other hand, the more there is to see. Neighborhoods like Staré Město, Nové Město, and Hradčany are replete with sights, while farther areas like Vinohrady and Žižkov feature fewer sights but a more authentically Czech experience.

ACCOMMODATIONS

Nové Město

MOSAIC HOUSE $$

Odborů 278/4   ☎221 595 350 www.mosaichouse.com

True to its name, art installations greet you before you even step through the doors of Mosaic House. Giant mushroom sculptures stand close to the entrance; sculptures of men with umbrellas hang above. Inside, sculptures of headless human figures display information. The hostel is pricier than other Nové Město and Prague places, but the quality of the hostel reflects the extra cost. The common spaces look like the apartment you always thought you'd have in your 20s before you realized you were broke. Mosaic House also features their own Music Bar and Lounge, La Loca, revolutionizing the concept of "staying in." A fun night starts right downstairs. Moreover, Mosaic House sets itself apart by its commitment to their green initiative, realized through their energy, insulation, and water systems. Not to mention how green with envy your friends at other hostels will be.

i B: Národní třída. Turn left onto Spálená and then right onto Odborů. The hostel is on the right. Dorms 400-550Kč. Laundry 280Kč. Check-in 3pm. Check-out 11am. Reception 24hr.

HOSTEL ANANAS $

Václavské nám. 846/1   ☎775 112 405 www.hostelananas.com

Located off of Wenceslas Square, Hostel Ananas is new to the hostel scene, having opened in 2015 as the latest in the fruit-themed hostel collection. Close to both New Town and Old Town sights, Ananas, and the 24-hour McDonald's on the same street, could not be more convenient. While some of McDonald's portion sizes may seem huge, nothing about Ananas' rooms could be described similarly. The 8-bed rooms seem better equipped to be four-bed-rooms—as of now, only one thin person can fit between some of the bunk beds. Moreover, while some of McDonald's snacks are disappointingly low on meat, at Ananas, the see-through shower doors bring meat in great abundance. If communal nudity is bonding, visitors to Ananas are the best of buddies. Regardless, Ananas offers 24-hour reception, remarkably reliable Wi-Fi, and laundry facilities, making it one of the best options in the area.

i A: Můstek – A. From the station, walk down towards 28. října. The hostel is on your right. Dorms 330-400Kč. Check-in 1:30pm. Check-out 10:30am. Reception 24hr.

HOSTEL ORANGE $

Václavské nám. 781/20   ☎775 112 625 www.hostelorange.cz

Another in the fruit hostel series, Hostel Orange can be found on Wenceslas Square, close to the New Town sights and reasonably close to the Old Town ones as well. Each floor of the hostel is painted in a different color, which is probably best for getting lost college-aged kids back to their proper rooms. Among its facilities, Hostel Orange counts a common room, Wi-Fi, free towels, 24-hour reception and laundry services. Orange you happy you chose to stay here? Orange puns not included.

i A: Můstek – A. From the station, turn left to stay on Václavské náměstí. The hostel is on the right. Dorms 320-500Kč. Check-in at 1pm. Check-out at 11am. Reception 24hr.

prague

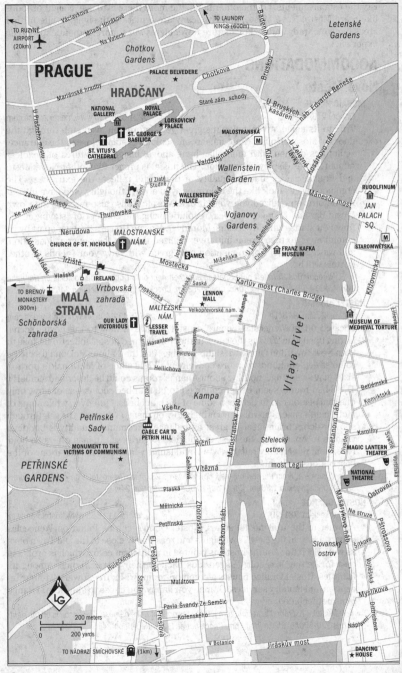

PRAGUE

HRADČANY

TO RUZYNĚ AIRPORT (20km)

Václavkova
Milady Horákové
Na Valech
TO LAUNDRY KINGS (600m)
Badeního
Chotkov Gardens
Letenské Gardens

Mariánské hradby
PALACE BELVEDERE
Chotkova
Bruskova
nábř. Edvarda Beneše

Staré zám. schody
U Bruských kasáren
U železné lávky
Kosárkovo nábř.

NATIONAL GALLERY
ROYAL PALACE
LOBKOVICKÝ PALACE
ST. GEORGE'S BASILICA
ST. VITUS'S CATHEDRAL
MALOSTRANSKÁ
M

U Prašného mostu
Zámecké Schody
Ke Hradu

Valdštejnská
Klárov

Wallenstein Garden

U Zlaté Studně
UK
Šporkova
Tomášská
WALLENSTEIN PALACE
Letenská
Vojanovy Gardens

RUDOLFINUM
Mánesův most
JAN PALACH SQ.
M
STAROMWĚSTKÁ

Thunovská
Nerudova
MALOSTRANSKÉ NÁM.
CHURCH OF ST. NICHOLAS

Jánský Vršek
Tržiště
Vlašská
IRELAND
US
Josefská
SAMEX
Mišeňská
U Lužického Semináře
Cihelná
FRANZ KAFKA MUSEUM

Mostecká
Lázeňská
Saská
Karlův most (Charles Bridge)
Křižovnická

TO BŘENOV MONASTERY (800m)
MALÁ STRANA
Vrtbovská zahrada
Prokopská
MALTÉZSKÉ NÁM.
LENNON WALL
Na Kampě
Velkopřevorské nám.

Schönborská zahrada
OUR LADY VICTORIOUS
LESSER TRAVEL
Karmelitská
Nosticova
Harantova
Pelcova
Hellichova
Nebovidská

MUSEUM OF MEDIEVAL TORTURE
Lihová

Petřínské Sady
Všehrdova
Újezd
Kampa
Vltava River

CABLE CAR TO PETRIN HILL
Říční
Šeříková
Seříková
Plaská
Mělnická
Petřínská
Zborovská

MONUMENT TO THE VICTIMS OF COMMUNISM
PETŘINSKÉ GARDENS
Vítězná
most Legií
Střelecký ostrov

MAGIC LANTERN THEATER
NATIONAL THEATER
Ostrovní
Smetanova nábř.
Divadelní
Karoliny
Pštrossova
Voršilská

Vodní
Malátova
Pavla Švandy Ze Semčíc
Kořenského
V Botanice

El. Peškové
Štefánikova
Preslova
Holečkova
Janáčkovo nábř.
Masarykovo nábř.
Slovanský ostrov
Na struze
Šítkova
Vodičkova

Myslíkova
Dittrichova
Náplavní

N
LG
0   200 meters
0   200 yards

TO NÁDRAŽÍ SMÍCHOVSKÉ (1km)
Jiráskův most
DANCING HOUSE

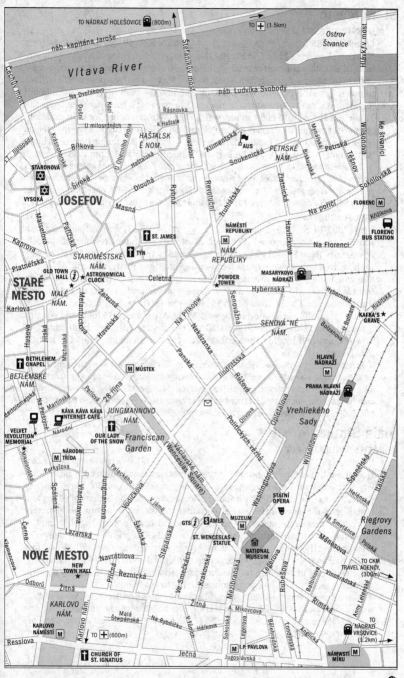

Staré Město

OLD PRAGUE HOSTEL $$

Benediktská 685/2   ☎224 829 058 www.oldpraguehostel.com

No funny business, kids. Old Prague Hostel sits right in front of a police station, next to a restaurant-club combo, and near a Korean restaurant. Any good night ends in handcuffs, but maybe it's best those aren't put on by a police officer. Two minutes from the Prague Beer Museum Pub and the club Roxy, for the alcohol inclined, it's not a long stumble home. Otherwise, it's four minutes from the Municipal House and eight minutes from the Astronomical Clock. In addition, as a sister hostel to Prague Square Hostel and Hostel Prague Týn, meager as it may be, breakfast is included. As college kids, this is a major turn on. Mmm. Something to think about while in those handcuffs, if you get our drift.

i B: Náměsti Republiky. Cross Na Poříčí, and continue onto Palladium. Keep walking as you pass Králdovorská/Truhlářská street. Pass Revoluční, pass Pizza Nuova and turn immediately after, keeping it on your right. Turn left onto Benediktská. The hostel is on the left. Wheelchair accessible. Dorms 560-700Kč. Security deposit 100Kč. Check-in 2pm. Check-out 10am. Reception 24hr.

HOSTEL PRAGUE TÝN $$

Týnská 1053/19   ☎224 808 301 www.hostelpraguetyn.com

Kid tested, nom approved. Free breakfast and an Indian restaurant literally downstairs from Hostel Prague Týn keep cranky travelers fed and well-tended to. Like wee babes, we require frequent feedings and distraction via Wi-Fi. Unlike wee babes, we require alcohol too. Prague Týn comes through on the first front with free Wi-Fi, as well as free lockers, linens and 24-hour reception. For the second, the Clock Tower Pub Crawl picks up from the hostel every night. Hostel Prague Týn is a four-minute walk to the Astronomical Clock, and equally, a four-minute walk to the Franz Kafka Monument. Accessible both from Old Town Square and Josefov, the location of this hostel is a major point of attraction for visitors.

i A: Staroměstská. Walk down Kaprova. Continue onto Nám Franze Kafky as Kaprova ends, passing in front of St. Nicholas Church. Continue as it becomes Staroměstské nám. As you reach the Ministerstvo pro místní rozvoj, turn right. Walk until you reach Týnská, turning left onto it. Turn left onto Týnská ulička, continuing as it becomes Týnská again. Hostel Prague Týn is on the left. Dorms 560-700Kč. Check-in 2pm. Check-out 10am. Reception 24hr.

Malá Strana

HOSTEL SANTINI PRAGUE $$

Nerudova 211/14   ☎257 316 191 www.hostelsantiniprague.com

Hostel Santini can be found on Nerudova, a street that couldn't get more touristy if it wore an I <3 Prague shirt. Actually, it sells those. But here, touristy translates to safe, and slightly inflated prices come with the benefit of shops and restaurants that crowd this street and cater to visitors. In a time of desperate hunger or desperate souvenir needs, Nerudova does not disappoint. Santini faces the Romanian embassy, recognizable by its sculptures of two muscular men holding the weight of the structure (men carrying their weight!). Breakfast in the morning—a pre-packed sandwich and cereal—are not always satisfying, but free. While in Malá Strana, Santini is remarkably close to Hradčany as well, making it an ideal choice for the tourist trying to cover both.

i A: Malostranská. From the Metro, take tram 12, 20, or 22 in the direction of Smíchovské nádraží, and get off at Malostranské náměstí. From here walk onto Malostranské náměstí and continue onto Nerudova. The hostel is on the left. Dorms 560-600Kč. Laundry 200Kč. Check-in 2pm. Check-out 10am. Reception 24hr.

HOSTEL MANGO $

Míšeňská 68/8   ☎775 112 625 www.hostelmango.cz

Part of the fruit hostel group, Hostel Mango is the Malá Strana one of the bunch. Close to Karlův Most and the Lennon Wall, the sweetest thing about this mango is its proximity to both Malá Strana and Staré Město sights. The bathrooms, admittedly, leave much to be desired – when the showers become unintentional baths, you learn the importance of carrying shower shoes. This isn't where Kim Kardashian would stay, but you aren't Kim Kardashian. Unless you are. Hey, Kim K! While more luxurious options exist, Mango is cheap and accessible. 24-hour reception, free Wi-Fi, free towels, and laundry services certainly sweeten the deal some.

i A: Malostranská. From the station, turn right onto Klárov. Continue onto U lužického semináře. Turn right onto Míšeňská. The hostel is on the right. Dorms 369-539Kč. Check-in 1:30pm. Check-out 10:30am. Reception 24hr.

Hradčany

ARPACAY BACKPACKERS HOSTEL $$

Nerudova 223/40   ☎251 552 297 www.arpacayhostel.com

Straddling Malá Strana and Hradčany, Arpacay is your girl Miley, in multiple-bed dorm form. The best of both worlds, Arpacay offers easy access to the Prague Castle, as well as the Charles Bridge. What we mean to say is that Arpacay is hella convenient. Planted on picturesque (and equally, touristy) Nerudova Street, Arpacay is in the part of Prague that ends up on postcards. Though the building that Arpacay occupies hails from the 16th century, its facilities have caught up to the needs of present-day. Arpacay serves all-you-can-eat breakfast for 130Kč, and boasts 24-hour reception, free towel rental, free padlock rental, and free Wi-Fi in its included services. Unlike much of its competition, Arpacay's rooms—even those with the most beds—embrace the idea of "personal space." Sardines no more, visitors have plenty of room to be.

i A: Malostranská. From the subway stop, turn right onto Klárov. Walk down this street for one block, then turn right onto Letenská. Continue onto Malostranské náměstí, and then onto Nerudova. The hostel is on the right. 10-bed dorm 440-490Kč; 4-bed dorm 540-590Kč. Laundry 149Kč. Breakfast 130Kč. Check-in 2pm. Check-out 11am. Reception 24hr.

Vinohrady

CZECH INN $

Francouzská 240/76   ☎420 267 267 612 www.czech-inn.com

Planted in trendy Vinohrady, the Czech Inn offers everything ranging from private singles to 36-bed dorms, and a comfortable first-floor lounge with alcohol and coffee to tie it all together. The shared facilities are sleek and modern, and the hostel is outfitted with a basement bar, laundry services, and the ever-essential Wi-Fi. If you're toward the 36-bed end of the range, the experience in the actual dorm room is about as pleasant as an experience with 35 other people can be. It's something like Russian Roulette, but chances are pretty good you won't get shot. Breakfast is served in the morning until noon for 150Kč, though there are also plenty of nearby cafes and restaurants for those willing to put on pants before eating.

i A: Náměstí Míru. Walk down Francouzská, which is on the southwest of the Metro station, near Retro Music Hall. The hostel is on your right. Dorms 400-500Kč, doubles 800-900Kč, singles 1800Kč. Check-in 3pm. Check-out 12pm. Reception 24hr.

Holešovice

⬛ SIR TOBY'S HOSTEL $

Dělnická 1155/24   ☎246 032 610 www.sirtobys.com

Equipped with a pub, breakfast for 150Kč, and reliable Wi-Fi, Sir Toby's is the whole package. Holešovice is at a distance from the center—accepting that, however, Sir Toby's is a solid deal. A well-kept kitchen and a nearby supermarket give thrifty travelers the option to cook rather than eat out. In addition, Sir Toby's offers 24-hour reception and free use of computers, hair dryers, converters, irons, and alarm clocks. Towels come at a 100Kč deposit and a 25Kč rental fee, but that's probably not a cost you'll want to skip out on. While "Sir Toby" may sound like a sex act, or something you'd name your miniature schnauzer, the hostel actually has pretty good vibes. All the shared rooms are reserved for those 18-39 years old, so there's a wealth of friends/drinking partners wandering about.

i C: Vltavská. Upon exiting the station, find Nábřeží Kapitána Jaroše on the south end of the station. Continue down this street onto Za Viaduktem and then onto Argentinská. Turn right onto Dělnická. The hostel is on the right. 12-bed dorms 400-500Kč; 4 or 5-bed dorms 500-800Kč. Self-service laundry 190Kč. Check-in 3pm. Check-out 11am. Reception 24hr.

PLUS PRAGUE $

Privozni 1   ☎220 510 046 plushostels.com/plusprague

Sauna and pool access win this hostel major points. And then a large lounge area, vending machines, and a nearby restaurant give this hostel the air of a nice hotel, but at broke backpacker prices. How else are you going to afford beer? It's at a bit of a distance from the center—approximately a 20-minute metro ride to the Astronomical Clock—but the facilities are nicer than what you'd find closer to Prague 1. 24-hour reception gives you the luxury of coming and leaving as you please and always finding staff available when you need them. Their restaurant and bar simplifies getting into bed after a crazy night; their 135Kč breakfast simplifies getting back out in the morning. For a little extra, you can get a padlock and a towel, and do your laundry here. Protect the bank; ward off the stank.

i C: Nádraží Holešovice. Upon exiting the station, turn left onto Plynární. Continue walking onto Ortenovo nám and then onto Přívozní. The hostel is on the left. Dorms 300-500Kč. Laundry 100Kč wash, 100Kč dry. Check-in 3pm. Check-out 10am. Reception 24hr.

SIGHTS

Nové Město

⬛ ALFONS MUCHA MUSEUM

Kaunický Palác, Panská 7   ☎420 224 216 415 www.mucha.cz

Much(a) to no one's surprise, the Alfons Mucha Museum exhibits a body of works by Alfons Mucha, as well as information on the artist and his life. Czech-born, Mucha's claim to fame came as he accepted a last-minute offer to create a poster for the Parisian actress Sarah Bernhardt. Bernhardt loved the poster, prompting Mucha's career. Mucha is best known for his representation of beautiful blonde women (in case you were wondering where Cosmo gets their ideals), within the Art Nouveau style. Okay, sometimes they're brunette. Mucha himself rejected this label, however, claiming that his style was not tied to the artistic style of the time, rendering Mucha the original hipster. After World War I, Mucha designed Czechoslovakian banknotes and stamps, featuring images of the Prague Castle found in Hradčany. The bills were widely circulated, granting Mucha a significant position in both the artistic and political history of the region. As fascism entered the scene, Mucha was arrested, interrogated,

czech republic

and then he died. The museum honors the artist's legacy, and like any decent establishment, has a gift shop with Mucha to offer.

i B: Můstek – B. From the station, walk down Jungmannovo nám. toward Na Můstku, and continue onto Na Příkopě. Take the pedestrian tunnel, from which you'll exit onto Panská. The museum is on your left. 240Kč, reduced admission 160 Kč. Open daily 10am-6pm.

WENCESLAS SQUARE (VÁCLAVSKÉ NÁMĚSTÍ)

Wenceslas Square, named after Bohemia's patron saint, Saint Wenceslas, functioned as a horse market in the Middle Ages. Quite a lot has changed since then—showering as a daily habit, for one, and the relevance of horse markets. Today's Wenceslas Square is a bustling block full of chain stores and vendors alike. The square serves as a central site in Prague, and fills regularly with tourists and locals passing through or visiting the National Museum, restaurants, or stores that stand on the Square. Throughout history, Wenceslas Square has held an important presence—in 1969, for example, Wenceslas Square was the site of Jan Palach's self-immolation protesting Soviet invasion. Today, Wenceslas is less about stirring up trouble, and more about stripping down. The Square is known for its strip clubs, and other similar services. During the day, it's much tamer however. Most tourists who visit New Town end up around the Square at some point. Stop by to see the statue of St. Wenceslas, and then check out David Černý's parody in the Lucerna Complex.

i A: Můstek – A. From the station, walk down Jindřišská.

DANCING HOUSE

Jiráskovo nám. 1981/6 ☎420 605 083 611

Nicknamed "Fred and Ginger," after the beloved dance duo in the early 1900s, the Dancing House presents a unique architectural feat. The building appears almost to be crooked or warped, and is said to resemble a pair converging together in dance, from where it gets its name and nickname. At the time of its construction, the building attracted significant criticism by critics who felt it clashed with its Art Nouveau surroundings. But buildings can have curves too, and public opinion has now grown to love and appreciate the Dancing House. At the top, the building features an international restaurant with a focus on French cuisine, appropriately named "Ginger & Fred" Restaurant. Precisely because the Dancing House was controversial at its inception, it has become a great tourist attraction and made an appearance on a series of architecture-themed 2000 koruna coins. Next in line: The Twerking House.

i B: Karlovo náměstí. From the Metro station, turn left onto Palackého nám. Turn right onto Rašínovo nábř. The building is on your right.

ST. HENRY'S TOWER

Jindřišská ☎420 224 232 429

The tallest freestanding belfry in Prague, St. Henry's Tower offers a view literally like that of no other bell tower. Despite its size, St. Henry's is often overlooked for other more out-there, in-your-face towers. St. Henry's has been reconstructed multiple times, following attacks and weather damage. The current tower stands at about 65 meters, composed of ten floors. Like any tourist site in Prague, St. Henry's has a restaurant, Zvonice, as well as a whiskey bar, a gallery, a museum, and an observation desk. St. Henry's Tower also features a carillon, and a bell preserved from 1518 on display in the restaurant.

i C: Hlavní nádraží. From the station, walk down Jeruzalémská. Turn left onto Senovážné nám. The tower is on the left. 100Kč, students 70Kč. Open daily Apr-Oct 10am-7pm; Nov-Mar 10am-6pm.

THE CHURCH OF OUR LADY OF THE SNOWS (KOSTEL PANNY MARIE SNĚŽNÉ)

Jungmannovo náměstí 753/18

The Church of Our Lady of the Snows was designed ambitiously, in the hopes of building a church comparable to the magnificent St. Vitus Cathedral. It never did

realize the goals of its creators, however, and that is a sentiment we relate deeply to. Sorry, mom. As legend has it, the Virgin Mary came to a merchant in a dream and told him that she would make it snow, despite the heat, and that he should construct a church on that site. Hence, The Church of Our Lady of the Snows. War wreaked havoc on the structure, and it has undergone several renovations throughout history. While not built according to the original plans, the church is still considered significant in Prague, and features a notably high altar and impressive vaulted ceilings.

i B: Můstek – B. The church is right outside the station. Open daily 9am-6pm.

FRANCISCAN GARDENS (FRANTIŠKÁNSKÁ ZAHRADA)

A little patch of hidden greenery, this park is lined with rows of roses, hedges, and benches. The Gardens offer respite from the chatter of Nové Město. While centrally located, the Gardens are easily overlooked, making it one of our favorite spots in the area. Previously a monastery, and a police station at one point, the site has now found its chill. Bringing a date here is highly recommended. Winking and whispering "I wanna see your secret garden next," not so much.

i B: Můstek – B. Turn left onto Jungmannovo nám. The gardens are on your left. Open daily Apr 15-Sept 14 7am-10pm; Sept 15-Oct 14 7am-8pm; Oct 15-Apr 14 8am-7pm.

EMMAUS MONASTERY (EMAUZSKÝ KLÁŠTER)

Vyšehradská 49/320   ☎224 917 662 www.emauzy.cz

The Emmaus Monastery was founded by Charles IV in 1348, and is associated with figures such as Jan Hus and Johannes Kepler. As legend has it, the monks of this monastery were so good that Hell sent the Emmaus Devil to distract them from their duties. Disguised as a cook, the Devil used food to interrupt the monks' piety, but was turned into a black cock when his intents were revealed. Never trust the cocks. Spared from destruction during the Hussite Wars, this building was briefly a Hussite monastery, though it has since been returned to the Benedictines. Despite the monastery's luck with the Hussites, Emmaus carries a history of trauma, like most significant Prague sites. Many of its monks were sent to concentration camps during World War II, and the structure was damaged by American bombings. The Emmaus Monastery has since been restored, however, and is notable for its preserved, elaborate frescoes and Gothic style.

i B: Karlovo náměstí. From the station, turn right onto Palackého nám and continue onto Zítkovy sady. Turn left onto nám. Pod Emauzy. Turn right on the next corner onto Pod Slovany. The monastery is on the left. 50Kč, reduced admission 30Kč. Open May-Sept M-Sa 11am-5pm; Oct M-F 11am-5pm; Nov-Mar M-F 11am-2pm; Apr M-F 11am-5pm.

Staré Město

CHARLES BRIDGE (KARLŮV MOST)

Bridge the gap between you and a date with a visit to Karlův Most, one of the oldest and most popular Prague attractions. Overlooking the Vltava River, the Charles Bridge offers a stunning view of lively Staré Město and Malá Strana, complemented by the calm of the river. There is something undeniably romantic about bodies of water, or so our YA novels have promised. It is said that Charles IV laid down the first stone for this bridge, back in the times where there was royalty who were "the Fourth" and people ran around marrying their uncles and shit. Old Charlie Boy married IV times—because monogamy was only in if you were a woman—and fathered 13 children. One too many to star in Cheaper by the Dozen. You overshot it, dude. The bridge today is lined with statues of saints, and its footpath is a hub for street vendors selling jewelry, portraits, and the like. This gothic bridge boasts a tower at each end of the bridge, and the kind of grim history that can only come with living alongside humanity. Floods and severed heads mark the past of the Charles Bridge, but the greatest threat you'll face today is a dress-lifting gust of wind or an errant selfie stick. Fear not, however, for the selfie you'll get out of it will definitely be worth it. Nothing says "I had a great time" like "I have a million pictures to prove it; believe me I had a great time."

i A: Staroměstská. Walk down Žatecká. Turn left onto Platnéřská and then another left onto Křižovnická. Follow Křižovnická, then turn right onto Křižovnické nám. Continue onto Karlův most. The bridge is within sight from here. Free.

ASTRONOMICAL CLOCK TOWER AND OLD TOWN HALL

Staroměstská náměstí   ☎236 002 629 www.staromestskaradnicepraha.cz

The Astronomical Clock, while a Prague favorite, may disappoint. (Read: small. Very small.) Hang around for a little longer though—the clock's got a little more than meets the eye. While the creator was first believed to be some poor fellow who was blinded so he could never make another clock like it, that is, in fact, nothing more than the product of some poor research. Oedipal themes aside, the real story is far tamer. The true creator was Miklaus of Kadan; it was made in 1410; no eyeballs were harmed in the construction of this clock. The clock features apostles that emerge every hour to figuratively wag their fingers at four figures representing Death, Greed, Pleasure, and Vanity. The clock is embedded in the Astronomical Clock Tower, part of the buildings that compose Old Town City Hall, notable for its historical function as a prison and damage at the hands of the Nazis. As a quick way to see the whole city at once, the view from the top of the Astronomical Clock Tower offers a magnificent glimpse into the happenings of the city, far above the red-shingled roofs.

i A: Staroměstská. Head down Kaprova toward Maiselova. Upon reaching Maiselova, turn left onto Nám. Franze Kafky, and continue down this street and make a slight right turn onto Staroměstské nám. Turn right around the corner, and the Astronomical Clock Tower will be on the right. Tower is wheelchair accessible. Astronomical Clock Tower 120Kč, students under 26 70Kč. Historical halls tour 100Kč, students under 26 70Kč. Tower open M 11am-10pm, Tu-Su 9am-10pm. Historical halls open M 11am-6pm, Tu-Su 9am-6pm.

CHURCH OF OUR LADY BEFORE TÝN (KOSTEL MATKY BOŽÍ PŘED TÝNEM)

Staroměstská náměstí

Prague's more goth than that choker you wore everyday in sixth grade. A softer side of the Gothic aesthetic, perhaps, the Church of Our Lady Before Týn is yet another Gothic church in Prague. You might have seen one around. Prague's kinda into them. This particular church resides in Old Town Square and replaced a similar predecessor, a replacement itself of a Romanesque church. The two spires of the church frame the skyline, though they are not of equal heights. One represents masculinity, the other femininity, and with a basic understanding of the patriarchy, you could probably guess which is which. Your mom always said that it's what's on the inside that counts, but this church is like Miley Cyrus—it's got the best of both worlds. The inside does not disappoint in the slightest. Sweeping high ceilings and gold-gilded errything, the building stands as a reminder that mankind produces beautiful things. It's rumored that the church inspired the architecture of the castle in Disney's Sleeping Beauty. Standing under its arches, it's quite easy to understand why. No prince in sight yet, but we'll definitely keep you updated.

i A: Staroměstská. Head down Kaprova toward Maiselova. Upon reaching Maiselova, turn left onto Nám. Franze Kafky. Make a slight right turn onto Staroměstské nám. Church of Our Lady Before Týn is on the left. Wheelchair accessible. Free. Tu-Sa 10am-1pm and 3pm-5pm, Su 10:30am-noon.

MUNICIPAL HOUSE (OBÉCNI DUM)   HALL

Nameští Republiky   ☎222 002 129 www.obecni-dum.cz

The Municipal House, the creation of artists in the early 1900s, today hosts a number of functions, among them Smetana Hall, a remarkable concert hall that plays a chief role in the music festival Prague Spring. Obécni Dum was built on the old site of the Royal Court, and in 1918, served as the location at which the new republic was declared. The Municipal House is known for its architectural style of Art Nouveau, a French term that translates directly to "New Art", proving once again that artistic talent does not extend to creative naming abilities. Like any attraction worth visiting, there's a restaurant inside, outfitted with the kind of chandeliers that imply you should probably find somewhere cheaper to eat. Enjoy a performance by the Prague Symphony Orchestra, and partake in the Prague Spring Festival if you're there in mid-May or early June. The official website encourages parents to bring their children, claiming that they will never forget "where the Royal Court was once located, which witnessed the proclamation of independent Czechoslovakia in 1918." They will most definitely forget this, but hey, you tried. That's almost enough.

i B: Náměstí Republiky. Tours 290Kč, students under 26 250Kč. Open daily 10am-8pm.

CHURCH OF ST. JAMES (SVATÝ JAKUB VĚTŠÍ)
Malá Štupartská 6

The Church of St. James was originally constructed in a Gothic style, but then it got Baroque-n. A fire in 1689 consumed the church, and it was rebuilt as a Baroque building. This gem of Prague serves as the resting place of Count Vratislav of Mitrovice, though he hardly rests in peace. They accidentally buried him alive—no one bothered to check, eh?—and for days after the count's burial, people heard noises coming from the tomb. As is logical, no one stopped to think, "Yo, maybe he's alive," and they just sprinkled holy water on him and went on with their days. Shit friends ya got, Count. If that's not creepy enough, a mummified arm hangs in The Church of St. James, supposedly the arm of a thief who tried to steal from the high altar of the church. Mary's got a side gig in law enforcement it seems, because legend has it she snatched the thief's arm and wouldn't release it until it had to be amputated. An interesting interpretation of "it'll cost you an arm and a leg," surely. A mural graces the top of the Church of St. James, and baby angels abound. Beautiful, yes, but the Church has got some skeletons in its closet. Literally.

i B: Náměstí Republiky. Free. Open Tu-Su 9:30am-noon and 2pm-4pm.

ESTATES THEATER (STAVOVSKÉ DIVADLO)
Železná 11 ☎224 901 448 www.narodni-divadlo.cz

A cultural center of Prague, the Estates Theater represents the caliber of the fine arts in Prague, presenting Opera, Ballet and Drama performances. Constructed in the 18th century, its architecture emulates a neoclassical style, and bears the motto "Patriae et Musis," proposed by its founder, Count Frantisek Antonin Nostitz-Rieneckwhich. This is a splendid name, the third part of which we can only imagine is pronounced "Nose Tits." Mozart's Don Giovanni premiered here in 1878, one of many fine works to be performed at the Estates Theater. Indecisive as ever, the theater has undergone many name changes, only to settle back down at where it started. Located near a major university, professors seem to have feared students would find performances at the theater more interesting than their lessons. What they seem to have overlooked is that essentially anything is more interesting than university lectures. The truth hurts, Professor.

i B: Můstek – B. Head down Na můstku and continue onto Na příkopě. Turn left onto Havířská and continue until you reach Ovocný trh. The Estates Theater is right around the corner, to your left. Open during performances. Ticket prices vary. Visit website for the most up-to-date information.

POWDER TOWER
Na příkopě

The Powder Tower, the result of a renovation on one of Prague's 13 original city gates, hearkens back to a time in which gates actually kept people out. Only

prague

true 11th century kids will understand. Once known as the New Tower, and for some time, Horská Tower, its name was changed to the Powder Tower when it started being used to store gunpowder. The Powder Tower, originally built in the Gothic style, was used for coronation ceremonies. The road from Kutná Hora also passed through here, connecting the city with Eastern Bohemia. Inside, a spiral staircase leads up 186 steps; a gallery near the top is accessible to the public and features an exhibition as well as a superb view of Prague.

i B: Náměstí Republiky. Head down Nám. Republiky onto Na příkopě. Make a slight right onto U Prašné brány. The Powder Tower is on the right. 95Kč, students 65Kč. Open daily Nov-Feb 10am-6pm, March 10am-8pm, April-Sept 10am-10pm, Oct 10am-8pm, .

ST. NICHOLAS CATHEDRAL (CHRÁM SV. MIKULÁŠE)
Staroměstské náměstí

If you Google, "St. Nicholas Church Prague," you'll pull up the one in Malá Strana instead, and that's probably what it feels like to have an older, much more successful sibling. St. Nicholas Cathedral—the one in Staré Mešto—stands as an architectural testament to the Baroque style. The green-spired cathedral, like almost any church in Prague, is a breath-taking sight; this one in particular serves a concert hall to the Czechoslovak Hussite Church, putting on performances everyday from April to November at 5pm and 8pm. On the inside; a large, flower-shaped crystal chandelier hangs, donated by Tsar Nicholas II.

i A: Staroměstská. Head down Kaprova toward Maiselova. Turn left onto Nám. Franze Kafky. Continue onto Staroměstské nám. St. Nicholas Cathedral is on the left. Free. Open M-Sa 10am-4pm, Su 11:30am-4pm. Mass at 10am on Sundays.

Josefov

A joint ticket (300Kč for adults, 200Kč reduced price) covers admission to the Pinkas Synagogue, the Maisel Synagogue, the Old Jewish cemetery, the Klausen Synagogue, the Ceremonial Hall, the Spanish Synagogue, and temporary exhibitions in the Robert Guttmann Gallery. Men are asked to cover their heads before entering the Jewish sites. All sights are within comfortable walking distance from the Information and Reservation Center of the Jewish Museum in Prague, where you can find tickets for tours and sites, as well as information maps and audio guides.

i A: Staroměstská. From the station, walk down Kaprova toward Valentinská, and turn left onto Valentinská. Turn right onto Široká. Walk down two blocks, and turn left onto Maiselova. The Information and Reservation Center will be on your left. Sites open Apr-Oct M-Th 9am-6pm, F 9am-Sabbath, Su 9am-6pm, closed Saturdays; Nov-Mar M-Th 9am-5pm, F 9am-Sabbath, Su 9am-5pm, closed Saturdays.

PINKAS SYNAGOGUE

The names of nearly 80,000 victims of the Holocaust cover the inner walls of Pinkas Synagogue, a memorial to the suffering borne by the Jews of Bohemia. Black and red prints span the synagogue, a visual reminder of the extent of tragedy the Holocaust brought. Additionally, the synagogue contains a permanent exhibit of children's drawings, kept from the concentration camp Theresienstadt. Originally a private prayer house, the Pinkas Synagogue is the second-oldest synagogue in Prague. Though closed during the Communist Era, the building was later reopened and now commemorates the loss of the Jewish community at the hands of the Nazis.

i From the information center, walk down Maiselova, and turn right onto Široká. The synagogue is on your right.

OLD JEWISH CEMETERY

About 12,000 tombstones fill the Old Jewish Cemetery, marking the remains of figures like Aaron Meshulam Horowitz, Mordecai Maisel, and Rabbi Judah Loew Ben Bezalel. The second oldest Jewish cemetery in Europe, demand for burials exceeded supply of plots, and much of the space now contains multiple bodies stacked on top of each other. The oldest tombstone at the site is marked with the year 1439, meaning the poor dude died during a time in which humanity still had not accepted that Earth revolves around the sun. Gray slabs stick out of the cemetery haphazardly like our teeth before braces and also after braces because we never wore our retainers. Pebbles lay at the base of the tombstones, commemorating the people who lay there in a Jewish tradition that swaps the perceived paganism of flowers for small stones. By the exit visitors will find the Ceremonial Hall, a two-floor museum on the history of Jewish burials.

i The entrance to the Old Jewish Cemetery is through the courtyard in the Pinkas Synagogue and behind the Information and Reservation Center.

SPANISH SYNAGOGUE

Complex geometric patterns outlined in red, green, and gold fill the interior of the Spanish Synagogue, known for its Moorish style produced by Josef Niklas and Jan Bělský. The youngest of the synagogues in Jewish Old Town, it is also perhaps the most beautiful, like the new kid at school that displaces the previously most popular. Better watch your back, Spanish Synagogue. The walls of the interior meet the ceilings at a curve, contrasting the straight lines of the floors and pews outlined with circular designs. The synagogue serves as both a concert hall and a museum, featuring exhibits on Czech Jewish history and silver artifacts.

i From the Information and Reservation Center, walk down Maiselova and turn left onto Široká. Walk down three blocks and at the roundabout, the Spanish Synagogue is to your left, right by the Statue of Franz Kafka.

OLD-NEW JEWISH SYNAGOGUE

Despite the name, the Old-New Jewish Synagogue is—as historians put it—hella old. The oldest operating synagogue in Europe, while actually new in the 13th century, the synagogue is now older than yo momma jokes. Like essentially all of Prague's churches, the synagogue was built in an early Gothic style. Legend claims that the remains of a golem, a protective monster in Jewish tradition lay in the attic of the Old-New Jewish Synagogue, after having been created by Rabbi Loew to defend the Prague Jews. Another tale posits that angels protect the synagogue from fire. So don't try dropping your mixtape here.

i From the Information and Reservation Center, walk down Maiselova. The Old-New Jewish Synagogue is on the right, by the corner between U starého hřbitova and Maiselova.

STATUE OF FRANZ KAFKA

This statue commemorating beloved Prague native, Franz Kafka, is the work of sculptor Jaroslav Rona, and features a large headless man with a small one riding on his shoulders (see also: Hagrid and his father, headless). The sculpture draws its subject matter from Kafka's own writing, a short story titled "Description of a Struggle." This memorial to Kafka, one of Prague's greatest, was given a Grand Prix award, and now stands near the site of Kafka's former home on Dušní Street. Though not directly related to the Jewish synagogues and cemetery, it happens to be remarkably close to the rest of the sites.

i From the Information and Reservation Center, walk down Maiselova, Turn left onto Široká. The statue is right by the Spanish Synagogue.

Malá Strana

🏞 PETŘÍN HILL

Prague has its highs and lows, and this is quite literally one of the highs. Petřín Hill, home to Petřín Tower, holds everything from a mirror maze to a memorial to the victims of communism. To the Czechs, it's just a nice park. The mirror maze, originating from the 1891 Jubilee Exposition, can be found near the tower, a favorite for children, narcissists, and people who just like mirrors, okay? For when Tinder pulls through, the Rose Gardens are the best place to break out into Shakespearean iambic pentameter. Success rate: mixed. On a similar topic, different direction, there's nowhere better than the observatory to break out the line "Are you from outer space? Because your butt is out of this world." Success rate: no data yet. With three telescopes and space exploration exhibits though, we'd say your chances look pretty good. At the base of the hill, you'll find a memorial to the victims of communism. If you're looking to spend a calm afternoon on the hill, bring along Milan Kundera's *The Unbearable Lightness of Being*. The hill is referenced multiple times in the novel, and that's some nice meta shit.

i A: Malostranská. Walk southwest toward the hill. Or, take the funicular. The funicular is considered part of the public transport system, and you can buy the same kind of ticket to use it (24Kč). The funicular starts at the Újezd tram stop.

▩ PETŘÍN TOWER

If being cheap has taught us anything, it's how to appreciate a good knockoff. The Eiffel Tower gets plenty of love, sure, but there's no reason to trek all the way to Paris when you can get (almost) the same thing right here in Prague. The structure of the tower is very deliberately modeled after that of the Eiffel Tower, resulting from a visit to Paris in 1889. 299 steps bring you to the top of the approximately 60-meter tower, shorter and fatter than the building that inspired it (see also: Angelina Jolie, us). The top floor offers a panoramic view of the city; the journey there offers quivering calves of steel. If the latter doesn't appeal, an extra 60Kč grants elevator access.

i Walk up Petřín Hill or take the funicular from Újezd. From the funicular stop, turn right and walk along the wall until you see the tower. Admission 120Kč, reduced admission 65Kč. Elevator 60Kč. Admission combined with Mirror Maze 190Kč. Open daily Apr-Sept 10am-10pm; Nov-Feb 10am-6pm; Mar-Oct 10am-8pm.

CHURCH OF ST. NICHOLAS (KOSTEL SVATÉHO MIKULÁŠE)

Malostranské nám.

The Church of St. Nicholas is considered one of the most beautiful examples of the High Baroque style. For the High Broke, admission isn't too bad either. One hundred years of construction went into the masterful structure that is now the Church of St. Nicholas. From the outside, the church is easily recognizable by its large green dome that stands tall against the Malá Strana skyline. On the inside, the ceilings are covered in elaborate frescoes—you've got your angels, your saints, your divine basics. Everything that could be gilded, is. For avid classical music fans, St. Nicholas Church holds frequent concerts.

i A: Malostranská. Turn right onto Klarov and follow Letenská to Malostranské náměstí. 70Kč, students 50Kč. Concerts 490Kč, students 300Kč. Open daily 9am-5pm. Concerts everyday except Tu 6pm-7pm.

LENNON WALL

Velkopřevorské náměstí

Everyone's favorite new cover photo, the John Lennon Wall came to be during the Czech Republic's communist era. Under the regime, western music was banned. The painting of Lennon's face onto a wall was an explicit act of defiance. Attempts to cover the face were all in vain; no matter how many times it was painted over, the Czech people replaced the image, expressing their hopes for peace through graffiti. This wall was, at its start, a countercultural symbol, art against the Man. Since then, the wall has gone the way of essentially everything notable ever: tourist magnet, beloved selfie background, cherished place to spray paint your name and that of your significant other. Put a big heart around it. The owners of the property have let the tourists and graffiti-ers have their way with the wall, filling it with, well, usually their names. Humans, we're a narcissistic people.

i From the Charles River, make a left turn onto Lázeňská after the bridge ends. Stay on it, then turn left onto Velkopřevorské náměstí. The wall is on the left. Free. 24hr.

WALLENSTEIN PALACE AND GARDENS

Valdštejnské nám. 162/3 ☎257 010 401

The Wallenstein Palace and Gardens bear the name of the nobleman who commissioned them, General Albrecht Vaclav Eusebius of Wallenstein, intending them to be his private residence. At the time of construction, the site occupied the space of over 20 houses. If that sounds excessive and unnecessary, that's because it totally was. Currently the site of the Czech Senate, the Wallenstein Palace and Gardens are still quite opulent and attract many visitors. The palace is built in an early Baroque style, and features stellar frescoes by Baccio del Bianco. Statues of muscular men wrestling stand alongside the rows of trimmed hedges in the gardens, no censorship in sight. One wall of the gardens is filled with artificial stalactites that contrast sharply with the rest of the carefully-kept area. At the end of the wall, an aviary stands.

i A: Malostranská. From the station, walk onto Valdštejnská. Turn left onto Valdštejnské nám. The palace is on the left. Admission free. Gardens open Apr-May M-F 7:30am-6pm, Sa-Su 10am-6pm; June-Sept M-F 7:30am-7pm, Sa-Su 10am-7pm; Oct M-F 7:30am-6pm, Sa-Su 10am-6pm. Palace open Apr-May Sa-Su 10am-6pm; June-Sept Sa-Su 10am-6pm; Oct Sa-Su 10am-6pm; Nov-Mar first weekend of the month 10am-4pm.

KAFKA MUSEUM

Cihelná 635/2b ☎257 535 373 www.kafkamuseum.cz

"The little mother with claws," said Kafka about Prague. It is now this mother that bears claim to Kafka, commemorating the writer's prolific legacy. In addition to the Kafka Statue in Old Town, Prague honors its city native with the Kafka Museum in Malá Strana. Outside the entrance of the museum stands one of David Černý's works, depicting two men pissing on the Czech Republic, moveable dicks in their hands. The top five reactions in this museum, in order: delight, shock, embarrassment, arousement, and apathy. Inside the museum, the designers create a Kafkaesque environment, as disorienting as the man's works. The museum exhibits a range of documents related to Kafka's life, including sketches, letters, and diary entries, with an emphasis on the interaction between Prague and Kafka's writing.

i A: Malostranská. From the station, turn right onto Klárov and continue onto U lužického semináře and then Cihelná. The museum is on the left. 100Kč, reduced admission 60Kč. Open daily 10am-6pm.

CHURCH OF OUR LADY VICTORIOUS (KOSTEL PANNY MARIE VÍTĚZNÉ)

Karmelitská 9 ☎257 533 646 www.pragjesu.cz

The first Baroque church in Prague—you read that right, Baroque—the Church of Our Lady Victorious dates back to the early 1600s. The church is not best known for its architectural style however, but for its figurine of the baby Jesus, donated by Polyxena of Lobkovic in 1628. The statue is believed to have healing powers, and to have served as a protectorate of the city during the Thirty Years' War. For this, the effigy has gained international recognition, receiving gifts from figures as famous as Pope Benedict XVI. All in all, the baby Jesus has amassed over 100 robes, a number that fills us with serious wardrobe envy. In the spirit of capitalism, take home your own replica from the souvenir shop.

i A: Malostranská. From the Metro, take tram 12, 20, or 22 in the direction of Radošovická , to Hellichova, which is 2 stops away. The church is right at the stop. Open M-Sa 8:30am-7pm, Su 8:30am-8pm.

prague

Hradčany

Around Prague Castle

The following sights are only a small sampling of what the castle complex has to offer. Both free and paid tours are available of this area. For the paid tour, two different possible routes. Route A (350Kč) covers: The Old Royal Palace, a permanent exhibition "The Story of Prague Castle," St. George's Basilica, the Golden Lane, the Powder Tower, St. Vitus, Wenceslas and Adalbert Cathedral, and the Rosenberg Palace. Route B (125Kč) covers: The Old Royal Palace, St. George's Basilica, the Golden Lane, St. Vitus, and Wenceslas and Adalbert Cathedral.

🏰 PRAGUE CASTLE

24 373 368; www.hrad.cz

Since the 10th century, Czech royalty and leaders have occupied the Prague Castle, the largest ancient castle in the world. In the castle complex remains the office of the President of the Czech Republic, and as such, is guarded by the Castle Guard. With all the contemporary enemies of the Czech Republic (like none), this position is primarily one of standing still in a fancy get-up without any of the fanbase of the beefeaters. Charles IV, of course, took his place in the Prague Castle for some time, and in 1918, the first President of the Czechoslovak Republic took up office here. During Nazi occupation, Reinhard Heydrich lived in the castle. Legend has it that anyone who unlawfully wears the crown jewels will die within a year. True or not, Heydrich fulfilled the legend, dying soon after wearing the jewels.

i A: Malostranská. From the station, walk down Klárov and continue onto Pod Bruskou. Turn left onto Staré zámecké schody, and follow the road to take the stairs towards Prague Castle. Open daily Apr-Oct 5am-midnight; Nov-Mar 6am-11pm.

🏰 ST. VITUS CATHEDRAL

Known colloquially as St. Vitus Cathedral, the building's full name is actually "The Metropolitan Cathedral of Saints Vitus, Wenceslaus, and Adalbert." We'd ask why Vitus gets all the credit, but with a name like Adalbert, the answer is pretty clear. Much to no one's surprise, St. Vitus Cathedral is an example of Gothic architecture and follows in the long history of multiple churches dedicated to St. Vitus, the first dating back to the year 930. St. Vitus Cathedral holds an important position in Czech history, and serves as the resting place of multiple queens, kings, and saints like Charles IV and his four wives. The Wenceslas Chapel is quite literally the gem of the site, adorned with 1300 gems, gold, original 14th century depictions of the Passion of Christ, and paintings of St. Wenceslas. The Czech Crown Jewels are also held in the chapel, though they are very infrequently accessible to the public and are protected by seven locks, the keys to which are in the possession of seven different Czech leaders. For a striking view of the city, head up the Great South Tower's 237 steps.

i A: Malostranská. The cathedral is slightly further behind the Prague Castle. To get there from the station, head down Klárov and continue onto Pod Bruskou. Turn left onto Staré zámecké schody and take the stairs. Continue onto U Svatého Jiří, then onto Hrad III. Nádvoří from which the cathedral is visible. Bell tower admission 150 Kč. Open Apr-Oct M-Sa 9am-5pm, Su noon-5pm; Nov-Mar 9am-4pm, Su noon-4pm. Last entry to cathedral is 20min. before close.

OLD ROYAL PALACE

"If it ain't broke don't fix it," is a saying best left to peasants. Royalty much prefer living by: "If it vaguely bores you, go ahead and get a new one"—a philosophy applied to servants, castles, and wives. While the Old Royal Palace was good enough for the likes of Charles IV and Vladislav Jagiello, later rulers just weren't feelin' it. The Old Royal Palace has remained relevant, nonetheless, resurfacing with different important functions. Vladislas Hall of the Old Royal Palace has served in the past as the site of tournaments and royal ceremonies and remains politically relevant. Vladislas Hall is perhaps best known by AP Euro and Latin students alike, however, for the Defenestration of Prague aka that time two Catholic governors were thrown out of a window. They survived the fall because of a pile of shit. Bullshit, if you ask us.

i A: Malostranská. The palace is right next to St. Vitus Cathedral. To get there from the station, head down Klárov and continue onto Pod Bruskou. Turn left onto Staré zámecké schody and take the stairs. Continue onto U Svatého Jiří, then onto Hrad III. Nádvoří from which the palace is visible. Open daily Apr-Oct 9am-5pm; Nov-Mar 9am-4pm.

Other Sights

STRAHOV MONASTERY (STRAHOVSKÝ KLÁŠTER)

Strahovské nádvoří 1/132   ☎233 107 704 www.strahovskyklaster.cz

Founded in 1143, the Strahov Monastery has survived wars, fires, and communism, and today you can go in to check out the library and gallery it houses. The works in the Strahov Book Collection number about 260,000, covering a diverse range of themes. In addition to books, the library houses a "cabinet of curiosities." which is quite different from your cabinet of curiosities next to your bed. Among the oddities are elephant trunks, a narwhal tooth previously believed to be a unicorn horn, and the remains of a dodo bird, a species that is now extinct. The Strahov Gallery, instead, features paintings from the 14th to 19th century. Expect a lot of paintings of landscapes, fruit, and constipated looking people. And if all this hasn't convinced you that monk lyfe can be fun, wrap up your time here with a beer at the monastic brewery.

i A: Malostranská. From the subway station, walk to the tram stop and get on the 22 tram going towards Bílá Hora. Ride for 4 stops and get off at Pohořelec. Walk down Pohořelec, and then continue onto Dlabačov. Turn right onto Strahovské nádvoří. The monastery is on the right. Gallery 100Kč. Library 100Kč. Gallery open daily 9:30am-11:30am and noon-5pm. Library open daily 9am-noon and 1pm-5pm. Brewery open daily 10am-10pm.

LORETO

Loretánské nám. 102/8   ☎233 310 510 www.loreta.cz

The Loreto in Prague holds great significance for Christians, and as such, is the starting site of many pilgrimages. A replica of the Santa Casa, or the "Holy House," stands as the focal point of the complex, believed by Christians to be the house in which the angel Gabriel visited Mary and announced her Immaculate Conception. The walls of the house were transported from Bethlehem to their current location at the Italian Loreto in the late 1200s, and a copy stands at the site in Prague. The site also incorporates the Church of the Nativity of Our Lord, notable for its 27-bell complex and beautiful carillon, as well as a treasury, which holds the "Prague Sun." This treasure holds 6,222 diamonds, making it quite a valuable artifact. Worldly goods are beautiful too.

i A: Malostranská. From the subway station, walk to the tram stop and get on the 22 tram going towards Bílá Hora. Ride for 4 stops and get off at Pohořelec. Walk down Pohořelec then continue onto Loretánské. Loreto is within sight after a block. 150Kč, students 110Kč. Audio guide 150Kč. Photo permission 100Kč. Open daily Apr-Oct 9am-5pm; Nov-Mar 9:30am-12:15pm and 1pm-4pm.

Vinohrady

VYŠEHRAD

V pevnosti 159/5b   ☎420 241 410 348 www.praha-vysehrad.cz

Vyšehrad, the site of a fortress overlooking the Vltava, dates back to about the 10th century, servicing Vratislav II and Charles IV at the height of its glory. Once a royal residence and military stronghold, Vyšehrad now lives out its days as a beautiful park with strIking views over Prague. Beloved by families and tourists alike, it's the Bob Ross of places. From war to tug-of-war, kings to engagement

prague

rings, Vyšehrad has now turned over to the peasants—a lovely, peaceful place to take a walk with kids or romantic prospects. Left over from its past are the St. Peter and Paul Church, the Devil's Column and the Vyšehrad Cemetery, where the Czech Republic's finest rest in peace. The graves of Antonín Dvořák and Alphonse Mucha, among others, can be found on the grounds. The Slavín tomb, the focal point of the cemetery, holds the remains of only the most important interred in the cemetery. The Devil's column, a pile of three small columns, is said to have resulted from a bet between the priest and the Devil. Why the Devil himself hasn't more important things to do (does hell run itself?) is beyond us.

i C: Vyšehrad. From the station, head north on Na Bučance. Turn right onto Lumírova. You will see Vyšehrad on your left.

Holešovice

LETNÁ PARK

The only kind of exercise you'll ever get us to do. A killer walk for a killer view, Letná Park sits atop a hill and offers the best view you'll ever get of the Vltava and of the city without getting on a plane. A bird-eye's view, no TSA-groping involved. The park is a popular destination for cyclists, skaters and runners—the winding paths and respite from the bustling streets offer a bubble of nature and calm in the heart of Prague. At the top, a large metronome marks the site where a Stalin statue used to stand. Up here, you can see the Vltava snake under bridges, red roofs in the background. It's Prague's best angle, and absolutely worth it.

i A: Malostranská. Upon exiting the station, walk down Nábřeží Edvarda Beneše. Letná Park is on your left.

PRAGUE ZOO

U trojského zámku   ☎296 112 230 www.zoopraha.cz

Petition to make elephants the dominant species. Do elephants bully others? Do elephants make others cry? Do elephants wear socks and sandals? They seem to be much more evolved than we are. The Prague Zoo is ranked as one of the best zoos in the world, making it a lovely place to visit in the afternoon. The baby chimp swings from rope to rope, egged on by audience amusement, while its parents lazily sunbathe. The giraffes stand perfectly still, seeing no reason to exert unnecessary energy. The polar bears swim laps all day because fitness is important. These animals have figured life out, and we have so much to learn. Spend a day among fur, claws, and scales and forget your obligations. They're social constructs anyway.

i C: Nádraží Holešovice. From the Metro, take bus 112. Take the bus seven stops and get off at Zoologická zahrada, or Prague Zoo. 200Kč, students 150Kč. Open daily June-Aug 9am-7pm; Sept-Oct 9am-6pm; Nov-Feb 9am-4pm; Mar 9am-5pm; Apr-May 9am-6pm.

DOX CENTRE FOR CONTEMPORARY ART

Poupětova 1   ☎295 568 123 www.dox.cz

Long gone are the days of vain Renaissance portraits and classical sculptures. Now is the age of—well, we're not sure. Photographs, yes, and twig and yarn sculptures. There's one of a twisted tire, another of a paper covered in ballpoint ink. There are murals, electrical schematics, and pornography covered in doodles. Contemporary art calls into question the substance of art itself. Is a twisted tire art? Is a piece of paper scribbled out art? Oh god, are we art? (We think you're a masterpiece btw). Find the answers to all these questions and more at the Dox Centre for Contemporary Art, a museum that houses the art the creative world is churning out nowadays, as well as a stellar cafe and design shop.

i C: Nádraží Holešovice. From the station, walk down Plynární. Turn right onto Osadní, and then after a block, turn left onto Poupětova. The Dox Centre is on your left. 180Kč, students 90Kč. Open M 10am-6pm, W 11am-7pm, Th 11am-9pm, F 11am-7pm, Sa-Su 10am-6pm. Closed Tuesdays.

NATIONAL GALLERY

Dukelských hrdinů 47   ☎224 301 122 www.ngprague.cz

Parts of the National Gallery can be found all over Prague, with the largest here in Holesovice. Like all great things, the National Gallery arose from a hint of elitism—an art collection formed by the doing of the "Society of Patriotic Friends of the Arts," with the aim of remedying the city's "debased artistic taste." The original hipsters, perhaps? The Veletržní palác is a functionalist building, with a wide space conducive to the exhibits it holds. Among the works displayed, you'll find names like Alphonse Mucha—the permanent exhibit emphasizes Czech artists while still including foreign talent, and centers on art in the 19th, 20th, and 21st century. With so many different National Gallery buildings out there, we're expecting to see a Buzzfeed quiz soon: "Which National Gallery is your spirit animal? And related Mean Girls gifs." This one may not be most relevant to your interests, but if the content does appeal, the site is sure to please.

i C: Vltavská. Walk down Heřmanova street. Turn right onto Dukelských hrdinů. The museum is on the left. Admission 200Kč. Open daily 10am-6pm.

FOOD

Nové Město

LEMON LEAF $

Myslíkova 260/14   ☎224 919 056 www.lemon.cz

Lemon Leaf is cheaper than it looks—in this case, that's a compliment. Large portions here will keep your energy up as you tour the city on foot. The dishes are altered to fit the European palate, but make for a lovely break from the traditional pork-heavy Czech cuisine. The restaurant's décor, unsurprisingly, is yellow-themed, is inviting, without being over-the-top. Less Kris Jenner, more Chris Pratt. For the picky eater, yes, there is Pad Thai.

i B: Národní třída. From the station, turn left onto Spálená. Two blocks down, turn right onto Myslíkova. The cafe is on the left. Noodle dishes 149-219Kč. Salads 189-199Kč. Alcoholic beer 39-59Kč. Open M-Th 11am-11pm, F 11am-midnight, Sa noon-midnight, Su noon-11pm.

GLOBE CAFÉ $$

Pštrossova 6   ☎224 934 203 globebookstore.cz

For when your attempts at Czech pronunciation have been laughed at just one too many times. Globe Café, an American expat favorite, is a taste of Prague with a nod toward the western. American foods dominate the restaurant's menu, English fills the air, and the bookstore works in Czech and English alike. Globe Café distinguishes itself further with cultural events at night, including film screenings, author readings, and live music. Escape the (dia)critics for a slice of America in the heart of Prague: wings, burgers, and grilled cheese sandwiches are all you need to feel at home. Star spangled banners not included. Healthcare, of course, also not included.

i B: Národní třída. From the station, turn left onto Opatovická. On the next corner, turn left onto Pštrossova where the cafe is on the left. Hot coffee drinks 45-80Kč. Pasta dishes 150-170Kč. Sandwiches 150-185Kč. Burgers 170-295Kč. Open M-F 10am-midnight, Sa-Su 9:30am-10pm. Kitchen open until 11pm. Happy hour M-F 5pm-7pm.

CAFÉ NEUSTADT $

Karlovo nám. 23/1   ☎775 062 795 www.cafeneustadt.cz

Wire sculptures dangle overhead; a piano stands next to them. Café Neustadt, a hip haven in the New Town Hall courtyard, boasts ample outside seating options and an equally charming inside. The chairs all seem semi-thrifted, but given Café Neustadt's clientele, this was likely on purpose. Neustadt has made a name for itself among the young and happening community, and keeps its cultured

trdelník

This street food is a sweet, doughy cylinder rolled in sugar, and you don't earn your Prague tourist badge until you've tried one. Staré Město, in particular, has plenty of *trdelník* stands lining Old Town Square and its outskirts. At about 60Kč, it's a little over $2, and well worth the price, at least once. A traditional Slovak treat, *trdelník* is hardly unique to Prague—in Hungary, it goes by *kürtőskalács*, *prügelkrapfen* in Austria, etc. If you're trying to figure out where to try the treat, the answer is definitely Prague. Who are you kidding? You can't pronounce *prügelkrapfen*.

reputation up with frequent concerts. Across the street from Mamacoffee, this is reason enough to drink more coffee. Stop by both, and bask in the glory that is a crippling caffeine dependence.

i B: Národní třída. From the station, turn left onto Spálená. Turn left onto Karlovo nám, where the cafe is on the left. Beer 25-38Kč. Wine 45Kč. Espresso drinks 38-57Kč. Open M-Th 8am-midnight, F 8am-4am, Sa 10am-4am, Su 10am-midnight.

Q CAFÉ $
Opatovická 166/12   ☎776 856 361 www.q-cafe.cz

We'll give it to you straight—Q Café is anything but. A rainbow flag flutters outside the establishment, and a line of rainbow light bulbs hang over the bar by the entrance. One of the walls displays artsy photos of naked men modeling together. The really naughty bits are all covered up, but if that's what you're looking for, you've probably heard of "the Internet." More than just an LGBT+-specific establishment, Q Café takes its commitment to the community seriously, and offers literature and products related to this topic, and more importantly, a safe space. While particularly loved by the gay male community, Q cafe is welcoming to all, within and outside of the community. Beers and queers, get your fill of both here.

i B: Národní třída. From the station, walk onto Ostrovní toward Spálená. Turn left onto Opatovická. The cafe is on the left. Nonalcoholic coffee 37-65Kč. Teas 37-80Kč. Salads 75-135Kč. Open daily 1pm-2am.

CAFÉ NONA $
Národní 1393/4   ☎775 755 147 www.cafenona.cz

Short for Nova Scena, or New Scene, the building containing Café Nona hosts modern theater performances, and looks like a physical manifestation of Jaden Smith's tweets. An ice-cube-alien-submarine something. The cafe occupies a floor of this space, and carries a confused public library aesthetic. Tables and comfortable couches are scattered throughout, illuminated by the light that streams through the waffle ceiling structure. The tables against the windows are particularly ideal for lunch dates, while the inner tables and couches are suited for reading or getting work done. At night, the patrons turn from caffeine to alcohol, the lights dim, and the place gets clubby.

i B: Národní třída. From the station, walk down Ostrovní toward Spálená. On the next corner turn right onto Mikulandská. Walk a block and then turn left onto Národní. The cafe is on the left. Coffee drinks 34-110Kč. Cocktails 70-120Kč. Beer 22-55Kč. Open M-F 9am-midnight, Sa-Su 11am-midnight.

Staré Město

EBEL CAFÉ $

Řetězová 9   ☎603 823 665 www.ebelcoffee.cz

The teacup pig of cafes. It's got two, maybe two-and-a-half coffee tables squeezed into a room that we imagine is comparable to Harry Potter's cupboard. And you'll love it. A visit to Café Ebel is probably the only time you'll get elbowed by another patron trying to pull out a chair and find it effing adorable. Small but mighty, Café Ebel serves quality espresso, desserts, and chocolate. A flyer on their coffee tables boasts Colombian coffee; their menu presents a United Nations spread of coffee beans for sale, hailing from Brazil to Zimbabwe. Phenomenal desserts proffer the sweet to coffee's natural bitter—try their apple pie (80Kč) with a cappuccino (55Kč). The small space isn't ideal for long stays, but free Wi-Fi keeps visitors to this cupboard of a cafe well-connected.

i A: Staroměstská. Walk down Kaprova in the direction of Maiselova. The cafe is on the left. Coffee 45-90Kč. Alcoholic drinks 40-295Kč. Pastries 80Kč. Open M-F 8am-8pm, Sa-Su 8:30am-8pm.

STANDARD CAFÉ

Karoliny Světlé 321/23   ☎606 606 806 www.standard-cafe.cz

A dented yellow canoe hangs from the ceiling of the middle room, and it's probably a symbol for something. Something deep. Nietzschean, surely. This slightly grungy cafe encompasses three rooms—the front naturally lit, the back two furnished with dim lamps, and all three filled with cigarette smoke. The artsy-fartsy vibes are strong with this one. The place boasts exposed pipes, mismatched chairs, an indie music selection, and aesthetic young people bent over journals and pints of beer. They all have cooler piercings than you and know like 34 bands you've never heard of. The menu offers a solid range of alcoholic, caffeinated, and none of the above drinks, in addition to dessert-y items, salads and paninis.

i B: Národní třída. Turn right onto Lazarská, and then right again onto Spálená. Follow Spálená until you reach Národni. Turn left onto Národni, and then turn right onto Karoliny Světlé. Standard Café is on the left. Coffee 29-75Kč. Cake 26Kč. Beer 20-70Kč. Salads 84-94Kč. Paninis 45-74Kč. Open M-F 10am-1am, Sa-Su 12pm-1am.

CHOCO CAFÉ U ČERVENÉ ŽIDLE $

Liliová 3/250   ☎222 222 519 www.choco-cafe.cz

A cup of Choco Café's hot chocolate running down your throat will bring you actual eye-rolling pleasure. Essentially a melted bar of chocolate, a mug of Choco Café's finest is no light dessert. Probably best to take on not-an-empty stomach but also not a too full one either to minimize ralphing potential. Strike the perfect balance and you'll achieve visceral satisfaction with Choco Café's hot chocolate with chili, orange, ginger or your favorite alcoholic indulgence. Complement your drink nicely with a croissant on the side (20Kč), and take it all in alongside vintage-y postcards. cats, gardens, crosses, and the like.

i A: Staroměstská. Turn right onto Platnéřská. Then turn left on Mariánské nám. Turn right on the first side street, and then turn left. Follow this street until you reach Karlova. Turn right and then immediately turn left onto Liliová. Choco Café is on the left. Hot chocolate 59-99Kč. Chocolate 89-195Kč. Coffee 39-95Kč. Hot alcoholic drinks 55-69 Kč. Open M-Sa 10am-9pm, Su 10am-8pm.

HAVELSKÁ KORUNA $

Havelská 501/23   ☎224 439 331 www.havelska-koruna.com

Not exactly Instagram material. The plastic trays and lunch-line serving style give off a middle school vibe, minus the trauma of puberty and bad haircuts. As a self-serve joint, enjoy authentic Czech eats here alongside real-life Czechs, not just selfie-happy Americans. You'll be handed a slip as you enter; as you order, the employees will write what you got on the slip. Unless you're finding your finances about 500Kč too solid, hold on to it. The menu is in both Czech and English, but most of the employees only speak Czech so go ahead and butcher their language a little. Whatever it gets you will probably be good anyway. And most importantly, cheap.

i A or B: Můstek. Follow Václavské nám as it becomes Na můstku. Turn right onto Rytířska, and then left onto Havelská ulička. Turn left onto Havelská. Havelská Koruna is across the street. Wheelchair accessible. Entrees 33-89Kč. Desserts 12-27Kč. Open daily 10am-8pm.

LA CASA BLŮ $

Kozí 857/15   ☎224 818 270 www.lacasablu.cz

Latin American eats? Let's taco 'bout it. Colorful knickknacks originating from various Latin American countries outfit the walls of Casa Blů, a restaurant that counts Argentinian chimichurri, Uruguayan beef, and tacos with pico de gallo among its offerings. Munching on Latin American cuisine in the Czech Republic minutes from the Jewish Quarter sounds like the start of some shitty joke—what do you get when you cross a Czech, a Jew and a churrasco? We didn't get around to making up a punchline to that, but anyway, globalization. A cultural hub, La Casa Blů played host to a 2000 Czech film, Samotáři, and regularly invites Latin American artists to perform or display their art. Swing by during happy hour to score a meal on the cheap (everyday until 5:30pm). The tacos chile con carne (175Kč, 120Kč during happy hour) are a huge hit and go nicely with a beer or Chilean wine. To be fair though, anything goes nicely with a beer or Chilean wine.

i A: Staroměstská. Turn right on Široká, and then left onto Kozí. The restaurant is on the left. Burritos 158-195Kč (Happy Hour 130-150Kč). Quesadillas 150-190Kč (Happy Hour 98-140Kč). Beer 21-44Kč. Open M-F from 11am, Sa from noon, Su from 2pm. Closing times vary. Happy Hour until 5:30pm.

KABUL RESTAURANT $$

Krocínova 316/5   ☎602 212 042 www.kabulrestaurant.cz

Culture in the form of a hunkering skewer of life-giving meat. The only Afghan restaurant in Prague, this place reps damn well. Arabic music videos play on the TV overlooking Afghan decorations. The famous National Geographic magazine photograph of a young Afghan girl hangs, framed. The seating is a mix of tables and chairs, and rugs with cushions circling a table. The food is, plainly put, delicious. Spring for one of the lamb dishes (220-290Kč) or a vegetarian dish (80-170Kč). The free Wi-Fi and (not-free) alcoholic drinks seal the deal. Is this true love or just lust? Who knows, but damn are we ready for that meat.

i B: Národní třída. Turn right onto Lazarská, and then right onto Spálená. Continue on this street and then turn left onto Národní and right onto Karoliny Světlé. Follow this street until reach a fork. Take the left fork onto Krocínova and arrive at Kabul Restaurant. Beef entrees 90-240Kč. Lamb entrees 220-290Kč. Vegetarian entrees 80-170Kč. Dessert 50-90Kč. Open daily 11:30am-11pm.

LOKÁL $

Dlouhá 33   ☎222 316 265 lokal-dlouha.ambi.cz

Size matters—and this place knows it. The restaurant spans the length of a block, but they don't seem to have trouble filling up. Cheap meals and quality tank beer draw in crowds looking for an authentic taste of Prague. If you didn't come to Prague for the absinth, maybe you came for the beer, and if PBR's all you've known till now, it's probably best you don't mention that. Czech out the beer (32-45Kč) and have a meal while you're at it. For vegetarians, the daily menus feature two salads and one non-salad vegetarian dish.

i B: Náměsti Republiky. Cross Na Poříčí, and continue on Palladium. Pass Pizza Nuovo and turn right immediately after. Follow this path as it merges with Benediktská. Turn left onto Dlouhá. Lokál is on your right. Wi-Fi available. Beer 32-45Kč. Sides 35-45Kč. Entrees 105-195Kč. Open M-Sa 11am-1am, Su 11am-midnight. Express meal available M-F 11am-3pm.

prague

Josefov

🏛 KAFKA SNOB FOOD $$

Široká 64/12   ☎420 725 915 505

In a swarm of overpriced tourist traps, Kafka Snob Food escapes the worst of it. The restaurant has an edgy industrial aesthetic, mixed with bright lights and KAFKA spelled out in big letters, should you forget for a moment where you are. Snobs or not—we'll leave that up to you to determine—the food does not disappoint. Should Josefov leave you tired out, this place has all the trappings of a cafe, and can make cappuccinos just as good as those of that minimalist Tumblr-looking cafe you probably prefer. A short walk from the sights, Kafka Snob Food is an ideal place to sit, recharge, and nom the ache in your feet away.

i A: Staroměstská. From the station, walk down Kaprova and turn left onto Valentinská. On the next corner, turn right onto Široká. The restaurant is on the right. Espresso drinks 55-80Kč. Entrees 195-350Kč. Open M-Sa 8am-10pm, Su 10am-10pm.

KOLONIAL $$

Široká 25/6   ☎224 818 322 www.kolonialpub.cz

Inexplicably, wheely attached to a bicycle theme. On Kolonial's windows are printed outlines of people on bicycles. The motif carries on to the interior as well with cycle pieces displayed throughout the space. Kolonial serves Czech cuisine and the kind of portion sizes you like to see when you've done more walking than your feet ever asked for. If you judge your food by literal height, go for one of the skewers. Served vertically, it gives the illusion of consuming a small edible tower; admittedly, somewhat amusing. Like Kafka Snob Food, Kolonial is quite close to the sights.

i A: Staroměstská. From the station, walk down Kaprova and turn left onto Valentinská. On the next corner, turn right onto Široká. The restaurant is on the right. Skewers 178-278Kč. Grill entrees 158-285Kč. Bottled beer 42-49 Kč. Open M-F 9am-midnight, Sa-Su 9am-midnight.

Malá Strana

🏛 CUKRKÁVALIMONÁDA $$

Lázeňská 7   ☎257 225 396

The name is the second best thing to have been on your tongue. First is their food. Come on, don't be dirty. A cafe-restaurant, Cukrkávalimonáda has all the trappings of a trendy Prague spot—magnificent chalkboard art, wooden stools and tables—with the menu of a restaurant to round it all out. Minutes from the Lennon Wall, Cukrkávalimonáda is the perfect place to unwind and process Lennon's revolutionary messages. If you're aching for Western ways, try the Camembert sandwich, a Czech twist on the classic American grilled cheese. Say yes to the dess(ert), and finish your meal with something sweet.

i A: Malostranská. From the station, turn right onto Klárov. Continue onto U lužického semináře. Turn right onto Saská, and then a left onto Lázeňská. The restaurant is on the right. Breakfast 69-249Kč. Sandwiches 159-249Kč. Coffee drinks 65-149Kč. Open daily 9am-7pm.

BAR BAR $$

Všehrdova 436/17   ☎257 312 246

Somewhat hidden, Bar Bar can be found on a street off of the main street in Malá Strana, and is truly a gem. Inside, wine bottles decorate the shelves built into one of the walls, imbuing the place with a sense of elegance. Sure, our collection of wine bottles is "concerning" and "a way of avoiding our problems," but Bar Bar's is "fancy" and "a nice touch." Anyway. The restaurant looks far more upscale than its prices reflect—the wine bottles and polished interior make a cheap meal feel like a splurge. The daily menu also often includes vegetarian options, which can be a difficult find in pork-loving Prague. If you're looking for drinks instead, Bar Bar is unsurprisingly, also a bar.

i A: *Malostranská. From the Metro, take tram 12, 20, or 22 in the direction of Radošovická , to Hellichova, which is 2 stops away. From the stop continue walking down Újezd. Turn left onto Všehrdova. The restaurant is on the left. Coffee and tea 37-54Kč. Entrees 155-235Kč. Burgers 180-190Kč. Open daily 11:30am-11:30pm.*

GREEN SPIRIT VEGETARIAN BISTRO & CAFÉ $
Hellichova 397/14   ☎257 317 459 www.greenspiritbistro.cz

Vegetarian food as delicious as this? Your friends will be green with envy. Meatless munchies can be difficult to track down in Prague, a city known for its meat-heavy cuisine. You'll pass restaurant after restaurant advertising pork knuckles, but very few vegetarian options, much less healthy ones. How many times can you eat fried cheese without having a heart attack? If you're looking for a vegetarian meal in Malá Strana, head to Green Spirit Vegetarian Bistro & Café, located a few blocks from Petřín Hill and the Church of Our Lady Victorious. Fettucine, tofu burgers, and paella are just some of the main dishes the restaurant offers, in addition to fruit cocktails to wash it all down.

i A: *Malostranská. From the Metro, take tram 12, 20, or 22 in the direction of Radošovická, to Hellichova, which is two stops away. From the stop, continue walking down Újezd. Turn right onto Hellichova. The restaurant is on the right. Coffee drinks 35-60Kč. Appetizers 60-65Kč. Entrees 129-159Kč. Open daily 10am-8pm.*

BELLA VIDA CAFÉ $
Malostranské nábř. 563/3   ☎221 710 494 www.bvcafe.cz

In Spanish, the name Bella Vida translates to "Beautiful Life," strikingly appropriate for a cafe that overlooks the Vltava. The outdoor seating of this establishment hangs over the quiet river, a view worth more than what you'll pay. On the inside, the décor is refined and elegant, filled with dark polished wood and a small collection of books. The establishment has a romantic ambiance—bring the cutest person you see along and let the place work its magic. We, for example, brought ourselves. #selflove. A meal here in their outside seating makes for the perfect lazy summer afternoon, a reminder that life is indeed beautiful.

i A: *Malostranská. From the Metro, turn right and onto Klárov. Continue onto U lužického semináře. Turn left onto Na Kampě. Continue onto U Sovových mlýnů, and then take the stairs and turn left onto Malostranské nábř. The cafe is on the right. Coffee drinks 50-145Kč. Salads 155-265Kč. Pasta 155-185Kč. Open daily 8:30am-10pm.*

Hradčany

KÁVARNA NOVÝ SVĚT $
Nový Svět 2   ☎242 430 700 kavarna.novysvet.net

Meaning "New World," Nový Svět is a short distance from the tourist-overrun sites in Hradčany, tucked just far away enough to escape the crowds of tourists. A New World, indeed. Nový Svět is your classic minimalist, delicate Prague cafe with drinks and desserts that put Starbucks to shame. To be fair, it doesn't take much to put Starbucks to shame. Located on a small winding cobble-stoned street, the cafe has a romantic small European town feel. Outdoor seating and indoor seating are both available, to suit your current outlook on nature, humanity, and how close you want to be to each. They don't have much on the menu besides caffeine and simple carbs; if your diet consists of more than that (why?), it's best to stop for a bite to eat beforehand.

i A: *Malostranská. From the subway station find the tram stop, and get on the 22 tram heading towards Bílá Hora. Ride this for 3 stops, and get off at Brusnice. From this stop, turn right onto Jelení. Turn left onto Černínská, then left onto Nový Svět. The cafe is on the left. Espresso drinks 35-45Kč. Beverages 35-38Kč. Savory food 38-68Kč. Open daily 11am-7pm.*

U ZAVĚŠENÝHO KAFE $

Úvoz 6   ☎605 294 595 www.uzavesenyhokafe.cz

Kindness is a universal concept, and one that reigns at U Zavěšenýho Kafe. This pub, a local favorite, sets itself apart from the flock of traditional Czech restaurants with its "pay-it-forward" coffee initiative. At U Zavěšenýho Kafe, patrons can pay for an extra cup of coffee or redeem an already-paid-for cup, as tracked by an abacus that hangs inside. Apart from their "hanged coffee" scheme, from which they derive their name, the pub displays comical, eclectic murals and equally odd sculptures. Not to mention their cult-like following. There are religions in this world with less devoted followers than this place. Salvation, U Zavěšenýho Kafe, does not promise—but good food and a relaxed quirky dinner atmosphere, yes.

i A: Malostranská. From the subway stop, turn right onto Klárov. Walk down one block then turn right onto Letenská. Follow onto Malostranské náměstí, then Nerudova, and then onto Úvoz. The cafe is on the right.Vegetarian dishes 85-145Kč. Entrees 65-175Kč. Salads 40-70Kč. Open daily 11am-midnight, kitchen closes at 10pm.

CRÊPERIE U KAJETÁNA $

Nerudova 278/17   ☎773 011 031

Crêperie U Kajetána knows its target group well: humans. Is there anything we love more than ourselves? Of course not, and Crêperie U Kajetána celebrates that charming narcissism. Black walls and chalk mean that every visitor and their favorite grandma can have their name written on the interior of the restaurant. The black walls are covered in the notes of everyone who stopped by recently, some reaching heights that make you question who stood on who and how. As for the food, U Kajetána successfully does not screw up one of the easiest foods to screw up. The crêpes—or palačinky, as the Czechs call them—come in sweet or savory variations, including toppings like chocolate and raspberries, goat cheese and pear, and grilled chicken and mushroom.

i A: Malostranská. Turn right onto Klárov. Walk down for one block then turn right onto Letenská. Continue onto Malostranské náměstí, and then onto Nerudova. The Crêperie is on the left. Sweet crêpes 99-149Kč. Savory galettes 129-169Kč. Trdelník 60 Kč. Open daily 9:30am-8pm.

Vinohrady

MONOLOK CAFÉ $

Moravská 1540/18   ☎739 018 195 www.monolok.cz

Metal abstract sculptures resembling twisted paper clips or tin foil after you unwrap your sandwich decorate the walls of this bright, naturally lit cafe. Art? Scrap metal? ¿Por qué no los dos? In addition to all that vitamin D, Monolok's menu provides plenty of healthy dining choices, among them a stellar open-faced salmon, spinach, lemon, thyme, and yogurt sandwich. When's the last time you put thyme in anything? We're not sure we could answer this question ourselves. Clean neutral tones dominate this cafe, and make it a lovely place to do work.

i A: Náměstí Míru. Walk down Korunní toward Blanická. Turn right onto Budečská. Walk down another block, and turn left onto Moravská. The cafe is on your right. Espresso 39-110Kč. Burgers 139-179Kč, Breakfast options 69-99Kč. Open M-F 8am-10pm, Sa-Su 10am-7pm.

MOZAIKA BURGER $

Nitranská 13   ☎420 224 253 011 www.mozaikaburger.cz

A classic for a reason. When all else goes wrong, beef and cheese do not. When trying new things leaves you battered and bruised, turn to an old comfort for the kind of love drunk guys in clubs will never give you. Mozaika Burger wins the burger award (does not exist, we think), and consequently, wins our hearts. They've got the tried and true burger varieties, but branch out with pesto, different kinds of cheese, cilantro, and the like. Cheesecake, cookies or ice cream, as these things tend to do, end your meal on a perfect, sweet note.

i A: Jiřího z Poděbrad. From the station, walk down Vinohradská toward Nitranská. Turn right onto Nitranská. The restaurant is on your right. Burgers 154-195Kč. Desserts 39-95Kč. Open M-Sa 11:30am-11pm.

CAFÉ MEZI ZRNKY $

Sázavská 19 ☎420 732 238 833

Your typical cute cafe with really, really good cappuccinos, Café Mezi Zrnky makes for a lovely stop in your day. Benches line the sides of the cozy room, and the baristas seem to have impeccable taste in American indie music. A chalkboard hangs above the kitchen part of the cafe listing the espresso options, the ceiling is covered by a draped white sheet, the wooden boards of the kitchen area are casually white-washed, and the entire thing looks vaguely like something we've seen on Pinterest. Yeah, we'd pin dat.

i A: Náměstí Míru. Walk down Korunní toward Blanická. Turn left onto Sázavská. The cafe is on your left. Open M-F 7:30am-6:30pm, Sa 9:30am-3:30pm.

DISH FINE BISTRO $

Římská 1196/29 ☎420 222 511 032

The name sounds like a bad translation or a poetic statement—and yeah, we'd spit a few verses for these burgers. Dish Fine keeps it short and sweet—burgers, salads and desserts, strong emphasis on the first one. For the stubborn (we prefer well-accustomed), you've got your basic beef-cheddar burger; for everyone else, combos like cured ham and eggplant, pickled shiitake mushrooms and spicy kimchi sauce, and rucola and sundried tomatoes. The restaurant itself is slightly upscale with nice wooden tables, which we'd describe as "good for pretending you're not just eating a burger." Denial is the best state of them all, friends.

i A: Náměstí Míru. Turn right onto Ibsenova. After a block, turn left at Římská. The restaurant is on your right. Burgers 165-195Kč. Open M-Sa 11am-10pm, Su noon-10pm.

U DĚDKA $$

Na Kozačce 12 ☎420 222 522 784 www.udedka.cz

Czech pubs abound, but some are better than others, and this is one of the best. U Dědka is more than meets the eye—chicken wings, duck confit, and quesadillas all find themselves on the same menu here. The pub is a little more upscale than one might expect for their prices, outfitted with paintings and complemented by Wi-Fi. One of the paintings is of a naked woman, which offends us deeply. Sure, when she's naked in the restaurant it's all "art" and "classy," but when we start taking off our clothes it's all "stop," and "please don't." Ugh.

i A: Náměstí Míru. Turn right onto Máchova, and then take the next left onto Rybalkova. Turn right onto Na Kozačce. The restaurant is on the left. Salads 140-145Kč. Main Dishes 140-235Kč. Desserts 80-85 Kč. Open M-F 11am-1am, Sa-Su 4pm-1am.

MAMACOFFEE $

Londýnská 122/49 ☎420 773 263 333 www.mamacoffee.cz

Mothers and coffee do indeed both give life, but so does Wi-Fi and on that front, Mamacoffee just doesn't come through. In the spirit of compensation, this cafe offers quality espresso drinks in delicate blue and white mugs with mild Martha Stewart vibes. You wouldn't think it if you saw it, but Mamacoffee is indeed a chain with multiple stores throughout Prague. The cafes maintain a small-cafe feel still, masking well their mitosis. In addition to prepared drinks, Mamacoffee sells a fine selection of beans and grounds so you too can engage in the process of quality caffeination.

i A: Náměstí Míru. From the station, turn right. Make a left onto Londýnská. Mamacoffee is on the right. Coffee 39-62Kč. Breakfast 45-75Kč. Entrees 105-135Kč. Open M-F 8:30am-8pm, Sa-Su 9am-6pm.

prague

KAFÉ KAKAO $

Americká 2   ☎777 903 902 www.kafekakao.cz

A relaxed coffee spot, Kafé Kakao drops all pretenses and does good food, good coffee, and good prices all within a pretty enough place. Kakao buys into none of the hipster thing, leaving abstract art and IKEA vibes to the young mustachioed crowd. A room of the cafe is dedicated to babies and kids, inviting families to stop by and let their snot-nosed miracles crawl around for a bit. Head to the adult section to enjoy a small meal and a coffee. Among the options are bruschetta, baked goat cheese, and couscous salad.

i A: Náměstí Míru. Walk down Americká for about for about five minutes. Kafé Kakao is on the left. Breakfast 45-92Kč, Salads 69-129Kč. Open daily 10am-7pm.

Holešovice

BIBLIOTECA DEL VINO $

Komunardů 894/32   ☎775 506 606 www.bibliotecadelvino.cz

Despite the name, there aren't really books, but there's plenty of alcohol. The semblance of class without any of the effort-consuming parts. The ceiling is detailed in graffiti, there's a wall entirely filled with wine bottles, and they serve damn good rosé. Pick your poison—in addition to wine, Biblioteca sells espresso drinks, delectable chocolate cake, and a respectable array of cheese. There's also salad, but we figured we'd start with the good things. On the downside, they're closed past 11pm and on weekends. On the upside, this is the perfect excuse for day drinking.

i C: Vltavská. Walk onto Nábřeží Kapitána Jaroše at the south end of the station. Continue onto Za Viaduktem and then onto Argentinská. Turn right onto Dělnická and then left onto Komunardů. Biblioteca is on the right. Wine by glass 70-90Kč. Espresso drinks 35-145 Kč. Chocolate cake 75 Kč. Open M-F 3:30pm-11pm.

OUKY DOUKY COFFEE $

Janovského 14   ☎266 711 531 www.oukydouky.cz

Ouky Douky doesn't look like much from the outside, but the inside is something like an espresso/book paradise. Shelves of worn books for sale line the walls, making this feel like a cafe plopped down in the heart of your favorite used bookstore. In addition, the expansive menu, which ranges from soup to sandwiches, mean that you could stay there all day, and finally make it through your summer reading. Refresh yourself and your soul with a visit to this literary hotspot. Read a book while enjoying your cappuccino and pretend you're Fitzgerald. Or substitute coffee for alcohol and pretend you're Hemingway.

i C: Vltavská. Upon exiting the station, turn left onto Heřmanova. Walk down this street and then turn left onto Janovského. The coffee shop is on your left. Espresso drinks 34-58Kč. Sandwiches 86-126Kč. Open daily 8am-midnight.

RESTAURANT BATERKA $$

Dělnická 71   ☎266 711 185 www.baterka.com

For those staying at Sir Toby's Hostel, Restaurant Baterka is but a short walk for large portions at reasonable prices. The restaurant's bright orange walls and tables look clean and nice, but the greatest appeal comes in Baterka's low prices. Perhaps not the best logic for picking a prostitute, but for a restaurant, it'll get you satisfied. This place serves respectable carb and crêpe options, two of our favorite c-words, right under "cocktails," and some other words we can't say. But if you're looking for a cheap and delicious dinner, stop by here.

i C: Vltavská. Upon exiting the station, walk onto Nábřeží Kapitána Jaroše. Continue onto Za Viaduktem. Continue walking onto Argentinská. Turn right onto Dělnická. The restaurant is on the left, about five blocks down the street. Pasta dishes 115-195Kč. Entrees 133-255Kč. Open M-Sa 11am-11pm, Su 11am-10pm.

czech republic

NIGHTLIFE

Nové Město

VINARNA U SUDU

Vodičkova 677/10 ☎222 232 207 www.usudu.cz

There's more to Vinarna U Sudu than meets the eye. Seemingly your typical Czech pub, a walk inside exposes room after room in this underground semi-maze. Several bars and tables fill the entirety of the space, as well as a small level filled with just foosball tables. More complex than you'd think (less, though, than your teen angst), Vinarna U Sudu has both the elements of a lively Czech pub and that of a hidden stone wine cellar. From outside, it's easy to overlook this gem of a pub, but this place is always full nonetheless. A wine bar, Vinarna U Sudu serves quality wine for anyone looking for something to add to their Snapchat story.

i B: Národní třída. From the station, turn right onto Purkyňova toward Vladislavova, and then turn right onto Vladislavova. Walk about a block and then turn left onto Lazarská. On the next block, turn the corner to the right and the pub is on your left. Beer 30-45Kč. Wine (by glass) 33Kč. Cocktails 80-84Kč. Open M-Th 9am-4am, F 9am-5am, Sa 10am-5am, Su 10am-3am.

JAMPA DAMPA

V Tůních 1770/10 ☎704 718 530

Lesbian? Lez Go. Jampa Dampa, an LGBT club and bar in the area shows love to the ladies who like showing love to the ladies. While open and inviting to all, the place keeps a solid Sapphic vibe, ideal for the female traveler who's even less straight than these Prague streets. A small dance floor takes up half of the lower level; tables occupy the rest. At night, women fill up the place, dancing together to pop-y songs and taking breaks at the tables. The atmosphere is lively, and more importantly, safe and welcoming to anyone inside or outside of the LGBT+ community.

i C: I. P. Pavlova. From the station, walk out and turn right Onto Sokolská. On the next corner turn left onto Ječná and then turn right onto V Tůních. The bar is on your right. Wine 42-240Kč. Beer 25-85Kč. Whiskey drinks 65-120Kč. Open Tu-W 6pm-4am, Th 6pm-2am, F-Sa 6pm-6am.

REDUTA JAZZ CLUB

Národní třída 20 ☎224 933 487 www.redutajazzclub.cz

Got the blues? Hop out of bed, and jazz things up with a trip to Reduta. Live musicians perform every night at this venue, in a luxurious red-clad, dimly lit lounge. The oldest jazz club in the city, Reduta has existed since 1957, but the aesthetic is that of the 1920s. Reduta is particularly famous for President Bill Clinton's 1994 sax performance at the venue (sex performance reserved for the American public). Reduta has brought to light many influential performers in the genre, and a night at the bar is a display of both history and talent.

i B: Národní třída. From the station, turn right onto Spálená. Walk a block and then turn left onto Národní. The bar is on the left. Entrance 225-350Kč. Open 9pm-midnight, performances start at 9:30pm.

Staré Město

ROXY

Dlouhá 33 ☎602 691 015

Men are always lying when they say, "It's bigger than you'd think." We're not. The outside of Roxy doesn't do the inside justice. Roxy rox pretty hard; it's easily one of the hottest clubs in the Josefov/Staré Mešto area, perhaps both literally and figuratively. The huge dance floor fills up quickly, and things heat up fast. Free Monday entrance gives us all a reason to look forward to the start of the week, because 9am lecture just ain't doing it. DJs got you dancing the night away, and it's almost like Tuesday will never come. It will, but that's a problem for future

prague

you. Roxy leans toward electronic and dance vibes, and easily attracts the young and hip of Prague.

i B: Náměstí Republiky. Walk down Havlíčkova. Turn left onto V Celnici, following it as it becomes nám. Republiky.Turn left onto Palladium. Turn right onto Benediktská, and then left onto Dlouhá. Roxy is on your right. Cover varies, usually either free or between 100-200Kč. Open daily 11pm-late.

KARLOVY LÁZNĚ

Smetanovo nábřeží 198/1 ☎222 220 502 www.karlovylazne.cz

A huge, five-story middle finger to the idea of quality, not quantity. Boasting the title of "the largest club in Central Europe," Karlovy Lázně is a one-stop shop for any tourist hoping to spend a night rubbing against sweaty college-aged kids. Each story of the club plays a different style of music—among them are radio hits, dance, oldies, hip hop, and chill out. Some floors have novelty elements like a dancing hologram skeleton and an oxygen bar; all floors offer horny masses. If you're willing to shell out extra, you can visit the Ice Pub inside of Karlovy lázně. It's cool as hell for maybe five minutes, cold as balls for the rest.

i A: Staroměstská. Head down Žatecká then turn right on Platnéřská. Follow Platnéřská onto Křižovnická and then onto Smetanovo nábř. Karlovy lázně is on the right. Cover Su-W 180Kč, Th-Sa 200Kč. Open daily 9pm-5am.

DRUNKEN MONKEY

U milosrdných 848/4 ☎773 683 003 www.drunkenmonkey.cz

This pub, founded by Americans, offers one of the main pub crawls in Prague: the Drunken Monkey Pub Crawl. Not to be taken literally—the hope is that you will still be able to stand by the end of a visit to pubs and clubs around town. Start off the night at the Drunken Monkey, and make your way through some of Staré Město's most popular watering holes. In a true American spirit, everyone plays fratty drinking games and gets smashed. Land of the free and all, but this crawl will set you back 500Kč. If you're feeling lonely or in need of guidance, cough up the dough and hand the reins over to a pro.

i A: Staroměstská. Head north on Žatecká toward Široká, turning right when you reach it. Turn left onto Dušní and walk down until you reach U milosrdných. The destination is on the right. Pub crawl 500Kč. Open daily noon-late night.

DÉJÀ VU

Jakubská 648/6 ☎222 311 743 www.dejavuclub.cz

You haven't déjà vu-ed a pub-club duo like this one. A two-story bar and club, Déjà Vu offers bright colored lights and a large image of Jim Morrison watching you get smashed. It's a great place to meet people, slurring their words as they hit on each other over Cuba Libres. From 6-9pm, indulge hedonistically in 50% off quality cocktails. The upper level, a bar, caters to those looking to talk and unwind; the lower level, a club, is for those looking to grind. Good vibes, literally and figuratively, this pub/club is known for its quality beats and ambiance.

i B: Náměstí Republiky. Walk down Nám. Republiky. Turn right onto U Obecního domu and right again onto Rybná. Then turn left turn onto Jakubská. Déjà Vu is on the left. No cover. Cocktails 105-185Kč. Bar open Su-Tu 6pm-2am, W-Th 6pm-3am, F-Sa 6pm-4am. Happy hour daily 6-9pm. Club open W-Th 8pm-3am, F-Sa 8pm-4am.

Malá Strana

🏠 U MALÉHO GLENA JAZZ AND BLUES CLUB

Karmelitská 374/23 ☎257 531 717

This pub serves up some serious talent—U Malého Glena has made a name for itself among the musical crowds. Take your beer with a side of beats; this is one of the classiest ways to spend a night drinking. If you're missing the Western world, the pub is owned by an American, and the menu knows it. Tex Mex in Prague? You bet. Live shows are put on every night in the lower part of the place, and the beer keeps flowing throughout. The venue is small, but it's all about the motion of the ocean, baby—and the talent is strong in this one. Sundays are jam sessions for any visitor who takes their music game past, "Anyway, here's Wonderwall."

i A: Malostranská. From the Metro, take tram 12, 20, or 22 to Malostranské náměstí. From the stop, turn left onto Karmelitská. The club is on the right. Cover M-Tu 200Kč, W-Th 170Kč, F-Sa 200Kč, Su 100Kč. Blues shows 130Kč. Grill items 159-199Kč. Salads 125-165Kč. Breakfast 95-159Kč. Open M-F 10am-2am, Sa-Su 10am-3am. Kitchen closes at midnight. Jazz/Blues Club doors open 7:30pm, shows start 9pm.

KLUB ÚJEZD

Újezd 422/18   ☎251 510 873 www.klubujezd.cz

Sea monsters greet you upon entrance (not a mirror, actually), setting the tone nicely for this bar. Klub Újezd is a multi-story bar with an eclectic character and equally unique client base. The basement is particularly interesting, with a quite literal underground vibe. Upstairs, the ambiance is more lounge-y and smoky. The décor is at best, odd, but the place is well-known and well-loved, giving hope to weirdos everywhere. Maybe high school just didn't get you, but this place does. The space is filled with peculiar original art, and the overall effect is very alt.

i A: Malostranská. From the Metro, take tram 12, 20, or 22 to Újezd. The club is right by the tram stop. Rum 46-220Kč. Whisky 60-140Kč. Beer 24-60Kč. Club open daily 6pm-4am. Bar open daily 2pm-4am.

POPOCAFEPETL

Újezd 19   ☎739 110 021 www.popocafepetl.cz

The Popos—so loved, they made more of them. As of now, there's the Újezd one, the Michalská one, the Na Struze one, and the Italska one. Each has a different personality, but all are student hotspots. This particular PopoCafePetl is more barlike, and has a relaxed ambiance. The décor is very underground cellar, as is the trend in Prague. Popo stays open quite late, if you find yourself with desperate needs at 3:30am. If you get a chance, swing by the other Popos to compare and contrast, and pick your favorite. If you happen upon a slow night, the place is quite close to Klub Újezd as well.

i A: Malostranská. From the Metro, take tram 12, 20, or 22 to Újezd. The club is right by the tram stop. Beer 22-45Kč. Rum 29-95Kč. Short cocktails 35-85Kč. Open daily 3pm-4am.

Vinohrady

RADOST FX

Bělehradská 234/120   ☎224 254 776 www.radostfx.cz

We can't promise you an orgasm, but at the very least, an Orgasm. Bols Amaretto, Finlandia Vodka, and Bailey's Cream—that's probably what sexual satisfaction feels like anyway. In addition to "Orgasms," Radost FX's list of cocktails features names like FX Spaceship, Ice Gimlet, and Make Love. Radost FX is everything weird still within the realms of not-creepy. Eclectic sofas, chandeliers, and mirrors compose the bulk of the place's décor, and make for a cool, chaotic ambiance. The second floor of Radost FX serves as a lounge, best for when you want to consume your alcohol in a sitting position. Standing takes so much effort.

i C: I. P. Pavlova. Turn left onto Legerova. Walk down about a block and turn right onto Jugoslávská. Turn left onto Bělehradská. The club is on the right. Club is free for women, 100Kč for men. Vodka cocktails 105-145Kč. Rum cocktails 90-145 Kč. Club open Th-Sa 10pm-5am. Lounge open daily 11am-2am. Café open daily 11am-midnight.

CLUB TERMIX

Třebízského 1514/4a   ☎222 710 462 www.club-termix.cz

A favorite for Prague's gay community, Club Termix is the universe's apology for Grindr. A small club with no cover charge, Termix fills up consistently with men looking for men. For the rest of the spectrum of people, the pickings are scarce—

the club attracts many more men than women—but for those who fall into the target group, the ratio couldn't be better. The club's space hangs odd things from the ceiling, but here, it's really what's on the inside that counts. Catering to the gay community, Termix fills a rare niche so that you can fill your rare niche (too far?), and for that, the club is beloved.

i A: Jiřího z Poděbrad. From the station, walk down Vinohradská toward U vodárny. Turn right onto Třebízského. The club is on the right. No cover charge. Beer 25-85Kč. Cocktails 30-130Kč. Open W-Sa 10pm-5am.

BAR & BOOKS
Mánesova 64   ☎222 724 581 www.barandbooks.cz

If drunk texting proves anything, it's that alcohol and words go together like Netflix, flunking your biochem final, and bitching about how unfair that curve was anyway. The inside of Bar & Books—the one in Mánesova, one of two Bar & Books in Prague with counterparts in Warsaw and New York City—is lined with shelves of books that whisper "culture" in soothing British accents. The dimly-lit bar has a romantic atmosphere, best for the couple with exquisite tastes looking for a relaxed, sophisticated night. The elegant décor transports visitors back to 1940s New York, and the bar hosts events including karaoke, live music, neo-burlesque, and complimentary cigars for ladies's nights.

i A: Jiřího z Poděbrad. From the station, head north and turn left onto Mánesova. Walk down about two blocks, and the cafe will be on your left. Cocktails 145-295Kč. Wine (by glass) 135-155Kč. Open daily 5pm-3am.

ZANZIBAR
Americká 152/15   ☎222 520 315 www.kavarnazanzibar.cz

A slightly upscale cafe + restaurant + bar, Zanzibar is your standard Czech pub plus better lighting, polished wood, and a touch of elegance. Patrons can find full meals, espresso drinks, and alcohol enjoyed alongside locals out with their friends or coworkers. Casually sophisticated, Zanzibar attracts clientele looking for a calm drink with friends, leaving behind the hordes of horny teens hoping to get plastered in Prague. Whether you're looking for a meal, a drink, or somewhere to go when your hostelmates are too annoying—Zanzibar has a little something for everyone.

i A: Náměstí Míru. From the station, walk down Americká for about 5 minutes. The cafe is on the right. Cocktails 129-139Kč. Wine (by glass) 32-45Kč. Beer 39-45Kč. Sandwiches 95-129Kč. Open M-Th 8am-11pm, F 8am-midnight, Sa 10am-midnight, Su 10am-11pm.

Holešovice

CROSS CLUB
Plynární 1096/23   ☎736 535 053 www.crossclub.cz

Decked out in more metal than a Hot Topic employee, Cross Club is Henry Ford's assembly line meets the Transformers meets drunk Europeans. Industrial vibes, complemented by electronic and alt music, dominate the bar/club/restaurant, meaning there are pipes everywhere and the entire thing feels like the coolest robot's body you've ever been in. More than just your average bar, however, Cross Club's ambiance, food, and drinks keep this place popular and one of Prague's best nightlife offerings.

i C: Nádraží Holešovice. Turn left onto Plynární. Cross Club is on the left. Cover varies. Bar open daily 2pm-2am. Club open F-Sa 6pm-7am, Su-Th 6pm-5am.

MECCA CLUB
U průhonu 799/3   ☎734 155 300 www.mecca.cz

A mecca of what remains unclear, but this club certainly is the center of a lot of attention. The décor of the club implies luxury and class, though it draws the same crowd as any other big Prague club. Open for only two days a week,

Mecca Club has got the exclusivity thing down on lock. Supply and demand, bitches. Equipped with five bars, Mecca keeps the alcohol flowing, like any respectable club should. International DJs fill the space with the kind of music ideal for rubbing against other people. If your money is just weighing you down too much, spring for a VIP table. One step closer to living out your dream of being a Kardashian.

i C: Nádraží Holešovice. Turn left onto Plynární and then right onto Osadní. Walk down this street until you turn left onto U průhonu. Mecca Club is on the left. Often no cover, but check website for specific events. Open Fr-Sa 8pm-6am.

FRAKTAL

Šmeralova 1 Praha 7   ☎222 946 845 www.fraktalbar.cz

Vera Bradley + the southwestern United States + the fashion sense of your aunt who did a lot of drugs in the 70s but is now a nice eclectic lady give this restaurant and bar happy vibes. Fraktal serves Mexican and pub food, and most importantly, plenty, plenty of beer. It's not a place for a rowdy night, but a nice spot to eat and drink among friendly people. There's outdoor seating for warm nights and a more casual ambiance. A nice respite from the throbbing music of clubs, a trip to Fraktal is worth it for everyone that understands it's so much nicer to consume alcohol sitting down.

i C: Vltavská. Walk down Heřmanova, then turn right onto Kamenická. Walk down half a block and turn left onto Městský Okruh/Pražský okruh/Veletržní. Continue until you reach Šmeralova. Fraktal is on your left. Nachos 110-155Kč. Burritos 155-145Kč. Beer 22-65Kč. Open daily 11am-midnight.

ESSENTIALS
Practicalities

- **TOURIST INFORMATION CENTRE** (Staroměstské náměstí 1, Staré Město. www.prague.eu. Open daily 9am-7pm.) Other branches in Wenceslas Square (Václavské náměstí. Open daily 10am-6pm) and Lesser Town Bridge Tower (Mostecká. Open daily 10am-6pm).

- **BANKS/ATMS:** ATMs can be found in the city center by Czech and international banks, of which many are located around Wenceslas Square. Cash machines in general can be found in large shopping centers as well as metro stations. Most accept regular international cards with Visa, Plus, Mastercard, Cirrus or Maestro symbols.

- **INTERNET:** Free Wi-Fi can be found in most McDonalds and KFC restaurants as well as Starbucks around Czech Republic. Look around for the 'Wi-Fi Zdarma,' or Free Wi-Fi signs on windows of cafes and restaurants to find Wi-Fi zones. There are also Internet cafes around the city for those unable to find Wi-Fi elsewhere. Click Internet Café (Malé nám. 13 Open daily 10am-11pm). Interlogic Internet Café (Budějovická 1123/13. Open M-F 9am-10pm, Sa-Su 11am-10pm.)

- **POST OFFICE:** Main Post Office (Jindřišská 909/14 ☎221 131 111; www.ceskaposta.cz. Open daily 2am-midnight.) Most other post offices are open M-F 8am-6pm.

Emergency

- **EMERGENCY NUMBER:** 112

- **POLICE:** 156 (city police), 158 (Police of the Czech Republic)

- **AMBULANCE:** 155

- **FIRE:** 150

- **RAPE CRISIS CENTER:** The White Circle of Safety (U Trojice 2. Hotline: ☎257 317 100. Open M-Th 5pm-8pm; F by appointment 9am-1pm)

- **HOSPITALS:** Public hospitals that treat foreigners without European insurance and have English-speaking staff and emergency care: University Hospital in Motol (V Úvalu 84 ☎224 431 111). Nemocnice Na Homolce (Roentgenova 37/2 ☎257 271 111).

- **PRIVATE CLINIC:** Poliklinika Na Národní (Národní 1010/9 ☎222 075 119). Unicare Medical Cente (Na Dlouhém Lánu 563/11 ☎420 608 103 050).

- **24/7 PHARMACIES:** Lékárna Palackého (Palackého 5 ☎224 946 982 / 222 928 220). Lékárna U Svaté Ludmily (Belgická 37 ☎222 513 396 / 222 519 731). Ústavní lékárna FTNsP (Thomayerova nemocnice, Vídeňská 800 ☎261 081 111 / 261 084 019).

Getting There

There are no direct trains or buses that will get you from the airport to the city center, but there are bus lines that will connect you to metro lines in the city. Tickets for buses or trams should be purchased at the Public Transport counters at the arrivals halls of Terminal 1 or Terminal 2, open from 7am-10pm. If they are closed, you can use the vending machines at the bus stop or purchase one from the driver. Note that the drivers will only accept small notes and change, and may require exact amounts.

Tickets are valid based on the amount of time passed since validating. A 32Kč ticket will be valid for 90 minutes for any type of public transport including transfers. You may need to purchase an extra half-price ticket for large pieces of luggage. Upon boarding the train, bus, or tram, make sure to validate your ticket by sliding your ticket into the yellow validating machines on the poles next to vehicle doors.

Bus 119 - leaves from Terminal 1 (Exit D, E, F) and Terminal 2 (Exit C, D, E). Get off at the last stop, Nádraži Veleslavín (Metro line A). The bus runs every 5 to 20min from 4:15am to 11:30pm, and the journey takes about 20min. From Nádraži Veleslavín, the Metro connects to Malostranská in Mala Strana, Staroměstské náměstí in Old Town or Můstek near Wenceslas Square.

Getting Around

Public Transportation

The same ticket is used for all forms of public transportation, and different tickets are valid for different amounts of time. A standard adult single ticket costs 32Kč and is valid for 90 minutes. Shorter tickets for 30 minutes can be bought 24Kč and longer tickets can be bought for 24 hours (110Kč), 3 days (310Kč), or 5 days (550Kč). Once the ticket is bought and you have boarded, be sure to validate your ticket by sliding it into the yellow validating machines that are next to poles on trams and buses and by the entrance of the metro station for metros.

Metro

The Prague Metro runs on 3 lines: A (green), B (yellow), and C (Red). It operates daily from 5am-midnight, and each train runs every 2-10 minutes. Maps of the metro system can be found in metro stations and in the trains.

Trams

Day trams operate between 4:30am-12:15am, and run every 8 minutes in the morning, and 10 minutes during the day. During the weekend, these intervals may increase to 15 minutes during the day. Night trams operate between 12:15am-4:30am and run every 30 minutes. The central point of night-time transfers is Lazarska.

Buses

Day buses operate between 4:30am-12:15pm, and run every 5-15 minutes in the morning, and 10-20 minutes during the day. During the weekend these intervals may increase to 10-60 minutes during the day. Night buses operate between 12:15am-4:30am and run every 30-60 minutes.

Taxis

Ubers are usually readily available, but taxis are also available in Prague. The maximum fare for taxis is 28 Kč/km, with a boarding fee of 40Kč. You can board taxis by waiting at taxi stands that can be found on roads including Jelení, Loretánské nám. 2, Malostranské nám., nám. Republiky, and more, but it is recommended that you order a taxi through a dispatching office where you can get information on fares in advance. Dispatching companies that speak English and also allow you to order a taxi online include AAA radiotaxi (☎222 333 222, www.aaataxi.cz/en), Citytaxi Praha (☎257 257 257 www.citytaxi.cz/en/praha), and Modrý anděl (☎240 727 222 333,www. modryandel.cz/en).

czech republic essentials

MONEY

Tipping and Bargaining

Like most European cities, Prague's policy on tipping is pretty relaxed: most locals will just round up. Aim for around 5-10% if you're satisfied with your service. Touristy restaurants in the center of town will expect a 15-20% tip, but it's best to avoid those places anyway. Bargaining is only done in open-air markets or antique shops.

SAFETY AND HEALTH

Local Laws and Police

You should not hesitate to contact the police in the Czech Republic. Be sure to carry a valid passport, as police have the right to ask for identification. Police can sometimes be unhelpful if you are the victim of a currency exchange scam; in that case, you might be better off seeking advice from your embassy or consulate.

Drugs and Alcohol

If you carry insulin, syringes, or any prescription drugs on your person, you must also carry a copy of the prescriptions and a doctor's note. The drinking age in the Czech Republic is 18. Avoid public drunkenness, as it will jeopardize your safety. The possession of small quantities of marijuana (less than 15g) was decriminalized in 2009. Carrying drugs across an international border—drug trafficking—is a serious offense that could land you in prison.

Smoking is incredibly popular in the Czech Republic. If you are sensitive to cigarette smoke, ask for a non-smoking room in a hotel or hostel or to be seated in the non-smoking area of restaurants.

SPECIFIC CONCERNS

Petty Crime and Scams

Scams and petty theft are unfortunately common in the Czech Republic. An especially common scam in bars and nightclubs involves a local woman inviting a traveler to buy her drinks, which end up costing exorbitant prices; the proprietors of the establishment (in cahoots with the scam artist) may then use force to ensure that the bill is paid. Travelers should always check the prices of drinks before ordering. Another common scam involves a team of con artists posing as metro clerks and demanding that you pay large fines because your ticket is invalid. Credit card fraud is also common in Eastern Europe. Travelers who have lost credit cards or fear that the security of their accounts has been compromised should contact their credit card companies immediately.

Con artists often work in groups and may involve children. Beware of certain classics: sob stories that require money, rolls of bills "found" on the street, mustard spilled (or saliva spit) onto your shoulder to distract you while they snatch your bag. **Never let your passport or your bags out of your sight.** Hostel workers will sometimes stand at bus and train arrival points to recruit tired and disoriented travelers to their hostel; never believe strangers who tell you that theirs is the only hostel open. Beware of **pickpockets** in large crowds, especially on public transportation.

Visitors to Prague should never enter a taxi containing anyone in addition to the driver and should never split rides with strangers. While traveling by train, it may be preferable to travel in cheaper "cattle-car" type seating arrangements; the large number of witnesses makes such carriages safer than seating in individual compartments. Travelers should avoid riding on night buses or trains, where the risk of robbery or assault is particularly high. *Let's Go* does not recommend hitchhiking and picking up hitchhikers.

czech republic

DENMARK

Straddling the border between Scandinavia and continental Europe, Denmark packs majestic castles, pristine beaches, and thriving nightlife onto the compact Jutland peninsula and its network of islands. Vibrant Copenhagen boasts busy pedestrian thoroughfares and one of the world's tallest carousels in Tivoli Gardens, while beyond the city, fairytale lovers can tour Han Christian Andersen's home in rural Odense. In spite of the nation's historically homogenous population, its Viking past has given way to a dynamic multicultural society that draws in visitors as it turns out Legos and Skagen watches.

greatest hits

- **#NOFILTER:** For one of the most iconic views of Copenhagen, take a walk down **Nyhavn** (p. 116), a famous waterfront area with colorful buildings.
- **UGLY DUCKLINGS UNITE:** Pay your respects to the man who invented your childhood at the **Hans Christian Andersen Museum** (p. 128) in Odense.

115

copenhagen

Most pollsters rank Denmark as the happiest country on earth. It's easy to brush that away. Happiness is so subjective, ya know? But then you'll get to Copenhagen, and it will slowly dawn on you: damn, these people are happy. As the capital city, Copenhagen is colorful, relaxed, and close to nature. Their greatest cultural creation is not the Vikings, but a concept called *hygge* that's best described as "being cozy with friends and family." It's is the kind of place where you can spend the day cafe-hopping in search of the perfect chai, or strolling through palaces and gardens before sampling the newest sushi-tapas fusion. It's a city where the old and the new have reached a harmony, and it may just be the liveliest place you visit. For foodies, the city has everything you can imagine, especially at massive "food halls" where dozens of stands hawk the latest trends in Nordic cuisine, dessert-making, and Middle Eastern street food. You can spend a month here and still not see everything, so whether it's art museums or coffee shops, bookstores or bars, we trust you'll get up to plenty of exciting adventures while you're here.

SIGHTS

CHRISTIANSBORG

Prins Jørgens Gård 1   ☎33 92 64 92 www.christiansborg.dk

Danes are absolutely in love with their royal family and now, for only 100 DKK you can take part in that experience. Walking through Christianslott is like being in a fairy tale: there's a Rapunzel-worthy tower overlooking the whole city, stables to house the royal ponies, and banquet halls that look like something out of fairy tale (though, presumably, with better mother figures and fewer talking animals). The best part: the tapestry room, showcasing eleven massive tapestries which depict Danish history from the beginning till now. Apparently each one has a small "mistake" for intrepid museum goers to find — so if you happen to catch a glimpse of Donald Duck above Hitler's head, congratulations!

i Combination ticket 120 DKK, students 100 DKK. Open 10am-5pm.

NYHAVN

Nyhavn 1-71   www.nyhavn.com

You've probably seen this place on postcards, but that's nothing compared to what it looks like in real life. Nyhavn (meaning "new harbor") is one of the main waterways in Copenhagen and it's surrounded by some very Nordic-looking buildings: almost every house overlooking the port is yellow, red, green, or blue. Like everything else Scandinavian, they look happy, old-fashioned and immaculately put together. From the port, you have the added bonus of being able to take guided tours of the harbor…because if anything screams "Eurotrip" it's canal boat ride selfie.

i Free. Open 24hr. Companies like Stromma offer sightseeing boat tours leaving from Nyhavn. Adults 80 DKK. Tours last an hour and depart one to four times every hour until 6pm. Check www.stromma.dk for more information.

KONGENS HAVE

Gothersgade 11

Kongens Have is the epitome of everything Danish: it's got nature, public drinking, and a metric ton of *hygge*. The park, one of Copenhagen's biggest and most centrally located, is an absolute must if you're looking to kick back and relax for any afternoon. The gardens are immaculately kept, there are often concerts there in summer, and it overlooks a number of beautiful Baroque buildings. Spend a day here and tell us the Danes aren't going to save the world.

i Free. Open daily 11am-7pm.

denmark

STATE ART MUSEUM (STATENS MUSEUM FOR KUNST)

Sølvgade 48-50   ☎33 74 84 94 www.smk.dk

Whether you want Renaissance landscapes or Greek statues, three-nippled goats or trippy expressionism, this has got to be the best art museum in Scandinavia. Even if you're not an art-lover, the roaming exhibits are bizarre and alarmingly fun to visit. The modern section houses Danish work from the last 50 years, and it's incredibly interesting to see how much they've changed. If you don't believe us, try explaining how else the country went from Virgin Mary to midgets riding toothless prostitutes in under a century.

i Permanent exhibitions free. Special exhibitions 110 DKK, students 90 DKK. Open M-Tu 10am-5pm, W 10am-8pm, Th-Su 10am-5pm.

get a room!

GENERATOR HOSTEL $

Adelgade 5   ☎78 77 54 00 generatorhostels.com/en/destinations/copenhagen

Generator has everything you could want in a hostel: comfy rooms, a restaurant and bar, a huge outdoor space, and, best of all, hammocks. Everywhere. The main floor is littered with blackboards giving advice on the best things to do in Copenhagen, and the staff seem particularly well-equipped to help you build an itinerary. Generator feels part hotel, part tourist agency, and it might just be the best decision you make while in town.

i Singles 480 DKK. Doubles 960 DKK. Dorms 150 DKK. Breakfast 70 DKK. Reception 24hr.

DOWNTOWN $$

Vandkunsten 5   ☎70 23 21 10 www.copenhagendowntown.com

Walk by this place and the first thing you'll notice is its guests: they're strewn out on beanbags or crashed on couches. Many are sipping Carlsbergs or pouring over maps in what looks like a commercial for budget cartography school, but this is just another day at one of Copenhagen's most popular hostels. With its sidewalk lounge area, free pasta, 2-for-1 happy hour, and a slew of other goodies specially tailored to backpackers, Downtown runs an operation that's hard to beat. Yoga? They got it. Free tours? Yep. Double shots for under 40 DKK? That's the price of half a beer in Norway—sign us up!

i Singles 686-931 DKK. 6-person dorm 225-284 DKK. 10-person dorm 200-236 DKK. Reception 24hr.

WAKEUP COPENHAGEN $

Borgergade 9

If the idea of spending the night with strangers doesn't float your boat, WakeUp will probably be the best (and most affordable) option for you in Copenhagen. With basic economy rooms going for around 500 DKK, it's certainly not ideal for those on a budget, but as FDR once said, "When you gotta splurge, you gotta splurge." The rooms at WakeUp are chic and well-designed, with comfortable mattresses, en suite bathrooms, and a TV, while the hotel itself is in a superb location right off of Gothersgade (around the block from Generator Hostel, Kongens Have, and many of the bars and restaurants listed here).

i Singles 500 DKK. Often 100 DKK cheaper if booked on their website. Reception 24hr.

copenhagen

christiana

Walking into Christiania is like taking a step into a different planet. From the moment you pass the giant wooden gates, there are three rules every traveller must abide by: 1) have fun, 2) don't run, and 3) for the love of God do not take photos. Often referred to as Freetown Christiania, this community is in a curious legal limbo that makes it an autonomous state with very... different practices from the rest of Copenhagen. From the moment you enter, you'll notice everyone is smoking a spliff in the open. Walk down the community's charmingly named Pusher Street, and you'll get a contact high stronger than a whiff of Bob Marley's dreams.

And while Let's Go in no way endorses the use of illegal drugs, there's a very important reason we're mentioning this place at all. Denmark is already one of the most progressive countries in the world. But when Christiania declared itself an independent commune in the 70s, it pushed the limits of what Danish society found acceptable. After dramatic clashes with police and organized crime in the 90s, the commune enacted a zero tolerance policy for selling or using hard drugs and has since then achieved a fragile de facto independence from Copenhagen and its police force. If you spend two seconds at any hostel in Copenhagen, someone is guaranteed to mention Christiania and how cool it is that they sell pot there. But we assume you're smarter than the average plebeian, so you should know that this place is much, much more than a drug haven. It's a self-sufficient community with fully-functional cafés, restaurants, markets, and a population that has equal say in its policies. Christiania is a real life experiment in anarchist living and, as long as you follow the rules, a perfectly safe and cool place to visit.

FOOD

◙ COPENHAGEN STREET FOOD $

Trangravsvej on PapirØen (Paper Island)

There are over 30 restaurants and food trucks on these premises, with everything from Moroccan barbecue to local ice cream to a place called "OK Thai" that serves pretty bitchin' Thai food. Our recommendations: go by Anatolia for some gozleme (flatbread with feta and eggs), Latinda for plantains with guacamole, Pølse Kompagniet for organic sausages, and end with a bucket of booze at the Bucket Bar. So get on over to PapirØen and prepare yourself for the culinary experience of a lifetime.

i Price varies based on restaurant. Most dishes under 80 DKK. Open M-Sa 11-10pm, Su 11am-8pm. Coffee available at 11am, food trucks open at noon.

◙ ZAFRAN $$

Blågårdsgade 9 ☎35 34 90 95

Zafran is one of Copenhagen's best Persian restaurants. Our personal favorite dish is the joojeh kebab—tender strips of marinated beef resting on a bed of buttery rice—though pretty much everything here is fresh and delicious. For starters, you can't go wrong with the mast-o-khiar (cucumber in mint yogurt) or the sabzi khordan (feta, dill, parsley, and onion scooped up with flatbread). Better yet, this place has a bring-your-own-wine policy because why not.

i Appetizers 40 DKK. Entrees 85-140 DKK. Open daily 5pm-10pm.

denmark

BEYTI KEBAB $

Blågårdsgade 1   ☎32 17 00 03

These guys are the MLB to the pee-wee league kebab shops you'll find in most Copenhagen neighborhoods. They have a huge menu (50+ items) and offer everything from your standard shish kebabs and hamburgers to vegetarian mixes and more esoteric Turkish specialties. The bigger dishes (~75 DKK) include juicy skewers of meat, rice, yogurt and pita bread soaked in various sauces. For the more broke among you, Beyti also whips up the classics like durum shish kebab and shawarma for under 40 DKK.

i *Entrees 75 DKK. Wraps and burgers 40 DKK. Salads 30 DKK. Open M-Th 11am-midnight, F-Sa 11am-6am, Su noon-midnight.*

TORVEHALLERNE $

Frederiksborggade 21   ☎70 10 60 70 www.torvehallernekbh.dk

There are a staggering 60 shops in Torvehallerne, so if you don't find something you like, there's a chance you are actually a lump of coal. While the center boasts too many places to list by name, we particularly enjoyed Banh Mi Daily (Vietnamese buns and spiced meat/herb baguettes; 58 DKK), Grøn (porridge is astounding) and Granny's House (Danish pastries—go for the peanut butter brownies and traditional rye bread; most under 30 DKK). Whether you're looking for coffee, sushi, wine or hand cream, you can be sure that a) they'll have it and b) it's more artisanal than a curated vegan cube of sustainably harvested oxygen.

i *Price varies based on restaurant. Most dishes under 80 DKK. Open M-Th 10am-7pm, F 10am-8pm, Sa 10am-6pm, Su 11am-5pm.*

SLIDERS $

Peblinge Dossering 2   ☎31 32 26 20

Sliders is like McDonald's older cousin who quit the fast food game and decided to make something of itself. That gamble has clearly paid off, as all nine burgers on the menu—from the BBQ pork to truffle cheese and hoisin duck—are leagues beyond what most places serve, and you can order them in batches of three. Though the restaurant can get packed, the communal table seems to turn over customers fast. If you're heading out for drinks in Nørrebro, Sliders is the perfect place to stock up on carbs and feel satisfied with your choices.

i *Single slider 45 DKK. Three sliders and a side 119 DKK. Open Tu-Sa 11am-10pm, Su 11am-9pm; closed Mondays.*

NIGHTLIFE

ALPEHYTTEN

Gothersgade 33A (in the basement)   ☎51 29 51 20 www.alpe-hytten.dk

This place is unapologetically simple, and that's the source of all of its charm. It's a small, local joint where everyone seems to know each other—the staff, in fact, seemed perfectly at home chatting up the regulars and playing beer pong as they were working behind the counter. On weekends, you can get endless refills on beer for 50 DKK, and, if you're clumsy enough to spill your drink, there's a high chance you'll have to take the Punishment: a skull-shaped glass jar packed with tequila, salt, and God knows what else. If you want a good taste of Danish hygge and place that'll go easy on your wallet, Alpehytten should be your go-to spot.

i *Drinks 40-90 DKK. Open Tu-W 8pm-3am, Th 8pm-4am, F 4pm-5am, Sa 9pm-5am.*

BUTCHER'S

Vestergade 10   ☎31 37 86 18 www.butcherscph.dk

Butcher's is great if you want a nightclub but hate the anonymity of 8,000 drunk teens humping in the dark. The lighting here is dim, but it's intimate enough to have a conversation, or at least make eye contact with the person you're grinding on. With admission at 30 DKK and most drinks below 80 DKK, it's not terrible on the wallet (though if you want to pop bottles, it's going to cost significantly more). For best results, drink somewhere cheap, come here on the later side, and spend the night bumping, twisting and twerking the night away.

i Cover 30 DKK. Beers 50 DKK. Mixed drinks 70-100 DKK. Th are 18+; F-Sa are 21+. Open Th 10pm-5am, F-Sa 9pm-5am.

NØRREBRO BRYGHUS
Baldersbuen 25   ☎46 55 04 70 www.noerrebrobryghus.dk

Microbreweries, like hula hoops and the Facebook, seem to be "all the rage" these days, so a trip here is definitely worth it if you want to see how the times they are a changin'. Bryghus seems to be a massive hit with the locals (making it difficult to get a table or even a spot on the floor during music performances) but it's profoundly worth it. The Bombay Pale Ale and Nørrebro Pilsner are both delicious, while you can also try a number of experimental flavors. If you're out on the town in Nørrebro, this may be the smartest decision you'll make all night.

i Beers: 25cl (small) 48 DKK; 40cl (medium) 69 DKK; 60 cl (large) 85 DKK. Brewery open M-Th 5:30pm-10pm, F-Sa 5:30pm-11pm.

KARUSELLEN
Ægirsgade 10   ☎35 83 29 16

Remember how we said there's nothing fancy about Alpehytten? Well, there's really nothing fancy about this place—yet many of the locals we met called it their favorite bar in Copenhagen. The atmosphere inside feels like a Viking mead hall: loud, smokey and pretty frickin' raucous. Its location in Nørrebro means that most of the crowd are locals, but both the clientele and staff are friendly and eager to chat. If you're looking for a slightly rough, no-nonsense spot, this is your place.

i Drinks 20-30 DKK. Open M-W 10am-2am, Th 10am-3am, F-Sa 10am-4am, Su 10am-8pm.

SUNDAY
Lille Kongensgade 16   ☎53 66 82 28 www.sundayclub.dk

If you're an Ibiza-type clubber and need a minimum of 2,000 people in the same room to feel comfortable, this is the place for you. In any event, all of that debauchery comes at a cost: most drinks are in the 100 DKK range and above, and the entrance can be steep. However, every city has that one club whose name is whispered with the same fear and admiration as "Voldemort" and, after a night here, you'll see why for Copenhagen, it's Sunday.

i Cover varies, usually over 100 DKK. Drinks 100 DKK. Open F-Sa 11:30pm-5am.

ESSENTIALS
Practicalities

- **TOURIST OFFICES:** Copenhagen Visitor Center (Vesterbrogade 5 ☎70 22 24 42; www.visitcopenhagen.dk. Open M-Sa 9am-7pm.)

- **TOURS:** Hostels such as Generator, Downtown, and Sleep in Heaven often arrange free walking tours in the mornings—simply ask reception for times and details. As Copenhagen is one of the most bike-friendly cities in the world, bike tours are very popular, but consult the Tourist Information Center website for full listings. **Grand Tour** (www.stromma.dk. Tickets for one hour boat tour 80 DKK): sightseeing by boat around Copenhagen's harbor and coastline. Leaves one to four times per hour from Nyhavn harbor until 6pm; tickets can be bought on-site. **Pub Crawl** Copenhagen (www.pubcrawlcopenhagen.dk. 140 DKK): A five-hour long pub crawl that comes with free entrance at night clubs, discounts on beers and mixers, and free shots. Meets at Black Memorial Anchor in Nyhavn every Tu and Th-Sa at 8pm.

- **CURRENCY EXCHANGE:** Possible at Copenhagen Airport, Forex stores, and most banks.

denmark

top danish foods you need to devour

1. STEGT FLÆSK: It's fried bacon, parsley sauce, and potatoes, and it's washed down with beer. Ain't nothing better (or more likely to give you a heart attack) than this classic Danish dish.

2. SMØRREBRØD: This Scandinavian classic is as simple as they come: it's an open sandwich with endless possibilities. Fish? Fo' sho. Meats and cheeses? Obviously. Chocolate? No, that's gross, but you can probably pay someone to throw some chocolate on there. No questions asked.

3. RUGBRØD: Don't ask us how to say this. Just know that it's absolutely delicious. Apparently all Danish children (and adults) eat this bread, and it's easy to see why: it's jampacked with seeds like it just survived a sunflower explosion, and the dough itself has a slightly acidic taste somewhere between sourdough and rye. It's tasty, healthy, and apparently available only in Denmark—so make sure you get a bite in before it's confiscated at border control!

4. FRIKADELLER: Meatballs. As in balls of meat. Rolled in breadcrumbs. Fried with onion and eggs. Served in mouthwatering garlic gravy. You can cry now.

- **ATMS:** You're never more than five minutes away from an ATM in Copenhagen. They are often in front of banks and especially visible around major pedestrian spots like Stortorget, Central Station, and Gothersgade.

- **LUGGAGE STORAGE:** Available at Copenhagen Airport (small box 50 DKK, larger box 75 DKK) and at Copenhagen Central Station (small box 50 DKK, large box 60 DKK. Open M-Sa 5:30am-1am, Su 6am-1am.)

- **GLBT SERVICES:** LGBT Denmark (Nygade 7 ☎33 13 19 48. Best to call on Thursdays 2pm-5pm. www.lgbt.dk.)

- **LAUNDROMATS:** Easily done at hostels such as Generator or Downtown, but there are laundromats (Danish: vaskeri) all over Copenhagen. One centrally located one is Renseriet (Borgergade 18 ☎33 14 04 53. Open M-F 8am-5pm.)

- **INTERNET:** Wi-Fi is available widely throughout Copenhagen, with hotspots in the Copenhagen Visitor Center, Kastrup Airport, many train stations, and most hostels and hotels. Additionally, many chain stores such as 7-11 and Baresso Coffee also have free connectivity.

- **POST OFFICE:** Posthus Købmagergade (Købmagergade 33 ☎70 70 70 30. M-F 10am-6pm, Sa 10am-2pm, closed Sundays.)

Emergency

- **EMERGENCY NUMBER:** ☎112

- **POLICE (NON-EMERGENCY):** ☎114

- **MEDICAL EMERGENCY:** ☎1813

- **SEXUAL ASSAULT:** Thora Center for Sexual Assault: ☎33 32 86 50

- **24 HOUR PHARMACIES:** Lyngby Svane Apotek (Lyngby Hovedgade 27 ☎45 87 00 96. Open 24/7.) Steno Apotek (Vesterbrogade 6C ☎33 14 82 66. Open 24/7.) Glostrup Apotek (Hovedvejen 101 ☎43 96 00 20. Open 24/7.)

- **PRIVATE DOCTORS:** Doctors at Laegelinien (☎25 96 93 75. www.laegelinien.dk.) Phone consultations and prescriptions from 130 DKK. House calls from 1200 DKK.

copenhagen

- **HOSPITALS:** Bispebjerg Hospital (Bispebjerg Bakke 23. 35 31 35 31.) Herlev Hospital (Herlev Ringvej 75 ☎38 68 38 68.) Hvidovre Hospital (Kettegårds Alle 30 ☎36 32 36 32.) Note: Foreign visitors are entitled to free medical treatment in case of an emergency.

Getting There

By Plane

Copenhagen Airport, also known as Kastrup, is the main airport servicing Denmark's capital city as well as much of southern Sweden. To get from the airport to Copenhagen Central Station takes less than 15 minutes by train. A one-way ride costs 48 DKK (if you're travelling to spots outside of the city limits, it's 75 DKK), and the train makes stops in Copenhagen at Central Station, Nørreport, and Østerport.

By Taxi

Taxis are much more expensive than public transportation and may take slightly longer. Most cab companies have fixed fares to and from the airport and can be booked in advance, but the 20min. ride will cost at least 250 DKK, often 300 DKK or higher.

By Train

All trains coming in from other parts of Denmark or Europe will arrive at Copenhagen Central Station (København H). The train from Malmö takes under 30 minutes and leaves at least twice per hour, at a cost of under 130 DKK. Central Station is also the drop off point for trains from other major Danish cities such as Odense (roughly 2hr. away, one-way tickets around 270 DKK) and Aarhus (roughly 4 hours away, one-way tickets around 600 DKK). Tickets can either be purchased at the station, online, or, for those with a European sim card, via the DSB app.

Getting Around

By Public Transportation

Copenhagen's transportation is run by the DSB, the Danish national railway company. To ride the metro, you can purchase tickets at most 7-11's and train stations, or with the app "Mobilbilletter Hovedstaden." Note: Transportation is on the honor system here, but know that if you are asked for a ticket and cannot produce one you can be fined up to 750 DKK. A single ride ticket for 2 zones (covers most of the city) costs 24 DKK; 24-hour ticket 80 DKK; 72-hour ticket 200 DKK.

The Copenhagen Card provides free admission to 74 museums, free public transportation, and discounts on restaurants and parking. 24 hours 360 DKK; 48 hours 500 DKK; 72 hours 590 DKK.

By Taxi

Taxis are more expensive than using public transportation, but given the size of Copenhagen, they are often your best choice on late nights out. You'll often find them lingering outside of popular tourist destinations or nightlife hotspots, but you can also book in advance. Taxa (☎35 35 35 35. www.taxa.dk.) Hailing off the street can have a base fee of 24-40 DKK and booking in advance will be 37-50 DKK. From there, it's 7 DKK per minute and 19.5 DKK per km.

Uber is widely available throughout Copenhagen, with a base fare of 40 DKK and a price of 4 DKK per minute and 20 DKK per km (minimum fare of 100 DKK).

copenhagen

aarhus

The second largest city in Denmark, Aarhus' main pedestrian walkways all follow the winding route of the Aarhus River, and most attractions are never more than ten minutes away from the ocean. With Parisian cafes and Viking cathedrals, Turkish kebab and massive Irish pubs, it's a city that straddles the old and the new. It has all the food options of an international city, alongside a vibrant Nordic cuisine culture, and you'll find cafes and coffee shops on nearly every block. In terms of nightlife, Aarhus can be as raucous as a frat house or as cool, calm and collected, as a scene from Mad Men—whatever your preference, you'll find it here. Perhaps most importantly, penny-pinching travellers will be happy to know that the city is not as expensive as Copenhagen, though the limited hostelling opportunities make budget hotels your best option.

get a room!

CABINN AARHUS $$
Kannikegade 14 ☎86 75 70 00 cabinn.com/CABINN-Aarhus-Hotel

Much like its Odense cousin, this Aarhus branch of the Danish hotel chain is pleasant, affordable, and located just steps from the Cathedral and Åboulevard. The hotel is in the process of doubling its capacity to 400 rooms, and we'd say it's best described as cheap and cozy without being cramped. Though the amenities may be simple—showers, Wi-Fi, TV, free coffee, and a bed—it's got a bang for your buck.

i Standard economy rooms 495 DKK. Larger rooms from 545 DKK. Book online to save 100 DKK. Reception 24hr.

HOSTEL CITY SLEEP-IN $
Havnegade 20 ☎86 19 20 55 www.citysleep-in.dk

City Sleep-In is a pretty simple place—clean, compact, and perhaps a bit drab in the lobby—but the price tag of 190 DKK makes it too attractive a bargain to pass up. It may not be the best place to socialize (it's about as quiet as watching an unexpected sex scene while at the movies with your parents), but there are plenty of good bars and restaurants nearby to make up for it.

i 6-bed dorm 190 DKK. Reception open M-F 8am-11am and 4pm-9pm, Sa-Su 8am-11am and 4pm-11pm.

SIGHTS

AARHUS CATHEDRAL
Store Torv ☎86 20 54 00 www.aarhusdomkirke.dk

It may be hard to wax poetic on cathedrals when you see them so often in Europe, but the Aarhus Cathedral is pretty remarkable. The building itself dates back to the 900s, a time when Aarhus was a B-list Viking city, and it's still one of the tallest buildings there today. The inside is open to the public on weekdays and it's beautifully decorated. The frescoes of Jesus are fabulous and the small boats hanging from the ceiling are de-lish. This is one of the most iconic spots in Aarhus, and as a good tourist, you absolutely must visit it.

i Free. Open M 9am-1pm, Tu 10:30am-1pm, W-Th 9am-1pm and 4pm-6pm, F 9am-1pm.

denmark

ÅBOULEVARD

Meaning "River Boulevard" (because Danish would call a river "Å"), this narrow walkway travels along the water and brings you past the main shopping attractions and cafes that define urban life in Aarhus. Whether it's parks full of smooching couples, teens breakdancing in a public square, or sidewalk coffee shops staffed by neckbearded baristas, a walk along the boulevard shows a slice of Aarhus that brings a whole new meaning to the concept of people-watching.

i *Free. Open 24/7.*

KUNSTMUSEUM (ART MUSEUM)

Aros Allé 2   ☎87 30 66 00 www.aros.dk

We imagine many visitors may be a bit shocked by a billboard of a naked woman pissing into a wine glass, but this newest ad for an art exhibition is just an everyday experience at the Aarhus Kunstmuseum. The white, angular awnings of the building's interior feel part Twilight Zone, part 2001: A Space Odyssey, and the exhibits mimic that diversity. Here you'll find French impressionists next to warzone photos, and it all feels weirdly zen. The biggest reason to stop by, though, is the rainbow panorama: a 360 degree walkway on the roof that overlooks the entire city and is covered by glass from every color on the spectrum.

i *90 DKK if under 28 years old, above 28 110 DKK. Free for under 18. Open Tu 10am-5pm, W 10am-10pm, Th-Su 10am-5pm; closed Mondays.*

VIKING MUSEUM

Sankt Clemens Torv 6   ☎87 16 10 16 www.moesgaardmuseum.dk/vikingemuseet

In case you needed a reminder that this country made its career pillaging and looting Europe, the Viking Museum has got you covered. The exhibits, located several feet underground in a basement darker than a Scandinavian winter, you can see the exploits of Denmark's first Christian king, the dentally-challenged Harald Bluetooth (and yes, he's the namesake for Bluetooth devices!). The museum gives interesting insight into Norse mythology and the founding of Aarhus, and its location directly across from the cathedral makes it a must-go on the list of sights to explore in the city.

i *Free. Open M-F 10am-5pm.*

DEN GAMLE BY

Viborgvej 2   ☎86 12 31 88 www.dengamleby.dk

Want to see what life was like in Ye Olde Denmark? Den Gamle By—Danish for "the old town"—is Aarhus's biggest attraction, and it's easy to see why. It's a massive, open air museum with recreations of life in the 1800s, 1920s, and 1970s. At each part, you can interact with park employees who discuss the relative merits of, we assume, burning coal, the Aryan race, and maybe LSD. While the 135 DKK adult price tag may seem a bit high, we trust there is nowhere else in Europe where you can feel what it was like to be Hans Christian Andersen, a World War I vet, and a commune hippie all in one day.

i *Entrance during the summer 135 DKK, students 70 DKK. Hours and prices vary each month, so check the website. Summer schedule listed here. Open Mar 28-June 26 10am-5pm; June 27-Aug 9 10am-6pm; Aug 10-Nov 13 10am-5pm.*

FOOD

JAKOB'S PITA BAR $

Vestergade 3   ☎87 32 24 20 www.jacobsbarbq.dk

Jakob's is more than a Pita Bar—it's a brand, it's an idea, it's a lifestyle. For 50 DKK, you can stuff toasty bread with tasty meats like lamb, falafel, or chicken all topped with a kaleidoscope of sauces. More importantly, you can enjoy your treat while sitting in Jakob's Café next door or having a drink at the bar.

i *Pitas 50 DKK. Open M-Th 5pm-11pm, F-Sa 5pm-midnight, Su 5am-10pm.*

MEXICAN GRILL BURRITOPLUS

$

Guldsmedgade 15 ☎22 30 92 48

Though critics and naysayers may opine that there's something rotten in the kingdom of Denmark, it's certainly not the burritos. This place serves up a tasty tortilla with chicken and all them fixings for only 49 DKK (add 20 DKK for guac) and, unlike whatever you told your prom date at 4am, it really is big enough. The place is located near one of Aarhus's biggest shopping streets and, for all of you who are aching under Europe's anti-Chipotle tyranny, it's a little taste of home.

i Burrito 49 DKK. Guac 20 DKK. Open daily 11am-9pm.

RESTAURANT RIVAS

$$

Fredensgade 22 ☎86 13 15 17 www.restaurantrivas.dk

Rivas is a taste of Iran in Denmark. The interior feels almost like an homage to golden-age Hollywood, though instead of Elizabeth Taylor they have photos of famous Persian stars from the same era. The wine selection is great, the prices aren't bad, and dishes like the jujeh kebab are juicier than any gossip you'll hear all month. If you're looking for Middle Eastern food with a touch of elegance and meat that's perfectly cooked, Rivas makes for a wonderful evening visit.

i Entrees 89-150 DKK. Open daily 4pm-9:30pm.

CAFÉ FAUST

$

Åboulevarden 38 ☎86 19 07 06 www.cafefaust.dk

Located right on the Aarhus River, Faust feels like the kind of place where you wile away the hours smoking cigarettes and plotting the overthrow of the Czar. That may just be the European romantic in us, but the cafe definitely seems to be a magnet for all kinds of Danes: students, pensioners, families—there's got to be a revolutionary or two in the mix! The 10am-2pm brunch may feel a bit pricey, but the scent of cheeses, smoothies, eggs, bacon, nutella, nuts, and more made us open our wallets faster than China, 1979.

i Brunch 115 DKK. Sandwiches 120 DKK. Open M-W 10am-midnight, Th 10am-1am, F-Sa 10am-2am, Su 10am-midnight.

NIGHTLIFE

WAXIES

Frederiksgade 16 ☎86 13 83 33 www.waxies.dk

Waxies advertises itself as "the biggest and best Irish pub in Aarhus," and it does have a certain charm when you spend enough time inside. Like a decadently alcoholic wedding cake, Waxies has three floors with three different bars and hosts activities like quizzes and music shows in case all that booze still can't get you to socialize. With pints of beer for as little as 30 DKK and weekend nights that last till 5am, this may be one of the best watering holes in Aarhus.

i Pints of beer 30-40 DKK. Drinks 50 DKK. Open M-T noon-2am, W-Th noon-3am, F-Sa noon-5am, Su noon-2am.

MEAT PACKERS

Skolegade 23 ☎86 93 77 27 www.meatpackers.dk

Meat Packers may not be the fanciest club, but, it's a cheap-beer, good-music kind of place, and it doesn't need to serve Cristal to deserve our write-up. In fact, it's better that this place doesn't serve Cristal, because then you and we probably couldn't afford it. With free entrance, 4-beers-for-50 DKK deals and latenight 2-for-1 cocktails, Meat Packers is affordable and packed as the party drags on. For those looking to get crunk in central Aarhus, the bumping beats and thankfully meat-free stench of Meat Packers makes it an ideal stopover as the sun is coming up.

i No cover. Beers 10-20 DKK. Shots 10 DKK. Ask about the happy hour deals. Open W 8pm-3am, Th-F 8pm-5am, Sa 10pm-5am.

ESSENTIALS

Practicalities

- **TOURIST OFFICES:** Visit Aarhus (Fredensgade 45 inside the bus station. www.visitaarhus.com. Open daily 7am-10pm.)

- **CURRENCY EXCHANGE:** A branch Forex Bank is located directly outside of Aarhus Central Station

- **ATMS:** ATMs can be found outside of Central Station, as well as along busy pedestrian walkways such as Park Alle, Rådhusplænen, or Østergade. Additionally, there is a Nordea Bank with an ATM directly across the street from the Aarhus Cathedral

- **LUGGAGE STORAGE:** Available at Aarhus Central Station from 30 DKK a day and up. Lockers take coins and cards.

- **GLBT SERVICES:** LGBT Danmark (located in Café Sappho, Mejlgade 71 ☎86 13 19 48 Open every Th 2pm-5pm.)

- **LAUNDROMATS:** Møntvaskeriet (Østbanetorvet 8 ☎86 27 73 84 Open daily 7:30am-10pm.)

- **INTERNET:** Internet is widely available in hotels, hostels, the train station, and coffee shops. Additionally, many places advertise free Wi-Fi on their shop windows—you'll see these especially along Sønder Alle, Åboulevard, and Jaegårdsgade.

Emergency

- **EMERGENCY NUMBER:** ☎112

- **NON-EMERGENCY POLICE NUMBER:** ☎114

- **MEDICAL EMERGENCY:** ☎1813

- **PHARMACY:** Løve Apoteket (Store Torv 5 ☎86 12 00 22. Open 24/7.)

- **HOSPITALS:** Aarhus University Hospital (Nørrebrogade 44 ☎70 11 31 31)

Getting There

By Plane

Aarhus is serviced by a small airport called Aarhus Lufthavn about 20 miles north of the city. There are less than a dozen flights a day and most go to Copenhagen or London. If you're coming from the airport, the airport shuttle bus leaves from directly in front of Aarhus Central Station (Aarhus H) on a schedule tailored to the flights coming in that day. The price of the bus is 100 DKK.

By Train

Trains from Copenhagen Central Station leave for Aarhus Central Station regularly. The ride is roughly 4 hours long, and a one way tickets costs around 600 DKK. Tickets can either be purchased at the station, online, or, for those with a European sim card, via the DSB app.

Getting Around

Public Transportation

Public transportation in Aarhus is run by a company called Midttrafik and the cost of a single ride is 20 DKK for 2 zones (which covers most of the city). You can buy tickets at the machines at bus stops or from the driver when you enter the bus.

The Aarhus Card offers free admission at 16 museums and 30% discount at the Old Town and Aros Art Museum. Cards can be bought at the Bus Station, City Sleep-in Hostel, most hotels and the Bruuns Galleri shopping center, among other locations. 24-hour card 129 DKK. 28-hour card 179 DKK.

Aarhus Taxa (☎89 48 48 48. www.aarhustaxa.dk.) Weekday rates start at 33 DKK and go up 7.81 DKK per km. At night, rates start at 44 DKK and go up 9.21 DKK per km.

odense

If New York City is the city that never sleeps, Odense is the city that took NyQuil and slept through all of its alarms. Though it's the third largest city in Denmark, it feels much more like a sleepy village than anything else: you can hit all of the main sights in a single day and your nightlife options are limited. Even so, the town has a special charm once you walk around: it's the childhood home of Hans Christian Andersen (the author of every fairy tale ever) and has a surprisingly large selection of cafés, restaurants, and stores. If you're looking for a quaint trip away from the hustle and bustle of Copenhagen, you're only two hours away from a town whose name means "Odin's Sanctuary." So let's go relax.

SIGHTS

⬛ HANS CHRISTIAN ANDERSEN MUSEUM

Bangs Boder 29   ☎65 51 46 01 www.museum.odense.dk/hcandersenmuseum

Hans Christian Andersen practically invented childhood: whether you like "The Little Mermaid" or "The Ugly Duckling," there's a fat chance you read this guy as a tot. He even inspired the movie *Frozen*…and while that might actually make you despise the man, please take your prejudice, let it go, and visit the quaint yellow house where he grew up. The displays tell his rags-to-moderate-income story as the son of a humble cobbler whose imagination and wordplay brought him international renown. While the entire museum will take you 30min. max, Danes get really, really excited about this guy—the least you can do is pay your respects (and 95 DKK for entrance).

i *95 DKK, children under 17 free. Open daily 10am-5pm.*

ST. CANUTE'S CHURCH

Klosterbakken 2   ☎66 12 03 92

You know how they say that death and taxes are the only unavoidable things in life? For Europe, they add one more category: churches. So if you truly want to experience Odense, you'll need to visit St. Canute's Church. It's medieval. It's huge. It's got more Gothic architecture than the entire Yale campus. Even better, the backstory to its construction reads like a Game of Thrones episode: murder, intrigue, kings blaming women for bad weather, and characters with unpronounceable names. What more could you ask for from a church? (besides, you know, spiritual salvation).

i *Free. Open M-Sa 10am-5pm, Su noon-4pm.*

KONGENS HAVE

Directly across from Odense Central Station

Kermit the Frog once famously opined that it's not easy being green. While we sympathize with his plight, we believe Kongens Have is a counterargument to this statement. In clear juxtaposition to the industrial-looking train station, this park hosts a sea of green grass, the majestic white pillars of the Odense Palace, and a clear view of nearby architectural wonders like the Odense Theater.

i *Free. Open 24hr.*

MUNKE MOSE

Was Kongens Have too small for you? Did the imposing architecture of the Soviet-style train station turn you off? Then consider that park your mistress and this

denmark

one your wife: Munke Mose is located on a gorgeous tree-lined river that looks like something out of the Shire, and the animal statues littered throughout the grounds resemble Aslan's camp from "The Lion, the Witch and the Wardrobe." This city is basically a living monument to nostalgia and this park continues that theme—just ten minutes south of Central Station, you can relive your favorite childhood adventures in this majestic setting.

i Free. Open 24hr.

FOOD

CAFÉ BIOGRAFEN $
Brandts Passage 39-41 ☎66 13 16 16 www.cafebio.dk

Biografen is a solid place to sip coffee, poke at your smoked salmon, and contemplate the inherent folly of Man. With both indoor and outdoor seating, and an interior theme that evokes Hollywood's Golden Age, this place is a local haunt for students and adults alike. Better yet, it's connected to an actual movie theater that shows films every day—because while Vince Vega may have bragged that you can buy beer at European movie theaters in Pulp Fiction, it's an entirely different experience when you do it firsthand.

i Coffee 25 DKK. Dishes 70 DKK. Open M-Th 10am-11pm, F-Sa 10am-midnight, Su 10am-11pm.

CAFE CUCKOO'S NEST $$
Vestergade 73 ☎65 91 57 87 www.cuckoos.dk

Cafe Cuckoo's Nest offers a fresh, delicious and professionally curated buffet. The bacon is crisp, the cheese selection is on point, and the salmon is more tender than your feelings. And they're right on the money with the tasty rugbrød, pastries, and fruit. It may all be a bit pricey (the brunch buffet will set you back 135 DKK) but why not treat yoself?

i All-you-can-eat brunch buffet 135 DKK. Coffee 25 DKK. Open M-Th 9am-11pm, F-Sa 9am-2am, Su 10am-10pm.

FROGGY'S CAFÉ $$
Vestergade 68 ☎65 90 74 47 www.froggyscafe.dk

Just off of Odense's main pedestrian walkway, this café is a hipster's wet dream: its English, Mexican, Indian, and Nordic menu is a taste of everything that is multicultural, and the late-night jazz and cocktails will have your fedora-wearing self quoting Allen Ginsberg until the wee hours of the morning. Whether you need a 4am nightcap or a late Sunday brunch, think of this place as an excellent spot to park your cash and escape from the real world for a bit.

i Entrées 90-140 DKK. Open M-W 9am-midnight, Th 9am-2am, F 9am-4am, Sa 9:30am-5am, Su 9:30am-midnight.

RED CHILLI $
Vesterbro 8 www.redchilli-odense.dk

In a town that's more Scandinavian than a socialized meatball dinner, this place is a surprisingly tasty injection of foreign culture. Most appetizers are in the 30 DKK range (we recommend the samosas) and the larger dishes are between 79 and 104 DKK. If you're looking for Indian food without the monsoons this summer, Red Chilli is the place for you.

i Appetizers 30 DKK. Entrées 79-104 DKK. Open M-Th 3pm-9pm, F-Sa 3pm-9:30pm, Su 3pm-9pm.

NIGHTLIFE

BLOMSTEN AND BIEN
Overgade 45 ☎26 11 76 58 www.blomstenogbien.nu

If you've ever seen *Inglourious Basterds*, you'll know Aldo Rayne's number one rule is that you never fight in a basement. Dancing in a basement, though, can be

CABINN ODENSE $$

Østre Stationsvej 9   ☎63 14 57 00 www.cabinn.com/en/hotel/cabinn-odense-hotel

This budget hotel is about as basic as a sorority girl with a pumpkin spice latte, but for the penny-pinching traveller it's a godsend. The rooms are compact—they take the term "Cabinn" quite literally here—but they're on the cheaper end of Odense accommodations and in a perfect location next to the train station. Every room has a TV, shower, and wifi, and most come with bunkbeds. The lobby has snacks, drinks, and computers and is a good launching point for a day of adventuring.

i Economy rooms 495 DKK. Larger rooms 545 DKK. Book online to save 100 DKK. Reception 24hr.

DANNHOSTEL ODENSE CITY $

Østre Stationsvej 31   ☎63 11 04 25 www.odensedanhostel.dk

This is the only hostel in central Odense, and what you see is what you get. Its location right next to the train station makes it ideal for backpackers, and the quality, services, and discounts they offer are identical to what you'll find in other Hostelling International locations throughout Europe. If you're only staying a night or two Odense, it may make sense to shell out the extra money for a single. You might not be able to fit you and your ego into the smaller 4-bed dorms.

i Singles 435 DKK. Doubles 570 DKK. Dorms 250 DKK. Reception daily 8am-noon and 4-8pm.

pretty fun. This particular basement is a nightclub offering music and libation that gives you time to kick back with an Old Fashioned or a Heineken as you compete with man-bunned Danes on the dance floor. Odense is a small town and it seems like half of the city comes here on Saturday nights, so plan on popping your collar, taking that cologne bath, and coming over before midnight if you want to beat the crowds.

i Cocktails 75 DKK. Beers 40 DKK. Open Th-Sa 10pm-5am.

BOOGIE DANCE CAFÉ

Nørregade 21   ☎22 30 43 39 www. boogiedance.dk

This is the place to be after 1am. The rooftop terrace is buzzing with young people until well after the sun has come up, and the dance floor and drink prices will have you screaming "Let's Go!" as you deftly slip our new European guidebook into your purse. Spend the night making friends and banging out 15 DKK shots in Hans Christian Andersen's hometown, and you'll never be able to describe your night with depressing adjectives like lonely.

i Cover 40 DKK. Beers 30 DKK. Shots 15 DKK. Open Tu-W 11pm-4:30am, Th-Sa midnight-5am.

ESSENTIALS

Practicalities

- **TOURIST OFFICES:** VisitOdense (Vestergade 2 ☎63 75 75 20; www.visitodense.com. Open M-F 9:30am-6pm, Sa 10am-3pm, Su 11am-2pm.)

- **CURRENCY EXCHANGE:** There is a Forex exchange center in Odense Central Station

- **ATMS:** ATMs can be found in Central Station, at the BankNordik one block east, and along major pedestrian paths such as Vesterbro and Kongensgade

denmark

- **LUGGAGE STORAGE:** You can use the lockers at Central Station at a rate of 40 DKK for 24 hours.

- **LAUNDROMAT:** Byens Møntvask (Nyborgvej 35 ☎40 11 15 51. Open daily 7am-9pm.) Washing a small load costs 35 DKK. Bigger loads cost 50 DK.

- **INTERNET:** You can get online at Central Station, certain buses, and many hotels. Additionally, you can go to the public library (Odense Centralbibliotek, Stationsvej 15 ☎66 13 13 72. Generally open daily 10am-4pm.)

- **POST OFFICE:** Posthus Odense City (Vesterbro 39. Open M-F 10am-6pm, Sa 10am-3pm.)

Emergency

- **EMERGENCY NUMBER:** ☎112

- **NON-EMERGENCY POLICE NUMBER:** ☎114

- **MEDICAL EMERGENCY:** ☎1813

- **PHARMACY:** Apoteket Ørnen (Filosofhaven 38B ☎66 12 29 70. Open 24hr.)

- **HOSPITALS:** Odense University Hospital (Søndre Blvd. 29 ☎65 41 21 00. Open 24hr.)

Getting There

Odense technically has an airport, but only offers a few flights a day—and, weirdly enough, none of those flights are domestic. If you come to the city, you will most likely do so by train.

All trains coming in to Odense arrive at Odense Central Station. The journey from Copenhagen takes around 2 hours and costs 240 DKK (270 DKK if you want to reserve a seat). Trains leave every 30min. or so from Copenhagen Central Station. Tickets can be purchased at the station, online or, for those with a European sim card, via the DSB app.

Getting Around

By Public Transportation

This town is the size of a hamburger and you can walk pretty much anywhere. However, there is a local bus system, for which single tickets cost 23 DKK, a 24-hour ticket costs 40 DKK, and a 10-trip ticket costs 150 DKK.

The Odense City Pass gets you free entrance in over a dozen museums, a 50% discount at the zoo, and free public transportation. A 24-hour pass costs 169 DKK.

By Taxis

Odense Taxa (☎66 15 66 31; www.odensetaxa.dk.) Fares on weekends and nights start at 36 DKK and go up 5.83 DKK per minute.

denmark essentials

VISAS

Denmark is a member of the EU. Citizens of Australia, Canada, New Zealand, the US, and many other non-EU countries do not need a visa for stays of up to 90 days. Denmark is a member of the Schengen area, so if you plan to spend time in other Schengen countries, note that the 90-day period of time you are allowed to visit without a visa applies cumulatively to all Schengen countries.

MONEY

Despite being a member of the EU, Denmark is not in the Eurozone and uses the Danish krone, (DKK or kr.) as its currency.

All service bills in Denmark tend to include a gratuity, so tipping is not expected. In restaurants, if no gratuity is added for some reason, you should tip your server 10%. If a gratuity is added, it is not uncommon to still leave a small tip in the form of rounding up the bill. Taxis in Denmark also often include a gratuity in the final charge, but if you would like to leave an extra tip, round up the bill.

ATMs in Denmark are common and convenient. They are often located in airports, train stations, and major pedestrian areas. The two major international money networks are MasterCard/Maestro/Cirrus and Visa/PLUS. To find out what out-of-network or international fees you may be subject to by using ATMs, call your bank.

ALCOHOL

The minimum age to purchase alcohol in Denmark is 16 for drinks below 16.5% ABV and 18 for drinks above 16.5% ABV. There is no minimum age to drink alcohol. To be allowed into bars, clubs, or discos that serve any kind of alcohol, you must be 18 or older. Remember to drink responsibly and to never drink and drive. The legal blood alcohol content (BAC) for driving in Denmark is under 0.05%, significantly lower than the US limit of 0.08%.

denmark

FRANCE

Think of a famous idea. Any famous idea. Or for that matter any brushstroke, article of clothing, architectural style, camera technique, great thinker that should have been medicated, or hip reason to brew a Molotov cocktail. If that idea is Western, then it is probably French (or at least hotly contested and contributed to a French intellectual movement). Your first walk around Paris will be defined by a paralyzing level of excitement. Your first party in Monaco might result in a Hangover-esque situation. It's no secret that young Americans "backpack" through France to lose their virginity and construct their identity at a safe distance from their parents. The successes of James Baldwin, Gertrude Stein, and Ernest Hemingway suggest that we couldn't have chosen a better spot; there is a pervading sense in France that everything is here.

Students might go to France to be fashionably disaffected artists in boho-chic corner cafes, but this isn't the land of berets and baguettes anymore: it's the land of sustainable energy and the 35hr. work week. As France wrestles with the economic and cultural ramifications of a globalized world, this is also, increasingly, the country of parkour and veil bans, sprawling Chinatowns and the Marie Leonie case of 2004. Nowhere is the cognitive dissonance of these cultural collisions more evident than in Marseille, whose burgeoning Little Algeria encroaches upon the city's Old World streets. In the midst of these transitions, the most sacred of French traditions remain gloriously preserved—you might eat a lot of kebabs while you're here, but you can still riot against The Man in the morning and commit adultery by noon.

greatest hits

- **WE'LL ALWAYS HAVE PARIS.** From the "metal asparagus" of the **Eiffel Tower** (p. 143) to the bars of **St-Germain**, you'll have plenty to do in France's capital.

- **THAT'LL DO NICELY. Nice** (p. 211) might be the best city on the Côte d'Azur for backpackers, and it's definitely the cheapest.

- **RAISE THE ROOF.** Dance the night away with a view overlooking two rivers and the entire city of Lyon at **Le Sucre** (p. 174), a bar sitting atop a defuncy sugar factory.

FRANCE

North Sea

Manchester

BRITAIN

Amsterdam
NETHERLANDS
Rotterdam
Münster

Düsseldorf

London

Bristol

Dover
Folkestone
Portsmouth
Dunkerque
Antwerp
BELGIUM
Brussels
GERMANY

Plymouth

English Channel
(La Manche)
Boulogne-sur-Mer
Calais
Lille
Arras
Mainz

Channel
Islands
Cherbourg
Le Havre
Somme R.
Amiens
LUX.
Metz

Roscoff
St-Malo
Bayeux
Caen
Rouen
Seine R.
Reims
Épernay
Nancy
Strasbourg
Sélestat

Brest
Mont-St-Michel
Dinan
Paris
Chartres
Marne R.
Troyes
Colmar

Quimper
Rennes
Le Mans
Mulhouse

Belle Ile
Angers
Loire R.
Tours
Amboise
Orléans
Fontainebleau
Dijon
Besançon
Pontarlier
SWITZ.
Bern

Ile d'Yeu
Nantes
Saumur
Blois
Loire R.
Nevers
Beaune
Haut-Jura Mts.
Lake Geneva

**ATLANTIC
OCEAN**
Poitiers
Vienne R.
Indre R.
Bourges
Cluny
Geneva
Annecy
A L P S

La Rochelle
Vichy
Lyon
Mont Blanc
4810m
Chamonix

Bay of Biscay
Limoges
Cognac
Gironde R.
Angoulême
Montignac
Clermont-Ferrand
Le-Mont-Dore
Rhône R.
Grenoble
ITALY

Les Eyzies-de-Tayac
Bordeaux
Sarlat
Dordogne R.
Castelnaud-la-Chapelle
▲ **Le Puy de Sancy**
Cévennes Mts.

Garonne R.
MONACO
Menton

Biarritz
Bayonne
St-Jean-Pied-de-Port
Avignon
Nîmes
Aix-en-Provence
Arles
Nice
Antibes
Cannes

Bilbao
Toulouse
Montpellier
St-Raphaël
St-Tropez
CÔTE D'AZUR

Adour R.
Lourdes
Cauterets
Carcassonne
Aude R.
Marseille
Toulon

Burgos
ANDORRA
Perpignan
Golfe du Lion
TO CORSICA

P Y R E N E E S

S P A I N

Zaragoza
Barcelona

N
L G

| TGV Line |

0   150 kilometers
0   150 miles

Mediterranean Sea

Valencia

Cap Corse

Calvi
CORSICA
Bastia
Corte
Ajaccio
Porto-Vecchio
Bonifacio
SARDINIA
(ITALY)

paris

Ah, Paris. The City of Lights. The City of Love. The City of American Projections of Luminosity and Lust. One of the most popular tourist destinations in the world, Paris remains, against all touristy odds, unabashedly Parisian. The city is packed to the brim with name-droppable, college-course-syllabus-worthy culture, and it shows. Here, you'll see people walking down the street with baguettes under one arm and a worn copy of Proust under another, sitting at cafes for hours—sometimes slipping out the occasional "ooh la la" and heading to the latest art gallery opening or ballet premiere.

You'll wind through iconic, elegant Haussmann boulevards as you find your way to both the predictable likes of the Louvre, where seemingly half the world piles in for a whopping dosage of culture, and the less crowded, equally French bakeries and brasseries that will do more than just about any Raphael can to make you feel like you're really having a Parisian experience.

But Paris is more than just the intellectual, effectual melange of dimly lit cafes and Caravaggios. It's an enormous, cosmopolitan city that's home to a global swell of cuisines and culture as rich as any. After your croissant, have some Kurdish; ramen may not pair well with macaroons, but you're damn right you should try it.

The subject of endless romanticizing and hyperbole, Paris can seem like an intimidating, even unfriendly, place to visit. A more eclectic, multicultural hub than what you'd imagine from the postcards, the City of Lights welcomes as it holds you to a certain standard. Just make sure to say *merci*.

ACCOMMODATIONS

▩ SMART PLACE GARE DU NORD $$$

28 Rue de Dunkerque   ☎01 48 78 25 15 www.smartplaceparis.com
Get smart at Smart Place Gare du Nord. You can put down the Descartes, though: The cheap prices and very convenient location (the major Métro artery! I can see it from my house!) will be more than enough material to have you feeling self-satisfied. With a nice little patio area and laundry facilities to complement the normal array of hostel amenities—free Wi-Fi, a common room—Smart Place certainly isn't dumb. Not that there will be too much to do or see in the area right around the hostel; it's just under a mile to Sacré Coeur. Just don't expect too much air-conditioning in the dorms—or breakfast.
i From Métro stop Gare du Nord, take a right on Rue de Dunkerque—you'll have to navigate a 6-way intersection, but you're essentially going straight. It will be on your right. Dorms €30-34. Free Wi-Fi, laundry facilities, and a small beer selection.

▩ VINTAGE HOSTEL GARE DU NORD $$

73 Rue de Dunkerque   ☎01 40 16 16 40 www.vintage-hostel.com
Here at *Let's Go*, we love all things vintage. Vinyl record players, 1970s football jerseys, the Beatles, the Watergate scandal—you know, all the great things that have happened in the last 70 or so years. And Vintage Hostel Gare du Nord is absolutely no exception. With affordable dorms, a location right next to a major Métro stop, free Wi-Fi, and free breakfast, this hostel will have you thinking, "Remember the Great Depression?" That's some vintage gold.
i From the Anvers Métro stop, take a short walk down Bd. de Rochechouart; the hostel is on the right. Dorms €25. Breakfast included. Free Wi-Fi in the lobby.

▩ ST. CHRISTOPHER'S INN CANAL $$

159 Rue de Crimée   ☎01 40 34 34 40 www.st-christophers.co.uk/paris-hostels-old/canal
Paris so nice, they did it twice. By "they" we mean the quite large and ever-present corporation, St. Christopher's, that has hostels all over Europe. By "so nice" we

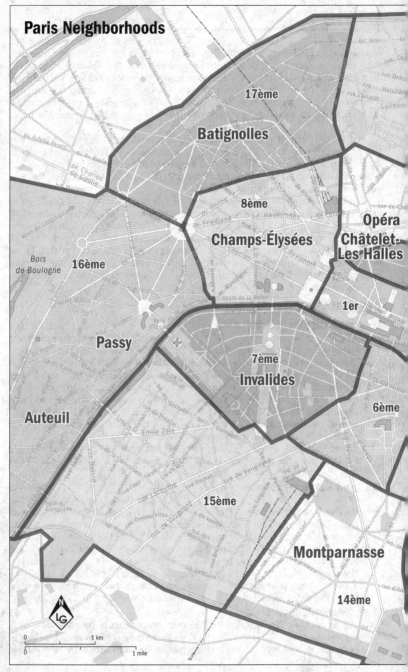

Paris Neighborhoods

17ème

Batignolles

8ème

Champs-Élysées

Opéra
Châtelet-
Les Halles

Bois
de Boulogne

16ème

1er

Passy

7ème

Invalides

6ème

Auteuil

15ème

Montparnasse

14ème

N

0   1 km
0   1 mile

france

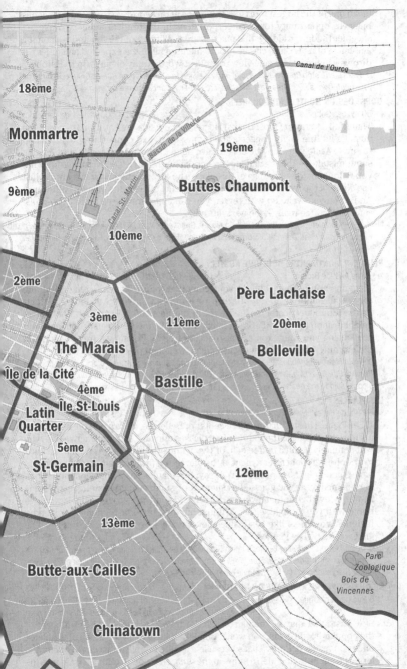

18ème

Monmartre

9ème

2ème

3ème

The Marais

Île de la Cité

4ème

Île St-Louis

Latin
Quarter

5ème

St-Germain

13ème

Butte-aux-Cailles

Chinatown

10ème

Canal St-Martin

Bassin de la Villette

Canal de l'Ourcq

19ème

Buttes Chaumont

11ème

Bastille

Père Lachaise

20ème

Belleville

bd. Diderot

Seine

12ème

Parc
Zoologique

Bois de
Vincennes

paris

mean one of the largest tourist destinations in the world, so a very advantageous business opportunity for large corporations in the tourism industry. Wake up, sheeple! Kidding, kidding: this place is great. With all of the fun and welcoming ambience of a St. Chris classic (not to mention all of the expected amenities), it throws in a nice canal-side view to make it worth a stay on any trip to Europe.

i *From Métro stop Crimée, take a right on Av. de Flandre. Take a left on Rue de Crimée; it will be on your right. Dorms €23. Breakfast included. Free Wi-Fi. A bar but no real kitchen.*

OOPS! DESIGN HOSTEL LATIN QUARTER $$$
50 Av. des Gobelins   ☎01 47 07 47 00 www.oops-paris.com

Thankfully, a stay at Oops! Design Hostel, just outside the Latin Quarter, isn't the mistake its title might suggest. The rooms, staff, and common room are all up to snuff. While you won't be able to turn up in the hostel and really start making some mistakes—that Canadian guy across the hall? He's not looking for what you're looking for—because of this place's no-alcohol rules, you can always just use some of the free Wi-Fi to make your own mistakes in the ensuite bathrooms. And when you wake up with regret, you can enjoy some free breakfast—croissants and coffee really—the next morning.

i *From Métro stop Les Gobelins, walk up Av. des Gobelins toward Pl. d'Italie away from the river. It will be on your right. Dorms €32. Breakfast included. Free Wi-Fi. No alcohol allowed in the hostel. No kitchen, either.*

PLUG-INN MONTMARTRE BOUTIQUE HOSTEL $$
7 Rue Aristide Bruant   ☎01 42 58 42 58 http://plug-inn.fr

Plugging is important. Plug in your computer, plug your ears, plug the drain; they're all important parts of a trip to Europe. Thankfully, at Plug-Inn Montmartre Boutique Hostel, nestled right in the heart of the winding Montmartre neighborhood (home to Paris's red-light district), you can do just about any kind of plugging you want. You can also access free Wi-Fi, enjoy a free breakfast in the morning, and sleep soundly in a clean, well-kept place.

i *From Métro stop Abbesses, take a right onto Rue des Abbesses. After 2 blocks, take a left onto Rue Aristide Bruant. It will be on your right. 6-bed dorms €22. Breakfast included. Free Wi-Fi. No alcohol sold in the hostel.*

LES PIAULES $$$
59 Bd. de Belleville   ☎01 43 55 09 97 www.lespiaules.com

If Les Piaules hostel, in the square center of Belleville, were a person, it would be a super cool (square-framed Ray-Ban glasses and all), super attractive one who will definitely go on a coffee date or two with you, but when you ask them back to your hostel room after a night at the bar, they'll probably smirk and tell you to have a good night. All of which is to say: Les Piaules has a dope common room/bar manned by a (you guessed it) super cool, super attractive staff; an awesome rooftop view; better-than-average dorms; and some sweet Wi-Fi. But it won't go home with you at night, either. Without any free breakfast, kitchen, or laundry facilities, you'll feel like Les Piaules never really loved you back. Still, you'll be glad you knew Les Piaules.

i *From Métro stop Belleville, head down Bd. de Belleville (slight decline, also toward the 20ème arrondissement). Dorms €33. Free Wi-Fi, pretty large bar, and a really nice view on the top floor. Small charge for breakfast, depending on what you order.*

ST. CHRISTOPHER'S INN GARE DU NORD $$
5 Rue de Dunkerque   ☎01 70 08 52 22
www.st-christophers.co.uk/paris-hostels-old/gare-du-nord

St. Christopher may be the patron saint of traveling, but for this installment of the popular hostel chain, you won't, thankfully, have to do too much of it, at least once you arrive in Paris. That's because it's quite literally adjacent to one of the largest train hubs and Métro stops in the area, so if you're taking a train into the

haussmann architecture

Building so nice, Paris did it twice. Building so nice, Paris did it thrice. Building so nice, Paris did it again and again until pretty much every building in the whole damn city looked essentially the same. Even if the only thing you've managed to do so far in Paris is find the nearest McDonald's for some Wi-Fi, you've seen this building: five stories tall, flat limestone white façade, and a blue roof, bending back from the front at a 45-degree angle.

How did this happen? Why is seemingly every building in the city identical, lining boulevards with such uniform proficiency that you're starting to feel a little suspicious? Was Paris designed in Sim City by a fifth-grader with OCD and an affinity for spokes and wheels?

The answer: yes. Turns out this monochromatic monotony is, essentially, the result of one man's urban design wet dream, endowing the city with an elegance that has become such a part of Parisian iconography that a Paris without this urban design seems like it could hardly be considered Paris. The man's name is Georges-Eugène Haussmann.

In the mid- to late 19th century, our man Haussmann set out to renovate and revitalize a Paris that was, to be blunt, getting a little stinky. At the behest of Napoleon III (yep, there were a few of those guys), he started clearing out huge swaths of the city (read: old, poor parts of the city) to create the long arterial boulevards, lined with our favorite limestone buildings, that now feel integral to Paris. Maybe unsurprisingly, this guy eventually became a little a controversial, but his architectural and design legacy lives on to this day. Look literally anywhere.

City of Lights, you could probably roll sideways a few times and find yourself here. With all of the moderately over-the-top accommodations of a chain hostel, St. Christopher's at Gare du Nord will probably be one of the better places in the city to meet other young travelers, all while enjoying free Wi-Fi, free breakfast, laundry facilities, and a nice bar.

i From Métro stop Gare du Nord, take a left. It's a straight shot from there; it will be on your right. Dorms €23. Breakfast included. Free Wi-Fi. There's a bar as well. No real kitchen.

LE VILLAGE HOSTEL MONTMARTRE $$$
20 Rue d'Orsel   ☎01 42 64 22 02 www.villagehostel.fr

If it takes a village to raise a child, well, you're out of luck. Le Village Hostel Montmartre isn't a daycare, so bring your bawling infants elsewhere. Instead, bunk with people who were babies 20 years ago and get ready for, well, a pretty standard hostel experience—just one that is very, very close to Sacré Coeur. You know, one of those places in Paris you're supposed to be seeing. And when you're done seeing it—the city! It's so pretty!—return to free Wi-Fi and a respectable, affordable place to rest your head.

i From Métro stop Anvers, walk up Rue de Steinkerque. After a block, take a left on Rue d'Orsel. It will be on your left. Dorms €30. Free Wi-Fi. No kitchen.

THE LOFT BOUTIQUE HOSTEL PARIS $$
70 Rue Julien Lacroix   ☎01 42 02 42 02 www.theloft-paris.com

In Paris, just about anything with the word boutique must cost a boatload, right? This is the world capital of expensive things with French-sounding names, isn't it? Thankfully, The Loft Boutique Hostel is not really a loft and not really boutique; it's cheap, convenient, and accommodating. You'll have Wi-Fi, breakfast,

paris

a kitchen, a bar, and a bed all within a few blocks from major Métro stops. And you won't even have to climb down from some loft.

i From Métro stop Belleville, walk down Rue de Belleville and take a right onto Rue Julien Lacroix after a few blocks; the hostel will be on your right. Dorms €20. Breakfast included. Free Wi-Fi. Open bar and kitchen.

LE REGENT MONTMARTRE HOSTEL & BUDGET HOTEL $$

37 Bd. Rochechouart   ☎01 48 78 24 00 www.leregent.com

With all of the glory (holes) of Montmartre just a few blocks away, a stay at Le Regent Montmartre is sure to be exciting. And that's not just because you'll be able to enjoy a free breakfast, some free Wi-Fi, and easy access to one of the city's most famous sights (Sacré Coeur, not whatever you'll be looking at in Pigalle). It's because, well, you'll be close to a bunch of sex shows. What fun!

i A few steps away from the Anvers Métro stop. Dorms €22. Breakfast included. Free Wi-Fi. Shared computers. Foosball.

YOUNG & HAPPY HOSTEL LATIN QUARTER $$$

80 Rue Mouffetard   ☎01 47 07 47 07 www.youngandhappy.fr

For the young and happy travelers that we are, a place that bills itself as also Young & Happy (ah ha HA HA, we are SO HAPPY) sounds like a match made in heaven, right? Sure enough, this place will have you feeling juvenile and joyous, with free Wi-Fi and breakfast on one of Paris's most adolescent and cheerful streets.

i From the Pl. Monge Métro stop, walk along Pl. Monge and continue onto Rue Ortolan. Turn left onto Rue Mouffetard, and the hostel will be on your right. Rooms €40. Free Wi-Fi. Breakfast included. Communal bar and game room.

MIJE PARIS FAUCONNIER $$$

11 Rue du Fauconnier   ☎01 42 74 23 45

www.mije.com/en/auberge-jeunesse-paris/fauconnier

One part of a three-part mega-hostel, MIJE Paris Fauconnier will make you think you can actually afford living in Le Marais. For a few days, anyway, you can. With free Wi-Fi, breakfast, and all of the interpersonal fun of a common room, this hostel does more than just put you in arguably the coolest part of the City of Lights. It's also a hostel, stocked with most of the things you hope and expect to find in a hostel. Imagine that.

i From the Pont Marie Métro stop, head southeast on Quai de l'Hôtel de ville toward Rue des Nonnains d'Hyères. Turn left onto Rue des Nonnains d'Hyères and then right onto Rue du Fauconnier; the hostel will be on your left. Dorms €34. Free Wi-Fi. Breakfast included. Lounge with board games.

GENERATOR PARIS $$$

11 Pl. du Colonel Fabien   ☎01 70 98 84 00

https://generatorhostels.com/en/destinations/paris

Too lazy to even leave the hostel to go get hammered? Do you want to ignore the fact that you traveled anywhere and just get completely sloshed with a bunch of other Americans in an English-speaking club-meets-bar-meets-frat-party? Don't worry, we have generated a solution for you! There's Generator Hostel Paris, party hostel among party hostels. The beds and Wi-Fi are almost afterthoughts.

i Just around the roundabout from the Colonel Fabien Métro stop. Dorms €30. Free Wi-Fi. A cafe and bars on the rooftop AND in the basement.

THREE DUCKS HOSTEL $$$

6 Pl. Étienne Pernet   ☎01 48 42 04 05 http://3ducks.fr

Duck, duck, duck, HOSTEL! Your childhood may be over, but your days of ducks and geese? They're just beginning. Take a break at Three Ducks Hostel in the 15ème arrondissement—free Wi-Fi, free breakfast, and reliable dorms will give you more than enough room to sit crisscross applesauce with some friends and chase each other in the circles. That's what the cool kids are doing these days, right?

i *A block from the Commerce Métro stop. Just walk down Rue du Commerce toward Rue des Entrepreneurs. Dorms €29. Free Wi-Fi. Breakfast included. You get a free drink on arrival.*

SIGHTS

🏛 NOTRE DAME

6 Parvis Notre-Dame, Pl. Jean-Paul II   ☎01 42 34 56 10 www.notredamedeparis.fr

Let's face it: there are some sights in Paris you're going to have to go and see. Thank the Lord that, in Paris, this doesn't suck—at least not most of the time. And what better place to thank the Lord than at one of those sights? And as far as You Have To See This tourist attractions go, Notre Dame just about tops the list: It's really old (dating from the 14th century), really holy, really pretty, and—what's that?—really free. The line, while long, doesn't even end up taking too much time to move through—besides, you'll have plenty of time to appreciate the beautiful front façade. (Be sure to check out the statue of the king without a head.) Basically, this is a blue-chip, bona fide home run of a tourist attraction.

i *From the Cité Métro stop, turn right onto Rue de la Cité and then left onto Parvis Notre-Dame/ Pl. Jean-Paul II. Open M-F 8am-6:45pm, Sa-Su 8am-7:15pm. Free.*

🏛 LOUVRE

4 Pl. du Louvre   ☎01 40 20 53 17 www.louvre.fr

Hopefully we're not the first ones telling you this: the Louvre is home to a bunch of influential and super famous artwork. Like, as famous as the *Mona Lisa*. Pretty much *exactly* as famous as the *Mona Lisa*, actually. So prepare your empty platitudes (does art imitate life or does life imitate art?) and pseudo-knowledge about the Renaissance ("Ah, yes, I know Michelangelo—he's an anthropomorphic turtle who fights crime with his brothers, Raphael, Leonardo, and Donatello") and descend into the glass pyramid that marks the beginning of the Louvre's cavernous collection. The world capital of tourists pretending to know anything about art, the Louvre is crowded, making the viewing experience for the most celebrated paintings more of a sophisticated breed of rubbernecking than it is your traditional museum-viewing fare. Not that this should stop you from visiting; if you're under age 30, snag a Carte Louvre Jeunes, which entitles the owner to one-year unlimited access without waiting in line and free access for the owner and a guest on Wednesday and Friday nights. There's so much here—from the Renaissance to ancient Egypt to just about everything in between—that you could easily spend that year exploring the beautiful palace halls. For those of you who are not art history savants and do not understand the difference between mutant ninja turtles and Renaissance painters, we recommend trying the audio tours. They come on cool Nintendo DSes!

i *From the Palais Royal/Musée du Louvre Métro, turn left onto Rue de Rivoli and look for the big glass pyramid. Open M 9am-6pm, W 9am-9:45pm, Th 9am-6pm, F 9am-9:45pm, Sa-Su 9am-6pm. €15, under 18 free.*

🏛 ARC DE TRIOMPHE

Pl. Charles de Gaulle   ☎01 55 37 73 77 www.arcdetriompheparis.com

What's a historic European city without some kind of arch, anyway? World War II and the awkward French surrender aside, France has a very rich military history. (We're not judging, France, but you could have lasted a little longer.) Remember Napoleon? The Little Corporal took Europe by storm 200 years before you did, bub. The Arc de Triomphe was Napoleon's pet project to commemorate his victories, but, in typical French fashion, he died before it could be completed. Today the monument remembers the French soliders who died doing Napoleon's dirty work (awkward) and in the French Revolution and also

paris

shakespeare & company

Any trip to Paris is incomplete without posing as an intellectual. (Oh, you've read Sartre? Tell us more.) And there's no better place to put on your proverbial scarf than Shakespeare and Company, an English-language bookstore shelved along the Seine near Pl. St-Michel. Between appearances in Hemingway's memoirs and the odd shoutout in Woody Allen movies, this green-toned, wood-framed store has got it all: name recognition; bespectacled, young employees who could out-hipster even the most insufferable person in your lit lecture; and oh-so-inspiring quotes on the wall about just how beautiful poetry is. But while all this may only seem to add to the snobbishness of a city that hardly needs more of it, the bookstore's charm and historical roots merit a visit for even the most casual fan of modernist fiction.

Founded by Sylvia Beach, a blue-chip American expat and literary persona, in the early 20th century, Shakespeare and Company started as a bookstore and creditor to many of the expatriates in Paris. For decades, Beach sold books and conversed with the likes of Ernest Hemingway, James Joyce, and F. Scott Fitzgerald (we figure you'll recognize at least one of these names). During World War II and the German occupation of Paris, the bookstore shut down, and Beach eventually died.

But like all things great and literary, the end of the original did not prevent the development of highly sophisticated (not to mention marketable) knockoffs. After the war, some of the old patrons of the bookstore got together to revive the old classic, purchasing the lot along the Seine where ol' Billy Shakes stands today.

Though you probably won't run into Ezra Pound or any Ezra Pounds-to-be (for your sake, we hope this does not happen), the contemporary store boasts an impressive array of fiction, all while providing and creating that literary charm you hoped for. There's a creaky staircase leading to an attic, rusting typewriters sprawling everywhere, and, yep, it's that kid from your lit lecture. So grab one of those Joyce novels you keep telling yourself you would read and maybe scratch out some self-serious prose. You're in Paris, after all.

serves as a point of pride for the modern French military. Not only does this big stone monolith stand testament to how powerful France is—look, we can build this big thing! Fear us!—and look really cool from the outside, but you can also go up this big stone monolith and see the city, for equally big of a price.

i Take the Métro to Argentine, Ternes, George V, or Kléber and walk toward the huge arch. Open daily Apr-Sept 10am-11pm; Oct-Mar 10am-10:30pm. €8, ages 18-25 €5.

■ SACRÉ COEUR

35 Rue du Chevalier de la Barre   ☎01 53 41 89 00 www.sacre-coeur-montmartre.com

That famous thing on the Paris skyline that is not the Eiffel Tower, Sacré Coeur, the cylindrical cathedral towering over the Montmartre district, both defines the view and provides views of Paris. Climb through the winding streets of Montmartre and enjoy the expansive lookout from the cathedral steps—look out for the men trying to make bracelets for you, though—or summit any number of the other viewpoints in the city and behold its smooth, white façade. (Don't expect to be able to see the Eiffel Tower from Sacré Coeur, though; we like to imagine these two monuments as rivals.) The views are this sight's main claim to fame, though; the cathedral itself, while free, is pretty run of the mill: big and grand and pretty. Overall, it's very much worth the stop, not least because you can

france

take a spin through the alternately quaint and kitschy side streets of the famed Montmartre district that surround the cathedral.

i From the Anvers Métro stop, walk up Rue Steinkerque and straight through Sq. Louise Michel. Open daily 6am-10:30pm. Free.

EIFFEL TOWER

Champ de Mars, 5 Av. Anatole   ☎08 92 70 12 39 www.toureiffel.paris

We really shouldn't have to tell you too much about this one. Seriously, if you were reading through this book, saw this blurb about the Eiffel Tower, and thought, "Huh, that looks interesting, I wonder what that is?" then you should probably look at your life, look at your choices. Spoiler alert—it's the big freakin' tower that's literally in every photograph, movie, postcard, keychain, T-shirt, Snapchat filter, or Morse code message about this city. Assuming you now want to climb this latticework of metal, prepare to wait in line and cough up some dough; it's more expensive if you want to go all the way to the top, and the views are still pretty damn good from the middle if you just do the cheaper walking option. The lines, while long, aren't actually as bad as you would think; expect to wait for about 45min. to 1hr. You might have heard, it's pretty popular.

i From Bir Hakeim Métro stop, take walk 10min. along Quai Branly. Open daily from mid-June to early Sept 9am-midnight; from early Sept to mid-June 9:30am-11pm. Lift to the top €17, ages 12-24 €14.50. Stair access to 2nd fl. €7, ages 12-24 €5.

CENTRE POMPIDOU

Pl. Georges Pompidou   ☎01 44 78 12 33 www.centrepompidou.fr

If art museums went to high school together, the Louvre would have been prom king, the Musée d'Orsay the valedictorian, and the French MoMA (in the Centre Pompidou) was that pale kid who smelled like Cheez Whiz and hissed at you that one time you spilled hot chocolate on his New Age prayer beads. But with 180 million visitors and counting, clearly that weirdo made a name for himself. The Centre Pompidou itself resembles a McDonald's PlayPlace on steroids: a massive, industrial mess of steel, glass, and plastic tubes so jarringly bright you may very well regurgitate your Royale with cheese. Wandering Pompidou's halls, you'll be struck with a flurry of pressing questions: Is that cow birthing a shovel? Whose toe is this, and is it flirting with me? Why is this clip of a bearded woman slapping her leg with a wooden spoon on an endless loop? Hush, child. This isn't the clearance aisle of a Target from the depths of hell—this is art. If you manage to make it to the top, you'll be treated to some absolutely gorgeous views of the city. Soak them in—you deserve it—then force your way through the array of mirrors and headless baby dolls to the exit.

i A block from the Rambuteau Métro stop along Rue du Renard. Open M-W 11am-10pm, Th 11am-11pm, F-Su 11am-10pm. €14.

MUSÉE RODIN

79 Rue de Varenne   ☎01 44 18 61 10 www.musee-rodin.fr

For one of the world's most socially acceptable ways to spend a few hours staring at a bunch of naked people, head to the Musée Rodin, a museum featuring the work of turn-of-the-century sculptor Auguste Rodin. Carved into the center of Paris's 7ème arrondissement, the museum features a bunch of stonework that you will vaguely recognize, including *The Thinker*. He and several other bodacious bods dot both an expansive garden outside and the interior of the fancy building, but his most famous works are all outside.

i From the Varenne Métro stop, head south on Bd. des Invalides; the museum will be on your left. Open Tu 10am-5:45pm, W 10am-8:45pm, Th-Su 10am-5:45pm. €10, ages 18-25 €7.

paris

PANTHÉON

Pl. du Panthéon   ☎01 44 32 18 00 www.pantheonparis.com

The Panthéon hulks over the Latin Quarter. Its Roman-columned front and spiraling dome endow the neighborhood with the grandiosity that, with the Luxembourg Gardens and some of the world's most famous universities, it so richly doesn't need. (We don't blame the Latin Quarter; when you're right next to Île de la Cité and Notre Dame, it can be easy to feel like you aren't historic and monumental enough.) A once-cathedral, now-monument to how dope France is, the Panthéon is the resting place for a number of great French luminaries, from Voltaire to Rousseau to Marie Curie. As one might guess from its name, the Panthéon has a very Classical vibe, and the beautiful secular cathedral dedicated to France paired with the marble tombs will just about have you humming "La Marseillaise" as you leave. A good stop for some history and for looking at some dead people, two of our favorite activities.

i *From the Cardinal Lemoine Métro, walk along Rue Monge and turn right onto Rue du Cardinal Lemoine. Turn right onto Rue Clovis and continue onto Pl. du Panthéon; it will be on your right. Open daily 10am-6pm. €7, ages 18-25 €4.50.*

LES INVALIDES

129 Rue de Grenelle   ☎08 10 11 33 99 www.musee-armee.fr

Let's face it—you wouldn't be a true American if you haven't made one or two really, really hilarious jokes about French defeatism ("French rifles for sale: never fired, dropped once!"). But a tour through Les Invalides, with its several museums and monuments dedicated to the French military, tell a slightly (OK, vastly) different tale. (Surprise! The French do not conceive of themselves as wimps!) From the 30 Years' War through Napoleon and both world wars, Les Invalides details everything from broad troop movements to the uniforms artillery troops wore on Napoleon's march into Russia. Oh, and there's Napoleon's grave, a giant marble tomb under the gold dome and the perfect endpoint for any first date. (Conquering Europe is a huge turn-on, trust us.)

i *Varenne and La Toure-Maubourg Métro stops are right outside. Open daily Apr-Oct 10am-6pm; Nov-Marc 10am-5pm. €11.*

CHAMPS-ÉLYSÉES

Av. des Champs-Élysées

Champs-Élysées is kind of like the Times Sq. of Paris: it's flashy, iconic, and cool for a maximum of 15min. This broad, crowded boulevard that stretches from the Louvre to the Arc de Triomphe seems to have collapsed in on itself. (Not physically speaking, unless you count large American Apparel stores as geographic destruction.) Nike stores and Starbucks appear to have replaced many of the high-end, French fashion boutiques you thought you could expect, making Champs-Élysées's main tourist attraction just that it is a famous tourist attraction, and not much else. Luckily, it doesn't cost any money to walk down a street, and it is fairly conveniently located, so it does end up being worth the stroll. Just expect to feel like you're in a fancy American strip mall, not at the heart of any kind of high fashion.

i *The Franklin D. Roosevelt and George V Métro stops are along the avenue.*

MUSÉE D'ORSAY

1 Rue de la Légion d'Honneur   ☎01 40 49 48 14 www.musee-orsay.fr

An old train station. A warm glow flowing out from the lights, which dangle from the ceiling. Windows that are also clocks. A museum. Famous paintings. Impressionism. (We tried painting you a painting to make some attempt at an in-joke about the artistic movement at the heart of this museum, but it didn't really work. We apologize.) The more accessible, almost-as-famous neighbor to the Louvre, the Musée d'Orsay boasts an authoritative collection of Impressionist

france

(and Neo-Impressionist, and Fauvist, and Pointillist, etc.) art that even the most uninitiated museum-goers among us will appreciate. Head to the fifth floor and tour through Monet, Manet, Cézanne, Degas, Van Gogh, and just about every other artist you vaguely remember learning about in middle-school art class. Once you're done, you can take a seat and just enjoy the building that hosts this art—we've always been a sucker for train stations, especially really big ones with a balcony view on the top floor.

i From the Solférino Métro stop, walk along Bd. St-Germain and turn right onto Rue de Belle-chasse. Continue onto Rue de la Légion d'Honneur; the museum will be in front of you. Open Tu-W 9:30am-6pm, Th 9:30am-9:45pm, F-Su 9:30am-6pm. €12, ages 18-25 €9, under 18 free.

SAINTE-CHAPELLE

8 Bd. du Palais ☎01 53 40 60 80 www.sainte-chapelle.fr

If you're one of those kids who likes to watch those kaleidoscope-style light shows on YouTube after a few hits of your drug of choice, a trip to Ste-Chapelle will be right up your alley. Watching pretty colors light up and blend with each other is not an entirely modern phenomenon, as it turns out. Way back in medi-

versailles

The gold-plated, tourist-infested ground zero of bougie excess, Versailles is too cool even for Paris. So cool and aloof, in fact, that Versailles— another one of those Parisian tourist attractions that you're basically obligated to go see—went ahead and did what everyone else seems to do when they come into enough money: they moved out to the suburbs. The old adage holds: once the palace for the kings of France, always high-maintenance, self-important, and undeserving of the praise it receives. (Louis XIV referred to himself as the Sun King, for Pete's sake.)

Sure, Versailles (the Palace of Versailles to you, you lowly peasant) is beautiful and historic. It was the seat of the French monarchy for more than a hundred years, home to more men in wigs than even the most populous drag shows. And while the nobles who lived there, doing their best to earn the favor of Louis S.K., likely did not engage in many gender-bending escapades or dancing, they did do their best to impress the man with their wit, charm, and general subservience. (A select group of nobles would watch the king wake up in the morning. Cute!)

At least until that absolute monarchy idea came crashing down harder than a guillotine blade on a hot summer day. Then, the enormous palace and its gardens, swampland that one of those Louises drained and turned into his personal hunting grounds, became both a symbol and artifact of those dark days when France had an authoritarian ruler. (Because an enlightened nation like this one would never again succumb to the supremely undemocratic notion of a dictator, right, Napoleon?) Somehow, the whole shebang survived political turmoil and monarchist revivals for decades until finally living up to its real potential: an enormous tourist attraction.

Enter you and every other dork with a map and a train ticket. These days, a tour through the palace itself—replete with a hall filled with mirrors, a Baroque-style chapel, and really big, cool paintings—more closely resembles your high-school locker room than anything remotely royal: it's smelly, sweaty, and filled with igno-rant tools. The more worthwhile treat is those gardens, just outside the royal palace. They're green, free, and large enough that you can finally get away from the crowds. Hmm, maybe Louis was onto something after all.

paris

eval times, a bunch of proto-stoner priests built this chapel and fit it with some stained glass that must have caused at least a few night epiphanies throughout time—just swap a Latinate cross around your neck with a huge earring. Watch as the light filters through these enormous windows and get in touch with your inner hallucination; you're going to have to if you want the €10 to feel worth it.

i From the Cité Métro stop, walk a block up Rue de Lutèce to the Palais de Justice; the entrance is on the left. Hours vary by season, but usually open daily 9:30am-6pm. €10.

LUXEMBOURG GARDENS

Rue de Médicis/Rue de Vaugirard ☎01 40 71 75 60 www.senat.fr/visite/jardin

[Cue the peppy pharmaceutical jingle:] Tired of walking and standing all day in Parisian museums? Are your feet sore and can't take another step? You may have a common condition known as Museum Foot. Luckily, there is a cure. Ask your doctor if Luxembourg Gardens® is right for you. Luxembourg Gardens is the once-royal, still-beautiful green space on the outskirts of the Latin Quarter. Stick a baguette under your arm (people do actually do this), lather on some sunscreen, and style yourself French; you'll fit right in among the young people here—many of whom are, in fact, posing for paintings. Side effects include drowsiness, a desire to run away from home and just live in Paris, and, if you happen to stray onto one of the forbidden lawns, a furious *flic* (police officer) yelling at you. As always, if you take a nap in Luxembourg Gardens® for more than 4hr., consult a doctor immediately.

i From the Odéon Métro stop, walk along Bd. St-Germain and turn right onto Rue Dupuytren. Walk around the Odéon Theatre de l'Europe. The garden will be in front of you. Hours vary widely depending on the season; generally open 7:30am-30min. before sunset. Free.

JARDIN DES TUILERIES

113 Rue de Rivoli ☎01 40 20 53 17

The Jardin des Tuileries blasts out from the famous Louvre across the 1er arrondissement. The proverbial palate-cleanser to a stuffy day spent in the museum, the famous garden is home to statues, small (and overpriced) cafes, and a view out toward the Champs-Élysées, Grand Palais, and Pl. de la Concorde. If you really need to get your heart rate back up after the enormous disappointment of the *Mona Lisa*, just head over to one of the small amusement-park rides on the garden's northern rim and spin yourself around until any piece of art will seem impressive. Free, beautiful, and essentially Parisian, this place is tailor-made for the Paris romantics among you.

i Directly off the Tuileries and Concorde Métro stops. Open daily June-Aug 7am-11pm; Sept 7am-9pm; Oct-Mar 7:30am-7:30pm; Apr-May 7am-9pm. Free.

PARC DES BUTTES CHAUMONT

1 Rue Botzaris ☎01 48 03 83 10

We get it: sometimes you need a vacation from your vacation. Those Haussmann buldings—are they all the same? What is going on here?—have a finite charm. But fret not; Parisians have got you on this. For something that doesn't resemble anything Parisian, touristy, French, or even particularly European, head to Parc des Buttes Chaumont. It's a bunch of trees and fields, and it's large enough to feel like you could get lost in its sprawling hills and streams. With a Roman-style temple perched on a hill at the center of the park, you can even tell yourself you went on a hike. Good for you.

i Right off the Botzaris and Buttes Chaumont Métro stops. Open daily 7am-9pm. Free.

MUSÉE DE PICASSO

5 Rue de Thorigny ☎01 85 56 00 36 www.museepicassoparis.fr

You've heard of him. You've seen him around a few times, you're Facebook friends, and you generally respect him. Still, if people ask you if you know him, you usually demur and respond with "I know *of* him." You don't want to get ahead of yourself. But now he's inviting you over for a real deal hangout, and you're basically there: you know Picasso. A journey through many of his earliest and some of his most famous works, Musée Picasso is just about as good of a primer on Picasso's work as you can hope to find (unless you're one of those "art history" majors). From the Blue Period to his rather bulbous sculpture work, you'll find yourself beginning to just maybe understand what all those cubes are about, and you'll get to enjoy the work of some of his best friends. In short, you'll be in with Picasso and his pals. Matisse, where you at?

i From the St-Paul Métro stop, walk up Rue Malher and take a slight right onto Rue Pavée. Continue onto Rue Payenne, then turn left onto Rue du Parc Royal. Continue around the curve and take a slight right onto Rue de Thorigny; the museum is on the left. Open Tu-Su 9:30am-6pm. €12.50.

CATACOMBS

1 Av. du Colonel Henri Rol-Tanguy   ☎01 43 22 47 63 www.catacombes.paris.fr

Nas may or may not have ever visited the Catacombs, but he could have: the line's a bitch and then you die. At first sight, the Catacombs may seem like another one of Paris's world-famous tourist attractions. But forget about the expected awe and wonder of wandering through centuries-old tunnels under one of the world's global cities. In fact, a stop at the Catacombs is a harrowing reminder of your own mortality. You wait and wait and wait until you're unsure why you're even there in the first place, and then, after maybe three full hours in line, you descend underground and look at a bunch of corpses. (Unless you pay premium and make a reservation to skip the line, but, again, Nas: "That's why we get high, cuz you never know when you're gonna go.") Don't worry, though: the tunnels and skulls are pretty sick.

i From the Mouton-Duvernet Métro stop, walk southeast on Rue Mouton-Duvernet; it will be on your right. Open Tu-Su 10am-8pm. €10.

MUSÉE DE L'ORANGERIE

Jardin des Tuileries   ☎01 44 77 80 07 www.musee-orangerie.fr

Maybe somewhat surprisingly, we found nothing about oranges in the Musée de l'Orangerie. Apparently, *les orangeries* have more to do with greenhouses and Impressionist art. Everyone we asked at the museum could not tell us if Monet liked oranges, and our attempts to paint in the small citrus fruits onto his *Water Lilies* canvases ended with a lot of pulpy nonsense. But if you can look beyond the abject absence of Vitamin C at this museum, located right on the edge of the Jardin des Tuileries, then you'll be able to enjoy Monet's famous *Water Lilies* (he did virtual reality first) and a host of other famous modern artists, including Matisse, Cézanne, Picasso, and the rest of the Paris art museum crew. Not quite as large or famous as some of its nearby art-museum buddies, this probably won't be your first stop on either an artistic or botanic tour of the city, especially given the somewhat weighty price. But art will always be good for your mind, if not your daily vitamin intake.

i From the Concorde Métro stop, walk straight through the Jardin des Tuileries toward the Seine. Open M 9am-6pm, W-Su 9am-6pm. €9, ages 18-25 €6.50.

FOOD

Paris can get expensive, and a lot of that expense comes from eating out here. Of course, the food here is incredible—they don't call it the City of Bites for nothing (OK, only we call it that)—but to save money once in a while, fill up with a meal of bread, bread, and more bread at any corner *boulangerie*. You can get a filling baguette for only a euro or two—plenty of dough for not a lot of dough.

boulangeries

Back home, the only bona fide baker you're likely to encounter is at the movie theater when you go see the newest *Hunger Games* movie. (#TeamPeeta.) But this is France, and in France, bread baking is a whole lot more than grist for young-adult dystopian fiction. It's the stuff of floury legal codes, national pride, and delicious breakfast. On just about every block in Paris, you'll come across one of those modern temples to the carb-heavy diet: a *boulangerie*. *Boulangerie*'s literal translation is bakery, but its loose translation is That Amazing Place Where You Go to Buy Buttery Goodness On The Cheap Cheap. At about a euro or so for baguettes, croissants, and a host of pastries, these places could suck and they'd be worth the cash. But Paris went ahead and threw us young backpackers a breadstick: at most *boulangeries*, this shit will be amazing.

Let's knead this dough a little more, though. Bakers—bakers who went to school for this, mind you; real educated bakers with baking licenses and all that—arrive at *boulangeries* at around 3am every morning to begin their work. And they're not just throwing anything together: to make a baguette or croissant or *pain au chocolat*, these educated bakers have to follow the law. That's right: the French government has strict legal codes about baking. If you want to sell baguettes, you'd better only use flour, yeast, water, and salt, or you can expect the French bread narcs to come crashing through the windows. So next time you fork over a whole €0.90 for a baguette, keep in mind that, well, the French take this stuff seriously.

LE PETIT VENDÔME $$
8 Rue des Capucines   ☎01 42 61 05 88

A far cry from the snooty fashion stores that define these few blocks of Paris, Le Petit Vendôme whips up affordable, tasty sandwiches that will feel both decidedly French and surprisingly familiar. Pull up a seat at the bar as the cast of characters—the knowledgeable waitress, the eccentric, absent-minded waiter, and the somewhat bumbling butcher—joke and mingle with the small crowd that will gather here for lunch. You can either build the sandwich yourself (to a somewhat deflated refrain of "just ham?" from the waiter) or order one of this place's specials (specifically, Le Spécial) at a bit more of a premium. Either which way, expect to drop between €4 and €7 on a hearty, protein-rich lunch. Or settle down in the cafe outside to enjoy a full French meal for a bit more than €15.

i From Pl. Vendôme, walk up Rue de la Paix (away from the river). Take a left onto Rue des Capucines.It will be on your right. Open M 8:30am-5pm, Tu-F 8:30am-2am, Sa 10:30am-2am.

LE POTAGER DU PÈRE THIERRY $$
16 Rue des Trois Frères   ☎01 53 28 26 20

OK, let's play a word-association game. French cuisine—go! *Escargots*, wine, croissants, baguettes. C'mon, work a little harder. Hint: they quack. You see them at the park. Duck! Lots and lots of succulent, savory, and saucy duck. Don't quack out: at Le Potager du Père Thierry, a small bistro that's cramped and crowded in just that French way, this duck is delicious and it's cheap. Tucked into the cobblestonedstreets the way you'll be tucked elbow to elbow with that sweaty French man next to you, Father Thierry's here hosts the rare mix of your favorite Montmartre tourist crowd and the ever-unimpressed Parisian local. The common denominator? Authentic French food, from foie gras (quack) to *confit*

france

de canard (quack) to, yes, pork, beef, fish, and lamb dishes that only run for about €12 a pop. The warm white-stone walls and English-friendly staff (and menu) might have you sticking around, though; a worthwhile endeavor when the *crème brûlée* and foie gras (this is also a dessert dish, apparently) are so reasonably priced, so delicious, and so absolutely French.

i From Métro stop Abbesses, head up Rue la Vieuville. Then take a left on Rue des Trois Frères—it will be on your left. Open daily 8pm-midnight.

HAPPY NOUILLES $

95 Rue Beaubourg   ☎01 44 59 31 22 www.happynouilles.com

The key to happiness, as it turns out, is actually quite simple. Forget meditating for hours every day; it's all about the noodles—the handmade "happy noodles" served in vibrant, steamy broth in the Le Marais district in Paris, to be precise. Human bliss is pretty cheap, too: €6-7 will get you a bowl (or plate) full of noodles and whatever kind of meat garnish you think will best help you achieve Nirvana. The journey to happiness is also less arduous than most people think: just walk about a mile (from Île de la Cité) along one of the main arteries in Le Marais or noodle your way through one of the neighborhood's charming side streets.

i From Métro stop Arts et Métiers, walk down Rue Beaubourg. It will be on your right. Open M 11:30am-10pm, Tu 11:30am-2:30pm, W-Su 11:30am-10pm.

URFA DÜRÜM $

58 Rue du Faubourg St-Denis   ☎01 48 24 12 84

Behold as fast-talking, no-nonsense men pile dough into the oven and throw meat sticks over a coal fire (they bake the bread and cook the meat as you order it) at Urfa Dürüm, home to maybe the best meal you'll have for under €10 in Paris. These Kurdish wraps, featuring the now-expected mix of lettuce, tomatoes, onions, and meat, land in your mouth with a flavor and spice that you'd hope for at a top-dollar restaurant. But the fraternity of fire-cookers and bread-raisers (you'll want to earn their begrudging respect, or maybe even a wry smile) don't take undue monetary advantage of their fresh, authentic offerings (or their Anthony Bourdain endorsement). The wraps cost €6-8, and you can enjoy them in the cool, almost comfortable squat chairs on the sidewalk outside. Its ethnic, affordable vitality means that you won't find this place in the heart of Le Marais, but it's well worth the 10min. walk north. This was the best wrap we had in Paris, and we ate a lot of wraps in Paris.

i From Château d'Eau, take a right. Then take a right onto Rue de Faubourg. The best wrap in Paris will be on your left. Open M-Sa 11:30am-10pm.

DONG HUONG $$

14 Rue Louis Bonnet   ☎01 43 57 42 81

It's a sad fact of life in Paris that not much that you eat will crunch. Sure, food may melt, sponge, linger, or just delight in your mouth, but rarely will you find food that will yield that satisfying cacophony of flavor that you know so well from back home. But Dong Huong, a Vietnamese restaurant in the heart of the Belleville neighborhood, has got you covered. For not much more than €10, the pho, vermicelli, and—maybe most importantly—the crisp, crunchy spring rolls will provide a fresh and refreshing break from the bready and pricey haunts you have been patronizing so far in the City of Lights. Make sure to get there on the early side, though: you'll be cheek to cheek with locals from across the city who are also hoping to trade *saucisson* for spring rolls.

i From the Belleville Métro stop, walk down Rue Louis Bonnet. Dong Huong will be on your right after a block. Open M noon-10:30pm, W-Su noon-10:30pm.

paris

LITTLE BRIEZH $$

11 Rue Grégoire de Tours   ☎01 43 54 60 74

Winding through the narrow, cobblestone streets near Pl. St-Michel can feel a lot like being a member of the Rebel Fleet at the end of *Star Wars*. The drinks will be overpriced, the food kitschy and underwhelming (and overpriced), and the TIE fighters—er, fanny packs—will be everywhere. In the words of Admiral Ackbar: it's a trap. But just like Luke Skywalker, you can find a way through this life-threatening situation and emerge victorious with an authentic, relatively cheap French meal in a pleasant, not-totally-garish ambience. At Little Briezh, the little brother to a larger cafe across the river, you'll find a host of crepe options that make for either a satisfying supper or a delicious dessert. For about €10, enjoy layers of goat cheese, ham, sausage, sardines, or just about anything else between the flakey, salty pancakes that will make you question if that floppy dough you bought on the street yesterday was anything more than some strips of cardboard. Still, tourist areas are tourist areas, and most of your fellow diners here will be asking the same questions in English you will, but the friendly, low-key staff and indisputably French food make it a worthwhile, affordable stop after a visit to some of Paris's high-traffic sites along the Seine.

i *From Mabillon Métro stop, take a right down Bd. St-Germain. Then stroll for 2 blocks and take a left on Rue Grégoire de Tours. Little Briezh will be on your right. Closed Sundays and Mondays. Open Tu-Th noon-2:30pm and 7-10:30pm, F noon-2:30pm and 7-11pm, Sa noon-3pm and 7-11pm.*

KADOYA $

28 Rue Ste-Anne   ☎01 49 26 09 82 http://kadoya.fr

Any kind of visit to the 1er arrondissement would be incomplete without a hearty bowlful of Japanese noodle soup—and you have plenty of options to choose from. For a ramen shop that won't have you have twiddling your thumbs for almost an hour but will have you squeezed in elbow to elbow with a noodle-loving neighbor, hit up Kadoya. For about €10, you'll enjoy a hearty, fatty bowl of broth and ramen noodles plus a savory row of gyoza dumplings. This spot may not be at the top of the surprisingly intense ramen scene in Paris (even a brief foray into Yelp reviews reveals vitriol and controversy and conflict—best ramen ever! Worst ramen ever!), but it gets the job done for about as little money as possible. So slurp that noodly goodness up and prepare to want to return soon.

i *From Pyramides Métro stop, take a left onto Av. de l'Opéra. After a block, take a right onto Rue Thérèse. You'll see Kadoya in front of you. Open M-F 11:30am-11pm, Sa 11:30am-11:30pm, Su 11:30am-11pm.*

SANUKIYA $$

9 Rue d'Argenteuil   ☎01 42 60 52 61

A Michelin-reviewed restaurant in Paris? Forget force-fed birds and hundreds of euros spent over hours in a dimly lit locale—but remember your chopsticks and about €15. The line for a seat in this crowded, chaotic udon noodle shop (most of the seats are along a series of bars rather than at tables, so it might not be the best place for a *tête-à-tête*) is more than worth the wait, to put it simply. Delightful broth floods textured, infinitely slurpable noodles that you can pair with a variety of toppings—tempura, pork belly, or just some hearty veggies. Your taste buds will sing, and your wallet will, too. The Michelin snobs may not have given this place any stars (what does a giant man made out of tires know about ramen, anyway?), but we'll give it a whole galaxy to make up for it. Who knew that you'd have some of the best Japanese food of your life in France? Funny how the world works.

i *From Pyramides Métro, take a left onto Av. de l'Opéra. After a block, take a right onto Rue des Pyramides and then a left onto Rue d'Argenteuil. Open daily 11:30am-10pm.*

france

KB CAFÉ $

53 Av. Trudaine   ☎01 56 92 12 41 www.facebook.com/CafeShopSouthPigalle

We get it. Sometimes you just want some filtered coffee, no more of those alternately bitter and massively over-sweetened espresso shots you've been gulping down in the rest of France. And sometimes you want a bespectacled, over-educated barista to deliver you your normal coffee (no, Americanos are not the same) in a coffeeshop that puts a modern, hip, dare we say American twist on the Parisian cafe. A little bit on the pricier side (knowing Proust by heart comes at a price, right?), KB Café looks out on a sloped Montmartre square—carousel, cafe awnings, and all—as it begins to remind you of the coffeeshops you loved to frequent at home (you know, those places where you pretended to do homework). English-speaking, hipster-type employees and coffee that they put *through a filter* (!!!) are not the only thrills that KB Café has to offer: solid sandwiches and pastries (no croissants or *pain au chocolat*, oddly) will fill you up for the first part of your day. Enjoy all of this sitting *en plein air*, albeit not in a wicker chair—the chairs, ever-hip, resemble those new deck chairs your brother-in-law just got for his Brooklyn patio.

i From Métro stop Pigalle, walk east down Bd. de Clichy. Then take a right on Rue des Martyrs—KB Café will be down a block, on your right. Open M-F 7:30am-6:30pm, Sa-Su 9am-6:30pm.

L'ILOT $$

4 Rue de la Corderie   ☎06 95 12 86 61 www.lilot-restaurant.com

Shuck, crack, and slurp your way to an authentic Parisian meal at L'Ilot, a small seafood restaurant in Le Marais. Sample oysters, prawns, crabs, and more as you squeeze your way into one of the deck-style chairs (you may just need one of the picks to dig yourself out at the end of the meal) on the crowded terrace outside. Plumbing the depths of the sea for the finest *fruits de mer* is a task, though, so don't expect it to come cheap. But don't feel like you have to have a full meal, either: the oysters are fewer than €2 apiece, making this a good spot for some early or late-night snacks. Again, you came to Paris: take a break from the meat and cheese at the grocery store every once in a while, OK?

i From Métro stop République, begin to walk down Rue du Temple. Quickly take a left on Rue Béranger. Walk a block, then take a right into Rue Charles-François Dupuis. Take a left onto Rue de la Corderie; it will be on your left. Open Tu-F 6:30-11:30pm, Sa 12:30-2:30pm and 6:30-11:30pm.

CHEZ ALAIN MIAM MIAM $

Marché des Enfants Rouges   www.facebook.com/ChezAlainMiamMiam

Sandwiched in between an assortment of eateries and *traiteurs* in the Marché des Enfants Rouges, Chez Alain Miam Miam makes for a hearty lunch stop with a dash or two of charisma. Alain, a grizzled man of maybe 50, works the food stand alone, tossing spices in neat flips onto the towering sandwiches before you and crooning *"Miam, miam"* ("Yum, yum"), with a hearty slice of self-deprecating charm. After mocking you for not knowing the difference between Cantal and Comté cheese—kids these days, what would your grandmother think?—he'll serve up one of the largest and most loaded sandwiches (the vegetarian options are wrapped in a freshly made crepe) that you'll likely find in Paris. The €8 for the sandwich—and €1.50 for a soda out of the stickered fridge—are a bit more than what you might find at your local *boulangerie*, but the loaded toppings and irresistible fun of this sandwich shop make it more than worth the slight premium.

i From Métro stop République, walk down Rue du Temple for a couple of blocks. Take a left onto Rue de Bretagne and continue for a couple of blocks. Wander into Marché des Enfants Rouges and you'll find it. Open W-F 9am-3:30pm, Sa 9am-5:30pm, Su 9am-3pm.

paris

L'AS DU FALAFEL $

34 Rue des Rosiers   ☎01 48 87 63 60

If imitation is the sincerest form of flattery, then L'As du Falafel has got to be pretty damn flattered. Not a block down Rue des Rosiers, just beyond the reach of the this falafel shop's stretching line, is a word-for-word copycat, color scheme and all. The mockingfalafelplace, called Thick Tchak by L'As du Falafel (do I hear a potential Harper Lee novel title?), probably has some self-esteem issues, but the less-than-sly attempts at culinary plagiarism are somewhat justified: L'As Du Falafel is awesome. As you wait in the almost too-long line, someone will take your order and give you ticket, your golden ticket to a wicked pita full of wicked falafel. Whether you take it away and wander Le Marais's vibrant streets or squeeze into a seat inside, this joint is well worth a stop on any trip to Paris, on any budget. It has its own Wikipedia page, for crying out loud.

i *From Métro stop St-Paul, take a left onto Rue de Rivoli. Then take a right on Rue des Ecouffes. It will be right in front of you from there—look for the place with the huge line. Open M-Th 11am-midnight, F 11am-6pm, Su 11am-midnight.*

CAFÉ DU MARCHÉ $$

38 Rue Cler   ☎01 47 05 51 27 www.cafe-du-marche.fr

They could very well call Café du Marché "Dime a Dozen" or "Baker's Dozen" or "Dime a Baker" or "Dozen's Dozen" or, well, you get the idea. What we mean is that everything here is €12, except for, well, the things that aren't, but that's only a couple of fancier items, like the steak, which are €16 (still, multiples of four! Maybe they could call this place the "House of Fours" or...). For this extraordinarily reasonable price, you'll enjoy a full selection of classic French cafe offerings, from *confit de canard* to tartare, all paired with some french fries or sauteed potatoes. Not far from Les Invalides or the Eiffel Tower, this place makes for a great lunch or dinner stop after sightseeing in Paris's loaded tourist district.

i *From Métro stop École Militaire, walk up Av. de la Motte-Picquet. Take a left onto Rue Cler, and it will be on your left. Open M 7am-11pm, Tu 6am-11pm, W-Th 7am-11pm, F 6am-11pm, Sa 8am-11pm, Su 6am-4pm.*

HUÎTRERIE RÉGIS $$

3 Rue de Montfaucon   ☎01 44 41 10 07 www.huitrerieregis.com

A light, refreshing change from the carb-heavy dining you'll find yourself eating in most of Paris (especially if you hit up a *boulangerie* for breakfast every morning), Huîtrerie Régis serves up oysters by the dozen at a not-inexpensive, not-unreasonable price. For €30, enjoy a dozen oysters, a glass of white wine, and a coffee at the end of the meal to have you feeling simultaneously Parisian and maybe even a little seaworthy. The whitewashed stone walls, young staff, and lingering taste of wine will make for a pleasant backdrop to your nautical ruminations and pedantic attempts at sophistication (Hemingway loved Parisian oyster bars, you know). But set sail for this *huîtrerie* before its 7pm opening time; its comparatively cheap prices and young vibe draw a crowd that quickly fills up its relatively small dining area. You told yourself you'd eat something nice and Parisian, right?

i *From Mabillon Métro stop, walk toward Bd. St-Germain. Right before you hit the main thoroughfare, take a right onto Rue de Montfaucon. It will be on your left. Open M-F noon-2:30pm and 6:30-10:30pm, Sa noon-10:45pm, Su noon-10pm.*

CHEZ LE LIBANAIS $

35 Rue St-André des Arts   ☎01 40 46 07 39 www.facebook.com/chezlelibanais

For better or for worse, cheap dining in Paris can often feel like a tour through French colonial projects in the 19th and 20th centuries, and Chez le Libanais, a Lebanese falafel joint in the center of the Latin Quarter, is certainly no excep-

france

tion. With blaring Lebanese music and sepia photos of Beirut streets along the wall, Chez le Libanais does its best to make you feel, well, at home with the Lebanese. And a welcoming home it appears to be: the no-nonsense men behind the counter will serve you warm, unusually flavorful (we've had so many at this point) shawarma wraps for €5-7. Vegetarian options also abound. While its location in the middle of one of the most garishly touristy parts of Paris may seem an initial deterrent, the Parisian and hungry line up here for cheap, authentic tastes of the Mediterranean. Good luck finding seats, though—the scant offerings fill up fast, leaving you heading down to the river, shawarma in hand, for a tasty, protein-rich, and cheap meal.

i From Odéon Métro stop, walk up Rue de l'Éperon. Then take a left onto Rue St-André des Arts. Chez le Libanais will be on your right. Open M-Th 11am-11pm, F-Su 11am-midnight.

LA TOUR DE BELLEVILLE $
15 Rue de la Présentation ☎01 48 05 92 80

Pop quiz, hot shot: what's less than €7 and homemade? In this city, not much—but there is La Tour de Belleville's bowl of hand-strewn noodles. Right in one of Paris's Chinatown neighborhoods, this joint serves up tasty, albeit simple, noodle dishes both in and out of broth. Pair it with a 64cL Chinese beer for €3, sit in the ungarnished, linoleum eating area, and watch as the staff wrings your noodles from pasty globs of dough. For something warm, tasty, filling, and cheap—above all, cheap!—that is not another kebab or baguette, look no further than this humble hole-in-the-wall eatery.

i From Métro stop Belleville, walk down Fauburg du Temple. Take a left on Rue de la Présentation—La Tour de Belleville will be on your left. They don't post formal hours because it's that kind of place, but it's open for dinner.

PANINO ROSSI $
12 Rue Notre Dame des Champs ☎01 45 48 19 90
www.facebook.com/Panino-Rossi-1423062267905193

Like Willy Loman, cheap lunches, especially cheap sandwiches, are just about a dime a dozen in Paris. Walk into any *boulangerie* and you'll get some good bread with some occasionally questionable ham shoved inside. Delicious decorations for that bread, and some warm delicious decorations at that, are less common, so a trip to Panino Rossi, an Italian sandwich shop on the edge of Paris's Latin Quarter, will have all the more appeal. A host of sandwich options run about €6, ranging from more Italian fillings like meatballs to familiar American ones like chicken tenders. The coffee here is also remarkably inexpensive at €1.50 for a shot of espresso (it's Paris, OK?), making Coffee-o just as appropriate a title. Young professionals and students alike cede some ground to Italian cuisine (French chefs are far more adept, we understand) here for lunch on a daily basis, so prepare to wait in a bit of a line or take your sandwich to go if you show up right around noon.

i From Métro stop St-Placide, walk down Rue Notre Dame des Champs. It will be on your right. Open M-Sa 9am-6pm.

LE SQUARE $$
31 Rue St-Dominique ☎01 45 51 09 03 www.restaurant-lesquare.com

Fortunately, a meal at Le Square will not make you a square. It will make you a savvy traveler with good taste. For under €20, you can load up on French classics at this slightly secluded cafe that looks out on a quiet, peaceful neighborhood square. Fries cut the thin way—man, are we glad we are not in Belgium any more—share the plate with tartare, duck, and other French delicacies. In this part of Paris, it can be hard to feel like you are even beginning to escape all things touristy. But here, the friendly, English-speaking staff will provide accessibility without the kitsch of an Anglophile invasion; everyone else here will be a

paris

very no-nonsense, serious Parisian who probably have four times as many taste buds as you do, so if they're eating here, you probably should try it.

i From Métro stop Solférino, head down Rue St-Dominique toward Les Invalides. It will be on your left. Open M-Sa 8am-11pm.

LE REFUGE DES FONDUES $$

17 Rue des Trois Frères   ☎01 42 55 22 65 www.facebook.com/lerefugedesfondus

Sometimes, the most important decisions you can make in life are the simplest ones. Paper or plastic? Credit or debit? At Le Refuge des Fondues, the quagmires and consequences of binary decision-making are cast into starker relief than even the perils of daily life. When you walk into this cave-like fondue bistro carrying hints of kitsch, a looming Frenchman will ask you two of the most fundamental, searing questions you may ever encounter: meat or cheese? Red or white? As you plumb your soul looking for an answer for this Obi-Wan Kenobi meets middle-school gym teacher of a waiter, soak in the colorful interior, where handwritten names and places sprawl all over the walls. In the end, the choice ends up a bit of a false one: the cheese is the medium in its eponymous fondue and bread is the dipping agent, while the meat fondue is for dipping meat in a boiling pot of oil. Maybe this is America talking, but where is our option for dipping meat in cheese? The "red or white" choice, meanwhile, refers to wine, and regardless of which one you choose, it's coming in a baby bottle. All of this runs for €22—not bad, considering you just had enough cheese to make the Cheetos cheetah kill himself.

i From Métro stop Abbesses, head up Rue la Vieuville. Then take a left onto Rue des Trois Frères—it will be on your right. Open daily 7pm-2am.

LE MAISON DU DIM SUM $$

4 Rue des Fossés St-Jacques   ☎01 55 42 03 44 www.lamaisondudimsum.com

This isn't just some dumb dim sum spot. It's the house of dim sum, and everyone knows you have to earn the ability to name your house—our attempts to call the Let's Go office "The House of Pain" were resolutely denied by God and the city zoning board. Enough semantics, though. The dumplings here? They're great. The other noshing options? They're also great. Ordering either straight from the menu or choosing the all-you-can-eat dim sum sampling option both make for a relatively affordable, highly delicious pivot from the bistros and brasseries around the city. For €17, you get a literally endless supply of dim sum options that the English-speaking staff will happily explain. A more surgical selection of individual plates will ring you up a cheaper bill at in this spot in the center of Paris's Latin Quarter. This is a win-win decision, though, and both will have you happy that most cultures do not eat in the sometimes-small, often-frustrating serving sizes you find in France (how many appetizers do they think we're going to order?).

i From Luxembourg Gardens, walk up Rue Soufflot, on the east side of the garden. Then hang a right onto Rue St-Jacques. Finally, take a left onto Rue des Fossés St-Jacques. Open M-Sa noon-2:15pm and 7-10:30pm.

NIGHTLIFE

Around Rue du Four and Rue de Canettes in the Latin Quarter, a cadre of bouncers stand sentinel for a bevy of nightlife options, including Chez Georges, a jazz bar. But if you're in a small group, don't speak the language, don't have friends who know the place, and didn't occasionally model when you were a teenager, then don't expect to have a lot of luck broaching these bastions of Parisian prestige and high society. Nightlife in Paris is as much about social status as it is about sexual success, so calibrate your expectations and maybe throw on a scarf or something to blend in. Even if you don't get into one of the more popular clubs, though, this block or so is

france

a fun area to check out and enjoy a beer after around 2am when the well-heeled and popular Parisian pricks start making their rounds. It's a good, potentially voyeuristic cap to a night spent at any of the neighborhood's excellent bars.

LE CROCODILE

6 Rue Royer-Collard   ☎01 71 93 49 68 www.facebook.com/LeCrocodileBar

Cocktail bar? More like croc-tail bar. Just short of needing a three-ring binder to hold its menu, Le Crocodile, lurking in the depths of the swamps of Paris's Latin Quarter, boasts a dizzying selection of mixed drinks with names ranging from the Misanthrope to the Pink Pussy. You won't even have to worry about this reptile ripping through your wallet: happy hour (really, 4hr. that all happen to be quite happy—with enough vodka) prices bring these freshwater brews down to a coldblooded €7. The seat safari is easier said than done when dozens of teeth-baring young professionals and students slink into this joint, so you may want to head over on the earlier side to beat the rush. In the end, though, the only bite at Le Crocodile you'll have to worry about comes from the drinks themselves.

i From the Luxembourg Métro, walk along Bd. St-Michel and turn right onto Rue Royer-Collard. Take a slight left to stay on Rue Royer-Collard, and the bar will be on your left. Open M-Sa 6pm-2am. Cocktails €6-9.

AUX FOLIES

8 Rue de Belleville   ☎06 28 55 89 40 www.aux-folies-belleville.fr

If you came all the way to Paris, you're probably looking for that wicker chaired, *en plein air* cafe to enjoy a few drinks, watch the world go by, and sniff in all of that French secondhand smoke. While you'll find one of these cafes on just about every street corner, locating one filled with the hip rather than the pretenders can be harder to find. Look no further than Aux Folies, a neon-lit, crowded bar not a block away from the Belleville Métro stop. Young locals crowd in on weekends (or just about any night, really), so prepare to dip, dodge, duck, and dive your way to a seat outside—or settle for the red-lit interior. Too mellow to make the center of your night and too loud to properly decompress or brood, Aux Folies is where you'd take a group of friends for some laughs and relaxation. All you need to do is actually make some friends.

i From the Belleville Métro, take a short walk down Rue de Belleville and it will be on your right. Open daily 5:30am-2am. Drinks €3-5.

LA DIVETTE DU MONTMARTRE

136 Rue Marcadet   ☎01 46 06 19 64

The TV show *Cheers* taught us that the best and most memorable part of a bar is the person (or people) who operate it. Towering over the bar with his six-foot-five frame, the bartender at La Divette du Montmartre is part opera baritone, part weathered sea captain whom you would probably trust with your life. With an amused, friendly eye, he'll serve you up shots of absinthe or pints of beer between renditions of something Italian and melodious. Only after you tear yourself away from his comforting presence will you find a lively soccer bar filled with young people (mostly men) excitedly debating the match or taking to one of the foosball tables in the all-green interior. Premonitions of Parisian priggishness quickly dissolve, and you'll quickly find yourself doing your best at a game of foosball with three Frenchmen at this bar not too from Sacré Coeur itself.

i From the Jules Joffrin Métro, walk down Rue Ordener and turn left onto Rue Duhesme. Turn right onto Rue Marcadet, and the bar will be immediately on your right. Open M-Sa 5pm-1am. Beer €2-4.

paris

LA FOURMI

74 Rue des Martyrs   ☎01 42 64 70 35 www.facebook.com/La-Fourmi-161609657184625

Maybe you're not up for Montmartre's red-light district tonight. Any other night, and you'd be committing all sorts of debauchery. But tonight? Tonight you just want to sit back, enjoy a few pints, maybe dink around at the foosball table, and push all memories of glittery strip poles out of your mind, at least for a few hours. Tall, well-lit ceilings, smooth hardwood floors, and reasonably priced beers make La Fourmi feel more like the set of a family-friendly sitcom (called *The Boys* or *The Guys* or something) than a bar situated in the middle of a red-light district. Filled with seemingly wholesome youth (well, as wholesome as you can find in Paris), this is a lively, conversation place to start the night with some pints, laughs, and foosball.

i From the Pigalle Métro, follow Bd. de Clichy and turn onto Rue des Martyrs; the bar is on your right. Open M-Th 8am-2am, F-Sa 8am-4am, Su 9am-2am. Burgers, salads, and entrees €10-14. Beer and wine €3-12.

LE PANTALON

7 Rue Royer-Collard   ☎01 40 51 85 85

Thought experiment: you have a bar. The bar is on a street in Paris, France. As you wade farther inside the place, popular with the students of the city's universities, you, again, find yourself on a city street. The place is set amid a "Tabac" sign, an eerie orange street light, and a working crosswalk machine (hi, little green man!). What do you call this magical bar? If you're the owner of Le Pantalon, the answer is "pants." Among the narrow streets of the Latin Quarter, Le Pantalon is a lively, conversational bar that will hopefully not having you thinking about or doing too much with your pants. At €5 for a pint of beer and €7 for cocktails, you'll have no trouble affording a night spent in this place that sometimes feels more like a French New Wave film set than the warm, friendly student bar that it is. Those Parisians, man—they mess with you.

i From the Luxembourg Métro, walk along Bd. St-Michel and turn right onto Rue Royer-Collard. Take a slight left to stay on Rue Royer-Collard, and the bar is on the right. Open M-Sa 3pm-2am, Su 3pm-midnight.

LIZARD LOUNGE

18 Rue du Bourg Tibourg   ☎01 42 72 81 34 www.cheapblonde.com/lizardlounge.html

At Lizard Lounge, a packed bar in Le Marais, you'll face the classic Friday night dilemma: do you want to be on top or on bottom? Both floors of the Lizard Lounge have something to offer. On weekends, this reptilian respite opens up its basement for live music and a rowdier, more drunken way to spend the evening—just lie back and let it happen to you. The first floor isn't too bad either, if a bit more work: the more controlled, more methodical, classier vibe here makes it a good place to enjoy a few of the reasonably priced happy hour drinks (€8 for a shot and a pint of beer).

i From the Hôtel de Ville Métro, head east on Rue de Rivoli and turn left onto Rue du Bourg Tibourg; the bar will be on your right. Open daily noon-2am. Drinks €5-8.

LATERASSE

145 Bd. St-Michel   ☎01 43 29 40 81 https://laterrassedu5.com

There is little in this world to match the pleasure of a cheap, cold beer, even in Paris. Laterasse, a crowded, neat cafe overlooking Luxembourg Gardens, serves up pints for €3.50, making it the home of such aesthetic and sensory beauty that you'll start to question which institutions really deserve the moniker "high art" in the city. Smooth, cool droplets of draft roll down your glass as students and people who look like they could be intellectual—he's wearing a fedora, he must be legit—lean back in wicker chairs and appear to debate something serious. Between the cheap beer and the pleasant, almost thoughtful ambience here, Laterasse is a worthwhile stop on a more low-key, wandering type of night—don't expect to start dancing. Even the guy wearing the fedora would be embarrassed.

i Open M-Sa 8am-2am.

FAUST

Pont Alexandre III   ☎01 44 18 60 60 www.faustparis.fr

Sell your soul to the devil, go over your Goethe notes, and head down to Faust, a restaurant meets bar meets club on the bank of the Seine in the 1er arrondissement. Whether you spend the night out on the packed terrace or wander into the depths of the club (€11), it's easy to raise at least a little hell over the course of a night here. With a lineup of DJs playing on Friday and Saturday nights, it can be a bit tricky to just walk into the club proper. Don't worry, though: the open-air terrace is free, and you can make a reservation for tickets online.

i From the Invalides Métro, walk toward the river along Rue Robert Esnault-Pelterie and turn left onto Quai d'Orsay. Take a right onto Pont Alexandre III; it will be on your left. Terrace open Th-Sa midnight-2am; club open F-Sa midnight-5am.

VIEUX LÉON

18 Rue de la Grande Truanderie   ☎01 42 21 17 38
       www.facebook.com/LE-VIEUX-LÉON-29873234388

At Vieux Léon, roar your way through a few drinks on a crowded, lively terrace space. With its reasonably priced drinks and young crowd, this spot makes for a good bookend to a night out in the neighborhood's livelier spots.

i From the Les Halles Métro, walk up Rue Pierre Lescot and turn right onto Rue de la Grande Truanderie; the bar is on your left. Open M-Sa 2pm-2am. Drinks €4-6.

LA CORDONNERIE

142 Rue St-Denis   ☎01 40 28 95 35

Do you like beer? Do you like cold beer? Do you like cheap beer? Well then, head on down to La Cordonnerie for the deal of a lifetime. Four euros are all you need to experience a one-of-a-kind classic: cold beer! Can you imagine? Beer, in Paris, that is cold and cheap. Look past the Comic Sans-decorated awning and head to La Cordonnerie for a fun, foamy night of drinks and dialogue with some friends in hand or friends to be. The friendly Francophone staff and crowd spilling out into the street will make it easy to spend your entire night here.

i From Métro stop Réaumur-Sébastopol, take a left on Rue Réaumur. Then take another quick left onto Rue St-Denis. It will be on your left. Open daily 8:30am-2am.

LE GUET APENS BAR

61 Rue Jean-Pierre Timbaud   www.facebook.com/leguetapensbar

In Paris, getting into a club can seem impossible. Your clothes aren't nice enough, you don't have the right gender ratio in your group (looking at you, solo clubbing dude), and you don't really speak French, so the bouncer ain't got no time for you. But if you still want to listen to house music as drunk Europeans squirm all over the dance floor, Le Guet Apens may just about do the trick. With hat-clad bartenders dressed in all black, a lights-out interior, and Kanye West blaring over large speakers, this place toes the line between club and bar as it makes space for people who don't have the money, inclination, or social cachet to actually go to a Paris club. A good stop on any decent Belleville bar crawl.

i From the Parmentier Métro, walk up Rue Edouard Lockroy and turn right onto Rue Jean-Pierre Timbaud. The venue is on your left. Open Tu-Su 5:30pm-2am. Beer and wine €2.50-3. Cocktails €5.

LE MAX BAR

6 Rue de la Petite Truanderie   ☎01 40 28 93 63 http://lemaxbar.fr

Before maxing out and humbly bumbling your way back home to say hello to your good old friend the toilet bowl, head to Le Max Bar, an affordable, surprisingly classy cocktail bar in Le Marais. Not quite the place to pound shots and

paris

holler for another one—trust us on this—you might consider taking that cutie from the hostel here for the respectable ambience.

i *From Métro stop Étienne Marcel, walk down Rue Mondétour; you should see the bar in the square in front of you after about a block. Open M-Th 4pm-2am, F-Su 2pm-2am. Cocktails €8.*

L'INTERNATIONALE

5/7 Rue Moret ☎01 42 02 02 05 www.l.international.fr

Live music? Moderately provocative imagery on the television screens? Rollicking bartenders (septum ring included) crushing that mint in a more than slightly suggestive way? L'Internationale has it all, making it a one-stop shop for a sexually charged, highly inebriated night of swaying to Whoever This Band Is. Maybe as to be expected, this place seems to mostly get going on the weekend, when music and vagina-lovers (we're sorry—they put them on the TV screen) alike go international. But for this trip, you can leave your passport at home; all you'll need is a very open mind and multiples of €8 for the cocktails.

i *From the Parmentier Métro, turn onto Av. de la République and take a slight left onto Rue Oberkampf. Turn left onto Rue Moret; the bar will be on your left. Open M-Sa 6pm-2am.*

ESSENTIALS
Practicalities

- **TOURIST OFFICES: Bureau Central d'Accueil** provides maps and tour information and books accommodations. (25 Rue des Pyramides. ☎01 49 52 42 63 www.parisinfo.com. Métro: Pyramides. Open daily May-Oct 9am-7pm; Nov-Apr 10am-7pm.) Also located at Gare de Lyon (☎01 43 33 24. Open M-Sa 8am-6pm), Gare du Nord (☎01 45 26 94 82. Open daily 8am-6pm), Gare de l'Est (Open M-Sa 8am-7pm), and Anvers facing 72 Bd. Rochechouart (Open daily 10am-6pm). There are **tourist kiosks** at the following Métro stations: Champs-Élysées-Clemenceau; Cité (in front of Notre Dame); Hôtel de Ville (inside the Hôtel de Ville); Anvers; and Bastille. All offices and kiosks have tourist maps, Métro, bus, and commuter rail maps, and walking guides to Paris produced by the Paris Convention and Visitors Bureau. Most hotels and hostels also offer these resources for free.

- **TOURS: Bateaux-Mouches** offers boat tours along the Seine. (Port de la Conférence, Pont de l'Alma. ☎01 42 25 96 10 www.bateaux-mouches.fr. Métro: Alma-Marceau or Franklin Roosevelt. Tours in English €12.50, under 12 €5.50, under 4 free. Cruise about 70min. Launches Apr-Sept M-F every 20-30min. 10:15am-10:30pm; Oct-Mar M-F every 11am-9pm, Sa-Su 10:15am-9pm every 45-60min.)

- **GLBT RESOURCES: Paris Gay Village** recommends GLBT accommodations, listings, and networking. There's also a map of GLBT-friendly establishments throughout Paris. A SKOPIK map can be found at most tourist offices. (61-63 Rue Beaubourg. ☎01 77 15 89 42 www.parisgayvillage.com. Métro: Rambuteau. English spoken. Open M 6-8pm, Tu-Th 3:30-8pm, F 1-8pm, Sa 1-7pm.) **Centre Gay et Lesbien** provides legal assistance and networking. (63 Rue Beaubourg. ☎01 43 57 21 47 www.centrelgbtparis.org. Métro: Rambuteau. English spoken. Open M 6-8pm, Tu 3-8pm, W 12:30-8pm, Th 3-8pm, F-Sa 12:30-8pm, Su 4-7pm.)

- **STUDENT RESOURCES: Centre d'Information et de Documentation pour la Jeunesse** provides information on temporary work, job placement, tourism info, and housing for students studying in Paris. (101 Quai Branly. ☎01 44 49 12 00 www.cidj.com. Métro: Bir-Hakeim. Open Tu-F 1-6pm, Sa 1-5pm.)

- **TICKET AGENCIES: FNAC** has several locations throughout Paris; check the website for more locations beyond this one. (74 Av. des Champs-Élysées. ☎08 25 02 00 20 www.fnacspectacles.com. Métro: Franklin D. Roosevelt or Châtelet/Les Halles. Open M-Sa 10am-11:45pm, Su noon-11:45pm.)

france

- **INTERNET: American Library in Paris** has computers and internet access for members or guests with day passes. (10 rue du Général Camou. ☎01 53 59 12 60 www.americanlibrary-inparis.org. Métro: École Militaire. Open Sept-June Tu-Sa 10am-7pm, Su 1-7pm; Jul-Aug Tu-F 1-7pm, Sa 10am-4pm.) There is also free Wi-Fi at **Centre Pompidou** and in its **Bibliothèque Publique d'Information.** (Pl. Georges Pompidou, 8 Rue Beaubourg. Métro: Rambuteau or Hôtel de Ville. Center open M 11am-9pm, W-Su 11am-9pm. Library open M noon-10pm, W-F noon-10pm, Sa-Su 11am-10pm.) There is also always free Wi-Fi at McDonald's and Starbucks as well as shaky Wi-Fi in public parks.

- **POST OFFICES: La Poste** runs the French postal system (www.laposte.fr). There are many post offices in Paris that are generally open M-F 8am-7pm, Sa 8am-noon. The most centrally located post offices are in **Saint-Germain** (118 Bd. St-Germain. Métro: Odéon. Open M-F 8am-8pm, Sa 9am-5pm) and **Châtelet-Les Halles.** (1 Rue Pierre Lescot. Métro: Les-Halles. Open M-F 8am-6:30pm, Sa 9am-1pm.) The **Paris Louvre** post office is also easily accessible. (52 Rue du Louvre. Métro: Louvre-Rivoli.)

Emergency

- **EMERGENCY NUMBERS:** General emergencies ☎112. Ambulance (SAMU) ☎15. Fire ☎18.

- **POLICE: Préfecture de la Police.** (9 Bd. Palais. ☎01 53 71 53 71. Métro: Cité. Across the street from the Palais de Justice. Open 24hr.)

- **CRISIS LINES: SOS Help!** is an emergency hotline for English speakers. (☎01 46 21 46 46.)

- **LATE-NIGHT PHARMACIES: Pharmacie Les Champs.** (84 Av. des Champs-Élysées ☎01 45 62 02 41. Métro: Franklin Roosevelt. Open 24hr.) **Pharmacie Européenne.** (6 Pl. de Clichy. ☎01 48 74 65 18. Métro: Pl. de Clichy. Open 24hr.) **Pharmacie Première.** (24 Bd. de Sébastopol. ☎01 48 87 62 30. Métro: Châtelet. Open daily 8am-midnight.)

- **HOSPITALS/MEDICAL SERVICES: SOS Médecins** is an on-call medical service that will bring doctors to you. (☎36 24. Open 24hr.) For emergencies, though, call a proper ambulance, or go to a hospital like the **American Hospital of Paris.** (Pedestrian entrance at 63 Bd. Victor Hugo, vehicle entrance at 84 Bd. de la Saussaye. ☎01 46 41 25 25 www.american-hospital. org. From Métro station Porte Maillot, take bus #82 to the last stop. Or from Ponte de Neuilly Métro, take bus #93 to Hôpital Américain. Or from Pont de Levallois-Bécon Métro, walk down Rue Anatole France, turn right onto Rue Baudin, walk 4 blocks, continue down Rue Greffulhe and Rue de Villiers, turn right onto Bd. du Château, walk 1 block, and turn right onto Bd. Victor Hugo; the hospital is on the left.) Finally, Paris can even help you out if you need a **dentist.** (☎01 43 37 51 00. Open daily 3-11pm.)

Getting There

How you arrive in Paris will be dictated by where you are traveling from. Those flying across the Atlantic will most likely end up at Charles de Gaulle airport, one of Europe's main international hubs. If flying from within Europe on a budget airline, you'll probably fly into Orly. Though it hardly counts as arriving in Paris, flying into **Beauvais** from other European cities will often save you a lot of money, even with the €16, 75min. shuttle ride into the Porte Maillot station in Paris. RER lines, buses, and shuttles run regularly from all three airports to Paris; however, times and prices vary with each airport. With its confusingly endless number of train stations, Paris offers options for both those coming from within France and those who are traveling by train from elsewhere in Europe.

By Plane

PARIS-CHARLES DE GAULLE (CDG)

Roissy-en-France   ☎01 70 36 39 50 www.adp.fr

Most transatlantic flights land at Aéroport Paris-CDG. The two cheapest and fastest ways to get into the city from Paris-CDG are by RER and by bus. The

paris

RER train services Terminals 1, 2, and 3. The RER B (€9.50; includes Métro transport when you get off the RER) will take you to central Paris. To transfer to the Métro, get off at Gare du Nord, Châtelet-Les Halles, or St-Michel. The **Roissybus** (☎01 49 25 61 87. €10. 45-60min.; every 15-20min. during the day, every 20-30min. at night) runs between Terminals 1, 2, and 3 (6am-11pm) and Opéra (5:45am-11pm). **Les Cars Air France** (☎08 92 35 08 20) departs from Terminals 1, 2, and 3 and connects to Étoile and Porte Maillot (Line 2) or Gare de Lyon and Gare Montparnasse (Line 4).

i *23km northeast of Paris.*

ORLY (ORY)

Orly   ☎01 49 75 15 15 www.adp.fr

Aéroport d'Orly is used by charters and many continental flights. From Orly Sud Gate G or Gate I, platform 1, or Orly Ouest level G, Gate F, take the **Orly-Rail** shuttle bus to the Pont de Rungis/Aéroport d'Orly train station, where you can board the RER C for a number of destinations in Paris, including Châtelet, St-Michel, Invalides, and Gare d'Austerlitz. Another option is the RATP █**Orlybus** (☎08 36 68 77 14. €7.20. 30min., every 15-20min.), which runs between Métro and RER stop Denfert-Rochereau and Orly's south and west terminal. RATP also runs **Orlyval** (☎01 69 93 53 00. VAL ticket €8.40, VAL-RER ticket €11.30), a combination Métro, RER, and VAL rail shuttle. The VAL shuttle goes from Antony (RER B) to Orly Ouest and Sud. Buy tickets at any RATP booth in the city or from the Orlyval agencies at Orly Ouest, Orly Sud, and Antony. See www.aeroportsdeparis.fr for maps of transportation between Orly and different locations in Paris. **Les Cars Air France** (☎08 92 35 08 20) connects from Orly Sud and Ouest terminals to Gare Montparnasse, Les Invalides, and Étoile (Line 1).

i *18km south of Paris.*

By Train

SNCF (www.sncf.com) sells train tickets for travel within France and abroad and offers *la carte jeune* for travelers ages 12-27, which guarantees reduced prices of up to 60% after you pay a one-time €50 fee. Other train companies that serve France, such as **Thalys** (www.thalys.com), also offer reduced prices for those under 26. **Rail Europe** (www.raileurope.com) also sells tickets for travel within France and abroad, but prices for US residents tend to be higher than those offered by SNCF.

There are several major train stations in Paris:

GARE D'AUSTERLITZ

85 Quai d'Austerlitz   ☎08 92 35 35 35

Gare d'Austerlitz services the Loire Valley, southwest France, Spain, and Portugal. Popular destinations include Barcelona (€135-170, 7-12hr.) and Madrid (€220-300, 12-13hr.). For trains to Spain, mainly book through www.sncf.com.

i *Métro: Gare d'Austerlitz. In the 5ème and 13ème arrondissements. Open daily 5:30am-midnight.*

GARE DE L'EST

Pl. du 11 Novembre 1918   ☎01 80 50 93 00

Gare de l'Est receives trains from eastern France, southern Germany, Austria, Switzerland, and Eastern Europe. Book overnight and daytime trains to Frankfurt (€89-119; 4hr.), Munich (€125-163; 9-10½hr.), and Prague (€118-172; 12-15hr.).

i *Métro: Gare de l'Est. In the 10ème arrondissement. Open daily 5:30am-1am.*

GARE DE LYON

20 Bd. Diderot   ☎08 92 35 35 35

Gare de Lyon runs to southeast France, Switzerland, and Italy. Hop a train to Lyon (€25-92; 2hr.), Marseille (€25-120; 3-4hr.), Nice (€25-125; 5½hr.), Florence (€135-170; 9-12hr.), Milan (€35-220; 10hr.), or Rome (€100-275; 12-15hr.). Book

france

through www.sncf.com to go to Geneva (€25-130; 3-4hr.). For overnight sleepers to Italy, book with www.thello.com.

i *Métro: Gare de Lyon. In the 12ème arrondissement. Open daily 3:30am-1:30am.*

GARE DU NORD
18 Rue de Dunkerque   ☎08 92 35 35 35

Gare du Nord is the arrival point for trains from northern France, northern Germany, Belgium, Netherlands, and the UK. To ride through the famous **Chunnel** to London (€42-183; 2½hr.) and the rest of the UK, book up to 120 days in advance at www.eurostar.com. For Brussels (€29-99; 1½hr.) and Amsterdam (€35-130; 3½hr.), use www.thalys.com. Trains go as far as Cologne (€99-120; 3-4hr.).

i *Métro: Gare du Nord. In the 10ème arrondissement. Open daily 5am-1am.*

Getting Around

By Métro

In general, the Métro is easy to navigate, and trains run swiftly and frequently. Most of Paris lies within zones 1-2, so don't worry about the suburbs in zones 3-5. Pick up a colorful map at any station. Métro stations themselves are a distinctive part of the city's landscape and are marked with an "M" or with *"Métropolitain,"* but, along the Champs-Élysées, they are unmarked stairs leading underground. The earliest trains start running around 5:30am, and the last ones leave the end-of-the-line stations (the *portes de Paris*) at about 12:15am during the week and at 2:15am on Friday and Saturday. In general, be at the Métro by 1am if you want to take it home at night. Connections to other lines are indicated by *correspondance* signs, and exits are marked by blue *sortie* signs. Transfers are free if made within a station, but it's not always possible to reverse direction on the same line without exiting. Hold onto your ticket until you exit the Métro and pass the point marked **Limite de Validité des Billets;** a uniformed RATP *contrôleur* (inspector) may request to see it on any train. If you're caught without a ticket, you will have to pay a €30 fine on the spot. It's a good idea to carry one more ticket than you need, although most, but not all, stations have ticket machines that now accept both bills and coins. Tickets cost €1.70 per journey, although it's much more useful to buy a *carnet* of 10 tickets for €13.30. You can also buy unlimited Métro passes for 1 day (€6.60), and, on the weekend, young 'uns under 26 can buy a day pass for €3.65. For longer visits, you can buy a week- or month-long (€19.80/65.10) **Navigo Découverte Pass,** which costs an additional €5 and requires a passport photo to attach to the card. Month-long passes begin the first day of the month, and week-long passes begin on Monday. You can also buy a **Paris Visite** pass (meant for tourists) for unlimited travel for 1-5 days at rather meager discounts (1-day pass €10.55; 2-day €17.15; 3-day €23.40; 5-day €33.70.)

When it's getting really late, your best chance of getting the train you want is heading to the biggest stations, like Gare du Nord, Gare de l'Est, and Châtelet-Les Halles. However, these stations are often full of tourists and pickpockets, so stay alert when traveling at night or avoid it altogether. If you must travel by public transport late at night, get to know the Noctilien bus (see below).

By RER

The **RER** (Réseau Express Régional) is the RATP's suburban train system, which passes through central Paris and travels much faster than the Métro. There are five RER lines, marked A-E, with different branches designated by a number. The newest line, E, is called the EOLE (Est-Ouest Liaison Express) and links Gare Magenta with Gare St-Lazare. Within central Paris, the RER works just like the Métro and requires the same ticket for the same price (if you have to transfer from the RER to the Métro or vice versa, however, you will need another ticket). The principal stops within the city that link the RER to the Métro are Gare du Nord, Nation, Charles de Gaulle-Étoile, Gare de Lyon, Châtelet-Les Halles, St-Michel, and Denfert-Rochereau. The electric

paris

signs next to each track list all the possible stops for trains running on that track. Be sure that the little square next to your destination is lit up. Trips to the suburbs require more expensive tickets that can also be bought at the automatic booths where you purchase Métro tickets. You must know what zone you're going to in order to buy the proper ticket. In order to exit the RER station, insert your ticket just as you did to enter and pass through. Like the Métro, the RER runs 5:30am-12:30am on weekdays and until 2:30am on weekends, but never wait until 2:30am to get to the Métro or RER. Again, if you must travel by public transportation late at night, get to know the Noctilien bus.

By Bus

Although slower than the Métro, a bus ride can be a cheap sightseeing tour and a helpful introduction to the city's layout. Bus tickets (€1.70) are the same as those used for the Métro and can be purchased in Métro stations or from bus drivers. Enter the bus through the front door and punch your ticket by pushing it into the machine next to the driver's seat. Inspectors may ask to see your ticket, so hold on to it until you get off. When you want to get off, press the red button so the *arrêt demandé* (stop requested) sign lights up. Most buses run daily 7am-8:30pm, although those marked **autobus du nuit** continue until 1:30am. The **Noctilien** runs all night (daily 12:30-5:30am) and services more than 45 routes throughout the city. If you plan to use this frequently, get a map of the routes from a Métro station and study it. Hard. Look for bus stops marked with a moon sign. Check out www.noctilien.fr or inquire at a major Métro station or Gare de l'Est for more information on Noctilien buses. Complete bus route maps are posted at the bus stops, while individual lines only give out maps of their own routes. Noctilien #2 runs to all the major train stations along the periphery of the city, while #12 and #13 run between Châtelet and Gare de Montparnasse.

By Taxi

Traveling by taxi in Paris can be intimidating. Parisian taxis usually have three fares that change based on the time of day and day of the week. Rush hours and early morning hours on the weekends are the priciest, while morning to midday fares on weekdays are the cheapest. Fares are measured out by the kilometer and only switch to waiting time if a trip is over an hour. The pickup base charge is €2.40, and minimum fare is €6.40. Each additional person after three passengers costs €3, and each additional piece of luggage after the first costs €1. A typical 20min. taxi ride costs €12-20, and a 40min. ride can be as much as €50. Taxis are easily hailed from any major boulevard or avenue, but stands are often outside major Métro intersections. If the taxi's green light is on, it is available. From the airport, prices skyrocket and begin at €50. It's never a bad idea to ask for a receipt at the end of your trip in case of dispute or lost property.

By Bike

If just don't feel like walking or gambling with timetables, bike rentals may be for you. There are many **Vélib'** stations around the city where you can rent a public bike for prices ranging from €1.70 for the day, €8 for the week, and €29 for the year. Each time you take it out, the first 30min. are free, the next 30min. are €1, the next 30min. are €2, and each additional 30min. thereafter are €4. You can return the bike at any Vélib' station. If you arrive at a station and there are no open spots, go to the machine, punch in your number, and receive an additional 15min. to find another open station. Stations at the top of hills are generally open, and those at the bottom are typically not; spots near major tourist destinations and the *quais* are often a safe bet. If you want to rent on the spot, you must have a credit card with a chip on it to use the automatic booths where you can rent a bike; otherwise, you can rent from www.velib.fr to receive a subscription code. **Paris Bike Tour** also offers bike rentals for

france

€20 for a 24hr. period; each extra day costs €10. The bad news is they also require a €250 deposit and a copy of your photo ID. (13 Rue Brantôme. ☎01 42 74 22 14. Open daily 9:30am-6:30pm.)

caen

A city almost entirely destroyed during World War II, Caen claims the inspiring narrative (if uninspiring aesthetic) of a city rebuilt and revitalized from ruins. A mix of post-war architecture and arching medieval structures—there's a huge castle near the middle of it—Caen shines because of the access it gives you as much as for what it contains within the city walls. Expect a lot concerning William the Conqueror—there's his castle, a cathedral with his tomb, and cathedrals with the tombs of the people who knew and slept with him. That's not to knock any of this; everyone loves a good castle and tomb every once in a while, especially when it's the tomb or castle of the guy responsible for conquering England and making the English language what it is today.

Leaving Caen for some of the surrounding sights is really the best part of your trip here, though. The beaches and memorials of the D-Day landings in Normandy make for an alternately haunting, relaxing, and refreshing experience. Mont St-Michel, the famous monastery in the bay, is also about an hour away by bus.

All in all, Caen is probably the best place to stay if you want to see Normandy. The prices are reasonable, the restaurants aplenty, and the ocean close. What more could you want?

SIGHTS

🗫 OUISTREHAM

Maybe it's telling that one of the best things you can do on a trip to Caen is leave Caen itself, but we're not here to make too many value judgments. You're in Caen, and you're gonna have a damn good time. The most accessible of the area's many beaches, the beaches around Ouistreham are a tad crowded, but for a good reason. The long, sandy stretch makes for a great place to catch up on some reading and gird yourself for a dip into the icy English Channel. Take a walk down toward Lion de la Mer for some more remote seaside imagery, or try a hot dog (they put it in a baguette, we kid you not) from one of the boardwalk shops. All in all, a sunny good time.

i Take bus #61.

get a room!

INTER HOTEL LE SAVOY $$$
106 Rue de Falaise   ☎02 31 82 28 50 www.hotel-le-savoy.fr

We hate to do this to you, recommending a hotel and all. But Caen isn't exactly a backpacker's destination, and every accommodation we could find in this city was missing that pesky little "s" and the budget prices we love so dearly. So all we have is Inter Hotel Le Savoy, a budget hotel that will still run you about €60 a night for room. Even if it does have all the trappings of a more upscale stay, including a private room and Wi-Fi and the rest, this is pretty expensive unless you're splitting the room with a friend or more-than-friend.

i Just off the intersection of Bd. Maréchal Lyautey and Rue de Falaise. Free Wi-Fi, TV, and a lounge. Rooms start around $60.

normandy beaches

The beaches of Normandy—beautiful and coastal since forever, world-famous since June 6, 1944—carve a crescent into the northeast coast of France, right across the Channel from England. For those of you who managed to miss one of the most monumental moments of the 20th century, the Allied powers launched the world's largest amphibious assault on these beaches as they began to liberate Europe from the Nazis in 1944. (Coincidentally, the name of our European escapades was Operation Overlord, and we can assure you that we liberated at least three small nations over the course of our adventures.) Once the sight of horrible death, destruction, and boatloads (literally) of military geekery, the beaches today—Omaha, Sword, Gold, and the rest—are pretty regular, beautiful spots. Given a photo of Omaha Beach and asked to identify which Spielberg movie was set there, you would probably guess *Jaws* well before *Saving Private Ryan*. In short, to everyone's benefit, there's a lot less blood and lot fewer dead people there today. (Thanks, America.)

Of course, the beaches, with all of their salty, historic grandeur, are not the only World War II-related memorials worth checking out in this part of the world. There's the bunker at Point du Hoc, where a bunch of Army Rangers engaged in a level of badassery that words can hardly describe; the American Cemetery, dotted with thousands of beautiful and haunting white graves; and the Memorial du Caen, a museum dedicated to the D-Day landings.

Ponying up (unfortunately, not literally getting on a pony) for a tour is probably the best way to knock out most of these landmarks. They're not exactly close together, and we'd be impressed if you have an automobile of your own to reach them. Granted, a few decades ago, people no older than us were scrambling onto these beaches to liberate a freaking continent, so you can figure out how to get yourself to some beaches for that Instagram.

CAEN CASTLE

☎02 31 30 47 60 http://musee-de-normandie.caen.fr

All right, so you went to beach, splashed around a little bit, maybe even tanned a bit. Everyone had a great time, even if it wasn't one of those topless French beaches you keep hearing about. Now you're back in Caen, and you're gonna have to do something—what about that big castle plopped right down in the middle of everything? The one-time haunt of William (née Guillaume) the Conqueror, the castle today is home to a few museums and some great views of the city. Check it out to learn about the history of Normandy (at the Normandy Museum) or history about Billy the Conks (guess which musuem this is at). Enormously historic, this castle will have you set up with all kinds of cultural enrichment to justify at least a few days of frying your brain and skin on the beach.

i Look for the big castle right by the University of Caen Normandy. Open M-F 9:30am-12:30pm and 2-6pm, Sa-Su 11am-6pm. €3.50-5.50, under 26 free.

france

FOOD

SASESU $

187 Rue St-Jean   ☎02 31 91 83 43 www.sasesu14.fr

What's the best meal to have after a long, hot day at the beach? Seafood! But you're a budget traveler, so you might as well forget about that. Instead, we offer you Vietnamese food—and boy is it cheap, and boy is it tasty. For €7.50, enjoy a bo bun, a rice bowl of business that they'll serve so quick you'll think you're at McDonald's. But you're not. You're eating savory vermicelli in Caen, France. Wake up, idiot.

i From the Church of St-Pierre, walk along Rue St-Jean toward the river for about 10min.; the restaurant will be on your left. Open M-Sa noon-2pm and 7-11pm, Su 7-11pm. Entrees €7-10.

LE CREP'USCULE $

60 Bd. des Alliés   ☎02 31 38 84 45 www.creperie-caen-lecrepuscule.fr

Nothing says French cuisine quite like a piping hot crepe, covered in all kinds of cheese and country ham, sitting on your plate. And nothing says a piping hot crepe, covered in all kinds of cheese and country ham, quite like a visit to Le Crep'uscule. Situated along the canal near the center of the city, Le Crep'uscule begins to strike an American diner-like-feel, except for the fact that none of the food is American, no one in the diner is speaking English, and (oh wait) it's not a diner. There's some white tiling, though. Decor aside, the food is here delicious and affordable—not to mention indisputably French and Norman. Before the sunset has you feeling to sleepy, you can also try some of the dessert crepes. Everything is better with ice cream, after all.

i From the Church of St-Pierre, turn onto Bd. des Alliés; the restaurant will be on your right. Open Tu-Su 11:30am-11pm. Crepes €7.

caen

NIGHTLIFE

Getting bombed is something of a tradition in Normandy; why not join in yourself? For the best nightlife drag in town, head to Rue Écuyere—a pedestrian street packed with different bars and clubs.

ESSENTIALS
Practicalities

- **TOURIST OFFICES:** You'll find helpful people and helpful guides at the **Office de Tourisme Caen.** (12 Pl. St-Pierre. ☎02 31 27 14 14. *i* Open M-Sa 9:30am-1pm and 2-6pm.)
- **CURRENCY EXCHANGE: Caen Change.** (115 Rue St-Jean. ☎02 31 30 18 87.)
- **INTERNET:** There are many cafes with free Wi-Fi in Caen—McDonald's is, of course, a sure bet. Try Fruit Café (28 Rue St-Pierre) for a smoothie and some smooth internet sailing.
- **POST OFFICES:** There's one right by Caen Castle. (63 Rue de la Pigacière. *i* Open M-F 9am-noon and 2-5pm, Sa 9am-12:15pm.)
- **POSTAL CODE:** 14000

Emergency

- **EMERGENCY NUMBERS:** General emergencies ☎112. Ambulance ☎15. Police ☎17.
- **POLICE:** 10 Rue du Dr Thibout de la Fresnaye. (☎02 31 29 22 22.)
- **LATE-NIGHT PHARMACIES:** Little green crosses demarcate most pharmacies in the city; visit www.ordre.pharmacien.fr to find the nearest open one.
- **HOSPITALS: University Hospital Caen.** (Av. de la Côte de Nacre. ☎02 31 06 31 06.)

Getting There

Caen has its own small little regional **airport,** with some international flights to a limited number of other European cities. It's about 3 mi. outside the city, and it looks like you're taking a taxi.

SNCF runs high-speed **trains** out of Caen station, and they're not too expensive. The station is about a mile outside the center of town, but there are nearby tram stations and bus stops to take you to where you need to go.

If you're traveling from somewhere else in France, taking the **bus** to Caen is probably your cheapest option, and it's just about as fast. Ouibus is the new bus option from our friends at SNCF, and it's the cheapest and most comfortable option. Flixibus is also great, if a little more expensive. Buses arrive at the same spot as the train station—about a mile outside the real center of the city.

Getting Around

Caens has a **tram** system—it has tires, but we're not going to linger on that—that spans over two lines. Tickets cost about €2 but depend on how far you're going. Caen is also home to a very convenient **bus** system that will take you around the city and to many of the surrounding towns. The main hub—where you can find all of the buses—is the Gare de Caen. You can buy tickets at the electronic kiosks or at some of the *tabacs* in town; the tickets are about €1.50.

france

rennes

We're going to be completely honest with you: Rennes is by no means the hot molten cultural and metropolitan center of the solar system. To tell the truth, it's probably not even inside the asteroid belt—just hanging out there with Saturn or Uranus or something. That's not to say it's not a great place to visit. Home to a university and an industrial center in its own right, Rennes makes up for its lack of star power with an acute sense of national and regional authenticity. Some of the medieval framed houses and cobblestone streets provide that eternal European charm, and you'll have some of the best crepes of your life here. The myriad green spaces and quaint municipal offerings will be more than enough to relax you, and the sea is only a bus ride away.

So if you're at all interested in seeing France as it exists, without the touristy varnish and glam of Paris, then a trip to Rennes is more than justified. You'll probably be the only English-speaking tourist you come across. And with a relatively cheap set of accommodations and meals, it's not too hard to justify the trip.

SIGHTS

PARC DES GAYEULLES

Rue du Professeur Maurice Audin   ☎02 99 67 11 11

Brittany kinda feels like the Maine of France, so you might as well get out and about while you're here. For a real bucolic and agrarian good time, head to Parc de Gayeulles, the large park in the city. There are cows, flowers, scenic lakes, and even the odd walking path or two. You'll quickly feel like you're out in the French countryside, and let's face it: you are out in the French countryside.

i Take the C3 bus to Gayeulles.

HÔTEL DE VILLE

1 Pl. de la Mairie   ☎02 23 62 10 10 http://metropole.rennes.fr

Granted, there are a lot of town halls in France, but Rennes's is worth a special look. This is a pretty dope building: cavernous halls, graceful marble architecture, and, if you're lucky, a cameo by [ominous attack-ad voice] the mayor of Rennes. Free tours take off at 4pm every day.

i From the République Métro stop, walk north on Passage de la Légion d'Honneur toward Pl. de la République. Continue onto Rue d'Orléans and then Pl. de la Mairie; it will be on the left.

get a room!

AUBERGE DES JEUNESSES DE RENNES $$

10 Canal St-Martin   ☎02 99 33 22 333 www.hihostels.com/hostels/rennes

Right along the main canal in Rennes, Auberge des Jeunesses de Rennes (translation: the Youth Hostel of Rennes) will have you feeling like you are, in fact, getting the seaside experience you came all the way out to Brittany for. But that's not to stop this hostel from actually being a pretty nice play to stay, all things considered. ("All things" being that you are in Rennes.) With free Wi-Fi, free breakfast, and, most importantly, a bed to sleep in (unfortunately, not free), you're all set.

i From Métro stop Anatole France, walk toward the canal and cross over to the other side. Then take a left onto Bd. de Chézy, continue for a few blocks, and take a right onto Rue St-Malo. It will be on your left near the canal. Dorms €20.

FOOD

LA BURGER ATTITUDE $$
13 Rue de St-Malo   ☎02 99 36 86 86 www.laburgerattitude.com

Little-known fact: hamburgers are the cornerstone of any authentic French meal. La Burger Attitude is one of those fancy, modern, and not-inexpensive burger joints that seem to be picking up ground in France (think Shake Shack, but with French waitresses). And while the pattie will weigh in at at least a quarter pound, don't expect a slice of lettuce here: You'll enjoy a French twist on the usual toppings. Think a cheeseburger with fancier cheese and sautéed onions. Oh, and get ready to eat that burger with a fork and knife. We apologize in advance.

i *From the Ste-Anne Métro stop, walk on Contour St-Aubin toward Pl. Ste-Anne. Turn right onto Rue de St-Malo; the restaurant will be on the left. Open Tu-Th noon-1:30pm and 7:30-10pm, F-Sa noon-1:30pm and 7:30-10:30pm. Burgers around €13.*

LA CREPERIE OUZH TAOL $
27 Rue St-Melaine   ☎02 99 63 36 33 www.facebook.com/Ouzh-Taol-292196157576016

Cut the crepe, will you? At Creperie Ouzh Taol, prepare to enjoy a crepe or galette (the technical term for a non-dessert crepe) that has got to be among the top 50 pancakes-for-dinner meals worldwide. Not only are you enjoying a crepe at a crepe restaurant in France, you are enjoying a crepe at one of the best crepe restaurants in the best crepe region in the best crepe country in the world. All for a pretty damn reasonable price. You're welcome.

i *From the Ste-Anne Métro stop, walk east on Contour St-Aubin toward Pl. Ste-Anne and turn right onto Rue de Bonne Nouvelle. Continue onto Rue St-Melaine; the restaurant will be on the left. Open Tu-Sa noon-1:30pm and 7:30-10pm. Crepes around €5.*

crepes

We all know crepes are another one of those French things you pretend to know about (wasn't it on the menu at Denny's that one time?) and enjoy. Well, sit down, young Padawan; you're about to get a crash course on the crepe course. Most of what you know (or think you know) is correct: yes, it is a very thin pastry made from wheat batter spread out over a massive hot plate. Yes, the crepe-making magicians do use a thin machete-style blade to flip it over as the batter pools out on the stove. And, finally, yes, you can enjoy crepes as dessert dishes, snacks, or a full-blown meal, if you throw in some egg, meat, or cheese and make this pastry dinner-worthy.

Crepes are a regional speciality in Brittany, the westernmost region in France. (Rennes is the capital of Brittany, and you just so happen to be in Rennes. Do your best to keep up.) That pancake heaped with Nutella on your plate actually goes back to the 12th century, when poor Bretons took everything they grew on their scraggly, coastal fields—buckwheat, for crying out loud—and tried to make it into something tasty. Centuries later, it's an international phenomenon, in no small part helped by the incorporation of white wheat flour in the 20th century, when it finally became affordable to, you know, the pancake-eaters of the world. Every year, on February 2, the French celebrate Candelmas, and everyone eats crepes like it's their job. In short, it's a big cultural deal, especially in Brittany. Now make sure you go actually taste a couple—they're quite good.

france

NIGHTLIFE

Just a stone's throw from one of the big cathedrals in town, Rue St-Michel is the perennial place for young people in Rennes. It's packed with bars, clubs, and, of course, kebab places. Getting sloshed is about as timeless of an activity as you can imagine, and a night out on Rue St-Michel just might be as close as you can get to a medieval blackout.

FOX AND FRIENDS

13 Rue de la Monnaie   ☎02 56 51 73 89 www.facebook.com/foxandfriendspub

Roald Dahl may not have intended for his children's novel to be recited from the top of a bar in Rennes, France, but what fun is Roald Dahl if you're not hammered? At Fox and Friends, if you're not getting a little bit foxy, then you're just not doing right. More a sports bar than anything else, this is the kind of place you would bring your friends for a casual hangout if you had friends and if you were allowed to go to nice bars back home. With a spacious terrace outside and reasonable prices, you're in for a good, relaxing time.

i From the Ste-Anne Métro stop, walk along Rue St-Michel and turn right onto Rue de la Monnaie; the bar is on the left. Open M-Th 11am-1am, Sa 9am-1am, Su 5pm-1am. Beer €4-6.

ESSENTIALS

Practicalities

- **TOURIST OFFICES:** You can find helpful English-language guides and a series of maps at the **Office de Tourisme de Rennes.** (11 Rue St-Yves. Near the République Métro stop. Open M-Sa 9am-7pm, Su 10am-1pm and 2-5pm.)

- **CURRENCY EXCHANGE: Bretagne Change** is near the Parliament building. (1 Rue Victor Hugo. Open M-F 9am-12:30pm and 2-5pm.)

- **INTERNET:** Why yes, **Cybernet On Line** does sound like a vaguely threatening line from the *Terminator* movies. (22 Rue St-Georges. ☎02 99 36 37 41.)

- **POST OFFICES:** There are 3 in town. (11 Pl. Ste-Anne, Pl. de la République, or 27 Bd. du Colobier. Open M-F 9am-5pm, Sa 9am-12:30pm.)

- **POSTAL CODE:** 35000

Emergency

- **EMERGENCY NUMBERS:** General emergencies ☎112. Ambulance ☎15. Police ☎17.

- **POLICE:** Headquarters lies at 22 Bd. de la Tour d'Auvergne. (☎02 99 65 00 22.)

- **LATE-NIGHT PHARMACIES:** Little green crosses demarcate most pharmacies in the city; visit www.ordre.pharmacien.fr to find the nearest open one.

- **HOSPITALS: Rennes University Hospital.** (2 Rue Henri le Guilloux. ☎02 99 28 43 21.)

Getting There

Rennes-Bretagne **airport** will be useful from some regional European flights, but not exactly on the cheap cheap. You'll also have to take a taxi from the airport to Rennes itself, so...

SNCF runs high-speed **trains** out of Rennes station, and they're not too expensive. The station is south of the true center of town, just a few Métro stops away.

If you're traveling from somewhere else in France, taking the **bus** to Rennes is probably your cheapest option, and it's just about as fast. Ouibus is the new bus option from our friends at SNCF, and it's the cheapest and most comfortable option. Flixibus is also great, if a little more expensive. Buses arrive at the train station.

rennes

Getting Around

Rennes has a **Métro** system that traces a single artery through the center of the system, which makes it pretty intuitive. Tickets are €1.50.

Lyon

When you think of glamorous vacation destinations in France, Lyon probably isn't the first that comes to mind. It's a little too quiet to be Paris. It's a little too loud to be Provence. It's way, way too far north to be the French Riviera. "Only the third-largest city in France? Eh, skip it," most backpackers might say. Those dopes. Nestled at the intersection of the Rhone and Saone Rivers, Lyon is so packed with culture and beauty that it comes close to bursting at its watery, cobblestone seams. It has a vibrant arts scene, including an annual film festival so outrageous that cinephiles call it "City of Lights." For the historically inclined, Lyon's Old Town (a UNESCO World Heritage Site that dates back to the Middle Ages) sits right on the outer bank of the Saone, and the ruins of two Gallo-Roman amphitheaters (built around 15 BCE) are a 10min. hike away. Best of all, Lyon is the gourmet capital of France (and, by some accounts, the world). Cheese, bread, wine, sausage—you name it, Lyon and its army of red-checked cafes/restos/*glaciers/bouchons* will feed it to you.

Of course, it takes a lot of space to fit in all this fun. Most of Lyon's downtown is squeezed into a compact little region called the **Presqu'île** (a peninsula bordered by rivers on three sides), but the rest of the city sprawls in all directions. We walked everywhere, but our aching feet have a message for you: use the Métro.

SIGHTS

▨ BASILIQUE NOTRE DAME DE FOURVIÈRE
8 Pl. Fourvière   ☎04 78 25 85 78 http://fourviere.org

If you look up, you'll see it—pearly spires glinting, stony pillars plunging, proud golden angel glaring atop its regal, vaulted seat. The basilica towers over Lyon, watching over every corner of the city. Don't leave Lyon without conquering your fears and staring this monolith right in its all-seeing, stained-glass eyes. Warm up with some crepes and light stretching in the Old Town, then tackle the difficult climb to Fourvière (or ride the slightly less difficult cable car for €2.80 round-trip). Up close, the basilica is everything it promised from afar (unlike your Tinder match). Gold leaf, mosaics, incense—the whole nine yards. Wake up in time for mass, and the basilica's spectacular acoustics will send traditional French hymns rumbling through your bones. After the service, make sure to save a few hours for the rest of Fourvière: the hill offers a spectacular rose garden, a close substitute for the Eiffel Tower, and ancient Gallo-Roman ruins.

i Free. Open daily 8am-6:45pm. Masses Sa 5pm, Su 7:30, 9:30, 11am, 5:30pm.

PARC DE LA TÊTE D'OR
Pl. Général Leclerc   ☎04 72 10 30 30

Pack sunscreen, goat cheese, and a baguette—the Parc de la Tête d'Or is a picnic lunch waiting to happen. Wander its miles of irregular, meandering pathways. Gape at the rose gardens and the occasional zebra.* Marvel at the fact that it's open on Sunday. Is this even France? Located less than 4km from Pl. Bellecour, directly behind the Museum of Contemporary Art, the park is accessible by bus, bike, or (tired and sweaty) foot. (*Note: there is a zoo in the park.)

i Free. Open daily Apr 15-Oct 14 6:30am-10:30pm; Oct 15-Apr 14 6:30am-8:30pm.

get a room!

SLO LIVING $$$
5 Rue Bonnefoi   ☎04 78 59 06 90

Live Slo, book fast—at Slo Living, rooms are in high demand, especially
in June when the annual soccer ("football") tournament comes to town.
This popularity is well earned: the hip open-air plaza (complete with
beanbags, twinkle lights, and a jazzy mural) is an acoustic jam sesh
waiting to happen, and the quaint little dinner table is a social space that
your college dormitory could only dream of. This tight community is Slo
Living's best feature. Weekly dinners, walking tours, and club outings
make it easy to meet other hostelers, and staffers are quick to recommend excellent bars and restaurants in the region. A free drink on entry
doesn't hurt, either. Ask your bunkmates how they like the hostel, and
you'll hear a chorus of affirmation: "The best, eh?" "Fab, mate," "Shh,
c'est minuit, ferme ta gueule."

i 8-bed dorms €28.

COOL & BED $$
32 Quai Arloing   ☎04 26 18 05 28 www.coolandbed.com

Cool & Bed is surprisingly, self-consciously fratty. Guests hail mostly from
the US, the UK, and Canada and are ready to party every day—an inclination that Cool & Bed is happy to indulge. Hostel staffers schedule events
nearly every night of the week, including regular beer-pong tournaments
and drinking games. The location isn't great—about a 40min. walk from
Pl. Bellecour or a 10min. walk to the nearest Métro station—but what
you spend on time you save on money. If your schedule says "Lyon," but
your heart and wallet say "Sigma Chi," the Cool & Bed might be for you.

i Breakfast included. 16-bed dorms €20.

LE FLANEUR GUESTHOUSE $$
56 Rue Sebastien Gryphe   ☎09 81 99 16 97 www.leflaneur-guesthouse.com

If Le Flaneur were a textile, it would be hemp. Exposed brick and a burgeoning backyard veggie garden give the building some distinct hippie
vibes, and the laid-back residents seem to have embraced the hostel's
official philosophy: "Le Flaneur" translates to "The Loafer." The chill staff
organizes equally chill in-house events (expect wine and board games).
If you're looking for a slightly more high-key experience, the hostel is an
easy 10min. walk from the heart of Lyon and only 5min. to Métro line D.
Though not exactly a luxurious choice—dorms can be a bit cramped and
dark—Le Flaneur does "downtown commune" with style.

i Dorms €19.

CROIX-ROUSSE MORNING FOOD MARKET
Bd. de la Croix-Rousse

Huge rounds of lavender cheese that taste the way first love feels. Glossy little
raspberries in dainty little cartons. Orchids bundled in brown paper. Whole
chickens roasting perfectly, dripping, flaking, wafting that golden-brown aroma.
Budget travelers fumbling with wallets, desperate to get their hands on it all.
Delightful.

i Up and down the entire boulevard. 23 vendors W-Th; 95 vendors Tu and F-Su. Open Tu 6am-
1:30pm, W-Th 6am-1pm, F-Su 6am-1:30pm.

lyon

OLD TOWN (VIEUX LYON)

Like Johnny Depp in the last *Pirates of the Caribbean* movie, Lyon's Old Town is beautiful, mysterious, and remarkably well preserved. Nestled between the slopes of Fourvière and the banks of the Saone, Old Town has been around since the Middle Ages, making it the second-most historic part of the city (after the Gallo-Roman ruins on the mountains just above). In recognition, it's been a UNESCO World Heritage Site since 1998. If the ancient French could live here for hundreds of years, you can afford 2hr. Fortify yourself with ice cream from one of the numberless *glaciers* (there is, almost literally, one at every stony ancient street corner). Wander into old churches. Most of all, explore the *traboules*—ancient, secret tunnels connecting the buildings. These can be a bit tricky to find on your own, so if you can tag along with a guided tour, do so.

FOOD

TERRE ADELICE $

1 Pl. de la Baleine   ☎04 78 03 51 84 www.terre-adelice.eu/glacierlyon

Fresh goat cheese. Organic tomato and basil. Buckwheat. Are we in Wisconsin? No, we're in a quirky little *glacier* in the heart of Old Lyon. Pay attention. Worth noting for its prime location alone, Terre Adelice offers the most astounding collection of ice-cream flavors you've ever seen. Ever wonder what violet petal tastes like? Terre Adelice has got you covered. Pine kernel? Ditto. For the slightly fainter of heart, the *glacier* also offers tamer flavors: the wild blackberry is like a crisp spring morning in your mouth, and we've heard good things about the chocolate.

i 1 scoop €2.60. Open May-Aug M-Th 1pm-midnight, F-Sa 1pm-1am, Su 1-11pm.

LE P'TIT BOUCHON $$

Rue de Créqui   ☎04 78 60 50 01 www.leptitbouchon-lyon.fr

Hot, meaty, and fatty enough to clog your arteries from two streets down—authentic Lyonnais food lives here. A tiny, red-checked terrace on a quiet street in the 3ème arrondissement, the restaurant is fully *bouchon*-certified and fully delicious. Order an aperitif on the terrace. Ponder the menu of strange French words you don't know. Brace yourself for the inevitable odd mouthful of tripe. Savor every salty, chewy bite.

i 1 course €16, 2 courses €21, 3 courses €28. Open M-W noon-2:30pm, Th-F noon-2:30pm and 7:30-10pm, Sa 7:30-10pm.

LE MUSÉE $

2 Rue des Forces   ☎04 78 37 71 54

It's 8pm. You're standing at the center of Rue de la République, exhausted after a long day of selfies with naked statues. You're lost, confused, and hungry for another Lyonnais *bouchon*—but you just don't have the energy to walk all the way to Le P'tit Bouchon or Old Town. By golly, you're going to find a place in Presqu'île, or you're going to march into that McDonald's you spotted back in Pl. Bellecour. No! No! Let's not get hasty. A cozy little hole in the wall across from the Printing Museum, Le Musée is like Le P'tit Bouchon but more convenient and more hands-on. The menu is a single handwritten piece of paper, and the server will take your order by bending down on one knee and reading you its entire contents out loud. If you're an Anglo, he will attempt to translate, freestyle, with lots of hand gestures (pointing at his veins means "blood sausage"). Thanks to its charm and in spite of its prices (good *bouchons* just aren't cheap), Le Musée is consistently packed. If you don't make a reservation, expect to be seated at an intimate table for two across from a nice older man from Provence who just wanted to eat his blood sausage in peace.

i Open Tu-Sa noon-2:30pm and 7-10:30pm.

france

LE PENJAB $$

25bis Quai Romain Rolland   ☎04 78 42 36 76 www.lepenjab-lyon.fr

Le Penjab is a roller coaster. You enter on a high. You're hungry, everything smells delicious, and your arteries just need a break from four consecutive days of Lyonnais *bouchons*. Then you hit your first low. You sit down and are immediately, gently chided. Ordering only water? Tsk. Skipping an appetizer? Tsk tsk. Eating only half your bread? TSK TSK TSK. You start to panic. How could you have gone so wrong? Why can't you just fit in? Just then, in the valley of your despair, the server emerges with your food. "You know what?" he says. You freeze. What did you do? "You know what?" he says again. Oh god, he's going to kick you out. He pauses. "ENJOY YOUR MEAL!" Later, you hear him go through this routine with four other tables. You ponder this strange, strange catchphrase and all the emotions it evokes. Then you take a bite of your chicken tikka masala. It tastes like tomato, and redemption. Mmmmmm.

i *Appetizers €4.50 and up. Entrees €6-16. Open daily 7:30pm-midnight.*

BRASSERIE GEORGES $$

30 Cours de Verdun   ☎04 72 56 54 54 www.brasseriegeorges.com

Like that one guy from high school, Brasserie Georges is kind of loud and obnoxious, but fun in large groups. Also like that guy, Brasserie Georges subscribes to the philosophy of "go big or go home." Founded in 1836, the restaurant is one of the oldest and the largest in Lyon. And we mean large—it measures its annual sauerkraut product in tons (44, to be precise) and holds Guinness world records for largest sauerkraut, largest baked Alaska, and largest Norwegian omelette. Why would it strive to achieve these records? Don't question; only marvel. The food is much classier than the vibe (try the *feuillantin au chocolat*), and if you and 12 hostelmates/new best friends are wandering reservation-less and hungry around downtown Lyon, Brasserie Georges is a decent bet.

i *Dish of the day €16.50. Multi-course menus €27.50. Open daily 11:30am-11pm.*

NIGHTLIFE

STAR FERRY

2 Quai Victor Augagneur   ☎04 72 60 97 18 www.star-ferry.com

"Shoot for the moon, land among the stars." Recall the wise words of your third-grade teacher. Look past their astronomical inadequacies (c'mon, Mrs. Gray, do better) and probe their deep philosophical lessons. If you aim high, how badly can you really fail? If you start the night at Star Ferry, how rapidly could it possibly devolve? Star Ferry—the beer garden, the land of 80 beers—is the place where you get to trade your cool vintage Polaroid for a cool vintage glass and temporary ownership of words like "vintage" and "hops" and "beer snob specialty term." Luckily for those less practiced in the art of beer snobbery (does beer pong count?), the bar makes this easy: drinks are categorized by country of origin and price. Try the Rhub'IPA—it's cheap, and it has a unique blend of vintage, uh, hops.

i *Beers €5.50-9.90. Open M-F 3pm-1am, Sa-Su noon-1am.*

LE SIRIUS

4 Quai Victor Augagneur   ☎04 78 71 78 71 http://lesirius.com

Enough with the beer already. You'll be too sloshy to dance. As the night progresses, make like a snowbird and migrate south—a few yards down the river, Le Sirius is turning up. Recommended by hostel staff everywhere (thanks, hostel lady!), this floating concert hall is where the river starts rockin'. Regular concerts take place at 10pm most Thursdays, Fridays, and Saturdays in the summer, and jazz jam sessions go down every Tuesday. Best of all, admission is free.

i *Open M-Sa 2pm-3am, Su 2-10pm.*

LA MARQUISE

20 Quai Victor Augagneur   ☎04 72 61 92 92

After nearly 20 years of experience, La Marquise knows how to throw a party. Dubbed "mythical" by native Lyonnais partygoers and "cool, bruh" by the Californians at our hostel, La Marquise features free live music every Friday and Saturday from 8pm to 11pm. When the night is no longer young and you're a bit live-musicked out (read: it's 3am and Le Sirius has kicked you out), La Marquise runs a little DJ action from 11pm to 5am. The oldest, the wisest, and also the closest to your hostel, La Marquise is the place to see the night to its bitter, bitter end.

i *Open daily 2pm-5am.*

BARBEROUSSE

18 Rue Terraille   ☎04 72 00 80 53 www.barberousse.com/ville/lyon

Located in the center of Presqu'île and guarded by two swashbuckling bouncers, Barberousse is a bar full of pleasant surprises, and also pirates. The first surprise is financial: entry is free, so you get to hold onto your dubloons. The second is architectural: once you get past the nondescript door, you are directed down a narrow wooden staircase to the ship's kee—we mean, the basement bar. The third is thematic: Barberousse really commits. Packed with barrels and nets and lined with a long wooden bar, the dance space is dark and warm and so packed with sweaty party people that the floorboards shake with the gentle rhythm of a ship at sea. Embrace your inner Jolly Roger—roll up your sleeves, wear your jacket like a bandana, and jump into the sweaty waves.

i *Shooters €2.50. Open Tu-Sa 9pm-3am.*

LE SUCRE

50 Quai Rambaud   ☎04 27 82 69 40 www.le-sucre.eu

Le Sucre is celebrated as the "best rooftop in all of France," and we're inclined to agree. The nightclub is perched on the rooftop of a now-defunct sugar factory on the southern tip of Lyon where the two rivers converge. Yeah, that's a sweet venue. Le Sucre is known for being something of an electronic mecca. Live DJs perform several nights per week, and the club is frequented by electro-snobs and EDM-fiends alike. You won't be an outcast here if you're not a diehard Radiohead fan; just don't start going off about how the music sounds like a malfunctioning elevator with a broken radio inside.

Any local with more than two friends will tell you Le Sucre is the best bet for clubbing in Lyon. The good news is that it's popular and will rarely, if ever, have a slow night. The bad news is that the club owner knows this and therefore charges admission; occasionally, Le Sucre even requires tickets for the more popular DJs. The tickets usually cost about €10, which isn't too bad, but you won't get a free drink with the cover charge like you might elsewhere. Check online before heading out to see if you can buy a ticket, as this will get you through the door much quicker and will save you some money by not having to buy a ticket at the venue.

i *Cover up to €10. Drinks €6-15. Open Th 10pm-midnight, F-Sa 11pm-5am, Su 3-10pm.*

ESSENTIALS
Practicalities

- **TOURIST OFFICES:** Pl. Bellecour. (☎04 72 77 69 69. Open daily 9am-6pm.)
- **LATE-NIGHT PHARMACIES:** Overnight pharmacy at 22 Rue de la République (☎04 72 56 44 14. Open daily 8pm-8am.)

Emergency

- **EMERGENCY NUMBERS:** General emergencies ☎112. Ambulance ☎15. Police ☎17. Fire ☎18.
- **POLICE:** For general inquiries, not emergencies, call ☎04 78 78 40 40.
- **HOSPITALS:** ☎04 72 11 69 53.

Getting There

Lyon's main **airport** is Lyon-St-Exupéry, the fourth-largest in France. Rhonexpress trains shuttle passengers from the airport into the main part of the city. (€14.70, ages 12-25 €13.20.)

Trains to Lyon run through Gare de Lyon Part-Dieu or Gare de Lyon-Perrache. Part-Dieu is the larger of the two and is where all national or international trains depart from. (5 Pl. Beraudier. Ticket desk open M-Th 8am-8pm, F 7am-10pm, Su 8am-8pm.)

Getting Around

Lyon is a big city, and it's only barely walkable. If you're just trying to navigate downtown, you can walk. If you're trying to get from Gare de Lyon-Perrache (the south end) to Croix-Rousse (the north end) or from Gare de Lyon Part-Dieu to anywhere, you're probably better off taking public transit. Public transportation in Lyon is run by TCL (☎08 20 42 70 00 www.tcl.fr), which administers **buses, trams,** and a **métro.** Tickets to any of the above cost €1.80 (€2 if purchased on the bus), and public transit runs from 5am-12:20am. Métro trains via line T1 run directly to Gare Part-Dieu. If you'd rather take a **taxi**, call Taxi Lyon. (☎04 72 10 86 86.) Lyon also has Velo'v **bike** stands all throughout the city where you can pick up or drop off rental bikes. Tickets can be purchased at the stand, online, or at the tourist office.

bordeaux

You hear "Bordeaux" and you think "wine." This is fair—Bordeaux is one of the most famous wine-growing regions in the world. These wines have intoxicated locals since the Romans planted the first vineyards sometime before 71 CE. These wines have intoxicated foreigners since Eleanor of Aquitaine married the English king in the 12th century. For a reasonable price (€2-4 per bottle for shit, €4+ per bottle for good shit), these wines can intoxicate you. "But you can buy Bordeaux wine pretty much anywhere," you say. "Why come here to do it?" Glad you asked. Even aside from the drank, Bordeaux is the best city in southwestern France. It has history—traces of the medieval city peek through the cracks of the modern one, resulting in weird fun facts like, "This giant door to nowhere marks the long-gone entrance to an ancient palace." It has youth—riverside hangars double as skateparks and art exhibitions, tram stops host city-sponsored concerts, and the "military wasteland" east of the Garonne has been transformed into an artsy eco-living complex called "Darwin." Best of all, it has beach access—world-class Atlantic beaches are only a bus ride away. This city is the total package.

SIGHTS

▨ MIROIR D'EAU
Pl. de la Bourse

Most water mirrors are fun. Big glimmering wading pools full of chubby little pumpkins and general summer fun—it's hard to go wrong, really. This water mirror is different. This water mirror is especially big. As a matter of fact, it's

AUBERGE DE JEUNESSE DE BORDEAUX $$

22 Cours Barbey   ☎05 56 33 00 70   www.auberge-jeunesse-bordeaux.com

Youth Hostel Bordeaux is the only youth hostel in Bordeaux. It's cornered the market. Complete monopoly. You, and every backpacker you've ever loved, are powerless ants beneath its feet. Luckily, Youth Hostel Bordeaux subscribes to a benevolent brand of economic tyranny, offering an excellent product for a reasonable price. Beds come with those little curtains so you can pretend you have actual privacy, and the "cafeteria" is a tame but pleasant social space if you decide to make friends or eavesdrop over dinner. There's even a kitchen that comes complete with everything you could possibly need to chop, bake, toast, or fry.

i Dorms €24.

the biggest (manmade) water mirror in the world—37,000 sq. ft. of pure water-mirror mastery. Like a cherry on top of a watery ice-cream sundae, the water park is also a functioning mirror: every 15min., when the fountains die down completely, the pool offers a breathtaking reflection of Pl. de la Bourse (the 18th-century building and square across the street).

i Free.

MONUMENT AUX GIRONDINS

Pl. des Quinconces

Speaking of "unnecessarily large"—the Monument aux Girondins is flippin' enormous. The 177 ft. tribute to the Girondins (martyrs of the French Revolution) was built at the end of the 19th century but looks like it could have been erected by mythical giants with something to prove. The larger-than-life sea people riding larger-than-life sea chariots led by larger-than-life sea horses in the fountain at the base drive the point a little bit further home. And the 31-acre gravel monstrosity of an esplanade (Pl. des Quinconces) that surrounds the monument? #compensation...

i Free.

PALAIS GALLIEN

Rue du Dr Albert Barraud   ☎05 56 00 66 00

Never seen the Colosseum? Now you'll never have to. That's right—you can get your dose of "ancient ruined amphitheater" right here in Bordeaux. Whew! What a relief! The Palais Gallien has stood since the second century, and though it's been dramatically weathered and damaged in the interim (you stand outside for two millennia and tell us how well your skin holds up), it remains staggeringly beautiful and breathtakingly Roman. Admire it from the street, then chat up the lady at the booth and climb right down into the site (this is allowed, so technically you don't have to chat her up). We particularly recommend the vomitorium.

i Free. Visible 24hr. Interior open daily 1-6pm. Free tours daily June-Sept.

BASILIQUE SAINT-SEURIN

Pl. des Martyrs de la Résistance   www.saintseurin.info

Of the gazillion churches in Bordeaux, the Basilica of St. Seurin is the one that really stands out among the haze of rose windows and flying buttresses that haunts our dreams and waking moments alike. The original basilica was begun on this site in the sixth century, and the existing basilica (a UNESCO World Heritage Site) was begun in the 11th. Home of St. Veronica's relics and conveniently located en route to Santiago de Compostela, the basilica became

france

a popular stop for pilgrims heading south throughout the Middle Ages. Students occasionally staff the church during off-hours—if you see them, ask for a tour of the crypt. Later, descend even deeper into the bowels of the earth and explore the archeological dig site/museum out front.

i Free. Open Tu-Sa 8:30am-7:45pm, Su 9am-8:15pm. Masses Tu 7:30am, 7pm, W-Th 7pm, F 7:30am, 7pm, Su 9:30, 11am, 7pm.

MUSÉE D'AQUITAINE
20 Cours Pasteur   ☎05 56 01 51 00

Aquitaine is the region of France that surrounds Bordeaux, and the Museum of Aquitaine tells its story. This large anthropological museum records the human history of Bordeaux from prehistory (including a cave painting or two) to modern times. It also includes a suite of rooms that record the Middle Passage and the shameful role that Bordeaux, as a major port, played in the sale and transport of slaves. While not always a particularly easy experience, the museum is comprehensive, honest, and fascinating. Block off 90min. and keep an open mind.

i €4, students €2, under 18 free. Open Tu-Su 11am-6pm.

FOOD

FUFU JAPANESE NOODLE BAR $
37 Rue St-Remi   ☎05 56 52 10 29 http://restaurantfufu.fr

FuFu is what it promises to be: a noodle bar in a French city famous for wine. That said, the place is consistently packed with people, and the ramen is salty, savory, and hot. Plus, if you manage to nab a seat, you get to watch the staff make everything from scratch in front of you. Sizzle on, little dumplings. Sizzle on.

i Noodles €8.50-10.50. Open M-Th 11:30am-3pm and 6:30-10:30pm, F 11:30am-3pm and 6:30-11pm, Sa 11:30am-3:30pm and 6:30-11pm, Su 11:30am-3:30pm and 6:30-10:30pm.

LA FROMENTINE $
4 Rue du Pas St-Georges   ☎05 56 79 24 10

In order to eat crepes at La Fromentine, you must complete two tasks: 1. Navigate the maze-like heart of Old Bordeaux to actually find the place. 2. Translate the menu. "Doesn't *gaufre* usually mean 'waffle'?" you ask sweetly. How cute. Within these walls, a *"gaufre"* is a savory crepe. What other lies fester unidentified, unknown, between the pretty French lines of this menu? Only fluent French speakers will ever know. Happily, if you can get past the games, La Fromentine is the precious frilly brunch place of your dreams. For €10, the afternoon *prix-fixe* menu will get you a cheese-and-meat-filled savory crepe the size of your head, a sugar-filled dessert crepe two-thirds the size of your head, and a garden salad about half the size of your head.

i Afternoon prix-fixe menu €10. Open M-F noon-1:30pm and 7-9:30pm, Sa 7-9:30pm.

LE CATERING $
4 Rue des Ayres or 12 Rue des Remparts   www.cateringbagels.com

Why does Bordeaux have so many bagel joints? This is not a phenomenon we have observed elsewhere in France. Does the salt air coming in off the Atlantic produce a craving for soft absorptive dough? Has the fishing industry created a salmon surplus that only daily servings of lox can possibly control? It's probably one of those two possibilities. But look past the bagel abundance. Don't be distracted by the lesser bagels; head straight for Le Catering. The exposed brick and the man juicing a carrot may be a little more Brooklyn than Bordeaux, but the lemons are zesty and the avocados are plentiful. Do lemons, avocados, and carrot juice really belong on a bagel? Tradition says no. Our taste buds say yes.

i All bagels €6. Open daily noon-11pm.

NIGHTLIFE

If you're in Bordeaux from June through September, don't miss (not that it would be possible to miss) ⚑**Metropolitan Summer**, a lineup of concerts, art exhibitions, and moonlit adventures that light up the city. "Dancing in the Streets" is a series of free outdoor concerts that run 6pm-1am and feature an eclectic, super-danceable mix of French and American music. When you're traipsing past a medieval church and its golden tower at midnight, do you expect to find three DJs and 200 drunken French people, several dozen of whom are dancing on the aforementioned golden tower? No. You don't expect that. Plan instead, by going online (http://etemetropolitain. bordeaux-metropole.fr) and perusing the summer lineup.

NAMA

24 Rue Lafaurie Monbadon ☎05 56 44 88 54/06 51 27 86 42 www.namawinerestaurant.com

Nama is only going to appeal to a niche crowd. If you're a broke student traveling alone and looking to get wasted on €4 or less, skip it. If you're traveling with a group of close friends, you've got some euros burning a hole in your pocket, you're not in a rush, you appreciate wine, and you've always dreamed of befriending a French sommelier, read on. In a sentence, Nama is a novelty wine bar. All guests must make reservations in advice, and there's a €10 cover. Once you enter, you become wino family: expert staff will befriend, entertain, and intoxicate you all night long. Wine recommendations? Blind tastings? The infamous "wine battle"? Check, check, and check.

i *Wine €1-5 by the glass. Prix-fixe menus €16-49. Open W-F noon-2pm and 7:30-10:45pm, Sa-Su 7:30-10:45pm.*

I.BOAT

1 Quai Armand Lalande ☎05 56 10 48 35 www.iboat.eu

Around 2am, most of Bordeaux starts to quiet down. The wine bars thin out; the public squares empty; the hooligans singing "Seven Nation Army" and driving in circles around Pl. de la Bourse get too tired to continue. To confused backpackers observing from downtown, it might seem like Bordeaux is shutting down. In a rare twist, those confused backpackers would be wrong. If they looked a little closer, they might notice that people are dispersing in a remarkably organized fashion. In fact, they're all boarding the B tram, outbound. And are they chanting... "boat"?

I.Boat is a floating club parked in a canal north of the city, and it's hands-down the city's best place to party. The €10 cover, while not cheap, gets you three decks (the highest for lounging, the middle for eating, the lowest for raging) and a rotating lineup of guest DJs from all over the country/continent/globe. The crowd is young (about 18-24), the bouncers are fairly lenient, and the dance floor is dark, crowded, and sweaty—just the way we like it. The only catch is location: I.Boat is almost 5km from the hostel, and the trams stop running at 2am. Luckily, there's a bike-rental station not far from the canal.

i *Cover €10. Beer before 1am €3.60-6, after 1am €6-10. Wine €3.50/6. Concerts 7-11pm. Club open daily 11:30pm-6am.*

ESSENTIALS
Practicalities

- **TOURIST OFFICES:** The central tourist office provides city guides to Bordeaux, maps, brochures, reservations, information on vineyard visits, and wine tastings. (12 Cours de 30 Juillet. ☎05 56 00 66 00 www.bordeaux-tourisme.com. Open M-Sa 9:30am-1pm and 2-7pm.)

Emergency

- **EMERGENCY NUMBERS:** General emergencies ☎112. Police ☎17. Fire ☎18.
- **HOSPITALS: Hôpital St-Andre.** (1 Rue Jean Burguet. ☎05 56 79 56 79.)

Getting There

Trains to Bordeaux arrive at Gare St-Jean (Rue Charles Domercq) from destinations like Lyon, Marseille, Nantes, Nice, Paris, Poitiers, and Toulouse.

Getting Around

Bordeaux isn't a huge city, but it can take a toll on your energy if you try to tackle the whole thing on foot. The **tramway** is the cheapest and most convenient way to get around Bordeaux, as trams depart every 5min. or so from the many street-side stops. To hail a **taxi,** call Taxi Tele. (☎05 56 96 00 34.)

    Buses depart from Réseau TransGironde and run to many smaller vineyard towns neighboring Bordeaux, which is the quickest way to get from the city to wine country. Bus stops and schedules are somewhat tricky within Bordeaux, so your best bet is to get a tutorial from the tourist office.

biarritz

Close your eyes. Picture the French seaside. The heat of the French sun. The smell of French sunscreen. Now open your eyes. Where are you? "The Riviera!" you squeal. No, you lovable goof, wrong seaside. This is Biarritz.

    A relatively small town on the coast of the Atlantic Ocean, Biarritz was made famous in 1855 when Napoleon and his wife Eugénie made it their summer residence. Since then, it's become a magnet for the international jet set—and, equally glamorous if slightly sweatier, the international surf set. Unlike most of the Riviera, Biarritz is home to giant crashing waves and both sandy and rocky shores, making it perfect for surfer folk who just want to ride some sick waves, bruh.

    For those less inclined to pit their flimsy human bodies against the raging gods of the sea, Biarritz also offers tamer pursuits. Think frolicking seals, morning mists over the Atlantic, and grassy crags that drop to the sea and look exactly like you've always imagined Middle Earth to look like. Plus, Biarritz is in Basque country. Have you ever tasted Basque food? Mmmmmm.

SIGHTS

☒ GRANDE PLAGE

Walking Biarritz's main beach at midnight was the most transcendent experience we have ever had. The glistening black sandy plains, the dark racing tide, the monstrous craggy boulders smashing against the sea—be glib, man, be glib. If you were born clutching a tiny surfboard, you'll probably spend most of your time at Biarritz's primary surf magnet, Basque Coast Beach. If you were born clutching sunscreen and a good book like the rest of us, Grande Plage is your best bet. Littered with colorful umbrellas, tan Biarrots, and (most importantly) sand, Grande Plage is the most accessible way to experience Biarritz's famous waves.

    i *Free.*

ROCHER DE LA VIERGE

Technically, the highlight of this attraction is the titular *vierge:* a statue of the Virgin Mary, gazing out to sea. She is beautiful, but also a little small and hard to see. Luckily, you have the *rocher* to keep you busy. This rocky outcropping

get a room!

AUBERGE DE JEUNESSE BIARRITZ $$

8 Rue Chiquito de Cambo ☎05 59 41 76 00

www.hifrance.org/auberge-de-jeunesse/biarritz.html

Auberge de Jeunesse Biarritz feels like sleepaway camp for the children of the urban elite. (We would feel totally comfortable letting Madison and Alistair spend eight weeks running around in the woods and grilling organic locally sourced beef over a campfire at this hostel.) It's located a little ways from town (OK, a 10min. walk and a 20min. ride on the #8 bus) but partially compensates for the inconvenience with charmingly park-like grounds. The interior is nice, too, with high wooden ceilings, a spacious cafeteria, and a half-decent *cafe au lait* machine. Downsides to the "rustic" vibe: we encountered a few bugs, and the Wi-Fi really only works in the lobby.

i Dorms July-Aug from €28.70; Sept from €23.50; Oct-June from €20.70.

SURF HOSTEL BIARRITZ $$$

Domaine de Migron, Bâtiment E ☎06 63 34 27 45 www.surfhostelbiarritz.com

The name says it all: Surf Hostel Biarritz is a place for serious surfers. Every bed comes with a surfboard (and a bike, to transport the surfboard), and the whole place has a salt-soaked feel that can only be produced by the continuous comings and goings of more than a dozen avid surf rats. Aesthetically, this is rad for even the least coordinated among us. Financially, the €40 per night price tag only makes sense for people who were actually planning on renting a board. Never surfed a day in your life and physically unable to tread water all day? Save your money. If you do surf and you do want to stay here, make sure to book ahead. Surf Hostel Biarritz books up quickly, and if you procrastinate you'll have to stay at its sister hostel Surf Hostel Bidart, which is basically identical but located waaaay farther away.

i 4-bed dorms €40; 2-bed €42. Reception M-Sa 8am-noon and 2-5pm. 3-night min. stay.

houses the statue and offers a more-than-180-degree view of the watery horizon. Gosh, the Atlantic is big.

i Located between Vieux-Port and Port des Pecheurs. Free.

MUSÉE DE LA MER

Plateau de l'Atalaye ☎05 59 22 33 34

The Marine Museum is directly behind the Virgin of the Rock. This is how you know it's good. Would Biarritz give real estate as prime as this to a marine museum that wasn't at the tippy-top of its game? No. Unsurprisingly, then, the Marine Museum is home to some underwater beasts that will (or at least should) send chills down your naive, land-dwelling spine. Example 1: the Caribbean eels, slippery green 8 ft. nightmares that may have slithered here straight from the Garden of Eden or the Chamber of Secrets. Example 2: the seals. Didn't think seals were scary? Take a seat and watch these ginormous, bullet-shaped sacks of meat, bone, and death dart around their giant, multi-floor aquarium. They will gnaw, they will gnash, they will look you right in the eye as they poop. Cold, man.

i €15, students €10.50. Open in summer daily 9:30am-midnight.

FOOD

⬛ LTB: LA TABLE BASQUE $$

4 Av. de la Marne ☎05 59 22 23 52 www.restaurant-ltb-biarritz.com

Think hearty everything. The sheep-cheese salad comes covered in chewy, savory charcuterie (surprise!). The main courses are all slabs of meat or fish, and the vegetable side is potatoes. The signature dessert, cherry Basque cake, is like a cross between cake and pie. Even the menu is written in three languages (Basque, French, and English), and comes with a brief history of the Basque people and Biarritz. Education and potatoes? Table for one, please.

i Starters €10. Mains €12-22. Prix-fixe menu €22. Open Apr-Oct M noon-1:45pm and 7:15-9:15pm, Tu 7:15-9:15pm, Th-Su noon-1:45pm and 7:15-9:15pm; Nov-Mar M noon-1:45pm and 7:15-9:15pm, Th-Su noon-1:45pm and 7:15-9:15pm.

HD DINER $$

46 Av. Edouard VII ☎05 59 22 07 37 www.happydaysdiner.com

HD Diner is pink like a piece of Hubba Bubba or a congealed cube of Pepto-Bismol. "Back to the fifties!" its sign screams, in English. You've never lived in the fifties, and you don't really buy into that brand of nostalgia, but you like English, so you wander inside and peer at the menu. The Mexican Wall Burger—"It's gonna be HUUUGE!"—peers back. You're equal parts tickled and frightened, so you buy the burger and a milkshake, then carry them upstairs where you sit at a vinyl booth and gaze dreamily at the Grand Plage far below. This is a good day.

i Burgers and salads €11-16. Pancakes €4-9. Bacon and eggs €9. Open daily 10am-11pm.

LA CASA DE JUAN PEDRO $$

48 Allée Port des Pêcheurs

La Casa de Juan Pedro is the quintessential seaside seafood shack. The place is simple and homey, with outdoor seating and a limited menu that nonetheless contains all the fishy treasures of your wildest dreams. Located directly on the coast, between the Port des Pêcheurs and the Rocher de la Vierge, Juan Pedro's also occupies one of the best locations in Biarritz. Unsurprisingly, this draws the crowds—expect to wait 20-30min. for a table. Luckily, the breathtaking view of the Atlantic should keep you busy while you wait.

i Food €9-16. Open April 1-Nov 15.

NIGHTLIFE

LE BAR BU

5 Rue Gaston Larre ☎05 59 22 24 79

"Le Bar Bu" is a pun on the French word for "beard," and the ownership must be really into beards (or puns) because the joint is plastered with photos of bearded men, the booths are full of bearded guests, and even the (male) staffers are significantly beardier than average. Other than beards, Le Bar Bu is notable for excellent music (mostly funk), surprisingly good sangria, and a very high number of motorcycle helmets per capita.

i Open daily 8am-2am.

LE CAFE CAFE BIARRITZ

10 Pl. Clemenceau ☎05 59 22 51 30 http://cafecafe-biarritz.com

Yes! A bar where people actually dance! If it's earlier than 1:30am (which is when the clubs in Biarritz really get going), but you're looking to shake something now, Le Cafe Cafe is your best bet. Granted, the space is a bit small and grubby. Granted, the DJ played "Uptown Funk" (let it die!). Whatever. At the end of the day, the dance floor is packed, the strobe lights are frantic, and the beer is mid-priced. What more do you want?

i Open daily noon-2am.

biarritz

ESSENTIALS

Practicalities

- **TOURIST OFFICES:** The tourist office offers same-day hotel reservations, campsite reservations, Guide Loisirs, Biarritzscope, and Hebergement city guides. (Sq. d'Ixelles. ☎05 59 22 37 10 www.biarritz.fr. Open July-Aug 9am-7pm.)

Emergency

- **EMERGENCY NUMBERS:** General emergencies ☎112. Police ☎17. Fire ☎18.
- **HOSPITALS: Centre Hospitalier Cote Basque.** (13 Av. Interne Jacques Loeb, Bayonne. ☎05 59 44 35 35.) **Médecin de garde** (doctor on call). (☎05 59 24 01 01.)

Getting There

Planes fly into Aeroport de Parme. Bus #6 runs directly to and from the airport, who offers flights within France and internationally to Dublin, London, Birmingham, Amsterdam, and Helsinki. (7 Esplanade de l'Europe. ☎05 59 43 83 83.) **Buses** drop off at Sq. d'Ixelles from regional destinations like St-Jean de-Luz, Hendaye, and San Sebastian.

Getting Around

Biarritz is small enough to make conquering the town on foot fairly simple. Be warned, however, that the town is very hilly, and if you're not one to enjoy walking up hills all day, you'd be wise to consult the bus schedule. VTAB **buses** run around the city and stop in front of the tourist office. For your own personal driver (aren't we fancy), call a **taxi** from Taxi de Biarritz. (☎05 59 03 18 18 www.taxis-biarritz.fr.)

toulouse

Toulouse has a lot of nicknames. Some call it the Pink City, after the rosy terra-cotta bricks that make up its centuries-old architecture. Others call it the Violet City, after the uniquely double-petaled "violet of Toulouse," sold in markets across town and throughout the world. We call it the Stained-Glass City, since old churches seem to outnumber both bricks and plants here. For real, throw a rock in any direction and you'll hit four medieval frescoes and a pew. Shaded by ancient leafy plane trees, dotted with public gardens and parks, watered on both sides by the banks of the Garonne—if you haven't clued in yet, Toulouse is one good-looking city.

But let's not be shallow. Toulouse has brains, too. The University of Toulouse is one of the biggest in France (and, founded in 1229, one of the oldest in Europe), and the large student population gives Toulouse major college-town vibes. Other people live here too: Toulouse is the fourth-largest city in the country. In fact, it has been called "the most dynamic in France." While Toulouse doesn't exist solely for tourists (*cough* St-Tropez *cough*), all the hustle and bustle make it a damn good place to be one.

SIGHTS

🏛 MUSÉE DES AUGUSTINS

21 Rue de Metz ☎05 61 22 21 82 www.augustins.org

The average fine-art museum earns about a 8.5 on the fun scale. Don't get us wrong—that's a good score. Old paintings? Old statues? Old pottery? We love that stuff. It's just that, after a while, one Roman bust starts to look a bit like the next one (kinda pale and marbly). We have to give credit where credit is due,

get a room!

SAINT-SERNIN $$
17 Rue d Embarthe   ☎07 60 88 17 17

St-Sernin skews a little bit nicer than average. For example, the Wi-Fi works in the lobby *and* the dorms (the ability to check your email from the comfort of your own bed? What is this, the Ritz?). Every bedroom is equipped with a kitchenette. (May Lucifer roast your bones if you try to microwave your stinky soup at 7am while your roommates are sleeping.) There's even an elevator and a ramp, making the whole deal unusually wheelchair-accessible. The single drawback to this centrally located, ivy-covered, generally top-notch hostel? No breakfast.

i 6-bed dorms €23.80.

FRIENDLY AUBERGE $$
31 Rue Gilet   ☎05 61 42 24 92

At first glance, Friendly Auberge makes sense. Sweet colorful shutters, pretty sun-filled rooms, a chef who makes "traditional" French food in-house—it's a recipe for success. At €19 a night, Friendly is even €4.80 a night cheaper than St-Sernin. What's not to like? Well, the location. Pull up Google Maps. Search "Colomiers." Note the fact that it's a suburb of Toulouse. It'll take you a full 2hr. to walk from the hostel to Pl. du Capitole, and nearly 1hr. by public transit. Don't stay here unless St-Sernin is booked solid.

i 8-bed dorms €19.

HABITAT JEUNES Ô TOULOUSE $
2 Av. Yves Brunaud   ☎05 34 30 42 80 www.otoulouse.org

Habitat Jeunes Ô Toulouse is part of the UNHAJ, a national organization dedicated to providing affordable housing to youths. As a result, it offers a lot of longer-term housing (the *"habitat jeunes"*) that you can't have. Fortunately, Ô Toulouse is also part of the FUAJ, a national chain of youth hostels. This means that it also offers some short-term housing (the *"auberge de jeunesse"*) you can have. Just make sure to book for two days and not two years, because good luck trying to get your money back. Bureaucrats. As with the rest of FUAJ, the hostel part of Ô Toulouse gets the job done. Beds are as cheap as they're going to get in southwestern France, and stuff is generally clean. It's a bit outside the city center, but you can get there in about 20min. by Métro, so it's doable. This is as much excitement as we can muster.

i 2-night min. stay.

though: the Musée des Augustins is a solid 10. Housed in a medieval Augustinian monastery, the museum's four sides enclose a central garden complete with a graceful ring of stone pillars that cast long shadows on the floor. Each chamber holds a collection of ancient statues (well, sometimes paintings, but usually statues) from a different era. In cases where the statues are not free-standing, the curatorial staff has worked cheeky, whimsical magic, erecting little seas of colorful pillars, laced throughout with ropes and hanging lanterns to illuminate each individually.

i €5, students free. Open M 10am-6pm, W 10am-9pm, Th-Su 10am-6pm.

toulouse

PLACE DU CAPITOLE

☎05 61 22 34 12

OK, so every city in France has a *hôtel de ville* (city hall) in the middle of a big square. Was every *hôtel de ville* built more than 800 years ago, in 1190 CE? Does every square feature a massive Occitan cross and sprawl across more than 129,000 sq. ft.? Is every hotel/square combo so stunning that the McDonald's next door agrees to hide the Golden Arches because they clash with the view? Yeah, we didn't think so. No matter what else you see or don't see in Toulouse, you're guaranteed to walk through the public square portion of Pl. du Capitole a half-dozen times during your stay. That's a given. We're not "advising" you to do that. We are advising you to slow down, think back to the last time you smelled a rose, and step inside the Capitole building. Frankly, it's worth it for the sheer quantity of gilt alone. So much gilt. Also, naked statues. There are even gilt-edged mirrors behind the naked statues so you can see their perfectly sculpted bums. It's 2016—this is important.

i Free. Open M-Sa 8:30am-7pm, Su 10am-7pm.

JARDIN DES PLANTES
Allée Jules Guesde

The Jardin des Plantes is the grassy green liver of Toulouse. It's not the most glamorous part of the city, the hottest destination, the densest patch of arteries and veins. But you know what? Not every organ can be the heart. Like the liver, the garden is a cleansing presence in the middle. Also, it's big. (Fine, that's the end of the metaphor.) Covering a huge tract of land south of the city (more than 17 acres, to be precise) since 1794, the Jardin des Plantes once served as a place for people to grow and gather medicinal herbs. Today, you'd be wise to gather your medicinal herbs elsewhere (there are many adorable, impressionable small children running around) but it's still a great place to relax and catch some rays. Begin with the Monument des Morts, a large arch erected in memory of World War I casualties, then continue down the Allées Forain-François Verdier to the Grand Rond, a circular park around a graceful central fountain. Snap some photos, refuel with a popsicle or two, then continue across the street

to a bigger park, the Jardin des Plantes. This massive public garden is dotted with a seemingly endless supply of marble statues, bumper cars, wild chickens, precious French babies, and natural history museums (well, one natural history museum), so bring your map and a taste for well-landscaped adventure.

i Free.

BASILIQUE SAINT-SERNIN

Pl. St-Sernin   ☎05 61 21 80 45 www.basilique-saint-sernin.fr

As we said before, Toulouse is a city of old churches. Of all the old churches in this old church city, though, we're telling you to go to this one. As the story goes, a Christian martyr named St. Saturnin died on this spot in the third century. In the fourth century, the first basilica was built above his relics and named in his honor. Conveniently located en route to Santiago de Compostela, the new basilica eventually became a major destination for Christian pilgrims. As the centuries passed and the other basilicas fell, this one stayed standing, and today it is the largest remaining Romanesque monument in Europe (and a UNESCO World Heritage Site). Charge your camera, do some neck stretches, and plan on spending 15min. (20min. if you're committed) looking at another big church. Ya gotta.

i Free. Masses M-Sa 9am, Su 9, 10:30am, 6:30pm. Guided tours Sa 10am-noon and 3-5pm, Su 3-5:30pm.

FOOD

🏠 RAJASTHAN VILLA $$

4 Rue de l'Esquile   ☎05 34 44 91 91 www.lerajasthanvilla.com

If Rajasthan Villa could try harder, it would. It can't, though. That's impossible. This perfect side-street Indian restaurant has reached Maximum Possible Effort. Servers are sweet, attentive, and juuust the right degree of flirty. The Chicken Népal is so creamy and sweet and spicy and mango-y that, once it was gone, we felt paradoxically both physically full and emotionally hollow. Best of all, free aperitifs and digestifs ("pre-food booze" and "post-food booze," respectively) are abundant. This is good business: a tipsy customer is a happy customer, and a happy customer is a tippy customer.

i Starters €4.40-9.30. Mains €9.20-17. Prix-fixe menus from €9. Open M-Th noon-2pm and 7-11pm, F-Sa noon-2pm and 7-11:30pm, Su noon-2pm and 7-11pm.

IL FORNO GUSTO $$

21 Rue Ste-Ursule   ☎05 61 21 81 53 www.fornogusto.com

Too hungry to buy pizza by the slice? Too afraid to buy pizza by the pie? Come to Il Forno Gusto and order pizza by the kilogram. You have three options: you can order a half-kilogram of a single type (i.e., a medium-size slab), you can order a full kilogram of a single type (i.e., a massive multi-person slab), or you can mix and match pieces of varying sizes and types and just pay by the weight at the end. The third option is the most exciting, and the riskiest, since mix-and-match availability basically depends on what other guests have been ordering. If somebody orders a half-kilo of The Rugby, the other half-kilo goes up for grabs. Don't want The Rugby? Suck it up. The Rugby is delicious.

i Pizzas €20-28 per kg. Salads €7.50-9.50. Lunch formulas €7.50-9.50. Open M-F 11:30am-3:30pm and 6:30-10:30pm, Sa 11:30am-11pm, Su 7-10pm.

LE FLORIDA $

12 Pl. du Capitole   ☎05 61 23 94 61 www.leflorida-capitole.fr

If the name didn't give it away, the piercing Boston accent two tables over should have: this place is for lost tourists. "Tourists? Gross!" you gasp. Well, that's true; thanks to Le Florida's tourist-trap status, prices can be high and service can be grumpy. But—though it's a bit of a close call—Le Florida redeems itself with location. Smack-dab in the middle of Pl. du Capitole, facing the Capitole building, it's as central as it gets. If you come early, order its impressively comprehensive breakfast (croissant, baguette, coffee, OJ, and good old-fashioned eggs and bacon) for €9, or stick to basics (just the eggs and bacon) for €3.50. If you come too late for breakfast, snag a table and sip a *café crème* and gaze out over the beautiful public square as you ponder all the life decisions that brought you to this dark, breakfast-less moment.

i Open daily noon-1am.

LE CHEVILLARD $$
4 Bd. du Maréchal Leclerc ☎05 61 21 32 02

If you're holding this book, you definitely cannot afford Le Chevillard for dinner. You might be able to justify Le Chevillard for lunch, though. The place offers a €15 multi-course menu on weekdays noon-2pm. That might not seem cheap, and it's not. But Le Chevillard is so quintessentially French that, when you arrive, you'll wonder if maybe you've fallen into a sepia-tone postcard. Red-checked tablecloths, check. Black-aproned waitstaff, check. Excessive quantity of goat cheese, check. If you do go for the lunch deal, plan on a late dinner. Portions are meat-based and massive, and everything comes with potatoes—just the way we like it.

i Main courses €8.50-27. Afternoon prix-fixe menu €15. Evening prix-fixe menu €24. Open M-F noon-2pm and 8-11pm, Sa 8-11pm.

ESSENTIALS
Practicalities

- **TOURIST OFFICES:** There's one in the Donjon du Capitole. (Sq. Charles de Gaulle. ☎08 92 18 01 80. *i* Open M 10am-7pm, Tu-Sa 9am-7pm, Su 10am-6pm.)

- **POST OFFICE:** 9 Rue Lafayette. (☎08 10 82 18 21. Open M-F 9am-6pm, Sa 9am-noon.)

Emergencies

- **EMERGENCY NUMBERS:** General emergencies ☎112. Ambulance ☎15. Police ☎17. Fire ☎18.

- **POLICE:** For non-emergencies, call the main police station at ☎05 61 12 77 77.

- **HOSPITALS: Centre Hospitalier Universitaire de Toulouse.** (2 Rue Viguerie. ☎05 61 77 22 33 www.chu-toulouse.fr.)

Getting There

Fun fact: Toulouse is the home of a major Airbus manufacturing site, making the city "the Airbus capital of France." Perhaps unsurprisingly, the **Toulouse-Blagnac Airport (TLS)** is one of the biggest in the country. It is connected to the city center by regular bus and tram service.

Trains to Toulouse arrive at Gare de Toulouse-Matabiau. The station is located at the south end of the city and is connected to the Métro.

Getting Around

Toulouse is served by Tisseo, a public-transit system made up of **buses** and a **métro.** Use the Tisseo website (www.tisseo.fr) to figure out directions and connections.

montpellier

If Montpellier were a French lady, she'd be a 20-something with three tasteful hoops in her left ear and jeans just high-waisted enough to be "hip" but not high-waisted enough to be "quirky." She would be the lead singer of a garage band, and when she passed you on the subway you would catch the faint static of painfully cool French indie rock. Consumed by curiosity, you would catch your breath and reach out a helpless hand, but she would have already slipped from your grasp, and your life. Mysterious French lady, who are you? Where did you find that leather jacket? What does this metaphor even mean?

It means that Montpellier is cool. Go thrift-shopping here. Find free outdoor concerts here. Buy buckets of takeout from independent side-street restaurants you didn't even Yelp here. And, after 11pm, join thousands of other party people and hit up the city's low-key but vibrant nightlife (read: you have to dress nice, but you don't have to wear heels). Just a long walk or a short bus ride from the coast of the Mediterranean, Montpellier even has easy beach access. Food, culture, sand… what else do you want? Economic and demographic growth? Well, Montpellier's got that too—the city's been growing exponentially for the last seven decades. This does not surprise us. We'd start a life here too.

SIGHTS

PROMENADE DE PEYROU

There's a lot going on in this outdoor promenade. At the entrance, a triumphal arch—the Porte de Peyrou—looms tall and ornate. Beyond, at the center of a smooth tree-lined esplanade, Louis XIV and his horse raise victorious stone limbs. In the distance, a wide pool reflects the pillars and arches of the water

get a room!

AUBERGE DE JEUNESSE HI MONTPELLIER $$
Impasse de la Petit Corraterie   ☎04 67 60 32 22
www.hifrance.org/auberge-de-jeunesse/montpellier.html

Though unassuming in most respects, this little government-funded hostel is the proud holder of one international title: Worst Shower in the Entire World. Picture it: a tap (no, not a showerhead, more like a rusty tube) jutting from a tiled wall. Below it, a single button with no means of temperature control. You hit the button and a lazy stream of frigid water trickles down the wall. You press your body against the wall and try to rub the water on yourself, but it's too late—it's been 15sec. and the water has automatically turned off. Though it's hard to look past the atrocity of the showers, the rest of the hostel is similarly euuughkk. Wi-Fi is weak and only works in the lobby. Breakfast ends at 9am. The first floor seems to be home to some kind of daycare, so babies scream loudly 3-5pm every day. Worst of all, the blankets. While we have accepted that blanket-washing is always a rare thing, we usually manage to forget that. The terrifying white substance on ours forced us to remember.

But after all that, you have to stay here anyway. There are no other hostels in town. If somebody opens one between the moment we write this and the moment you read it, though, go stay there.

i Just off Rue des Écoles Laïques. Dorms June-Sept €22.60; Oct-May €21.40. Reception 8am-noon and 2pm-midnight.

montpellier

monument, tinged purple, pink, or deep blue depending on the light. The whole affair stretches from east to west, basically guaranteeing stunning vistas at any hour of the day, but we recommend coming at sunset. That's when the indie bands and men with accordions come out to play. It's also when the sun dips directly in line with Aqueduct St-Clement (yep, there's an 18th-century aqueduct too).

i Free.

MUSÉE FABRE

13 Rue Montpelliéret   ☎04 67 14 83 00 http://museefabre.montpellier3m.fr

The Musée Fabre is the best fine-art museum in Montpellier and one of the better fine-art museums in France. Thanks to major renovations in 2003-2007, the place is now huge: it covers nearly 100,000 sq. ft. and offers pretty thorough coverage of Western art of the last 600 years. We were particularly impressed by its 17th-century Dutch collection. Dead chickens, dead bulls, angry dogs killing chickens and bulls—the Musée Fabre has it all.

i Free. Tours €8, students €5.50. Open Tu-Su 10am-6pm.

PLACE DE LA COMÉDIE

Did you go see Pl. Massena in Nice, Pl. Bellecour in Lyon, or Pl. du Capitole in Toulouse? This is like that. It's a masterwork of urban planning and architecture. Lights, stones, humongous allegorical statue. Big fountain, beautiful city hall, people-watching. It's a public square in France. You get the gist.

i Free.

FOOD

🍴 CHE BOLUDO EMPANADAS ARGENTINAS $

10 Rue Boussairolles

Mmmmmmmmmmmmmm. The deliciousness of these empanadas is best expressed in the form of an extended groan of sheer gustatory ecstasy. Flaky, crunchy, meaty, and above all piping hot—a Che Boludo empanada is everything an empanada should be. The Argentine pastries come in a wide range of varieties and sell for a flat rate of €3.50 each. We ordered three but regret not ordering more, partially because they were so delicious and partially because they're only medium-size. Count on four, unless you're really hungry, in which case you should add a dessert empanada at the end.

i Empanadas €3.50. Open daily 7-11:30pm.

BAGEL & U $

66 Rue de l'Aiguillerie   ☎04 67 56 38 78
7 Rue en Gondeau   ☎04 34 81 65 70

Much as we dislike the name (does "Bagel & U" sound like a tween clothing store to anyone else?), this little bagel store is an absolute gem. The bagels are fairly large to begin with, and they're made larger when the staff stuffs them chock-full of fresh veggies, cheeses, and meats (we recommend anything with bacon). The natural result of being so delicious, the tiny Montpellier chain has two locations: on Rue de l'Aiguillerie, which is conveniently close to Montpellier's only hostel, and on Rue en Gondeau, which isn't too far from Pl. de la Comédie. Best of all, coffee is self-serve, and the staff seems quite loosey-goosey about when/how much you can have.

i Bagels €5.50-6.80.

PLAYFOOD $

16 Bd. Louis Blanc   ☎04 34 22 61 52 www.playfood.fr

Playfood gets too much credit for originality. We'll admit: on the surface, the concept (called "*verrines*") does seem new and fresh. Tiny portions? Of strange gourmet foods? Served in shotglasses? Cool, we're adventurous, sign us up. But probe that a little deeper. Doesn't "tiny portions designed for sharing" sound a little bit... familiar? It's just tapas in a glass, friends. That aside, Playfood's dishes are both strange and enticing. For just €2 a pop, you can sample dishes like beet risotto, sweet potato soufflé, and salmon mousse. There are about 12 savory and 12 sweet varieties to choose from on any given day, and while there doesn't seem to be any official menu, staff are willing to recite (and re-recite) names and ingredients in both English and French at the drop of a hat. Taste-wise, the *verrines* can be hit and miss. We would enthusiastically recommend the pineapple upside-down cake; we would not recommend the thing with the lentils. Visually, though, Playfood is a guaranteed win. Bring your DSLR and your quirkiest Warby Parkers—these dainty colorful glasses have "100 likes" written all over them.

i *Verrines €2.20. Open M-W 7:30-10:30pm, Th-Sa noon-1:30pm and 7:30-10:30pm, Su 7:30-10:30pm.*

NIGHTLIFE

THE SHAKESPEARE PUB

12 Rue de la Petite Loge   ☎04 67 60 22 25 www.shakespearepub.fr

To beer or not to beer? That is the obligatory joke. Unlike that cringe-inducing Shakespeare pun, the Shakespeare Pub is actually good. In fact, it is a warm, beery, English-speaking oasis in the midst of a cool, winey, French-speaking desert. Located in a narrow alley just up the road from the hostel, the pub attracts expats from all kinds of English-speaking countries, especially the UK (Brits know how to drink). This is probably, at least in part, because of the programming: Monday is poker night, Tuesday is quiz night, and Thursday is €2 shots. We also noticed a very lively game of Twister. If you're feeling a bit lonely/nostalgic/desperateto-play-Twister-with-your-Anglo-brothers-and-sisters, the Shakespeare Pub is where it's at.

i *Open June 21-Aug 31 M-F 4pm-2am, Sa 2pm-2am, Su 4pm-2am; Sept 1-June 20 M 4pm-midnight, Tu-F 4pm-1am, Sa 2pm-1am, Su 4pm-midnight.*

GRAND CAFE RICHE

8 Pl. de la Comédie   ☎04 67 54 71 44

It's midnight. You're sitting in a woven linen chair, holding a glass of red wine in one hand. Crowds of French—in black jumpsuits and high heels, in blue jeans and black tees—clatter across the smooth flagstones of Pl. de la Comédie, back-lit against the watery blue lights of the fountain. You take a drag on your long cigarette. Now you, too, are French.

i *Wine €2.80-3.80. Small beer €3-3.70; large €5.40-6. Cocktails €8. Open daily 7am-midnight.*

ESSENTIALS

Practicalities

- **TOURIST OFFICES:** 30 Allée Jean de Lattre de Tassigny. (☎04 67 60 60 60. Open M-Sa 9:30am-7:30pm, Su 10am-5pm.)

- **POST OFFICES:** 15 Rue Rondelet. (☎04 67 34 51 11. Open M-W 9am-6pm, Th 9am-noon, F 9am-6pm, Sa 9am-12:30pm.)

Emergency

- **EMERGENCY NUMBERS:** General emergencies ☎112. Ambulance ☎15. Police ☎17. Fire ☎18.

- **POLICE:** For non-emergencies, call the police station at ☎04 99 13 50 00.

- **LATE-NIGHT PHARMACIES: Pharmacie de la Gare.** (2 Rue Serane. ☎04 67 58 37 68. Open 24hr.)

montpellier

- **HOSPITALS: Centre Hospitalier Régional Universitaire de Montpellier.** (191 Av. du Doyen Gaston Giraud. ☎04 67 33 67 33 www.chu-montpellier.fr.)

Getting There

Fly into Montpellier–Méditerranée Airport (MPL), a mid-size airport a few miles outside the city. **Trains** arrive at Montpellier St-Roch station. From there, take Tram 2 into the city center.

Getting Around

Montpellier is a sizable city—count on using public transit. Fortunately, TaM (Montpellier's **tram** system) covers most of the city, and its trams are quick, clean, and reliable.(www.tam-voyages.com.)

avignon

Avignon is a city with a strong medieval flavor. Ringed by massive fortifications, filled with soaring Gothic cathedrals, and crisscrossed by narrow cobblestone streets, the place looks like it could be an artist's recreation of the year 1322.

There's a reason for that. Though Avignon has thousands of years of history, it reached its heyday in the 14th century, when it was briefly the seat of the Catholic Church. Yes, that's right—from 1309 to 1377, seven popes and two anti-popes (it's complicated) lived in a massive Gothic palace in the center of the city. For 14th-century serfs and bishops, this represented a seismic moment in church history. For 21st-century tourists, this represents a seismic selfie, and probably also a tour.

A piece of advice: treat Avignon as a (deeply historical) timeout from your raging speed-of-light Eurotrip. Avignon is, after all, a small town. It's no Paris, it's no Lyon. Yes, tour the Popes' Palace—yes, walk the Pont d'Avignon—but do so slowly, with an ice-cream cone held loosely in one hand. Once you're done, take a dip in your hostel's inexplicable Olympic-size pool. Maybe window-shop a little. It's the French countryside. It's gucci.

SIGHTS

⬛ PALAIS DES PAPES

Pl. du Palais   www.palais-des-papes.com

Yes, you've already been to Vatican City. Yes, tickets are expensive. Yes, you saw six historical monuments last week. We don't care, Jeffrey. You're going to the Popes' Palace and THEN you can eat ice cream. The Popes' Palace is the reason that Avignon is famous—it's one of the most popular monuments in France—and a visit there is absolutely non-negotiable. Built in 1335, it's the largest Gothic palace in Europe (the size of about four standard Gothic cathedrals). More importantly, through the 14th and 15th centuries, it was home to seven popes and two anti-popes, leaders of a western movement to challenge the authority of the Italian popes. Made up of 25 rooms ranging from chapels to treasuries to the popes' private chambers, the palace is a masterpiece of medieval architecture and is basically littered with spectacular 600-year-old frescos and statues. While the Popes' Palace is certainly gorgeous, it's important more for its history than its visuals. For the full historical-soap-opera experience, fork over the extra €2 for an audio tour.

i €11, students €9. Combination ticket with Pont d'Avignon €13.50/10.50. Open daily July 9am-8pm; Aug 9am-8:30pm; Sept-Oct 9am-7pm; Nov-Feb 9:30am-5:45pm; Mar 9am-6:30pm; Apr-June 9am-7pm.

france

a tale of two (well-armed) cities

Today, Avignon might seem tame: a sleepy little touristy city. Somewhere to buy ice cream and postcards and little sachets of lavender to put in your sock drawer to make your socks smell nice. Those massive city walls? Those tiny arrow slits? The strange preponderance of giant mountaintop fortresses in the immediate vicinity? Probably decorative.

Not even close. Over the last several thousand years, this little vacation destination has seen some shit. Occupied since the Neolithic Period and named Avignon (well, Avenion) around 539 BCE, Avignon was conquered and reconquered on repeat for thousands of years. Walls kept getting busted up. Houses kept getting razed. Vineyards kept getting burned. By the 14th century, things hadn't gotten much better. Perched right on the Rhone River (which was the border between two major empires), Avignon technically belonged to the Holy Roman Empire but was within eyesight of the Kingdom of France. This proximity freaked everybody out—and when Pope Clement V moved to Avignon beginning in 1309 and the city became the seat of the Holy Roman Empire, it got serious.

The Holy Roman Empire got things going by building the Popes' Palace, with giant walls even more massively reinforced than the humongous city walls already were. The Kingdom of France responded by building Fort St-André in Villeneuve-lès-Avignon, a monster of a hilltop fortress with an excellent view of the Popes' Palace. Crenellations, arrow slits, barbicans—though these two behemoths never actually engaged in battle with one another, they were not kidding around. Nearly 800 years later, the two fortresses still perch on their respective hilltops, glaring angrily across the Rhone.

FORT SAINT-ANDRÉ

Rue Montée du Fort, Villeneuve-lès-Avignon   ☎04 90 25 45 35 www.fort-saint-andre.fr

A selfie taken from the ground, set against the bottom half of a medieval papal palace: not bad. A selfie taken squeezed between the crenellations of the highest tower of an ancient French fortress, set against a gorgeous pastoral vista and the silhouetted spires of the aforementioned medieval papal palace: really not bad. For the most breathtaking view in all of Avignon, leave the city center and walk, bike, or bus 3km to Fort St-André. Built from 1291 and used to defend the border between the Kingdom of France and the Holy Roman Empire (i.e., the popes living in the palace across the river), Fort St-André is no prissy *château*. Instead, this massive fort sprawls tall and muscular across the top of a big-ass hill, offering panoramic views of the surrounding countryside. Explore the cavernous medieval architecture. Eyeball centuries' worth of graffiti (including mysterious scripts, Templar crosses, and some rather ominous inscriptions by someone named "Dragon," circa 1790). Best of all, climb the winding stone staircases all the way to the end and emerge—solitary, regal, triumphant—at the top of the towers. Pro tip: on your way back down, scan the towers' outer walls for latrines. The stains are hard to miss.

i €5.50, students €4.50, under 18 free. Open daily June-Sept 10am-6pm; Oct-May 10am-1pm and 2-5pm.

avignon

PONT D'AVIGNON

☎04 32 74 32 74

The main takeaway of this tourist attraction is, "It used to be really hard to build a bridge." According to legend, the Pont d'Avignon was first completed in 1185 by St-Bénézet, who had received direct orders from God. Unfortunately, the strong current of the Rhone soon washed portions of the bridge away. For centuries afterward, the residents of Avignon tried to rebuild the bridge, but always it was washed away. Even today, "the bridge to nowhere" juts only halfway across the Rhone River.

Unfortunately, while the view of the half-bridge wreathed in morning fog is hauntingly beautiful, you can't actually see the Pont d'Avignon while you're on the Pont d'Avignon. The view is much better from the nearby, free Daladier Bridge or from the far side of the river. On the other hand, the Pont d'Avignon is more than a view—it's also a mildly interesting piece of history. If you're already planning to visit the Popes' Palace (which you are), you might as well buy the Palace/Bridge combo ticket for an extra €1.50 and stop by the Pont d'Avignon.

i €5, students €4. Combination ticket with Palais des Papes €13.50/10.50. Open daily July 9am-8pm; Aug 9am-8:30pm; Sept-Oct 9am-7pm; Nov-Feb 9:30am-5:45pm; Mar 9am-6:30pm; Apr-June 9am-7pm.

ROCHER LES DOMS
Montée des Moulins

Like Jennifer Lawrence at the Oscars, Rocher Les Doms is a quick, reliable trip. A rocky cliff on the side of the Rhone topped by a small public garden, Rocher Les Doms features tiny waterfalls, a duck pond, and panoramic views of the city and river. Peer into the horizon and you'll even spot Fort St-André. Best of all, unlike every other tourist attraction in this supremely touristy city, this cliffside garden is free. Bring a book, buy a popsicle (ahh, they got you after all), and spend 30min. enjoying the shade and the view.

i Off Pl. du Palais. Free. Open daily June-Aug 7:30am-9pm; Sept 7:30am-8pm; Oct 7:30am-6:30pm; Nov 7:30am-6pm; Dec-Jan 7:30am-5:30pm; Feb 7:30am-6pm; Mar 7:30am-7pm; Apr-May 7:30am-8pm.

FOOD

🏵 LE COCHON BLEU
$$

9 Rue d'Annanelle ☎04 90 82 95 10

This is the French food you've always dreamed of. Le Cochon Bleu is a spectacular little restaurant located just 5min. from Rue de la République. Stay in a cheap hostel and splurge on a three-course meal so delicious you'll never enjoy your meal plan again—we ordered buttered *escargots* as an appetizer (so creamy!), duck fillet with cherries and crunchy polenta as a main course (so tender!), and roasted St. Marcellin cheese with honey for dessert (so GOOD!). For a better bargain, come at noon and order the lunch menu: two courses and a glass of wine for €15. Sit on the terrace if you can, or venture inside for a view of the restaurant's eponymous blue glass pigs.

i Lunch menu €15. Dinner menu €29. Open Tu noon-2pm and 7:30-10pm, W-Sa noon-2pm and 7-10pm.

COUSCOUSSERIE DE L'HORLAGE
$$

18 Pl. de l'Horlage ☎04 90 85 84 86

This *couscousserie* is a Moroccan restaurant with three charms. 1) Location. If you're within Avignon's city walls, Couscousserie de l'Horlage is probably convenient. Right at the base of the Popes' Palace, smack-dab in the middle of Pl. de l'Horlage, this little place could make a strong claim for the best location in Avignon. 2) Value. Portions are well priced and massive (seriously, you could

france

POP HOSTEL $$
17 Rue de la République   ☎04 32 40 50 60 www.pophostel.fr

Staying at Pop Hostel is kind of like adopting a golden retriever—both are almost perfect. Pop Hostel is located in the absolute heart of Avignon, just steps away from some of the city's best food, sights, nightlife, and shopping. The bathrooms are spacious and clean; the common space is colorful and centrally located; the bedrooms are neat and airy, all with big metal lockboxes and plenty of outlet space. Best of all, the bar is hoppin' (or should we say poppin'): happy hour takes place every day 5-8pm, with glasses of wine for €1 and half-pints of beer for €1.80. The whole shebang is even moderately priced, with beds starting at just €24 per night. Like a good puppy, Pop Hostel can satisfy almost all of your emotional needs. But—we say "almost." Underneath all of their beauty and energy and inspirational zest for life, golden retrievers are heart-wrenchingly inbred critters. Similarly (?), Pop Hostel has bad Wi-Fi. Yep, you heard us. The Wi-Fi doesn't work at all. Accept this, and email your mom on one of the available desktop computers instead.

i Dorms from €24.

AUBERGE BAGATELLE $
25 Allée Antoine Pinay   ☎04 90 86 30 39 www.auberge-bagatelle.com

Auberge Bagatelle has no frills. Soap? Frill. Lockbox? Frill. Top sheet on your bunk bed? Frill. Bagatelle is first and foremost a campground—most people come with an RV and a family—and the *auberge* (hostel) part seems like more of an afterthought. Thanks to the camping culture, expect very little in terms of amenities. There's an upside to this austerity, though: with beds starting at €13 a night, the place is super, super, super cheap. More practically, Bagatelle is just on the far bank of the Rhone River, so it's very walkable (about 1km to the city center). Stay here if you plan on spending €40 on dinner and need to offset the cost.

i On Île de la Barthelasse. Dorms €13-15.

YMCA AVIGNON $$
7bis Chemin de la Justice   ☎04 90 25 46 20 www.ymca-avignon.com

The YMCA is a lovely hostel with a very misleading name. This hostel is located more than 2km outside Avignon, in the similarly named but distinctly different village of Villeneuve-lès-Avignon. It's a doable commute (just follow the highway), but it is a commute. Location aside, though, the place is lovely. Private bedrooms (with shared bath) are clean and spacious, there's an airy restaurant with a pool table and games for use as a common space, and the terrace offers a gorgeous view of the surrounding landscape. Best of all, the whole building is structured around a massive, pristine pool. Thanks to this, most hostelers seem to be able to overlook YMCA Avignon's locational shortcomings: the place is frequently booked solid.

i High-season singles €30; doubles €39.

avignon

split this with a friend). A monster plate of couscous and an even larger bowl of veggies and broth cost €10, and a giant, perfectly seared chicken breast makes it €13. When the waiter brought our food, we thought they'd misplaced a decimal. 3) The Yum Factor. Salty, savory, melt-in-your-mouth tender—this place is a win. Couscous, veggies, and meat come separately, so that the eater controls the breakdown of each in every bite. At first, we found this intimidating—the perfect combination of chickpeas, couscous, and perfect juicy chicken is an elusive thing. Upon further reflection, we appreciate the challenge.

i Veggie couscous €10. Couscous with meat from €13. Open daily 11am-3pm and 6pm-1am.

JEAN LE GOURMAND $
15 Rue St-Agricol   ☎04 90 22 09 58

The only bad thing we have to say about Jean le Gourmand as a breakfast spot is that it also sells ice cream, forcing us to make a tough choice before noon. That aside, this is a solid and cheap way to find real breakfast in Avignon. A small open-air creperie just next to Pl. de l'Horloge, Jean le Gourmand offers enormous crepes on the cheap. The crepe-making process is fully machine-operated (a little mechanical arm swivels around and flattens the batter to perfection), so breakfast isn't exactly made with love, but it is made with cool tech—and, in the end, are the two really so different? Order a ham and cheese crepe the length and width of your arm for €3, or shake it up with tomato pesto or salmon.

i Crepes €1-4. Open M-Sa 11am-7:30pm, Su 2-7pm.

LES TROIS BONHEURS $$
5 Rue des Trois Carreaux   ☎04 90 82 08 69

Though slightly off the beaten path, this second-floor walkup Chinese restaurant is worth a bit of map-reading and direction-asking. Small, quiet, and dotted with tapestries and paper lanterns, Les Trois Bonheurs offers a decent range of Chinese dishes at a reasonable price (especially before 9pm, when you can order an appetizer and a main course off the house special menu for €7.50). Portions are small to mid-size, and menus are in French, but if you're tired of *escargots* and just want a moderate quantity of pineapple chicken, this is your best bet in Avignon.

i Special menu €7.50 before 9pm. Regular dishes €7-15. Open M-Tu 11:45am-2:45pm and 7-11pm, Th-Su 11:45am-2:45pm and 7-11pm.

NIGHTLIFE

ARTEBAR
25 Rue St-Jean le Vieux   ☎07 86 17 83 76

Contrary to its name and its deceptively sleek black-and-white exterior, Artebar is not a particularly artsy bar. People don't come here to have a quiet glass of wine or discuss the latest film noir, nor could they if they wanted to. The flashing colored lights are dazzlingly distracting, and the thumping bass in the background drowns out all speech more enlightened than "Heyyyy." Pubby, rowdy, and tacky in a fun way, Artebar is one of the busiest bars in Pl. Pie, which is in turn one of Avignon's best late-night hotspots. Avoid the energetic/seizure-inducing interior and snag a table with everybody else on the terrace. Come early, though—like most bars in Avignon, Artebar closes at 1am.

RED SKY
21 Rue St-Jean le Vieux   ☎04 90 85 93 23

Red Sky's vibe is an equal mix of 1970s disco America and 1870s distinctly less disco Germany. Pass the heavy wooden façade and you'll be greeted by a close darkness lit, in part, by blinking red numbers on the wall. As you watch, they change. 82… 83… 82… Equal parts quirky and ominous, this display keeps track of the volume of the pounding bass. Spoiler: it stays loud. Don't let this scare you away, though—as with Artebar, which is just a couple doors down, the best ambience is on the terrace. Order a "Pink Chloe" (cocktails come with free glowsticks) and use its phosphorescent light to guide your way outside.

i Cocktails €7. Open daily 9am-1:30am.

LE CID CAFÉ

11 Pl. de l Horloge   ☎04 90 82 30 38 www.lecidcafe.com

Le Cid Café is the place you and your girlfriends take Miranda when she's totally over him but she's had a hard week and she just needs some red wine and a martini, OK?! Centrally located right on Pl. de l'Horloge, Le Cid Café is gold, glittery, and chic all over. Order a moderately priced beer or a ritzy-glitzy cocktail: we recommend the Globe Trotteur (vodka, Soho, pineapple juice, and grenadine). If you prefer your alcohol in dessert form, finish the evening with a Grand Marnier crepe. Le Cid Café isn't really a place to turn up, but then again neither is Avignon. Have a few drinks here, then go home, and take a hot bath.

i Beer €3.20-5. Cocktails €10. Crepes and waffles €3.20-6.50. Open daily 6:30am-1am.

ESSENTIALS

Practicalities

- **TOURIST OFFICES:** 41 Cours Jean Jaurès. (☎04 32 74 32 74. Open July daily 9am-7pm; Aug-Oct M-Sa 9am-6pm, Su 10am-5pm; Nov-Mar M-F 9am-6pm, Sa 9am-5pm, Su 10am-noon; Apr-June M-Sa 9am-6pm, Su 10am-5pm.)
- **POST OFFICE:** Cours Président Kennedy. (☎04 90 27 54 10. Open M-F 8:30am-6:30pm, Sa 8:30am-noon.)

Emergency

- **EMERGENCY NUMBERS:** General emergencies ☎112. Ambulance ☎15. Police ☎17. Fire ☎18.
- **POLICE:** For non-emergencies, call the local police at ☎04 90 16 81 00.
- **HOSPITALS: Centre Hospitalier Henri Duffaut.** (305 Rue Raoul Follereau. ☎04 32 75 33 33 www.ch-avignon.fr.)

Getting There

Avignon has a small international **airport** (AVN), but flights may be cheaper out of nearby Marseille (MRS). From Marseille, the trip to Avignon is an easy train or bus ride. **Trains** arrive at Gare d'Avignon-Centre, which is just across the street from Avignon's city walls and Rue de la République. TGV (high-speed) trains service the city from a farther-away station, Gare d'Avignon TGV.

Getting Around

Avignon is a very small city. It has **bus** service, but if you're within the city walls and if you're able, it's probably easier to walk. Pick up a map from the tourist office and plan to tackle the city on foot.

aix-en-provence

Wander into the center of Aix-en-Provence and take a deep whiff. Go ahead, breathe it in. The first thing you'll notice is the strong scent of French countryside. Pine, olive, maybe a hint of lavender. The region of Provence is famous for its natural beauty and sleepy pastoral vibe, and Aix manages to strike the perfect balance between "quaint rural village" and "city large enough to actually have things to do."

Now, take a second sniff. Is that—turpentine? Thanks to all that natural beauty, Aix has been the playground of famous artists and intellectuals like Paul Cézanne, Émile Zola, and Ernest Hemingway. Wander through any Impressionist/Fauvist/Cubist art gallery in the world, and you'll probably spot Aix, immortalized beautifully and

get a room!

AUBERGE DE JEUNESSE JAS DU BOUFFON $$

3 Av. Marcel Pagnol   ☎04 42 20 15 99 www.auberge-jeunesse-aix.fr

If you're looking to visit Aix-en-Provence and you don't want to rent a hotel room or camp in the woods, Auberge de Jeunesse Jas du Bouffon is your only bet. Luckily, Jas du Bouffon isn't half-bad, considering that it's completely cornered the market and can basically do what it wants. Many bedrooms come with little balconies overlooking the parking lot, and there are three large common spaces—a breakfast room, a restaurant, and the aforementioned parking lot—which means lots of gathering spaces for your soon-to-be best friends. More strangely, the hallways also tend to become social spaces: each bedroom has only one outlet, so anybody looking to charge a cell phone (i.e., everyone) ends up migrating to the hall. Think of this as an (annoying) opportunity. Located right on the edge of the Aix-en-Provence city center, Auberge de Jeunesse Jas du Bouffon is about a 30min. walk from downtown. Fortunately, there's also a bus stop right outside the hostel. If the bus is running late, wander down the street and check out Bastide du Jas du Bouffon—the childhood home of Paul Cézanne—while you wait.

i Take bus #2 and get off at Vasarely. High-season dorms €23-27; low-season €19-23.

weirdly, at least once. Wander through an Aixois art gallery, and you'll see it about a gazillion times.

But that's not all. Sniff one last time. What is that—that lingering, dusty, faintly green smell? It reminds you of Beverly Hills... of the Upper East Side... Ah! Old money. In the 17th century, Aix oozed wealth like a perfect *éclair* oozes cream, and its stunning *grand siècle* urban design and architecture show it. In fact, its main street (Cours Mirabeau) was built when the town's wealthy demanded a new place to promenade their expensive carriages led by their expensive horses with their expensive families inside. Spend two days in Aix, and dress nice.

SIGHTS

COURS MIRABEAU

Cours Mirabeau is basically the jugular of Aix-en-Provence. A wide, pedestrian-heavy street dotted with plane trees, Cours Mirabeau runs all the way through the middle of downtown Aix. Fountains dating back as far as the 17th century divide the street every 100m or so, making for excellent selfie stops (especially the "mossy fountain," whose warm water flows directly from a hot spring). Once you've done your first lap, join tourists and locals alike and nurse a drink on one of the many terraces that line the street. Pro tip: Cours Mirabeau is great for day-drinking, but a bit too touristy for day-eating. For that, venture further into Old Aix.

GRANET MUSEUM

Pl. St-Jean de Malte   ☎04 42 52 88 32

Have you ever wanted to see the shattered remnants of a statue of an ancient Gallic warrior gripping the severed heads of his enemies? Have you ever wanted to see said statue in a museum located only a few miles from the site where it was built, broken, and buried for thousands of years? What a coincidence! The Granet Museum has such a thing! This museum has both a small but mighty wing of local ancient history and a world-class collection of 18th- to 20th-century art. Block out some serious time for its temporary exhibitions (the recent Camoin exhibit was so lovely we cried) and even longer for the permanent ones (Cézanne? Giacometti? Picasso? Yeah, you've met).

i €5.50, students and under 18 free. Open Tu-Su in summer 10am-7pm; in winter noon-6pm.

PAVILLON DE VENDÔME

13 Rue de la Molle ☎04 42 91 88 75

The Pavillon de Vendôme is a quiet French paradise located on the northern edge of town. Originally built in 1652 as a gift from a wealthy duke to his lover, today the quaint house and garden stand as a testament to old-timey French love. Dainty rose curtains flutter in every window; excessively geometric shrubs line every path; a perfectly manicured lawn stretches from wall to wall without a dandelion in sight (seriously, somebody's got a team of gardeners on this). For a historically accurate self-guided tour, stand in a balcony and chuckle at the plight of the hungry 17th-century peasants. For a slightly less cynical experience, bring that hostel hottie you've been eyeing and canoodle on one of the many low stone benches. Either way, when you're done, make sure to pop inside and check out the art collections currently on display.

i Garden free. House €3.50, students and under 25 free. Open M 10am-12:30pm and 1:30-6pm, W-Su 10am-12:30pm and 1:30-6pm.

ATELIER DE CÉZANNE

9 Av. Paul Cézanne ☎04 42 21 06 53 www.atelier-cezanne.com

Like anyone with an Instagram account, Paul Cézanne understood the importance of good lighting. In fact, the artist was notoriously light-obsessed and designed his *atelier*—studio—to reflect that. The box-like hilltop studio faces north for the steadiest possible light, and its walls have been painted (and repainted, and repainted) the perfect shade of non-reflective bluish-gray. It's also home to many vases, jugs, and mannequins now memorialized in his work as well as an easel still stained with blue paint from one of his most famous works, *The Bathers*. Take a perfectly lit selfie, join the English tour at 5pm, then take the #5 bus (or walk—it's not too far) back to the city center.

i €2.50.

SAINTE-VICTOIRE MOUNTAIN

Route du Tholonet ☎04 42 29 05 37

A short drive from the city center, Ste-Victoire Mountain looms white, balding, and approachable like an igneous Joe Biden. Strap on your hiking shoes, pack your swimsuit (mountain lakes, people!), and take bus #110 or #140 to Aix-en-Provence's most popular daytrip. Paths are clearly marked and meticulously maintained, but it's a lengthy climb, so you'll want to block off a whole day. If Cézanne could paint this mountain a bajillion times, you can spend a day wandering on top of it.

FOOD

🍴 SPY'S $

2 Rue d'Italie ☎08 99 86 88 03

A colorful little stand with a small terrace near the center of Old Aix, Spy's is a safe bet for a moderately sized, moderately priced midday pick-me-up. Wraps come hot, grilled, and surprisingly gourmet ("Le Saumon" includes smoked salmon, guacamole, fresh goat cheese, grilled almonds, and olive oil), and their prices peak below €7. Vive la cheap lunch!

i Wraps €5-6.30. Open M 3-7pm, Tu-Th 10am-10pm, F-Sa 10am-11pm.

PIZZA CAPRI $

48 Rue Espariat   ☎04 42 24 84 73 www.pizza-capri.fr
1 Rue Fabrot   ☎04 42 38 55 43 www.pizza-capri.fr
48-50 Pl. Richelme   ☎04 42 21 49 01 www.pizza-capri.fr

Pizza Capri is so popular among tourists and locals alike that it has three locations in Aix-en-Provence. We have three hypotheses for this popularity. 1) They're all fairly centrally located and easy to find. 2) They sell pizza by the slice, which is weirdly rare (come on, southern France, we don't want to eat an entire pizza by ourselves, but we will if we have to). 3) Dessert pizza. Yeah, we like the concept too. Unfortunately, as much as we value sugar-based creativity, "Nutella and almond pizza" should probably stay conceptual—it's just not as yummy as it sounds. By all means, come to Pizza Capri, but keep it savory. You can always order a crepe after.

TONKIN FOOD $

11 Rue Boulegon   ☎06 75 32 86 50 www.tonkinfood.fr

The best reason to come to this teensy Vietnamese restaurant is the owners' teensy Vietnamese child. She seems to have free rein over the joint and spends her evenings running around pointing and laughing adorably. For real, that smile melted our cold, dead hearts. Wave at the small child, order a big bowl of pho to go (Tonkin is primarily a takeout joint, although there are also tables in-house), then eat perched on the edge of the nearest 17th-century fountain.

i   *Pho €8. Open M 6-9:45pm, Th-Su 6-9:45pm.*

JARDIN D'AMALULA $

7 Rue Mignet   ☎04 42 63 04 05

We don't know who Amalula is, but we suspect she has tiny wings and lives in a buttercup, because Jardin d'Amalula feels like a fairy garden. Nestled within a canopied backyard oasis, this little gem of a restaurant specializes in breakfasts, desserts, and unadulterated childlike joy. Order a tart with meringue in the shape of a perfectly toasted rose or a basket of fluffy bread and an array of tiny jams.

i   *Breakfast €4.50-8.10. Dessert €6-9.50. Open M-Sa 9:30am-5pm.*

NIGHTLIFE

AU P'TIT QUART D'HEURE

21 Pl. Forum des Cardeurs   www.auptitquartdheure.fr

Aix-en-Provence isn't a rowdy-neon-club kind of city. Aix-en-Provence isn't a splashy-sticky-pub kind of city. No, wealthy, genteel, and just a little bit self-satisfied, Aix-en-Provence is a wine bar kind of city—and the best wine bar in this wine bar city is Au P'tit Quart d'Heure. The bar itself is way too small for indoor seating, but it opens onto Pl. Forum des Cardeurs, so nab a table outside and sip your wine in the twinkliest nighttime square in Aix.

i   *Wine of the month €2.50. Small beer €2.50-3.50; large €5-6.50. Open Tu-Sa 10am-1pm and 3-9pm.*

O'SULLIVAN'S

61 Pl. des Augustins

So you're a pint-o'-beer kinda person in a *verre-du-vin* kinda city. Don't despair—Aix has a decent range of pubs, O'Sullivan's first among them. Located slightly outside the main nightlife region of Old Aix (which is a good thing, because Old Aix is a maze at night), O'Sullivan's occupies a tiny plaza off Cours Mirabeau. It's this plaza that makes the bar unique: while the interior is traditionally pubby, the terrace is much calmer. In fact, the outdoor seating surrounds a burbling fountain that's just loud enough to mask the loud, drunken sportsiness inside. It's still an Irish pub, but with a slightly Provençal take.

i   *Open M-Sa 11am-2pm, Su 1pm-2am.*

23 Cours Sextius

"I wanna go where the locals goooo," you croon in your best *Little Mermaid* impression. Stop. Think. How many locals have you actually befriended in southern France? Zero. French locals are cool, and French, and already have their own cool French local friends. They don't need you. Tourists, on the other hand, are exactly as friendly/desperate as you are. IPN knows this and makes it work. As the name implies, IPN is a basement club that caters almost exclusively to tourists. Expect a preponderance of hairy backpackers, American music, and sweat. Hopefully, you're into all three, because if you're looking to turn up in Aix and you don't want to go to a strip club or Le César (€1 shots, and no, that's not a good thing), IPN is your best bet.

i Open Tu-Sa 6pm-4am.

ESSENTIALS
Practicalities

- **TOURIST OFFICES:** The tourist office is in **Les Allées Provençales.** (300 Av. Giuseppe Verdi. ☎04 42 16 11 61. Open Apr-Sept M-Sa 8:30am-7pm, Su 10am-1pm and 2-6pm; Oct-Mar M-Sa 8:30am-6pm.)

- **POST OFFICES:** Sq. Colonel Mattei. (☎36 31. Open M-W 9am-6:30pm, Th 9am-noon and 2:15-6:30pm, F 9am-6:30pm, Sa 9am-noon and 2-5pm.)

Emergency

- **EMERGENCY NUMBERS:** General emergencies ☎112. Ambulance ☎15. Police ☎17. Fire ☎18.

- **LATE-NIGHT PHARMACIES: Pharmacie des Precheurs.** (2 Rue Peyresc. ☎04 42 38 18 60. Open 24hr.)

- **HOSPITALS:** ☎04 42 33 90 28.

Getting There

To get to Aix by **plane,** fly into nearby Marseille (MRS). From Marseille, take the train or bus to Aix-en-Provence Centre. **Trains** to Aix-en-Provence are operated by SNCF and arrive at one of two stations: Aix-en-Provence Centre (which is walking distance from the city center) or Aix-en-Provence TGV (which is a long cab ride from the city center). For maximum convenience, make sure your train arrives at the former.

Getting Around

Aix-en-Provence is fairly walkable, with a single exception: the city's only hostel is several kilometers from the city center.

cassis

Cassis is the sweet spot of southern France. Snuggled on the southern edge of Provence, it seeps pastoral sweetness from every colorful clay pore. Arguably the westernmost point of the Riviera, it offers sweeping vistas, endless skies, and blue, blue, blue sea. The winding streets are fringed with hibiscus and bougainvillea. The air is fresh and salty. The people are kind. Best of all, Cassis is less than 20 mi. from Marseille. This is exactly close enough that intercity travel is easy (just 20min. by train), and exactly far enough that the smell doesn't carry over.

cassis

SIGHTS

CALANQUES

The lobby of the Empire State Building is pretty nice, but you don't come for the lobby. No, you hustle through the lobby so that you can stand on that little platform and take blurry panoramas while throwing pennies at the unsuspecting dorks below. Similarly, sweet as downtown Cassis may be, it's not really the point of Cassis. You don't come here for the ports, the churches, or the nightlife (hahahahaha). No, you come for the *calanques*.

Although *calanque* translates to "cove" or "creek," the term is unique to Provence and Corsica, and you should just call them *calanques* (cah-LONKS). Basically, *calanques* are long watery valleys edged by steep rocky cliffs. Picture shallow bays the color of emeralds and sapphires, hidden beaches of tiny pebbles and sand, and towering ledges, bluffs, and crags. The coast from Cassis to Marseille is basically littered with these, but the most common daytrip involves the nearest three to Cassis: Port-Miou, Port-Pin, and En Veau.

No matter how many *calanques* you plan to see, make sure to prepare—the route there is fairly well marked and well maintained, but it's still going to take a couple hours of hiking. Bring comfortable shoes, because blisters would be annoying. Pack water, because gasping with thirst on an abandoned country road would be unpleasant. Charge your camera, because walking through the

get a room!

AUBERGE CASSIS HOSTEL $$$
4 Av. du Picouveau   ☎06 85 65 10 92/09 54 37 99 82 www.cassishostel.com

Why are the hostels in Cassis so nice? Wait, it's because they're €35 a night. Auberge Cassis Hostel feels like a five-star resort with bunk beds. The linens are the expensive kind of beige. The staff is unnaturally tall and attractive. The front yard is an infinity pool. The only real downside is the elevation: a little less than 10min. from downtown, the hostel perches at the top of a tall hill, making getting there a bit of a workout. On the bright side, this makes the view from the infinity pool all the more spectacular. Did we mention there's an infinity pool?

i High-season dorms from €30; mid-season €26; low-season €24.

MINI HOSTEL AU PETIT CHEZ SOI $$$
2 Rue Auguste Vidal   ☎06 71 81 37 44

Mini Hostel au Petit Chez Soi might be our favorite hostel in France. The place isn't especially luxurious—it's actually quite small, and it's a bunk-bed situation—but that doesn't matter, because it feels like home. Just 1min. from the port, the hostel is next to a beautiful old church and ringed by a leafy wall. The 12 beds are divided between two "apartments," each with its own bathroom and kitchen, but most evenings everyone eats together on the shared terrace. The owner, Anne-Marie ("Mimi"), and her spouse check in regularly and bring fresh bread and jam every morning. At €38 a night, it is considerably more expensive than the generic *auberge de jeunesse* located 100,000 mi. from town and slightly more expensive than the Auberge Cassis Hostel located a few minutes up the hill, but we spent the extra money and we'd do it again. This is the hostel your mother always wanted for you.

i High-season dorms €38; low-season €35.

france

most stunning natural beauty you've seen in your entire life and not keeping a record would be fucking tragic.

i Free.

LES ROCHES PLATES
Impasse du Littoral

This natural phenomenon has three names, some more appropriate than others. "The Flat Rocks": very clear. There are rocks. They are flat. "The White Rocks": fine. The rocks are also white. "Blue Beach": there is no "sand" here. There are no "pebbles" here. There are only giant boulders here. What about that says "beach" to you, Cassis? For the record, Les Roches Plates are a stony outcropping about 5min. from Port-Miou. A little smaller and more easily accessible than the *calanques*, they are the ideal place to nap in the sun or scream crazily and leap into the perfect azure sea—splash! Thanks to this versatility, the rocks are a hub for reckless kids, adrenaline-happy teens, and sun-hungry adults alike. Consider them a rest stop en route to the *calanques* or a destination in and of itself.

i Free.

FOOD

RESTAURANT LE CHAUDRON $$
4 Rue Adolphe Thiers   ☎04 42 01 74 18

Cash in those student loans, take out that second mortgage, and treat yourself to a meal at Le Chaudron. Start with the cheese assortment, two flaky pastry bundles of melted mozzarella and goat cheese, plus a salad. Fill up with a steak topped with caramelized onions, with roasted red peppers on the side. Finish with *crème caramel*, topped with real whipped cream and a swirly-twirly gingerbread wafer. Is this a meal appropriate for a college student on a budget? Frankly, no. But it will change you. And isn't that part of what travel is really about? (If your answer to that is "no," perhaps we can interest you in Les Frangines next door, a nearly as delicious and marginally cheaper version of Le Chaudron.)

i Open M 7-11pm, W-Su 7-11pm.

SNACKING LES CALANQUES $
1 Av. Victor Hugo   ☎04 42 01 73 13

For the uninitiated, "Snacking" is a word the French use to indicate any meal eaten after breakfast and before 7pm. In the case of Snacking Les Calanques, this means kiosk food: crepes, ice cream, panini, the whole shebang. The place has excellent real estate, directly on the port, and it is also reliably the busiest place in Cassis. Why? Either people are lazy, people are broke, or people genuinely dig this kiosk. We suspect it's some combination of the three. After all, though Snacking Les Calanques works cheap, it works well. In particular, we've gotta hand it to the waffles—golden brown, crunchy, and swimming in melted chocolate, just the way we like them. OK, our Belgian friend said she'd had better—but she had to think about it first.

i Crepes from €2. Waffles from €3. 1 scoop of ice cream €2.40. Open daily 8am-5pm.

NIGHTLIFE

BIG BEN
Pl. Georges Clemenceau   ☎06 11 83 20 30

Of Big Ben, Charles Dickens wrote, "It was the best of clubs. It was the worst of clubs. It was the only club." Big Ben doesn't measure up to the clubs further down the coast. There are no world-famous DJs here, no multi-million-dollar sound systems, no hordes of the young and the beautiful. Picture more of a "dark basement" vibe. It is, however, the only club in Cassis—and with a bit

cassis

of optimism and determination it can almost be a good time. For example, Big Ben sits right along the harbor, so at least you don't have to walk very far to be disappointed. For example, the empty dance floor means plenty of space to break out that new move you've been working on. For example, well... OK, two's all we've got.

i Beer €5. Shots €5. Open daily 11:45pm-5am.

CENDRILLON
Pl. Georges Clemenceau   ☎04 42 01 70 24

Cassis may have only one club, but it has a couple of places to buy alcohol. Of these, by far the best is Cendrillon. Compared to its competition (a handful of back-alley pubs where "cocktail" apparently gets translated as "glass full of tequila and literally nothing else"), Cendrillon is surprisingly bright, clean, and modern. Sip your moderately priced beer in the shiny interior or carry it out onto the terrace, which (say it with us now) faces out onto the harbor. The place is also right next door to Big Ben, which makes it the best place to drink—and drink, and drink, and drink—until the club seems good.

i Beer €3.40-8.40. Open M-Sa 7:30am-1:30am, Su 7:30am-midnight.

ESSENTIALS
Practicalities
- **TOURIST OFFICES:** Quai des Moulins. (☎08 92 25 98 92 www.ot-cassis.com. Open in summer daily 9am-7pm.)

Emergency
- **EMERGENCY NUMBERS:** General emergencies ☎112. Police ☎17. Fire ☎18.
- **POLICE:** For non-emergencies, call ☎04 42 01 17 17.
- **HOSPITALS: Centre Hospitalier La Ciotat.** (1 Bd. Lamaritine. ☎04 42 08 76 00.)

Getting There
Getting into Cassis by **train** is the easiest way to access this seaside village. The train station is only 20min. from Gare St-Charles in Marseille, making Cassis an easy spot to get to. Trains run between Marseille and Cassis every 30min. or so, and tickets are refreshingly cheap.

Buses run from the Gare SNCF into the town center roughly every 20min. The easiest stop to get off and hit the town center is at La Poste (Rue l'Arene). One trip costs €0.80, and the bus runs daily 7am-7pm.

Getting Around
Cassis is small. As such, everywhere within the town is accessible by foot. The longest walk you'll have to take is that from the center of town to the first *calanque*, and that will only take you 30min. maximum. **Buses** run from the Gare SNCF to the center of town every 20min. Beyond that, taking a bus anywhere else in Cassis would be foolish if not impossible, considering how small the city is. **Taxis** can be had by calling (☎04 42 01 78 96), but you're better off hoofing it, as everywhere within the town limits is easily within walking distance.

saint-tropez

There's a good reason why the oil barons vacation in St-Tropez. Unlike roaring Nice, unlike flashy Cannes, St-Tropez is quiet. Though it's been more than half a century since Brigitte Bardot starred in *And God Created Woman* and the world's wealthiest 1% began coming here to party, St-Tropez still feels pristine. Peaceful. Calm. A sleepy, sun-drenched haven carved in terra-cotta and jewel tones. Of course, none of it is real. St-Tropez not a place to live. No, St-Tropez is a place to park your yacht while you tan on a €200-an-hour beach bed and drink a bottle of wine that costs more than your last three facelifts combined. The city dies almost completely every winter and only revives in June when the entire population of southern France floods in to work at the touristy restaurants and hotels. Make no mistake: St-Tropez is a yacht-owner's town.

Luckily, there are ways for the yachtless among us to cope. If it's always been your dream to walk among the rich and famous but you don't have the cash up front, we've got you covered. St-Tropez is (sort of) within reach.

SIGHTS
None of the museums in St-Tropez is free for students. This is symbolic. Know what else is symbolic? City maps cost €2.

get a room!

There are no hostels in this city. There are no motels in this city. There aren't even any cheap hotels in this city (the cheapest single is going to run you at least €150 a night). Your best bet is to book an Airbnb far, far in advance. If you're too young and foolish to plan your trip more than 48hr. in advance, just accept the things you cannot change and bus in from a nearby city.

For maximum convenience, you could theoretically stay at the BedNGo in La Croix Valmer (about a 30min. bus ride from St-Tropez), although we find that we cannot ethically recommend it to you. Why doesn't the front door lock? Why doesn't the bedroom door lock? Why was it possible for us to wander in from the highway at 4am and stumble past three unlocked doors directly into our beds? Also, the shower has no curtain. This is exactly as nightmarish as it sounds.

If you value your person or any of your possessions, you can also stay in the semi-nearby town of Ste-Maxime or slightly less nearby Fréjus or St-Raphael. These are not super convenient, nor are they particularly cheap, but St-Tropez is just a one-day visit. Get in, take a photo, accidentally spend a small fortune, get out.

▨ SAINT-TROPEZ HARBOR
Marina Port Harbor

It is literally impossible to visit St-Tropez and miss the harbor—St-Tropez *is* the harbor. In fact, the harbor's five quays (Quay Hippolyte Bouchard, Quay Gabriel Péri, Quay Suffren, Quay Jean Jaurès, and Quay Frédéric Mistral) are basically the beating heart of the city—home to many of the city's restaurants, most of its artists, and all of its yachts. Fun fact: the value of a yacht is supposedly five million dollars per meter in length, but after walking along this port we realized that can't possibly be true. No one on earth could possibly have that much money. Right?

i Free.

PLAGE DE PAMPELONNE
Route des Plages

Unlike most of the cities in this neck of the woods, St-Tropez is not built around a beach. Whoa, whoa! Don't panic! There totally is a beach. Pampelonne Beach is massive and world-class—it's just located in Ramatuelle, about 6km south of the St-Tropez city center. If you manage to get there, Pampelonne Beach stretches for miles along the coast in a big sandy half-moon. It's hugely popular (probably because everybody in St-Tropez but you has a car, or a chopper), so expect big crowds in the summer. Pampelonne is divided between public and private beaches, but like in the rest of southern France, the private beaches are expensive and totally unnecessary. Also like the rest of southern France, the beaches are generally top-optional (although we'd suggest you look up the rules of your specific beach and/or follow the lead of those around you).

i Bus #7703 travels between St-Tropez and Plage de Pampelonne every few hours. Beach free.

PLAGE DE LA PONCHE

For the less long-bus-ride-inclined, there is a nearer, smaller alternative to Pampelonne. Ponche Beach is located just steps from the center of St-Tropez along the eastern coast. It's a little rockier and a lot smaller, but if you just want to splash around and soak up a little sun, it gets the job done. Hot tip: while a bit sub-par as a daytime destination, Ponche Beach is just two minutes from the

france

Caves du Roy and faces almost directly east, making it an ideal place to be in the wee hours of a Sunday morning.

i Free.

LA CITADELLE DE SAINT-TROPEZ

1 Montée de la Citadelle   ☎04 94 97 59 43

If you're ever bored in southern France, climb the nearest mountain. Guaranteed, there's a fortress up there. Even St-Tropez has one: La Citadelle, which perches atop a low mountain within easy walking distance of the port. Built in the 16th century, when religious conflict between the French and the Spanish led Tropezians to fear an attack from the sea, La Citadelle comes complete with battlements, towers, and a moat. Its outer pavilion offers a decent overhead view of the city (albeit slightly obstructed by trees), and in places its interior walls are low enough to climb, tan, and nap on. For the nautically inclined, there's even an absurdly comprehensive marine museum at the fortress's very center. Expect enough nets, barrels, and ocean noises to last a lifetime.

i €3. Open daily Apr-Sept 10am-6:30pm; Oct-Mar 10am-5:30pm.

CHANEL STORE

1 Av. Général Leclerc   ☎04 94 49 07 47

Housed in a giant manor at the west end of town, the Chanel Store is guarded by a wrought-iron gate and an army of suit-clad, sunglasses-wearing bouncers. Do said bouncers actually bounce? Difficult to say. We got in wearing sneakers, but it felt like a close call. Beyond the tasteful "Chanel" signs and curving stone staircases, a diamond-encrusted paradise awaits. Velvet cushions flaunt pointy shoes with price tags higher than your little cousin can count. Hidden spotlights showcase leather bags with gems so big they look fake but probably aren't. Out back, the store opens onto a manicured lawn and a pool. At this point, you may become overwhelmed with inadequacy and/or suddenly reminded of how long it's been since you bathed or washed your clothes. Resist the urge to sponge off in the pool. Instead, consider this an exercise in humility. When you hit up the clubs later, you'll appreciate the warm-up.

i Entry: free. Clothing: not free. Open daily 10am-1:30pm and 3:30-8:30pm.

MUSÉE DE L'ANNONCIADE

2 Rue de l'Annonciade   ☎04 94 17 84 10

A high-ceilinged converted chapel located right on the edge of the port, the Musée de l'Annonciade has a small but mighty collection of 19th- and 20th-century French art. Unsurprisingly, this involves a lot of Fauvism. (Seriously, the French really like Fauvism.) The place isn't huge—plan on about 30min.—but it is convenient, air-conditioned, and one of the only museums in St-Tropez. Also, it has bathrooms. Know what else isn't free in St-Tropez? Public bathrooms.

i €6, students €4. Open M 10am-1pm and 2-6pm, W-Su 10am-1pm and 2-6pm.

FOOD

LA BARAQUE DES LICES $

Pl. du 15ème Corps   ☎04 94 43 87 42

We're not going to say St-Tropez has bad food. St-Tropez has delicious food—delicately grilled veal steaks, fresh-caught seafood, homemade ravioli and fettuccine—you just can't afford it. For that reason, we direct you to La Baraque: St-Tropez's most popular (and only?) fast-food joint. Centrally located and open 24hr. a day, this versatile kiosk works for every meal. Breakfast? Crepes with apricot jam. Lunch? Ham and cheese panini. Dinner? Kebabs. Thanks to its great hours and location (right in the center of the well-lit and well-supervised Pl. des Lices), La Baraque is also a safe and popular post-club destination.

i Open 24hr., though it appears crepes stop being made sometime around 4am.

saint-tropez

LA TARTE TROPEZIENNE

$$

36 Rue Georges Clemenceau   ☎04 94 97 71 42 www.latartetropezienne.fr
13 Av. du Général Leclerc   ☎04 94 97 46 99 www.latartetropezienne.fr

Of course St-Tropez gets its own pastry. St-Tropez gets what it wants. Soft, flaky, and filled with swirly cream, the Tropezian tart reaches *éclair*-level deliciousness. It's widely available across southern France, so you could theoretically have your first in Aix or Nice, but you're better than that—do it here, in this city, in this patisserie. To make glutting yourself on sugar and butter maximally convenient, La Tarte Tropezienne even has two branches in St-Tropez: a big storefront near Pl. des Lices and a stand near the bus station. The only real difficulty is size: Tropezian tarts are usually prepared family-size. What's a solo traveler to do? Buy and eat a pastry the size of our head? Perish the thought.

i Tropezian tarts €4.40-32, depending on size. Breakfast combo (coffee and pain au chocolat) €2. Open daily 6:30am-9:30pm.

NIGHTLIFE

The nightlife in St-Tropez is really, really famous. It is also really, really exclusive. While most clubs don't technically charge a cover, there are only two ways to get in: dress like you have money (Michael Kors or better) or prove that you have money (bribe the bouncer). For that reason, St-Tropez is kind of a difficult city to go out in. Instead of trying to club-hop along the port, we suggest putting all your eggs/bribe money in one basket—Les Caves du Roy.

LES CAVES DU ROY

Av. du Maréchal Foch   www.lescavesduroy.com

Money crinkles as it passes from palm to palm. Louboutins flash on the dance floor. A woman orders a €150,000 bottle of champagne, which comes with a flaming torch and a silver platter. An hour later, she orders another. This is Les Caves (or possibly the set of a French gangster movie). Perched at the top of a long flight of stairs, Les Caves is guarded by two groups of bouncers. Pass the first and you get to approach the club. Pass the second and you get to enter. It's easier said than done. Exceptionally glamorous women and/or people who can afford to slip the bouncer €50 are in. Everybody else should expect to wait at least 45min. in line. But Les Caves is worth a wait. Inside, strategic mirrors create the illusion of low, cavernous halls, and the thickest fog you've ever seen turns the dance floor into a pulsing den of smoke and iniquity. Drinks start at €26, so you can't refresh your buzz unless you take that leering 40-something up on his offer (dude, c'mon, how old are you?), but the energy runs so high here that you won't need alcohol to stay awake.

i Open Apr 22-June F-Su 8pm-5am; July-Aug daily 8pm-5am; Sept F-Su 8pm-5am.

ESSENTIALS

Practicalities

- **TOURIST OFFICES:** 8 Quai Jean Jaurès. (☎08 92 68 48 28. Open M-Sa 9:30am-12:30pm and 2-6pm.)

- **POST OFFICES:** Pl. Alphonse Celli. (☎36 31. Open M-F 9am-noon and 2-5pm, Sa 9am-noon.)

Emergency

- **EMERGENCY NUMBERS:** General emergencies ☎112. Ambulance ☎15. Police ☎17. Fire ☎18.

- **POLICE:** For non-emergencies, contact the local police at ☎04 94 54 86 65.

france

- **LATE-NIGHT PHARMACIES: Pharmacie du Port.** (9 Quai Suffren. ☎04 94 97 00 06. Open 24hr.)
- **HOSPITALS: Centre Hospitalier de Saint-Tropez.** (Rond Point du Général Diégo Brosset, Gassin. ☎04 98 12 50 00 www.ch-saint-tropez.fr.)

Getting There

If you're approaching St-Tropez from the east, hop the **train** and ride it as far as St-Raphael. (Apr-May M-Sa 9:30am, 2:30pm, Su 2:30pm; June daily 9:30am, 2:30pm; July-Aug daily 9:30, 11:30am, 2:30, 5, 8pm; Sept daily 10:30am, 5:15pm; Oct Tu-Sa 10:30am, 5pm.) At St-Raphael, get off, walk 5min. to the harbor, and climb aboard the blue **ferry** docked there. "Les Bateaux de St-Raphael" make regular circuits between St-Raphael and St-Tropez, and, while they're a little pricey, they will save you from a loooong bus ride around the bay. Also, the ferry ride is breathtaking. (☎04 94 95 17 46 www.bateauxsaintraphael.com. €15, round-trip €25.) If you'd prefer the **bus,** the Var bus line services St-Tropez and surrounding areas. From St-Raphael, take bus #7601 to St-Tropez. (€3. 70min.)

Getting Around

Most people in St-Tropez travel by yacht. If you don't have a yacht, expect to walk while inside the town. When you need to leave the town center, count on the Var **bus** line. All rides are €3, and the different routes will take to beaches and surrounding small towns (where you should probably find lodgings).

cannes

Unpack your ritziest swimsuit. Get out your glitziest shoes. Slick on your fanciest sunscreen. Cannes is one of the hottest (in all senses) cities on the French Riviera, and its average tourist has money to burn. Actually, thanks to its annual film festival, Cannes is less of a city and more of a giant nonstop party where shipping magnates and people with Oscars drink Verve Clicquot by the beach. If you're not a shipping magnate or a person with an Oscar, Cannes can be tough to navigate. The place just doesn't cater to backpackers. Sunbathers on La Croisette will eye your giant pack with suspicion, and when you ask that guy on the Vespa for directions to a hostel, he will laugh and speed away. If you're very lucky (read: you snag the city's cheapest bed and subsist on canned beans and crepes), you might be able to see Cannes on €50 a day. Bank on €70.

So is it worth it? Two words: sandy beach. Cannes is blessed with one of the only sandy beaches in this neck of the woods, and it is absolutely world-class. Seventeen more words: bobbing yachts, purple sunsets, and a ring of far-off mountain ranges fade gently into the breathtaking horizon. Strangely, despite the intensely beachy vibe, we even didn't notice that many seagulls. Guess they can't afford it.

SIGHTS

LA CROISETTE

Promenade de la Croisette

J'adore Weitzman, habillez-moi;
Louis, Dolce Gabbana, Alexander McQueen, et oh!
Merde, j'aime ces Manolos.

Is this a dated Gaga song or the internal monologue of the lady in the Mercedes idling outside the Pucci store? Either way, if you're within a 5 mi. radius of La Croisette, it's appropriate. Bordered by the sandy shores of the Mediterranean on one side and the diamond-encrusted storefronts of every major fashion house

VILLA SAINT-MICHEL
$$

1 Impasse des Deux Églises ☎04 93 60 58 37

You know that weird dream you have sometimes where everything is normal except your car is nicer, your hair is better, and also you're tied up with the mob? It's not a bad dream, exactly. The mob money is great, and your mob friends are chill, and breaking kneecaps is actually kind of a thrill if you look at it the right way. It's just a bit weird. Similarly, Villa St-Michel is great but surreal. After all, Cannes is notorious for being the city with no hostels. Why would this place—a three-story inn in a quiet neighborhood just 5min. from the beach—defy expectations and rent out a dorm? Clean, private, and spacious—it should definitely charge more than €35 a night (yes, that's super cheap for Cannes). We have some theories. First, it's a ladies-only dorm, which reduces the market (sorry, fellas). Second, though it's close to the beach, it's about a 15min. walk from the city center. Third, it gave us spooky vibes. Though we stayed in the middle of the summer, the entire place was empty. The other beds stayed unrumpled, the other lights stayed off, the hall bathroom stayed pristine. We did not see a soul for three days except the guy who let us in on the first day. On one hand, the privacy was pleasant. On the other...

i High-season dorms €35. 3-night min. stay.

HOTEL ATLANTIS
$$$

4 Rue du 24 Août ☎4 93 39 18 72

Given that Hotel Atlantis falls into the species of *Crappius motelus*—as does everything else in Cannes under €80 a night—it's pretty good. Thanks to the nature of *Crappius motelus*, beds are large and free from snoring roommates, making this a good place to catch up on your beauty sleep. Also, rooms come with cable TVs, air-conditioning units (which sometimes work!), and a single yellow rose (which is a damn nice touch).

i Singles from €49.

on the other, La Croisette is the perfect boardwalk. Tired? Rent a €200 beach bed and soak up that Riviera sun. Bored? Wander into the nearest Escada and spark up your wardrobe with this season's bucket bag. Can't afford to do either of those things? Console yourself with a fresh crepe at one of the eight gajillion kiosks that line the water.

i Free if you're "just looking."

PLAGE DU MIDI

Bd. Jean Hibert

By some miracle of nature or imported goods, Cannes has sandy beaches. Unfortunately, most of them are private. This leaves you with two options: buy the cheapest drink at the cheapest beach bar and play the game by their rules or walk a little farther for a public space. We recommend the second (screw The Man, man). The beaches at the east and west corners of the harbor are both public, and though they get insanely crowded on sunny days and weekends, they're generally good bets.

But you know what? Sometimes "good" isn't good enough. Sometimes you don't want "good," or "easy," or "safe." At some point in a person's life, it comes time to STAND UP FOR WHAT YOU BELIEVE IN. For that, hike a little farther east to Plage du Midi. Quiet, peaceful, and just as sandy as its more centrally

france

located brethren, the Plage du Midi is a gem. Come at midday, as the name suggests, or reject conformity and arrive around 7-8pm to catch the famous "golden hour." Sunsets at this west-facing cove are unforgettable.

i Free.

MUSÉE DE LA CASTRE

Pl. de la Castre ☎04 89 82 26 26

Like all good things, the Musée de la Castre is located at the top of a very tall hill. If you can handle the incline, though, the museum contains an impressively diverse collection of art and artifacts, ranging from tiny things carved in stone a long time ago to big things painted on paper not that long ago. Some of the items concern us slightly (how does a tiny museum in France obtain that many ceremonial Tibetan masks?), but we're sure it's all ethical (right?). After checking out the exhibits inside the museum, make sure to climb the massive tower out back. The winding staircase is a bit precarious and unfortunately not wheelchair-accessible, but if you can make it to the top you'll be treated to a mindboggling 360-degree view of Cannes.

i €6, ages 18-25 €3.50. Open Apr-June Tu-Su 10am-1pm and 2-6pm; July M 10am-7pm, W 10am-1pm and 2-9pm, Th-Su 10am-7pm.

FOOD

🖼 URBAN CAFE $

3 Rue Hoche ☎09 84 34 51 46

The eternal mystery. The futile question. "Where do I find breakfast?" Ah, this bacon-forsaken country. Well, suffer no more—your quest ends today with a *croque madame*. An eggy spin on a French classic, the *croque madame* is basically a grilled-cheese sandwich with a slice of ham in the middle and a fried egg on top. It's got protein; it's got fiber; it's got crunch and squish and the yum factor. Basically, it's the closest you're going to get to scrambled eggs and bacon without leaving the continent. But the *croque madame* takes a delicate touch. The bread can't be too soft or the cheese too thick. Luckily, Urban Cafe takes this task seriously, and its *croque madame* is perfect. The egg comes dusted with fancy herbs, for goshsakes. Urban Cafe also does more than just the *croque madame*. *Croque de Paris, croque d'Italie, croque de Provence*—you name the region, Urban Cafe has it in grilled-cheese-sandwich form.

i Croques €5-6. Smoothies €4-4.50. Salads €9. Open M 9am-6pm, Tu-F 8am-6pm, Sa 8am-7pm.

CREPERIE DE LA CROISETTE $$

82 Bd. de la Croisette ☎04 93 94 43 47 www.creperiedelacroisette.com

You know what? We might've jumped the gun on the breakfast situation. Maybe we shouldn't be trying to make French breakfast conform to our narrow breakfast ideals. Maybe we should slow down, take a breather, and really examine what else this proud nation has to offer. Crepes, for example. Crepes count as breakfast, as long as you put jam on them. This is where Creperie de la Croisette comes in. Centrally located and full of both crepes *and* jam, the creperie is an ideal place to people-watch and start your day. It's also a good place to work. Plunk yourself down, pull out your notebook, and spend an afternoon eating warm, flaky crepes.

i Crepes €3.80-8.50. Pancakes €5-16.50. Open Apr 15-Oct 15 daily from 8:30am; Oct 16-Apr 14 Tu-Su from 8:30am.

NIGHTLIFE

Cannes is the best party city in southern France. More glamorous than Nice, slightly less exclusive than St-Tropez (emphasis on "slightly"), Cannes is the perfect mix of Wealthy Enough To Blow Your Mind and Chill Enough That You Might Get In. That

said, you gotta dress up. Shirts should have buttons. Shoes should have stilettos. Take it from us: rejection stings, friends.

BAOLI

Port Pierre Canto, Bd. de la Croisette   ☎04 93 43 03 43 https://baolicannes.com

While Cannes has tons of clubs, especially downtown, two emerge as the very best. The first, and perhaps slightly more famous, is Baoli. Located halfway along the peninsula at the east end of town, the club is fairly difficult to find, which is probably an intentional strategy to screen for tourists and the very drunk. (Joke's on Baoli, though: tourists have maps!) The outer ring of the club is open-air and surprisingly chill, with a tropical theme—bamboo umbrellas, wooden tables, fountains, and pools. At the club's center, though, the theme falls away. In fact, the heart of Baoli is a giant mirrored cube ("dance floor"). This cube is almost completely soundproof until someone opens the door to enter or leave, at which point the entire club is assaulted with a wall of screamy, house-music bass. Lethal as this may sound, the dance floor is where the party's at. Gird your loins, accept your inevitable hearing loss, and enter this decadent den of auditory excess.

i Open daily 8pm-5am.

GOTHA

Pl. Franklin Roosevelt   ☎04 93 45 11 11 http://gotha-club.com

Frankly, while Baoli might be about 2% more internationally renowned, we had more fun at Gotha. First of all, it's a little bit bigger. "Size doesn't matter," you say. OK, we'll give you that. But it's also a little bit younger. In fact, unlike many of the ritziest clubs in Cannes, Gotha doesn't feel like a private club for 40-something Armani investors. Instead, it's more like an especially wild concert

france

venue. This vibe is accentuated by its world-class DJ lineup: past A-listers have included Steve Aoki.

i No official cover, but this seems to be at the discretion of the bouncers. Open daily midnight-7am.

ESSENTIALS
Practicalities
- **TOURIST OFFICES: Palais des Festivals.** (1 Bd. de la Croisette. ☎04 92 99 84 22. Open daily 10am-7pm.)
- **POST OFFICES:** 22 Rue Bivouac Napoléon. (☎04 93 06 26 50. Open M-F 8am-7pm, Sa 8am-noon.)

Emergency
- **EMERGENCY NUMBERS:** General emergencies ☎112. Ambulance ☎15. Police ☎17. Fire ☎18.
- **POLICE:** Reach the central police station at ☎04 93 06 22 22.
- **HOSPITALS: Centre Hospitalier de Cannes.** (15 Av. des Broussailles. ☎04 93 69 70 00 www. ch-cannes.fr.)

Getting There
Fly into the large, international Nice Cote d'Azur airport, then take the train or a bus to Cannes. **Trains** to Cannes run through two stations: Cannes and Cannes La Bocca. Make sure to use only the former, as Cannes La Bocca is miles out of town.

Getting Around
Cannes does not have a subway system, but the Palm Bus fleet runs regular **buses** around the city. Tickets are €1.50 per trip or €10 for 10 journeys. You can also buy a weekly pass for €11. Cannes has many **taxi** services, but they tend to be expensive, even by French Riviera standards. If you do choose to call a cab, ask the price before you get in. In the end, though, Cannes is a very walkable city. Just hoof it.

nice

Nice is a city of tourists. That's not a bad thing—we're tourists, and we find ourselves quite charming—but it's a real thing. Restaurants are filled with tourists. Public squares are filled with tourists. The tourist office is filled with tourists (bet you didn't see that one coming). After all, Nice is no ritzy Cannes, no inaccessible St-Tropez. Vibrant, beautiful, affordable—Nice is the most backpacker-friendly city on the French Riviera.

Some people come for the location. Nice squats right on the border of France, making it a natural stopping point for those doing the Spain-France-Italy sprint. For the slightly less mobile among us, Nice is just €1.50 and a scenic bus ride away from the scenic villages of Villefranche, Cap-d'Ail, and the village/independent country Monaco.

Others come for the culture. Nice has been occupied since prehistory, and ancient Gallo-Roman ruins dot the hills to the north. In slightly more recent history, world-class art museums have overrun the city like locusts or overly sexed bunnies. (Seriously, blink and this place has birthed another one.) Try and fail to see them all, or strap on your running shoes and shoot for four: the Museum of Fine Arts (for the Rodin), the Chagall and Matisse Museums (for the Chagall and the Matisse), and the

get a room!

Nice has a lot of hotels and hostels. Really—so many. Unfortunately, all this competition for your gracious presence doesn't produce super-cheap rates like you might expect (how do you even say supply and demand in French?). Even the cheapest beds generally run in the €25-30-per-night range, and this can fluctuate much higher depending on the season, the demand, and the weather.

ANTARES HOSTEL
$$
5 Av. Thiers   ☎04 93 88 22 87 www.antaresnice.hostel.com

Among Nice's shifting sea of options, one emerges as the safest, cleanest, and (generally) cheapest: Antares Hostel. It's one of the larger hostels in town but manages to stay intimate and comfy-cozy thanks to two social spaces (a dining room and a basement lounge) and a robust air-conditioning system (to counteract the body heat). If you start feeling claustrophobic, you can also loosen up with free wine and chips 7-10pm most nights in the summer. Located in Nice's unofficial hostel district (i.e., everywhere within a half-mile or so of the train station), Antares is about a 15min. walk to the beach. That said, it's only a 15sec. walk to a delicious €4 kebab place that we may or may not have eaten at four times. Compromise.

i Dorms €20-26; prices vary by the date. Cash only.

BACCARAT
$$
39 Rue d'Angleterre   ☎04 93 88 35 73

Baccarat is owned by the same management as Antares and is nearly identical in size, architecture, and geography (the two hostels are close enough to access each other's Wi-Fi). As a result, choosing between the two depends on your priorities. If you're looking for straight-up comfort, Antares has a little more space, a little more quiet, and a little more class. If you're looking to climb up on a balcony, chant some kind of Scottish sports anthem, then spray beer all over the ceiling and 20 tipsy backpackers, then consider Baccarat. Though its narrow, box-like "chill-out room" is BYOB and technically supervised by hostel staff, hostelers seem to party there pretty much every night of the week, peaking at about 11pm before people leave for the bars or the beds. Our advice: pull a Hannah Montana and get the best of both worlds by staying at Antares but coming to Baccarat to party.

i Dorms €20-26; prices vary by the date. Cash only.

HOSTEL ALTEA
$$
3 Bd. Raimbaldi   ☎04 93 85 15 22 www.hostelaltea.com

If you've got a couple extra euros, splurge on Baccarat or Antares. If you really need to do Nice on the tightest possible budget, though, Altea is OK. Just be prepared for some tradeoffs. For example, beds are terrifyingly triple-bunked, but hostel staff compensates by decorating female dorms with prints of Marilyn Monroe and distinctly labial flowers. Shower rods lack even suction cups to keep them attached to the walls, but the suspense of wondering when the shower curtain is going to fall down makes you feel alive. Staff members are harried and cranky, but sometimes they'll forget to ask you to put down your €20 deposit.

i Dorms €20-24. Book on its website to save €1 per night.

france

Museum of Contemporary Art (for the humbling experience of complete and utter incomprehension).

The most important reason to come to Nice, though, is the beach. Let's face it: Nice is a beach town. You can "see the sights" and "visit the museums" and "soak up the culture" as much as you want, but in the end you're just going to spend most of your time working on your tan. Don't fight this.

SIGHTS

★ PROMENADE DES ANGLAIS

The Promenade des Anglais traces the southern coast of Nice from the airport to Castle Hill, providing easy access to Nice's many, many beaches. Beau Rivage Beach, Blue Beach, Opera Beach, Ruhi Beach, Hi Beach... are these beaches actually different, or are they just arbitrary chunks of one large beach? That's for you to decide—no, actually, it's not, they're definitely the same. Regardless, we suggest that you make it your personal goal to sunbathe on every public beach you can get your sweaty, salty hands on. They're all rocky, but we have a hunch that the beaches at the west end may involve sliiightly smaller rocks. "Ew, rocks," you say. First, you're wrong. No sand equals no sand in your nooks and crannies. Second, the promenade is more than just beach access. It's also a panoramic view of the ocean, a walking tour waiting to happen, and the city's best place to people-watch. Nab some ice cream and a bench and keep your eyes peeled.

i Free.

PLACE MASSENA

Plunked right at the intersection of the beach, Old Nice, and the road that leads to the train station, Pl. Massena is a natural gathering place for tourists, locals, and street performers. It is also the biggest, nakedest public square in Nice. Massive statues of naked Poseidon and his naked water-lady friends dominate the south end. A stunning water park (the Miroir d'Eau) full of arcing water and gleefully clothes-free small children stretches to the east. And seven glowing, crouching men in their birthday suits perch on sky-high pillars throughout the center of the square. According to a tiny plaque in a distant corner of the square, this last installation is a metaphor for world peace (each naked man represents a continent). Yeah, it's over our heads as well. Ponder the symbolism as much or as little as you like, but make sure to walk through Pl. Massena at least once during your stay.

i Free.

CASTLE HILL

Montée du Château

Question: what's the only thing better than the beach? Answer: a breathtaking panoramic view of the beach—the endless glittering pebbly coast of the Mediterranean—from high above the city. If you only leave the beach once during your stay in Nice, it should be to climb Castle Hill. This can be a bit daunting at first—even the first lookout is several hundred steps above the ground—but if you're able and equipped with comfortable shoes, it's at most a 10min. trek. Stop for a breather at the Panorama of the Baie des Anges, a circular platform about two-thirds of the way up that provides a stunning 270-degree view of the coast—then do some light stretches and continue on. At the top of the hill, you'll find Roman ruins, a waterfall, and a series of balconies overlooking the eastern port where adorable couples cuddle against the setting sun. Take a seat next to them and ponder the beauties of nature and solitude. Alternatively, gag audibly and take surreptitious photos that you'll later post to Instagram alongside the

nice

caption "BAE des Anges" and certain heavy implications about your personal romantic success. Your call.

i Free. Open daily Apr-Sept 8:30am-8pm; Oct-Mar 8:30am-6pm.

CHAGALL MUSEUM

36 Av. Dr Ménard ☎04 93 53 87 20

Whether you've ever heard of Marc Chagall, whether you've ever cared about Marc Chagall, the Chagall Museum is an excellent place to spend an hour. The museum itself isn't massive—the collection is, after all, limited to one dude—but the paintings are, and the audio tour is so thorough and interesting that you can easily spend 5-10min. staring at each giant canvas. Spin slowly in the center of the Song of Songs exhibit, an interactive, musical, pentagonal little space tucked to the side of the museum and dedicated to love and the story of David and Bathsheba. Nap in the gentle blue light of the theater as the Chagall documentary plays softly in the background. When you wake up, continue north to the Matisse Museum to make the afternoon a double-header.

i €8, non-EU citizens 18-25 €6, EU citizens 18-25 free. Open M 10am-6pm, W-Su 10am-6pm. Documentary screened free in English daily noon, 2, 4pm.

MATISSE MUSEUM

164 Av. des Arènes de Cimiez ☎04 93 81 08 08 www.musee-matisse-nice.org

Unlike the Chagall Museum, the Matisse Museum is free for students. Also unlike the Chagall Museum, the Matisse Museum contains very few paintings. "Hold up," you say in surprise and derision. "Henri Matisse was a painter." Well, apparently, he was also a sculptor and a crafter—and while Nice couldn't quite get its hands on many of the Post-Impressionist canvases that made him famous, they did get some of his earlier realist works, many of his famous cutouts, and most of his statues. After all, the guy did spend the last years of his life in Nice in the Regina Hotel, which stands just minutes from the site of the museum. Check it out on your way to the museum, and then afterward check out the Gallo-Roman ruins of Cimiez just behind the museum. They're totally unrelated, but they're free and they're cool.

i €10, under 18 and students free. Open M 10am-6pm, W-Su 10am-6pm.

france

FOOD

▨ ILLIA PASTA $

4 Rue Droite ☎06 52 82 95 52

Picture it: you're perched under the windowsill of a tiny resto in the east end of Old Nice. On your right stretches the narrow cobblestone street, quiet but for the occasional French pedestrian or pair of heart-eyed honeymooners. On your left hangs a black chalkboard with a list of the day's sauces, a few crossed out. *"Votre ratatouille!"* your waiter says, breaking your reverie. He places a ceramic bowl of house-made farfalle on the table before you. It looks soft, savory, and so, so fresh. You laugh triumphantly, because, though Illia Pasta is generally a takeout place, you broke the system and ate *sur place*. Also because the whole shebang cost less than €10.

i Pasta €8-9. Open M noon-7:30pm, Tu-Th 11am-7:30pm, F noon-7:30pm, Sa 11am-7:30pm, Su noon-7:30pm.

POP O THYM $

20 Cours Saleya ☎04 93 27 22 20

Cours Saleya, the wide pedestrian-only street that runs parallel to the beach along the south end of Old Town, is the touristy food capital of the touristy city capital of southern France. On the upside, the street itself is easy to find—just follow the ritzy older couple in white linen and Botox. On the downside, good food on the street is not. Fortunately, within the tacky, affluent desert that is Cours Saleya, Pop O Thym is a crepe-y oasis. Savory crepes stuffed with meats, veggies, and cheeses are large enough to function as a whole meal, but for the very hungry, the *prix-fixe* menu includes two crepe courses (one savory, one sweet) as well as alcohol and coffee. On their own, none of the crepes is necessarily mind-blowing, but the brilliance of Pop O Thym is its respectability. Here, you get to sit at a table on a nice street, eat nothing but crepes for an hour straight, and—at the end of the day—call it a square meal.

i Crepes €4.80-12. Prix-fixe menu €15.50. Open daily 11am-7:45pm.

PIZZA PILI $

24 Rue Benoît Bunico ☎04 93 54 18 31

Pizza Pili is pretty persistently packed. Every night of the week, a crowd loiters by the little stand, eyeing the long menu of possibilities. They chat in French, English, Spanish, Italian, a veritable everything pizza of locals and tourists alike. "Do I go with the Eggplant? Or maybe the Texan? Keep it classy and opt for the Reine?" Happily, their anxieties are for naught: Pizza Pili is the best takeout pizza in Nice, so they can't really choose wrong. They also can't choose small. Like everywhere else on this part of the map, Nice's pizzerias have no patience for that "buy by the slice" nonsense. Buy an entire pizza, carry it down to the beach, and eat the whole thing by yourself. Nobody's watching.

i Pizza €7. Special daily pizza €9. Open daily 11am-midnight.

FENOCCHIO $

2 Pl. Rossetti ☎04 93 80 72 52 http://fenocchio.fr
6 Rue de la Poissonerie ☎04 93 62 88 80 http://fenocchio.fr

Fenocchio is a strong contender for best ice cream in southern France. Behind the low glass counter of this little open-air *glacier* in Old Nice, tub after tub of ice cream stretch to delicious infinity. The classics are present, but don't order them—you're having an adventure, for goodness's sake. Try the chocolate orange, the Grand Marnier, the lavender, the rose, or the violet. For €2.50, you can have a single scoop of creamy, pure, smooth happiness.

i 1 scoop €2.50; 2 scoops €4. Pl. Rossetti location open daily 9am-midnight. Rue de la Poissonerie location open M 9am-midnight, W-Su 9am-midnight.

nice

PAPILLA $

1 Bd. Carlone   ☎04 93 96 18 38 http://papilla.fr/papilla-nice

OK, yes, this is another ice-cream place. What can we say—Nice has cornered the ice-cream market. Located at the south end of Pl. Massena, barely 100m from the beach, Papilla offers a mid-size range of flavors so simultaneously pure and complex that you'll be forced to question everything you thought you knew about dairy—and yourself. Sample a few: portions are big, and even a small cone buys two flavors. We recommend the lemon tart (which involves chunks of actual lemon tart!) and the coconut (actual coconut!). In 2015, TripAdvisor declared Papilla the best ice cream in France. We understand that you might find this confusing. "Didn't you say Fenocchio is the best?" you inquire sweetly. Ah, our darlings. It's never so simple, is it? Just eat both.

i 1 scoop €2.50. Open daily 8am-11pm.

NIGHTLIFE

WAYNE'S

15 Rue de la Préfecture   ☎04 93 13 46 99 http://waynes.fr

At Wayne's, people dance on the tables and chairs. Not "sometimes." Not "on a good night." Always. In fact, they're supposed to. Sturdy wooden furniture takes up the whole dance floor, leaving only narrow aisles of floor space for coming and going. A caution: it's quite tough to dance on tables and chairs, so drinks will get spilled, and you will get sticky. Live bands play a mix of American top 40 and '90s throwback jams, and they take requests, meaning that if a roomful of your drunk peers start chanting "Wonderwall," you're going to hear "Wonderwall." That said, Wayne's is the best, and most memorable, bar in Nice.

i No cover. Small beer €3.80-4.30; large €6.50-7.20; large during happy hour €4.50-5. Shots €6. Cocktails €8; during happy hour €5. Open daily 10am-2am. Happy hour 5-8pm.

BULLDOG PUB POMPEII

16 Rue de l'Abbaye   ☎06 31 24 53 99

If you just want to sit back and drink a beer without scalawags jumping around trying to "nae-nae" or "macarena" or whatever it is the youths are doing these days, mosey on down to Bulldog Pub Pompeii. While this two-story pub does feature loud live music, it does so within a distinctly cozy-brown-couch kinda space. Climb the stairs to meet the eponymous wooden bulldog, but beware the second-floor smoking room. The glass doors may claim to trap the smoke, but our nostrils say otherwise.

i Open daily 11pm-6am.

NEW BLISS

12 Rue de l'Abbaye   ☎04 93 16 82 38 http://newbliss-nice.com

New Bliss is as minimalist and weird as it sounds. The club is hardly big enough to hold a DJ and a bar. To distract patrons from the size, owners seem to have invested in a very zealous fog machine. Seriously, that thing works overtime; picture a shed-sized glass box of pulsing blue smoke. Even if you don't find that image appealing, New Bliss is worth checking out for the music. During the summer, the club hosts an ever-changing lineup of guest DJs and performers—Billie Well and Mystic Voodoo Ladies, anybody?—in genres that are mostly house, hip hop, and pop but might occasionally surprise you. New Bliss isn't particularly glamorous, clean, or nice, but it's loud and unpretentious. Check the website for upcoming events or just show up.

i No cover. Concert times vary. Open Tu-Sa 8pm-2am.

france

OBSESSION

65 Quai des États-Unis ☎06 50 40 18 20

Obsession is the rowdiest club in Nice. For whatever reason, everybody here seems to be slightly sweatier and slightly drunker than anybody anywhere else. This is the place where three bald men get so drunk they waltz; where a post-Brexit Brit wraps himself in the Union Jack and gyrates patriotically among his peevish neighbors; where you dance with your hands in the air because there's nowhere else to put them. More important than the club's sloppy interior, though, is its location. If you're going to party in Nice, you owe it to yourself to party on the beach at least once—and Obsession faces almost directly onto the Mediterranean. This is an optimal post-party skinny-dipping opportunity. Carpe that diem.

i Shots €5. Open daily 5pm-5am.

ESSENTIALS
Practicalities

- **TOURIST OFFICES:** The tourist office at **Gare SNCF** is incredibly convenient, as it's located directly outside of the train station in Nice. The office provides maps, brochures, and other touristy information. (Av. Thiers. ☎08 92 70 74 07 www.nicetourisme.com. Open daily 8am-8pm.)

- **CONSULATES: United States.** (7 Av. Gustave V. ☎04 93 88 89 55. Open M-F 9-11:30am and 1:30-4:30pm.)

- **POST OFFICES:** The main location is at **21 Av. Thiers.** (Open M-F 8am-7pm, Sa 8am-noon.) Additional post offices are scattered all throughout the city.

- **POSTAL CODE:** 06000

Emergency

- **EMERGENCY NUMBER:** ☎112.

- **POLICE: Nice police station.** (1 Av. Maréchal Foch. ☎04 92 17 22 22.)

- **HOSPITALS: Hospital Saint-Roch.** (5 Rue Pierre Devoluy. ☎04 93 62 06 91.)

Getting There

Flights to Nice land at Nice-Cote d'Azur airport. (☎08 20 42 33.) Shuttles from the airport to the train station run every 30min. **Trains** from Cannes, Marseille, Monaco, and Paris arrive at Gare SNCF Nice-Ville. (Av. Thiers. ☎04 93 14 82 12 www.sncf.com.) **Bus** #100 runs from Nice to Monaco/Menton to the Gare Routiere. Tickets are €1.50. (5 Bd. Jean Jaurès. ☎04 92 00 42 93.) Corsica Ferries also runs **ferries** from, yup, Corsica. (☎04 92 00 42 93 corsicaferries.com.)

Getting Around

Vélo Bleu is the Nice **bike**-sharing company. Rent a bike for roughly €1 per hour and return it to any Vélo Bleu stand in Nice. (www.velobleu.org.)

nice

france essentials

MONEY

Tipping

By law in France, a service charge, called "service compris," is added to bills in bars and restaurants. Most people do, however, leave some change (up to €2) for sit-down services, and in nicer restaurants it is not uncommon to leave 5% of the bill. For other services, like taxis and hairdressers, a 10-15% tip is acceptable.

Taxes

The quoted price of goods in France includes value added tax (VAT). This tax on goods is generally levied at 19.6% in France, although some goods are subject to lower rates. Non-EU visitors who are taking these goods home unused may be refunded this tax for purchases totaling over €175 per store. When making purchases, request a VAT form and present it at a Tax Free Shopping Office, found at most airports, road borders, and ferry stations, or by mail. Refunds must be claimed within six months.

SAFETY AND HEALTH

Drugs and Alcohol

Although any mention of France often conjures images of black-clad smokers in berets, France no longer allows smoking in public as of 2008. The government has no official policy on berets. Possession of illegal drugs (including marijuana) in France can result in a substantial jail sentence or fine. Police may arbitrarily stop and search anyone on the street.

There is no drinking age in France, but restaurants will not serve anyone under the age of 16, and to purchase alcohol you must be at least 18 years old. Though there is no law prohibiting open containers, drinking on the street is considered uncouth. The legal blood-alcohol level for driving in France is 0.05%, which is less than it is in the US, UK, New Zealand, and Ireland, so exercise appropriate caution if operating a vehicle in France.

KEEPING IN TOUCH

Cellular Phones

In France, mobile pay-as-you-go phones are the way to go. The two largest carriers are SFR and Orange, and they are so readily available that even supermarkets sell them. Cell-phone calls and texts can be paid for without signing a contract by using a Mobicarte prepaid card, available at Orange and SFR stores, as well as tabacs. You can often buy phones for €20-40, which includes various amounts of minutes and 100 texts. Calling the US from one of these phones is around €0.80 a minute, with texts coming in at around €0.50.

france

GERMANY

Anything that ever made it big is bound to attract some stereotypes, and Germany is no exception. Beer, crazy deaf composers, robotic efficiency, sausage, Inglourious Basterds—just to name a few. Germany has some of the best collections of art in the world, incredible architecture, and a history that makes it clear no one bosses Germany around. Whether giving the ancient Romans a run for their money or giving birth to Protestantism, Germany has always been a rebel. Even behind its success as a developed country, it hasn't given that up.

The damage from World War II still lingers in city skyscapes, and the country is keenly embarrassed of its Nazi and communist pasts. Even though its concrete wall has been demolished, Berlin, the country's capital, still retains a marked difference between east and west after decades of strife, tempering the picturesque castles and churches of earlier golden ages.

Plenty of discounts, cheap eats, and a large student population make Germany an exciting place to visit and study. It's also incredibly accessible for Anglophone visitors, as many Germans have no qualms about slipping from their native tongue into English. The nightlife and culture of Berlin or Munich will grab you and never let you go, while thriving smaller university towns will charm you into wanting to stay another semester.

greatest hits

- **COLD WAR KIDS.** Admire the Berlin Wall murals painted by artists from around the world at the **East Side Gallery** (p. 237).

- **BEAMER, BENZ, OR BENTLEY.** Sport the classiest threads you own, and head to the **BMW Welt and Museum** (p. 285) to test drive a new whip.

- **DOWN IN ONE.** Pace yourself and avoid using the vomitorium at Munich's most famous beer hall, **Hofbräuhaus** (p. 288).

GERMANY

berlin

So you've decided to visit Berlin. Congratulations. Your pretentious friends went to Paris. Your haughty friends went to London. And your lost friends went to Belarus. But you decided on Berlin. You've probably heard that Berlin is the coolest city in the world, or that it has one of the best clubs in Europe, or that it sleeps when the sun comes up. Well, don't believe the hype. It's not the coolest city in the world; it's several of the coolest cities in the world. It doesn't have one of the best clubs in Europe; it has 10. And to top it off, Berlin never sleeps.

Berlin's rise began with some normal history, taken to epic heights. King Friedrich II and his identically named progeny ruled from canal-lined boulevards, built palaces like middle-fingers to all the haters, and developed Prussia into an Enlightened

European powerhouse, with Berlin at the helm. But after centuries of captaining Europe, Berlin went crazy in the 20th. As the seat of Hitler's terror and with World War II drama in its streets, Berlin rebooted in the '50s, only to become a physical manifestation of Cold War divisions. The Berlin Wall rose in 1961, slicing the city and fueling the enmity of a radical student and punk population. Ten years after the Wall crumbled in 1989, the German government decided to relocate from Bonn to Berlin. And from there, Berlin became today's European champion of cool.

Sorry about your friends.

ORIENTATION

Charlottenburg

Should you tire of the immense bustle or forget that Berlin was an old European capital, venture into Charlottenburg. Originally a separate town founded around the grounds of Friedrich I's palace, it became an affluent cultural center during the Weimar years and the Berlin Wall era thanks to Anglo-American support. The neighborhood retains its original old-world opulence, from the upscale Beaux-Arts apartments to the shamelessly extravagant **Kurfürstendamm,** Berlin's premiere shopping strip. **Ku'damm,** as the locals call it, runs from east to west through southern Charlottenburg. Popular sights include the Spree River in the northwest and the absurdly splendiferous **Schloß Charlottenburg** to the north, both of which bolster Charlottenburg's old-Berlin appeal. Aside from the sights, the neighborhood's high rents keep out most young people and students, so the Charlottenburg crowd tends to be old and quiet and prefers the sidewalk seating of expensive Ku'Damm restaurants to crazy ragers in the area's few clubs.

Schöneberg and Wilmersdorf

South of Ku'damm, Schöneberg and Wilmersdorf are primarily quiet residential neighborhoods, remarkable for their world-class cafe culture, bistro tables, relaxed diners, and coffee shops spilling out onto virtually every cobblestone street. Also, nowhere else in Berlin, and perhaps in all of Germany, is the GLBT community quite as spectacularly ready to party as in the area immediately surrounding **Nollendorfplatz.** To the west lies one of Berlin's most convenient outdoor getaways: **Grunewald** rustles with city dwellers trading their daily commute for peaceful strolls with the family dog among the pines. But if you don't have the time for the 20min. bus or tram ride—or if a palm reader once predicted that you would be mauled by dogs in a German forest—then Schöneberg and Wilmersdorf offer a gracious handful of shady parks scattered among their apartment façades, where you can sit in the grass and kick back the cups of joe.

Mitte

Mitte lives up to its name. Literally, Mitte means "center" in English, and every second you spend in Mitte will remind you that it is, in fact, the center of everything in Berlin. You're going to find thousands of tourists in Mitte, and you'll also find anything and everything political, historical, and cultural. Southwest Mitte boasts the **Brandenburg Gate,** the **Reichstag,** and the exceedingly famous **Jewish Memorial.** At the very center of it all, you'll find **Museuminsel,** literally an island of museums that piles some of the world's most awe-inspiring sights practically on top of each other. In the north, Mitte borders **Prenzlauer Berg** starting at **Rosenthaler Platz.** This area has Mitte's cheapest eats and tons of techno clubs you're sure to encounter. Some of the world's most famous performance halls, including the **Berlin Philharmonic** and the **Deutscher Staatsoper,** grace this cultural capital. Then, of course, there's the forest-like **Tiergarten** at the center of Mitte, which shelters sunbathers, barbecuers, pensive wanderers, and probably several breeds of magical creatures. The main street cutting through the Tiergarten,

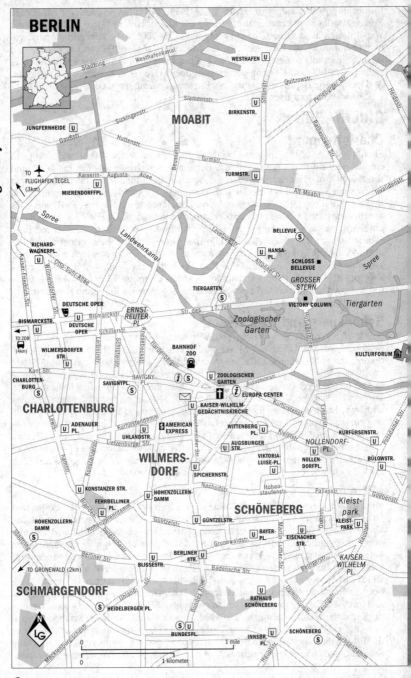

BERLIN

WESTHAFEN Ⓤ

Westhafenkanal

Stadtring

Quitzowstr.

MOABIT

Siemensstr.

Sickingenstr.

BIRKENSTR. Ⓤ

Stromstr.

Perleberger Str.

JUNGFERNHEIDE Ⓤ

Gaußstr.

Huttenstr.

Turmstr.

Rathenower Str.

Heidestr.

TO ✈
FLUGHAFEN TEGEL
(3km)

Kaiserin- Augusta- Allee

TURMSTR. Ⓤ

Alt-Moabit

Invalidenstr.

MIERENDORFFPL.

Spree

Beusselstr.

Levetzowstr.

BELLEVUE Ⓢ

RICHARD-
WAGNERPL. Ⓤ

Landwehrkanal

Altonaer Str.

HANSA-
PL. Ⓤ

SCHLOSS
BELLEVUE ■

Spree

Otto-Suhr-Allee

GROSSER
STERN

Kaiser-Friedrich-Str.

Wilmersdorfer Str.

TIERGARTEN Ⓢ

VICTORY COLUMN ■

Tiergarten

DEUTSCHE OPER 🎭 Ⓤ
Bismarckstr.

ERNST-
REUTER-
PL.

Str. des 17. Juni

Hofjägerallee

BISMARCKSTR. ←

DEUTSCHE
OPER Ⓤ

Schillerstr.

Zoologischer
Garten

TO ZOB →
(4km)

WILMERSDORFER
STR. Ⓤ

Leibnizstr.

Kneseckstr.

Hardenbergstr.

BAHNHOF
ZOO 🚆

KULTURFORUM 🏛

Kant Str.

Schlüterstr.

ℹ Ⓢ

ZOOLOGISCHER
GARTEN Ⓤ

Budapesterstr.

CHARLOTTEN-
BURG Ⓢ

SAVIGNYPL.

SAVIGNY
PL. Ⓢ

✉

✝

EUROPA
CENTER ℹ

CHARLOTTENBURG

KAISER-WILHELM-
GEDÄCHTNISKIRCHE

Kurfürstenstr.

Potsdamer Str.

ADENAUER
PL. Ⓤ

Kurfürstendamm

$ AMERICAN
EXPRESS

Lietzenburger Str.

Joachimstaler Str.

WITTENBERG Ⓤ
PL.

Kleiststr.

NOLLENDORF-
PL.

KURFÜRSTENSTR. Ⓤ

Einemstr.

Leon Str.

Konstanzer Str.

hansig

UHLANDSTR. Ⓤ

AUGSBURGER
STR. Ⓤ

NOLLEN-
DORFPL. Ⓤ

BÜLOWSTR. Ⓤ

WILMERS-
DORF

SPICHERNSTR. Ⓤ

VIKTORIA-
LUISE-PL. Ⓤ

Nachodstr.

Hohen-
staufenstr.

Pallasstr.

Goebenstr.

KONSTANZER STR. Ⓤ

FEHRBELLINER
PL. Ⓤ

HOHENZOLLERN-
DAMM Ⓤ

Hohenzollerndamm

GÜNTZELSTR. Ⓤ

SCHÖNEBERG

Kleist-
park

KLEIST
PARK Ⓤ

HOHENZOLLERN-
DAMM Ⓢ

Stadtring

Berliner Str.

Mehlitzstr.

Güntzelstr.

Grunewaldstr.

BAYER. Ⓤ
PL.

Martin-Luther-Str.

EISENACHER
STR. Ⓤ

Gothtstr.

Haupstr.

Belziger Str.

KAISER
WILHELM
PL.

BERLINER
STR. Ⓤ

BLISSESTR. Ⓤ

Badensche Str.

TO GRUNEWALD (2km) ←

Uhlandstr.

Bundes Allee

Dominicusstr.

Feurigstr.

Sachsendamm

SCHMARGENDORF

RATHAUS Ⓤ
SCHÖNEBERG

Mecklenburgischestr.

Ⓢ HEIDELBERGER PL.

Ⓢ Ⓤ

BUNDESPL.

INNSBR. Ⓤ
PL.

SCHÖNEBERG Ⓢ

Haupstr.

N
🧭

0 ——————— 1 mile

0 ——————— 1 kilometer

germany

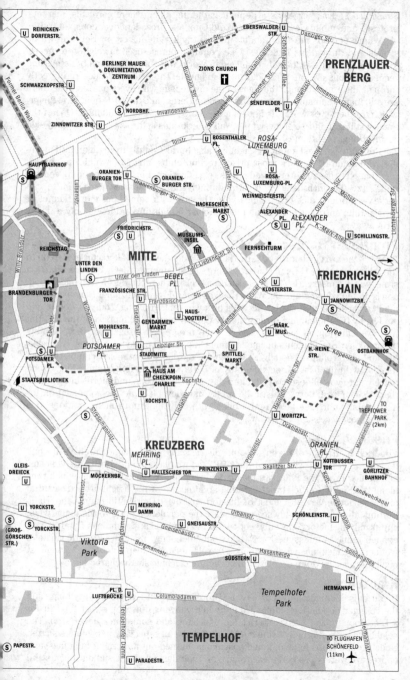

Straße des 17 Juni, serves as a popular gathering place where carnivals, markets, protests, and public viewings of the World Cup take precedent over constant traffic.

What's perhaps most fun about Mitte is tracing the history of Berlin down its streets and through its buildings. One common phrase used in relation to nearly every sight in Mitte is "heavily damaged in World War II," and original buildings and reconstructions are often difficult to distinguish. The **Berlin Wall** once ran directly through Mitte, and, though the signs of the divide fade with every passing year, there are still many remnants of a more fragmented Berlin, like the DDR-built **Fernsehturm,** which, for better or worse, is Mitte's most incessantly visible landmark. One of the longest still-standing stretches of the Wall deteriorates in the south, an unsightly sign of unsettling recent times.

But Mitte isn't just about the sights; it also burns brightly from night until morning with some of Berlin's most prized techno clubs, many of which are named, for whatever reason, after baked goods (e.g., **Cookies**). Plus, with shopping centers both ritzy (**Friedrichstraße**) and intimidatingly hip (**Hackescher Markt**), Mitte can serve as a pricey place to replace your threads with something more flannel or form-fitting; entry into the sometimes exclusive nightlife options is only a flashy strut away.

Prenzlauer Berg

P'Berg is the area just north of Mitte that runs from the edge of **Rosenthaler Platz** up to the **Schönhauser Allee** U-Bahn station. P'Berg's most famous street is **Bernauer Strasse,** a street which runs east(ish) to west(ish), parallel to where the Berlin Wall once stood, and is dotted with memorials. When the Wall came down, Prenzlauer Berg was pretty much a ghost town. But after decades of lower rents drawing students, youth, and vitality, by the millennium, Prenzlauer Berg had become the hippest of the hip. But hip, by definition, never lasts, and as time progressed, Prenzlauer Berg steadily began to gentrify: students became parents, hippies gave way to yuppies, and parks became playgrounds. Though it's changed, Prenzlauer Berg hasn't completely lost its cool: with the best bar scene of any of Berlin's neighborhoods, including a wine place where you choose how much to pay, a ping-pong bar, and more vintage sofas than *Mad Men*, P'Berg can still be pretty unbelievable. One recommendation for maximizing your time here: rent a bike. With only about four metro stations, this Berg is most accessible on two wheels.

Friedrichshain

Friedrichshain is one of Berlin's cheaper districts. It's rough around the edges, it won't let you forget that it was part of the DDR, and it's plastered in graffiti, metal-heads, and punks. From the longest still-standing remnant of the Berlin Wall, which runs along the Spree, to the stark, towering architecture of the neighborhood's central axis, **Frankfurter Allee**, the ghost of the former Soviet Union still haunts the 'Hain. Fortunately, this ghost only seems to scare the population out into the night, when any crumbling factory, any cobwebbed train station, and any complex of graffiti with enough grime is fair game for F'Hain's sublimely edgy nightlife. Friedrichshain is wonderfully inexpensive and unique. Travelers should keep a lookout, though, at night, because its often desolate infrastructure can hide shady characters.

Kreuzberg

If Mitte is Manhattan, Kreuzberg is Brooklyn. Graffiti adorns everything, and the younger population skulks around while chowing down on street food fit for a Last Supper. The parties start later, end later, and sometimes never stop. The neighborhood's alternative soul sticks around like an especially persistent squatter. Underground clubs in abandoned basements, burned-out apartment buildings, and oppressive warehouse complexes shake off their dust when the sun disappears and rage until well after it reappears. The area is also home to most of Berlin's enormous Turkish population (hence the nickname "Little Istanbul"). *Döner* kebabs, the salty scraps cut from those gigantic meaty beehives in every other storefront, go for €2-3 all across this district, and the **Turkish Market** along the southern bank of the **Landwehrkanal** is one of the most exciting, raucous, cheap, and authentic markets in Western Europe. If you want to learn about Berlin, head to Mitte. If you want to not remember what you learned, come to Kreuzberg.

ACCOMMODATIONS
Charlottenburg

HAPPY GO LUCKY HOTEL $
Stuttgarter Platz 17   ☎30 327 09 072

The Germans tend to be straightforward, and this quiet hostel is no exception. With friendly staff and friendlier prices, Happy Go Lucky is just that. We appreciated the festive graffiti (did you know you were in Berlin?), over-ate from the €6 breakfast buffet, and filled the peaceful courtyard with cigarette smoke. Although it's far from the rush of the city's center, its proximity to cute cafes, cheap eats, and the U-bahn and S-bahn will certainly make you happy (though you might not get lucky). Until recently, this stop was called the Berolina Backpacker, and much of the integrity of the original backpacker's oasis remains the same. Large groups (like high-school field trips) commonly book here, so it might be worth it to book ahead of time.

i Dorms from €9. Singles €38. Doubles from €65. Reception 24hr.

ALETTO KUDAMM $
Hardenbergstr. 21   ☎30 233 214 100

Though the logo frightens us (we think it was inspired by a bad trip in a sex shop), the Aletto Hotel and Hostel makes up for this colorful cactus-dildo with immaculately clean rooms (personal air-conditioning and a TV?!), inviting staff, and more ballsy activities in the common spaces than we have time for (quite literally: foosball, futballs, ping-pong balls, billiard balls, and metal balls in a sand pit are just the start). A 2min. walk from the Zoologischer Garten, the Aletto Kudamm is an ideal location for less-than-ideal Charlottenburg. Aletto also has this wonderful hotel/hostel combination in Schoeneberg and Kreuzberg, so it maintains high standards that give this contemporary stop an almost sanitized feel.

i Dorms €12. Singles €39. Doubles €49. Reception 24hr.

Schöneberg and Wilmersdorf

GRAND HOSTEL BERLIN $
Tempelhofer Ufer 14   ☎30 200 95 450

Though technically this hostel is located in neighboring Kreuzberg, it's only a 10min. walk from the heart of Schöneberg (and 10 seconds from Mockenbrucke station) and well worth the commute. Upon arrival at the grand 19th-century building, you'll be greeted with a complimentary beer or coffee while you're waiting to get checked into your room. On top of this unexpected hospitality, the reception is warmly welcoming and adjacent to a cozy bar/library where you'll find many of the hostel's residents working while they drink or drinking while they work.

JUGENDHOTEL BERLINCITY $$
Crellestr. 22

Nestled in a cozy nook of peaceful Schöneberg, Jugendhotel Berlincity is a great option for travelers looking to cafe-hop by day and avoid the clubs by night.

Our only hesitation is the lack of dormitory option; the only choice is to book a private room regardless of whether you are a one-woman wolfpack or a six-person group. Given the location and private-room-only option, this hotel is better suited for older couples or younger groups who are traveling for the first time.

i *Singles from €35. Doubles from €50.*

Mitte

HEART OF GOLD HOSTEL $
Johannisstr. 11   ☎30 2900 3300

Heart of Gold has the answer to the ultimate question, and it's 42. If you're confused, don't panic! You'll soon discover that Heart of Gold is *Hitchhiker's Guide to the Galaxy*-themed, and Google will help you with any references you don't get. The rooms are so large they feel like deep space, but they're much cleaner than the atmosphere. The wall-sized windows and quaint courtyard provide the perfect vantage points for stargazing or day drinking, whichever you prefer. You won't leave saying, "So long, and thanks for all the fish," but you will be thanking the Heart of Gold for much more.

i *Dorms from €17. Reception 24hr.*

ST. CHRISTOPHER'S HOSTEL $$
Rosa-Luxemburg-Straße 41   www.st-christophers.co.uk

St. Christopher's embodies the backpacker's spirit. The culture is youthful and energetic, and the vibrant common areas attract a lively crowd. The best part of St. Christopher's might be Belushi's, which is its famous UK-style sports pub that runs great happy hours and is the perfect start to any night out in Berlin. The rooms uphold the same standard of spaciousness and cleanliness as just about every other hostel chain, so you won't have any surprises except how much fun you're going to have. Enjoy.

i *Dorms €20-27. Reception 24hr.*

BAXPAX DOWNTOWN $
Ziegelstr. 28   ☎30 2787 4880 www.baxpax.de

Baxpax Downtown has got it goin' on. They've figured out everything a youthful traveler could want or need and set a new standard for the all-inclusive hostel. It has a bar and lounge downstairs with enough cheap snacks to satiate your whole group for under €10, and there's even a club in the basement. On top of that, they have two pop-up pools for the summertime heat waves. Brightly colored walls and wooden floors give Baxpax Downtown plenty of character, and comfortable rooms promise a much-deserved night's rest.

i *Dorms €15-23. Reception 24hr.*

Prenzlauer Berg

EASTSEVEN HOSTEL BERLIN $$
Schwedter Str. 7   www.eastseven.de

East Seven is cozy and opinionated, and we absolutely love it. Nestled on a quiet street in Prenzlauerberg (which is everywhere, but you get the idea), East Seven caters to the backpacker who has taste. With an indoor lounge and beautiful patio area equipped with a grill, this place understands how to make travelers feel at home. Rooms are spacious with hardwood floors, elegant windows, and subtle-hued stripes that your grandmother would approve of. The young, knowledgeable staff makes checking-in welcoming and easy; just make sure you take advantage of their expertise of all things Berlin.

i *Dorms from €23. Reception 7am-midnight.*

ALCATRAZ HOSTEL
$

Schönhauser Allee 133A   www.alcatraz-backpacker.de

If the real Alcatraz took some lessons from this hostel, they'd never again have problems with people trying to escape because no one would want to leave. The staff is friendly and accommodating, the common spaces (a.k.a. the chillout room and common kitchen) are tidy and outfitted with foosball along with some well-worn couches, and the location is uber-close to the U-bahn. The only commonality we can find between this Alcatraz and the prison is that the hostel rooms err on the cozier side and the decorations are pretty minimal. Instead of sitting in your room contemplating these similarities, take a stroll into the central courtyard or enjoy the bright murals lining the walls.

i Dorms from €12. Reception 7am-1am.

Friedrichshain

U INN BERLIN HOSTEL
$

Finowstr. 36   ☎30 330 24410 www.uinnberlinhostel.com

In one of the busiest nightlife districts in Berlin, U Inn Berlin Hostel is a restful refuge, quiet sanctuary, and peaceful perch amid the never-ending nocturnal abyss that is Friedrichshain. Though still proximal to the busiest parts of the nightlife districts, U Inn Berlin is nestled on one of the quieter streets in northern Friedrichshain and is only a stone's throw from the best restaurants and cafes anywhere in Berlin. Exceptionally friendly staff will invite you to cook dinner with them, similarly congenial travelers will invite you to party with them, and this cozy hostel will definitely look forward to having you back.

i Dorms €18. Singles €34. Doubles €54. Reception 7am-11pm.

EASTERN COMFORT HOSTELBOAT
$

Mühlenstr. 73-77   ☎30 6676 3806 www.eastern-comfort.com

That's right. This hostel is on a boat. We don't even really care about anything else—we're happy enough that we're floating and get to spend the night. Especially given the potential for this to be the most kitschy, gimmicky tourist trap known to traveler-kind, we were delighted that the accommodations were surprisingly acceptable. You can even camp on deck and have a view of the East Side Gallery. We wouldn't not do it again.

i Camping €15. Dorms from €16. Reception 24hr.

Kreuzberg

THE CAT'S PAJAMAS
$

Urbanstr. 84   www.thecatspajamashostel.de

The Cat's Pajamas is the cat's meow; seriously, this fabulous feline hostel is far from a flophouse. Modern, minimalist, and magnificently clean, the Cat's Pajamas is the attenuated accommodation in an ideal location. Right on the border of New Age Neukolln and creative Kreuzberg, the Cat's Pajamas is equipped with every amenity a backpacker could need or want. This hostel puts the icing on the cake with artful decor that continues to convince you you're in one of the most creative and progressive places in the world, with one of the hippest hostels to boot.

i Dorms from €15. Singles €49. Doubles €60. Reception 24hr.

THREE LITTLE PIGS HOSTEL BERLIN
$

Stresemannstr. 66   www.three-little-pigs.de

The big bad wolf of Berlin is a daunting beast. The Three Little Pigs Hostel has outsmarted its perpetrator, though, with a location that locals are envious of. The hostel is equidistant from both the cultural epicenter of Mitte and the nocturnal haven of Kreuzberg and Friedrichshain. If you have to see everything

Berlin has to offer in little to no time, the Three Little Pigs Hostel will be a perfect perch from which to explore the city. The hostel is much more than just a location, though, with amenities that are far from a pig sty. This place isn't just for youthful swine; appreciate their taste in decor, knack for cleanliness, and overall hospitality that will make you proud to be a little pig.

i *Dorms from €13. Reception 24hr.*

SIGHTS

Charlottenburg

OLYMPIASTADION

Olympischer Platz 3   ☎30 306 88 100

Originally erected for the 1936 Olympics, the Olympiastadion operates today as, well, a stadium. Occasionally hosting major sporting events (such as the 2006 FIFA World Cup final) and concerts, the stadium generally functions as a tourist attraction for those interested in seeing one of the three Nazi-built monumental structures, but really the stadium acts as an unofficial monument to Jesse Owens. If you've never heard of him, he was an African American track and field athlete in the 1936 Games who won four gold medals, but some dude with a mustache refused to recognize his wins due to his race. Because of the significance of the fact that Germany hosted the Olympics in 1936, it is definitely worth the trip out west to check this place out and reflect on the turbulence Berlin has experienced throughout the last century.

i *€7, students €5.50. Audio guide €4. Guided tour €11, students €9.50. Open daily Apr-July 9am-7pm; Aug 9am-8pm; Sept-Oct 9am-7pm; Nov-Mar 10am-4pm.*

SCHLOSS CHARLOTTENBURG

Spandauer Damm 20-24   ☎30 320 911

Sprawling extravagance shouldn't repel you from this garish Baroque palace, but man does strolling through the inside make your wallet feel thin. Not only does entrance cost €12 (€8 for students), but there is so much rich people stuff on the inside, you'd think they would be more careful about who they let in. From the outside this place is no joke either. Commissioned as a gift for his wife in the 1600s, Friedrich I must have screwed up bad if he built a palace to get out of the doghouse. Be sure to stroll along the beautiful and immaculately maintained garden, which spans for acres behind the palace (all for free!). The weaving network of paths wrap around gardens, fountains, and even a summer residence called Belvedere (tours from €4). All of this makes it the perfect destination for a summer picnic or romantic stroll.

i *€12, students €8. Photo pass €3. Audio tour free. Garden free from sunrise to sunset. Open Tu-Su 10am-6pm.*

MUSEUM BERGGRUEN

Schloßstr. 1

Need a break from the beautiful faces all around Berlin? Soak up Picasso in all of his asymmetrical glory and gain some appreciation for those good-lookin' folks at your hostel. There are two whole floors dedicated to Picasso's work, so even if you're not a Picasso enthusiast you might be by the time you leave. Along with the expansive Picasso collection, Museum Berggruen has a room dedicated to Matisse, some Paul Klee scattered about, and a few creepy humanoid statues made by Alberto Giacometti (one extra-tall one standing guard as you walk in—look out).

i *€10, students €5. Audio guide free. Open Tu-F 10am-6pm, Sa-Su 11am-6pm.*

BROHANMUSEUM
Schloßstr. 1a

You'll never again forget what Art Deco means, but you might want to after sponging up so much functional Cubism. The Brohanmuseum houses an expansive collection of furniture, paintings, sculptures, and posters highlighting the origins and progressions of the Art Nouveau and Art Deco era (roughly 1889-1940). For those of us rusty with art history, this essentially means that every item at the cat lady's eclectic garage sale can be found here. Seriously. This place is like the collection of leftovers from the set of *That 70's Show*.

i €6, students €4. Open Tu-Su 10am-6pm.

KATHE-KOLLWITZ MUSEUM
Fasanenstr. 24

Though not as large as many of the museums in Berlin, the Kathe-Kollwitz Museum is one of the most moving. Through WWI and WWII, Kathe Kollwitz was a member of the Berlin Sezession, and through her haunting depictions of wartime suffering, she became one of the most prominent German artists of the 20th century. Her illustrations and sculptures are tonally dark and elicit equally dark feelings from emotionally trying times. You can feel the presence of death and suffering in each of her pieces, which is both an incredible feat and emotionally draining. The experience is not one to miss.

i €6, students €3. Open daily 11am-6pm.

C/O BERLIN
Hardenbergstr. 22-24   ☎30 284 441 662

C/O Berlin is one of Berlin's newest museum additions. It operates as both a performance space and photography museum. The installations rotate every few months but attract a diverse range of artists and photographic styles. Whether you're a fine-art photographer or daily selfie-stick user, C/O Berlin is worth a visit. In addition to its neatly curated photo spaces, it also has a quaint cafe bustling with aspiring artists. We recommend C/O Berlin for a lunch-break museum tour and coffee or for one of its many events (which are often free!).

i €10, students €5. Open daily 11am-8pm.

Schöneberg and Wilmersdorf

Schöneberg sights are a mix of pastoral parks and whatever cultural bits and pieces ended up in this largely residential neighborhood. Travelers with limited time in Berlin should note that attractions here are few and far between and aren't easily and efficiently visited. If you want to see them all, attack these sights in groups.

▨ GRUNEWALD AND THE JAGDSCHLOSS
Am Grunewaldsee 29 (Access fromPücklerstr.)   ☎030 813 35 97 www.spsg.de

This 3 sq. km park, with winding paths through wild underbrush, gridded pines, and a peaceful lake, is popular dog-walking turf and a great change from the rest of bustling Berlin. About a 1km walk into the woods is the **Jadgschloß**, a restored royal hunting lodge that houses a gallery of portaits and paintings by German artists like Anton Graff and Lucas Cranach the Elder. The one-room hunting lodge is worth skipping, unless you find pottery shards particularly enthralling. Instead, walk around the grounds or take a hike north in the forest to **Teufelsberg** ("Devil's Mountain"), the highest point in Berlin that was made from WWII rubble piled over a Nazi military school.

i U3 or U7: Fehrbelliner Pl., or S45 or S46: Hohenzollerndamm, then bus #115 (dir. Neuruppiner Str. or Spanische Alle/Potsdamer): Pücklerstr. Turn left onto Pücklerstr., follow the signs, and continue straight into the forest to reach the lodge. Check the Jadgschloß visitor center for a map. Hunting lodge €4, students €3. Tours in German €1) offered on weekends. Open spring-fall Tu-Su 10am-6pm, last entry 5:30pm; winter Sa-Su 10am-4pm, last entry 3:30pm.

BRÜCKE MUSEUM

Bussardsteig 9   ☎030 831 20 29   www.brueckemusuem.de

The Brücke (The Bridge) houses a number of brightly-colored oil paintings which you'd think were put together by Monet. Think again. For us non-artistic folk, no-names line every wall of this museum. Their works are part of *Die Brücke* movement, which showcases thick brushstrokes, super-bright yellows, and other energetic colors. This museum is tiny and extremely far from almost everything else, but for anyone who's heard of *Die Brücke* before, it'll be worth the trek. It's not often you get to experience your passion in a modern building nestled at the edge of a German wood.

i U3 or U7: Fehberlliner Pl., then bus#115 (dir. Neuruppiner Str. to Spanische Allee/Potsdammer): Finkenstraße, then walk back up Clayallee about 50ft. and turn left onto the footpath leading into the woods. Look for signs. €5, students €3. Cash only. Open M 11am-5pm and W-Su 11am-5pm.

ALTER SANKT-MATTHÄUS-KIRCHHOF

On Großgörschen Str.   ☎030 78 11 850

We're fairly sure Hansel and Gretel and the mean-nasty witch they killed are all buried in this cemetery. Well, maybe not, but both of the Grimm brothers are. This *Kirchhof* is an expansive and sloping retreat from the city around, and it's isolated from the bustle by tall trees and hushed gardens. Besides the infamous Brothers Grimm, this cemetery is the eternal resting place of Romantic composer Max Bruch. A grand, mid-19th-century chapel juts out from the shrubbery, as do a number of gigantic and increasingly impressive structures that old Berlin families built for their deceased. After you've spent an hour grave hunting, stop by the cafe and flower shop to ease yourself back into the hassles of the living.

i U7, S2, S25: Yorckstr. Open in summer M-F 8am-8pm, Sa-Su 9am-8pm; winter M-F 8am-4pm, Sa-Su 9am-8pm. Hours vary by month. Cafe open M-Sa 9am-6pm.

VIKTORIA-LUISE-PLATZ

Intersection of Motzstr. and Winterfeldstr.

Come young, come homeless! Like the best German *Plätze*, Viktoria-Luise-Platz just seems to bring everyone together during those blissfully sunny afternoons. There's probably a kid trying out his new skateboard tricks on one side and a young mother watching her child take its first steps on the other. This oasis of a park is named after Wilhelm II's daughter and, in keeping with its name, channels the extravagance of an older, pre-war, bourgeois Berlin, with a central geyser of a fountain and a Greco-Roman-looking row of columns standing guard at one side. Take advantage of the lack of an open container law and bring your booze collection and a blanket to sip lazily amid the perfectly green grass and flowers.

i U4: Viktoria-Luise-Pl.

RATHAUS SCHÖNEBERG

John-F.-Kennedy-Pl. 1

The *Rathaus* (literally, "courthouse") here is pretty unremarkable, being the stark, early 19th-century building that it is (so many straight lines!). Still, JFK came here to establish that he was a jelly-filled doughnut during his Translation 101 case study-worthy speech in which he declared, "Ich bin ein Berliner." But this place isn't just a dull and historical courthouse. It also houses a flea market every Saturday and Sunday on the *Platz* out front bearing Jack's name. Even if you come here midweek, the huge park is an ideal spot to romp around, catch some sun, and nibble on whatever foodstuffs you happen to bring with you.

i U4: Rathaus Schöneberg. Flea market open Sa-Su 10am-6pm.

GAY MEMORIAL

Just outside the Nollendorf U-Bahn station

Don't blink! You might miss it. This slightly hidden memorial is shaped like a Crayola crayon, with six ultra-neon colors running down its sides. The small

monument commemorates homosexuals killed during World War II. There's not a whole lot to see here—the memorial is tiny, and the markings are virtually nonexistent. Still, it's worth turning your head if you happen to pass by on the way to the Nollendorfplatz U-Bahn stop.

i U1, U3, U4, or U9: Nollendorfpl.

Mitte

PERGAMON MUSEUM

Bodestr. 1-3

We aren't kidding when we say that people come all the way to Berlin just to check this place out. Here's why: Pergamon was the capital of a Hellenistic kingdom, and the museum reconstructs its temple to nearly its full size, so you can walk up its steep steps. The awe-inspiring battle relief on the wall displays jagged toothed snakes ripping off heroes' arms while titans tear lions' mouths apart. The Mesopotamian Ishtar Gate, reconstructed tile-by-tile from the original, rises 30m into the air, then stretches 100m down a hallway. You'll hardly believe it, so come see it. But wait! The Pergamon Museum is under renovation until 2019, so if you want to get the full effect you should wait to book your tickets until then. The closures affect the Pergamon Altar, the North Wing, and the Hall of Hellenistic Architecture. The Market Gate of Miletus, the Ishtar Gate and Processional Way from Babylon, and the Museum of Islamic Art will remain open during this time.

i €12, students €6. Museum Island Pass (Museuminsel ticket; €18, students €9) is a one-day pass to all of the museums on Museum Island (hint: it's worth it). For an even better deal, get the Museum Pass, which is a 3-day (consecutive) ticket to all of the National Museums of Berlin (Staatliche Museen zu Berlin) and a few others (hint: it's even more worth it). €24, students €12. Open daily 10am-6pm.

MEMORIAL TO THE MURDERED JEWS OF EUROPE

Cora-Berliner-Straße 1

Simple, haunting, and beautiful, the Memorial to the Murdered Jews of Europe is well worth a visit. Stark concrete blocks arranged in a grid pattern over an entire city block, the location is not one you'd expect for a place of reflection. As you walk deeper into the grid, though, you'll become surrounded by towering blocks in a maze of gray and the noise of the city will recede into silence. After losing yourself among the concrete labyrinth, head below ground for a moving, informative exhibit on the history of Judaism during World War II. Especially devastating is the "family" room, which presents pre-war Jewish family portraits and then investigates the individual fates of the family members. The last room continuously plays one of the thousands of compiled mini-biographies of individuals killed in the Holocaust.

i Free. Open Tu-Su 10am-7pm; closed Mondays.

BRANDENBERG GATE

Pariser Pl.   ☎030 250 02 333

You've already seen its image obnoxiously covering the windows of every passing U-Bahn train, but upon approaching the real Brandenburg Gate for the first time, trumpets may still blare in your head. During the day, tourists swarm this famous 18th-century gate; however, the wise traveler will return at night to see it ablaze in gold. Friedrich Wilhelm II built the gate as a symbol of military victory, but Germans these days prefer to shy away from that designation. A system of gates (and, independently, a certain famous wall) once surrounded it, but today only this most famous gate remains.

i S1, S2, or S25: Brandenburger Tor.

BERLINER DOM
Am Lustgarten

As one of Berlin's most magnificent buildings, this landmark is impossible to miss and would be a mistake not to visit. Unfortunately, you have to pay a small fee to enter the church, but the grandeur of the inside will quickly wipe your memory bank of any fiscal resentment. After thoroughly exceeding your aesthetic expectations, take a walk up the stairway to heaven (it never ends), stop to gaze at the museum of the church's construction along the way, and then enjoy a stroll around the dome itself and find some spectacular views of the city. Just don't fall down the stairway on your way down—you wouldn't want to end up in the spooky crypt beneath the church.

i €7, students €5. Open M-Sa 9am-8pm, Su noon-8pm.

NEUES MUSEUM
Bodestr. 1-3

Ironically, the Neues Museum (literally translated to New Museum) houses one of the best collections of ancient artifacts in the world. In addition to the incredible collection of sarcophagi, jewelry, and sculptures throughout the space, the museum itself is a remarkable work of modern architecture and worth a visit by itself. Don't miss Nefertiti—she's kinda famous. Then learn about your origins from the "time machine" and massive collection of prehistoric artifacts. Wander into the central chamber on the second floor, and you might just feel like the slab of granite you're standing on is floating through some esoteric Egyption incantation. Given that the Neues Museum is one of the best museums in Berlin, it manages to attract quite a crowd, so get here early or reserve tickets online to avoid lines.

i €12, students €6. Open M-W 10am-6pm, Th 10am-8pm, F-Su 10am-6pm.

ALTE NATIONALGALERIE
Bodestr. 1-3

This expansive collection of late-19th- and early-20th-century, mostly German artwork pays its dues to *fin de siècle* greats such as Adolph von Menzel, Paul Cezanne, Auguste Rodin, Caspar David Friedrich, and many more. The first floor is an ode to Realism with canvases depicting everything from France to feet, while the second floor reminds us of artwork that could be on the cover of some elven fantasy novel (apparently they call that Romanticism). Additionally, there's a small collection of works by the French Impressionist masters like Monet, Manet, Munet, Bidet (OK, maybe not the last two), and Renoir.

i €12, students €6. Open Tu-W 10am-6pm, Th 10am-8pm, F-Su 10am-6pm; closed Mondays.

ALTES MUSEUM
Am Lustgarten

Standing as a pillared fortress across the courtyard from the Berliner Dom, the Alte (meaning "old") Museum has an expansive collection of things that are, well, pretty darn old. With mostly Roman and Etruscan antiquities like vases, sculptures, jewelry, and tons of other artifacts from the daily lives of the long-dead, the Altes Museum can be a bit overwhelming after visiting the much more grandiose Pergamon and Neues Museums. Don't brush this one under the rug, though, because it has a world-famous collection of Greek sculptures, terracotta, and ancient coins that is worth checking out.

i €10, students €5. Open Tu-W 10am-6pm, Th 10am-8pm, F-Su 10am-6pm; closed Mondays.

BODE MUSEUM
Am Kupfergruben

The Bode Museum houses a gigantic collection of sculptures dating back to the Middle Ages. Basically, this means there are a ton of crazy fold-out nativity scenes made out of wood, more sculptures of Jesus than you'd expect to find in the Pope's house, and a whole range of Byzantine art. The museum itself is gorgeous, but after walking through the whole place you'll definitely appreciate a beer and a seat in Monbijou Park. You'll realize that the Bode Museum is pretty darn good-lookin' from the outside, too.

i €10, students €5. Open Tu-W 10am-6pm, Th 10am-8pm, F-Su 10am-6pm; closed Mondays.

NEUE WACHE
Unter den Linden 4   ☎030 250 023 33

Neue Wache (literally "New Watch") originally housed the royal palace guards. In 1969, after both devastating World Wars, an unnamed soldier and an unnamed concentration camp victim were laid to rest here. The memorial is nothing short of eerie, with a small amount of light propagating from the roof toward a mesmerizing sculpture by Käthe Kollwitz. The sculpture is aptly titled "Mother with her Dead Son." Aside from this grand adornment, the room is empty. There's little so affecting as the echo of a footstep within this room.

i U2: Hausvogteipl. From the metro, walk north along Oberwallstr. Free. Open daily 10am-6pm. The interior of the monument is still visible when the gate is closed.

FERNSEHENTURM
Panoramastr. 1A   ☎030 247 575 875 www.tv-turm.de

At 368m the Fernshehturm (literally "TV Tower") trumps all other sky pokers in the EU. It's shaped like a lame 1950s space probe on purpose: the East Berliners wanted their neighbors to the west to remember Sputnik every time they looked out their windows in the morning. For better or for worse, capitalism has since co-opted the DDR's (East Germany's) biggest erection, giving you the chance to rocket up into the tower's crowning Christmas ornament for a steep fee. Fortunately, in spite of the hordes of tourists that will inevitably get in your way, the view is incredible and especially worth checking out at the end of your stay, once you have a working vocabulary of Mitte's sights. Otherwise, it's just a big, beautiful mess of towers and roofs.

i U2, U5, or U8: Alexanderpl. €13, ages 3-16 €8, under 3 free. Entrance requires you to pass through security, so be sure to leave any pocket knives at your hostel. Open daily 10am-midnight.

KULTURFORUM
Matthäikirchplatz

Located right next to Potsdamer Platz, Kulturforum is a collection of significant architectural buildings that house some of Berlin's most prominent museums and event halls. The most notable among this group is the Neue Nationalgalerie, which has been temporarily closed for renovations with expectations to re-open around 2018. That said, the Kulturforum is absolutely worth visiting, with both the Gemaldegalerie holding one of the world's most expansive and important collections of European paintings. There are 2700 paintings covering the time and styles between the 13th and 18th centuries, so bring your walking shoes and thinking cap—you'll be sure to need them. In the same vicinity are both the Art Library and Museum of Decorative Arts, which both warrant their own visit. Often, though, the Art Library will have temporary exhibits like work from photographer Mario Testino. Oh, and on your way out, make sure to take a stroll by the Berlin Philharmonie, which is a landmark for unique architecture in Berlin and will entice you to snap a few photos.

i Prices and hours vary at each of the museums, but the Museum Pass is accepted at all of them except at special exhibits.

HAMBURGER-BAHNHOF MUSEUM
Invalidenstr. 50-51

Although this used to be a major train station connecting Berlin to Hamburg, the space has nothing to do with transportation. Instead, the building has been transformed into the museum for contemporary art, exhibiting a mixture of

berlin

paintings, sculptures, photography, and mixed-media installations from a variety of noteworthy artists (there's some Warhol in there, just to namedrop). You'll find yourself confused, exhausted, inspired, and reborn through your trek around this gigantic exhibition space; just make sure you don't get too frustrated with the conceptual nature that is modern art.

i *€14, students €7. Open Tu-W 10am-6pm, Th 10am-8pm, F-Su 10am-6pm; closed Mondays.*

THE KENNEDYS

August Str. 11-13   ☎030 206 53 570 www.thekennedys.de

The Kennedys is half museum, half art gallery. It houses an exhibit of photographs and rare memorabilia— JFK's suitcases, matches, and pens—and shows museum-goers the Kennedys' progression from Irish immigrants to America's political elite. Berlin seems to be extremely fond of the Kennedys, and not just for JFK's über-famous *"Ich bin ein Berliner"* comment—the city's relationship with the Kennedys started what the museum repeatedly refers to as the great German-American friendship. You may end up learning more about the Kennedys than you ever wanted to know, and the exhibition can often seem far too starry-eyed for its handsome protagonist, but the photographs are engaging, especially the ones you don't recognize. Anticipate seeing hundreds of pics of the Kennedys playing with their children, but don't expect to see any snaps of JFK wearing his reading glasses. After learning about the Germans' American hero, treat yourself to an American delicacy at Mogg & Melzer on your way out—you won't regret it.

i *S1, S25, or U55: Brandenburger Tor. From the metro, walk west toward Brandenburg Gate, then turn right into the square immediately before the Gate. €5, students €2.50. Open Tu-Su 11am-7pm.*

Prenzlauer Berg

Prenzlauer Berg isn't the place for sightseeing. There are a couple of treasures, namely **Mauerpark** and random bits of the remaining Berlin Wall, but this part of the city is mostly about hip bars, boutiques, and cafes.

▨ MAUERPARK

Extends north of the intersection between Eberswalder Str. and Schwedter Str.

Mauerpark is the heart and soul of Prenzlauer Berg. It's a grungy, sprawling, all-in-one park: you'll find a flea market, a stadium, some unique graffiti (if your name is Alex, there's even a marriage proposal!), day-drinking, a huge playground, men walking their dogs, and Sunday afternoon karaoke. In summary, Mauerpark is a park designed to exemplify the very essence of Berlin—perhaps as a thesis, spoken through a loudspeaker. We don't recommend taking a nap here, but we do recommend spending some time appreciating everything it has to offer.

i *U2: Eberswalder Str. From the metro, walk west on Eberswalder Str. Mauerpark extends far to the north after you pass the stadium. Free.*

▨ BERLINER MAUER DOKUMENTATIONSZENTRUM

Bernauer Str. 111   ☎030 467 986 666 www.berliner-mauer-gedenkstaette.de

A remembrance complex, museum, chapel, and entire city block of a preserved portion of Berlin Wall (complete with watch tower) come together in this memorial to "victims of the Communist tyranny." The church is made of an inner oval of poured cement walls, lit from above by a skylight and surrounded by a transparent skeleton of two-by-fours. The museum has assembled a comprehensive collection of all things Berlin Wall, including original recordings, telegrams, blueprints, film footage, and photos. Climb up a staircase to see it from above.

i *U8: Bernauer Str. From the metro, walk north on Brunnen Str., then turn left onto Bernauer Str. The church and memorial are on the left before Ackerstr., and the Dokumentationszentrum and exhibition are on the right immediately after Ackerstr. Free. Open Apr-Oct Tu-Su 9:30am-7pm; Nov-Mar 9:30am-6pm.*

JÜDISCHER FRIEDHOF

Schönhauser Allee

Prenzlauer Berg was one of the major centers of Jewish Berlin during the 19th and early 20th centuries. This ivy-covered Jewish cemetery contains the graves of composer Giacomo Meyerbeer and artist Max Liebermann and is studded by impressively high, dark tombs under towering trees. It's currently in a disappointing state of disrepair, with countless overturned tombstones and fallen trees, but it's still a beautiful grove worth wandering through. Nearby,**Synagogue Rykstrasse** (Rykestr. 53, right next to the Wasserturm) is one of Berlin's loveliest synagogues and one of the few spared on *Kristallnacht*. Since the synagogue still operates as a school, visitors aren't allowed to enter, but the red-brick, turn-of-the-century façade is impressive enough to warrant a visit.

i U2: Senefelderpl. From the metro, walk north on Schönhauser Allee. The gate to the cemetery is on the right, near the Lapidarium. Free. Open M-Th 8am-4pm, F 8am-1pm.

ZEISS-GROSS PLANETARIUM

Prenzlauer Allee 80   ☎030 421 84 50 www.astw.de

In 1987, this spherical planetarium opened as the most modern facility of its kind in the DDR. Would you believe that they had technology as advanced as the radio? The technology paled in comparison to what was going on in the West at the time, but today it can still show you the stars, sometimes with accompanying Bach or commentary for children. There are no exhibits, only shows, so check the website or call ahead for times.

i S8, S41, S42, or tram M2: Prenzlauer Allee. From the metro, the planetarium is across the bridge, on the left €5, students €4. Shows Tu-Th 9am-noon and 1-5pm, F 9am-noon and 1-9:30pm, Sa 2:30-9pm, Su 1:30-5pm.

Friedrichshain

▨ EAST SIDE GALLERY

Along Mühlenstr.   www.eastsidegallery.com

The longest remaining portion of the Berlin Wall, this 1.3km stretch of cement slabs has been converted into the world's largest open-air art gallery. The Cold War graffiti is unfortunately long departed; instead, the current murals hail from an international group of artists who gathered in 1989 to celebrate the Wall's fall. One of the most famous contributions is by artist Dmitri Wrubel, who depicted a wet, wrinkly political kiss between Leonid Brezhnev and East German leader Erich Honecker. The stretch of street remains unsupervised and, on the Warschauer Str. side, open at all hours, but vandalism is surprisingly rare.

i U1, U15, S3, S5, S6, S7, S9, or S75: Warschauer Str. or S5, S7, S9, or S75: Ostbahnhof. From the metro, walk back toward the river. Free.

▨ VOLKSPARK FRIEDRICHSHAIN

Volkspark Friedrichshain isn't the largest park in Berlin; it loses out to the **Tiergarten** in Mitte in terms of both size and class. But this brings us to the age old question: does size really matter? Volkspark compensates by attracting tons of people, from dog-walkers to kite-fliers to sunbathers. Monuments have popped up around the park as well, the most popular being the **Märchenbrunnen,** or the "Fairy Tale Fountain," a fountain that depicts 10 Grimm characters around a tremendous cascade of water. **Mount Klemont** gained its mass from the enormous pile of rubble swept beneath it in 1950 from two bomb-destroyed World War II bunkers; today, it occasionally serves as a platform for open-air concerts and movie screenings.

i S8 or S10: Landsberger Allee or U5: Strausbgr. Pl. From Strausbgr. Pl., walk north on Lichtenberger Str. Bounded by Am Friedrichshain to the north, Danziger Str. to the east, Landsberger Allee to the south, and Friedenstr. Str. to the south.

STASI MUSEUM

Ruschestr. 103, Haus 1   ☎030 553 68 54 www.stasimuseum.de

It's odd to imagine that this was once the most feared building in all of Germany: the Stasi Museum is housed in the gigantic headquarters of the East German secret police, the **Staatssicherheit**, or **Stasi**. During the Cold War, the Stasi kept dossiers on some six million of East Germany's own citizens, an amazing feat and a testament to the huge number of civilian informers in a country of only 16 million people. Since a 1991 law made the records public, the "Horror Files" have rocked Germany, exposing millions of informants and destroying careers, marriages, and friendships at every level of German society. The museum exhibition presents a wide array of original Stasi artifacts, among which is a mind-blowing collection of concealed microphones and cameras. All we want to know is how nobody noticed the bulky microphone concealed under a tie.

i U5: Magdalenenstr €6, students €4.50. Exhibits in German; English info booklet €3. Open M-F 10am-6pm, Sa-Su 11am-6pm.

Kreuzberg

None of Kreuzberg's sights are essential, especially compared to their glamorous cousins in Mitte, but if you're interested in something other than grunge, there are several museums, parks, and buildings you should consider stopping at. In addition to the sights we've listed, Kreuzberg also has several beautiful 19th-century churches that are worth a peek, including **Saint-Michael-Kirche** (Michaelkirchpl.), the **Heilig-Kreuz-Kirche** (Zossener Str. 65), and **Saint Thomas-Kirche** (Bethaniendamm 23-27).

🏛 DEUTSCHES TECHNIKMUSEUM BERLIN

Trebbiner Str. 9   ☎030 902 54 0 www.sdtb.de

With 30 full-size airplanes, 20 boats—including a full-size Viking relic—and a train from every decade since 1880, this museum could be a city in itself. Its permanent exhibitions cover everything from aerospace to road traffic to photo technology, but the special exhibitions also manage to be enticing. Most recently, Technikmuseum showed off 30 years in 30 photographs, a small but incredibly charming tour of the museum's technological prowess. But if photographs don't appeal, we find it hard to believe that World War II planes used for the Berlin Airlift, a U-boat, and a WWII rocket won't please.

i U1 or U2: Gleisdreieck. From the metro, head east on Luckenwalder Str. and turn right onto Tempelhofer Ufer. Walk under the train tracks and turn right onto Trebbiner Str. The entrance is about¾ of the way down Trebbiner Str. Many exhibits in English. €8, students €4; after 3pm, admission is free for children and students under 18. Open Tu-F 9am-5:30pm, Sa-Su 10am-6pm.

🏛 TOPOGRAPHY OF TERROR

Niederkirchner Str. 8   ☎030 254 50 90 www.topographie.de

The Topography of Terror takes you way back to 1930, and from then it takes you to explore the development of Nazi-/Gestapo-/Secret Service-induced terror. Seriously, prepare to be terrorized. The main exhibit consists of an extended series of maps, graphs, photographs, and an enormous amount of context—you could spend an entire afternoon reading through all the captions and explanations, which are fortunately provided in both German and English. That said, the images are so consistently powerful—and the exhibition so unbelievably exhaustive—that it is a must for any nuanced understanding of the development of Nazi terror. Outside, a newer exhibition of the development of Nazi influence in Berlin runs along the block-long remaining segment of the Berlin Wall.

i U6: Kochstr., or U2: Potsdamer Pl. From the metro, head east on Leipziegerstr. and take a right onto Wilhelmstr. Free. Open daily 10am-8pm.

BERLINISCHE GALLERY
Alte Jakobstr. 124-128

Berlin is a modern city, and a modern city needs a good museum for modern art. Despite the fact that the majority of Berlin has acted as a canvas for contemporary artists over the last 50 years, the Berlinische Gallery does a pretty good job keeping us entertained. With rotating exhibits, there's always something waiting to surprise us. There's also a concise collection outlining the history of architectural progression after the war along with some paintings highlighting the rebelliousness of an era.

i €8, students €5, under 18 free. Open M 10am-6pm, W-Su 10am-6pm.

SOVIET WAR MEMORIAL
Treptower Park

This memorial, a commemoration of Soviet soldiers who gave the ultimate sacrifice during the Battle of Berlin, is humongous. At 20,000 sq. m, it puts Mitte's **Soviet Memorial** to shame. Two jagged triangular slabs, each bearing the hammer and sickle, guard a tremendous rectangular square lined by exquisitely cut shrubs and surrounded by marble reliefs of Soviet soldiers helping the poor and the huddled. Quotes from Stalin in the original Russian and in German surround you at every step. But the most impressive piece stands at the end of the square: a tremendous, grassy mound bears a giant bronze statue of a Soviet soldier crushing a broken swastika and lugging a sword.

i U1 or U15: Schlesisches Tor. From the metro, walk southeast on Schlesische Str. Cross both canals and continue until you reach a fork in the road, between Puschkinallee and Am Treptower Park. Take Puschkinallee and walk along the park until you reach a large, semicircular courtyard with an entrance gate. Turn into this courtyard; the memorial is on the left. Free. Open 24hr.

JEWISH MUSEUM
Lindenstr. 9-14   ☎030 259 93 300 www.jmberlin.de

You'd know the Jewish Museum was important just from a single glance from outside the building: traffic blockades and security personnel swarm around the place, and you have to go through a security checkpoint to enter the museum. The building itself plays a significant role in the portrayal of its exhibitions: Daniel Libeskind designed the building to reflect the discomfort, pain, and the inherent voids in Jewish history, manifesting these characteristics as tremendous, triangular shafts, inaccessible rooms, and uneven floors. It's an amazing museum that actually succeeds at being experiential: it's disorienting, frightening, and historical.

i U1 or U6: Hallesches Tor. From the station, head east on Gitschinerstr. and take a left at Lindenstr. €7, students €3.50, under 6 free. Audio tour €3. Open M 10am-10pm, Tu-Su 10am-8pm. Last entry 1hr. before close.

CHECKPOINT CHARLIE
Zimmerstr. and Friedrichstr.

Though we really don't like this place, we can't leave it out: Checkpoint Charlie is incredibly popular, absurd, and has hundreds of tourists and multiple Starbucks cafes (which practically don't exist in Berlin) on one street. Never, ever have we seen more of a tourist trap. Though Checkpoint Charlie was once important to Berlin as the entrance to the American sector of West Berlin, today it's nothing but a mock entrance point, with German men dressed as American soldiers. You guessed it—you can take your picture with them for two badly-spent euro. A set of placards along Kochstr. provides a somewhat interesting history on the checkpoint and the various escapes it witnessed. Skip the museum: with admission at €12.50, you're better off buying a few beers.

i U6: Kochstraße. From the metro, walk north on Friedrichstr. Free. Museum €12.50, students €9.50. Open 24hr.

PRINZESSINNEN GARTEN

Prinzenstr. 35-38   www.prinzessinnengarten.net

This difficult-to-pronounce public garden is a rags-to-riches story. Left as abandoned wasteland by the city for years, a group of volunteer friends and neighbors transformed the unused space into a blooming and booming public garden and social space. In addition to the ecologically diverse landscape, the space also is host to diverse exhibitions and vendors that not only set the example for urban gardening projects around Europe, but also finance the rent of the space from the city. Impressive. Delicious. Trendy. Green. Pay a visit and appreciate the progressiveness of Berlin's public spaces.

i Free. Open daily 11am-6pm.

FOOD

Charlottenburg is not known for its budget-friendly fare, so head north to Moabit for cheap, authentic Turkish or Vietnamese food. Check out Schöneberg's relaxed cafe culture around the intersection of Maaßenstr. and Winterfeldstr. In Mitte, it's best to avoid overpriced restaurants and cafes near major sights. Prenzlauer Berg is another cafe capital: check out Kastanienallee or the streets around Helmholtzpl. for the highest concentration of caffeine. Some of Friedrichshain's narrow cobblestone streets are lined with cheap cafes, ice cream joints, and reasonably priced restaurants. The intersection of Simon-Dach-Str. and Grünbergerstr. is a good place to start. For the best international cuisine in a city known for cheap ethnic fare, head to Kreuzberg, where incredible restaurants line Oranienstraße, Bergmannstraße, and Schlesische Straße.

Charlottenburg

KASTANIE $
Schloßstr. 22

If you've been dreaming about the idyllic German meal of meat, Wießbier, and more meat, make this your first stop. Best enjoyed on a sunny afternoon, settle into the classic wooden table and chairs beneath the shade of kastanie trees, dig your feet into the gravel courtyard, and indulge in Bavarian specialties like six Nürnberger sausages, served with a side of pretzel, mustard, and an enthusiastic "Guten tag." You can self-diagnose an extreme case of gout upon departure, but it will be worth it.

i Food €2-10. Beer €3. Breakfast €3-8. Open daily 10am-2am.

LONMENS NOODLE HOUSE $
Kantstr. 33   ☎30 3151 9678

We know you didn't come to Berlin for Taiwanese food, but maybe you should have. Authentic and dirt-cheap, LonMens is a hidden gem that fills its hole-in-the-wall status with the freshest dumplings west of the East. We guarantee that everything you order will be delicious, and it won't break your already-suffering bank account. Though not on the menu, the chili wontons are divine and will leave you salivating until you return the next night. The best part? You can strut your steamed duck buns (not kidding—order them) right by the tourists disappointed in their less authentic, more expensive Chinese food right next door (we're talking about you, Good Friends).

i Food €4-8. Open daily noon-11pm.

WUSTEREI $
Hardenbergstr. 29d

It's tough to recommend currywurst stands in Berlin because they're all so damn delicious, cheaper than using the toilette, and more common than Starbucks in Manhattan. Wusturei caught our attention just because it seemed to have the perfect sauce: not too ketchupy, with just enough kick, and we didn't feel too much like a giant sausage after eating it. *Das ist gut!* If for whatever inhuman reason you don't enjoy indulging in this version of Germany's fast-food staple, walk across the street and try it again at Curry 36, which we also found to be amongst the best of the 'wurst. Regardless of what you choose, grab a Berliner Kindl, ask for extra mayo on the *pommes frites*, appreciate the posture-correcting standing barrel-tables, and enjoy the view of the Kaiser-Wilhelm Memorial Church while you gorge yourself like the pig you're eating.

i Food €4-10, but you should realistically get out of there too full to walk on about €7, including the beer (€3). Open M-Th 10am-midnight, F-Sa 10am-3am, Su 10am-midnight.

WINDBURGER
$
Windscheidtstr. 26 ☎30 437 27 177

As we're sure you will discover, Berlin has a bit of an obsession with New Age burger joints. There seems to be one around every corner, and we aren't complaining. If you find yourself missing good old-fashioned American food, head to WindBurger. You can snag a burger and fries on the go here for just a euro or two more than you'd spend at a doner kebab or currywurst stand. Meat not your thing? You should probably leave Germany, or at least order the veggie burger. The homemade fries will bring you right back to all that time you've never spent sitting at those classic American sports bars.

i Food €6-12. Open M-Sa noon-10pm.

CAFÉ AM NEUEN SEE
$
Lichtensteinallee 2 ☎30 254 4930

If you came to Berlin yearning for Oktoberfest-like biergartens only to discover that the authentic ones are in Bavaria, this place will grant you reprieve. Perched on the Neuen See Pond in the southwest of the Tiergarten, this cafe and biergarten could have been Disney's inspiration for Epcot Germany. Best enjoyed on a sunny afternoon when you're craving a romantic setting and an unromantic amount of beer, Café am Neuen See is a peaceful refuge hidden from the rush of the Ku'damm just 5min. away. The best thing about this biergarten is that no matter how much beer you've had, they'll still let you rent a rowboat (€5 per 30min.). Dissatisfied with the selection? Compare beer, garden, and biergarten at the Schleusenkrug on the northern side of Tiergarten, only a 15min. walk away.

i Pizza, pretzels from €5. Beer €3-6. Open M-F 11am-late, Sa-Su 10am-late.

SCHWARZES CAFÉ
$
Kantstr. 148 ☎30 3138 038

Craving absinthe at 4am? This is your place. Schwarzes serves up an extravagant menu 24hr. a day, but don't be fooled: Schwarzes is not your average late-night drunken pitstop. Its range is expansive and eclectic, from homemade hummus to indulgent dessert crepes, but it doesn't sacrifice quality for quantity. Enjoy the antique decor, contemporary artwork, indie music, and diverse crowd while you decide whether absinthe is more like an alcohol or a drug. Be careful—your bill will rise faster than the sun.

i Food €6-13. Drinks €3-7. Open daily 24hr., except closed Tu 3-10am.

Schöneberg and Wilmersdorf

CAFÉ BILDERBUCH
$
Akazienstr. 28

Whoever opened Café Bilderbuch seemed to have a conflict between starting an antique shop or a cafe. Well, the cafe won out, and we're glad it did. Though the cafe was seemingly designed by an eclectic Francophile and collector of regal antiques, you'll overlook the fringed lamps and well-worn leather couches for the delicious brunch menu, which is printed on the restaurant's own press.

Anything you order will undoubtedly be great, but you can't go wrong with a plate of fruit and cheese accompanied by a coffee and a bread basket.

i Breakfast and brunch options €5-8. Open daily 9am-11pm.

IMREN GRILL $
Hauptstr. 156

This is the best doner kebab place you'll find in Schöneberg, hands down. The durum (they make their own bread) is €4, the Turkish pizza is €3, and the endless, guilt-free joy you and your tastebuds will experience is priceless. Perfect for a late-night snack or a lunch on the go, Imren Grill has got you covered.

i Food €3-6. Open daily 10am-11pm.

EULE'S CAFÉ $
Über die Parkeingänge

Nestled among gardens on the west side of Gleisdreieck Park, Eule's Café is a safe haven for parents, children, cyclists, skateboarders, and park-goers alike looking for a Milchkaffee and pastry. The tiny shack might not be all that impressive, but the ambience makes up for the appearance. With a sign out front stating: "No Wi-Fi, talk to each other, pretend it's 1993, live!" and a crowd who couldn't be happier to be enjoying their coffee off the grid, Café Eule is a perfect oasis away from the hustle and bustle of the city next door. So sit back, relax, and enjoy your cappuccino while you watch fashionable moms push very impressive strollers all around Gleisdreieck.

i Food €2-6. Open daily 10am-6pm.

CARAMIA FOCACCERIA $
Goltzstr. 32

Simple and unassuming, Caramia Focacceria served us the best personal-sized pizzas for €2.50 we've ever had. We ordered one, and then we ordered one more (OK, OK, we ordered one after that, too). Nobody in there speaks English, but everyone speaks the language of Italian delicacies, so point and smile, then eat and enjoy. If you have any room left over in your stomach, you will definitely give in to temptation with gelato staring at you while you ravenously scarf down Berlin's best impression of NYC's dollar pizza.

i Pizza €2.50-5. Open daily 11am-midnight.

Mitte

DJIMALAYA $
Invalidenstr. 159

The combination of affordability, location, atmosphere, and unbelievable hummus makes Djimalaya one of our top stops for a relaxed lunch or low-key dinner in Mitte. The wraps are killer and on a different planet from even the best doner kebab stands. We opted for the fried cheese hummus wrap and wish we could have eaten ten. On a hot summer day, order a pitcher of the homemade lemonade and sit curbside; you won't want to leave.

i Food €4-10. Open daily noon-11pm.

CHAY VIET $
Brunnenstr. 164

The amount of authentic, delicious Vietnamese food in Mitte will astound you. Chay Viet is no exception, but stands out from the most trafficked Vietnamese spots because it's a bit farther away from bustling Rosenthaler Platz. As a result of being a bit off the beaten path, Chay Viet serves up delicious, affordable vegetarian soups and curries with a more peaceful atmosphere that is well worth the five-minute walk.

i Food €6-14. Open M-F 11:30am-10pm, Su 1-10pm.

1. CURRY 36: This place is so popular they started selling their own t-shirts. Though they're speckled all over the city, the one right outside of the Zoologischer Garten almost always has a line for a reason. Order it any time of the day, but try it ohne darm (without casing—it's the Berliner style)

2. WITTY'S: Bio-markets are around every corner, but Bio-wurst? You'll have to go to Witty's. Promising all organic meat and oils, Witty's is your best bet when you are environmentally and health conscious.

3. WURSTEREI: Some claim that the best currywurst is all about the sauce. Those people go to Wursterei. Not too spicy, not to sweet, just enough pizazz, and still dirt-cheap.

4. KU'DAMM 195: If you want your currywurst served up with a bit of class, head to Ku'damm 195. Need some champagne to wash it down? They've got you covered.

5. BRUTZELSTUBCHEN: Delivered fresh from the butcher every morning, the sausage here is incredible. Plus, the name is so fun to say it doesn't even matter how good the food tastes.

germany

DUDU $$
Torstr. 134

We are going to skip all of the immature Dudu jokes that you know we want to make and cut straight to the chase. Sure, this place might seem like just another chic, Asian-fusion trend-follower that attracts gullible yuppies into its makeshift jungle, but stave off your judgments until you take your first bite. Its yellow coconut curry over rice was da bomb, and its sushi was some of the best we've ever had. If you're pinching pennies, you can walk away only spending €10, but you won't want to. The cocktails are pretty damn tasty, too.

i Food €10-20. Open M-Sa noon-midnight, Su 1pm-midnight.

NOLA'S AM WEINBERG $$
Veteranenstr. 9

Talk about picturesque. Then pay for it. We're only kind of kidding. Nola's is a Swiss restaurant that does Sunday brunch particularly well. Apparently it does fondue too, but we'd really only recommend coming here for a lazy Sunday brunch when you don't mind forking over €12 for a beautiful (all-you-can-stuff-your-face) buffet of meats, cheeses, eggs, and pastries. Perched on the top of the hill overlooking Weinsburgsweg Park, Nola's is a pretty idyllic spot to enjoy a sunny Sunday afternoon.

i Food €8-18. All-you-can-eat brunch €12. Open daily noon-1am.

MOGG & MELZER $$
Auguststr. 11-13

Sometimes you just need a good ol'-fashioned sandwich. Well, this place doesn't have anything like that. Instead, they have mountains of thick-sliced pastrami towering between slices of homemade bread. We're not really sure these behemoths are really sandwiches, but they're effing delicious. They also come with coleslaw so tasty you won't even know it's coleslaw. The only downside to Mogg & Melzer is that the sandwich options come in two styles: "there-goes tomorrow's budget" expensive and it has "Well, damnit, now I'm homeless" expensive. We chose the latter, and it was well worth it. Could you spare any change?

i Food €8-15. Open M-Sa 10am-10pm, Su 7am-8pm.

CURRY MITTE

$

Torstr. 122

There are simply too many currywurst stands in Berlin to choose a favorite. For us, Curry Mitte has the perfect balance of sweet and spicy sauce, fresh meats, and proximity to the late-night scene that deems Curry Mitte the best of the 'wurst. It really doesn't get any better when your midnight raving gives you a midnight craving. So go indulge in Berlin's favorite fast food and forget about feeling guilty.

i Food €3-7. Open M-Th 11am-midnight, F-Sa 11am-6am.

EISMANUFAKTUR

$

Auguststr. 63

To our pleasant surprise, Berlin's ice-cream culture is nearly as strong as its coffee culture (and that's really saying something). The ice cream at every place we tried was incredible and often had delicious flavors we'd never heard of and will never forget. However, Eismanufaktur stood above the rest with ice cream, gelato, and sorbet only fit for gods and goddesses. We tried the guava and mango flavors, and then went back for the rhubarb. Rhubarb? That's right: rhubarb. Get it; you won't regret it.

i Ice cream €2-5. Open M-Th 1-8pm, F-Sa 1-9pm, Su 1-8pm.

Prenzlauer Berg

Prenzlauer Berg is smitten with its cafes: nearly every street hides a cafe (or six), so a cheap, tasty cup of joe or a small, inexpensive meal are never hard to come by. Check out **Kastanienallee, Kollwitzstrasse,** or the streets around **Helmholtzplatz** for the highest concentration of caffeine. If your place is kitchen equipped, stock up at any of the several **REWE** stores around P'Berg.

PIZZA NOSTRA

$$

Lychener Str. 2

Seriously delicious pizza at a reasonable price? Yes please. Sometimes you just gotta stuff your face with pizza, so why not make it the best pizza in Prenzlauer Berg? What makes Pizza Nostra so damn delicious is its history; run by two Italian dudes with roots going back to a Napoli bakery over a century ago, this place has Italian style in its DNA. Using their family dough recipe, they serve up unique slices with pick-your-own toppings from the simple to the extravagant—all for a decent price.

i Pizza €7-12. Open M-Sa noon-midnight, Su 1pm-midnight.

W-DER IMBISS

$$

Kastanienallee 49

This place should be on your radar from the second you step foot in Berlin. Signifying their mission in a simple act of rebelliousness, W-Der Imbiss is easily identified by the upside down McDonald's logo. You'll understand more about this stance against shitty food more once you taste the Mexi-Indi-talian fusion goodness. Basically, they've taken naan and used it as a burrito wrap, pizza dough, bread dip, and, well, just naan. It's all great, so make sure to bring a friend in order to taste more of the menu.

i Food €6-12. Open M-Th noon-10pm, F-Sa noon-11pm, Su noon-10pm.

CAFÉ KRONE

$

Oderberger Str. 38

Café Krone embodies Prenzlauer Berg's cafe culture in one meal. Elegant yet relaxed, this cafe is the perfect place to enjoy a lazy morning's breakfast and coffee while watching the hoards of Berliners walking to Mauerpark flea market. Just know that you're getting the better deal with delicious charcuterie plates, pancakes, or muesli. You'll have as hard of a time deciding as we did. The chef apparently has a sweet spot for egg dishes as well, and the egg salad redefined the dish for us. Give it a try, fellow egg-lovers.

i Food €4-14. Open M-F 9:30am-6:30pm, Sa-Su 10am-7pm.

Friedrichshain

GOODIES
$$

Warschauer Str. 69   ☎30 8965 4973 www.goodies-berlin.de

Anything that was directly on Warschauer Str. we turned a blind eye to, assuming that it would either be overpriced or catering to tourists. After one particularly long night (read: it was 10am) we sacrificed our food-tegrity and ate at this funky-looking grocery store/cafe right on the busiest part of the street (you can see both Berghain and the Warschauer train station from here). Goodies was exactly what we needed to replenish after a long night of Club Mate and beer. Organic smoothies, vegan breakfast wraps, and tempting cookies just scratch the surface of their extensive, though expensive, menu. Think Whole Foods, but more German.

i Food €4-10. Open M-F 7am-8pm, Sa-Su 9am-8pm.

REMBRANDT BURGER
$$

Richard-Sorge-Straße 21   ☎30 8999 7296 www.rembrandt-burger.de

We know, we know. Another burger place?! You came all the way to Berlin to eat shitty American-style food? Well, friends, rid yourself of your dubiousness or you shalt be duped. Not only was Rembrandt one of the craziest-ass mofos with a cool hairdo to run the art world, Rembrandt Burger is his modern-day equal in burger form. Their burgers are damn good, and their fries are even better. We had the Old Amsterdam Burger in the spirit of Rembrandt's hometown, and we weren't disappointed. Why don't Americans think of burger combinations like this?

i Food €8-12. Open daily noon-10pm.

Kreuzberg

MUSTAFAS GEMUSE KEBAP
$

Mehringdamm 32

If we could, we'd smuggle the mountain of meat responsible for filling Mustafa's kebabs home with us and eat durum every day for the rest of our lives. It's seriously good and the most filling, delicious lunch you'll have for €4. As far as doner kebab stands go, we think Mustafa's may very well be the best in Berlin, if not the whole world. Go. Eat. Enjoy.

i Food €3-8. Open daily 10am-2am.

GASTHAUS FIGL
$$

Urbanstr. 47   www.gasthaus-figl.de

There are places to grab a quick pizza pie all over Berlin. Gasthaus Figl is not one of these places. For Figl, Pizza is their craft, created with only the utmost care and freshest ingredients. They make each of their pies with a hefty dose of love, and we love eating it. Rumor has it that Figl makes the best pizza in Berlin, and we'd be lying if we said we didn't believe it. If you don't think they make the best pizza, you can't deny that they have the best website. Get hungry at gasthaus-figl.de.

i Food €8-15. Open Tu-Su 6pm-midnight.

HALLESCHES HAUS
$

Tempelhofer Ufer 1

Hallesches Haus is like an all-in-one store for hipsters. Not only is it a third-generation coffee shop serving up pristine brews and super sandwiches, it's also a general store selling all sorts of handmade appliances for the young urban professionals who appreciate thoughtfully designed silverware. What's not to love? Even if you're not into hand-crafted knives or self-bound books, Hallesches Haus is the perfect place to start your day with a cappuccino and croissant.

i Coffee €2. Pastries and sandwiches €2-6. Open M-F 9am-7pm, Sa 11am-4pm; closed Sundays.

NIGHTLIFE

If you're reading this section and thinking, "I'm not sure I want to go clubbing in Berlin," then stop it. Stop it right now. Take a hint from Lady Gaga, patron saint of Berlin, and just dance... you won't regret it. The true *Diskotheken* await in the barren cityscape of Friedrichshain and the notoriously nocturnal Kreuzberg. Mitte does not disappoint, either—its tremendous multi-room clubs filled with exquisitely dressed 20-somethings are generally worth their hefty covers. The major parties in Schöneberg are at the GLBT clubs in the northern part of the neighborhood. For tamer nightlife, try the jazz clubs in Charlottenburg or the bar scene in Prenzlauer Berg.

Charlottenburg

Don't go to Charlottenburg expecting a wild time. We're pretty sure you won't be able to get *that* crazy here, since Charlottenburg is known for its residential feel, quiet cafes, and the 30-somethings who are busier starting families than throwing crazy ragers. The neighborhood is great for a mellow evening or some live jazz, but the real parties are eastward. The **Ku'damm** is best avoided after sunset, unless you enjoy chatting up drunk businessmen.

DAS KLO

Leibnizstr. 57 ☎30 437 27 219

Translating to "The Loo," Das Klo takes its shit seriously. Well, kind of. Food is served in mini porcelain toilets, and beer is served in urine collectors (never used—don't worry). Every kitschy antique neglected by upscale antique shops has been claimed and vomited onto Das Klo's walls, only adding to the confusion you'll feel after being squirted by water when walking through the door and insulted in German by its DJ/comedian/porcelain-priest. If you don't take yourself too seriously and have always wanted to eat out of the toilet, it might be worth the experience.

i Beer €4-8. Open M-W 7pm-2am, Th-F 7pm-4am, Sa 7pm-2am.

QUASIMODO

Kantstr. 12a ☎30 318 04 560

Great music every night of the week with genres from blues to jazz to funk, or some eclectic combination of each. The only problem is that the crowd tends to be representative of Charlottenburg, which means older and boring. If you want deep house until the sun comes up, you should go somewhere else, but if you don't mind getting funky next to a 40-something who has to put the kids to bed after the next song, Quasimodo is the place for you!

i Tickets €8-15. Doors open at 9pm. Restaurant open M-F 4:30pm-midnight, Sa-Su noon-1am.

A-TRANE

Pestalozzistr. 105 ☎30 313 2550

Unless you're a passionate jazz fan, you shouldn't board the A-Trane. For those of you who enjoy hearing the brass wail and the strings dance, then A-Trane is definitely worth stopping by. Though small in size, the internationally acclaimed jazz club attracts some big names (Herbie Hancock, Wynton Marsalis, just to name a couple) and has been the recording site for many live albums. Expect to groove well into Sunday morning with a crowd that has been doing the same thing since '92.

i Cover €10-20. Doors open at 9pm.

Schöneberg and Wilmersdorf

Schöneberg is Berlin's unofficial gay district, so most of the nightlife here caters to the GLBT community. A couple of distinctive cocktail bars may be worth visiting in the interest of broadening your buzz, but the neighborhood's real parties happen at the GLBT clubs and bars in northern Schöneberg.

KUMPELNEST 3000
Lützowstr. 23

Imagine every person you've ever seen who you've looked at and thought, "Wow, that person looks crazy." Now imagine them all in the same place. Well, Kumplenest 3000 is that place. In what used to function as a brothel, Kumpelnest 3000 now acts as a disco-themed dive bar and attracts everyone from shirtless transvestites to the average college partygoer—even on Wednesday nights. German for "nest of friends," the Kumpelnest is surprisingly friendly—and we mean really friendly. When you're ten Pilsners deep and it's 3am (and only then), you should venture to the Kumpelnest for an experience you probably won't forget or won't remember one second of.

i *Drinks €4-12. Open M-Th 7pm-6am, F-Sa 7pm-8am, Su 7pm-6am.*

THE GREEN DOOR
Winterfeldtstr. 50

Step behind the green door and enjoy some of the most creative cocktails in Schöneberg. You'll have to ring the bell to be let in, but unless you look like you're going to attempt something crazy, you shouldn't have any problems. The inside of the bar exudes cool, with simple, funky decor straight from a '70s porno. Speaking of porno, the bar is a reference to the movie, Behind the Green Door, which is a kitschy porno from way back when lava lamps were trending. You'll never guess that from the much classier inside, but it's always worth getting references. The classed-up inside comes at a cost, though, with cocktails tending toward the expensive side.

i *Drinks €8-15. Open M-Th 6pm-3am, F-Sa 6pm-4am, Su 6pm-3am.*

MISTER HU'S COCKTAIL BAR
Goltzstr. 39   ☎30 217 2111

Our favorite part about Mister Hu's was that, at 2am on a Thursday, there were tons of people chilling in the outdoor seating. The cocktails are good but not terribly original or impressive. The bar and music were pretty standard, but the crowd enjoying the laid-back atmosphere is what makes this place great. If you're looking to sit down and drink for an extended period of time without a worry in the world, we recommend checking out Mister Hu's.

i *Drinks €7-13. Open daily 6pm-3am.*

Mitte

Mitte's techno clubs often offer the height of Berlin's dance scene. Nowhere else will you find clubs so well attended by exquisitely dressed locals in their early 20s, and, despite high covers, these tremendous multi-room clubs rarely disappoint. Most of these places are pretty close to **Rosenthaler Platz**, but some club is always just around the corner in Mitte. Don't expect to get a full night's sleep; the parties generally don't heat up until 2am.

MUSCHI OBERMAIER
Torstr. 151

Named after the iconic sex symbol from left-wing Berlin in the late '60's, Uschi Obermaier, this place reeks of grit, grunge, and rock-and-roll. The place is dark, sweaty, and saturated with cigarette smoke, and we suspect it hasn't changed much since its prime. The music makes up for the tiny dance floor, and the crowd ranges from young and naïve to old and weathered. Everyone seems to have the same idea, though, which is to have a damn good time. The drinks aren't particularly special, but the atmosphere is unique enough to pay it a visit.

i Cover varies but usually under €5. Open M-Sa 8pm-2am.

MEIN HAUS AM SEE

Torstr. 125

Vintage decor, well-worn couches, a miniature cafe next to the bar, and a constant horde of youngsters teeming with angst make Mein Haus am See a popular destination for backpackers passing through Mitte. In addition to a range of funky seating upstairs, there is also a downstairs with a club-like atmosphere and club-like lighting (a.k.a. no lighting). Not your scene? Grab a book and latte at 4am because this joint plays 24/7 and used to be a library. Don't misinterpret us though—most don't come here to catch up on literature.

i Usually no cover unless there's a live music event. Beer €2.50. Cocktails €6-8. Open 24hr.

NEU ODESSA

Torstr. 89

The bright entrance light will guide you straight into some of the better cocktails in Mitte. The vintage parlor look and smoke stained couches give Neu Odessa its upscale atmosphere and attract a group of night-owls who aren't just there to get hammered. The well-dressed hipsters who frequent this bar know to order the whiskey and stay away from the overpriced beer, but either way you aren't going to get out of here on a budget.

i Beer €4. Cocktail €8-15. Open daily 7pm-late.

KITTY CHENG

Torstr. 99

Kitty Cheng might be disguised as an antique, posh bar, but it has much more soul than it alludes to. One of the only bars that regularly bumps to old-school and new-school hip-hop, it has created one of the more interesting spots for higher-end cocktails in Mitte but they know it and make you pay for it. It's pretty stringent about the guy-to-girl ratio, so if you're a group of excited dudes, you might want to think about bringing a date or you won't be let in. And maybe spiff up a bit—they don't take too kindly to sloppily dressed partygoers.

i Beer €4. Cocktails €8-15. Open M-Th 9pm-2am, F-Sa 9pm-5am.

Prenzlauer Berg

Prenzlauer Berg has one of the highest birth rates in all of Germany, meaning that you aren't going to find many crazy clubs that rage until the sun comes up. There's less techno, more lounging, and far earlier quiet hours (starting around midnight) than other parts of Berlin. Prenzlauer Berg's nightlife is calm but still worth checking out. The bars are some of the most unforgettable in town, and, since they fill and empty a bit earlier, they're perfect before you head out to later, clubbier climes.

☒ THE WEINEREI: FORUM

Fehrbelliner Str. 57   ☎030 440 69 83 www.weinerei.com

With its dim lighting and kitschy, mismatched, super comfy furniture, Weinerei Forum dillies up some of the best and cheapest coffee and food in the neighborhood. Wait, it gets better. From 8pm to midnight, this place holds Berlin's most lively wine tasting: you pay €2 for a glass, you try any of their several wine varieties, and at the end of it all, you put as much money as you "think you owe" in a jar. Now, if you just read this as "€2 for unlimited wine!!!" you're not the kind of cool cat the forum is trying to attract. As you leave without putting any money or just a few euro cents in that jar, you'll get scowled at and possibly called out. Weinerei Forum wants you to be the judge of the value of your wine and food;

while that's totally awesome and a great way to spend an evening, it doesn't mean it's a freebie.

i U2: Senefelderpl. From the metro, exit by the northern stairs, then head west on Schwedter Str. Turn left onto Kastanienalle, then veer right onto Veteranenstr., a block down the hill. The bar is on the corner of Veteranenstr. and Fehrbelliner Str. Cash only. Open daily 10am-late. Wine flows 8pm-midnight every night, so let that guide you.

SCOTCH AND SOFA
Kollwitzstr. 18   ☎030 440 42 371

Retro. Stylish. Classic. Scotch and Sofa defines what a bar should be, with comfortable spaces to lounge about. Come to Scotch and Sofa to sip your scotch or whiskey, talk about something intellectual, and osmose the coolness of the atmosphere. Take some advice, though: if you aren't already experienced in the whole classy-scotch-drinking game, pick the cheapest option on the mile-long menu. It all tastes good, and your wallet will thank you.

i U2: Senefelderpl. From the metro, exit by the northern stairs, then head southeast on Metzer Str. After passing the grocery store, turn left onto Kollwitzstr. The bar is on the right, half a block up Kollwitzstr. Scotch from €5. Open daily 6pm-very late. Happy hour daily 6-7pm; cocktail of the day €3.80.

WOHNZIMMER
Lettestr. 6   ☎030 445 54 58 www.wohnzimmer-bar.de

This bar is laid back, and when we say that, we mean grab a beer (€2.60) and lie on a chaise lounge or one of the many super comfy couches in the "living room." Wohnzimmer is a smoking bar, so the patrons tend to be in their late 20s and exude philosophical vibes. Nostalgia abounds.

i U2: Eberswalder Str. From the metro, head east on Danziger Str., turn left onto Lychener Str., then right onto Lettestr., just past the park. The bar is on the left, at the corner of Lettestr. and Schliemannstr. Beer €2.50-3. Cocktails €4-5. Cash only. Open daily 10am-late.

Friedrichshain

Barren factory-scapes, heavily graffitied walls, and blinding floodlights may not be the most inviting obstacles to navigate in the dead of night, but such is the environment that hides some of Friedrichshain's—and Berlin's—biggest and most bangin' techno clubs. The old warehouses along **Revaler Strasse** hold the lion's share of sprawling dance floors, but you might want to branch out a little to avoid a double-digit cover.

BERGHAIN AND PANORAMA BAR
Am Wriezener Bahnhof   www.berghain.de

Even if we told you not to, we know you're going to end up going to Berghain. It's the unofficial electronic epicenter of the world—a techno temple that offers a church service for house worshippers from Friday until Monday. If this is your culture and you came to Berlin to go to Berghain, you must go. For those of you who didn't know what Berghain was until now, you should think about going somewhere else. The line to get in (even at 3am on Saturday or 10am on Sunday) is usually over two hours long (should be named Berg-line, amirite?), and there's a good chance Sven will shake his head in disapproval and you'll be sent packing. Oh, if you decide to go, make sure you wear all black.

i Cover €14. Drinks €4-10. Open F-Sa noon-late.

CASSIOPEIA
Revaler Str. 99   ☎30 4738 5949 www.cassiopeia-berlin.de

Cassiopeia is in the RAW Temple, which still stands as an act of defiance to the gentrification of Berlin. The party zone bordering the train tracks is filled with broken bottles, graffiti, and industrial buildings giving off the vibe of third-world country meets clubbing sanctuary. You might see the lights shining out of Cassiopeia like the queen in her starry chair, beckoning you to come and take a shot, but we reckon you'll hear Cassiopeia before you get anywhere close enough to see it. This place is just as raucous as the rest of 'em and will give you a hell of a night if you show up with the right attitude.

i Cover €5-15. Beer €2-4. Shots €2-5. Cocktails €5-10. Hours vary, usually open 11pm-late. Check website for the most up-to-date times.

Kreuzberg

If you came to Berlin for nightlife and you've visited some places in other neighborhoods, you've probably been left wondering why on earth Berlin has the reputation it boasts. And the answer, dear friend, is Kreuzberg. Kreuzberg is world-renowned for its unbelievable techno scene. Converted warehouses, wild light displays, destructive speaker systems, and packed dance floors cluster around **Schlesisches Tor,** but some of the best spots are scattered more widely. Kreuzberg is one of Berlin's most nocturnal neighborhoods, so expect parties to rage from 2am to well past dawn.

berlin

TRESOR

Köpenicker Str. 70   www.tresorberlin.com

Housed inside an old, derelict heating plant, Tresor is a modern techno tabernacle and legendary labyrinth of some of the best electronic music to come out of Berlin. With an industrial dance floor in the basement and more laid-back house lounge upstairs, the sheer size of the space will impress you. Globus on the third floor produces some of the smoothest house vibes we've found, +4 is the laboratory where the techno-technicians experiment, and the vault is where Tresor's signature sound staves off the morning and then charges straight through to the next day. Anywhere within this once-machine-filled maze makes for the perfect place to dance the night away, and a crowd with similar interests puts Tresor at the top of our list of clubs to visit in Kreuzberg.

i Cover varies, usually €7-15. Open W and F-Sa midnight-late.

LIDO BERLIN

Cuvrystr. 7   www.lido-berlin.de

Lido is one of the most renowned institutions for live music in Berlin. What? Not another techno-house factory? Yup, that's right. Lido has been hosting some of the greatest indie rock bands to come out of and visit Berlin for the last decade. Housed in a 1950s style movie theater, the venue is a welcome change of pace from the industrial drum-and-bass warehouses, with a stage and dance floor big enough for you and a couple hundred of your newfound friends and an outdoor lounge that is the perfect place to rest your ears and your feet. If live music is your thing and techno doesn't float your boat, Lido will be your flagship.

i Cover varies, usually €4-10. Hours vary depending on the concert; check website for the most up-to-date schedule.

LUZIA

Oranienstr. 34   ☎030 817 99 958 www.luzia.tc

Kreuzberg is covered with clubs, but where are all the bars? Well, they're superfluous because Luzia is such a great bar that they'd all fall short in comparison. Luzia is huge and tremendously popular with the Kreuzberg locals, most of whom are UK transplants who think of themselves as German artists. Whatever, this is still a great bar. Gold-painted walls glow softly in the light of flickering candles. The huge, L-shaped design allows for long lines of vintage, threadbare lounge chairs, cafe tables, and a bar so long that it can easily serve the crowd that swarms here at peak hours.

i U1 or U8: Kotbusser Tor. From the metro, head northeast up Aldabertstr. and turn left onto Oranienstr. The bar is on the right. The only sign is a large, black rectangle with a gold coat of arms in the middle. Beer €2.50-3.50. Long drinks €5-6. Absinthe €3-7. Cash only. Open daily noon-late.

SO36

Oranienstr. 190   ☎030 614 01 306 www.so36.de

SO36 was probably amazing in 1970. For one thing, seeing David Bowie on a dance floor might make your heart stop. But today, SO36 is less of a club and more of a relic, a tribute to better music and better times. The various parties, live shows, and cultural presentations that fill this huge hall attract a mixed gay/straight clientele whose common denominator is that they like to party hardy. Gayhane, a gay cabaret that performs the last Saturday of every month, has become a staple of the Berlin GLBT scene and can get pretty epic.

i U1 or U8: Kottbusser Tor. From the metro, walk north on Adalbertstr. and turn right onto Oranienstr. The club is on the right. Cover varies. Shots €2.20. Beer €2.80-3.50. Wine €3. Long drinks €5.50, with Red Bull €6. Cash only. Hours vary, but usually open F-Sa 10pm-late.

ROSES

Oranienstr. 187   ☎030 615 65 70

At first glance, it might look like a kink shop, but, rest assured, the fuzzy pink walls and the omnipresent cheetah print make this gay bar a sight for sore eyes. Gay men, some lesbian women, and a couple of straight groups (there to camp out in campy glory) join together for small talk over some clean electronic. The bar's small size makes mingling easy, and the endless assortment of wall trinkets (glowing mounted antlers, twinkling hearts, a psychedelic Virgin Mary) keep everyone giggling.

i U1 or U8: Kottbusser Tor. From the metro, head northwest on Oranienstr. past Mariannenstr. The bar is on the left. Beer €2.50. Cocktails €5, with Red Bull €6. Cash only. Open daily 9pm-late.

ARTS AND CULTURE

As the old saying goes, "Where there be hipsters, there be Arts and Culture." Though the saying's origins are unclear, it certainly applies to Berlin. Whether it's opera, film, or Brecht in the original German that you're after, Berlin has got you covered.

Music and Opera

BERLINER PHILHARMONIE

Herbert-von-Karajan-Str. 1   ☎030 254 88 999 www.berlin-philharmoniker.de

If you fancy yourself to be a fan of classical music, you'd better have heard of the **Berlin Philharmoniker.** Led by Sir Simon Rattle, the Philharmoniker is considered one of the world's finest, if not the finest, orchestras. Concerts take place in the Philharmonie, a decidedly huge and weird-looking concert hall near Potsdamer Platz. The bright yellow building was designed to be pitch perfect: every member of the audience gets an adequately full view and incredibly full sound. With most concerts selling out about a month in advance, it can be pretty tough to get a seat, so check the website for availability. For sold-out concerts, some tickets and standing room may be available 90min. before the concert begins, but only at the box office. Stand in line, get some cheap tickets if you're lucky, and enjoy some of the sweetest sounds known to mankind.

i S1, S2, S25, or U2: Potsdamer Pl. From the metro, head west on Potsdamer Str. Tickets for standing room from €7, for seats from €15. Open from Jul-early Sept. Box office open M-F 3-6pm, Sa-Su 11am-2pm.

DEUTSCHE STAATSOPER

Unter den Linden 7   ☎030 203 54 555 www.staatsoper-berlin.de

The Deutsche Staatsoper is notorious for its splendor. Though its presence and patronage suffered during the years of separation, this opera house is rebuilding its reputation and its repertoire of Baroque opera and contemporary pieces. Unfortunately, its exterior is under extensive renovation, and the usual opera house is closed until mid-2014. Until its main building reopens, the Staatsoper presents performances in the sticks—Schiller Theater in Charlottenberg.

i U6: Französische Str. Or bus #100, 157, or 348: Deutsche Staatsoper. Tickets €14-260. For certain seats, students can get a ½-price discount, but only within 4 weeks of the performance and only at the box office. Unsold tickets €13, 30min. before the show. Open Aug through mid-Jul. Box office open daily noon-7pm and 1hr. before performances.

FESTSAAL KREUZBERG

Skalitzerstr. 130 ☎030 611 01 313 www.festsaal-kreuzberg.de

Free jazz, indie rock, swing, electropop—you never know what to expect at this absurdly hip venue. A tremendous chasm of a main hall accommodates acts of all shapes and sizes, plus an overflowing crowd of fans packed together on the main floor and the mezzanine. A dusty courtyard out front features a bar and novelty acts like fire throwers. Poetry readings, film screenings, and art performances fill out the program with appropriately eclectic material, making this one of Berlin's most exciting venues.

i U1 or U8: Kottbusser Tor. From the U-Bahn, head east on Skalitzerstr. The venue is on the left. Tickets €5-20. Shots €2. Long drinks €6. Hours vary. Usually open F-Sa 9pm-late.

COLUMBIAHALLE

Columbiadamm 13-21 ☎030 698 09 80 www.c-halle.com

Any venue that features Snoop Dogg, The Specials, and Bon Iver in a matter of a couple months has a special place in our hearts. With a wildly eclectic collection of superstars and indie notables from all over the world, Columbiahalle's calendar is bound to make you gasp and say, "I definitely wanna see that," at least twice. Once a gym for American service members in south Kreuzberg, Columbiahalle may look dated and innocuous, but its standing-room-only floor and mezzanine sure can rage.

i U6: Platz der Luftbrücke. From the metro, head east on Columbiadamm. The venue is in the 1st block on the right. Tickets €20-60, depending on the act. Hours and dates vary, but concerts tend to start at 8pm. Check the website for more details.

Film

Finding English films in Berlin is almost as easy as finding the Fernsehturm. On any night, choose from over 150 different films, marked **O.F.** or **O.V.** for the original version (meaning not dubbed in German), **O.m.U** for original version with German subtitles, or **O.m.u.E.** for original film with English subtitles.

LICHTBLICK KINO

Kastanienallee 77 ☎030 440 58 179 www.lichtblick-kino.org

Lichtblick is a charming cinema. The 32-seat theater presents avant-garde films and radical documentaries, as well as a wildly eclectic range of movies. English films are intermixed with all sorts of other international fare, and all films are shown with the original sound and accompanied by German subtitles, so you won't need to perform any amazing feats of lip-reading for any of the many English films. With a bar in the main entrance and a couple guys reading philosophical novels by candlelight, this is the quintessential art house experience.

i U8: Eberswalder Str. From the metro, walk southwest on Kastanienallee, past Oderberger Str. The theater is near the end of the next block on the left. Tickets €5, students €4.50. 2-5 films shown every night, check the website for a calendar. Usually 5-10pm.

ARSENAL

In the Filmhaus at Potsdamer Pl. ☎030 269 55 100 www.arsenal-berlin.de

Run by the founders of Berlinale and located just below the **Museum for Film and Television,** Arsenal showcases independent films and some classics. Discussions, talks, and frequent appearances by guest directors make the theater a popular meeting place for Berlin's filmmakers. With the majority of films in the original with English subtitles, non-Germans can watch easy.

i U2, S1, S2, or S25: Potsdamer Pl. From the metro, head west on Potsdamer Str. and go into the building labeled "Deutsche Kinemathek." Take the elevator down to the 2nd basement level. Tickets €6.50, students €5. 3-5 films shown each night. Films usually start 4-8pm. Check the website for a full calendar.

Theater

ENGLISH THEATER BERLIN

Fidicinstr. 40 ☎030 693 56 92 www.etberlin.de

Though all the shows here are presented in English, it's hard to find a theater that is more "Berlin." From 10min. skits to full-out festivals, the English Theater tries out every edge of the spectrum, and, boy, is this place ever edgy. We hear that most shows feature naked people and cabbages.

i U6: Pl. der Luftbrücke. From the metro, head north on Mehringdamm for 2 blocks and turn right onto Fidicinstr. The theater is on the left, within the 1st block. €13, students €8. Box office opens 1hr. before show. Shows are at 8pm unless otherwise noted. Check the website for a calendar of performances.

DEUTSCHES THEATER

Schumann Str. 13a ☎030 284 41 225 www.deutschestheater.de

Built in 1850, this world-famous theater was once controlled by legendary director Max Reinhardt and is still a cultural heavy hitter in Berlin. With even English dramas in translation (Shakespeare and Beckett are rockstars here), Anglophones shouldn't expect to understand any of the words. Fortunately, the productions are gorgeous enough that they're worth seeing in spite of the language barrier.

i U6: Oranienburger Tor. From the U-Bahn, head south on Friederichstr., take a right onto Reinhart-str., then another right onto Albrecthstr €5-30. Box office open M-Sa 11am-6:30pm, Su 3-6:30pm. Shows are at 8pm unless otherwise noted.

VOLKSBÜHNE

Linienstr. 227 ☎030 24 06 55 www.volksbuehne-berlin.de

Originally established to house productions of Socialist Realism at prices accessible to the working class, this imposing "people's theater" looks like it came straight out of a utopian sci-fi thriller. While the enormous stage goes dark during the summer, alive with concerts, German and English theater, and touring performances and festivals from Sept-May. Productions range from Büchner to Brecht to an interactive contemporary work called "Revolution Now!"—you'll probably leave more convinced of capitalist injustice than ever before. Before and after the shows, crowds gather in the beautiful plaza to smoke and talk.

i U2: Rosa-Luxemburg-Pl. From the metro, walk south down Rosa-Luxemburg-Str. Tickets €6-30. Students get a 50% discount on certain performances; check the website. Box office open daily noon-6pm and 1hr. before performances. Shows are at 8pm unless otherwise noted.

SHOPPING

Books

Finding English books in Berlin is about as easy as finding someone who speaks English: they're everywhere, but they're not always very good. Secondhand is the best way to offset the extra cost of English books.

🏴 ST. GEORGE'S BOOKSTORE

Wörterstr. 27 ☎030 817 98 333 www.saintgeorgesbookshop.com

You'd be hard-pressed to find a better English-language bookstore on the continent. St. George's owner makes frequent trips to the UK and US to buy the loads of titles that fill the towering shelves. The books are stacked from the floor to the ceiling, and picturesque ladders stretch upward. Over half of the books are used and extremely well-priced (paperbacks €4-8), with a number of books for just €1. Pay in euro, British pounds, or American dollars (oh my!).

i U2: Senefelderpl. From the metro, head southeast on Metzerstr. and turn left onto Prenzlauer Allee. Follow Prenzlauer Allee 3 blocks, then turn left onto Wörtherstr. The bookstore is halfway down the block, on the right. Used hardcovers €10. Open M-F 11am-8pm, Sa 11am-7pm.

ANOTHER COUNTRY

Riemannstr. 7   ☎030 694 01 160   www.anothercountry.de

Browsing this cluttered secondhand English bookstore feels a little like walking around some guy's house, but a wide and unpredictable collection rewards your searching, especially since all books are €2-5. Another Country doesn't just want to be that forgettable place where you can buy a cheap copy of *Twilight* (which is in stock; €5); it wants to be a local library and cultural center. A small percentage of the books are labeled "lending only," meaning they're priced a little higher (around €10), and you get back the entire price, minus €1.50, when you return them. Plus, live acoustic performances, readings, and trivia add further incentive to return again and again. Check out the wide selection of "Evil Books," which includes a copy of L. Ron Hubbard's *Dianetics*, a book entitled *The Quotable Richard Nixon*, and *Bradymania*.

i U7: Gneisenaustr. From the metro, walk south on Zossener Str. Turn right onto Riemannstr., and Another Country is on the left. Open Tu-F 11am-8pm, Sa-Su noon-4pm.

Music

⚄ SPACE HALL

Zossenerstr. 33, 35   ☎030 694 76 64   www.spacehall.de

They don't make them like this anymore in the States—maybe they never did. With two addresses (one of just CDs, the other strictly vinyl), Space Hall makes it nearly impossible *not* to find what you're looking for. The vinyl store never misses a beat, with the longest interior of any Berlin record store (painted to resemble a forest, of course) and easily one of the widest selections to boot. They also have an inspiring collection of rubber duckies.

i U7: Gneisenaustr. From the metro, head south on Zossenerstr. The record store is on the left. CDs regular €10-20, discounted €3-10. LPs €10-30. Open M-W 11am-8pm, Th-F 11am-10pm, Sa 11am-8pm.

⚄ HARD WAX

Paul-Lincke-Ufer 44a   ☎030 611 30 111   www.hardwax.com

Walk down a silent alleyway, through an eerily quiet courtyard, up three flights of dim, graffitied stairs, and suddenly, you're in one of Berlin's best record stores for electronic music. Bare brick and concrete walls make it feel aggressively nonchalant, while an entire back room dedicated to private listening stations for patrons proves that Hard Wax is dedicated to helping you get out of the House. Here, you'll find dubstep, IDM, ambient, and subgenres upon subgenres. Fortunately, nearly every CD and LP bears a short description in English courtesy of Hard Wax's experts, so you'll never feel like you're randomly flipping through a lot of crap. Though the selection is small compared to some of Berlin's other electro-record stores, the offerings seem hand-picked.

i U1 or U8: Kottbusser Tor. From the U-Bahn, head south on Kottbusserstr. Take a left just before the canal, then enter the courtyard on the left just after crossing Mariannenstr. Records €5-30; most €8-12. CDs €10-20. Open M-Sa noon-8pm.

berlin

ESSENTIALS
Practicalities

- **TOURIST OFFICES:** Now privately owned, tourist offices merely give you some commercial flyer or refer you to a website instead of guaranteeing human contact. Visit **www.berlin.de** for reliable info on all aspects of city life. **Tourist Info Centers.** (Berlin Tourismus Marketing GmbH, Am Karlsbad 11 ☎030 25 00 25 www.visitberlin.de. On the ground floor of the Hauptbahnhof, next to the northern entrance. English spoken. *Siegessäule, Blu,* and *Gay-Yellowpages* have GLBT event and club listings. Transit maps free; city maps €1-2. The monthly *Berlin Programm* lists museums, sights, restaurants, and hotels as well as opera, theater, and classical music performances, €1.75. *Tip* provides full listings of film, theater, concerts, and clubs in German, €2.70. *Ex-Berliner* has English-language movie and theater reviews, €2. Open daily 8am-10pm.) **Alternate location.** (Brandenburger Tor S1, S2, S25, or bus #100: Unter den Linden. *i* On your left as you face the pillars from the Unter den Linden side. Open daily 10am-6pm.)

- **STUDENT TRAVEL OFFICES: STA** books flights and hotels and sells ISICs. (Dorotheenstr. 30 ☎030 201 65 063. S3, S5, S7, S9, S75, or U6: Friedrichstr. From the metro, walk 1 block south on Friedrichstr., turn left onto Dorotheenstr., and follow as it veers left. STA is on the left. Open M-F 10am-7pm, Sa 11am-3pm.) **Second location.** (Gleimstr. 28 ☎030 285 98 264. S4, S8, S85, or U2: Schönhauser Allee. From the metro, walk south on Schönhauser Allee and turn right onto Gleimstr. Open M-F 10am-7pm, Sa 11am-4pm.) **Third location.** (Hardenbergstr. 9 ☎030 310 00 40. U2: Ernst-Reuter-Pl. From the metro, walk southeast on Hardenbergstr. Open M-F 10am-7pm, Sa 11am-3pm.) **Fourth location.** (Takustr. 47. ☎030 831 10 25. U3: Dahlem-Dorf. From the metro, walk north on Brümmerstr., turn left onto Königin-Luise Str., then turn right onto Takustr. Open M-F 10am-7pm, Sa 10am-2pm.)

- **TOURS: Terry Brewer's Best of Berlin** is legendary for its vast knowledge and engaging personalities, making the 6hr.+ walk well worth it. Tours leave daily from in front of the Bandy Brooks shop on Friedrichstr. (☎017 738 81 537 www.brewersberlintours.com. S1, S7, S9, S75, or U6: Friedrichstr €12. Tours start at 10:30am.) **Insider Tour** offers a variety of fun, informative walking and bike tours that hit all the major sights. More importantly, the guides' enthusiasm for Berlin is contagious, and their accents span the English-speaking world. (☎030 692 3149 www.insidertour.com. Tours last 4hr.)

- **CURRENCY EXCHANGE AND MONEY WIRES:** The best rates are usually found at exchange offices with **Wechselstube** signs outside, at most major train stations, and in large squares. For money wires through Western Union, use **ReiseBank.** (M: Hauptbahnhof ☎030 204 53 761 Open M-Sa 8am-10pm.) **Second location.** (M: Bahnhof Zoo ☎030 881 71 17.) **Third location.** (M: Ostbahnhof 030 296 43 93.)

- **LUGGAGE STORAGE:** In the M: Hauptbahnhof, in "DB Gepack Center," 1st fl., east side €4 per day). Lockers also at M: Bahnhof Zoo, M: Ostbahnhof, and M: Alexanderpl.

- **INTERNET ACCESS:** Free internet with admission to the **Staatsbibliothek.** During its renovation, Staatsbibliothek requires €10 month-long pass to the library. (Potsdamer Str. 33 ☎030 26 60 Open M-F 9am-9pm, Sa 9am-7pm.) **Netlounge.** (Augustr. 89 ☎030 24 34 25 97 www.netlounge-berlin.de. M: Oranienburger Str. €2.50 per hr. Open daily noon-midnight.) **Easy Internet** has several locations throughout Berlin. (Unter den Linden 24, Rosenstr. 16, Frankfurter Allee 32, Rykestr. 29, and Kurfürstendamm 18.) Many cafes throughout Berlin offer free Wi-Fi, including **Starbucks,** where the networks never require a password.

- **POST OFFICES: Bahnhof Zoo.** (Joachimstaler Str. 7 ☎030 887 08 611. Down Joachimstaler Str. from Bahnhof Zoo on the corner of Joachimstaler Str. and Kantstr. Open M-Sa 9am-8pm.) **Alexanderplatz.** (Rathausstr. 5, by the Dunkin Donuts. Open M-F 9am-7pm, 9am-4pm.) **Tegel Airport.** (Open M-F 8am-6pm, Sa 8am-noon.) **Ostbahnhof.** (Open M-F 8am-8pm, Sa-Su

10am-6pm.) To find a post office near you, visit the search tool on their website, www.standorte. deutschepost.de/filialen_verkaufspunkte, which is confusing and in German but could help.

- **POSTAL CODE** 10706.

Emergency

- **POLICE:** Pl. der Luftbrücke 6. U6: Pl. der Luftbrücke.

- **EMERGENCY NUMBERS:** ☎110.

- **AMBULANCE AND FIRE:** ☎112.

- **NON-EMERGENCY ADVICE HOTLINE:** ☎030 466 44 664.

- **MEDICAL SERVICES:** The American and British embassies list English-speaking doctors. The **emergency doctor** (☎030 31 00 31 or ☎018 042 255 23 62) service helps travelers find English-speaking doctors. **Emergency dentist.** (☎030 890 04 333)

- **CRISIS LINES:** English spoken on most crisis lines. **American Hotline** (017 781 41 510) has crisis and referral services. **Poison Control.** (030 192 40) **Berliner Behindertenverband** has resources for the disabled. (Jägerstr. 63d ☎030 204 38 47 www.bbv-ev.de Open W noon-5pm and by appointment.) **Deutsche AIDS-Hilfe.** (Wilhelmstr. 138 ☎030 690 08 70 www.aidshilfe.de) **Drug Crisis Hotline.** (☎030 192 37 24hr.) **Frauenkrisentelefon.** Women's crisis line. (☎030 615 4243 www.frauenkrisentelefon.de Open M 10am-noon, Tu-W 7-9pm, Th 10am-noon, F 7-9pm, Sa-Su 5-7pm.) **Lesbenberatung** offers counseling for lesbians. (Kulmer Str. 20a ☎030 215 20 00 www.lesbenberatung-berlin.de) **Schwulenberatung** offers counseling for gay men. (Mommsenstr. 45 ☎030 194 46 www.schwulenberatungberlin.de.) **Maneo** offers legal help for gay victims of violence. (☎030 216 33 36 www.maneo.de Open daily 5-7pm.) **LARA** offers counseling for victims of sexual assault. (Fuggerstr. 19 ☎030 216 88 88 www.lara-berlin.de Open M-F 9am-6pm.)

Getting There

By Plane

Capital Airport Berlin Brandenburg International (BBI) is currently under construction and will be opened at an unknown future date. Until then, **Tegel Airport** will continue to serve travelers. (☎018 050 00 186 www.berlin-airport.de. Take express bus #X9 or #109 from U7: Jakob-Kaiser Pl., bus #128 from U6: Kurt-Schumacher-Pl., or bus TXL from S42, S41: Beusselstr. Follow signs in the airport for ground transportation.)

By Train

International trains (☎972 226 150) pass through Berlin's **Hauptbahnhof** and run to: Amsterdam, NTH (€130. 7hr., 16 per day); Brussels, BEL (€140. 7hr., 16 per day); Budapest, HUN (€140. 13hr., 4 per day); Copenhagen, DNK (€135. 7hr., 7 per day.); Paris, FRA (€200. 9hr., 9 per day.); Prague, CZR (€80. 5hr., 12 per day); Vienna, AUT (€155. 10hr., 12 per day.)

By Bus

ZOB is the central bus station. (Masurenallee 4. ☎030 301 03 80. U2: Theodor-Heuss-Pl. From the metro, head southwest on Masurenallee; the station is on the left. Alternatively, S4, S45, or S46: Messe Nord/ICC. From the metro, walk west on Neue Kantstr. The station is on the right. Open M-F 6am-9pm, Sa-Su and holidays 6am-8pm.)

Getting Around

By Public Transportation: The Bvg

The two pillars of Berlin's metro are the **U-Bahn** and **S-Bahn** trains, which cover the city in spidery and circular patterns, (somewhat) respectively. **Trams** and **buses** (both part of the U-Bahn system) scuttle around the remaining city corners. (BVG's 24hr. hotline ☎030 194 49 www.bvg.de.) Berlin is divided into three transit zones. **Zone A** consists of central Berlin, including Tempelhof Airport. The rest of Berlin lies in **Zone B.Zone C** covers the larger state of Brandenburg, including Potsdam. An **AB** ticket is the best deal, since you can later buy extension tickets for the outlying areas. A **one-way** ticket is good for 2hr. after validation. (Zones AB €2.30, BC €2.70, ABC €3, under 6 free.) Within the validation period, the ticket may be used on any S-Bahn, U-Bahn, bus, or tram.

Most train lines don't run Monday through Friday 1-4am. S-Bahn and U-Bahn lines do run Friday and Saturday nights, but less frequently. When trains stop running, 70 night buses take over, running every 20-30min. generally along major transit routes; pick up the free *Nachtliniennetz* **map** of bus routes at a **Fahrscheine und Mehr** office. The letter "N" precedes night bus numbers. Trams continue to run at night.

Buy tickets, including monthly passes, from machines or ticket windows in metro stations or from bus drivers. **Be warned:** machines don't give more than €10 change, and many machines don't take bills, though some accept credit cards. **Validate** your ticket by inserting it into the stamp machines before boarding. Failure to validate becomes a big deal when plainclothes policemen bust you and charge you €40 for freeloading. If you bring a bike on the U-Bahn or S-Bahn, you must buy it a child's ticket. Bikes are prohibited on buses and trams.

Single-ride tickets are a waste of money. A **day ticket** (AB €6.30, BC €6.60, ABC €6.80) is good from the time it's stamped until 3am the next day. The BVG also sells **7-day tickets** (AB €27.20, BC €28, ABC €33.50) and **month-long passes** (AB €74, BC €75, ABC €91). The popular tourist cards are another option. The **WelcomeCard** (sold at tourist offices) buys unlimited travel (AB 48hr. €17, ABC €19; 72hr. €23/26) and includes discounts at 130 sights. The **City TourCard** is good within zones AB (48hr. €16, 72hr. €22) and offers discounts at over 50 attractions.

By Taxi

Call 15min. in advance for a taxi. Women can request female drivers. Trips within the city cost up to €30. (☎030 261 026, toll-free ☎0800 263 00 00)

By Bike

Biking is one of the best ways to explore the city that never brakes. Unless your hostel is out in the boonies, few trips will be out of cycling distance, and given that U-Bahn tickets verge on €3 and that the average long-term bike rental costs €8 per day, pedaling your way can be a better deal and a simpler way to navigate. **Fat Tire Bike Rental** (Panorama Str. 1a ☎016 389 26 427)and **Prenzlberger Orange Bikes** (Kollwitzstr. 35 ☎030 240 47 991 www.berlinfahrradverleih.com) are both great options.

hamburg

As the waterway to the North Sea, some claim that Hamburg has 2579 bridges, but the official count is "more than 2300." Whichever way you count, Hamburg has more bridges than Venice, London, and Amsterdam combined. And that's really something; the city's water is breathtaking. But if water, water, and more water isn't your thing, Hamburg's also the perfect place to try donning high heels on cobblestone streets. Or just take a break and explore Hamburg's copper roofs, fantastic parks, awesome boating opportunities, chic shops, and old factories. Like any good quintessential German city, Hamburg has been burned, bombed, and bisected with nightlife trashier than garbage (again outdoing Venice, London, and Amsterdam combined). Still, the city has somehow managed to draw in corporations, lawyers, and a whole bunch of immigrants. Maybe it's the nightlife. Hamburg is a port, after all.

ORIENTATION

Hamburg's geography is notoriously complex, so consider pulling out a map to look over as you read through this. Hamburg lies on the northern bank of the **Elbe River.** The city's **Altstadt,** full of old façades and labyrinthine canals, lies north of the Elbe and south of the **Alster lakes. Binnenalster,** the smaller of the two Alster lakes, is located in the heart of the Altstadt, with the bustling **Jungfernstieg** on the south corner. The much larger **Außenalster,** popular for sailing in the summer and skating in the winter, is slightly farther north, separated from the Binnenalster by the **Kennedy- and Lombardbrücken.**

Five unique spires outline Hamburg's Altstadt. Anchoring the center of the Altstadt is the palatial **Rathaus,** the ornate town hall, and its exquisite doorstep and regular home to both political protests and farmers' markets, the **Rathausmarkt. Alsterfleet Canal** bisects the downtown, separating Altstadt on the eastern bank from the **Neustadt** on the west. The city's best museums, galleries, and theaters are within these two districts.

The **Hauptbahnhof** lies at the eastern edge of the city center, along **Steintorwall.** Starting from the **Kirchenallee** exit of the Hauptbahnhof, Hamburg's gay district, **St. Georg,** follows the **Lange Reihe** eastward. Outside the Hauptbahnhof's main exit on Steintorwall is the **Kunstmeile** (Art Mile), a row of museums extending southward from the Alster lakes to the banks of the Elbe. Perpendicular to Steintorwall, **Mönckebergstraße,** Hamburg's most famous shopping street, runs westward to the **Rathaus.** Just south of the Rathaus, **Saint Pauli** bears long waterside walkways and a beautiful copper-roofed port along the towering cranes of the Elbe's industrial district. Horizontally bisecting St. Pauli is the infamously icky **Reeperbahn** (disingenuously pronounced "RAPER-bawn"), which is packed with strip joints, erotic shops, and a tourist mecca of clubs on the pedestrian off-shoot **Große Freiheit.**

To the north of St. Pauli, the **Schanzenviertel** is a radically liberal community on the cusp of gentrification. Here, rows of graffiti-covered restaurants and a busy, late-night cafe and bar scene show little edge but attract fleets of bargain-hunting students. In late summer, the **Schanzenfest** illegal street market consistently breaks out into a full-fledged war of Molotov cocktails and tear gas between cops and civil discontents. On the westernmost side of Hamburg, **Altona** celebrates with a mini-Schanzenviertel nightlife and restaurant scene; the area was an independent city ruled by Denmark in the 17th century before Hamburg absorbed it. Altona's shop-lined pedestrian zone, the **Ottenser Hauptstrasse,** runs west from the Altona train station.

SIGHTS

⬛ PLANTEN UN BLOMEN

Next to the Hamburg Messe   ☎040 428 232 125 www.plantenunblomen.hamburg.de
This park is fantastic. It's huge, it's laden with lily pads and manicured gardens, and it has something for everyone. There's a real botanical garden, a greenhouse growing things which we thought could only grow south of the Equator, coffee and bananas among them. There's a Japanese garden. There's a charming little rose garden. There are a whole handful of cafes and ice cream stands. There are wading pools. There are fountains. For the Harry Potter enthusiast, a giant (though inanimate) chess set is the arena of competition for many a muggle.

get a room!

Accommodations in Hamburg can get freakishly expensive, especially in the summer months. But like the good, cheap food, the good, cheap hostels are located in the Schanzenviertel and out west in Altona.

INSTANT SLEEP $$

Max-Brauer-Allee 277   ☎040 431 82 310 www.instantsleep.com

Instant Sleep combines the feel of a summer camp and the set-up of an institution: the beds aren't bunked, but they feel like cots and are all quite close together. Instant Sleep keeps a fully stocked kitchen and an awesomely social common room. Expect to find foosball, hammocks, and a comfy loft with bean bags and a television. A young backpacking crowd gathers here to hang out or fans out onto the balcony for a smoke.

i U3, S11, S21, or S31: Sternschanze. Free Wi-Fi. Linens included. Laundry available. 12-bed dorm €15; 6- to 8-bed dorms €17; 4- to 5-bed €21; singles €39; doubles €54; triples €72. Cash only. Reception open M-W 8am-11pm, Th-Sa 8am-2am, Su 8am-11pm. Balcony open until 10pm.

SCHANZENSTERN ALTONA $$

Kleiner Rainstr. 24-26   ☎040 399 19 191 www.schanzenstern.de/hotel/altona

Altona has a hotel atmosphere, with a silent courtyard, a residential street, and a lack of common space. Still, the rooms here are tremendous, the beds are comfy and rarely bunked, every room comes with its very own bathroom, and the wide view of Altona will make you swoon. With the Altstadt and the Schanzenviertel each about a 5-10min. train ride away, the location can feel a little remote. Good thing there's a bustling shopping and nightlife center nearby.

i S1, S2, S3, S11 or S31: Altona. From the metro, exit at Ottenser Hauptstr. and head west along the pedestrian walkway. Turn right at Spritzenpl. and take the right fork in the road. Turn left onto Kleiner Rainstr.; the hostel is on the left, just before the bend in the road. Free Wi-Fi and internet terminals available. Breakfas €6.50. Linens included. Dorms €19; singles €44; doubles €59-69; triples €74; quads €84; apartments €79-100. Cash only. Reception 24hr. Common room open 7am-2am.

Daily performances by groups ranging from Irish step dancers to Hamburg's police choir fill the outdoor Musikpavillion Sundays at 3pm May-Sept. The nightly Wasserlichtkonzerte draws crowds to the lake with fountains and choreographed underwater lights.

i S11, S21, or S31: Dammtor. Or U1: Stephanspl. Open daily 7am-11pm. Hours of the other attractions (Japanese garden, botanical garden, golf course, etc.) vary.

HAMBURGER KUNSTHALLE (HALL OF ART)

Glockengießerwall   ☎040 428 131 200 www.hamburger-kunsthalle.de

The Kunsthalle is the Louvre of Germany. The museum is stately, massive, and located on prime Hamburg turf. Staring at every piece of artwork for 10 seconds each would take a few days, and just running quickly through the place sucks up a good two hours. Either way, it's time well spent. With an incredible collection of canvases from every period in art history—from early medieval religious paintings through Modernism—arranged chronologically across its spacious, skylit halls, this museum is freakishly gorgeous. After you've gotten your fill of everything pas, enter the cafe and take the underground passage behind you to the *Galerie der Gegenwart* (Gallery of the Present) for an expertly curated series of contemporary art exhibits, which may include anything from photographs to the skins of stuffed animals.

i *Turn right from the "Sitalerstr./City" exit of the Hauptbahnhof and cross the street. The Kunsthalle has the domed ceiling. €12, students €6, under 18 free. Audio tour €2. Open Tu-W 10am-6pm, Th 10am-9pm, F-Su 10am-6pm.*

RATHAUS

Rathausmarkt ☎040 428 312 064

With more rooms than Buckingham Palace, the 1897 Hamburger Rathaus is an ornately carved stone monument to Hamburg's long history as a wealthy port city. Today, we have the privilege of seeing the post-fire original: during the extensive Allied bombing of the Innenstadt, a bomb fell on the Rathausmarkt just out front, but, due to the quick thinking of some invisible, architecture-loving time traveler, it never exploded. Accessible only with a thorough 40min. tour, the lavish chambers of the Rathaus overflow with expansive murals, disorienting ornate molding, and wedding-cake chandeliers.

i *U3: Rathaus. Tours don't run on days that the state government convenes. Even on open days, certain rooms may be closed due to meetings, so call ahead. Tours €3, under 14 €0.50. English tours M-Th every hr. 10:15am-3:15pm, F 10:15am-1:15pm, Sa 11:15am-5:15pm, Su 11:15am-4:15pm.*

MUSEUM FÜR KUNST UND GEWERBE

Steintorpl. ☎040 428 134 880 www.mkg-hamburg.de

This museum aims to confuse: the complex is a concoction of 19th-century and hyper-modern construction, and the exhibited art and design is similarly varied. Works hail from everywhere and anywhere: a hall of 17th- and 18th-century pianos borders a room of Middle Eastern carved tile; Art Deco pottery squares off against a gigantic collection of 18th-century porcelain arranged by region of origin; and a hallway of late 20th-century chairs challenges your backside to figure out how to sit in them. And this is just the permanent collection. Special exhibits range from 1980s and '90s Japanese fashion to Art Nouveau advertisements. Yes, it's a disorienting jumble, but it's a pleasing one.

i *S1, S2, S3, S11, S21, S31, U1, U2, or U3: Hauptbahnhof. Leave through the Hauptbahnhof's south exit; the museum is across the street. €10, students €7, under 18 free. Admission €5 on Th after 5pm. Open Tu-W 10am-6pm, Th 10am-9pm, F-Su 10am-6pm.*

Outside Central Hamburg

KZ-GEDENKSTÄTTE NEUENGAMME

Jean-Dolidier-Weg 75 ☎040 428 131 500 www.kz-gedenkstaette-neuengamme.de

It's quite a trek from Hamburg, but it's one you should make: seeing the complex that once housed a concentration camp is nothing short of a chilling experience. Since the camp lies out in the rolling Hamburg countryside, a visit will take at least three hours, but this lesser known center of Nazi terror is a humbling experience worthy of the trip. Between 1938 and 1945, this camp held more than 100,000 forced laborers. Close to half the occupants died from overwork, disease, or execution. Walk around the camp buildings, from the cafeteria and dorms—now reduced to stark piles of rubble—to the work camps, and browse the thorough and moving collection of photographs and artifacts, which includes artwork by some of the prisoners.

i *S21: Bergedorf. Then take bus #227 or #327: KZ-Gedenkstätte, Ausstellung (about 35-45min.). Buses leave the train station and the camp M-Sa every 30min., Su every 2hr. Free. Museum and memorial open Apr-Sept M-F 9:30am-4pm, Sa-Su noon-7pm; Oct-Mar M-F 9:30am-4pm, Sa-Su noon-5pm. Paths open 24hr. Tours in German Su noon and 2:30pm.*

FOOD

▓ RISTORANTE ROCCO $$$
Hofweg 104   ☎040 22 31 88

From the outside, with its spot next to a small canal and outdoor tables tiered
to approach the water, Ristorante Rocco looks way too cla$$y for budget trav-
elers. Even on weekdays, Rocco always hosts business peeps out on date night.
Despite the pretentious atmosphere, though, the food is unpretentious and
the prices unassuming. For the local all-time favorite, opt for the *lasagne* (€9),
which is baked in its own little dish and covered in deliciously-crispified cheese.

i *U3: From the metro, walk north on Winterhuder Weg for 3 large blocks. Then keep left as Win-*
terhuder Weg splits off of Herderstr. Turn right onto Hofweg, and the restaurant is on the right,
right next to the canal. Pasta €8-10.50. Entrees €10.50-18. Open M-F noon-3pm and 6-11:30pm,
Sa-Su 6-11:30pm.

▓ AZEITONA $
Beckstr. 17-19   ☎040 18 00 73 71

They say that Hamburg is famous for its €2.50 falafel, and we think Azeitona
scored the reputation for the whole city. This cafe is tiny and all vegetarian,
and the falafel is pretty darn good. For the perfect sandwich, add some of
Azeitona's antipasti for €0.50. The restaurant is decorated like a little slice of
the Middle East, and even the benches are carpeted.

i *U3: Feldstr. From the metro, walk north on Sternstr. After a short block, turn left onto Beckstr.*
Azeitona is on the right. Entrees €2.50-6. Caipirina €4. Open M-Th noon-11pm, F-Sa noon-late,
Su noon-11pm.

▓ EISCAFE AM POELCHAUKAMP $
Poelchaukamp 3   ☎040 27 25 17

It's just an ice cream parlor, but it's an exceptionally good one. The owners are
Italian, and the *eis* is authentic, too. Get a couple scoops—the rum flavors, rum
truffle and *malaga* or rum raisin, are the best. Take it to explore the nearby
residential neighborhood.

i *U3: Sierichstr. From the metro, walk south on Sierichstr. for about 10min. Then turn right*
onto Poelchaukamp, and the Eiscafe is on the left near the canal. Each scoop €1. Open daily
11am-10pm.

LA SEPIA $$
Neuer Pferdemarkt 16   ☎040 432 24 84

When in Hamburg, eat seafood. It's simply a must, and this Spanish and
Portuguese restaurant serves some seriously generous portions at seriously
affordable prices (at least in comparison to similar cafes). The low prices justify the interior, which is impersonal and loaded up with tanks of crustaceans.
Avoid the expensive dinner entrees and catch the lunch special (noon-5pm) for
around €5-7, or try the fish sampler (€6) to get the full cornucopia of Hamburg's
Meeresfrüchte (fruit of the sea).

i *U3, S11, S21, or S31: Sternschanze. Entrees €7.50-22. Soups €4.50. Open daily noon-3am.*

HATARI PFÄLZER CANTINA $$
Schanzenstr. 2   ☎040 43 20 88 66

You'll be glad to hear that the word "eclectic" sums this cafe up quite nicely:
it's decorated with Chinese **dragons** and hunting trophies. Students flock here
for hamburgers (€7.80-8.20) and Hamburger-watching on the busy street corner. Hatari also serves German specialties, including *schnitzel* (€11-12) and
Flammkuchen (€7.30-8.30), or "French pizza," a Bavarian thin crust spread
with thick cream and piled with toppings.

i *U3, S11, S21, or S31: Sternschanze. Entrees from €7. Cash only. Open daily noon-late.*

Schulterblatt 16 ☎040 594 53 402

This veggie diner is fittingly dog-friendly. As you enter, you might hear one of the servers adoring a dog: *"Wasser für den Hund."* If you're intimidated by meaty German classics, this is your chance to fill up on veggie versions of Deutschland staples. Hin&Veg serves dishes like vegetarian currywurst (€3) and *döner* (€4), all with vegan sauces. Also, a delicious collection of veggie burgers makes for a light, refreshing way to gain the requisite Hamburg/hamburger bragging rights.

i U3, S11, S21, or S31: Sternschanze. From the metro, head south on Schanzenstr. and take the 3rd left onto Schulterblatt. The restaurant is on the right. Burger €2-4. Pizza €5.90-7.50. Cash only. Open M-Th 11:30am-10:30pm, F-Sa 11:30am-midnight, Su 12:30-10pm.

NIGHTLIFE

▧ AUREL
Bahrenfelderstr. 157 ☎040 390 27 27

Aurel identifies itself as a *Kneipe*, which is basically a pub. Despite the prevalence of beer drinking, one of the main attractions at Aurel is their delicious mojito special (€6.50 before 9pm). An early crowd sticks around Aurel until bedtime. A small, beleaguered bar keeps tabs on the incessantly large crowd, which packs the small tables and inevitably spills out onto the sidewalk. Check out the stained glass on the back wall (don't worry—we don't get it either).

i S1, S3, or S31: Altona. From the metro, exit onto Ottenser Hauptstr., walk east, then turn right onto Bahrenfelderstr. The bar is on the left at the corner of Bahrenfelderstr. and Nöltingstr. Beer €2.60-3.50. Mojitos €8 after 9pm. Mixed drinks €6-8. Cash only. Open daily 10am-late.

▧ SHAMROCK IRISH BAR
Feldstr. 40 ☎040 432 77 275 www.shamrockirishbar.com

Our researchers were mystified by the outdoor flower garden at this punk bar: how, oh how, could leather-clad, whiskey-drinking old boys frequent this dark, smoky Irish bar without treading on them? True to its Irish heritage, Shamrock often fills to capacity with Guinness-drinking English-speakers. Irish football banners hang from the ceiling, and some of the funniest bartenders this side of the Channel fill huge steins with Guinness, Kilkenny, and Irish Car Bombs. Come Thursday nights at 9pm for a hilarious pub quiz and watch Germans mutter to each other in broken English about topics ranging from Bolshevism to Batman to beer.

i U3: Feldstr. From the metro, head east on Feldstr. The bar is on the left. Guinness and Kilkenny 0.3 €2.90, 0.4L €3.80. Open Tu-Th 6pm-1am, F 5pm-late, Sa 1pm-late, Su 6pm-midnight.

ROSI'S BAR
Hamburger Berg 7 ☎040 31 55 82

In an area famous for debauchery, Rosi's sets the standard. Though this bar is located on a strip of seemingly identical bars, nowhere else comes close to Rosi's age-old(going on 60 years) notoriety, fame, or motley collection of DJs. Come for soul one night and return for goth-rock the next; no two evenings are alike. Rosi, the one-time wife of Tony Sheridan, became the bar's manager at the tender age of 18 and still runs it now with her son. Dark wood walls are dressed up with a single disco ball and layers of music posters, all of which contribute to Rosi's wild nights.

i S1, S2, or S3: Reeperbahn. Go east on Reeperbahn, take a left onto Hamburger Berg, and walk about 75m. DJs most nights from 11pm. Beer €2.50-3. Cocktails €5. Cash only. Open M-Th 9pm-4am, F-Sa 9pm-6am, Su 9pm-4am.

CAFÉ GNOSA

Lange Reihe 93   ☎040 24 30 34   www.gnosa.de

Café Gnosa is a Hamburg institution. It's a great cafe and perfect for a visit during the day, but it's most famous for its fabulous GLBT nightlife. Full of bright lights and decorated with dark wood, Café Gnosa has been serving warm and cold drinks and famous cakes since World War II. Hamburg's first gay bar attracts an older crowd—gay and straight—who remember its early days, plus some younger faces eager to enjoy the exquisite cakes and talk with the refreshingly friendly staff. You can also pick up free GLBT publications like *hinnerk* and Hamburg's Gay Map here.

i *From the north entrance of the Hauptbahnhof, follow Ernst-Mecke-Str. as it becomes Lange Reihe. Beer €2.70-3.60. Cocktails €5.50-8. Champagne €8.70. Coffee €1.90. Cakes €2-5. Cash only. Open daily 10am-1am.*

KYTI VOO

Lange Reihe 82   ☎040 280 55 565   www.kytivoo.de

Red neon lights and loud electro suggest a small club, but Kyti Voo is really a large, chic gay bar with an insatiable hunger for heavy beats. The bar inside is massive and many-sided, so it's too bad no one uses it in the summer, when 20- to 40-somethings snatch up the extensive outdoor seating. By about 10:30pm, Kyti Voo's sidewalk is one of the most popular places in St. Georg. Sip coffee or cocktails or chow down on a steaming hot *Flammkuchen* (€6.90-8.90).

i *From the north entrance of the Hauptbahnhof, follow Ernst-Mecke-Str. as it becomes Lange Reihe. The bar is on the right, about halfway down the block. Espresso €1.60. Beer on tap 0.3L €2.80, 0.5L €3.60. Cocktails €5.50-8. Wine €3.40-6.50. Cash only. Open M-F 9am-late, Sa-Su 10am-late.*

YOKO MONO

Marktstr. 41   ☎040 431 82 991   www.yokomono.de

Yoko Mono is situated on the edge of a trash-covered, motor-biker-frequented park. The crowd that gathers here is student heavy and generally under 25. Yoko Mono is pretty much the ideal place to chat to someone about how much you love Bon Iver. A pool table heats up the side room, while the small main bar is dark, cozy, and packed. With all the cool, attractive friends it encourages you to meet, this bar could've easily broken up the Beatles.

i *U3: Feldstr. From the metro, head north on Laeiszstr., then west on Marktstr. Wine €2.50-2.80. Beer €2.80-3.50. Cash only. Open daily noon-2am or later.*

FABRIK

Barnerstr. 36   ☎040 391 070   www.fabrik.de

Fabrik used to be a factory for machine parts. Complete with a rusted crane on the roof, Fabrik is perhaps the only appropriate place to do the robot. Actually, no one does the robot, even here, though you can engage in some Fabrik boogie woogie. For years, crowds have packed this two-level club to hear live DJs, big-name rock acts, and an eclectic mix of other bands, with styles ranging from Latin to punk.

i *S1, S3, or S31: Altona. From the metro, exit at Ottenser Hauptstr., walk along the pedestrian walkway to the east, turn right onto Bahrenfelderstr., and walk north until you reach Barnerstr. The club is on the right. Check the website for a schedule of events. Live DJ most Sa nights at 10pm. The club hosts a "Gay Factory" night each month. Cover €7. Tickets €17-36. Hours vary, and most acts start at 9pm.*

ESSENTIALS
Practicalities

- **TOURIST OFFICES:** Hamburg's main tourist offices supply free English-language maps and pamphlets. All sell the Hamburg Card (€8.90), which provides discounts for museums, tours, and particular stores and restaurants, plus unlimited access to public transportation. The Hauptbahnhof office books rooms for a €4 fee and offers free maps. (☎040 300 51 300. In the Wandelhalle, the station's main shopping plaza, near the Kirchenallee exit. Open M-Sa 9am-7pm, Su 10am-6pm.) The Sankt Pauli Landungsbrücken office is often less crowded than the Hauptbahnhof office. (Between piers 4 and 5. ☎040 300 51 203. Open M-W 9am-6pm, Th-Sa 9am-pm.)

- **CURRENCY EXCHANGE:** ReiseBank arranges money transfers for Western Union and cashes traveler's checks. (☎040 32 34 83. 2nd fl. of the Hauptbahnhof near the Kirchenallee exit. Also sells telephone cards. Other branches in the Altona and Dammtor train stations as well as in the Flughafen. 1.5% commission. €6.50 to cash 1-9 checks, €10 for 10 checks, and €25 for 25 checks. Exchanges currency for a fixed charge of €3-5. Open daily 7:30am-10pm.) Citibank cashes traveler's checks, including AmEx. (Rathausstr. 2 ☎040 302 96 202. U3: Rathaus. Open M-F 9am-1pm and 2-6pm.)

- **GLBT RESOURCES:** St. Georg is the center of the gay community. Hein und Fiete, a self-described "switchboard," gives advice on doctors, disease prevention, and tips on the gay scene in Hamburg. (Pulverteich 21 ☎040 240 333. Walk down Steindamm away from the Hauptbahnhof, turn right onto Pulverteich ,and look for a rainbow-striped flag on the left. Open M-F 4-9pm, Sa 4-7pm.) Magnus-Hirschfeld-Centrum offers film screenings, counseling sessions, and a gay-friendly cafe. (Borgweg 8 ☎040 278 77 800. U3: Borgweg. Cafe open M-Th 5:30-11pm, F 5pm-late, Su 3-8pm.) Magnus-Hirschfeld-Centrum also offers gay and lesbian hotlines. (Gay hotline ☎040 279 00 69. Lesbian hotline ☎040 279 0049. Gay hotline open M-W 2-6pm and 7-9pm, Th 2-6pm; Lesbian hotline open W 5-7pm, Th 6-8pm.)

- **INTERNET ACCES:** Free Wi-Fi is available in Wildwechsel (Beim Grünen Jäger 25 Open daily 4pm-late), at the Altan Hotel (Beim Grünen Jäger 23. You don't have to be a guest to use internet in the lobby/bar. Open 24hr.), and at Starbucks. (Neuer Jungfernstieg 5 Open M-F 7:30am-9pm, Sa-Su 8am-9pm.) Staats- und Universitätsbibliothek has computers on the 2nd floor, but internet access is limited to library cardholders. (Von Melle-Park 3 ☎040 428 38 22 33. Library car €5 per month, €13 per 6 months. Open M-F 9am-9pm, Sa-Su 10am-9pm.)

- **POST OFFICE:** Hauptbahnhof. (At the Kirchenallee exit. Open M-F 8am-6pm, Sa 8:30am-12:30pm.)

- **POSTAL CODE:** 20095.

Emergency

- **EMERGENCY NUMBERS:** ☎112.

- **POLICE:** 110. (From the Kirchenallee exit of the Hauptbahnhof, turn left and follow signs for"BGS/Bahnpolizei/Bundespolizei." Another branch is located on the Reeperbahn, at the corner of Davidstr. and Spielbudenpl., and in the courtyard of the Rathaus.)

- **PHARMACY:** Adler Apotheke.(Schulterblatt 106 ☎040 439 45 90. Schedule of emergency hours for Hamburg pharmacies out front. Open M-F 8:30am-7pm, Sa-Su 9am-4pm.) Hauptbahnhof-Apotheke Wandelhalle. (☎040 325 27 383. In the station's upper shopping gallery. Open M-W 7am-9pm, Th-F 7am-9:30pm, and Sa-Su 8am-9pm.)

Getting There

By Plane

Air France (☎018 058 30 830) and **Lufthansa** (☎018 058 05 805), among other airlines, serve Hamburg's **Fuhlsbüttel Airport** (HAM; ☎040 507 50). **Jasper Airport Express** buses run from the Kirchenallee exit of the Hauptbahnhof directly to the airport. (☎040 227 10 610. €5, under 12 €2. 25min. Every 10-15min. 4:45am-7pm, every 20min. 7-9:20pm.) Alternatively, you can take U1, S1, or S11 to Ohlsdorf, then take an express bus to the airport. (€2.60, ages 6-14 €0.90. Every 10min. 4:30am-11pm, every 30min. 11pm-1am.)

By Train

The **Hauptbahnhof,** Hamburg's central station, offers connections to: Berlin (€56; 2hr., about 1 per hr.); Frankfurt (€109; 4hr., 1 per hr.); Hannover (€40; 1½hr., 2 per hr.); Munich (€185; 6hr., about 1 per hr.); and Copenhagen (€80; 5hr., 6 per day). The efficient staff at the **DB Reisezentrum** sells tickets (Open M-F 5:30am-10pm, Sa-Su 7am-10pm), which are also available at the ticket machines located throughout the Hauptbahnhof and online at. **Dammtor** station is near the university, to the west of Außenalster; **Harburgdorf** is to the southeast. Most trains to and from Schleswig-Holstein stop only at **Altona,** while most trains toward Lübeck stop only in the Hauptbahnhof. Stations are connected by frequent local trains and the S-Bahn.

By Bus

The **ZOB** terminal is across Steintorpl. from the Hauptbahnhof. (☎040 24 75 76 Open M-Tu 5am-10pm, W 5am-midnight, Th 5am-10pm, F 5am-midnight, Sa-Su 5am-10pm.)

Getting Around

By Public Transportation

HVV operates the efficient U-Bahn, S-Bahn, and bus network. Tickets are validated upon purchase according to the station or time you buy them. Short rides within downtown cost €1.30, and one-way rides farther out in the network cost €0.80; when in doubt, use the starting point/destination input tool on any ticket machine to figure out which of the one-way tickets will suffice. Two different day cards may cause confusion: the **9-Uhr Tageskarte** (9hr. day card €5.50) works for unlimited rides midnight-6am and 9am-6pm on the day of purchase. A **Ganztageskarte** (full-day pass; €6.80) works for unlimited rides at any point throughout the day of purchase until 6am the next morning. A **3-Tage-Karte** (3-day ticket; €16.50) is also available. Passes are available for longer time periods, though anything over a week requires a photo. Frequent riders can bring a photo or take one in the nearby ID booths for €5.

By Ferry

HADAG Seetouristik und Fährdienst AG runs ferries. (☎040 311 70 70. Departs the docks at St. Pauli Landungsbrücken. 21 stops along the river. Price included in HVV train and bus passes; €2.60 for a new ticket. All 21 stops 75min., every 15min.) Take the HVV-affiliated ferries in lieu of the expensive tour boats for an equally impressive view of the river Elbe.

By Taxi

All Hamburg taxies charge the same rates. Normally, it's about €2.70 to start, then about €1.80 per km for the first 10km and €1.28 per km thereafter. Try **Autoruf** (☎040 441 011), **Das Taxi** (☎040 221 122), or **Taxi Hamburg**. (☎040 666 666)

By Bike

Hamburg is wonderfully bike-friendly, with wide bike lanes on most roads. Rent a bike at **Fahrradstation Dammtor/Rotherbaum** (Schlüterstr. 11 ☎040 414 68 27. €4-8 per day Open M-F 9am-6:30pm) or **Hamburg City Cycles**. (Bernhard-Nocht-Str. ☎040 742 14

420. Offers guided bike tours €12 per day, €23 per 2 days, €7 per day thereafter. Open Tu-F on request, Sa-Su 10am-6pm.)

cologne

Many know the name Cologne because of Eau de Cologne, a perfume that was all the rage in the 18th-century and now makes for the perfect passive-aggressive gift. Fewer know Cologne itself, which manages to earn the title of the fourth largest in Germany (after Berlin, Hamburg, and Munich), while feeling decidedly provincial: its famous cathedral owns all the other buildings in town, and the locals speak their own funky dialect called Kölsch.

Cologne's city center was meticulously reconstructed after being razed by bombings during World War II, and the city never regained the power it had in the Middle Ages, but that doesn't mean that it lives in the past. Cologne is home to many art museums and the nightlife scene stays vibrant thanks to the presence of the University of Cologne (Universität zu Köln), one of Germany's largest. Known as the "Gay Capital of Germany," Cologne is also the site of an enormous Pride parade every summer. Don't be fooled: Kölsch beer may be served in the smallest glasses you'll find in Germany, but people here like to enjoy life in big gulps.

SIGHTS

☒ COLOGNE CATHEDRAL

Domkloster 3 ☎0221-17940555 www.koelner-dom.de

Just how old is Cologne Cathedral? It's a tough question to answer. Construction began on the present-day structure in the mid-13th century, and it was left unfinished in 1473. It wasn't until the 19th century that work resumed and the cathedral's enormous spires were built. Long story short: When you're looking at the Cologne Cathedral, you're looking at a near-millennium-long labor of love—one that happens to be one of Europe's highlights of Gothic architecture. If you're feeling up to it, climb the 533 steps up the Südturm (southern tower) and catch a glimpse of what Cologne's skyline looks without the "Dom."

i Cathedral free. Tours €8, students and children €6. Cathedral open daily May-Oct 6am-9pm, Nov-Apr 6am-7:30pm. Tower open daily May-Sept 9am-6pm, Oct 9am-5pm, Nov-Feb 9am-4pm, Mar-Apr 9am-5pm. English tours M-Sa 10:30 and 2:30, Su 2:30.

☒ MUSEUM LUDWIG

Heinrich Boll Platz ☎0221-22126165 www.museum-ludwig.de

If you thought Cologne was too focused on its past to collect modern art, you were wrong. The exterior of the Museum Ludwig is itself a work of art that contrasts beautifully with the historical cathedral next door. Still, the metal curves are nothing compared to the astronomic collection of 20th-century art inside. You'll find almost 800 works by Pablo Picasso (the world's third largest collection), and the bottom floor is dedicated to the biggest names in Pop Art: Andy Warhol, Roy Lichtenstein, and Robert Rauschenberg, and their ilk. Also not to be missed are the Expressionists and Russian avant-garde that dominate the permanent collection.

i €11, students €7.50, "children" under 18 free. Half price 5pm-10pm on the 1st Th of the month. All other days open Tu-Su 10am-6pm.

☒ TWELVE ROMANESQUE CHURCHES

Throughout city center ☎0221-22125302 www.romanische-kirchen-koeln.de

One outstanding Romanesque church is cool; twelve is just greedy. Still, these (mostly reconstructed) medieval masterpieces served a purpose back in the day: to protect Cologne against invaders and, more importantly, sin. The Dom dwarfs germany

☒ DIE WOHNGEMEINSCHAFT $$

Richard-Wagner-Strasse 39   ☎0221-39760904 www.die-wohngemeinschaft.net

It would be easy to spend four times as much on a hotel room that wouldn't be half as comfortable as the dorms in Die Wohngemeinschaft. Each bunk comes with an enormous mattress, privacy curtains, a light, and an outlet—so yeah, you can sleep in the buff, if that's your thing. As a bonus, the first floor of DW is a trendy bar where hostel guests nab a 10% discount. If you're in search of a more laid-back place to drink, the common room includes beer and wine paid for on the honor system, as well as unlimited free coffee and tea.

i Dorms €20-30. Reception 8am-10pm; after that, go to the bar for help.

☒ STATION - HOSTEL FOR BACKPACKERS $$

Marzellenstrasse 44   ☎0221-9125301 www.hostel-cologne.de

This five-floor backpacker haven has the best location of any hostel in town and a lively atmosphere to match. The "What's On" part of their website and the knowledgeable staff will direct you to all the cool places in Cologne. The bar and lobby are on the smaller side, but the upstairs seating area with a great kitchen makes up for it.

i Dorms €20-25. Free Wi-Fi. Reception 24hr.

---

them all, but the most memorable of the twelve—St. Ursula, St. Gereon, and St. Martin—attest to the glory and immense wealth of what used to be the most important city north of the Alps. Fortunately, that wealth isn't increasing at your expense: Entry is free.

i Free. Hours vary; most open daily during daylight hours.

FOOD

☒ BRAUEREI ZUR MALZMÜHLE $$

Heumarkt 6   ☎0221-92160613 www.muehlenkoelsch.de

Malzmühle's revolving door entrance is low-key enough that most tourists probably miss it; inside, however, locals nosh on enormous cuts of meat and typical Rhenish snacks (the halve hahn, a sandwich of gouda on buttered rye, is a must-try). Of course, it's pretty much mandatory to wash down all of this with a glass or four of the house-brewed kölsch, served in small glasses that one of Malzmühle's many blue-clad waiters will refill as soon as you finish.

i Snacks €3-8. Mains €8-15. Kölsch €1.90/0.2l. Cash only. Open M-Th 11:30am-12am, F-Sa 11:30-1:30am, Su 11:30am-11pm.

☒ ZÜLPICHER DÖNER $

Zülpicher Strasse 3   ☎1578-5148269

Zülpicher serves up Cologne's best döner kebab, hands down, and is worthy of a visit even if not suffering from a case of the drunchies. We never thought we'd be praising a kebab joint for its attention to detail, but Zülpicher's fresh-baked bread, perfectly spiced meat, and generous toppings help to elevate Europe's most common sandwich into an uncommonly delicious experience.

i Sandwiches €4-6. Cash only. Open daily 11am-5am (exact closing time depends on mood).

WEINHAUS VOGEL $

Eigelstein Strasse 74   ☎0221-1399134 www.weinhaus-vogel-koeln.xregional.de

Don't be fooled by the name or the wine glasses in the window: Weinhaus Vogel is an authentic local restaurant, and beer is king. If you're still not convinced, take a look around at the enormous collection of beer posters. Daily local food specialties go for €6-7, but we also recommend entrees from the main menu, especially the delicious schnitzel.

i Mains €6-18. Daily specials €6-7. Kölsch €1.60. Cash only. Open M-Th 10am-midnight, F-Sa 10am- 2am, Su 10am-midnight.

NIGHTLIFE

GLORIA

Apostelnstrasse 11   ☎0221-660630 www.gloria-theater.com

Gloria is a landmark of Cologne's LGBT scene. Not your typical cafe+club, this former movie theater offers the best of all worlds and hosts events from parties to films to stand-up comedy. Although the cafe is nice, the real deal is the multi-purpose theater in the back, with red velvet walls and clusters of disco balls. Call or visit the website for the schedule of events; in the past, big names such as Sufjan Stevens and Coldplay have performed here.

i Cover €8-15. Beer €1.90, cocktails €6-7. Cash only. Cafe open M-Sa noon-8pm; club hours vary based on events.

DAS DING

Hohenstaufenring 30-32   ☎2233-714206 www.dingzone.de

Das Ding, or "The Thing," is a smoky student disco with a bunch of neon lights everywhere, making it the best place to show off your dance moves to your new hostel friends. It's also incredibly budget friendly, with dirt-cheap specials every night of the week. Tuesdays, for example, offer €1 vodka energy shots in addition to free-beer-o'clock from 9-11pm. And it doesn't stop there: the club has a birthday-week special that includes 10 free shots, a bottle of champagne, and party goods. Student IDs are not required, but the bouncer outside keeps the crowd young.

i Beer €1.20. Shots €1.50-3. Cash only. Open Tu-W 9pm-3am, Th 10pm-4am, F-Sa 10pm-5am.

ESSENTIALS

Practicalities

- **TOURIST OFFICE:** KölnTourismus. (Kardinal-Höffner-Platz 1, across from the Dom. ☎0221-346430. www.koelntourismus.de. Open M-F 9am-8pm, Sa-Su 10am-5pm.)

- **CURRENCY EXCHANGE:** Reisebank. (Inside the Hauptbahnhof. ☎0221-134403. www.reisebank.de. Open daily 7am-10pm.)

- **POST OFFICE:** Deutche Post. (Breite Strasse 6-26, near Appellhofpl. Open M-F 9am-7pm, Sa 9am-2pm.)

Emergency

- **EMERGENCY NUMBERS:** ☎112. Police: ☎110.

- **PHARMACY:** Dom Apotheke (Bahnhofsvorplatz 1, between the Dom and the Hauptbahnhof. ☎0221-20050500. www.dom-apotheke-koeln.de. Open M-F 8am-8pm, Sa 9am-8pm.)

Getting There

By Plane

Flights from **Köln-Bonn Flughafen** (☎02203 40 40 01 02 www.koeln-bonn-airport.de), located halfway between Cologne and Bonn, serve most major European cities, in addition to Turkey and North Africa. The airport is also a budget airline hub. The **S13** runs between the Cologne Hauptbahnhof and the airport. *i* €2.50. 15min., every 20-30min.) A taxi from Cologne to the airport costs no more than €30.

By Train

The Cologne Hauptbahnhof is located right by the Dom in the Altstadt-Nord. Trains go to: **Berlin** (€109. 5hr., 1-2 per hr.); **Bonn** (€6.80. 30min., 2 per hr.); **Frankfurt** (€64. 1½hr., every hr.); **Munich** (€129. 5hr., every hr.); **Amsterdam** (€58. 3hr., every 2hr.); **Basel** (€111. 4hr., every hr.); **Brussels** (€46. 2hr., 4 per day); **London** (€400. 5hr., 2 per day); **Vienna** (€154. 10hr., 5 per day.) Prices may be lower if booked at least three days in advance.

Getting Around

By Public Transportation

Cologne's buses, trams, and subways are served by the **KVB,** or Kölner Verkehrs-Be-triebe (☎0221 26 313 www.kvb-koeln.de). A **Kurzstrecke** ticket (€1.70, ages 6-14 €1) is good for a ride of four stops or less. A ride to anywhere in the city is €2.50 (ages 6-14 €1.30), but you can save money by buying a carnet of four (€9/4.90). A day pass is €7.30 for individuals, and €10.70 for groups of up to five. Validate tickets at the validating machines before boarding or face a €40 fine.

By Ferry

Köln-Düsseldorfer leaves from the dock in the Altstadt, between the Deutzer and Ho-henzollern bridges, and offers trips up and down Rhein. (☎0221 208 83 18 www.k-d. de *i* To the Mainz €55, round-trip €60; to Bonn €14/16. Up to 50% discounts for students with valid ID. 1hr. panoramic cruises up and down Rhein in the Cologne area €7.80. 2hr. afternoon cruises €12. Panoramic cruises Apr-Oct daily 10:30am, noon, 2pm, and 6pm. Afternoon cruises 3:30pm.)

By Gondola

Kölner Seilbahn sells scenic gondola trips across the Rhine, from the Zoo to the Rhe-inpark. (Riehlerstr. 180 ☎0221 547 41 83 www.koelner-seilbahn.de *i* U18: Zoo/Flora. 1-way €4; round-trip €6. Open Apr-Oct daily 10am-6pm).

By Bike

Cologne is a big city, and renting a bike can help you conquer the distances more easily. Pay attention to the direction of bike traffic, as bike lanes are often one-way. In general, keep to the right side of the street. **Radstation** offers bike rental near the Hauptbahnhof. (Breslauer Pl. ☎0221 139 71 90 *i* Exit the Hauptbahnhof through the rear exit, then turn right. €50 deposit. €5 per 3hr., €10 per day, €40 per week. Open M-F 5:30am-10:30pm, Sa 6:30am-8pm, Su 8am-8pm.)

düsseldorf

Düsseldorf has an inferiority complex, and it's entirely undeserved. Long overshadowed by the size and double spires of its nearby rival Cologne, the city has recently emerged as a European leader in contemporary art and architecture, as a quick stroll through its futuristic Media Harbor will show. The city's famous amber Altbier is served by the barrel in Düsseldorf's Old Town, which transforms into "the longest bar in the world" at night.

SIGHTS

▓ K21 STÄNDEHAUS

Ständehausstrasse 1 ☎0211-8381204

If the thought of walking slowly around a huge gallery filled with impressive paintings feels so 20th century, then head over to the K21, which focuses on contemporary installation art. Most rooms in the K21 are restricted to a few visitors at a time, so be prepared to wait in line within the museum if it's busy. The highlight of the K21 is the American artist James Turrell's minimalist piece Grey Dawn, which requires at least 20 minutes to really appreciate (it's located in a dark room, so your eyes will need to adjust). We promise—this is one of the only artworks in the world you won't get in trouble for trying to touch. The associated K20 gallery, a short walk or shuttle ride away from the K21, is more painting-oriented, with a noteworthy collection of works by Paul Klee, Frank Stella, and Max Ernst.

i €12.50, €10 students; combo ticket with K20 €18, €14 students. Free on the first Wed of each month from 6-10pm. Open Tu-F 10am-6pm, Sa-Su 11am-6pm.

▓ MEDIA HARBOR AND RHEINTURM

Stromstrasse 20 www.guennewig.de/en/rheinturm-duesseldorf

Featuring not one, not two, but three wavy buildings by the star American architect Frank Gehry, the constantly-in-construction Media Harbor is like a Petri dish for experimental urban planning. It may not make sense (see: multicolored human statues scaling a building), but the future is here, and it's in Düsseldorf.

get a room!

BACKPACKERS DÜSSELDORF $$

Fürstenwall 180 ☎0211-3020848 www.backpackers-duesseldorf.de

Backpackers can feel oddly residential—travelers who seem to have been staying there for weeks might throw shade if you sit in their preferred spot, and it's not uncommon to share a dorm with entire families. Still even with the Hotel California vibe, the free breakfast and comfy beds make it a worthwhile place to stay.

i Dorms €20-25. Cash only. Reception 8am-10pm.

A&O DÜSSELDORF HAUPTBAHNHOF $

Corneliusstrasse 9 ☎0211-339944800 www.aohostels.com/duesseldorf/

There are always "nicer" places to stay than an A&O. But it's here in this guide—and here, like, in a general sense—because the value can't be beat. Dorms run just €15-20, for which you'll receive a clean bed, internet, and pretty much nothing else. Interaction with your fellow travelers? Free breakfast? Forget about it; that'll be €7. The breakfast, that is—you can't buy friendship.

i Dorms €15-20. Reception 24hr.

The nearby Rheinturm, an enormous telecommunications tower, provides stomach-flipping views of the city from its revolving restaurant/observation deck at a height of over 500 feet.

i Media Harbor free. Elevator to Rheinturm is €9, €5 before 11am or after 10pm. Media Harbor open 24hr. Rheinturm open F-Sa 10am-1am, Su-Th 10am-midnight.

FOOD

🍴 CURRY $
Hammerstrasse 2   ☎0211-3032857 www.curry-deutschland.de

Currywurst is hard to make classy (see also: wifebeaters and tramp stamps), but these guys nearly do it. Media Harbor's Curry offers a range of sausage and sauce flavors, as well as addicting double-fried pommes frites. If the place is crowded, grab any available seat, or watch them get snapped up by no-nonsense locals. All's fair in love and wurst.

i Mains €8-10. Cash only. Open daily 11:30am-11pm.

🍴 SPATZ UP $
Mertensgasse 23   ☎160-8567613

We're still trying to figure out whether Spatz Up's name is supposed to be an English-language pun, but no amount of semantic sketchiness can take away from the tasty noodles served up by this Carlsplatz cafe. Spätzle, long known by vegetarian travelers as "the only dish I can eat at most German restaurants," is the focus here, and comes alongside a range of goulashes, veggies, and flavorful sauces. We give this place a few spatz on the back.

i Mains €7-10. Cash only. Open daily 12pm-7pm.

NIGHTLIFE

Düsseldorf's Alstadt essentially turns into one enormous and continuous bar most nights and weekends, so the best strategy for a night out is to head there in the evening and pick a place that looks lively. A heads up: you'll likely get served a glass of Altbier immediately upon arrival at most traditional bars and breweries, so if you're planning to pace yourself, you'll have to be vocal.

🍴 ZUM UERIGE
Bergerstrasse 1   ☎0211-866990

Once you're cocooned within Uerige's cozy interior, it can be hard to leave—maybe it's the atmosphere, or maybe it's the many glasses of superb Altbier that its lightning-fast waiters start serving as soon as you enter. The kitchen serves up a range of sausage and rye-based snacks and sandwiches, as well as heartier fare such as pork knuckle and schnitzel for those with a case of the Düsseldorf drunchies.

i Beer €1.80, Snacks €3-5, Mains €10-15. Cash only. Open daily 10am-midnight.

🍴 CUBANITOS
Kurzestrasse 14   www.cubanitos-bar.de

Cubanitos is a rare blend of mixology and dancing that's especially unexpected in beer-soaked Düsseldorf. If you're into a specialty liquor, it's probably on the shelf at Cubanitos. Grab a Melon Cool (€9) and hit the dance floor—or, show up a few hours earlier and sample a few €5 cocktails at the 6-9pm Happy Hour.

i Cocktails €8-9, €5 during happy hour. Cash only. Open Tu-Th 6pm-1am, F-Sa 6pm-4am. Happy hour 6-9pm.

ESSENTIALS
Practicalities

- **TOURIST OFFICE:** Tourist Information Office Alstadt (Markstrasse 6. ☎0211-17202840. www.duusseldorf-tourismus.de/en/tourist-information-offices. Open daily 10am-6pm.)

- **POST OFFICE:** Deutsche Post (Heinrich-Heine-Allee 22. ☎228-4333112. Open M-F 9am-6pm, Sa 10am-1pm.)

Emergency

- **EMERGENCY NUMBERS:** ☎112. Police: ☎110.

- **HOSPITAL:** University Hospital of Düsseldorf. (Moorenstrasse 5. ☎0211-8100. www.uni-duesseldorf.de.)

frankfurt

When you think of Germany, do you imagine timber houses, cobblestones and castles, Lederhosen, or Oktoberfest? Forget all that: Frankfurt has none of it. Allied bombs destroyed Frankfurt's Old European style, and all that remains is "Mainhatten," a local slang term for the city that references its location on the Main River and its utter domination by banking and skyscrapers. Is Frankfurt worth visiting? With all of the other impressive cities nearby in Germany, probably not. But you're probably going to end up in Frankfurt because of a layover, and the city does have some worthwhile sights and museums, as well as a relatively laid-back feel in the neighborhoods south of the Main.

SIGHTS

The Altstadt, Frankfurt's tiny old town, features some leftovers from its medieval glory days, including adorable reconstructions of those half-timbered houses you've set as your computer's background and an exquisite Gothic cathedral, which, by the glory of luck or a chance deity, survived the Allied bombing of 1944. The Main River, which splits Frankfurt in two, offers some gorgeous views that almost make you forget the steel phalluses scraping the sky around you.

🏛 MUSEUM FÜR MODERNE KUNST

Domstrasse 10   ☎069-21230447 www.mmk-frankfurt.de

The Museum für Moderne Kunst is one of the best ways to spend a couple of hours in Frankfurt. Sure, the collection could be located anywhere, but this modern city does modern art pretty damn well. MMK has a little something for everyone: plastic, yellow mini skyscrapers; paintings of bound and nude women; rooms full of messy "found art" sculptures; video installations, including one of an elephant doing all its elephant things as it's circled by a camera; and works by some of the great pop artists, including some of Andy Warhol's iconic Campbell's soup cans. Be sure to check out the temporary exhibitions at the MMK's other branches around Frankfurt (MMK2 and MMK3).

i €10, students €5. Last Sa of the month free. Open Tu 10am- 6pm, W 10am-8pm, Th-Su 10am-6pm.

🏛 PALMENGARTEN

Siessmayerstrasse 61   www.palmengarten.de

When Frankfurt is feeling too bland, corporate, and/or dangerous, a walk in one of Europe's largest (and most beautiful) botanical gardens can be just what the doctor ordered. It's easy to spend a few hours exploring the art exhibitions,

get a room!

Squeamish or inexperienced travelers will probably want to avoid staying anywhere within a ten-minute walk of the Hauptbahnhof, an area infamous for encompassing most of Frankfurt's sex industry and public drug use.

▨ HAUS DER JUGEND $

Deutschhernufer 12   ☎069-6100150 www.jugendherberge-frankfurt.de

Haus der Jugend is in the best location of all the hostels in Frankfurt. It's right on the river and only a five minute walk from Frankfurt's best sights, including the Altstadt and the Museumsufer, not to mention Sachsenhausen's nightlife. Unfortunately, Haus der Jugend does maintain a curfew, which limits the awesomeness of its closeness to Sachsenhausen. Despite gorgeous river views, like any hostel with over 400 beds, Haus der Jugend feels more like a hospital than a B&B. Still, anonymity is a small price to pay for good amenities and an unrivaled location.

i Dorms €18-20. Reception 24hr. Curfew 2am.

FIVE ELEMENTS HOSTEL $$

Moselstrasse 40   ☎069 240 05 885 www.5elementshostel.de

Five Elements is in the middle of Frankfurt's red light district, so we weren't expecting much by way of homeyness. Thankfully, we were pleasantly surprised. Every night is special at Five Elements, which offers a free pasta night, free barbecue night, free movie night, and a constantly updated list of free surprises. If this weren't enough, the rooms are superior, with tall metal bunks, plenty of floor space, and huge windows looking out on the skyscrapers. Reserve ahead of time, as Five Elements fills early in the summer.

i Dorms €20-25. Free Wi-Fi. Reception 24hr.

EASYHOTEL $$$$

Dusseldorferstrasse 19   ☎069-17489220 www.easyhotel-frankfurt.de

easyHotel is run by the same company as easyJet, and it shares the airline's ruthless dedication to stripping away amenities. You'll pay for Wi-Fi (€6/day), and even the in-room TVs won't turn on without payment. Solo travelers will be better off opting for a hostel, but easyHotel offers the best private room rates in Frankfurt (€40-50/night for doubles), and those rooms are clean—if tiny. Be warned that easyHotel is located only a couple minutes' walk from the Hauptbahnhof, an area that isn't going to win any awards for its safety or lack of drug abuse.

i Private rooms €40-70. Wi-Fi €6 per day. Reception 24hr.

---

grottos, and—of course—plants at the Palmengarten, which also makes an ideal location for a picnic lunch. Just don't try to eat it in the cactus nursery, or things might get prickly.

i €7, students €3. Open daily Feb-Oct 9am-6pm; Nov-Jan 9am-4pm.

▨ STÄDEL

Schaumanikai 63   ☎069-6050980 www.staedelmuseum.de

The Städel Museum, with its collection dating back to 1300, is probably one of the most successful and complete museums you'll find in Germany. Masters like Botticelli, Rembrandt, and Dürer dominate one end of the timeline, while modern gods like Renoir, Kirchner, and Picasso command the other. The contents of this museum were hidden in a Bavarian castle during World War II, and

(sidebar) germany

everything survived except the main gallery, which was rebuilt in 1966. Excellent presentation, curatorial decisions, and organization will turn you into an art history beast after a single visit.

i *€12, Students €10. Open Tu 10am-6pm, W-Th 10am-9pm, F-Su 10am-6pm.*

STADTWALD

The Stadtwald, a 80km forest in the south of Frankfurt, is wasted on the city's corporate types. Filled with densely packed birches and winding footpaths, the Stadtwald is one of the largest city forests in Europe, and also one of the least crowded. Follow the signs for the Stadtwaldhaus to find a delightful museum and zoo, and hunt down the wooden Goethe Tower (Goetheturm) for a climb that ends with panoramic views of the Frankfurt skyline. Then, celebrate the fact that you're not stuck in one of those buildings.

i *Take Tram 12 to Oberschweinsteige, directly in the center of Stadtwald. Free.*

DOM SANKT BARTHOLOMÄUS

Domplatz 14   ☎069-13376184 www.dom-frankfurt.de

This cathedral is practically the only sight in Frankfurt that isn't shiny and new. Amazingly, the 66m spire survived the Allied bombing of 1944. Back when the Holy Roman Empire was still neither holy, Roman, nor an empire, seven electors chose continental Europe's most influential emperors here, and the glorious coronation ceremonies that followed filled the Dom's Gothic halls with splendor. Unfortunately, the church had to be reconstructed after an 1867 fire, but the resulting Gothic tower is among Germany's most famous.

i *Cathedral free. Museum €3, students €2. Tours €3/2. Cash only. Cathedral open M-Th 8am-8pm, F noon-8pm, Sa-Su 9am-8pm, except during services. Museum open Tu-F 10am-5pm, Sa-Su 11am-5pm. Haus am Dom open M-F 9am-5pm, Sa-Su 11am-5pm. Tours (in German) Tu-Su 3pm.*

FOOD

MERAL'S IMBISSBOOT $

Schaumainkai 35   ☎0162-4353304 www.meral-event.de

Of all the thousands of döner kebab joints in Germany, we're pretty sure this is the only one on a boat. Anchored on the south bank of the Main, near Frankfurt's hip Saschenhausen neighborhood, Meral's serves up a range of creative döner-style sandwiches, including fish-based and vegetarian options. Enjoy your sloppy sandwich on the riverbank, and don't forget to wash it down with a cup of ayran (€2) that's better than any we sampled in Istanbul.

i *Sandwiches €4-5. Cash only. Open daily noon-11pm.*

NUY'S THAI IMBISS PATTAYA $

Taunusstrasse 17   ☎069-234356 www.pattaya-imbiss.de

No one ever said that eating well had to be glamorous. Sure, at Nuy's, you're likely to share a tiny standing table with hungry businessmen on a lunch break. The restaurant staff might even wash your utensils in front of you. Still, digging into an enormous curry for the price of an appetizer at Frankfurt's ritzier Thai restaurants (€4-7) feels pretty good.

i *Most mains €4-7. Soup €3-4. Cash only. Open M-F 11am-9pm, Sa 12-6pm, Su 2-9pm.*

BIZZI-ICE $

Wallstrasse 26   ☎069-94942550 www.bizzi-ice.com

Finding good gelato in Europe is about as difficult as finding an all caps tweet on Kanye's timeline. That's why, at Let's Go, we generally don't review eis joints (as they're known in Germany). Bizzi-Ice, an organic gelato shop in the heart of Frankfurt's Sachsenhausen neighborhood, deserves an exception. Delivering huge scoops of outside-the-box flavors like cardamom-almond and elderflower, Bizzi-Ice is a gem among the gelato masses.

i *Scoops €1.50. Cash only. Open daily 11am-10pm.*

ADOLF WAGNER

$$

Schweizerstrasse 71   ☎069-612565 www.apfelwein-wagner.de

Saucy German dishes and some of the region's most renowned Apfelwein (0.3L €1.80) keep patrons jolly at this Sachsenhausen icon. Sit with regulars and try some of the Grüne Soße (green sauce) that you keep hearing about, preferably slathered atop the Frankfurter schnitzel (€12). The sauce is creamy and sour, and the wine fills your mouth with a lingering apple aftertaste. As you drink and digest, bask in either of the two sunny courtyards.

i *Entress €7-14. Open daily 11am-midnight.*

NIGHTLIFE

■ PULSE AND PIPER RED LOUNGE

Bleichstrasse 38a   ☎069-13886802 www.pulse-frankfurt.de

Pulse and Piper features two dance floors, two lounges, a restaurant, and a beer garden. It's the ultimate all-in-one nightlife paradise. Despite its size, the club maintains some coziness: bartenders greet regulars on their way in. Piper, the smoking section, comprises a separate bar with loads of lounge space and is one of the largest of its kind in Frankfurt. Officially a gay club, Pulse attracts a clientele both gay and straight with its sublimely social spaces and hair-splitting house music that prompts patrons to dance far more wildly than the usual German two-step.

i *Beer €2.50-3.80. Cocktails €8-10, happy hour €4-5. Restaurant entrees €6-22. Pulse open M-Th 11am-1am, F 11am-4am, Sa 10am-4am, Su 10am- 1am. Piper Lounge (entry within Pulse) open daily 6pm and closes with Pulse. Happy hour M-W 7-9pm, Th 6pm-1am, F-Su 7-9pm. All martini €5 on Mondays. Kitchen open until 11pm.*

COCOON CLUB

Carl-Benz-Strasse 21   ☎069-900200 www.cocoon.net

Cocoon is in the middle of nowhere. It'll cost you €20 to get there with a taxi (alternatively, you can take a tram), but despite the hassle and the cover, those looking for a legit night out won't want to miss it. The complex is gigantic and makes you feel like you're descending into the lair of a monstrous, postmodern spider; the decor is so weird that it's impossible not to deem cool. The main floor, which pumps house music at maximum volume with one of Europe's best sound systems, is enclosed by a gargantuan white-plastic lattice: the cocoon, where your spasms may metamorphose into dancing. Outside the inner sanctum, expensive cocktail bars greet you at every curve in the halls, and couples get cozy in comfy indentations punched into the cocoon's exterior. The bouncers are picky about wardrobe, but this is Frankfurt's premiere club.

i *Accessible via Trams 11 or 12. Cover €10. Cocktails €8-12. Open F-Sa 9pm-6am.*

KING KAMEHAMEHA

Hafeninsel 2   ☎069-48003790 www.king-kamehameha.de

King Kamehameha, much like Cocoon, is in the middle of nowhere, but at least it's less in the middle of nowhere. This place lies in Frankfurt's southeast industrial district, where, by day, businesspeople shop for new kitchen interiors and schmancy new Benzes. However, on Friday and Saturday nights, devastatingly loud house music from seasoned DJs threatens to shake this former brewery (with smokestack still standing) to the ground. Thursdays feature the renowned King Kamehameha Club Band, which ignites crowds with everything from '60s dance hits to top 40. Next to the packed main dance floor, a partially covered "garden" is the perfect place to take a break from the dancing, drinking, and steam.

i *Cover €10. Shots €4. Beer €4-5. Cocktails €10. Cash only. Open Th 9pm-4am, F-Sa 10pm-5am.*

ESSENTIALS
Practicalities

- **TOURIST OFFICES:** Tourist Information Hauptbahnhof has your back. (Inside Hauptbhanhof. ☎069-21238800. Near the main exit, next to the car rental. Brochures, tours, and map €0.50-1. Will book rooms for a €3 fee; free if you call or email ahead. Open M-F 8am-9pm, Sa-Su 9am-6pm. Alternate location at Römerberg 27 open M-F 9:30am-5:30pm, Sa-Su 10am-4pm.)

- **CURRENCY EXCHANGE:** ReiseBank in the Hauptbahnhof has slightly worse-than-average rates, but, unlike most banks, stays open on Saturday. (In the Hauptbahnhof. ☎069-24278591. Descend the stairs inside the main entrance and walk down the hallway to the right. Open M-F 7am-6:30pm, Sa 10am-6pm.)

- **INTERNET ACCESS:** Plenty of Internet-Telefon stores can be found on Kaiserstr., directly across from the Hauptbahnhof. The Starbucks offers unlimited free Wi-Fi without a password, so you don't even need to buy an expensive drink.

- **POST OFFICE:** Yup, there's one of these inside the train station too. (Inside Hauptbahnhof, opposite track 22. Open M-F 7am-7pm, Sa 9am4pm.)

- **POSTAL CODE:** 60313.

Emergency

- **EMERGENCY NUMBERS:** ☎110. Fire and Ambulance: ☎112.

- **POLICE:** City Police (Adickesallee 70. ☎069-75500. Take the U1 or U2 to Miquel Adickesallee and head east; the station is on the left.)

- **PHARMACY:** Apotheke im Hauptbahnhof. (Station's Einkaufspassage. ☎069-233047. In the Hauptbahnhof, take the escalators heading down toward the S- or U-Bahn trains, then turn left. Open M-F 6:30am-9pm, Sa 8am-9pm, Su 9am-8pm.)

heidelberg

There's no way around it: especially during the summer, Heidelberg is absolutely packed with tourists. Attempting to navigate around fanny-packing American pensioners in the old town's cobbled streets can make you feel like you're in some grown-up version of Disney World, a comparison that extends to the extortionist food prices. However, there's still a solitude and beauty to be found in Heidelberg, one in which the city's many famous philosophers and poets have revelled for centuries. It might be hard to find, but it's there.

get a room!

🏨 LOTTE – THE BACKPACKERS $$
Burgweg 3   ☎06221-7350725 www.lotte-heidelberg.de

If you manage to snag a spot at Heidelberg's tiny Lotte (book early!), you'll be treated to free cereal in the morning, a cozy bed, and an unbeatable location at the base of the hill that leads up to Heidelberg Castle. Strong Wi-Fi, plentiful outlets, and free luggage storage are other key benefits that make Lotte an essentially perfect place to make your base in Heidelberg. But again: book now.

i Dorms €25-30. Reception 8am-10pm.

SIGHTS

■ HEIDELBERG CASTLE

Schlosshof 1   ☎06221-658880 www.schloss-heidelberg.de/en

Looking at the enormous ruins of Heidelberg Castle from below, it's impossible to imagine that it took the locals until the late nineteenth century to start selling tickets. The castle's enormous complex, which was most recently destroyed by lightning in 1764, is a hodgepodge of reconstructed Renaissance palaces and medieval towers, the interiors of which are accessible only via guided tour (€5, or €2.50 for students). The castle's basement also contains Europe's largest wine cask—capable of holding over 50,000 gallons of wine—which must've made for some killer games of slap the barrel. Don't skip the Deutches Apotheke Museum housed in the castle, which makes the history of the German pharmacy as interesting as it could possibly be.

i €7, €4 students; guided tour €5, €2.50 students. Open daily 8am-6pm.

THE PHILOSOPHERS' WAY

Less a path than a state of mind, the Philosophers' Way runs along the side of the Heiligenberg Hill, across the river from Heidelberg's Old Town. Throughout the city's history, romantic poets and stern philosophers have prized the solitude and views of the Neckar River and Heidelberg Castle afforded by this moss-covered route. If you're up for a bit of a hike, take a detour further up the hill to see the chilling ruin of an enormous Nazi thingstatte, or outdoor amphitheater, built on the hill in the 1930s.

i Cross the old bridge and walk toward the hill; follow the signs for the "Philosophenweg." Free.

FOOD

■ PALMBRÄU GASSE $$

Hauptstrasse 185   ☎06221-28536 http://palmbraeugasse.de

Embrace your inner elderly tourist and head to Palmbräu Gasse for heaping dishes of authentic Swabian and Bavarian food, both of which are all about sausages, spätzle, and sweet beer. Sitting in the city's bustling Marktplatz, Palmbräu Gasse isn't the cheapest place to grab a meal (most mains run between €10-20), but it's comfortable, almost always full, and open late (3am on Fridays and Saturdays, 1am on other days). By that time, the median age will probably be a little closer to yours.

i Mains €10-20. Beer €3-5. Open Su-Th 11:30-1am, F-Sa 11:30-3am.

NIGHTLIFE

■ MARSTALLCAFÉ

Marstallhof 1   ☎06221-540

Instead of attempting to hunt down a reasonably priced bar in the Old Town (it ain't gonna happen), head to where the University of Heidelberg's 30,000 students hang out. Beer costs less than €3 at Marstallcafé, and it's best enjoyed at one of the many picnic tables outside, where you can befriend an eclectic mix of tipsy students. If you happen to be around on a Sunday, don't miss the special tarte flambeées (a regional specialty similar to pizza) served up by the guest chefs for under €5 each.

i Beer €3. Cash only. Open M-F 9am-11pm, Sa 2:30-8:30pm, Su 1:30-10pm.

ESSENTIALS
Practicalities

- **TOURIST OFFICES:** Tourist Information Centers can help with most tourist issues. (Willy-Brandt-Platz 1. ☎6221-5844444. Open Apr-Oct M-Sa 9am-7pm, Su 10am-7pm; Nov-Mar M-Sa 9am-6pm.)
- **INTERNET:** Free Wi-Fi is often easily accessible in the city center and at most cafés.

Emergency

- **EMERGENCY NUMBERS:** ☎112. Police: ☎110. Ambulance: ☎089-19222.
- **HOSPITALS/MEDICAL SERVICES:** University Hospital Heidelberg is a world-renowned medical center. (Im Neuenheimer Feld 400. ☎6221-566243. www.heidelberg-university-hospital.com)

stuttgart

The long-time cradle of the German automobile industry (Mercedes and Porsche are based here), Stuttgart is delightfully far from the corporate city you might expect. World-class museums, lush parks, and a laid-back pace of life are Stuttgart's calling cards, and you'll probably get to enjoy them free from other travelers, most of whom are probably in Heidelberg instead.

SIGHTS
In Stuttgart

▨ MERCEDES-BENZ MUSEUM

Mercedesstrasse 100   ☎0711-1730000

www.mercedes-benz.com/en/mercedes-benz/classic/museum/

If you leave Stuttgart's massive Mercedes-Benz Museum wondering whether the company's engineers and designers could solve global warming if they set their minds to it, the relentless self-promoting propaganda offered up by its exhibits has worked. Still, not every car company invented the car—as you'll often be re-minded here—so we'll give them a pass. Housed in a seven-story complex to the north of Stuttgart, the Benz museum features over a century's worth of classic cars, including several owned by celebrities (now's your chance to see John Paul II's original bulletproof Popemobile). The self-guided audio tour makes it easy to pick and choose what to learn about from the seemingly infinite exhibits—it'd be possible to spend an entire day here, but most people take 2-3 hours.

i €8, students €4. Free with StuttCard. Open Tu-Su 9am-6pm.

▨ WEISSENHOF ESTATE

Rathenaustrasse 1-3   ☎0711-2579187 www.weissenhofmuseum.de

House-hunting and tourism have finally become one. As Stuttgart grew in the early 20th century, it experienced a serious shortage of low-income housing, which inspired many well-known Modernist architects to design and build a complex of homes atop a hill to the city's north during the late 1920s. Nowadays, the building designed by architectural gods Le Corbusier and Mies van der Rohe is a museum dedicated to the project, complete with recreated living spaces (including beds stored in cabinets during the day to avoid clutter). If you decide you want to move in, many of the surrounding homes in the Weissenhof Estate are now private residences. Bring your checkbook.

i €5, students €2.50. Free with StuttCard. Cash only. Open Tu-F 11am-6pm, Sa-Su 10am-6pm.

get a room!

JUGENDHERBERGE STUTTGART INTERNATIONAL $$

Haussmannstrasse 27   ☎0711-6647470 http://stuttgart.jugendherberge-bw.de

This enormous hillside hostel definitely has a "thirty-somethings who didn't want to shell out for a hotel room" feel. Still, the views of Stuttgart can't be beat, especially when you're enjoying them over Jugendherberge's surprisingly excellent free breakfast. Don't expect to pay less than €25 for a bed, but as a bonus, you'll probably only be sharing a room with a few other people.

i Dorms €25-30. 1 hour free Wi-Fi per day. Reception 24hr.

A&O STUTTGART CITY $

Rosensteinstrasse 18   ☎0711-25277400 www.aohostels.com/en/stuttgart/
stuttgart-city/

Like most branches of Europe's A&O chain of hostels, Stuttgart's is aimed at those who prioritize economy over ambience and cleanliness over character. This makes them a middling bet in most cities, but in the hostel-sparse Stuttgart area, A&O's faults seem pretty minor, and its benefits (€15-20/night for a bed in the 8-man dorm)…well, your wallet will thank you.

i Dorms €15-20. Free Wi-Fi. Reception 24hr.

STAATSGALERIE

Konrad-Adenauer-Strasse 30-32   ☎0711-470400 www.staatsgalerie.de

The lime green piping-meets-classicism façade of the Staatsgalerie was famously described as the "epitome of Postmodernism," a quote which might be the epitome of pretentiousness. Like the building or not, it houses a truly excellent collection of modern and contemporary art—entire rooms are devoted to Picasso, Oskar Schlemmer, and Paul Klee—and a pleasant but skippable gallery of works dating from 1300 to 1800.

i €10, students €8. Free with StuttCard. Open Tu-Su 10am-6pm.

PORSCHE MUSEUM

Porscheplatz 1   ☎0711-91120911 www.porsche.com/museum

Slightly overshadowed by the grandiose Mercedes-Benz Museum, the Porsche Museum attempts to distinguish itself in the same way its namesake company always has: attention to technical detail. While you don't need to know anything about cars to appreciate the Porsche Museum, it really helps in maintaining your interest in exhibits on efficient crankshafts and carbon-fiber chassis construction. Or, you can just gaze longingly at the timeless original 911s from the '50s and '60s—until someone hits you in the face with a selfie stick.

i €8, students €4. Half-price until 11am; free with StuttCard. Open Tu-Su 9am-6pm.

Outside Stuttgart

HARBURG CASTLE

Burgstrasse 1   ☎09080-96860 www.die-harburg.de

For those traveling via train or car between Munich and Stuttgart, we strongly recommend making a side trip to Harburg Castle, a magnificently preserved medieval castle overlooking its namesake tiny Bavarian village. Don't skip the guided tour, which is full of choice anecdotes, like how the castle's rulers once survived an attack by holing up in a sealed tower for a month, or how it took workers an hour to draw a bucket of water from the extremely deep well in the middle of the castle grounds. From Harburg, it's not far to Nördlingen and Donauwörth, two picturesque towns along Southern Germany's so-called "Romantic Road" (which we generally think of as a tour bus slogan). The cheaper and more fun way is to buy a daily Bayern (Bavaria) Ticket, which gives you unlimited access to trains in the region for a day (€23 for a single rider, €5 more for each additional rider).

i From the train station, walk into town and follow the signs for the "Burg" (about a 20-minute walk). Admission €2, guided tour €2 extra. Open daily Mar-Oct 9am-5pm.

FOOD

▨ DIE METZGEREI $$
Elisabethenstrasse 30   ☎0711-63329271 www.metzgereistuttgart.de

Despite (or because of) its near-total lack of online presence, Metzgerei is almost always swarmed by locals, many of whom are perfectly okay with eating while standing outside. Enormous salads and pasta dishes (€8-13) are the name of the game here, and each comes with a suggested wine pairing (€4-6). If this sounds like fine dining to you, the setting is considerably more laid-back: dogs are allowed inside the restaurant, and the beer flows freely.

i Mains €8-13. Beer €3. Wine €3-6. Cash only. Open daily 9am-12am.

▨ MÓKUSKA CAFFÈ $$
Johannesstrasse 34   ☎0711-93329039 www.mokuska-caffe.de

At first, it's easy to dismiss Mókuska as a German imitation of those trendy, overpriced New York coffee shops. That is, until you actually try the coffee, and realize that, unlike at those other coffee shops, it's actually worth €3-4. Mókuska is closed on Mondays so that its staff can roast the week's beans using the enormous contraption in the corner, and the result is a fresh and flavorful brew.

i Drinks €3-4. Cash only. Open Tu-F 8:30am-6:30pm, Sa 10am-6pm.

▨ STUTTGARTER STÄEFFELE $$
Buschlestrasse 2   ☎0711-664190 www.staeffele.de

Those in search of traditional Swabian food should look no further than Stuttgarter Stäeffele. Named after the sets of stairs ("stäeffele") that litter Stuttgart's hilly landscape, this old-school restaurant specializes in dishes like maultaschen, a noodle dumpling filled with spinach, pork, and onion sauce. Although there's an English menu available and plenty of travelers to be found here, Stäeffele is no tourist trap: most dishes run under €10 and are big enough to make you feel like you should find the nearest set of stairs and run up and down them a few dozen times.

i Mains €9-12. Cash only. Open M-F 11am-2:30pm, 6-10:30pm; Sa-Su 6-10:30pm.

NIGHTLIFE

TEQUILABAR STUTTGART
Steinstrasse 15   www.tequilabar-stuttgart.com

The drinking scene in Stuttgart is about as unpretentious as they come, a result of the city's long-held status as a center of manufacturing. Accordingly, a visit to Tequilabar will likely be one of the cheapest nights out you'll experience this side of the Iron Curtain—every beer comes with a shot of tequila. Just remember the rhyme in order to drink them in the right order: Beer before liquor, nothing is slicker. Wait, is that it?

i Beer €3. Cash only. Open daily 24hr.

AER CLUB
Büchenstrasse 10   ☎0175-8089633 www.aer-club.de

Everyone in AER seems to think that they're in a music video, including the theatrical DJs who gyrate around their laptops on stage every Saturday night.

hip to (eat) squares

Germany's favorite brand of budget chocolate, Ritter Sport, has been produced in the Stuttgart area for over a century. It comes in hefty, square bars wrapped in varying colored labels for each flavor, most of which run between €0.50-1.50 at grocery stores. Some of these flavors and fillings are standard (hazelnut, coffee), while others will seem a bit strange to those who came up under the hegemony of Hershey's (blackberry yogurt, tortilla chip, white chocolate coconut). We're impressed by the strawberry yogurt flavor, which tastes eerily like those gas station frozen shortcake bars, and the biscuit-filled bar, which puts your standard sans-marshmallow s'more to shame. But there's a clear winner of the coveted Let's Go thumbpick here: the "Olympia" bar, consisting of an improbably delicious combination of honeycomb, yogurt, nuts, and chocolate.

Still, even self-conscious style is style, and the techno-loving Stuttgarters who populate AER have it in spades. Expect to pay a hefty cover (€10-15) depending on whether there's a special event, and don't forget to dress to impress.

i Cover €5-15. Drinks €7-12. Cash only. Open F-Sa 11pm-5am.

ESSENTIALS
Practicalities

- **TOURIST OFFICES:** i-Punkt provides tourist information and advice. (Königstrasse 1. ☎711-2228100. www.stuttgart-tourist.de/a-tourist-information-i-punkt-stuttgart. Open daily 9am-6pm.)

- **INTERNET:** Free Wi-Fi is often accessible in the city center (under UnitymediaWiFi) and can be found at most cafes.

- **POST OFFICE:** Deutsche Post will take care of all your snail mail needs. (Arnulf-Kett-Platz 2. ☎228-4333112. www.deutschepost.de. Open M-F 8am-8pm, Sa 9am-4pm.)

Emergency

- **EMERGENCY NUMBERS:** ☎112. Police: ☎110. Ambulance: ☎089-19222

- **HOSPITALS/MEDICAL SERVICES:** Marienhospital Stuttgart (Böheimstrasse 37. ☎0711-64890. www.marienhospital-stuttgart.de).

munich

If you ask the average traveler about this Bavarian capital, you'll hear beer, beer, and more beer. The birthplace of Oktoberfest, Munich is the third largest city in Germany and one of the country's most expensive. Less worthy of celebration, Hitler's first attempt to seize power took place in Munich, and the Führer spoke at some of the very beer halls that you can visit today. The first Nazi concentration camp, Dachau, is just 30 minutes away from the city. Today, Munich has put most of this history behind it, and has become a thriving center of European commerce, with world-class museums, parks, and architecture.

get a room!

GSPUSI BAR HOSTEL $$$

Oberanger 45 ☎089-24411790 www.gspusibarhostel.com

With its massive planks of unsanded wood flanking each bed and its free, rustically scented soaps, Gspusi feels like a budget hunting lodge. It's not the cheapest hostel in Munich, but Gspusi's central location, strong Wi-Fi, and clean bathrooms are worth the extra euros. Also refreshing is the fact that most dorms house only 3 or 4 beds, as opposed to the standard 8 or 10. The bar/reception area is a great place to grab a relatively cheap beer in the evening and meet a few beer garden buddies to drink a few more with.

i *Dorms €25-35. Reception 24hr.*

EURO YOUTH HOSTEL $$

Senefelderstrasse 5 ☎089-59908811 www.euro-youth-hostel.de

Euro Youth Hostel has some of the most luxurious reception and common areas in the city. The 12-person dorms are surprisingly cheap, so make sure to book in advance, as beds fill up very early. The lounge and its wrap-around bar are the site of many entertaining nights, which range from quizzes to '80s dances to karaoke. Euro Youth Hostel's location near the Hauptbahnhof is great for a quick escape, but not so great for nearby nightlife (unless you prefer a döner kebab crawl to a pub crawl).

i *12-bed dorms €12-25, private rooms €40-100. Breakfast €4.50. Free Wi-Fi. Reception 24hr.*

THE TENT $

In den Kirschen 30 ☎089-1414300 www.the-tent.com

When Munich prepared to host the 1972 Olympics, the government kicked out all the hippies camping out at the English Garden, who then skipped out to the northeast corner of town to set up permanent camp here. Thus, the not-for-profit Tent was born. Two tents are filled with bunk beds, while the third makes space for the bravest travelers: those who sleep on a thin, rainbow-colored mat on the floor. This is by far the cheapest place to stay in Munich, but it's quite far outside the city center, so we hope you like hiking as well as camping.

i *Tram 17: Botanischer Garten. Take a right onto Franz-Schrankstrasse and a left at the end of the street. Free Wi-Fi. Lockers available. Floor space €7.50 (including floor pad and blankets). Beds €11. Camping €5.50 per person; €5.50 per tent. Bike rental €9 per day. Cash only. Open Jun-Oct. Reception 24hr.*

SIGHTS

PINAKOTHEKEN

Barerstrass 40 ☎089-23805284 www.pinakothek.de

Don't let the whole "five museums" thing scare you away from Pinakotheken: think of all these museums as just one giant and super impressive art gallery. The five buildings are part of the Kunstareal, a museum district in Maxvorstadt that comprises the bulk of Munich's art museums. The highlight of the five is the Pinakothek der Moderne, which houses 20th-century and contemporary art (including works by Dalí, Max Beckmann, and German legend Joseph Beuys) in an impressive, spacious interior. The Neue Pinakothek, which touts itself as the world's first contemporary art gallery, focuses on art that was contemporary when it opened—namely 19th-century paintings—while the Alte Pinakothek reserves itself for the Old Masters. The Pinakotheken can be a lot of art all at once, so consider visiting over several days—or run (not literally) through the museums on Sundays, when admission is only €1.

i U2: Theresienstr. Walk east on Theresienstr. until you see the big museum complex. Museum Brandhorst, Alte (currently partially open while undergoing renovation), and Neue Pinakothek each €7, students €5; Pinakothek der Moderne €10/7; Sammlung Schack €4/3; 1-day pass to all 5 €12/9; 5-entry pass €29. All museums €1 on Su. Alte Pinakothek open Tu 10am-8pm, W-Su 10am-6m. Neue Pinakothek open M 10am-6pm, W 10am-8pm, Th-Su 10am-6pm. Pinakothek der Moderne open Tu-W 10am-6pm, Th 10am-8pm, F-Su 10am-6pm. Museum Brandhorst open Tu-W 10am-6pm, Th 10am-8pm, F-Su 10am-6pm. Sammlung Schack open daily 10am-6pm.

🏛 ENGLISCHER GARTEN

☎089-38666390

Strolling through the open emerald fields and leafy paths of the enormous Englischer Garten is one of the most relaxing things to do with a summer day in the city. The park is one of the largest metropolitan public parks in the world, dwarfing both Central Park in New York and Hyde Park in London. The amazingly fit residents of Munich do everything from ride their bikes to bathe in the sun here. Some choose to do the latter in the nude, in areas designated FKK or Frei Körper Kultur ("Free Body Culture"). In the southern part of the garden, a former Nazi art exhibition space, Haus der Kunst (Prinzregentenst 1. 089-21127113. www.hausderkunst.de), is now Munich's premier venue for contemporary art, with changing international and domestic exhibitions.

i U3: Universität, Giselastr., or Münchner Freiheit. Park free. Haus der Kunst €5-12. Student discounts available. Haus der Kunst open M-W 10am-8pm, Th 10am-10pm, F-Su 10am-8pm.

🏛 DACHAU CONCENTRATION CAMP MEMORIAL SITE

Alter Römerstrass 75 ☎081-31669970

The first thing prisoners saw as they entered Dachau was the inscription "Arbeit Macht Frei" ("Work will set you free") on the camp's iron gate—a lie. One of the most moving parts of the memorial site is actually part of the audio guide: Survivors tell their life stories and describe the unimaginably inhumane life in the camp. The barracks, originally designed for 5,000 prisoners, eventually held 30,000—two have been reconstructed for visitors, and gravel-filled outlines of the others stand as haunting reminders. It is impossible to prepare yourself for the camp's crematorium and gas chamber, which were built a few hundred meters away from the main camp to hide their existence from prisoners, and which have been restored to their original appearance. The extensive museum at the Dachau Memorial Site, housed in the former maintenance building, examines pre-1930s anti-Semitism, the rise of Nazism, the establishment of the concentration camps, and the lives of prisoners.

i Accessible via train and S-Bahn from Munich Hbf. Once you've arrived at Dachau station, take bus #726. Museum and memorial grounds free, audio tours €3.50, students €2.50. Memorial grounds open daily 9am-5pm. Museum and information office open Tu-Su 9am-5pm.

🏛 ASAMKIRCHE

Sendlingerstrass 32 ☎089-23687989

The shiny, overflowingly Baroque interior of Munich's Asam Church resembles an episode of Hoarders set in the 1700s. Originally built as a private chapel by the artsy Asam brothers (one was a sculptor, the other a painter), the church is now open to the public, but not fully: you'll have to admire the ornate statues and ceiling frescoes from behind an iron gate at the back.

i Free. Open daily 9am-5pm.

BMW WELT AND MUSEUM
Am Olympiapark 1   www.bmw-welt.com

Do you know what BMW stands for? Regardless of your answer, you have to stop by the BMW Welt and Museum. (BMW stands for "Bayerische Motoren Werke," by the way.) The amazing, futuristic architecture of the entire BMW complex alone would make a visit worthwhile. However, you can also jump into all sorts of cars, play racing computer games, and watch shows of handsome Germans driving motorcycles up and down stairs while you're here. And all this is only in the BMW Welt, which is the company's showcase. The museum is almost as cool (although perhaps not as interactive), with state-of-the-art exhibits detailing the history, development, and design of Bavaria's second-favorite export. Frosted glass walls and touch-sensitive projections lead visitors past engines, chassis, and concept vehicles with exhibits in both English and German.

i U3: Olympiazentrum. BMW Welt is the large steel structure visible upon exiting the metro; the museum is located across the street. BMW Welt free. Museum €9, students €6, family €12. €7 with Olympiapark ticket or the City Tour Card. BMW Welt open daily 7:30am-midnight. Museum open Tu-Su 10am-6pm; last entry 30min before close. English tours daily 11:30am and either noon or 4pm. Factory and BMW Welt tours available only with a reservation.

OLYMPIAPARK
Spiridon-Louis-Ring 21   ☎089-30670

Built for the 1972 Olympic Games, the lush Olympiapark contrasts with the curved steel and transparent spires of the Olympic Stadium and the 290m Olympiaturm, Munich's tallest tower. The Olympic area (including the stadium) can be accessed for free, but you can buy a self-guided audio tour for in-depth information about the various structures. Otherwise, three English-language tours are available. The Adventure Tour gets you into many of the buildings and introduces you to Olympiapark's history; the Stadium Tour focuses just on the stadium; and the Roof Climb lets you unleash your inner Spider-Man and climb the stadium's roof with a rope and a hook. The building where Palestinian terrorists captured Israeli athletes during the Munich Massacre is in the northern half of the park.

i U3: Olympiazentrum. Audio tours and tickets for tours can be purchased at the information desk in the southeast corner of the park. Audio tour €7, deposit €50. Adventure Tour €8, students €5.50. Stadium Tour €7.50, students €5. Roof climb €41, students €31. Tower and Rock Museum €5.50, under 16 €3.50. Admission includes discounts at Sea Life and the BMW Museum. Audio tour available 9am-5pm. Tower and Rock Museum open daily 9am-midnight. Guided tours daily Apr-Nov: Adventure Tour 2pm, Stadium Tour 11am, Roof Climb 2:30pm (weather permitting).

MARIENPLATZ

The pedestrian area around Marienplatz is the heart of Munich. Its name comes from the Mariensäule, a 17th-century monument to the Virgin Mary that sits at the center of the large square as a tribute to the city's miraculous survival of the Swedish invasion and the plague. The square is dominated by the impressively ornate Neo-Gothic Neues Rathaus, or new city hall, which was built in the early 20th century. Camera-toting tourists gawk at its central tower during the thrice-daily Glockenspiel mechanical chimes displays, which may be one of the most underwhelming tourist attractions you'll ever see or hear. At the eastern end of the square, the Altes Rathaus (Old Town Hall) houses a small and somewhat boring toy museum.

ALTER PETER (SAINT PETER'S CHURCH)
Rindermarkt 1   ☎089-210237760

As the poster inside explains, Alter Peter was severely damaged during World War II. The Gothic-inspired church was then meticulously rebuilt, but most of the interior walls remain plain and white. However, you can still see an original

surfing the eisbach

As the world of science and technology progress, surfing has begun to break free from its coastal constraints and penetrate parts of the world previously relegated for farming. In Munich, a structural anomaly has created a standing wave in the heart of the city and in the shallows of the Eisbach. Even more anomalous is the surf culture that has flocked to it. Just minutes from some of the busiest parts of the city, long-haired surfer dudes and shredding surfer chicks make a daily commute to get their surfing fix as if Munich were on the coast of California.

On either side of the river wave, surfers wait their turn to plunge into the water. Given the difficulty of staying on the wave itself, surfers only last an average of 20 seconds before they're swept away in the rapid current. What makes the wave unique for surfers is that it operates unconditionally; 365 days a year and 24 hours a day, the Eisbach wave is flowing as usual.

For the traveler visiting Munich, the experience of viewing this city-wave and experiencing the culture is a must. For those who are more courageous, there are two other standing waves in the city that are much more manageable for beginners. One is in the Englischer Garten and the other is by the Zoo. Talk to the surfers at Santoloco Surf Shop and get yourself a board, wetsuit, and instructions. It's an experience you won't forget.

cannonball lodged in the church wall (behind the church, take the steps leading up to Cafe Rischart and look around the top right corner of the window frame). Also check out the freakish, gem-studded skeleton of St. Munditia, exhibited in a glass case that looks more like a diamond ad gone wrong than holy remains. The church's tower offers a bird's-eye view of Munich and is definitely worth climbing. However, the ascent to the almost-heavens is challenging, as the 306 steps are too narrow for two-way traffic. Watch out for others and observe the decades of cool signatures and stickers on the walls.

i Tower €1.50, students and children €1. Cash only. Tower open in summer M-F 9am-6:30pm, Sa-Su 10am-6:30pm.; in winter M-F 9am-5:30pm, Sa-Su 10am-5:30pm.

FOOD

◪ TIAN $$$
Frauenstraße 4   ☎089-885656712 www.taste-tian.com

The best pizza in Munich—and possibly all of Germany—is made in an upscale vegetarian restaurant that has a "Philosophy" section on its webpage. Okay, it's not exactly pizza, but the wood-fired tarte flambée (€13-14) at Tian is a can't-miss, featuring a crispy crust and flavor combinations such as asparagus-taleggio-truffle oil. Like its Michelin-starred counterpart in Vienna, Tian serves up affordable lunch menus during the week (€15 two-course, €19 three-course) that show just how delicious the joining of fresh veggies and molecular gastronomy can be.

i Casual clothing acceptable. Pizzas €13-14. Open M 6pm-midnight, Tu-Sa noon-midnight.

◪ NAGE UND SAUGE $$
Mariannenstraße 2   ☎089-298803 www.nageundsauge.de

If a restaurant that serves mostly salads can thrive in the sausage-and-dumpling culinary biome of Bavaria, it must be doing something right. Quirky flavor combinations and heaping portions make Nage und Sauge a top destination for locals in search of tasty and filling meals that'll make their doctors uncharacteristically proud. Don't worry, though: if all the greens start making you feel guilty, there's plenty of excellent beer on tap.

i Mains and salads €9-13. Cash only. Open daily 5:15pm-1am.

▨ TEGENSEER TAL $$
Tal 8 ☎089-222626

Lying just a stone's throw from the Alter Peter, Tegenseer is a refuge for locals in search of traditional food in a traditionally touristy area. Tegenseer is almost as lively and not as suffocatingly crowded as many of Munich's better-known beer halls—as well as slightly cheaper. However, it's still a beer hall in the Old Town, so expect to pay €4 for a half-liter of beer and €10-15 for a meal.

i Beer €4. Mains €10-15. Cash only. Open Su-W 9:30am-1am, Th-Sa 9:30am-3am.

▨ RUFFINI $$
Orffstrasse 22-24 ☎089-161160 www.ruffini.de

The plain white walls, large mirrors, and stacks of simple, clear glasses makes this enchanting cafe a nice break from the (also awesome) Bavarian over-decoration. This cooperative cafe, located on a quiet residential street, buzzes with locals chatting or reading the morning paper. Order a frothy cappuccino and a flaky croissant and carry them to the sunny terrace upstairs. For lunch, there are many vegetarian options, and the meat dishes usually come from eco-friendly sources. Ruffini is owned collectively by over two dozen people, ranging from designers to policemen, who all put in hours working at the cafe. If you're in a hurry, you can also stop by the small bakery that sells beautiful cakes and fancy wines.

i Breakfast €6-9. Dinner €8-14. Cash only. Cafe open Tu-Su 10am-midnight. Shop open Tu-F 8:30am-6pm, Sa 8:30am-5pm, Su 9am-5pm.

▨ CAFÉ RISCHART $
Marienplatz 18 ☎089-231700320 www.rischart.de

Budget travelers can always count on Cafe Rischart: it's cheap, fast, and simple. There are two cafes on Marienplatz that have touristy outside seating areas, but there are also multiple locations at subway stops and train stations where even locals stop by to grab something to go. The delicious sandwiches are made from mouthwatering bread, with plenty of tasty German or Italian fillings inside (€3-4). A scoop of gelato (€1.20) is also obligatory on sunny days.

i Locations on the southeast corner of the square and behind Alter Peter. Coffee €1.80-3. Sandwiches €4. Cash only. Open M-Sa 6:45am-9pm, Su 9am-9pm.

NIGHTLIFE

▨ HOFBRÄUKELLER
Innere-Wiener-Strasse 19 ☎089-4599250 www.hofbraeukeller.de

Lying a short walk across the Isar River from its tourist-dominated counterpart (the Hofbräuhaus), the Keller has an unbeatable ambience, especially when it's warm enough to sit in its enormous beer garden. Grab a Maß (liter) of beer from the self-service station in the corner, try to find an open spot at one of the picnic-style benches, and watch the locals drain mugs faster than you can say "It's a Wednesday." It's also worth looking (and drinking) inside the Hofbräukeller's richly decorated beer hall, where a young Hitler delivered one of his first political speeches.

i Beer €8. Self-service food €5-10. Pretzels as big as your head €4. Cash only. Open daily 10am-12am.

BAR GABÁNYI

Beethovenplatz 2 ☎089-51701805 www.bar-gabanyi.de

Long overlooked by beer-thirsty travelers, Munich's cocktail bar scene has recently emerged in style, with the help of a system of mixology apprenticeships that would make early Americans jealous. After a couple of decades spent at Munich's famous Schumann's American Bar, the master bartender Stefan Gabányi opened this namesake joint, a favorite among discerning locals who prefer their cocktails to have no fewer than six ingredients. Splurge on the "Pinky" (absinthe, triple sec, lemon juice, maple syrup, rhubarb nectar, and apple juice, €10) or simply tell the bartender your liquor and flavor of choice.

i Cocktails €7.50-11. Cash only. Open W-Th, Su 6pm-3am; F-Sa 8pm-5am.

BACKSTAGE

Wilhelm-Hale-Strasse 38 ☎089-1266100 www.backstage.eu

Backstage may be a converted gas station, but the abundance of trees and plants (lit up with vibrating green lights) makes this venue much cooler than you might think. The complex features live music from the underground indie scene. The local crowd varies depending on the act, but during the summer, you can always expect a crowded Biergarten with one of the better beer deals in town (€6.80 liters). The entire area includes three performance venues and multiple outdoor seating areas.

i Liter of beer €6.80. Cash only. Check the website for event schedules. Summer beer garden open M-Th 5pm-1am, F-Sa 5pm-5am, Su 5pm-1am.

HOFBRÄUHAUS

Platzl 9 ☎089-290136100 www.hofbrauhaus.de

We could easily list the Hofbräuhaus under Sights—no trip to Munich is complete without a visit to its most famous beer hall. This is "das original" Hofbräuhaus beer hall that gave rise to dozens more imitators around the world. Figures like Lenin, Hitler, and Mozart are mere footnotes in the long history of the place, which was royalty-only until King Ludwig I opened it to the public in 1828. Beer here comes in liters (€8.20); if you try to ask for anything less, they'll chortle and probably bring you a Maß anyway. By the end of the night you'll either be singing at the top of your lungs or singing a different tune at the famous vomitorium. Be sure to check out the ornate hall upstairs, where an English-language museum describes the storied history of the Hofbräuhaus.

i Liters of beer €8.20. Live Bavarian music at 7pm (arrive early to guarantee a spot). Open daily 10am-11:30pm.

maß extinction

Over the past decade, Munich has experienced growing influence from the American craft beer craze, but it remains a "quantity over variety" city when it comes to the suds. Most beer halls and gardens in the city only serve a few types of draft beer, mostly in 0.5L and 1L (Maß) mugs—and you're going to feel some pressure to go with the bigger size. Typically, one of each of the following Bavarian beer specialties will be on tap: a hell (or helles), a pale, sweet, not-hoppy lager; a weiss (or weizen), a cloudy wheat beer that's typically sweet and malty; and a dunkel, a dark, malty lager that often tends toward the sweet. If you've noticed a trend here, that's no accident—Bavarian beers tend to eschew heavy hopping, which makes them both sweeter and more gulpable.

ALTER SIMPL

Türkenstrasse 57 ☎089-2723083 www.eggerlokale.de

The gothic letters, wooden tables, hundreds of old posters, liters of beer, and great Bavarian food make Alter Simpl a genuinely great place for a bite or beer any time of the day. Founded in 1903, the bar takes its name from an old satirical magazine called Simplicissimus, with the magazine's iconic logo of a dog breaking the chains of censorship reworked into a dog breaking open a champagne bottle. For more of the dog, see the red statue inside the establishment. Although the bar was once a second home to Munich's artists and intellectuals, it is now a lively hangout packed with students and a young crowd.

i Beer €4. Snacks and entrees €6-16. Cash only. Open daily 11am-3am.

ESSENTIALS

Practicalities

- **TOURIST OFFICES:** Tourist Offices house English-speaking staff who will book rooms for free with a 10% deposit. München Ticket, a booking agency for concerts, theater, and other events, has locations at each tourist office. (Bahnhofsplatz 2, ☎089-23396500. www.muenchen. de. Open M-Sa 9am-8pm, Su 10am-6pm.) or (Marienplatz 2, inside Neues Rathaus. ☎089-23396500. www.muenchen.de. Open M-F 10am-7pm, Sa 10am-5pm, Su 10am-2pm.)

- **CURRENCY EXCHANGE:** ReiseBank has decent rates, and Western Union will cash traveler's checks at a 1.5% commission. (Hauptbahnhof. ☎089-551080. www.reisebank.de. Open daily 7am-10pm.)

- **LUGGAGE STORAGE:** Lockers are in the main hall of the Hauptbahnhof. (☎089-13085036. €5 per day. Max. 3 days. Open M-F 7am-8pm, Sa-Su 8am-6pm.)

- **GLBT RESOURCES:** Gay & Lesbian Information Line (Men ☎089-2603056; women ☎089-7254272. Open F 6-10pm.) LeTra is a resource for lesbians. (Angertorstrasse 3. ☎089-7254272. www.letra.de. Hotline M 2:30-5pm, Tu 10:30am-1pm, W 2:30-5pm.)

- **INTERNET:** Free Wi-Fi is often easily locatable in the city center and by the Hauptbahnhof, but for a dependable source of Wi-Fi, try one of the many San Francisco Coffee Company locations around the city.

- **POST OFFICE:** Hauptbahnhof Post Office. (Bahnhofsplatz 1, yellow building opposite the train station. www.deutschepost.de. Open M-F 8am-8pm, Sa 9am-4pm.)

Emergency

- **EMERGENCY NUMBERS:** ☎112. Police: ☎110. Ambulance: ☎089 19 222.

- **CRISIS LINES:** Frauennotruf Muenchen operates a rape crisis hotline. (Saarstrasse 5. ☎089-763737. www.frauennotrufmuenchen.de. Available M-F 10am-midnight, Sa-Su 6pm-midnight.)

- **PHARMACIES:** Bahnhofplatz 2. (☎089-59989040. www.hauptbahnhofapo.de. Exit the train station and take a right. Open M-F 7am-8pm, Sa 8am-8pm.)

- **HOSPITALS/MEDICAL SERVICES:** Klinikum Schwabing (Kölner Platz 1. 089-30680. www.klinikum-muenchen.de) and Red Cross Hospital Neuhausen (Nymphenburgerstrasse 163. ☎089-12789790. www.swmbrk.de) both provide 24hr. emergency medical services.

Getting There

By Plane

Munich's international airport, Flughafen München (Nordalee 25 ☎089 975 00 www.munich-airport.de) is a 45min. train ride from the city center. Take S1 or S8 to Flughafen. (€9.80 on a Streifenkarte. Every 10-20min. 4am-1:30am.) A cab ride to the airport from the city center cost €60.

By Train

Munich's central train station, München Hauptbahnhof (Hauptbahnhof 1 ☎089 130 81 05 55 www.hauptbahnhof-muenchen.de. S1, S2, S3, S4, S6, S7, S8, U1, U2, U4, or U5: Hauptbahnhof), has arrivals and departures to a host of European cities. Connected cities include **Berlin** (€120 6hr., 2 per hr.); **Dresden** (€100 6hr., 2 per hr.); **Frankfurt** (€91 3hr., 2 per hr.); **Hamburg** (€129 6hr., every hr.); **Köln** (€129 5hr., 2 per hr.); **Amsterdam**,NHE (€150 6hr., every 2hr.); **Paris**, FRA (€150 6hr., every 2hr.); **Prague**, CZR (€60 6hr., 2 per day.); **Zurich**, CHE. (€70 4hr., 3 per day.) These prices are the official ones if you purchase the day of departure; you can often get heavy discounts (30-40%) by buying a ticket between three months and three days in advance.

Getting Around

By Deutsche Bahn

The S-Bahn is under the operation of the Deutsche Bahn (DB) network, which means that Eurail, InterRail, and German rail passes are all valid. Before beginning your journey, validate your ticket by getting it stamped in the blue boxes. DB officers often check for validation, and those without properly validated tickets are charged a heft €40 fine. The S-Bahn generally runs between 3:30am and 1:30am.

By Public Transportation

The U-Bahn, trams, and buses are all part of the city's MVV network (☎089 41 42 43 44 www.mvv-muenchen.de) and require separate ticket purchases. Pick up maps at the tourist office or at the MVV Infopoint office in the Hauptbahnhof. Transportation schedules vary, but the U-Bahn opens around 4:30am and closes around 1am during the week (2am on weekends). Nachtlinien (night trams) run every 30min. and cover most of the city. Tickets come in multiple forms based on how far you're traveling and how long the pass is valid. The simplest form is the single Einzelfahrkarte (€2.50), which is good for 2hr. for a trip in one direction. All other trips depend on the distance, for which the Munich area is split into 16 different zones of concentric circles around the city center. For short trips (within the same zone), get a Kurzstrecke (€1.20). For multiple rides, buy a Streifenkarte (stripe ticket; €12), which usually comes with 10 stripes. The zones are further grouped into four different colors (white, yellow, green, and red), for which you can get one-day or three-day passes. For the most part, tourists will stay within the white zone, for which a one-day pass costs €5.40 and a three-day pass €13.30. Partner tickets can save you money if you're traveling in a group. There are several cards available:

- **ISARCARDS:** An IsarCard is a week- or month-long pass that can be even cheaper than the three-day pass. One-week passes cost €12.30-17.60, depending on whether you pick two, three, or four zones. IsarCards, however, are only valid during the week or the month proper (e.g., a weekly pass will only work from Su to Su, and 1-month passes work for specific months), so plan accordingly.

- **CITY TOUR CARDS:** This card gets you transportation, along with some tiny discounts to attractions in Munich. That said, these attractions are not always the most popular ones in town. The City Tour card probably isn't worth it if you're not getting the partner ticket.

- **BAYERN TICKET:** The Bayern Ticket gets you access to any public transportation within Bavaria for an entire day. (€21. Valid M-F 9am-3am, Sa-Su midnight-3am.) The ticket also covers neighboring cities, including Ulm and Salzburg, making it perfect for day trips. The greatest savings can be achieved by getting a group Bayern Ticket, which covers up to five people for just €29.

By Taxi

Taxi-München-Zentrale (☎089 216 10 or ☎089 19 410 www.taxizentrale-muenchen. de) is a large taxi stand just outside the Hauptbahnhof. Taxi stands are located all around the city. The pricing algorithm is complicated, but there is a flat fee of €3.30, and shorter distances generally cost €1.70 per km.

By Bike

Munich is extremely bike-friendly. There are paths on nearly every street, and many locals use bikes as their primary mode of transportation. Renting a bike can be a great way to see a lot of the city in just a few days. Remember to stay within the bike lanes and that many lanes are one-way.

germany essentials

MONEY

Tipping

Service staff are paid by the hour, and a service charge is included in an item's unit price. Cheap customers typically just round up to the nearest whole euro, but it's customary and polite to tip 5-10% if you are satisfied with the service. If the service was poor, you don't have to tip at all. To tip, mention the total to your waiter while paying. If he states that the bill is €20, respond "€22," and he will include the tip. Do not leave the tip on the table; hand it directly to the server. It is standard to tip a taxi driver at least €1, housekeepers €1-2 a day, bellhops €1 per piece of luggage, and public toilet attendants around €0.50.

Taxes

Most goods in Germany are subject to a value added tax—or mehrwertsteuer (MwSt)—of 19%, which is included in the purchase price of goods (a reduced tax of 7% is applied to books and magazines, food, and agricultural products). Non-EU visitors who are taking these goods home unused may be refunded this tax for purchases totaling over €25 per store. When making purchases, request a MwSt form and present it at a Tax Free Shopping Office, found at most airports, road borders, and ferry stations, or by mail. Refunds must be claimed within six months. For more information, contact the German VAT refund hotline (☎0228 406 2880 www.bzst.de).

SAFETY AND HEALTH

Local Laws and Police

Certain regulations might seem harsh and unusual (practice some self-control city-slickers, jaywalking is €5 fine), but abide by all local laws while in Germany; your embassy will not necessarily get you off the hook.

Drugs and Alcohol

The drinking age in Germany is 16 for beer and wine and 18 for spirits. The maximum blood alcohol content level for drivers is 0.05%. Avoid public drunkenness; it can jeopardize your safety and earn the disdain of locals.

Needless to say, illegal drugs are best avoided. While possession of marijuana or hashish is illegal, possession of small quantities for personal consumption is decriminalized in Germany. Each region has interpreted "small quantities" differently (anywhere from 5 to 30 grams). Carrying drugs across an international border—drug trafficking—is a serious offense that could land you in prison.

Prescription Drugs

Common drugs such as aspirin (Kopfschmerztablette or Aspirin), acetaminophen or Tylenol (Paracetamol), ibuprofen or Advil, antihistamines (Antihistaminika), and penicillin (Penizillin) are available at German pharmacies. Some drugs—like pseudoephedrine (Sudafed) and diphenhydramine (Benadryl)—are not available in Germany, or are only available with a prescription, so plan accordingly.

GREAT BRITAIN

What is the coolest country in the world? Everyone will have his or her own answer to this question—Hollywood wannabes will say America, sappy romantics will say France, and bold (possibly crazy) adventurers will say Nepal. But the answer just might be Britain. Name anything you love, and Britain has it. Music? The Beatles. The arts? The Edinburgh Festival. Learning? Oxford and Cambridge. History? On every street corner. Sports? "Football." Literature? Shakespeare. Celebrity gossip? The royal family.

Britain has everything a traveler could want, and it's one of the most accessible countries in the world. There's no language barrier, the waiters aren't judging you,and everything is crammed into a convenient island-sized package. But don't think Britain is resting on its laurels. This country continually invents and inspires, as musicians create new beats, modern-art museums deliver mind-blowing spectacles, and boy wizards save the world. In 2012, the Olympic Games even came to London for a record third time. Whether you spend your trip touring all of London's free museums or curled up in front of the BBC with a cuppa, you'll be experiencing British culture at its best. Forget about Nepal, get over France, and bid good day to the USA, because Britain is where it's at.

greatest hits

- **DRINKING WHISKEY AND RYE.** You'll have to shell out for a pricier ticket to get more than one sample, but visit the **Scotch Whiskey Experience** (p. 350) to get a healthy dose of Alcohol 101.

- **STREET WHERE THE RICHES OF AGES ARE STOWED:** While in Notting Hill in London, check out the wares on **Portabello Road** (p. 313).

- **OPEN YOUR TEXTBOOKS:** It's time for British History 101 at the **People's History Museum** (p. 336) in Manchester, which focuses on the more social aspects of the nationa's past.

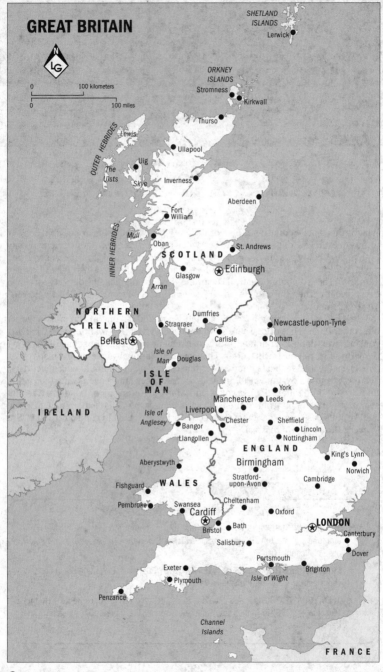

GREAT BRITAIN

N

0   100 kilometers

0   100 miles

SHETLAND ISLANDS

Lerwick

ORKNEY ISLANDS

Stromness

Kirkwall

Thurso

OUTER HEBRIDES

Lewis

Ullapool

Uig

The Uists

Skye

Inverness

Aberdeen

Fort William

INNER HEBRIDES

Mull

Oban

SCOTLAND

St. Andrews

Edinburgh

Glasgow

Arran

Dumfries

NORTHERN IRELAND

Stranraer

Newcastle-upon-Tyne

Carlisle

Durham

Belfast

Isle of Man

Douglas

ISLE OF MAN

IRELAND

York

Manchester   Leeds

Liverpool

Isle of Anglesey

Chester

Sheffield

Bangor

Lincoln

Llangollen

Nottingham

ENGLAND

Aberystwyth

King's Lynn

Birmingham

Norwich

Stratford-upon-Avon

Cambridge

Fishguard

WALES

Cheltenham

Pembroke

Swansea

Oxford

Cardiff

LONDON

Bristol

Bath

Canterbury

Salisbury

Dover

Portsmouth

Exeter

Brighton

Plymouth

Isle of Wight

Penzance

Channel Islands

FRANCE

great britain

london

A screaming comes across the sky: the sound you make, realizing, as jet plummets into unfussed sprawl of the Big Smoke, you don't have a clue what to expect now the anticipation's frenzy rushes in past your continent, the ocean, its transitioning air, the unfamiliar molecules scattering and Europe's gravitational tug—tweed and tea? pubs, prowling flanges of wanton party bros pirouetting madly within the wee English night? the perpetual loosing of the river around and again around the land's fang? walking, grayscale, along the cement and loaded sky, to library, museum, cathedral, across a churchyard, the wet fingers of British rain flexing along the pavement like the living roots? towers and apartments this blond brick, this food that tastes like blond brick? the handsome strangers of the open road, the secret, sacred cross-pollination of two souls in stuffed isolation? then the wintry gush of Death's own parted lips, beckoning, lingering in the lap of July?

Well, stop yelling, dude. We wrote this book for you.

London (see above) is busy. Each of its 32 boroughs have distinctive characters and are themselves filled with distinctive characters, making the so-called city feel more like a conglomerate of neighborhoods and villages. The feisty independence and unceasing currents in and around each haul the London "buzz" in a new direction every few years, with the city's epicenter for groovy scenes and freaky happenings constantly on the move—previously disregarded neighborhoods are always on the verge of bursting into prominence.

There are, of course, many mainstays as well, and even the top sights' resigned touristiness is navigable if you know how and where to get in line, pay less, cut corners, avoid clichés, and, broadly, live it up. Every day in London brings something new, so finish your pint and Let's Go!

ACCOMMODATIONS

City of London

YHA LONDON ST. PAUL'S $$
36 Carter Ln.   ☎01629 592 700 www.yha.org.uk/hostel/london-st-pauls

Less a hostel, more a self-contained summer camp, this massive accommodation features more than 200 beds, a restaurant/bar for mom and pop, and a prime location around the corner from its namesake, God's favorite hang. As such, its appeal is largely to families and travel groups, though YHA pledges its hospitality to all ages of traveler. If you don't mind (or would prefer, though that's a little weird) kicking it amid kiddies, book well in advance for a terrific deal.

i Dorms £17-25. Reception 24hr.

Hyde Park and Notting Hill

SMART HYDE PARK VIEW $
16 Leinster Terr.   ☎20 7402 4101

It's hard to say what exactly is supposed to be so cerebral about Smart Hyde Park View, but with clean, uncramped rooms (the beds in the larger ones are innovatively curtain-covered to afford extra privacy), you could certainly do much worse for a place to sleep. Just don't expect to bump into any Isaac Newtons, or much of anyone else, for that matter, as the pop-radio-booming lobby/bar and underutilized common room provide little in the way of social space.

i Dorms £16-24. Doubles £80-100. Reception 24hr.

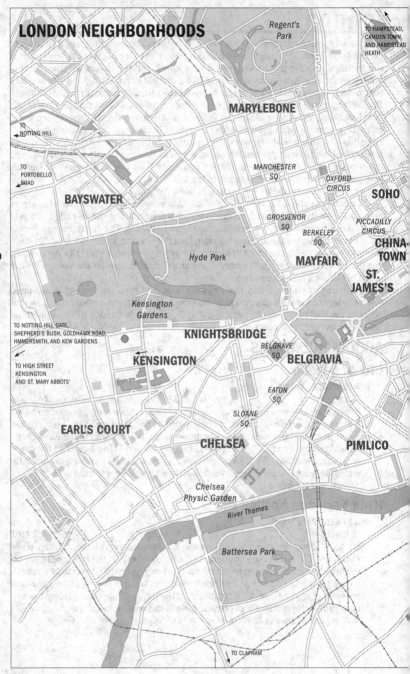

LONDON NEIGHBORHOODS

TO HAMPSTEAD, CAMDEN TOWN, AND HAMPSTEAD HEATH

Regent's Park

MARYLEBONE

TO NOTTING HILL

TO PORTOBELLO ROAD

MANCHESTER SQ.

OXFORD CIRCUS

SOHO

BAYSWATER

GROSVENOR SQ.

BERKELEY SQ.

PICCADILLY CIRCUS

CHINA TOWN

Hyde Park

MAYFAIR

ST. JAMES'S

Kensington Gardens

TO NOTTING HILL GATE, SHEPHERD'S BUSH, GOLDHAWK ROAD, HMMERSMITH, AND KEW GARDENS

KNIGHTSBRIDGE

BELGRAVE SQ.

BELGRAVIA

KENSINGTON

TO HIGH STREET KENSINGTON AND ST. MARY ABBOTS'

EATON SQ.

SLOANE SQ.

EARL'S COURT

CHELSEA

PIMLICO

Chelsea Physic Garden

River Thames

Battersea Park

TO CLAPHAM

great britain

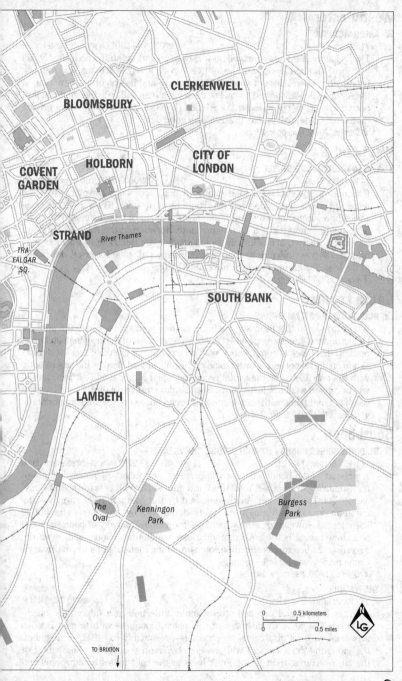

BLOOMSBURY

CLERKENWELL

HOLBORN

CITY OF
LONDON

COVENT
GARDEN

STRAND   River Thames

TRA-
FALGAR
SQ.

SOUTH BANK

LAMBETH

The
Oval

Kenningon
Park

Burgess
Park

TO BRIXTON

0   0.5 kilometers
0   0.5 miles

N

LG

london

Westminster

✦ ASTOR VICTORIA $$
71 Belgrave Rd.   ☎020 7834 3077 www.astorhostels.com

This is a very good hostel: excellent location, gregarious staff who instantly call you "bro" and belt along with the lobby's Top 40, lovely bedrooms, and a strong friend vibe. There's less of an established clan—and less alcohol—here than at the Astor Hyde Park across town, but deep hangs can still be achieved if you puff out your touristy chest and make friends (however that works). More private than most hostels of its size, this is a very good deal.

i Dorms £20-27. Reception 24hr.

West End

YHA LONDON OXFORD STREET $$
14 Noel St.   ☎0800 0191 700 www.yha.org.uk

If London's hostels had a food chain—which, poor tasty traveler, we're not necessarily saying they don't—YHA would be at the apex. The variety of accessories here, including excellent kitchen, assortment of board games, colorfully festooned common space, and, importantly, location in the thick of London's touristiest district, are definitely aimed at the clan, though solo travelers may find themselves drawn to the menagerie; in terms of value for price, this is one of the best hostels in London. A hip hang it's not.

i Dorms £20-25. Reception 24hr.

South London

✦ PUBLOVE @ THE STEAM ENGINE $
Who is to say, in this futuristic age of machinery and space, where the publove begins and the steam engine ends? One of the very best of the growing pub/hostel market, this place is comfortable, with a cozy but not cramped feel—it doesn't skimp on the hostel part in order to favor the pub; indeed, it takes the best of both, with the pub itself, like the hostel reception, open 24hr. a day. That means food whenever you want it. Clean rooms, forthcoming staff, and a pretty good location south of Southbank, with transit close by, round out a very solid accommodation.

i Dorms £10-12. Reception 24hr.

Southbank

✦ ST. CHRISTOPHER'S INNS - LONDON BRIDGE: THE VILLAGE $
161-165 Borough High St.   ☎020 7939 9710 www.st-christophers.co.uk

A stalwart of the London party-rocking scene, and singularly unabashed about its "Gonna Make You Lose Your Mind" intentions, The Village is the hostel equivalent of an LMFAO song. As underscored by the comparatively shrug-worthy common room, the venue's energy is dominated by the open-to-the-public karaoke bar downstairs, atop which is set a winding hallway of bedrooms and abandoned wine bottles. Accommodations are quite spacious, with even the cavernous 24-bed rooms affording some breathing room (if not a ton of privacy). Come here to smang or be smung.

i Dorms £17-20. Reception 24hr.

✦ THE WALRUS $
172 Westminster Bridge Rd.   ☎020 7928 4368

A funky little hostel perched atop a funky little pub in a funky little neighborhood. The sheer Englishness of this place (complete with framed Beatles artwork—we'll let you guess which song—presumably to offset, or augment, the mounting Funk Factor) will ceaselessly charm you. Do not be afeared of the fab overtures, though: the Funk halts at the hallway, with bathrooms and lodgings delightfully clean. Free Wi-Fi, lockers, padlocks, adapters, and towels, along with a good location and convenient Tube access, make this one of the best deals in town.

i Dorms £26-28. Reception 7:30am-11:30pm.

Marylebone and Bloomsbury

CLINK 78 $
78 Kings Cross Rd.

In the era before the decision to just ship them all to Australia, England tried and imprisoned her criminals in two-for-one courthouse-jails like the one now converted into the popular hostel known as Clink 78. The theme has stuck around to cute effect—the TV and computer spaces, each a former courtroom, retain their bench, bar, jury box, and signposts for defendant and press, though we assume the plush padding has been added more recently. In the larger dorms, though, the tightly stacked bunks recall the building's original purpose with a little too much gusto. Of particular note is the basement's Clash Bar, where ubiquitous backpacker party bros shoot pool and pool their shots; DJs, karaoke, and beer pong are among the frequent diversions.

i Dorms £17-26. Reception 24hr.

ASTORS MUSEUM HOSTEL $
27 Montague St.

There are hostels that smell like feet and hostels that don't; Astors ["It's-Not-A"] Museum ["It's-A"] Hostel does not at all. Take that as a ringing endorsement of this homey hostel situated across the street from the British Museum. A few hostelgoers may be seen to chill their weary asses in the ground-floor TV lounge, watching British standup comics say British jokes in British accents. (It's very funny, Let's Go is informed.) Downstairs, the recently revamped kitchen is equipped for culinary sorcery, though you'll have to provide your own ingredients. Less rowdy than its cousins in the bar-hostel clan, though by extension also less communal, Astors offers a cheap, clean, classy place for trekkers to crash.

i Dorms £18-26. Reception 24hr.

South Kensington and Chelsea

BARMY BADGER BACKPACKERS $
17 Longridge Rd.   ☎020 7370 5213 www.barmybadger.com

A strong contender for the coveted Let's Go Most British Name Award, this homey hostel, run by the marmiest mum around and her faithful arthritic pooch, is also in the running for best accommodation in the area. Clean, spacious rooms make even the triple bunks comfortable (each level bedecked with hella memory foam and power outlet), and everything—from Wi-Fi to a personal locker and safe—is free except laundry. The drably upscale neighborhood's nothing to wave a weasel at hangout-wise, but the Earl's Court Tube stop is within spitting distance for a good-sized polecat.

i Dorms £25-27. Reception M-Sa 7:30am-5am, Su 9am-8pm.

West London

MONKEYS IN THE TREES $
49 Becklow Rd.   ☎020 8749 9197 www.monkeysinthetrees.co.uk

The kitchen's first-aid kit expired in 2014, the Wi-Fi resets every half-hour, and the wooden-frame bunks are cramped and cramping, but Monkeys in the Trees has one significant ace in its hole: the people you'll meet here. Its distance from central London means the backpackers who come here are getting set for the longer haul, finding jobs, writing screenplays, and taking breaks from school, making the downstairs pub a solid hang during the day. In terms of cozy, unique community, it's second to none.

i Dorms £9.50-16.50. Check-in 2-11pm. Check-out noon.24hr.

East London

THE DICTIONARY HOSTEL $$
20 Kingsland Rd.   ☎207 613 2784 www.thedictionaryhostel.com

If you're a certain type of elaborate-facial-hair-sportin' bro or ripped-tights-bleached-hair chicka, Shoreditch is where you're gonna want to be in London, and The Dictionary is where you're gonna want to be within where you're gonna want to be. Tube access isn't great, but you'll barely want to leave the neighborhood—well-amenitied, pretty well-cleaned, and oozing vibe, The Dictionary will make you feel like you never left Brooklyn(/Portland/Austin)—and all with a helpful wall-size lobby map and directions about where to eat, drink, listen, watch, and party in the here and now's happenin'est hood.

i Dorms £17-27. Reception 24hr.

North London

ST. CHRISTOPHER'S INN, CAMDEN $$
48-50 Camden High St.   ☎0208 600 7500 www.st-christophers.co.uk

Like the other St. Christopher's hostels, the Camden branch thrives on its conjoined Belushi's Bar, which is where the action takes place. Decor-wise it's the best in faux-artiness (like Camden itself), including motivate-you-to-travel wall slogans (like, guys—we're already here, you don't have to convince us) and a huge mural, inexplicably featuring American blues singer Robert Johnson alongside English mainstays Brian Jones and Amy Winehouse, which serves as a terrific metaphor for the St. Christopher's philosophy of "good times without thinking too hard."

i Dorms £18-20. Reception 24hr.

SIGHTS

City of London

ST. PAUL'S CATHEDRAL
St Paul's Churchyard   ☎0207 246 8350 www.stpauls.co.uk

Sweet Christ of the Hay and Reaper, this is one of the few A-listers in London where our parsimonious Let's Go penny-pinchers have to admit the elaborate site is worth the elaborate price: the interior combines the best of London's mu-

city limits

What's the deal with the City of London? I thought all of London was a city! Like a pretty big one! Like a pretty big one! . . . right? So, like, what makes this part more city-like? Time to get schooled on the town, whiz kid traveler, so sit your peasant ass down and whip out the ol' quill and scroll: the City of London refers to the "Square Mile" of oldest settlement at the heart of London, dating at least as far back as 47 CE, when it was a site of Roman chilling at the northwest corner of their empire, though some historians believe the party started even earlier, with Welsh legend describing the mythic public works projects conducted by an opportunistic city planner/monarch named Lud, who may have given the area its name: Lundain. As is wont to happen over the course of two millennia, a lot of people have since come and gone, with the most recent conquering wave comprised mainly of lawyers and businesspeople, though many of these are commuters from elsewhere in the (lowercase) city—only about 7,000 people live in the City-city. And they put up with you tourists every day.

seums, churches, towers, and pretty buildings, with every angle of sight, facing in, out, or up, worthy of long-standing contemplation. That the grounds have been churchland for nearly 1500 years comes across in the myriad styles and forms, from Henry Moore's futuristic neo-sculpture *Mother and Child* to the terrifying Greek-style statues of British war heroes (of which there are many. There's an equally all-star cast memorialized in the crypt, including the cathedral's architect, Christopher Wren, visionary poet/artist William Blake, and, our favorite, Sir Arthur Sullivan, musical partner to comic lyricist W. S. Gilbert. Midway up the inner dome (there are a bunch, we're told, a bit over-proudly) is the Whispering Gallery, where it's very rude to shout, and for one of the city's best views, keep walking upstairs (and keep walking, and keep walking).

i £18, online tickets £15.50. Students £16, online tickets £13.50. Open M-Sa 8:30am-4:30pm.

🖾 OURTAULD GALLERY

Strand   ☎020 7848 2526 www.courtauld.ac.uk/gallery

The Courtauld Gallery shares the National Gallery's predilections for historical Christian art and well-known Impressionists and is free for students, but the similarities end there: forgoing the bustle of London's more popular museums, this is one of the best and most underrated collections in the area. Set in cool stone within the magnificent Somerset House, its spiral staircases lead to a few quiet rooms of fantastic beauty. You'll be glad you came.

i £7, students free. Open daily 10am-6pm.

THE TEMPLE

2 King's Bench Walk   ☎020 7353 8559 www.templechurch.com

Interestingly enough, Dan Brown wasn't the first author to feature this formerly obscure church complex in the climactic scene of a European thriller named for the secret messages of a famous Renaissance artist—our own *The Michelangelo Cipher* beat him to the punch by about four months. Not that we care or anything. We are legally obliged to assert that the Knights Templar, who founded the original church in 1185, have since "disbanded." Nowadays the Temple is a combination of law offices, gardens, ancient churchspace, and soaring ceilings—an unholy blend of divine allure and savvy management that explains the church's recent adoption of a £5 ticket fee. Check online before

you go, as the opening hours fluctuate with what seems like almost deliberate wildness.

i £5, unless you just want to pray, in which case it's free. But do you really want to tempt a wrathful Lord? Hours often vary, so check the website for the most up-to-date schedule.

TOWER BRIDGE

Tower Bridge Rd. ☎020 7403 3761 www.towerbridge.org.uk

If missed your chance to order service from our on-call Let's Go Bridge Mechanics Correspondent, you'll have to make do with this engaging exhibit perched atop one of London's more out-of-the-way river crossings. The bridge's history is explored in several installments, some with flashy animation and some a little more old-school, all of which gives way to the vertigo-inducing glass floor. For best results, plan your visit to coincide with a bridge lift, the times for which are listed on the website. Furthermore, tickets cross over that indefinable line between too expensive and within reason if you purchase them online.

i £9, students £6.30. Open daily Apr-Sept 10am-5:30pm; Oct-Mar 9:30am-5pm.

TOWER OF LONDON

☎844 482 7777 www.hrp.org.uk/TowerOfLondon

Legend has it that if you wait until deep into the blackest night, you may hear issuing forth from high atop the hoariest parapet a ghastly choir of tortured voices—the song of the many tourists fooled into spending nearly £20 to get into this old-ass castle. Don't be tricked by the name—there is definitely more than one tower going on here, each with a distinct history, which we'll save you the aforementioned fee and summarize forthwith: the oldest pylon, White Tower, was built by William the Conqueror; the Bloody Tower is where the least fun king in English history, Richard III, killed off his competitors, Edward V and his brother ["Li'l"] Richard, possibly proceeding to stuff their bodies in a closet; the Wakefield Tower is allegedly infested with mythologically significant crows; and the Jewel House, interestingly, houses the jewels. All in all, if you're very keen on masonry, lapidary, or the strange, slightly sexual tension arising from standoffs with ubiquitous beefeaters, make this a high priority.

i £24.50, online ticket £23.10; students £18.70, online ticket £17.70. Open Mar-Oct M 10am-5:30pm, Tu-Sa 9am-5:30pm, Su 10am-5:30pm; Nov-Feb M 10am-4:30pm, Tu-Sa 9am-4:30pm, Su 10am-4:30pm.

MUSEUM OF LONDON

150 London Wall ☎020 7001 9844 www.museumoflondon.org.uk/london-wall

This oddly catch-all museum isn't exactly boring, covering a solid 10,000 years of area history, but for all its Roman burial pits, 18th-century pox-ridden longhorn cattle skulls, weirdly "middle school video book report"-esque clips of ancient terrain and gladiatorial fistfights, and ubiquitous references to the Thames as a "sacred stream," it's not altogether that exciting, either. Let's Go enjoys dioramas explaining the Black Plague, Great Fire, execution of Charles I, and reinstatement of Charles II like 10 years later (the populace was having trouble making up its mind at that point) as much as the next student budget travel guide, but for all the wealth of information represented here, it could do with some paring down and reorganization. Totally free, so there's that—best to come here, hit a few highlights, and be on your way without delving too deep into the geological past. Though that rocks too.

i Free. Open daily 10am-6pm.

Hyde Park and Notting Hill

HYDE PARK

It's big and it's a park. Got it. Bigger and more jungley than the majestic Regent's Park to the north, Hyde Park consists of miles of tangled pathways meandering through small forests, along water features, and across enchanted prairies, though it should be noted that all trails inexorably lead into the dens of malevolent gremlins. We recommend the spaces least-overrun with faeries and other sprites, such as the Kensington Gardens, which is strictly flowers and statuettes, and the Round Lake, from which all merfolk were peaceably eradicated beginning in the 1950s. The whole park is bisected vertically by West Carriage Dr. (technically, everything west of this is Kensington Gardens, though you'd never know and we suspect this is just the Brits having a laugh at us again), which runs parallel to the picturesque and boat-friendly Long Water. There are no herons, and the utter lack of reed vegetation makes this an unlikely site for the future settlement of herons.

i Free. Open 5am-midnight.

SPEAKERS' CORNER
Hyde Park

"Komrades!" hissed the Voice of Insurrection as Let's Go approached the northeast corner of Hyde Park. "The blood of our revolution was for naught. Hark my doomful tale!" As explained to us, Let's Go discovered London's strongest bastion of free public discourse to be the site of aggressive cyclists and an even more aggressive pair of 15-year-old co-fondlers. Where the likes of Marx, Lenin, and Orwell once pontificated, glazed-over tourists now stare into smartphones. "Blood alone moves the wheels of history!" wheezed the Voice. "Also, don't forget to visit the Speaker's Corner Café for an assortment of espresso and pastries before you go!"

i Free. Open 5am-midnight.

West End

🏛 NATIONAL GALLERY
Trafalgar Sq. ☎020 7747 2885 www.nationalgallery.org.uk

Christ may have only wept twice, but here, you can relive those moments hundreds of times—if the contents seem surprisingly Jesus-y, bear in mind that the collection mostly spans the centuries when there wasn't much else to paint, and that to do so was to beg for allegations of witchery. To balance out the assorted diptychs, panels, nativity scenes, and frescos of the Lord and his chums sprawled on outcroppings, the wide-ranging collection includes an engaging array of pagan sex rites and antiquated divine assault. The elusive wing of Very Famous Impressionists deserves a whole visit to itself.

i Free. Open M-Th 10am-6pm, F 10am-9pm, Sa-Su 10am-6pm.

🏛 TRAFALGAR SQUARE
Let's Go is impressed by the gumption of our home country, which direct-mailed a statue of George "Let's Kick Some Redcoat Ass" Washington to the British government in 1924, which, sighing and shaking their heads, installed him along the back edge of Trafalgar Sq. a few years later. The rest of the square is less passive-aggressive, featuring a variety of fountains, stone beasts, tourists, and street entertainers, the latest generation of whom seem to have gained powers of levitation through selective inbreeding and/or Force-awareness. The corners of the park are decorated with four "plinths," three of which bear statues of famous British men, while the northwesternmost plinth features a changing exhibition spotlighting contemporary sculptors, which (sort of) explains the skeletal were-dog currently presiding from the column, gazing impassively, its eyeless stare frozen as Death's.

i Free. Open 24hr.

NATIONAL PORTRAIT GALLERY

St. Martin's Pl.   ☎20 7306 0055 www.npg.org.uk

We know, we know: this is not the most compelling museum. Almost entirely devoted to illustrations of centuries-old British aristocrats you've never heard of, this gallery's central location and free admission make it worth a quick stop early in your trip—you can blaze through the interesting parts (the oldest portraits, circa 1200s, and the newest, circa 1960s-present) in 45min. or less, and you'll pick up a little Albion history through osmosis while you're at it. Keep an eye out for the hidden gem, a grandly disinterested description of the American Revolution next to some familiar-looking former Brits.

i Free. Open M-W 10am-6pm, Th-F 10am-9pm, Sa-Su 10am-6pm.

ST. MARTIN-IN-THE-FIELDS

Trafalgar Sq.   ☎020 7766 1100 www.stmartin-in-the-fields.org

OK, sure, ancient Anglican church with beautiful internal stone- and glasswork, sanctuary of regal tranquility, an intriguing loop of underlying tombs purportedly built on the site of pre-Christian (i.e., devil-related?) ceremonies just a couple steps off the main hubbub of Trafalgar Sq.—but honestly, the most practical reason you should keep this place in the back of your mind is that its subterranean bathroom is the cleanest and most convenient in the area. Call us crass, but that's important to know. Check the website for upcoming performances, or just wander on over for some quiet—it's the kind of place where you can spend five minutes or two hours. (The crypts are not extensive, especially compared to the adjoining Crypt Café and gift shop.)

i Free. Open M-Tu 8:30am-1pm and 2-6pm, W 8:30am-1:15pm and 2-5pm, Th 8.30am-1pm and 2-6pm, F 8:30am-1pm and 2-6pm, Sa 9:30am-6pm, Su 3:30-5pm.

Westminster

WESTMINSTER ABBEY

20 Dean's Yard   ☎020 7222 5152 www.westminster-abbey.org

We've been hoping for a spectacularly God-tier throwdown between this and St. Paul's Cathedral for a long time, but so far, neither has shown an inclination to do anything but be stately churches. More Gothic than its crosstown rival, Westminster Abbey was built in the 11th century by Edward the Confessor, whose resplendent tomb is featured alongside countless sepulchers of fellow English royalty. Bedecked accordingly, the whole abbey drips tradition. Its welcoming layout, free audio tour, and all-star cast of memorials encourage you to weave in and out of the history without knocking anything over. (Don't be fooled by the Poet's Corner, though—a few greats, like Chaucer and Dickens, are buried here, but 90% of the busts and inscriptions are for writers whose remains lie elsewhere.) And it's not just a tourist trap—Westminster Abbey is still a place of worship: its hourly intercom-broadcasted prayers are introduced with messages of welcome to sightseers and pilgrims alike. You can skip the pricier daytime and come to a free Evensong instead.

i £20, students £17. Open M-Tu 9:30am-3:30pm, W 9:30am-6pm, Th-Sa 9:30am-3:30pm.

CHURCHILL MUSEUM/CABINET WAR ROOMS

King Charles St.   ☎020 7930 6961 www.iwm.org.uk

If you're like Let's Go—and good gracious, are we relying on that to sell these books—there's a small but vocal part of you still disappointed you never got to kick Hitler's ass. While only dreams can satisfy your deepest caprices, the adjoined Churchill Museum and Cabinet War Rooms are the next-closest you'll get. Used as the British strategic headquarters beginning in 1939, the current installations do an incredible job of blending the contemporary with the retrospective, including wartime memorabilia and recordings, and a preserved

Map Room at the museums' heart; the Churchill wing explores the man with microscopic focus (all the better for clueless Americans who think FDR won the war. Pfah! we say).

i £16.35, students £14.40. Open daily 9:30am-6pm.

HOUSES OF PARLIAMENT

Parliament Sq.   ☎20 7219 3000 www.parliament.uk

In the years since the American Revolution (in Britain, the "IDGAF We Still Have Canada Conflict"), the singularly English balance between the elite and the salt of the earth has shifted again and again, from monarchs and ministers to Lords and Commons to the current proportionally elected three parties. Parliament has been at the core of every step along this grand democratic experiment, and its layout—a thoroughly modern administration housed within an extraordinarily ornate edifice—demonstrates the best of modernity and history. To get your gummint on, we recommend attending a debate, committee meeting, or Question Time (though, as an non-UK citizen, you get bottom priority for tickets). Tours are also available but, again, aren't aimed at foreigners, who can only attend when Parliament isn't in session on Saturdays or over the summer. (What are they hiding?)

i Tours available on Saturdays or on weekdays when Parliament is on recess. Check the website for more visiting and booking information. Audio tours £18, students £15.50. Guided tours £25, students £20.

BUCKINGHAM PALACE

☎020 7766 7300 www.royalcollection.org.uk

Dang. Queens have it made. Surrounded by guards (some with sweet hats, some AK-47s), brimming with porcelain, furniture, paintings, and miscellaneous treasure, and comprising a variety of stables and regal tearooms, Buckingham Palace is the place to be, especially if you are royalty and get to live here. Everyone else will have to make do with the attractions: the vivaciously decorated State Rooms, where the Queen hosts formal events; the Royal Mews, where horses (not Pokémon) and associated carriages are kept; and the Queen's Gallery, where the treasure—from photos of the first Antarctic expeditions to original da Vincis—is. Out front is where the famous Changing of the Guard ceremony takes place, albeit at a distance—arrive before 11:30am to get a good spot for viewing the 40min. spectacle, and as with everything else in London, the weekends are busiest, so we recommend the less-crowded middle of the week.

i Combined ticket for the State Rooms, Buckingham Palace, the Queen's Gallery, and the Royal Mews £35.60, students £32.50. Open daily Jul-Aug 9:30am-7:30pm; Sept 9:30am-6:30pm. Hours vary monthly, so check website for most up-to-date schedule.

BIG BEN

While we hate to have to correct the pedants who insist that "Big Ben" refers not to the tower or clock on the north end of Parliament, but the 8ft., 13½-ton bell inside it—our Let's Go Temporal Mechanics Correspondent has recently unearthed evidence that "Big Ben" refers to the 600-year-old man whose godforsaken task it is to ring said chime every 15min. (the ironic thing being measuring in at only 6'1", Ben is by modern standards no longer the giant he once was).

i Tours only open to UK residents.

South London

SOUTH LONDON GALLERY

65-67 Peckham Rd.   ☎020 7703 6120 www.southlondongallery.org

Sprawling galleries like the Tate Modern force time-sensitive visitors to flit indecisively between their thousands of masterpieces as the perennially undiscovered ghost beckons from the next room. The more modestly ambitious South

abbey road studios

While it's easy to get caught up in the mindless thrill of cat-and-mouse, many of the clueless tourists haphazardly dodging pissed-off drivers miss the real significance of Abbey Road—the studio itself. While still a functioning recording workspace and therefore not open to the public, Abbey Road Studios (or, as it was known before the iconic album cover catapulted it to global fame, EMI Studios) is, of course, best-known for being the site where The Beatles produced virtually all of their songs. In fact, the studio was briefly a kind of mecca for cosmic musical freaks, with the Fab Four's psychedelic peers, including Pink Floyd, The Zombies, and The Hollies, recording a cluster of significant albums in the 1960s. So, yes, click a quick pic before traffic kicks your dick, but Let's Go encourages you to blow your mind in other ways, too: bring your iPod and DJ your own summer of love.

London Gallery, by contrast, with its couple of installation pieces, practically begs unhurried stretches of meditation from languid viewers. Remarkably casual and inviting, you may be your only company during your visit, which makes the immersive experience so much the better. Complete with lovely adjoining cafe and niche shop, this is a must for the open-minded.

i Free. Open Tu 11am-6pm, W 11am-9pm, Th-Su 11am-6pm; closed Mondays.

Southbank

▨ TATE MODERN

Bankside   ☎020 7887 8888 www.tate.org.uk

Millennia later, galactic historians still wonder at the year 2115: the onset of humanity's pure symbiosis with machine, their subsequent colonization of the Milky Way's western spiral arm, and the rapid spiritual evolution of these motorized demigods as they became one with the very fabric of the cosmos. They needn't speculate; indicators of coming transcendence were right before our eyes at the Tate Modern. Freaky dreamscapes, distorted nudes, fleetingly recognizable industrial structures, and some of the biggest names in 20th-century art are all here, totally for free. If you don't "get" modern art—screw you, for one—go anyway; everyone could use some time spent in quiet reflection at this temple to the playful, fantastic, and nightmarish.

i Free. Open daily 10am-6pm.

▨ IMPERIAL WAR MUSEUM

Lambeth Rd.   ☎020 7416 5000 www.iwm.org.uk

At the other end of the spectrum is the brutally real Imperial War Museum. Its five floors contain artifacts spanning more than a century's worth of conflict, including World War II-era machinery, wreckage from the Twin Towers, and exhibitions of anti-war protest art. Deeply moving without descending to moralization, this is one of the most underrated museums in London.

i Free. Open daily 10am-6pm (last entry 5:30pm).

SHAKESPEARE'S GLOBE

21 New Globe Walk   ☎020 7902 1400 www.shakespearesglobe.com

All the world's a stage, but this playhouse arguably a little more so. The original Globe Theatre burned to the ground in 1613—something involving cannon fire and a thatched roof—but was rebuilt twice, once the following year and once more in 1997. Though the tour guides and subterranean exhibition space are cool, you'll enjoy seeing a real play even more, and feel marginally less touristy besides. (Standing tickets are only £5 and totally worth it.)

i *Tickets for performances vary, but standing tickets are typically £5. Tickets for exhibition and tour £13.50, students £11. Exhibition open daily 9am-5:30pm. Tours leave every 30min. M 9am-5pm, Tu-Sa 9:30am-12:30pm, Su 9:30am-11:30am.*

DESIGN MUSEUM

28 Shad Thames   ☎020 7403 6933 www.designmuseum.org

Things look good here. Rotating exhibits feature beautiful examples of the ubiquitous (when we were there, an entire floor of designer shoes) and ubiquitous examples of the beautiful (a room of furniture arranged just so). But the real gem is the Design of the Year awards, in which mind-boggling innovations, from ocean cleanup infrastructure to rebooted feminist magazines to the next inexorable step toward the manufacture of our robot to-be overlords, are displayed in the top floor gallery. Prices are a little steep, but if you like pretty, they got pretty. (Sketchbooks encouraged.)

i *Note: relocating to the former Commonwealth Institute Building in Kensington in 2016. £13, students £9.75. Open daily 10am-5:45pm (last entry 5:15pm).*

Marylebone and Bloomsbury

BRITISH MUSEUM

Great Russell St.   ☎20 7323 8299 www.britishmuseum.org

The jaw-dropping scale of the British Museum will be impressed upon you from the instant you enter. A Euclideanly weird checkered-glass ceiling ripples above the yawning marble interior, the whole dazzling rotunda raising an unsubtle middle finger to the faraway and Euclideanly pretty straightforward Louvre, whose checkered-glass triangles are comparatively tiny. Seen one way, the British Museum is a jarring reminder of the colonialist agenda that ransacked the globe for hundreds of years. Seen another, this is where all gods and men come to prove their mettle or die. The museum pits the best against the best in one beautiful, badass building: here are the primo depictions of ancient Mesopotamian military strategists, the best busts of early Buddhist transcendental beings, and the finest mausoleum you'll ever see indoors on a Tuesday afternoon. The whole thing is totally free, though donation bins beseech you like Dickens indigents at seemingly every turn. ("Please, sah, a bit more for the imperialist regime?")

i *Free. Suggested donation €5. Audio guides £5, students £4.50. Maps £2 suggested donation. Open M-Th 10am-5:30pm, F 10am-8:30pm, Sa-Su 10am-5:30pm.*

REGENT'S PARK

Chester Rd.   ☎300 061 2300

In the early 19th century, throngs of insufficiently damp Londoners found it impossible to further their acquaintance with the English rain. Alarmed at the prospect of so many citizens remaining so dry, the desperate Prince Regent turned to architect John Nash, whose park-shaped solution has been exposing the umbrella-less to the elements since 1835. It's a beautiful, sprawling scene: the middle section of the park is dotted with athletic fields ("pitches," Let's Go is informed), three children's playgrounds deliver significant frolicking potential, and the southwesterly boating lake has no confirmed deaths since 1867. A triumph both of sporting and shrubbery, 10,000 wildflowers bloom among the park's 50 beautiful acres, while, not to be outdone, royal gardeners have produced more than 30,000 roses in Queen Mary's Garden. (O, the hubris of Man!) *i* *Free. Open daily 5am-9pm.*

BRITISH LIBRARY

96 Euston Rd.   ☎30 333 1144 www.bl.uk

Sure, Leonardo's notebook, Shakespeare's First Folio, and Handel's handwritten *Messiah* are impressive, but what really makes the British Library so fascinating are the gems hiding in plain sight—here, a 15th-century Italian astrological guide (Capricorn, and everyone else: beware diseased rats); there, the first collection of female biographies (though it's not exactly an antique treatise of feminism—the 104 subjects are represented by only 56 images, many of which the author unashamedly reuses); and there, the handwritten lyrics to early Beatles songs (from before their post-White Album phase in which Yoko instructed the entire fab quartet to scream incoherently). To access the reading rooms, you'll need two pieces of ID (one with signature, one with home address) and a nerd drive that goes above and beyond. The library also hosts various exhibitions, which, though lavish, can cost upward of £10. Our advice: Skip the exhibition, soak up the Ritblat Gallery's peerless wow factor, then sip espresso like an intellectual on the first-floor cafe.

i Free. Special exhibition prices vary. Open M-Th 9:30am-8pm, F 9:30am-6pm, Sa 9:30am-5pm, Su 11am-5pm.

South Kensington and Chelsea

VICTORIA AND ALBERT MUSEUM

Cromwell Rd.   ☎020 7942 2000 www.vam.ac.uk

We understand: the British Museum's a tease. If you crawled away from its collections all hot and bothered, begging for release, it's time you turned yourself over to the V and A's loving embrace. This is as intimate as museums get, though it still covers a surprising breadth of cultures and times; wander betwixt massive sculptures of naked dudes carrying off wives as they see fit and just murdering the hell out of every Philistine, but stumble into the next room and you might find Middle Eastern ruggery or the clothing of South Asia. Upstairs, there's a huge room where you can familiarize yourself with Raphael's cartooning phase. If you try you just might get what you need.

i Free. Special exhibit prices vary. Open M-Th 10am-5:45pm, F 10am-10pm, Sa-Su 10am-5:45pm.

NATURAL HISTORY MUSEUM

Cromwell Rd.   ☎020 7942 5000 www.nhm.ac.uk

Though pitched at wide-eyed kids more than sexually frustrated 20-somethings (oh, how we know our readership), the Natural History Museum has one trump card: dinosaurs were raw as hell. ROAWRRWHRHGHHG. Laid out in a sprawl of color-coded zones so you can hone in on a particular pursuit—"Volcanoes and Earthquakes"; "Fishes, Amphibians and Reptiles" (though not "Oxford Commas")—it's worth a peek regardless of your age. Try not to spend too much on stegosauruses in the gift shop.

i Free. Special exhibit prices vary. Open daily 10am-4:50pm (last entry 4:30pm).

SAATCHI GALLERY

Duke Of York's HQ, King's Rd.   ☎020 7811 3070 www.saatchigallery.com

When Let's Go visited this spiffy gallery, there were thousands of gleaming watches on display. (We kept expecting the staff to all start laughing, pull down a curtain, and go "Just kidding! Here's the real art gallery!" But it was all just watches. Everywhere we looked, more watches. Spooky effing watches.) You never know for sure what you'll find at Saatchi, unless you check its website or whatever; overflowing with helpful, snappily dressed staff, it's the best free modern gallery in the area.

i Free. Open daily 10am-6pm (last entry 5:30pm).

CHELSEA PHYSIC GARDEN

66 Royal Hospital Rd.   ☎020 7352 5646 www.chelseaphysicgarden.co.uk

Definitely the Physic Garden, and not the Psychic Garden, this is where you can come to see all manner of plants used in medicine, not mind-control. Founded in 1673 by the Worshipful Society of Apothecaries, the site is home to about 5,000 plants of curative, comestible, or beneficial purpose. The Garden's features, including an after-hours Secret Garden (definitely not Secret Powers) tour and historical talks, are beyond the mind's comprehension.

i Free. Open Apr-June Tu-F and Su 11am-6pm; Jul-Sept Tu-W 11am-10pm, Th-F and Su 11am-6pm; Oct Tu-F and Su 11am-6pm; Nov-Mar M-F 9:30am-4pm.

West London

ROYAL BOTANIC GARDENS, KEW

Kew Rd.   ☎020 8332 5655 www.kew.org

But sweet damn are there a solid deal of gardens, parks, greeneries, clearings, commons, meadows, floral arenas, and summery anti-tundras in and around this city. Make no mistake: despite its regal claims, this is indeed another park, albeit a more dedicatedly pruned specimen than its more popular neighbors to the north. With this identification in mind, the winding paths, bridged lake, Japanese garden, and greenhouse jungle (with its uninspiring subterranean floor of fish tanks) might not merit the £14 student entry fee—unless you are extremely keen on hipster flowers or paintings thereof, hedges, and/or golf course grass. The herons at the gardens were haughty and aloof but authorized momentary glimpses.

i £15, online tickets £14; students £14, online tickets £13. Gardens open daily at 10am. Closing times vary depending on the day and season, so check the website for the most up-to-date information.

HAMPTON COURT PALACE

East Molesey, Surrey   ☎020 3166 6000 www.hrp.org.uk/HamptonCourtPalace

There are two ways of looking at the one-stop catch-all funganza that is the Hampton Court Palace. One goes: Come on, dude. The royal family hasn't even lived here since King George II was busy spanking his grandkids. (True story; thanks, Wikipedia.) The other goes: This place is spooky as hell, with a maze, figurines of hella freaky animals, much architecture from a 500-year history of crazy anecdotes (another good one: King James hammered out the particulars of Bible production here), like a bazillion green acres, more stained glass and old-ass tapestry than Let's Go would know what to do with, and to top it all off, a mid-June festival featuring all manner of bardic hijinks. We say go.

i Tickets Mar-Oct £19.30, online £18.20; students £16, online £14.90. Tickets Nov-Feb: £18.20, online £17.10; students £15.40, online £14.30. Maze only £4.40. Garden only £5.80, students £4.90. Open daily Mar 29-Oct 24 10am-6pm; Oct 25-Mar 28 10am-4:30pm.

East London

ROYAL OBSERVATORY GREENWICH

Blackheath Ave.   ☎020 8858 4422 www.rmg.co.uk

The hilltop Royal Observatory Greenwich, the best part of the parkwide conglomerate featuring the National Maritime Museum and the Queen's House Gallery, is a well-hyped but ultimately disappointingly earthbound destination. The best parts are the downstairs planetarium (which costs extra) and adjoining Astronomical Photographs of the Year gallery, which feature the best efforts of amateurs with their heads in the clouds. Also of note is the well-denoted Prime Meridian, where you can take your picture with like six other people as you all prove how very multihemispherical you are. Even our *Let's Go Astrophysics* Correspondent was a little underwhelmed by the "bang for the buck" ("pow for

london

the pound"?) factor—we suggest doing the Astronomy Centre (free) and Planetarium (£6.50) by themselves if you're particularly stoked on stars, or just climb the hill for a nice view of eastern London.

i Observatory £9.50, students £7.50. Planetarium shows £7.50, students £6.50. Combo ticket for both £12.50, students £9.50. Open daily 10am-5pm.

WHITECHAPEL GALLERY
77-82 Whitechapel High St.　　　　　　　　☎020 7522 7888 www.whitechapelgallery.org

Carved into the sheer stone and ancient tombs of Whitechapel is this fabulous exhibition space, composed of several galleries and cinema rooms, themselves harboring a veritable "what is or soon will be up" of art, most of it modern, but with a terrific sense of the retrospective (with OG art films intermingled with the currently cutting-edge), itself produced by a variety of artists of a variety of nationalities and creeds, not to mention ages, and let's not even get into the political persuasions and disciplines, all of which can be sampled, even absorbed—we recommend blocking off a solid chunk of time to dig into the surprisingly voluminous gallery—for £0. Do.

i Free. Open Tu-W 11am-6pm, Th 11am-9pm, F-Su 11am-6pm; closed Mondays

North London

CAMDEN MARKET
Camden High St.　　　　　　　　　　　　　www.camdenmarket.com

Camden Market has veered ever closer to the mean clankings of commercial machinery in recent years, but the core of the bazaar remains relatively human, especially its central food stands, which deliver an incredible variety of meals at unbeatable prices. Other Camden Market goodies include a stand selling 100-year-old photography equipment (though we were disappointed by the way its seller assured us the contents would transfer easily to .jpegs), an all-neon clothing boutique, and miscellaneous CD shops of varying quality (go deeper to find the best ones).

Open daily 10am-6pm.

HAMPSTEAD HEATH
Oh, dogg, but you know it is time for some strolling. You know this. Rural though it may seem, Hampstead Heath is only four miles from the heart of London, making its wild terrain of beauty easily accessible for wanderers who enjoy entrapping themselves in the illusion of nature. Its top feature is Parliament Hill, which has nothing to do with Parliament but is a commendable outcropping with a wide view of the whole city. Sprinkled throughout with patches of forest, walking paths, benches, and cafes, one could easily while the day away here. Hampstead Heath has achieved marked success where herons are concerned.

i Free. Open during daylight hours.

FOOD

City of London

⚐ CITY CAPHE　　　　　　　　　　　　　　　　　　　　　　　$
17 Ironmonger Ln.　　　　　　　　　　　　　　www.citycaphe.com

"Sandwiches," mm-mm-mmmh—Let's Go may never have heard of this tasty bread-based dish before our arrival in London, but now we can't get enough of this little-known food genre. Near as we can tell, City Caphe makes some of the best and cheapest around—this no-frills (though colorfully decorated) French/Vietnamese sandwichery up an unassuming side street is sure to whet your appetite for the unfamiliar "sandwich"!

i Food £4-7. Open M-F 11:30am-4:30pm.

portabello road

This charming street fronts shitty tourist shops at its southern end before a gradual northwesterly slope transforms it into a valley of paradise for the vintage shopper, bar crawler, or coffee fiend. Say a fervent prayer against temptation before embarking, as enticements—from Belgian waffles to made-before-your-eyes crepes, from secondhand clothing to umpteenth-hand soul records—will do their best to seduce you from all sides. (Some of it's cheap, some of it's not.) It's not all indie heaven, either, as the odd American Apparel or burger chain has crept in to sully the alt mix, and a few white-haired gents roam around calling each other "Reg." A calculatedly easy place to spend an afternoon, not to mention the carefully-budgeted contents of your coffers, Portobello Road is a definite don't-miss of the Hyde Park-Notting Hill region.

CLERKENWELL KITCHEN $
27-31 Clerkenwell Cl. ☎20 7101 9959 www.theclerkenwellkitchen.co.uk

Lots of places will do you an English breakfast, but few will do it with the smiley zeal of this trendy pop-up. The coffee is best avoided, but the desserts are so fine and the soups luscious, providing a tantalizing diversion from the ultra-hip/yuppie-tastic neighborhood—it's a solid people-watching location, too.

i Food £4.50-11. Open M-F 8am-5pm.

Hyde Park and Notting Hill

SEE CAFÉ $$
4d Praed St. ☎20 7724 7358 www.seesushi.com/

If you're hankering for some Japanese cuisine, this restaurant will see to it that your desire is met. It's a little tricky to find, given its location behind a post office, but you'll see See Café as soon as you round the corner. Once you've had your seat, you'll see the towering metallic buildings reflected in the Paddington Basin, a curious waterway that must be seen to be believed. Well laid out and insightfully designed, See Café is a delight to the sight (not to mention taste); it's easy to see why so many hungry sightseers flock to see See. Seeing as See isn't seen by the sea, the scene's set with several selections of sustenance—some saltwater snacks, some slightly slippery sides; simultaneously sushi, sashimi, sake, satay, and Thai.

i Entrees £7-18. Bento boxes £9-12. Noodles £8-9.50. Open M-F noon-3pm and 6-11pm.

CRAZY HOMIES $$
125 Westbourne Park Rd. ☎020 7727 6771 www.crazyhomies.com

Imagining Mexican food in London is almost as difficult as saying the name of this restaurant with a straight face; luckily, Crazy Homies took our skepticism and punted it across the Atlantic like a deflating football. The ground floor, decorated with the, shall we say, imprecise perception Brits seem to have of Mexico—that is, camp movie posters in which sumptuously-breasted broads flee a grim reaper clutching halfheartedly at his motorcycle's ghostly handlebars—is pretty cramped, though this only encourages you to check out the cool bar area downstairs (dark, neon lights). The burritos are of the knife-and-fork variety, filling and intriguingly spiced. Not even our Let's Go Nautical Correspondent was brave enough to find out what a "wet burro" was—in part because it costs an extra $2 on a bill that already adds up quickly if drinks are involved.

i Burritos, enchiladas, taco salads £7.75-14.95. 6 churros £5.50. Drinks £4-13. Open M-Th 6am-11pm, F 6am-11:30pm, Sa noon-10:30pm; closed Sundays.

MIMO'S CAFÉ $

19 London St.   ☎020 7706 7175

In all directions, expensive restaurants and grubby tourist shops scratch themselves and snicker at the same lackadaisical pranks. Fools! In the heart of squalor, Mimo's Café silently forges its empire. What seems on the outside like any of the innumerable delis dotting the area north of Hyde Park, Mimo's Café's ample room, homey air with cheerful regulars, and—most importantly—inexpensive menu of terrific food have earned it the coveted Let's Go Eat Breakfast There recognition. Options later in the day include a variety of dirt-cheap sandwiches, salads, and more significant pasta dishes.

i Breakfast £3.50-4.50. Salads £4.75-6. Pasta £5.50-6.50. Sandwiches £4. Open daily 7am-10pm.

West End

JUMBO EATS $

59 Brewer St.   ☎020 7494 2133

Long have we toiled and traversed, searching unsatisfied in our wicked and wandering ways: lore tells of a length of time, of utter upheaval and ubiquitous unrest, before the beginning of the bringer of the unbelievable: the wondrous, awesome, worthy wrap. That time is now. We found the place where the wrap came from, the origin of the wrap, the setting of the wrap's creation myth, and it was right here in the West End all along. (Don't know how we could have missed it.) With amazing prices for about a billion options, veggie and meat and beyond, fantastic service, extremely j-chilling of a vibe, they never run out of seating, and "Gangsta's Paradise" spits on the PA—though even Coolio doesn't know everything: this is no mere paradise. This is the birthplace of the wrap.

i Wraps £4.50-5.50. Drinks £1-3. Open M-F 8am-8pm, Sa-Su 9am-8pm.

NORDIC BAKERY $

14a Golden Sq.   ☎020 3230 1077 www.nordicbakery.com

The word's out—despite their website's self-promotion as a place where "visual clutter and noise is eliminated," our favorite hinterlandian transplant is no longer the temple of peace it alleges to have been. No matter: the food's good, and pretty damn Nordic, and with a prime location opposite Golden Sq. in Soho, there's plenty of room to escape the bustle. Prices are good for the neighborhood—OK for the billowing maelstrom of demand and satisfaction that is life in this age of machinery. Try the pancake, avoid the quiche.

i Food £1-6. Drinks £2-3. Open M-F 8am-8pm, Sa 9am-7pm, Su 10am-7pm.

Westminster

▨ POILÂNE $

46 Elizabeth St.   ☎0207 808 4910 www.poilane.fr

This first English iteration of the famous Parisian bakery chain set out to conquer new territories, Norman-style, in Pimlico, and we've never had Stockholm syndrome so bad. The bakers live above the shop, waking in the wee hours of each bready morning to go about their solemn craft, toiling in the dough, in the flour, in the heat of a thousand wood stoves. Everything from the pain au chocolat to the more complicated confections is to die for.

i Food £1.50-6. Open M-F 7am-7pm, Sa 7am-3:30pm.

SPICY FOOD PLUS $

83 Wilton Rd.   ☎020 7834 8068

This might actually be the cheapest food in London—we're talking "no website" cheap, "served in a tin dish" cheap—but you wouldn't know it for the flavors involved. Filling portions of curry, rice, veggies, and some of the best naan in all of London make this hole in the wall a must for Pimlico's hungry.

i Drinks £1-3. Food £2-5.50. Open M-Sa noon-3pm and 4:30-11pm.

South London

▨ SNACKISTAN @ PERSEPOLIS $
28-30 Peckham High St.   ☎020 7639 8007 www.foratasteofpersia.co.uk

You know where those cookie-cutter "ethnic" stores like Urban Outfitters steal "authentic" rug designs from? This is what the whole industry aspires to be. Hang of the hippies and hip, home to cheap, delicious desserts, Snackistan doesn't give a damn about their posted hours—they'll stay open however long people are partying in their relaxed, sugary way. Only the occasional two seconds of shrill emergency exit alarm, ignored by everyone in the room, punctuates the ambience—yet somehow still adds to it. Bedecked with funny signs and with a staff ranging from friendly to Christ-like, this "Land of the Peckish" is a must for anyone in south London.

i Foods £3-5. Nonalcoholic drinks £1.50-3. Open daily 10:30am-9pm.

CAFÉ EAST $
100 Redriff Rd.   ☎20 7252 1212 www.cafeeastpho.co.uk

Tucked away along a sleepy stretch of southeast London asphalt—across the parking lot is a bowling alley and movie theater—Café East buzzes like a dining hall; you may have to wait up to 15 minutes for a table when they're at their busiest (they don't take reservations). The food is terrific, though, and in huge portions, and don't even think about asking for tap water—partly because the drinks are so tasty (the Che Ba Mau sweet drink is particularly fetching), and partly because they will not give you any.

i Entrees £8-9. Drinks £1.50-4. Open M and W-F 11am-3pm and 5:30pm-10:30pm; Sa 11am-10:30pm; Su noon-10pm; closed Tuesdays.

Southbank

PIE MINISTER $
Gabriel's Wharf, 56 Upper Ground   ☎0207 928 5755 www.pieminister.co.uk

Surely, when Robert Plant sang "Ooh, your custard pie, yeah, sweet and nice / When you cut it, mama, save me a slice," he was referring to this quaint pie shop a stone's throw from the Thames. Quite cheap and utterly satisfying, with veggie and dessert options, this homey sanctuary is a must for travelers overwhelmed by the surrounding Southbank's weary commercialism. (Finding it can be slightly tricky—it's in there among the clothing boutiques.)

i Pies £4.50, with one side £6.50, with two sides £7.50. Drinks £1.60-2.30. Open daily 10am-6pm.

THE TABLE CAFÉ $
83 Southwark St.   ☎0207 401 2760 www.thetablecafe.com

Like a sci-fi Denny's from the hipster future where their food is really good and the furnishings are made from uncommon trees. Table isn't cheap, but, two Christs and half a Jesus, is this where we got the best lemon pancake we've ever had. The staff, led by one dude whose own mustache overwhelms him, are a well-heeled lot, knowledgeable and innovative. Bi-weekly Thursday Jazz Nights liven up an already friendly scene. Eat here and be glad you have done so.

i Food £6-15. Open M 10am-4:30pm, Tu-F 7:30am-10:30pm, Sa-Su 8:30am-4pm.

Marylebone and Bloomsbury

FORK DELI PATISSERIE $

85 Marchmont St.   ☎020 7387 2680

Mother Earth is cruel to her soft-bellied children. Fork Deli Patisserie, an oasis of affordable pap, beckons. Much more than mere bean-toting cafe, FDP combines the best of coffeehouses (drinks are artisanal in every way but price), sandwich shops (with coveted vegetarian options, though sometimes in short supply), and dessert bar (have you ever had panini-pressed banana bread? YUM). The range of quality munchies, including various gluten-free sweets, outstrips most cafes and yielded a garbanzo salad our Let's Go correspondent called "absurdly tasty." FDP's location, midway between the British Library and Museum, allows even the raggedest of paupers a chance to refuel before once again attempting the ladder of high culture. Take note that it closes at 4pm on weekends.

i Drinks £1.70-2.70. Pastries £1.70-3. Open M-F 7:30am-7pm, Sa 8:30am-4pm, Su 9am-4pm.

MEAT LIQUOR $

74 Welbeck St.   ☎20 7224 4239

This charmingly-named burger joint aims to win fans by overwhelming them with sheer 'tude. Lit dimly, splashed with graffiti, and crawling with 20-some-things (with whom you may end up sharing a table), it's the fast food equivalent of a rock concert—though "fast" may be putting it strongly, as lines spill out the main door frequently enough to merit the positioning of instructions-laden signposts. The food is good. Getchyer taste of America while in London, mate.

i Burgers £7.50-8.50. Beer £3-4. Cocktails £7.50-10. Open M-Th noon-midnight, F-Sa 11am-2am, Su noon-10pm.

South Kensington and Chelsea

KENSINGTON CREPERIE $

2-6 Exhibition Rd.   ☎020 7589 8947 www.kensingtoncreperie.com

This chilling place is haunted by tortured souls who come in for the savory crepes, stay for the gelato, then want sweet crepes to go with the gelato, need another savory crepe to cleanse their palate, follow it with a scoop of gelato, and so on. It took our Let's Go Aerospace Correspondent three full weeks to extradite herself from the Crepe Cycle, but the info provided us was invaluable: while not inexpensive, the crepes are extensive and artfully crafted, and well worthy of a full meal—this ain't snack food. The gelato is, though, and yummy at that. A touristy location makes this a solid outpost for people-watching, too.

i Crepes £4-10. Ice creams £3-6. Drinks £3-9. Open daily 8:30am-11:30pm.

VQ CHELSEA $

325 Fulham Rd.   ☎020 7376 7224 www.vq24hours.com

Conveniently located a few blocks from Chelsea-Westminster Hospital, VQ Chelsea—the Diner That Does Not Close—has done its part to greasen up the community for close to two decades. Snug but not uncomfortable, it can get elbowy around dinnertime, but there's always the rest of the time that isn't dinnertime. Its 24hr. breakfast outdone only by its corresponding 24hr. alcohol license, this last holdout against the merciless conquest of time will be your go-to for diner food until your last breath.

i Food £4-12 depending on extravagance. Beer £4-5.50. Nonalcoholic drinks £3.50. Open 24hr.

West London

SUFI RESTAURANT $$

70 Askew Rd.

It's worth eating at this tucked-away Persian restaurant on the strength of the unbelievable naan bread alone. This is bread to die for, bread genuine as the

great britain

seven dials

Nestled in the part of Covent Garden where wealthy people go to make their hands smell fragrant is the heptagonal death trap known as Seven Dials. Scores of lotus eaters are forever entombed in a waking half-life, not by choice, but due to the eerie arrangement of uneven cobblestone, perpetually cycling and darting traffic, the tourists' own recently-acquired confectionaries, and the ever-tested will not to die. Let's Go honors them.

For drivers, this is your fairly typical central statue-looping roundabout, albeit with several options beyond the norm for eventual de-circumvention. To pedestrians, Seven Dials is a polydimensional, perverted game of Frogger, with oncoming traffic subject to unfamiliar laws and irregular patterns as yet undescribed by the natural sciences or reason. Many unlucky or unwise enough to attempt an underprepared journey across the square's intermediate rings of desolation do not return; for even if the eye of the hurricane is breached in one direction, it may be weeks—twenty months, in the case of our erstwhile Let's Go Urban Planning Correspondent—before the vulturelike circulation of cabs and shipping vehicles realigns to allow safe passage, the poor interloper with only the dying heat of their overpriced pastry to warm them against a frigid moon hung amidst all the violence of space.

tears of Christ, bread made in a kiln right before your child-stealin' eyes. The rest of the menu is delicious and filling and pretty middle of the road, price-wise; top it off with an authentic dessert and you've got one kickass meal in a classy venue.

i Starters £3-4. Entrees £8-14. Drinks £1.50-3. Wines £4-6. Open M-Sa noon-11:30pm, Su noon-10:30pm.

MR. FALAFEL $

New Shepherd's Bush Market, Uxbridge Rd. ☎779 8906 668 www.mrfalafel.co.uk

Hey, Mr. Falafel man: Sing a song for me. Or give me a large falafel wrap plus drink (yummy salted yogurt, mm-hmm-mmm) at this friendly, no-frills restaurant for less than £8. Up to you, man. Bonus: visit the "Videos" tab on their website for some Tim-and-Eric-style throwback footage.

i Wraps £4.50-6.80. Open M-Sa 11am-6pm.

East London

THE BIG RED PIZZA BUS $

30 Deptford Church St. www.bigredpizza.co.uk

Straight-up, that's what this is. Seeing its next-door neighbor's "eccentric aunt" vibe and raising it a "sixties hippie bus," this pizzeria, bar, community space, and double-decker blast from your LSD-laden past is an absolute must in East London. Food and drink—yes, indeed, the bus serves you drinks; ohhh, yes—are reasonably priced, with a nice selection of desserts (the brownies are real fine). What makes this joint stand apart, aside from, you know, being a bus, is the entertainment: live comedy on Tuesdays, jazz on Fridays, and "busker night" on Wednesdays—strum a song, earn a pint.

i Food £4-12. Drinks £1.50-4.50. Open Tu-Th 5-11pm, F-Sa noon-past midnight, Su noon-11pm.

☒ THE LITTLE SQUARE OF FOOD TRUCKS OFF DRAY WALK $

Rather than trying to choose just one of the excellent options we've sampled here, Let's Go invites you to do a little exploring, albeit within about 200 sq. ft. Tucked away amid chic boutiques and stalwart record store, Rough Trade, is this constellation of cheap and delicious eats: pizza, buffalo wings, BBQ, and much more. All of it is incredibly cheap, in generous portions, authentic—well, as authentic as buffalo wings get—and will make you feel cool as hell. Bonus: picnic tables for unabashed hipster-watching.

i Prices vary, food usually £3-9. Drinks £1.50-4. Hours vary, generally daily 11am-midnight.

North London

☒ YUMCHAA TEAS $

35/37 Parkway   www.yumchaa.com

Cozy as can be, this loose-leaf tea gem is one of a micro-chain that's spread successfully throughout London. Spaciously designed and bedecked with an assortment of old-fashioned garden chairs, couches, and what appear to be dozens of different couples' wedding photographs (not sure what the story is there), Yumchaa is as wonderfully British as it gets, though with an unplaceable exotic edge. We cannot recommend the raspberry vanilla tea highly enough, and the chocolate velvet cake is not of this world.

i Teas £5-8. Open M-F 8am-8pm, Sa-Su 9:30am-8pm.

☒ LALIBELA $$

137 Fortress Rd.   ☎020 7284 0600 www.lalibelarestaurant.co.uk

If you've never had Ethiopian food before, we kindly, but firmly, demand that you go here. Arguably the best in the city at what it does, it isn't cheap, but won't break the bank, either—and portions are generous; you can stuff yourself for as little as £8 for veggie options and a little more for various meats.

i Food £4-15. Drinks £2. Open M-Th 6-11pm, F-Su noon-3pm and 6-11pm.

NIGHTLIFE

City of London

YE OLDE CHESHIRE CHEESE

145 Fleet St.   ☎020 7353 6170 www.cheshirecheeselondon.co.uk

This is one of those fairly typical-seeming homey London bars with a fantastic history: Great Fire notwithstanding, there's been a pub at this location since 1538, when, to be fair, there wasn't much else to name your pub after besides dairy products. Charles Dickens alludes to it in *A Tale of Two Cities*, regulars at various points included Mark Twain, PG Wodehouse, Alfred Tennyson, and Sir Arthur Conan Doyle and, for four decades, an African gray parrot named Polly. Prices on food aren't amazing—we wouldn't be surprised if Polly died crackerless—but there are (fast-food-esque) combo deals to be had.

i Food £5.75-10.95. Drinks £4-19.95. Open M-F 10am-11pm, Sa noon-11pm; closed Sundays.

JAMAICA WINE HOUSE

St. Michaels Alley   ☎020 7929 6972

Another City mainstay (since circa 1652) with a friendly vibe, this relaxed saloon gets solid daps for its downstairs wine bar, which serves mysterious appetizers (what are fritters?) alongside pub classics and mouth-cidering ciders. The prices are nothing amazing compared to what you'll find elsewhere in the city, but for the City itself, they're pretty good.

i Wines £3-6. Beers £2-4. Open M-F 11am-11pm.

Hyde Park and Notting Hill

NOTTING HILL ARTS CLUB

21 Notting Hill Gate   ☎020 7460 4459 www.nottinghillartsclub.com

Underground in the first, second, third-part-A, and third-part-B definitions of the word (Merriam-Webster, 2011), this deep bohemian hang lies behind a set of massive warehouse doors and two huge dudes possibly named Leroy. If you can find it—the unmarked entrance, wedged in between a Tex-Mex joint and several banks, easily escapes detection—descend the steep staircase into a hella chill lair of hipness. The club is live almost every evening of the week, hosting everything from straightforward DJ-steered dances to more exotic happenings like Funk Night and '90s garage revivals, so it's worth checking the online schedule to find something to match your taste.

i *Cover varies depending on show, usually between £5-12. You can pay at the door or get tickets ahead of time (latter option is cheaper—check website for guestlist options). Beers £3.80-5.50. Wine £4.30-4.60. Shots £4. Open M-Th 7pm-2am, F 6pm-2am, Sa 4pm-2am, Su 6pm-1am.*

PIX PINTXOS

185 Portobello Rd.   ☎0207 727 6978 www.pix-bar.com

Though it may sound like a more appropriate method for pricing male prostitutes, Pix Pintxos has produced an ingenious method for keeping its customers satisfied: grab as you go and pay later according to the size of the wooden knob sticking out. The gimmick is cool, and portions are big enough that you don't have to run up a massive bill to get stuffed. Spanish in vibe and cozy in feel, "PP" sports a live DJ on some weekends and a convivial staff; aim for the very limited open-air seating in the back for a bit of privacy and quietude.

i *Wine by glass £5-9. Beers £4.50. Cocktails £9. Open M noon-10:30pm, Tu-Th noon-11pm, F-Sa noon-midnight, Su noon-10:30pm.*

West End

LA BODEGA NEGRA

16 Moor St.   ☎0207 758 4100 www.labodeganegra.com

The entrance to this subterranean spot is cleverly disguised as a sex dungeon, for the purpose of, uh… well, we're not totally sure what the story is there, but if you're brave enough to head downstairs, you'll be delighted to find a loud, dark, mad groovy bar (or, at other times of day, restaurant; and, at the adjacent location, cafe). Less "strip club," as it turns out, and more "old-school saloon with modern touches," La Bodega Negra has an extensive cocktail menu and live DJs at night, though there's no room to dance.

i *Cocktails £8-9. Open M-Sa 6pm-1am, Su 6pm-midnight.*

THE LOOP

19 Dering St.   ☎020 7493 1003 www.theloopbar.co.uk

Everything about The Loop is massive, stirring a long-submerged claustrophobia deep within Let's Go: three floors, four rooms, awesome decor, lots of things that light up or go dark, ubiquitous stag and hen parties, dudes probably a bit too comfortable in whipping out the rock horns, and a worthy menu—food is amazingly enough pretty reasonable pricewise, with the appetizers even—dare we say—cheap. We recommend checking their website, maybe even a few days in advance, as therein you can find all manner of complex and pre-packaged deals and loopholes for free drinks and fractioned drinks and entry of oscillating prices before or after precise hours.

i *Food £4-11. Drinks £2.75-9. Open M noon-11pm, Tu noon-midnight, W noon-1am, Th-Sa noon-late; closed Sundays.*

london

CELLAR DOOR

Aldwych   ☎020 7248848 www.cellardoor.biz

Featuring everything from Monday drag queens to a Tuesday open mic (hosted by an infamous gent known as "Champagne Charlie") to cabaret and burlesque, this is one of the weirder nights out in London. Cellar Door brings an old-school 1930s New York vibe to London, with a wide-ranging drinks menu that includes absinthe and snuff. Not cheap, but worth the price.

i Food £3-5. Drinks £4-9. Open M-Sa 4pm-midnight; closed Sundays.

Westminster

CASK

6 Charlwood St.   ☎0207 7630 7225 www.caskpubandkitchen.com

Beer, beer, beer; beer—beer, beer, beer; beerbeerbeer-beer (beer beer—beer!)... beer, beer. Discover all this and more at Cask. A great stop for tenderfoots and brew buffs alike, the spacious pub was established in 2009 to make a huge variety of pints available to everyone. The knowledgeable, friendly staff is happy to take the edge off the beer intimidation factor, shrugging off even the most incriminating mispronunciations with smiles. But do not step to these masters, ye beer trivia bros, for a bitter iciness borne of years of slow maturation lurks beneath their warm, frothy facades.... mmmm....

i Pints start at £3.95. Open M-Sa noon-11pm, Su noon-10:30pm.

THE RED LION

48 Parliament St.   ☎020 7930 5826 www.redlionwestminster.co.uk

Just up the road from 10 Downing St., generations of prime ministers downed keggers here until Edward Heath never showed in the '70s. Since his absence, you're unlikely to find the current PM, but The Red Lion's location across the way from Parliament ensures that some lesser politicos continue to trickle in. So do hordes of tourists, making its three-floor setup very necessary and often well used—but, steeped in tradition as it is, it's worthy of a stop, even if it doesn't become your go-to for your trip. The pies are extremely popular.

i Pints start at £3.90. Food £5.25-14.

South London

🏛 MINISTRY OF SOUND

103 Gaunt St.   ☎0870 060 0010 www.ministryofsound.com

Among other artistic things (Shakespeare, etc.) London has been the land where freaky electronic wizards of the 1990s came to do battle. Their chief fortress was known as the Ministry of Sound. Stocked with what's said to be the "world's best sound system," on a sheer musical level this is perhaps the premier club in England; it's almost worth coming here just as a tourist for the musical history. Though catching those sonic sorcerers can cost a pretty penny, this venue makes it worthwhile.

i Tickets generally £15-20. Open F 10:30pm-6am, Sa 11pm-7am.

THE LOST HOUR

217-219 Greenwich High Rd.   ☎020 8269 1411 www.thelosthourgreenwich.co.uk

Are not all hours lost once gone by, irretrievable? Or does hope spring in the mewling of a newborn babe? Ruminate all night at this great pub: spacious and modern, the Lost Hour retains the traditional pub feel without descending into clichés. With excellent value for your pounds, both for food (all day breakfast: yaasss) and drink, this makes a terrific destination on your night out—especially on Fridays, when live DJs help you lose time quicker—or as an early stop on your party train.

i Shots £1+. Beers 2 for £6-7. Cocktails £5+. Food £3-11. Open M-Sa 11am-11:30pm, Su 11am-11pm.

Southbank

THE HIDE

39-45 Bermondsey St.   ☎020 7403 6655 www.thehidebar.com

The Hide is a cocktail aficionado's paradise. Its stated goal: "not to get you drinking more, but better." While Let's Go does not believe these categories are mutually exclusive, it's nice to know such a place exists; here, it's all the perks of a classy night out without the need to actually be classy, and with a broad clientele besides (backpacking bums are slumped into leather couches alongside chic jazz cats).

i Beers £5 for a pint, £2.70 for a half-pint. Cocktails £9. Food £3-11. Open Tu 5pm-midnight, W-Th 5pm-1am, F-Sa 5pm-2am.

SOUTHWARK TAVERN

22 Southwark St.   ☎020 7403 0257 www.thesouthwarktavern.co.uk

London's really into its punitive institutions, and you should be, too. Rather than paying to go on the London Dungeon tour, though, you should chill in this former prison and drink beer while you're at it. You can relax in the main area or claim your own cell in the basement (choice seems pretty clear to us). The food's excellent, with the Sunday afternoon roasts particularly lauded for their selection and taste.

i Food £3.50-15. Drinks £4-10. Open M-Th 11am-midnight, F-Sa 11am-1am, Su noon-midnight.

Marylebone and Bloomsbury

THE SOCIAL

5 Little Portland St.   ☎0207 636 4992

By day, it's a Wi-Fi cafe, and by night, it is a bar. The upstairs section is shrug-worthy, though with above-average food—we're particularly delighted to see hot dogs catching on outside baseball stadiums—but things get more exciting as you move downstairs (don't they always?). Come to the club for its more fully fledged bar and themed nights, including a Wednesday new bands showcase and a Thursday hip-hop karaoke our Let's Go correspondent declared "scrupulously happenin'."

i Beers £4.50-6. Ciders £5-7. Food £3-12. Open M-W 11:30am-midnight, Th-F 11:30am-1am, Sa 6pm-1am; closed Sundays.

South Kensington and Chelsea

THE TROUBADOUR

263-267 Old Brompton Rd.   ☎0207 370 1434 www.troubadour.co.uk

Trust us; there will come a point in your stay when you'll long to hear a British Neil Young sing cheerful ballads of death. At such an occasion, look no further than this underground club (the top bit's a normal restaurant; just ask for the downstairs), where the genre formerly known as folk music has expanded its horizons to include soul, indie rock, and even forays into electronic gadgetry, six nights a week—hard to say if you'll peep the next James Taylor or James Blake. Also with a two-for-one happy hour on drinks 8-10pm and a broader-than-usual food menu.

i Cover £6-8. Cocktails £6-8. Burgers, salads, snacks £3.95-13.25. Open M-Th 9am-midnight, F-Sa 9am-2am, Su 9am-midnight.

THE DRAYTON ARMS

153 Old Brompton Rd.   ☎020 7835 2301 www.thedraytonarmssw5.co.uk

Fairly typical as pubs go, the Arms is saved from anonymity by its inspired performances every night of the week in its black box theatre. Shows are a little pricey but are an intimate counterpoint to the scores of big-budget productions elsewhere in London. The bar area is comfortably laid out and homey, with elegant touches (it is Chelsea, after all).

i Drinks starting at £4. Food £6-8. Open M-F noon-midnight, Sa-Su 10am-midnight.

THE BLACKBIRD

209 Earls Court Rd.　　　　　　　　☎020 7835 1855 www.blackbirdearlscourt.co.uk

"Blackbird singing in the dead of night," warbles Paul. "There are no wings here, broken or otherwise, but the pies are great and the sandwiches cheaper than you'll find at other pubs in the area. All your life, live music by local musicians every Friday at 9pm, unassertive rock 'n' roll the rest of the time. You were only waiting for this pub to arrive in Kensington near Earls Court."

i Drinks starting at £3.50. Food £6.75. Open M-Sa 9am-11:30am and noon-10pm, Su 9am-11:30am and noon-9:30pm.

606 CLUB

90 Lots Rd.　　　　　　　　☎020 7352 5953 www.606club.co.uk

On the more established, and therefore pricier, side of the live music club spectrum, this venue attracts a world-class roster of mostly jazz acts matched only by its crosstown rival, Ronnie Scott's. Booking using its online form (on an old-school Flash website) can be a bit of a hassle. So can getting your mind blown by the insane melodic wizardry of a traveling sax man who understands only the wordless aura of the blues. But that's life.

i Cover and times are subject to change depending on the show. General cover £10, F-Sa nights £12. Shows M-Th 7-11:15pm, F-Sa 8pm-12:45am, Su 12:30-3:30pm and 7-11:15pm.

West London

THE DOVE

19 Upper Mall　　　　　　　　☎020 8748 9474 www.dovehammersmith.co.uk

Hit up this fine young (actually, apparently been around since forever—a list of famous diners includes Ernest Hemingway, Charles II, and James Thompson, writer of the Royal Navy's unofficial anthem "Rule Britannia!" in 1740) pub for its beautiful terraced riverside view and bang-up menu. That it features the Guinness Book-certified world's smallest bar-room gives you a sense of its slightly eccentric character—though there's plenty of room outside of that cell, and the outside's the best bit. Food is expensive, but the pub's worthwhile for the beer.

i Drinks £4-10. Food £6-22. Open M-Sa 11am-11pm, Su noon-10:30pm.

BUSH HALL

310 Uxbridge Rd.　　　　　　　　☎020 8222 6955 www.bushhallmusic.co.uk

The British music scene's obsession with the young, glitzy, and attitudinal is a bit beyond Let's Go, but if you want to see a vicious young band of up-and-comers, this is certainly the place to do it. It's best to check online for whatever might tickle your fancy (and to make sure tix are still available, and that a wedding won't be going on that night). There's an affiliated dining room next door, with full and "pre-gig" menus for those in a rush to get musicked.

i Ticket prices usually between £15-25. Hours vary based on the act. Check the website for the most up-to-date prices and times.

East London

THE VANBRUGH

91 Colomb St.　　　　　　　　☎20 8305 1007 www.thevanbrugh.co.uk

The website claims it's "Greenwich's Best Kept Secret," but there might be good reason for that—down an overlookable side street at the bottom of a long hill, you could be forgiven for mistaking this joint for a Miami villa garden. Once you're in the door, though, you'll dig the comfy couches, bumping soundtrack, and spacious outdoor seating. The food's a little spendy, but the desserts sublime and the drinks totally affordable.

i Pints £3.50+. Open M-F noon-3:15pm and 6-9:45pm, Sa noon-4:45pm and 6-9:45pm, Su noon-8:45pm.

93 FEET EAST

150 Brick Ln.   ☎20 7770 6006 www.93feeteast.co.uk

Wait, do they even use feet in England? It definitely originates from something about kings and the lengths of their sandals, right? These questions will not be resolved at this popular dance club, but it will, for at least a few moments, help you forget your units-of-measurement-related worries (or maybe just introduce new ones?). With a top-notch events calendar geared mostly toward DJs, you can also check the website for listings re: bands, film screenings, and poetry slams.

i Pints £4. Burger and chips £4.90. Open M-Th 5-11pm, F-Sa 5pm-1am, Su 5-10:30pm.

North London

🏛 SOUTHAMPTON ARMS

139 Highgate Rd.   www.thesouthamptonarms.co.uk

Its website, in icy Courier New, bitches out the alleged sign-design-thieves at a rival pub, the next page painstakingly delineating what does and does not constitute a "proper emergency" (i.e., the circumstances in which you are allowed to telephone them, basically limited to fires, floods, suicide bombers, and over-eager chimpanzees—we're not making this up). Desiccatedly dry British hipster pub wit aside, this is a delightful neighborhood pub. The challenging bit about blending in with the locals is finding a place to sit down.

i Pints £4. Open daily noon-midnight.

SPIRITUAL CAIPIRINHA BAR

4-6 Ferdinand St.   ☎02 0748 56791

Ooooooh, spiiiiiiiiritualllllll. This bar/concert venue/record label's most prominent wall, or mosaic of Polaroids, dangles guitars behind the stage; weird art is to be found in just about every corner. Singer-songwriters strum earnestly most nights of the week, with open mics and happenings galore rounding out a very cool lineup. It's like being at the cool local music space your hometown never quite managed to get rolling—but it serves alcohol, too (caipirinhas are £4.50 during happy hour).

i Cocktails £7. Open M-Sa 6pm-1am, Su 6pm-midnight.

ESSENTIALS

Practicalities

For all the bombastic hostels, cafes, museums, and bars we list, we know some of the most important places you visit during your trip might actually be more mundane. Whether it's a tourist office, free Wi-Fi hotspot, or post office, these practicalities are vital to a successful trip, and you'll find all you need right here.

- **TOURIST OFFICES:** There are zillions of tourist information centers in London, and the visitlondon.com website can direct you to the nearest one (www.visitlondon.com/tag/tourist-information-centre); if you're thinking of exploring beyond the city, its sister site, visitbritain.com, offers droves of knowledge and will welcome you with a flattering quail. An easy place to start is by tracking down one of the blue- or magenta-shirted Team London Ambassadors loitering about in Trafalgar Sq.—they've volunteered to answer your questions about London, from travel advice to listings of "What's on" to bathroom directions.

- **LGBT RESOURCES:** The LGBT Tourist office near the Leicester Sq. Tube stop offers information on everything from saunas to theater discounts. (25 Frith St., www.gaytouristoffice.co.uk/): Boys (http://boyz.co.uk) lists gay events in London as well as an online version of its magazine.

Gingerbeer (www.gingerbeer.co.uk) is a guide for lesbian and bisexual women with events listings. Time Out London's magazine and website (https://timeout.com/london) also provide a good overview of the city's LGBT establishments and the city in general.

- **INTERNET:** Wi-Fi abounds in this speed-of-tech city. Most cafes provide internet access. Chains like Starbucks and McDonald's almost always have free Wi-Fi, though you may pay a karmic debt or be reincarnated as a lesser being for consistent Wi-Fi squatting (though using these neo-corporatist freebees to plot the downfall of Western capitalism is encouraged). Other chains with Wi-Fi include The Coffee Republic (www.coffeerepublic.co.uk), Wetherspoon (i.e., the IHOP of pubs, www.jdwetherspoon.co.uk), and Pret a Manger (www.pret.com). Public areas also have Wi-Fi. The area between Upper St. and Holloway Rd., also known as The Technology Mile, is the longest stretch of free internet in the city.

- **POST OFFICES:** There are a lot of them, and they're easily Googled. Hostels also can point you in the right direction. Here's one, off the top of our heads: Trafalgar Sq. Post Office. (24-28 William IV St. ☎020 7484 9305. Charing Cross Tube stop. Open M 8:30am-6:30pm, Tu 9:15am-6:30pm, W-Th 8:30am-6:30pm, F 8:30am-6:30pm, Sa 9am-5:30pm, closed Su.)

- **BANKS/ATMS:** It's almost always cheaper to withdraw cash from ATMs than exchanging dollars for pounds via individual credit/debit transactions or at (heavens no!) tourist-manipulating money changers. ATMs also allow you to withdraw more dough in one go, meaning that you're only paying a single flat fee to take out large sums, rather than having a bank fee tacked on every time you swipe your plastic for a venti fat-free almond turtle mocha. Legend holds that there are as many ATMs in London as there are stars above the Albion sky—no matter where you are, there most likely will be a cash machine within a few blocks. Keep an eye out for free ATMs, though be aware that while the machine itself may not levy a few pounds for the transaction, your bank from home will probably still enact its standard debit withdrawal fees. You should be able to get by fine without ever setting foot in a London bank, but in case you do, keep an eye out for the larger ones, such as Barclay's, Natwest, Lloyd's, and the Royal Bank of Scotland. For tourist purposes, these are all essentially the same, unless your home bank has a special relationship with one of them.

Emergency

- **EMERGENCY NUMBER:** ☎999—that's for fire, medical, police, etc.
- **POLICE:** Emergency ☎999. Non-emergency ☎101. For hearing-impaired people using a Textphone, ☎18000.
- **RAPE CRISIS CENTER:** For women, with connections for organizations to help men as well: ☎0808 802 9999.
- **HOSPITAL:** University College Hospital (☎20 3456 7890), St. Thomas Hospital (☎20 7188 7188), St. Bartholomew's Hospital (☎20 7377 7000).
- **PHARMACY:** There are like 1000 pharmacies in London. "Boots" is a chain that's similar to an American Walgreens/CVS/etc. Zafash Pharmacy in Chelsea is one of the only 24hr. pharmacies. (☎20 7373 2798)

Getting There

By Plane

London's main airport is Heathrow (☎0844 335 1801 heathrowairport.com), and it's one of the busiest in the world. The cheapest way to get from Heathrow to central London is on the Tube. The southwestern end of the Piccadilly Line arrives from central London and loops around Heathrow. (Time depends on where you're coming from, but takes about 1 hour, comes every 5min., M-Sa 5am-11:54pm, Su 5:46am-10:37pm). Heathrow Express (☎084 5600 1515 www.heathrowexpress.com) runs between Heathrow and Paddington station four times per hour. The trip is signifi-

royal albert hall

In 1861, Prince Albert, a real man of the people, died. This was a huge bummer for his bae slash first cousin, Queen Victoria, who in her mourning saw fit to open a gigantic concert hall ten years later. The hall's acoustics were terrible; the standard joke was that the RAH was the only place in Britain a composer could be sure to hear their concert twice. Renovated on and off during the remainder of its history, the Royal Albert Hall has become one of the most famous performance venues in Europe, holding concerts, ballets, operas, film screenings, circus shows, poetry recitals, and a variety of sporting events, including London's first-ever sumo wrestling tournament in 1991.

London is really into the "making people with less money stand whilst the upper classes gloat in their plump chairs" thing—see also Shakespeare's Globe—but if you see an ad for something that interests you, we urge you to take advantage of the offer and get tickets for the uppermost level of the Hall. Ad-hoc communities form in the jostling crowd peering down from the rafters as the pilgrims and pariahs of society merge; indeed, sometimes entire micro-civilizations rise and fall, Lord of the Flies-style, over the course of a three-hour concert. Besides, up here, there's more room to dance.

cantly shorter (though comparably pricier) than many of the alternatives, clocking in around 15-20min. (£21.50 when purchased online or from station, £26.50 on board. 1st train departs daily around 5:10am.) The Heathrow Connect (www.heathrowconnect.com) also runs to Paddington but is cheaper and takes longer, since it makes five stops on the way to and from the airport. There are two trains per hour, and the trip takes about 25min.

The National Express (☎08717 818 178 www.nationalexpress.com) bus runs between Victoria Coach Station and Heathrow three times per hour. Though cheap and often simpler than convoluted Underground trips, the buses are subject to the slings and arrows of outrageous London traffic. Posing a similar traffic threat, taxis from the airport to Victoria cost around £60 and take around 45min.—in short, they aren't worth it.

Getting to Gatwick Airport (LDW; ☎0844 335 1802) takes around 30min., making it less convenient than Heathrow but less hectic, too. The swift and affordable train services that connect Gatwick to the city make the trip a little easier. The Gatwick Express train runs nonstop service to Victoria station, leaving approximately every 15min. (less frequently in the middle of the night). You can buy tickets in terminals, at the station, or on the train itself. (☎0845 850 1530 www.gatwickexpress.com. 1-way £17.70; round trip £31.05—round-trip ticket valid for a month.)

National Express runs buses from the North and South terminals of Gatwick to London. The National Express bus (☎0871 781 8178 nationalexpress.com) takes approximately 90min., and buses depart for London Victoria hourly. Taxis take about 1hr. to reach central London. EasyBus (☎084 4800 4411 easybus.co.uk) runs every 15min. from North and South terminals to Earls Court and West Brompton.

By Train

Europe has left the one-time railroad-obsessed States far behind—London in particular offers several ways to easily reach other European destinations via train. Multiple companies pass through the city; the biggest are Eurostar (☎08432 186 186 www.eurostar.com), which travels to Paris and Brussels (and, thereby, beyond),

london

and National Rail (☎08457 48 49 50 www.nationalrail.co.uk), which oversees lines running throughout the United Kingdom. Train travel in Britain is generally reliable but can be unreasonably expensive. Booking tickets weeks in advance can lead to large savings, but spur-of-the-moment train trips to northern cities can cost upward of £100.

By Bus

Bus travel is another, frequently cheaper, option. Eurolines (☎08717 818 181 www. eurolines.co.uk Phone lines open daily 8am-8pm) is Europe's largest coach network, servicing 500 destinations throughout Europe. Many buses leave from Victoria Coach Station, at the mouth of Elizabeth St. just off Buckingham Palace Rd. Many coach companies, including National Express, Eurolines, and Megabus, operate from Victoria Coach. National Express is the only scheduled coach network in Britain and can be used for most intercity travel and for travel to and from various airports. It can also be used to reach Scotland and Wales.

Getting Around

There's nothing quite so smug as the sound of a Transport for London operator using the intercom to intercom everyone in the station that there is "good service" on a particular line—and even when there are interruptions to service, TFL does a good job of keeping travelers aware. Each station will have posters listing interruptions to service, and you can check service online at www.tfl.gov.uk or the 24hr. travel information service (☎08432 22 12 34). The website also has a journey planner that can plot your route using any public transport service. Memorize that website. Love that website. Though many people in the city stay out into the wee hours, the Tube doesn't have the same sort of stamina; when it closes around midnight, night owls have two options: cabs or night buses.

Travel Passes

Travel passes are almost guaranteed to save you money. The passes are priced based on the number of zones they service (the more zones, the more expensive), but zone 1 encompasses central London and you'll probably seldom need to get past zone 2. If someone offers you a secondhand ticket, don't take it. There's no real way to verify if it's valid—plus, it's illegal. (Utilizing a complex succession of logical proofs, our *Let's Go Philosophy* Correspondent has informed us that illegality is bad.) Under-16s get free travel on buses, passengers ages 11-15 reduced fare on the Tube with an Oyster photocard. Students 18 and older must study full time (at least 15hr. per week over 14 weeks) in London to quality for the Student Photocard, which enables users to save 30% on adult travel cards and bus passes. It's worth it if you're staying for an extended period of time (study-abroad-sters, we're looking at you).

Oyster cards enable you to pay in a variety of ways, and you should get one if you plan on being in London for any decent length of time. Fares come in peak (M-F 6:30-9:30am and 4-7pm) and off-peak varieties and are, again, distinguished by zone. Oysters let you "pay as you go," meaning that you can store credit on an as-needed basis. Using an Oyster card will save you up to 50% off a single ticket. Remember to tap your card both on entering and exiting the station. You can use your card to add Travelcards, which allow unlimited travel on one day. This will only be cost-effective if you plan to use the Tube a lot; they cost £6.40 for day travel (on- or off-peak, doesn't matter) within zones 1 and 2. You can top up your Oyster at one of the ubiquitous off-licenses, marked by the Oyster logo, scattered throughout the city.

Season tickets are weekly, monthly, and annual Travelcards that work on all public transport and can be purchased inside Tube stations. They yield unlimited (within zone) use for their duration. (Weekly rates for zones 1-2 £32.10.)

By Underground

Most stations have Tube maps on the walls (though they may be placed in frustratingly out-of-the-way corners) and free pocket maps. The Tube map in no way reflects an above-ground scale, though, and should not be used for even the roughest estimation of walking directions. (Seriously.) Platforms are organized by line and will have the colors of the lines serviced and their names on the wall. The colors of the poles inside the trains correspond with the line, and trains will often have their end destination displayed on the front. This is an essential service when your line splits. Many platforms will have a digital panel indicating ETAs for the trains and sometimes type and final destination. When transferring within a station, just follow the clearly marked routes.

The Tube runs from Monday to Saturday from approximately 5:30am (though it depends on station and line) until around midnight, and less frequently on Sundays, with many lines starting service after 6am. If you're taking a train within 30min. of these times (before or after), you'll want to check the signs in the ticket hall for times of the first and last train. Around 6pm on weekdays, many of the trains running out of central London are packed with the after-work crowd, so if you don't want to wait for train after train before one with enough room for you finally arrives, it's best to avoid these lines at this time of day.

You can buy tickets from ticket counters (though these often have lines at bigger stations) or at machines in the stations. You need to swipe your ticket at the beginning of the journey and then again to exit the Tube. Random on-train checks will ask you to present a valid ticket to avoid the £50 penalty fee (reduced to £25 if you pay in under 21 days).

The Overground is a newish addition to the London public transportation scene. It services parts of the city past zone 1 where Tube lines are sparse and is particularly useful in East London. Fares and rules are the same as the Tube; you can just think of it as another line, except with a better view.

By Bus

While slower than the Tube for long journeys (thanks to traffic and more frequent stops), the buses that crawl antlike over London's every inch are useful for traveling short distances covered by a few stops (and several transfers) on the Tube. Bus stops frequently post lists of buses serving the stop as well as route maps and maps of the area indicating nearby stops. These maps are also very helpful for finding your way around a neighborhood. Buses display route numbers. The highest-traffic buses are being installed with LED signs which display the arrival times of incoming buses.

Every route and stop is different, but buses generally run every 5-15min. beginning around 5:30am and ending around midnight. After day bus routes have closed, night buses take over. These typically operate similar routes to their daytime equivalents, and their numbers are prefixed with an N (N13, for instance). Some buses run 24hr. services. If you're staying out past the Tube's closing time, you should plan your night-bus route or bring cab fare (single rides £2.20).

cambridge

If you think touring colleges is reserved only for prospective students and their over-eager parents, you clearly haven't been to the right schools. Take Cambridge's King's College, for example, which has been around for nearly 600 years, but only started accepting 'commoners' in large numbers in the last 200. Or perhaps Trinity College, where famous alumni include A.A. Milne, creator of Winnie the Pooh; John Winthrop, first governor of Massachusetts; and a guy named Isaac who theorized a little about

get a room!

YHA CAMBRIDGE $
97 Tenison Rd. ☎0845-371-9728 www.yha.org.uk/hostel/cambridge

YHA Cambridge is guaranteed to be your favorite hostel in town—of course, that mostly stems from the fact that it's the only hostel in Cambridge. You might think that lack of competition would mean lack of quality. Fortunately for all you hopeful young backpackers, YHA is a huge chain in Europe, meaning across the board standardization (i.e. they have to stay on top of their shit). Expect the usual YHA amenities here—beds with personal power ports, self-catering kitchen and laundry, and a common room and café on site. The hostel boasts a friendly staff who can help with directions and most buses make a stop around the corner at the train station. Because it's the only game in town, rooms book out pretty far in advance. Be sure to book ahead.

i Dorms generally £16-20, Singles from £60.

FAIRWAY GUEST HOUSE $$
143 Cherry Hinton Rd. ☎0122-324-6063 www.fairwaysguesthouse.com

If you've ever wanted to pretend to be a struggling NYC writer working at a small-time newspaper to pay the bills so you can continue to work on your novel, living in a pint-sized room because that's all you can afford, then you'll feel right at home here. That's not to say that you won't be comfortable though, but it's basic living at its best. Your room has a bed, a desk, a closet, and (if you dish out extra) a private bathroom all contained in a room you couldn't really swing a golf club in. The narrow staircases and halls are "BnB chic" (lots of floral carpets and varying shades of brown and tan), but the cheap rooms, nearby bus stop, and Cambridge Leisure Center up the road mean you'll be set for seeing all the sights.

i Singles £35-40, en-suite £45-60; doubles £55-65, en-suite £68-95.

something we like to call 'gravity'. Well, that's interesting, you say, but I'm a tourist, not a time traveller. But even without all the history, Cambridge is pretty stunning to look at. Think centuries old buildings, cobblestone walking streets, and more than one impressive chapel. Whether you're trying to blend in by riding a bike (and avoiding getting crushed by the thousand other people cycling around) or cruising along the Backs in a punt, you'll find Cambridge to be a place to relax and enjoy a college town without all that college stress.

SIGHTS

THE CAM RIVER

Like every great British city (and a lot of fairly average British cities), Cambridge is located on the banks of a river. Although the Cam isn't on par with the waterways of Venice or Amsterdam when it comes to size, its old-fashioned charm makes it better for aimlessly floating along. The most popular way to get down the river is to be punted, which is more pleasant than it sounds. It involves flat boats, propelled along by long sticks rather than swift kicks to the rear. If you'd prefer a workout, you can hire your own punt and steer yourself downstream, but guided punts offer a more relaxing way to enjoy the ride with decreased risk of bumping into something and falling into the water. Just make sure you go on a weekday, as weekends are often crowded by tourists who do nothing more than ram into one another and piss off the ducks.

MUSEUM OF CAMBRIDGE

2/3 Castle Street   ☎0122-335-5159 www.folkmuseum.org.uk

Remember when you used to go with your grandma to visit her zany friend Ms. Catterwall and marveled at the amazing amount of old stuff that she had in every nook and cranny of her house? No? Well, visiting the Cambridge museum is a bit like that, except you don't have to put up with Ms. Catterwall pinching your cheeks constantly and reminding you how she knew you when you were "this big." The building itself is an antique, serving as the local inn for over 300 years while maintaining its 16th century design (including the creaky floorboards and tiny winding staircases). More impressive is the amount of antiques that have been jam-packed inside. If you can think of some obscure antediluvian item, they'll probably have it on display. Candle boxes, kettles, pianos, sewing machines, ice skates, hat-making tools, vacuum cleaners, courting tokens, eel traps, creepy china dolls and jelly molds– find it all here. The museum might not have the glitz and glamor of the Fitzwilliam Museum, but its eclectic display make it an interesting visit for more dedicated history buffs or antique fiends.

i £4, students £2. Open Tu-Sa 10:30am-5pm, Su noon-4pm; last admission 30min. before closing.

FOOD

◪ AROMI $$

1 Bene't St.   ☎0122-330-0117 www.aromi.co.uk

This isn't just your regular pizza, pasta, pretending-to-be-authentic Italian restaurant. This is the straight outta Sicily, family–run Italian eatery that offers up classics like arancini, pizza siciliana, spianata, and other hard-to-pronounce Italian words that sound great when English people say them. As a popular local restaurant and gelato stop, it can get busy, but the friendly staff never hesitates to dish up delicious and generous portions to all. The affordable prices will have you loading up on carbs faster than Regina George in Mean Girls (and probably with a similar sense of denial). Make sure to save room for a cannoli, some tiramisu, or a scoop of gelato before you leave.

i Open Su-Th 9am-7pm, Fr-Sa until 8pm.

CREPEAFFAIRE $

66 Bridge St.   ☎0122-336-2662 www.crepeaffaire.com/uk

When we think crepes, we think sweet, syrupy goodness with a generous portion of chocolate in the mix. Others might think of cheesy, more savory crepes stuffed with veggies and meats. Whatever you're thinking, you can try it at Crepeaffaire, where they have a delicious selection of crepes that run from the healthy super-veg to the mouth-watering "I'll have what she's having" (and with strawberries and Nutella, you will). With most crepes hovering around the £5 mark, you can indulge your tastebuds and spare your wallet. When the cashier asks if you want a scoop of ice cream with your crepe, don't let any onlooking health nuts judge you—say yes (and cast a sidelong glance at their aloe-infused guava spritzers). Who cares if it's 10am in the morning? Live your life.

i Open M-F 8am-8pm, Sa-Su 9am-8pm.

NIGHTLIFE

THE MILL $

Granta Pl.   ☎0122-331-1829 www.themillpubcambridge.com

A number of classic pubs line the river in Cambridge, but The Mill is easily the coziest. Sure, it doesn't have a history that involves Watson and Crick or Pink Floyd, but the old name of the pub (Hazards Arms) has something to do with two men who hated each other (and that's just about as good). There's some large-sized booths and a wood-paneled back room where you can grab a pint with friends new and old while wasting a rainy afternoon with a beer and board games. On a warm day you can ask for your beer in a plastic cup and go sit by the water's edge to participate in the city's pastime— watching tourists crash their punts into the walls along the river. Is there a better way to spend an afternoon?

i Open Su-W 11am-11pm, Th-Sa until midnight.

THE CAMBRIDGE BREW HOUSE $$
1 King St.   ☎0122-385-5185 www.thecambridgebrewhouse.com

1 King St. seems to be as cursed as the Professor of Dark Arts position at Hogwarts—in the last 20 years, four different pubs have stood at this site. Whether or not Cambridge Brewery House outlasts the rest remains to be seen, but in the meantime, it serves as a good watering hole/chill-out spot for those in need of a drink. A large open room decked out with wooden tables and bus seat booths covers the first floor, along with a view into the microbrewery, the brews of which you can order at the bar. More privacy and sports can be found upstairs where there's a large projector screening football (the European kind, of course), and a small terrace that offers views of a parking lot and soggy benches. Maybe just stick to the inside. The menu consists of mostly British-style tapas you can nibble on, though there's a selection of slightly pricier mains if you need a serious feeding.

i Open Su-Th 11am-11:30pm, F-Sa until midnight.

ESSENTIALS
Practicalities

- **TOURIST OFFICE:** Cambridge Visitor Information Center will help with bookings for sights in and around Cambridge. (Peas Hill, ☎0122-379-1501. Open M-Sa 10am-5pm, Su 11am-3pm in the summer, closed in the winter.)

- **ATMS:** There is a local HSBC bank branch, which has ATMs as well as desk services available. (63-64 St. Andrews St.)

- **POST OFFICE:** For that letter addressed to Mom. (57-58 St. Andrews St. ☎0845-722-3344. Open M-Sa 9am-5:30pm, Su Closed.)

Emergency

- **EMERGENCY:** ☎999 (UK/Ireland) or ☎112 (Europe-wide)

- **PHARMACY:** Boots Pharmacy (28 Petty Cury. ☎0122-335-0213. Open M-Sa 8am-8pm, Su 11am-5pm.)

- **HOSPITAL:** Addenbrooke's Hospital (Hills Rd. ☎0122-324-5151.)

Getting There
By Train

The only significant starting point for trains to Cambridge is London. Trains arrive at **Station Road.** (*i* 20min. walk southeast from the town center. Ticket office open M-Sa 5:10am-11pm, Su 7am-10:55pm.) You can catch trains at London King's Cross (£22. 50min., 2 per hr.) and **London Liverpool St.** (£15.30. 1¼hr., 2 per hr.)

By Bus

The bus station, mostly for short-distance buses, is on **Drummer Street.** (Ticket office open M-Sa 9am-5:30pm.) Airport shuttles and buses to more distant destinations run from **Parkside.** Buses arrive from: London Victoria (Transfer at Stansted. £12.70. 3hr., every hr.); Gatwick (£34. 4hr., every 2hr.); Heathrow (£28.60. 3hr., every hr.); Stansted (£10.50. 50min., every 2hr.); Oxford. (Take the X5 bus. £12.50. 3¼hr., every 30min.)

Getting Around

By Bus

CitiBus runs from stops throughout town, including some on **Saint Andrew's Street, Emmanuel Street,** and at the train station. The most useful routes are C1 (from the station) and C2 (goes out along Chesterton Rd.). Single rides cost ₤2.20. **Dayrider Tickets** (unlimited travel for 1 day; ₤3.90) can be purchased on the bus; for longer stays, you can buy a **Megarider** ticket (unlimited travel for weeks; ₤13 per week).

By Taxi

For a taxi, call **Cabco.** (☎01223 312 444 Open 24hr.)

By Bike

You'll see students on bikes everywhere in Cambridge. To fit in, go to **City Cycle Hire.** (61 Newnham Rd. ☎01223 365 629 www.citycyclehire.com. ₤7 for 4hr., ₤10 for 8hr., ₤12 for 24hr., ₤17 for 2-3 days, ₤25 for 4-7 days, ₤35 for 2 weeks, ₤80 for up to 3 months. Open Easter-Oct M-F 9am-5:30pm, Sa 9am-5pm; Nov-Easter M-F 9am-5:30pm.)

stonehenge

As the Stonehenge audio tour will explain, Stonehenge is not only an enigma, but a mystery (jury's out on whether either one is wrapped in the other). But the question remains: what is it all for? Is it a calendar? A status symbol? A sacrificial altar? Proof of extra-terrestrials? We're sad to inform you that merely visiting will not leave you with one definitive answer. However, whatever its purpose or maker, the stone circle really does inspire a sense of wonder—and that's enough of a reason for 21st-century tourists to visit.

🏛 STONEHENGE

Amesbury ☎019 8062 2833 www.english-heritage.org.uk

A trip to Stonehenge paired with a stop in Salisbury—the nearest major city—is a full-day event that basically repeats the message of Ken Follett's *The Pillars of the Earth*: building stuff is hard. Stonehenge itself is a tricky customer. While only 30 years ago, the place was an out-of-the-way tourist spot that only very thorough travelers would attempt to visit, there are now bus tours that drop thousands of visitors next to the highway that Stonehenge overlooks. For casual appreciation of pagan architecture, an hour is all you need; the audio tour will walk you through the materials, construction, layout, and purpose of the pi-shaped masonry. Surprisingly, even though you'll share your magical experience with hundreds of people, the design of the walkway is expertly shaped so that you can get as many mystical selfies as your heart deigns without someone in a red windbreaker wandering into the shot. If you have more time and money saved up, traveling here via Salisbury instead of via the A303 is a nice way to get a more rounded survey of British history (and pre-history).

i By train: take the National Rail from Waterloo to Salisbury (around £40). Once in Salisbury, the Stonehenge Bus leaves from the train station for the site every 30min. from about 9:30am-6pm in summer and 10am-2pm in winter (£12). By bus: tours leave the city (£30 with price of admission). Adult £8, concessions £7.20. By barge, with 50-ton rocks: leave that to the pagans. Open daily Jan-Mar 15 9:30am-4pm; March 15-May 9:30am-6pm; Jun-Aug 9am-7pm; Sept-Oct 15 9:30am-6pm; Oct 15-Dec 9:30am-4pm.

york

People flock to London, hoping to find the authentic British experience in its sprawling streets and robust metro system. But if you want to go old school British, look no further than York. Much like your great-aunt's taste in home décor, the streets seem to have barely changed since the 13th century. This all means you can expect lots of narrow alleyways with medieval houses hovering above them like over-protective mothers, with the possible addition of indoor plumbing, so there's no threat of local residents dumping their chamber pots onto your head. Just because it's old though doesn't mean York can't get with the times—a collection of swanky cocktail bars, independent coffee shops, and fine-dining restaurants make that apparent. Whether you're looking to immerse yourself in York's history or just want to chill out and enjoy a nice cuppa (or maybe a cuppa something else), you'll probably find it in one of York's cobblestoned enclaves.

get a room!

SAFESTAY YORK $

88-90 Micklegate ☎0190-462-7720 www.safestay.com

York is an old town, and it seems like everywhere you go there's another medieval-ish home that used to be the House of Lord So-and-So in the year something something. You can get your own slice of medieval history and poshness at Safestay York. The building has a long history you can read about in the foyer, but the bottom line is that this is an old house that manages to maintain some of its original charm even though it's been decked out in the latest in home improvements, like electricity and running water. Each dorm is outfitted with comfy bunks, en-suite bathrooms, personal reading lights, and enough plugs to charge your phone and computer at the same time without pissing off the whole room. And after weeks of enduring the sight of male roommates walking around in their underwear, your Let's Go researcher especially enjoyed the blackout curtains on the bed that can be drawn to block out 90% of light and 100% of weird hostel mates. That's some quality living right there.

i Dorms from around £20.

YHA YORK $

Water End. ☎0190-465-3147 www.yha.org.uk/hostel/york

YHA is a far cry (about a 20-minute walk) from York city center, but considering York is about the size of your little finger, that's not really saying much. That being said, you won't get space like this at any other hostel in York— we're talking about the grounds themselves actually, not the rooms which are of average size. Along with the large kitchen and onsite restaurant comes a backyard big enough to actually qualify as a backyard. Dorms average at eight beds per room and offer individual lights and power stations as well as the option of an en-suite bathroom. With 200 beds you should be able to find a friend even though the hostel also caters to big groups and families. All in all, not a bad place to settle down, but if you want proximity more than space, try Safestay or Fort Boutique instead, which are located within the castle walls.

i Dorms from £10; private rooms from around £30.

SIGHTS

▨ YORK CASTLE MUSEUM

Eye of York   ☎0190-468-7687 www.yorkcastlemuseum.org.uk

If there's one thing we love more than finding a meal for under £5, it's museums that do re-creations. So going to York Castle Museum was comparable to finding an all-you-can-eat buffet for a fiver in terms of their smorgasbord of props. And, like a good buffet, there didn't seem to be a really unifying theme tying it all together besides, well, history. Sample a little bit of everything here—different kitchens, some from the 1700s to one resembling your grandma's; a collection of toys, that combines a 1800s plastic toy with early 2000s Sonic the Hedgehog; and even a mash-up of memorabilia from the 60s. And of course, the pièce de résistance, the roasted pig with the apple in its mouth at the center of the table, is their full size 19th century street, where you can wander in and out of candy stores, stumble into a police station, and even see a replica of an outhouse complete with (hopefully) fake poop. You gotta love that attention to detail.

i £10; students £5. Open M-Su 9:30am-5pm.

YORKSHIRE MUSEUM

Museum Gardens   ☎0190-468-7687 www.yorkshiremuseum.org.uk

York has had more ruling powers than Taylor Swift has had boyfriends, and you can experience all the highlights of that roller coaster of rulers in the Yorkshire Museum. Opting for an in medias res tactic, the museum throws you right into the thick of Roman times, with lots of pottery, old vases, and stone statues with vague descriptions of what Roman life was like. Follow through to see roman influence on York in the form of pottery, sculpture, and skulls that have all been dug up nearby, including a stone carving of a "phallus"— they say it was a sign of birth, we see it as evidence that guys have always been drawing (or carving) dicks onto stuff. Underground you'll find history in York after Roman times, and after Anglican rule, and after the Vikings, and after the Norman empire—we weren't kidding about York's long list of exes.

i £7.50; students £4. Open M-Su 10am-5pm.

YORK ART GALLERY

Exhibition Sq.   ☎0190-468-7687 www.yorkartgallery.org.uk

Welcome to the York Art Gallery, or perhaps the 'I Heart Ceramics' Institute. The museum's biggest permanent display is a collection of 10,000 ceramic bowls stacked high on scaffolding that reaches the ceiling, as well as an adjacent room that has probably the most visually-pleasing, color-coded wall of ceramics in the world. Not a huge pottery fan? Beyond their collection of all things breakable, the museum also has the Burton Room, a compilation of paintings and sculptures that, in a freak twist of events, you're actually encouraged to touch. The museum itself is pretty small but makes a great stop for a rainy afternoon, especially if you have the YMT access card, which gives you free, year-long access to the museum as well as the Yorkshire Museum and the York Castle Museum.

i £7.50, students £4. Open M-F 10am-5pm, Sa 10am-6pm, Su 11am-4pm.

FOOD

▨ BREW & BROWNIE $

5 Museum St.   ☎0190-464-7420 www.brewandbrownie.co.uk

Unfortunately for the American traveller, the International House of Pancakes is all a lie—they aren't as international as they claim to be and calling it THE house of pancakes seems to be stretching the truth a bit. However, there is a place in York that will dish up some delicious pancakes for you all hours of the day, and neither claim to be so cosmopolitan nor the last word on pancakes, and we appreciate that honesty. We also appreciate the fluffy sweet delectableness that is their much loved all-American pancake stacks. Besides pancakes, the café also offers up a selection of sandwiches, soups, and delicious pastries you can chow on while sipping some of their specially-sourced coffee.

i Open M-Sa 9am-5pm, Su 10am-4pm.

HENSHELWOODS DELICATESSEN $

10 New St.　　　　　　　　　　☎0190-467-3877 www.deliyork.co.uk

Henshelwoods Deli is, of course, a deli, specializing in meats and cheeses. However, they also specialize in shoving those meats and cheeses into buns and serving them up picnic style to the hungry locals of York at a deliciously- reasonable price. Choose from their eccentric list of cheese, veggie, and meat sandwiches (the soft cheese, apple, date combo makes a delicious and sweet offering, while the applewood cheddar with chili jam is for the more adventurous eaters) or just make your own. There's no seating inside or out, so you'll have to just grab and go, but just outside the narrow street is an open square with plenty of park benches on which to feast.

i Open M-Sa 9am-5pm, Su 11am-4pm.

great britain

NIGHTLIFE

▒ EVIL EYE $

42 Stonegate　　　　　　　　　☎0190-464-0002 www.evileyelounge.com

From the outside, Evil Eye is a little intimidating—the outer appearance of a bottle shop with a named based on a killer look adorned with the paintings of horned demons are all probably equally to blame. But brave you must be and you'll be pleasantly surprised with the laidback vibe and probably a little shell shocked at the amount of liquor stacked on the shelves. For a town that seems to be founded on pubs, the focus is surprisingly on cocktails; they've got classics like long islands and cosmos as well as a selection of "evil creations"—wrinkly squid, apple strudel, and the elusive green fairy. And if you're going for the "drunken-tourist-passed-out-in-a-gutter award," you could try the Snakes and Ladders and shots game on the menu (though we feel like this game has no real winners).

i Cocktails £6-7; shots £3; food £4-10. Open M-Th 10am-midnight, F-Sa 10am-1am, Su 11am-midnight.

CITY SCREEN PICTUREHOUSE $

13-17 Coney St.　　☎0871-902-5726 www.picturehouses.com/cinema/York_Picturehouse

It's time to take a break from all the boozing and experience some arts, my friend. If you're feeling fancy, you could hit up York Theatre Royal, where you can see a number of plays and musicals, but for something more alternative, try City Screen and the adjoining venue, The Basement. The movie theatre plays a lot of commercial films, but also shows art house and documentary films regularly, as well as occasionally offering streaming services of major performances taking place elsewhere in the world, which is probably the only way you'll ever see a performance in the Sydney Opera House (while eating popcorn too!).

i Tickets £7-11; student £7-10. Discounts available. Basement tickets vary from free to £20.

ESSENTIALS
Practicalities

- **TOURIST OFFICE:** Visit York. (1 Museum St. Open M-Sa 9am-5pm, Sun 10am-4pm.)

- **ATMS:** The most centrally-located ATMs are in the shopping district on Piccadilly and Coney Sts.

- **POST OFFICE:** Yes, they still have these. (22 Lendel St. Open M-Sa 9am-5:30pm, Su closed.)

Emergency

- **EMERGENCY:** ☎999 (UK/Ireland) or ☎112 (Europe-wide)

- **PHARMACY:** Boots. (43 Coney St. ☎0190-465-3657. Open M-W and F-Sa 8:30am-6pm, Th 8:30am-7pm, Su 11am-5pm.)

- **HOSPITAL:** The York Hospital (Wigginton Road. ☎0190-463-1313.)

Getting Here & Getting Around

York is a city where the pedestrian rules supreme. Inside the city walls are small cobblestones streets, some for cars, some walking only. There are, however, 5 major bus lines that run through town: the white line to Askham Bar, the yellow line to Grimston Bar, the red line to York Designer Outlet, the silver line to Monks Cross, and the green line to Rawcliffe Bar. Singles start at only £1 and a weeklong pass is just £12. For more information, visit the Bus and Visitor Information Point at the Railway Station.

manchester

Depending on where you start, you may develop a very different first impression of Manchester. Find yourself in the Central district and you'll think of the city as a busy metropolis with a convenient park where people go to nap during the middle of the day. Start in the Northern Quarter and you'll think the entire town is a collection of vintage stores, trendy cafes and bars, and the odd adult movie store or two. If you're in Castlefield, down by the wharfs, you'll probably think that the city is an industrial-style Amsterdam with lots of canals that criss-cross past old railway storage buildings. But Manchester is really just a collection of all these little regions, mashed up into one confusing, but entertaining and satisfying experience. Whatever part of town you end up in, and however that shapes your opinion of Manchester, you'll leave knowing that there's a lot more to the city than just their famed football teams (although they're definitely worth checking out, too).

SIGHTS

▨ PEOPLE'S HISTORY MUSEUM

Left Bank, Spinningfields   ☎0161-838-9190 www.phm.org.uk

British history tends to read like a good Game of Thrones episode – a bunch of people with lots of power and some fancy costumes stomp around plotting to kill one another, while we watch from the corner wondering if anyone has actually checked in on the citizens. To shed some light on how the other half (i.e. those kill-happy kings) lived, there's the People's Museum, which focuses on the very long and storied history of England from the perspective of, well, the people. Although it only covers 400 years of British history, it's still a lot to take in: the gallery is broken up into pre-1940 and post-1940 (not quite equal, but hey). The walk through the gallery consists mostly of posters, pictures, and banners that cover multiple revolutions, from the fight for a more democratic nation back in the 18th century to the recent coal miners strike of the 1980s and everything in between.

i Free. Open M-Su 10am-5pm.

YHA MANCHESTER $

Potato Wharf, Castlefield ☎0845-371-9647 www.yha.org.uk/hostel/manchester

We are unable to confirm, but feel pretty certain, that YHA is on some sort of mission for world domination, as you can find one in just about every city you visit. But since this world domination also features comfortable beds and solid amenities at a reasonable price, we're not really complaining. Expect clean and compact en-suite rooms, a large downstairs common area with book exchange and board games, and an onsite restaurant. It all makes for a great recipe to chill out, which is mostly what you'll be doing here—the location is at the far southwest end of town, not exactly in amidst the most bumpin' bar scene.

i Rooms from £10.

HATTERS ON NEWTON STREET $

50 Newton St. ☎0161-239-9500 www.hattershostels.com/manchester-newton-street

There's a class of hostels you seek out as a retreat from the crazy outside world, where you can get a hot shower and disappear into a comfy bed for a restful night. Hatters Newton is not one of those hostels. Should you try to disappear into your bed early on a weekend, the sounds of everyone else in the Northern Quarter partying it up in the street will remind you what you're missing. But you shouldn't be in bed anyway with all the pubs in the neighborhood, and Hatters puts you in prime location to hit them all. Too long, didn't read: if you're trying to have a relaxing stay in Manchester, maybe try elsewhere. But if your sightseeing plans generally involve heading out after 9 pm, you'll fit in just fine.

i Dorms £13-18, but rise to £20-30 on weekends; private rooms £35-45, weekends £70-90.

MANCHESTER ART GALLERY

Mosley St. ☎0161-235-8888 www.manchesterartgallery.org

From the outside, you might expect the Manchester Art Gallery to be merely a collection of rooms that showcase paintings of old men in bulbous trousers alongside decaying fruit. And though that most definitely is the case in some areas, the museum also curates a number of temporary exhibits that lean toward something more modern. 2016 was dominated by fashion, as Vogue and designer dresses took over the first and third floors, but the future promises a more diverse exhibition that isn't centered on pictures of Kate Moss (making you regret eating all those scones with extra butter). The permanent exhibit isn't anything to shrug off either, featuring talented (if not well known) artists and spanning over 200 years of art that go far beyond men in fancy pants with bowls of fruit.

i Free. Open M-Su 10am-5pm.

MUSEUM OF SCIENCE AND INDUSTRY

Liverpool Rd. ☎0161-832-2244 www.msimanchester.org.uk

Every city has their crowning age of achievement; for Manchester, that was the age of industry and cotton production. The museum is as engaging as it can be considering it's housed in a railway storage house and it's about a time period where kids under ten could be working over twelve hours a day. The museum also has an exhibit on the city's history as a huge cotton industry mainstay, where you can look at an old cotton machine and check out the different types of fabrics used in making clothes. And if trains are your thing, you can also ride on a train, along with a bunch of very excited eight-year-old kids.

i Free. Open M-Su 10am-5pm.

FOOD

THE KITCHENS $
Irwell Sq., Leftbank, Spinningfields   ☎0770-345-5347 www.thekitchensleftbank.com
What do we want? We don't know! Why don't we know? Too much pressure! Let your stress go and hit up The Kitchens in Spinningfields, where you can either choose between five different traders serving up street food from around the world, or just go ahead and sample a little somethin' somethin' from each one. Want flavor? Chaar Cart has a selection of curries you can sample. Looking for something greasy and delicious? The hip-hop chip shop will serve you up a basket of fish, fries, and peas with some old school music. Take your meal to the grassy outdoor eating space adorned with tropical plants and string lights. With most filling meals at just £5-6 pounds, you'd be hard pressed to find a better deal in the area, or better shop names—beef dishes available at aptly-named Well Hung. We'll take a burger though.

i Dishes £5-10. Open M-W noon-3pm, Th-Su noon-9pm.

DOGS 'N' DOUGH $
Bow Ln.   ☎0161-834-3996 www.dogsndough.com
When Google Maps tells you to go down a weird side street to find Dogs 'n' Dough, you'll probably think, "maybe I'll just stick to this Subway right here." Don't deprive yourself, though, of the opportunity to gorge yourself on some all-American artery clogging goodness. The basement bar/restaurant somehow manages to make tacky American bars look cool, with its low lighting and fresh-looking booths. And though the atmosphere certainly adds to the experience, that's not why you're here; the menu offers over a dozen different kinds of dogs or pizzas with combinations that include combining beef and bun with Doritos or, alternatively, doughy pizza goodness with mac and cheese. Pair your meal with a milkshake or American soda for a classic taste, or choose from their long list of cocktails to make eating that sauce-slathered dog even more challenging.

i Hot dogs £5-10; pizza £7-11. Open M-Th 4pm-10pm, F-Sa noon-11pm, Su noon-9pm.

SOUP KITCHEN $
31-33 Spear St.   ☎0161-236-5100 www.soup-kitchen.co.uk
You might think that the endorsement of a soup kitchen means Let's Go has sunk to a new low in searching for a cheap meal. Yet, instead, we were chasing a new high in the soup-and-sandwich business—a worthy lunch combo if there ever was one. Past the lunch table-style dining, populated with a mostly bearded clientele enjoying soft rock, you'll find a large blackboard advertising the available fare along with the odd curry or wrap. Fresh ingredients make for a tasty lunch, sweet pastries for a great dessert, and the fully-functioning bar for a good time. Soup Kitchen stays open late and offers live shows and DJs on the reg, which you can check out on their website or at the table of posters on site. Just remember: this isn't actually a soup kitchen, and you will have to pay for your food (preferably cash, as there's a 50p charge for paying by card).

i Open M-Sa noon-9pm, Su noon-7pm.

NIGHTLIFE

▨ NIGHT AND DAY CAFÉ $

26 Oldham St.   ☎0161-236-1822 www.nightnday.org

Not many pubs get their own Wikipedia page, but since Night and Day Café has been hosting live music acts long before the Northern Quarter filled up with trendy bars, they earned that honor. They've also had the honor of hosting past performances from Jessie J, Snow Patrol, and Arctic Monkeys, making it an integral part of the city's live music scene. You can check out upcoming shows by looking on the website; generally, you'll have to get tickets in advance to get inside, but you're almost guaranteed to see a stellar live performance if you do.

i Cocktails £7; shots £3; beer £4-5. Open Tu-Su 11am-2am, M closed.

THE COMEDY STORE $

Arches 3-4, Deansgate Locks   ☎0161-839-9595 www.thecomedystore.co.uk/manchester

They say that British humor is something that Americans just can't get. Whether they're referring to the dry, somewhat depressing jokes, or the varied and sometimes unintelligible accents, we're just not sure. However, now is your chance to decide for yourself. The Comedy Store Manchester is a branch of a comedy club of the same name in London, offering up class acts Thursday and Friday in an attempt to tickle your funny bone the right way. Tickets generally run in the £15-20 range, with options that include dining or your own personal pizza, but come Sunday the club offers discounted tickets for about £2. The catch is that the comedians are trying out their new stuff, which means you'll either be laughing at some great new material or laughing at how awkward the silence is.

i Open M-W 11am-6pm, Th 11am-midnight, F-Sa 11am-2am, Su 10am-midnight.

THE LIARS CLUB $

19A Back Bridge St.   ☎0161-834-5111 www.theliarsclub.co.uk

Perhaps the name is some muddled reference to pirates and their deceitful lives in the Caribbean, because once you descend the steps into this little cocktail bar, you'll find yourself in a full-on tiki hideaway—the tables are barrels, the ceiling is covered in beach movie posters, and drinks are served in treasure chests. The cool reggae music and fancy-themed cocktails reveal a great place to enjoy a drink with friends, but if you want to go full pirate, you can buy an entire bottle of rum and get free mixers to go with it. (You don't have to drink it all in one night though, as they'll store it behind the counter for a return visit. Or do drink it all in one go, Blackbeard.)

i Cocktails £7-9; shots £3.50. Open M-Sa 5pm-4am, Su until 3am.

ESSENTIALS

Practicalities

- **TOURIST OFFICES:** Manchester Visitor Information Center. (1 Piccadilly Gardens. ☎0871-222-8223. Open M-Sa 9:30am-5pm, Su 10:30am-4:30pm.)

- **ATMS:** Not that hard to come by in Manchester; there are a few right outside Piccadilly gardens, just outside the Northern Quarter and not far from the tram system and train station.

- **POST OFFICE:** For all those postcards. (26 Spring Gardens. ☎0845-722-3344. Open M-F 9am-6pm, Sa 9am-5:30pm, Sun closed.)

Emergency

- **EMERGENCY:** ☎999 (UK/Ireland) or ☎112 (Europe-wide)

- **PHARMACY:** Boots. (11-13 Piccadilly Gardens. ☎0161-834-8244. Open M-F 7:30am-8pm, Sa 9am-6:30pm, Su 11:30am-5:30pm.)

manchester

• **HOSPITAL:** Manchester Royal Infirmary. (Oxford Road. ☎0161-276-1234.)

Getting There

From Manchester Airport, you can catch the TransPennine Express into Manchester Piccadilly. From there, you can grab a tram, bus, or taxi to wherever you need to go.

Getting Around

Manchester has two main intra-city transport systems: the tram and the bus. The tram has nine different routes which can take you all the way to Manchester Airport if you need, but you'll probably stick to the city zone, which will run you about £1.20. Alternatively, you could utilize the Metroshuttle which operates between all the main rail stations and central areas in town for free. That's right, for free! Look for the buses/bus stops that are green, purple, and orange or the routes that say Metroshuttle 1, 2, or 3. A map of the routes can be found at www.tfgm.com/buses/Pages/metroshuttle.aspx. Also of note is that there is WiFi on the buses, so you can always just jump and ride around for a bit while you check Facebook.

liverpool

Liverpool may never again be as cool as it was in the early sixties, when Lilipudlian bands topped the charts worldwide (despite names like "The Swinging Blue Jeans."). But let's face it—most cities never attain that level of coolness anyway, and the city on the Mersey still has plenty to recommend it. From the staggering museums in the Cultural Quarter to the beautiful canals of Albert Dock, Liverpool is a city filled with vibrant attractions, most of which emphasize the city's varied history. As a major port, it imported items from all over the world; as a major pop music producer, it started exporting hits.

Whether you're having a pint at one of the city's many craft beer bars or sampling some great grub in the small but electrifying Chinatown, you'll soon discover that there's much more to this place than the Beatles—though if that's all you're interested in, you won't lack for places to visit.

SIGHTS

THE BEATLES STORY

Britannia Vaults, Albert Dock ☎0151-709-1963 www.beatlesstory.com

You might have heard of a little band that got their start in Liverpool a few years back, called the Beatles. If not, this museum/shrine will set you straight. A walkthrough will take you all the way back to when the Beatles first met in their teenage years, and will let you live it all again via the various recreations of places the band played, worked, and spent time together. Some of the exhibits make perfect sense, like the Abbey Road Studio and the Yellow Submarine, but others, like Matthews St., not so much (you can literally walk down the same street today and see it hasn't changed too much). But hey, this is the Beatles story, so you just gotta include it. It's a cool and in-depth experience of the Beatles musical career; the exhibits are entertaining to peruse, while the audio guide provides a lot of information about the band, so you can finally learn about their tours in Germany and why George Best got the boot in the end.

i £14.95, students £11.50. Open M-Su 9am-6pm.

liverpool

EURO HOSTEL LIVERPOOL $

54 Stanley St. ☎0845-490-0971 www.eurohostels.co.uk/liverpool

Formerly known as Hoax (and still showing up that way on a lot of maps), Euro Hostel Liverpool is the newest in the chain of Euro Hostels and probably the best yet. The location straddles the bar scene on Matthews St. and the shopping center of Liverpool One, which puts you in prime location for sightseeing and bar-hopping. But you might not want to leave with the downstairs bar and restaurant, clean en-suite bathrooms, and a comfy bed that gets made every day while you're out, just like Ma used to do. Since the hostel is part of a chain, most things not immediately present in the room will cost extra (including WiFi), but what is available is more than enough on which to get by.

i Dorms from £14 per night; private rooms from £40.

HATTERS HOSTEL $

56-60 Mount Pleasant St. ☎0151-709-5570 www.hattershostels.com/liverpool-mount-pleasant

If you're disappointed upon entering Hatters Hostel about not being greeted by a character from Alice in Wonderland (we know we were), maybe some of the hostel's amenities will make you feel better—free breakfast and occasionally free dinner, free tea and coffee at all hours of the day, movie nights, pub crawls, and en-suite bathrooms. If that doesn't make up for the lack of hats we don't know what will. A short walk from Lime Street Station, the hostel has a bar on the first floor that serves more than just communal wine. Rooms tend to run on the "cozy" side (read: small) but there's enough room in the downstairs chill-out lounge or upstairs bar to make up for it.

i Dorms from £12; private rooms from £40.

MARITIME MUSEUM

Merseyside Maritime Museum, Albert Dock ☎0151-478-4499
www.liverpoolmuseums.org.uk/maritime

Liverpool was, and is, first and foremost a port city. In case you hadn't noticed, all the museums you've been wandering through are located on the docks. One of those museums happens to be the Maritime Museum, the sole focus of which seems to be reminding you "ships are our jam." The exhibits here examine that from every perspective and probe every glorious maritime era that can be crammed into the four-story building.

Downstairs you'll find a re-creation of a ship from the 19th century and an exhibit on smuggling, or "how'd that monkey get in my suitcase?" The museum is also home to the sobering International Slavery Museum, which looks at how Liverpool's history as a port city also made it a key player in the slave trade. This includes exhibits on early slavery and how it remains a problem even to this day. The museum is located on Albert Dock, next to the Tate Modern Art Museum and on the opposite side of the Beatles Story. And if you just can't get enough ships even after all that, the Mersey Ferries are a four-minute walk away on Pier's Head.

i Free. Open M-Su 10am-5pm.

FOOD

🐒 MOWGLI $

69 Bold St.   ☎0151-708-9356 www.mowglistreetfood.com

What was it that drew us to Mowgli? The delicious smells wafting out the door? The promise of a lassi shake with our meal? A deep-seated childhood fascination with The Jungle Book and the picture of a Monkey outside? Whatever it was, it lured us from the cold streets into its embrace of fresh Indian food in a cozy atmosphere. The restaurant offers up "tiffin," a light- style meal in India, and basically translates to Indian tapas. Portions tend to be small, but if you've been playing your cards right (i.e. gorging on toast at the hostel breakfast in the morning), you can easily fill up with one or two dishes and a side of carbs, like Puri, Roti, or Rice. Also notable is Mowgli's special-diet menus, which offer up either gluten-free or vegan options in similar number to their regular menu. Wash it all down with a lassi and call it a day before hitting up the bars and clubs on Fleet and Seel Sts.

i Dishes £4-8. Open M-W and Su noon-9:30pm, Th-Sa noon-10pm.

ZIFERBLAT $

Unit 7, The Colonnades, Albert Dock   ☎0151-709-0771 www.ziferblat.co.uk/albert-dock.html

If you're the kind of person who can only work effectively under a time crunch, you have to check out Ziferblat. The term café applies loosely here; the cavernous room seems to be an extension of someone's grandmother's house, as comfy couches, plush armchairs, and throw blankets abound. The kitchen is self-service and has everything you need to make tea, coffee, toast, or hot chocolate, as well as serving a selection of cakes, biscuits, and soup. And it's all free. Whaaaaaat? Yup. But like much of life there is a catch. Every minute you spend in Ziferblat will cost you 8p. Time is money here, so if you're so inclined you can check in, stuff your face with breakfast and tea foods, and get out for a pound (12.5 minutes for the mathematically challenged among us). But if you're looking to chill out for a bit, you can make yourself a tea or peppermint hot chocolate (yum), grab a board game or hop on the WiFi and just take a moment.

i 8p per minute. Open M-Su 10am-7pm.

AMERICAN PIZZA SLICE $

52 Whitechapel   ☎0151-707-1333 www.americanpizzaslice.co.uk

If you're a solo traveller, you will inevitably face the struggle of wanting pizza really badly but not needing a whole pie for yourself. We feel your pain. We suggest you hit up American Pizza Slice, which will make all your cheese- and dough-infused dreams come true. For under £3, you can pick up a slice from the tiny pizzeria, and for £2 more throw in some garlic bread and a bottle of soda (because bottle soda is the best soda). But if you do decide that you want the whole pie for yourself (you go girl!), try their 8-slice special, which is just a collection of whatever 8-slices you want in an 18" pizza. Let the inviting glow from their pizza display draw you in and chow down on some serious dough at their outdoor tables, while you jam out to the pop music playing at the convenience store next door.

i £2-2.20 per slice; £8-12 for small pie; £14-17 for big pie. Open M-Su 11am-11:30pm.

NIGHTLIFE

🐒 MOTEL $

5-7 Fleet St.   fleetstreetmotel@gmail.com / www.motelbarliverpool.com

Motel gets the Let's Go award for 'Bar that Doesn't Care What You Think'. A neon sign outside introduces you to the Motel. The door itself advertises cocktails and fried chicken, complete with a sign confirming, "no, not that kind of motel."

top places to be a beatles groupie

1. PENNY LANE: Apparently the street sign here has been stolen so many times that the city eventually decided to just paint it on the wall because it was too expensive to keep replacing it. You can't steal it anymore (would you even manage to get it through airport security?), but you can join the legions of other visitors and just graffiti it instead.

2. STRAWBERRY FIELD Childhood hangout of singer/songwriter John Lennon. Also happens to be the name of a somewhat famous song. Snag that selfie at the red gates outside. Are they real?

3. CAVERN CLUB: Big name in the Beatles history, and cavern club knows it. As the venue where the Beatles used to frequently play, this club sits below the bustling nightlife-centric Matthews St. and still gets many live performances each week.

4. JACARANDA: The first venue the Beatles managed to gig at, and also recently reopened to house future musical talent in the basement bar/club.

5. ST. PETER'S CHURCH: Picture a young Paul McCartney rolling up to hear local band The Quarrymen, lead singer John Lennon, about 60 years ago. If you can't be bothered, then try your best to find Eleanor Rigby's grave in the graveyard out back.

Plow through meat locker curtains into a room that's not quite sure what it wants to be, so it decided to be everything. The interior is rustic, with brick walls and long wooden tables pushed against the wall like something's goin' down. Neon signs, pinball machines, everything seems to be glowing in this place. Sounds like a relaxing place for a drink, except punk-pop music on lock from the DJ, the smoke machines and flashing strobe lights. Is there dancing? Maybe. Are people just drinking? Probably. Does what's happening make sense? Not really, but that's kind of the point—Motel mixes whatever parts of a club and pub it feels like.

i Pints £3-5; cocktails £7 (£5 before 10 on weekdays). Open M-Th 5pm-1am, F 5pm-3am, Sa-Su noon-3am.

SHIPPING FORECAST $

15 Slater St.   ☎0151-709-6901 www.theshippingforecastliverpool.com

Weekend nightlife in Liverpool seems to fall into a few different categories, including: karaoke pubs filled with 40-year-olds singing Shania Twain; hectic clubs packed with stag-and-hen parties twerking on the dance floors; and places that are empty but still play loud music with daring hope. The Shipping Forecast falls into none of these categories, which makes it a breath of fresh air in the area. The music is loud, but not too loud; there's ample seating to grab a drink with some friends; and the multi-level setup prevents any twerking from taking place, but does allow for lots of nooks and crannies to hunker down with a brew. The beer selection leans more towards craft brews, but there's also a selection of mean cocktails to go with it and a rotating selection of ales if you're looking to try something new. The downstairs basement also hosts different music performances (check their Facebook page), along with other food and drink deals.

i Pints £3-6; cocktails £5-7. Open Su-Th noon-midnight, F-Sa noon-3am.

CAMP AND FURNACE $

67 Greenland St.   ☎0151-708-2890 www.campandfurnace.com

Is Camp and Furnace a bar, a restaurant, or a music venue? The answer is yes (yes and yes), which means you can expect pretty much anything to be on offer here. Access to their front room, the lobby, is available every day and offers a lumber-sexual space complete with logs stacked behind the bar and a fireside set of couches on which to enjoy a brew and a bite to eat. But if you want the full experience, try to make it one of their weekly events that take place in the massive warehouse space behind the lobby. Friday is Food Slam, which is basically a food market with different stalls selling food and cocktails to a club soundtrack—unusual mix, but a great excuse to try that, and that, oh, that looks good! Or you could try some serious steaks at their meat market on Saturdays; try the Sunday roast, or get tickets to their Thursday Night Bingo which is way too popular to be as lame as it sounds.

i Pints £3-5; cocktails £6-7; food £4-12. Open M-Sa 10am-late, Su 10am-6pm.

ESSENTIALS
Practicalities

- **TOURIST OFFICE:** Albert Dock Visitor Centre. (Anchor Courtyard, Albert Dock, near the Beatles Story. ☎0151-223-2008. Open M-Su 10am-5:30pm.)

- **ATMS:** ATMs are clustered in Liverpool One, the big shopping area that goes from Liverpool Lime Street Station to Albert Docks. There is also an ATM right outside the Beatles Story at the docks.

- **POST OFFICE:** In case you need snail mail. (1-3 South Johnson St. ☎0151-707-6606. Open M-Sa 9am-5:30pm, Su 11am-3pm.)

Emergency

- **EMERGENCY:** ☎999 (UK/Ireland) or ☎112 (Europe-wide)

- **PHARMACY:** Boots. (9-11 Church St. ☎0151-709-3149. Open M-Fr 8:30am-8pm, Sa 8:30am-7pm, Su 11am-5pm.)

- **HOSPITAL:** The Royal Liverpool University Hospital. (Prescot St. ☎0151-706-5806.)

Getting There & Getting Around

The main train station in Liverpool is Liverpool Lime Street, and it's only a short walk away from the docks, Liverpool One, and the central city sights. The airport for Liverpool is the John Lennon Airport—the 500 bus will take you from the airport to Liverpool One. The bus is the best way to get around Liverpool (after your own two feet, of course) and the central bus station is located at the end of Liverpool One right before the docks, at the end of Hanover St. Bus fares vary depending on how far you want to go, but generally range between £2-4 for central bus travel.

glasgow

Glasgow is renowned for many things: it is Scotland's biggest city, a UNESCO city of music, the 1990 European Capital of Culture, and home to probably the most intense local football rivalry in the UK (only here would sports be so political). The city has historically been riding a 'proverbial' roller coaster, from her days as the second city of the empire to her role in bearing the brunt of the 1920s economic depression.

Nowadays, Glasgow is known as a cultural hub, hosting a plethora of live music venues, museums and historical buildings, a famously large shopping center, and one of the most distinctive accents of the UK. But if culture isn't your thing (what are you doing in Europe?), Glasgow also has some pretty great restaurants and bars hidden in the winding streets and sloping hills, perfect for spending rainy afternoons. Whether you're checking out the trendy cafes along the West End or ducking into stylish pubs in Merchant City, you're sure to find a gem hidden in the rough that suits you just fine.

SIGHTS

KELVINGROVE ART GALLERY AND MUSEUM

Argyle St.   ☎0141-276-9599 www.glasgowmuseums.com

Glasgow has a host of different museums that cater to all kinds of tastes—the Gallery of Modern Art, the Riverside Museum, the Burrell Collection, among others. But if you're the kind of person who struggles with the existential crisis of soup or salad for a lunch side, you'll want to go to Kelvingrove, which has one of the most eclectic collections you'll find in Scotland.

The building itself is gorgeous enough, with high ceilings, rising columns, and chandeliers giving the place a Night at the Museum-feel. Add in everything from a Spitfire airplane to a life-size stuffed giraffe, and you'll get a sense of the mismatched displays that await you inside (and that's just the first room). The museum has a staggering collection of art, taxidermy, and historical artifacts spanning the globe from Egypt to France to the Netherlands; and yes, and healthy focus on Glaswegian and Scottish history and art. Exhibits don't always flow smoothly from one to the other (ah yes, I immediately associate the

get a room!

SYHA GLASGOW YOUTH HOSTEL $

8 Park Terrace   ☎0141-332-3004 www.syha.org.uk

The SYHA used to function as an old-timey hotel, and it shows. The grand wooden staircase leads up through three floors of generic wallpaper and hotel-style rooms that have traded in their king and queen beds for bunks. As a guest, this can mean some great things—all rooms are en-suite, meals can be purchased on site, and the average bed count in each room is six, so you don't have to be cramped in a room with 20 other sweaty bodies. SYHA also offers up a TV room, a games room, and a lounge room for relaxing, as well as a conference room for when you need to have that heart-to-heart with your snoring roommate. Its location makes it ideal for exploring the University of Glasgow and the West End, but it can be a bit of a hike from the central shopping area of Glasgow and a few of the museums and other top sights.

i Dorms from £20; private rooms from £50.

EURO HOSTEL $

318 Clyde St.   ☎0845-539-9956 www.eurohostels.co.uk/glasgow

Euro Hostel has the market cornered on location, as it's across from the River Clyde, about two minutes from Central Station, and situated smack-dab in the bustling center of Glasgow's shopping district. For those looking to cut expenses in the accommodation and travel department, this is probably your best bet, but the cost of those cheap prices and central location is a lack of hostelling experience. In some ways, Euro Hostel is more like a low-budget hotel that has decided to turn some of the rooms into dorms; you really can't expect too much outside of a bed, toilet, shower, and locker. It's perfect for the traveller spending a few days in Glasgow and looking to see as much as possible, but if you want to stay for longer in a more comfortable room, check out SYHA in the West End.

i Dorms from £10, private rooms from £30.

the duke of wellington

Erected in 1844, the Duke of Wellington statue in Glasgow was created by Italian artist Carlo Marochetti to honor Arthur Wellesley, the first Duke of Wellington and blah blah blah—honestly, what you'll really notice about this statue is the traffic cone on its head. At first glance, you'll probably think it's just the result of mixing a drunken stag party and a traffic diversion. Although that might be true, there's more history to it than that. People have been putting traffic cones on the Duke's head since the '80s for reasons that still aren't clear to anyone at all, especially the Duke. The tradition has become so ingrained in Glasgow culture that a plan in the early 2010s to raise the height of the statue so the Duke could no longer be crowned in orange was canned after even the suggestion provoked strong public backlash. Although you may not understand it, you gotta appreciate a city that takes its history with a dash of humor.

Holocaust with ancient armor), but the whole experience will be interesting and disorienting enough that you might not even notice the organ recital happening above your head. (Hint: on Sundays there are organ recitals.)

i Free. Open M-Th and Sa 10am-5pm, F and Su 11am-5pm.

WELLPARK BREWERY TOUR

161 Duke St.   ☎0141-202-7145 www.tennentstours.com

Walking up to Wellpark Brewery is a bit like taking a glimpse into some sort of Willy Wonka Beer Factory—the walls leading up to it are graffitied with slogans and advertisements for the beer. Beyond that brick wall barrier, you can see the golden towers that are responsible for producing millions of gallons of amber liquid each day. From there, the comparison just about ends. But even if you don't get to drink from a river of beer or watch that one snarky girl on the tour get transformed into a pint glass doesn't mean you won't enjoy the tour.

Where Guinness has created a museum that gives you a look back through their history and a feast for the eyes, Tennent's provides an educational experience into running a brewery. After donning the required safety gear (pro tip: bring a hat, unless you want to buy a cap or really like hairnets for some reason), you'll be led through the grounds to the site where they make the good stuff, past the bottling and canning location, and finally, back to the visitor center for a tasting. Along the way, you'll learn about how Tennent's is made, what hops actually look like, and how nobody in the 1970s gave a damn and everyone was drunk on the job. Of course, the highlight is probably at the end, when you get a pint of one of Tennent's brews from the bar. Taste some of the rarer strains of beer they create while checking out the different types of cans that have existed over the years.

i £7.50, students £5. Open M-Sa 9am-6pm, Su 10am-6pm.

FOOD

▨ POMMES FRITES $

476 Sauchiehall St.   ☎0141-332-0860 www.pommesfritesuk.com

If you're the kind of person who loves to order humongous amounts of fries but hates the shame associated with that sort of diet, 1. We feel your struggle and 2. We've found a solution. Pommes Frites is a Belgian-inspired food stop on Sauchiehall Street that offers up fries, fries, and more fries. That might sound pretty simple, but add in their huge selection of seasonings and sauces to your salty snack and the combinations are almost limitless. If you're looking for something a little more filling than just potatoes, they also offer hot dogs and Belgian waffles (but if you don't get fries with that, then what are you doing here?). Its location and late-night hours make it a perfect drunk food stop when you're stumbling back from a pub in the wee hours of the morn, and for that, we thank the French fry gods and the powers that be.

i Open M-Sa noon-4am, Su 1pm-4am.

MONO'S $

12 Kings Ct.   ☎0141-553-2400 www.monocafebar.com

There's really no shortage of hipster joints in Scotland that try to appeal to your inner indie-cravin' and animal-lovin' soul, and Mono just might take the cake. First, the surrounding neighborhood is mostly art galleries or vintage second-hand stores...you know, to get you in the mood. Second, the café/bar venue also doubles as a record store and music venue. Yup, once you make it past the skylight dome ceiling and big stage, you'll see the CD/record shop at the back of the room, decked out in string lights and full of trendy locals. And third, all the food is vegetarian or vegan. From the vegan sausage pizza to the raw ice cream scoops, you won't find any of your favorite woodland critters on the menu, a refreshing contrast to the constant overload of pub food and burger joints in town, and one that yields delicious results. Whether hipsterdom is your religion or you're more basic than an IKEA futon, Mono's aims to please.

i Sandwiches £6, mains £8-9, sides £3-4. Open Su-Th 11am-11pm, F-Sa 11am-1pm.

MUNRO'S $

185 Great Western Rd.   ☎0141-332-0972 www.munrosglasgow.co.uk

Visiting pubs outside normal drinking hours is generally frowned upon, but in a country where you'll find people regularly drinking before 1pm, it's totally acceptable. If you're looking for a local vibe and want to get a pint before you've had your côffee, Munro's is a pretty good place to do it. The decor is slightly chic (compared to most pubs anyway) and the menu offers a good mix of classic pub grub with more unusual offerings like falafel and sweet potatoes with naan. Come earlier in the day and you'll be dining with a mostly older crew of gentlemen who relax at the large round bar tables watching whatever sports happen to be on. So take a page from their book, order yourself a pint and whatever looks good, and cheer and boo at the TV while your scarf down your meal.

i Pizza and dogs £7-8; burgers £8-10. Open M-F noon-midnight, Sa-Su 11am-midnight.

NIGHTLIFE

⌧ BAR HOME $

80 Albion St.   ☎0141-552-1734 www.homeglasgow.co

Bar Home really does have a homey feel, if your idea of home is a 45ft. high room that has a bar, a balcony, and a large selection of cocktails. Not exactly the home we grew up in either, but we just might trade up for this bar. And despite the large space, Bar Home does have a laid-back atmosphere, emphasized by lush leather couches, wraparound cushioned booths, and liberal use of blinking string lights. On weekdays you can cozy up to one of their special discount cocktails (only £3.25) or if you're feeling bold try to make it through their "7 Deadly Gins" (we recommend doing them over several nights). Make yourself at home while you while away a few hours here sipping cocktails and watching sports projected onto the wall—just not too at home, because the other patrons might not find your pajama pants and slippers as enjoyable as you do.

i Cocktails £6-8; beers £3-5. Open M-Su noon-midnight.

HILLHEAD BOOKCLUB $

17 Vinicombe St.   ☎0141-576-1700 www.hillheadbookclub.co.uk

There's a lot you might immediately notice when walking into Hillhead Bookclub. "Look at the ceiling, it's so ornate!"; "Check out the booths and armchairs, they look super comfy"; "Yeah, but what about the ping pong and foosball tables?"; "Dude, that moose's head is glowing!" But the funky-funk atmosphere doesn't stop there, my friends. This low-lit late-night lair has enough trendy vintage décor spread over its two levels to make Zooey Deschanel weep with joy. Where else can you sip cocktails while learning to cross-stitch, or get a bowl of punch served in a gramophone? Maybe it's a bit too much, but since their cocktails run less than £6, we really aren't complaining.

i Cocktails £3-6; beer £3-5. Open M-F 11am-midnight, Sa-Su 10am-midnight.

FLAT 0/1 $

162 Bath St.   ☎0141-331-6227 www.flat01.co.uk

When was the last time you went to a house party? If the answer falls in the "too long ago" category, take yourself over to Flat 0/1. Nestled in among the other clubs and pubs on Bath St., Flat 0/1 does the opposite of stand out, as the only sign outside that even advertises its existence says "for rent." But inside, it's not your average low-lit base-bumping bar. The room is designed like, well, a flat —a kitchen-style bar lines one wall while TVs showing psychedelic cartoons, hanging chairs made from bathtubs, and plain-old couches take up the back of the bar. Early weekday nights might find you lacking in company, but weekends see the place fill up, and if there's a special performance or guest DJ on prepare for some crowded party-rocking to be happening. The friendly bar staff offer up a cheap selection of beers and spirits to get the night going, and you don't have to worry about the police shutting the place down—all the neighbors are too busy throwing their own parties.

i Beer £2-5; liquor £2-3, prices go up on the weekend. Open Tu 9pm-3am, W-Th 8pm-3am, F-Sa 6pm-3am, Su-M closed.

ESSENTIALS

Practicalities

- **TOURIST OFFICE:** Basement of the Gallery of Modern Art. (Royal Exchange Square. Open M-W and Sa 10am-4:45pm, Th 10am-7:45pm, F and Su 11am-4:45pm.)

- **ATMS:** The main roads of the city center serve as a huge shopping district, which means there are ATMs left and right. Just make sure you check before slotting in your card as some charge for transactions.

- **POST OFFICE:** 59 Glassford St. (Open M-Sa 8:30am-5:30pm, Sunday closed.)

Emergency

- **EMERGENCY:** ☎999 (UK/Ireland) or ☎112 (Europe-wide)

- **PHARMACY:** Superdrug. (66 Argyle St. ☎0141-221-9644. Open M-W and F 8am-7pm, Th 8am-8pm, Sa 8am-6:30pm, Su 9:30am-6pm.) Also available is Lloyd's Pharmacy. (147 Great Western Rd. ☎0141-332-1478. Open M-F 9am-6pm, Sa 9am-5pm, Su closed.)

- **HOSPITAL:** Glasgow Royal Infirmary. (84 Castle St. ☎0141-211-4000.)

Getting There

Route 500 goes direct from Glasgow Airport to the city center for £7. There are two main train stations in Glasgow city center, Central Station and Queens Street, that both serve to greater Scotland and the UK.

Getting Around

Glasgow has an extensive bus service that runs by zones, and most popular locations are served by the first zone which means tickets will run you about £1.40. The routes are pretty complicated but can be studied at www.firstgroup.com/greater-glasgow. You could also try Glasgow's underground subway, which is probably one of the world's smallest and easiest to understand. It runs in a six mile loop through central Glasgow, down to the south and out to the University of Glasgow in the west starting at £1.40. You never have to worry about missing your stop because it'll just circle back around eventually. Alternatively, you could try the "subcrawl" which entails buying a day pass for the metro and getting out at every stop to have a pint (15 pints in total). Not for the weak hearted, but a great way to see the city (even if you don't remember it).

edinburgh

Edinburgh is many things—a well-preserved medieval city, a college town, a cultural center—but it doesn't feel defined by any of those narrow labels. It feels more like something out of a fairy tale—some mystical place where all the homes are townhouses, all the streets are cobblestoned, and vast cliffs and forests jut into the city center. Indeed, to go for a walk in Edinburgh—whether it's through the stunning

get a room!

CALEDONIAN BACKPACKERS $

3 Queensferry St.   ☎131 226 2939 www.caledonianbackpackers.com

Caledonian Backpackers is a bit removed from Edinburgh's Old Town, where it can seem like there's a hostel on every corner. But that doesn't mean you're far from where the action is. Princes Street Gardens, Stockbridge, and the old town itself are all within walking distance. Breakfast is available until noon, which basically eliminates the need for lunch. There's a bar on the premises, and the amount of additional social space is overwhelming. Be sure to check out the Cucumber Room, which might be more accurately titled "The Big, Shoes-Optional Room with a Lot of Couches and a Guitar," as well as the Beanbag Cinema.

i Dorms from £13. Reception open 24hr.

BUDGET BACKPACKERS $

37-39 Cowgate   ☎131 226 6351 www.budgetbackpackers.com

Usually, great location comes with an obscene price tag. But that tried-and-true formula is turned on its head by Budget Backpackers, a hostel minutes away from Edinburgh Castle, the University of Edinburgh, and the Scotch Whisky Experience. You can easily book a bed for £9 a night (provided it's not during the Edinburgh Festival Fringe, where prices skyrocket around the city). "We beat the pants off everyone else for value," the hostel proudly proclaims.

i Dorms from £9 a night. Reception open 24hr.

valleys of Princes Street Park or the awe-inspiring peaks of Calton Hill—is to be astonished. The locals are blasé but prideful. "Everything here is old and magnificent," one says. "People will say 'oh, that's only 600 years old.'"

Your sense of amazement will likely continue whether you're quaffing a pint in an eccentric pub or visiting one of the city's many museums. There's a reason this is the UK's most popular tourist destination after London.

SIGHTS

THE SCOTCH WHISKEY EXPERIENCE

354 Castlehill   ☎131 220 0441 www.scotchwhiskyexperience.co.uk

Perhaps because it's not affiliated with a specific brand, the Scotch Whisky Experience doesn't beat you over the head the same way the Guinness Brewery and the Old Jameson Distillery do (both of those Dublin attractions, while certainly worth visiting, are not intended for those who want a fair and balanced appraisal of Guinness and/or Jameson). Make no mistake—these guys love everything about whisky—its history, its taste, and, most visibly, its color. The in-house restaurant is called "Amber," the staffers all wear amber ties, and there's even a light yellow glow in some rooms. But they also recognize that some people may not know very much about whisky, and that others might not even like it all that much. For that reason, the tour is a primarily educational experience, albeit one that will appeal to the novice and to the seasoned drinker who's looking to find out more.

You start by getting strapped into a barrel and undergoing a process designed to teach replicate the process of making whisky—it's kind of like a Disney ride combined with an unnatural fascination with alcohol. And while parts of this ride are cheesy, other segments are just plain nuts. Get excited for the yeast room.

The meat of the tour, however, is the whisky tasting. Unless you spring for a pricier ticket (the costliest option includes a three-course meal), you'll only be able to sample one of the four major types of Scotch whisky. This can be a fear-inducing choice, especially since the wrong whisky might well be nausea-inducing. Thankfully, the guides will provide you with a scratch and sniff card, allowing you some insight into the four major flavors. To top it all off, they've got the world's largest collection of Scotch whisky upstairs, seemingly rivaled only by the gift shop's selection.

i *Silver tour £13.50, £10.50 for students and seniors, £6.75 for children. Golden tour £23.50, £20 for students and seniors. Platinum tour £27. Open daily 10am-6pm.*

NATIONAL GALLERY OF SCOTLAND

The Mound   ☎131 624 6200 www.nationalgalleries.org

The Scottish National Galleries are beautiful. The buildings themselves are models of neoclassicism, all situated on pristine grounds, be it Princes Street Park or an old estate. And the art inside's pretty good too.

The flagship museum is the National Gallery of Scotland, located in the city center, close to Edinburgh Castle, the Scott Monument, and other frequent tourist destinations. Here, you'll see masterpieces by Rubens, Memling, Titian, and some Scottish artists who have been inexplicably confined to the basement. How's that for national pride?

Though the building is on the smaller side, don't be fooled when you think you've gone through the whole thing in an hour—certain galleries can only be reached through less-than-central passages. Although there's free Wi-Fi in the building, Google Maps can't help you find your way to the early Netherlandish painting room—you'll have to pick up one of the free maps to navigate the space.

edinburgh festivals

Edinburgh attracts artists all year round—the university and museums tend to do that—but what really brings creative types to Scotland's capital are the festivals.

The most famous, of course, is the Edinburgh Festival Fringe, an arts festival held at the end of July and beginning of August. It's the world's largest, and today regularly features over 2000 different performances. There's no selection process, so it's somewhat of a mixed bag—still, the diversity is totally unparalleled. Great for theater and comedy—Tom Stoppard's famous play *Rosencrantz and Guildenstern are Dead* premiered at the Fringe in 1966, and Steve Coogan, Flight of the Conchords, and Demetri Martin have all performed here.

Lesser-known but up-and-coming is the Edinburgh International Film Festival, which occurs at the end of every June. It lacks the red carpet glamour of Cannes and the indie chic of Sundance, but it does have an impressive stock of independent films from around the world, many of which you'll likely have trouble finding again. Be sure to check out a screener or three—when the director makes it big, you'll be able to tell your friends you got in on the ground floor.

Most of the films are followed by question-and-answer sessions, which feature not only obscure directors but TV stars like Parks and Recreation's Aubrey Plaza. What's not to like?

If one of the works appeals to you (you'll probably find at least one that really catches your eye), the downstairs gift shop has a truly massive selection of postcards and prints to choose from. It's a cheap, easy-to-transport souvenir (if you get the postcard—prints can get a fair bit pricier).

i Free. Open M-W, F-Su 10am-5pm. Th 10am-7pm.

SURGEON'S HALL MUSEUM

Nicolson St.   ☎131 527 1711 www.museum.rcsed.ac.uk

No one wants to visit a hospital while they're on vacation, but there's nothing wrong with checking out a museum of medical history and curiosities. That's just what you'll get at Edinburgh's Surgeon's Hall, which houses the Royal College of Surgeons of Edinburgh as well as a museum that dates back to 1699.

The collections range from the grisly (check out the Greig Collection of deformed skeletons) to the historic (they've got an original Squire inhaler, which was used to knock patients out with ether in the early days of anesthesia). You'll see plenty of organs and the like in jars (aortas, lymph vessels, and cranial nerves all pop up). Again, the emphasis is on the unusual—one heart has a massive hole caused by a bullet that went straight through it. Cue "You Give Love a Bad Name" by Bon Jovi. The strangest exhibit might well be the Dental History Collection, which traces dentistry back to ancient times. If you think getting your wisdom teeth out stinks, wait 'til you see what they did for toothaches in the Middle Ages.

If all this medical history inspires you, the museum has an interactive exhibit where you get to take on the task of keyhole surgery. After trying your hand at that, marvelous at the bizarre case of Robert Penma, who grew a 72 ounce tumor in his mouth that had to be removed without anesthetic. Really puts your appendix operation into perspective.

i Closed until Summer 2015.

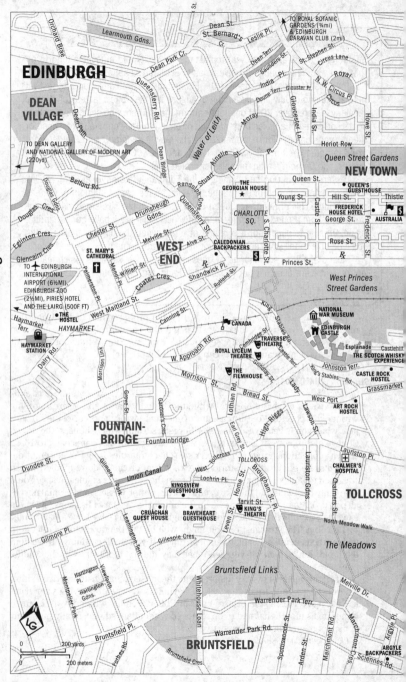

EDINBURGH

DEAN VILLAGE

NEW TOWN

WEST END

HAYMARKET

FOUNTAIN-BRIDGE

TOLLCROSS

BRUNTSFIELD

The Meadows

Bruntsfield Links

West Princes Street Gardens

Queen Street Gardens

great britain

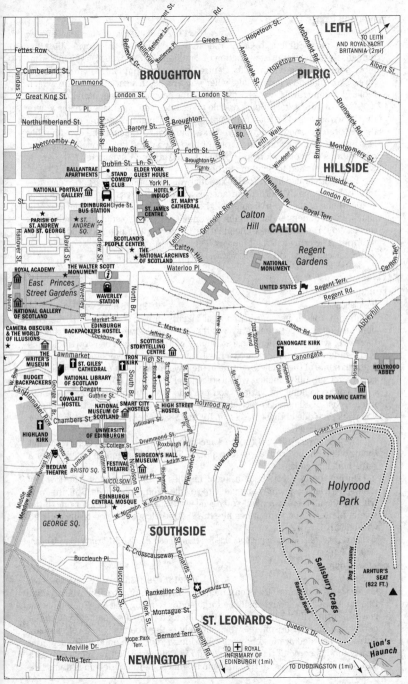

EDINBURGH CASTLE

Castlehill   ☎131 225 9846   www.edinburghcastle.gov.uk

You can't miss Edinburgh Castle. Located at the end of the Royal Mile, this immensely popular tourist attraction (1.2 million visitors in 2011) is visible from most points in Edinburgh's City Centre, especially from Old Town or Princes Street. You may do a double take when you first catch sight of the castle, which looks like some rural fortress dropped into the heart of cosmopolitan Edinburgh.

And you might keep doing double takes once you get inside. This is where the Crown Jewels of Scotland are kept, and as you might expect of crown jewels, they're pretty darned opulent. If you like your royal artifacts to be considerably less photogenic, check out the Stone of Destiny, a giant, gray stone used during coronations of Scottish kings. Though it kicked around England for 700 years, it was finally returned to Scotland in 1996.

The Castle's also home to the National War Museum, and for good reason—this site has arguably more importance as a military fortress than as a residential castle. Being at the top of a steep hill helps a lot. Though the National War Museum places understandable emphasis on history, it's also startlingly modern at times—you'll see things like chemical warfare suits right alongside 18th century uniforms. The army had a lot more style back then.

i £16, students and seniors £12.80, children £9.60. Open daily 9:30am-6pm.

FOOD

TANJORE $

6-8 Clerk St.   ☎131 478 6518   www.tanjore.co.uk

Edinburgh, for all its charms, can get slightly dreary sometimes. If the gray buildings, gray streets, and gray weather gets you down (an unholy trinity if there ever was one), a spicy meal at Tanjore will get you right back on track. This South Indian restaurant, located a few blocks past the University of Edinburgh, features some of the liveliest cuisine in the city. Go nuts with one of their famous curries, all helpfully labelled with a spice level. Be daring.

If you're looking for variety, you can't do much better than thali, a South Indian feast of 10 courses served on a giant metal platter. During the weekday, you pack pick one of these babies up for just £8 at lunch; you'll be set for dinner with this amazing deal.

The restaurant's BYOB (no corkage charge, so go crazy on that front) but their non-alcoholic drink menu's no slouch. Try their homemade lime soda or a refreshing mango lassis.

During the day, you'll see a lot of families or older couples. The low-key atmosphere isn't especially amenable to rowdier, younger crowds. Still, the food will provide all the excitement you need—especially if you spring for one of the spicier platters. And with prices like the £8-for-thali special, you really can't go wrong with Tanjore.

i Starters about £3, Mains from £7-10. Open weekdays noon-2:30pm, 5-10pm. Weekends noon-3:30pm, 5-10pm.

ROAMIN' NOSE $$

14 Eyre Place   ☎131 629 3135   www.theroaminnose.com

Given the weird name, the small menu, and the paintings of Bill Murray that fill up the wall, you could easily be forgiven for thinking that the Roamin' Nose is a joint primarily for hipsters, and that the food plays a secondary role to the cooler-than-thou atmosphere. Well, not only is the Roamin' Nose refreshingly devoid of bearded scenesters who will criticize your style and music taste, the hearty food is some of the best you'll find in Edinburgh. With a focus on pasta and other Italian dishes, the small menu is still chock-full of delicious items like spaghetti and clams. The specials list is nearly as long as the menu—go for the venison burger if it's available.

While you'll have to trust the staff when it comes to the menu—don't worry, it pays off—you'll have your pick of drinks. The selection of wines and beers is remarkably exhaustive, and they've got quite a few house cocktails as well. These are particularly worth taking note of, as they're seriously well-priced for Edinburgh. You can expect to pay as much as £10 for the drinks at hot bars around town. But you don't need to order a drink for the Roamin' Nose to be worth it (even if it's a seriously well-priced drink). Just sink your teeth into one of their delicious meals—after taking a whiff, of course.

i Starters £3-4, Mains £10-14. Open M 9:30am-5pm, Tu-F 9:30am-10pm, Sa 10am-10pm, Su 10am-5pm.

OINK $

34 Victoria St.   ☎777 196 8233 www.oinkhogroast.co.uk

There's absolutely no ambiguity about what OINK is selling. If the name didn't tip you off, the giant roasted hog in the window sure will. This tiny restaurant sure knows how to make a pulled pork sandwich. And with all prices under £5 (even for the largest roll), the price is right.

Even if you're not a vegetarian, OINK might be slightly off-putting. The smallest sandwich, after all, is named "piglet." Winnie the Pooh fans, visit at your peril. And the fact that you can get your sandwich with haggis may not be appealing to most. As a side note, this is a great opportunity to try the infamous haggis without committing to a full plate of the stuff.

But if you do go in and get a nice and toasty hog roll, your taste buds will be thanking you all the way home. The impressive speed of the servers belies the exceptional care put into these flavorful sandwiches. Try it with some apple relish to add sweetness.

Somewhat curiously for a sandwich joint, OINK sells souvenir postcards, and that's a testament to just how much of a local fixture it is. Located on Victoria Street, near Grassmarket, OINK is surrounded by tourist hotspots but maintains a staunchly local flavor. Maybe the pig in the window scares off outsiders.

i Sandwiches £1.80-4.50. Open daily 11am-5pm.

NIGHTLIFE

BREWDOG

143 Cowgate   ☎131 220 6517 www.brewdog.com/bars/edinburgh

There are a number of hostels up and down Cowgate, and consequently there are a lot of Cowgate Bars that cater to the international party going crowd. BrewDog Edinburgh is not one of those bars. The first thing you see is a giant sign that reads "NO LIVE SPORT, NO FOOTBALL, NO SHOTS, NO STELLA." Under that, in smaller font: "but we do have board games!"

That they do. If you want a good pub quiz but can't find one, why not come here and play a round of Trivial Pursuit? They've got tons of games, along with a remarkable selection of beers on draught and in bottles. With guest beers like Mikkeler Black (16.8% ABV), who needs shots? And with numerous booths and large tables, you'll actually be able to sit down and play some of these board games. If for some reason you're carrying around old boxes of Monopoly or Candyland, bring them here—you'll get a pint for every board game you turn in. Relatedly, there are more than a few thrift stores in the area, some of which stock board games. Use that as you will.

But despite the lack of shots and the older crowd that populates BrewDog during the day, the atmosphere gets admirably rowdy at night. Craft beer gets the crowd just as wild as normal brews do—and since their motto is Beer for Punks, they're not opposed to thinks getting a little loud.

i Pints are generally from £3-5, but specialty brews can cost as much as £8. The wide selection of bottles is also highly variable in terms of price. Nearby: Budget Backpackers, OINK. M-Sa noon-1am, Su 12:30-1am.

HOLYROOD 9A

9a Holyrood   ☎131 556 5044 www.theholyrood.co.uk

Holyrood 9a looks like a fairly traditional pub; wood paneled walls, amber-tinged lighting, old beer signs on the walls, all that jazz. Then you see the area behind the bar. This gleaming array of metal, glass, and mirrors looks like a space-ship has crash-landed in a typical Edinburgh pub, bringing with it a host of obscure spirits and over 20 varieties of beer.

From another planet or not, the variety of beers available at Holyrood 9a will certainly overwhelm you. They've even been known to commission special brews for special events; for their fifth birthday party, they served "Hollyrood" ale.

Moreover, the large space and big tables mean this is a social space, and not just a place for beer geeks to bug out over rare brews. It also means that if all your friends are beer geeks, you should grab a table as soon as you get to Edinburgh.

The food menu is no slouch either—the burgers are known as being some of the best of Edinburgh. Whether you stop by for an early afternoon drink or just want a few calories in your system before last call, ask to see the menu. You'll be pleasantly surprised.

Given the quality of the food and liquor, it's no surprise that Holyrood 9a gets pretty busy in the evening. You'll need to come early to snag a table, but if you get there during a busier hour, the attentive staff will make sure you're not without a drink for long. Best of all, finding the place couldn't be easier—the name is the address.

i Pints £3-£5. Open M-Th, Su 9am-midnight, F-Sa 9am-1am.

52 CANOES

13 Melville Place   ☎131 226 4732 www.facebook.com/52canoes

Edinburgh's drink of choice will always be scotch, but 52 Canoes is proof that the city can branch out in a big way. This tiki bar boasts many varieties of rum, available to sample by themselves or in one of the many fruity cocktails on the menu (52 in total). Edinburgh's a long way from Polynesia, but the tropical decor and exotic soundtrack make this the perfect place to grab a Mai Tai or a Zombie (both of which are set aflame before being served to you) And if the weather outside's got you down, check out one of their warmers—cocktails made with hot tea, coffee, or other substances guaranteed to raise your body temperature. But the menu isn't limited to Polynesian drinks—you can also get Caribbean classics like the piña colada or daiquiri. Every Thursday from 6pm onwards, they host a reggae night. If you're enjoying Edinburgh but can't help but be dismayed by the lack of Bob Marley, this is the place to go.

Perhaps the most surprising thing about 52 Canoes, however, is the quality and variety of the food. You'll be able to order anything from beef skewers to Belgian waffles. Whatever you drunkenly crave will probably be available on the menu in some capacity, and the staff will be happy to cook it up for you. At heart, this outrageous tiki bar is just a friendly neighborhood pub, albeit one with leis and tiny umbrellas everywhere.

i Cocktails £7-9, warmers £4-6. Nearby: Caledonian Backpackers, The Roamin' Nose. Open M-F 11am-1am, Sa-Su 9am-1am.

ESSENTIALS
Practicalities

- **CASH:** There are ATMs up and down Princes Street, including a number of Royal Bank of Scotland ATMs located near the end of Princes Street and the beginning of Queensferry Road. There is also a Royal Bank of Scotland building with several ATMs.
- **INTERNET CAFÉ:** Here! Internet (23 Leven Street. M-F 10am-7:30, Sa 10-6, Su 10-5.) Filament Coffee (5 India Buildings, Victoria Street. Open daily 8am-7pm.)
- **POST OFFICE:** The post office at 40 Frederick Street has a 24 hour ATM. The post office is open M 9-5:30pm, T 9:30-5:30, W-F 9-5:30, and Sa 9-12:30. The post office on 33 Forrest Road offers currency exchange. Open M-F 8:30-6, Sa 9-5:30.

Emergency

- **EMERGENCY NUMBER:** 999
- **HOSPITALS:** Royal Edinburgh Hospital, Morningside Place. ☎131 537 6000.
- **PHARMACY:** Boots Pharmacy (40-44 North Bridge, Edinburgh. M-F 8-7pm, Sa 8:3-6:30pm, Su 10-6pm.)

Getting Around

Edinburgh has a bus and tram system. Tram tickets cost £1.50 for city zone travel—the main line runs along Princes Street and terminates at Haymarket. The bus system, Lothian Buses, has several routes; the 24 is easiest for getting from the North Town to the Old Town (and thus avoiding the numerous hills in between).

great britain essentials

VISAS

Britain is not a signatory of the Schengen Agreement, which means it is not a member of the freedom of movement zone that covers most of continental Europe. Fortunately, its visa policies are fairly simple (for casual travelers, at least). EU citizens do not need a visa to visit Britain. Citizens of Australia, Canada, New Zealand, the US, and many other non-EU countries do not need a visa for stays of up to six months. Those staying longer than six months may apply for a longer-term visa; consult an embassy or consulate for more information. Because Britain is not a part of the Schengen zone, time spent here does not count toward the 90-day limit on travel within that area. Entering to study or work will require a visa. Check www.ukvisas.gov.uk for more information.

MONEY
Tipping and Bargaining

Tips in restaurants are sometimes included in the bill (it will appear as a "service charge"). If gratuity is not included, you should tip your server about 10%. Taxi drivers should receive a 10% tip, and bellhops and chambermaids usually expect £1-3 per night. To the great relief of many budget travelers, tipping is not expected at pubs and bars in Britain (unless you are trying to get jiggy with the bartender). Bargaining is practically unheard of in the upscale shops that overrun London. Don't try it (unless you happen to be at a street market or feel particularly belligerent).

Taxes

The UK has a 20% value added tax (VAT), a sales tax applied to everything but food, books, medicine, and children's clothing. The tax is included in the amount indicated on the price tag. The prices stated in Let's Go include VAT unless otherwise mentioned. Upon exiting Britain, non-EU citizens can reclaim VAT (minus an administrative fee) through the Retail Export Scheme, although the process is time-consuming, annoying, and may not be worth it, except for large purchases. You can obtain refunds only for goods you take out of the country (not for accommodations or noms). Participating shops display a "Tax-Free Shopping" sign and may have a minimum purchase of $50-100 before they offer refunds. To claim a refund, fill out the form you are given in the shop and present it with the goods and receipts at customs upon departure (look for the Tax-Free Refund desk at the airport). At peak times, this process can take up to an hour. You must leave the country within three months of your purchase in order to claim a refund, and you must apply before leaving the UK.

SAFETY AND HEALTH

Police

Police are a common presence in Britain and there are many police stations scattered throughout the city. There are two types of police officers in Britain: regular officers with full police powers, and police community support officers (PCSO), who have limited police power and focus on community maintenance and safety. The national emergency number is ☎999.

Drugs and Alcohol

The Brits love to drink, so the presence of alcohol is unavoidable. In trying to keep up with the locals, remember that the Imperial pint is 20oz., as opposed to the 16oz. US pint. The legal age at which you can buy alcohol in the UK is 18 (16 for buying beer and wine with food at a restaurant).

Despite what you may have seen on Skins, use and possession of hard drugs is illegal throughout the United Kingdom. Do not test this—Britain has been cracking down on drug use amongst young people in particular over the past few years. Smoking is banned in enclosed public spaces in Britain, including pubs and restaurants.

Terrorism

The bombings of July 7, 2005 in the London Underground revealed the vulnerability of large European cities to terrorist attacks and resulted in the enforcement of stringent safety measures at airports and major tourist sights throughout British cities. Though eight years have passed, security checks are still as thorough as ever. Allow extra time for airport security and do not pack sharp objects in your carry-on luggage—they will be confiscated. Unattended luggage is always considered suspicious and is also liable for confiscation. Check your home country's foreign affairs office for travel information and advisories, and be sure to follow the local news while in the UK.

MEASUREMENTS

Britain uses a thoroughly confusing and illogical mix of standard and metric measurement units. Road distances are always measured in miles, and many Brits will be clueless if you give them distances in kilometers. For weights, don't be surprised to see grams and ounces used side-by-side. There's also a measurement called a "stone," equal to 14lb., that is regularly used for giving body weights. Paradoxically, meters and centimeters are the most common way to give body heights. How the British ever accomplished anything in this world when they can't settle on a consistent system of measurements, we'll never know.

GREECE

Greece is a land where marble comes standard issue, circle-dancing and drinking until daybreak are time-tested rites of summer, and the past is inescapable. Tourists flock to hear the whispers of long-dead statesmen and playwrights echoing off the magnificent ruins of ancient civilizations. At the center of Greece's past and present is Athens. Though hemp-wearing backpackers and fanny pack-laden tourists have replaced the chiton-robed philosophers of the past, Athens maintains its position as a cultural hub of the Mediterranean. After centuries of foreign domination, Athens is now a world-class international capital, where the past and present sit comfortably side by side. It is also the gateway to the sun-drenched Cyclades, defined by white and blue stucco buildings, notorious nightlife, and fabulous beaches. Mix some hangovers with all your history by heading to Mykonos and Ios, then check in on Santorini's world-famous sunsets and peaceful mountain villages. They're just a short ferry ride away. Even with all those thousands of years of history, Greece remains constantly dynamic, and you'll always find something new to discover in this ancient land.

greatest hits

- **CHEAP EATS.** Eat souvlaki in **Monastiraki Square** (p. 364) in Athens. It's the most touristy fun you'll have for less than €2.

- **PRAISE THE GODS.** Channel your inner Zeus atop **Mt. Olympus** (p. 370) near Thessaloniki—or, pray you don't collapse after the long trek to the top.

- **JUST KEEP SWIMMING.** Morning coffee? Afternoon snacks? Nighttime beers? You can have it all—24hr. a day—at **Reef** (p. 374) in Volos.

GREECE

Mediterranean Sea

athens

If you come to Athens for an Acropolis picture and inspiration for your frat's next toga party, you'll stay for the bright colors, rich history, vivacious nightlife, and delicious food. Vine-shaded benches, orange trees, and lazy stray cats set the laid-back mood, and welcoming locals are willing to show you around the city's different neighborhoods. Tour the impressive museums and archaeological sites of the Plaka area in the day, then grab some souvlaki and head out to experience the city's nightlife, or visit the student cafes of Anarchist Exarchia. And sure, your toga party could use some authentic Athenian shot glasses from Monastiraki's flea market anyway.

ORIENTATION

Accommodations in **Monastiraki** offer the closest proximity to the main tourist attractions, so you'll have access to the widest variety of tacky and distasteful toga-esque tee shirts. It's also home to a variety of busy hostels, an extensive flea market, and no shortage of rooftop bars. Ermou pedestrian shopping street runs between Monastiraki square and the central Syntagma square and Parliament building, making it easy to access other parts of the city from there.

South of Monastiraki lies **Plaka,** Athens' most historical neighborhood, situated directly beneath the Acropolis. If you're skipping the Greek islands, Plaka can give you a taste of the quaint and romantic island vibe, and is guaranteed to bring out your basic side due to the ample opportunities for cute pics. You can't miss the typical Greek architecture and the closely packed cafés lining the steps up the hill. It's the perfect place to take a note from the city's stray cats and dogs and sun yourself between the yellow and blue buildings.

If Plaka is the sophisticated mother of the city, **Exarchia** is the rebellious and angsty teen. What the neighborhood lacks in historical sights it makes up for in a different kind of charm: denim vests and leather jackets, record stores, and Anarchist graffiti. The nearby university makes for a young and hip crowd to replace the flocks of tourists in Monastiraki, and the area's cafés and bars offer good deals for students. Exarchia also provides a gateway from the city center out to the National Archaeological Museum, Victoria Square, and Areos Park of the Mouseio neighborhood.

Even if you're staying elsewhere, the nightlife in **Gazi** makes it worth the excursion. You can go deaf from the high-volume music, lose your voice from singing along to the Greek words that you make up as you go, and wear holes in your shoes from dancing like a complete idiot, but it's all worth it for the booze-fueled romp that is a night in Gazi. A few of the clubs right outside of the main square are more exclusively for the locals, so you can sidle on up to some single Greeks and see if they'll escort you through the entrance. By day, the area is a popular spot for musicians to hold concerts, and a hub for modern art.

SIGHTS

LYCABETTUS HILL

Stairs accessible from Kleomenous St

Lycabettus Hill is the perfect spot for a panoramic view of Athens, stretching to all the landmarks you saw the day before and out to the water. Getting to the top of the hill takes about half an hour for an average person. If your environmental morals don't prevent you from doing so, you can add your name to the carvings on the flowered cacti lining the way up. At the top, snap a picture of the view, wander inside the Byzantine church, and enjoy a freddo cappuccino at the café. If you're staying in a central location near the Acropolis, this is also a good opportunity to head down the other side of the hill and explore the less touristy neighborhoods.

WALKING TOUR OF ATHENS

If you have limited time in Athens, you should regret missing more opportunities for *souvlaki*, but don't fear missing the main sights. First of all, you can basically throw a rock from anywhere in Athens and hit some sort of ancient monument (and Socrates probably pissed on that rock you threw). And secondly, most of the noteworthy locations can be tackled in a day-long walking tour.

A good place to start is the **Ancient Agora**, right near Monastiraki square. The Agora includes multiple buildings and structures, the highlight of which is the remarkably intact **Temple of Hephaestus.** The reduced student fare will also allow you to see an ancient Athenian prison, the remains of a Roman house, the Stoa of Attalos (a covered walkway reconstructed in the 1950s), a Byzantine church, and a large assortment of ancient stones/sculptures/inscriptions scattered across the grounds.

Once you've wandered the area, head uphill for the holy grail of Athens: the ▨**Acropolis.** Built as a temple to the city's namesake goddess Athena, the Parthenon dominates the citadel, but you can also see the **Propylaea,** the **Temple of Athena Nike,** and the **Erechtheum.** It's easy to follow signs up the hill, but taking a more circuitous route through some side streets on your way up is a good way to take in the picturesque cafe-lined staircases strewn throughout the Plaka neighborhood. Once you get up to the entrance, take advantage of the reduced rate for students with IDs, and the option of purchasing a ticket that gets you into six other landmarks too for only €5 more. Poking around at the top, you'll find the monuments impressively maintained, and the details of the architecture extraordinarily precise. After making a round at the top, head down the southern slope past the **Theater of Dionysus,** where a stray dog might replace the players of the past as your performers.

From there it's a straight shot down to the **Acropolis Museum.** Only €3 for students, the museum features three levels of exhibitions and glass floors so that you can see the excavation done below. It will become clear that the ancient Greeks gave credit to Athena for pretty much everything, like an ancient Beyoncé or something. Highlights include the third floor array of fighting centaurs, the statues recovered from the pediments of the **Parthenon,** the Acropolis replica made of Legos because why the fuck not, and the trendy-feeling balcony café. The next stop is the **Temple of Zeus,** best for snapping a quick picture and maybe taking a quick break while you bask in the ancient glory of the King of the Gods. You'll need it before you head to the **Panathenaic Stadium,** where you'll be obliged to make a lap of the track and take in the full view of the expansive stadium from the very top. The free audio guide is painfully cheesy, but will enlighten you to the magical **Cave of the Fates,** where young Greek girls once danced naked around bonfires to gain luck for finding husbands and old women stood guard to keep the ancient pervs away. You can also take a posed photo on top of the podium to show that you got first place in being a tool.

To complete the loop, head North through the **National Gardens,** where you can pause to relax under a canopy of ivy surrounded by orange trees. This will bring you to the **Parliament building.** If you've timed it right, you'll be able to see the hourly changing of the guards, complete with pom-pommed shoes and complex choreography. At noon on Sundays there's an extended version that

greece

ATHENSTYLE (MONASTIRAKI) $$

Agias Theklas 10   ☎210 332 50 10 info@athenstyle.com

Athenstyle is Monastiraki's most popular hostel. The rooftop bar is frequented by guests and locals alike for its low prices, daily happy hour,
and breathtaking glimpses of the Acropolis. Right in the heart of classical
Athens, the hostel is just a quick walk from sights like the Ancient Agora,
Monastiraki's flea market, Ermou pedestrian shopping street, and an
abundance of sidewalk cafes and lively bars.

i *Checkout at 10am; 24hr. desk service, free maps, free wifi, offer day trips booked
through desk.*

ATHENS STUDIOS $

On other side of Acropolis   ☎210 923 5811 www.athensstudios.gr

A free shot of ouzo upon arrival sets the party mood at Athens Studios.
You'll also have easy access to the rooftop bar of Athens Backpackers,
the Studios' twin hostel located just a few blocks away. The rooms are
inviting and feel more like a hotel than a hostel, with wide sliding doors
leading to small balconies, and a few kitchen appliances so you can
choose to cook for yourself. The prime location right under the Acropolis
will give you easy access to the metro station, Acropolis Museum, and the
bar scene of the Plaka neighborhood. But because of the fun pub and fun
people, it's not clear that you'll even want to leave this place.

i *Right near Acropolis station in Plaka. Includes breakfast. Access to laundromat for a
few euros. Free wifi. Air conditioning, heating in rooms. Checkout at 10:30.*

ZORBAS HOTEL $

Victoria Square, 10 Gkyilfordou Street   ☎210 82 24 927

Located a stone's throw from Victoria Square, Zorbas Hotel provides an
alternative to staying in the tourist-packed areas closer to the Acropolis.
While you won't run into as many camera and fanny pack-toting foreigners, you'll still have easy access by foot to the National Archaeological
Museum and the Victoria metro station. Walk Southeast from the hostel
to experience the student nightlife in nearby Exarchia. Although the
minimal decor reflects some shopping at whatever is the next step down
from Ikea, the facilities are clean and functional, and you'll save major
euro: a space in a dorm goes for as little as €13 a night. A social crowd
hangs out at the indoor and outdoor common spaces downstairs, but if
you're looking for a party you'll need to head out into the city around
11pm, when management may ask you to quiet the common spaces down
for those sleeping in the dorms through the wall.

i *24 hour reception. Provides sheets and towels-for-hire, wifi, maps, showers, computers, safes for valuables, laundry service available. €13 for 6 bed mixed dorm up to €52
for 4 bed private.*

athens

closes part of the street and involves a great deal of fanfare from the elderly
crowd whose tour buses have deposited them there. Crossing **Syntagma Square**
and walking down the crowded Ermou shopping street will bring you back to
the Monastiraki area, where you can shove that well-deserved *souvlaki* into your
face.

1. SOUVLAKI: Cheap, fast, and delicious at €2 to €3, souvlaki kicks other street foods' collective ass. It's skewered meat and sometimes veggies, potatoes, and pita.

2. SAGANAKI: Fried cheese. Need we say more?

3. MOUSSAKA: One of the most traditional Greek dishes made from eggplant, ground meat, and bechamel sauce, moussaka will always be remembered for the scene from My Big Fat Greek Wedding when a bully makes fun of the main character for eating moose kaka. Well that girl was mean and this food is delicious.

4. KOLOKITHI KEFLEDES: Usually it's advisable to try and order in the local language, but these fried zucchini balls with feta cheese are best left to English, since incorrect pronunciation means you will be saying "ass meatballs."

5. GEMISTA: Hollowed peppers and tomatoes stuffed with rice provide further evidence that two good things become even better when one is stuffed inside the other.

6. YAOURT KEBAB: Kill two birds with one stone and then feel a stone settle in your stomach as you sample both delicious Greek yogurt and greasy, flavorful kebab at the same time.

7. DOLMADES: You won't feel more Mediterranean than when you chow down on these grape leaves stuffed with meat or rice.

FOOD

greece

⬛ YIASEMI $
Mnisikleous 23   ☎21 3041 7937

Yiasemi will undoubtedly fulfill all of your romantic preconceived notions of gallivanting around Greece to quaint, colorful, vine-adorned street cafes. This can't-miss restaurant is a slice of the Greek islands tucked into a narrow cafe-lined stairway. Sit outdoors between locals directly on the steps and sample one of the five-euro entrees or delicious desserts. The atmosphere is lively and charming at all times of the day, but the colors are especially vibrant when lit up at night.

i Open daily 10am to 2am.

⬛ FLORAL $$
Themistokleous 80   ☎21 0380 0070 www.floralcafe.gr

Do you resent the man? Are you tired of being a part of the system? Do you just want an affordable sandwich? If you answered yes to any of the above, Exarchia's popular student cafe and bookstore Floral may suit your needs. Walk past the tattooed and pierced youth wearing ripped denim vests and painting anarchist symbols on the square's statues, and enter Floral's wide patio doors to where students working on laptops try to bring down the system from the inside while enjoying a fresh salad. Large black and white vintage photos and rose images cover the walls and menus, giving the cafe a more bohemian vibe than some of the neighborhood. During the daytime, it's a popular lunch spot, and in the evening university students take advantage of the beers on tap and extensive eight-euro cocktail menu.

BOLIVAR $
Alimos 115 77   ☎697 036 7684

Ingredients of The Longest Island cocktail: Rum. Vodka. Lemon. Everything else the bartender can find. Regrets. There's nothing like chilling amongst the tiki lounges at Bolivar, cocktail in hand and delicious four euro bruschetta or pizza close by, and soaking in the rays of Athens' southern beaches. A trip to the beach club is well worth the thirty minute tram ride from Sintagma square. Just hop off at the Kalamaki station and pay the five euro entry fee for access to the lounge chairs, umbrellas, and beachside service. You'll also get a complimentary view of the old Greek men playing Bat and Ball in their Speedos nearby (we're hoping there are some tan lines under there). And who knows, the offer of an ice bucket full of Alpha, a Greek beer, might even attract a few fellow travelers to tag along with you.

DIO DEKARES I OKA $
Dimitrakopoulou   ☎21 0922 0583

As you enter the restaurant, you're met with a sight for hungry eyes: all the food is on display, and the very welcoming waitress will walk you through each dish before you make your selections. The service here is outstanding, with a staff that will explain the ingredients, make sure that you try the most delicious and traditional Greek cuisine, and remind you not to fill up on bread. The lamb is a house specialty, and the accompanying sauce can be used to soak your french fries.

i Open daily 12pm to 12am, also offer free delivery. Dishes are €5 to €8 for large and filling portions.

OFF WHITE $
Aiolou 10a   ☎211 4087310

If the typical Athens eateries just aren't hipster enough for you, bring your typewriter and cuffed skinny jeans over to Off White, an artistic restaurant, bar, and gallery right across from Hadrian's Library. If you're really going through hipster withdrawals, you can try to administer one of their many delicious and well-known teas or healthy juices intravenously. A great spot for Greek yogurt and breakfast, Off White also has snacks, cheap meals, and great desserts. Plus, they offer 5 euro mojitos and caipirinhas to go because stationary drinking is just too mainstream.

SAVVAS $
Ermou 91   ☎21 0321 1167 www.savvas-restaurant.gr

After a few days in Athens, you've probably consumed dangerous amounts of yogurt kebab, but it's worth the risk of developing an actual brick in your stomach to have it again at the rooftop of Savvas. Boasting excellent food at midrange prices, three levels of seating, and, at the risk of sounding like a broken record, a superb view of the Acropolis, this restaurant is perfect for a nice dinner and ouzo with your hostel pals. Although the crowd is typically a bit older, the bright furnishings contribute to a stylish atmosphere. Or if you choose not to stay, you can grab their gyros to go for €2.50. The enormous platters of falafel, hummus, and pita will keep everyone satisfied, meaning you can even bring your vegetarian friends.

i Open daily 9am to 2am

AISCHYLOU GRILL HOUSE $
Aischylou, 14-16 Psiri Sq.   ☎210 3244117-8

Aischylou Grill House is like the set of a scene from My Big Fat Greek Wedding: cream colored stone, a canopy of vines and lights covering the outdoor seating area, and live traditional music. Whether or not your crazy family is ruining your nuptials, you'll want to stop here to soak in the atmosphere. Located in Psiri out of the way of the most touristy areas, you can enjoy your meal in peace without being trampled by old folks on tours trying to capture the essence of Greek cuisine in an inevitably dark and blurry photo. Try the giant mixed grill platter, or share some traditional Greek appetizers like fried cheese or zucchini balls. The two-euro souvlaki is also a delicious option if you want to save some cash but still experience the atmosphere.

NIGHTLIFE

AKANTHUS

Alimos 174 55   ☎21 0968 0800 http://www.akanthus.gr/gr/home

Wednesdays should just be referred to as Akanthursday from now on, since those are the days of the beach club's wild "Sex Me Up" parties. You'll pay a higher price for drinks and transportation down to Acanthus, but it's one of the biggest and arguably the best parties in Athens and you'll be the only non-local there. In fact, they can be strict about letting foreigners in, so try to sweet-talk some Greeks into splitting a table with you and your hostel mates or letting you tag along through the main entrance behind them. In the event of a strike-out with the bouncer, you can head further down the beach to Bolivar. If you do make it in though, you'll get to see the half-naked dancers, the lit-up Sex Me Up sign, and the Greek people out in their nighttime finery.

i Cover €15.

GAZI

Gazi, about a ten minute walk from Monastiraki square, is known as the center of nightlife in Athens. Rooftop bars like The Hive and clubs pumping Greek music line a square where you can buy cheap burgers at the end of the night, or rather, the morning. The area really gets going around 2am, when the locals arrive to shout random lyrics and dance until the sun comes up. Drinks in Gazi are pricier, but kiosks in the square sell cheap beers, and the lack of open container laws means the world's your stage when it comes to pregaming. If you get lucky enough to befriend some Greek locals while you're out, they may even take you to one of the locals-only clubs like Socialista right outside of the square. After a night out, you can catch a cab back, which may be subject to the higher nighttime fare. Or, if it's been really wild, the Scottish guy from your hostel can fireman-carry you out of there.

360 DEGREES

Ifestou 2   ☎21 0321 0006

If you like looking at the Acropolis as much as advertisements for nearby establishments think you do, you'll have to take advantage of this centrally located rooftop bar. A large young crowd and trendy light and water fixtures contribute to a 360 degrees hip vibe, and it stays busy throughout the week, making it the perfect place to grab a drink before heading to a more rowdy bar or club, or just hanging when things aren't as lively elsewhere. The steeper prices reflect its higher altitude, but the cocktails are creative, pretty strong, and aesthetically pleasing (hello, Insta-likes). A word of warning: if you stay late into the night, couples tend to start taking advantage of the romantic view and making out next to you. *Winks at cutie from hostel.*

CINE PARIS

Kidathineon 22   ☎21 0322 2071

We're all familiar with the issue: you're treating yourself to some relaxation time with your favorite movie when you think to yourself, "Tom Hanks is killing this role, but there just aren't enough centuries-old landmarks in this film." Well, my friend, Cine Paris has the solution for you. Built in the 20s by a Greek hairdresser who once lived in France, the outdoor theater provides views of your favorite films to the front and of the Acropolis to the left. If the movie is especially cheesy, you can always rotate your chair slightly or grab some popcorn and drinks. And don't worry, it won't all be Greek to you; the films are shown in English with Greek subtitles.

i Cover €8, reduced price of €6 Tu and W.

ESSENTIALS
Practicalities

- **TOURIST INFO:** Greek National Tourism Organization (GNTO): 18-20 Dionyssiou Areopagitou St.
- **TOURIST POLICE/INFO:** Call ☎1571, 24hr.

Emergency

- **FIRE SERVICE:** ☎199
- **FIRST AID/AMBULANCE:** ☎166
- **HELLENIC POLICE:** ☎100

Getting There

From Athens International Airport, "Eleftherios Venizelos," you can directly take the metro to downtown, or the bus if you arrive late at night. You can also take a taxi into town for a set fare of €38. Otherwise, the daytime meter rate (which you should double check when you enter the cab by making sure the meter is set to "1" and not "2" for the nighttime rate) is €0.32 per kilometer.

Getting Around

Public transport is simple and accessible in Athens, with the option of buses and bus trolleys, the metro, or the tram. The metro is easy to take all over town, and runs from 5:30am to midnight M through Th, and until 2am on F and Sa. The metro also runs to Piraeus port, the point from which boats go back and forth to the islands. Some of the stops display artifacts from the subway excavations. Metro maps are available at the GNTO or at Syntagma station. A single ticket is €1.40 (make sure to validate it at the station, as fines for non-validation are large) and a day pass is €4. These can also be used for the bus, or you can find one of the various kiosks around the city selling bus tickets. Check out Athens Urban Transport Organization website at www.oasa.gr (English version available) for bus schedules and maps, which, spoiler alert: are very confusing. Air-conditioned trams go from downtown to the coast for beach access.

santorini

Crazy Australian tourists staying up all night, hundreds of donkeys, fabulous wineries, a volcano, and the most amazing island sunset views you'll ever see: Santorini really has it all. You can rent quads at one of the dozens of rental places on the island and check out the Ancient City atop narrow twisting roads, or head to the black sand beach of Perissa and run on your tiptoes into the cool, clear water. Take a boat to the volcano that created the island and lather yourself in mud at the nearby hot springs (white swimsuits not recommended). Take in sunset views in the picturesque Oia or while tasting fine wines at Santos winery (our thoughts: hmm....that one tastes red), and top it all off with a wild night out in Fira.

FOOD

TRANQUILO $$
Beach front, Perissa ☎22 86 08 52 30

Tranquilo is just that: so, so tranquil(o). You can't miss the bright orange building adorned in colorful tapestries, and you won't want to. Their open-air patio looks

out onto Perissa beach, and features body-enveloping couches, hammocks,
burlap sacks, and more. Anything comfortable to sit on, they've got it! The staff
is as calm as the setting. We're not sure if having dreadlocks and slouchy elephant print pants is a requirement to work there. Their salads are mountains of
greenery and delicious fresh fruits, and we think their signature dip would make
even yesterday's leftover fish taste great.

NIGHTLIFE

KOO CLUB
Santorini 847 00   ☎22 86 02 20 25
You know it's a good club when even an eighty-year-old man is still partying at
5:30am. Dance on any elevated surface available. Inside you'll find two rooms
of bars, shrouded in purple lighting and blaring top 40 hits—the perfect vibe for
some crazy dancing. Outside, lounge under couches shaded by palm trees where
another bar provides a place to chill between dance sessions.

BROTHERS BAR
Dekigala, Thira 847 00   ☎22 86 02 30 61
Yes, this bar was founded by two brothers. And yes, two brothers are still running
the show. You may wander inside after hearing its blaring house music. Though
the commotion inside is an attraction on its own, the best part is the bar's the
signature "head shot." Essentially, you pay the bartender €2 to slap a helmet on
you, give you a shot of vodka, and whack you on the head with a stick. Recipe
for a concussion? Perhaps. Seems like a great idea after a few drinks? Definitely.

thessaloniki

What do you get when you cross thousands-of-years-old archaeology with hundreds
of bustling bars and clubs? Probably some "hold my beer" moments, but also the city
of Thessaloniki. Its citizens head west of the university and into the city center for
wild, late-night parties in Ladadika every day of the week. In the daytime, locals sip
on Thessaloniki's specialty frappes at cafés along the waterfront, shop in the fish and
meat market off of Aristotelous Square, or walk the city streets under the various
large-scale instances of commissioned street art. Head north of the city center and
into the old town of Ano Poli to see the ancient castle and still-intact city walls, or
gtfo for a day and hike on the nearby Mt. Olympus. After all the partying you'll be
doing, a visit to one of the city's many churches or museums might be a good way to
save your soul.

SIGHTS

ARISTOTELOUS SQUARE/STREET

If you love hunting for bargain bars of soap, buying fly swatters, or smelling raw fish (doesn't everyone?), you need to check out the open air market off of Aristotelous Street. Primarily a meat and fish market, it's best to photograph (and smell) early in the morning, when goods are fresh and well stocked, but it's best to shop in the late afternoon, when vendors slash prices. You can also find flowers, fresh fruits, and other goods if observing raw meat isn't your idea of fun. You also have the option of taking a scenic stroll down the rest of the manicured and palm-lined Aristotelous Street, which features a view of the water reaching ahead and the old town stretching up behind. At the end is Aristotelous square, where fashionable cafés and bars are in abundant supply. It even has a Starbucks for those who want to overpay for coffee in every corner of the world.

ROTUNDA

The student fee of €1 is well spent seeing the Rotunda, with its meters-thick walls, centuries-old (and impressively intact) mosaics, and innumerable stray cats. Some original paintings are still remarkably visible, and the large domed ceiling retains its awe-inspiring effect. The informative signs are actually interesting, unlike the White Tower's, and even if you're not a history buff, you can

get a room!

◼ LITTLE BIG HOUSE $
Andokidou 24   ☎6944 397 864 www.littlebighouse.gr

After embarking on a death march up to the Old Town with your unfathomably heavy pack, you might just cry when you see the slice of heaven that is Little Big House. The colorful reception, adorned with cute travel posters and hand-painted murals, must've been designed by a fairy godmother who shops at Pottery Barn. Upon arrival, you'll be greeted with a smile and a free ice cold frappe. Rooms are not only spacious and clean, but also feature a full kitchen and balcony with a stunning view of the city. We're getting emotional thinking about it. In the morning, participate in the €2 breakfast buffet, and in the evening, head to the terrace for a delicious cocktail. That's it. We're making Little Big House the godparent to our first-born child.

i Reception open 8am to 11pm, quiet hours start at 11. Included towels, hair dryer, other amenities. Computer available downstairs. Free walking tours. Pets welcome.

STUDIOS ARABAS $
Sachtouri 28 (Ano Poli)   ☎6944 466 897 www.hostelarabas.gr

We didn't think it was possible to perch a hostel on a street that slopes (what feels like) 80 degrees, but Studios Arabas proved us wrong. Halfway up the hill, you may consider simply dropping your bag and falling asleep on the ground; however, the friendly international staff, homemade wine and cheap cocktails, and comfortable bed in a spacious room should be enough incentive to continue the climb. Visit the fish and meat market in the city center at some point during your stay, since Arabas has a common kitchen and outdoor barbecue that you're welcome to use. As your resident Gordon Ramsay, we recommend that you stick some lemon slices in a fish, wrap it in foil, throw it on the barbecue for 20 minutes and pair it with some €1 white wine from reception.

i Reception open 8am-11pm, quiet hours start at 11pm.

pretend to read them until someone starts singing from the center of the church to test the echo. Make sure you don't miss the arch at Kamara on the way up, with intricate carvings that have stood the test of time.

WHITE TOWER

Going to Thessaloniki without seeing the White Tower is like going to Paris without seeing the Eiffel Tower. It's not only the symbol of the city, but the walk there along the water also provides stunning scenery, and the 360 degree view of Thessaloniki and the Aegean sea from the top is unbeatable. The Museum of the City is inside the tower, but unless you speak Greek the informative posters won't mean much to you. You can also take a free audio tour, but the commentary is a little bland, so don't feel too guilty about being a tourist and just going for the panoramic pics. Beware of the numerous ripoffs centered around the tower, like the "free" boat tours that nail you with expensive drinks and the horse-drawn carriages that are more sweaty and saddening than romantic.

i €2 entrance for students.

mt. olympus

After a trip to Mt. Olympus, you may end up naked and sweaty, and not because Zeus "showed you his thunderbolt." You'll be sweaty because the trek up Mt. Olympus feels like someone put a Stairmaster in a sweat lodge, and you'll be naked because the cold and crystal clear water at the bottom provides an opportunity for a refreshing nude plunge.

Those staying in Thessaloniki can consider spending the night in the mountainous village of Litohoro and climbing the entire mountain the following day, or opt to take the bus to the village in the morning and make a day trip of it for a slightly less victorious, but still beautiful, hike. It's hard to resist the temptation to have coffee and sit around at one of the adorable cafés nestled at the mountain's base, but eventually you should cross the river and head up to the peaks. By stumbling around and asking some elderly Greek folk for directions you can find the trail leading up to Prionia, the village further up the mountain.

Upon emerging from the trees a few kilometers up, you'll see that a paved road leads directly to the lookout where you'll be standing, and some tourists will no doubt have driven their Volkswagen straight up there while you slaved away on the hillside. Well, what you put in is what you get out, there's no elevator to success, grind hard stay humble, etc. Plus, you'll have the advantage of getting to make up Greek myths to entertain yourself as you hike. With the amazing views and sheer size of the mountain, you can see why the ancient Greeks thought this place was the home of the Gods. You may also believe that the river running through the valley was the result of Athena putting Apollo's hand in warm water while he slept as revenge for telling the other gods she had syphillis. (Yes, we made that one up.)

If you fall short of the 11 kilometers to Prionia, you can always sit at a scenic overlook and eat a chocolate bar before heading back down the mountain in time for the late afternoon bus back to Thessaloniki. However, you should take a few moments to strip down and dive into the crystal clear water near the bottom, which we're fairly confident is not actually Apollo's piss. The people near you on the bus may be slightly offended that you're both smelly and dripping everywhere, but the unappreciative glances are well worth the experience.

FOOD

◪ CAFÉ AITHRIO $$

Tzachila 7, Thessaloniki 54634

If you can summon the willpower to make a trip up Thessaloniki's hills to the old town, you deserve a refreshing treat. Luckily, the summery cocktails at Café Aithrio will do the trick. The leafy trees shading the outdoor terrace will provide a welcome respite from the heat as you enjoy a plate of Greek cheeses and meats. This garden setting, with its green and white furniture and potted plants, is the perfect break from a hot day of castle-spotting in Ano Poli. Live out an actual fairy tale as you listen to jazzy music in and pause to gaze at the vine-covered brick. The happily ever after that is Café Aithrio is waiting for you.

JOIN THE JUICE CO. $

Victory Avenue 73 ☎2310250792

You'll learn very quickly that the main source of variety in Greek cuisine is which kind of animal you'll be consuming. Indeed, in a country known for its meat skewers and fried cheese, it can be hard to get around as a vegan or vegetarian. Join the Juice Co. provides vegan and gluten free options for those who are less fried-meat-and-bread inclined, and throws in a waterfront view at an affordable price, too. At Join the Juice Co., you can experiment with fresh and interesting juices, like orange mint elderflower for only €2.60 or enjoy a gluten free sandwich or salad for less than five.

2ND STORY BLUES $$

Right above the Roman Forum

The only thing more hipster than the blue fluorescent lights, bare light bulb fixtures, and metal interior of 2nd Story Blues is deciding you're too cool for this interior and sitting in the tree-lined courtyard overlooking the Roman Forum. This outdoor setting is guaranteed to satisfy even if you never lay eyes on the inside of the café. It's a popular spot with a stylish, mature crowd, and the prices reflect it, so this place is best for a cold afternoon coffee overlooking one of Thessaloniki's famous archaeological sites. And you can't have a café in this city without an extensive cocktail menu, so pay a visit at night, too, if Thessaloniki's party scene has rubbed off on you.

NIGHTLIFE

⊠ LADADIKA

While we're not your physician, we know that spending a few nights in a row at Ladadika can't be good for your health. On busy nights (which, in Thessaloniki, is every night), the club-lined streets get up to dangerous decibels, and the constant cigarette smoke spilling out of the clubs will cling to your clothes for days. But sometimes you have to live a little dangerously, and Ladadika is the perfect place to let loose and take a ride on the wild side. Most of the clubs in the area play a mixture of Greek and American pop and house music, but side streets can be home to a more alternative crowd. If you want to get out of the main fray try City Bar Tokyo, where graffiti on the way up warns you that eating meat is murder and the red-light-brick-wall-weird-ass-art decor will conjure up feelings of some underground Berlin-style stuff. We hope you like techno.

THE PULP BAR

Al. Svolou 8 ☎231 027 0830

If skin-tight leopard print, overpriced vodka, and Greek techno aren't for you, leave the Ladadika clubs in the dust and head over to The Pulp Bar instead, a cool spot with more of a dive bar feel thanks to its vintage posters and pop art logo. The real hook is its selection 135 different beers. If you can lift the encyclopedia of a menu, you can take a break from the usual Greek Budweiser equivalents like Alfa and Mythos and find anything from midrange Greek IPAs like Voreia to the locally microbrewed Ali.

DOGS

4 Polytechneiou ☎6947 377749 / 6944 863248

Dogs Club is certainly more German Shepherd than Jack Russell. It's sleek, large, and as muscular as a club can be. Although you'll spot the occasional septuagenarian getting down in the VIP section, the other two floors of the club are packed with a young crowd. Mirrors adorning the walls add to the impressive impact and also will undoubtedly confuse the shit out of you after a few (slightly overpriced) drinks. In the local fashion, this place is more about standing and drinking with friends than getting wild and dancing, so bring good company and snag your own table with drinks and complimentary snacks.

ESSENTIALS

Practicalities

- **THESSALONIKI TOURISM ORGANIZATION:** Egnatia, Thessaloniki (☎231 027 928)

Emergency

- **POLICE:** ☎100. Tourist Police in English, French, and German: ☎23 10 55 48 71

Getting There

From Macedonia, the main bus station, you can easily connect to one of the local buses that goes into the city center or up to the old town. Regular tickets are €1.10. The train station is also a busy stop for the local buses. The airport is served 24 hours a day by the Thessaloniki Urban Transport Organization. Taxis from the airport to the city center cost €15 to €20, with increased rates late at night.

Getting Around

The bus is the primary form of public transport. Lines run all over the city, as well as out to the beach and other attractions. The main sights are clustered around the city center, and the best places to eat and go out are all within walking distance. Walking up from the waterfront to the Ano Poli takes about 20 minutes.

volos

Home to the University of Thessaly, Volos is now the domain of the students, full of bustling cafes and lively clubs. Though there aren't many accommodation options for visiting youth, the lack of hostels ensures that you'll get to know local students and have a genuinely Greek experience. You can walk on the waterfront with the families and off-leash dogs at sunset, explore the shopping on Ermou Street, visit one of the city's many historic churches, or head up Mt. Pelion to the scenic old villages of Portaria and Makrinitsa.

SIGHTS

LOFOS GORITSA

Walk past the beaches to the East of the city center, and follow the road up North past a pool and track before it twists around to the top of the hill. You can go in the late afternoon and watch the sun set over the city and then scramble down before it gets too dark and reward yourself with an ice cold beer on the waterfront. You'll need it after the somewhat strenuous hike up.

MAKRINITSA

A stay in Volos wouldn't be complete without an excursion to the petite and scenic old village of Makrinitsa. Everything about it, from its traditional inns and Museum of Folk Art to the stray animals, vine-covered trellises, and spice shops, will make your eyes widen and sparkle. It's just. So. Cute. You can catch the bus from behind the info center in Volos, and enjoy the scenic, if a bit perilous, journey up Mt. Pelion with views of the wealthier residential areas and then the whole expanse of the city below. At the top, you can sit in the village's small square, shaded by a massive hollow tree, and pity the little ant-sized people below.

FOOD

🏠 ART CAFÉ MAKRINITSA $

Unnamed Rd ☎697 438 4488

Can you even call yourself a village if you don't have a quaint, ivy-trellis covered, rose-adorned café? In Makrinitsa, an old village North of Volos, Art Café fits the bill. The white stone and strawberry plants are reminiscent of the "simpler days" that silver-haired women in the sauna are always talking about, and the shady deck will make you feel like you're sitting in the garden of the sweetest grandmother in the world. Look out from your spot on Mt. Pelion on the Greek flag flying over the city of Volos as you enjoy a fruit-filled Greek yogurt, delicious

HOTEL PHILIPPOS VOLOS $

Solonos 9 ☎24 21 03 76 07 http://www.philippos.gr/en

Are you sick and tired of towels that don't actually dry you, using your phone's flashlight as a legitimate light source, and making your own bed? It's time to take a break from hostels and treat yoself. Volos doesn't have any hostels, so you don't really have a choice. Instead, there's Hotel Philippos Volos, an affordable three star hotel located right next to the waterfront. It's hard to beat the view of the gulf from the rooms' balconies, effective air conditioning, and sweet sweet privacy. Hotel Philippos is within easy walking distance of the bus stop, city center, clubs, restaurants, you name it. With its professional staff and comfortable rooms, you'll never want to go back to hostel life again.

i Offers breakfast daily for €4 euros from 7am to 10:30am. Free maps.

traditional pie (I assume the cute grandmother is baking in the back), or a refreshing coffee drink. Thanks, grandma.

i €4-7 for food and drinks, €2-3 for coffee.

URBAN DAY AND NIGHT $

T.Oikonomaki 51 ☎24 21 10 57 18

With its Campbell's Soup Can lighting fixtures, funky mismatched chairs, and painted tables, Urban Day and Night looks more like a modern artist's studio loft than a café. Exposed brick and the black and white map covering the back wall may even inspire you to start wearing a beret and journaling. On the busy Oikonomaki street near Agios Nikolaos, it's the perfect place to sit outside, have a coffee and toasted sandwich, and watch the world go by. And by the world we mean cute dogs and attractive Greek people on motorbikes. They have mostly coffee and drinks, not many food options, on the menu, but what's a starving artist all about anyway?

i Open daily 9:30am to 3am.

ISALOS $$

Plastira Nikolaou ☎698 330 5178

A place that has both banana-walnut-chocolate pancakes and lots and lots of booze? Sounds too good to be true. Add a view of the gulf and some colorful and comfortable couches and you have Isalos, the inviting restaurant/bar combo to rule all restaurant/bar combos. The staff of friendly students will explain the Greek menu to you as you relax under the bamboo roofs and tapestries in the morning or enjoy a cocktail and take in the scenery in the evening. Just a few minutes' walk past the city center, there's seating right out on the water, and the young and friendly crowd will give you an opportunity to meet some local students.

i Open daily M-Su 9am to 3am.

NIGHTLIFE

⌧ **REEF**

Αργοναυτών & Γαμβέτα ☎2421 024168

If you thought card games were for the retirement home, Reef is here to prove you wrong. It's a 24-hour cycle: coffee in the morning, groups of students drinking freddo cappuccinos and playing cards at the couches and low tables in the afternoon and evening, and a stylish bar in the night and back into the

AM. Even when the rest of the waterfront restaurants are dead, Reef is always bustling. Their fairly priced beers and delicious shakes and snacks guarantee a constant flow of young people, and the low-key music sets a relaxed but social atmosphere.

i Open daily 24 hours.

VENICE

The newest club in town, and made for a smaller crowd than clubs like Amaze and White, Venice is the baby of the family when it comes to Volos' nightlife. But isn't it always the younger sibling who goes on to be more annoyingly successful? Located right on the port, Venice is home to Volos' hottest and most stylish. The interior is fresh and artistic, contrasted with the mix of traditional Greek and revamped 90s music. The smaller capacity gives it more of an intimate feeling than the factory-like grandeur of some of its neighbors, perfect for making new acquaintances and getting up close and personal with the DJs.

ESSENTIALS

Practicalities

- **TOURIST OFFIE:** Located West of the port on Sekeri & Lambraki str. (Phone and Fax: ☎24 21 03 09 30, 40. voloinfo@otenet.gr, http://www.volos-city.gr. Open M-Su 8am-9pm in summer.)

Emergency

- **HOSPITAL PHONE:** ☎2421094200
- **TOURIST POLICE:** ☎2421076987
- **POLICE** ☎100
- **FIRE DEPARTMENT:** ☎199

Getting There

From Athens, take the bus for about €30. From Thessaloniki, it's about €20. The bus station is within easy walking distance of the city center, depending on how heavy your backpack is. Volos also has its own train station within close proximity to the city center, but the nearest airport is about a 40 minute drive.

Getting Around

It's easy to get around on the bus, but most sights are within walking distance. To go to the old neighborhoods, take the bus from the main station across from the info center. A ticket is €1.80.

greece essentials

MONEY

Tipping

In Greece, it's normal to include around a 10% gratuity to the bill if the service warrants it. More than that is just showing off your elevated social class. With revolutionary times in Athens and surrounding areas, revealing bourgeois sympathies is not a good idea. There is no need to tip for other services, although rounding up the price to the nearest euro is not unusual.

Taxes

With the EU continually bailing Greece out of its tar pit of debt, the value-added-tax (VAT), applied to all consumer goods, will increase to a maximum 23%. Also, Greece introduced a 10% excise tax on tobacco, fuel, and alcohol. The Greek inflation rate is currently the second highest in the European Union, but rates seem to be on the path to leveling out.

SAFETY AND HEALTH

Local Laws and Police

Greek police are used to having foreigners around, but that does not mean they allow them to break the law. The purchase of pirated goods (including CDs and DVDs) is illegal; keep your receipts for proof of purchase. Taking objects or rocks from ancient sites is forbidden and can lead to fines or prison sentences. Drunk driving and indecent behavior can also result in heavy fines, arrest, and imprisonment. Although legal in Greece since 1951, homosexuality is still frowned upon socially. GLBT individuals are not legally protected from discrimination. That said, destinations like Athens, Ios, and especially Mykonos offer gay and lesbian hotels, bars, and clubs.

Drugs and Alcohol

Visitors of all ages generally have very little difficulty obtaining alcohol in Greece. In contrast, drug laws are very strict. Conviction for possession, use, or trafficking of drugs, including marijuana, will result in imprisonment and fines. Authorities are particularly vigilant at the Turkish and Albanian borders.

Natural Disasters

In one of the world's most seismically active areas, Greece experiences frequent and occasionally large **earthquakes.** The most recent serious quake, in 1999, wreaked an estimated US$3 billion worth of damage and caused nearly 150 deaths and 2000 injuries in Athens. Earthquakes are unpredictable and can occur at any time of day. If there is a strong earthquake, it will probably only last one or two minutes. Protect yourself by moving under a sturdy doorway, table, or desk, and open a door to provide an escape route.

Demonstrations and Political Gatherings

Strikes and demonstrations occur frequently in Greece, especially during the never-ending economic crisis. Although generally orderly and lawful, they frequently spiral out of control: most recently, May 2011 riots and violent demonstrations involving destructive vandalism, fire, stun-grenades, tear gas, and forceful clashes between civilians and the police rocked Athens. The protests continued into summer 2011, ranging from violent, concentrated protests to city-wide strikes. Disruption of public services, such as public transportation and air traffic control, occur unexpectedly due to union strikes. Common areas for protest include the Polytechnic University area, Exharia, Omonia, Syntagma Sq. and Mavii Sq. in Athens. If a demonstration does occur during your trip, you should avoid these areas and stick to the quieter parts of the city. The islands are generally more peaceful.

EUROPE 2017

SIFNOS ISLAND, GREECE

FLORENCE, ITALY

VENICE, ITALY

Venice: city of intrigue, of loving by lamplight, of fading frescoes and Persian arches fronted by jade-green waters, of leathery artisans shaping glass and weaving lace, of laundry fluttering drowsily before pastel shutters, of children tripping over soccer balls. Wander, get lost, stop for gelato, and, most of all, pity the postmen.

BARCELONA, SPAIN

ALHAMBRA
GRANADA, SPAIN

The historic Albayzín neighborhood. The caves
overlooking the city. The Alhambra—oh, man, the
Alhambra. Elegant yet edgy, Granada has no shortage
of beautiful vistas and historic architecture. Snack on
fresh tapas while watching a rousing flamenco show;
meander through graffiti-covered walls and bustling
outdoor markets; smoke just inches away from a
Moorish castle.

MUNICH, GERMANY

Like beer? So does Munich—so much that they've devoted an entire month to drinking it. Much more than a cliché tourist junket, Oktoberfest is a window into Bavarian sights, sounds, smells, and tastes just as frothy and fun as it was at its 1810 inception. But while Oktoberfest might bring you to Munich, the world-class museums, parks, and architecture—and its more sobering World War II history—will keep you around.

page 282

LONDON, ENGLAND

page 295

LONDON, ENGLAND

London is, simply put, busy. On one corner, Harry, Ron, and Hermione dash off to Diagon Alley; on another, Sherlock Holmes finds another clue; on one bank, Shakespeare's words are recited for the 54,932nd time in 400 years; on the other, Churchill's are emblazoned as a permanent reminder. Yet the city of so many stories is always adding new ones, and the London "buzz" is constantly on the move.

PARIS, FRANCE

Ah, Paris. The City of Lights. The City of Love. You'll wind through iconic, elegant Haussmann boulevards to both the predictable likes of the Louvre, where seemingly half the world piles in for a whopping dosage of culture, and the less crowded, equally French bakeries and brasseries that will do more than just about any Raphael can to make you feel like you're really having a Parisian experience.

LISBON, PORTUGAL

A mosaic of neighborhoods with their own indelible character, Lisbon is as full of surprises as it is of history. To experience the city to its fullest, get lost. Let your nose lead you to sizzling fish; stumble through an alleyway to find an architectural marvel; talk to the locals at the hole-in-the-wall and take their advice.

page 613

STOCKHOLM, SWEDEN

ATHENS, GREECE

If you came to Athens for a selfie with the Acropolis, you'll stay for the vibrant colors, incredible history, mouthwatering souvlaki, and vivacious nightlife. Vine-shaded benches, orange trees, and lazy stray cats set a laid-back mood, while the welcoming locals will be more than willing to show you the city's distinctive neighborhoods with their distinctive character.

page 360

COPENHAGEN, DENMARK

Copenhagen is the kind of place where you can
spend the day cafe-hopping in search of the perfect
chai or strolling through ornate palaces and gardens
before sampling the newest sushi-tapas fusion. Follow
Copenhagen's unceasing currents of cool wherever
they lead you: art museum or coffee shop, bookstore
or bar. You can spend a month roaming the city and
still not see everything.

LUCERNE, SWITZERLAND

Lucerne is often relegated to the role of convenient rest stop, a less expensive bed for aspiring Alpinists whose real objects are mountains such as Pilatus, Rigi, and beyond. While these high-altitude daytrips are well worth the splurge, the city proper is replete with natural and rustic Germanic charms. Gabled wooden bridges (including the famous Kappellbrücke in the city center), earthy painted façades, and turreted medieval walls of your childhood fairy tales await you here.

page 780

MAKE THE MOST OF YOUR TRAVELS

DISCOVER AND BOOK AMAZING
THINGS TO DO

PLACEPASS.COM/LETSGO

HUNGARY

Throughout Hungary, the vestiges of Ottoman and communist rules can be found on the same block. Castles stand staunchly and thermal baths pool beside concrete Soviet monuments, overlooking the graves of 20th-century writers and medieval poets. Döner kebabs, bockwurst, and cheeses are peddled side by side, while Budapest locals frequent Turkish bathhouses.

But Hungary's real draw may be the freewheeling youth and a relentless drive toward the modern. Streets are packed with hip hangouts and their patrons exude a vehemently chill attitude, making this city one of the best student urban destinations in Europe. And even though the locals might be too cool for school, they do appreciate a tenacity to learn about their culture. So make the effort and immerse yourself in all that is Hungary, with endless plates of goulash, sleepless nights at ruin pubs, and countless cups of coffee with some newfound friends.

greatest hits

- **TAKE A DIP.** Your childhood self would laugh if they knew you'd fly across the globe to take a bath. But in Budapest—at the **Széchenyi Medicinal Bath** and **Király Baths** (p. 382)—you can soak up an afternoon of relaxation.

- **BURN BABY BURN.** For an authentic, old-world Hungary experience, head northwest out of Budapest to **Győr** (p. 389), which means "burnt city."

- **GET OUTTA TOWN.** Your Eastern Europe excursion doesn't have to end in the land of goulash and palinka: **Bratislava, Slovakia** (p. 392) is only two hours from Budapest.

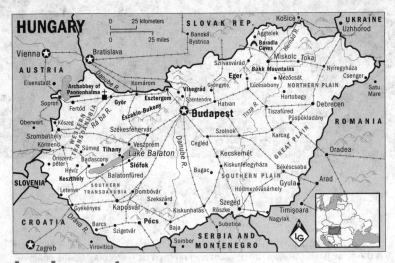

budapest

From its river to its ruins, Budapest's magnificence is impossible to escape. Situated over lush hills and gushing thermal springs, the city is crowned with stunning edifices like the impressive Parliament of Pest and the grand Buda Castle. These gems don't bandage Budapest's bloody history but instead stand as testaments to it—they remind us of what once was, even as the city moves continually toward a brighter future. The relaxed pace of daily life along the Danube river, which divides the city, finds its foil in a vibrant, fast-paced nightlife that features teeming ruin pubs and internationally infamous shots of pálinka. International travelers, young and old, come to Budapest en masse to explore one of Europe's most beautiful and walkable cities, giving its streets and dance floors a language of their own.

SIGHTS

Budapest's key sights offer a tale of two (formerly separate) cities: the hills and castles of Buda offer up stunning, panoramic views, while Pest houses the majority of the city's quirky museums and opulent architecture. Many of Budapest's more touristy attractions (St. Stephen's Basilica, the Great Market Hall, the Széchenyi Chain Bridge) are centrally located and are free or nearly free, meaning that you can check them out fairly quickly and move onto even better things.

🏛 CITADELLA / GELLERT HILL

Budapest's best aphrodisiac (not the shots of palinka, which tend more toward the soporific side) is watching the sunset from the top of Gellert Hill. A steep, 20-minute hike from the banks of the Buda side will take you up to the nineteenth-century Citadella, which provides panoramic views of the inner city, including Buda Castle and the Parliament Building. Sure, the hordes of tourists imitating the pose of the hill's enormous Liberty Statue might be a bit of a turn-off, but when the sun sets on the Danube, you and your SO/past one-night-stand/future one-night-stand might just be spellbound.

i Free. From the Pest side, cross the Elisabeth Bridge and take the stairs immediately opposite. The paths going up Gellert Hill often diverge, but unlike Robert Frost you won't wish you could've traveled both, because they all lead to the same place. There's a bar atop the hill, but you can also save a few forints and BYOB. Bathrooms available atop the hill until 8pm—after that, well, you're in a forest.

MUSEUM OF APPLIED ARTS (IPARMŰVÉSZETI MÚZEUM)

1091 Budapest, Üllői str. 33-37.   ☎1 456 5107 http://www.imm.hu/en/contents/informacio

The most jaw-dropping building in Budapest isn't the Hungarian Parliament Building (too try-hard) or St. Matthias Church (Gothic? How passé...), but this Art Nouveau stunner that houses Budapest's material arts museum. The Mughal-inspired interior is worth the small price of admission alone (900 Ft for students), but the exhibits are excellent too, centering on luxury objects owned by the kinds of people who wouldn't be caught dead holding a *Let's Go* guide. Tiffany vases abound.

i 2000 Ft, 3500 Ft for temporary exhibitions, students ticket 900 Ft/1750 Ft. Open Tu-Su 10am-6pm. Cash or credit. Free Wi-Fi available in the café on the ground floor.

HUNGARIAN PARLIAMENT BUILDING

Kossuth Lajos tér 1-3   ☎1 441 4000 http://latogatokozpont.parlament.hu/en

"The motherland does not have a house," the Hungarian poet Milhaly Corosmarty lamented in 1846; luckily, he wouldn't have to wait too long for this mega-mansion to arrive. Built in response to the growing Hungarian nationalist movement of the nineteenth century, this palatial Gothic building looks more like a cathedral than a seat of government. The building is the largest in Hungary and third largest parliament in the world, towering at 96m—a number which references the date of Hungary's millennial anniversary.

While the Parliament's exterior provides more than enough material for a good eyegasm, tours of the interior are also offered every day in Hungarian and English. Decked in gold and marble, the building has 692 rooms and once required more electricity than the rest of the city combined to operate; if you're patient, you'll even catch a glimpse of the original Holy Crown of Hungary.

i 5400 Ft, students 2800 Ft. Open Apr-Oct M-F 8am-6pm, Sa-Su 8am-4pm; Nov-Mar M-Su 8am-4pm.

MATTHIAS CHURCH

2 Szentháromság tér.   ☎1 488 7716 http://www.matyas-templom.hu/

Decked out with a colorful tiled roof and steeples, this Gothic church atop Castle Hill is one of Budapest's most photographed sights. Turn your back on the church and the view is just as stunning: the hill overlooks the Pest side of the Danube and is the perfect setting for a travel selfie that'll rake in the likes.

While the exterior of the church no longer reflects its original 13th century state, you can still find little pieces of history scattered around inside. While facing the altar, turn left in order to see the tombs of King Bela III and his first wife, the only tombs in the church to survive the Ottoman occupation. Archeologists stripped the corpses of their royal jewelry a few years back in order to display the gems in the National Museum. Ghostly royal wrath resulting from the de-jeweling has yet to be felt, so be sure to only speak words of admiration while viewing the replica of the Hungarian crown upstairs in the church's Museum of Ecclesiastical Art. You'll want to be in good favor with Old Bela when he arises to take back his beloved jewels.

i 1500 Ft, students 1000 Ft. Open M-Sa 9am-5pm, Su 1-5pm.

DOHÁNY STREET SYNAGOGUE / JEWISH MUSEUM

Dohány u. 2, 1074   http://www.greatsynagogue.hu/gallery_syn.html

Although it's the largest synagogue in Europe, this Moorish Revival-style masterpiece hardly looks the part. Featuring a cavernous interior, stained glass, and a massive organ (played by a Gentile to keep its Neolog congregation in line with Shabbat), the 150-year-old structure is the closest thing to a church this side of a bacon cheeseburger. Skip the guided tour, which consists of exactly two long-winded stops, and instead head over to the Jewish Museum found inside the synagogue complex. Here there's a superb collection of Judaica, ranging

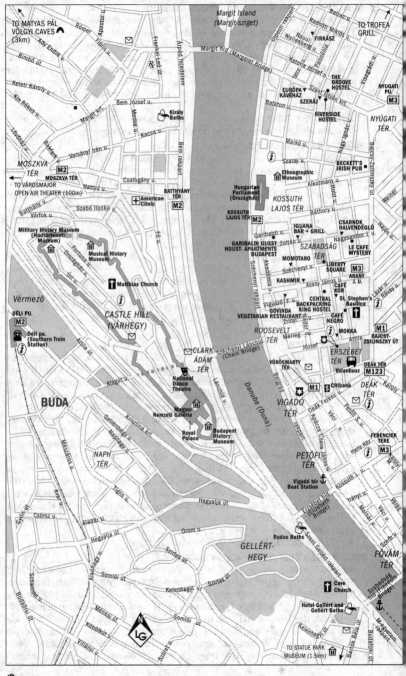

Margit Island
(Margit-sziget)

TO MATYAS PÁL
VÖLGYI CAVES
(3km)

TO TROFEA
GRILL

Margit híd (Margaret Bridge)

THE
GROOVE
HOSTEL

NYUGATI
PU.
M3

EURÓPA ▼
KÁVÉHÁZ

SZERÁJ

RIVERSIDE
HOSTEL

NYÚGATI
TÉR

Király
Baths

BECKETT'S
IRISH PUB

MOSZKVA
TÉR
M2
MOSZKVA TÉR

TO VÁROSMAJOR
OPEN AIR THEATER (100m)

BATTHYÁNY
TÉR
M2

Hungarian
Parliament
(Országház)

Ethnographic
Museum

KOSSUTH
LAJOS TÉR

American
Clinic

KOSSUTH
LAJOS TÉR
M2

CSARNOK
HALVENDÉGLŐ

Military History Museum
(Hadtörténeti
Múzeum)

IGUANA
BAR + GRILL

GARIBALDI GUEST
HOUST- APARTMENTS
BUDAPEST

SZABADSÁG
TÉR

LE CAFE
MYSTERY

Musical History
Museum

MOMOTARO

LIBERTY
SQUARE

Matthias Church

KASHMIR ▼

M3

ARANY
J. U.

CAFÉ
KÖR

Vérmező

CENTRAL
BACKPACKING
KING HOSTEL

St. Stephen's
Basilica

CASTLE HILL
(VÁRHEGY)

GOVINDA
VEGETARIAN RESTAURANT

CAFÉ
NEGRO

DÉLI PU.
M2
Déli pu.
(Southern Train
Station)

ROOSEVELT
TÉR

MOKKA

M1

BAJCSY-
ZSILINSZKY ÚT

CLARK
ÁDÁM
TÉR

Széchenyi Lánchíd
(Chain Bridge)

ERZSÉBET
TÉR

DEÁK TÉR

DEÁK
TÉR

VÖRÖSMARTY
TÉR

Volanbusz
M123

BUDA

National
Dance
Theatre

Danube (Duna)

M1

Citibank

VIGADÓ
TÉR

Magyar
Nemzeti Galéria

Royal
Palace

Budapest
History
Museum

PETŐFI
TÉR

FERENCIEK
TERE
M3

NAPH
TÉR

Vigadó tér
Boat Station

Hegyalja út

Erzsébet híd
(Elizabeth
Bridge)

GELLÉRT-
HEGY

Rudas Baths

FÖVÁM
TÉR

Cave
Church

Szabadság híd (Freedom
Bridge)

Hotel Gellért and
Gellért Baths

TO STATUE PARK
MUSEUM (1.5km)

N
LG

hungary

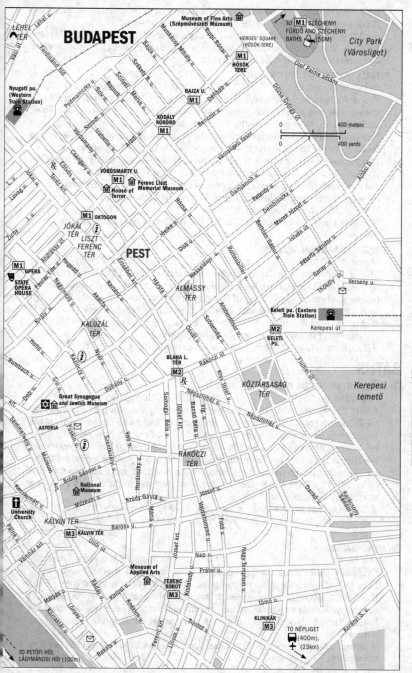

from 16th century ceremonial swords to a diary of a Hungarian Jew during the Holocaust—and not a single droning tour guide to be seen.

i *3000 Ft, students with ISIC card 2000 Ft. Guided tours an additional 700 Ft. Open Th 10am-7:30pm, F 10am-4:30pm, Su 10am-7:30pm. The synagogue closes three hours earlier in winter. Cards accepted. Free Wi-Fi in the Jewish Museum.*

PINBALL MUSEUM (FLIPPER MUZEUM)

Radnóti Miklós utca 18.   ☎30 900 6091 http://www.flippermuzeum.hu/en/

You don't have to have a supple wrist to enjoy the 130+ working pinball machines collected at the recently-opened Pinball Museum in Újlipótváros. Housed underground, the museum (really an arcade, since there's no history of pinball to be found) has themed machines ranging from Hollywood classics (Star Wars and Indiana Jones) to some truly odd science-fiction-inspired sets from Germany. Playing any of the machines is totally free and is unlimited with your ticket, so don't worry if you're not a wizard—Player 1 is always up to shoot here. Although the museum's more devoted (read: even nerdier) patrons often play well into the evening, the noise and flashing lights created by all the sets may turn you into Tommy: deaf, dumb, and blind.

i *2500 Ft, students from EU 1200 Ft. Open W-F 4pm-midnight, Sa 2pm-midnight, Su 10am-10pm. Cash only.*

HUNGARIAN NATIONAL MUSEUM

Múzeum krt. 14-16   ☎1 338 2122 http://hnm.hu/en

The one museum in Budapest where you're more likely to run into locals than tourists, the Hungarian National Museum is an exhaustive (and sometimes exhausting) chronological survey of Hungary's material culture from the Stone Age to the present day. Stuffed with literally thousands of well-described artifacts that trace Hungary's historical contact with the Romans, Ottomans, and Soviets, the museum rewards those who are willing to wander.

i *1600 Ft. Open Tu-Su 10am-6pm. Wi-Fi available. Cash or credit.*

BATHS

⬛ SZÉCHENYI MEDICINAL BATH

Állatkerti út. 9-11, 1146   ☎1 363 3210 http://www.szechenyibath.hu/

Easily the wettest labyrinth in the world, the enormous complex of swimming pools, steam rooms, thermal baths, and saunas that make up Széchenyi takes several relaxing hours to wade through. To be fair, exactly how relaxing those hours are will depend on how comfortable you are around large, speedo-wearing Hungarian men—but following them around helps provide a method to the madness that is Széchenyi. Be sure to bring a towel, or you'll have to rent one (1000 Ft). Flip-flops and a plastic bag to put your wet items in afterwards are also highly recommended.

i *Daily ticket with locker 4700 Ft. on weekdays, 4900 Ft. on weekends. Outdoor baths open daily 6am-10pm. Thermal baths open 6am-7pm. Extra for private cabin and/or massages. Cash or credit.*

⬛ KIRÁLY BATHS

Fő u. 84   ☎1 202 3688 http://en.kiralyfurdo.hu/

Originally built during the 16th century when Budapest was still under Ottoman rule, the interior of Király looks like it hasn't been renovated since. What this local hangout lacks in opulence (and English-speaking staff) compared to Széchenyi, it makes up for in smaller crowds and a tidy appearance. As an added bonus, Király's student discount means you can get clean without cleaning out your wallet.

i *Student ticket with locker 1800 Ft, standard ticket with locker 2400 Ft. Open daily 9am-9pm. Cash or credit.*

◪ BIG FISH HOSTEL $

Erzsébet krt. 33 ☎70 302 2432 http://www.bigfishhostel.com/budapest/

Located a few minutes from all of Budapest's major ruin pubs, Big Fish is an ideal place for travelers who want to turn both up and down. There's a pregame to be found every night in the hostel's combination kitchen/living room, which features a blackboard updated daily with nightclub recommendations by Big Fish's laid-back staff.

i Dorms $15-20. Cash only. Wi-Fi available, but cuts out often. Laundry service available for extra. Reception open 24hr.

◪ ADAGIO HOSTEL 2.0 $$

Andrássy út 2 ☎1 950 9674 http://adagiohostel.com/

Housed in a retro building straight out of a Wes Anderson flick, this grand Budapest hostel has been updated for the 21st century, featuring loads of natural light and a spacious, modern interior. Reasonably priced for its location (spitting distance from St. Stephen's Basilica), Adagio provides lodgers with a kitchen and free coffee.

i Dorms $20-25. Laundry service available for extra. Reception open 24hr.

◪ CARPE NOCTEM ORIGINAL $$

Szobi u. 5, 1067 ☎20 365 8749

If you have any desire to get a good night's rest and have a productive early morning, 1) why are you in Budapest? and 2) do not stay at Carpe Noctem. This party hostel lives up to its name, leading travellers out every night to one of Budapest's ruin pubs or clubs. The staff are young, friendly and international, a dynamic shared by the lodgers themselves: Carpe Noctem has a policy of not allowing any groups of more than three people to stay the night, meaning that most of the guests are young solo travelers looking to meet new friends. There's only 20 beds, so chances are you'll get to know your neighbors.

i Dorms $20-25. Reception open 24hr.

MAVERICK HOSTEL $$$

Ferenciek tere 2 ☎1 267 3166

With its marble walls, wrought-iron stairs, and most importantly, extremely clean facilities, it's no wonder why Maverick Hostel has long been considered one of Budapest's best. Even in a 10-bed mixed dormitory, each traveler and his or her backpack have room to spread out. Maverick offers lockers for valuables, although its familial atmosphere feels safe and secure. Its prime location (only a block from the Danube) makes it easy for even the drunkest of customers to find their way home—just head to the Elizabeth Bridge.

i Dorms $30-35. Reception open 24hr.

budapest

FOOD

Eating on a budget in Budapest is as easy as eating; due to the city's low prices, many sit-down meals can be enjoyed for less than 1000 Ft a pop. Eating well is only slightly more challenging—in general, avoid restaurants that accept euros, which tend to cater to out-of-the-loop tourists who don't know goulash from pálinka. For best results, steer clear of the overpriced traps along Vaci utca in Pest and avoid eating anything substantial in Great Market Hall.

BORS GASZTROBÁR $

Kazinczy u. 10   ☎70 935 3263

In the world of Budapest street food and its tempting döner kebabs, Obi-Wan Kenobi's warning rings true: "Your eyes can deceive you. Don't trust them." Fortunately, whether you're suffering from low blood sugar or high midi-chlorians, there's one cantina in Budapest that's dedicated to serving up delicious (yet cheap) soups and baguette sandwiches: Bors GasztroBár. While it might be nice to have C-3PO alongside you to translate Bors' entirely Star Wars-themed and almost entirely Hungarian menu, the protocol droid server taking your order will be happy to offer a few forceful suggestions, just as soon as he's done picking out an even more aggressive Hungarian rap track to blast from his iPod. While Bors never quite becomes a wretched hive of scum and villainy, it does get crowded around dinner time, so anyone with a pressing need to get to Tosche Station to pick up some power converters should consider skipping the sandwiches—which don't exactly come out at light speed—and go for the soup instead (540 Ft) And remember: even when you leave Budapest, the Bors will always be with you.

i Soup 540 Ft. Sandwiches 540-780 Ft. Open daily 11:30am-9pm. Cash or credit. No Wi-Fi.

FRICI PAPA KIFOZDÉJE $

Király utca 55   ☎061 351 0197 www.fricipapa.hu

Casting aside decades of Food Network dogma, Frici Papa displays no interest in carefully plating its dishes. You see, that might limit the portion size—and the main goal of this traditional Hungarian café is to gorge its customers on mouth-watering stew, meat, potatoes, and pastries. The price of Frici Papa's daily three-course lunch menu (napi menü, 999 Ft) can't be beat. Quality and quantity: who said it was a tradeoff?

i Lunch menu (Napi menü) 999 Ft. Mains 700-800 Ft. Drinks 300-400 Ft. Open M-Sa 11am–11pm. Cash or credit. Wi-Fi available. Pro tip: Pay at the counter after you're finished.

TÖLTŐ $$

Wesselényi u. 31   http://www.tolto.net/

Catering to the drunk at heart, TöLTő serves up luxury sausages at affordable prices. The restaurant's made-to-order creations (lime-ginger chicken sausage with ponzu sauce, coconut balls, and radishes; chili pork sausage with ratatouille sauce and kumquats) generally take around 15min. to prepare—fast food it ain't. But what TöLTő lacks in immediate gratification, it makes up for with mouthwatering flavors and generous portions. This might be the one time that "nine inches" isn't an exaggeration.

i Sausages 1200-1300 Ft. Open M-F noon-8pm, Sa-Su noon-midnight. Cash or credit. Wi-Fi available (just ask).

RUSZWURM CUKRÁSZDA $

1014 Budapest, Szentháromság u. 7.   ☎1 375 5284 www.ruszwurm.hu

Despite displaying all the trappings of a tourist trap—location next to a major monument, swarms of English-speaking customers—Ruszwurm evades the category in the most delicious way possible, serving up traditional Hungarian pastries and cakes at prices that don't seem to have risen much since the bakery's opening in 1827. For a classic treat, try the dobostorta (a layered sponge cake); the lip-puckering sour cherry strudel also can't be missed. If the café is full—and it probably will be—order your goodies to go and enjoy them in the park adjacent to the Fisherman's Bastion.

i Cash only. No Wi-Fi. Standing in front of St. Matthias Church, turn around and walk down the main street.

NAPFÉNYES ÉTTEREM $$

Ferenciek tere 2   ☎20 311 0313 http://www.napfenyesetterem.hu/

Eating in a country in which the standard serving size is four chicken breasts can be a shock to the gastrointestinal system. Enter Napfényes, a restaurant that accomplishes the miraculous feat of transforming traditional Hungarian dishes into vegan delights. Dig into crispy oat fritters, stuffed cabbages, and seemingly endless potatoes while sipping on a glass of Napfényes' signature ginger lemonade. It might not taste like chicken, but you've probably had enough already.

i Mains 1500-2500 Ft. Open daily noon-10:30pm. Cash or credit.

KICSI CSÁNGÓ MAGYAR KONYHA $$

Alagút u. 1, 1013   ☎30 338 6888

Sometimes, eating like a true Hungarian means doing it yourself. Not cooking (the horror) but ordering à la carte from the offerings of one of Budapest's many cafeteria-style local joints, in which different types of meat, potatoes, and salads sit behind glass like delicious puzzle pieces. Unlike many of the city's sit-down cafés advertising "Traditional Hungarian Food," there's often very little English spoken at these places, so take a deep breath and get ready to point your way to a meal. Kicsi Csángó, located a stone's throw away from the non-Danube side of Castle Hill in Buda, is a convenient and tasty option for those looking to eat like a local in one Budapest's most tourist-heavy zones. Specializing in homemade vegetable stew (főzelék), roasted chicken, and potluck-style cold salads, Kicsi Csángó might not be the most delicate way to fill one's stomach in Budapest, but it's one of the more satisfying.

i Meals with drink and dessert 1700-2300 Ft. Open daily 24hr. Wi-Fi Available. Cash or Credit.

NIGHTLIFE

If you're reading this section, then we don't have to tell you to go to Budapest's ruin pubs—enormous, multi-room complexes that attract a mix of internationals and locals. While the clubbing in Budapest is rightfully legendary, don't overlook the significantly cheaper bars and pubs that populate Erzsebétváros, where drink deals can help you pre-game for the till-dawn parties of the ruin pubs at a third of the price. Or, there's always the least expensive and most traditionally Hungarian option: buying your own bottles and cans at an ABC store and drinking them on the street. No open container laws? Time to open some containers.

INSTANT

Nagymező utca 38   ☎1 311 0704 http://instant.co.hu/en

Instant is a psychedelic maze of optical illusions, flashing lights, and stuffed animal heads whose eyes may or may not be following the drunk patrons. While that may sound like your worst nightmare, Instant is a must-go for those looking to experience the best of Budapest's nightlife. Close your air passages while crossing the barrier of smoke that serves as Instant's greeting—its long entryway is the only smoker-friendly room in the joint—and then open your mind to Budapest's adult funhouse. With over 20 rooms and four stories, everyone is guaranteed a spot on one of Instant's many dance floors, each with its own DJ and bar. The music changes from room to room: anything from the archetypal American turn-up jams (which you know by heart) to European drum and bass (which you don't) blasts through the halls of this ruin pub. While very popular amongst tourists, Instant is also a go-to for locals.

i Beer 680 Ft. Mixed drinks 980-1400 Ft. Open daily 4pm-6am. No cover. Cash only.

STIFLER BAR

Erzsébet krt. 19   ☎20 200 1000 http://legjobbkocsma.hu/pub/bemutatkozas/stifler_bar

Stifler edges out the many near-identical bars that line Budapest's Erzsébet krt. thanks to its slightly lower drink prices, fanatical dedication to all things sports,

Budapest is one of Europe's best cities for English-language bookstores, which cater to both plot-starved travelers and locals trying to buff up on their (already quite excellent) foreign language skills. Let's Go recommends **Massolit Books** and **Libra Books,** both located on the Pest side, which sell used copies of everything ranging from classics to Twilight at reasonable prices. If you feel like a taste of local literature, both also sell works in translation by contemporary Hungarian literary superstars like Péter Nádas, László Krasznahorkai, and Sándor Márai.

and internal passageway to a burger joint. No spot in the sprawling, multi-story bar has a view of fewer than four flat-screen televisions, which also makes Stifler an ideal place to catch a game with friends. Beer and spirits are self-service (not frozen yogurt-style self-service, you dolt; we mean there are no waiters).

i Beer 390-600 Ft. Drinks 290-800 Ft. Open M-Sa 9am-5am, Su 9am-midnight. Cash only. No Wi-Fi.

SZIMPLA KERT

Kazinczy utca 14 ☎20 261 8669 www.szimpla.hu

Budapest's first and most famous ruin pub ranks among the most trippy hangout spots on any night out in the city. Fruit-flavored hookah smoke will assault your nose before you even step within Szimpla's graffitied arches. The extra dollar or two that you spend on your drink here seems to fund the entertainment, which ranges from experimental films screened in the pub's very own cinema-themed room to screaming girls spraying each other with whipped cream. The bar fills up fairly early with an international crowd, but if you're looking to really throw down on the dance floor Szimpla may not be the spot. Instead, chill with friends in one of Szimpla's cave-like rooms; with its relaxed, low energy, Szimpla is an ideal first stop on a night of bar-hopping.

i Beer 700-900 Ft. Mixed drinks 900-1500 Ft. No cover. Open daily 12pm-4am. Cash or credit.

BOBEK CAFÉ

Kazinczy u. 53 ☎1 322 0729 www.bobek.hu

Half ruin pub, half beer garden, Bobek is the perfect place to beat the crowds (and prices) of Budapest's more popular pubs and clubs. Sitting at Bobek's picnic tables, patrons can sip on gargantuan glasses of Hungarian wine (300-500 Ft/dl, usually served in 3dl portions). Planning to pregame at Bobek is a dangerous move, because you might not make it to the actual game.

i Beer 500-800 Ft. Mixed drinks 900-1300 Ft. Open M-Th 1pm-midnight, F 1pm-2am, Sa 3pm-2am.

ESSENTIALS

Practicalities

- **TOURIST OFFICES:** Tourinform arranges tours and accommodations (Suto utca 2, ☎01 429 97 51, open M-F 9-6:30pm, Sa 9am-2:30pm). The Budapest Card provides discounts, unlimited public transportation, and free or discounted admission to most museums, but unless you're planning to make it to most of its applicable sights, we recommend skipping it.

- **ATMS:** English-language ATMs from which you can withdraw forints and euros can be found on almost every corner. Be careful using the most common Euronet ATMs, as these often have hidden fees and poor exchange rates; the ATMs located within Hungarian banks generally provide better deals. Currency changing businesses are also widely available, and generally

hungary

have decent exchange rates—just check before you change your money to avoid getting ripped off by a few of the bad apples.

- **LGBT RESOURCES:** Check http://www.budapestgaycity.net/ for updates on LGBT activities and LGBT-friendly businesses in Budapest.

- **LAUNDROMATS:** Self-service laundromats are relatively rare in Budapest, but there are a few located in Pest under the name Önkiszolgáló mosoda. Otherwise, your hostel or hotel will generally be willing to do your laundry for a small fee.

- **INTERNET:** Wi-Fi is widely available in cafés and restaurants in Budapest. Generally, you just need to ask the cashier for the password. Public Wi-Fi tends to be a little spottier and can be found near most of the major tourist attractions in Buda.

- **POST OFFICES:** Post offices in Budapest are generally open Monday to Friday 8am-6pm, though some hours vary. To inquire about specific hours call ☎06 40 46 46 46. Postal services in Budapest are run by Maygar Post. Their website is all in Hungarian, so to find the post office nearest you, your best bet is use Google Maps. The main office is on Petöfi Sandor St., though there are many post offices in Budapest in each of its districts, all offering the same services.

Emergency

- **GENERAL MEDICAL EMERGENCY:** ☎112
- **DOMESTIC INQUIRIES:** ☎198
- **INTERNATIONAL INQUIRIES:** ☎199
- **IN CASE OF FIRE:** ☎112
- **24HR. MEDICAL ASSISTANCE IN ENGLISH (FALCK SOS HUNGARY):** ☎06 1 2000 100
- **POLICE:** ☎01 438 80 80. The office for tourist police is located inside the Tourinform office at Suto utca 2. You can get here through the metro lines: M1, M2, or M3 at the Deak ter stop. Or, you can reach them by phone at ☎01 438 80 80. The office is open 24hr. a day.

- **LATE-NIGHT PHARMACIES:** Look for green signs labeled Apotheke, Gyogyszertar, or Pharmacie. Many pharmacies and drugstores are not open 24hr. Déli Pharmacy (XII district, Alkotás út 1/b), Óbuda Pharmacy (II district, Vörösvári út 84), Szent Margit Pharmacy (II district, Frankel Leó út 22), and Teréz Pharmacy (VI district, Teréz krt. 41) are all 24hr. pharmacies. The website budapest-moms.com also has a full list of 24hr. pharmacies.

- **MEDICAL SERVICES:** The majority of hospitals and clinics in Budapest have English-speaking personnel. Two sure-bet 24hr. clinics are FirstMed Center (Hattyú utca 14, 5th floor; ☎06 1 224 9090) and Rózsakert Medical Center (Gábor Áron u. 74-78; ☎ 06 1 392 0505). The US embassy also maintains a list of English-speaking doctors. Call 112 if faced with a serious emergency. You should not hesitate to contact the police in Budapest if you are the victim of a crime. Be sure to carry a valid passport, as police have the right to ask for identification. Police can sometimes be unhelpful if you are the victim of a currency exchange scam; in this instance, it may be better to seek advice from your country's embassy or consulate.

Getting There

The Budapest international airport, Budapest Ferihegy Airport, is 16km southeast of downtown Budapest. For general information regarding the airport, call ☎36 1 296 9696; regarding flight details, call ☎36 1 296 7000. The airport has ATMs and many exchange bureaus, but avoid exchanging currency at the airport as nearly every block in downtown Budapest has an exchange station that offers far better rates.

There are many ways to get into the city from the airport. All major car rental companies have stations inside the airport. The airport also offers a cheaper minibus service that will take you to your final destination in the city. Prices vary depending on your address, but as a rule of thumb the minibus price will be less than a taxi

hungary

and more than a standard bus. If public transportation is the right choice for your wallet, the BKV bus number 200E goes to M3 station Kőbánya-Kispest (blue line), about 20min. away. You'll need to transfer from here to the metro, which will take you straight into the city center. You can buy a transfer ticket (500 Ft) at the airport, but be sure to validate your ticket on the bus and on the metro! For those flush with cash, a final option is one of Budapest's infamous taxis—the fastest way of getting to the city center, but also the most expensive.

Getting Around

By Taxi

Taxis are widely available in Budapest. Note that taxi rates are not regulated by the government, so frequent use might spell disaster for your pocketbook. Independent taxis are especially dangerous in this regard, but not always easy to spot. Ask your hostel or hotel for the number of a reliable taxi company which you can call if you need a taxi's services. While it may look glamorous to flag down a cab, this may just be your bank account's swan song in Budapest.

Public Transportation

Almost no sight or activity is a far walk in Budapest. In fact, Let's Go recommends walking as often as possible—it's the best way to experience the city's unique architecture and varied landscape. For rainy days, Budapest's public transportation company, BKV, offers bus, trolley bus, tram, and metro services, making it easy to maneuver the city for the time- or movement-impaired. BKV's services run daily from 4:30am-11pm; ticket are cheap at 300 Ft (€1) per trip. Tickets must be bought and presented before entering the bus or station. If you plan on using public transportation a lot, look for deals like 24hr. or 72hr. unlimited or 10-ticket passes. These can be found at all metro stations where regular tickets are sold, along with maps of the BKV network. The main station downtown is Deák tér Station, where all lines interconnect. Budapest also offers a night bus, which runs every 15min-1hr. from 11pm-4am. Tickets are bought on board the night bus, and security officers now stand guard to make sure every party animal pays—so be sure to validate your tickets by sticking them in the orange machines, or you'll have to pay a hefty (8000 Ft) fine! All information on public transportation, specific pricing, and schedules can be found at www.bkv.hu/en.

győr

The original city of Győr (which means "burnt city") was razed to the ground during the 16th century by its commander Kristóf Lamberg in a slightly misguided attempt to keep the city from the claws of the invading Turkish army. It was soon resurrected in Renaissance style and retains its cobblestone streets and delicately molded buildings to this very day. Despite its charm, Győr hasn't quite made it onto the tourist circuit yet; English is a rarity here and most of the visitors are small-town locals from the surrounding area. To the outsider Győr's intimacy may seem intimidating, but its old world charm is undeniable. Travelers on the road between Budapest and Vienna should consider stopping here for an afternoon.

SIGHTS

Győr has very few traditional "sights", so the best way to experience the city is to wander the old town surrounding Széchenyi Square and the Raba River. The Rado Holm island in the middle of the Raba is a small, secluded getaway for many local couples and teenagers looking to escape the (very relative) hustle and bustle of Győr's city center.

FOOD

VEGABONA BÜFÉ $
Árpád út 26   ☎20 230 1356

The fact that Vegabona has survived within the meat-dominated culinary landscape of small-town Hungary is a testament to its tastiness. This small café serves up vegan burgers made from a variety of non-animal things (mushroom, oat, beet), accompanied by homemade potato chips (combo 1200 Ft). The portion sizes are hardly Hungarian—but then again, hardly anything about Vegabona is.

i Open M-Sa 11am-8pm. Cash or card. Wi-Fi available.

CAFÉ FREI $
Czuczor Gergely utca 6   ☎20 373 7408

If eating gelato is an occasional treat in Budapest, it's an obsession in Győr. Let's Go recommends eating as much as possible (we're not your doctor), and Café Frei should be your first stop. Scooping creative flavor combinations like mango ginger, caramel orange, and yuzu currant, Café Frei also sacrifices the ostentatious piles of gelato of other purveyors in order to chill its cream properly in covered cylinders. The result is perfectly refreshing.

i Scoops 220 Ft. each. Open Th 10am-10pm, F-Sa 10am-midnight, Su 10am-10pm. Cash only.

PALFFY ITALIA $$
Kenyér köz 1

Full of families and ladies who lunch, Palffy Italia hosts possibly half the population of downtown Győr on any given sunny day. Palffy deserves its own popularity but is not a place for a quick bite. While perhaps most popular for its thin, family-size gourmet pizzas, its menu offers a range of pastas, salads, and meats—most featuring everyone's favorite artery blocker, mozzarella cheese. Although the wait staff may not perfectly understand English—and most certainly won't comprehend your horrid attempts at sounding out Hungarian—they are patient and excellent hosts.

i Pizzas 1800 Ft. Entrees 2000-4000 Ft. Open daily 9am-midnight. Cash or card.

NIGHTLIFE

NAPSUGÁR OLD BAR
János Pál tér

If you're in Győr to party, it might be quicker to hop a train to Budapest than to hunt down the club scene in this sleepy town. A light buzz is easier to find, and the array of cocktails served up by Napsugár Old Bar make the hunt delicious. Order a properly dirty martini (made, as the menu notes, from the original recipe in Jerry Thomas's 1862 Bar-Tender's Guide) and sit out on the patio—at only 1200 Ft, you've got a license to spill.

i Cocktails 1000-2000 Ft. Open W-Sa 5pm-midnight. Cash only. No Wi-Fi.

ESSENTIALS

Practicalities

- **TOURIST OFFICES:** Tourinform arranges tours and accommodations. The Tourinform office in Győr is located between the train station and the downtown area at Baross Gábor út 21 (☎96 33 68 17).

- **ATMS:** Readily available on most streets near the city center. Cash change stations are also available near the train station.

- **POST OFFICES:** The main post office in Győr can be found at Bajcsy-Zsilinszky út 46, right across from the Győr National Theatre. It's open Monday to Friday 8am-6pm.

◪ **GRÓF CZIRÁKY PANZIÓ GYŐR** $$$
　Bécsi kapu tér 8　　　　　　☎96 52 84 66 www.hotelcziraky.hu/?lang=en

Tucked away in a secluded corner that's only a 3min. walk from Széchenyi tér, Győr's main square, this hotel is the perfect blend of peace and proximity. The quaint yellow building embodies the best of the old world feel that Győr has to offer, with charming single rooms with their own small private bath and television. Besides the luxury of having your own personal shower, Gróf Cziráky Panzió serves a complimentary breakfast spread each morning down in its basement, which also operates as a restaurant at night.

i Dorms €35; doubles €45. Reception open 6am-7pm.

Emergency

- **GENERAL MEDICAL EMERGENCY:** ☎112

- **HUNGARIAN POLICE DEPARTMENT:** ☎107

- **INTERNATIONAL COUNTRY CODE:** ☎36

- **FIRE:** ☎105

- **24HR. MEDICAL ASSISTANCE IN ENGLISH (FALCK SOS HUNGARY):** ☎06 12 00 01 00.

- **TOURIST POLICE:** There is no tourist police office in Győr, but the Győr City Police are ready to assist in an emergency. The Győr City Police office can be found at Zrínyi utca 54; their telephone number is ☎96 52 00 00.

- **PHARMACY:** Look for green signs labeled Apotheke, Gyogyszertar, or Pharmacie. There are six pharmacies in Győr, three of which are clustered around the Győr National Theatre. Aranyhajó gyógyszertár (Jedlik Ányos utca 16) has a selection of medicines and is open Monday to Friday 7am-6pm and Saturday 7am-2pm. Most pharmacies are not open on weekends, and none are open 24hr. For serious medical emergencies, call 112.

- **MEDICAL SERVICES:** Because English is not widely spoken in Győr, the Petz-Aladár Teaching Hospital, which offers all services besides open-heart and transplant surgery, is recommended for tourists. It is one of the biggest hospitals in Hungary and is located at Zrínyi utca 13 (☎96 418 244).

- **LOCAL LAWS AND POLICE:** You should not hesitate to contact the police if you are the victim of a crime. Be sure to carry a valid passport, as police have the right to ask for identification. Police can sometimes be unhelpful if you are the victim of a currency exchange scam; in this instance, it may be better to seek advice from your country's embassy or consulate.

Getting There

The Győr International Airport, Győr-Pér Airport, has not been in use since December 2013. The closest airport is the Budapest international airport, Budapest Ferihegy Airport, 16km southeast of downtown Budapest. For general information regarding the airport call ☎12 96 96 96; for information regarding flight details call ☎12 96 70 00. Győr is about a 1hr. 30min. drive from Budapest. Highway M1 connects the city with the capital. Check out www.elvira.hu to see train listings from Budapest to Győr. Trains and buses between the two cities depart fairly regularly and usually cost under 2500 Ft. Győr is also an hour's bus ride from Bratislava, Slovakia—for cheap bus tickets between the two, see https://www.regiojet.sk/.

excursion: bratislava

Often overlooked in favor of nearby European capitals (Vienna is an hour away; Budapest, two), Bratislava is beginning to make a comeback as a destination rather than a stopover. The city's compact and well-preserved old town, which dates back to its days as medieval Pressburg, is a maze of narrow alleyways, grand royal buildings, and even grander churches, all nestled alongside the slowly rolling Danube. Bratislava is a city where kings (and queens) were once crowned, and it's not difficult to see why.

SIGHTS

All of Bratislava's important sights are clustered within or near the radius of its old town. Most, like the reconstructed castle that overlooks the city, are best to simply admire from the outside—but you'll still have plenty at which to marvel.

▧ ST. MARTIN'S CATHEDRAL
Rudnayovo námestie 1

Lying just a few steps away from the city's infamous "UFO Bridge," St. Martin's Cathedral encapsulates Bratislava's lengthy, proud, and oft-troubled history. Completed in 1452, the church was the coronation site for the rulers of Hungary in 1563, and continued in that capacity until 1830. Maria Theresa (one of the original girls to rule the world) was crowned here in 1741, and Bratislava hosts an annual festival in June to celebrate the event. Entrance is cheap and includes access to the crypts, which house the remains of Bratislava's best and brightest (and dead).

i €2. Open M-Sa 9-11:30am and 1-6pm, Su 1:30-14pm.

FOOD

Slovakian food will be familiar to anyone who's experienced Hungarian, Czech, or Austrian food—plenty of dumplings, pork, and more pork. The most prevalent traditional dish here is bryndzové halusky, or potato and sheep cheese dumplings topped with crispy bacon.

▧ SLOVAK PUB $
Obchodná 613/62   http://www.slovakpub.sk/index.php/en/

Boasting a sixteen-page menu of traditional Slovakian food and nearly as many rooms filled with tipsy locals, Slovak Pub offers a tasty and cheap opportunity to try out the local delicacies, which tend toward the sour (sauerkraut and sausage soup, sheep's cheese, and more). The house-brewed beer flows easily at just €1.50 a pint, and since Slovak Pub is just a few minutes' walk from Bratislava's Old Town you can afford to have a few without worrying about getting lost.

i Mains €5-10. Beer €1.50-2.50. Wine €2-4. Open M-Th 10am-midnight, F-Sa 10am-2am, Su noon-11pm. Cash or credit.

NIGHTLIFE

NU SPIRIT BAR
Štúrova 19/3

Ironically, it's best to watch out for the spirits at Bratislava's surprisingly atmospheric (for a basement) Nu Spirit Bar. Order a mixed drink and the bartender might make a move toward the top shelf, at which point it's appropriate to wave your Let's Go guide at him and remind him that you're broke. But when the price is right (usually €5 for mixed drinks), it's right, and Nu Spirit has some low-key mixologists on staff. Live DJs begin spinning drum n' bass and house music at 9pm each night.

i Cocktails €5, Beer €3-4. Open W-Sa 8pm-5am. Cash only.

get a room!

WILD ELEPHANTS HOSTEL $$

Františkánske námestie 413/8   ☎908 821 174 http://www.elephants.sk/

You can't buy friendship, but it comes at a discount in dirt-cheap Bratislava's hostel scene, especially at Wild Elephants. Catering to solo travelers and small groups (4 or less), this laid-back, bare-bones hostel takes its friendliness seriously, organizing nightly vegan-friendly dinners and pub crawls for its crowd of student travelers. Wild Elephants is no insomniac Budapest party hostel, but don't expect to have an early night—your newfound friends will see to that.

i Dorms €16-20. Reception open 24hr.

ESSENTIALS

Practicalities

- **TOURIST OFFICES:** The central tourist center in Bratislava is located at Klobučnícka 2 and is open daily 9am-7pm.

- **ATMS:** Readily available on most streets near the city center.

- **POST OFFICES:** The main post office in Bratislava can be found at Námestie SNP 35. It's open Monday to Saturday 7am-8pm.

Emergency

- **GENERAL MEDICAL EMERGENCY:** ☎112

- **SLOVAKIAN POLICE DEPARTMENT:** ☎158

- **INTERNATIONAL COUNTRY CODE:** ☎421

- **IN CASE OF FIRE:** ☎150

- **PHARMACY:** Look for green signs labeled Apotheke. For serious medical emergencies, call ☎112.

- **MEDICAL SERVICES:** The two main emergency hospitals in Bratislava are Policlinic Ruzinov on Ruzinovska Street 10, open 7pm to 7am and Policlinic Strecnianska on Strecnianska Street 13, open 7pm to 7am.

- **LOCAL LAWS AND POLICE:** Bratislava is a relatively safe city and has less petty crime than more touristy capitals. However, you should not hesitate to contact the police if you are the victim of a crime. Be sure to carry a valid passport, as police have the right to ask for identification. Police can sometimes be unhelpful if you are the victim of a currency exchange scam; in this instance, it may be better to seek advice from your country's embassy or consulate.

Getting There

Bratislava's airport is M. R. Štefánik Airport; Slovakia has no national airline, but the airport is a hub for Ryanair (which is partly why you'll see so many Brits in Bratislava). From the airport you can take bus 61 to Račianske Mýto, then tram 5 to the city center. Be sure to validate your ticket once you get on the bus. Bratislava is about a 1hr. drive from Vienna (fun fact: they're the closest two capital cities in Europe), and buses and trains run frequently between the two cities—see https://www.regiojet.sk/ for more information. Bratislava is also 2hr. away from Budapest by car.

hungary essentials

MONEY

Although part of the European Union, Hungary's official currency is the forint (Ft).

Currency Exchange

Hungary is part of the European Union, so euro are widely accepted, though its official current is the forint (Ft). Tipping: a 10% tip is customary in all situations where the customers and service workers come face to face. Most tips, however, are already added on to the bill. Taxes: goods, products, and services in Hungary are subject to a value-added tax of 25% (a reduced tax of 12% is applied to basic consumer goods). Ask for a VAT return form at points of purchase to enjoy tax-free shopping. Present it at customs upon leaving the country along with your receipts and the unused goods. Refunds can be claimed at Tax Free Shopping Offices, found at most airports, road borders, and ferry stations, or by mail.

Tipping and Taxes

Tipping is customary in all situations where the customers and service workers—waiters, taxi drivers, and hotel porters—come face to face. Depending upon how satisfied you are with the service, plan to tip 10-15%. Goods, products, and services in Hungary are subject to a value added tax (VAT) of 27% (a reduced tax of 18% is applied to basic consumer goods). Non-EU visitors who are taking these goods home unused may be refunded this tax for purchases totaling over 48,000Ft per store. When making purchases, request a VAT form and present it at a Tax Free Shopping Office, found at most airports, road borders, and ferry stations, or by mail. Refunds must be claimed within six months.

SAFETY AND HEALTH

Local Laws and Police

You should not hesitate to contact the police in Budapest if you are the victim of a crime. Be sure to carry a valid passport, as police have the right to ask for identification. Police can sometimes be unhelpful if you are the victim of a currency exchange scam; in this instance, it may be better to seek advice from your country's embassy or consulate.

Drugs and Alcohol

Avoid public drunkenness as it will jeopardize your safety. In Hungary, drinking is permitted at age 18. Marijuana is entirely illegal throughout the country. Carrying drugs across an international border—considered to be drug trafficking—is a serious offense that could land you in prison.

Smoking is incredibly popular in Budapest. If you are sensitive to cigarette smoke, ask for a non-smoking room in a hotel or hostel, or to be seated in the non-smoking area of restaurants.

IRELAND

If you haven't yet heard that Ireland is the land of shamrocks, shillelaghs, and 40 shades of green, you should probably purchase a television, a copy of Darby O'Gill and the Little People, or a guide to Western culture since 1855. Surprisingly prominent in the international imagination for an island of sixmillion people, Ireland is a place that the rest of the world feels it understands very well, and the Irish themselves find much more complex. Their native country was originally chopped up into several dozen regional kingships, and today it's still split between two different countries, two different religions, and 11 different Wikipedia disambiguations. (Eight-seven percent of native Irish find that last division to be the most contentious.)

OK, we made that last statistic up. It's still no wonder, though, that Ireland and "Irishness" can be difficult to categorize. Its two capitals—Belfast in the North, and Dublin in the Republic—are at once the least and most "Irish" cities on the island. Belfast, home to the island's largest Orangemen parade and some its strongest pro-British sympathies, is Ireland's second-largest city and the one-time centerpiece of the iconic, tragic Troubles. Dublin, capital of the Republic and site of the Easter Rising, is increasingly urban and international, making it feel more like modern London than magical Glocca Morra. However, these cities' entanglement with issues of national identity, history, and globalization is a lot more Irish than that Claddagh ring your friend paid €50 for. Like pouring a perfect stout, dancing with Michael Flatley, or spelling a one-syllable word in Gaelic, visiting Ireland should be a wonderfully complicated experience—otherwise you're not doing it right.

greatest hits

- **THE ROYAL TREATMENT.** It would be a bit of a crime to visit Ireland and not see at least one castle, and if you're going to see one, it better be the **Dublin Castle** (p. 396).

- **CLUBLIN.** When you're fully saturated with Guinness and want to abandon the pubs for the clubs, look no further than **Copper Face Jack's** (p. 404), one of the best ways to end a night in Dublin.

- **PRIDE OF BELFAST.** Immerse yourself in the history of the *Titanic* in Belfast's **Titanic Quarter** (p. 405). As they proudly say, "It was fine when it left us."

dublin

Dublin is not particularly green. You won't see endless undulations of clover or cliffs plummeting westward to America. The only Irish you'll see will be on menus and kitschy gift items. But Dublin is more than just a way station to the rest of the Emerald Isle. A capital for millennia, a resentful colonial city and later site of rebellion, a small city whose writers and performers have produced art all out of proportion to its size: the city is all of these things.

Nowadays Dublin embodies "craic"—the Irish word for fun, gossip, lively talk, a good time. Walkable, friendly, alive, you can't skip it. Get lost in its winding side streets, stumble upon hidden pubs shops, try an Irish beer that isn't Guinness—there's a lot more to Dublin than meets the eye.

SIGHTS

📷 TRINITY COLLEGE
College Green   ☎01 8961000 https://www.tcd.ie

Trinity College is just like any ol' college campus, if that campus happens to be four centuries old, home to one of the oldest manuscripts in the world, and alma mater of chumps like Jonathan Swift, Bram Stoker, and Oscar Wilde. Trinity, the sole college in the University of Dublin, is often counted the finest university in Ireland, but if that doesn't impress you, the beautiful and historical campus should. You can take a stroll through the three main squares of Trinity College, including the misnamed New Square (now two centuries old). Or fight your way through a sea of tourists to get a glance of the famous Book of Kells, a beautifully illuminated nineteenth-century manuscript of the Gospels. Soothe your OCD in the Long Room of Old Library, where books are ordered by size rather than author. To learn more, try one of the student-run tours, which offer history, fun facts, and Irishmen wearing scholarly capes. If all else fails, grab a coffee at the Arts Café across from Old Library and pretend for one blissful moment that you're a student here.

i Tours €13, students €12 for students, €6 without access to Book of Kells. Tours leave every 45min. from 10:15am-3:15pm. Book of Kells Open M-Sa 9:30am-5pm, Su 9:30am-4:30pm.

DUBLIN CASTLE
Dame Street   ☎01 6458813 www.dublincastle.ie

If you're in the market for a castle, be sure to add Dublin's to your wish list. Not only are the rooms here massive and richly decorated—they house some serious history, serving at various times as a Viking military base and a Red Cross hospital for wounded soldiers. Self-guided tours are an option for casing the joint (and choosing your bedroom), but if you want a more in-depth look, take the guided tour of the cathedral and medieval undercroft (a cellar with a river running through it).

i Self-guided tour €6.50, students €5.50. Guided tour €8.50, students €6.50. Open M-Sa 9:45am-4:45pm, Su noon-4:45pm.

CHRISTCHURCH CATHEDRAL
Christchurch Place   ☎01 6778099 http://christchurchcathedral.ie

Although it's the oldest cathedral in Dublin, Christchurch has changed shape over the years due to the Restoration, various regime changes, and your run-of-the-mill collapsing wall. All this makes Christchurch an eclectic mixture of different eras in Dublin's history.

  The most interesting part is the surprisingly large underground crypt that is original from the church's beginnings. Here you can look at the Treasures of Christ exhibition and check out the mummified bodies of a cat and a rat that got caught in an organ pipe in the 1800s (nicknamed "Tom and Jerry," of course). Other notable dead people include Strongbow, leader of the Anglo-Normans, and the less impressively named Charles Lindsay, last bishop of the church.

Myriad tickets are available. For the short and sweet visit, opt for the regular admission to the cathedral and crypt. If you're interested in a more interactive experience, book ahead for a tour of the belfry and chance to ring one of the nineteen bells.

i Admission €6, students €4.50. Open summer M-Sa 9am-7pm, other seasons it closes an hour or two earlier. Check the website for Sunday hours, which accommodate religious services.

NATIONAL LIBRARY OF IRELAND
Kildare St.   ☎01 6030200 http://www.nli.ie

The National Library of Dublin is one of several free exhibits in the Trinity College area, and home to the Genealogy Advisory Service, where you can drop in and get help digging up those long-lost Irish roots. Even if you're not interested in finding out your great-grandpater came from Roscommon, check out the reading room on the top floor or the William Butler Yeats exhibition on the bottom floor, where you can learn about his torrid romances and occult religious beliefs. (We also hear he wrote some poems.) Next door are the National Museum of Ireland Archeology and the Natural History Museum, and behind is the National Gallery, making this area ideal for a rainy afternoon.

i Admission free. Open M-W 9:30am-7:45pm, Th-F 9:30am-4:45pm, Sa 9:30am-12:45pm.

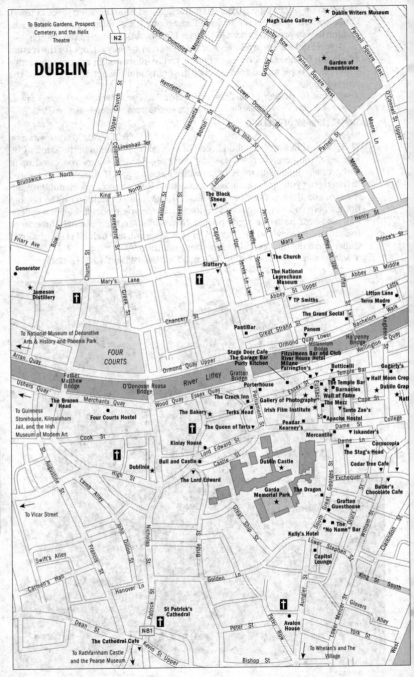

DUBLIN

To Botanic Gardens, Prospect
Cemetery, and the Helix
Theatre

N2

★ Dublin Writers Museum
Hugh Lane Gallery ★

Granby Row

★ Garden of
Remembrance

The Black
Sheep ▼

Slattery's

■ The Church

The National
Leprechaun
Museum

TP Smiths

Litton Lane
Terra Madre

The Grand Social

PantiBar

Panem

Stage Door Cafe
The Garage Bar
Purty Kitchen

Fitzsimons Bar and Club
River House Hotel
Milano
Farrington's

Botticelli
Gogarty's
Half Moon Crep

Porterhouse

The Temple Bar
Barnacles
Wall of Fame

Dublin Grap

The Czech Inn

Gallery of Photography
Irish Film Institute

The Mezz
Tante Zoe's

Nati

The Bakery
Turks Head

Apache Hostel

Peadar
Kearney's

Mercantile

Iskander's

Cornucopia

The Queen of Tarts ▼

Dame

The Stag's Head

Kinlay House

Cedar Tree Cafe

Bull and Castle

Dublin Castle

Butler's
Chocolate Cafe

Dublinia

Castle

The Lord Edward

Garda
Memorial Park

The Dragon

Grafton
Guesthouse

Generator ●

★ Jameson
Distillery

To National Museum of Decorative
Arts & History and Phoenix Park

FOUR
COURTS

Father
Matthew
Bridge

O'Donovan Rossa
Bridge

River Liffey

Grattan
Bridge

Ha'penny
Bridge

Ushers Quay

The Brazen
Head

Merchants Quay

To Guinness
Storehouse, Kilmainham
Jail, and the Irish
Museum of Modern Art

Four Courts Hostel

Cook St

The
"No Name" Bar

Kelly's Hotel

Lower Stephen St

To Vicar Street

Capitol
Lounge

St Patrick's
Cathedral

N81

Avalon
House

The Cathedral Cafe

To Rathfarnham Castle
and the Pearse Museum ▼

Bishop St

To Whelan's and The
Village

ireland

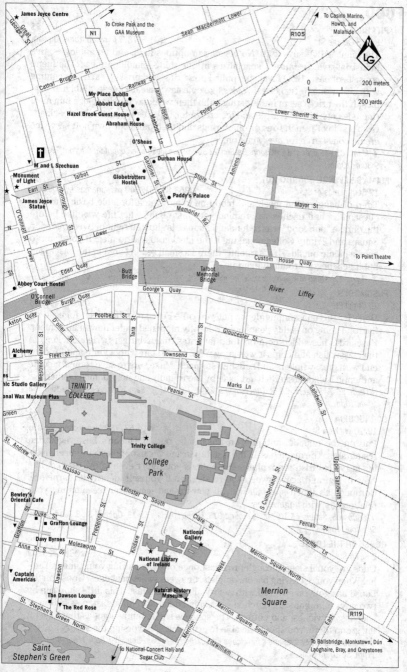

James Joyce Centre

To Croke Park and the
GAA Museum

N1

Great George's St

Cathal Brugha St

Sean MacDermott Lower

R105

To Casino Marino,
Howth, and
Malahide

N
LG

0   200 meters
0   200 yards

Railway St

James Joyce St

My Place Dublin
Abbott Lodge
Hazel Brook Guest House
Abraham House

Marlboro Ln

Foley St

Lower Sheriff St

O'Sheas

Gardiner St Lower

Durban House

Globetrotters
Hostel

Store St

Amiens St

Mayor St

M and L Szechuan

Talbot

Paddy's Palace

Monument
of Light

Earl St

James Joyce
Statue

Marlborough St

O'Connell St Lower

N

Abbey St Lower

Memorial Rd

Custom House Quay

To Point Theatre

Eden Quay

Abbey Court Hostel

O'Connell
Bridge

Burgh Quay

Butt
Bridge

Talbot
Memorial
Bridge

George's Quay

River   Liffey

Aston Quay

D'Olier St

Poolbeg St

Tara St

Moss St

City Quay

Gloucester St

Alchemy

Westmoreland St

Fleet St

Townsend St

Marks Ln

Lower Sandwith St

ic Studio Gallery
onal Wax Museum Plus

Green

TRINITY
COLLEGE

Pearse St

St Andrew St

Trinity College

College
Park

S Cumberland St

Boyne St

Upper Sandwith St

Nassau St

Leinster St South

Clare St

Fenian St

Denzille Ln

Bewley's
Oriental Cafe

Duke St

Grafton Lounge

Davy Byrnes

Molesworth St

Frederick St

Kildare St

Dawson St

National
Gallery

Merrion Square North

Captain
Americas

Anne St S

The Dawson Lounge

The Red Rose

National Library
of Ireland

Natural History
Museum

Merrion St

West

Merrion Square
North

Merrion
Square

R119

St Stephen's Green North

Saint
Stephen's Green

To National Concert Hall and
Sugar Club

Merrion Square South

Fitzwilliam Ln

To Ballsbridge, Monkstown, Dún
Laoghaire, Bray, and Greystones

Merrion St

East

dublin

FOOD

⚑ PITT BROS. $$
84-88 George St.   ☎01-6778777 www.pittbrosbbq.com

The giant "BBQ" says it all. No vegetarian options here, and no apologies; this industrial-style restaurant specializes in one thing—smoking meat. The menu consists of basic BBQ faves like pulled pork, ribs, and brisket, each one coming with either one or two classic sides like coleslaw, mac n' cheese, and hush puppies. If the prices seem intimidating, grab their weekday lunch meal: a bun meal (includes one side), a drink, and ice cream for €10. Feeling just a little peckish? Grab a side of french fries or onion rings and then pull your own soft serve ice cream cone—free for every customer.

i Meals €10-16. Open M-F at noon, Sa-Sun 12:30pm; "we close when our meat runs out," usually 9:30 or 10pm.

MAMA'S REVENGE BURRITO HUT $
12 South Leinster St.   ☎353-87 4512340 www.mamasrevenge.com

Tired of bangers and mash and blood pudding? The affordable basic burritos, quesadillas, and nachos will remind your taste buds what life was like before the phrase "pub food" was redundant. Mama's is situated right between Merrion Square and Trinity College, making it the ideal grab-and-go meal if you want to have a picnic outside. If it's raining, there's a small seating area in the basement, but it gets hectic around lunchtime.

i Mains 4-8. Open M-F 8am-8pm, Sa noon-6pm.

FUSCIARDI'S $
10 Capel St.   ☎01 4411333

Don't let the unassuming decor put you off—Fusciardi's has been focused on the food going on eighty years now. Recently reopened under new management, Fusciardi's has added comfort food favorites (pizza, burgers, fried chicken) to the classic fish and chips it was known for. You'll start with a knife and fork but end with greasy fingers and satisfied stomach. Make sure to save room for some authentic Italian desserts handmade by the friendly and helpful management.

i Fish €6-7. Burgers €3-6. Other mains €5-8. OPen M-Th 9am-10pm, F-Sa 9am-1am, Su 10am-10pm.

CORNUCOPIA $$
19/20 Wicklow St.   ☎01 6777583 www.cornucopia.ie

Pub on the outside, anti-pub on the inside: one of Dublin's best vegetarian restaurants. The menu has all the vegetarian and vegan option you've been missing in typical Irish food, plus some options you didn't even know existed, like "raw living" and agave-sweetened food. Even if you self identify as carnivore, Cornucopia's lunch specials will fill you up and leave you reevaluating your relationship with vegetables.

i Soups €5. Salads €5-10. Mains around €13. Lunch specials €9-13. Open M-Sa 8:30am-11pm, Su noon-11pm.

GOOSE ON THE LOOSE $
2 Kevin St. Lower   ☎086 1529140

Odds are you'll sleep through breakfast once or twice during your time in Dublin. When you're craving bacon, omelets, or sweet sweet pancakes, Goose on the Loose has got you covered with hearty all-day breakfast. This little shop run by two guys in a pint-sized kitchen serves, in addition to breakfast, a selection of soups, sandwiches, and coffees. The space is small, but as long as there isn't a big group there, you should be able to get a seat and worship the savory gods.

i Breakfast €2-7. Salads and sandwiches €4-6. Open M-Tu 8am-5pm, W-F 8am-11pm, Sa 10am-11pm, Su 10am-5pm.

ireland

get a room!

TIMES HOSTEL CAMDEN PLACE $$

8 Camden Pl. ☎01 4758588 www.timeshostels.com/dublin/camden-place/the-hostel

At first the distance to Temple Bar and its beery nectar may be a turn-off—ten whole minutes, rather than five—but it more than makes up for it. The rooms, though small, are clean and brightly lit and come with private bathrooms. Much of the hostel follows the usual formula of common room, kitchen, and computer space, but how many hostels can boast ice cream parties and wine-and-cheese nights? Add in the Street Fighter arcade game and you've got yourself a winner.

i Breakfast included. Kitchen available. Towels and laundry €5. 2- to 10-bed dorms with ensuite bath €16-30, private room €70-90.

KINLAY HOUSE DUBLIN $$

2-12 Lord Edward St., Temple Bar   ☎01 6796644 www.kinlaydublin.ie

Backpacker arts-and-crafts vibe: the walls are all brightly painted and decked out with movie and music posters. The common room offers a pool table, couches aplenty, and a TV room where you can Netflix (and chill?). All is guarded by Tito, the tiny hostel turtle at the front desk. Out behind the kitchen is a beer garden belonging to Darkey Kelly's Pub (named after a brothel madam executed in 1761), the back entrance of which is accessible from this area. Just down the road from Temple Bar, Kinlay gives the option of being near all the action, but not quite inside of it, so it still offers a good night's sleep.

i Breakfast included. Kitchen and bike rental available. Dorms €15-25. Reception 24hr.

SPIRE HOSTEL $$

90-93 Marlborough St.   ☎01 8734173 www.spirehostel.com/find-us

The good thing about Spire Hostel is that you won't get lost. Just look for the 400-foot spire on O'Connell St., head west, and hang a right on Marlborough Rd. (Good for tipsy walks home from the pub.) Beyond its location, Spire offers "free drink night" every Saturday, so you can get the night started without leaving the building, and maybe some friends in the process. The hostel also offers three common rooms, one of which leads to an outdoor balcony area, with an outdoor barbeque for those rare sunny days. Rooms come either with or without a private bathroom, although it can be worth it to shell out for a private bathroom to get some more consistency with the hot water.

i Breakfast included. Kitchen and luggage storage available. Dorms 15-30 euros (prices skyrocket on the weekends). Reception 24hr.

EGALI HOSTEL $$$

146 Parnell St.   ☎01 5580882 www.egalihostel.com.br/en

Wooden pallets as decor and funky murals that line the halls here—Egali has budget chic down. Although the building itself is narrow, Egali makes use of its limited space with a homey kitchen, game room with pool table and TV, and an adorable petit terrace, possibly designed with leprechauns in mind. Its location, just two minutes from O'Connell Street and ten minutes from Temple Bar, makes it perfect for the ideal Dublin Day: sightseeing during business hours, squeezing in a late afternoon nap, and heading back out to drink in the beers and sights of Dublin at night.

i Breakfast included. Lockers and kitchen available. Dorms range from weekdays €15-25, weekends €25-35. Reception 24hr.

dublin

SKINFLINT
19 Crane Ln. $

☎01 6709719 www.joburger.ie/skinflint

No sign flags this restaurant's location in a hidden alleyway, so look for the distinctive red pillars. Inside is a mix of industrial workspace and antique decor. Skinflint offers several starters and meatballs, but their specialty is the long thin crust pizza. Try their lil' pizza (which isn't actually that little) and its combination of poached pear and sweet pickled onion, or the vonie, which comes with serrano ham and a hen's egg on top. After 7 a DJ imbues the pizzeria with a club atmosphere. Before 3pm, there's a soup and sandwich deal (€7).

i Starters €4-8. Meatballs €7. Pizzas €9-15. Open M noon-9pm, Tu-Th noon-11pm, F-Sa noon-11:30pm, Su noon-9pm.

NIGHTLIFE

☒ P.MAC'S
30 Stephen St. Lower   ☎01 4053653

If a teashop and an Irish pub mated, this would be the offspring. Every table has red candles in silver candelabras. Old-fashioned lampshades feature heavily, along with a of a goldfish in the back and a vintage rocking horse on the bookshelf. Snag an enclosed booth with swinging doors for some intimacy, or claim the mismatched couches in the corner to get access to the TV. If you look lonely enough they might even throw some bar snacks your way.

i Pints €5-6. Open M-Th noon-midnight, F-Sa noon-1am, Su noon-11:30pm.

THE GEORGE
89 South Great George St.   ☎01 6713298 www.thegeorge.ie

The George describes itself as "the first port of call for young gay people in Ireland." Once you make your way past the bouncers, you enter one of Dublin's more modern late night social spaces. Purple and pink lights reflect off the wall while pop music plays in background. Everyone's here: minglers alongside the bars on both the bottom and balcony levels, couples nesting in cozy booths near the back of the club. But the dominating feature of the space is the large stage, which takes up a quarter of the bottom floor. It features the nightly events at the George, ranging from live musical performances to Sunday Bingo (subtract your grandma, add a drag queen cabaret show). As the night wears on, the crowd gets larger and the space becomes more dance friendly, so don't be afraid to kick loose.

i No cover M-Th; F-Su free before 10pm, €5/10 thereafter. Pints €5-6, mixed drinks €7.50. Open M-F 2pm-2:30am, Sa 12:30pm-2:30am, Su 12:30pm-1:30am.

WHELAN'S
Wexford St.   ☎01 4780766 www.whelanslive.com

Camden Street houses a lot of pubs and clubs, but Whelan's is king when it comes to live rock music, as attested to by the posters on the wall exhibiting past performances from musicians such as the Arctic Monkeys, Ed Sheeran, and Nick Cave. There are two different stages in Whelan's—a smaller, more intimate venue with seating space is upstairs, while the larger concert stage dominates the back of the lower level. Tickets are available ahead of time around the corner; buy ahead, as they're cheaper and you won't risk being turned away at the door. If you're not feeling a live music performance, drop by later. Up front you might find a small band playing, with patrons chatting in booths and around the bar. In the back a DJ plays your favorite indie/alternative rock on the lower level as aristocrats on the balcony sit in luxurious leather chairs looking at the dancers below.

i Pints around €6. Music tickets €5-20. Open M-Sa 5pm-3am, Su 5pm-2am.

dublin

COPPER FACE JACK'S
29-30 Harcourt St.   ☎01 4255300 http://copperfacejacks.ie

Copper Face Jack's is the kind of club that provokes a strong reaction from people who know it, but not a universal one. Love it or hate it, there's no denying that on any given night the place will be bumpin'. The two-level club is massive but consistently packed as music pulses over the neon-lit black walls. Doors open at 11 and entrance is free until midnight, but the crowd doesn't usually show up until they've had time to prepare. If you want to lose yourself in the anonymity of a thousand dancing sweaty bodies until the wee hours, you've come to the right place.

i Pints around €5. M-Th and Su 21+, F-Sa 22+. Open M-Th 11pm-late, F-Sa 10pm-late, Su 11pm-late.

ESSENTIALS

Practicalities

- **TOURIST OFFICES:** Tourist Office Dublin. (37 College Green Southside ☎01 41 00 700 Open M-W 8:30am-6pm, Th-Su 8:30am-10pm.) Discover Ireland Center. (14 Upper O'Connell St. Open M-Sa 9am-5pm.)

- **EMBASSIES:** U.S. (42 Elgin Road, Ballsbridge. ☎01 66 87 122; https://ie.usembassy.gov.)

- **ATMS:** ATMs can be found near most banks in Ireland, including at the top and bottom of O'Connell Street, and at the Bank of Ireland across from Trinity College.

- **POST OFFICES:** An Post, General Post Office. (O'Connell Street Lower ☎01 70 57 000 Open M-Sa 8:30am-6pm.)

Emergency

- **EMERGENCY NUMBERS:** ☎999 (Ireland/UK); ☎112 (Europe-wide)

- **CRISIS LINE:** Irish Tourist Assistance Service, for tourists who are victims of crime. (7 Hanover St. East ☎1 890 365 700 Open M-Sa 10am-6pm, Su noon-6pm.)

- **PHARMACIES:** Hickey's Pharmacy. (21 Grafton St. ☎01 67 90 467 Open M-W 8:30am-8pm, Th 8:30am-8:3-pm, F 8:30am-8pm, Sa 9am-7:30pm, Su 10:30am-6pm.) City Pharmacy. (14 Dame St. ☎01 67 04 523 Open M-F 9am-9pm, Sa 11am-7pm, Su noon-6pm.)

- **HOSPITALS:** St. James Hospital. (James's St. ☎01 41 03 000.)

Getting There

The Dublin Bus #747 is probably your best option for getting from the Airport to Dublin proper. One-way €6, return €10 return; it stops at all the major stops in town.

Getting Around

Leap Cards are a reloadable smart cards that offer discounted fares on bus, Luas, and DART. Getting one is probably only worth it if you plan on using transportation frequently.

By Bus

Dublin is easiest seen on foot, as most attractions, restaurants, and clubs are within fifteen minutes' walking distance. If you grow footsore, the Dublin Bus has a huge number of different routes; routes and timetables available at the tourist offices or online. You can buy a card ahead of time at convenience stores displaying a bus logo, or just get one on the bus, but be warned: only exact change is accepted. (www.dublinbus.ie. Zones 1-3 €2, 4-13 €2.70, beyond €3.30.)

By Luas

Luas is the other Dublin transportation option. Luas is a tram system that runs on two lines, the red and the green. Tickets and maps are available for purchase at Luas stations. Luas is also undergoing construction anticipated to end in late 2017, so prepare for potential changes in routes. (Single tickets €1.90-3.10, round-trip €3.50-5.60.)

By Train

Dublin also has a train system called DART that offers cheaper way to get to the nearby seaside villages of Dublin. (One trip tickets €2.80-€5.90, one-day pass €11.40.)

belfast

Say goodbye to the villages of Ireland and hello to the mini metropolis that is Belfast. Though it was once known (rather infamously) for the Troubles, Belfast has changed dramatically in the last two decades, exploding with new hotels, shops, and restaurants to cater to the tourists. That doesn't mean that Belfast has forgotten where it came from (the many murals and memorials make sure of that) or turned into a kitschy tourist trap. The bars are bumping, the streets are bustling, and the city is on its way up.

SIGHTS

☒ TITANIC BELFAST

1 Olympic Way, Queen's Rd.   ☎28-9076-6386 http://titanicbelfast.com

Everyone knows it ended up in Davy Jones' locker; fewer know the Titanic was built in Belfast. Not that it's a surprise if you've spent more than a minute in Belfast; after all, there's a whole section of town named the "Titanic Quarter." If you have any interest at all in the construction, sinking, or rediscovery of the Titanic, make your way to Titanic Belfast.

    The gallery, which stands at the site of the old shipyard, has four floors dedicated to teaching visitors all about the ship's construction and demise, as well as the mission that located the Titanic on the bottom of the ocean floor. But Titanic Belfast is less of a gallery and more of an amusement park with a historical angle; one gallery includes a historical roller coaster ride as part of the exhibit. On your way out, stop by the SS Nomadic, the Titanic's little sister and the last White Star Vessel in existence, to get a feel for what ships in the early 1900s were like. Don't worry: the ship's tied up and there's a "No Icebergs Allowed" sign out front.

i Adults £17.50, students M-F £12.50, Sa-Su £14.50. Open Jan-Mar 10am-5pm, Apr-May 9am-6pm, June-Aug 9am-7pm, Sept 9am-6pm, Oct-Dec 10am-5pm.

BELFAST CASTLE AND CAVE HILL PARK

Antrim Rd.   ☎28-9077-6925 www.belfastcastle.co.uk

Even if you have castle fatigue, don't skip this one. It's on top of a really big hill, so the views of Belfast alone make the trip worth it. The garden is gorgeous, with people constantly dropping by to have a picnic in the shade of the structure; look for the hidden cats while you're here. Once you're done with the castle itself, wander around Cave Hill Park and its numerous hiking trails.

i Free. Open M 9am-6pm, Tu-Sa 9am-10:30pm, Su 9am-6pm.

belfast

GLOBAL VILLAGE $

87 University St. ☎28-9031-3533 http://globalvillagebelfast.com

Like most hostels in Belfast, Global Village is located in the Queen's District (by the college) and the vibe here is "totally chill, man." To that end, Global Village does have a lot chill stuff you can do, like play pool or foosball, strum guitar, or just hang out on the outdoor deck. They even have a slab of wood on just to convert the pool table into a platform for drinking games—yeah, that kind of place. So join a game and make a few friends, or maybe just snag a novel from the book exchange and while away the night that way.

i Breakfast included. Dorms start from £14.

VAGABOND $

9 University Rd. ☎28-9023-3017 www.vagabondsbelfast.com

The two common spaces at Vagabonds are decked out in plush couches and beanbags, making them perfect for a movie night. If that's not your thing, Vagabonds also offers a pool table, a ping pong table, and a barbecue set-up in their massive beer garden out back. Still not enough? The hostel also puts you right in between the cafe-heavy Queen's District and the bustling city center, each one about a ten-minute walk away. If you don't know where to start in Belfast, the friendly, international staff are ready to help.

i Breakfast included. Kitchen and laundry available. 4- to 8-bed dorms £14.50-16.50. Doubles £44.

CITY HOSTEL $

53-55 Malone Ave. ☎28-9066-0030 ibackpacker.co.uk

Apart from a few murals dedicated to some Belfast icons like the Big Fish, the peace wall, and Samuel L. Jackson in Pulp Fiction (one of these is not like the other), City Hostel is pretty standard. Dorms come with big mattresses and marshmallow pillows, and everything is brightly lit and cleaned on the regular. The hostel seems to foster a strong community—you can often find one of the staff chatting with people and enjoying a brew at the outside tables. The location puts it within five minutes of Queen's University, meaning most of the surrounding houses are full of college kids partying it up—don't be surprised to hear a house party when you walk down the street at night.

i Breakfast included. Lockers and luggage store available. Reception open 8am-11pm. Dorms £15; double with bath £40. Check for discounts online.

FOOD

🍴 ACTON AND SONS $$

17 Brunswick St. ☎28-9024-0259 www.actonandsons.com

After hitting up fish-and-chip joints and the hostel kitchen, Acton and Sons is a step up. In an area dominated by generic pre-theater menus, this place stands out for its chic but relaxed rustic design and reasonable prices for great food. The meat cuts are great. Keep an eye out for weekly food specials like Fizzy Fridays (three small plates and a bottle of prosecco £25). If you still have room and a little cash at the end, don't say no to the gooey, sticky sundae dessert options (£5-6).

i Beef cuts £18-26. Other mains £10-14. Open M-Th 11:30am-9:30pm, F-Sa 11:30am-10pm.

ireland

LITTLE WING PIZZERIA $

10 Anne St.   ☎28-9024-7000 www.littlewingpizzeria.com

Each slice of pizza at Little Wing has the oily goodness of something that's home-made with real ingredients and baked in a modern pizza oven. Cozy up with one of their lunch specials ($5) or get a couple friends together and grab a 24-inch circle of deliciousness.

i Small pizzas £6-10; large pies £17-20. Open M-W 11am-10pm, Th-Sa 11am-11pm, Su 11am-10pm.

CONOR $

11a Stranmillis Rd.   ☎28-9066-3266 www.cafeconor.com

With its high ceilings, airy feel, and massive skylight on the roof, Conor feels like an artist's studio, which in fact it was. But 11a Stranmillis has stopped creating works of visual art and now produces gastronomical pieces for the residents of the Queen's District. The large lunch menu includes breakfast from all day long (9am-5pm). Fear not, vegetarians—there's a big veggie breakfast, so you don't have to choose between pricey oatmeal and pushing the sausage and bacon to the side of your Irish breakfast.

i Starters £3-4. Breakfasts £6. Burgers £9. Mains £7-12. Open M-Sa 9am-10pm, Su 9am-9pm.

SLUMS $

25 Bruce St.   ☎28-9031-5164 www.slums.co

Welcome to Slums, a "unique new dining concept" featuring fast food-style Indian dishes in a "Shanty Town style interior." The menu is basic: choose between a wrap, bowl, or salad and add some meat, sauce, and veggies. The food is good and fast and the prices are low. Wash it all down with a lassi shake ($2.50).

i Wraps and bowls £5-6. Open M-Sa noon-9pm.

NIGHTLIFE

▓ THE NATIONAL GRANDE CAFÉ

62-68 High St.   ☎28-9031-1130 www.thenationalbelfast.com

Is it a cafe or a club? Both, of course. During the day this multi-purpose pur-veyor of food and drink offers up pastries, sandwiches, and breakfast for the brunch-going residents of Belfast. But after the kitchen closes, it transforms into a hub of activity that spreads itself over all four floors including, but not limited to, a beer garden, a rooftop garden, a nightclub, and a warehouse-style bar. Drink prices aren't anything special, but the place still fills up with all kinds of people looking to unwind after hours.

i Beers and spirits £4-6. Cocktails £8. Cover for club floor £5 after 11pm. Open M-F 8:30am-1am, Sa-Su 9:30am-1pm.

FILTHY QUARTER

45 Dublin Rd.   ☎28-9024-6823 www.thefilthyquarter.com

Actually four spaces in one, one of which is charmingly called "Filthy McNas-ty's." McNasty's low lighting and comfy couches makes it ideal for grabbing a beer and singing along to the loud music playing overhead. Other quarters: Secret Garden, a two-level beer garden with a bird cage gazebo where most of the bar patrons flock; Filthy Chic, styled like a trendy cafe; and Gypsy Lounge, a nightclub. The place may feel a little disjointed, but much like the large crowd that gathers here on any given night, the four spaces together give the place a energetic, if somewhat eclectic, atmosphere.

i Pints £3-5. Open M-Sa 1am-1pm, Su 1pm-midnight.

EGLANTINE BAR

32 Malone Rd.   ☎28-9038-1994 http://eglantinebar.com

Forget the pub; throw on a nice shirt and sit down for a cocktail. This once-pop-ular student bar has been completely renovated for a classier look, complete

belfast

with an-all black exterior and whitewashed brick walls. But just because they've changed their appearance doesn't mean they're trying to drive off student customers—half-price cocktails on Thursday and Friday and 20% student discounts make sure of that.

i Pints £4. Cocktails £7. Open M-Tu 11:30am-midnight, W-Sa 11:30am-1am, Su 11:30am-midnight. Check their website for more special promotions during the week.

DIRTY ONION
3 Hill St.   ☎28-9024-3712 www.thedirtyonion.com

Beer gardens are a big thing in Belfast, but no one does it quite like the Dirty Onion. Enter through their wooden archway into a jam-packed outdoor area and direct your eyes to the huge wooden scaffolding at the edge of the garden. It's the remnants of the original whiskey warehouse that stood on this site from the 18th to 20th centuries. Now one of the busiest nightspots in Belfast's city center, the Dirty Onion offers its clientele a large beer selection that draws a swarm of bodies to the beer garden. The Onion also houses Yardbird, a chicken joint, where you can buy some wings to soak up the beer.

i Pints £3-5. Open M-Sa noon-1am, Su noon-midnight.

ESSENTIALS

Practicalities

- **TOURIST OFFICES:** Visit Belfast. (9 Donegall Sq. North ☎28 9024 6609 Open M-Sa 9am-8pm, Su 11am-4pm.)

- **ATMS:** The most centrally located ATMs are out front of city hall; if you're facing it, they'll be on the street to the left and to the right. The city center also happens to be right by a shopping center, which also has ATMs. If you're near Queens University, there is one on the other side of the street from the main entrance from the school.

- **POST OFFICES:** Belfast City Post Office. (12-16 Bridge St. Open M 9am-5:30pm, Tu 9:30am-5:30pm, W-Sa 9am-5:30pm.)

Emergency

- **EMERGENCY NUMBERS:** ☎999 (Ireland/UK); ☎112 (Europe-wide)

- **PHARMACIES:** Urban Pharmacy. (56 Dublin Rd. 28-9024-6336 Open M-F 8am-8pm, Sa 9am-5:30pm, Su 1-5:30pm.) Botanic Pharmacy. (98 Botanic Ave. ☎28 9032 5509. Open M-Sa 9am-5:30pm.)

- **HOSPITALS:** Belfast City Hospital. (51 Lisburn Rd. ☎28 9032 9241.)

Getting There

Belfast has two airports: Belfast International Airport and Belfast City Airport; make sure you know which one you want. The Airport Express 600 (£2.50, round-trip £3.80) goes to Belfast City Airport and the Airport Express 300 goes to Belfast International (£7.50, round-trip £10.50) and they both run every 15-20 minutes to the city center.

Getting Around

The main bus system is called the Metro. Tickets for the bus (usually £1-3, depending on distance traveled)can be purchased on West Bedford Street; if you're facing city hall, look to your left for a small collection of pink ticket booths. You cannot buy tickets onboard. There are twelve major lines that run from the city center to the various reaches of Belfast and the information center across the road from the bus ticket center can give you a map of their routes. You can also find them online (www.translink.co.uk/Services/Metro-Service-Page/Timetables).

galway

Galway is a city with a split personality, but unlike Jekyll and Hyde, the two sides work well together. On the east side of the River Corrib is busy and energetic Quay St., with pubs and tourist shops on every corner jammed with locals and visitors alike. On the west side people lunch, read a book, or take a nap on the grassy banks of the river. Regardless of which side of the river you find yourself on, you're guaranteed good food, good pubs, and a good time in what locals call Ireland's "most Irish city."

SIGHTS

GALWAY CITY MUSEUM
Spanish Parade   ☎91 532460 www.galwaycitymuseum.ie

The City Museum is a pleasant surprise, housing exhibits that take you back into Irish history through the lens of Galway City. The first floor houses Neolithic history, including ancient artifacts and a huge Galway Bay ship hanging from the ceiling. For the really interesting stuff, head upstairs to the exhibit on more recent history. Here you can learn about Ireland's two-century struggle for independence as well as the meaning behind all those popular street names (hint: it has to do with famous rebels). The top floor houses a portrait gallery of Galwegians, but more importantly an exhibit on the science of the sea, which is geared toward children but features a mini model submarine that will transform you into your ten-year-old self. After you've had your fill of Galway history, head to The Kitchen, the museum cafe frequented less by museumgoers and more by locals in search of good brunch.

i Down Merchants Rd. to the River Corrib. Free. Open Tu-Sa 10am-5pm, Su noon-5pm.

ARAN ISLANDS

Strictly speaking the Aran Islands are not in Galway, but once you've seen the city, you may realize that some of the best it has to offer lies outside the city itself.

If you've ever wanted to live in a Wes Anderson movie, Inis Mór is probably as close as you'll get—a landscape of stone walls and rugged green plains. At the docks there are a few brightly painted restaurants and pubs, as well as a sandy beach and some of the clearest water this side of the Atlantic. But what you'll really want to do is escape the cutesy main part of the island and make your way along the winding roads that run along the coast. Once there, you could get a tour bus, hop in a horse-drawn buggy, or even hoof it, but this is probably the most movie-montage bike ride you'll ever take, so we recommend renting some wheels.

Popular activities on the Island include visiting Dún Aonghasa, a prehistoric fort at the opposite end of the island where the brave can stand near the edge of the sheer cliffs (€4, students €3); enjoying close-up animal experiences with cute horses and donkeys; and exploring various old ruins. If you're feeling hungry after a day on the island (which you will, if riding that bike is the first exercise you've done since getting to Ireland), try a meal at Pier House by the main docks. It can be a little pricey, but you're guaranteed a delicious meal. Then hop back on the ferry and sleep the whole way back, dreaming of the greenness and blueness of Inis Mór's hills and waters.

Inis Meáin and Inis Oírr are the other two islands in the Arans. They're smaller but equally beautiful and feature similar sights and ancient ruins. The Aran Island Ferry leaves from Ros an Mhíl (Rossaveal); ferry tickets €25, students €20. A shuttle leaves from Eyre Sq. for the ferry dock; €7, students €6. Island merchants mostly deal in cash, so make sure to bring some with you.

get a room!

GALWAY CITY HOSTEL
Frenchville Ln., Eyre Sq.   ☎91 535878 www.galwaycityhostel.com   **$$**

One of the newest hostels in town, Galway City Hostel knows what budget backpackers want, and they deliver: a breakfast of fresh-baked bread and scones, universal plugs in dorm rooms, and Wi-Fi that promises to be there for you when your hostel mates aren't. Oddly, the building's most private room is probably the 16-bed dorm, where each bed comes in its own little cubicle, complete with a curtain you can draw back to block out the rest of the world. Plus, it's also the only room with an ensuite bathroom attached. Add in the fact that it's right by the train and bus stations, and you've booked yourself a solid stay in Galway.

i Wi-Fi. Breakfast included. Lockers, laundry, kitchen available. 4- to 16-bed dorms available; they average about €20.

SNOOZLES
Forster St.   ☎91 530064 www.snoozleshostelgalway.ie   **$$**

Easily identifiable by the large sign on the side of the building, Snoozles delivers on the hostel essentials: good rooms and a good social scene. Dorms are small but spacious and clean, all with ensuite bathrooms . Downstairs, guests can spend the morning munching on pancakes in the dining room, the afternoon relaxing on the outdoor wooden patio, and the evening knocking back a few in the common room while playing pool, singing karaoke, or watching a movie on the big-screen TV. And if you need help figuring out what to do with your time in Galway, the huge chalkboard by reception offers a list of activities—just ask one of the helpful staff about them.

i Breakfast included. Kitchen available. 4-, 6-, and 10-bed dorms.

FOOD

🖾 JUNGLE CAFÉ
29 Forster St.   ☎91 562858   **$**

Ireland is a beautiful country, but sometimes old stone building after old stone building gets tiresome. If you're starting to feel gloomier than the weather, escape to Jungle Café, in what might be Ireland's only Little Brazil. The cafe more than lives up to its name. Their outdoor seating offers reggae music, comfy bamboo couches, and tropical plants that really drive home the tropical vibe. The main offerings here are coffee- and tea-based, but they do offer soups, sandwiches, and crepes if you're feeling a bit more peckish. The smoothies aren't half bad either.

i Coffee and tea €2-3. Juice/smoothies €4.50. Sandwiches €7-8, soup. Breakfasts (until noon) €8. Open M-W 9am-7pm, Th 9am-8pm, Su 10am-5pm "depending on the weather."

🖾 THE PIE MAKER
10 Cross St. Upper, Galway   ☎91 513151   **$**

In a shaded road off Quay Street sits a pie shop that's one part submarine, one part cellar, and wholly delicious. The eclectic design of the place is one thing—stuffed pheasants on the walls, a roof that looks to be made of copper planks, and a chandelier made from a teapot and several hats. The food is another thing altogether. Offering up a selection of savory vegetable and meat pies, as well as sweet pies, this shop boasts handmade organic pies produced with local ingredients, perfect for the locavores and environmentally conscious among us. For those who couldn't care less: the pies are fresh, delicious, and filling. If you're looking for a full meal, opt for the pie with all the sides (mashed potatoes, peas, cabbage), but if not you can just grab a pie on its own. Wash it all down with an interesting selection of drinks, ranging from elderflower lemonade to blood orange sparkling juice, or take it to go and have a picnic lunch down by the River Corrib.

i Pies €8-9. Sweet pies €5. Meal and pie €11-12. Open daily noon-10pm.

NIGHTLIFE

☒ RÓISÍN DUBH

Dominic St.   ☎91 586540 www.roisindubh.net

This is the most Irish-sounding pub you'll go to, even though they don't always offer the most Irish of music. That doesn't mean it'll disappoint—the Róisín Dubh has a history of hosting great performers, with names from Two Door Cinema Club to Franz Ferdinand stopping by to play. Although they do offer some free live music, a lot of concerts require tickets, which are usually available at the door. Not in the mood for a live performance? Drop by later as the space fills out, or enjoy its cavernous downstairs area or the large patio on the upstairs level.

i Midweek silent disco. Open-mic night Su. Drinks €5. Open M-Su 6pm-2am.

SALLY LONGS

33 Abbeygate St.   ☎91 565756

If you want to experience an Irish pub in full swing, check out any of the major pubs along Quay Street—there's more than enough to slake your thirst for crowds and loud music (and beer). If you want something a little more low-key, head to the sidestreets for Sally Longs. This small pub has all the fixings of a good Irish rock hall without the hordes of people spilling out the door. In back you can enjoy live rock music every night of the week; if you're looking to commune with a pint instead, the front has couches to accommodate you.

i Pints €4-5.

CARBON

19-21 Eglinton St.   ☎91 449204 www.carbongalway.ie

Carbon checks all the important boxes that make a club clubby: dark foggy interior lit by neon lights, drinks served from a bright white bar, and a big dance floor with a DJ playing thumping music all night. Scattered around the fringes are cocktail tables and couches where you can spend a moment enjoying a beverage between sessions busting a move. If you're hoping for a crowd, wait a little after it opens, as it can be dead earlier in the night.

i 18+. Cover M-Th €3-5, Sa-Su €8, Su €3-5. Drinks €6. Open M-Th 11pm-2am, F-Sa 11pm-2:30am, Su 11pm-2am.

ESSENTIALS

Practicalities

- **TOURIST OFFICES:** Áras Fáilte. (Forster St. at Fairgreen Rd. ☎91 53 77 00 Open M-Sa 9am-5pm.)

- **ATMS:** There are several ATMs in Eyre Square, including 43 Eyre Square (by the taxi line) and 24 Eyre Square (next to the pub on the west side of the square). There's also one on Shop Street by Lynch's Castle.

- **POST OFFICES:** An Post. (3 Eglinton St. ☎91 53 47 27 Open M 9am-5:30pm, Tu 9:30am-5:30pm, W-Sa 9am-5:30pm.)

galway

Emergency

- **EMERGENCY NUMBERS:** ☎999 (Ireland/UK); ☎112 (Europe-wide)

- **CRISIS LINE:** Irish Tourist Assistance Service, for tourists who are victims of crime. (☎1 890 365 700 Open M-Sa 10am-6pm, Su noon-6pm.)

- **PHARMACIES:** Boots. (35 Shop St. 91 561022 M-W 9am-7pm, Th-F 9am-9pm, Sa 9am-7pm, Su 11:30am-6pm.) Whelan's Careplus Pharmacy. (11 Williamsgate St. ☎91 56 22 91 Open M-Sa 9am-6pm.)

- **HOSPITALS:** University Hospital Galway. (Newcastle Rd. ☎91 52 42 22)

Getting There

By Bus & Train

The bus and train stations in Galway are right off Eyre Square in the center of town and provide services to most major cities within Ireland. Train tickets booked in advance cost as little €15 from most cities in Ireland, €20-30 if booked later. Students get a discount. Buses similarly cost €15-20 when booked in advance.

By Plane

The nearest airports to Galway are about a one-hour drive from the city. Only one of them (Shannon Airport) serves international destinations.

Getting Around

Like most Irish cities, Galway is easily accessible by foot. If you're heading for the farther reaches of the city, take Bus Éireann. Routes, timetables, and fares are available online. (www.buseireann.ie/inner.php?id=459.) Fares run €2-3.)

cork

Cork is Ireland's second city, Dublin's kid brother—smaller and quieter, with an earlier bedtime. Up and down the hills lie the colorful homes of locals, while the city center bustles with a hundred different shops and eateries. Cork makes a good vacation stop on its own, but it also serves as a launching pad to everything else that southern Ireland has to offer. You might think of giving it a miss in favor of bigger towns like Belfast or Galway, but don't cross Cork off yet: it might surprise you.

SIGHTS

■ BLARNEY CASTLE

Blarney   ☎21 4385252 www.blarneycastle.ie

The trip up to kiss the Blarney Stone isn't for the faint of heart—it takes you up 100 steps to the very top of the castle, where you lean off the edge of the castle and reach your lips towards a stone that's just a little too far away for comfort. (But hey: before the safeguards were added, someone held you by the ankles while you leaned out to kiss it.) Legend says that kissing the stone gives you the "gift of gab," the Irish knack for talk, eloquence, and poetry. Whether or not this is sheer... blarney remains to be seen, but it's a time-honored tradition and it'd be a waste to miss out on it.

Despite the strangeness of the activity, Blarney Castle is one of the top tourist destinations in Ireland, and for good reason. The castle is nestled in the picturesque countryside of County Cork, and the entire estate sprawls over sixty acres with a multitude of gardens, forest trails, and views of green country. If hanging over heights and kissing old stones isn't your bag, the surrounding area offers a number of alternatives. Right next to the Castle is Ireland's only "poison garden," where remedies and draughts straight out of Harry Potter—wolfsbane and mandrake—abound. Or you can choose to take one of the scenic walks through the grounds and partake in other local traditions, like walking backwards with your eyes closed down the Wishing Steps, with your deepest wish in mind. One could easily spend a whole day perusing the grounds.

i The Castle is about 8 km from Cork and is accessible by the 215 bus. Open summer M-Sa 9am-7pm, Su and holidays 9am-6pm; in other seasons it closes an hour or two earlier. Last entry 30min. before close.

CORK CITY GAOL

Convent Ave., Sunday's Well   ☎21 4305022 www.corkcitygaol.com

If you missed out on Kilmainham Gaol in Dublin, fear not: Cork has its own old prison for tourists to walk through. Cork Gaol looks a bit like castle from the outside, but the inside offers a look at what prison life was like in the 1800s through the individual stories, interactive prison cells, and creepy lifelike mannequins. Each cell tells a tale about a prisoner that lived here and reveals the brutal conditions that often caused prisoners to go insane. There's even a chance

get a room!

BRÚ BAR & HOSTEL $$
57 MacCurtain St.   ☎21 4550667 www.bruhostel.com

If the name didn't make it obvious, this is a bar first and a hostel last. This doesn't mean that the hostel is lacking in quality—just be prepared for locals to come by after dark, grab a drink, and listen to the live music that plays every night. On the bright side, you're never too far from a good pub and the discounted drinks that come with having a room here. It can, however, get a bit noisy if you're on one of the lower floors. The hostel itself is pretty standard, with a small common space, a kitchen, and private bathrooms in every dorm, but staying here comes with a bunch of discounts to local eateries, sights, and pubs, as well as pay-as-you-go access to a gym and pool right down the road (€10 per visit). Only a five-minute walk from the central part of town makes Brú a pretty solid bet for a quality stay in Cork.

i Breakfast included. 4- and 6-bed dorms €15-18; doubles €18-20; triple M-Th & Su €48, F-Sa €60.

KINLAY HOUSE $
Bob and Joan's Walk, Shandon   ☎21 4508966 http://kinlayhousecork.ie

Located in the shadow of St. Anne's Church and her famous bells, Kinlay House offers some of the cheapest rooms in Cork that are still within good walking distance of the sights and without the addition of a pub below your room, making it ideal for those seeking peace and quiet. It seems like none of the rooms in Kinlay are the same, with singles and doubles occasionally having in-room sinks and wardrobes, while dorms tend to be barebones with only bunk beds and the occasional in-suite bathroom. The eccentric room setup gives the place personality, but may be reason to book a private room. The location puts you in the midst of a quieter part of town, so if you want to get a taste of regular life in Cork, Kinlay is a good place to do it, but it's a little farther from the action closer to the river.

i Dorms €16-17; 6-bed dorm with bathroom €18; double €25, with bath €28; single with bath €45.

cork

to step into a cell yourself and see what it was like to be caught committing a crime in 19th-century Cork (and make you suddenly appreciate the luxury of your hostel). Upstairs you'll find a short exhibit on 6CK Radio Broadcasting, one of the most important radio networks in Ireland, which used the gaol as its home base from 1927-1957. The long hike up the hill to the gaol is a good excuse for a pint afterward.

i Take the 201 bus to Hollyhill, a 10min. walk away. €8, students €7. Open daily Oct-Mar 10am-4pm, Apr-Sept 9:30am-5pm.

SAINT FIN BARRE'S CATHEDRAL
Dean Street   ☎21 4963387 www.cathedral.cork.anglican.org

From the top of the hill in Cork, countless spires poke through the skyline, but Saint Fin Barre's gothic steeples stand out. Up close, the intricate structural work is more striking. The cathedral itself is young compared to some of Europe's other cathedrals, clocking in at just over 150 years old, but the grounds have been a sight of worship for fourteen centuries, a simple monastery now the great church that stands here. It's not a huge space, but it beautifully incorporates color and intricate detail in its stained glass windows, the sanctuary ceiling mural, and the mosaic floor of the altar. Europe is plagued by cathedrals, but Cork County's own mother church is worth a visit.

i €5, students €3. Open M-Sa 9:30am-5:30pm, Su Apr-Nov 1:30-2:30pm & 4:30-6pm.

FOOD

◨ O'FLYNN'S GOURMET SAUSAGES $
14 Winthrop St.   ☎21-427-4422 www.oflynnsgourmetsausages.ie

What's more Irish than a footlong sausage? For €5 you can experience one of O'Flynn's hot dog sensations, ranging from the salsa and jalapeño Latino Dog to the classic Cork Boi (pronounced BO-YEE), and for €10 you get twelve inches of prime pork with your choice of a side. If you can't make it to Winthrop Street, check out their stall in the English Market or keep your eyes peeled for their food truck on Grand Street.

i Sausage €5, with side €8. Footlong €10. Open M-Th 9am-5:30pm, F 9:30am-8pm, Sa 9am-6pm, Su 10am-6pm.

UNCLE PETE'S $$
40 Paul St.   ☎21 4274845 www.unclepetes.ie

Although it's considered the second city of Ireland, Cork seems to be the first one to bed: most places close around 5 or 6pm. For late-night warriors in need of food, the answer is Uncle Pete's. Pizza? Got it. Burgers? No problem. Pasta, falafel, he serves everything. Uncle Pete also offers a surprising amount of gluten-free and vegetarian options. Come for the Greek diner-style panoply of food options, stay for the homey movie-poster ambience.

i Mains €9-13. Burgers €9. Small pizzas €6-11, large €16-18. Open M-Sa 8am-late, Su 10am-late.

NIGHTLIFE

◨ REARDEN'S
26 Washington St.   ☎21 4658100 www.reardens.com

Sometimes all you need is a pub. Rearden's is, for the most part, pretty standard. The music is loud and modern. One end of the room is dominated by a wooden stage, but beyond that—grab a pint, grab a booth, contemplate the memorabilia lining the walls, and enjoy the live music on the weekends. The mild vibrations you may see jostling your pint are from the bass at Havana Browns, the club upstairs and one of Cork's finest, where you can head if you're done peacefully sipping and want to get down.

i Pints €5-6. Open daily 9am-2am.

BIERHAUS

Pope's Quay   ☎21 4551648 http://thebierhauscork.com

Tired of Guinness? Worry not, blasphemer. Bierhaus offers 200 beers and a large selection of spirits. You may need a magnifying glass to read the list of beer styles and offerings on the chalkboard, hailing from countries around the world. If you're having trouble deciding, close your eyes and point at a random spot on the wall: every square inch is covered in beer memorabilia.

i Drinks €5-6. Open M-Th 3-11:30pm, F-Sa 3pm-12:30am, Su 3-11pm.

ESSENTIALS
Practicalities

- **TOURIST OFFICES:** Fáilte Ireland. (Grand Parade. ☎21 42 55 100 Open M-Sa 9am-5pm.)
- **ATMS:** Clustered in the central area of Cork in the shopping district. Also one located by the New Bar on the University of Cork Campus.
- **POST OFFICES:** An Post. (15/16 Washington St. ☎21 42 73 645 Open M-F 9am-5:30pm, Sa 9am-1pm.)

Emergency

- **EMERGENCY NUMBERS:** ☎999 (Ireland/UK); ☎112 (Europe-wide)
- **CRISIS LINE:** Irish Tourist Assistance Service, for tourists who are victims of crime. (☎1 890 365700 Open M-Sa 10am-6pm, Su noon-6pm.)
- **PHARMACIES:** Phelan's Midnight Pharmacy. (2 Kinsale Rd. ☎21 43 10 132 Open 10am-midnight.) Phelan's Late Night Pharmacy. (9 Patrick St. ☎21 42 72 511 Open 10am-9pm.)
- **HOSPITALS:** Mercy University Hospital. (Greenville Pl. ☎21 42 71 971.)

Getting There

Bus Éireann serves Cork. The 226 bus will get you from Cork Airport to the bus or train station. From here, walking to the city center is easy, but if you're carrying a bit of luggage the 205 bus from the train station will get you to Patrick Street, the main shopping street running through central Cork, and the bus station at Parnell Place.

Getting Around

Cork is fairly accessible by foot, but if you want to see the further reaches of the country, Bus Éireann is probably the best way to go. Routes, timetables, and fares are available online. (www.buseireann.ie/inner.php?id=458.) Leap Cards, reloadable fare cards, are an option for discounted travel in Cork.

ireland essentials

VISAS

Citizens of almost all major developed countries (including Australia, Canada, New Zealand, the UK, and the US) do not need visas to enter the Republic of Ireland. Citizens of these countries can stay for up to 90 days without a visa, but after this period will have to apply for a longer-term visa. Note that the Republic of Ireland is not a signatory of the Schengen Agreement, which means it is not a part of the free movement zone that covers most of the EU. The advantage of this is that non-EU citizens can visit Ireland without eating into the 90-day limit on travel within the Schengen area. Some travelers have been known to use Ireland as a convenient location for"stopping the Schengen clock" and extending their Eurotrip. The only real disadvantage of Ireland's non-Schengen status is that you will be subject to border controls on entry, so don't forget your passport.

Those hoping to study or work in Ireland will have to obtain special visas to do so; consult your nearest Irish embassy or consulate for information on applying. You will generally need a letter of acceptance from a university or company in order to apply. You can find more information on all visa questions at the website of the Irish Department of Foreign Affairs and Trade (www.dfa.ie).

Since Northern Ireland is in the United Kingdom, its visa rules are the same as for Britain. For information on these policies, see the Great Britain chapter.

MONEY

Tipping and Bargaining

Some restaurants in Ireland figure a service charge into the bill; some even calculate it into the cost of the dishes themselves. The menu often indicates whether or not service is included. If gratuity is not included, consider leaving 10-15%, depending upon the quality of the service. Tipping is not necessary for most other services, such as taxis and concierge assistance, especially in rural areas. In most cases, people are usually happy if you simply round up the bill to the nearest euro. But if a driver is particularly courteous and helpful, consider tipping 5-10%. Hairdressers, at least for women, are typically tipped 10% of the bill. Never tip in pubs—it's considered condescending. In general, do not tip bartenders, though some bartenders at hip urban bars may expect a tip; watch and learn from other customers.

Taxes

The Republic of Ireland has a 23% value added tax (VAT), although some goods are subject to a lower rate of 13%. Northern Ireland edges its southern neighbor with the UK VAT rate of 20%. The prices stated in *Let's Go* include VAT unless otherwise noted. Given the Irish government's serious cashflow problems, don't be surprised if the rates increase even more.

SAFETY AND HEALTH

Although Ireland has a long history of serious sectarian violence and terrorism, the situation has improved considerably in the last 15 years. It is still probably best to avoid incendiary discussions with strong opinions on the Northern Ireland question or by stating your undying love for Oliver Cromwell (this will not go down well). Always be aware of your surroundings and don't assume that the Troubles are completely over: there are still many fringe groups who are prepared to commit acts of terrorism.

Drugs and Alcohol

The Republic of Ireland and Northern Ireland both regulate the possession of recreational drugs, with penalties ranging from a warning to lengthy prison sentences. Possession of marijuana results in a fine, though repeated offenses can result in prosecution. Harder substances are treated with severity. If you carry prescription drugs with you, have a copy of the prescription and a note from a doctor readily accessible at country borders. The drinking age, 18 in both the Republic of Ireland and Northern Ireland, is more strictly enforced in urban areas. While there is no national legislation prohibiting drinking in public, local authorities may pass by-laws enforcing such a policy. Drinking is banned in many public places in Northern Ireland. Contact the local authority for more information.

ITALY

For the home of the papacy, Italy certainly knows how to do sensual pleasures right: stylish Vespas, intoxicating vino, vibrant piazze, and crackling pizzas covered in garden-fresh produce will light up your eyes, ears, nose, and taste buds as you make your way across the Mediterranean's favorite boot. In a country where la dolce far niente ("the sweetness of doing nothing") is a national pastime, you will nonetheless find yourself with a wealth of opportunities to pursue la dolce vita. And as a student traveler, you are uniquely situated to experience Italia in all its ridiculousness and sublimity. Striking out on your own, likely on a budget, you will open yourself up to what someone who stays in the swankiest hotels and eats at all the five-star restaurants will miss: making connections with the people and the way of life in Italy's many storied cities and towns.Wander your way along the canals in Venice and marvel at the famed mosaics of Ravenna. Try to dodge the sharp glances of the fashionistas in Milan and discover the moving stories of the flood-ravaged Ligurian Coast as you make your way along the Cinque Terre. Eat pizza in Naples, climb the Duomo in Florence, and explore ruins in Sicily. With its Renaissance art, Roman grandeur, and religious relics, Italy presents curious and intrepid travelers with an experience that is at once cultural, historical, and truly divine.

greatest hits

- **ANCIENT ANTIQUES.** The relics of ancient Rome pop up all over the place. **Rome** (p. 420) is obviously the place to start, but even cities like **Verona** (p. 485) and **Milan** (p. 452) share this fascinating history.

- **WHERE REBIRTH WAS BORN.** Thanks to the Renaissance, there's more art in Italy than even a Medici can handle. Get the best possible primer at the king of Italian museums: Florence's **Uffizi Gallery** (p. 507).

- **GIVE THE MAINLAND THE BOOT.** Once you've made it down the Mediterranean coast, hop on a ferry to see a whole other side of Italy in Sicily, including the Byzantine-influenced **Palermo** (p. 539) and the ruins of **Syracuse** (p. 548).

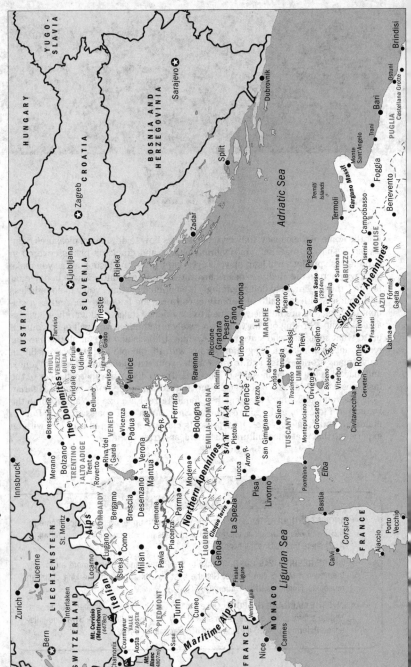

italy

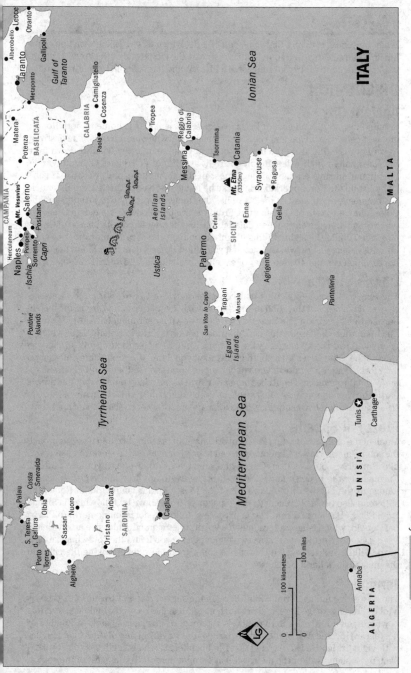

ITALY

Ionian Sea

MALTA

Gulf of
Taranto

Lecce
Otranto
Alberobello
Taranto
Gallipoli
Metaponto
Matera
Potenza
BASILICATA
CALABRIA
Camigliatello
Cosenza
Paola
Tropea
Reggio di
Calabria
Taormina
Catania
Mt. Etna
(3350m)
Syracuse
Ragusa
Enna
SICILY
Gela
Cefalù
Palermo
Agrigento
Messina
Aeolian
Islands
Ustica
San Vito lo Capo
Trapani
Marsala
Egadi
Islands
Pantelleria

CAMPANIA
Herculaneum
Mt. Vesuvius
Salerno
Naples
Positano
Ischia
Sorrento
Pompeii
Capri
Pontine
Islands

Tyrrhenian Sea

Mediterranean Sea

Carthage
Tunis

TUNISIA

Palau
Costa
Smeralda
S. Teresa
Olbia
d. Gallura
Porto
Torres
Sassari
Nuoro
Arbatax
Alghero
Oristano
SARDINIA
Cagliari

100 kilometers
100 miles
0
0

Annaba

ALGERIA

italy

rome

When in Rome, "If it ain't Ba-roque, don't fix it." Which is why Rome won't be cleaning up its streets anytime soon, but it's also why the city is one of the greatest places to experience the relics and ruins of art, history, and humanity in the entire world.

ORIENTATION

Ancient City

Situated just south and east of Piazza Venezia, Ancient City is home to both Rome's greatest collection of ancient ruins and its most overwhelming crowds. The best way to get here is either from the metro stop at M Colosseum or by walking down from Via Nazionale, which will spit you out right at the foot of Trajan's Column. Via dei Fori Imperiali runs straight through most of the sights here, starting with Trajan's Column and the Fori Imperiali, which can be found just east of the Vittorio Emanuele II Monument; to the west of the street lies the Roman Forum, and at its end loom the Colosseum and Arch of Constantine. From the arch, walk down Via di San Gregorio, where you'll find the entrance to Palatine Hill and, farther along, the far end of Circus Maximus. While the sights in this neighborhood are the area's major draw, wander into the streets just off Via Cavour, and you'll find Rome's delightful Monti neighborhood, which is home to a number of excellent restaurants and aperitivo spots.

Centro Storico

The tangle of vias and vicolos that comprise much of Centro Storico isn't always easy to navigate, but the good news is that nearly every twist and turn in this neighborhood will lead you to a historic church or down a charming, narrow side street. The main thoroughfare in this neighborhood is Corso Vittorio Emanuele II, which is connected to Piazza Venezia in the east via Via del Plebiscito and runs all the way west to the Tiber River. Just south of this road you'll find the Area Sacra and Campo de' Fiori; wander a bit north and you'll happen upon the Pantheon and Piazza Navona. While the sights and churches here are worth a visit at any time of day, this area is particularly good for an evening stroll, as both Campo de' Fiori and many of the side streets immediately west of Piazza Navona are great for food, drinks, and aperitivo.

Piazza di Spagna

Much of the area surrounding Piazza di Spagna is all ritz and glitz, and if you approach the square along Via dei Condotti, you can feast your eyes on the storefronts of shops like Burberry, Louis Vuitton, Gucci, and a bunch of other places you can't afford. Fortunately, the piazza's famed Spanish Steps are totally free and a great place to lounge in the middle of the day. One of the most popular landmarks in Rome, the steps can also be easily reached via M Spagna or from above by following Via Sistina from Piazza Barberini. From Piazza di Spagna, follow V. del Babuino north to Piazza del Popolo, which is also a terminus for Via di Ripetta and the massive artery that is Via del Corso. Northeast of these two major piazze, you'll find the sprawling gardens of the Villa Borghese, which is home to some great views overlooking the city and the must-visit Galleria Borghese.

Termini

The area surrounding Termini Station is, on the surface, kind of trash. As in, there is a lot of literal garbage here, and not a whole lot of sights or pretty buildings. But this is where you'll find a lot Rome's hotels and most of its cheap hostels. A number of hostels are located east of the station, so if you're staying in one of those, get familiar with Viale Enrico De Nicola and Piazza Indipendenza, which you'll use to get to and from most sights and/or the metro stop at Termini Station. To the west of the station you'll find a lot of kebab shops, but wander a little farther and you'll happen upon Basilica di Santa Maria Maggiore, the gem of the neighborhood. Walk north from here, and you'll hit Piazza della Repubblica, which is home to the Basilica di Santa Maria degli Angeli and one end of the Baths of Diocletian. Don't eat too many dinners in and around Termini if you can help it, but if you're in a pinch and are looking for good food close to your hostel, wander up to Via Venti Settembre and some of the streets farther north for better options. And while you're up there, absolutely do get gelato at Gelateria La Romana. And while buses #40 and #64 will become your best friend if you're staying near Termini, it's also perfectly safe to walk back to your hostel here at night as long as you keep your wits about you.

Vatican City

Besides the crowds that flood and wind their way around the walls of the Vatican and St. Peter's Square during the day, the neighborhood surrounding the Vatican is relatively quiet, local, and residential compared to some other areas of Rome. Accessible by both M Ottaviano and M Lepanto, the streets of this neighborhood lie on what could almost count as a grid, and some of the area's wide boulevards include Viale Giulio Cesare, Via Candia, and Via Cola di Rienzo. In many cases in this area, all roads lead to the Vatican and St. Peter's, and even if they don't, just look for the basilica's massive dome or the daunting, slanted walls of the Vatican if you need to orient yourself. Although the area gets a bit quieter after the major sights close in the evening, you can still find some great, understated food if you're willing to look hard enough (be sure to check out Pizzarium for lunch, Sciascia for coffee, and Fa Bio for sandwiches). The eastern perimeter of the neighborhood is marked by the Tiber and its many impressive bridges—you'll find a number of Bernini sculptures adorning the Ponte Sant'Angelo, across from which sits the Museo di Castel Sant'Angelo—and if you follow Lungotevere south along the river, you'll eventually reach Trastevere.

Trastevere

Tucked into a bend just west of the Tiber, Trastevere's name is derived from the Latin Trans Tiberim, which literally means "beyond the Tiber." This little neighborhood is a charming mix of twisting streets, yellowed buildings, stray cats, and crawling ivy. The busy, beating heart of the neighborhood is Piazza Santa Maria in Trastevere, where tourists sit on the steps of the square's central fountain and musicians riff on guitars late into the night. From here, you can wander the narrow side streets and discover many good, affordable restaurants. Home to John Cabot University and a number of college students, Trastevere also boasts Rome's largest concentration of trendy bars and hip hangout spots, many of which are centered around Piazza Trilussa. Trastevere is bisected by the busy Viale di Trastevere, and while the area to the west is often busy with tourists, to the east you'll find quieter streets and quainter, more authentic Roman restaurants nestled into a number of hidden piazze. And if you've had enough of all the eating and drinking (which is, admittedly, the main draw of the area), you can head up Via Garibaldi to Gianicolo Hill or take a breather under the palm trees of the Orto Botanico.

ACCOMMODATIONS

Ancient City

◪ CESARE BALBO INN $$
V. Cesare Balbo 43 ☎06 98 38 60 81 www.cesarebalboinn.com
Given its unique location, reasonable rates, and some of the friendliest service you're likely to encounter in Rome, Cesare Balbo Inn might just be the best value accommodation the city has to offer. Tucked away on the quiet V. Cesare Balbo, the inn is just down the road from the stunning Basilica di Santa Maria Maggiore

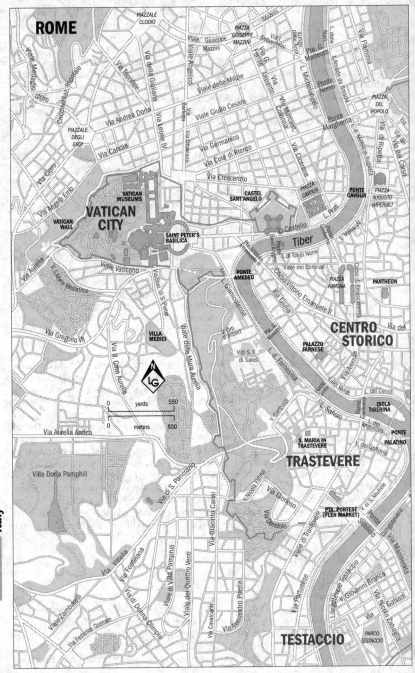

ROME

PIAZZALE
CLODIO

PIAZZA
GIUSEPPE
MAZZINI

PIAZZALE
DEGLI
EROI

VATICAN
MUSEUMS

VATICAN
WALL

VATICAN
CITY

SAINT PETER'S
BASILICA

CASTEL
SANT'ANGELO

PIAZZA
CAVOUR

PONTE
CAVOUR

PIAZZA
AUGUSTO
IMPERIALE

PIAZZA
DEL
POPOLO

Tiber

PONTE
AMEDEO

PIAZZA
NAVONA

PANTHEON

CENTRO
STORICO

VILLA
MEDICI

LG

PALAZZO
FARNESE

yards   550

meters   500

ISOLA
TIBERINA

PONTE
PALATINO

S. MARIA IN
TRASTEVERE

TRASTEVERE

Villa Doria Pamphili

PTA. PORTESE
(FLEA MARKET)

TESTACCIO

PARCO
TESTACCIO

italy

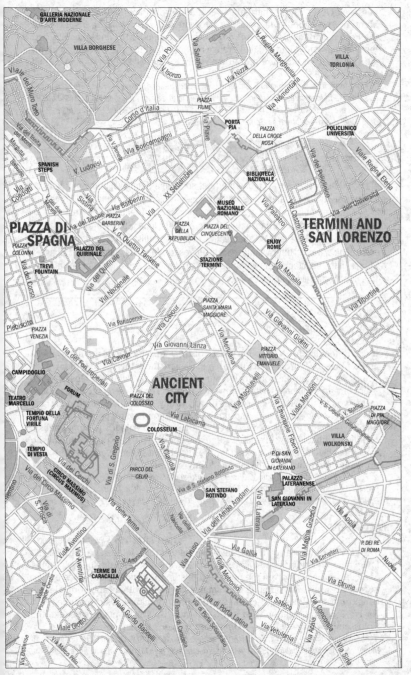

GALLERIA NAZIONALE
D'ARTE MODERNE

VILLA BORGHESE

VILLA
TORLONIA

Viale del Muro Torto

Via Po

V. Isonzo

Via Salaria

Via Nizza

V. Regina Margherita

Via Nomentana

Corso d'Italia

PIAZZA
FIUME

Via Piave

PORTA
PIA

PIAZZA
DELLA CROCE
ROSA

POLICLINICO
UNIVERSITA

Via del Policlinico

Viale Regina Elena

Via Boncompagni

Via Veneto

V. Ludovisi

SPANISH
STEPS

Via dei Monti
Meguria

Via
Condotti

Viale due Macelli

Via
Sistina

Via Barberini

XX Settembre

BIBLIOTECA
NAZIONALE

Via Castro Pretorio

Via Palestro

Via dell'Università

Via del Tritone

PIAZZA
BARBERINI

V. d. Quattro Fontane

PIAZZA
DELLA
REPUBBLICA

PIAZZA DEL
CINQUECENTO

MUSEO
NAZIONALE
ROMANO

TERMINI AND
SAN LORENZO

PIAZZA DI
SPAGNA

PIAZZA
COLONNA

PALAZZO DEL
QUIRINALE

Via del Quirinale

ENJOY
ROME

Via Marsala

TREVI
FOUNTAIN

Via Nazionale

STAZIONE
TERMINI

Via del Corso

Via Tiburtina

Plebiscito

Via Panisperna

Via Cavour

PIAZZA
SANTA MARIA
MAGGIORE

Via Giovanni Giolitti

Via Merulana

PIAZZA
VENEZIA

Via dei Fori Imperiali

Via Cavour

Via Giovanni Lanza

PIAZZA
VITTORIO
EMANUELE

CAMPIDOGLIO

ANCIENT
CITY

Via Machiavelli

Viale Manzoni

V. S. Croce in Gerusalemme

V. Statilia

PIAZZA
DI PTA.
MAGGIORE

TEATRO
MARCELLO

FORUM

PIAZZA DEL
COLOSSEO

Via Labicana

Via Emanuele Filiberto

TEMPIO DELLA
FORTUNA
VIRILE

COLOSSEUM

VILLA
WOLKONSKI

TEMPIO
DI VESTA

Via di S. Gregorio

Via Claudia

PARCO DEL
CELIO

P. DI SAN
GIOVANNI
IN LATERANO

Via Appia

CIRCO MASSIMO
(CIRCUS MAXIMUS)

Via del Cerchi

Via di S. Stefano Rotondo

SAN STEFANO
ROTONDO

PALAZZO
LATERANENSE

P. DEI RE
DI ROMA

Aventino

Via del Circo Massimo

Via delle Terme

Via della
Navicella

Via dell'Amba Aradam

SAN GIOVANNI IN
LATERANO

Via d. Laterani

Via Magna Graecia

Via Cerveteri

Nuola

Via di
S. Prisca

Viale Aventino

Via Aventina

V. Antoniana

Via Druso

Via Gallia

Via Metronio

Via Etruria

Via Piramide Cestia

TERME DI
CARACALLA

Via di Porta Latina

Via Satoco

Via Concordia

Via Adaia

Via Sinta

Viale Guido Baccelli

Viale di Terme di Caretella

Via di Porta Sebastiano

Via Vetulonia

Viale Ostiense

Viale Giotto

Via Marco Polo

rome

and even closer to the charming streets and stylish aperitivo spots of Rome's Monti neighborhood (which also situates guests a short walk from Via Cavour, the Forum, and the Colosseum). Rooms are clean, colorful, and spacious, with high ceilings and bright red and orange bedspreads. Plus, the charming, chipper guys at the front desk are more than ready to answer any questions you may have.

i From Termini Station, exit onto V. Giovanni Giolitti and proceed down V. Cavour. Turn right onto V. di Santa Maria Maggiore, which becomes V. Panisperna, then turn right onto V. Cesare Balbo. The inn is on the right. Singles €60. Doubles €70. Quads €80. Breakfast included. Reception 8:30am-6pm. Guests arriving later than 6pm must pay a small fee.

lungo il tevere

You should really take a walk along the Tiber sometime during your time in Rome, and why not do it when there's also a lot of beer available for purchase along the way? From June-August, the city sets up a long stretch of tents on the west side of the river where you can booze and cruise all night long. Sure, it's touristy, but as Death Cab for Cutie said so eloquently, "You Are a Tourist." So have at it. Eat *al fresco*, drink *al fresco*, buy overpriced skirts *al fresco*. Alternately, just wander along and take in the spectacle after grabbing more quality food and drinks up the stairs and across Lungotevere in Trastevere.

CASA DI SANTA PUDENZIANA $

V. Urbana 158

If you're looking for a temporary taste of the monastic life, make like Ophelia and get thee to Casa di Santa Pudenziana. Despite those threats your mom made when you were a rebellious teen, your stay here is probably the closest you'll ever come to living in an actual convent. (Bonus: The *casa*'s women-only policy means you won't even have to deal with any whiny, existentially frustrated Hamlets during your stay here!) And don't worry if you haven't prayed the rosary recently—this *casa* is a perfect, welcome retreat for saints and sinners alike, complete with a homey breakfast room and courtyard. The elderly woman who runs this place might not speak a lot of English, but if you're staying here, you probably prefer things on the quiet side anyway.

i From Termini Station, exit onto V. Giovanni Giolitti and proceed down V. Cavour. Turn right into P. dell'Esquilino, then turn left down V. Urbana. The casa is on the right. Dorms €26. Singles €40. Doubles €52. Breakfast included. Curfew M-F 10:30pm, Sa midnight, Su 10:30pm. Reception 7am-10:30pm.

HOTEL ROSETTA $$

V. Cavour 295 B/1   ☎06 47 82 30 69 www.rosettahotel.com

The courtyard where you'll find the stairs leading to Hotel Rosetta, with its yellow walls and laundry hanging from various windows, is surprisingly charming and quiet, especially given the noisy and bustling V. Cavour that rushes by just beyond its walls. The hotel itself is small and quaint, with a cabinet of trinkets behind the front desk and clean, basic rooms. Breakfast is not included, but Rosetta's central location (just a few minutes' walk from major sites like the Colosseum) will make it easy to find plenty of good food nearby.

i M: Colosseum. Walk down V. dei Fori Imperiali and turn right onto V. Cavour. Hotel Rosetta is on the left. Singles €60. Doubles €80. Email info@rosettahotel.com for reservations. Reception 24hr.

italy

Centro Storico

ALBERGO POMEZIA $$

V. dei Chiavari 13   ☎06 686 13 71 www.hotelpomezia.it

Situated on the charming Via dei Chiavari, Albergo Pomezia's biggest selling point is clearly its real estate, although a breakfast room and bar add extra value to the convenience of this hotel's location. Reception and the clean, basic rooms radiate a warm yellow light that you can wander back to after an evening spent exploring the wine bars in and around Campo de' Fiori. Although breakfast is included, consider popping downstairs one morning for some fresh bread from Forno Marco Roscioli, a neighborhood favorite located just across the street.

i From Campo de' Fiori, walk down V. dei Giubbonari and turn left onto V. dei Chiavari. The hotel is on the right. Singles €80. Doubles €120. Breakfast included. Reception 24hr.

Piazza di Spagna

▨ HOTEL PANDA $$

V. della Croce 35   ☎06 678 01 79 www.hotelpanda.it

Sure, a single with a shared bathroom at Hotel Panda will run you about double the price of a night in a hostel dorm, but given this hotel's excellent location amid the glitz and ritz of the streets surrounding Piazza di Spagna, the rates here are actually quite reasonable. Rooms are sometimes small but have a real European, boutiquey feel about them, with rosy bedspreads, stone sinks, and dark wood fixtures. If you're looking for the convenience of its prime location, a break from the hostel life, or the simple privacy of a night to yourself (#nonew-friends), Hotel Panda is a great option.

i From P. di Spagna, walk down V. della Croce. Hotel Panda is on the left. Buzz for entry. Singles from €65. Doubles from €95. Triples from €125. Reception 24hr.

Termini

▨ THE BEEHIVE HOTEL $

V. Marghera 8   ☎06 44 70 45 53 www.the-beehive.com

Tucked in behind the walls of a colorful courtyard on Via Marghera, the Beehive Hotel is the epitome of cute and offers a quiet alternative to the bumpin' party hostel scene that surrounds much of Termini Station. And while the place isn't exactly buzzin', the Hive (the hotel's eight-bed, mixed-gender dorm room) offers a chance to get to know your fellow travelers while enjoying the comfort, amenities, and stellar service of a smaller and more intimate hostel. Although hostelers don't have access to a kitchen or fridge while staying in the Hive, breakfast (made with fresh, organic ingredients €2-7) is available in the morning, and snacks and drinks (whether coffee, wine, or beer) can be enjoyed al fresco in the secluded peace of the front courtyard at any time. Who needs drunk Eurotrippers when you can hang out under a banyan tree all day?

i From Termini Station, exit onto P. dei Cinquecento and turn right onto Vle. Enrico De Nicola, then right onto V. Marsala. Turn left onto V. Marghera and the Beehive is on the left (look for the sign under some leaves and vines). Dorms €25. Privates with shared bath €70. Privates with ensuite bath €80. Book early to secure a spot in the dorm. Reception 7am-11pm. Check-in 2pm.

▨ ALESSANDRO DOWNTOWN $

V. Carlo Cattaneo 23   ☎06 44 34 01 47 www.hostelsalessandro.com

Despite being located closer to the bustle of Termini Station than its sister hostel, Alessandro Palace, Alessandro Downtown is actually the less rowdy of the two establishments. But with splashes of color on the walls and plenty of seating and vending machines in the large common area, the Downtown is still a great place to meet fellow globetrotters. Tailored specifically to the needs of young budget travelers, the hostel offers great nightly rates (exempt from the

rome

Rome tourist tax!) and opportunities to book discounted tours of all the city's major sights. And perhaps most importantly, if your clean underwear supply is reaching critical levels, there are laundry facilities available for guest use.

i From Termini Station, exit onto V. Giovanni Giolitti and walk down V. Gioberti. Then turn left onto V. Principe Amedeo, then right onto V. Carlo Cattaneo. Alessandro Downtown is on the left. Dorms €24-30. Private doubles from €88. Breakfast tickets €4. Laundry €4 wash, €4 dry, €1 detergent. Reception 24hr.

Vatican City

COLORS HOTEL
, HOSTEL

V. Boezio 31 ☎06 686 79 47 www.colorshotel.com

The distinguishing principle of this hotel isn't exactly high concept, but Colors certainly commits to its titular bit and delivers with green walls, orange bathrooms, pink bedspreads, and a yellow breakfast room. One of the few hotels with dorm rooms that you'll find this close to the Vatican, Colors is a little bit like living inside a crayon box, and it's all so sunny and bright that you might be distracted from the fact that the dorms don't have lockers and the breakfast is a bit expensive at €6.50. Still, bunking up here means you'll enjoy the amenities of a hotel (the cleaning staff will remake your bed, change out your towel, and leave a fresh bottle of water on your pillow every day), and rooms and bathrooms are incredibly clean.

i M: Ottaviano. Walk down V. Ottaviano and turn left onto V. Cola di Rienzo, then right onto V. Terenzio. Colors is on the corner of V. Terenzio and V. Boezio. Less than a 10min. walk to both St. Peter's and the Vatican Museums. Dorms from €28. Reception 24hr.

PENSIONE PARADISE
$

Vle. Giulio Cesare 47 ☎06 36 00 43 31 www.pensioneparadise.com

Conveniently located just across the street from the Lepanto metro station, Pensione Paradise is tucked into its quiet, charming courtyard almost as tightly as you'll be tucked into its tiny rooms. And even though the wooden bed frames and close walls might make you feel like a Borrower living in a cupboard for a few days, it's all very cozy and comfortable. Reception is friendly and helpful, and all rooms (even those with shared bathrooms) come equipped with stone sinks that add to the boutique feel of the pensione.

i M: Lepanto. Pensione Paradise is across the street on Vle. Giulio Cesare. Singles from €50. Doubles from €70. Reception 8am-9pm. Check-in 2pm.

Trastevere

Despite the many tourists who wander the picturesque streets of Trastevere at all hours of the day, the neighborhood has remained largely devoid of more traditional accommodation establishments like big hostels and hotels. What Trastevere does have in abundance is very small guest houses, bed and breakfasts, and apartments travelers can reserve for their stay.

✉ ORSA MAGGIORE FEMALE ONLY HOSTEL
$

V. di San Francesco di Sales 1a www.foresteriaorsa.altervista.org

Orsa Maggiore is basically your mom (or domestically minded dad! we here are Let's Go are gender-inclusive!): it feeds you breakfast free of charge, makes your bed for you every morning, and even does your laundry (alas, that last one will cost you €7). Adding to these comfort-of-home amenities, the dormitories at this female-only hostel also provide guests with personal nightstands and nightlights, along with lockers that are really more like very secure closets. me! The only downside may be the hostel's lack of air-conditioning and in-room Wi-Fi, but with its abundant and Wi-Fi-equipped common areas (from the large breakfast room to the couch- and bookshelf-lined hallways to the courtyard filled with tables and benches), Orsa Maggiore makes up for the inconvenience.

i From Ponte Sisto, cross Lungotevere della Farnesina and walk left down the stairs to V. della Lungara, then turn right onto V. di San Francesco di Sales. Orsa Maggiore is on the left. Dorms from €28. Breakfast included. Reception 24hr.

SIGHTS

Ancient City

▓ COLOSSEUM

ROME

P. del Colosseo

The first thought that'll cross your mind when you walk up to the Colosseum will be something along the lines of, "Oh my god," followed shortly by, "Oh, the humanity." And while the sheer mass of selfie stick-carrying bodies that pour into the Colosseum each day might leave you feeling a little overwhelmed, at least it will give you some idea of what the stadium looked like on the day of a gladiator fight nearly 2000 years ago, when more than 70,000 Roman citizens crowded into the building to watch the Russell Crowes of antiquity fight it out for box office glory (or something like that).

Start your visit on the second level, where you can wander through the exhibition space set up in the building's outermost hallway and brief yourself on all the history of the Colosseum. Look down at the stage where spectacles of all varieties took place, the grand arches through which gladiators, prisoners, and other performers entered the arena, and the cross that marks where the emperors and important people of Ancient Rome used to sit. Up close, the stadium certainly doesn't fail to impress. What's perhaps even more breathtaking, however, is those moments when you glimpse it from farther off, unexpectedly, looming in the distance like the mammoth and enduring ghost of Ancient Rome that it is.

i M: Colosseum. The line for the Colosseum is almost more shocking than the thing itself, but if you buy your ticket at either the Roman Forum or Palatine Hill, you can enter through the left queue and bypass half a mile's worth of sorry suckers on your way inside. €12 combined with the Roman Forum and Palatine Hill. Ticket is valid for entrance to the Colosseum and the Forum/Palatine Hill for two consecutive days. Audio guide €5.50. Video guide €6. Open daily 8:30am to one hour before sunset.

PALATINE HILL

ROME

Perhaps the least popular site of the three included in the Colosseum-Forum-Palatine Hill ticket, Palatine Hill deserves a little more recognition. Mostly because, you know, this is where the city of Rome was born (according to legend, the cave where Romulus and Remus were nursed by the she-wolf was located on this hill, and the hill's Casa Romuli is allegedly where Romulus made his home after founding the city). And although people lived on Palatine Hill as early as 1000 BCE, if you were a citizen during the hill's later years, you likely would have been willing to kill somebody Caesar-style for a piece of real estate up here. As the Beverly Hills of the Republican and Imperial periods, Palatine Hill (from which we get the word "palace") was home to all the city's hottest property, and today you can see the ruins of centuries' worth of temples, the houses of Augustus and Livia, and the Imperial Palace, whose apartments once overlooked Circus Maximus.

i M Colosseum. Entrance on V. San Gregorio. You can also reach Palatine Hill from the Roman Forum. €12 combined with the Roman Forum and the Colosseum. Ticket is valid for entrance to the Colosseum and the Forum/Palatine Hill for two consecutive days. Open daily 8:30am to one hour before sunset.

italy

THE ROMAN FORUM

Your visit to the Roman Forum will probably leave you thinking, "Wow, this city is really falling to pieces." But by this point, you've probably realized that that's Rome's calling card: making tourists pay too many euro to see a bunch of dirt and old bricks. Still, what was once the center of Roman public life has become the center of Roman tourism, and a walk through the Forum is an essential part of any first visit to this city. The ends of the Forum are marked by the Arch of Titus (near the entrance) and the Arch of Septimius Severus (near the far exit at the foot of Capitoline Hill), and in between you'll find other highlights that include the Tempio di Romolo, the Tempio di Antonino e Faustina, and the House of the Vestal Virgins.

i M: Colosseum. Entrance to the Forum is on V. dei Fori Imperiali or V. San Gregorio (directly opposite the Colosseum). You can also enter the Forum from Palatine Hill. €12 combined with Palatine Hill and the Colosseum. Ticket is valid for entrance to the Colosseum and the Forum/Palatine Hill for two consecutive days. Open daily 8:30am to one hour before sunset.

FORI IMPERIALI

V. dei Fori Imperiali

A funny thing happened on the way to the forum—namely, you probably stumbled across a whole other set of fora. And while they might not be The Forum, you will probably come to know Fori Imperali as The Free Fora, which is almost better. Lining the V. dei Fori Imperiali between the Vittorio Emanuele II Monument and the Colosseum, these fora once served as the business district of Rome and are now home to many a ruin and lingering column, all of which can be admired from the various spots along the street. Overshadowing it all, however, is Trajan's Column, located at the far end of the Trajan Forum. Built to commemorate the emperor's victories in the Dacian Wars (and to tell the world, "Hey, guys, I have a big dick!"), Trajan's Column stands 98 ft. tall and is decorated with a single continuous frieze magnificent enough to distract you from all the phallic overcompensation.

i M: Colosseum. Walk down V. dei Fori Imperiali; the ruins and Trajan's Column are on the right. Free.

ARCH OF CONSTANTINE

V. San Gregorio

Standing just across the street from the Colosseum, the Arch of Constantine is a bit dwarfed by its mammoth neighbor. In fairness, it's hard for any structure to compete with the Colosseum for people's attention, but we're pretty sure the Arch of Constantine is sitting there thinking, "At least I still have my youth and all my marble, god." The arch straddles the Via Triumphalis, the road used by emperors when they returned home after totally slaughtering the competition at away games. It was dedicated in 315 CE to celebrate Constantine's victory (and complete inability to work well with other people) over his co-emperor Maxentius in 312 CE. An architectural wonder in its own right, the arch is often admired in passing as everyone makes his or her way over to the Colosseum, but take a moment to pause and marvel at the friezes depicted on nearly every surface of the structure.

i M: Colosseum. The arch is right across from the Colosseum; you can't miss it. Free.

CAPITOLINE HILL

Tucked around the back side of the Vittorio Emanuele II Monument, Capitoline Hill converges around Piazza di Campidoglio, which was designed by Michelangelo and is punctuated by an equestrian statue of Marcus Aurelius. If you mount the hill from the central stairs on the west side Piazza Venezia, you'll be welcomed by two naked guys and their horses (alas, statues, although they do make you reconsider the logistics of bareback riding). Surrounding the piazza are the Capitoline Museums, which are home to the world's oldest public collection of ancient art. The back end of Capitoline Hill overlooks the Roman Forum, so wander around and take in the view of the ruins and the Arch of Septimius Severus from that vantage point, then seek out one of the hill's shady retreats to rehydrate before heading back out into the sun.

i From P. Venezia, facing the Vittorio Emanuele II Monument, walk right down V. Teatro Marcello, then look for the stairs on the left and head up the hill. Free.

THE VELABRUM   ROME

This sunken section of the ancient city lies in a valley between Palatine Hill, Circus Maximus, and the Tiber and features the lesser-known ruins of the Teatro di Marcello and the Arco di Giano, among others. The only reason most people wander down here, however, is to visit the Chiesa di Santa Maria in Cosmedin. If you're wondering what the giant line outside this otherwise random church is for, it's a crowd of people who are trying to capture the lingering essence of Audrey Hepburn and Gregory Peck, who famously visited the church's Bocca della Verita ("Mouth of Truth") in *Roman Holiday*. Although entrance to the actual church is free, most people just come here for a picture with the mouth (which, according to legend, will bite off the hand of a liar). So proceed with caution, prepare for a long wait, and just remember: you are not secretly a princess, and the sweaty guy in front of you in line is most definitely not Gregory Peck. Mostly, you stood in line for 30min. and all you got was a photo with the Bocca's ugly mug.

i From P. Venezia, facing the Vittorio Emanuele II Monument, walk right down V. del Teatro Marcello and continue as it turns into V. Petroselli. The Velabrum and its sights are in the flat region as the base of the hill. Church located in P. Bocca della Verita. Free. Church open daily 9:30am-5:50pm.

Centro Storico

⛪ PANTHEON   ROME
P. della Rotonda

You've probably heard excellent things about the Pantheon and its legendary unsupported dome—the largest of its kind 1889 years running. And man, this church really holds up to all the hype (and, you know, to gravity and time). Built in the second century CE, this temple to the gods (all of them) remains one of Rome's most impressive and best-preserved relics from the ancient period. While the building's 16 Corinthian columns are shocking enough in their size and girth, it is the Pantheon's richly colored interior and rotunda that will truly leave you dumbfounded. Try to preserve for yourself that moment when you first walked inside and caught of glimpse of the rotunda's central oculus and the blue sky beyond—try to remember the awe and smallness that you felt in that moment because it's pretty singular.

i From P. Navona, exit onto Corsia Agonale, then turn left onto Piazza Madama, then take a quick right onto V. dei Salvatore. Turn right onto V. Della Dogana Vecchia, then left onto Salita de Crescenzi and proceed to P. Della Rotonda. Free. Open M-Sa 8:30am-7:30pm, Su 9am-6pm.

PIAZZA NAVONA

If you're not looking for a selfie stick or an overpriced watercolor of the Colosseum, the main draw for the swarm of tourists who congregate in Piazza Navona is Bernini's famous Fontana dei Quattro Fiumi, which depicts personified versions of each major river of the four continents that were under papal control when fountain was constructed in 1651. Look for the Danube (Europe), the Ganges (Asia), the Rio de la Plata (America), and the Nile (Africa). Overlooking the fountain, you'll find the Chiesa di Sant'Agnese in Agone, a magnificent Baroque church designed by Bernini's rival, Francesco Borromini (take time to pop inside and admire the frescoes and gold leaf of the church's domed interior). The piazza is certainly popular among tourists, but after you've taken the time to admire the Bernini and the Borromini, make your way to the more charming side streets, where you'll find plenty of restaurants, wine bars, and gelaterias lining the narrow cobblestones.

i From Corso Vittorio Emanuele II, turn into P. San Pantaleo and turn right into V. della Cuccagna and walk through Palazzo Braschi to P. Navona. Piazza and church free.

VITTORIO EMANUELE II MONUMENT
P. Venezia

The Vittorio Emanuele II Monument is also known as Italy's "Altar to the Fatherland," and from its position overlooking the busy traffic circle of Piazza Venezia, everything about it seems to be saying, "Bow down, tourists." And you will, because its sprawling steps, enormous white columns, and imposing equestrian statue of V-Manny himself are just that impressive. Constructed in 1885 to celebrate nationalism and unification, the monument also features Italian flags that are almost as big as the American ones you'll find outside most Hummer dealerships. And even if most Italians refer to it as "The White Typewriter" or "The Wedding Cake," damn if it isn't a tasty slice. You can catch glimpses of the monument from almost every spot in Rome, and while each stolen glance never ceases to impress, nothing quite rivals walking right up to it. Don't forget to climb up the many steps on the west side of the monument to take in all of Rome from its panoramic terrace. The exhibits inside are only worthwhile if you're a Vittorio Emanuele II fanboy/fangirl. They have his trousers. What more convincing do you need?

i P. Venezia. You can't miss it. Free. Monument open daily 9:30am-5:30pm.

CHIESA SAN LUIGI DEI FRANCESI
P. San Luigi dei Francesi 5

When you walk up to this 16th-century church and consider its relatively generic gray exterior, you might wonder, "Haven't I walked past this before?" Probably not, although the Chiesa San Luigi dei Francesi and its understated facade do look pretty run-of-the-mill (at least by Roman standards). And although the church distinguishes itself by being French, its real draw is entirely Italian: namely, the three famous works by Caravaggio that can be found here. Interestingly, the church's magnificent, gilded altar and intricate ceiling sculptures (turn around and check out the angels holding up the massive organ) take center stage here, while Caravaggio's *The Calling of Saint Matthew*, *Saint Matthew and the Angel*, and *The Crucifixion* are all crammed into the same corner chapel. Still, these Baroque masterpieces won't be hard to find—just look for the crowd of eager-beaver art students gathered in the upper-left-hand corner of the church. While admiring Caravaggio's supreme mastery of chiaroscuro, you can consider the play of light and shadow in more ways than one, as the church turns its chapel lights on and off every few minutes. Life imitates art, ya know?

i From P. Navona, exit onto Corsia Agonale, then turn left onto C. del Rinascimento, then right onto V. Santa Giovanna d'Arco. Free. Open daily 10am-12:30pm and 3-7pm.

AREA SACRA
Bordered by V. di Torre Argentina, V. Florida, and Largo di Torre Argentina

Some people might say that the Area Sacra has really gone to the dogs in recent years. Or maybe to the cats—as in, part of this ancient ruin is literally a cat sanctuary. A tribute, perhaps, to some dangerously catty politicians? Because lo—this is also the place where a bunch of senators decided, in the immortal words of Gretchen Wieners, to "totally just stab Caesar" on the Ides of March, 44 BCE. The tall tree near the ruins of the Theatre of Pompey mark the place where Caesar's blood was spilled and the trope of stabbing your

take me to church

"But all Italian churches look the same!" said the beleaguered, world-weary American tourist after seeing one too many fancy gilded ceilings. Fair enough: if you're one of those travelers who can't appreciate the finer details of fine art, here are a few churches in Rome that house artwork famous enough for you to actually give a damn about.

- **CHIESA DI SAN LUIGI DEI FRANCESI:** The understated facade of this church belies the fact that it is home to three of Caravaggio's most celebrated paintings, including *The Calling of Saint Matthew.*

- **BASILICA DI SAN PIETRO IN VINCOLI:** Located near V. Cavour in Rome's Monti neighborhood, this church houses Michelangelo's famous High Renaissance sculpture of Moses.

- **CHIESA DI SANTA MARIA DELLA VITTORIA:** Although Bernini's fingerprints are all over St. Peter's Basilica, the artist's moving *Ecstasy of Saint Teresa* can be found in this church, tucked just up the road from P. Barberini.

- **BASILICA DI SANTA MARIA DEL POPOLO:** Often overlooked by tourists who visit Piazza del Popolo, this church houses two works by Caravaggio and also features gold frescoes painted by none other than Raphael.

friend in the back (yes, you, Brutus) was born. Admire the ruins from the street and reflect on all the CW show plotlines that owe so much to this place.

i From P. Venezia, walk west down V. Plebiscito, which turns into Corso Vittorio Emanuele II; walk until the street meets Largo di Torre Argentina. Free.

PALAZZO VENEZIA

V. del Plebiscito 118   ☎06 678 01 31 www.museopalazzovenezia.beniculturali.it

The Palazzo Venezia could have been called "The House of Creepy Babies," or perhaps the "Let's Normalize Public Breastfeeding Museum." Indeed, much of the 14th-to-18th-century artwork you'll find here features plenty of wooden mothers and questionable interpretations of what infants look like. (You know how all parents think their babies are adorable even if they actually look like a squashed melon? That's also a symptom of a lot of the artists whose little darlings are housed here. Maybe these tots could grow into their weird, bulbous heads, but in this case, time will not tell.) Be aware: a lot of this museum is religious panel painting, plus some ceramics and one incongruous room of 18th-century portraits that are all pink cheeks and powdered wigs. Constructed during the Renaissance, the building itself features a dimly lit but imposing staircase and encompasses an impressive garden of palm trees, where it's easy to picture Mussolini dreamin' and schemin' his way to infamy (the palace once housed his offices, and its balcony served as stump for many of his speeches).

i From P. Venezia, walk down V. del Plebiscito. The museum entrance is on the left. €5, reduced €2.50. Open Tu-Su 8:30am-7:30pm.

Piazza di Spagna

🏛 BORGHESE GALLERY

Ple. Scipione Borghese 5   ☎06 84 13 979 www.galleriaborghese.it

Cardinal Scipione Borghese knew a thing or two about how to pimp out a villa. An early patron of Gian Lorenzo Bernini and a devoted Caravaggio

italy

fanboy, Scipione sketched out plans for this gallery as a place to house his extensive art collection. Constructed in the 17th century and opened to the public in 1903, the Borghese Gallery is now home to some of the greatest Bernini sculptures in existence and the world's largest concentration of works by Caravaggio. Bernini highlights include everything from the masterful *Apollo and Daphne* to the mythic and moving *Aeneas, Anchises, and Ascanius* to the heartbreaking *The Rape of Proserpina*; the museum also houses Bernini's *David*, a more dynamic and Baroque take on the myth that Michelangelo so immortalized in his own famous statue. Give yourself plenty of time to circle each sculpture a few times—every angle reveals a new detail and serves as testament to Bernini's supreme skill (it's really no wonder he was such an egomaniac). Among the collection of Caravaggio paintings housed here, you'll find *David with the Head of Goliath, Sick Bacchus*, and *Boy with a Basket of Fruit* (who, if you think about it, is really kind of a tart). The 20 rooms of the gallery, spread out across two floors (sculptures on the first floor, paintings on the second), are a marvel in themselves, stuffed to the brim with statues and columns, adorned with intricate molding and gold leaf, and splashed with staggering ceiling frescoes.

i Located in the Villa Borghese Gardens, at the crossroads of Vle. dell'Uccelliera and Vle. del Museo Borghese. Reservations required. Book online or in person up to two weeks in advance. Bags of all sizes must be checked downstairs before you enter the gallery. €11, EU citizens 18-25 €6.50. Audio guides €5. Open Tu-Su 8:30am-7:30pm. Ticket office closes at 6:30pm.

VILLA BORGHESE GARDENS

The Borghese Gardens are no Central Park. For one thing, they're a lot older and more legit than Central Park, having been first built up by Scipione Borghese starting in 1605 and later restyled and perfected in the English taste in the 19th century. And perhaps that's why, in some ways, they look a little worse for the wear. But what this 148-acre park lacks in manicured lawns and frisbee-tossing yuppies it makes up for in purple wildflowers, fountains on fountains, the occasional horse track (casual), and long grass and towering trees that seem to defy the urban insanity of the surrounding metropolis. Located just above Piazza del Popolo, the sprawling gardens are crisscrossed by gravel trails and paved paths, and it seems like all roads lead to some pond or statue or obelisk (or, you know, the Galleria Borghese). As usual, when in Rome, no opportunity goes unexploited to try to sell stuff to tourists; said stuff here includes gelato carts, bike and *bici pincio* rentals, and overpriced cafes and restaurants within the grounds of the park.

i M Flamino or M Spagna. There are multiple entrances to the park: Porta Pinciana, Ple. Flaminio, Vle. Belle Arti, V. Mercadante, and V. Pinciana. Free. Open 24hr.

PIAZZA DI SPAGNA AND THE SPANISH STEPS , PIAZZA

P. di Spagna

If we're going to boil things down to their most basic elements, Piazza di Spagna is one big celebration of all the stuff rich people can buy, plus a Bernini fountain and a Keats museum that probably no one ever visits. And yeah sure, the Spanish Steps are historic (all 135 of them) leading to a sparse church, but they're also a giant audience of people looking out at a bunch of stores they can't afford. But don't worry—if you didn't factor Gucci and Prada into your backpacking budget, you can always console yourself with a selfie stick. At least Bernini's Fontana della Barcaccia (literally, "Fountain of the Ugly Boat") provides an opportunity to contemplate whether Bernini was being unduly hard on himself or if he was a just an egotistical bastard who knew that even if he made a shitty statue, people would still be taking pictures of it hundreds of years later.

i M: Spagna. Free. Open 24hr.

TREVI FOUNTAIN
P. di Trevi

The only time to really see Trevi Fountain is at 4am, when the moonlight hits the water just right and you can fawn over its majesty while ignoring the guy reading a newspaper next to you. Because yes, it's always crowded. Full of tourists, shop vendors, or policemen making sure you don't pull a *La Dolce Vita* and hop in, Trevi is one of those iconic Roman places you have to see. Nicola Salvi's beautiful fountain cut from rock and stone depicts an enormous Neptune surrounded by the goddesses of abundance and good health, as well as two brawny horsemen chilling out just because. Do as the Roman tourists do and save up on those one-cent coins to toss in here: one ensures a prompt return to Rome, two will bring you love in the Eternal City, and three will bring about your wedding.

i From P. di Spagna, walk down V. Propaganda (right if facing the Spanish Steps) and veer right as it turns into Largo del Nazareno. Turn left onto V. Poli and continue on to where High Expectations meet Supreme Disappointment at P. di Trevi. Free. Unless you toss a coin into it.

PIAZZA DEL POPOLO
P. del Popolo

Piazza del Popolo is ostensibly the "People's Square," but really, this place belongs to the massive Egyptian obelisk of Ramses II that dominates its center (the structure was first brought to Rome in 10 BCE and erected, like the giant phallic symbol that it is, in this square in 1589). Home to the church of Santa Maria del Popolo (worth a look), the piazza is also centrally located near Piazza di Spagna and the Villa Borghese Gardens, both a short walk away, and is situated at the opposite end of V. del Corso from Piazza Venezia—look straight down the street to catch a glimpse of the Vittorio Emanuele II Monument at the other end.

i M: Flamino. Or from P. di Spagna, proceed down V. del Babuino (left if facing the Spanish Steps). Free.

MUSEO DELL'ARA PACIS
V. della Frezza 43   ☎06 06 08 www.arapacis.it

Consecrated on January 30, 9 BCE, and ostensibly dedicated to the Roman goddess of peace (but mostly to Augustus, to commemorate some of his not-so-peaceful conquests in Spain and Gaul), the Ara Pacis was buried underground for several centuries before being rediscovered and excavated in the early 20th century. (Because, you know, that kind of thing can happen in a city that's literally older than dirt.) Today, the Ara Pacis is the main (and nearly the only) attraction in this museum, which you might not have realized until after you paid €10.50 for the ticket. If you're particularly familiar with the reign of Augustus or can appreciate a nice frieze or two (the ones adorning the altar are quite stunning and well preserved), then this museum certainly warrants a look. For everyone else, it might not be worth the entrance fee, although the juxtaposition of ancient and modern architecture is a sight to see (made all the more intense by the fact that both the altar and its museum radiate varying shades of stunning white). If you're feeling ambivalent about whether or not it's worth your while (or your euro), the good news is that you can still catch a glimpse of the altar through the museum's large glass windows and sit for a spell next to the fountain outside the main entrance.

i From P. di Spagna, walk down V. del Babuino (left if facing the Spanish Steps) and turn left onto V. Vittorio. Continue several blocks as V. Vittorio turns into V. dei Pontefici, then turn left onto V. di Ripetta. The museum is on the right. €10.50, reduced €8.50. Open Tu-Su 9am-7pm.

italy

Termini

BASILICA DI SANTA MARIA MAGGIORE

P. di Santa Maria Maggiore 28

Basilica di Santa Maria Maggiore is really feelin' itself. Forget about charity and humility, man: this church is all about the gold leaf life and, true to its Baroque style, architectural gluttony. Originally constructed in the fifth century as one of the first churches dedicated to the Virgin Mary (because apparently it took 500 years for this chick and her magic womb to finally get some recognition #yesallwomen), the basilica has undergone several restorations since then, including an interior renovation in the late 1500s. Located just a few blocks from Termini Station, the basilica is a must-see for anyone who possesses even the most basic appreciation of pretty stuff. The church also has an adjoining museum that you can visit for a fee, but once you've seen the altar and the columns and the ceiling (and, come to think of it, even the floor) of the church's interior, you've already seen the best part for free.

i From Termini Station, exit onto V. Giovanni Giolitti and turn right down V. Gioberti. Continue to P. di Santa Maria Maggiore. Modest dress required. Basilica free. Museum €4, reduced €2. Museum open daily 9:30am-6:30pm. Basilica open daily 7am-7pm.

CHIESA DI SANTA MARIA DEGLI ANGELI

P. della Repubblica

This famous church isn't fronting. Granted, that's mostly because it doesn't have a facade with which to front. Its less-than-impressive exterior and location amid the hustle of Piazza della Repubblica, however, doesn't mean you should overlook the Chiesa di Santa Maria Degli Angeli, because—spoiler alert—it was designed by Michelangelo (yeah, that guy). The vaulted ceilings and red granite columns of this shockingly large "theater of light" were designed by the master himself in 1563 after he was recruited to adapt part of the ruins of the ancient Baths of Diocletian. Don't forget to check out the meridian line that runs from the east transept to the altar and the signs of the Zodiac that surround it.

i M: Repubblica. Located on the northeast side of Piazza della Repubblica. Modest dress required. Free. Shawls available for €1. Open daily May-Sept 7:30am-7pm; Oct-Apr 7:30am-6:30pm.

BATHS OF DIOCLETIAN

Vle. Enrico De Nicola 79   www.archeoroma.beniculturali.it

For a sight as old and as cool as the Baths of Diocletian, the city of Rome sure makes it hard for you to figure out where the hell they are. Do you see those signs for the baths in Piazza della Repubblica? Nope, the baths aren't actually here. Did you make it as far as buying a ticket to the National Museum and are now lost somewhere in Michelangelo's Cloister? Nope, no baths here, either. Although the cloister and its many sculptures are worth a stroll (note: the rest of the museums are not), the ruins of the ancient baths are what you came here to see, so upon leaving the ticket counter, hightail it through the bookshop and proceed through a door on the left, and you'll eventually find the towering walls of the age-old baths. You'll be rewarded with a nearly private viewing (congrats: no one else could figure out how to get here, either!). Indeed, the baths are shockingly quiet and empty, which only serves to accentuate the gravity of the massive ruins; the lack of other tourists also makes it a little easier to imagine ancient Romans flocking to these sumptuous pools nearly 2000 years ago.

i From Termini Station, exit onto P. dei Cinquecento and cross the street to Vle. Enrico De Nicola. Look for the signs for the Museo Nazionale Romana; the entrance for the museum and the baths is on Vle. Enrico De Nicola. €7, €3.50 EU students 18-25. Ticket provides entry to the Baths of Diocletian, Museo Nazionale Romano, Palazzo Altemps, and Crypta Balbi; valid for 3 days. Open Tu-Su 9am-7:45pm.

rome

Vatican City

THE VATICAN MUSEUMS

Vle. Vaticano 97   ☎06 69 88 38 60 www.museivaticani.va

A visit to the Vatican Museums is a real test in avoiding oversaturation and, perhaps more critically, in maintaining your sanity and affection for humankind in general. Because you will be tested, both by the museums' more than 7km of galleries and by the hundreds of swarming tour groups, all of whom have determined to either elbow you in the kidney, step on your toes, or form one giant unmoving mass that will trap you in a corner of the Raphael Rooms. But avoid the herds if possible and take your time as you make your way through the Vatican's sprawling and truly astounding collection of some of the greatest art in the world. The museum is one continuous loop, so you won't miss anything if you just follow the crowds (it certainly won't be hard to spot them). Try to take in the sculptural spread that is the Galleria Chiaramonti, with its concentration of more than 1000 statues collected in a single corridor. Admire the Belvedere Torso (a true butterface if there ever was one) in the Sala delle Muse and the giant, gilded bronze statue of Hercules in the red Sala Rotunda. Perhaps the most famous rooms here, however, are the Raphael Rooms, where you can see the legendary School of Athens (which is basically just the Raphael's Renaissance take on celebrity photobombing) and several of the master's other incredible frescoes.

i M: Ottaviano. Walk down V. Ottaviano, turn right onto V. dei Bastioni di Michelangelo, and follow the wall until you see the end of the line for the museums. Entrance on Vle. Vaticano. Make a reservation online in advance if you want to skip the lines. €16. Free last Su of each month. Audio guides with map €7. Museums open Mar-Oct M-F 10am-6pm, Sa 10am-4pm; Nov-Feb M-F 10am-3pm. Museums open last Su of every month 9am-2pm for free. Last entry 1hr. 15min. before close.

ST. PETER'S BASILICA

At the end of V. della Conciliazione   ☎06 69 88 16 62 www.vaticanstate.va

Citizens of Renaissance-era Rome certainly didn't have to wonder where all their taxpayer tithes were being spent. Just one look up at St. Peter's ornate, mind-blowingly intricate ceiling and you can almost hear the coins in the coffer ringing and a thousand souls from purgatory springing. And while the Catholic Church's historical excess and overindulgences of more than one variety may be a little gross, fortunately for you, the price of admission to the basilica today will cost you little more than some time spent in line (which, in fairness, could be upward of 2hr. if you don't plan well).

the pope's general audience

Every Wednesday when the Pope is in town, he holds a general audience that anyone with a ticket can attend. And in a surprise twist, the Catholic Church won't even charge you for it, which is an especially good deal now that we finally have a pope that people can get excited about. Indeed, seeing Pope Francis (or as we like to call him, Dope Francis) is almost like seeing a celebrity, so pick up a ticket. You can reserve tickets in advance online, or you can just walk up to one of the Swiss guards at the Bronze Doors of St. Peter's and ask for one (Tu 3-7pm, W 7-10am). And no need to feel awkward if you're not Catholic—that just means you're one of those lost sheep who are extra welcome.

The church itself, which was constructed over a period of more than 100 years during the late Renaissance, is so cavernous, sprawling, and richly decorated that it'll be hard to know where to look. Generally speaking, "anywhere" is a pretty foolproof strategy, although be sure to take note of Bernini's twisted baldacchino, which dominates the center of church and marks both the pope's altar and the spot just above St. Peter's tomb. To the right of the basilica's entrance, you'll also find Michelangelo's Pietà—the artist's famous, moving rendition of the Virgin Mary and Jesus shortly after the Crucifixion. (Since the dawn of the smartphone, Mary and her son have basically become the Beatles of St. Peter's, so try to make your way through the dense crowd of tour groups and iPhones held eagerly aloft to get a closer, more intimate look at Mary's mournful visage through the bulletproof glass.) And while a few of the chapels here are reserved for prayer, don't expect to find much peace or time for spiritual reflection while wandering through the rest of the basilica: this place is crawling with tour groups. But even these tour groups get swallowed up by the sheer size of this enormous basilica.

i M: Ottaviano. Walk down V. Ottaviano and follow the walls of the Vatican to the square. Or walk down V. della Conciliazione. Knees and shoulders must be covered. Arrive early in the morning (before 8am) to avoid the crowds. And if you're not oversaturated after visiting the church, you can also pay a visit to St. Peter's Tomb and the Vatican Grottoes during your trip to St. Peter's. Basilica free. Cupola €5. Basilica open daily Apr-Sept 7am-7pm; Oct-Mar 7am-6pm. Cupola open daily Apr-Sept 8am-6pm; Oct-Mar 8am-5pm.

PIAZZA DI SAN PIETRO

At the end of V. della Conciliazione ☎06 69 88 16 62 www.vaticanstate.va

St. Peter's Square sits in front of St. Peter's Basilica (of all things) and can be approached from a number of different directions, although the most dramatic is certainly walking up to it along V. della Conciliazione. Designed by Bernini, the sweeping elliptical piazza is encompassed by enormous Tuscan colonnades topped with 140 statues of saints that, in the artist's own words, were intended to welcome visitors into "the maternal arms of Mother Church." (Kind of ironic syntax for an institution full of a bunch of dudes wearing funny hats.) The columns stand four rows deep, and if you look on either side of the square's central obelisk (yes, another one of those—Rome was even more into Egypt than you were in third grade), you'll find a circle marked "Centro del Colonnato" where, if you stand directly on it, all the columns line up perfectly. Because Bernini was artsy and good at math! The piazza is best visited at night, when the fountains and basilica are all lit up and when the line of people and sunbrellas waiting to get into the church has dissipated.

i M: Ottaviano. Walk down V. Ottaviano and follow the walls of the Vatican to the square. Or walk down V. della Conciliazione. Free. Piazza open 24hr.

MUSEO NAZIONALE DI CASTEL SANT'ANGELO

Lungotevere Castello 50 ☎06 68 19 111 www.castelsantangelo.com

Rome isn't exactly known for its old-school castles, but in case you've gotten sick of ancient ruins, Renaissance churches, or the overindulgence of Baroque art in general, this one's for you. Originally built as a mausoleum for Hadrian's super-important ashes (pardon his dust), the Castel Sant'Angelo was repurposed as a military fortress in the fifth century and later used as a papal castle and refuge starting in the 14th century. As a result, the current structure is composed of distinct levels that include the mausoleum, prisons and warehouses, military patios, papal apartments, and a panoramic terrace. So make like Bowser and roam the halls of this seemingly endless castle. Don't miss the Hall of Urns in the center of the castle (the room that is believed to have held Hadrian's ashes) or the winding, cavernous Rampa Diametrale in the dungeon-like inner halls (the lights along the passageways aren't quite torches, but the effect is close enough). Then contrast the dark, chilly vibe of the castle's bowels with the stunning sunlight and sweeping vistas you'll encounter with each new level of the structure, from the parapet walk (keep an eye out for the Borgo Passetto, the protected papal passageway that leads to St. Peter's) to the upper terrace to the final exposed roof of the fortress, from which you can look out over St. Peter's, Ponte Sant'Angelo, and all of Rome.

i The castle is at the end of V. della Conciliazione, at the intersection with Ponte Sant'Angelo. €10.50, reduced €7. Open Tu-Su 9am-7:30pm. Last entry 6:30pm.

Trastevere

GIANICOLO HILL

Fun fact: Gianicolo Hill isn't actually one of the seven hills of Rome. Not that you were going to scale all of them anyway (it's too damn hot for that nonsense). But as the second-tallest hilltop in the modern city, Gianicolo (alternatively Janiculum) is worth the relatively quick climb up V. Garibaldi from the west side of Trastevere. Wind your way up the road, or take a shortcut up a steep flight of stone steps; either way, feel free to refresh yourself after the climb at the rushing waters of the Fontana dell'Acqua Paola, where you can also enjoy a preliminary view of the city. Then make your way down Passeggiata del Gianicolo along a leisurely avenue of sycamores to P. Giuseppe Garibaldi, where you can perch yourself on a ledge and look out over nearly all of Rome (from the other side of the piazza, you can see St. Peter's Basilica through the trees). Relax and enjoy the view: the foreground may be littered with empty beer bottles, but the backdrop is harder to sniff at.

i From P. San Egidio, turn left onto Vicolo del Cedro and climb the stairs, then take a left onto V. Garibaldi. Free.

ORTO BOTANICO (BOTANICAL GARDENS)

Largo Cristina di Svezia 24   ☎06 49 91 71 07 web.uniroma1.it/ortobotanico

Bordering the lower perimeter of Gianicolo Hill, Trastevere's Botanical Garden is a 30-acre sanctuary of paths, park benches, and more than 7000 species of plants, all of which are protected from the traffic, crowds, and litterbugs of Rome. It sounds different here: the quietude, and the sound of your own feet shuffling along the gravel paths, is almost unsettling. And while you can never fully escape the sounds of city police sirens and mopeds ripping down the surrounding streets, the chorus of birds in the trees and wind tossing the leaves creates a calmer kind of uproar here. The entire garden is a loop, so start at one end, make your way around the main pathway, and feel free to take detours along the meandering side trails. Wander through the garden's grand palm trees and admire its shady ginkgos, wind your way up to the Japanese garden and into a thicket of bamboo, and tiptoe your way down the different levels of the rose garden. There are plenty of benches along the way, so if you want to make an afternoon of it, bring a book or some music and spend a couple hours under the cover of the dense flora. Every now and then, look out through the trees to see the domes and rooftops of Rome peeping through breaks in the branches.

i Walk to the end of V. Corsini until you reach Largo Cristina di Svezia. €8, reduced €4. Open May-June Tu-Su 9am-6:30pm; July-Aug Tu-Sa 9am-6:30pm; Sept-Oct Tu-Su 9am-6:30pm; Nov-Apr Tu-Sa 9am-6:30pm.

FOOD

Ancient City

PIZZERIA DA MILVIO $

V. dei Serpenti 7 ☎06 77 20 13 61

If you're starting to feel hangry after hours of sightseeing in the hot Roman sun, up your spirits and your blood sugar with a quick stop at Milvio. Located just off V. Cavour near the Colosseum, Milvio offers an assortment of pizzas, panini, and pastas whose quality far exceeds their budget prices. Order at the counter and then grab an orange, Jetson-esque plastic seat at one of the many tables at the back of the pizzeria. It's not the fanciest food you'll find in the city, but at this point in the day, you're probably a sweaty mess who's just looking for some carbs and a bathroom, dammit. For a cheap, fast, and satisfying meal in the middle of the day, Milvio fits the bill on all fronts.

i *M: Colosseum. Walk down V. dei Fori Imperiali and turn right onto V. Cavour, then left onto V. Serpenti. Milvio is on the left. Pizza €9-15 per kg. Panini €7. Pasta €5. Open daily 8am-midnight or later.*

LA CARBONARA $

V. Panisperna 214 ☎06 48 25 176 www.lacarbonara.it

At La Carbonara, the writing's on the walls—and that's a good thing. With more than a decade's worth of notes and dedications scrawled on the walls from fans all over the world, La Carbonara certainly doesn't need TripAdvisor to assure you that you're going to have a good meal with the anti-TripAdvisor signs in the window—bold move, La Carbonara). Service is brusque but friendly, and the random assortment of posters, horse busts, and glass orbs scattered around the walls give the restaurant a cluttered, lived-in feel. You get the sense that La Carbonara isn't trying to impress you; rather, it sets the tone and makes the rules (one of which is "People with good taste talk in a low voice"—they even spelled it out in English for all you loud, ugly Americans). In return, you order some of their delicious pasta (classics like the *cacio e pepe* are foolproof) and go home happy.

i *From Basilica di Santa Maria Maggiore, proceed down V. di Santa Maria Maggiore, which becomes V. Panisperna. La Carbonara is on the left. Get here right when the restaurant opens if you don't have a reservation and want to get a table. Antipasti €5-10. Primi €6-10. Secondi €9-22. Drinks €3-5. Open M-Sa noon-3:30pm and 7-11pm.*

Centro Storico

IL FORNO CAMPO DE' FIORI , BAKERY $

Vicolo del Gallo 14 www.fornocampodefiori.com

Forno means "oven" in Italian, and chances are you've seen a lot of these signs all over the city (and not because Italy is really into its appliances). Perhaps no *forno* pronounces itself so boldly as this one, but besides the giant lettering over the entrance, that's pretty much where the bakery/pizzeria's self-marketing ends. Despite being located in the northwest corner of Campo de' Fiori, it stands a bit aloof from the many mediocre restaurants lining the square and has no designated guy out front trying to pimp out the bakery; instead, it lets business come to its door. And with good reason. The baked goods, pizza, and focaccia here are fresh, fantastic, and shockingly cheap. Even if you're just passing through the Campo, stop for a bag of precious, perfect little pieces of biscotti that will run you just over €1.

i *Located in the northern corner of Campo de' Fiori. Pizza €10-17 per kg. Open M-Sa 7:30am-2:30pm and 4:45-8pm.*

rome

GELATERIA DEL TEATRO
$$
V. dei Coronari 65   ☎06 45 47 48 80 www.gelateriadelteatro.it

In contrast to Frigidarium, Gelateria del Teatro aims for more subtle flavors and carefully selected ingredients when whipping up its fresh, homemade gelato. And although it's incredibly popular and busy, this place takes its time, so grab a ticket at the front door and feast your eyes on all the options—you'll need some time to wrap your head around artisanal flavors like cherry and cheese, white chocolate and basil, and yogurt al lemon grass, and fortunately for you, there's no rush. Then take your milky, refreshing cup of *pistacchio di bronte* outside and enjoy it from one of the ceramic tables tucked just off the charming V. dei Coronari. It all might seem a little bougie to you (it's prices certainly are), but after a few bites, you might also realize that you don't care—because you're sophisticated, dammit.

i From P. Navona, turn left onto V. dei Coronari and walk a few blocks. The gelateria is on the left. Gelato €2.50-8. Open M-Th 10:30am-11pm, F-Sa 10:30am-11:30pm, Su 10:30am-11pm.

FORNO MARCO ROSCIOLI
$
V. dei Chiavari 34   ☎06 686 40 45 www.anticofornoroscioli.it

One of the most popular bakeries in the neighborhood, Marco Roscioli is yet another *forno* near Campo de' Fiori that makes for a great lunch spot (even though once you walk inside, all you might want for lunch is a pastry of some sort). Order panini on the right and pizza on the left, where the guy behind the counter will serve up your slice with a sound thwack of his knife. Take your lunch to go and walk around the corner to San Carlo ai Catinari, where you can enjoy your lunch from the steps of the church.

i From Campo de' Fiori, exit onto V. dei Giubbonari and turn left onto V. dei Chiavari. Marco Roscioli is on the left. Pizza €10-18 per kg. Open M-Sa 7am-7:30pm.

L'ANTICA SALUMERIA
$
P. della Rotunda 4

We're not exactly sure how this place has (allegedly) held up since 1375, but who knows—its direct view of the Pantheon may have provided some divine inspiration. And given that most of the food you'll find just outside the Pantheon is trash, Salumeria is a surprising find and a solid place to grab a midday panino. Although the penis pasta for sale might scream tourist trap, the smell of fresh baked goods and pistachio cookies wafting from Salumeria's open door should be enough to persuade you (and may even distract you momentarily from the square's main attraction). Get a panino to go and eat it from the steps facing the Pantheon and wonder how your life ended up so great.

i P. della Rotunda; on the right when facing the Pantheon. Pizza €2-4 per etto. Panini around €5. Pastries €1.80-4. Open daily 8:30am-2am.

DAR FILETTARO A SANTA BARBARA
$
Largo dei Librari 88   ☎06 686 4018

Flying in the face of Italian tradition and history in more ways than one (no pasta or pizza to be found here!), Dar Filettaro is something of an anti-Renaissance man. It does one thing and does it to perfection—and doesn't waste time trying to build dumb flying machines. So if Dar Filettaro's menu looks a little fishy to you, that might be because its sole entree is just a piece of fried fish. And if you feel a little underwhelmed when your single portion of golden brown cod arrives ungarnished on a white plate, that's totally normal. We thought the same thing. But beauty, as it turns out, is skin deep and then some—take a taste, and you might find yourself wondering why you've been eating pasta all week when Dar Filettaro has been just down the street from Campo de' Fiori the whole time. Service is brisk and bare-bones (ask for a napkin and you shall receive a piece of paper), and the small collection of tables here are crammed in tight, so either arrive early or take it to go.

i *From Campo de' Fiori, walk down V. dei Giubbonari and turn left onto Largo dei Librari; Dar Filettaro is on the right. Cod €5. Antipasti €5. Salad €4.50-5. Dessert €3.50. Open M-Sa 5:30-11:30pm.*

Piazza di Spagna

▨ PASTIFICIA $

V. della Croce 8

It is a truth universally acknowledged that most of the food surrounding the Spanish Steps is a scam. Pastificio, however, is another (almost) age-old Roman institution that will make a visit to P. di Spagna worth your while. Cooking up unbelievably cheap, fresh pasta daily since 1918, Pastificio makes up for its lack of variety (only two types of pasta are available every day) with its absolute mastery of the craft. Just close your eyes and point—seriously, you really can't go wrong here. There's no seating (only a little counter space), so get your pasta in a box to go and enjoy the al dente noodles al fresco.

i *From P. di Spagna, walk down V. della Croce. Pastificio is on the first block on the left. Fresh pasta €4. Dry bags of pasta starting at €6. Open daily 10am-9pm. Fresh pasta ready at 1pm.*

CIAMPINI $

P. di San Lorenzo in Lucina 29   ☎06 68 76 606 www.ciampini.com

Ciampini's uniformed waiters, marble countertops, and gold placards listing all its gelato flavors may have you thinking, "I'm so fancy," but you should know that a small cone (which is actually a pretty big cone and entitles you to three scoops) will only run you €2.50. Life in the fast lane has never been so cheap (can't you taste this gold?). Lunch sandwiches are equally affordable and worth the slight walk from P. di Spagna for quality food in the middle of a long day of sightseeing. If you're interested in resting your dogs for a bit longer, Ciampini also has a full, sit-down menu and plenty of outdoor seating in the middle of Piazza di San Lorenzo.

i *From P. di Spagna, walk down down V. del Condotti and turn left onto V. del Leoncino. Gelato €2.50-6.50. Sandwiches €4. Primi €10-13. Secondi €13-20. Open M-Sa 7:30am-10pm, Su 9:30am-10pm.*

CAFFETERIA CAMBI $

V. del Leoncino 30   ☎06 687 80 81

Located just around the corner from the busy shoppers and bustling mopeds of V. Tomacelli, this understated gem of a caffeteria is tucked under a nondescript awning that doesn't actually even say "Cambi." (C'mon, Cambi, have some self respect! You're worth it!) A short walk from P. di Spagna, Cambi is a great place to stop for a quick, authentic, and shockingly cheap piece of fold-up pizza. A variety of tarts, pastries, and panini are also available, but with more than a dozen varieties of white and red pizzas to choose from on any given day, the slices of pie here might be too good to pass up.

i *From P. di Spagna, walk down V. del Condotti, take a slight right onto V. Tomacelli, and turn left onto V. del Leoncino. Cafeteria Cambi is on the right. Cash only. Very limited counter seating. Pizza priced by weight (approximately €2.50 per piece). Open M-Sa 8am-8pm.*

Termini

▨ GELATERIA LA ROMANA $

V. Venti Settembre 60   ☎06 42 02 08 28 www.gelateriaromana.com

Despite its clean lines, light wood, and modern aesthetic, La Romana has actually been serving up incredible gelato since 1947 and now boasts several locations through Italy. And given its history (and, perhaps more importantly, the line of young Italians that spills out the door after dinner hours), La Romana is really the only gelato you should be eating on this side of town. Especially because a small cone (which includes two flavors and a finishing dollop of whipped cream) only costs €2. Flavors are listed on the wall in Italian, so if you're flummoxed and don't know what to order (note: you will be, and it's all amazing), just tell the girl at the counter to give you the two best flavors, and goddammit, she will.

i From P. della Repubblica, continue down V. Vittorio Emanuele Orlando and turn right onto V. Venti Settembre. La Romana is located on the left, on the corner of V. Venti Settembre and V. Piave. Gelato from €2. Open M-Th 11am-midnight, F-Sa 11am-1am, Su 11am-midnight.

RISTORANTE DA GIOVANNI $
V. Antonio Salandra 1

Ristorante da Giovanni has been ahead of the game for a while, serving up simple and delicious Italian meals since 1948. Tucked in the basement of a building just off V. Venti Settembre, da Giovanni's white wood walls, plaid tablecloths, and old-fashioned Coca-Cola signs provide a quiet retreat from the city outside. The dishes here are understated but authentic (you can't go wrong with a classic like *cacio e pepe*), and the waiters' limited English will only add to your conviction that this place is the real deal.

i From P. della Repubblica, continue down V. Vittorio Emanuele Orlando and turn right onto V. Venti Settembre. Continue several blocks and turn left onto V. Antonio Salandra. Ristorante da Giovanni is on the right. Primi €6-7.50. Secondi €5.50-14. Dessert €4. Open daily noon-3pm and 7-10:30pm.

THE BRAMBLE BAR & KITCHEN $
V. Vicenza 40   ☎06 44 70 21 62 www.bramblebar.com

If you're staying near Termini Station and are looking for solid food close to home, skip the restaurant portion of the Yellow Hostel and Bar and head around the corner to the Bramble; prices for breakfast, lunch, and dinner are comparable, and the food is astronomically better. The Bramble services a mostly tourist crowd, and while the food isn't the best you'll have in the city, it's actually quite good. And because the mysteries of Italian breakfast (does it even exist??) remain opaque to many a tourist throughout their time in Rome, the Bramble is a particularly good option for travelers who can't get hip to the "espresso and go" style of most Italian mornings and just want some sit-down coffee and toast.

i From Termini Station, exit onto P. dei Cinquecento and turn right onto Vle. Enrico De Nicola. Walk through P. dell'Indipendenza and turn right onto V. Vittorio Bachelet, then left onto V. Vicenza. The Bramble is on the left. Free Wi-Fi. Guests staying at Alessandro Palace or Downtown get discounts. Primi €7.50-10. Secondi €9-18. Pizzas €7-9.50. Hamburgers €9-11. Breakfast €3-7. Open M-Sa 7am-midnight, Su 6pm-midnight in summer. Lunch menu available starting at noon.

FASSINO $
V. Bergamo 24   ☎06 854 91 17

This creperie and gelateria is located a bit farther into Northern Rome than you're likely to be wandering, but if you want a chance to explore a less touristy area of the city, head for Piazza Fiume and enjoy cappuccino and gelato al fresco at Fassino. The staff here will be lookin' swanky (hello, bow ties), as will the granite table tops, vintage black-and-white photos on the walls, and piles upon piles of fancy pastries, but the prices here don't lie: this place is dirt cheap and has been since 1880. And that, we think, is worth the walk.

i From P. della Repubblica, continue down V. Vittorio Emanuele Orlando and turn right onto V. Venti Settembre. Continue several blocks and turn left onto V. Piave to P. Fiume. From the piazza, turn right onto V. Bergamo. Fassino is on the right. Gelato €1.80-3.50. Pastries from €2. Aperitivo €6.50. Open daily 7:30am-12:30am.

Vatican City

❧ PIZZARIUM $

V. della Meloria 43   ☎06 39 74 54 16

After a whole morning of walking through the Vatican Museums, the idea of eating your lunch standing up might not sound particularly appealing, but prioritize your stomach over your feet, and Pizzarium will make it worth your aching arches. Because while the high tables at this white-walled, open-doored pizza counter don't come furnished with any actual chairs, Pizzarium does have some of the best, crispiest square pizza in the city. And it's pretty gourmet, too: you'll find everything from giant peppers to dollops of ricotta cheese to fold upon fold of freshly sliced meat piled high on these slices of pie. Pick out a couple varieties and wait while the staff pops them back into the piping oven for a few minutes. And while the Catholic Church may have pinched a pretty penny out of you earlier today, Pizzarium is a total steal—a couple slices will generally run you less than the price of the Vatican Museums' €7 audio guide.

i *From the Vatican Museum, walk down the steps to V. Tunisi and turn left onto V. Candia. Veer left onto V. Angelo Elmo and turn right onto V. della Meloria 43. Pizzarium is on the left. Pizza €17.50-30.50 per kg. Open M-Sa 11am-10pm, Su noon-4pm and 6-10pm.*

❧ OLD BRIDGE GELATERIA $

Vle. dei Bastioni di Michelangelo 5   ☎32 84 11 94 78 www.gelateriaoldbridge.com

The only bridge you'll find here is the one that spans the gap between your dreams and reality. Located just across the street from the slanting, defensive walls of the Vatican, Old Bridge serves up gelato that's almost as divine as the Holy See itself. There's almost always a line, and you won't have a lot of time to decide what flavors you want once you get up to the counter, but don't stress too much—you really can't go wrong with any of the options here. Seriously, this stuff is so good, it should probably be taken as a daily sacrament (also, it might be made out of the Body of Christ). And as a final touch, Old Bridge's light, not overly sweet whipped cream is heavenly enough to have been blessed by Pope Francis himself.

i *Just off P. Risorgimento, across the street from the line for the Vatican Museums. Gelato €2-5. Open M-Sa 9am-2am, Su 2:30pm-2am.*

SCIASCIA CAFFÈ $

V. Fabio Massimo 80/A   ☎06 32 11 580

Little known to tourists, Sciascia is a super local coffee shop that takes pride in its *caffè con cioccolato* (espresso with chocolate) and, probably, in its lack of foreigners. Not much English is spoken here, but the guys in bow ties at the counter will still serve you up one of the best cups of coffee you'll have in Rome (and they already know you're a stupid American, so have no shame—go ahead and order that post-11am cappuccino!). Then settle in at a table with your perfectly foamy cup of cultural faux pas and watch the local Italians file in, toss a euro to the girl at the counter, down their shot of espresso, and then head back out into the world. It's like all the tables and chairs in here are just for show (and for you, because you're a tourist who finally found a place in Italy where you can sit down with a cup of coffee).

i *M: Ottaviano. Walk down Vle. Giulio Cesare and turn right down V. Fabio Massimo. Sciascia is on the left. Espresso and cappuccino €1-3.50. Open M-Sa 7am-8pm.*

FA BIO $

V. Germanico 43   ☎06 64 52 58 10 www.fa-bio.com

Sandwiches and smoothies? Fresh fruit and organic ingredients? Pressed juice? Did you take a wrong turn out of the Sistine Chapel and somehow end up in L.A.? No, you just found your way to Fa Bio. It's like your favorite American sandwich shop (complete with a modern interior, green and orange color

rome

scheme, and faux-blackboard menus on the wall), except these sammies come with fresh mozzarella and Italian pesto in addition to your standard summer tomatoes and avocados. Just a few minutes' walk from the Vatican, Fa Bio is a surprisingly hip hole in the wall (there a couple small tables in back, plus a few more seats at the counter), and although you'll have to wait a while for your food, it's because everything here is made entirely from scratch. So add a smoothie to your order because it's fresh and delicious (and you probably need some more Vitamin C in your life anyway).

i M: Ottaviano. Walk down V. Ottaviano and turn left onto V. Germanico. Fa Bio is on the right. Ingredients run out later in the day, so arrive earlier if you want a full selection of all it has to offer. Sandwiches €4-5.50. Salads €5. Juice and smoothies €2.50-5. Open M-F 11am-5:30pm, Sa 11am-4pm.

SU E GIU CUCINA ROMANA $

V. Tactio 42   ☎06 32 65 03 52 www.suegiucucinaromana.blogspot.com

Su e Giu Cucina Romana is proof positive that not all of the area surrounding the Vatican is a culinary wasteland. Located on a less than scenic stretch of Via Tacito, this restaurant may not look like much, but the simple, straightforward Roman dishes here speak for themselves. Served on basic white earthenware with paper napkins, the fare here is kind of like the delicious but unshowy comfort food that somebody's mom would serve when you visited her at home (if you actually had cool friends from Italy, that is). Try the bruschetta with sausage or the fried artichokes when they're in season, and you certainly can't go wrong with a classic plate of spaghetti carbonara. Tourists in the know tend to flock here around dinnertime, so arrive early if you're hoping to get one of the few tables outside.

i M: Lepanto. Walk down V. Ezio, which turns into V. Tacito. Su e Giu Cucina is a few blocks down on the left. Antipasti €2-14. Primi €8-11. Secondi €9-15. Dessert €5-8. Open M-Sa 12:30-2:30pm and 7:30-11:50pm.

Trastevere

🔳 LA RENELLA $

V. del Moro 15   ☎06 581 72 65

La Renella doesn't mess around. This *forno* is fairly basic: just a countertop full of pizza and panini and a row of dark wood stools along the wall, but with sandwiches and biscotti this good, it doesn't really need to pander to customers with anything fancier (or with overly friendly service for that matter). Tourists and local Italians alike swing by for a panino on the go, and you should, too. Savor the perfectly salted bread and fresh mozzarella of a caprese panino, or go for something a little more adventurous—either way, you won't be paying much more than a few euro for a really sizable sandwich. Then stop by after dinner for a late-night piece of biscotti.

i From P. Trilussa, walk down V. del Moro. La Renella is on the left. Panini €3-3.50. Pizza €12-14 per kg. Open M-Th 7am-10pm, F-Sa 7am-3am, Su 7am-10pm.

🔳 FRUTTERIA ER CIMOTTO

P. di San Giovanni della Malva 6   ☎06 580 64 60 www.fruterriaercimotto.com

Just because all those negronis you've been drinking are garnished with an orange wedge doesn't mean your Italian diet of pizza, pasta, and little else will prevent you from developing a nice case of scurvy while abroad. Fortunately, Frutteria Er Cimotto is here to help keep your teeth from falling out. Not your average mini-market, Er Cimotto has been providing Trastevere with fresh fruit and vegetables of all varieties since 1890. And while you can brown-bag it and load up on some much-needed fresh produce, you can also order fresh-pressed juices, homemade soups, and robust salads here. Pop in in the afternoon and

With its evening tradition of *aperitivo*, Italy has basically found an excuse for its citizens to pregame dinner every single night. Not really, but this pre-dinner period is still a great way to get the fermented juices flowing before sitting down for a later meal (Italians normally don't eat dinner until 8:30 or 9pm, so aperitivo is a good way to tide yourself over between lunch and the last meal of the day). Although the tradition originated in northern Italy, *aperitivo* has made its way to Rome and trickled all the way down to the lowly tourists who frequently enjoy *aperitivo* in and around Campo de' Fiori, Piazza Navona, and Trastevere. Usually enjoyed anytime between 7 and 10pm, *aperitivo* is a great time to sample Italy's incredible cheeses, cured meats, and, of course, wine. Traditionally, patrons are expected to order one round of drinks per dish of food, so don't go ham on the *vino* unless you're planning on ordering more proscuitto, too.

walk away with a small bag of perfectly plump peaches for just a couple euro—a nice, healthy alternative for your midday snack (or maybe just a palette cleanser between rounds of gelato).

i *From P. Trilussa, walk up V. Benedetta to P. di San Giovanni della Malva. Frutteria Er Cimotto is on the left. Fruit €3-20 per kg. Open M 7:20am-9pm, Tu-Sa 7:20am-10pm, Su 8:30am-9pm.*

BISCOTTIFICIO ARTIGIANO INNOCENTI $

V. della Luce 21 ☎06 580 39 26

Tucked away on the quieter side of Trastevere, this bakery is pretty inconspicuous and doesn't look like much. But pass through the strips of old plastic in the doorway into the plain white interior and let the scents and taste of fresh-baked cookies stimulate your other senses. The woman who works here is incredibly friendly, so swing by for a sweet pick-me-up as you wind your way through the rest of the neighborhood.

i *From Ponte Garibaldi, walk into P. Sidney Sonnino and turn left onto V. della Lungaretta, then right onto V. della Luce. The bakery is on the left. Prices vary; everything here is generally very inexpensive and will only run you a few euro. Open daily 8am-8pm.*

DA ENZO $$

V. dei Vascellari 29 ☎06 581 2 260

For a more local taste of the tourist-heavy Trastevere, head away from the crowds in Santa Maria, across Vle. di Trastevere, and over to the quieter side of the neighborhood, where you'll find Da Enzo. From the outside, this small restaurant may look like just another Italian eatery: all plaid tablecloths, cramped seating, canvas umbrellas, and wine bottles on the wall. But Da Enzo is a lot harder to get into than your average Trastevere tourist trap, mostly because this place cooks up classic Roman cuisine that's more than worth a reservation (or a long wait for a table at dinnertime). Try their fried artichokes and spaghetti alla carbonara. And if you want to beat the rush, either come early for dinner and try to get a table when the restaurant opens at 7:30pm or swing by for a late lunch.

i *From Ponte Garibaldi, cross Lungotevere and walk through P. Sidney Sonnino down Vle. di Trastevere, then turn left down V. dei Genovesi. Turn left onto V. dei Vascellari; Da Enzo is on the right. Primi €9-11. Secondi €9-15. Open M-Sa 12:30-3pm and 7:30-11pm.*

PIZZERIA NERONE $
V. del Moro 43   ☎06 58 30 17 56 www.pizzerianerone.com

Pizzeria Nerone is kind of like Rome's version of a greasy pizza place, but in this case, "greasy" really just means more olive oil and more flavor. So stop by this underrated pizzeria and try to ignore all the touristy kitsch on the walls (although if you didn't have the patience to wait in line and stick your hand in the real Mouth of Truth, you can stick your finger in a miniature version here). Sure, the Roman statues in the corners may not be legit, but the woodfired oven in the middle of the restaurant certainly is. Your pizza will arrive still steaming, with plenty of gooey cheese and a chewy crust cooked to perfection. And while you'll find plenty of tourists here, there's also a steady flow of locals who stop by to take away a pizza or sit in the "regulars" section of the restaurant in back.

i From P. Trilussa, walk down V. del Moro. Pizzeria Nerone is on the right. Antipasti €3-8. Pizza €6.50-10. Calzones €8. Open daily 7pm-12:30am.

NIGHTLIFE
Ancient City
AI TRE SCALINI
V. Panisperna 251   ☎06 48 90 74 95 www.aitrescalini.org

Perfectly placed in the dip of Via Panisperna (if you're having trouble finding it, just look for the wire of hanging ivy just outside the door), Ai Tre Scalini is a popular aperitivo spot for tourists and locals alike. "Snacks" start at just €3, so enjoy some olives or truffles with a pre-dinner drink in the dimly lit interior and sit back as your conversation mingles with the soft notes of the bar's jazzy background music. The bar is open until late (1am), and although a lot of hip locals and businessmen may be chilling outside with beers and glasses of wine, you're probably not cool enough for that, so look for a table inside instead.

i From Basilica di Santa Maria Maggiore, proceed down V. di Santa Maria Maggiore, which becomes V. Panisperna. Ai Tre Scalini is located at the dip in the road. Snacks €3-5. Aperitivo €7-16. Primi €7-8. Secondi €7-10. Open daily 12:30pm-1am.

SCHOLARS LOUNGE
V. del Plebiscito 101   ☎06 69 20 22 08 www.scholarsloungerome.com

Just down the road from Italy's altar to itself is a small corner of town where you can swap out the Eternal City for the Emerald Isle. A traditional Irish sports pub transplanted to the heart of Italy, Scholars Lounge offers Guinness on tap and over 250 varieties of whiskey (which, the last time we checked, was definitely a Scottish thing, but in this case, cultural appropriation works in your favor). The staff is mostly young internationals from the UK, and the dark wood interior, meat pies, and pictures of Samuel Beckett on the wall will have you thinking and drinking like a real Irishman (that is to say, a lot). A popular spot situated on a busy street, Scholars Lounge is a great place to wander into as you're making your way home on Corso Emanuele late at night or if you just need a break from sightseeing in the middle of the day.

i From P. Venezia, walk west down V. del Plebiscito. Scholars Lounge is on the right. Free Wi-Fi. Live music M, Th, F. Karaoke Tu, W, Su. Pints €6-7. Half-pints €4.50-5.50. Wine €4.50-5.50. Cocktails €8. Shots €5. Irish pie of the day €10.50. Open daily 11am-3:30am.

italy

Centro Storico

CUL DE SAC

P. Pasquino 73   ☎06 68 80 10 94 www.enotecaculdesac.com

Cul de Sac is part gastronomical delight, part circus spectacle. Watch the guys at this incredibly narrow wine bar partake in a grand balancing act as they pluck bottles down from the ceiling with long instruments that could only be classified as wine claws. Then go back to your plate of freshly sliced cured meat and cheese because, despite the waiters' unending juggling act, the wine and aperitivo here is the real star of the hour. Select a glass or bottle from a list of more than 1,500 available every day and tuck in.

i *From P. Navona, exit onto V. Pasquino and proceed to P. Pasquino; Cul de Sac is on the left. Cold cut meat €7-13. Cheese €7-9. Primi €8-10. Secondi €7-11. Wine starting at €4 per glass. Open daily noon-4pm and 6pm-12:30am.*

LA BOTTICELLI

V. di Tor Millina 32   ☎06 686 11 07

Just because La Botticelli has been around for more than 100 years doesn't mean it's not hip enough to figure out how to project a Red Sox game on the back wall of the bar. You wouldn't have guessed it from the fancy Italian name, but La Botticelli is Rome's spin on an American sports bar, which means you'll find statues of saints wearing football helmets and Steelers pennants hanging from the towering antique bar here. So if you're looking for the comfort of home (or just need to see how your favorite team is doing), grab a table in the dimly lit interior, a stool at the bar, or a seat at one of the tables outside.

i *From P. Navona, exit onto V. di Tor Millina. La Botticelli is on the left. Beer €5. Cocktails €6. Shots €3.50. Open daily 5pm-2am.*

ABBEY THEATRE

V. del Governo Vecchio 51   ☎06 686 13 41 www.abbey-rome.com

How an Irish bar managed to secure such prime real estate just beyond the reach of Piazza Navona is a mystery. That being said, Abbey Theatre certainly makes the most of it. With its six rooms, multiple bars, and 16 immense television screens showing everything from women's FIFA to curling, Abbey Theatre is a great tourist pub for sports- and beer-loving internationals of all varieties (although it certainly keeps things green with the Guinness on tap, €11 Irish specials, and pictures of famous Irishmen painted on the walls). People often spill out the door and hang out on the street later in the evening, mingling with the crowd that gathers around Frigidarium across the street.

i *From P. Navona, exit onto V. Pasquino and continue through P. Pasquino to V. del Governo Vec-chio. Abbey Theatre is on the right. Summer drinks €5. Irish specials €11-15. Open M noon-2am, F noon-3am, Sa 11am-3am, Su 11am-2am.*

FLUID

V. del Governo Vecchio 46   ☎06 683 23 61

Of all the fluids in your life (cleaning, lighter, bodily, etc.), this one is probably the hippest you've come across. Amid all the restaurants and Italian wine bars surrounding Piazza Navona, this self-consciously trendy cocktail lounge is a bit incongruous and looks like it got lost somewhere on its way from Tokyo to New York. That being said, if you're a hip millennial in search of a cocktail in a sea of red wine and prosecco (you're young, and sometimes you just need to get hard... at least with your liquor), this place might be the spot for you. If the glowing white cubes in the front window aren't enough to entice you, just walk toward the purple light at the back of the bar.

i *From P. Navona, exit onto V. Pasquino and continue through P. Pasquino to V. del Governo Vec-chio. Fluid is on the right. Cocktails starting at €8. Open daily 7pm-2am.*

Termini

THE YELLOW BAR

V. Palestro 40   ☎06 49 38 26 82 www.the-yellow.com

The Yellow Bar is here to remind you that getting blitzed in Europe has gotten a lot more fun since World War II. So what is the difference between the Yellow and every loud, sloppy American college party you've ever been to? Besides the currency and the international crowd, not a whole lot. Alcohol flows continuously here, mostly because it's so goddamn cheap (even the cocktails that run upward of €7 and boast cheeky names like "Adios Motherfucker" contain more than your money's worth of liquor). While there's plenty of seating both inside and out, the bar area itself is small and always crowded, as is the dance floor downstairs, so cozy on up to your fellow travelers, make some new friends, and see if you can remember any of it in the morning.

i From Termini Station, exit onto P. dei Cinquecento and turn right onto Vle. Enrico De Nicola. Walk through P. dell'Indipendenza and continue straight down V. San Martino della Battaglia, then turn right onto V. Palestro. The Yellow Bar is on the left. Beer €2.50-4. Cocktails €4-7. Open 24hr. Happy hour daily noon-9pm.

TRIMANI WINE BAR

V. Cernaia 37/B   ☎06 446 96 30 www.trimani.com

You're probably not going to make many new acquaintances at the quiet Trimani Wine Bar, but who needs friends when you have a nearly endless selection of wines by the glass to keep you company? (You, Andre, and Franzia may go way back, but now that you're in Rome, it might be time to reevaluate your relationships and upgrade to a more sophisticated crowd.) In the wine business since 1821, Trimani will help you achieve your most ambitious #squadgoals. And if you're a bad judge of character and have no clue what to order, the helpful waitstaff can point you in the right direction. At the very least, you can always pair one of the fancy desserts with a nice, friendly glass of Moscato.

i From Termini Station, exit onto P. dei Cinquecento and turn right onto Vle. Enrico De Nicola. Cross the street to the left side of P. dell'Indipendenza and turn left onto V. Goito, then right onto V. Cernaia. Trimani is on the right. Wine by the glass €5-18. Primi, secondi, and antipasti €5-24. Dessert €8. Open M-Sa 11:30am-3pm and 5:30pm-12:30am.

BAR OASIES

V. Villafranca 1/A

Bar Oasies is a low-key, local alternative to the international Eurotripping that's going on at nearby hostels. And while there's nothing particularly special about the food or drinks here, there is a strange, stripped-down charm to this bar's total lack of self-promotion. It's just sitting there, doing its thing—green walls and red tablecloths and generic menu and all—and so is Dominico, one of the Italian bartenders who will happily use you as a specimen upon which to practice his English. Grab a seat outside and relax with a beer before reentering the fray at the Yellow Bar around the corner.

i From Termini Station, exit onto P. dei Cinquecento and turn right onto Vle. Enrico De Nicola. Walk through P. dell'Indipendenza and continue straight down V. San Martino della Battaglia, then turn right onto V. Villafranca. Bar Oasies is on the right. Wine €3-5. Beer €3-5. Cocktails €6. Primi €6-7. Secondi €5-8. Pizza €3-8. Open daily 7am-late (after 1am).

Trastevere

FRENI E FRIZIONI

V. del Politeama 4-6   ☎06 45 49 74 99 www.freniefrizioni.com

Who knew chandeliers and mason jars looked so good together? Freni e Frizioni did, but then again, this repurposed auto body shop seems to know a thing or two about design and hipster shit. From its high industrial ceiling to its movie-poster-inspired menu to the carefully curated clutter on its walls, Freni e Frizioni is about as hipster as Rome gets. Fortunately, it's so popular and such a good deal that you won't even have time to roll your eyes at its self-conscious trendiness while you make a beeline for the buffet table. Come by for aperitivo, when the crowd of young travelers and students spills out onto the patio and, more importantly, when the purchase of one drink gives you free range over a spread of unlimited bread, pasta salad, hummus, carrots, vegetables, and rice dishes.

i *From P. Trilussa, walk down the tiny V. del Politeama and look for the steps (and the crowd) on the left. Beer €6. Long drinks €7. Cocktails €10. Lower prices after 10pm. Open daily 6:30pm-2am. Aperitivo 7-10pm.*

MECCANISMO ROMA (CAFE FRIENDS)
P. Trilussa 34 ☎06 581 61 11 www.meccanismoroma.com

It's a youthful hangout spot in Trastevere, which means it must be—you guessed it—modern and trendy! Meccanismo will be your friend at all hours, but especially during aperitivo, when you can get a drink and some finger food for just €8 (even if you don't opt for the food, the waitstaff here will still bring you some potato chips in a hip little brown paper bag). There's plenty of outdoor seating here, so enjoy your drinks al fresco along the edge of Piazza Trilussa. And if you're feeling a little tender the next day, Meccanismo is open early and has coffee, tea, and a full American breakfast to help you soak up the hangover.

i *From Ponte Sisto, walk across the street and into P. Trilussa. Meccanismo is on the left. Wine €3.50-4. Beer €4.50-7. Cocktails €7-9. Aperitivo €8. Open daily 7:30am-2am. Aperitivo 6:30-9pm.*

BIR E FUD
V. Benedetta 23 ☎06 589 40 16 www.birefud.it

Beer lovers rejoice: you won't be drinking any more red wine or spritzers tonight. Instead, you can add even more carbs to your Italian diet by sampling the many yeast-y offerings of Bir e Fud. In keeping with the modern design of the many hip hangouts in Trastevere, this bar has clean lines, a sleek bar with a row of impressive bronze taps, and some kind of modern art on the wall that looks like a metallic version of those plastic six-pack rings that dolphins get their noses stuck in. Fortunately (or unfortunately), you'll be thinking more about wheat than wildlife conservation when your beer is served to you with a full, perfectly foamy head. Enjoy it outside, at a stool along the bar, or with some bruschetta at a table in back.

i *From P. Trilussa, turn right onto V. Benedetta. Bir e Fud is on the left. Draught beer €5-6. Bruschetta €3-6. Pizza €6-12. Open daily noon-2am. Kitchen closes at 1am.*

ESSENTIALS
Practicalities

- **TOURIST OFFICES:** Comune di Roma is Rome's official source for tourist information. Green PIT info booths, located near most major sights, have English-speaking staff and sell bus and metro maps and the Roma pass. (V. Giovanni Giolitti 34 in Termini, P. delle Cinque Lune near Piazza Navona, P. Sidney Sonnino in Trastevere, and V. dei Fori Imperiali. ☎06 06 08 www.turismoroma.it. Most locations open daily 9:30am-7pm; Termini location open daily 8am-8:30pm.)

- **LUGGAGE STORAGE:** Termini Luggage Deposit. (☎06 47 44 777 www.romatermini.com. Below Track 24 in the Ala Termini wing. Storage for bags up to 20kg. Max. 5 days. 1st 5hr. €6, €0.90 per hr. for 6th-12th hr., €0.40 per hr. thereafter. Open daily 6am-11pm.)

- **POST OFFICES:** Poste Italiane are located through the city. (☎800 160 000 www.poste.it) The main office is located at Piazza San Silvestro 19. (☎06 69 73 72 16 Open M-F 8:20am-7pm, Sa 8:20am-12:35pm.)

Emergency

- **POLICE:** Police Headquarters. (V. di San Vitale 15 ☎06 46 861; M Repubblica.) Carabinieri have offices at V. Mentana 6 (Near Termini ☎06 44 74 19 00) and at P. Venezia 6 (☎06 67 58 28 00) City Police. (P. del Collegio Romano 3 ☎06 46 86)

- **LATE-NIGHT PHARMACIES:** The following pharmacies are open 24hr.: Farmacia Internazionale (P. Barberini 49 ☎06 4871195); Farmacia Risorgimento (P. del Risorgimento 44 ☎06 39738166); Farmacia Fargion (V. Cola di Rienzo ☎06 3244476)

- **HOSPITALS/MEDICAL SERVICES:** Policlinico Umberto I. (Vle. del Policlinico 155 ☎06 49971 www.policlinicoumberto1.it M Policlinico or bus #649 to Policlinico. Emergency treatment free. Open 24hr.) International Medical Center is a private hospital and clinic. (V. Firenze 47 ☎06 48 82 371 or ☎06 0862 441 111 www.imc84.com M Repubblica. Call ahead for appointments.) Rome-American Hospital. (V. Emilio Longoni 69 ☎06 22 551 for emergencies, ☎06 22 55 290 for appointments www.hcir.it. Well to the east of the city; consider taking a cab. To get a little closer, take bus $409 from Tiburtina to Ple. Prenestina or tram #14 from Termini. English speaking. Private emergency and laboratory services. 24hr. emergency care.)

Getting There

If you're traveling to Rome from an international destination, you'll probably arrive at Da Vinci International Airport and take a train into the center of Rome. Trains from the airport arrive at Termini Station during the day, although if you're traveling by night you may have to transfer to a bus. For travelers on a budget, Rome Ciampino Airport is the closest budget airport, although getting to Rome will be a bit slower, as no trains run from here to the city center. If you're heading to Rome from elsewhere in Italy, take advantage of the train network that runs throughout the country.

By Plane

Commonly known as Fiumicino, **Da Vinci International Airport** (30km southwest of the city ☎06 65 951 www.adr.it/fiumicino) oversees most international flights. To get from the airport, which is located right on the Mediterranean coast, to central Rome, take the Leonardo Express train to Termini Station. After leaving the airport's customs, follow signs to the Stazione Trenitalia/Railway Station, where you can buy a train ticket to Termini Station at an automated machine or from the ticket office. (€14. 30min. every half hour.) The FL1 rail line runs regional trains to and from other stations in Rome, including Rome Tiburtina and has departures every 15min. Don't buy a ticket from individuals who approach you, as they may be scammers. If you arrive after the ticket windows have closed, you'll have to use an automated machine. Before boarding the train, make sure to validate the ticket in a yellow box on the platform; failure to do so may result in a fine of €50-100. To get to Fiumicino before 6:30am or after 11:30pm, the easiest option is to catch a taxi.

   Rome Ciampino Airport (CIA; 15km southeast of the city ☎06 65 951 www.adr.it/ciampino) is a rapidly growing airport that serve budget airlines like Ryanair and EasyJet. There are no trains connecting the airport to the city center, but there are some buses. The SIT Bus Shuttle (€4, 40min.) and Terravision Shuttle (€4, 40min.) run from the airport to V. Marsala, outside Termini Stations. For easy and cheap access to the Metro, the COTRAL bus runs to M Anagnina.

By Train

Trenitalia (www.trenitalia.com) trains run through Termini Station, central Rome's main transport hub. International and overnight trains also run to Termini. City buses C2, H, M, 36, 38, 40, 64, 86, 90, 92, 105, 170, 175, 217, 310, 714, and 910 stop outside in

P. del Cinquecento, so you definitely aren't short on options for the next leg of your journey. The station is open 4:30am-1:30am; if you arrive in Rome outside this time frame, you will likely arrive in Stazione Tiburtina or Stazione Ostiense, both of which connect to Termini by the night bus #175. Trains run from: Bologna (€35-55, 2-4hr.); Florence (€20-50, 2-5hr.); Naples (€12-40, 1-3hr.); Venice (€50-80, 3hr. 30min.-6hr.); and Milan (€67-79, 2hr. 40min-3hr. 30min.).

Getting Around

By Bus

The best way to get around the city other than walking is by bus. Dozens of routes cover the entire city center as well as the outskirts. Bus stops are marked by yellow poles and display a route map for all lines (regular and night lines) that pass through the stop. Useful lines include #40 (Termini, P. Venezia, Argentina, P. Pia), #64 (Termini, P. Venezia, Argentina, Vatican), #62 (Repubblica, Spanish Steps, P. Venezia, Argentina, Vatican), and #81 (Vatican Museums, Spanish Steps, P. Colonna, P. Venezia, Circo Maximo, Colosseum). Tickets cost €1.50 for 75min. and can be purchased at tabaccherie, bars, or vending machines at metro stations. Although Let's Go does not condone freeloading, inside sources tell us that inspectors don't check tickets after 9pm.

By Metro

Rome's Metro system consists of two lines: Line A, which runs from Battistini to Anagnina (passing through P. di Spagna and Ottaviano near the Vatican) and Line B, which runs from Laurentina to Rebibbia (passing through the Colosseum, Ostiense, and southern Rome). The lines intersect at Termini Station. While the Metro is fast, it doesn't reach many areas of the central city and is best used when trying to get from one end of the city to the other. Stations are marked by poles with a red square and a white "M". Tickets can be purchased with cash at machines or sometimes with cards at ticket windows (€1.50 for 1 60min. ride). Validate your ticket at turnstiles upon entering the station. The Metro usually operates 5:30am-11:30pm (until 1:30am on Saturdays).

By Tram

Trams make many stops but are still an efficient means of getting around. A few useful lines include #3 (Trastevere, Piramide, Aventine, P. San Giovanni, Villa Borghese, P. Thorwaldsen), #8 (Trastevere to Largo Argentina),#9 (P. Venezia, Argentina, Trastevere), and #19 (Ottaviano, Villa Borghese, San Lorenzo, Prenestina, P. dei Gerani).

By Bike

ATAC runs Bikesharing. Purchase a card at any ATAC ticket office (06 57 003 M A: Anagnina, Spagna, Lepanto, Ottaviano, Cornelia, or Battistini or M B: Termini, Laurentina, EUR Fermi, or Ponte Mammolo. Bikes can be parked at stations around the city. Cards are rechargeable. Initial charge €5, €.050 per 30min. thereafter. Bikes available max. 24hr.) Other companies also rent bikes, including Bici and Baci.

By Taxi

Given the scope of Rome's bus system, taxis should only be reserved for desperate or time-sensitive affairs. Legally, you may not hail a cab on the street--either call RadioTaxi (06 3570 www.3570.it) or head to a cab stand (near most major sights). Ride only in yellow or white cars and look for a meter or settle on a price before the ride. If the cost of your ride seems especially high, write down the license number and contact the company. Tips are not expected.

rome

milan

A certain one-time Disney sensation once warbled, "Everybody's in stilettos. Guess I didn't get the memo." Same, Miley—same. Good thing Milan is well paved, as the rustic cobblestones of other Italian cities might spell disaster for the stilettoed pedestrians of this fashion capital. Prepare to look especially shabby during your stay in Milan; in addition to residents' pointy shoes come skin-tight trousers and chic blazers with elbow patches, to recount a couple of the more conventional ensembles you'll see during your strolls through the city's glitzy streets. While Milan has its own share of important Renaissance art and a fancy, stunning Duomo, this northern metropolis distinguishes itself from other popular Italian cities by being just that—a metropolis. We're talking skyscrapers and metros, immigrants and authentic ethnic restaurants, and edgy youths in bold outfits who transition seamlessly from their daytime perches at hipster cafes to the dark rooms and booming rhythms of Milan's famed nightclubs. Get back into the fast lane—whip out your cleanest T-shirt, smooth back that under-conditioned traveler's hair as best you can, and join the glammed-up masses.

SIGHTS

Museums in Milan are closed on Monday. Free entry offered at civic museums every day 1hr. before close and on the first Sunday of each month. The Milan Card gives you free public transport and not-super-generous discounts to various landmarks. Probably not worth it unless you plan on going to every single museum in town. Buy card online or at the airport or train station (24hr. €7, 48hr. €13, 72hr. €19).

▧ THE LAST SUPPER (CHIESA DI SANTA MARIA DELLE GRAZIE)

V. Giuseppe Antonio Sassi, 3   ☎02 467 6111, ticket office ☎02 92800360
                                        http://legraziemilano.it/il-cenacolo

The Mona Lisa is smaller than expected. Michelangelo's David has really anatomically correct junk that kind of ruins the majesty of it all. Famous works of art have a knack for being somewhat underwhelming in person, but that trend ends with Leonardo da Vinci's The Last Supper, which can be found on the wall of Milan's Chiesa di Santa Maria delle Grazie. Depicting the moment directly after Jesus reveals that one of his disciples will betray him, the painting fairly glows with the realness of suspended emotion (shock, in most cases, and something more sinister from traitor Judas's profile). The work's survival, given the circumstances, is as spiritual as its subject matter: da Vinci painted it directly on the drywall instead of on wet plaster (as is the case with most frescos), so the paint began deteriorating within six years of the work's completion. Furthermore, during WWII, a bomb fell on the chapel, destroying three of the room's walls and miraculously leaving The Last Supper unharmed. You'll want to book tickets at least three months in advance.

i From the Cadorna metro stop, turn onto Ple. Luigi Cadorna (which turns into V. Giovanni Boccaccio); at the roundabout, take 2nd exit onto V. Caradosso, and turn right onto V. Giuseppe Antonio Sassi. Located in Chiesa di Santa Maria delle Grazie. Tickets €10. Book at least 3 months in advance. Iif you can't secure a ticket but are set on seeing it, there are more expensive tours that include entrance to The Last Supper. Open Tu-Su 8:15am-7pm.

▧ DUOMO

P. del Duomo   ☎02 7202 2656 www.duomomilano.it/en

Mandatory tourist destination. This cathedral is the third largest in Europe after Westminster and Seville (St. Peter's Basilica in Vatican City is also larger but technically not in Europe—let the Milanese have this, okay?). It took 479 years to build (as expected, Italy) and features 3400 marble statues fastened to its exterior. Stats aside, don't miss the disgustingly sinuous sculpture of St.

italy

get a room!

OSTELLO BELLO GRANDE $$$
V. R. Lepetit 33   ☎02 670 5921 www.ostellobello.com

More like a six-floor playground for backpackers than a hostel, Ostello Bello Grande is well worth its relatively high price tag. The laundry list of amenities (€6 laundry service among them) includes free breakfast and dinner, AC, abasement lounge, free toiletries and towels, a kitchen stocked with ingredients up for grabs, and wireless modems to keep you connected while adventuring. The staff posts lists of their favorite restaurants and bars on the walls and offers whenever-you-feel-like-it check-in and luggage storage even after check-out. The 24hr. bar is actually listed as a nightlife destination, and in the evenings it's packed with both guests and regretful backpackers who couldn't book a bunk. One last word of praise: the hostel is located three minutes away from the Centrale train station and metro stop, providing easy access to the city and at least some incentive to not sunbathe all day on the rooftop terrace.

i *Turn left out of Centrale Station. Cross the street and take the 1st right. Dorms from €38; singles from €89; twins from €110. Breakfast included. Laundry €6. Reception open 24hr. Check-in 2pm. Check-out 11:30am.*

MADAMA HOSTEL AND BISTROT $$$
Vle. Regina Margherita, 9   ☎02 3656 4959 www.madamahostel.com/en

Once a police department, this airy structure on the east side of town has since been overrun by sultry, glossy-haired vixens—the staff is entirely made up of strong, Italian women. Fend off the Milan heat in air-conditioned rooms (ask to get the air turned on) furnished with bunks and lock boxes made entirely from recycled materials. Buffet breakfast and dinner are provided—you'll share the latter with patrons of the affiliated bistro for aperitivo, so the food is quite good.

i *From Centrale Station take the MM3 metro (Yellow Line toward San Donato) for 8 stops. Get off at Lodi T.I.B.B. and walk 3min. until you reach Madama Hostel. Dorms from €32; doubles from €99. Breakfast included. Laundry €3. Reception open 24hr. Check-in 2pm-midnight. Check-out 11am.*

GOGOL'OSTELLO & CAFTÈ LETTERARIO $$
V. Privata Chieti, 1   ☎02 3675 5522 www.gogolostellomilano.com

Perhaps deterred by the "literary cafe" subheading, young backpackers are scarce at this hostel, which instead houses middle-aged couples and lithe bicyclists in Spandex. Clear of drunken juveniles, Gogol'Ostello offers clean white rooms and a touch of culture: enjoy your complimentary breakfast of off-brand Nutella while perusing the well-stocked bookshelves (+1 for Slaughterhouse Five, -1 for Twilight) and listening to '70s rock. An ancient TV in the corner of the common area has the exhortation "READ INSTEAD!!!" scrawled across the screen. Presiding over the reception and distributing scalding cups of black tea is Italian Bellatrix Lestrange, complete with wayward curls and dramatic eyeliner (and only a bit less intimidating).

i *From Centrale Station, take the metro Line 2 (Green Line) two stops to Garibaldi, change to Line 2 (Purple Line) and ride three stops to Gerusalemme. Take V. Fauche' and turn left onto V. Chieti. The hostel is at the end of the street. Dorms from €26; twin privates from €75. Breakfast included. Laundry €3.50. Reception open M-Fr 8:30am-9:30pm, Sa 8:30am-11:30pm, Su 9:30am-9:30pm. Check-in 12:30-10:30pm. Check-out 11am.*

milan

Bartholomew, who was skinned alive, in the back right of the main sanctuary. The cross hanging high above the altar supposedly contains nails from Christ's crucifixion, and once in a blue moon, the head priest gets hoisted up in a decorative basket (bet that wasn't in the job description) to bring them down for public veneration. You'll probably want to get the package ticket that provides access to the cathedral, museum, and terrace (€11)—the ticket office behind the structure is significantly less crowded. Come with shoulders and knees covered.

i Located in P. del Duomo (it's hard to miss). €11, €15 for terrace with lift. Church open daily 8am-7pm. Museum open 10am-6pm, Th-Su 10am-6pm.

HANGAR BICOCCA

V. Chiese 2   ☎02 6611 1573 http://hangarbicocca.org

Don the most obnoxious outfit in your limited backpacker's closet (preferably some variety of oversized glasses will be involved) and bus it 20min. outside the city limits to this relic of Milan's manufacturing days, which is now a free contemporary art museum. This cluster of cavernous hangars house three temporary exhibits at any given time—the featured installation during the summer 2016 season was a series of displays by German phytopathologist Carsten Höller that explored themes of boredom, dreaming, love, and art. One interactive installation entitled "Two Flying Machines" hung participants from a slowly rotating mechanical arm so they could "experience embarrassment, suspended in the air like a bag of potatoes." Your standard ridiculous but interesting contemporary art stuff. If your head starts spinning from the insufferable art lingo and meta-ness, at least the clean restrooms are something we can all understand.

i From the V. Chiese bus stop, take 2nd exit at roundabout onto V. Sesto San Giovanni; destination is on the left. Free. Open Th-Su 10am-10pm.

L.O.V.E.

P. Degli Affari

For all the unemployed youths who chose righteous poverty over selling their souls to Wall Street (and are now regretting it from their parents' basements), this is the public F.U. to capitalism that we've (yes, we're included in this—we spend our summers drinking around the world, for Pete's sake) been searching for. No, literally—this is an enormous statue of a raised middle finger by Italian artist Maurizio Cattelan, planted directly in front of the Milan stock exchange building. Erected during the 2010 financial crisis, this statue understands our unemployed pain and, blessedly, can be viewed free of charge. If you look closely, you'll notice that the other fingers aren't clenched but severed—the hand in its entirety would thus resemble a communist salute.

i Located in P. Degli Affari. Free. Open 24hr.

CASTELLO SFORZESCO

P. Castello   ☎02 846 3700 www.milanocastello.it/en

After visiting a few Italian cities, you'll begin to notice this trend where super wealthy, all-powerful medieval families holed themselves up in uncomfortable-looking castles that have since been opened to the public as museums. The Milanese have the Castello Sforzesco on the edge of Sempione Park—the city's largest centrally-located green space. A walkthrough of the castle grounds is free of charge and available for the daydreaming pleasures of tourists and locals alike. The interior of the castle houses various museums, most notably the tiny Museo Pietà Rondanini-Michelangel, which houses Michelangelo's final sculpture. Probably intended to decorate his gravestone, the unfinished work depicts a crucified Jesus in the arms of Mary and is an interesting point of contrast to a younger Michelangelo's famous (and finished) Pietà in the Vatican.

i Located in Parco Sempione. Castle free. Museum €5 (free every Tu after 2pm and W-Su 1hr. before close). Castle open daily 7am-7pm. Museum open Tu-Su 9am-5:30pm (last entry 5pm).

FOOD

In Milan, lunch typically runs from noon-3pm; aperitivo from 6-8pm (and sometimes as late as 10pm; see Navigli area); and dinner from 8-10pm. Aperitivo exists everywhere in Italy, but it's bigger and better in Milan—not only is it a lot more substantial than what you'll find in other cities, but it often serves as dinner and social hour for the city's young people. At most aperitivo spots, you can expect to pay for one drink (usually around €8) and then get access to an array of buffet food. Traditional Milanese food includes risotto (with saffron), cotoletta alla Milanese (breaded veal chop fried in butter—"alla Milanese" generally refers to things fried in butter), and panettun (Christmas cake). As is the case in Europe, tip is factored into the listed prices, but sit-down restaurants also charge a €2 per person service tax.

🍕 PIZZA AM $

Corso di Porta Romana, 83   ☎02 551 0579 www.pizzaam.it

With its bright, Keith Haring-themed interior, this pizzeria positions itself precisely at the intersection of value and quality. Enormous, handmade personal pizzas topped with various permutations of fresh tomato sauce, veggies, and cheeses range from €6-9. The relatively limited menu, itself shaped like a pizza, offers seven options in total, and all of them are vegetarian (and for all you carnivores out there, you'd be surprised at the power of garlic and the region's San Marzano tomato sauce once you take meat out of the equation). You shouldn't need a reservation but might have to wait in line on particularly busy nights.

i From the Crocetta metro stop, walk down Corso di Porta Romana; destination is on the left. Pizza €6-9. Open Tu-F noon-3pm and 7-11pm, Sa 1-3pm and 7-11pm, Su 7-11pm.

🍦 IL MASSIMO DEL GELATO $

V. Lodovico Castelvetro, 18   ☎02 349 4943 http://ilmassimodelgelato.it

Given the high density of gelato shops throughout Italy, the impressive queues outside Il Massimo must mean somethin' good. Fight your way inside through clusters of every demographic—sticky children, stoic old people, leggy ladies with perky butts (that infuriatingly remain so despite their eating gelato at 10pm)—and grab a number; the lines are formidable but move quickly. The interior bears testament to this gelateria's celebrity status: you'll find plenty

(window) shopping

Prolific, animated fashion designer Edna Mode held her fashion show in "Milan, darling, Milan," and where fashion thrives, shopping is sure to follow. At the top of the food chain are the designer brands, for your window-shopping and (if you're daring enough to enter in your sensible walking shoes) perfume-sampling pleasure–these stores are concentrated in the Galleria Vittorio Emanuele and the Quadrilatero della Moda, a square of side-by-side luxury establishments. For stuff that you maybe have a chance of affording, try Rinascente, the seven-floor department store alongside the Duomo. Sure, you've got your floors of Gucci children's wear, but you can also pick up a €10 coffeepot or €5 packaged pastas. More our speed is Humana Vintage–a retro secondhand store with a lot of shoulder pads and a mission: all proceeds go to charity. Shopping needn't be limited to clothing: Eataly is a Whole Foods on steroids, consisting of three floors of artisan foods sourced from farms around Italy. Peruse jars of pesto and organic teas alongside bespectacled aging hipsters and harried new parents still committed to organic baby food. In general, shops open from 10am-7:30pm or from 9am-1pm and 3pm-7:30pm and are typically closed on Sundays and Monday mornings.

milan

of framed awards and newspaper features on the walls, along with a haughty grandmother manning the register. Be warned: high-quality gelato generally means extra-rich and super-dense—the chocolate flavors in particular are not for the faint of stomach.

i From the Gerusalemme metro stop, turn right onto V. Poliziano, left onto V. Giovanni Battista Fauchè, and left onto V. Lodovico Castelvetro; destination is on the left. Gelato €2.80-3.20. Cash only. Open Tu-Sa noon-midnight, Su noon-midnight.

BAR LUCE $

Largo Isarco, 2   ☎02 5666 2611 www.fondazioneprada.org/barluce-en

Wes Anderson devotees unite! Everyone else, come here for the photogenic pastries (€1.20-4) and waiters in bowties (also photogenic). The imaginative director of The Grand Budapest Hotel designed this cafe for local hipsters and the Prada Institute (itself an imposing concrete structure housing an unimportant contemporary art gallery). Slurp your espresso (€1) at a snail's pace to have enough time to appreciate the delightfully retro interior, inspired by the Galleria Vittorio Emanuele and historic Milanese cafes from the '50s and '60s. The color palette is pale blues and greens (see Moonrise Kingdom). Don't miss the custom-made pinball machines against the wall—one is The Life Aquatic-themed, while the other is designed after Anderson's short film Castello Cavalcanti.

i From the Lodi T.I.B.B. metro stop, walk down Corso Lodi, turn right onto V. Brembo, then left onto V. Orobia; destination is on the right. Espresso €1. Croissants €1.30-1.50. Tarts €3.50. Tiramisu €4. Open M 9am-9pm, W-Th 9am-9pm, Fr-Su 9am-10pm.

IL CAMINETTO $$

V. Felice Casati, 22   ☎32 9891 9331

If you're looking to taste authentic Milanese cuisine, make this your one not-so-budget meal. While this homey family operation is definitely on the cheaper end of sit-down restaurants, classics like cotoletta alla Milanese (breaded veal chop fried in butter) and risotto will inevitably run €18 and €20, respectively. It is, however, possible to get pastas for €7-8 and some meat dishes for as little as €10. The portions are generous, and the service is warm and relaxed. Tips are pre-factored into the list prices, but expect a €2 per person service tax.

i From Centrale, head down V. Mauro Macchi, turn left oton V. Napo Torriani, right onto P. Cincinnato, right onto V. Lazzaretto, and left onto V. Felice Casati; destination is on the left. Antipasti €9-12. Primi €7-14. Secondi €10-20. Dessert €5. Drinks €4-8. Open M-Sa 5-10:30pm.

PAVÈ $

V. Felice Casati, 27   ☎02 9439 2259 www.pavemilano.com/en

If you're homesick for your local hipster coffee shop, don your horn-rimmed specs and sip espresso (€1-1.10) under Pavè's Mason jar lights. Select something to eat from a variety of freshly-made, French-inspired pastries, which are widely acknowledged as Milan's best. At €2.50-5, the pastries are on the pricey side, so make it worth your while by sticking around for the quiet cafe atmosphere and free Wi-Fi. Italian at heart, Pavè naturally serves alcohol (€5), as well as teas (€2.50), soft drinks (€2-4), and cold cuts (€9-12).

i From Centrale, turn left onto V. Napo Torriani; at the roundabout, take second exit onto V. Carlo Tenca and turn left onto V. Felice Casati; destination is on the right. Espresso €1. Pastries from €2.50-5. Aperitivo €5-12 (noon-3pm). Open Tu-F 8am-8pm, Sa-Su 8:30am-7pm.

LUINI $

V. S. Radegonda 16   ☎02 8646 1917 www.luini.it

After wandering the hallowed halls of the Duomo and fending off the pigeons out front, take the edge off your hunger with a snack from this crowded bakery (just a 5min. walk from P. del Duomo). Their featured product is panzerotti, thick shells of dough wrapped around sweet or savory fillings and baked. The extensive menu on the wall doesn't provide prices, but each panzerotti is rough-

italy

ly €2.50. Collect your takeout bag and join the locals munching while squatting on the pavement.

i From P. del Duomo, pass through Galleria Vittorio Emanuele II, continue onto V. Giovanni Berchet, and turn left onto V. Santa Radegonda; destination is on the right. Panzerotti approx. €2.50. Open M 10am-3pm, Tu-Sa 10am-8pm.

NIGHTLIFE

NOTTINGHAM FOREST

Vle. Piave, 1   www.nottingham-forest.com

"A mercurial oasis where you can hear the echo of the world." No, you're not in a hookah lounge but Nottingham Forest, headquarters of a decidedly spiritual mixologist who might be on a power trip, convinced that his experimenting with solid and liquid elements of cocktails taps into "the real law of the cosmos" (we were similarly confused about this). Drinks are expensive at €12 (€10 during happy hour), but with good reason: the hefty menu consists of inventive concoctions combining chemistry with ethnic influences and pop culture. One of the most visually distinctive is the "Sephora," served in a small bathtub and topped with white peach liquor foam and an aromatic rubber duck. Expect to wait 30min. or more for a table before the impassive visage of a decidedly sulky bouncer; reservations are not accepted.

i From the Piazzata Venezia metro stop, turn right onto Vle. Piave and continue 10min.; destination is on the right. Drinks €12 (€10 from 6-9pm). Open Tu-Sa 6:30pm-2am, Su 6pm-1am.

VINILE

V. Tadino 17   ☎02 3651 4233 www.vinilemilano.com

When Milanese men-children want to drink something other than their mothers' chocolate milk, they emerge from their basement lairs and stagger to this home away from home. The theme is retro-geek: Hulk dolls share shelf space with R2-D2 models and old radios under the kindly gaze of a life-sized C-3PO cutout. Take a seat at what looks suspiciously like an elementary school desk (presumably for the comfort of the men-children), and scan the menu by the dim light of a drowsily rotating disco ball.

i From the Lima metro stop, walk down Corso Buenos Aires, turn right onto V. S. Gregorio, then left onto V. Alessandro Tadino; destination is on the right. Salads €7-8. Piadina €7. Beer €4-7. Wine €5-7. Drinks €5-8. Open Tu 6:30pm-midnight, W-Th 6:30pm-1am, F-Sa 6:30pm-2am, Su 6:30pm-midnight.

CINEMA MEXICO

V. Savona, 57   ☎02 4895 1802 www.cinemamexico.it

One of the few theaters in Milan that shows movies in their original languages (primarily English) with Italian subtitles. Catch a few American blockbusters or, more likely, one of those somewhat artsy, Oscar-bait type flicks—check the website for featured films and showtimes. The cinema is famous for its outrageous Rocky Horror Picture Show on Friday nights, in which the Tim Curry film plays while live actors in requisite gold speedos do the Time Warp on a stage in front of the screen. Audience participation is a given, and past attendees have described the experience as "de-virginizing." Make of that what you will. The show does not run in the summer.

i From the Ple. Genova F.S. metro stop, turn left onto Piazzale Stazione Genova, right onto V. Ventimiglia, left onto V. Tortona, right onto V. Cerano, and left onto V. Savona; destination is on the left. Tickets €7.50. Open daily 4pm-12:30am.

GINGER COCKTAIL LAB

V. Ascanio Sforza, 25   ☎335 569 0779

True to its name, this bar specializes in inventive cocktails incorporating intense spices; for example, the "Strawberry Fields," consisting of strawberry alcohol,

milan

lake clooney

Lake Como, of Hollywood and rich-people-through-the-ages fame, is a mere 1hr. trip from Milan (take the train from Centrale to Varenna). Besides the natural beauty of the lake and surrounding mountains, which have a distinctly Swiss feel that befits the lake's location on the border of Italy and Switzerland, this playground for the wealthy offers a number of historic villas open to the public for around €10 (student discounts available with ID). Villa Carlotta is known for its extensive gardens, which include a small man-made rainforest. Reenact the mushy scenes from Star Wars: Episode II (or wish the whole film never happened) on the balcony of V. del Balbianello, where Padmé and Anakin were secretly married. Finish off your daytrip with a sunset lurk around Villa Oleandra, which was purchased by George Clooney in 2002 as his private vacation home—the dim lighting will provide some cover from security cameras.

basil, and ginger ale (€8), or the "Mescalina," with grapefruit and lime juice and a whole pepper dangling off the rim (€8)—'cause the kick of liquor isn't enough. Ask the tattooed bartender for breakdowns of the drinks—chances are he'll throw in a healthy dose of bar gossip (apparently there's this whole feud between the head bartender and the owner, and it's a big deal and very dramatic). The prime location along the Naviglio Pavese (the smaller of Milan's two canals) is ideal for people-watching, and there are countless nearby watering holes if you want to turn the evening into a bar crawl.

i From the bus stop at P. Ventiquattro Maggio, walk toward Naviglio Pavese, then continue down V. Ascanio Sforza; destination is on the left. Wine €5-6. Drinks €7-9. Open Tu-Su 6:30pm-3am.

ESSENTIALS
Practicalities

- **TOURIST OFFICE:** Galleria Vittorio Emanuele II. (P. della Scala. ☎0288455555 www.turismo.milano.it. Open M-F 9am-7pm, Sa 9am-6pm, Su 10am-6pm.)

- **POST OFFICE:** Milano Centrale. (☎02 67072150. Open M-Sa 8:35am-7:10pm.)

- **ATMS:** Located throughout the city.

Emergency

- **HOSPITALS/MEDICAL SERVICES:** 24hr. Emergency ☎02 34567.

- **POLICE:** 112 (carabinieri), ☎113 (local police). Police Headquarters. (V. Fatebenefratelli, 11 ☎02.62261, http://questure.poliziadistato.it/Milano)

Getting Around

Milan, unlike Rome or Florence or Venice, doesn't really reward walking around on foot because most parts of the city aren't that beautiful. Plus, Milan is really big. So public transportation is the best way to go. Run by ATM, one metro ticket (also valid on bus and tram) is €1.50, valid for 90min. after validation (this does not mean you can leave the metro and do your thing and hop on again; it means you can hang out in the metro for up to 90min. and still be able to validate the same card a second time to get out of the metro). A carnet of 10 tickets is €13.80; a 1-day ticket is €4.50 (worth it if you plan to take four or more rides); and a 48hr. ticket is €8.25 (worth it if you plan to take six or more rides). Purchase individual tickets at machines in the metro or at tabaccheria; purchase special passes and carnets at offices in metro.

The Metro consists of four lines: M1 (red), M2 (green), M3 (yellow), and M5 (purple), all of which are clearly marked, easy to navigate, and well run (although M5 is the nicest). M1, M2, and M3 run approx. 6am-12:30am, while M5 runs from 6am-midnight. After midnight, night buses take over the M1/M2/M3 routes and run every 30min. Be on the lookout for strikes.

General survival note: 2-5pm is unbearably hot during the summer months, so make like a local and consider a siesta.

genoa

In 1492, Columbus sailed the ocean blue. But before leaving Spain for the New World, the traveling bastard set out from his hometown of Genoa in search of funding, and a walkthrough of the city presents one theory as to the source of the plagues that wiped out much of the Americas' native people. Some 500 years after Columbus, Genoa is still a bit of a cesspool, the labyrinthian streets of its old town spawning graffiti, bird poop, mysterious damp patches, and really bad Asian restaurants ("Japanese spaghetti" just isn't the same thing as ramen, okay?). Malodorous exteriors and Columbus affiliation aside, Genoa has its share of maritime museums and historic palaces and is particularly heavy on fantastic, affordable cuisine (provided you steer clear from the pseudo-Asian options). Its coastal location is well within daytripping distance of idyllic fishing towns like Boccadasse and Nervi, and during the summer, the swimming is just fine.

SIGHTS

Most museums and attractions are closed on Mondays. If you intend on going to a good number of museums, the Museum Card provides free admission to 25 museums, along with discounts to other sights (€12 for 24hr., €15 for additional free bus access; €20 for 48hr., €25 for free bus access). Purchase at participating museums or IAT Tourist Offices.

SPIANATA CASTELLETTO

Belvedere Luigi Montaldo

We recommend this lookout at night, when the cooler temperatures will ward off perspiration as you make the 10min. trek uphill. Also, let's face it, Genoa looks better in the dark. If you're set on visiting during the day, though, don't sweat it—an Art Nouveau elevator will shuttle you up for only €0.90. From the top, enjoy 360-degree views of the old town, port, and Lanterna lighthouse. A number of restaurants and bars are nestled at the top, including popular gelateria Don Paolo.

i Take the stairs up from V. Garibaldi, turn right onto Salita di S. Francesco, left onto Spianata di Castelletto, then turn right and climb until the stairs end. Free. Open 24hr.

VIA GARIBALDI AND MUSEI DI STRADA NUOVA

V. Garibaldi 11   ☎010 5572193 www.museidigenova.it/it/content/musei-di-strada-nuova

Via Garibaldi aka Strada Nuova aka La Via Aurea (but most commonly known as Via Garibaldi nowadays). This avenue of palaces bisecting the center of the old city dates back to the 16th century, when Genoa's nobility decided to create their own neighborhood—because societal inequality and unbridled wealth and the 1% and stuff. Take a stroll down this wide, posh avenue—the looming palaces on either side keep the sun off your face as you scrutinize their ornate facades. If you like what you see, visit the Musei di Strada Nuova, composed of Palazzos Rosso, Bianco, and Tursi. The interiors feature tapestries, underwhelming paintings by Italian and Genoese artists, porcelains and Ligurian pottery, and fancy furniture. The Palazzo Tursi also houses Paganini's violin.

i *From the P. del Portello bus stop, turn left onto V. Antonio Brignole Sale, then right onto V. Garibaldi. €9 for entrance to all 3 museums. Free with Genoa Card. Open Tu-F 9am-7pm, Sa-Su 10am-7pm.*

FOOD

Many restaurants are closed on Mondays.

ZIMINO $

Vico delle Scuole Pie 4R, da P. Cinque Lampadi ☎010 403 0321

Authentic Genovese food in an authentic Genovese location—that is, tucked away in a narrow alleyway that's nearly impossible to find. The staff is made up of two amiable brothers who cook, take orders, and collect payments at breakneck pace to keep up with the crowds of locals who flow in for lunch and the €1 tiramisu. Order at the open window that overlooks the kitchen before snagging a table in the cramped interior. The menu changes daily and features Genovese classics like minestrone (€5), pesto lasagna (€6), and fried catch of the day (€8).

i *From the Cathedral of San Lorenzo, walk down V. San Lorenzo, turn right into P. San Lorenzo, then right into P. Invrea, and left into P. delle Scuole Pie; destination tucked away by the Express market. Dishes from €5-8. Open M-Sa noon-8pm.*

IL MASETTO: HAMBURGERIA NAZIONALE $

V. di Canneto Il Lungo, 111 ☎342 961 9673 www.facebook.com/ilmasetto

If you're tired of Genoa's trademark pesto and seafood, make like a local college student and join the queue at this hopping burger joint. Il Masetto is far more than a glorified McDonald's; constructed with fresh, regional ingredients, their burgers have a distinctly Italian taste. In fact, locals who recommend this place make it a point to explain that these are "Italian-style" burgers, perhaps to distance themselves from American fast-food and the culinary taint of the word "burger." The cheapest option is a mere €2.80 (add €2.40 for fries and a drink), which is one of the best values in the city. Be warned: the red condiment bottle does indeed contain ketchup, but the yellow squirts mayonnaise instead of mustard.

i *From P. Giacomo Matteotti, head down Salita Pollaiuoli and turn left onto V. di Canneto Il Lungo; destination is on the left. Burgers €2.80-6. Open M-Th noon-3:30pm and 6:30pm-10:30pm, F-Sa noon-3:30pm and 6:30pm-2am.*

CAVOUR 21 $

P. Cavour, 21 ☎393 851 1140

At Cavour 21, you'll find typical Genovese food and a cozy restaurant setting for unbelievably low prices. Tuck into generous portions of surf and turf plates, including all the Ligurian classics like pesto over trofie (€6), penne and octopus (€6.50), and peppered mussels (€4). To secure a table for dinner, you'll want to show up a little before their opening hour at 7pm or put your name down for the queue the day before. Once inside, expect to wait a bit for your food as friendly-but-swamped servers take orders and shuttle stacks of plates from table to table. To pass the time, doodle on your brown paper place mat—your ungainly masterpiece might get added to the collection on the walls.

i *From the San Giorgio metro stop, walk inland and turn right onto V. Filippo Turati, which leads to P. Cavour; destination on left up a flight of stairs (opposite side of freeway from port). Antipasti €3-7.50. Primi €2.50-15. Secondi €3.50-9.50. Dessert €2.50-3. Open Tu-Su noon-3:30pm, 7-9:30pm.*

ABBEY HOSTEL
$$

Vico di Santa Fede 8-10   ☎010 4033223 www.thehostel.it

This converted abbey is equipped with all the conveniences the early monks had to do without, including Wi-Fi, squashy armchairs, an elevator, and AC units. Carried over from monastic times are bewildering rings of old-fashioned keys—for the front entrance, the other front entrance, bedroom, and lockers—that'll eventually have you battering down doors like a soldier in the Inquisition. The chain-smoking locals loitering just outside might seem menacing but are a (generally) harmless fixture of the narrow alleyways along the port.

i From the Principe train station, exit to P. Acquaverde and walk straight ahead to V. Balbi. Continue along V. Balbi until the end of the street. As soon as the street opens up to the roundabout, turn right and then right again. You will see a street sign Vico Nuovo (it is a narrow street that looks more like a footpath rather than a street). Take Vico Nuovo as it turns left and continue until you see the hostel straight ahead of you. Dorms from €20. Reception open 8am-midnight. Check-in 3pm-midnight. Check-out 10:30am.

OSTELLIN GENOA
$$

Vico dei Parmigiani 1/3   ☎010 098 1928 www.ostellingenova.it

Colorful industrial lighting and handmade wooden shelving modernize the still-visible ceiling frescos of this old building just off V. Garibaldi and P. de Ferrari. The obliging receptionist heartthrob will hopefully distract from both the three flights of stairs up to the entrance and the inconvenience of Wi-Fi that, with any luck, at least works in the common room. If you're too slow, or too selfless, to monopolize your room's fan, choose between throwing the windows open to tempt the sea breeze or roasting in mosquito-free heat.

i From P. De Ferrari, take V. XXV Aprile; at the corner of P. Fontane Marose, turn right onto Vico dei Parmigiani. Dorms from €22. Reception open 8:30am-11pm. Check in 2pm-10pm. Check-out by noon.

ROMEO VIGANOTTI GELATO
$

Salita del Prione 12R   ☎010 251 4061 www.romeoviganotti.it

It gets increasingly difficult to review gelato shops because they are, for the most part, all really good, and we can only write, "Much yum, very wow" so many times. The centuries-old Viganotti Gelato, unanimously recommended by travel guides and locals alike, blessedly provides new fodder for this listing with their unconventional flavors, including pineapple and ginger, beer, and mixed berries with Jamaican rum. The more exotic concoctions run out by the end of the night, so be sure to stop in on the earlier side for your double scoop (€2.30). If you're looking to flirt with diabetes, this gelateria also owns the adjacent pastry shop and cioccolateria.

i From P. delle Erbe, walk up Salita del Prione approx. 1min.; destination is on the left. Gelato €2.30. Open M-Tu noon-8pm, W-Sa noon-midnight.

PINSACCIO
$

V. di S. Bernardo, 33   ☎010 247 7445 www.facebook.com/pinsaccio

The kindly grandpa shooting the breeze out front transforms into a badass pizza maestro with a twinkle of the eye, slicing sausage with his pocketknife and deftly shunting discs of dough in and out of the oven. Select from a variety of cream and tomato-based flavors, including vegan options, ranging from €1.50-4.50. The

genoa

coastal day trip

When you Google "Genoa," you'll likely come across quaint pictures of orange and yellow walkups sheltering an intimate, crystal-clear lagoon. This, uh, actually isn't Genoa, but rather the neighboring fishing village of Boccadasse, 30min. away by train. Once you've exhausted the palaces and Christopher Columbus relics of the city center, pack your swimsuit and take a day trip to the place you thought you were going to all along. While you're at it, 30min. further east takes you to the edge of the Genoa region, called Nervi, which features a breathtaking waterside walk that was favored by the European aristocracy in the 19th and 20th centuries. If you're not quite ready to return to the slums—we mean Genoa proper—20min. further east takes you to Santa Margherita Ligure, a resort town that is home to a Baroque church and Grand Budapest Hotel-esque buildings.

pizzas do run a bit small, even for personal pan sizes, so you might want to order one more than the number of people in your party to be safe. If you're feeling adventurous, try one of the (more expensive) seasonal specials like salmon pâté or prosciutto with figs.

i From P. San Giorgio, head down Vico del Fumo, turn right onto Vico di Santa Rosa, then left onto V. di San Bernardo; destination on right. Pizza €1.50-4.50. Wine €1.50-2. Cash only. Open Tu-Th 11:30am-11pm, F-Sa 11:30am-12am, Su 11:30am-11pm.

NIGHTLIFE

PORTO ANTICO

Calata Molo Vecchio 15 - Magazzini del Cotone, Modulo 5 ☎010 2485711 www.portoantico.it

By day, the old port is popular for its various tourist attractions, like the (extremely expensive) aquarium and panoramic elevator. By night, locals congregate along the boardwalk at various bars and clubs; for dancing, try Banano Tsunami (go for the beer pong and toga parties, not the food). Summertime ushers in a host of free concerts, typically centered in the port's outdoor venue, Arena del Mare (check online for the schedule). Our favorite option, particularly if your savings are running low, is to stock up on beers from the nearest grocery and swig on the dock, legs dangling over the water.

i Porto Antico bus stop. Prices vary. Open 24hr.

KAMUN LAB

V. di S. Bernardo, 53 ☎347 122 1775 www.kamun.it

For a cultured night out, warm a seat at this den of beer enthusiasts (beer can be cultured, right?). This pub serves the products of its affiliated artisan brewery (located a few miles outside the city), which boast sophisticated nicknames like "Nocturna" (€3) and "Fabula" (€3). Talk craft beers with the chill bartender as he deftly scrapes the foam from the rim of your mug, or subtly watch the waitress not-so-subtly moon over said bartender. On cooler nights, the rustic second floor seating area is open. Check the website for tasting events.

i From P. de Ferrari, turn left onto V. Cardinale Pietro Boetto, right onto P. Giacomo Matteotti (which turns into Salita Pollaiuoli), then right onto V. di San Bernardo; the destination is on the left. Drinks €2.50-5.50. Cash only. Open M-Th 6pm-1am, F-Sa 6pm-2am, Su 6pm-midnight. Kitchen closes at 10pm.

italy

ESSENTIALS

Practicalities

- **TOURIST OFFICES:** V. Garibaldi 12 R. (☎010 5572903. Open daily 9am-6:20pm.) V. al Porto Antico 2. (☎0105572903. Open Apr-Sept daily 9am-6:20pm, Oct-Mar daily 9am-5:50pm.)
- **POST OFFICE:** V. Dante 4B/r. (Open M-F 8:00am-6:30pm, Sa 8:00am-1:30pm.)

Emergency

- **HOSPITALS:** The 24hr. emergency number is ☎118. Azienda Ospedaliera Villa Scassi Ospedale Civile Sampierdarena. (Corso Scassi, 1 ☎010 84911 www.villascassi.it) Ospedale Evangelico Internazionale. (Corso Solferino, 1A ☎010 55221 www.oeige.com) Ospedali Civili Di Genova. (Vle. Benedetto, XV ☎010 352859 www.hsanmartino.it)
- **POLICE:** Polizia di Stato (civil national police). (V. Armando Diaz, 2 ☎113 www.poliziadistato.it) Comando Poliza Municipale (local police). (V. di Francia ☎0105570 www.pmgenova.it)

Getting Around

The Old town of Genoa contains most of the city's sights and is a maze of narrow streets. The easiest way to navigate is on foot. If you don't want to walk, public buses, trains, the sole metro line, and ferryboat are all run by AMT (single ticket €1.50, valid for 100min. throughout the entire city network; sold at stations, tabaccheria, pubs, stores, and newsstands). The Genova Pass, valid for 24hr., is sold at IAT office for €4.50

cinque terre

Apparently, Italians curse Rick Steves for "discovering" the Cinque Terre. His comprehensive guides to the area, the first of their kind, put this craggy coastline on the tourist map, infecting the previously hidden gem with all the side effects of sightseers: crowds, rising prices, and flabby beach bods. Still, the government does what it can to preserve this UNESCO World Heritage site—it's nearly impossible to obtain building permits, most towns severely limit motor traffic, and large boats can't dock in the harbors. At the end of the day, even without the regulations, there's only so much we wee, weeing-in-the-ocean humans (even hoards of us armed with selfie sticks) can do to mess up plumes of sea spray fanning around craggy rocks or the sun sinking beneath the horizon and staining the water blood orange. The sunburned hordes elbowing their way into trains and trailing Band-Aids in the lagoon are irksome, but a succulent mussel or the crusty feel of seawater evaporating from your hair has a knack for filling your senses until there isn't room for anything else. Before we start sounding like ol' Ricky: give it go, and remember that taking the train between cities is okay and is perhaps preferable to passing out on the trail.

SIGHTS

CHIESA DI SANTA MARGHERITA D'ANTIOCHIA
P. Matteotti

On some undoubtedly dark and stormy night ages ago, a small chest containing the finger bones of St. Margherita d'Antiochia supposedly washed up on the rocks that front Vernazza's harbor. Now, how the townspeople identified the soggy, decaying digits as the remains of this particular saint is beyond us (heck, who this particular saint even was is beyond us), but they felt sure enough to build a church commemorating the relic's landing. The bones have since been lost, but the church remains: a poetic stone structure at the water's edge, with a

OSTELLO CINQUE TERRE MANAROLA $$

V. Riccobaldi 21, Manarola ☎331 5471593 www.hostel5terre.com/manarola.html

☎0187 920039, when closed

The Cinque Terre consists of five relatively small and immensely popular towns precariously erected on the craggy Italian shoreline—not the most auspicious location for budget accommodations. With that in mind, a €25 bed located within the limits of one of the cities (thus eliminating long train rides and restrictive curfews) can get away with quite a lot. Weigh the benefits of this hostel's prime Manarola location against the not-so-convenient spotty Wi-Fi, sparse outlets, and tepid atmosphere. Chances are you'll be spending most of your time gorging on seafood or working on your tan anyway, so suck it up and book away—just be sure to bring shower shoes.

i From the Manarola train station, take tunnel to the village center and turn right up the hill. Follow the road to the church square; turn left at the church, and the hostel is the large green building behind the church. Dorms from €25. Twins from €70. Quads from €108. Reception open daily 8am-noon, 4-8pm. Check-in 10am-1pm, 4pm-8pm. Check-out 10am. Daily lockout from 10am-noon.

dim, no-frills interior that befits a swashbuckling maritime town. Take a seat inside before staggering up the trail from Vernazza to Monterosso—the start of the trail is a little ways behind the church.

i Built right at the edge of the water; walk from the Vernazza train to the harbor, and the church will be on the right. Free. Open M-Sa Mass 5:30pm and 6pm, Su Mass 11am, 3:30pm, 5:30pm, and 6pm.

FOOD

Regional foods include pesto, focaccia, and seafood.

◙ GASTRONOMIA SAN MARTINO $

V. S. Martino, 3, Monterosso al Mare ☎338 5699017

Don't be fooled by the low prices and plastic cutlery—this restaurant is fully entitled to the "Gastronomia" in its name. Just behind the not-even-in-your-wild-est-dreams fine dining institutions of the Cinque Terre's most touristy town, this family operation serves really good food (like, really good) for €6-10. The menu changes daily and draws heavily from local ingredients, including trofie with pesto (€6) and tagliatelle in seafood sauce (€9). The interior is sweltering (forget what the meditative chef intones about "heat as a frame of mind"), so you'll want to wait for an outdoor table or get your food to go and nom on the beach.

i From P. Garibaldi, take V. Fegina (which turns into V. Roma) away from the shore, turn left toward V. Emanuele, then take a right onto V. Emanuele; the destination is on the left. Plates €6-10. Cash only. Open M-F 10am-3pm and 6-9:30pm, Sa 10am-3pm and 6-10pm, Su 10am-3pm and 6-9:30pm.

IL PESCATO CUCINATO $

V. Colombo 199, Riomaggiore ☎339 262 4815

Tourists meandering up V. Colombo clutching brown paper cones precede this popular friggitoria. Fish 'n chips in the Cinque Terre means fries with a medley of freshly-caught sea critters that include calamari, shrimp, mussels, anchovies, and cod. At Il Pescato, whatever they haul in from the sea that morning gets fried up and served in piping hot small (€5) or large (€7) cones. If the sight of whole

italy

battered fishies will bother you as you fork down steaming calamari, you might ask to hold the anchovies.

i Riomaggiore. From P. Vignaiole, walk up V. Colombo 1min.; destination is on the left. Large €7, small €5. Cards only. Open daily 11:30am-8:30pm.

LUNCH BOX $

V. Roma 34, Vernazza ☎338 908 2841

If the Italian staples of pasta and bread have got your insides all gummed up, pop in here for a quick detox—but one that actually tastes good. Fresh salads (€5-7) and customizable green juices (€3.5-5), coupled with tanned tourist clientele in board shorts and aviators, will have you thinking you're in a SoCal juice bar until the genial couple in charge properly orients you with the very Italian exhortation to eat more. If embarking on the 2 ½ hour-long hike from Vernazza to Monterosso, grab a panino (€3.5-7) for the trail.

i Vernazza. Walk down V. Roma and the destination is on the left up a few stone stairs. Panini €3.50-7. Salad €5-7. Fresh juice €3.50-5.

NIGHTLIFE

The best nightlife can be found in Riomaggiore and Monterosso.

BAR CENTRALE

V. Colombo, 144, Riomaggiore ☎0187 76 00 75

If not completely KO'd from hitting the trails all day, knock back a few at the Cinque Terre's best attempt at nightlife. Bar Centrale is a bit of a tourist institution, known for being among the area's most lively watering holes, with a prime people-watching location on Riomaggiore's main road. Open from 7am onwards, this bar also serves coffee, gelato, and shamelessly Americanized Italian food. Rest assured, though—this is first and foremost a bar, and the booze flows freely throughout the day, so enjoy a shot of tequila with your morning pancakes (if it's ever possible to enjoy tequila).

i Riomaggiore. From P. Vignaioli, head up V. Colombo and the destination is on the left. Drinks €6. Open daily 7am-1am.

ESSENTIALS

Practicalities

- **TOURIST OFFICES:** Found at the train station for each city and La Spezia. (www.parconazionale5terre.it)

manarola

Manarola has a reputation for being the town without a reputation—it can't claim a superlative like "prettiest" (Vernazza) or "most locals" (Riomaggiore). Perhaps for that reason, this middling middle child feels a bit less crowded than the others (excepting Corniglia, but those 365 stairs up are just ridiculous). To escape the tourist jam, try Manarola's easy-on-the-eyes, easy-on-the-thighs Vineyard Walk. Hoof it to the upper end of the town, which flattens out at the Church of San Lorenzo square; the start of the walk is marked with a wooden railing a few feet below the church. The neat dirt path wends its way through local gardens, providing superb views of the town and, as you go further, the sea. Soothe any scrapes with aloe plucked along the trail, and admire the grapes that make the region's famous white wine. The trail ends at a fork: right takes you to Corniglia, and the sharp left brings you to a shady playground and nearby graveyard with some of the best views of Manarola.

cinque terre

- **POST OFFICES:** Riomaggiore (V. Pecunia, 7), Manarola (V. Discovolo, 216), Corniglia (V. della Stazione, 5), Vernazza (V. Gavino, 30), Monterosso (V. Roma, 73).

Emergency

- **HOSPITALS:** The nearest hospital is in Levanto. (V. Nuestra Senora della Guardia ☎800409)
- **POLICE:** Station in Monterosso. (V. Buranco, 64)

Getting Around

The Cinque Terre consists of five cities along the coast, each about a 10min. train ride from one to the next (or a 2hr. Hike, although that varies depending on the hike). The islands are, in order from south to north: Riomaggiore (the biggest island with the highest concentration of locals), Manarola (middling, has a little bit of everything), Corniglia (the smallest and highest island—you have to climb 365 steps to get it—famous for itswine), Vernazza (supposedly the prettiest), and Monterosso al Mare (the flattest of the islands and home to the best beaches).

The best way to see the Cinque Terre is to hike it on the many sentieri, or footpaths. The blue paths (coastal paths or sentiero azzurro) are part of the CT National Park and run right along the coast; they are also generally shorter and easier (30min.-2hr., €7.50 for one day). Footpath 2 (from Riomaggiore to Corniglia, one of the most popular and easy, nicknamed Lover's Lane) is currently closed due to landslides. The red paths are free but longer (2-4hr.) and take you further from the coast into the mountains.

The Cinque Terre Pass gets you unlimited train travel between villages (and La Spezia in the south and Levanto in the north—useful if you're staying in the cheaper accommodations of either), access to blue trails, and use of ATC buses within villages. Validate your card only once, when you take your first train ride. Does not include boat access. (1-day €16, 2-day €29, 3-day €41.) Trains runs until around midnight and cost €4 one-way without a pass. Buses run within each village but have limited routes, €2 one-way.

There are also ferries that run between the villages (except Corniglia because no water access), apparently they provide nice views of the towns from the front, not affiliated with the national park. Day pass 32euro per person.

turin

The engine of the Piedmont region and the former capital of the country, Turin nevertheless is not a terribly well-worn tourist stomping ground. Still, its world-class museums (which blessedly shy away from Italy's standard depictions of ugly medieval babies in favor of more interesting subjects like Egypt and cinema), markets (1kg of white peaches for €2, anyone?), and mysterious religious relics (you might say, shrouded in mystery) make it well worth a visit. The numerous universities keep the city's arteries pumping with students and their bars and clubs, and the wide, posh avenues give Turin a reputation for being the most French or Austrian of Italian cities. Also, expect a generous smattering of dog-lovers (we might have entered a promising cafe, only to find it serving exorbitantly priced treats for our canine friends). Below are some tips for tourin' Turin.

SIGHTS

Museums are usually closed on Mondays; free entrance 1st Sunday of the month. Save money with the Torino + Piemonte Card, which gives free or discounted access to various sights and public transportation in Torino and the larger Piemonte area. On sale in tourist information offices and online. Any Torino + Piemonte card can

park it right there

Sprawling industrial metropolis though it may be, Turin nevertheless invests in beauty beyond its ornate palaces and makes space for the green stuff with numerous city parks. Two of the most interesting are the Parco del Valentino and the Parco Dora. The former is a long, skinny number that stretches the whole length of the San Salvario neighborhood. Concealed in its verdant embrace are a baroque castle (Castello del Valentino) and a model of a medieval village, but the park is most prominently advertised as the city's best smooching locale, either for its secluded pockets of rustic charm or its name's association with a certain sickly sweet holiday. The climbing vines and bold street art of Parco Dora blanket the concrete and rust red skeleton of a defunct Fiat and Michelin factory. Part of the old roof remains, providing a wide shady space complete with a skate park at one end. Otherwise, the park resembles the set of Maze Runner, with bladed columns towering over rough graffiti-scrawled shelters in which teens do sketchy things.

be combined with the Pass of the Tourist Services (€6) that lasts three days and gives free access to the panoramic lift in Mole Antonelliana (€7, or €5 with student discount), boats on the River Po, and some shuttles and trains. Purchase at tourist office or online.

MOLE ANTONELLIANA AND CINEMA MUSEUM

V. Montebello, 20 ☎011 8138 563 www.museocinema.it/museo.php

The Eiffel Tower of Turin is the Mole (pronounced MOL-ay) Antonelliana, whose distinctive narwhal-esque silhouette dominates the skyline. Originally intended as a synagogue, the cavernous dome instead became a celebrated national museum dedicated to cinema. The religious intentions of its shell permeate the museum's design: the yawning central chamber is referred to as "Temple Hall" and is arrayed with luxurious reclining seats of plush movie theater red, which proffer their occupants before a flickering screen overhead. Around Temple Hall are ten "chapels," each dedicated to a different moment in cinema history. For example, a tasteful recreation of "Caffe Turin" shows Italian films. For "Love and Death," a sensuous bedchamber with red silk hangings, has visitors lie on velvety cushions and view clips of various romance films in the supine. In a zany tribute to absurdity in film, The Phantom of Liberty plays on loop before rows of those iconic toilet seat chairs, all in a giant refrigerator. The upper floors present interactive exhibits on optical illusions, shadow play, sets, costumes, etc. Running through the middle of the Mole is a great glass elevator, which shuttles visitors to an open-air observation deck. Ease back into reality by enjoying 360-degree views of the old city.

i 10min. from P. Castello; turn right onto V. Giuseppe Verdi and left onto V. Montebello; destination on right. Museum €10, students €8. Lift €7, students €5. Combined ticket €14, students €11. Open M 9am-8pm, W-F 9am-8pm, Sa 9a-11pm, Su 9am-8pm.

CATTEDRALE DI SAN GIOVANNI BATTISTA AND MUSEO DELLA SINDONE

V. XX Settembre, 87 (church) ☎011 436 1540 www.duomoditorino.it/en
V. San Domenico 28 (museum) ☎0114365832 www.sindone.it

Behold, one of Christendom's most prominent and controversial relics. Well, you can't actually behold the supposed burial shroud of Jesus Christ (also called the Shroud of Turin), seeing as it's locked away in a fancy climate-controlled box in the Turin Duomo, presented for public veneration once in an undisclosed blue moon. Nevertheless, pilgrims daily flock to the cathedral, praying and

TOMATO BACKPACKERS HOTEL $$

V. S. Pellico 11   ☎011 020 9400 www.tomato.to.it

This is the city's most centrally located hostel, a mere 10min. walk from the Porta Nuovo train station, in the newly fashionable San Salvario neighborhood alongside the skinny Parco Valentino that hugs the Po River. You'll appreciate the convenient location when stumbling back late at night after visiting one (or two, or three) of the many bars in the area. The white rooms are cool, clean refuges from the broiling Turin heat, and the common area and garden on the ground floor provide similar respite from excessively chatty bunkmates.

i From Central Station, walk 4 blocks south on Corso Vittorio Emanuele II, turn right onto V. Principe Tommaso, continue 4 blocks on V. Principe Tommaso, and turn left onto V. Silvio Pellico. Dorms from €25. Singles from €38. Doubles from €61. Laundry €4. Reception open 8am-midnight. Check-in 4pm. Check-out noon.

BAMBOO ECO HOSTEL $$

Corso Palermo 90/d   ☎011 235084 www.bambooecohostel.it

This hostel can be summed up by its name. Bamboo is the aesthetic of choice, from the decals on the front windows to the stumps dangling from the room keys. Touting their numerous sustainability awards, the obliging staff adorns the communal kitchen and bathroom walls with friendly reminders to shut off the water and lights. The rooms, similarly decorated with exhortations to save electricity, feature rows of sturdy, unvarnished pine bunks, done over in sheets that very much feel reused (but clean). Complimentary breakfast includes soymilk and organic breads; thankfully, Nutella is deemed sufficiently sustainable and is included in the spread.

i Dorms from €22. Doubles €60. Check-in 3-7pm. Check-out 11am. 10min. bus ride to city center (#4, 18, 27, or 57) or 20-25min. walking. From Porta Nuova Train Station, take tram 4.

OPEN011 $

Corso Venezia, 11   ☎011 250535

Think hospital or Sunday school for a Korean mega church, neither of which are pleasant prospects. This hostel, more popular with businessmen than backpackers, features a clean, no-frills interior obstinately devoted to an odd, orange-and-green color scheme. Two major downsides are the common room-only Wi-Fi and the location way up in the northern outskirts of the city, but if you're looking for last minute, under-€30 accommodation, this is your best bet.

i From Dora train station, head up V. Errico Giachino, take a slight right to stay on V. Errico Giachino (changes into Corso Venezia), and the destination is on the left. Dorms from €24. Breakfast €2.50. Reception open 24hr. Check-in 3:30-10pm. Check-out 10am.

italy

swooning before the shroud's ornate container. For the rather less faithful and/or imaginative, the Museum of the Holy Shroud, a 10min. walk from the church, helpfully features a full-sized reproduction of the concealed cloth, as well as comprehensive historical background, from its discovery in the early 1400s to the many photographic experiments intended to prove its legitimacy. Religious or not, the mystery surrounding the shroud is intriguing: What could account for the corpse of Christ—or any corpse—leaving an imprint on cloth? Does the shroud enable us to construct and behold the face of God? Let us know what you think.

i Museum €6, students €5. Church free. Museum open daily 9am-noon and 3-7pm. Church open daily 8am-12:30pm and 3-7pm.

CONVENTO DEL MONTE DEI CAPPUCCINI

Ple. Monte dei Cappuccini, 3 ☎0116604414 www.cappuccinipiemonte.it

Directly across the river from P. Vittorio Veneto, albeit atop a rather steep hill, is this secluded church, mostly unmolested by tourists or locals out for a morning dog walk. The 20min. hike up is somewhat strenuous but blessedly shady, and the summit hosts a spigot to replenish depleted bodily water levels recently spent as sweat. Eye-level with the few high rises of the city, take in the spread of rooftops beneath your feet until you almost feel a curl of smoke rising from the roasting exposed scalp of your hair part; the slender wooden cross beside you provides scant shade. Retreat to the surprisingly small interior of the chapel, which possesses the standard church fare: elaborate marble altars, painted domes, and good acoustics.

i About a 15min. walk from P. Vittorio Veneto; cross Ponte Vittorio Emanuele I, turn right onto Corso Moncalieri, left onto V. Vittorio Amedeo Gioanetti; then turn right toward V. Gaetano Ettore Giardino and follow until it turns into Salita al C.A.I. Torino, then take a sharp left to stay on Salita al C.A.I. Torino and follow to Ple. Monte dei Cappuccini. Free. Lookout open 24hr.

GALLERIA CIVICA D'ARTE MODERNA (GAM)

V. Magenta, 31 ☎011 4429518 www.gamtorino.it/it

Perhaps to maintain its self-proclaimed alternative street cred or perhaps because it couldn't secure any of the treasures of the Renaissance, Turin is a patron of modern art, and the Galleria Civica d'Arte Moderna is its flagship. Rebuilt in 1959 after heavy bombing during WWII, the imposing concrete structure wears modernness on its sleeve, from its slanted orientation along the sun's zenith course over Turin (intended to challenge the city's rigid grid layout) to the exterior lettering declaring "All Art Has Been Contemporary." The featured works, ranging from 18th-century canvases to a few Picassos and Warhols, are somewhat forcefully arranged according to four themes: infinity, velocity, ethics, and nature. For those puzzling over the lengthy and pretentious exhibit descriptions, you'll appreciate the work Spatial Concept by Lucia Fontana, done in "oil, tears and graffiti on white canvas"—we feel your pain, Lucy. Be sure to catch the quirky doodles by Nedko Solakov, dubbed Eight Ceilings, done on the ceilings of the museum's staircases, and the video archive in the basement, which screens the short film The Well Shaven Cactus by Ger Van Elk (portraying, obviously, a cactus getting the shave of its life that subsequently ends its life).

i From Re Umberto metro stop, head down Corso Vittorio Emanuele II, turn left onto Corso Re Umberto, right onto Corso Vittorio Emanuele II, left onto Corso Galileo Ferraris, and right onto V. Magenta; destination on left. €10, €8 for students. Free 1st Tu of the month. Open Tu-Su 11am-7pm. Ticket office closes at 6pm.

FOOD

Restaurants and cafes are usually closed on Sundays.

🍴 CURRY & CO $

V. Verdi 45/a ☎3932760383

A troupe of unironically bandanna-ed Italians on a mission to share their Southeast Asian fetish with the world—in the form of inexpensive Thai takeout, all the better to corner the student market from the nearby University of Turin. Choose from four types of curry (€4.50) or daily specials like pad Thai (€5) and yaki udon (€5); vegetarian and vegan options are also available. Scan the National Geographic-style pictures of Thailand's spice markets on the walls as you listen to the crackle of something fabulous getting stir-fried. If still not convinced of this place's quality, get a whiff of the peppery condiments wheeling formidably by on a Lazy Susan. Heck, they even offer chopsticks.

i *From P. Vittorio Veneto, turn right onto V. Giulia di Barolo, left onto V. Giuseppe Verdi, and destination is on the right. Curry with noodles or rice €4.50, specials €3.50-5. Open M 11am-4pm, Tu-F 11am-4pm and 7-9:45pm.*

🥪 L'ACCADEMIA DEL PANINO $$

V. Sant'Ottavio 27 ☎011 19694708 www.accademiadelpanino.com

Widely renowned as one of the city's best paninoteche, this unassuming shop offers over 60 varieties of simple but hearty sandwiches. The menu is in Italian, but the free Wi-Fi makes it so you can translate, and then Google, all the esoteric cheeses. Peer around stacks of chewy, floured bread to place your order with the jovial shop owners, who deftly construct panino after panino at lightening speed. Best of all, most options will cost you a mere €2.50-5.

i *From the University of Turin, head down V. Giuseppe Verdi, turn left onto V. Sant'Ottavio, and the destination is on the left. Panini from €2.50-17 (most are €2.50-5). Cash only for purchases under €10. Open M-F 8am-6pm, Sa 10am-3:30pm.*

POOR MANGER $

V. Maria Vittoria 32/D ☎388 942 6771 www.poormanger.it

"Baby, you're all that I want / When you're lyin' here in my arms / I'm findin' it hard to believe / We're in heaven," Bryan Adams croons overhead as part of this joint's clutch playlist. When your steaming baked potato (€5-8) heaped with cheese and cured meats is placed in front of you, you'll find yourself mouthing the same sweet words between bites. "Poor eating?" Feh! The wealthy don't know what they're missing or are also here, seated at the creaky wooden tables alongside boisterous college youths.

i *From the National Cinema Museum, head down V. Alessandro Riberi, turn right onto V. Giuseppe Verdi, left onto V. Montebello (which turn into V. S. Massimo), and left onto V. Maria Vittoria; destination on right. Dressed baked potatoes from €5-8. Cash only. Open daily noon-3pm and 7:15-11pm.*

SOUP & GO $

V. San Dalmazzo 8/A ☎011 19887604 www.soupandgo.it

The vibe of this soup shop is wooden porch furniture, tousled potted plants, and bespectacled university students. The rusticity preserves the authenticity of the place, so it just avoids teetering over the edge from committed organic eatery to pretentious haunt of Instagramming college students. Select from four seasonal soups, served in squat jam jars, and/or the verdant pickings of a self-serve salad bar; one portion of either starts from €5.50. As expected, the staff also offers organic juices (€2) and is generous with free bread and condiments.

i *From P. Castello, turn right onto V. Giuseppe Barbaroux, then right onto V. S. Dalmazzo. Soups from €5.50. Salads from €5.50. Open M noon-3pm, Tu-Sa noon-10pm, Su noon-3pm and 7-10pm.*

GELATERIA POPOLARE $

V. Borgo Dora 3 ☎348 670 8713 www.gelateriapopolare.it

Something fresh to clean the dust of the ages from your mouth after haggling over antiques at the V. Borgo Dora flea market. Catch the acoustic Italian folk music issuing from this crowded gelateria. The pierced and tattooed ice cream scoopers are going for a countercultural, '60s vibe, with the full text of Martin Luther King, Jr.'s "I Have a Dream" speech and a printout of John Lennon framed on the walls. The flavors are seasonal and prepared from all-natural ingredients, which are proudly detailed on the menu.

i *Located at the very end of V. Borgo Dora. Gelato €2-3.50. Granita from €2. Open daily noon-11pm (later in summer).*

a pear of markets

The northern end of the old city is open market territory! The Piazza della Repubblica daily hosts the Mercato di Porta Palazzo: a sprawling oasis of stand after stand of fresh produce, where the going rate is roughly €1 per kilo of fruit. Pyramids of peaches and heaps of mint perfume the air, which is suffocatingly warm by the time the market closes around noon (on Saturdays, sales don't stop until 6pm). Once you extract yourself from yet another fruit stand, arms laden with produce, you might breeze through pop-up shops peddling the inedible, from dog accessories (this city is dog-obsessed) to tacky clothing. A few minutes further north takes you to the rather shabbier V. Borgo Dora, which on Saturdays is a street-long flea market offering furniture, art, clothing, and jewelry. Every second Sunday of the month is the Grand Balon flea market: don't miss this sale of antiques and vintage goods on a grand scale.

NIGHTLIFE

⚑ ASTORIA

V. Berthollet 13   ☎3897663731 www.astoria-studios.com

"This place is so cool!" "... I know." We felt our faux pas as severely as the kick from our extremely alcoholic cocktail—never admit admiration to a waitress with blunt bangs and gauges. Such are the games you play at this alternative watering hole. Dispassionately sip your drink, the contents of which could easily remove a layer of said waitress's nail polish (black, obviously), and sink deeper into a deliciously gloomy mood prompted by the indie folk rock playing overhead. Excepting the summer months, the basement beneath the bar is open as a concert venue and breathless dance floor.

i *From Porta Nuova train station, head toward P. Carlo Felice, turn left onto Corso Vittorio Emanuele II, right onto V. Goito, and left onto V. Berthollet; destination on left. Drinks €7-8. Beer €3-4. Shots €2.*

HIROSHIMA MON AMOUR

V. Bossoli 83   ☎011 3176636 www.hiroshimamonamour.org

Named for the groundbreaking 1959 film that launched the French New Wave, this self-proclaimed "cultural association" similarly defies categorization. Hiroshima Mon Amour is a rock club, an art gallery, a comedy venue, a concert hall, a discotheque, a hub of cultural events, and a magnet for local and international artists alike. Check the website for the packed schedule of upcoming events, many of which require you to buy tickets in advance. Discounts are available for guests at the nearby Ostello Torino, and free drinks are pressed on all who arrive by bike.

i *From the Torino Lingotto stop, walk down V. Carlo Bossoli, pass through the roundabout, and the destination is on the right. Prices vary. Hours vary.*

CAFÉ DES ARTS

V. P. Amedeo N. 33/F   ☎339 3630945

Café des Arts is, literally, a cafe dedicated to the arts, from the painting of a giant snail by a local artist exhibited on the wall to the live bands featured every Thursday night on the little stage in the back room. Though the joint attracts its fair share of grandfathers in for the €1 coffee and complimentary helping of gossip, evening sees the cafe transformed into a hipster jazz haunt. Follow the

turin

advice of Bob Marley and the Wailers warbling their bit on the running jazz and blues soundtrack: order a drink or two and "Simmer Down!"

i From National Cinema Museum, head toward V. Giuseppe Verdi, turn right onto V. Giuseppe Verdi, left onto V. Montebello (turns into V. S. Massimo), and left onto V. Principe Amedeo; destination on left. Drinks €2-6. Wine €3-4. Coffee €1. Open M-Sa 7:30am-midnight, Su 9am-8pm.

THE BEACH

V. Murazzi del Po, 22   ☎392 288 3024 www.thebeachmurazzi.it

Extensive busing to the shores of the Mediterranean not required—this club is so dubbed for its location on the bank of the River Po, in the thick of the frenetic nightlife around P. Vittorio Veneto. This is a quintessential club of the sort every teenager dreams of attending, until they actually do and realize that getting sloshy with strangers isn't all that fun, and the weird male-female courtship/power dynamics give them the fantods. Needless to say, we joined the cluster of sensitive losers chatting in the corner. If you're cooler than us (and it would be difficult not to be), whip out your sheer tops and ripped jeans and bob about on one of Turin's most popular dance floors.

i From P. Vittorio Veneto, head toward the River Po; at the bridge (Ponte Vittorio Emanuele I), take the stairs on the left down to bank of river; destination on left. Drinks €6. Open F-Sa 11pm-4:30am.

ESSENTIALS

Practicalities

- **TOURIST OFFICES:** Ufficio del Turismo. (P. Carlo Felice Torino. ☎011535181 www.turismotorino.org. Open daily 9am-6pm.) Another major tourist office is located on V. Garibaldi Torino in P. Castello.

- **ATMS:** Located throughout city.

- **POST OFFICES:** Turin's main post office (V. Alfieri 10) is located just west of P. San Carlo at V. Alfieri 10 (☎011 506 0265). Open M-F 8:30am-6:30pm, Sa 8:30am-noon. A list of central post offices and opening times can be found at www.quartieri.torino.it.

- **BATHROOMS:** Public restroom can be found at train stations.

- **WATER:** Tap water potable. Spigots around city.

Emergency

- **HOSPITALS:** Call ☎118 for emergencies. Ospedale Mauriziano Umberto I. (Largo Filippo Turati 62. ☎011 508 1111 www.mauriziano.it. Open 24hr.

- **POLICE:** ☎112 (carabinieri), ☎113 (local police). Central police headquarters located at Questura Torino near Stazione di Porta Susa. (Corso Vinzaglio 10 ☎011 55 881. Open M 9am-1pm, Tu 9am-1pm and 3-6pm, W-F 9am-1pm.) 24hr. police headquarters located at V. Grattoni 3 (☎011 558 8615 640).

Getting Around

Most people get around Turin on foot, although public transportation (run by GTT) is available. The metro, trams, and buses all take same ticket (90min. urban ticket €1.50, urban + suburban €1.70, carnet of 5 tickets €6.50). Tickets valid for 4hr. from validation (between 9am and 8pm) is €3, a daily ticket is €5 (urban and suburban), 2-day tickets are €7.50, 3-day €10. Buy tickets at any tobacconist, newspaper shop, or machine in metro stations. You need to validate on board; If found on public transport without a ticket, the fine is €25.

Bus and tram lines run from roughly 5am-midnight. The night service on weekends (including Friday) is called "Night Buster" and runs from the central bus terminal in P. Vittorio Veneto (stops close to main nightlife), ending around 1am on Sundays. The metro runs daily from approx. 6am-midnight.

Taxis cost €3.50 to start and then €1.44/km (€2.50 after 10pm). A ride between the city and airport costs a flat rate of €34.

venice

Venezia or Veniceland? City of intrigue, of loving by lamplight, of fading frescoes and Persian arches fronted by jade-green waters, of leathery artisans shaping glass and weaving lace, of laundry fluttering drowsily before pastel shutters, of children tripping over soccer balls? Or, oversized amusement park of kitschy knick-knack vendors, of cigarette butts caught between cobblestones, of cruise ships, of vaporetti stops clinging barnacle-like to riverbanks, of gondolas for hire? The longest lasting independent republic in history, once the customs house between East and West, the fiercely patriotic birthplace of the grandest parties and a regional tongue? Or, soon-to-be ghost town, pushing residents to the mainland with tourist traffic and high prices, and peddling glass beads, canals, and its very history until its last breath? Wander, get lost, stop for gelato, and decide for yourself. Whatever you do, pity the postmen.

ORIENTATION

Venice consists of anywhere from 116 to 124 islands (apparently no one has done an official count) connected by 428 bridges. To make some sense of this fish-shaped labyrinth, Venetians divide their city into six sestieri (neighborhoods): Cannaregio in the north, Santa Croce in the west, San Polo in the center, San Marco just below San Polo, Dorsoduro in the south, and Castello at the eastern tail end. Addresses are formulated not with street names but with the sestieri followed by a number from 1 to 7000. Tell which sestieri you're in by looking at street lamps—each bears a small white card below the shade with the sestieri initials.

ACCOMMODATIONS

GENERATOR VENICE $$
Fondamenta della Croce, 84-86, Giudecca   https://generatorhostels.com

If Urban Outfitters had a hostel line (they might as well at this point—what don't they sell?), this would be its flagship location. The only true hostel in the city itself, Generator's enormous common space is decked out in mismatched armchairs, psychedelic wallpaper, and avant-garde chandeliers. Guests—mostly of the youthful variety, hoisting oversized packs and bobbing along to Spotify jams—snake around the bar in the center of the lobby or seriously suck at pool. The location on the secluded Giudecca island five minutes from San Marco Square is a mixed bag: on the one hand, you'll have to take the vaporetti between Generator and the main island. On the other, the odd tourist bachelor party still going strong won't wake you up at 2am. Key card room access and lockers keep your valuables safe from whoever you just schooled at pool.

i Located on Giudecca Island (take a 5min. boat ride across the bay from Zaccaria to Zitelle, then walk 3min. along the waterfront; destination is on the left marked with lightning bolt decals. Dorms from €18. Private rooms from €42. Reception open 24hr. Check-in 2pm. Check-out 10am.

PLUS CAMPING JOLLY, VENICE $$
V. G. de Marchi, 7   ☎04 192 0312 http://plushostels.com/it/pluscampingjolly

For those of you who believe that accommodations are places to crash for the night and maybe splash your armpits once every three days, camping outside of Venice is the way to go. Tents at Camping Jolly are as low as a third of the

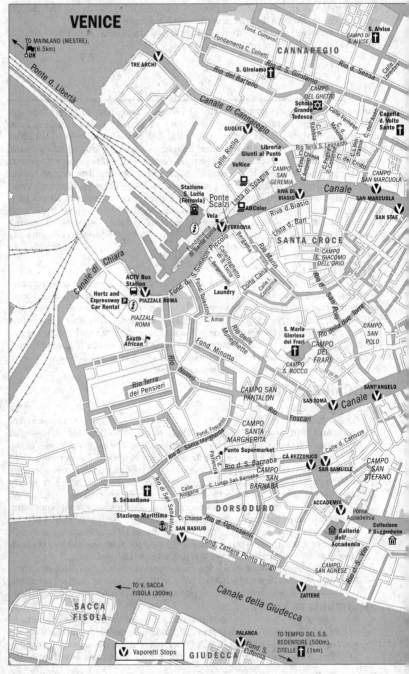

VENICE

TO MAINLAND (MESTRE), (6.5km)
DUK

Ponte d. Libertà

Canale di Cannaregio

TRE ARCHI

Fond. Contarini

Fondamenta C. Colletti

CANNAREGIO

Rio d. S. Girolamo

S. Girolamo

Rio del Battello

Rio d. Sensa

Calle Loretan

S. Alvise
CAMPO DI
S. ALVISE

Schola
Grande
Tedesca

CAMPO
DEL GHETTO

Calle Farnese

Calle d. Rabbia

C. d. Masena

C. d'Italia
C. d'Orbens

Capella
d. Volto
Santo

GUGLIE

Calle Riello

Libreria
Giunti al Punto

VeNice

Rio Terra S. Leonardo

C. Vari
C. Priuli

C. Pesaro
C. Colonne

CAMPO
SAN MARCUOLA

C. Emo
C. Chiesa

C. del Cristo

Stazione
S. Lucia
(Ferrovia)

Ponte
Scalzi

Lista di Spagna

CAMPO
SAN
GEREMIA

RIVA DI
BIASIO

Canale

SAN MARCUOLA

Vela

ABColor

Riva d. Biasio

SAN STAE

i

FERROVIA

Bergama

Lista d. Bari

Fondamenta
di Santa Lucia

Fond. d. S. Simeon Piccolo

C. Calle Bergama
C. Bergamasco

Rio Marin

SANTA CROCE

CAMPO
S. GIACOMO
DELL'ORIO

Canale di Chiara

ACTV Bus
Station

PIAZZALE ROMA

Corte Canal

Calle 1.
Contarina

Rio d. San Polo

Hertz and
Expressway
Car Rental

i

PIAZZALE
ROMA

Fond. d. Tolentini

Laundry

Rio della due Torre

CAMPO
SAN
POLO

South
African

C. Amai

Rio delle
Munighette

S. Maria
Gloriosa
dei Frari

CAMPO
DEI
FRARI

Fond. Minotto

Rio Nuova

Rio Terra
dei Pensieri

CAMPO SAN
PANTALON

CAMPO S. ROCCO

Rio
Foscari

SAN TOMÀ

Canale

SANT'ANGELO

Fond. Foscarini

CAMPO
SANTA
MARGHERITA

Rio d. Santa Margherita

C. d.
Pazienza

Punto Supermarket

Rio d. S. Barnaba

Calle d. Carrozze

Calle
Avogaria

C. Lunga San Barnaba

CAMPO
SAN
BARNABA

CÀ REZZONICO

SAN SAMUELE

CAMPO
SAN
STEFANO

Rio di San Sebastiano

S. Sebastiano

S. Basilio

C. Chiesa

DORSODURO

Rio d. Ognissanti

ACCADEMIA

Ponte
Accademia

Stazione Marittima

SAN BASILIO

C. Chiesa

Gallerie
dell'
Accademia

Collezione
P. Guggenheim

Fond. Zattere Ponto Lungo

Rio d. S. Vio

CAMPO
SAN AGNESE

TO V. SACCA
FISOLA (300m)

SACCA
FISOLA

Canale della Giudecca

ZATTERE

PALANCA

Fond. S.
Eufemia

TO TEMPIO DEL S.S.
REDENTORE (500m),
ZITELLE (1km)

V Vaporetti Stops

GIUDECCA

italy

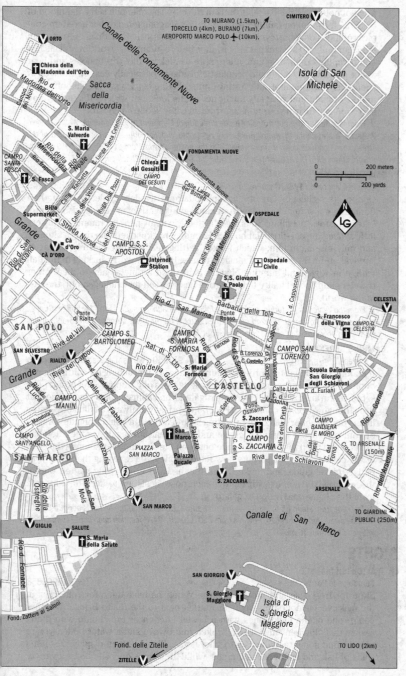

TO MURANO (1.5km),
TORCELLO (4km), BURANO (7km),
AEROPORTO MARCO POLO (10km),

CIMITERO

ORTO

Canale delle Fondamente Nuove

Isola di San
Michele

Chiesa della
Madonna dell'Orto

Sacca
della
Misericordia

S. Maria
Valverde

FONDAMENTA NUOVE

Chiesa
del Gesuiti
CAMPO
DEI GESUITI

CAMPO
SANTA
FOSCA

S. Fosca

0   200 meters

0   200 yards

Billa
Supermarket

Strada Nuova

OSPEDALE

CÀ
D'ORO

CÀ
D'ORO

CAMPO S.S.
APOSTOLI

Internet
Station

Ospedale
Civile

Grande

S.S. Giovanni
e Paolo

CELESTIA

Rio d. San Marina

Barbaria delle Tole

S. Francesco
della Vigna
CAMPO DI
CELESTIA

SAN POLO

Ponte
di Rialto

Ponte
Rosso

SAN SILVESTRO

RIALTO

CAMPO S.
BARTOLOMEO

CAMPO
S. MARIA
FORMOSA

CAMPO SAN
LORENZO

Grande

Riva del Vin

Riva del Carbon

Rio della Guerra

S. Maria
Formosa

Scuola Dalmata
San Giorgio
degli Schiavoni

CASTELLO

CAMPO
MANIN

CAMPO
SANT'ANGELO

Fond
Osmarin

S. Zaccaria

CAMPO
BANDIERA
E MORO

TO ARSENALE
(150m)

SAN MARCO

PIAZZA
SAN MARCO

San
Marco

Palazzo
Ducale

S. S. Provolo

CAMPO
S. ZACCARIA

Riva   degli   Schiavoni

S. ZACCARIA

ARSENALE

SAN MARCO

TO GIARDINI
PUBLICI (250m)

Canale   di   San   Marco

GIGLIO

SALUTE

S. Maria
della Salute

SAN GIORGIO

S. Giorgio
Maggiore

Isola di
S. Giorgio
Maggiore

TO LIDO (2km)

Fond. Zattere al Saloni

Fond. delle Zitelle

ZITELLE

venice

price of bottom-of-the-barrel hostels in the city. The clientele is the definition of eclectic, from full-on families driving station wagons to edgy, leathered-up couples rolling in on motorcycles to the standard American, Canadian, or Australian teenager making the backpacking rounds before joining the workforce. This last demographic dominates, and you're sure to pick up day trip buddies and hear about past lives of mundane scholastic drudgery heroically cast off in favor of spontaneity and alcohol and "testing limits." Your electricity might shut off in the middle of night and your key might not fit the lock, but with all the money you save, you can drown your housing woes in triple scoops of gelato.

i From Ple. Roma, take bus #6 going in the direction of Marghera to V. Paleocapa. Walk left down V. Beccaria and continue approx 8min. Turn right onto V. della Fonte and walk to the end of the street, then continue down a small walkway to the hostel. Dorms from €12.90 (tent), €19 (cabin). Privates from €45. Reception open 8am-midnight. Check-in 2pm. Check-out 10am.

SMARTHOLIDAY $$$
Calle Dell'Anconeta 1981, Cannaregio ☎327 331 1249

One of the cheapest in-city accommodations available, ideally located in Cannaregio just minutes away from canal-side nightlife and the Jewish Ghetto. Like its historic neighbor, Smartholiday has too many people crammed into very little space. The one-floor flat houses 12 budget backpackers at a time, a kitchen, and only one bathroom, which makes getting ready in the morning a sort of survival of the fittest-themed musical chairs. But don't worry, lurking in the hall with your towel and bursting bladder is as good a time as any to meet other travelers and to feel guilty that America has pressed its language upon the rest of the world.

i From the Venice train station, turn left and follow the "Rialto" sign. Cross the 1st bridge (Guglie), and just before you reach the 2nd bridge, the hostel is on the right. Mixed or female-only dorms €38. Cash only. Check-in noon-11pm. Check-out 10am.

CAMPING SERENISSIMA $
V. Padana 334/a,, SR 11 ☎041 921850 www.campingserenissima.com/en

If man-made canals and hordes of tourists have got you aching for a little nature, book a bunk under the damp, signal-blocking trees of Camping Serenissima. The setup, featuring rows of adjacent corrugated iron cabins, makes you realize that even though you can't connect to Facebook, privacy is always an illusion—listen in on your neighbor's account of getting strip searched in Milan from the comfort of your own bed. Camping is cheap and more than makes up for the €1.50 bus ticket you'll need for the 30min. ride between the site and Ple. Roma at the edge of the canals. Tell your parents how much money you're saving thanks to your budget travel guide, and make it rain for the things that really matter: one of those Carnevale masks with the five-inch nose, designed to keep doctors safe from the plague, and heaps of gelato.

i Take bus from stand B6 in Ple Roma toward Padova, Dolo, or Stra; the hostel is about a 30min. bus ride away. Dorms from €16. Privates from €20. Laundry €4. Reception open until 11pm. Check-in 2pm. Check-out 10am.

SIGHTS

▨ RIALTO FISH MARKET
Campo de la Pescaria ☎0412960658

Shop for fresh fish and produce as the Venetians have done for centuries: in the massive, cacophonous open-air market next to the Rialto Bridge. Whether you're one of the lucky ones with a hostel kitchen or the chump who didn't realize that "kitchen" meant one broken microwave and a water boiler, you're sure to find some tasty morsel to take home. Burly seamen display glistening slabs of fish and feebly stirring crabs, while the stands opposite boast a variety

of fruit that'll make the banana-apple-orange routine of your college dining hall seem like a bad dream. Bring cash and covered shoes.

i *Located right along Rialto Bridge; follow yellow signs to get to bridge. Prices vary. Cash only. Open M-Sa 7am-2pm.*

CHIESA DI SAN GIORGIO MAGGIORE AND BELL TOWER

Isola di S.Giorgio Maggiore ☎041 524 0119 http://en.turismovenezia.it/

For those of you with a hankering for high places, skip the Campanile di San Marco—the popular tower in San Marco Square—and head out to the church of San Giorgio Maggiore for better views, shorter lines, and a cheaper price tag. The tower entrance is through the church itself, but before you complain about having yet another church thrust before your sore eyes, this one is appealingly hushed, with the sacred musty smell of old libraries that'll temporarily mask your traveler's BO. The bell is accessible by elevator only, confounding your best intentions to make this leg day—no complaints here. Enjoy panoramic views of both the main and outer islands, and follow the intricate dance of vaporetti and private motorboats crisscrossing the bay. Spot the high density of foolish tourists at the foot of the tower in St. Mark's, and feel smug—until the shattering tower bell that rings every half hour suggests you return back to earth.

i *From Ple. Roma or Ferrovia, take waterbus line 2 to Isola di San Giorgio. €6, €4 students and under 26. Open Apr-Oct daily 9am-7pm, Nov-March daily 8:30am-6pm. Last entry 20min. before close. Visits suspended Su from 10:40am-noon during holy mass.*

PEGGY GUGGENHEIM MUSEUM

704 Dorsoduro ☎041 240 5411 www.guggenheim-venice.it/inglese/default.html

What did fabulously wealthy 20th-century American heiresses do with their free time (aka, their time)? If they were named Peggy Guggenheim, they purchased prime canal-front real estate in Venice, decorated it with valuable contemporary art, diddled around a bit with valuable contemporary artists, and opened their house to the public as this stunning gallery. For a respite from fresco after fresco of ugly Jesus babies, take a couple hours to soak up avant-garde snootiness and puzzle over the distinctions between Cubism, Neo-Cubism, Neo-Impressionism, Surrealism, and the dreaded Purism. Eavesdrop on gushing art devotees while privately wondering how a collection of gray squares translates into a couple dancing the ragtime. If utterly lost, read the painting descriptions that helpfully suggest emotions the works ought to inspire: for example, "The floating bells, filling the sky, evoke a feeling of uncertainty and disbelief. Yet nothing will happen: the irony of Magritte's imagery is that it implies a story that will never unfold—a narrative suspended in our imaginations." This is for a painting of, uh, floating bells. Plus one for the suspension pun.

i *Located on the Grand Canal between the Accademia Bridge and the Church of Santa Maria della Salute. €15, seniors €13, students €9. Open M 10am-6pm, W-Su 10am-6pm.*

PIAZZA SAN MARCO

P. San Marco

On occasion, the tourists get it right and flock to landmarks that are famous for good reason; the veritable tourist worship of the square dedicated to St. Mark, the patron saint of Venice, marks one such occasion. The only official square on the island, this open space makes for a welcome respite from the typical to-pography of narrow alleys, though here the canals are replaced with less swiftly flowing streams of sightseers. First among the square's treasures (which include several museums, a library, and the Doge's palace) is St. Mark's Basilica. This luxurious structure is the product of both Byzantine and Renaissance aesthetics and features mosaic domes, statues of the apostles, and an enormous bejeweled mural. St. Mark's is the lowest spot on the island and frequently floods at high tide—at night, the arches of the palace, illuminated with the soft yellow glow of

Reserve one of the days of your 72hr. vaporetti pass for a jaunt through the outer islands of the Venetian archipelago. Murano and Burano are the celebrities of the lagoon: the former is home to a number of glass forges that produce everything from cheap strings of glass beads and little hedgehog figurines to elaborate chandeliers and Bohemian horseheads priced at thousands of euro. The latter's artisan export is lace, handmade by the local grandmothers and sold in the cool white establishments of effusive saleswomen. The government regulates the coloring of buildings on Burano, so you'll skim past brilliantly colored storefronts on your way to the next lace shop. Mazzorbo and Torcello are both located along the vaporetti routes to Murano and Burano but are often skipped over, so be the intrepid traveler who disembarks on their strange shores. You'll find idyllic silence, a lone fisherman scraping barnacles off the hull of his boat, local toddlers learning to bike ride, and creaky wooden churches in which you'll be able to send your prayers upward unfettered by tourist jostling.

lamps, cast quivery reflections on the floodwaters that'll almost make you forget about rising sea levels and global warming.

i Follow posted yellow signs that will lead you to the piazza from almost anywhere on the island.

FOOD

First, a quick vocab lesson: bacari = cafe/restaurant-type joints that serve cicchetti (Venetian tapas, each €1-2) and drinks; osterie = casual, more local, less expensive restaurants, often specializing in fish.

BIGOI $

Calle Crosera, 3829   ☎80 0960 553

When your head starts spinning from hours of unsuccessful navigation through devilish Venetian streets, pop into the deliciously simple Bigoi. This casual joint features freshly made bigoli (the city's official pasta, like spaghetti but thicker) topped with one of nine sauces, each for €5. The one-woman band chef and cashier closely resembles Mary of Downton Abbey, if Lady Mary would ever deign to wear a crisp white apron and cap, and doles out substantial servings with characteristic efficiency. Snag a standing spot at the counters between sappy tourist couples and genial locals, or chow on the road.

i From Campo San Pantalon, walk down Calle San S. Pantalon and turn right onto Calle Crosera; Bigoi is on the right. Street food €5. Open daily 11:30am-10pm.

LA ZUCCA $$

S. Croce 1762   ☎041 524 1570 www.lazucca.it

Can caramelized onions change your life? At La Zucca, you bet your grossly swollen belly they can. Creative concoctions of seasonal vegetables are the name of the game here; though the menu features a few meat plates, the signature seafood of Venice is absent. The dishes themselves are difficult to decipher, unless you're very well-versed in Italian names for vegetables (our shared Latin roots are less helpful than you'd expect), but the genial waitresses will translate. Walk-ins are apologetically turned away, so reserve at least a day in advance.

i From the San Stae vaporeti stop, walk down Salizada San Stae, turn right onto Calle del Tintot, then left onto Calle dello Spezier; destination is on the left. Starters €10. Primi €9-12. Secondi €19-21. Dessert €2-8. Wine by the bottle €18-70. Open M-Sa 12:30-2:30pm, 7-10:30pm. Make reservations either in person or by phone one day in advance.

venice

GELATERIA CÀ D'ORO $
Cannaregio 4273/B   ☎036 5313 0272

Its convenient location on a crowded tourist thoroughfare might deter you, but
rest assured, you're in for an authentic scoop (or three) at this gelateria. Fat
dollops of melon and Mediterranean pistachio teach life lessons about tough
decision-making, namely, that compromising sucks—but at least you're burning
calories while getting lost, right?

i *From the Cà d'Oro vaporetti stop, walk up Calle Cà d'Oro and turn right onto Str. Nova; destina-*
tion is on the right. Gelato €1.8-4.50. Cash only. Open daily 11am-11:30pm.

PASTICCERIA TONOLO $
Calle S. Pantalon, Dorsoduro   ☎037 0449 0279

The Italian evening meal might be three massive courses drawn out well into the
night, but for breakfast, locals crowd into steamy standing room only bakeries
for a cup of coffee and a pastry to pad their paunches. The rows upon rows of
bright, geometric confections at Tonolo's are every perfectionist's dream, and
the €1 prices will shamelessly enable your stomach's urgings to not hold back
and break the fast like a boss—an obese, happy boss. Open until 8pm, there's no
need to confine your indulging to the morning, since pastries are an all-day kind
of food (right?).

i *From Campo St. Pantalon, walk down Calle St. Pantalon 1min. Pastries €1-1.20. Coffee €1-2.50.*
Wine €1-2.50. Open Tu-Sa 7:45am-8pm, Su 7:45am-1pm.

OSTERIA ALBA NOVA DALLA MARIA $$
Lista Vecchia Dei Bari, Santa Croce   ☎041 524 1353 www.osteriaalbanova.it

Eat like the Doge for plebeian prices! Tuck into Venetian classics like spaghetti
with cuttlefish in a sauce of its own ink (€14.90) or sweetbread (cow brains)

simmered in red wine (€15.80). Quirky inventions of maritime Italy share the table with more standard fare, but rest assured, this polysyllabic osteria is the culinary antithesis of its degenerate American spawn, the Olive Garden. If your wallet is feeling more plebe than Doge, skip the antipasti and select from the primi and secondi menus. Wash down your authentic Venetian meal with a glass of the regional spritz (pronounced "spreetz-ah," add hand-waving for emphasis).

i From the Riva di Biasio vaporetto stop (lines 1, 5.2, 5.1), walk away from the canal and turn left onto Lista Bari; continue for 2min. and the restaurant is on left. Antipasti €12-15. Primi €12-18. Secondi €15-18. Wine and beer €2-3. Open daily 12-2:30pm, 7-10pm.

UN MONDO DIVINO $

Cannaregio, 5984/A ☎041.5211093

Tired of polite conversation with plump, wine-and-sun-flushed tourists? Tired of conversation? Make a pit stop at this bacari, whose authenticity is verified by its clientele of the local grandpas, uniformly clad in sweater vests over polos and aviator glasses with inch-thick lenses. These are the sort of old people who, in the words of Sophie from Howl's Moving Castle, just want to "stare at the scenery." In this case, the scenery is your foreign and (hopefully) non-sweater vested self puzzling over the array of 40+ fine wines (€1.50-5 by the glass). Pair your fermented grape juice with a plate of cicchetti (€1.50-3), including marinated artichokes, sarde in saor (sardines in onion marinade), and local favorite bacalà (salted cod).

i From Campo Santa Maria Nova, turn left onto Salizada S. Canzian and continue for 1min.; destination is on the left. Chiccetti €1.50-3. Wine €1.50-5. Beer €2 from 3-6pm. Cash only for orders under €10. Open Tu-Su 10am-10pm.

NIGHTLIFE

Nightlife in Venice is not the stuff of Roman ragers (for that, you'll probably have to get out to the mainland). Instead, young people chat in the campos with glasses of spritz or listen to live music at intimate jazz bars (mostly found in Dosoduro).

BÀCARO JAZZ

San Marco 5546 ☎041 528 5249 www.bacarojazz.com

Fall madly in love with the outrageously flirtatious antics of the bartender here, who closely resembles a middle-aged Zorro and concocts spectacular cocktails with all the flair of that skillful swordsman. No surprise, he's chosen to decorate the bar's ceiling with a colorful array of bras gifted by past patrons, from the massive leopard print number (the back problems!) to one that reads Greg + Emily (what better medium for immortalizing love than hanging lingerie in a Venetian bar?). Decor aside, the youthful crowd and central location make this bar among Venice's most hoppin'. If worried about the steep €10 price tag on your pina colada, visit during happy hour from 4-6pm, or sit at the bar: Mario periodically presses free shots to those nearest.

i From Rialto Bridge, turn left onto Calle del Fontego, then left onto Salizzada del Fontego dei Tedeschi; destination is on the right. Shots €4.50-6. Cocktails €10. Beer €4.50-9. Wine €4.50-7. Open daily noon-2am. Kitchen closes at 1am. Happy hour 4-6pm.

IL PARADISO PERDUTO

Fondamenta de la Misericordia, Cannaregio 2540 ☎041 720581 https://it-it.facebook.com/osteriaparadisoperduto

Pricey seafood restaurant by day, popping venue for eclectic live music and poetry readings by night. Named for Milton's epic poem written to "justify the ways of God to men," this historic restaurant—featuring steaming fried seafood cicchetti and weekly appearances by local musicians—needs no such justification (and trust us, you don't want to read our poetry anyway). Check the Facebook page for announcements about upcoming concerts, and call ahead to reserve a

venice

table in the cramped interior near the intimate wooden stage. Otherwise, get a glass of wine to go and settle by the canal to observe the amorous intrigues of lanky college students and honeymooning tourists.

i *8min. walk from the S. Marcuola-Casino vaporetti stop. Antipasti €8-29. Primi €12-17. Secondi €18-55. Dessert €5-7. Wine €2-4.50. Cash only. Open M 10am-midnight, Th-Su 10am-midnight. Reservation recommended.*

SOTTOSOPRA

Dorsoduro 3740/1 ☎041 52 42 117

Quintessential Venetian nightlife (read: intimate bar for chatting and moderate drinking, gasp!) in the artsy Dorsoduro district. Squint to read the chalkboard drinks list by the light of a retro '90s neon, and grab a seat next to a pop-art poster of John Lennon. You might encounter the American oaf on holiday, who views Venice as an exotic extension of his breeding ground, but as the location is appealingly off the beaten tourist trail and beyond the pitiful map skills of said bumbling American, you'll likely stir your caipirinha (€6) and watch the game beside local university students in for a cheap drink.

i *From C. Santa Margherita, follow C. della Chiesa, cross the bridge and continue right until you reach C. San Pantalon. Keep walking until you hear the music. Drinks €6-7. Beer €3-6. Shots €3. Open M-F 11am-midnight. Sa, 6pm-midnight.*

DEVIL'S FOREST PUB

San Marco, Calle Stagneri 5185 ☎041 520 0623 www.devilsforestpub.com

Frat house meets hunting lodge in this testosterone-filled altar to male mid-life crises. Bro-y bartenders toot their own horns with aggressive decor, like the tree stump that reads, "Please be patient with the bartender. Even a toilet can serve only one asshole at a time." Truth. The dark wood paneling and enormous mounted elk head would age the place were it not for the blasting soundtrack of heavy metal and American rap. Select from an impressively lengthy and international list of mixed drinks (€5-7.50) and feel like a real man or, alternately, slightly embarrassed for men everywhere.

i *From Rialto Bridge, turn right into Campo S. Bortolomio, then turn left at the Disney store; the pub is on the right. Drinks €5-7.50. Wine €2.50-5€. Light lunch €10-12 from noon-3pm. Cash only. Open daily 11am-1am.*

VENICE JAZZ CLUB

Dorsoduro 3102, Ponte dei Pugni ☎041 523 2056 http://venicejazzclub.weebly.com

What's sexier than jazz? Live jazz, played by Venetian hunks grooving it up on piano, drums, double bass, and vibraphone. The in-house quartet at Venice Jazz Club performs five nights a week by the light of flickering candles and enflamed, lusty hearts. The sultry bartender-pianist-MC both announces pieces and jokes lightly in English for the benefit of the international crowd. Even with the first drink included, the €20 entrance fee is steep, but you're in for a solid two hours of number after number, and when you lock eyes with that drummer, thoughts about budgets (and all thoughts in general) miraculously evanesce. Check out the website for concert schedules (from Miles Davis tributes to bossa nova nights) and reservation info.

i *From Campo San Barnaba, turn left onto Fondamenta Gherardini and cross the bridge; destination is on the right. Tickets €20 (includes 1 drink). Drinks €3-8. Dinner €8 per person. Open M-W 7pm-11pm, F-Sa 7pm-11pm (dinner from 7:30-9pm, concert from 9-11pm).*

ESSENTIALS
Practicalities

- **TOURIST OFFICES:** Head to one of the four main tourist information branches in Venice for the Venice Card, maps (€2.50), museum passes and more. Though the tourist information booths can at times be helpful especially for buying more prolonged vaporetto passes the website should answer most of your questions (info@turismovenezia.it, www.turismovenezia.it). **Venezia San Lucia Train Station Tourist Office** (☎041 52 98 711 for Tourist Contact Center) is open daily 9am-1:30pm in front of the station overlooking the Grand Canal in a white kiosk and 1:30pm-7pm alongside Track 1. **Ple. Roma Tourist Office** (☎041 24 11 499) is open daily 9:30am-2:30pm. Additional offices are near P. San Marco (San Marco 71) and San Marco Giardinetti.

- **PHARMACIES:** Pharmacies throughout the city are marked with bright green crosses.

- **BATHROOMS:** Blue or brown signs marked "WC" lead to public bathrooms, usually €1.50 for use.

Emergency

- **HOSPITALS/MEDICAL SERVICES:** Call ☎118 for an ambulance. Ospedale SS. Giovanne e Paolo. (Pedestrian entrance on Campo SS. Giovanni e Paolo; emergency entrance on the water, next to the Ospedale waterbus stop.)

- **POLICE:** ☎112 for emergencies.

Getting Around

The cheapest way to get around and the best way to see the city is by walking. Walk on the right side of the street; the high volume of tourist traffic is unsurprisingly annoying to locals, and further clogging the streets by occupying the wrong side of the road might incite Venetian ire.

Alternatives include vaporetti (water buses), run by the local transportation department ACTV, that shuttle along the Grand Canal and also provide access to neighboring islands. One-way is a shamelessly extortionate €7.50 (sold in front of all

free walking tours

The walls of the ticket office at Piazzale Roma are draped in tempting tour advertisements of all varieties: Take a boat down the Grand Canal for €50! Hire a guide for the full St. Mark's Square experience for €100! Sell your soul for less! Tours and local guides can add educational fiber to your stay and, more importantly, point you off the beaten tourist trail towards local gems, but their services are well beyond the wallets of budget travelers...or so it would seem. Enter the gift of St. Anthony (patron saint of travelers—you learn these things while going around Italy) to backpackers everywhere: free walking tours. It just so happens that Venetian locals who are altruistic, fiercely patriotic, and/or coaxed by the local government run daily tours of the various sestieri—all you have to do is reserve a spot online and show up at the designated starting point. Guides talk history and local folk myths and point out their beloved childhood gelateria and osteria. The tours are completely free, though the guides won't say no to a €5 bill surreptitiously concealed in a farewell handshake. Venice Free Walking Tours and Free Walk in Venice are two solid agencies.

Italy

vaporetti stops), so you'd best get an ACTV package, sold in front of or around major vaporetti stops (Ple. Roma, Santa Lucia, Burano, etc.). The best value is a 72hr. pass for €28 if you're a student or under 29 (otherwise it's €40); the pass also provides unlimited land bus access and Rolling Venice benefits (which provides discounts at participating museums and restaurants). The 72hr. pass will not get you transport to and from the airport, which is €8, €15€ roundtrip. For shorter stays, there are 12hr. boat passes for €20. Vaporetti run for 24hr., with more limited night routes, and buses run until midnight (if you're staying outside the city, do not miss the last bus—taxis to campsites 20min. away will cost at least €40). One-way bus tickets are €1.50, sold at ACTV stands throughout city, airports, most hostels, and occasionally on buses themselves. You've got to wave down buses (land ones) because multiple lines stop at each stop and those apathetic drivers will pass you by otherwise. Note: It might be tempting to hitch a ride without a ticket because it appears that no one watches the validation points and bus drivers don't seem to give a damn, but there are random searches and huge fines for those caught without tickets.

There are also the traghetti, or gondolas, that cross the Grand Canal at seven different points. ACTV passes do not work for these, but the charge is just €0.50 one-way. These are the only boats that locals take.

Private gondolas are too expensive to take seriously (at least €80 for 40min.); also, none of the gondoliers sing that well anyway.

verona

Behold! As we walk across this stage, we will extoll the virtues of fair Verona. Verona of citizens made comatose by summer heat, slowly roasting in Piazza Bra. Verona of sleek Vespas and expensive cars careening down narrow cobblestoned roads. Verona of shady walks along the Adige, tart granita in hand. Verona of obscure medieval frescos depicting the baby Jesus with middle-aged male faces. Verona of old people and intimate nooks and crannies and an agèd beauty.

SIGHTS

If you're planning to see most of the sights in town, consider purchasing the Verona Card, which grants access to almost all the monuments, churches, and museums in Verona (along with a little balcony you might have heard about). Passes can be purchased at the tourist office or at most of the major sights. A 24hr. pass costs €18, while a 48hr. pass is €22; considering that the Arena alone will run you €10, the Verona Card is probably worth the upfront investment.

⬛ ARENA DI VERONA

Piazza Bra 1 ☎045 800 51 51 www.arena.it

Constructed in 30 CE and once able to seat 30,000 spectators, Verona's Arena isn't quite the Colosseum, although it did play host to its fair share of gladiator fights back in the day. It's also the third-largest ancient Roman amphitheater in the world, so give it a little bit of credit. Since the 18th century, the Arena has become renowned for a slightly more sophisticated and humane form of entertainment, replacing dramatic fights to the death with the drama of opera. If you're in town on the night of a summer performance, you should try your best to purchase last-minute tickets; while an afternoon romp up and down the stadium seats and through the cavernous bowels of the amphitheater might keep you entertained for about 20min., the true glory of the Arena can be better appreciated in the evening, when the stage is set and the seats are filled to capacity.

i Located on the north end of P. Bra. Hard to miss. €10, reduced €7.50. Free with Verona Card. Open M 1:30-7:30pm, Tu-Su 8:30am-7:30pm.

TORRE DEI LAMBERTI

V. della Costa 1   ☎045 927 30 27

Part of a group of towers constructed near the Palazzo della Ragione, the Torre dei Lamberti is the only one of the original four that remains standing at full height today. The climb up the 300+ steps here will take you right into the heart of the bell tower, where you can stop on the first landing and look out over the entire city before scaling the final twisting staircase to the tippy top. Way up

get a room!

B&B ALLE TORRI
$$$$

V. Fratelli Rosselli 9   ☎340 996 2801

Once you've swallowed the bitter reality of needing to shell out for Verona accommodations, especially during opera season, embrace the whimsy of this B&B and its host. Vittorio's sleek shaved sides and muscle tees belie his penchant for floral decals, fantasy novels, and kpop. He's more than happy to chat about any of the above, in addition to pointing out favorite attractions and eateries on a free city map, showering you with Italian candies, and doing your laundry. Sleep soundly in one of three lavishly (if a bit outlandishly) decorated doubles, from a nautical room with hanging seashell mobiles to a Louis XIV-esque vision.

i *About a 20min. walk to the city center. Doubles from €55. Cash only. Check-in 2-10pm (arrange arrival beforehand). Check-out 11am.*

VILLA FRANCESCATTI
$$

Salita Fontana del Ferro n° 15   ☎045 590360 www.ostelloverona.it/english.html

For by far the cheapest Verona accommodation, hit up the lone youth hostel in the northern hills of the city, next to the Teatro Romano and Castel San Pietro. A converted 16th-century villa, this hostel affords all the quiet nights and cool temperatures its elevated mountain location suggests (and your aching glutes won't let you forget it). The sulky staff is a bit wacky, from their restrictive curfews to this unnecessarily specific line off their website: "The hostel welcomes also underage boys with their parents" (we're hoping something crucial was lost in translation). Fellow bunkers are kind enough, though, from backpackers questing for Shakespearean romance to elderly opera-goers looking for a cheap siesta spot before curtain time.

i *From P. Isolo bus stop, follow the signs to the youth hostel. Dorms €18. Cash only. Open 7am-midnight.*

B&B DOLCECASA
$$$

V. Campostrini 13   ☎045 8325196

The kindly family man at the head of this establishment takes the phrase "service with a smile" to heart—seriously, he never puts those pearly whites away, and when you reciprocate, it all degenerates into an anxiety-inducing contest of pleasantness. Relax your fiercely flexed cheek muscles in the privacy of your clean room and take advantage of the only somewhat spotty Wi-Fi (well done, Italy!). The major downside is the location 40min. outside the city center—the bus ride into town is simple enough, but if you miss your ride, you'll have to wait an hour for the next #21 to come around.

i *About a 40min. bus ride from Verona; take 103 or 21, and the hostel is a 3min. walk from the bus stop. Singles from €26. Doubles from €44. Cash only. Check-in 5-9pm. Check-out 10:30am.*

italy

a night at the opera

When in Verona, do as the powdered, orthopedically-shod do and go to the opera. Verona isn't just about Shakespeare, as every guidebook and travel website is fond of noting to prove their off-the-beaten-trail street cred. Late June to early September marks the annual period in Verona when hostel prices skyrocket and museums suspend discounts—aka, opera season. During this time, the grand Arena off P. Bra once again opens its gates to panting spectators intent on witnessing brutal slaughter—here, the fictional demises of eponymous protagonists (Carmen from Bizet's Carmen and Aida from Verdi's Aida, to name two on the 2016 roster). For those of you who think culture is dead, just observe the damp, malodorous hundreds who pack into the outdoor theater for four-plus hours in 80-degree heat to watch a show accompanied by a live orchestra and subtitles. Tickets run from €226 for gold members (these guys roll up in ball gowns and tuxes) to €16.50 for unassigned seats in the outer stone stalls (gates open at 7pm for the 9pm show; expect to start lining up by 6:45pm to get good seats). It doesn't really matter where you sit, though, as the theater has fantastic acoustics throughout. Purchase tickets at the office opposite Gate 63 (V. Dietro Anfiteatro 6/8, ☎045 80 05 151, biglietteria@arenadiverona.it, www.arean.it).

here, lovers linger as they look out over the city through some netting while tangled in each others' arms. Adding to the romance already in the air, the walls of this topmost level are covered in the names of couples who have probably already broken up by now.

i *From P. delle Erbe, walk down V. della Costa. The ticket office is on the right (enter the tower through the giftshop). Elevator available for part of the climb. €5. Free with Verona Card. Open M-F 10am-6pm, Sa-Su 11am-7pm. Last entry 45min. before close.*

CASTEL SAN PIETRO
Regaste Redentore

You can't actually go inside the castle that lies at the top of this hill, but the views of Verona and the Adige River from San Pietro make it more than worth the climb up here. After crossing the river over the Ponte di Pietro, scale the many steps that lead you winding your way up to the tree-lined terrace where you sit and admire the entirety of Verona from a sunny bench or ledge. The gates remain open until midnight, so you can take in the beauty of the city lit up at night, although we recommend visiting during the day if you want to avoid all the Romeos and Juliets who hike up here after dinner to "let lips do what hands do" under the cover of darkness.

i *From Ponte di Pietro, cross the street and climb the set of stairs directly across from the bridge. Free. Open daily 6:30am-midnight.*

PIAZZA DELLE ERBE

At the end Via Mazzini and its many upscale shops lies Piazza delle Erbe, Verona's most popular square and once the site of its forum during the Roman Empire. Today, the piazza is still stuffed with plenty of market stalls that sell everything from fruit cups to party masks, although amid all the bartering going on, you'll also find a white marble column topped off with St. Mark's Lion and a fountain featuring a statue of Madonna Verona. The other major focal point of the piazza is the Torre dei Lamberti, whose massive clock tower looms over the whole square. And although Juliet's famous balcony may be located just down the street, the beautiful buildings of Piazza delle Erbe boast their own collection

verona

of iron-wrought balconies and Baroque decorations that adds to the timeless charm of the square.

i *From P. Bra, walk down V. Mazzini to the piazza, on the left. Free.*

CASA DI GIULIETTA

V. Cappello 23   ☎045 803 43 03 www.casadigiulietta.verona.it

Allegedly the home of Juliet Capulet, Literary Character Who Didn't Actually Exist, the Casa di Giulietta is a popular stop for tourists who seem to have forgotten that Romeo and Juliet is a work of fiction. Still, you should probably drop by and see her balcony just for the ritual of it. If you've already paid for the Verona Card, a quick turn through the rooms here isn't a complete waste of your time; in addition to snapping a picture of yourself standing out on Juliet's balcony, you can also admire multiple artists' rendition of Romeo, Home Intruder, along with the bed where cinematic love was consummated in the 1968 film version of the play. Other than that, just stick to the ivy-covered courtyard, where you'll find vandals of all varieties leaving letters to Juliet on the walls of the archway leading to the house. In the far corner of the courtyard, there's also a statue of young Juliet whose right boob has been groped by way too many tourists (she's 13, you guys!).

i *From P. delle Erbe, walk down V. Cappello. The archway leading to Juliet's house is on the left. €6, reduced €4.50. Free with Verona Card. Open M 1:30-7:30pm, Tu-Su 8:30am-7:30pm.*

DUOMO

P. Duomo 21   ☎045 59 28 13 www.cattedralediverona.it

Although the striking white bell tower of Verona's Duomo is probably the first thing you'll notice about this church (that and the fact that it's basically located in a parking lot), its exterior also features two Romanesque porches and a charming little statue of an angel robed in blue. Inside, there's even more going on, from the large orange columns lining the central nave to the black tiling on the floor to the curved marble surrounding the central altar. Thanks to a great deal of restoration work, the frescoes surrounding the church's many chapels are remarkably intact. Don't leave without making a quick pass through the baptistry and a second church that now serves as an interesting archaeological site.

i *From P. delle Erbe, walk down Corso Sant'Anastasia to Chiesa di Sant'Anastasia, then turn left onto V. Duomo. €2.50. Combined admission to Duomo, S. Anastasia, S. Zeno, and S. Fermo €6. Free with Verona Card. Open M-F 10am-5:30pm, Sa 10am-4pm, Su 1:30-5:30pm.*

FOOD

Verona is red wine country—try the Amarone or the Bardolino.

🍴 GELATO BALLINI $

V. S. Maria Rocca Maggiore 4/A   ☎8476 0235

According to experts (in light of all the gelato we've consumed, we consider ourselves experts), the best gelato isn't heaped in glistening mounds to tempt the sweaty passerby but rather is concealed in cans with flat metal lids. That said, Gelato Ballini is legit. Choose from a variety of fruity and creamy flavors, including a tart passionfruit and a rice number problematically named JAP (we're hoping that's a rice-related acronym in Italian). Though located a bit outside the city center, these cans of gelato at the end of your weary backpacker's rainbow are easy to find thanks to a personalized street sign that points the way from Ponte Nuovo del Popolo.

i *From Ponte Nuovo del Popolo (opposite side of the bank from the city center), head down the street away from the bridge and turn left onto V. Santa Maria Rocca Maggiore; destination on right. Gelato €1.50-4. Granita €2.50-3.50. Open M-F 1pm-10pm, Sa-Su noon-1:30pm and 2-10pm.*

italy

PARMA A TAVOLA
$$

Corso Santa Anastasia 20   ☎045 8012001 www.parmatavola.com

This family operation reels you in with their open kitchen on the ground floor and a pasta-making station strategically placed by the window for the ogling pleasures of hungry pedestrians. The dining area, lit by pseudo-quaint mason jar lights, is on the second floor, just through a stairway decorated with rave reviews from past customers and ungainly cartoon animals drawn by said customers' children. The service is on the slower side, but true art—here, hand-carving slabs of yellow dough into fresh ravioli—is a painstaking labor of love. Pasta offerings change daily and range from roughly €9.50-16.50.

i From the Church of Sant'Anastasia, head down Corso Sant'Anastasia 1min.; destination on left. Pasta €9.50-16.50. Open Tu-Th 9am-10pm, F-Sa 9am-midnight, Su 9am-10pm.

GUSTO PIADINERIE
$

Stradone Porta Palio, 4   ☎042 6267 0237 www.piadineriagustoverona.it

This might be the only place in all of Italy, with its tortoise-beats-hare-life-is-a-marathon meal philosophy, that gladly lets you take away leftovers, probably by force of habit: the hunks of crusty bread, mozzarella, and freshly-sliced prosciutto they call sandwiches have even the bulkiest of locals requesting takeout baggies. Skip the build-your-own piadine, or flatbreads (€4-6), in favor of one of 14 enormous panuozzo (€5.50-7 for a half, €11-13 for a whole) or a panini on pizza dough.

i From San Zeno Church, turn right onto Stradone Antonio Provolo, left onto Vicolo Pietrone, and left onto Stradone Porta Palio. Piadine €46. Cassoni €3.50-4. Panuozzo €5.50-13. Open daily 11am-11pm.

NIGHTLIFE

▓ OSTERIA BOTTIGLIERIA ZAMPIERI – LA MANDORLA

V. Alberto Mario, 25   ☎045 59 7053

Just this once, suspend your seasoned traveler's instinct to avoid eateries within close proximity of major landmarks. This rustic wine bar is about a 3min. walk from P. Bra (allowing for time to get lost), but its outdoor seating is regularly packed with locals and savvy tourists. The well-worn wooden interior, lined with wine bottles and sepia prints, confirms its authenticity, as does the wide selection of local liquors (€1.50-7) and snacks, including regional favorite horse meatballs (does not taste like chicken, but is quite indistinguishable from beef).

i Just a few minutes off P. Bra, turn left onto Piazzetta Scalette Rubiani, then turn right onto V. Alberto Mario; destination on right. Beer €2.50. Wine €1.50-7. Open M-F 11am-2pm and 5pm-midnight, Sa-Su 11am-2pm and 5pm-1:30am.

ART&CHOCOLATE

Vicolo Cavalletto, 16   ☎045 923 0141 www.artandchocolate.it

You know your annoying nemesis from high school—the one who got straight A's, played three instruments, and was thinking of picking up a fourth, just for the heck of it? This is their cafe/bar/coffee shop/chocolatier/art gallery incarnation. Typically in the restaurant business, an establishment with too broad a menu is tagged to fail. Art&Chocolate, however, manages its wide range of culinary and artistic offerings with delectable success. True to its name, this "gallery cafe" features bonbons and chocolate drinks in a cultured museum cafe-esque setting, with local art on the walls between hanging incandescent light bulbs. The joint also offers salads and pastas, pastries, coffee and tea, cocktails, wine, and craft beers. If you can stomach the slightly inflated prices and hipster clientele, try a tea-based cocktail or a glass of wine (free of chemical fertilizers and herbicides, of course).

i From the Church of Sant'Anastasia, walk down V. Don Bassi, turn slightly right onto Corso Sant'Anastasia, then left onto Vicolo Cavalletto; destination on left. Coffee €1. Wine €2. Pasta €7. Open M-Th 7:30am-10pm, F-Sa 7:30am-1:30am, Su 8am-6pm.

verona

ESSENTIALS
Practicalities

- **TOURIST OFFICES:** Central Tourist Office. (V. degli Alpini 9. ☎045 80 68 680. Walk south from Arena di Verona into P. Bra. The tourist office is on the left. Open M-Sa 9am-7pm, Su 10am-4pm.)
- **LUGGAGE STORAGE:** Porta Nuova Station. (Located on the ground floor of the station. 1st 5hr. €6, 6-12th hr. €0.90, €0.40 per hr. thereafter. Open daily 8am-8pm.)
- **CURRENCY EXCHANGE:** There is a Forexchange currency exchange point near P. delle Erbe on V. Cappello. (V. Cappello 4. Open M-Sa 11am-7pm.)
- **ATMS:** Located throughout the city. There is a Unicredit ATM located in the corner of Piazza Bra, near V. Roma. (P. Bra 26/E, ☎045 487 1304.)
- **POST OFFICES:** Poste Italiane. (V. Carlo Cattaneo 23. From P. Ba, take V. Fratta and turn left onto V. Carlo Cattaneo. Open M 8:30am-1:30pm, Tu-F 8:30am-7pm, Sa 8:30am-12:30pm.)

Emergency

- **POLICE:** Polizia di Stato. (Lungadige Antonio Galtarossa 11. ☎045 80 90 411. From P. Bra, continue as it becomes V. Pallone. Cross over the river and turn right onto Lungadige Antonio Galtarossa.) Carabinieri. (V. Salvo D'Acquisto 6. ☎045 80 561. From the city center, walk along Corso Porta Nuova and turn right onto V. Antonio Locatelli.)
- **HOSPITALS/MEDICAL SERVICES:** Ospedale Civile Maggiore. (Ple. Aristide Stefani 1. ☎045 81 21 111. www.ospedaleuniverona.it.)

Getting There

Aeroporto Valerio Catullo Villafranca (VRN; ☎045 80 95 666 www.aeroportoverona. it) is Venice's small international airport. Flights are available through smaller airlines such as Ryanair and Vueling from many cities in Italy, including Rome and Naples, along with other major European cities. An Aerobus shuttle runs from the airport to the train station every 20min. (€6.) Verona Porta Nuova station (Ple. 25 Aprile. ☎199 89 20 21 www.grandistazioni.it) is where most travelers arrive in Verona. You can get to Verona by bus, but the train is by far the best and most common option. Trains arrive from Padua (€7-18, 45min.-1hr.); Milan (€13-22, 90min.-2hr.); Venice (€9-22, 1-2hr.); and Rome (€60-100, 3hr.).

Getting Around

Verona is an incredibly walkable city, and it is unlikely that you will need anything but your own two feet to get around town. That being said, city buses operated by ATV are available and run all across the center of Verona and through the surrounding area (☎045 80 57 811 www.atv.verona.it). Tickets can be purchased from tobacco shops or onboard (buying a ticket onboard will cost you €0.80 extra and you must pay with exact change). Lines and routes are posted outside each bus stop; pay attention to the schedules, as Sunday, holiday, and night service have different bus numbers and routes. Most buses run from Verona Porta Nuova, where you can catch the regional bus to Lago di Garda. RadioTaxi also has 24hr. taxi service (☎045 53 26 66 www.radiotaxiverona.it) clustered around P. delle Erbe and P. Bra. Bike shares are another option, and stations are scattered throughout the city (☎800 89 69 48 www.bikeverona.it).

italy

padua

On the well-worn Italian tourist trail, Padua lives in the shadow of the glamorous Venice (a mere 30min. away by train), and not without good reason—unless you're very much into Galileo, 14th-century frescos, and/or St. Anthony, you might be, well, bored out of your mind here. That said, traveling is exhausting business, and Padua is the ideal rest stop: it's stocked with enough history to convince your mom that you don't just hit the bottle all day but small enough to explore in a couple afternoons, leaving your evenings free to binge a season of Modern Family and pine for good ol' 'Murica. If you are actually drinking your way through Europe, college students from the illustrious University of Padua make for chic drinking buddies, at least until the Cinderella-esque bus system bids you home by midnight.

SIGHTS

Save money with the Padova Card, which grants free access to all public transportation and discounted or free entry to the most important monuments for 48hr (€16) or 72hr. (€21).

🏛 BASILICA DI SANT'ANTONIO

P. del Santo, 11   ☎049 860 3236 www.santantonio.org/en

Join the stream of pilgrims who throng here to fervently pray and flash creepy pictures of the Pope over the interred remains of Anthony of Padua. Ol' Tony is the patron saint of many things, including travelers, lost articles, starvation, and Tigua Indians—all relevant to the budget backpacker. You will get dress coded if not up to Sunday school standards, even in your baggy quick-dry athletic shorts that certainly aren't inspiring any forbidden feelings in this house of God, so be sure your knees and shoulders are covered. This multi-domed church, colloquially referred to as "Il Santo," is in that vaguely rustic, old European church style known as Romanesque Gothic and features your standard lineup of frescoes, statues, and altars. Pause in the shady courtyard to refill water bottles and rest your legs next to a tacky gift shop peddling wooden llamas and your own complete priest vestment for the unmerciful price of €340.

i Located in P. del Santo, across from the Botanical Gardens. Free. Open daily Jan-Mar 6:20am-6:45pm, Mar-Oct 6:20am-7:45pm, Nov-Dec 6:20am-6:45pm.

SCROVEGNI CHAPEL

P. Eremitani, 8   ☎049 2010020 www.cappelladegliscrovegni.it/index.php/en/

This is Padua's version of the Sistine Chapel, about which the city is possibly even more proud than the Catholic Church is about the Vatican. The interior is entirely covered with Giotto's famed fresco cycle depicting the life of Christ, crowned with an enormous illustration of the Last Judgment on the west wall. As bemused parents with middle school spawn in tow soon realize, just because art is from the 14th century and religious does not guarantee a PG rating—Giotto's brainchild features butt-naked sinners graphically sawed, roasted on spits, and crushed under Satan's genitalia (clothing is not a thing in Hell).

i Located in P. Eremitani. €13, €8 for members and groups of 10 or more, €6 for children, students, and 65 or older. Ticket grants access to chapel and adjacent museum. Open 9am-7pm, but you must book in advance at the tourist office or at the chapel itself.

FOOD

🍴 DALLA ZITA $

V. Gorizia 16   ☎049 654992

Warning: not for the indecisive. The menu at this bustling panini shop consists of 143 (not including daily specials) permutations of various cheeses and cured meats, helpfully deconstructed (albeit in Italian) and nicknamed on colorful

get a room!

Believe it or not, there aren't too many young budget backpackers who make Padua a part of their trip, so traditional youth hostel options are pretty slim. What you're left with are pricey hotels in the city or B&B-type establishments a bus ride away. We prefer the latter. As a warning, B&B's usually don't take credit cards, so be sure to load up on cash.

B&B GREEN FIELDS GUESTHOUSE $$$
V. Oderzo, 2   ☎347 70 56 494

With hostel pickings pretty slim, B&B's may be your best option while poking around Padua. Book a bed over in the greener pastures of this guesthouse, named either for the surrounding vegetable patch and orchard or the slightly garish green carpeting. This home away from home is a 20min. bus ride from the city center and offers privacy, motherly hosts, and free laundry—all sorely missed while making the party hostel rounds (you can only rinse your socks in the sink so many times). The owners and clientele are both of the older variety, so you won't have much luck finding 2am drinking buddies. You will, however, encounter companions with whom to discuss Islam as you rustle up a dinner of kale and quinoa. It's cooler than it sounds.

i From the train station, take the 22 bus from Vle. Codalunga and ask the driver to stop at the Madria Church. From here, follow the passage after the butcher shop down to V. Ca Rasi and head straight down a small rocky road. The B&B is the 2nd white house on your right. Singles from €35. Doubles from €55. Cash only. Check-in 1pm (contact reception before arrival). Check-out 11am.

OSTELLO CASA A COLORI $$
V. del Commissario 44   ☎049 680332 www.casaacoloripadova.com

This bare bones hostel is among the cheapest you'll find in the Padua area. Sure, the sickly orange wallpaper and long linoleum hallways might suggest the place's previous function as an insane asylum or low-income retirement home, but at least standards of medical cleanliness have persisted. Everyone from balding businessmen to families book rooms here, but if you sift through the age-inappropriate rabble, you'll likely be able to unearth a backpacker buddy or two to split a bottle of supermarket wine.

i From the train station, catch bus 3 and ask to get off at V. Bembo in front of the Chiesa del Crocefisso. V. del Commissario is across the street from the stop. Dorms from €18. Singles from €39. Privates from €54. Cash only. Check-in 4-10pm. Check-out 10am.

notecards that paper the wall. Try the Hemingway for a tabasco-spiced munch or, if homesick, the pepperoni-laden Mississippi (this is what the rest of the world thinks of us, and we can't say it's inaccurate). Whatever portion of pork you choose, the meat is carved from hunks before your eyes. So pop out your Google translate and puzzle a bit, but, in the words of one impatient local, "You ah-can't-ah go-ah wrong."

i From P. della Frutta, turn left onto V. Marsilio da Padova, then right onto V. Gorizia. Panini €3.30-5.80. Cash only. Open M-F 10am-7:30pm.

SUGO PADOVA $
di Davide Curcio, Via del Santo, 7   ☎342 9310831

Chipotle with fresh pasta and salads instead of burrito bowls and…food poisoning. Build your meal from a variety of pastas (including a gluten free option), greens, sauces, and/or toppings. As is the case at its TexMex cousin, at Sugo's, chefs construct personalized dishes before your eyes, sautéeing with impeccable wrist technique and plucking basil from a hardy little plant in the corner. The cozy space attracts locals of all ages, from the ravenous college student to the grandmother with a to-go order of giant meatballs (€1.50/per). Best of all, the piping hot or cool n' crunchy contents of your takeout container will cost no more than €6.

i From Padova University, turn right onto V. Zabarella, left onto V. San Francesco, then right onto V. del Santo. Pasta €3-5.50. Salads €4-6. Open M-Tu noon-3pm, W-Sa noon-3pm and 6:30-10:30pm, Su noon-3pm.

GOURMETTERIA $$
V. Degli Zabarella 23 ☎049 659830 www.gourmetteria.com/padova

For those of you who enjoy window-shopping at Williams-Sonoma, this quirky cross between a restaurant and gourmet market is precisely your cup of tea. Savor gnocchi that'll teach you the true potential of potatoes (€8-11.50) while scanning the jars of sauces and whimsical kitchen supplies for sale on the floor-to-ceiling shelves. If you're feeling guilty about ordering a burger (€12-13.50) while abroad, rest assured: the foppish chefs at Gourmetteria add a twist to the American classic by topping the beef patty with your choice of Italian cured meat. Everyone wins, except maybe your cholesterol.

i From Padova University, walk down V. Cesare Battisti and turn right on V. Zabarella. Antipasti €8-12. Primi €8.50-12. Secondi €13-19. Open daily 10am-midnight.

NIGHTLIFE

◪ ALEXANDER BAR
V. San Francesco 38 ☎049 876 2908

In this drowsy town of respectable museums and historic universities, it's no surprise that the nightlife sounds like indistinct chatter and the tinkle of wine glasses—which renders the feverish punk rock issuing from this dive bar all the more appealing. Sip a spritz (€3) or vodka sour (€4) with the entire University of Padua student body while shouting to be heard over live music. The bar frequently redecorates to match its themed concert series (advertised on the Facebook page), from reggae parties to a bizarre three nights dubbed "Alex in Wonderland," in which giant playing cards are hung from the walls and Alice in Wonderland (the original Disney version) is played on loop.

i From the university, turn right onto Riviera dei Ponti Romani from V. Cesare Battisti, then left onto V. S. Francesco; destination on right. Wine €2. Drinks €3-5. Aperitivo 7-9pm. Open daily 4pm-2am.

IL GOTTINO
V. Delle Piazze 16 ☎348 427 1900

Stave off hunger before Italy's 8pm dinnertime with aperitivo (Italy's version of happy hour) at this collegiate wine bar. Classic movie posters affixed to the pale pink walls and stacks of vintage trunks impart a classy academic vibe, while the sloshy university students taking the Euro Cup way too seriously remind you why you can't wait to leave school. If the athletic jingoism gets too loud, take your glass of wine or inventive blackberry-adorned cocktail outside and listen to the band rehearsing in the garage next door.

i From the University, walk 3min. and turn left onto V. VIII Febbraio, right onto V. S. Canziano, and left onto V. delle Piazze; destination on right. Drinks €2-5. Open M-F 6pm-2am, Sa 11am-3:30pm and 6pm-2am, Su 6pm-2am.

padua

cycle city

Though Padua's city center, home to most of the city's sights, is small enough to conquer on foot, these streets were made for biking. The most densely populated areas around the university have traffic restrictions, so bikes replace cars at the top of the transportation food chain. On wheels, free of aching feet and inconsistent public transportation, Padua's horizons expand to include, for example, the nearby Tronco Maestro River; regular bike paths ensure safe passage through traffic. In the south lies Prato della Valle—this elliptical square is the largest in Italy and makes for a shady nap spot between bookish marble statues and a central fountain. More relevantly, the park is ringed with a flawlessly flat concrete track ideal for both reckless races and getting more familiar with life on two wheels. Frequent spigots around the square provide water for hydrating and/or rinsing your novice biker wounds. The city offers several bike rental services, including Good Bike Padova, which offers plans starting at €8 for 4hr.. Their office is at V. Altinate 70.

CAFFÈ PEDROCCHI
V. VIII Febbraio 15 ☎049 8781231 www.caffepedrocchi.it

Connect butt-to-butt with the generations of literary luminaries who planned revolutions and praised the eggnog (€6) from these velvety seats, earning this cafe its own Wikipedia page. The clientele nowadays are just as bougie as past patron Lord Byron, if less literarily-inclined—as no one really discusses politics or shares poetry nowadays, evenings at Caffè Pedrocchi include live music and costume parties (detailed on the website). The establishment's eclectic mish-mash of architectural styles is the work of some famous designer about whom the snooty waiters, suspiciously eyeing your scuffed sneakers and backpacker's sleeve tan, will undoubtedly provide a mini-lecture. Try the Pedrocchi Coffee (€3) for a minty twist on your usual caffeine fix.

i Located in Piazzetta Cappellato Pedrocchi. Coffee €3-5euro. Drinks €6-10euro. Snacks €3.50-10. Open daily 8am-11pm.

ESSENTIALS
Practicalities

- **TOURIST OFFICES:** IAT. (Stazione Ferroviaria Railway Station, P. della Stazione 14. ☎049 201 0080. Open M-Sa 9am-7pm, Su 10am-4pm.)
- **PHARMACIES:** Pharmacies are marked with green crosses.
- **POST OFFICE:** Corso Garibaldi, 25. (☎049 8772209)
- **WATER:** Spigots can be found around town, particularly around Prato delle Valle, and provide potable drinking water. You should also try the Fanta because it's delicious.

Emergency

- **HOSPITALS:** ☎118 is the catchall emergency number. Complesso Clinico Ospedale Civile e Cliniche Universitarie. (V. Giustiniani, 1. ☎049 8211111) Ospedale S. Antonio. (V. Facciolati, 71. ☎049 8216511) Ospedale Militare. (V. S.G. Verdara, 115. ☎049 8722411 or ☎049 723106)
- **POLICE:** ☎112, ☎113 (local police)

Getting Around

It takes about 30-40min. to walk the entire length of the town, from Prato delle Valle in the south to the train station in the north. Essentially all of the major sights are concentrated between Prato delle Valle and the Scrovegni Chapel (5min. south of the train station), so Padua is very much a walkable city (and its bus/tram system is rather inconsistent and not recommended).

bologna

La dotta, la grassa, la rossa. To spend any time in the capital of Emilia-Romagna is to understand the three defining characteristics of the city's identity. *La dotta*: the learned. Bologna is, first and foremost, a university town (and by first and foremost, we really mean it—the University of Bologna is the oldest in the world still in operation, having been founded way back in 1088). Where other Italian cities teem with tourists and their beloved selfie sticks, Bologna's streets are animated by a more vital and local spirit—all those people reading newspapers outside cafes in the middle of the afternoon are actual residents of Bologna, and those kids sitting along the curbs of bar-filled streets every night are students from the university. *La grassa*: the fat. While the people of Bologna aren't actually packing on a lot of extra pounds, they do know how to indulge in excellent, rich food at all hours of the day. The city is known for its tortellini, lasagna, and, of course, tagliatelle bolognese (which, heads up, ain't your mama's Chef Boyardee ragu). Sample as many traditional dishes as you can during your stay here because, as one local told us, to know the cuisine of Bologna is to understand the city. *La rossa*: the red. Bologna's final distinctive trait may refer to the anti-Fascist spirit and communist sympathies you'll find among many of its residents, but it also reflects, quite literally, the color and character of the city and its streets. Indeed, the endless maze of portico-lined medieval streets here will have you seeing new shades of red (and orange and rust and umber) with every twist and turn. Bologna truly is a city unlike any other, and to visit here is to abandon the usual rhythms of the tourist life and surrender yourself to the food, the architecture, the friendly people, the park benches, and the slower pace of real Italian life that you will discover under Bologna's many covered archways.

ORIENTATION

With a population of over 375,000, Bologna is actually a fairly large and sprawling modern city. Most of the places you'll be visiting during your stay, however, are located within the historic *centro*. The focal point of the city center is Piazza Maggiore, where you'll find the massive Basilica di San Petronio, several of the city's palazzos, and the popular Fontana del Nettuno. Directly to the north, the wide, commercial street of Ugo Bassi runs through the center of town to the Two Towers, the other major (if slightly off-kilter) landmarks with which to orient yourself. From here, Via Zamboni stretches northeast to the university area of town, while Via Castiglione runs south to the Giardini Margherita, just outside the city center, and also forms one perimeter of the Quadrilatero, a site of medieval markets that is now home to a concentration of bakeries, jewelers, and other shops (Piazza Maggiore, V. Rizzoli, and Piazza della Mercanzia constitute the other boundaries of the district). While you can find good food throughout the city, Via Pratello and Via Mascarella are filled with restaurants and bars that particularly popular among Bologna's younger crowds. West of the city center, the Portico di San Luca begins at the Arco del Meloncello and runs 3.5km uphill to the magnificent Santuario della Madonna di San Luca.

SIGHTS

Enjoy the many towers, churches, and palazzos of Bologna's historic *centro*, but venture outside the old city walls to add a little greenery to *la rossa*'s landscape of red roofs and endless maze of orange porticos.

SANTUARIO DELLA MADONNA DI SAN LUCA

V. di San Luca 36   ☎051 614 23 39 www.sanlucabo.org

If there are two things you need in your life right now, it's probably a little more exercise and a little more Jesus. (Well, maybe not the last one—you have seen your fair share of Madonna and Childs lately.) But regardless of your current level of physical fitness and/or the present state of your soul, make the pilgrimage up to the Santuario della Madonna di San Luca, a massive basilica that dominates a hilltop on the outskirts of Bologna. You may be escaping the city, but you can never escape its distinctive penchant for porticos; indeed, the real draw here, almost more than the basilica itself, is the 3.5km continuous portico that leads up to the church. The longest of its kind in the world, the Portico di San Luca is composed of 666 arches that ambitious tourists, locals in exercise gear, and little old ladies with swinging rosary beads pass under on their way up the hill. If you have a free afternoon, this is certainly a highlight—just make sure you have the hours and energy to commit to it.

i *The portico begins at Porta Saragozza, outside the city center. Walk all the way up the portico to the church at the top of V. di San Luca. Free. Open daily 7am-12:30pm and 2:30-7:30pm.*

BASILICA DI SANTO STEFANO

V. Santo Stefano 24   ☎051 22 32 56

At the Basilica di Santo Stefano, you get seven churches for the price of one (which, in Bologna, is still blessedly "free"). A Russian nesting doll of a Catholic church, the basilica was constructed over many centuries and is composed (in the order that you will likely walk through them) of the Church of St. John the Baptist (constructed in the eighth century and still the primary place of worship in the church today), the dark and haunting Church of the Holy Sepulcher (fifth century), the Church of the Saints Vitale and Agricola (first built in the fourth century but reconstructed in the 12th), the Courtyard of Pilate (13th century), the Church of the Trinity (13th century), the Cloister, and the Chapel of the Bandage (which now also houses a free museum). The entire complex, with its quiet brick courtyards and gloomy old altars, is quite striking and unlike most churches you'll come across in Italy—take a turn through its many component parts before admiring the beauty of the sum total from the piazza outside.

i *From the Two Towers, walk down V. Santo Stefano to the piazza. Free. Open daily 7am-noon and 3:30-6:45pm.*

PIAZZA MAGGIORE

As Bologna's main square, Piazza Maggiore is a good place to orient yourself within the *centro* and is also home to many of the city's most magnificent buildings, including the Basilica di San Petronio and Palazzo Comunale. In the summer months, the piazza hosts a series of a free outdoor film screenings. Adjoining the main piazza is Piazza del Nettuno, named after its popular fountain that depicts Neptune lording over a bevy of fat water babies and a bunch of maidens who are quite literally feelin' themselves by the water's edge.

i *From the crossroads of Ugo Bassi and V. dell'Indipendenza, walk across P. del Nettuno to P. Maggiore. Free.*

BASILICA DI SAN PETRONIO

P. Galvani 5   ☎051 23 14 15 www.basilicadisanpetronio.it

With its towering rows of brown stone stacked on top of pink and white marble, the unfinished facade of San Petronio certainly makes a strong statement as

get a room!

ALBERGO PANORAMA $

V. Giovanni Livraghi 1   ☎051 22 18 02 www.hotelpanoramabologna.it

With singles starting at just €40 per night, you can't do much better than Albergo Panorama, whose central location just off Ugo Bassi makes it a comfortable and convenient place to spend your time in Bologna. Breakfast here is served on a tray every morning, and although you'll be the one dishing it up and carrying it back to your room, the abundance of croissants and fresh fruit make it more than worth the self-service (and hey, breakfast in bed is still breakfast in bed). The sign downstairs may say that Albergo Panorama is located on the fourth floor, but if you're good at counting, you'll soon realize that it's actually on what Americans would call the sixth (we recommend that you take the lift and skip the 120 steps it takes to get up to your room). Fortunately, the high altitude at this *albergo* means that, although the views in each room aren't quite panoramic, they do feature a beautiful backdrop of rooftop gardens and the yellows and oranges of Bologna's colorful buildings.

i Walk down Ugo Bassi away from the Two Towers and turn left onto V. Giovanni Livraghi. The hotel is on the right. Singles with shared bath €40. Doubles from €55. Check-in noon-9pm.

ALBERGO CENTRALE $

V. della Zecca 2   ☎051 22 51 14 www.albergocentralebologna.it

At Albergo Centrale, the name says it all: rooms here are a few minutes' walk from the heart of Bologna and start at just €45 per night. And while the prime location and cheap rates are the primary draw here (rooms themselves are clean and comfortable but fairly basic), Albergo Centrale has the added draw of incredibly friendly reception and a couple of nooks and seating areas where you can enjoy the hotel's complimentary breakfast.

i Walk down Ugo Bassi away from the Two Towers and turn left onto V. della Zecca. The hotel is on the left. Singles with shared bath €45. Double with shared bath €65, private bath €72. Reception 24hr.

the focal point of Piazza Maggiore and might leave you with a hankering for some Neapolitan ice cream. Inside, this Gothic church adheres to what we're now assuming must be the Official Color Scheme of Bologna, with long, striking reddish-orange columns that line the three naves of this absolutely cavernous church (and it would have been even bigger—the city originally had plans to build a church that would surpass St. Peter's in size, but then the po-pope shut that shit down). Still, this church comes in at a respectable 15th largest in the world and is impressive in its own right. Soak it up and remember how stunning it all looks, because a Kodak moment here will cost you €2.

i It's the bigass church in P. Maggiore. Free. If you want to take pictures, a pass costs €2. Open daily 7:45am-1:30pm and 3-6:30pm.

TWO TOWERS

P. di Porta Ravegnana   ☎051 647 21 13

You might be surprised to learn that Pisa isn't the only town in Italy with a leaning tower. Technically, Bologna has two, although the majorly off-kilter Garisenda (which once stood at 60m but had to be cut down to 48m in the 14th century to prevent it from completely falling to pieces) makes the taller Asinelli look

bologna

fairly straight by comparison. Scale the 97.2m of the Torre Asinelli, however, and you might get a sense of its tipsiness from the narrow and often slanted wooden steps (497 total) that lead up to the top of the tower. After the seemingly endless climb, you'll be rewarded with breezes from the surrounding hills and great views of the city, which will give you a better sense of the *centro*'s layout. Note the five long, straight streets that run, like spokes in a wheel, from the towers out to the five gates of the old city walls. Fun fact: University of Bologna students never climb the tower due to an urban legend that those who do won't graduate (even more superstitiously—and impractically—they also never cross Piazza Maggiore on its diagonal).

i Located at the far end of Ugo Bassi. Torre Asinelli €3. Torre Asinelli open daily 9am-7pm.

PINACOTECA NAZIONALE
V. delle Belle Arti 56 ☎051 42 09 411 www.pinacotecabologna.it

It really should come as no surprise that a university town as old and storied as Bologna would have a great art museum. But still—the overachieving collection of work at the Pinacoteca Nazionale is really gunning for that A. And with its collection featuring works by greats such as Giotto, Raphael, Titian, and others, it definitely earns it. The 29 rooms of this excellently curated museum will carry you through the rich history of Italian (and often specifically Bolognese) art history, starting in the 13th century with a number of ornate, gilded altarpieces and working its way through the Renaissance and all the way up to the powdered wigs of the 18th century. The collection is certainly worth an hour or two of your time, and the walk down to the museum will also take you through the university area of town.

i From the Two Towers, walk down V. Zamboni until it meets with V. delle Belle Arti; the art museum is right near the intersection of the two streets. €4, reduced €2. Open Tu-W 9am-1:30pm, Th-Su 11am-7pm.

GIARDINI MARGHERITA
P. di Porta Santo Stefano

The Giardini Margherita perfectly exemplifies the local vitality of Bologna. While this 64-acre park located just south of the centro is certainly a nice place for tourists to take a stroll, it is primarily filled and buzzing with locals. From the joggers who make their way along the curving roads and paths to the vast, grassy field where teenagers kick around soccer balls to the tiny go-carts and swings where little kids bump around under the eyes of watchful parents, the park is a locus for Bolognese of all ages, sizes, and activity levels. And it's large enough to accommodate everyone's choice of afternoon diversion (even yours, which will probably involve buying some gelato at one of the stands in the park and engaging in an aggressively un-aerobic sprawl underneath a shady tree).

i From the city center, walk all the way down V. Castiglione; entrance to the gardens is located through Porta Castiglione and across Vle. Giovanni Gozzadini. Free.

PALAZZO DELL'ARCHIGINNASIO
P. Galvani 1 ☎051 27 68 11 www.archiginnasio.it

This 16th-century palace once served as the seat of the University of Bologna from 1563 to 1805 and now houses the more than 800,000 volumes of the Biblioteca dell'Archiginnasio. Although the library is not open to tourists, you can come here and admire the coats of arms of more than 5000 former university teachers and students that cover the walls and ceilings of the central courtyard and stairwells here. You should also consider throwing down the €3 it costs to visit the Anatomical Theatre upstairs where medical classes were once held. The entirely wooden interior of this small lecture hall features bodies crawling on the ceiling (look, there's Apollo suspended among the creepy crawlers) and rows of benches where we can only assume students once took copious notes during dissections (because back in the day there wasn't any Facebook to browse when they should have been paying attention). And unlike the buff, totally swole statues you find throughout the rest of Italy, the skinless statues that flank the lectern here know it's (literally) what's on the inside that counts (namely, your tendons and ligaments).

i From P. Maggiore, walk down V. Archiginnasio (to the left of San Petronio when facing the church). The palazzo is on the left. Courtyard free. Anatomical Theatre €3. Anatomical Theatre open M-F 10am-6pm, Sa 10am-7pm, Su 10am-2pm.

FOOD

As locals will tell you, pick any trattoria or osteria in Bologna, and you're guaranteed an excellent meal. Absolutely order a platter of cheese or meat (or both) and a basket of crostini (thin, flaky, and flavorful, it's like bread but even better), then dig into one of Bologna's renowned pasta dishes—don't leave town without trying the tortellini, lasagna, or, of course, tagliatelle bolognese.

LA SORBETTERIA DI CASTIGLIONE

V. Castiglione 44   ☎051 58 21 78 www.lasorbetteria.it

For the best gelato in Bologna, walk a little farther out from the center of town to La Sorbetteria Castiglione, whose silver canisters of gelato gleam in the lavender interior of this adorable pasticceria. Flavors here are listed in Italian, and although the place is frequented by locals, the friendly guys and gals behind the counter will still flash a winning smile at bumbling tourists like yourself. And good news for all you people who have trouble deciding between cones and cups—at La Sorbetteria, they're one in the same, so you can have your coppetta and eat it, too.

i From the city center, walk down V. Castiglione. La Sorbetteria is a few blocks down on the left. Additional location at V. Saragozza 83. Gelato from €2.50. Open daily 11am-midnight.

OSTERIA AL 15

V. Mirasole 15 $

☎051 33 18 06

A bit of a trek from Bologna's more central eateries, the walk over to Osteria al 15 will take you winding through portico after portico to this quieter side of town. Tucked under an archway on an otherwise empty street, it's not easy to find this restaurant if you're not looking for it, which means you'll likely be one of the few tourists here. Indeed, step into this cozy, cluttered osteria, and you'll find yourself among tables crowded with Italian families chattering away animatedly while passing around plates of pasta. The homestyle food and friendly

mortadella: it ain't no baloney

Forget Oscar Mayer. In Bologna, our baloney has a first name, and it's *m-o-r-t-a-d-e-l-l-a*. But the pink American lunch meat that you're probably most familiar with does, indeed, descend from a popular Bologna sausage called mortadella. Made from finely ground pork, mortadella is a cold cut meat that looks a lot like its bastardized American cousin, save for its distinctive white squares of pork fat and, occasionally, pieces of green olive that add a little texture to the mix. The meat is flavored with black pepper and myrtle berries, which give it its unique flavor, and although the little pieces of lard may have scared off the U.S. government (American baloney is not allowed to have any chunks of pork fat visible in the sandwich meat), don't let it freak you out because it's really good. Try mortadella in a sandwich or as an appetizer with some crostini.

manager here add to the sense of comfort and family, so order some traditional Bolognese ragu and settle in among the pots and pans hanging from the walls, the cabinets full of colorful owls, and the old brown magazine pages plastered on the ceiling.

i From P. Maggiore, walk down V. Massimo D'Azeglio several blocks, turn left onto V. delle Tovaglie, right onto V. Paglietta, then left onto V. Mirasole. The restaurant is on the right. Primi €8-9. Secondi €9-10. Open M-Sa 7:30pm-1am.

MOUSTACHE $

V. Mascarella 5 ☎051 23 54 24 www.moustachebologna.com

To eat among some real Italians, head over to Moustache on V. Mascarella. This laid-back restaurant and bar serves up authentic Bolognese dishes at student-friendly prices. Come here and eat the way Italians do—pass around a basket of crostini and a plate of cheese and meat, relax, eat slowly, tuck into some richy, meaty pasta, and just hang out for a while as you make your way through a couple bottles of wine. On weekends in the summer, sit outside and enjoy live street music late into the night.

i From V. Marsala, turn onto V. Mentana, then veer right onto V. delle Belle Arti, then left onto V. Mascarella. Moustache is on the right. Primi €6-9. Secondi from €7. Open M 6pm-midnight, Tu-Th 6pm-1am, F-Sa 8pm-1:30am.

PIZZERIA DA CIRO $

V. De Gessi 5 ☎051 22 69 17

If you've had enough ragu to satisfy your craving for a while and are looking for a cheap, familiar slice of pizza, head to Pizzeria da Ciro, where the thin-crust pies are made fresh, hot, and crispy. The plain white walls and pale green tablecloths here don't make much of a first impression, but what this pizzeria lacks in interior design it makes up for in the warm chatter of Italian families and couples that crowd in here for simple, no-fuss plates of pizza and pasta. The waiters don't speak much English, but luckily for you, the point-and-smile method of ordering goes over pretty well here.

i From Ugo Bassi walking away from the Two Towers, turn right onto V. Calcavinazzi and continue onto V. de Gessi. The pizzeria is on the right. Pizza €6.50-8. Primi €7-8. Secondi €9-16.

NIGHTLIFE

Unlike most cities, the summer months in Bologna are actually on the quieter side, as the drain of students from the city leaves its streets and bars emptier in July and August than they are during the school year. That being said, there's still plenty happening all year round, and visiting in the summer does mean you might have a chance to catch the live music lineup that plays in V. Mascarella on weekends. In addition to the street music, V. Mascarella is also lined with a number of restaurants, bars, and jazz clubs (check out Cantina Bentivoglio and Bravo Caffè). For more popular late-night options, head down to V. del Pratello, where young people gather under the porticos with drinks and cigarettes in hand outside the many bars on this street. At the end of the night, make your way to one of the squares in town, where you're guaranteed to find young locals hanging out on the curbs and under archways as dusk bleeds into dawn.

▨ PUB MUTENYE

V. del Pratello 44

The wooden furniture and warmly lit interior of this bar is a welcoming variation from the dark walls and green lights you find in so many Italian pubs. Although Mutenye's cozy front bar and back room provide plenty of space for patrons to mill about, on warm summer nights, most of the locals who frequent this pub enjoy pints at tables or under the porticos outside. And if the many varieties of beer available here aren't enough, there's always the pinball machine in the corner to help keep you entertained throughout the night.

i Walk down Ugo Bassi away from the Two Towers to where it ends, then cross the street and veer slightly left onto V. Pratello. Pub Mutenye is a few blocks down on the left. Beer from €3. Wine from €3. Open daily 5pm-3am.

OSTERIA L'INFEDELE

V. Gerusalemme 5

☎051 23 94 56

The walls here may display a few famous international names and faces (hey look, there's Obama in full red-white-and-blue "Hope" mode, right under a poster of his BFF, Vladimir Putin), but the crowd here is mostly local Italians who greet the bartenders and each other upon entry and then proceed to hang around until the wee hours of the morning. Tuck into a seat at one of the wooden tables and let your eyes flicker over the bar's assortment of old magazine covers and black-and-white photos on the walls, or step outside and enjoy some fresh night air with the crowd gathered out on the curb.

i From P. Santo Stefano, walk down V. Gerusalemme. The bar is on the left. Beer €3.50-4.50. Cocktails €6-7. Whiskey and rum €5-7. Shots €2. Open M-Sa noon-3am, Su noon-midnight.

BARAZZO

V. del Pratello 66b

☎328 796 73 13 www.barazzo.it

If you find yourself far from V. Mascarella and are looking for some live music to go with your Saturday-night spritzers, stop in at Barazzo, whose main stage hosts a variety of musical acts throughout the week. While the bar also offers a full menu, the tunes and atmosphere here are the main draw, so pop in after dinner for a beer or cocktail and get ready to sit back, relax, and face the music (in a literal, totally non-ominous kind of way).

i Walk down Ugo Bassi away from the Two Towers to where it ends, then cross the street and veer slightly left onto V. Pratello. Barazzo is a few blocks down on the left. Open Tu-Su 6pm-3am.

ESSENTIALS

Practicalities

- **TOURIST OFFICES:** IAT provides information and is the starting point for walking and bus tours. (P. Maggiore 1E ☎051 23 96 60. Open M-Sa 9am-7pm, Su 10am-5pm.)

- **LUGGAGE STORAGE:** Stazione Centrale. (Located on the ground floor. Open daily 7am-9pm. 1st 5hr. €6, 6-12th hr. €0.90, €0.40 per hr. thereafter.)

- **ATMS:** There is a Unicredit ATM located at V. dell'Indipendenza 11.

- **POST OFFICE:** Poste Italiane. (P. Minghetti 4 ☎051 275 67 36. Open M-F 8am-6:30pm, Sa 8am-12:30pm.)

Emergency

- **POLICE:** Polizia di Stato. (V. degli Agresti 3 ☎051 23 76 32)

- **HOSPITALS/MEDICAL SERVICES:** Policlinico Sant'Orsola Malpighi. (V. Pietro Albertoni 15 ☎051 63 62 111. www.aosp.bo.it. Follow V. San Vitale to V. Giuseppe Massarenti and turn right. Open 24hr.)

Getting There

For those arriving by plane, Aeroporto Guglielmo Marconi (BLQ; V. Triumvirato 84 ☎051 64 79 615 www.bologna-airport.it) is northwest of the city center. ATC operates the Aerobus, which runs from the airport to Stazione Centrale (€6, every 15min.). For those arriving by train, Stazione Centrale services Florence (€19-24, 35min.), Milan

(€17-40, 1-3hr.), Venice (€12-30, 90min.-2hr.), and Rome (€49-56, 2hr. 15min.), among other smaller cities.

Getting Around

Bologna is most easily navigated on foot, although ATC does operate a comprehensive bus system throughout the city. Tickets cost €1.30 if purchased before getting on the bus or €1.50 if purchased on board.

florence

The capital of Tuscany and birthplace of the Italian Renaissance, Florence may not be able to lay claim to the thousands of years' worth of ruins and ancient history that you can wander through in Rome, but its legacy is something else entirely. Ruled by the storied Medici family and home to many great artists and thinkers, Florence boasts a history both Shakespearean in its political drama and unparalleled in the wealth of art that it created. Just as the city's artistic giants—from Michelangelo to Botticelli to Donatello—mastered space, lines, and geometry to create some of the greatest buildings, paintings, and sculptures in human history, so, too, does the city itself seem to be a purposeful work of art, with its bright palette of yellow and orange buildings, its cohesive architecture, and its clean, tourist-friendly streets. In every respect, Florence is a city of high culture—from the masterpieces of the Uffizi and the Galleria dell'Accademia to the dresses and trousers on display in the windows of fashion houses to the DOCG-stamped bottles of Chianti that you can sample in the vineyards that surround the city. The spell of Florence's perfection can very occasionally be broken by the crush of tourists flooding Piazza del Duomo or snaking along the walls of the city's museums—and sitting low in a valley surrounded by the far off Apennine mountains, Florence is particularly susceptible to hot summer days that leave tourists and their cones of gelato dripping under the Tuscan sun. It is this same cradled position, however, that makes the city so stunning when viewed from the high perches of spots like Piazzale Michelangelo or the Forte di Belvedere. When the sun begins to retreat behind the distant peaks and the pink haze of the sunset envelopes the low-lying city, the iconic orange Duomo and the bridges of the Arno take on new hues and new beauty—and despite its feast of towers, cathedrals, and Renaissance treasures, the entire spread of the city itself is perhaps Florence's greatest marvel.

ORIENTATION

The heart of the city and its most popular sights are concentrated in Piazza del Duomo. Slightly to the north in San Lorenzo lies the Basilica di San Lorenzo, the San Lorenzo outdoor market, and the many food stalls and eateries of Mercato Centrale. From this neighborhood, Stazione Santa Maria Novella is easily reached via the busy Via Nazionale. Wander farther south to Santa Croce, a popular nightlife neighborhood that surrounds the basilica from which it takes its name. The second -busiest square in the city is Piazza della Signoria, where you'll find plenty of statues, stringed orchestras, and the towering Palazzo Vecchio. Just around the corner sits the Uffizi Gallery and the distinctive gray architecture and long galleries of Piazza degli Uffizi. From here, cross the famed Ponte Vecchio (or any of the city's lesser bridges) to the Oltrarno (literally "beyond the Arno"). On this side of the river, you'll find Palazzo Pitti, the sprawling Boboli Gardens, and the popular restaurants and bars of Piazza Santo Spirito to the west and Piazzale Michelangelo and San Miniato al Monte looming high above the rest of the neighborhood in the east.

ACCOMMODATIONS

OSTELLO GALLO D'ORO $$
V. Cavour 104   ☎055 552 2964 www.ostellogalldoro.com

This may be the hostel of the "golden cockerel," but the only roosters you'll find here are the ones in the Wi-Fi passwords. One of Florence's smaller hostels, Gallo D'Oro comprises just one floor, but its single, twisting green hallway is decorated with letters from and pictures of happy hostel guests, all of whom proclaim their collective love of cock (sorry—it was too easy!). The close quarters here means that you'll get to know both your fellow travelers and the wonderful staff quite well (shoutout to the awesome Matteo and Martina!). Adding to the family feel of this hostel are the omnipresent snacks in the common area, the books available to browse on the shelves in the hallways, and a bountiful breakfast spread featuring fresh, homemade breads and tarts.

i From the Duomo, walk down V. Cavour several blocks. The hostel is a 10min. walk down the street, on the right. Dorms from €30. Breakfast included. Laundry machine available. Reception 24hr.

WOW FLORENCE HOSTEL $$
V. Venezia 18/b   ☎055 579 603 www.wowflorence.com

You always wanted to be a superhero, and WOW Florence Hostel just might be your chance. At the very least, the color blocking and countless posters of comic book heroes at this hostel will make you feel like you're living inside the pages of a Marvel (or DC!) comic book. The rooms here are just as colorful as reception, and the hostel offers plenty of spaces to hang out with your fellow travel avengers (whether it be the high-ceilinged common room, breakfast area, or sunny smoking patio). WOW is located all the way up on the fifth floor, so either whip out those Spidey web-slinging powers or, you know, just take the elevator.

i From the Duomo, walk down V. Cavour several blocks and turn right onto V. Venezia. The hostel is on the left. Dorms €29. Singles €50. Breakfast €5. Check-in 2pm.

PLUS FLORENCE HOSTEL $
V. Santa Caterina D'Alessandria 15   ☎055 628 6347 www.plushostels.com

The giant lettering and sliding doors that usher you into the cool, sprawling lobby of this massive hostel makes Plus feel more like a giant corporate hotel (or maybe even a convention center) than a youth hostel. With multiple locations throughout Europe, this behemoth of a hostel features an internet cafe, fitness center, restaurant, and even an outdoor swimming pool and bar. And if that wasn't enough, it has beds and toilets, too! Now you know where the "plus" in the name comes from.

i From the Santa Maria Novella train station, walk through P. Adua onto V. Bernardo Cennini, then turn left onto V. Faenza, then right onto V. Pratello. Continue a ways before curving right on V. Cosimo Ridolfi, walk through P. dell'Indipendenza, and turn left onto V. Santa Caterina D'Alessandria. Dorms from €25. Reception 24hr. Check-in 2:30pm.

HOSTEL ARCHI ROSSI $$
V. Faenza 94r   ☎055 290 804 www.hostelarchirossi.com

The cool-colored murals that cover the walls of reception might make you feel like you're living inside a full-sleeve biker tattoo, but fortunately for you, this hostel is a little bit cozier than an easy rider's bicep. In addition to the chill guys at the front desk, the lobby will also greet you with vending machines and a full breakfast buffet every morning. And while rooms are comfortable but basic, they do glitz things up a bit with gold metal bunk frames.

i From Santa Maria Novella train station, walk through P. Adua and onto V. Bernardo Cennini, then turn right onto V. Faena. The hostel is just a few steps away, on the left. Dorms €28-30. Reception 24hr. Check-in 2:30pm.

florence

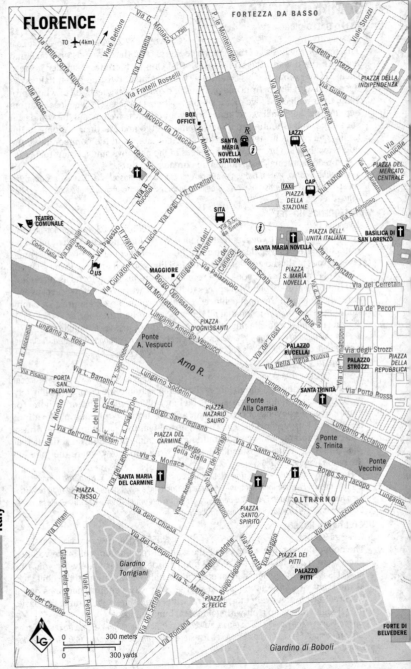

FLORENCE

TO ✈ (4km)

FORTEZZA DA BASSO

PIAZZA DELLA INDIPENDENZA

Via G. Monaco
V.J. Pili
Viale Belfiore
Via delle Porte Nuove
Alle Mosse
Via Cittadella
Via Fratelli Rosselli
Via Jacopo da Diacceto
P. le Montelungo
Via Strozzi
Viale Strozzi
Via della Fortezza
Via Faenza
Via Gualfa
PIAZZA DEL MERCATO CENTRALE
Via della Scala
Via B Rucellai
Via degli Orti Oricellari
Via Alamanni
Via Valfonda
Via Fiume
Via Nazionale
Via Panicale
Via dell'Ariento
Via S. Antonino

BOX OFFICE
SANTA MARIA NOVELLA STATION
LAZZI
TAXI
CAP
PIAZZA DELLA STAZIONE
SITA
Via S.C. da Siena

TEATRO COMUNALE
Corso Italia
Via Garibaldi
Via Montebello
Il Prato
Via Palazzuolo
Via Curtatone
Via Solferino
Via S. Lucia
Via della Spada
Finiguerra
Via dell'Alloro
Via de' Cimatori
Via del Palazzuolo
Via de' Canacci
Via della Scala

US
MAGGIORE
Borgo Ognissanti
PIAZZA D'OGNISSANTI
Lungarno Amerigo Vespucci

SANTA MARIA NOVELLA
PIAZZA DELL' UNITA ITALIANA
BASILICA DI SAN LORENZO
PIAZZA S. MARIA NOVELLA
Via de' Panzani
Via de' Cerretani
Via de' Pecori
Via del Sole
Via del Belle Donne

Ponte A. Vespucci
Lungarno S. Rosa
Via d. Ardiglione
Via Pisana
Via L. Bartolini
PORTA SAN FREDIANO
V. S. Onofrio
Lungarno Soderini
Arno R.

PALAZZO RUCELLAI
Via della Vigna Nuova
Via de' Fossi
Via de' Tornabuoni
Via degli Strozzi
PALAZZO STROZZI
PIAZZA DELLA REPUBBLICA

SANTA TRINITÀ
Lungarno Corsini
Via Porta Rossa
Lungarno Acciaiuoli

Via L. Ariosto
Via dell'Orto
V. d. Cardatori
P. dei Nerli
V. d. Piaggione
V. d. Tessitori
V. d. Leone
Borgo San Frediano
PIAZZA NAZARIO SAURO
Ponte Alla Carraia
Ponte S. Trinita
Ponte Vecchio
Borgo San Jacopo
Lungarno

PIAZZA DEL CARMINE
Borgo della Stella
Via S. Monaca
SANTA MARIA DEL CARMINE
PIAZZA T. TASSO
Via del Campuccio
Via della Chiesa
Via dell'Orto
Via S. Agostino
Via S. Spirito
Via di Santo Spirito
PIAZZA SANTO SPIRITO
OLTRARNO
Via de' Guicciardini
Borgo San Jacopo

Giardino Torrigiani
Giano Della Bella
Via Villani
Via del Leone
Via del Serragli
Via delle Caldaie
Via S. Maria
Via Mazzetta
Borgo Tegolaio
Via Maggio
PIAZZA DEI PITTI
PALAZZO PITTI
PIAZZA S. FELICE

N
LG
0 — 300 meters
0 — 300 yards

Via del Casone
Viale F. Petrarca
Via Romana
Giardino di Boboli
FORTE DI BELVEDERE

italy

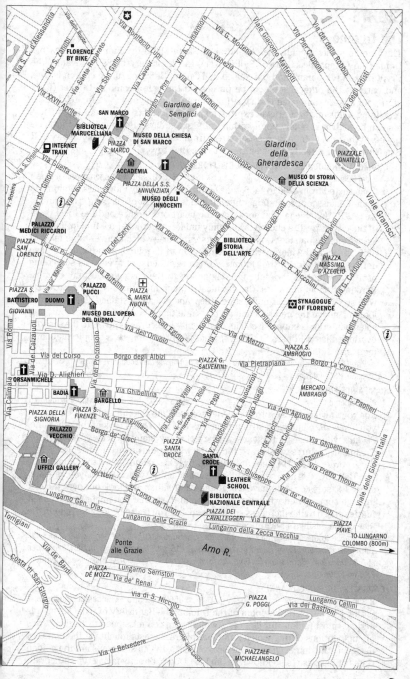

FLORENCE BY BIKE

Via delle Ruote

Via S.C. d'Alessandria

Via S. Zanobi

Via Santa Reparata

Via San Gallo

Via XXVII Aprile

Via Cavour

Via Giorgio La Pira

Via Bonifacio Lupi

Via A. Lamarmora

Viale Giacomo Matteotti

Via G. Modena

Via Venezia

Via P.A. Michelli

Via della Robbia

Via Pier Capponi

Via degli Artisti

Giardino dei Semplici

SAN MARCO

BIBLIOTECA MARUCELLIANA

INTERNET TRAIN

Via della Dogana

Via Guelfa

Via de' Ginori

Via Ricasoli

Via Cavour

Via S. Orsola

V. Rosina

MUSEO DELLA CHIESA DI SAN MARCO

PIAZZA S. MARCO

ACCADEMIA

Via Gino Capponi

Via Giuseppe Giusti

Giardino della Gherardesca

PIAZZALE DONATELLO

MUSEO DI STORIA DELLA SCIENZA

Viale Gramsci

PALAZZO MEDICI RICCARDI

PIAZZA SAN LORENZO

Via de' Pucci

Via de' Martelli

PIAZZA DELLA S.S. ANNUNZIATA

MUSEO DEGLI INNOCENTI

Via dei Servi

Via della Colonna

Via Laura

Via della Pergola

Borgo Pinti

BIBLIOTECA STORIA DELL'ARTE

Via G.B. Niccolini

V. Luigi Carlo Farini

PIAZZA MASSIMO D'AZEGLIO

Via G. Carducci

Via degli Alfani

Via Bufalini

PALAZZO PUCCI

PIAZZA S. MARIA NUOVA

Via della Mattonaia

PIAZZA S. BATTISTERO GIOVANNI

DUOMO

MUSEO DELL'OPERA DEL DUOMO

Via dei Calzaiuoli

Via Roma

Via San Egidio

Via dell'Oriuolo

Borgo Pinti

Via Fiesolana

Via di Mezzo

Via dei Pilastri

SYNAGOGUE OF FLORENCE

PIAZZA S. AMBROGIO

Via del Corso

Borgo degli Albizi

Via D. Alighieri

Via del Proconsolo

PIAZZA G. SALVEMINI

Via Pietrapiana

Borgo La Croce

ORSANMICHELE

Via Calimala

BADIA

BARGELLO

Via Ghibellina

Via Giuseppe Verdi

Via delle Seggiole

Via Isola delle Stinche

Via de' Pepi

V.M. Buonarroti

Borgo Allegri

Via dell'Agnolo

MERCATO AMBROGIO

Via F. Papfieri

PIAZZA DELLA SIGNORIA

PIAZZA S. FIRENZE

PALAZZO VECCHIO

Via dell'Anguillara

Borgo de' Greci

Via de' Macci

Via delle Casine

Via Ghibellina

Via della Giovine Italia

UFFIZI GALLERY

Via dei Neri

Via de' Benci

Via del Corso dei Tintori

PIAZZA SANTA CROCE

Via del Pinzochere

SANTA CROCE

Via S. Giuseppe

Via delle Conce

Via Pietro Thouar

Via de' Malcontenti

LEATHER SCHOOL

BIBLIOTECA NAZIONALE CENTRALE

Lungarno Gen. Diaz

PIAZZA DEI CAVALLEGGERI

Via Tripoli

Lungarno della Zecca Vecchia

PIAZZA PIAVE

TO LUNGARNO COLOMBO (800m)

Torrigiani

Ponte alle Grazie

Arno R.

Costa di San Giorgio

Via de' Bardi

PIAZZA DE' MOZZI

Lungarno Serristori

Via de' Renai

Via di S. Niccolo

PIAZZA G. POGGI

Lungarno Cellini

Via dei Bastioni

Via del Monte alle Croci

Via di Belvedere

PIAZZALE MICHAELANGELO

florence

SIGHTS

The Duomo

The Duomo sights include the Cathedral of Santa Maria del Fiore, Brunelleschi's Dome, the Campanile (Giotto's Bell Tower), the Baptistery of San Giovanni, the Crypt of Santa Reparata, and the Museo dell'Opera. Entrance to the church is free, and entry to the other sights can be purchased through a combined ticket (€15); after your ticket is activated upon visiting your first sight, you have 24hr. to visit the remaining sights until your ticket expires, so plan your sightseeing accordingly. Tickets can be activated at any point within the first six days after purchase. Purchase tickets at the ticket office (across the street from the entrance to the Baptistery in P. San Giovanni) or directly at the entrance to the Bell Tower.

DUOMO (CATHEDRAL OF SANTA MARIA DEL FIORE)

P. del Duomo   ☎055 23 02 885 www.operaduomo.firenze.it

Constructed from 1296 to 1436, the Duomo was basically Florence's version of a giant, Renaissance foam finger intended to tell the rest of Tuscany, "Hey, guys—we're #1! Also, Siena, you suck!" As the heart of Florence and the focal point of the cityscape, the church is certainly unlike any other you'll find in Italy—at least from the outside. Compared to its exterior—which is a veritable feast of pink, green, and white marble, all leading up to its stunning and iconic orange dome—the interior of the Duomo is often regarded by travelers as something of a letdown. And certainly, in comparison to the absolute gluttony of most Baroque Roman churches, this basilica is much more modest and restrained, with simple white walls, understated tiles, and just a few stained-glass windows looming above the central altar. At the same time, its massive, cavernous, and solemn interior is impressive in its own right—indeed, as opposed to the sensory overload that is Rome's St. Peter's, what's impressive here is simply the mammoth size of the church.

i P. del Duomo. Entrance is through the left door when facing the facade. Free. Open M-Sa 10am-5pm, Su 1:30-4:45pm.

CAMPANILE AND DOME

P. del Duomo   ☎055 23 02 885 www.operaduomo.firenze.it

For your own up-close, bird's-eye view of both the Duomo and the Bell Tower, you'll need to climb each structure in order to get a good look at the other one. So kick your glutes into gear—you've got some stairs to scale. Although the Campanile features two-lane traffic all the way up and down the tower (tuck into those corners!), its 414 steps are still slightly less strenuous than the Dome's 463. The Bell Tower is also separated into several levels, which means you can stop every 100 steps or so to have a seat, take a breather, and look out over the city through some grated windows. At the top of the tower, you might find yourself fully exposed to the merciless summer sun, but you'll also be looking right in the face of the basilica's magnificent orange Dome.

i Entrance to the Dome is on the north side of the Cathedral (via the Porta della Mandorla). Entrance to the Bell Tower is pretty easy to spot. €15 with Duomo sights ticket. Dome open M-F 8:30am-7pm, Sa 8:30am-5:40pm (last entry 40min. before close). Bell Tower open daily 8:15am-6:50pm.

BAPTISTERY OF SAN GIOVANNI

P. San Giovanni   ☎055 23 02 885 www.operaduomo.firenze.it

Sitting just opposite the doors of the Duomo, the Baptistery of San Giovanni is perhaps most famous for its doors, which were commissioned through a series of competitions during which a number of great artists fought for the honor of designing the doors. Of the three sets of doors, the most famous are the golden Gates of Paradise (also known as the East Doors, directly facing the cathedral), which were designed by Lorenzo Ghiberti and include a number of panels depicting the life of Christ. Inside, the dark, cave-like interior of the Baptistery provides a shocking contrast to the building's white marble facade, although if you crane your neck upward and have a look at the ceiling mosaics, you'll discover a brighter array of colors (including more gold!) and the looming visage of an enormous Christ at the Last Judgment.

i Entrance on the north side of the Baptistery in P. San Giovanni. €10 with combined ticket for Dome, Campanile, Baptistery, and Reparata. Open M-F 8:15-10:15am and 11:15am-6:30pm, Sa 8:15am-6:30pm, Su 8:15am-1:30pm.

Piazza della Signoria

THE UFFIZI GALLERY

Piazzale degli Uffizi 6   www.uffizi.org

The Uffizi Gallery comprises two U-shaped floors that house some of the greatest artwork in all of Italy and the world. After you make your way through the infamous line outside, you'll begin your visit upstairs on the first floor, where the numbered rooms of the gallery begin just off the First Corridor, which is lined with busts and portraits of famous Florentines and plenty of Medicis (in case you forgot who they were). From here, make your way into Room 2, where you'll find a lot of large gilded altarpieces whose main theme seems to be "Madonna and Child" (what else?). Rooms 3-4 features Gothic artwork from Siena (which rival Florence seems to have reluctantly let slip into the collection). Starting in Room 7 (which features the debut of perspective!), watch as the Renaissance unfolds before your eyes. In Room 8, you'll see the familiar profiles of Piero della Francesca's *Portraits of the Grand Dukes of Urbino*. Room 15 features early works by Leonardo da Vinci (including his *Annunciation*), while Room 35 (with red walls that denote 16th-century artwork) houses pieces by Michelangelo. Depending on the time of year (and time of day) that you visit the Uffizi, the line for entry can take quite a while. If you haven't made a reservation before you arrive, check the electronic sign outside entrance #2 that displays the current average wait time. If the wait is only 60-90min. and you have a good book or podcast with you, it's worth standing in line (don't worry if it seems like the line isn't moving very quickly—that's because they only let new batches of people in every 30min. or so). Going later in the day sometimes means that you'll encounter shorter lines, but make sure that the wait will still leave you at least two hours to tour the museum before it closes.

i Right around the corner from P. della Signoria. €12.50, with reservation €16.50. Open Tu-Su 8:15am-6:50pm. Ticket office closes at 6:05pm, museum begins closing at 6:35pm.

THE BARGELLO

V. del Proconsolo 4   ☎055 23 88 606

A visit to the Bargello will require much less of your time than most other museums in Florence, and it will also demand a lot less of your money. For just a few euro, you can enter this palace and wander through one of the city's greatest collections of sculpture work and pieces by early Renaissance artists, including Brunelleschi and Ghiberti. While the inner courtyard is lined with impressive statues and coats of arms, some of the museum's most famous sculpture work is located upstairs. The largest and most impressive room here is the Salone di Donatello, which was inaugurated in 1886 on the 500th anniversary of the artist's birth and now houses several of his most celebrated statues. Watch as the Gothic influences of the early 15th century give way to the classically inspired stylings of the early Renaissance, a shift perfectly exemplified in Donatello's two statues of David. Downstairs, you can swing through another room of sculptures on your way out; this collection features statues from the later years of the Renais-

florence

sance and includes four works by Michelangelo, including his *Apollo-David* and a decidedly tipsy Bacchus.

i From P. del Duomo, walk toward the river down V. del Proconsolo. Entrance to the museum is on the left. €4, reduced €2. Open daily 8:15am-4:50pm. Last entry 30min. before close. Closed 1st, 3rd, and 5th Monday and 2nd and 4th Sunday of each month.

PIAZZA DELLA SIGNORIA

Known to most tourists as "that square with all the statues," Piazza della Signoria is home to a number of sculptures that you can see without having to pay any entrance fees or wait in any lines (imagine that!). You'll find most of these statues in the square's Loggia, which is home to Giambologna's impressive *Rape of the Sabine Women* and Benvenuto Cellini's *Perseus with the Head of Medusa*. Perhaps even more popular, however, is the square's famous statue of Poseidon, which is situated outside the Palazzo Vecchio just a few feet away from a reproduction of Michelangelo's *David* that stands in the exact spot where the original was once installed. You'll probably pass through this piazza without even trying to several times during your time in Florence, especially if you're planning to visit the palazzo, but try swinging by in the evening, when you can catch some live music in the square and see the statues all lit up at night.

i This is the main piazza north of the Uffizi. Free.

PALAZZO VECCHIO

P. della Signoria   ☎055 27 68 465

If you spent all morning and afternoon waiting in lines for the Uffizi and the Galleria, the good news is that you'll still have time in your day to visit the Palazzo Vecchio, which is one of the few museums in town that stays open after dark. The town hall of Florence, the Palazzo and its tower is the central fixture of Piazza della Signoria. Buy your tickets on the ground floor, drop your bags at the cloak room, and start your visit in the Tracce di Firenze where you can take a look at some paintings of Florence throughout the years, including some more contemporary ones depicting the damage inflicted on the city by WWII and the flood of 1966. After this brief visual history lesson, head upstairs to the rooms of the palace. Highlights include the Apartments of Leo X on the first floor and the Apartments of the Elements on the second floor; the floor plans of both levels line up perfectly, and the second-floor rooms dedicated to individual deities each correspond to a Medici family member whose room lies below (note, for example, how the Ceres Room is the room of Cosimo Il Vecchio—because just as Ceres provided for man by blessing him with the fruits of the earth, so did Cosimo bring prosperity to the city of Florence).

i The huge building in P. della Signoria. Museum €10, reduced €8. Tower and battlements €10, reduced €8. Archaeological tour €4. Museum and tower combined ticket €14, reduced €12. Museum open Apr-Sept M-W 9am-11pm, Th 9am-2pm, F-Su 9am-11pm; Oct-Mar M-W 9am-7pm, Th 9am-2pm, F-Su 9am-7pm. Tower and battlements open Apr-Sept M-W 9am-9pm, Th 9am-2pm, F-Su 9am-9pm; Oct-Mar M-W 10am-5pm, Th 10am-2pm, F-Su 10am-5pm. Nighttime tour of the tower and battlements 9-10:30pm.

PONTE VECCHIO

Try walking anywhere along the north side of the Arno, and you'll likely find yourself tangled up in throngs of tourists trying to capture a perfect selfie with this famous bridge. While the structure itself is impressive—it spans the narrowest section of the Arno river and is believed to have been first constructed by the Romans, although the current iteration dates back to the medieval period—what's less mesmerizing is the crush of tourist crowds that you'll encounter if you ever try to cross it. Where the bridge was once home to merchant stalls and butcher shops, it is now lined with gold shops and vendors selling everything from paintings to laser pointers. Still, the Ponte Vecchio is an iconic symbol of

Florence and is the only bridge in the city to have survived the devastation of World War II and the Nazi occupation (according to local legend, the protection of the Ponte Vecchio was an express order from Hitler himself). Despite its history and enduring power, however, the bridge is still best seen and admired from afar.

i From the Uffizi, walk to the river and turn right. It's the bridge with all the shops on it.

Santa Maria Novella

☒ MUSEO DI FERRAGAMO

P. Santa Trinita 5r ☎055 289 430 www.museoferragamo.it

If you can't afford any actual Ferragamo shoes and are too sweaty to even browse the store, you're still more than welcome to pay the €6 entrance fee to this museum (located in the basement of Palazzo Spini Feroni) and explore the history of Salvatore's much sought-after kicks. Each year, a different exhibit is featured in this museum, and you might be disappointed to find out that the majority of it has nothing to do with shoes. In 2015-16, the exhibit traced the history of the Palazzo Spini Feroni itself, and although the collections here are quite interesting and carefully curated, you came here to drool over heels you will never own. Fear not: regardless of the rest of the exhibition, the first couple rooms of the museum always focus on Ferragamo and feature shoes from his collection of dainty prototypes made throughout the first half of the 20th century.

i Enter at P. Santa Trinita on the side of the building that faces away from the river. The museum is in the basement of Palazzo Spini Feroni. €6. Open daily 10am-7:30pm.

BASILICA DI SANTA MARIA NOVELLA

P. Santa Maria Novella 18 ☎055 21 92 57 www.chiesasantamarianovella.it

Another gaping, white-walled Florentine church, the Basilica di Santa Maria Novella at least had the originality to add a little stripey pizazz to its ceiling. The huge frescoes covering the walls of the church's chapels also make up for its otherwise basic interior (you can even walk around the central chapel here and check out the intricate altar that features a miniature Duomo). For even more frescoes (in case you haven't had enough of those things), take a turn through the Chapter House and the Green Cloister, which also features scenic views of a lot of dead grass.

i From Santa Maria Novella train station, walk south through P. della Stazione and onto V. degli Avelli. The church is in P. Santa Maria Novella. €5, reduced €3.50. Open Apr-Oct M-Th 9am-7pm, F 11am-7pm; Nov-Mar M-Th 9am-5:30pm, F 11am-5:30pm.

San Lorenzo

☒ MEDICI CHAPEL

P. Madonna degli Aldobrandini 6 ☎055 238 86 02

The dome of this chapel is perhaps the second-most prominent in Florence's cityscape, but it's surprising how few tourists actually make it inside. Which is a shame because it's basically one giant vault of dead Medicis. Pass through security, and you'll find yourself right in the crypt of the building, where you can brush up on your Medici family tree and try to connect the dots between the artifacts on the walls and their owners buried in the ground below your feet. The real gem of the building, however, is the Chapel of Princes, whose decadent polychrome marble walls and semi-precious stone floor come in rich shades of greens, browns, blues, and maroon. In case you couldn't guess from the chapel's name (or from all the COSMVSes written in massive Latin letters on the walls), this extravagant mausoleum was constructed for the extra-special remains of the Medici grand dukes, six of whom are buried here in elaborate tombs that look kind of like giant bathtubs.

i Located just behind the Basilica di San Lorenzo. From the church, walk down P. di San Lorenzo and turn left onto V. del Canto de' Nelli. Entrance to the chapel is on the left. €8, reduced €4. Open daily 8:15am-5pm. Last entry 20min. before close. Closed on the 1st, 3rd, and 5th Monday and 2nd and 4th Sunday of each month.

BASILICA DI SAN LORENZO
P. San Lorenzo 9 ☎055 21 66 34

First consecrated in 393 CE and later rebuilt during the 14th century, the Basilica di San Lorenzo was Florence's very first cathedral. It's also a pretty good place to start your sightseeing in the city. Not only will the white walls and slate-gray columns here introduce you to the restrained architecture and subdued aesthetics of many Florentine churches (a shocking contrast to the Baroque gluttony of Rome's basilicas), but the church also highlights the work of some of Florence's most celebrated artists: Brunelleschi's clean designs feature heavily here (although his sacristy is punctuated by flashier polychrome contributions from Donatello, who is also buried in the crypt), while the Library of Cosimo Medici (also housed in this complex) was designed by none other than Michelangelo. You can either buy a ticket for just the church or for the church, library, and crypt; we recommend the latter ticket if you want to brush up on some of your Medici family history in addition to getting your prayer on.

i From the Duomo, walk up through P. San Giovanni (past the Baptistery) and turn right onto Borgo San Lorenzo. The church is on the left in P. San Lorenzo. €4.50, for basilica and library €7.50. Open M-Sa 10am-5pm, Su 1:30-5pm.

PALAZZO MEDICI RICCARDI
V. Cavour 1

Of all the Medici property in town (which is, admittedly, most of Florence), the Palazzo Medici Riccardi is probably the most skippable. That being said, if you have an extra 30min. in your day and a few euro in your pocket, take a swing through the palace where some of these ruling dukes actually lived. The highlights are the palace's central courtyard (which you can get a peek into from the street) and the beautiful Chapel of the Magi, whose colorful fresco is chock-full of Medici faces and looks like something straight out of a fairytale storybook.

i From P. di San Lorenzo, walk down V. Cavour. The palace is on the left; entrance is at V. Cavour 3. €7, reduced €4. Open M-Tu 9am-7pm, Th-Su 9am-7pm.

San Marco

GALLERIA DELL'ACCADEMIA
V. Ricasoli 58 ☎055 238 86 12 www.polomuseale.firenze.it

Visitors to Florence line up outside the Galleria dell'Accademia for hours to witness the glory of Italy's most famous Renaissance man (and his equally famous manhood). Michelangelo's *David*, however, is more than just the sum of his parts (although those parts are pretty impressive, too). There's a gravity and haunting magic to him that you'll get a taste of the moment you round the corner of the museum's introductory room and catch your very first glimpse of the world-famous statue standing in his own private tribuna at the end of a long gallery. For a slayer of giants, the 17 ft. *David* is a behemoth in his own right. Walk a little closer and gaze up his mammoth hands, his huge toe nails, and every curl of his giant head—then take a moment to consider the smaller details of this masterpiece, like the veins on *David*'s arms, the outlines of his ribs, and the dimple of a belly button in the ripple of his rock-hard abs. Indeed, it's hard to admire Michelangelo's unparalleled artistry without also taking time to admire *David*'s killer bod ("Holy V-lines, Batman!").

i *From P. del Duomo, walk down V. Ricasoli. Entrance to the museum is on the right; pick up reserved tickets at the office on the left. The length of the lines here, coupled with the relatively short amount of time you're likely to spend in the actual museum, make the Galleria a good place to splurge on a reservation. €8, with reservation €12. Open Tu-Su 8:15am-6:50pm. Ticket office closes at 6:20pm, museum begins closing at 6:40pm.*

Santa Croce

GREAT SYNAGOGUE OF FLORENCE

V. Luigi Carlo Farini 6 ☎055 234 66 54

Hozier may want to take you to church, but at this point in your trek through Italy, your own personal tune may have changed to something like "Please, God, don't take me to another church." So if you've had your fill of crucifixes, Madonna and Childs, and New Testament frescoes, seek out the Great Synagogue of Florence, whose oxidized copper dome stands out like a Gatsby-esque green light in a sea of Catholic churches and red Tuscan roofs. Constructed in the late 1800s, the synagogue's towering palm trees, pink pomato stone, and Moorish influences provide a welcome contrast to most of the church facades you've seen thus far. Inside, the synagogue takes on a different color scheme all together—the walls of the temple are entirely covered in hand-painted blue, red, and brown arabesques. The beauty of the synagogue is even more remarkable when you consider that it was almost entirely lost during the German occupation of Italy during World War II, when the Fascists seized the synagogue and turned it into a garage, then rigged it with explosives during their evacuation of the city.

i *From P. del Duomo, walk down V. dell'Oriuolo, turn left onto Borgo Pinti, then right onto V. di Mezzo, left onto V. dei Pepi, right onto V. dei Pilastri, then left onto V. Luigi Carlo Farini. €6.50, reduced €5. Open June-Sept M-Th 10am-6:30pm, F 10am-5pm, Su 10am-6:30pm; Oct-May M-Th 10am-5:30pm, F 10am-3pm, Su 10am-5:30pm. Last entry 45min. before close.*

BASILICA DI SANTA CROCE

P. Santa Croce 16 ☎055 246 61 05 www.santacroceopera.it

At the Basilica di Santa Croce, it's never #toosoon to cash in on dead famous people. You'll find a lot of them here, and you'll have to drop a few euro if you want to see their final resting places. Dante's tomb is massive (and, spoiler alert, contains no Dante—he rests in Ravenna), while Machiavelli's is a little less grand than you might expect for such a prince. The two most impressive tombs, however, are Michelangelo's and Galileo's (located on opposite sides of the nave near the front doors of the church). Both tombs feature polychrome marble and easily recognizable tributes to each titan: Michelangelo's is decorated with statues representing painting, sculpture, and architecture, as well as a bust of the artist himself, while Galileo's is adorned with a sculpture of the scientist with the world in his hand.

i *Located on the far east end of P. di Santa Croce. €6, reduced €4. Open M-Sa 9:30am-5:30pm, Su 2-5:30pm. Last entry 30min. before close.*

West Oltrarno

PALAZZO PITTI

P. de Pitti 1 ☎055 294 883 www.uffizi.firenze.it

The Palazzo Pitti certainly isn't shy about announcing itself—not only is the palace itself quite daunting in size, but the huge plaza out front will also give visitors plenty of time to admire the mammoth structure while they truck it across the bare expanse of asphalt on their way up to the ticket office. The palace, once the primary residence of the Grand Dukes of Tuscany and later a base

florence

used by Napoleon, now houses a number of museums and galleries: the Galleria Palatina, Galleria d'Arte Moderna, and Appartamenti Reali can all be visited by purchasing the palazzo's Ticket 1, while the Museo Degli Argenti, Galleria del Costume, and Museo della Porcellana are included in Ticket 2. The biggest draw of the palace complex, however, is actually its sprawling grounds, which comprise the enormous and beautiful Boboli Gardens. Entrance to the gardens is included in Ticket 2.

i *Cross the Ponte Vecchio to Oltrarno and follow V. de' Guicciardini to P. de' Pitti. Ticket 1 €13, reduced €6.50. Ticket 2 €10, reduced €5. Open daily 8:15am-6:50pm. Last entry 45min. before close.*

BOBOLI GARDENS
Palazzo Pitti   ☎055 229 87 32 www.uffizi.firenze.it

Although there are a number of gates to the garden along its extensive perimeter, the easiest way to enter the Boboli Gardens is through the Palazzo Pitti (where you'll likely be purchasing your ticket anyway). From the courtyard of the palazzo, a left turn will lead you along a number of sunny paths and hedgerows; walk straight ahead, and you'll find yourself climbing up a set of steps to the central fountain of Neptune and some crisp brown lawns; continue farther up, and you'll reach the pretty gardens of the Porcelain Museum, which also provide some nice overlooks onto the surrounding Tuscan hills. Perhaps the nicest, shadiest paths of the park, however, are farther to the east (a right turn from the main entrance); here you'll find a number of green, canopied paths, hidden fountains and statues, and the garden's impressive, sloping Cypress Alley.

i *Enter through Palazzo Pitti. €10 with Ticket 2. Open daily 8:15am-6:50pm. Last entry 45min. before close.*

FORTE DI BELVEDERE
V. di San Leonardo 1

For an incredible view of Florence from West Oltrarno that won't cost you €10 (looking at you, Boboli Gardens), hike your way up to Forte di Belvedere (where you can, quite literally, look down on the Boboli Gardens, as well as out over the entirety of the city). Constructed by order of the Medicis in the late 16th century, the fortress now hosts contemporary art exhibitions and the occasional celeb wedding (Kim + Kanye 4ever, y'all). Roam the grounds and walk around the fortress for views of the city and the Tuscan countryside in every direction.

i *Cross the Ponte Vecchio to Oltrarno, then turn left onto V. de' Bardi. Veer right onto Costa dei' Magnoli and follow it uphill as it curves right becomes Costa San Giorgio. When the road forks, veer right onto V. del Forte di San Giorgio. Free.*

SANTA MARIA DEL CARMINE (BRANCACCI CHAPEL)
P. del Carmine   ☎055 21 23 31

The sole draw of the understated Santa Maria del Carmine, located in a quiet corner of West Oltrarno, is the church's famous Brancacci Chapel. It even acknowledges as much, roping off the entirety of the cathedral's beige interior save for the chapel and allowing visitors to enter this tight corner of the church through a single side door. Often regarded as the Sistine Chapel of the Early Renaissance, the Brancacci Chapel features a cycle of frescoes depicting stories from the life of St. Peter, including a depiction of the Temptation of Eve that you'll probably recognize from one of your high school history textbooks (you can check out the perpetuation of the "women ruin everything" trope on the far right wall).

i *Cross Ponte alla Carraia to Oltrarno and continue straight along V. dei Serragli, then turn right onto V. Santa Monaca and follow it to P. del Carmine. €6, reduced €4.50. Open M 10am-5pm, W-Sa 10am-5pm, Su 1-5pm. Last entry 45min. before close.*

East Oltrarno

PIAZZALE MICHELANGELO

Perched high above the city and across the river in East Oltrarno, this piazzale boasts some of the best views of Florence you're likely to find in the whole city. The only downside is that it's not exactly a well-kept secret. Throughout the day and well into the evening, tourists of all sorts make the long trek up the stairs to this square (the grade is gently sloping at first and then turns into flight upon flight of steps). Piazzale Michelangelo is particularly popular in the evenings, when countless tourists crowd along the edge of the square to watch the sun dip below the mountains. As night sets in, young people gather on the steps at the top of the square and listen to live musicians while nursing cheap bottles of beer and wine (you can either BYOB or purchase something from the bar or refreshment stands up here). Start trucking your way up here about 45min.-1hr. before sunset to get a good spot for the light show and the changing colors of Florence and the Arno at dusk. And if you can tear your eyes away from the cityscape for a moment or two, take note of the green David standing tall and proud in the center of the piazzale.

i *From pretty much any bridge, bear east along the river until P. Giuseppe Poggi, where the base of the steps is located. If you're not wearing walking shoes, take bus #12 or 13. Free.*

FOOD

The Duomo

MESOPOTAMIA $

P. Salvemini 14

This Mesopotamia is neither the cradle of human civilization nor the cradle of authentic Tuscan food. But everyone gets drunk sometimes, and this little kebab shop will do the trick when you get a case of the late-night drunchies. But if, fair reader, you fancy yourself a little classier than the Eurotrippers who stumble in here as late as 5am, Mesopotamia is also a nice place to stop for a quick lunch in the middle of a day of sightseeing (it's just down the street from the Duomo and professes to serve the best kebabs in Florence).

i *Follow V. dell'Oriuolo from the southeast corner of P. del Duomo. Mesopotamia is on the left when the street opens onto a piazza. Kebabs €4-7.50. Falafel €4-5. Open daily 11am-5am.*

Piazza della Signoria

DA VINATTIERI $

V. Santa Margherita 4r   ☎055 29 47 03 www.davinattieri.it

The hot, toasted panini at Da Vinattieri get Let's Go's vote for the best sandwiches in the city. Located just down the road from Casa di Dante, this tiny shop just might be the ninth circle of Sandwich Heaven and is tucked far enough away from Piazza della Signoria that it escapes the crush of tourist crowds at more centrally located lunch spots. And with sandwiches ringing in at just €4 a pop, you won't be feeling salty about these prices—although you will be enjoying some sea salt sprinkled on Da Vinattieri's excellent, crusty bread. The long list of panini offered here includes options like lard, goat cheese, and walnuts and salami, gorgonzola, and sun-dried tomatoes.

i *From P. della Signoria, walk down V. dei Magazzini (away from the river), turn right onto V. Dante Alighieri, then make a quick left onto V. Santa Margherita. Da Vinattieri is on the right. Sandwiches €4. Wine €3-6 per glass. Open daily 10am-5pm (although they stop serving sandwiches whenever they run out of bread).*

florence

PIZZERIA O'VESUVIO $

V. dei Cimatori 21r

☎055 28 54 87 www.ovesuviofirenze.com

The only thing that might erupt here is your stomach, and if it does, it will be in the name of a worthy cause. O'Vesuvio serves up hot, perfectly thin Neapolitan pies out of the volcanic wood-fired oven in the middle of the restaurant, and you have the option to order your pizza with stuffed crust. And not the Domino's kind, either—these crusts come stuffed with creamy ricotta, which is pretty much what dreams are made of. And while the decor and ambience of this restaurant leave a little to be desired—what do some California Highway Patrol badges, a single *Scarface* poster, some soccer jerseys, and a lone hanging cluster of plastic grapes have in common, besides the fact that they're all here?—you'll probably be too distracted trying to finish your pizza to notice. (Yes, it will all fit in your stomach, so just keep going, and leave some room for the Nutella pizza dolce to top things off.)

i From P. della Signoria, walk down V. dei Calzaiuoli and turn right onto V. dei Cimatori. O'Vesuvio is on the right. Pizza €7-9.50. Calzones €6.50-9. Open daily 11:30am-4pm and 6:30-11:30pm.

ALL'ANTICO VINAIO $

V. dei Neri 74r

☎055 238 27 23 www.allanticovinaio.com

All'Antico Vinaio isn't exactly a well-kept secret—the line of tourists here around lunchtime often rivals the one just around the corner at the Uffizi. But that's because the giant sandwiches here are so damn cheap—for just €5 euro, you'll get two floppy, floury pieces of focaccia stuffed with mozzarella, meat, and other fresh ingredients listed on the wall of this tiny sandwich shop. It's a good thing college parties taught you how to double fist like a pro because the giant square sandwiches here are so big you'll need to hold onto them with both hands. Order one of their popular panini (try the Summer Sandwich) or make your own. As the signs will remind you, "Don't mix meats! It's blasphemy!!" and "Don't mix cheeses, is not pizza!!" (Sure, the guys here are a little totalitarian about the whole sandwich-crafting thing, but if you're OK with your culinary creativity being stifled, All'Antico is worth it and knows what it's doing.)

i From the Uffizi, walk right down V. della Ninna and onto V. dei Neri. All'Antico is on the right. Panini €5. Open Tu-Sa 10am-4pm and 6-11pm, Su noon-8pm.

San Lorenzo

⊠ FRUTTA SECCA (DRIED FRUIT AND NUTS) $

Mercato Centrale

Your campfire gorp doesn't even come close to the kind of trail mix you could throw together at Frutta Secca. In addition to all your standard almonds, walnuts, peanuts, and cashews, this market stall of fruity dreams also has almost every variety of dried fruit you could think of: swing by and pick up some pineapple rings, banana chips, dried cherries, blueberries, or raspberries, or go out on a limb and throw in some ginger and dried kiwi into the mix. Just make sure your eyes aren't bigger than your pocketbook—the grams add up faster than you'd think.

i Located inside Mercato Centrale. From main entrance on V. dell'Ariento, turn left; the stall is in the far corner on the ground floor. Dried fruits €1-4 per 100g. Nuts €2-5 per 100g.

TRATTORIA MARIO $

V. Rosina 2r

☎055 21 85 50 www.trattoria-mario.com

Just because you can't see inside this restaurant doesn't mean it's a particularly hidden gem. Indeed, what's obscuring the front windows of this tiny but insanely popular lunch spot are all the "recommended by" stickers it has earned from countless critics and guidebooks over the years (including a few from yours truly). If you can even manage to open the door and push your way inside, you'll

italy

One reason to brave the wasteland that is Florence's clubbing scene is a chance to grab a 3am chocolate croissant from one of the city's "secret bakeries." Which aren't actually much of a secret among Florence's study abroad crowd. But that doesn't mean you shouldn't follow in the sorority girls' footsteps and make your way to one of the bakeries in town that will slip a few piping hot pastries to drunk travelers who stop by in the early hours of the morning (when the chefs are already awake and cooking up fresh batches of the day's baked goods). One such bakery is tucked into V. del Canto Rivolto; stop by around 2 or 3am, knock on the door, and slide a euro to the guy who answers it. Keep quiet and be respectful, and they should grant your requests for croissants, cannoli, or whatever else they happen to be baking up in the wee hours.

probably be looking at at least a little bit of a wait—fortunately, the traditional Tuscan dishes here are certainly worth the tight squeeze.

i Located behind Mercato Centrale (around the corner from Trattoria Zà Zà). Primi €5-6.50. Secondi €6.50-14. Open daily noon-3:30pm.

DA NERBONE $

Mercato Centrale

Amid the maze of meat counters and crates of fresh produce on the ground floor of Mercato Centrale sits Nerbone, a Florence institution since 1872. This permanent lunch stall serves up fresh pasta, risotto, and other specialities on ceramic plates that posted signs warn you not to take upstairs. Instead, place your order, grab a tray, collect your food, and find a seat at one of the marble tabletops just across from the counter. Enjoy your lunch amid the buzz and chatter of the market and under Nerbone's clusters of plastic hanging flowers.

i Located on the ground floor of Mercato Centrale. Look for its distinctive green wooden signs overhead. Panini €3.50-4. Primi €4. Secondi €7. Open M-Sa 7am-2pm.

ANTICA GELATERIA FIORENTINA $

V. Faenza 2A   www.gelateriafiorentina.com

Piazza del Duomo is lined with plenty of either crappy or overpriced gelateria. Just a few blocks away, however, Antica Gelateria Fiorentina's cups and cones of creamy, high-quality gelato start at just €1.50. Try the deep, dark black chocolate ("a good choice," as the guy behind the counter will tell you) and park yourself outside on one of the wooden benches.

i Just around the corner from the Medici Chapel on V. Faenza. Gelato €1.50-5. Open daily noon-midnight.

San Marco

ITIT IL SANDWICH CAFE $

V. Cavour 45r   ☎339 619 15 44

ITIT really wants you to review them on TripAdvisor (they appreciate every review—"especially 5 star reviews!"). And you might judge them for making their Wi-Fi password "tripadvisorplease" if you weren't so effing excited to find an Italian coffee shop with free working Wi-Fi, an abundance of outlets, and baristas who won't give you the stink eye if you pull out a laptop and decide to sit and work while finishing off your cup of Americano. They will definitely charge you for it—at ITIT, "for here" also means "that'll be an extra €0.50"—but at least they won't judge you openly. Grab a sandwich and order yourself an iced

florence

cappuccino, a latte macchiato, or something fun like the Shakerativo and settle in for a while.

i From the Duomo, walk down V. Cavour. The cafe is on the left. Drinks €1-4.50. Open M-Sa 8am-8pm, Su 10am-8pm.

East Oltrarno

🏆 GELATERIA LA STREGA NOCCIOLA

V. de Bardi 51   ☎055 238 2150 www.lastreganocciola.it

The best gelato in Florence is just a stone's throw from the Ponte Vecchio and flies shockingly under the radar. While tourists ogle the jewelry shops on the bridge and then wander starry-eyed into the overpriced gelaterias nearby, Strega Nocciola sits quietly by with its covered canisters of gelato waiting to be discovered by people in the know. With more exotic flavors like lavendar, blood orange, and Aztec (white chocolate cinnamon), along with classics like chocolate and pistachio, this is definitely the place to splurge on multiple scoops. If you vacillate long enough about how you will ever possibly decide, your scooper might even offer to let you sample a number of the options before you take your deep dive into an incredibly light and flavorful cup of Strega gelato.

i Cross the Ponte Vecchio and turn left onto V. de Bardi. Strega Nocciola is a few doors down on the right. Gelato €2.50-5. Open M-F 11:30am-midnight, Sa-Su 11am-midnight.

West Oltrarno

GUSTA PIZZA $

V. Maggio 46r   ☎055 28 50 68

Some of the best pizza in Florence is also some of its most popular (who'd have thunk?). Come here around dinnertime, and you'll find this tiny pizzeria packed with tourists and buzzing with locals who drop by to pick up boxes of 'za to go. You won't find a lot of different varieties of pizza here, but that's because Gusta's pizza is so good that they don't need to get overly fancy with their toppings (stick to the classics and you'll do just fine). Crowd around the wooden barrels and glass tabletops inside if you can; alternatively, take your pizza to go and enjoy it from the steps of the Chiesa di Santo Spirito just down the road.

i From the Ponte Santa Trinita, walk straight down V. Maggio a few blocks. Pizza €4.50-8. Open Tu-Su 11:30am-3pm and 7-11pm.

OSTERIA SANTO SPIRITO $

P. di Santo Spirito 16r   ☎055 238 23 83 www.osteriasantospirito

For some excellent Tuscan fare in the quaint setting of Piazza Santo Spirito, wander across the river to this popular osteria in West Oltrarno. There are plenty of tables outside in the piazza, so have a seat on one of the pastel-colored chairs and people-watch while munching on bread served in a metal colander. The pastas here are excellent (we especially recommend the oven-baked gnocchi with truffle oil, which comes out hot enough to scald your fingers and your tongue). Dishes at this restaurant might be on the pricier side, but the good news is that you can order reduced portions of any primo for a few bucks less. (NB: Service can be pokey, so if it seems like your food is taking a while, don't be afraid to give your waitress a little nudge to help speed up the process.)

i From the Ponte Santa Trinita, walk through P. de' Frescobaldi and take a right onto V. di Santo Spirito, then a quick left onto V. del Presto di San Martino. Turn right into P. di Santo Spirito; the restaurant is in the corner of the piazza. Arrive early if you don't have a reservation. Antipasti €5-15. Primi €4-16. Secondi €8-25. Dessert €6. Open daily noon-11:30pm.

(side margin) italy

NIGHTLIFE

Despite its large population of study abroad students, Florence doesn't boast one of Italy's most bumpin' late-night scenes. At some point during your stay here, truck it up to Piazzale Michelangelo for drinks on the steps while watching the sunset. Piazza della Signoria is a good place to stop earlier in the evening for live music (enjoy a bottle of wine or two to the soundtrack of a live full-string orchestra). As the night wears on, the bars and streets surrounding Santa Croce and, on the other side of the Arno, Santo Spirito are generally Florence's most exciting nightlife spots.

KING GRIZZLY BIRROTECA
P. dei Cimatori 5

For some really good draft beers or a wee dram of whiskey, seek out King Grizzly, which doesn't do much to announce itself on the corner of P. dei Cimatori. A rather small Irish bar, Grizzly manages to fit a few giant barrels into its dark wood interior, along with a collection of tables and barstools that line the floor-to-ceiling, open-air windows (which one might just call "no walls"). While a number of in-the-know Americans gather here for a pre-dinner drink, it's never overly crowded; if you really want to hang with the cool kids, head for the tiny back patio, where a number of Italians lounge about with pints and cigarettes.

i *From P. della Signoria, walk down V. dei Calzaiuoli and turn right onto V. dei Cimatori. King Grizzly is in the corner of P. dei Cimatori, on the right. Beer from €3. Rum and whiskey €5-7. Open daily 6pm-2am.*

CAFFE SANT'AMBROGIO
P. Sant'Ambrogio 7r   ☎055 247 72 77

On first glance, Caffe Sant'Ambrogio might just look like a collection of packed tables and chairs outside a pharmacy in an otherwise empty piazza. But the actual bar is there, too, just across the street. But if you're visiting Florence in the summer, you won't be spending much time in the sleek, blue-lit interior; instead, ask to be seated outside and settle in for a few drinks with the young travelers and Italians who flock here late into the evening. Alternatively, enjoy your drink and a cigarette on the steps of the Chiesa Sant'Ambrogio (we're pretty sure God won't judge you for it).

i *The cafe is in the piazza at the end of V. Pietrapiana. Wine from €4. Mixed drinks from €6. Open daily 10:30am-2am. Aperitivo 6-9pm.*

RED GARTER
V. de' Benci 33r   ☎055 248 09 09 www.redgarteritaly.com

If a sorority girl falls off the karaoke stage, but it's too loud in the bar for anyone to hear it, does she make a sound? The kids at Red Garter will never know, and everyone is probably too drunk to remember it in the morning anyway. But that's what makes the Red Garter the perfect place to let go of your inhibitions and bust out that karaoke rendition of "Party in the U.S.A." that you've had in your back pocket this whole trip. Full of young, English-speaking travelers and college students passing around pitchers of beer and mixed drinks, Red Garter is one of the best spots to have a decidedly non-local experience and turn up in Florence (because isn't that what #Eurotripping is really all about?). Crowd into a table downstairs, try to find a seat up on the balcony, or claim your rightful place up on the karaoke stage.

i *From P. di Santa Croce, walk down V. de' Benci. Red Garter is on the right. Beer €4-6, pitchers €18-21. Cocktails €7.50, pitchers €36. Open M-Sa 4pm-4am, Su 11:30am-4am.*

LION'S FOUNTAIN
Borgo degli Albizi 34r   ☎055 234 44 12 www.thelionsfountain.com

In case you couldn't tell from all the "I <3 Lion's Fountain" signs everywhere, this bar really wants you to love it. And even if you may not fall head over heels for this fairly standard Irish pub, you will appreciate its wide variety of cheap drinks, its outdoor seating in a little piazza, and its free Wi-Fi. Sports fans in particular might even develop a little crush on its collection of large television screens, which broadcast football matches every day (check the schedule outside to see who's playing whom).

i From the back of the Duomo, walk south down V. Proconsolo, then turn left onto Borgo degli Albizi. Lion's Fountain is near the end of the street, on the left. Beer €4-7. Cocktails €6-8. Whiskey €6.50. Shots €4. Open daily 10am-2:30am

DOLCE VITA

P. del Carmine 5 ☎055 28 45 95 www.dolcevitafirenze.it

Life really is sweet when you're sipping spritzers al fresco with a full view of the Chiesa di Santa Maria del Carmine just across the piazza. With a sleek white design both inside and out, throbbing, moody music, and bartenders in button-down shirts, Dolce Vita is a more grown-up option for aperitivo or late-night drinks in Florence. Come for the cocktails and stay for the sophisticated crowd and secluded setting in Piazza del Carmine.

i Cross Ponte alla Carraia and walk straight down P. Nazario Sauro, then turn right onto Borgo San Frediano and left into P. del Carmine. Dolce Vita is on the left side of the piazza when facing the church. Cocktails from €7. Open M-W 7pm-1:30am, Th-Sa 7pm-2am, Su 7pm-1:30am.

EASY LIVING

P. Poggi ☎335 663 03 41 www.easylivingfirenze.it

Let's go to the beach—or at least to the banks of the Arno. At Easy Living, an outdoor bar and restaurant that overlooks the river in East Oltrarno, you can crowd in with fellow travelers and young Italians for aperitivo, provided you can find a seat amid the sea of packed plastic tables and chairs here. Alternatively, you can saddle up to the bar, grabs a few drinks, and find a place to perch on the ledge overlooking the river. The food here isn't anything to write home about, but the atmosphere is more than worth the trek—it's also a good place to land after you make your way down from watching the sunset up at Piazzale Michelangelo.

i Cross Ponte alle Grazie and turn left onto Lungarno Serristori. Easy Living is located along the river in P. Poggi. Drinks from €5. Open daily 10am-1:30am.

ESSENTIALS
Practicalities

- **TOURIST OFFICES:** Uffici Informazione Turistica (www.firenzeturismo.it) has its primary office at V. Manzoni 16. (☎055 23 320 Open M-F 9am-1pm.) Other locations include P. Stazione 4 (☎05 21 22 45 Open M-Sa 8:30am-7pm, Su 8:30am-2pm), V. Cavour 1r (☎055 29 08 32 Open M-Sa 8:15am-7:15pm, Su 8:30am-1:30pm), and Borgo Santa Croce 29r (☎055 23 40 444).

- **CURRENCY EXCHANGE:** There are a number of currency exchange points in and around P. del Duomo. Look for offices at the corner of V. Cavour and P. del Duomo and the corner of V. Roma and P. di San Giovanni. There are also a currency exchange offices on V. di San Lorenzo and V. dei Calzaiuoli.

- **ATMS:** BNL has locations at V. Giuseppe Giusti 2, V. dei Cerretani 28, and V. le Spartaco Lavagnini 27. You can also find ATMs on V. Cavour and in P. di San Lorenzo.

- **LUGGAGE STORAGE:** At Stazione di Santa Maria Novella. (Near platform 16 on the ground floor. 1st 5hr. €6, 6th-12th hr. €0.90 per hr., €0.40 per hr. thereafter. Open daily 6am-11pm.)

- **POST OFFICES:** Florence's main post office is located at V. Pellicceria 3, south of P. della Repubblica. (☎055 27 36 481 Open M-F 8:30am-7pm, Sa 8:30am-12:30pm.) There are additional post offices around town, including one office at V. Pietrapiana 53.

florence

chianti

You may have imbibed your fair share of red wine in college, but now that you're in Tuscany, it's time to swap out those boxes of Franzia for a more sophisticated bottle of Chianti. In addition to enjoying a nice glass with dinner every night, try to squeeze a wine tour into your visit to Florence, which is situated just north of the Chianti wine region that lies between the Florence and Siena. A visit to a winery and the vineyards of Chianti will not only give you a legitimate excuse to get tipsy in the afternoon but will also offer you a chance to see the beautiful Tuscan countryside that surrounds the city of Florence. A wine tour will also teach you how to sip vino like the classy broad that you aspire to be (hold that glass by the flute!) and recognize a nice bottle of Chianti (look for the black rooster and the DOCG label). If you're lucky, your tour will also include samples of aged cheese, balsamic vinegar, and grappa (a 60% alcohol Italian "digestive" that tastes something akin to gasoline). A popular and reliable company through which to book an afternoon in wine country is **My Tours**, which operates daily tours. (☎39 055 284770 www.mytours.it *i* Tours €42; include two tastings and transportation to and from Santa Maria Novella train station. Tours run 2:30-7:45pm) If you're interested in booking longer, fancier (read: more expensive) tours, book online or talk to your hostel or hotel for recommendations.

- **POSTAL CODE:** 50100

Emergency

- **EMERGENCY NUMBER:** ☎118

- **POLICE:** There is a police station at V. Pietrapiana 50r (In P. dei Ciompi ☎055 203911 Open M-F 8am-2pm). Urban Police Helpline is available 24hr. at ☎055 32 83 333. The emergency Carabinieri number is ☎112.

- **LATE-NIGHT PHARMACIES:** Farmacia Comunale. (P. Stazione Santa Maria Novella 13 ☎055 21 67 61 Open 24hr.) Farmacia Molteni. (V. dei Calzaiuoli 7r, just north of P. della Signoriav ☎055 215472 Open 24hr.)

- **HOSPITALS/MEDICAL SERVICES:** Ospedale Santa Maria Nuova is northeast of the Duomo and has a 24hr. emergency room (P. Santa Maria Nuova 1 ☎055 27 581). Tourist medical services can be found at Via Lorenzo II Magnifico 59, in the north of the city, near P. Liberta. (☎055 47 54 11 Open M-F 11am-noon and 5-6pm.)

Getting There

How you arrive in Florence will be dictated by where you come from. Florence may have named its Amerigo Vespucci airport after the guy who in turn gave the Americas their name, but that doesn't mean the city has any flights from the USA. Those flying across the Atlantic will have to transfer at another European airport. If flying from within Europe, it will probably be cheaper for you to fly into the budget-airline hub that is Pisa Airport. Buses run regularly from Pisa Airport to Florence; they take just over 1hr. and cost about €10. If coming from within Italy, you will most likely catch a train, which will bring you into Santa Maria Novella station. If traveling locally, buses may be useful.

By Plane

Aeroporto Amerigo Vespucci is Florence's main airport. (V. del Termine 11 ☎055 30 615 www.aeroporto.firenze.it) From the airport, the city can be reached via the VolainBus shuttle. You can pick up the shuttle on the Departures side. (Exit the airport to the right and pass the taxi stand. Dropoff is at Santa Maria Novella station. €6. 20-30min., every 30min. 6am-8:30pm and every hour 8:30-11:30pm.) A cab from the airport to the city center costs around €25.

By Train

Santa Maria Novella train station dominates the northwest of the city. (www.grandistazioni.it Open daily 6am-midnight.) You can purchase tickets from the fast ticket kiosks or from tellers. There are daily trains from Bologna (€19, 40min.), Milan (€44-55, 2hr.), Rome (€34-39, 1hr. 30min.), Siena (€9, 1hr. 45min.), and Venice (€39-45, 2hr.). For precise schedules and prices, check www.trenitalia.com.

By Bus

Three major intercity bus companies run out of Florence's bus station. From Santa Maria Novella train station, turn left onto V. Alamanni—the station is on the left by a long driveway. SITA (www.sitabus.it) runs buses to and from Siena, San Gimignano, Chianti, and other Tuscan destinations. LAZZI buses connect to Lucca, Pisa, and many other regional towns. CAP-COPIT (www.capautolinee.it) runs to regional towns. Timetables for all three companies change regularly, so check online for schedules.

Getting Around

The main thing you should know is that Florence is a small city. Most visitors simply walk everywhere without any need for public transportation. This is ideal for the budget traveler, as you won't rack up any metro or bus fares like you would in many other European cities. That being said, if you're looking to avoid the hike up to Piazzale Michelangelo or are planning to venture elsewhere outside the compact city center, Florence has got you covered.

By Bus

As the city's only form of public transportation, Florence's orange buses are surprisingly clean, reliable, and organized. Operated by ATAF and LI-NEA, the extensive bus network includes several night-owl buses that take over regular routes in the late evenings. The schedule for every passing line is posted on the pole of each well-marked bus stop, complete with the direction the bus is going and a list of every stop in order. Most buses originate at P. Stazione or P. San Marco. Buses #12 and #13 run to Ple. Michelangelo; bus #7 runs to Fiesole. You're unlikely to need to use the buses unless you're leaving the city center. You can buy tickets from most newsstands, ticket vending machines, *tabaccherie*, or the ATAF kiosk in P. Stazione (☎800 42 45 00; 90min. ticket €1.20). You can also sometimes buy tickets directly from the bus driver, but they cost more and there is no guarantee the driver will have tickets. Stamp your ticket when you board the bus; you then have the length of time denoted by the ticket to re-use it. Be careful—if you forget to time-stamp your ticket when you board the bus (and can't successfully play the "confused foreigner" card), it's a €50 fine.

By Taxi

To call a cab, call Radio Taxi (☎055 4390, ☎055 4499, ☎055 4242, or ☎055 4798). Tell the operator your location and when you want the cab and the nearest available care will be sent to you. Each cab has a rate card in full view, and the meter displays the running fare. If you're traveling far or are nervous, it never hurts to ask for an estimate before boarding. There are surcharges for Sundays, holidays, luggage, and late nights. Unless you have a lot of baggage, you probably won't want to take a taxi during the day, when traffic will make the meter tick up mercilessly. Nevertheless,

florence

cabs are a manageable late-night option if you're outside the city, and especially if you're in a group and can split the fare with friends. Designated cab stands can be found at P. Stazione, Fortezza da Basso, and P. della Repubblica. Cabs can also often be found at Santa Maria Novella and in P. del Duomo.

By Bike

It takes some confidence to bike in the crowded parts of central Florence, but cycling is a great way to check out a longer stretch of the Arno or to cover a lot of territory in one day. Bikes can be rented from Florence By Bike (V. San Zanobi 54r ☎055 488 992 www.florencebybike.it Open Apr-Oct M-F 9am-1pm and 3:30-7:30pm, Sa 9am-7pm, Su 9am-5pm; Nov-Mar M-Sa 9am-1pm and 3:30-7:30pm). The company rents out a range of bikes, including city bikes (€3 for 1hr., €9 for 5hr., €14 for 1 day) and mountain bikes (€4 for 1hr., €18 for 5hr., and €23 for 1 day) and also offers guided tours.

pisa

Given Pisa's rich ancient history and charming modern cityscape, it's almost a shame that this thriving university town is so thoroughly overshadowed by its slightly off-kilter tower. An important port city since the days of Ancient Rome, Pisa became a preeminent maritime capital and commercial center during the Middle Ages. Indeed, its medieval history is evident in its imposing city walls and the architecture of its central monuments in Piazza dei Miracoli (which have, collectively, been named an UNESCO World Heritage Site). And while the Arno River that bisects the city is no longer the central artery of Italian trade and commerce that it once was, it remains lined with the colorful pink, yellow, and orange pillbox buildings that are so characteristic of Pisa. Certainly, those who keep their visit to Pisa limited to a photocall with the Leaning Tower might leave the city convinced that it's little more than a stomping ground for flocks of tourists, but visitors who delve a little deeper will discover that Pisa is, in actuality, a college town. Once the site of studies by hometown hero Galileo, who attended the University of Pisa and allegedly used the Leaning Tower as a means of studying gravity, the city is today home to more than 50,000 students whose presence has resulted in a rather vibrant (if not raucous) collection of local eateries and late-night bars. So spend your morning in Pisa taking obligatory selfies with that cattywampus tower before heading south to the Arno and its surrounding streets to explore what else the city has to offer.

ORIENTATION

Although you'll likely arrive in Pisa via the train station, which is located on the south side of town, the city's most famous sights are located across the Arno River and farther north in P. dei Miracoli. Here you'll find the Duomo, the Battistero, Camposanto, and the famous (infamous?) Leaning Tower. You can approach this piazza and its sweep of shockingly green lawns along the wide, pedestrian V. Santa Maria, which is lined with a number of touristy restaurants and hotels. For better culinary options, veer off this well-beaten path to the charming P. dei Cavalieri and the winding, criss-crossed streets beyond. For after-dinner activities, look to the north shore of the Arno, just across from Ponte di Mezzo; here you'll find a lot of nightlife and restaurants centered around P. Garibaldi, Borgo Stretto, and the surrounding *piazze* and side streets. And once you've taken enough terrible pictures of yourself with the Leaning Tower, head to the riverfront and the little streets that run parallel and perpendicular to it; a walk along the water, criss-crossing bridges and wandering down adjacent alleyways, makes for a surprisingly beautiful and relaxing afternoon after a morning of more hardcore sightseeing.

SIGHTS

PIAZZA DEI MIRACOLI

Most of Pisa's major sights are centered in the P. dei Miracoli (literally, the Square of Miracles), whose monuments include the Leaning Tower, the Duomo, Camposanto, and the Battistero. And while the tower is forever flooded with throngs of posers, the rest of the piazza and its clean, perfectly manicured grounds take on an almost university-like feel, with plenty of students and tourists seeking out patches of grass in the shade of the monuments or the city's walls. After the sun sets, groups continue to lounge and loiter on the lawns, while couples retreat to the crooks and crevices of the various monuments under the cover of night.

i Free. Open 24hr.

LEANING TOWER

You may have seen the Leaning Tower on hundreds of pizza boxes throughout your life, but nothing quite compares to seeing it in its pearly marble flesh, looming over the buildings and walls of Pisa in its charmingly off-kilter way. Indeed, the tower's famous, fantastic tilt is a marvel that might have you wishing you had brought your protractor to Italy (or at least wishing you remembered how to use a protractor). Fun fact: the Leaning Tower is also the site of the highest incidents of accidental photobombing in the world—walking around the tower, you will be ruining or in the background of somebody else's cheesy photo at pretty much any given moment. And although this tower may be the tipsiest in Italy, it hasn't quite reached the point of falling-down-drunk, which means you can climb it if you so desire. Just keep in mind that scaling these slanted, slippery steps is likely the most expensive thing you'll do in Pisa (it'll run you €18 and requires a reservation that you can make at the ticket office), while a corny picture outside the tower is priceless in more ways than one.

i P. dei Miracoli. Just follow the crowds. Reservations to climb the tower must be made in advance. Steps are narrow and slippery, and those under the age of 18 must be accompanied by an adult. €18. Open daily Apr-Sept 8am-8pm; Oct 9am-7pm; Nov-Feb 10am-5pm; Mar 9am-6pm. Last entry 30min. before close.

BATTISTERO

We would nominate Pisa's Battistero as the actual best-looking monument in Piazza dei Miracoli. If you take a second to tear your eyes away from the Leaning Tower, let them come to rest on this bulbous little baptistery. Constructed in 1152, the marble structure looks almost like the dome of a great cathedral, minus the actual church (because everyone knows that, just like muffins, the best part of a church is the top). And although the Battistero's interior is a little plain, its circular geometry makes for perfect acoustics. Be sure to stop inside and catch a demonstration of the building's flawless resonance once every 30min., when a guard closes all the doors, orders everyone to shut the hell up, and sings a few long notes that continue to reverberate and echo throughout the Battistero for the next several minutes. The guards themselves are pretty nonchalant about the whole thing, but the lingering echoes of the simple song are quite beautiful and haunting for visitors.

i P. dei Miracoli. €5. Combined ticket with 1 other monument/Museo delle Sinopie €7. Combined ticket with 2 other monuments/Museo delle Sinopie €8. Open daily Apr-Sept 8am-8pm; Oct 9am-7pm; Nov-Feb 10am-5pm; Mar 9am-6pm. Last entry 30min. before close.

DUOMO

If you're quickly approaching the "every goddamn church looks the same" quota of your Italian sojourn, Pisa's Duomo just might push you past your breaking

get a room!

HOSTEL PISA TOWER

$

V. Piave 4

☎050 520 2454 www.hostelpisatower.it

From the random guitar in the living room to the faded flowery sheets in the dorms to the endless supply of Twinings tea in the kitchen, this place often feels more like a house than a hostel. And who knows, by the end of your short stay here, the nice people who run this place—including the guy at the front desk who might offer you apricots one afternoon and the white-haired man who'll ask you to turn off the lights in the living room whenever you decide to go to bed—just might feel like a weird little family. But if bonding with strangers isn't your thing, a) why are you traveling? and b) walk out the front door, and one look at the Leaning Tower looming over the city walls just down the road should be enough to convince you that this is a supremely convenient place to shack up for a night or two.

i From the monuments, walk east and turn left down V. San Ranierino. Walk through the archway and turn left onto V. Contessa Matilde, then right onto V. Piave at the traffic light. Hostel Pisa Tower is on the right. Breakfast not available, although there are vending machines and an espresso machine available for 24hr. use. Dorms from €23. Check-in 2pm-12:30am. Check-out 10:30am.

HOTEL HELVETIA

$

V. Don G. Boschi 31

☎050 553 084

When you consider how close a bed here will position you to P. dei Miracoli, Hotel Helvetia's rates for single rooms are almost as mind-boggling as the physics of the Leaning Tower itself. Tucked around a corner just off V. Santa Maria, rooms here are basic but clean—and really, who cares about interior design when you're paying this little to sleep in a room where you're guaranteed to be the only person snoring? If the privacy and prime location weren't enough, the staff here is also very helpful and friendly. And although breakfast is not provided, there is a courtyard and common area whose painted walls will remind you to go see Pisa's Keith Haring mural at some point during your stay.

i From the monuments, walk down V. Santa Maria and turn left onto V. Collegio Ricci, then right onto V. Don G. Boschi. Singles with shared bath €45, with ensuite €54. Doubles with shared bath €54, with ensuite €64. Reception 8:30am-midnight.

point. While its interior houses some richly colored Renaissance paintings and its altar offers a large, lively depiction of Jesus that might catch your eye, the rest of the cathedral is the same massive columns, gilded ceilings, and antiquated "cover those blasphemous bare shoulders" rules that you'll find in most other churches in Italy. That being said, entry is free, so you really should take a turn through the Duomo's shady interior at some point between photo ops with the tower outside. The most impressive views of the church, however, are really from outside; stand back and admire its intricate and impressive facade, which, when paired with the complementary white exteriors of the Leaning Tower, the Battistero, and Camposanto, is truly stunning against the backdrop of the verdant, manicured lawns of P. dei Miracoli.

i P. dei Miracoli. Free. Open daily Apr-Sept 10am-8pm; Oct 10am-7pm; Nov-Feb 10am-5pm; Mar 10am-6pm. Last entry 30min. before close.

MUSEO DELLE SINOPIE

There's not a whole lot to see at the Museo delle Sinopie besides some faded biblical frescoes, a little bit of the history of P. dei Miracoli, and a 3D virtual tour of the monuments that looks like it was made sometime in the late '90s. Still, entry to the museum is included in most tickets for the monuments, so take a pass through here whenever you find yourself most in need a spot of A/C in the middle of your day of sightseeing. And depending on the exhibit, the contemporary art displayed on the second level might be worth a visit.

i Located on the south end of P. dei Miracoli, across from the lawns. €5. Combined ticket with 1 other monument €7. Combined ticket with 2 other monuments €8. Open daily Apr-Sept 8am-8pm; Oct 9am-7pm; Nov-Feb 10am-5pm; Mar 9am-6pm. Last entry 30min. before close.

GIARDINO SCOTTO

Lungarno Leonardo Fibonacci ☎050 910 111

For a little green space free of leaning tourists, stroll east down the Arno and take a turn through the Giardino Scotto, a local park where you'll find some shady paths, park benches, playground equipment, and palm trees, along with the occasional amorous couple finding a little splendor in the grass. Enclosed on one side by some old Roman walls, the park is now home to more modern attractions, like a permanent outdoor movie theater and some in-ground trampolines that you're definitely too old to jump on.

i Located on the south side of the Arno, across from Ponte della Fortezza. Free. Open daily May-June 9am-8pm, July-Aug 8am-8:30pm, Sept 9am-8pm, Oct 9am-7pm, Nov-Jan 9:30am-4:30pm, Feb-Mar 9am-6pm, Apr 9am-7pm.

ORTO BOTANICO DI PISA

V. Luca Ghini 5 ☎050 221 1310 www.biologia.unipi.it/ortobotanico

There's not much to this botanical garden that you haven't already seen, but there's also not much in the way of an entrance fee, so for a quick return to nature, have a stroll through the garden's palm trees, around its lilypad-covered fish pond, and between its impressive thickets of bamboo. We would say have a seat and enjoy the shade of the trees for a while, but the mosquitoes here will probably suck you dry before your bum hits the park bench.

i From the monuments, walk down V. Santa Maria and turn right onto V. Luca Ghini. The entrance to the gardens is through the building on the left. €2.50, reduced €1.50. Open M-F 8:30am-5:30pm, Sa 8:30am-1pm.

FOOD

ANTICA TRATTORIA IL CAMPANO $$

V. Domenico Cavalca 19 ☎050 580 585 www.ilcampano.com

You might have heard a thing or two about Pisa pizza, but for some genuinely authentic regional cuisine, stop by Trattoria Il Campano. The waiters here don't speak much English, and you won't find any pizza on the menu, but that's how you know you're in for a real deal Tuscan meal. Order some of the fresh pasta and indulge in the simple, understated flavors of the local specialties. The lunch and dinner menu might be a little more than you're used to spending, but if you're planning to indulge anywhere in Pisa, it should be here (and not, let's be honest, on the €18 that it costs to climb the Leaning Tower). Sit outside against the brick walls of this secluded restaurant and enjoy a late lunch under a dark canopy of hanging plants.

i Antipasti €5-10. Primi €7-9. Secondi €15-18. Light lunch menu €15. Dinner menu €30. Open M-Tu 12:30-3pm and 7:30-10:45pm, Th 7:30-10:45pm, F-Su 12:30-3pm and 7:30-10:45pm.

pisa

top 5 foods to try in tuscany

Tuscany doesn't specialize in Pisa pizzas, so when you find yourself in the Italian Hillz, head for a local trattoria and try some of these regional specialties.

1. TORTELLI LUCCHESE. It may look like standard meat ravioli, but this egg-based pasta primi isn't your average Chef Boyardee. In addition to being served in a meat sauce, this pasta is also stuffed with even more meat and can be served in a variety of fashions. Try one of them at Anne e Leo (Lucca).

2. CECINA. Cecina is basically a chickpea pancake that's often served up in triangular, pizza-like slices. Hummus lovers will wonder why the hell they didn't think of this before. Give it a go at Pizzeria Il Montino (Pisa) or Pizzeria Da Felice (Lucca).

3. WILD BOAR. Siena doesn't mess around with hot dogs and lunchmeat and pulled pork. Instead, you'll find wild boar on the menu at pretty much every sandwich shop and restaurant in town.

4. BUCCELLATO. A Lucchese speciality, this lightly sweetened bread is made with currants and anise seeds and can be found at every bakery in town. Pick up a piece at Pasticceria Pasquinelli (Lucca).

5. WINE. You're in Italian wine country! So grab yourself a nice Chianti and some fava beans and enjoy.

PIZZERIA LE MURA $

Largo del Parlascio 33/34   ☎393 225 7773 www.pizzerialemura-pisa.it

For a simple and satisfying slice of pizza near the Leaning Tower, head down to Pizzeria Le Mura, where Mrs. Elena and her family have been serving up hot, fresh, bready pies for more than 40 years. Cute little instructions on walls and the menu will show you how to order (spoiler alert: order your pizza at the counter, then grab a seat either inside in the A/C or outside on the patio and wait for your food to arrive). The charming cartoons of Mrs. Elena and her beloved pizza oven are almost as charming as Elena herself, whom you'll find behind the counter, still running the show more than four decades after she rolled her first dough.

i From the monuments, walk down V. Cardinale Maffi Pietro to Largo del Parlascio. Le Mura is on the right. Pizzas €5-12. Individual slices also available. Open for lunch and dinner Tu-Su.

LA BOTTEGA DEL GELATO

P. Garibaldi   ☎050 575 467

Plopped down just north of the river in P. Garibaldi, La Bottega Del Gelato serves up smooth, creamy gelato at all hours of the day, making it a perfect spot for a mid-afternoon pick-me-up or a late-night treat (or both, let's be honest). With its flavors listed outside, La Bottega gives you some time to contemplate your flavor choices before you get up to the crowded counter. The gelateria has a few tables outside, but there's also seating under the statue in the center of the piazza; you could also take your gelato for a nice little walk along the Arno, but then again, that would be healthy and unnecessarily aerobic, so maybe not.

i On the west side of P. Garibaldi, across the street from Ponte di Mezzo. Gelato €1.50-3. Open daily 11am-1am.

PANINERIA L'OSTELLINO $

P. Cavallotti 1   ☎050 00 000 www.lostellinopisa.com

For a fast lunch just down the road from the Leaning Tower, this panineria does the job. In case you couldn't tell from all the pigs and pork paraphernalia cluttering up the walls, you should probably order a sandwich that features L'Ostellino's special Tuscan ham. You also can't go wrong with some of the spicy salami or any of the many cheeses here. Sandwiches are served on thick, crunchy bread and wrapped in yellow paper, so if you can't grab a spot at one of the handful of tables in the tiny interior, you can always walk back down the road to Piazza del Duomo and pop a squat in the shade outside the cathedral.

i From the monuments, walk down V. Santa Maria and turn left onto P. Cavallotti. The panineria is on the left. Sandwiches €3.50-5.50. Open daily noon-10pm.

NIGHTLIFE

BAZEEL
Lungarno Pacinotti 1   ☎340 288 1113 www.bazeel.it

You may not fully realize the meaning of a crowd "spilling into the street" until you come to Bazeel during aperitivo. Indeed, the throngs that gather here for cheap drinks and a buffet of fried finger food certainly spill (and in more than just the "sorry my wine is now all over your shirt" sense). As the evening progresses, young folks pour out the doors of the bar, into p. Garibaldi next door, and all the way across the street, where they sit along the walls of the Arno with drinks and cigarettes in hand. Maybe it's because they're not into the cat videos being projected onto the back wall of the bar's large, open interior, or maybe it's just that Bazeel offers so much outdoor seating that it's hard to resist frozen cocktails outside on a warm summer night.

i On the west side of P. Garibaldi, across the street from Ponte di Mezzo. Beer €3-6. Wine €3.50. Cocktails €5.50. Frozen cocktails €6.50. Open M-Th 7:30am-1am, F-Sa 7:30am-2am, Su 8am-1am. Aperitivo 7-9:30pm.

SUD
V. delle Case Dipinte 21/23   ☎347 889 0864 www.senzaunadirezione.it

Sud is a hip and happening little gem that's particularly popular with 20-somethings looking for a good deal on aperitivo. And while the name might imply that this place is primarily for foamy suds-lovers, you might consider skipping your standard beer for a taste of one of the bar's many varieties of Italian liqueurs. (Or do both and just remember that beer before liquor, never sicker...or is it beer after liquor? Either way, you're young and don't get really bad hangovers yet, so just dive in.) Order through the walk-up window outside (it's like a drive thru without the cars!) and try to land a seat under one of the umbrellas or squeeze in on the wooden benches near the front door.

i From P. Garibaldi, walk down Borgo Stretto and turn right onto V. Mercanti, then left onto V. delle Case Dipinte. Sud is on the left. Drinks €1-4.50. Panini €4. Open M-Th 7pm-12:45am, F-Sa 7pm-1:45am, Su 7pm-12:45am. Aperitivo 7-9pm.

ORZO BRUNO
V. delle Case Dipinte 6   ☎050 578 802 www.orzobruno.it

Beers lovers can't do much better than Orzo Bruno, whose yellow walls and cartoons of beer pints painted on its glass windows help it stand out from the crowd of other bars along V. delle Case Dipinte. Wooden blocks on the walls provide the details of the many varieties of beer you can sample here, which will delight connoisseurs and overwhelm and confound college students who thought a Corona with lime was the apex of the fermented yeast experience. The crowd here is a little older, but grab a spot at one of the many dark wood tables and relax with a pint while staring out the floor-to-ceiling glass windows at all the youths drinking spritzers and shitty beer across the street.

i From P. Garibaldi, walk down Borgo Stretto and turn right onto V. Mercanti, then left onto V. delle Case Dipinte. Orzo Bruno is on the right. Beer €3-4. Cocktails €4.50. Whiskey and rum €4-6. Bruschetta €3. Panini €4.50-5.50. Open M-Th 7pm-1am, F-Sa 7pm-2am, Su 7pm-1am.

italy

ESSENTIALS
Practicalities

- **TOURIST OFFICES:** The office in P. Vittorio Emanuele II provides maps, an events calendar, and other assistance (P. Vittorio Emanuele II 16 ☎050 42 291 www.pisaunicaterra.it Open daily 10am-1pm and 2-4pm.). Second office in Piazza del Duomo (☎050 550100 www.pisaunicaterra.it Open daily 9:30am-5:30pm.).

- **ATMS:** To withdraw cash near the monuments, there are two ATMs on V. Santa Maria next to the Hotel Duomo, as well as other cash machines around town.

- **LUGGAGE STORAGE:** In the train station. At the left end of Binario 1.

- **POST OFFICES:** P. Vittorio Emanuele II 7/9, on the right side of the *piazza* (☎050 51 95 14 Open M-Sa 8:15am-7pm.).

- **POSTAL CODE:** 56100

Emergency

- **POLICE:** Polizia Municipale (V. Cesare Battisti 71/72 ☎050 91 01 11).

- **LATE-NIGHT PHARMACIES:** Lungarno Mediceo 51. On the north shore of the river, so the east (☎050 54 40 02 Open 24hr.).

- **HOSPITALS/MEDICAL SERVICES:** Santa Chiara. V. Roma 67, near P. dei Miracoli; entrance is adjacent to V. Bonanno Pisano (☎050 99 21 11).

Getting There
By Plane

Galileo Galilei Airport (☎050 84 93 00 www.pisa-airport.com) is practically within walking distance of the city, but the train shuttle takes only 5min. The shuttle arrives at platform 14 in Pisa Centrale (€1.10). The airport is a major budget airline hub for all of Tuscany, including Florence. Apart from a few flights to Morocco and northern Africa, no intercontinental flights serve Galileo Galilei, but you can fly directly to Pisa from most European cities.

By Train

Pisa Centrale will be your main port of entry from other Italian destinations (P. della Stazione, South of P. Vittorio Emanuele II ☎050 41 385 Ticket office open 6am-9pm, but there is always a long line; check out the 24hr. self-service machines.) Trains run to and from Florence (€9, 1hr. 15min.), Rome (€30-50, 3hr.), and Lucca (€4, 30min.). If leaving from San Rossore, Pisa's secondary station is in the northwest part of town; buy tickets at a local *tabaccheria*.

By Bus

SITA (☎043 62 28 048 www.sitabus.it) and Terravision (☎44 68 94 239 www.terravision.eu) run buses betweens Pisa's airport and Florence, while Lassi (☎058 35 84 876 www.lazzi.it) and CPT (☎050 50 55 11 www.cpt.pisa) run buses that leave from and arrive in P. Sant'Antonio. Buses leave from Florence's Santa Maria Novella bus station. (From the train station, take a left onto V. Alamanni; the station is on the left by a long driveway. €10, 1hr. 15min.) Buses to Lucca leave from Pisa Airport and run to and from P. Giuseppe Verdi in Lucca (30min.).

pisa

Getting Around

On Foot

There's little need for anything but your feet while you're in Pisa. From the train station to P. dei Miracoli—the longest diameter of the city and also the route you're most likely to take—is about a 20-25min. walk.

By Bus

LAM Rossa runs a loop between the airport, train station, tower, and several other points in Pisa every 20min. Most buses stop at P. Sant'Antonio, just west of P. Vittorio Emanuele II. You can purchase bus tickets (€1 for 1hr.) at a *tabaccheria* or at ticket machines at Pisa Centrale and Galileo Galilei Airport.

siena

Siena is, in many ways, Tuscany at its finest and most essential. Climb up to the top of the Torre della Mangia (or scale any street in the city center, really) to see what we mean: while the highest peaks and towers of the city reveal sweeping views of red roofs, stacks of tan Tuscan buildings, and an unrelenting patchwork of hills and fields in every direction, the narrow streets of the city itself are also built directly into the dips, slopes, and steep grades of the region's difficult topography. But Siena is worthy of the sweat you'll sacrifice to it. Once a thriving republic of the Middle Ages before being devastated by the Black Death, Siena today retains a charming mix of medieval heritage and modern Tuscan culture, from the winding layout of its historic centro (which has been designated an UNESCO World Heritage Site) to the green of its surrounding hillsides to its penchant for panini packed with boar meat. While the bars and restaurants stacked and teetering along steep Siena streets are in themselves a sight to see, the city's actual historic and artistic landmarks (you know, the ones you have to pay to see) are flat-out staggering, particularly in the case of its Duomo, whose striped, geometrically-intricate interior makes it one of the most stunning churches in all of Italy. The true spirit of Siena is most palpable twice a year each summer, when Il Palio di Siena—the city's historic medieval horse race—is held on July 2 and August 16 in Piazza del Campo. The days leading up to the race sees Siena's streets decorated in the flags of the city's 17 neighborhoods (*contrade*, singular *contrada*), while locals and tourists alike take part in the traditional ceremonies and spectacles of the centuries-old race. Even outsiders who can never fully grasp the magnitude of the race and the intense meaning it holds for the Sienese will still find themselves powerfully moved by the excitement, despair, and insanity that the Palio brings out in the city's passionate people.

ORIENTATION

The sloping streets of Siena are built directly into the hills and dips of its Tuscan setting, and you can feel it everywhere, whether you're racing around a steep bend on one of the city's free-flying buses or dragging your way up and down the narrow streets of the centro on stiff calves. Most of Siena's buses pass through P. Gramsci, which is located just north of the city's stadium and east of the Fortezza Medicea. An easy way to get from bus stops to the city center is to find V. Montanini and follow it south to Il Campo, the thriving heart of the old city. Here you'll find not only the race track that hosts Siena's Palio twice a year but also the Palazzo Pubblico and its Torre del Mangia—perhaps the city's most iconic and recognizable structure. The campo is lined with restaurants and bars and gives way to a number of tiny *vicoli* that boast even more tucked-away eateries. From Il Campo, follow the many signs to the fantastic, striped Duomo and its accompanying sights. Nearby, V. Fontebranda

HOTEL ALMA DOMUS $$

V. Camporegio 37 ☎0577 44 177 www.hotelalmadomus.it

Sitting quietly along a set of sloping stairs just down the road from San Domenico, Hotel Alma Domus offers a surprisingly varied range of rooms and rates. Decide whether or not you're Covergirl worth it and consider your many options, from sparse economy singles, which provide a neat and tidy place to sleep but little else, to superior doubles whose balconies and pillowy beds make for a cloud-like retreat from which to gaze out onto some incredible views of the city. Whether you choose to live like a deity or a dormouse, all guests are free to enjoy the complimentary breakfast, plentiful common spaces, and sunny courtyard dotted with clusters of red flowers. Popular among students, the economy singles are a great way to snag a cheap room in the middle of Siena's city center.

i *From Basilica San Domenico, walk down V. Camporegio; Hotel Alma Domus is around the bend in the road, on the left. Economy singles €51. Classic singles €55. Superior doubles €80-90. Breakfast included. Reception 24hr.*

ALBERGO BERNINI $$

V. della Sapienza 15 ☎0577 289 047 www.albergobernini.com

Located just a few twists and turns from the heart of Siena's centro, Albergo Bernini boasts the antique furniture, rustic tiled floors, and flowery bedspreads that you'll find in many a boutique hotel. The only difference here is that the quaint, homey decor doesn't translate to pint-sized living space. Instead, the rooms and beds here are enormous (at least by Italian standards). And although you might not be in the company any actual Baroque masterpieces while staying at Bernini, the abundance of space (bolstered by the hotel's breakfast room, courtyard, and several seating areas) means you'll have plenty of room to get splashy, flashy, and dynamic (and, you know, sculpturally exquisite) all on your own. You may not be in Florence yet, but ask for a room with a view and wake up to the Siena skyline and its towering Duomo every morning.

i *From the city center, walk down V. d. Terme and turn left onto V. della Sapienza. Albergo Bernini is on the left. Doubles with shared bath €65, with ensuite €85. Breakfast €5. Reception 8am-11pm.*

leads down to the city's medieval fountain, while a bit farther north, V. Sapienza will drop you off at the doors of San Domenico. Siena's centro, which is confined within the city's medieval walls, is closed off to cars, making things a little easier for foot-travelers; that being said, the twists and turns and steep grades of these streets can get confusing, so bring a well-marked map and don't be surprised if you make a wrong turn that sends you traipsing down a steep hill only to realize you've made a terrible mistake and have to turn around and climb back up.

SIGHTS

DUOMO

P. Duomo ☎0577 283 048 www.operaduomo.siena.it

And you thought all churches in Italy looked the same. Sure, this Duomo has the cavernous ceilings, mammoth columns, and decorative floors of your standard over-the-top Catholic church, but just when you thought a leopard can't change its spots, Siena's Duomo surprises with an abundance of stripes and goes straight zebra. Moreover, its aforementioned ceiling is a deep blue and spotted with gold stars, its dichromatic columns aren't your standard Corinthian, and its floors, rather than being covered in familiar mosaics, are decorated with cartoon-like drawings that will remind you more of a comic book than Bible stories of old. The entire church is truly a marvel, mostly because of its dense layers of atypical geometry: the interior is an optical illusion of steps, curves, and lines, and some of the tiling on the floor is very proto-Escher in style. Follow the suggested itinerary around the perimeter of the church (and stay inside the red ropes!) and take note of works by Donatello and Bernini..

i Follow the signs in the city center to P. Duomo. You can't miss it. €7. Opa Si Pass Mar-Oct €12; Nov-Feb €8. Pass is valid for three days and includes entry to the Duomo, the Crypt, the Baptistery, and the Museo dell'Opera and Facciatone. Open daily Mar-Oct 10:30am-7pm; Nov-Feb 10:30am-5:30pm.

PIAZZA DEL CAMPO

Siena's most central and celebrated square, Piazza del Campo is impossible to miss—pretty much the second you get off the bus in the city center, you'll see signs on every corner pointing toward Il Campo. Twice a year, it becomes the pulsating center of Italy's most famous horse race, the Palio di Siena. And while the square is decidedly less exciting for the other 363 days of the year, it is where you'll find plenty of restaurants, bars, and side streets to explore in the evening. And if you're not here when the Palio is happening, you can always walk around the racetrack and imagine what it feels like when the horses and their jockeys come thundering around the corners of the piazza in pursuit of local glory.

i Follow the ubiquitous signs that point to Il Campo. Free.

PALAZZO PUBBLICO AND TORRE DEL MANGIA

P. del Campo 1   ☎0577 292 614

If the ticket booth smells a little bit like horses, that's because this is where Siena's prized thoroughbreds storm out into Il Campo on the day of the Palio. Every other day of the year, however, the palace and its Civic Museum (which can be visited for a fee of €9) are a little less showstopping. The highlight here is truly the Torre del Mangia, which dominates Il Campo from below and, from above, offers the absolute best views of Siena's rooftops, the Duomo, and the surrounding Tuscan hills. The trip up to the crown of the tower itself will be one of simultaneous splendor and Hitchcockian horror; wind your way up the narrow staircase like the Jimmy Stewart that you wish you were and prepare to redefine your definition of vertigo upon reaching the very top and getting a glimpse of the tiny Il Campo below. And to make the whole thing even more classically cinematic, enjoy the shrieking, swooping birds that circle the tower tirelessly.

i It's that tall thing at the bottom of Piazza del Campo. Tower €10. Civic Museum €9, reduced €8. Tower open daily Mar 16-Oct 10am-7pm; Nov-Mar 15 10am-4pm. Civic Museum open daily Mar 16-Oct 10am-7pm; Nov-Mar 15 10am-6pm. Ticket office closes 45min. early.

CRYPT

P. Duomo   ☎0577 283 048 www.operaduomo.siena.it

Although these subterranean rooms are called the Crypt, you won't be seeing any dead people here. Unless you count Jesus, who is depicted on the walls of this cavern in a series of frescoes that capture the moments before, during, and after the Passion. For a series of cave paintings that were completely forgotten until just recently, when they were accidentally discovered during excavations under the Duomo in 1999, the frescoes here are remarkably well preserved and shockingly vibrant in hue. Despite the bright reds and rich blues of these frescoes, however, their mournful subject matter is actually quite somber and moving if considered in the right mood. Note, in particular, the depiction of

Joseph of Arimathea removing the nails from Jesus's feet after the Crucifixion and Mary holding her lifeless son in her arms after his painful sacrifice. Although a visit here won't take up much of your time, the crypt is included in the Opa Si Pass and is worth a stop.

i Just past the Duomo sights ticket office, on the left. €6. Opa Si Pass Mar-Oct €12, Nov-Feb €8. Pass is valid for three days and includes entry to the Duomo, the Crypt, the Baptistery, and the Museo dell'Opera and Facciatone. Open daily Mar-Oct 10:30am-7pm; Nov-Feb 10:30am-5:30pm.

MUSEO DELL'OPERA AND PANORAMIC FACCIATONE

P. Duomo   ☎0577 283 048 www.operaduomo.siena.it

The Museo dell'Opera is a whole lot of wooden sculptures and panel painting (along with the super old throw pillow here and there), and none of it will be of much interest for non-art-history students (hey, it's OK—you're a student of life, man). Still, most of the rooms here are air-conditioned, so maybe take a little while to ponder those dusty pillows while giving all that back sweat some time to dry. Even more critically, you'll need to wind your way up through the museum to reach the Facciatone, which you'll find at the end of the Hall of Vestments. Wait your turn to climb up to this panoramic overlook and take in a sweep of Siena and Tuscany that rivals that of the Torre del Mangia. Heads up for people who are afraid of heights—the guardrail at the top isn't particularly high.

i To the right of the Duomo sights ticket office. €7. Opa Si Pass Mar-Oct €12, Nov-Feb €8. Pass is valid for three days and includes entry to the Duomo, the Crypt, the Baptistery, and the Museo dell'Opera and Facciatone. Open daily Mar-Oct 10:30am-7pm; Nov-Feb 10:30am-5:30pm.

BAPTISTERY

P. San Giovanni   ☎0577 283 048 www.operaduomo.siena.it

Located at the bottom of a steep flight of stone steps at the back of the Duomo, the Baptistery is almost like a miniature version of the church itself, complete with the signature stripes, cool colors, and even more ceiling frescoes. It's also much smaller and easier to take in than the cathedral, so have a seat and look heavenward (for insights, answers, God's grace...or just a nice view). Despite the rich, dense detail of the frescoes and the ornate baptismal fount, the whole thing

il palio

On two days in the middle of the hot Tuscan summer, the city of Siena comes alive as horses, men in medieval tights, and thousands of overheated spectators flood Piazza del Campo during the Palio di Siena. Held twice a year—first on July 2 in honor of Madonna of Provenzano and again on August 16 to celebrate to the Assumption of Mary—Siena's historic medieval horse race sees the city's 17 districts battle it out for local glory in a sporting event that dates back to the Middle Ages. While the week leading up to the race sees the horses paraded through Il Campo and members of the various *contrade* gathered together for neighborhood dinners, the day of the Palio itself is unparalleled in the emotions, intensity, and fanaticism it stirs up in the passionate Sienese. And then, after nearly two hours of parades in which members of each contrada march around Il Campo in traditional medieval garb, the cannons sound, and 10 of the 17 *contrade* thunder around the Campo's track in a blistering, exhilarating bareback race that often sees jockeys fall off their horses and thoroughbreds crash on their way around the tight bends in the track. For days after the race, you can hear members of the winning *contrada* celebrating their victory throughout the streets of the city, and the parades, dinners, and victory banquets continue as long as six months after the race.

siena

is a bit dark and chilly for a place meant for welcoming/dunking babies into the Kingdom of God.

i At the bottom of the steep steps behind the Duomo. €4. Opa Si Pass Mar-Oct €12, Nov-Feb €8. Pass is valid for three days and includes entry to the Duomo, the Crypt, the Baptistery, and the Museo dell'Opera and Facciatone. Open daily Mar-Oct 10:30am-7pm; Nov-Feb 10:30am-5:30pm.

BASILICA CATERINIANA SAN DOMENICO

P. San Domenico 1   www.basilicacateriniana.com

If you look out over Siena from any high point in the city, you'll likely see San Domenico looming in the distance, a giant brick block of a church located farther west and north of the more central sights. And while the Gothic basilica, built in the 13th century and later enlarged, is most impressive when viewed from afar, if you find yourself nearby, it doesn't hurt to pop your head inside and have a look at the church's massive, gaping interior. Quite sparse in comparison to many Italian churches, San Domenico does boast the remains of some frescoes on its walls and some more recent stained glass behind its altar.

i From the city center, walk west down V. della Sapienza to P. San Domenico. Free. Open daily Mar-Oct 7am-6:30pm, Nov-Feb 9am-6pm.

FONTEBRANDA

V. di Fontebranda

Fontebranda is less of a fountain in the modern (or even Renaissance) sense and more of a random watery cave that you might happen upon while looking for something a little grander. But lo, this is it! Constructed in 1081 and rebuilt in 1246, the three basins of this medieval watering hole were once used to supply good old H2O for animals, mills, and the local Sienese, but now, like your great-aunt in a nursing home, they pretty much just sit here being old. The Fontebranda may look like something out of the *Chamber of Secrets* (don't look the fish directly in the eyes!) but was, in fact, featured in Dante's *Inferno*.

i From P. del Campo, cross V. di Citta and follow V. di Fontebranda down to the fountain. Free.

FORTEZZA MEDICEA

P. della Liberta

You might end up wandering around this fortress's high, mossy walls wondering where the hell the entrance is. Just keep walking and eventually you'll find it. Although this structure was once used to fight off invading forces from Siena's archrival Florence, today the biggest spats the city has to deal with are the ones between its own *contrade*, and so the Fortezza Medicea is now mostly a bunch of hot gravel surrounded by some high walls. Still, the upper perimeter of the fortress offers some shady trees, purple flowers, and park benches, so have a stroll around and look out on Siena from a variety of angles. The fortress also hosts outdoor movies in the summer as part of Siena's Cinema in Fortezza program, and if you're visiting in the afternoon, consider stopping at Antica Enoteca Italiano for a glass of real Italian wine.

i From P. Gramsci, walk west down Vle. C. Maccari to the fortress. The entrance to Fortezza Medicea is on the left. Free.

FOOD

GINO CACINO DI ANGELO $

P. Mercato 31   ☎0577 223 076 www.ginocacinodiangelo.blogspot.it

For a fast, affordable, and delicious lunch near Il Campo, veer away from the overpriced V. Citta and head for the square hidden just behind Palazzo Pubblico; here, in the corner of P. Mercato, under a canopy of purple flowers, you'll find Gino Cacino. Step inside and the floral scents will be quickly replaced by the rich aromas of the aged cheese and freshly sliced meat that crowd the counter of this small and cluttered deli. If you can, find a stool and order a plate of cheese

italy

and meat, which will be brought out on a wooden board. Otherwise, you can't go wrong with one of its panini, made fresh and served hot on a crusty bun (yes, that is cheese rind in your sandwich, and it's awesome); take it to go and eat it in the shade on one of the benches in the center of the piazza.

i From P. del Campo, walk to the back of the square (behind Palazzo Pubblico) to P. Mercato. Gino Cacino is on the left under the purple flowers. Panini €3.50-7. Cheese and meat plates €6-9. Open daily 7:30am-8pm.

OSTERIA LA CHIACCHERA $

V. Costa Sant'Antonio 4   ☎0577 280 631 www.osterialachiacchera.it

For simple, authentic, and memorable Tuscan dishes, wander through Siena's winding streets to Osteria La Chiacchera, which sits nestled into the side of the steep V. Costa Sant'Antonio. Seating here can get tight when the restaurant is busy, but the closeness, combined with the brick-walled interior and friendly warmth of the waiters, makes for a cozy atmosphere in which to enjoy the homestyle Italian cuisine. And if you get here early enough, try to snag a seat outside—the tables are staggered on the hillside, so you can spend your evening looking down onto V. Costa Sant'Antonio as it dips and falls away from the restaurant (like eating your meal at the top of a rollercoaster, but without the nausea).

i From the city center, walk down V. d. Terme and turn left onto V. della Sapienza, then left down V. Costa Sant'Antonio. The osteria is on the right. Antipasti €3.50-9.50. Primi €6-8. Secondi €7.50-9.50. Dessert €4-4.50. Open M noon-3pm and 6:30-10pm, W-Su noon-3pm and 6:30-10pm.

GROM $

V. Banchi di Sopra 11   ☎0577 289 303

Sitting amid the many clothing stores that line V. Banchi di Sopra, on first glance, Grom's tall glass storefront and gaping, white-walled interior looks less like an ice cream shop and more like just another shopping outlet. But slow down and stop in for a cup of Grom's cheap and ethical gelato (and its perhaps even more ethical and humane A/C). Part of an Italian chain, Grom makes its gelato with exclusively all-natural ingredients and uses only Carrubba flour as its primary thickening ingredient. And if you don't really know what that means, just know that it tastes great.

i From P. del Campo, walk up to V. Banchi di Sopra. Grom is on the left. Gelato €2.50-3.50. Open M-Th 11:30am-midnight, F-Sa 11:30am-1am, Su 11am-midnight.

LA FONTANA DELLA FRUTTA $

V. delle Terme 65-67   ☎0577 40 422

In addition to its many overpriced eateries, Siena's centro is also home to a number of little markets, deli counters, and produce shops. Of the latter, La Fontana Della Frutta just might be the best. Stop in for some lasagna and pasta salad, or just to stock up on some much-needed fruits and vegetables (you know, for all those vitamins and minerals you haven't been consuming). And if you're a thirsty bitch, order your fruits and veggies juiced—La Fontana will slice, dice, and press its produce for you in a number of different combinations, including grapefruit-apple-papaya and avocado-celery-lime.

i From the city center, walk down V. delle Terme. La Fontana Della Frutta is on the left. Open daily 8am-7:30pm.

NIGHTLIFE

CAFFE DEL CORSO

V. Banchi di Sopra 25   ☎0577 226 656

Skip the restaurant upstairs and go straight for Caffe del Corso's comprehensive cocktail list. Divided into easily consumable categories, this mixed drink menu allows you to browse lists of short drinks, long drinks, and after-dinner drinks,

siena

all of which could be grouped together under the single umbrella of "cheap drinks" (because that's the one you really care about). And with Caffe del Corso's open-air windows and plentiful outdoor seating in an alley just off V. Banchi di Sopra, you can drink in both your frozen daiquiri and the Siena summer night, all to the tune of Justin Timberlake and other top pop hitmakers.

i From P. del Campo, walk down V. Banchi di Sopra. Caffe del Corso is on the left. Cocktails €5. Open Tu-Su 8:30am-3am.

ANTICA ENOTECA ITALIANA

P. della Liberta 1 ☎0577 228 811 www.enoteca-italiana.it

Built into the walls of the Fortezza Medicea, Enoteca Italiana offers an Italian wine-tasting experience that couldn't get more Tuscan if a lovelorn Diane Lane showed up. With its curved brick archways, dim lighting, and wine bottles displayed carefully on its walls, Antica Enoteca Italiana is worth the trek it will take to get over here, as visitors can enjoy the unique experience of sampling authentic Italian wine from a collection of more than 1500 varieties. While you can certainly make a reservation for a wine tasting, you can also keep things low-key and just stop by and sip a glass on the terrace. And if you get the munchies with your drunchies, the enoteca also has a restaurant where you can enjoy a full meal or the rotating tasting menu in addition to your *vino*.

i From P. Gramsci, walk west down Vle. C. Maccari. Antica Enoteca Italiana is inside the entrance to the Fortezza Medicea, on the left. Wine by the glass starting at €1.50. Antipasti €10-12. Primi €10-12. Secondi €13-18. Enoteca open Tu-Sa 3-8pm. Restaurant open M-Sa noon-midnight.

ESSENTIALS

Practicalities

- **TOURIST OFFICES:** APT Siena provides maps for a small fee. It also has brochures and a bookstore. Facing the tower in P. del Campo, it's on the left side of the piazza. (P. del Campo 56 ☎0577 28 05 51 www.terresiena.it Open daily 9am-7pm.)

- **CURRENCY EXCHANGE:** Forexchange (V. di Citta 80).

- **ATMS:** Monte dei Paschi at V. Banchi di Sopra 84 near Il Campo.

- **LUGGAGE STORAGE:** The underground bus station in P. Gramsci has luggage storage.

- **POST OFFICES:** Poste Italiane (P. Matteotti 37 ☎0577 21 42 95). Just past the main bus stops. Additionally, stamps can be purchased and letters posted at a number of the tobacco shops in the city center.

Emergency

- **POLICE:** V. del Castoro. ☎0577 201 111. Near the Duomo.

- **LATE-NIGHT PHARMACIES:** Several pharmacies in the centro share a late-night rotation. Visit any one of them to check the schedule outside and get the number of the pharmacy on duty. The easiest to find is Farmacia del Campo (P. del Campo 260 ☎0577 28 02 34). Facing the Torre del Mangia, it's on the right side of the Campo, nestled between some restaurants.

- **HOSPITALS/MEDICAL SERVICES:** Santa Maria alle Scotte; take bus #3 or 77 from P. Gramsci (Vle. Mario Bracci 16 ☎0577 58 51 11 Open 24hr.).

Getting There

Traveling to Siena from Florence is easy enough, but if you're arriving in the city from elsewhere, you'll likely have to transfer trains or buses at least once.

By Bus

Although traveling to Siena by rail is a popular option, the bus station is significantly closer to the center of Siena than its far-flung train station. The TRA-IN/SITA bus is also faster than the train and runs directly to Siena's P. Gramsci from Florence. From Florence, the #131 bus will take you to Siena; you can catch either the #131O regular bus (€8, 1hr. 35min.) or the #131R rapid bus (€8, 1hr. 15min.).

By Train

If bumpy roads make you feel like you're trapped in a popcorn bag, the train may be a better option for you. Trains arrive at the Siena train station in P. Rosselli, a 15min. walk outside Siena's centro or a 10min. ride via bus #3, 4, 7, 8, 10, 17, or 77. Trains arrive from Florence (€9, 90min.), Poggibonsi (€4, 30min.), and Chiusi-Chianciano (€9, 90min.). Those traveling from Rome will need to transfer at Chiusi-Chianciano.

Getting Around

Once you're within the walls of Siena's historic centro, the best and virtually only way to get around is on foot (unless you really enjoy biking up and down steep hills). Siena's extensive bus system will only really be useful for travelers who are staying far outside the city center (i.e., at the Siena Hostel). Bus tickets cost €1.20 per ride and must be validated on the bus. Nearly all buses end their routes in P. Gramsci, northwest of the centro, and its underground station sells tickets for bus trips to other towns. Many buses also pass through the Siena train station. In the evenings, Siena switches over to a night bus system. Check the schedules outside the bus stops or in P. Gramsci.

pompeii

If Rome isn't Roman enough for you, take a daytrip to Pompeii, the city buried in time. Sailing around the Bay of Naples, you'll see Mt. Vesuvius lurking formidably over nearly all vistas. On August 24, 79 CE, the volcano erupted, blanketing Pompeii in a cloud of ash. Though tragic for the residents of this ancient metropolis, the eruption created a gold mine for archaeologists and a historical playground for tourists. Streets covered in stone blocks, fading frescoes, chipped mosaics, and a labyrinth of small rooms may get repetitive after a few hours but nonetheless inspire thoughts about how different life was nearly two millennia ago.

ORIENTATION

The ruins cover 66 hectares of land, although only 45 are accessible to the public. The area around the Circumvesuviana, the Porta Marina entrance, and Piazza Esedra is full of expensive restaurants and souvenir shops. A 20-25min. walk down V. Plinio and then V. Roma leads to the modern city's centro. From here, the Trenitalia train station is down V. Sacra in P. XXVIII Marzo. Inside the ruins, the most important sights are located on the western side, closer to the Porta Marina entrance. These sights include the Forum and the House of the Faun. A little to the east is the old city's brothel, and at the far eastern corner, you'll find Pompeii's amphitheater. Working your way back from there toward the entrance, you'll pass the Great Theater on the southern edge of the ruins.

SIGHTS

One ticket gives you the run of an entire ancient city. But touring the ruins is no simple undertaking—Pompeii was a true metropolis, complete with basilicas, bars, and brothels, and that kind of scope can be intimidating. Plenty of tour guides will try to coerce you into joining their group, which will cost €10-20. Rather than shelling out to become one of the crowd, opt for an informative audio tour (€6.50, 2 for €10). While both options will teach you a lot, one of the most fun ways to experience Pompeii is to navigate its maze-like streets solo—even with a map, you're likely to get lost. Of course, the pleasure of going at it alone can be mitigated when the city is packed, and at times, it's hard to walk down one of Pompeii's cobbled streets without running into another visitor. Come in the early summer or the fall for a slightly less crowded experience. If you plan on seeing more sites, a combined ticket allows entry to Herculaneum, Oplontis, Stabia, Boscoreale, and Pompeii over the course of 3 days. (*i* €11, EU citizens ages 18-24 €5.50, EU citizens under 18 and over 65 free; combined ticket €20/10/free. Cash only. Open daily Apr-Oct 8:30am-7:30pm; Nov-Mar 8:30am-5pm. Last entry 1½hr. before close.)

Near the Forum

As soon as you enter through Porta Marina, you can get down to business at the main market district in Pompeii, complete with the Basilica, Temple of Venere, and Forum. Stand in the middle of the Forum and look left, and you'll get a beautiful view of Mt. Vesuvius looming above the city. Next, wander into the Granai del Foro, which has plaster body casts, including the famous one of the dog. But if these are all too mortal for your divine tastes, walk into the Tempio di Apollo, which has copies of the statues of Apollo and Artemis that once dominated the area (the OG versions are at the Naples's Museo Archeologico Nazionale). If you're feeling dirty (because the showers in your hostel are always full), check out the well-preserved baths in the Terme del Foro. It can count as your proper hygiene care for the week.

Near the House of the Faun

To see more luxuries than you're getting at your one-star hostel, invite yourself over to the Casa del Fauno, an enormous and impressive ancient Roman home. With a bronze faun statue explaining the name and various mosaics, the lack of the famous Alexander Mosaic may be heartbreaking, but it's still a spacious, luxurious old home. For more tastes of wealth, go to the House of the Small Fountain, which has a fountain (no plot twist there). But also take a look at the frescoes, mosaics, and small sculptures while you're here. To see things on a larger scale, go to the House of the Vettii, where you'll find the famous frescoes of a well-endowed Priapus, who holds his place as the elephant in the otherwise gorgeous red room.

Near the Brothel

If ruins and an ancient city haven't left you all hot and bothered, you're probably just hard to please. But go to the ancient brothel, the Lupanare, and try to not be a little turned on (by history, of course). The explicit frescoes on the wall displaying various sex positions were either used to get the clientele excited or to give them a list of services provided. Various stone beds (which were covered with mattresses) occupy the surrounding rooms that were once sprinkled with graffiti about the ladies (and their various) there. Nearby, the Stabian Baths have a body cast and more mosaics for those who prefer non-pornographic images.

Near the Great Theater

To make your visit to Pompeii even more dramatic, head to the Great Theater, where rowdy Romans once gathered to watch bawdy plays and summer rock and roll concerts. Or something like that. Nearby, the Small Theater was built for the hipsters in the city to gather and listen to poetry readings in an acoustically impressive structure. The Botanical Garden next door offers some natural wonders of the area (because nature isn't all explosions and volcanoes).

Near the Amphitheater

To see what Pompeii residents did for fun when they weren't dying, check out the massive amphitheater where they gathered to watch others die. Holding 20,000 spectators during gladiator battles, it's almost large enough to accommodate all the tourists getting in your personal space. The Great Palaestra nearby is a lovely place for respite where you can sit under some trees and feel one with nature before you head to the Garden of the Fugitives to dampen your mood with some more plaster casts of the less-than-fortunate Pompeii-ers. But if you're set on ending things on a happier note, walk through the House of Octavius Quartio and House of Venus before you leave, where horticulture will give you some symbolic understanding of man's control over nature. And maybe convince you to take up gardening. (Your mom will be so proud.)

ESSENTIALS

Practicalities

- **TOURIST OFFICES:** Offices at P. Porta Marina Inferiore 12 (☎081 53 63 293) and at V. Sacra 1 (☎081 85 07 255) offer free maps of Pompeii, tickets for sightseeing buses around Campania, and pamphlets about area museums. (www.pompeiturismo.it Open daily 8:30am-6:30pm.)

- **LUGGAGE STORAGE:** Bag check at the archaeological site is free and mandatory for large bags.

Emergency

- **POLICE:** Carabinieri in Pompei Centro at V. Lepanto 61. (☎081 85 06 163)

Getting There

The best way to get to Pompeii's archaeological site is to take a train to Naples's Stazione Centrale from Termini Station. (€11-45. 1-3hr., 50 per day 4:52am-9:50pm.) Once in Naples, go to the lower level to catch the Circumvesuviana train (€2.90. 20-30min., every 15min.) toward Sorrento. Get off at Pompei Scavi. From the train, the ruins' main entrance, Porta Marina, is to the right. If you proceed down V. Villa dei Misteri, you can head through the less crowded entrance at P. Esedra (although audio tours are not available here). Alternatively, you can take a Trenitalia train from Naples. (€2.90. 20-40min., every 30min.) The train drops you off in modern Pompeii's centro. From the station, walk up V. Sacra until you reach P. Bartolo Longo. Turn left down V. Colle San Bartolomeo. It's a 20-25min. walk to the archaeological site's main entrance; it's better to enter at the less crowded P. Anfiteatro, a short way down V. Plinio.

palermo

Gritty, bustling, historic, and real. Palermo takes thousands of years of history under Greek, Byzantine, Norman, and Spanish influence, fills its streets with gorgeous theaters and churches, and then walks by them all without looking twice. Though a popular tourist city, it never feels like one. The famous buildings all look worn, and the cobblestone streets by the markets are littered with shrimp tails. Palermo is not a historic relic. It's still a living, thriving city full of fishermen, immigrants, students, and businessmen all going about their days in the shadow of breathtaking Byzantine cathedrals. At night, the city comes alive with huge crowds gathering at bars and discos, filling open squares with chatter and street food, and dancing until the early hours of the morning.

Palermo is the kind of city that could swallow you up with its slightly grimy building facades and winding narrow streets. To situate yourself, know the three main streets: Via Roma, Via Vittorio Emmanule and Via Maqueda, which will take you pretty much anywhere you want to go. Palermo's famous street markets, which fill up old streets with everything from swordfish heads to sassy Italian t-shirts, are at Ballaro, Vucciria, and Capo. Head down Via Maqueda and you'll get to the famous Teatro Massimo, the second largest theater in Europe that could house operas with elephants. Head down Via Roma and you'll reach the Politeama, an enormous piazza with another large theater. Along the way, numerous churches with golden Byzantine mosaics covering every inch or spiraling Baroque columns or Arab style roofs done by master craftsmen line the streets, so always be sure to peek in. In between all the culture and history and zooming Vespas, you'll catch a glimpse of Palermo in all its raw, gorgeous glory.

SIGHTS

CAPPELLA PALATINA AND PALAZZO REALE

P. Indipendenza ☎091 626 2833 www.federicosecondo.org/en/norman-palace

Sometimes having a palace just isn't enough. If you're like the Norman kings in Sicily, you'll want a drop dead gorgeous chapel as well. A visit to the Palazzo dei Normanni, also known as the Royal Palace, will make you feel lowly in more way than one. It's like the building form of middle school, but with its beautiful architecture and mosaics, it's well worth a visit.

The main attraction of the entire palace is the Palatine Chapel. Built in the 1100s, this chapel is one of the most beautiful you will see in all of Sicily. Every inch is covered with Byzantine-style mosaics, leaving all the walls a shimmering gold in the light. Every arch and every corner is filled with brightness and beautiful artistry. The mosaics represent everything from the Signore, Jesus Christ himself, to acts of the apostles to beautiful flora and fauna.

The most beautiful aspect of this chapel, however, is its seamless integration of Norman, Byzantine, and Arab works. Built in a Norman palace with Norman architecture and doors with Latin inscriptions, the chapel opens up to gorgeous Byzantine mosaics and Greek text; then, as you look up, you'll see the Arabic arches and roof with Arabic script. Multiculturalism, bitches.

As you walk out of the chapel, be sure to check on the chapel's left, where there's an inscription written in Latin, Greek, and Arabic, capturing all the styles represented here. Afterwards, head up to the more palace-y part of this palace. Walk through some beautiful halls and rooms filled with paintings of everything from Hercules and his labors in parliament (damn that bureaucracy) to portraits of the viceroys. Though the palace part may pale in comparison to the shimmery chapel, it's still worth a look. It's all higher society, after all.

i €8 M, €7 Tu-Th, €8 F-Su. Open M-Sa 8:15am-5:40pm, Su 8:15am-1pm.

MONREALE

About 15km south of Palermo lies the beautiful medieval city of Monreale. Serviced regularly by Palermo city buses 389 and 309, which drop you off steps away from a free shuttle into Monreale proper, make the trip down here if you have a couple hours to spare.

Located high up on a mountain, this city offers stunning views of Palermo and the sea below. It's also full of winding cobblestone streets that eventually give way to a small, pulsing city that exists apart from the tourist world. Small bakeries and pizzerias line all parts of town. Find somewhere a little off the beaten road for a good meal. Some of the "fast food" options are surprisingly delicious in this city.

AI QUATTRO CANTI
P. del Ponticello, 1   ☎339 266 0963 www.aiquattrocanti.hostel.com

Ai Quattro Canti, named after the nearby baroque square of the same name, is an adorable little hostel with bright colors, comfy couches, and boards advertising past crazy tequila parties. Which captures everything anyone ever wanted from a hostel.

It's rather small, with only two rooms and two bathrooms, but if you can snag a room here, take it. The prices are cheap, the beds are comfy, and the hostel owner, Giuseppe, is amazing. He fosters a close environment, encouraging new people and old to go out to dinner or grab really cheap beers together, and he is always willing to make you an espresso. Take it. Then go out with a bunch of your new hostel friends and relish in that backpacking life.

The hostel also has a decently-sized kitchen and enough utensils to cook your own food. The hostel is steps away from V. Maqueda and V. Vittorio Emanuele, too, so good cheap food isn't hard to find in this area. The great location right in the center of everything will make you want to walk everywhere in Palermo, but the kitchen walls lined with possible excursion destinations and information about how to get there might give you enough wanderlust to head to more gorgeous beach resorts for a day. So if you're looking for a fun, social place to stay with pink couches, flowery '70s curtains in some doorways, and blue waves on the walls, come here.

i Dorms €16. No curfew. Reception hours vary.

A CASA DI AMICI
V. Dante 57   ☎091 765 4650 www.acasadiamici.com

Who doesn't like houses and who doesn't like friends? That's why the concept behind A Casa di Amici is brilliant. Add in squeaky clean rooms, comfortable beds, air conditioning, and a great social atmosphere, and you've got a winner.

Bright, spacious rooms, hardwood floors, and a sleek, artsy aesthetic make this hostel an ideal place to stay. The large common areas and social atmosphere also make this an ideal place to have a kickass time in Palermo. The facilities are great. Free breakfast and access to musical instruments? We feel like that's something every hostel should start to offer. Because after some drumming lessons, you'll finally find an appropriate way to beat it in a hostel, thus solving an age old problem.

Located a little off V. della Liberta, you'll still be within walking distance of the main streets and sights in Palermo. Add to that free Wi-Fi, free towels, and free TV, and you might be so overwhelmed that you'll have to use the yoga and meditation room. This hostel is always prepared. Once you've collected yourself, head out into Palermo, which isn't as clean as your hostel, but it's still got that fun charm.

i Dorms €16-20. Reception 24hr.

palermo

Take some time wandering around Monreale, then go off to see the main attraction itself. Impossible to miss (kinda because the bus drops you off right there) is the enormous cathedral. As one of the greatest examples of Norman architecture, this Duomo is a breathtaking sight. Inside, everything is shimmering gold. Beautifully crafted Byzantine mosaics cover every part of the ceiling, making sure you spend a lot of time looking up. Gilded, shining figures float in golden backgrounds. A famous and large Christ Pantocrator stares severely from the apse. Scenes from the Bible, such as Noah's Ark, surround the rest of the interior.

It's one of those rare creations where everything is pretty. The blue and gold ceilings, the Corinthian columns, the back door which is so high it almost opens up the entire church. If you time your visit here, you might be able to wedding crash one of the many lucky couples who get to be married in this marvelous cathedral. During these adorable moments, maybe you can even catch stern Jesus looking a little happier. He practically glows.

i Cathedral entrance free. Open M-Sa 8:30am-12:45pm and 2:30-5pm, Su 8-10am and 2:30-5pm.

SAN GIUSEPPE DEI TEATINI
C. Vittorio Emanuele, at Quattro Canti

One of the churches in the beautiful baroque square of Quattro Canti, San Giuseppe del Teatini is a hidden gem in the midst of the loud, gritty city. The weathered facade gives way to a gorgeous and untouched Sicilian Baroque church from the 17th century.

Step inside and be taken aback first by how beautiful the red and green marbles and twisting columns are, and then by the fact that there's practically no one here. Every corner is decorated with rich marbles and stunning frescoes. Take a look up at the elaborate ceiling painted with soft pastels. Then look down at the lovely marble floor. The statues decorating the church are masterfully made, and some, like the Virgin Mary, are done in a flowered marble.

The altar is breathtaking and will make you keep looking up as cherubs and angels peer out in high relief. The twisted baroque columns and cherub'd columns and bright marbles all give the building itself a sort of movement. But then the interior is silent. Here is a ruin kept in perfect condition, in all its grandeur, with very few people to come admire it. And within all that, it captures an essence of the forgotten beauty in Palermo. It's enough to make you start writing poetry or something. We can respect that.

i Free. Open daily 8:30-11am and 6-8pm.

PALAZZO CHIARAMONTE
P. Marina, 61   ☎091 607 5306

One of the more unusual sights in Palermo, this historical castle turned Spanish Inquisition prison turned museum is a somber and eye-opening look into the past. Once home to the powerful Sicilian lord, Chiaramonte, this castle built in the 14th century has had quite the life beyond that. During the late-15th century to early 16th, this castle fell under the rule of the Spanish, who destroyed many of the symbols of Chiaramonte. Then from 1600 to 1782, it was the home to the tribunal and many prisons for the Spanish Inquisition. Now both the prisons and a few rooms of the palace are open to the public as a museum that can only be visited along with a guide.

First, a guide will take you into the archaeological site where artisans quarters from the 10th century have been dug up (i.e., this is where you can check out some cool pots—no museum in Sicily is complete without those). Next is the Interrogation room where a Spanish inquisitor was killed, which seems super badass. Unfortunately, now it's just a room.

After this introduction, the tour takes a turn for the dark and twisted. It heads into the prisons where much graffiti from the prisoners remains. The Poet's Cell is famous for having verses scribbled on the walls. Other sections have elaborate sketches and drawings of wide-eyed saints and slightly inaccurate maps of Sicily. The walk through the cells is like a walk through an intellectual asylum. Terrifying, heartbreaking, beautiful. Many write on the walls asking for death. Other create gorgeous human figures. One of the last rooms may pull some heartstrings, since it was home to an Englishman who wrote his graffiti in English.

Following the prisons, turn into the palace. All the symbols of Chiaramonte were destroyed by the Spanish, but the two visible rooms here are still beautiful. Note the Arab influences in the doors and take a look at the gorgeous painted ceilings. The palace is a short visit with looks only into two large rooms, but it's also home to Renato Guttuso's painting, Vucciria. Then let the guide lead you back out into the sunset and take a couple moments to figure out what the hell just happened. History, that's what.

i €5. Open Tu-Sa 9am-6:30pm, Su 10am-2pm.

DUOMO

P. di Cattedrale   ☎091 33 43 73 www.cattedrale.palermo.it

As the most important church in Palermo, we guess this is worth a visit. As you're walking down V. Vittorio Emanuele, stop at the Duomo to go see a building undergoing an intense architectural identity crisis while also embodying in stone the confusing history of the city.

To get the true scope of the Duomo's rich architectural diversity, we'll have to start way, way back. In 1184, the Archbishop of Palermo had this grand old idea to build a cathedral. Perché, non? He chose the site where it stands today because there used to stand an old mosque from the ninth century which itself had been built over an old Christian basilica. This place was just ripe for some more building. The story goes that the archbishop wanted to build a cathedral that would rival the one in Monreale. Well, he failed. Sorry, Palermo. Monreale is widely recognized as a more beautiful church. But all is not lost—the Duomo still stands as quite the masterpiece.

Starting in 1184, the Duomo was built in a Norman style. In the 13th and 14th centuries, however, like any good angsty teen, the facade started its Gothification. In the 15th century, the Spanish brought their Catalan style to mix with the Gothic. In the 18th century, the cathedral underwent a neoclassical phase. So now as you walk in, the main facade is Gothic. Step in and you'll enter a scavenger hunt for history. Look out for columns inscribed with Qur'an verses and the south porch done in the Catalan style. The interior has a stark neoclassical appearance, which is quite different from the bedazzled interiors of the Duomo at Monreale. Still, the sheer size, history, and self ascribed-importance make this Duomo incredible.

Inside are also the tombs of past Italian kings. For a modest fee, you can go see the royal pantheon and some impressive tombs, including that of Roger II, the first king of Sicily. If bling's your thing, also stop by the treasury full of gold and crowns. Take that, Monreale. You don't have to be the prettiest when you've got the bling.

i Free. €2 for crypts. €3 for crypts and treasury. €7 for crypts, treasury, and roof. Open M-Sa 9am-5:30pm, Su 7:30am-1:30pm and 4pm-7pm.

FOOD

ANTICA FOCACCERIA DEL MASSIMO $

V. Bara all'Olivella 76   ☎091 33 56 28

Want to know where all the locals eat? Look no further than Antica Focacceria del Massimo. Don't let its proximity to Teatro Massimo fool you. Authentic local food, authentic locals, and some of the best food around can be found here.

Let your counter-cultural personality rejoice at the lack of tourist menus here. This large restaurant has a cafeteria-esque feel with tables scattered everywhere and everyone from workers to students trying to get a glimpse of what's on today's menu. This busy restaurant specializes in pasta. Walk in and head toward the counter in the back where there's a menu posted. Delicious meals range from ravioli to spaghetti to probably some of the best lasagna in Palermo. All for around €3-4.

Head to the cash register, pay for your meal, and then go to the back counter of pastas, give your receipt to the chef, and wait around 5min. for your freshly-made pasta to come to the table where you sit down. Oh, and then breathe. It's not that complicated. Trust us.

The pasta comes in large portions, so one plate could easily fill you for lunch and keep your wallet filled for the rest of the day. The al dente is perfect, the sauces are fresh, and after you take one bite, you, too, will realize why locals flock here for lunch at all hours.

i Pasta €3-4. Panini €2.50-4. Open daily 8am-4pm.

MOUNIR $

V. Giovanni da Procida 19 ☎091 77 30 005

Most of the time, you really shouldn't wander into small alleyways in Palermo. But make an exception for Mounir. For some incredible (and incredibly cheap) pizza in Palermo, veer a little off your trusted V. Roma and go to Mounir. A small pizzeria with plenty of outdoor seating, this is a popular venue among the young crowd thanks to its delicious food, large servings, and bargain prices.

Walk into the storefront, and you'll see Mounir himself tossing pizza dough and ceremoniously dumping delicious toppings like prosciutto and tomatoes on fresh-baked pizza. There's a modest menu hanging up on the wall where you can choose which pizza you'd like to be made right on the spot. If pizza isn't what you're craving, you should really get that checked out, but there's also a decent kebab menu. Can't decide? Go for a kebab pizza.

Delicious choices include prosciutto and cheese, quattro formaggi, or capricciosa when you're feeling a little gluttonous and just want it all. Order, then

grab a table outside. Not enough tables? One of the waiters will set one up for you. There is usually a wait because all the pizzas are made fresh, and it can take some time on a busy Friday night. But it's always worth it.

i *Pizza €4-8. Open daily 7pm-1am.*

PASTICCERIA CAPPELLO

$

V. Colonna Rotta, 68   ☎091 48 96 01

There are a lot of words to describe Palermo. Sweet isn't usually one of them. That's until you decide to haul ass up to Pasticceria Cappello, at which point Palermo is just a slightly more Mafia-riddled version of Candyland.

Walk into this pastry shop and you'll be surrounded on all sides by pastries, tarts, cannoli, gelato, and pretty much anything else one could need to satisfy every desire behind glass counters. If you're in the mood for gelato or granita, head to the right, where a counter of smooth, fresh gelato will parade a rainbow of flavors in front of your eyes. If your dreams are a little more solid, take your pick of pastries everywhere else in the shop.

Delicious cannoli with sweet ricotta, tart pastries made with fresh berries, and delicious cream cakes topped with fresh and exotic fruits like kiwi, mango, and pineapple—you really can't go wrong here. And with most of the small pastries costing less than €0.50, it would just be wrong not to try almost all of them.

i *Pastries €0.20-2.50. Open M-Tu 7am-9:30pm, Th-Su 7am-9:30pm.*

AL GELONE

$

V. Giuseppe Puglisi Bertolino, 23   ☎091 36 36 04

You know what you need? Gelato. Obviously. So go to Al Gelone. Venture a little beyond P. Sturzo, and you'll be rewarded with some fresh, delicious (and cheap!) gelato. Modern quirkiness at its finest, the bright colors, neon spoon decor, and tables in the shape of giant spoons are something to look at. If you can bear to look away from the large selection of gelato, that is.

On the right wall as you enter, there's a giant picture of a chef magically pointing with his finger as fresh ingredients swirl about. Which, okay, is a little weird, but this gelato is pretty damn magical. We think that's the message of the mural.

Flavors range from fresh pistachio to coffee where you can still taste the grounds to anise because why the hell not. Cones are cheap, at €2 for a medium, so don't be afraid to ask for two flavors. If you want something a little lighter and more refreshing, head to the counter on the far end for some granita, which is like ice cream but made with water instead of cream, meaning it will quench your thirst a little better. So we think you should just have both. Order, pay, then take your gelato, sit on one of the white stools filled with sand (really, don't ask questions—it's modern art) and enjoy the loveliness of smooth, cold gelato that you just have to devour before it melts all over you. The brain freeze is worth it.

i *Gelato €1.50-3. Open daily 11am-1am.*

ANTICA FOCACCERIA SAN FRANCESCO

$$

V. Alessandro Paternostro 58   ☎091 32 02 64 www.anticafocacceria.it

Since 1834, Antica Focacceria San Francesco has been serving up delicious street food in a charming little cobblestone piazza next to a church. For five generations, this restaurant has seen everyone from weary travelers to hungry locals to mob bosses to carabinieri at its doorstep. But nothing has stopped this family from making some of the best food in Palermo.

Enjoy the rustic charm of the enormous brown and gold doors, walk by the kitchen where all the magic happens, and take a seat outside where you can admire the prettiness of old Sicilian buildings and churches outside. Then get ready to feast.

palermo

The menu is divided into two parts: the street food and the food for fancy shmancy travelers (which is still reasonably priced). As far as street food goes, try some of the delicious and filling arancini, fried rice balls filled with meat and cheese in a way that will almost make you never want to eat regular off-the-street arancini again. There's also unsurprisingly focaccia at this focacceria, which is a type of Italian flatbread that can be filled with tomatoes and cheeses.

If eating street food in a sit down restaurant is a little too crazy, there's also a great selection of pastas and seafood. Try the rigatoni, which is al dente at its perfection. You also can't go wrong with anything plus sardines in Palermo.

i Street food €3-4. Entrees €8-15. Open daily 11am-12am.

NIGHTLIFE

NOGA WINE BAR
V. dei Chiavettieri

Located on the popular V. dei Chiavettieri, which is lined with bars, Noga Wine Bar stands out. Walk by during aperitivo hours and you'll see that this place has the perfect mixture of ambient street seating and delicious, generous portions of aperitivo food. How could you pass it up?

The waiters are the perfect mixture of helpful and sassy. If you ask for a menu, they'll probably inform you that they are the menu. Know some good aperitvo drinks off the back of your hand. Can't decide? Spritz is always a safe option. Or if you're feeling a little classier, this is a wine bar. Ask a waiter for their recommendations on the best wine.

After you buy your drink, congratulations. You've gained entrance to an amazing aperitvo buffet. Try delicacies ranging from rice with salmon to those little rolled up hot dogs that Italians seem to love so much. The food is very well done and much better than the chips and peanuts you might get in America. Chickpeas and bread, grilled eggplants, salads with olives—if you aren't careful, this place turns into dinner. Call it a chiusitivo instead.

The drinks are delicious, the aperitivo is reasonably priced, and the seating on V. dei Chiavettieri (since there isn't much room inside the actual bar) will give you the perfect chance to people watch. And laugh at how measly everyone else's aperitivo seems. You are so winning right now.

i Drinks €5-8. M-F 6pm-2am, Sa 6pm-3am, Su 6pm-2am.

AI BOTTAI
V. Bottai, 62   ☎091 774 67 86

As you cross V. dei Chiavettieri onto V. Bottai in your late night Palermo adventures where crossing streets is a life threatening sport, you'll stumble into an enormous crowd sitting, talking, and singing in the streets. Welcome to Ai Bottai.

A lively pub in Palermo, there's always something happening here. Football game, live music, wild Tuesday night—everything's a reason to celebrate. This place is popular, so crowds usually fill the area on Friday and Saturday nights. Try to snag a table to meet some of the friendliest bartenders in the area while downing delicious drinks. If that's as impossible as getting laid in Palermo (… not your best odds), just stand.

Most of the time, you won't even see the bar inside, since everyone prefers to hang out on the pedestrian-only road here. TVs are set up outside during game days; otherwise some jazzy music may blast. Either way, the traffic here is always astonishing. Try one of the drinks, and you'll begin to understand why. With good beers, great cocktails (some even colored to look like the Italian flag!), and reasonable prices, this is one of the go-to pubs in Palermo. Ravers will be disappointed, but if you just crave some company and crowds, wiggle yourself

italy

in here. Because everyone needs some close human contact + alcohol every now and then.

i Drinks €4-8. Open daily 4pm-3am.

VUCCIRIA

Off V. Roma, near V. Argenteria area.

As bustling as the vucciria, or marketplaces, are in the morning, a different sort of crowd fills them up on weekend nights. Fish stands give way to burgers and beer stands, and the shoppers leave to make room for students looking to turn up. Popular among the youth in Palermo for their large open spaces, loud music, and, of course, cheap, cheap beer, if you're looking for a fun night out with your friends, hit up a marketplace

For some good fun, head to the aptly-named marketplace, Vucciria. Here, crowds gather for late-night food as stands pop up and cook meat right in front of you, filling the streets with a hazy, delicious smoke. Get at us, smoke machines in discos. Plenty of bars line this area, so as the night progresses, the crowd gets rowdier and takes up much of the square behind the marketplace as well. Everyone mingles as music blasts, and no one really knows what bar they're at, but that just sounds like an ideal Friday night.

LA CHAMPAGNERIA DEL MASSIMO

V. Salvatore Spinuzza, 59 ☎091 33 57 30

For a wild night of drama, intrigue, and fun fun fun, go to Teatro Massimo. Then take a sharp turn and head straight for the bars. In case operas don't seem like your ideal wild night out, Palermo's got you covered. Right outside the theater are plenty of bars filled with people who have found a different kind of entertainment: good alcohol. Now that's where the party starts.

Head to La Champagneria Del Massimo, which is steps outside the theater, and welcome to a boozy haven. You just have to try to act a little classy. As a wine bar, there's always an incredible selection of wine (and other, stronger drinks) lining the walls inside. Bottles on bottles on bottles. On almost every wall. Challenge accepted.

If you wanna be a champagne master, you've gotta catch 'em all (or something like that). Come here and walk inside, where you'll be met by a classy wooden bar surrounded by wine bottles and wine glasses hanging from the ceiling. If you come in the evening, you'll make aperitivo hours. Grab a glass of something (it'll probably be good) and enjoy the wonders of free food with any alcohol purchase. Come by at night, and you'll see a little more fun. A popular place to come and drink, people fill up these tables, bathe in the kindness and generosity of the owners and servers, and drink away. Though a quieter, calmer place to spend the night, it's in the area of some rowdier bars and clubs if your wine tasting adventure goes a little crazy. It happens.

i Drinks €6-10. Open M-Sa 9am-3am.

DON CHISCIOTTE

V. Candelai 52/54 ☎349 59 23 650

Plenty of places have loud music blasting on V. Candelai. Don Chisciotte actually has a dance floor to go along with it. Success. Walk into a bright, neon-lit room with an enormous bar on the left. You can grab a drink of anything that you need to get you over to start dancing. The art here will be trying to get the bartender to hear you over the bar's own deafening music.

After a couple shots, turn your attention to the right. The doorway opens up to one of the larger dance floors in Palermo. There's no lighting except for some strobe lights, which are covered up by the smoke machine. Is there anyone else here? Nobody really knows.

palermo

If you come by too early (i.e., midnight), the dance floor is still prepared for you, with benches along the sidelines where you can sit and check out the sexy shadows coming and going into the room until the place turns a little rowdier. Twerking might not be everyone's favorite activity at this bar, but since it is one of the few places in Palermo with a legitimate dance floor, if any young Italians want to dance, they'll probably end up here by the end of the night. So take a seat, go slightly deaf from all the electronic beats, and when the party gets a little more turnt up (or you get a little more turnt up), do that smoke and neon light some justice and hit the dance floor with some sweet moves that no one will ever really see.

i *Drinks €5-8. Open daily 6pm-2am.*

ESSENTIALS

Practicalities

- **POST OFFICE:** Mail is handled by Poste Italia. The central post office is at V. Roma 320 (open M-Sa 8:20am-7:05pm).

- **INTERNET:** Wi-Fi can be hard to find outside of your hotel. Check for cafes or restaurants that offer complimentary Wi-Fi.

Emergency

- **EMERGENCY NUMBERS:** The emergency number in Italy is 112 for police, fire department, and ambulances.

- **PHARMACIES:** Look for a big green "+" sign anywhere, and you'll find a pharmacy. Late-night pharmacies can be a little difficult to find. Closed pharmacies will usually list where the nearest open pharmacies are.

Getting There

Falcone–Borsellino Airport is the airport in Palermo. Transport from the airport to the city is easily done by the Prestia Comandé bus, which costs around €6-7 and departs from the airport every 30min. and goes to Stazione Centrale, the main train station in Palermo. If you arrive by ferry, the bus 139, which stops right outside the port, will take you from the port to Stazione Centrale.

Getting Around

Palermo is a mammoth of a city, but the main tourist area between the train station and Politeama is walkable. The main bus stations are at Stazione Centrale (where you can also catch trains heading to other cities), Piazza Independenzia, and Piazza Sturzo. Bus tickets cost €1.40 and can be bought in Tabaccherie.

syracuse

From the tiny cobblestone streets in the island of Ortigia to the sprawling ruins in the archaeological park to gorgeous sunsets by the ocean, Syracuse has all the charm you could ask for in a small Italian town. And then there's the food. All the delicious cannoli, gelato, and signature pizzolo will keep your stomach satisfied. Should you hunger for some knowledge and history, this ancient town of Archimedes will take care of you with its museums and sites.

To orient yourself, start at the train and bus station, where you'll probably be arriving. From here, always head east. (There's nothing but sunsets and cowboys in the west.) The main street, Corso Umberto, will take you anywhere you'd like to go.

Follow it to Corso Gelone to get to the archaeological park or keep heading straight and to get to the bridge that leads to the island of Ortigia and the old part of the city. Here, the winding narrow roads lead into beautiful open piazze like Piazza del Archimede and the famous Piazza del Duomo. Walk in any direction long enough and you'll reach the bluest water over which you can watch breathtaking sunsets.

SIGHTS

DUOMO DI SIRACUSA

Piazza Duomo   ☎093 16 53 28

Enter the Piazza Duomo and its namesake will steal the scene. Always surrounded by paparazzi and always looking flawless, this celebrity cathedral is famous for a reason. First of all, it's drop dead gorgeous. Soaring white Corinthian columns, large arched windows, towering statues. Could it be any more of a cathedral? Built in two different periods, this cathedral displays both Baroque and Rococo styles which come together in a gorgeous fluid façade that's full of fun movement.

The statues outside start with St. Peter on the lower left, St. Paul on the lower right, San Marciano, the first bishop of Syracuse on the upper left, Santa Lucia, the patron saint of Syracuse on the upper right, and everyone's favorite virgin who isn't you in the center. Take a walk through the columns to see the inside. Remember to be modestly dressed and then pay a modest fee – it's all about the modesty in here. Except for the ridiculously elaborate doors with their swirling columns. Did we mention that this cathedral has got some good moves?

Once you step in, however, you'll see the Duomo's most famous secret: it was once an ancient Greek temple. Large stone arches line both sides of the nave giving it an ancient feel. Probably because it is ancient. The Duomo is built on an ancient doric temple to Athena. According to Cicero, this used to be a gorgeous marble and gold temple to the virgin goddess (still not you). Athena's shield once graced the doors in bright gold and helped ships navigating from afar. Good goddess Athena.

Much like many ancient temples, it became repurposed as a Christian church and this one now celebrates another virgin. The old columns of the temple were reused providing quite a physical link between the past and the present. The main altar displays more beautiful white Corinthian columns and a painting of the Virgin with child. Walk around the main nave then take a look inside the little chapels. There is small but beautiful one dedicated to Santa Lucia. And before you leave, be sure to look down as you're walking around as well. There are some great mosaics that might even floor you.

i Admission €2. Open daily 7:30am-7:30pm.

THE ARCHAEOLOGICAL PARK OF SYRACUSE

Entrance at intersection of Corso Gelone and Via Paolo Orsi

If you like old shit, you're in the right country. And if you're in Syracuse, get your ass over to the Archaeological Park. A vast area filled with ancient Greek and Roman ruins, this is a place no history buff or saw-300-and-got-really-excited-kind-of-person can miss.

About a 10-min walk from the new city or 20-min if you're posh enough to stay in Ortigia, head up and once you start seeing wheat fields and such you're either stuck in the Gladiator movie, or you've arrived. The strangely difficult to find ticket office is located past all the souvenir shops by the bus parking area. It may cost you a pretty penny, but if you plan on visiting the Archaeological Museum as well, buy a combined ticket and save some euros.

The entrance to the park is right across the street. The first couple stops are actually free and open to the public. Turn left after entering through the main

LOLHOSTEL $

V. Francesco Crispi 92-96 ☎0931 465 088 www.lolhostel.com

Stay at LolHostel, and you can ROTFLOL at the prices everyone else is paying to stay in Syracuse. This is the only hostel in town, and if you're a world weary backpacker, you'll probably be staying here. But you can be assured that you won't be complaining.

Located on the V. Crispi, you'll be a minute away from the bus and train station that'll bring you in and only 10-12min. away from the archaeological park and the city center in Ortigia, so you can #brb quite often. And it's also right off Corso Umberto, which is full of delicious and cheap noms.

Walk in, and you'll be greeted by friendly reception and given a map with more recommendations than you'll be able to cope with. On the ground floor is a fully functional IKEA-esque kitchen where you'll assure yourself you'll cook once you get the motivation to go to a supermarket (so probably never). There's also a lounge with fluorescent colored chairs and a full bar next to the kitchen that serves the cheapest drinks around. Complimentary breakfast is served every morning, and if you're up before 11am, make sure you go because delicious pastries. Take some marmalade-filled cornetti out to the garden, and it will be one of your better morning experiences.

All the bedrooms are located upstairs. The 20-bed loft is an impressive feat, but the eight-bed rooms are also large and spacious. With windows on the ceiling, the rooms can be a little dimly lit, but everyone looks better in dim lighting. The beds are standard, but the blankets are ridiculously soft.

The hostel caters to a young student crowd but isn't much of a party hostel, so you might have to be the party sometimes. But still, after a busy night in Ortigia, the walk back will never be bad, and you'll <3 being able to stay here. Maybe even <4.

i Dorms €20-23. Reception 24hr. May-Aug.

gate and you'll get to the ruins of a Roman amphitheater. See the giant stone ruins pop up through the overgrown field and try to imagine what it would be like to watch people fight to the death here. Yeah, gladiator battles were weird. Walk down and as you avoid the large tour groups, you'll see the Ara di Lerone on your left, which was used by the Greeks for animal sacrifices. Now largely in ruins, it's still a pretty cool sight before you head into the ticketed area of the park.

Once you're in, head down and the stone ruins will give way into a lush jungle of palm trees. Also the temperature will drop by like five degrees which is nice too. This is the Latomia del Paradiso. Once an ancient quarry site, it's been filled with trees ever since and is now a beautiful paradise. Inside here you'll find the Ear of Dionysus. Before you cry out that's the strangest thing you've heard, calm down. It's only a cave. A very pretty cave at that. In the shape of a very big ear and with incredible acoustics that you can try out for yourself, legend has it that the tyrant king Dionysus used to keep prisoners here so he could hear everything they said. We don't know how the prisoners didn't see it coming since they were being kept in a giant ear.

italy

Head back up and out of the gardens and you'll see the steps leading to the Greek theater. As one of the world's largest, this is still indeed a functional theater where dramas are performed in the summer. An impressive 455 feet in diameter, it's still surprisingly in tact. Used for plays in ancient days, the Romans weren't always willing to put up with your drama so it was sometimes filled with water for mock sea battles. On a hot day, filling the theater with water doesn't seem like a bad idea. Just saying.

i €10. Combined ticket with museum €13.50. Open daily 9am until 2 hours before sunset

PAOLO ORSI REGIONAL ARCHAEOLOGICAL MUSEUM

Viale Teocrito, 66   ☎093 14 89 511 www.regione.sicilia.it/beniculturali/museopaoloorsi/

If the archaeological park wasn't able to convince you of how much history Syracuse has, hit up the museum for a more air-conditioned tour of the past. Located about five minutes away from the park, the museum is in a beautiful little garden with swaying palm trees and all about dat Mediterranean life.

Walk in to a pretty modern museum with plenty of windows looking out at the funky Sanctuary of the Madonna of Tears and get ready to see more history than you'll ever be ready for. The museum itself is divided into four major sections which like your grades go from A to D. The first section takes you way way back. Start with a geological foundation of Syracuse. Various rocks and some fossils of pygmy elephants make sure you realize what kind of island climate you're dealing with. Also pygmy elephants are just fun. The section begins to challenge you when you claim how much you love pot, because holy shit there are a lot of pots here. Everything from potsherds to pots big enough that you could sit in them, you're bound to find one pot you like.

Section B will take you a little further into history with the Greek colonies. Plenty of kouroi and korai, statues of young men and women, as well as beautiful remains from Greek temples. Along with a very silly gorgon. Section S is home to findings from Hellenized subcolonies aka more pots and some pretty statues. Section D will take you up and towards the height of sculpture in this museum.

Admire some flowing beards, expressive faces, and of course the beautiful Landolina Venus which apart from boobs is a very beautiful and delicate statue. While you're up in D, be sure to walk around on the second floor to see the famous Sarcophagus of Adelphia. A marble sarcophagus that is a great example of art from late antiquity, this sarcophagus shows plenty of Biblical scenes using adorable little figures in the sarcophagus, and with Christianity wraps up our long trek through the ancient world in this museum that has proved to you that history is cool. And that people used a shit ton of pots.

i €8. Combined ticket with park €13.50. Tu-Sa 9am-6pm, Su 9am-1pm.

PIAZZA DUOMO
Piazza Duomo

There's nothing quite like being lost in the tiny alleys and streets in Ortigia only to have the road open up to the breathtaking Piazza del Duomo. Considered one of the more beautiful piazze in Italy by, well, anyone who has actually visited it, Piazza del Duomo will take you in with its irregular but fascinating semioval shape filled with twisting Baroque buildings and of course the Duomo itself and make you fall in love with a square that isn't your first boyfriend.

The most eye-catching building of all is the Duomo, a stunning cathedral built out of a Greek temple to Athena. High Corinthian columns, large arched windows, gorgeous statues, and great steps to sit on and watch Syracuse pass you by.

Next to the Duomo on the left is the Archbishop's Palace, which is sadly not open to the public. Thanks a lot, archbishop. Across on the right is the Palazzo Beneventano dal Bosco, a rather boxish but still beautiful baroque palace with large rectangular windows. In the furthest end of the piazza is the Church of Santa Lucia alla Badia which, with its high white façade and columns is yes, also baroque (with a touch of rococo). You might be seeing a trend here. There are many restaurants and bars in this area as well, but as a well-travelled backpacker you'll realize that famous piazza aren't the best places to get deals.

So grab some gelato from the side streets and then come sit here. Enjoy the over the top whimsy, the not quite straight up and down, and the large arches and windows of the baroque and rococo. Huzzah.

FOOD

LA VOGLIA MATTA $
C. Umberto I, 34 ☎093 16 71 18

Let's be real. The #1 reason you've come to Italy? History, beaches, the gorgeous men? Nope. Even better: gelato. So when you're in Syracuse, be sure to hit up one of the best gelaterias in town...like, a couple times a day. La Voglia Matta: translated as "The Crazy Desire," it pretty much sums up all your feelings about gelato. Come in and let your dreams be realized.

Located right on Corso Umberto and just minutes before the bridge to Ortigia, stop here for a cone to make your entrance onto the beautiful island even sweeter. You'll probably have tp walk by the counter a couple times before you can come up with the winning combination of the many flavors on hand. With everything from classic lemon and pistachio to Kinder, all these are artisanal and handmade gelati. To act like a true Italian, get the ricotta penne and ciocolato nero, which is ricotta with sweet fruit and dark chocolate (it's a specialty of this gelateria).

La Voglia Matta also sells delicious espresso if you need a wake up shot. There aren't a whole lot of places to sit in the small shop, but try to snag one from the collection of white tables inside. Otherwise, take your gelato and go. Walk across the bridge to Ortigia, take look at the water below, and enjoy the beauty of gelato. And Syracuse, too.

i Gelato €2-5. Open daily 9am-2pm, 4pm-midnight.

BAR MIDOLO $
C. Umberto I, 86 ☎093 16 80 46

Pizza. Arancini. Cannoli. All in one place? With everything you've ever wanted from Italy under the same roof, we're pretty sure Bar Midolo is some small bar form of heaven. In an unassuming storefront on a corner of Corso Umberto, at Bar Midolo you'll find a line of locals waiting for anything from morning coffee to a fast lunch to some delicious pastries. Join them. Take a walk inside and browse the counters lined with delicious Italian treats, like various kinds of arancini—little but surprisingly filling rice balls stuffed with ragu, cheese, and all other kinds of savory goodness. We recommend the arancini prosciutto.

Though known for its arancini, Bar Midolo also sells various types of delicious pizza and other bready treats, all for extremely reasonable prices. If you have more of a sweet tooth, go to the counter right by the pizzas and find a delectable selection of dolce: small fruit tarts, little pies with nuts, and, of course, cannoli.

Bar Midolo has some of the best and cheapest cannolis in all of Syracuse. As if you needed an excuse to buy a cannoli here. Try the little ones. They're like two bites of pure deliciousness, and you can pop them in your mouth as you walk around Ortigia. And so, for a quick lunch and dessert, be sure to do as the locals do and pop into Bar Midolo. Then come back here for your three mandatory afternoon snacks. You need that energy, after all.

i Pizza and arancine €1-2.50. Pastries €0.50-1. Open daily 6am-11pm.

NIGHTLIFE

IL SALE
V. Amalfitania 56 ☎093 14 83 666

In a small alley off a small alley in Syracuse, Il Sale is about as Ortigia as you can get. Look for the chalkboard advertising drinks and live music on V. Amalfitania and take the narrow path leading you up. You'll emerge victorious in a gorgeous, cavernous bar.

Rock hewn and more stoned than you'll ever be (hopefully), this large bar charms with its cave-like appearance. There's outdoor seating on a rocky platform and plenty of locals gather here to sit at tables, grab a drink, and talk the night away.

The lights are low while jazzy music plays, and it's casual and peaceful here, tucked away from the busy P. del Duomo.

The interior is swanky, with a shiny bar and an eye-catching display of liquors. Cocktails here are a little on the pricier side, which might be why people here don't drink to get tipsy. Though full of people, this isn't a wild bar but is instead a charming, ambient place to stop by with a friend or two and talk about how much you love Syracuse. Because, really, what else is there to talk about in Syracuse?

i Drinks €5-10. Open M-Th 7pm-3am, F-Sa 7pm-4am, Su 7pm-3am.

syracuse

PUB LES CREPES

9 V. Maniace

www.lescrepespub.altervista.org

Hungry? Of course you are. This Saturday night, combine your two favorite things—beer and chocolate—by coming to Pub Les Crepes. Bright orange walls, wooden tables, and Nutella. Perfection. A quiet but delicious place to start the night, take a seat on a bar stool and ogle the crepe choices. Anything from a sweet Nutella and Baileys to a more savory Salmon and Philadelphia cream cheese, we never said choices on wild nights out were going to be easy.

Service is friendly, the food is great, and the cozy and casual atmosphere will make you feel no shame as you get melted chocolate gooeyness all over your turn-down-for-what clothes. No one will notice in the dark anyway. And the prices? Mmm—delectable.

So after you finish your third crepe, turn your attention to the adorable wooden bar with teapots on it. Oh, and it's also lined with liquor. As one of the cheaper places to get a shot or a cocktail, we recommend you spend a decent amount of time here before heading out to some of the classier places in Ortigia. If you're feeling brave, go for the tequila shots. Otherwise a small beer will run you up €3 or so.

Come with your friends, eat crepes, drink some €5 cocktails. If you're feeling adventurous, ask about table games like Taboo that you can rent out (in Italian, of course—it'll be a learning experience). And after you've had your fill of delicious food, bright walls, and wooden tables, head out for the night to somewhere grungier. Or maybe somewhere with more late night food. Pick your own adventure.

i Crepes €4.50. Shots €3-5. Beer €2.50-4. Cocktails €5. Open Tu-Su 9pm-2am. Open for lunch M-F 12:30-3pm.

DAIQUIRI LOUNGE

Piazza Duomo

☎320 785 71 29

And sometimes, when you're by the Duomo on a Saturday night, you just need a little advance on your Eucharist. Come to Daiquiri. A wine and cocktail bar right in P. Duomo, this swanky bar will make drinking on some steps look downright classy.

If you haven't noticed yet, Taormina's kind of on a mountain. Steep inclines and rock hewn stairs make up most of the side streets. While you might be sure that this geography stands to screw you over, Daiquiri uses it to its advantage. Located on some large stone steps leading up from P. Duomo, to get a seat, you'll have to back that ass up onto one of the luxurious white cushioned chairs or couches with sleek white tables set out on the stairs themselves.

The interior of the bar is pretty much just the bar itself. Most people who come here find a table outside and enjoy the beautiful view of the Duomo at night. Catering to a slightly posh crowd (i.e., everyone in Taormina), you'll have to wear a dress or put on some slacks if you want to come here. Don't worry, drinks here are relatively cheap by local standards, so trying to look nice will pay off.

Listen to jazzy music, enjoy the comfy white chairs, and try some of the delicious drinks. This place never gets crazy, but it's a good place to chill after a day at the beach.

i Drinks €4-8. Open daily 7pm-3am.

italy

ESSENTIALS

Practicalities

- **POST OFFICES:** Mail is handled by Poste Italia. Postcards and letters from Greece to outside Europe cost €0.85. The central post office is at P. Riva della Posta right across the bridge into Ortigia (open M-F 8:20am-7:05pm, Sa 8:20am-12:35pm).

- **INTERNET:** Wi-Fi can be hard to find outside of your hotel. Check for cafes or restaurants that offer complimentary Wi-Fi. There is free Wi-Fi from the city available outside the Tempio di Apollo in Ortigia.

Emergency

- **EMERGENCY NUMBERS:** The emergency number in Italy is 112 for police, fire department, and ambulances. More specific numbers are listed below.

- **POLICE:** 113

- **AMBULANCE SERVICE:** 118

- **FIRE BRIGADE:** 115

- **PHARMACIES:** Look for a big green "+" sign anywhere, and you'll find a pharmacy. Late night pharmacies stay open on a rotating basis. Check www.comune.siracusa.it/index.php/it/farmacie to find out which ones are open overnight.

Getting There

The closest airport to Syracuse is Catania. From Catania, you can take an AST or Interbus regional bus that will take you from the airport to Syracuse for around €6.

Getting Around

Luckily for you, Syracuse is not a big town. From the bus station to the island of Ortigia takes about 15min. walking, and the Archaeological Park to Ortigia takes about 20min. There are no cars allowed on Ortigia, so your best bet in Syracuse all around will be walking.

italy essentials

MONEY

To use a debit or credit card to withdraw money from an ATM (*Bancomat* in Italian), you must have a four-digit Personal Identification Number (PIN). If your PIN is longer than four digits, ask your bank whether you can use the first four or if they'll issue you a new one. If you intend to hit up ATMs in Europe with a credit card, call your credit card company before your departure to request a PIN.

The use of ATM cards is widespread in Italy. The two major international money networks are MasterCard/Maestro/Cirrus and Visa/PLUS. Most ATMs charge a transaction fee, but some Italian banks waive the withdrawal surcharge.

In Italy, a 5% tip is customary, particularly in restaurants (10% if you especially liked the service). Italian waiters won't cry if you don't leave a tip; just be ready to ignore the pangs of your conscience later on. Taxi drivers expect tips as well, but luckily for oenophiles, it is unusual to tip in bars. Bargaining is appropriate in markets and other informal settings, though in regular shops it is inappropriate. Hotels will often offer lower prices to people looking for a room that night, so you will often be able to find a bed cheaper than what is officially quoted.

SAFETY AND HEALTH

Local Laws and Police

In Italy, you will mainly encounter two types of boys in blue: the *polizia* (☎113) and the *carabinieri* (☎112). The *polizia* are a civil force under the command of the Ministry of the Interior, whereas the *carabinieri* fall under the auspices of the Ministry of Defense and are considered a military force. Both, however, generally serve the same purpose, to maintain security and order in the country. In the case of attack or robbery, both will respond to inquiries or desperate pleas for help.

Drugs and Alcohol

The legal drinking age in Italy is (drumroll please) 16. Remember to drink responsibly and to **never drink and drive.** Doing so is illegal and can result in a prison sentence, not to mention early death. The legal blood alcohol content (BAC) for driving in Italy is under 0.05%, significantly lower than the US limit of 0.08%.

Travelers with Disabilities

Travelers in wheelchairs should be aware that getting around in Italy will sometimes be extremely difficult. This country predates the wheelchair—sometimes it seems even the wheel—by several centuries and thus poses unique challenges to disabled travelers. **Accessible Italy** (☎378 941 111 www.accessibleitaly.com) offers advice to tourists of limited mobility heading to Italy, with tips on subjects ranging from finding accessible accommodations to wheelchair rental.

italy

THE NETHERLANDS

There are few places in the world that can pull off the Netherlands's unique combination of reefer-clouded progressiveness and folksy, earnest charm. This part of Europe somehow manages to appeal both to tulip-loving grandmas and ganga-crazy, Red-Light-ready students. So, like everyother college student, come to Amsterdam to gawk at the coffeeshops and prostitutes, but don't leave thinking that's all there is to this quirky country. Take some time to cultivate an appreciation for the Dutch masters. Obviously, most Dutch people aren't pot-heads—they'll tell you that if marijuana was legalized in the states, 700,000 fewer people would need to be incarcerated annually. Consider what it would be like to live in a place where hookers are unionized and public works like windmills, canals, and bike lanes define the national character, and get ready to go Dutch!

greatest hits

- **LET'S (VAN) GOGH:** The area around Museumplein in Amsterdam features not one, but two of Europe's greatest art museums. Savor the Dutch Golden Age at the **Rijksmuseum** or *Sunflowers* at the **Van Gogh Museum** (p. 562).

- **DAM GOOD BARS: Leidseplein** is a nightlife haven, with laidback and musical bars littering the streets (p. 568).

- **IT'S ELECTRIC!:** **Electric Ladyland** (p. 566) the world's "First Museum of Fluorescent Art," will take you on an unforgettably weird trip into the world of glowing rocks and "participatory art."

amsterdam

"Quit smirking!" is your unfortunate follow-up every time you tell someone you're going to Amsterdam. "I mean, sure there are hookers and weed, but the city's got so much more to it! Like—like—like history. And. . . um. . . canals, a-and bikes! And the Anne Frank house!"

Relax, fidgeting traveler. We wrote this chapter for you.

The Netherlands' shall-we-say-permissive attitudes are the product of a long tradition of liberalism and tolerance that dates back far before the advent of drug tourism and prostitutes' unions. One of the few areas in Europe to fall outside the influence of the all-powerful Vatican, Amsterdam was for centuries a refuge for Protestants and Jews, with the wealth of its tremendous trading empire—stretching from New York (er, New Amsterdam) to Indonesia—incubating the artistic achievements of the Dutch Golden Age and nurturing the political and economic birth of modern Europe. Nowadays, this diverse and progressive city is as famous for its art museums and quaint canal-side cafes as for its coffee shops and women of the night.

The most subtly satisfying aspect of your trip will be strolling the streets, every route bringing unpredictable glimpses of this pretty city's culture and vitality. Quite compact for all its riches, Amsterdam can be biked or even walked in a day, rambling from the peaceful canals of the Jordaan to the gaudy peepshows of the Red Light— though to plow directly through would be to miss out on all the density's offerings. So drop that J, pack along this book, and Let's Go!

ACCOMMODATIONS

COCOMAMA
$$

Westeinde 18   ☎020 627 2454 www.cocomama.nl

It's all about decadence here at the award-winning Cocomama: check-in is accompanied by your choice of water, tea, or champagne, and the triple-tiered bunks feel fit for Dutch royalty (those flower-flaunting fools). A lavishly-decorated basement kitchen, with garden-y backyard, lends the whole thing a communal feel that's cozier than a Dutch monarch is to his tulips.

i Dorms €40-50. Reception open 9am-9pm.

STAYOKAY STADSDOELEN
$$

Kloveniersburgwal 97   ☎020 624 68 32 www.stayokay.com

With "only" 200 beds, this Stayokay is less than half the size of its less centrally-located sibling, and feels like a correspondingly more friendly and relaxing place to hang out. Less of an emphasis is placed on groups and families, meaning that individual backpackers can come here and dip into the social scene. A friendly staff and clean rooms round out this very worthy accommodation.

i Dorms €30-35. Reception 24hr.

SHELTER CITY
$

Barndesteeg 21   ☎020 625 3230 www.shelterhostelamsterdam.com

Just a short drunken swerve from the Red Light District is this outpost of godliness, where even ye, sinner that ye are, have a chance to repent—it's the larger and more centrally-located of the two Christian hostels known as Shelter, although its increased size won't make you anonymous in the eyes of staff (or God). With good rooms and a koi fish pond to boot, this is a wonderful sanctuary for people of all, or no, faiths.

i Dorms €20-30. Reception 24hr.

the netherlands

THE NETHERLANDS

0 ___ 25 miles
0 ___ 25 kilometers

Schiermonnikoog
Terschelling
Ameland
Vlieland
Wadden Islands
Waddenzee
Texel
North Sea
Den Helder
Leeuwarden
Harlingen
Heerenveen
Groningen
Assen
Hoogeveen
IJsselmeer
Hoorn
Alkmaar
Zaanse Schans
IJmuiden
Edam
Meppel
Vecht R.
Zwolle
Haarlem
Amsterdam
Zandvoort aan Zee
Noordwijk aan Zee
Lisse
Aalsmeer
Apeldoorn
Scheveningen
Leiden
Utrecht
DE HOGE VELUWE NATIONAL PARK
The Hague
Delft
Amersfoort
Hoek van Holland
Gouda
Rijn R.
Arnhem
Rotterdam
Waal R.
Nijmegen
Maas R.
Rhine R.
Breda
Maas R.
GERMANY
Eindhoven
Antwerp
Roermond
Cologne
BELGIUM
Brussels
Maastricht

TO NEWCASTLE, ENGLAND

TO HARWICH, ENGLAND AND HULL, ENGLAND

FLYING PIG DOWNTOWN $$

Nieuwendijk   ☎100 020 420 6822 www.flyingpig.nl

EDM thrums in the main common room/bar of this classic party hostel. A notch above the surrounding competition in terms of staff, cleanliness, and décor, the Flying Pig Downtown offers a safe place to crash, and its welcoming atmosphere ensures you'll meet some cool compatriots.

i Dorms €30-45. Reception 24hr.

FLYING PIG UPTOWN $$

Vossiusstraat 46/47   ☎020 400 4187 www.flyingpig.nl

Well-staffed and -décor'd—the common room/bar looks handsome with its warm woodiness. Paintings of (non-Amsterdammer 27-Clubbers) Jimi Hendrix, Kurt Cobain, and Amy Winehouse adorn the walls. The Flying Pig Uptown's massive size, with more than 200 beds, can be a little overwhelming for those who're looking for a cozy relaxing place to make cozy relaxing friends. If your goal is partyrockin', however, look no further.

i Dorms €30-45. Reception 24hr.

SHELTER JORDAN $

Bloemstraat   ☎179 020 624 4717 www.shelterhostelamsterdam.com

If your time in Amsterdam leaves you feeling morally and spiritually bankrupt, look no further than this Christ-tastic outpost in the middle of one of the city's hipper areas. Well-cleaned, comfortable, and our-smiles-never-skip-a-beat

amsterdam

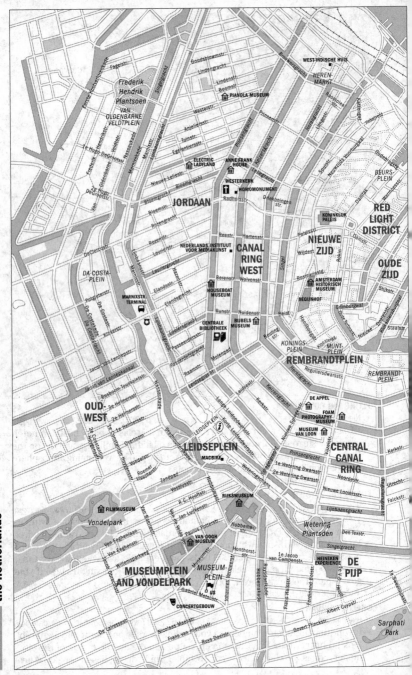

the netherlands

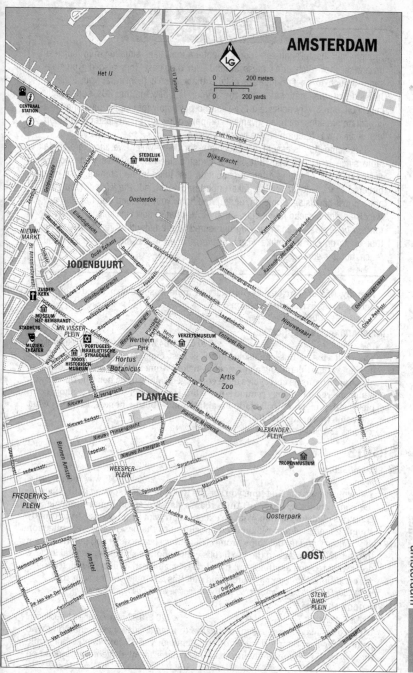

hagelslag

Though your hostel's austere complimentary toast-jam situation may suggest otherwise, the Dutch don't mess around with breakfast. They also dig on desserts—though to be fair, name a culture that doesn't. (Lookin' at you, Iceland. Just kidding—their national pastry, the *snuour*, is kingly.) In the '30s, supposedly in response to a very persistent five-year-old boy who wrote letters pleading for a chocolate breakfast item, an inventive company of plucky Dutch upstarts came up with a great way to combine the two: *hagelslag*.

This confection is essentially chocolate sprinkles—which, we know, are kinda lame since ten years ago. But seriously, don't sleep on this—it's your socially acceptable way of eating a ton of chocolate first thing in the morning. Take your buttered toast, add *hagelslag*. Take unbuttered toast, add *hagelslag*. (You may not eat just *hagelslag*. Come on, dude.) And know your product: don't accept any *hagelslag* with a cacao rating of less than 35%—that's known in Holland as "cacao fantasy *hagelslag*." As in, *hagelslag* unmoored to the tenants of reality, *hagelslag* that exists only in dreamlike wisps, a mirage deep in the mind's recesses: you reach, but it is gone.

friendly, this is your best opportunity to build in some structured Bible study between massive sinning sessions.

i Dorms €20-30. Reception 24hr.

INTERNATIONAL BUDGET HOSTEL
$$
Leidsegracht 76 ☎020 624 2784 www.internationalbudgethostel.com

The chill vibe of this canalside hostel is best emblemized by the 2nd floor's aerosol wall art depicting a curvaceous naked women toking on a fat doob like all nature's patterns and cycles have converged calmly upon her. The downstairs hangzone-reception may remind some a little too strongly of a coffee shop, complete with a menu of grill-made breakfast food—but be honest, isn't this what you came to Amsterdam for?

i Dorms €30. Reception 24hr.

SIGHTS

🏛 RIJKSMUSEUM
Museumstraat 1 ☎0900 07 45 www.rijksmuseum.nl

You won't forget the first time you see the Rijksmuseum's soaring gothic façade: the commanding exterior of Amsterdam's flagship art museum bespeaks the centuries of history within. With an excellent array of Dutch works, from frankly stunning medieval and religious compositions to the basement-level collection of weaponry and model ships; from 17th century landscapes and portraits from the Dutch Golden Age to the top floor's contemporary and experimental art (we don't want to spoil anything, but the phrase "vagina bed" will be bandied about). Air conditioned and immaculately laid out, this is a must-see for your trip.

i €17.50. Free with Museumkaart (€59.90, valid for one year). Open daily 9am-5pm.

🏛 VAN GOGH MUSEUM
Paulus Potterstraat 7 ☎020 570 5200 www.vangoghmuseum.nl

It's hard to imagine a museum dedicated to a single artist, especially one who painted for less than a decade, offering enough variety and depth. But while the works of everyone's favorite bad boy painter/facial surgeon are indeed on display at this gorgeous museum, the famous paintings are just one dimension of what's offered here: different exhibits examine the artist's correspondence and letters, shed light on his fascinating biography, or contemplate his complicated personal life. Interspersed with the van Goghs are paintings by the artists who influenced him, and others by those he influenced. We think it's the best museum in Amsterdam, but unfortunately, so does everyone else; discouragingly busy at peak hours, it's worth the wait, so get here early.

i €17. Free with Museumkaart (€59.90, valid for one year). Open M-Th 9am-6pm, F-Sa 9am-10pm, Su 9am-6pm.

EYE FILM INSTITUTE
IJpromenade 1 ☎020 589 1400 www.eyefilm.nl/en

Like Sauron of old does this futuristic white building turn its vengeful socket upon the city and towards all we hold dear. Only a minute's ferry ride from Centraal Station, the Institute screens a wide breadth of artful programming, from cinematic retrospectives to up-and-coming docu-makers (and, with the student discount, often for cheaper than seeing a current release in downtown Amsterdam). The in-institute bar-restaurant will seduce you with its quaint view of the IJ, but will take all your money and leave you waiting, wanting, lusting for more—hit up an eatery up the street if you're looking to nibble before a film.

i Movie tickets €10, students €8.5. Exhibition €9, students €7.5. Exhibition free with Museumkaart (€59.90, valid for one year). Exhibition open M-Th 11am-7pm, F-Sa 11am-9pm, Su 11am-7pm.

TASSEN MUSEUM OF BAGS & PURSES
Herengracht 573 ☎020 524 6452 www.tassenmuseum.nl

An entire museum comprised of pouches, sacks, satchels, briefcases, luggage, and the forlorn-looking boyfriends who have been dragged along to look at it all (poor souls: their journey is over, their battle fought and lost)—if this sounds up your alley, and God help you if it does, you won't be let down. Yes, signs on the wall will try to frame it in terms of the fundamentally human quest for beauty, or the twin axis of style (Minimalist vs Maximalist; Classicist vs Eccentrist), or the surprisingly interesting historical evolution of the bag, but don't be fooled: this is, in the end, about purses, purses, and more purses.

i €12.50; students €9.50. Free with Museumkaart (€59.90, valid for one year). Open daily 10am-5pm.

FOTOGRAPHIEMUSEUM AMSTERDAM (FOAM)
Keizersgracht 609 ☎020 551 6500 www.foam.org

One of the best-curated museums in Amsterdam, the "FOAM" offers terrific breadth, from showcases of up-and-coming talents to revivals of famous works from the past. Its twisting white halls and chambers go on for a deceptively long time (you could easily spend a whole afternoon here), and it's all set inside an understated exterior that blends right in with the surrounding apartments, making this truly a treasure of the city—nowhere else could you find such aloof elegance.

i €10, students €7.50. Free with Museumkaart (€59.90, valid for one year). Open M-Th 10am-6pm, F-Sa 10am-9pm, Su 10am-6pm.

PIANOLA MUSEUM
Westerstraat 106 ☎20 627 9624 www.pianola.nl

This was about the point where we went, "Come on, how many museums does this city have, anyway?" But for all the furrowedness of our brooding eyebrows, this turned out to be one of the most enchanting museums in Amsterdam. Dedicated to the player piano, or pianola, a little-remembered playback instrument from wayyy back even before records (do ya know what a record is, sonny? Heh heh, well, back in my day…) which beginning at around 1900 automatically played paper "rolls" containing different songs, kind of like the hand-cranked cylindrically-operated miniature gift shop harps so beloved by the youths of today. The museum archives contain over 25,000 of such rolls, so browse around for your favorite prewar jingle and let the entertainment-machines do the rest.

i €5. Open July-Aug Th-Su 2pm-5pm; Sept-June Su 2pm-5pm.

HUIS MARSEILLE, MUSEUM FOR PHOTOGRAPHY

Keizersgracht 401 ☎0 20 531 8989 www.huismarseille.nl

Presenting a homier, quirkier feel than the nearby FOAM, the Huis Marseille absolutely holds its own in terms of sheer excellence of artwork—you can get lost here amidst the six exhibition spaces, each with its own distinct feel, and interconnected by old school Dutch passages. One of the lesser-frequented spots for tourists, this museum is a great place to immerse yourself.

i €8, students €4. Open Tu-Su 11am-6pm.

HOMOMONUMENT

Westermarkt www.homomonument.nl

The Homomonument is the culmination of a movement to erect a memorial honoring homosexual victims of Nazi persecution—but it's also meant to stand for all people, past and present, who've been oppressed for their sexuality. Designed by Karin Daan and opened in 1987, the monument consists of three connecting pink granite triangles—in remembrance of the symbol the Nazis forced homosexuals to wear—which represent the past (one triangle points toward the Anne Frank House), the present (pointing toward the National War Monument in Dam Square), and the future (pointing toward the headquarters of the COC, a Dutch gay rights group, which, founded in 1946, is the oldest continuously operating gay and lesbian organization in the world). Look for the engraved words "Naar Vriendschap Zulk een Mateloos Verlangen" ("such an endless desire for friendship"), a line from the poem "To a Young Fisherman" by the gay Dutch Jewish poet Jacob Israel de Haan (1881 - 1924).

i Free. Open 24/7.

AMSTERDAM SEX MUSEUM

Damrak 18 ☎020 622 8376 www.sexmuseumamsterdam.nl

Unless you were previously unaware of sex—like, as a concept—there's not that much new information in this museum. (The brief "Sex Through the Ages" presentation is hilariously simplistic, though the elegant British-accented narration is priceless.) But who needs information when you've got smut? Museumgoers' reactions differ widely to the contents; some leave slightly offended by the hardcore porn-and-fetish room, while others find the farting dolls titillating. If you really want to see a parade of pictures of people having sex, you could just visit a sex shop in the Red Light District. Or, you know, use Incognito Mode on Chrome.

i €4. Open daily 9:30am-11:30pm.

ANNE FRANK HOUSE

Prinsengracht 263-267 www.annefrank.org

Don't balk at the two-plus hours you'll spend waiting outside—this could very well be the most meaningful thing you do on your trip. After World War II, Anne's father Otto, the sole Frank family member to survive the Holocaust, published the now-famous diary and helped establish a foundation to prevent the house's demolition. The modern museum preserves the building's amazing history, augmenting excerpts from Anne's diary with interviews with Otto and the Franks' helpers—non-Jewish coworkers who hid and supplied the family during their years in the secret annex. The meditative journey through the museum is perfectly designed and deeply moving without a trace of heavy-handedness.

i €9. Free with Museumkaart (€59.90, valid for one year). Open Apr-June M-F 9am-9pm, Sa 9am-10pm; Su 9am-9pm; Jul-Aug daily 9am-10pm; Sept-Oct M-F 9am-9pm, Sa 9am-9pm, Su M-F 9am-9pm; Nov-Mar M-F 9am-7pm, Sa 9am-9pm, Su 9am-7pm.

the netherlands

WESTERKERK

Prinsengracht 281   ☎20 624 7766 www.westerkerk.nl

B-b-big towers! Cool, man! Way up there above the rest of the city, it'll take you half an hour just to scale the thing, which might've been the whole idea back when Europeans were invading each other's churches with more consistency. A bombastic selection of bells in the tower belfry—we've been looking forward to using that word for the whole book: belfry—is just icing on the cake; the best view in Amsterdam is really what's waiting at the top. Somewhere down below the church, Rembrandt is buried, though due to oversights, no one's totally clear just where. The tower tour is a must, but you can also come for free at any point, and a calendar of upcoming concerts is on their web site.

i Free. Tours €7. Open M-Sa 10am-3pm.

VONDELPARK

Vondelpark, Vondelpark, we long for your greens. Dubbed by everyone around the "Central Park of Amsterdam," the comparison's understandable if not totally apt—while it is indeed the citizenry's favorite parkspace, and on summer days the whole town seems to descend upon it, the park's actually located decently far from the center of things (though thanks to Amsterdam's compactness, none of the city's destinations are that remote from each other). Besides, you can't toke a doob in the middle of Manhattan. Named for 17th-century poet and playwright Joost van den Vondel, a.k.a. the "Dutch Shakespeare" (competitive much? what is it with these comparisons?), the park boasts an open-air theater, which puts on free concerts in the summer, and should that not prove entertainment enough, as of 2008 it is legal to have sex [thumbs up] in the park, provided you stay away from the playgrounds (duh, perv) and dispose of condoms.

i Free.

ELECTRIC LADYLAND

Tweede Leliedwarsstraat 5   ☎0 20 420 3776

The "First Museum of Fluorescent Art" begs many questions (namely, what was the second?); its passionate and eccentric owner, Nick Padalino, will gladly spend hours explaining the history, science, and culture of fluorescence to each and every in-the-dark visitor crossing the doorstep into his one-room basement, which is where the museum is located. We promise it's way better than we're making it sound: the true spirit of Amsterdam is alive and well here, from the globally-harvested collection of glowing rocks to the hands- and feet-on brightly-colored stalactites. (Though all the psychedelia raises another question—how'd this dude dodge Jimi's copyright lawyers?)

i €5. Open Tu-Sa 1pm-6pm.

FOOD

⬛ EETSALON VAN DOBBEN $

Korte Reguliersdwarsstraat 5-7-9   ☎020-6244200 www.eetsalonvandobben.nl

If you're on the prowl to "eet" the cheapest meals in the entire city, put this on your list—most sandwiches are in the €2.50-4 range, and frankly you wouldn't know it for their taste, and the traditional croquette is a delicacy. Smallish and friendly, with purported historical ties dating back to the 1950s, the place's vibe is pleasantly neighborhoody. And did we mention €3 sandwiches?

i Sandwiches €2.50-5. Open M-W 10am-9pm, Th 10am-1am, F-Sa 10am-2am, Su 10am-8pm.

⬛ LOUIS $

Singel 43

For your hardworking Let's Go team, the question with places like this one is always whether to call it a bar, a restaurant, or a cafe: Louis combines the best of all food and drink categories, serving up ravishing (yet affordable) sandwiches to compliment the long list of brews and mixed drinks. The décor is perfectly laid-back, with framed photographs of rusting automobiles and a wide selection of Dutch-edition Dan Brown novels. Be aware that facing out the window near the back end of the venue makes it likely that you'll be locking eyes with a hooker all day/night. Which is a plus or a minus, depending on your tastes.

i *Sandwiches and salads €4-11. Drinks €2.50. Open M-Th 11am-1am, F-Sa 11am-2am, Su 11am-11pm.*

IJSSALON TOFANI
Kloveniersburgwal 16

$

☎0 20 624 3073

You heard it here first—roll through for some of the city's top gelato. As you'll no doubt notice in your gamboling and wayfaring, not every two-bit self-proclaimed dessert server in the downtown is worth stopping by, but this place absolutely is. A nice array of flavors ranges from the classic to the esoteric. Outdoor seating seals the deal.

i *Sandwiches €4.50-7. Drinks €2-5. Open daily noon-midnight.*

ZUIVERE KOFFIE
Utrechtsestraat 39

$

The wonderfully Dutch expression "dat is geen zuivere koffie" translates literally to "that's no pure coffee," but really means something like "I smell a rat," or "something's fishy," or "there's fungus among us." This cozy store is the opposite of all those things, submitting croissants and sandwiches for your deep pleasure (and don't get us started on the apple pie). And the coffee itself is, indeed, pure.

i *Sandwiches €5. Drinks €2-4. Open M-F 8am-5pm, Sa 9am-5pm.*

what's up with the tulips, anway?

Chances are, you'll meet some tulips in Amsterdam, and—getchyer mind outta the gutter—we mean the plant specimen. The bulb has a complex history in Amsterdam: introduced to Europe as a gift from the Ottoman Empire in the mid-1500s, tulips became especially popular in the Netherlands for their hardiness in the famously low-lying area. As Holland gained independence and stoked its economic prospects, citizens clamored for the exotic-looking flower, which came to be a powerful status symbol. Prices for individual bulbs skyrocketed, with local taverns becoming the epicenter of what the Dutch came to term *windhandel*, or "wind trade." As the wanton whims of the tulip bubble thrashed ever onward, after a certain point no flowers were actually changing hands—it became more lucrative just to resell the tulips one had recently "acquired" on paper. Even people who had never seen tulips with their own eyes were getting in on the action.

Eventually—some speculate due to a particularly nasty outbreak of the Bubonic Plague, which kept death-fearing auction-goers from participating—prices crashed and the bubble burst spectacularly, though not before ten acres of land had been offered in exchange for a single bulb. "Tulip mania" remains a figure of speech for the self-perpetuating insanity of unrestrained economics, seen recently in accounts of the dot-com bubble and 2008 subprime mortgage crisis. The moral of the story, of course, is to get in early, play the market born seemingly overnight around the craze for a little-understood foreign import, wait until the last possible second, leap out, resettle in South America with your fortune, and live out your days in luxury.

amsterdam

PLLEK

$

Tt. Neveritaweg 59   ☎020 290 0020 www.pllek.nl

We have no idea how it's pronounced, either, but Pllek offers a dash of industrial/rustic beauty up north of the city and the Lake IJ. A variety of programming makes the trek totally worthwhile—Movie Nights by the water on Tuesdays are particularly charming, and while a dish involving squid can never be described as "charming," we enjoyed it (although the specialty here is definitely drink-grabbing, not extensive meals). Busy on nice days.

i *Sandwiches €6.50-8.50. Open M-Th 9:30am-1am, F-Sa 9:30am-3am, Su 9:30am-1am.*

WINKEL 43

$

Noordermarkt 43   ☎020 623 022 www.winkel43.nl

Pie, pie, pie. Is that all anyone cares about anymore? Get outta here, old man! At Winkel, the answer's obviously yes: don't be surprised if everyone here has a slice, along with an (un)healthy dollop of whipped cream. There's food here, too, but that's a little beside the point.

i *Slices €4.50-7.50. Open M 7am-1am, Tu-Th 8am-1am, F 8am-3am, Sa 7am-3am, Su 10am-1am.*

CAFÉ CHRIS

$

Bloemstraat 42   ☎020 624 5942 www.cafechris.nl

The oldest pub in Jordaan (opened 1624) remains a perennial favorite for its relaxed and welcoming air—free from tourist swarms, the staff will treat you like one of Amsterdam's own, even instructing you on how to order your drink in Dutch. The jukebox goes and goes.

Open M-Th 3pm-1am, F-Sa 3pm-2am, Su 3pm-9pm.

'T KUYLTJE

$

Gasthuismolensteeg 9 HS   ☎020 6201045 www.kuyltje.nl

This avocado-colored cafe will serve you some of the best "broodjes" (sammie rolls), hot or cold, in Holland. Humming with cheerful banter and activity, 't Kuyltje, in spite of its edgy use of punctuation, provides further evidence that family-run cafes are the friendliest places wherever in the world you're traveling.

i *Sandwiches €4.50. Open M-F 7am-4pm, Sa 10am-4pm; closed Sundays.*

BLACKGOLD

HOUSE $

Korte Koningsstraat 13   www.blackgoldamsterdam.com

For further proof that the Dutch are the planet's most culturally advanced civilization, look no further than this coffee shop/record store. Simultaneously oozing cool and caffeine, you can at once get wired and mellow out with the latest beats. Vinyl might be a little hard to store in your luggage, but holy shit, man, look what I just found. . . [pulls a record so obscure it lacks even a name].

i *Espresso €2.50. Open M 9am-5pm, Th-F 9am-5pm, Sa 10am-5pm, Su 11am-5pm. Closed Tu-W.*

TOMATILLO

$

Overtoom 261   ☎020 683 3086 www.tomatillo.nl

Tacos in Holland? Strange as it may seem, it's a thing, and for years now Tomatillo's been pulling of their Tex-Mex trick with aplomb, avoiding the overcheesiness synonymous with many Gringo attempts at the cuisine. Reasonably priced and quite clean in its small, open space, this'll do ya right.

i *Burritos €9-12. Beer €4. Open M-Th 4pm-10pm, F-Su noon-10pm.*

NIGHTLIFE

BITTERZOET

Spuistraat 2   ☎020 42 123 18 www.bitterzoet.com

The area immediately around Centraal Station isn't exactly known for being the epicenter of cool, but maybe it's the low expectations that came together to form something unpretentiously rad here at Bitterzoet. Sometimes DJ'd, sometimes with live acts, this is a dependable party close enough to city center for you to eventually stagger back to your nearby hostel.

i Tickets vary €8-18. Open M-Th 8pm-3am, F-Sa 8pm-4am, Su 8pm-3am.

CAFÉ BRECHT

Weteringschans 157   ☎020-6272211 www.cafebrecht.nl

The cozy and AC'd cool Café Brecht (named for German writer, poet, and thespian Eugen Berthold Friedrich Brecht) drops you straight into a relaxed Berlin-style "living room cafe" from prewar decades of yore—frumpy regulars vape in the back as table lamps glow. The drink menu is a little pricey, but offers a mouth-watering assortment of exotic brews, from Czech beers to intriguing fruit/cider combinations to Italian coffee. It's equally easy to while away an afternoon or an evening (or both) here in the company of pals or a good book.

i Drinks €2-7+. Open Su-Tu noon-1am, F-Sa noon-3am.

COFFEESHOP EN MUZIEKSTUDIO DE GRAAL

Albert Cuypstraat 25   ☎20 471 1791

Tucked sneakily between restaurants and cafes, this truly dank coffee shop has just the right combination of old chairs, slow rap, and reptile tanks to keep you occupied for hours. The shopkeepers are chill as all get, happy to instruct, and help maintain the place's lovable calm—you'll always have a place to sit here. There's a cat, too. Nice.

i Marijuana €7-12 per gram. Open daily 10am-1am.

PRIK

Spuistraat 109   ☎0 20 320 0002 www.prikamsterdam.nl

"Amsterdam's favorite gay bar," which just celebrated its 9th birthday, is actually named for the Dutch word for "bubble," you naughty-minded traveler, and features cocktail specials all day on Thursday, not to mention cock specials basically always. Service is great, DJs spin the night away on weekends, and a variety of special and themed nights are advertised on the web site.

i Beers €3.50. Open M-Th 4pm-1am, F-Sa 4pm-3am, Su 4pm-1am.

LA TERTULIA

312 Prinsengracht   ☎0 20 623 8503 www.coffeeshoptertulia.com

Remember, Let's Go never recommends drug use—all we're saying is, while you totally could come all the way to Amsterdam and not try a "Ganja Shake," what will the cool rebel kids back home you're trying to impress think? Better enjoy this not-that-unlikely-seeming combination at La Tertulia, a split-level coffee shop that's a cut above for its attention to the non-weed things: friendly service, leafy ambiance, bang-up food, and outdoor, canal-side seating.

i Marijuana €8-12 per gram. Open Tu-Sa 11am-7pm

HILL STREET BLUES BAR

Warmoesstraat 52 A   ☎020 638 7922 www.hill-street-blues.nl

A favorite amongst the tourist crowd for its ambiance, including a soundtrack that specializes in drum & bass and jungle music, Hill Street Blues Bar is nothing to turn your hip young nose up at—they know their cannabis. Like virtually every other coffee shop in Amsterdam, seating can be limited, so try to think not like a stoner (for once) and show up when the others aren't around. Or be content to stand for a bit.

i Marijuana €7-12 per gram. Open M-Th 9am-1am, F-Sa 9am-3am, Su 9am-1am.

HANNEKES BOOM

Dijksgracht 4   ☎020 419 9820 www.hannekesboom.nl

This derelict-looking shack ain't frontin' when it claims to be in the "best place in Amsterdam"—perched on an outcropping with a beautiful view of the Oosterdok canal, this is where the city's young and handsome descend on hot summer days, plop their flirty selves down on benches, stools, and tree branches, and dangle their smooth/hairy legs from the wharf. Pleasantly busy without feeling chaotic, Hannekes Boom provides ever-flowing drinks at reasonable prices on through afternoon and evening.

i Drinks €4+. Food €11-20. Open M-Th 10am-1am, F-Sa 10am-3am, Su 10am-1am.

DULAC
Haarlemmerstraat 118   ☎020 624 4265 www.restaurantdulac.nl

Bizarre sculptures crowd in among the world-weary students congregating at this bar; as it's some of the only nightlife in the area, you might have to put up with some inanimate company (though if you happen to make a friend here, chances are he'll not made of stone). A 50% student discount on food helps seal the eating deal.

i Beer €2.50. Food €10+. Open M-Th 3pm-1am, F 3pm-3am, Sa noon-3am, Su noon-1am.

BIMHUIS
Piet Heinkade 3   ☎020 788 2188 www.bimhuis.com

Up north of the city, this imposing black skyward cube doesn't exactly call to mind the jazz of your grandparents' youth, but that's because that bland shit is dead, cat, dig? Tickets can be expensive, but if you treat yourself, you'll get to hear some of the leading innovators in the unstoppable artform—as an already-up and still-coming cultural magnet, Amsterdam attracts all the biggest names, and venues like Bimguis are why.

i Hours and tickets vary (usually between €20-30) depending on the show. Check website for schedule.

ESSENTIALS
Practicalities

- **TOURIST OFFICES:** VVV is the main tourist office in Amsterdam (Zeestraat 37. Open March-Sept M-Sa 10am-5pm, Su 11am-4pm; Oct M-Sa 10am-5pm; Nov-March M-Sa 10am-3pm.)

- **MUSEUMKAART:** This Museum Card allows entrance to over 400 museums in Amsterdam including the Anne Frank House, Van Gogh Museum, and Rijksmuseum. It costs €59.90 for adults and €32.45 for youth up to 18. The card is valid for one year.

- **BANKS/ATMS:** There are so, so, so many ATMs in Amsterdam. You can't walk down the street without tripping over like three. And a lot of them are feeless, too. It's almost like they want you to take out money so you can spend it. You can also pay for most things with a debit/credit card (i.e. without drawing cash), especially at stores, though some restaurant/cafe places have a minimum or don't accept plastic.

- **GLBT:** GAYtic is a resource center endorsed by VVV. (Spuistraat 44 ☎020 330 1461; www.gaytic.nl. Open M-Sa 11am-8pm, Su noon-8pm.)

- **INTERNET:** Openbare Bibliotheek Amsterdam has free Wi-Fi and computer access (Open daily 10am-10pm). The Mad Processor, a favorite of gamers, also offers Wi-Fi for €1 per 30min (open daily noon-2am, ☎020 612 1818; www.madprocessor.nl).

- **POST OFFICE:** The main branch of the post office is located at Singel 250 (☎020 556 3311. Open M-F 7:30am-6:30pm, Sa 7:30am-5pm.)

Emergency

- **EMERGENCY NUMBER:** ☎112
- **EMERGENCY DOCTOR:** ☎088 003 0600
- **POLICE (NON-EMERGENCY):** ☎0900 8844
- **RAPE CRISIS CENTER:** ☎31 887 555 588

1. Road Where a Canal Would've Done Just as Well

2. Street Where Van Gogh Went One Time For a Beer, Though He Swore He'd Never Do It Again

3. Alleyway Where the City's Reptilian Citizenry Go to Shed Their Beautiful, Blonde Skin

4. Cursed Overpass Where Only Tourists Who Stop at at Least Five Canalside Cafes May Pass Safely

5. Street Wherein Famed Early Dutch City Planner Johannes Hans Van Shnockleck Designed the Bulk of His Streets

- **HOSPITAL:** Academisch Medisch Centrum (Meibergdreef 9 ☎20 566 9111; tourist medical service: ☎020 592 33 55.)

- **PHARMACIES:** There isn't a single pharmacy open 24-hours all the time, but each night, there should be at least one that is open. Call ☎020 694 8709 for information about what's open.

Getting There

By Plane
Schiphol Airport is the major airport. The train from the airport to Centraal station costs €4.40. A train leaves 4-10 times per hour except between 1am and 6am, when it leaves once per hour. It's a 15-20 minute ride.

By Train
Taking the train is a good way of getting around within the continent. Trains arrive from all over and almost always end up at Centraal station. Rail Europe can be a good resource for comparing prices.

By Bus
Taking the bus is another way of getting around the continent and the UK. Eurolines (020 560 87 88) is the best choice.

Getting Around
While the tram and buses exist for those who are in a rush, Amsterdam's small size makes it very easily walkable if you have time to spare. In short, the Metro isn't that useful. A single journey costs €2.90, which can be paid in cash or by using a chipkaart—just make sure to tap your card on and off or you'll be charged hella euro. Trams run 5am-midnight, and night buses fill in the intermediate hours.

the netherlands essentials

SAFETY AND HEALTH

Drugs and Alcohol
It hardly needs to be stated that attitudes toward conscience-altering substances are quite different in Amsterdam than in other areas of the world, though the city is taking active measures to change this image. The Dutch take a fairly liberal attitude toward alcohol, with the drinking age set at 16 for beer and wine and at 18 for hard liquor. Public drunkenness, however, is frowned upon and is a sure way to mark yourself as a tourist.

When it comes to drugs other than alcohol, things get a little more interesting. Whatever anyone standing outside of a club at 4am might tell you, hard drugs are completely illegal, and possession or consumption of substances like heroin and cocaine will be harshly punished. Soft drugs, such as marijuana, are tolerated, but consumption is confined to certain legalized zones, namely coffeeshops (for marijuana) and smartshops (for herbal drugs). However, the age of the coffeeshop is, in some ways, coming to a close. Under new laws passed by the Dutch government, only Dutch residents over the age of 18 will be allowed to enter coffeeshops. As of 2012, customers will have to sign up for a one-year membership, or "dope pass," in order to use the shops, which have been blamed in recent years for encouraging drug trafficking and criminal activity.

Prostitution

The "world's oldest profession" has flourished in the Netherlands, particularly in Amsterdam's famous Red Light District. Legal prostitution comes in two main forms. Window prostitution, which involves scantily clad women tempting passersby from small chambers fronted by a plate-glass window, is by far the most visible. Another option is legalized brothels. The term usually refers to an establishment centered around a bar. Women, or men, will make your acquaintance—and are then available for hour-long sessions.

The best place to go for information about prostitution in Amsterdam is the Prostitution Information Centre. (Enge Kerksteg 3, in the Red Light District behind the Oude Kerk ☎020 420 7328 wwww.pic-amsterdam.com. Open Sa 4-7pm. Available at other times for group bookings, call ahead.) Founded in 1994 by Mariska Majoor (once a prostitute herself), the center fills a niche, connecting the Red Light District with its eager visitors.

GLBT Travelers

In terms of sexual diversity, in Amsterdam, anything goes—and goes often. Darkrooms and dungeons rub elbows with saunas and sex clubs, though much more subdued options are the standard. Despite this openness, certain travelers—including drag queens and kings, other cross-dressers, and transgendered visitors more generally—should take extra caution walking the streets at night, especially in and around the Red Light District. All GLBT visitors to Amsterdam should also be aware that, though the city is a haven of homosexual tolerance, the recent infusion of fundamentalist religiosity into the Dutch political dialogue has created an environment detrimental to complete acceptance of GLBT behaviors and visibility.

Minority Travelers

Despite Amsterdam being known for its openness, there's a lot of hullabaloo about ethnic minorities coming into the Netherlands. Immigrants aren't always welcomed with open arms. Although foreign tourists of all stripes are sometimes treated with suspicion, it's mostly non-white visitors who occasionally encounter hostility. Muslims, or those who appear Muslim, seem to run into the most problems. The city is still generally tolerant, but sadly racism is not unheard of.

the netherlands

NORWAY

Norway's rugged countryside and remote mountain farms gave birth to one of the most feared seafaring civilizations of pre-medieval Europe: the Vikings. Modern-day Norwegians have inherited their ancestors' independent streak, voting against joining the EU in 1994. Currently, Norway enjoys one of the highest standards of living in the world. Its stunning fjords and miles of coastline make the country a truly worthwhile destination—but sky-high prices may challenge even the best-prepared budget traveler.

greatest hits

- **GET CULTURED:** Pay a visit to Oslo's **National Art Gallery** (p. 576) to see classics like Edvard Munch's Scream and works by your boys Picasso and van Gogh.

- **BEER WITH US HERE:** Though the name may sound like something you got by banging your keyboard, **Schouskjelleren Mikrobryggeri** (p. 580) is easily the best microbrewery in Oslo.

- **PINING FOR THE FJORDS:** No trip to Norway is complete without some fjords. Hop on a boat in **Bergen** (p. 585) to see these natural wonders.

oslo

Oslo might not be a cultural capital in the style of Paris, London, or Berlin, but it has a unique identity as an international city smack in the middle of nature. A short train ride can often bring you from bustling, modern shopping centers to wilderness so pristine Columbus would claim it for the Spanish Crown. It's a place where night-clubs spill out into botanical gardens, and kebab, Thai, and gourmet burgers are all available five minutes from your camping site.

Due to high taxes, high incomes, and a high standard of living, there's no cheap anything in Oslo; it vies with Tokyo and London every year for the title of world's most expensive city. Even the stingiest backpackers will find it hard to get by on less than $100 a day if they want to eat full meals and experience everything, but we hope the tips and tricks in this book help guide you in the right direction. Oslo is a place with such a collage of identities—young, Nordic, punk, American, European, African, and more—that it would be a real shame to miss blowing through some money here while you're in Europe.

CAMPING

Even Oslo's cheapest accommodations are at least 250 NOK a night. Think for a second what you could do if you saved that money. You could save up for college, you could pay off your debt...you could even afford a real Norwegian beer! So give your wallet and mental health a break and make the smart choice—sleep in the great outdoors!

LANGØYENE CAMPING
Langøyene Island

Head to Langøyene Island in the Oslofjord and you'll find a nude beach, volley-ball courts, and enough campground to lie back and sleep without the person next to you causing a fuss! Cost of entry is free (though you have to bring your own tent) and as long as you don't scream, murder, or litter, you can stay here as long as you want. Bathrooms, hiking, and a coffee shop on the island make it a convenient place to spend the night, but be sure to check the ferry schedule so you don't get stranded.

i Take the B4 ferry from Radhusbrygge/behind City Hall to Langøyene Island (requires a valid NSB metro pass or the Oslo Pass). Free. Ferries leave for the island about every 15 min during the summer, but be sure to check the schedule. You must bring your own tent. Quiet hours 11pm-7am.

EKEBERG CAMPING
Ekebergveien 65   ☎221 98 568 www.ekebergcamping.no

As opposed to the free-for-all of Langøyene, Ekeberg is a structured, profession-al camping site that charges for everything it provides. It has room for about 600 "units" and specializes in accommodating mobile homes, though visitors are also welcome to use tents (they're just not as likely to get a spot near a power outlet for the night). The amazing view and proximity to Oslo's downtown (about 15min. by bus) is a huge advantage, but when you add up the price of entrance, showers, and any snacks you buy on site, you're likely to find that this place costs roughly the same as a hostel, but with a higher chance of bug bites. Our recommendation: if you're the kind of person who cries at the beauty of the Grand Canyon, spend a night here; if you're only pitching a tent because your wallet is empty, head to Langøyene and camp for free instead.

i Take bus 34 to the Ekeberg Camping stop. Tent or caravan with car 270 NOK. Tent (up to 2 people) 185 NOK. Motorhome 255 NOK. Shower (6min.) 15 NOK.

OSLO CENTRAL HOSTEL $$

Kongensgate 7 ☎231 00 801 hihostels.no/en/hostel/oslo-central-hostel

This place is like a hostel on steroids. It has a new, modern building with every service a traveler could need: among them, laundry, breakfast, and heated bathrooms (that last one may not sound impressive, but after you use it, you'll find our own bathrooms barbaric by comparison). Each room comes with sockets by the beds, ensuite bathrooms, and free Wi-Fi—short of reading you a bedtime story, this place does it all. The price alone should convince you to stay, but if not, know that HI members get a 10% discount and there's always a colorful cast of characters in the rooms.

i From Oslo S, walk three blocks south to Radhusgata. Walk west until building #7. Dorms 395-445 NOK. Reception 24hr.

ANKER APARTMENTS $

Københavngata 10 ☎229 93 000 www.ankerapartment.no

Hopping hostels is a hit-or-miss situation, and our researcher was so down on his luck when he entered Anker Apartments that the most articulate thing he could say was, "Wow!" Indeed, the apartments might be the best money you spend while in Oslo, as 220 NOK gets you a spot in a spacious four-bed unit with a kitchen and bathroom in one of Oslo's coolest neighborhoods. The lobby is massive and nicely furnished, with a TV, foosball tables, and IKEA furniture so artsy it'd make Andy Warhol throw up. If that's not enough, the building is connected to a cheap, fully stocked grocery store, making it the perfect base of operations as you head out to explore Grünerløkka.

i Take Bus 30 to Daelenenga. Walk down Københavngata. The apartments are on the left. Dorms 220-250 NOK. Singles 500 NOK. Doubles 700 NOK. Reception 24hr.

SENTRUM HOSTEL $

Tollbugata 8 ☎223 35 580 www.sentrumhostel.no

Sentrum is three short blocks from Karl Johans Gate, which means there's no need for a cab at the end of your late-night boozing and ke-bab-ing. Towels and linens are included in the price, and the communal kitchen and rec room make it easy to meet other hostelers. All the rooms come equipped with comfortable single mattresses, but know that this place is a bit of a labyrinth: bathrooms and showers are communal and on different floors. For the area and the price you're paying, though, it's as good a bargain as the Louisiana Purchase.

i Oslo S. Walk down Karl Johans gate. Turn left onto Skippergata, then right onto Toll-bugata. Dorms 260 NOK. Reception 10am-midnight.

SIGHTS

▣ KON-TIKI MUSEUM

Bygdøynesveien 36 ☎230 86 767 www.kon-tiki.no

As the descendants of Vikings, it's no surprise that Norwegians are crazy about boats—but that thalassomania (look it up; it's a real word!) pushes its own limits at Bygdøy's Kon-Tiki museum. Erected in honor of Thor Heyerdahl, the intrepid, shirtless Norwegian who sailed a balsa raft across the Pacific in 1947, the muse-um hosts the original Kon-Tiki boat and enough memorabilia to make you want to dive overboard. For just 60 NOK, you can uncover the story of Heyerdahl's raft, which beat the odds to sail on for 101 miraculous days; watch our hero go from scientist to seafarer to environmentalist; or just revel in the man's John Stamos-level sex appeal.

i Take bus 30 directly to the museum. 90 NOK, students with ID 60 NOK. Open daily June-Aug 9:30am-6pm; Sept-Oct 10am-5pm; Nov-Feb 10am-4pm; Mar-May 10am-5pm.

NATIONAL ART GALLERY (NASJONALGALLERIET)

Universitetsgata 13 ☎219 82 000 www.nasjonalmuseet.no

Wherever they go in Europe, most people feel the need to visit at least one institution of higher culture. What's Paris without the Louvre, after all, or London without its famed British Museum? Lucky for you, Oslo has one of the most impressive art collections in Europe. Located right off Karl Johans Gate, the National Gallery is home to such classics as Edvard Munch's *Scream* (no photographs allowed) and a number of impressive works by Picasso and Van Gogh. There's something for everyone, whether portraits, landscapes, or pieces that draw a fine line between modern art and vomit on a canvas.

i Oslo S. Walk down Karl Johans gate. Turn right onto Universitetsgata. The museum is on the left. 50 NOK, students 30 NOK. Free on Sundays. Backpacks and purses must be checked in lockers for a fee of 20 NOK. Open Tu-W 10am-6pm, Th 10am-7pm, F 10am-6pm, Sa-Su 11am-5pm, closed Mondays.

NORWAY'S RESISTANCE MUSEUM (NORGES HJEMMEFRONTMUSEUM)

Bygning 21, Akershus Festning ☎230 93 138

Like much of Europe during World War II, Norway was forced to play host to the worst guests of the century when the Nazis invaded in 1940. As the museum imparts, that five-year saga involved painful collaboration, starvation, and murder—but also *Avengers*-level resistance. Visitors may be surprised to learn that Norwegian crack troops stopped Hitler from building an atomic bomb, or that they saved over half the country's Jewish population by smuggling them into Sweden. The exhibit is well planned and remarkably honest in its presentation of the facts. (Best done in conjunction with the Kon-Tiki museum, as the ferry to the Bygdøy area departs from Aker Brygge, five minutes away from where the Resistance Museum is.)

i Tram 12 to Aker Brygge. Walk east toward the medieval fortress overlooking the harbor (Akershus). Follow the signs to the museum once there. 50 NOK, students 25 NOK. Open Jun-Aug M-Sa 10am-5pm, Su 11am-5pm; Sept-May M-F 10am-4pm, Sa-Su 11am-4pm.

FROGNER PARK AND VIGELAND SCULPTURES

Kirkeveien/Middelthuns Gate

If you have a secret Freudian fantasy of being trampled by tourists, Frogner is the place for you. The park looks like Norway's take on Versailles, though with more sculptures and less decapitating the monarchy. The main path takes you through a number of fountains and gates until you reach the "Monolith" sculpture installation; to both the left and right are grassy fields where you can sit back with a book and wonder how there are 150 different species of roses in one park but you're still single. As long as you're not suffering from irritable bowel syndrome (in which case, have fun paying money to use the toilets here) there's really no reason not to visit.

i Tram 12 to Frogner Park (Frognerparken). Free. Open 24hr.

VIKING SHIP MUSEUM

Huk aveny 35 ☎221 35 280

The Vikings were like the Danny Zucco of the Middle Ages, though instead of smoking cigarettes and singing "Grease Lightning" they were plundering Europe and exploring the boundaries of the known world. If you're craving a taste of their swashbuckling exploits, head to the Viking Ship Museum and marvel at the three massive ships on display. Though you may leave wondering if they were built to compensate for something, the sheer size of these puppies will have you going berserk. Ha. (Best done in conjunction with the other Bygdøy museums like Kon-Tiki or the Norwegian Folk Museum, as all are within walking distance of one another.)

i Take the B4 ferry from Aker Brygge Harbor (55 NOK roundtrip) to the Viking Museum stop in Bygdøy. Alternatively, take bus 30 to the Vikingskipshuset stop. 80 NOK, students 50 NOK. Open daily May-Sept 9am-6pm; Oct-Apr 10am-4pm.

OPERA HOUSE

Kirsten Flagstads Plass 1   ☎214 22 121 www.operaen.no

The Opera House rises aggressively out of Oslo Harbor to throw a giant middle finger to indie music and traditional architecture. It's massive, shiny, and tilted at a 45-degree angle. The outside is a good place for a picnic or hanging with friends, while those with a bit more cash on their hands can venture inside to see the very blonde (and very talented) Norwegian Opera and Ballet.

i Oslo S. Turn left onto Langkaia. Turn left onto Operagata. The opera house is impossible to miss. Tickets from 100 NOK. Box office open M-F 10am-8pm, Sa 11am-6pm, Su noon-6pm.

HOLMENKOLLEN

Kongeveien 5   ☎229 23 200 www.skiforeningen.no

If Norwegians are slaves to a cult of skiing, then Holmenkollen is their high temple—literally. It's over 1000 ft. above sea level and hosts one of the world's largest ski jumps. If heights aren't your thing, visitors can set foot in the Ski Museum or step into the ski simulator to experience nausea in 3D. If you're willing to shell out some serious bank—we're talkin' 50 Cent-style "In Da Club" bank—then try your hand at Holmenkollen's 1200-foot zipline. To clarify, that's the height of the Empire State Building. On a zipline. All you need is 120 NOK for museum entrance, 590 NOK for the ride, and an extra pair of underwear just to be safe.

i Take the 1 train from Oslo S to the Holmenkollen stop. Walk down Holmenkollveien for about 15min. Turn left onto Kongeveien. Ski Museum 120 NOK, students 100 NOK. Ski simulator 50 NOK. Overwhelming sense of vertigo: priceless. Ski Museum open daily June-Aug 9am-8pm; Sept 10am-5pm; Oct-Apr 10am-4pm; May 10am-5pm.

NOBEL PEACE CENTER

Brynjulf Bulls plass 1   ☎483 01 000 www.nobelpeacecenter.org

The Nobel Peace Center has rolling exhibits on recent recipients of the prize. There's an enormous amount you can learn about past winners and the organization itself if you spend a good 20 minutes walking around. Though it might not be as impressive as places like the National Gallery, the Nobel Peace Center's later hours and location near Oslo's main sights makes it an ideal spot to stop by at the end of a long day.

i Take bus 30/31 to Radhuset. The museum is directly next to Aker Brygge harbor. 90 NOK, students 60 NOK. Open May-Aug M-W 10am-6pm, Th 10am-8pm, F-Su 10am-6pm; Sept-May Tu-Su 10am-6pm, closed Mondays.

FOOD

◼ MATHALLEN $$

Maridalsveien 17   ☎400 02 409 www.mathallenoslo.no

This place might just be God's gift to Oslo. It's a collection of pop-up restaurants and stands directly below a culinary school, and even the stingiest of stingy travelers would be amiss if they didn't drop a little dough here. The selection is too big to count, but some wallet- and palate-pleasing choices would have to be Noodles, Obento Box, and French Bakery, while Hopyard has a big enough beer selection to put Germany to shame. Free Wi-Fi and an

enormous amount of free cheese makes this Let's Go's favorite place to spend the day eating in Oslo.

i *Take bus 34 to Telthusbakken. Walk down Maridalsveien. The restaurants are on the left. Prices vary. Cheaper options 100 NOK. Sit-down restaurants 200 NOK. Open Tu-F 8am-late, Sa-Su 10am-late.*

ILLEGAL BURGER

$$

Møllergata 23 ☎222 03 302

"You miss 100% of the shots you don't take." We believe John Wilkes Booth said that, and he could not have been more correct. You may think a restaurant with a name like Illegal Burger is just another yuppie get-up trying to be edgy—the estranged cousin of bars named Pepto Bismol—but this is the kind of place God would have made on the third day and called "good." Though it's generally packed out the door, you won't be sorry you waited: burgers like the bacon and guac Hot Mama Deluxe, or the smokey Illegal Special, are so tasty they could make the Grinch love Christmas.

i *Oslo S. Walk down Karl Johans Gate. Turn right onto Møllergata. Walk five blocks, and the restaurant is on your left. Burgers 95-200 NOK. Open M-Th 4-11pm, F-Sa 4pm-3am, Su 3-10pm.*

CARMEL GRILL

$

Dronningens gate 27 ☎224 16 769

For the cash-strapped traveler, Middle Eastern food will be your best friend in Oslo. Even among the hundreds of kebab stores in Oslo, Carmel sets itself apart with the size of its portions (hint: they're huge) and the number of items available. The 70 NOK "kebab i pita" is one of the best deals in the area and may have the only vegetables you'll eat all day; the hummus and shish kebab are so authentically Middle Eastern they're on an FBI watch list (just kidding).

i *Oslo S. Walk down Karl Johans gate. Turn right onto Dronningens gate. The restaurant is on a raised brick platform among other stores. Entrees 60-120 NOK. Open daily 9am-3:30pm.*

HAI CAFÉ

$

Calmeyers gate 6 ☎222 03 872

Craving pho, banh mi, or other words you can't properly pronounce? Hai Café is about as cheap as it gets. With appetizers going for 60 NOK and entrees in the 120 NOK range, you can eat tasty food here without having to splurge. Hell, with the money you'll save, you can even order a bottle of its alcohol-free wine (and wonder where your life went so wrong). The place is generally packed, and the menu has numbers on it for the linguistically challenged.

i *Oslo S. Walk down Lybekker gate. Turn right onto Calmeyers Gate. The restaurant is on the left. Entrees 120-300 NOK. Open M-Sa 11am-10pm, Su noon-10pm.*

MUNCHIES

$

Thorvald Meyers gate 36a www.munchiesoslo.no

Beneath the pretty exterior of scenic mountains and breathtaking vistas, there is a bitter and angry conflict simmering on Oslo's streets: who has the better burger, Munchies or Illegal? Out of respect for the natives we will remain silent on our ruling, but here are the facts: the Munchie Burger (112 NOK) is juicy and packs an incredible punch with its blue cheese and bacon. The veggie burger (98 NOK) is similarly large and comes with a delectable mango curry, while the fries with aioli dip might just be the best in town.

i *Nybrua. Walk up Thorvald Meyers gate. The restaurant is on the right. Gluten-free and vegetarian options available. Burgers 96-150 NOK. Open M-W 11am-10pm, Th 11am-midnight, F-Sa 11am-3am, Su 11am-10pm.*

BARI

$

Torggata 23 ☎221 11 965

There are a million places to get Middle Eastern food in Oslo, but Bari has something special—it's either the creamy naan gyros, the curry and french fry pizzas, or the Dorian Gray-style paintings on the inside. The place tends to be packed (especially on weekends), but you will quickly forget the wait once you unwrap the foil on your greasy treat and realize that this is high art in culinary form. Can you find somewhere in Oslo with better taste and portions for the price? To quote Wallace Shawn in *The Princess Bride*, "Inconceivable!"

i Oslo S. Walk down Karl Johans gate. Turn left onto Torggata. The restaurant is on the right. Entrees 69-79 NOK. Pizza 75-110 NOK. Open M-Th noon-midnight, F-Sa noon-3am, Su noon-midnight.

CAFÉ SARA $$
Hausmanns gate 29 ☎220 34 000 www.cafesara.no

If an album drops in the woods and no one is there to hear it, will a hipster still claim it's his favorite? We all know the answer is yes, but just to be sure you can ask the clientele at Café Sara in Oslo's trendy Grünerløkka neighborhood. The restaurant has a young and vibrant feel, and its menu reflects that—it serves everything from kebabs and burritos to salads and tzatziki, with a great craft beer list on top of that. Much like Williamsburg, this place is a bit pricey. Our favorite dish, the Iskender Kebab, seemed to be a cheaper option at 134 NOK, so consider it for drinks or snacks rather than a full-on meal if you're on a budget.

i Take bus 34 to Jakob Kirke. The cafe is right across from Kulturkirken Jakob. Appetizers 84 NOK. Entrees 130-160 NOK. Beer 10-60 NOK. Open M-Sa 11am-3:30am, Su 1pm-3:30am.

HEALTHY LIVING ASIAN EXPRESS $
Karl Johans gate 24

This place is cheap and big-portioned. If you're craving Chinese in Oslo, Asian Express serves quick, affordable, and (allegedly) healthy takeaway. The tasty noodles and fried rice come with large portions of meat, and the cheap price range means that you can add on an appetizer without having to ask for an IMF bailout. With its chic, box-like setup right in the middle of Karl Johans, this is the perfect place to fuel up before an afternoon at the National Gallery.

i Oslo S or Nationaltheatret. Pop-up stand in the middle of Eidsvolls plass. Appetizers 55-70 NOK. Entrees 89 NOK. Open M-F 11am-7:30pm, Sa noon-7pm, Su 1-7pm.

NIGHTLIFE

▨ MIKROBRYGGERI $
Trondheimsveien 2 ☎213 83 930 www.schouskjelleren.no

Though the name may sound like something you got by banging your keyboard, Schouskjelleren is easily the best microbrewery in Oslo. The bartender is a zany, chatty Englishman with impeccable taste in the beer he brews. If you're looking for a suggestion, you can't go wrong with the James Blond or Empress of India, both 78 NOK. If that's not enough, it's in a vaulted cellar that looks like a Viking mead hall. You can't get more Scandinavian than that.

i Take bus 30/31 to Heimdalsgata. Turn left onto Trondheimsveien. The brewery is on the right. Beers 80 NOK. Imported beers 90-110 NOK. Open M-Tu 4pm-1am, W-Th 4pm-2am, F-Sa 4pm-3:30am, Su 4pm-midnight.

▨ GUDRUNS
Karl Johans Gate 10

Gudruns is a hit with locals and tourists alike, so prepare for weekend waits of up to 30min. if you're trying to get in. The ground floor is stocked with dusty books and sofas straight out of a Victorian novel, as well as a bar about 30 ft. long. Keep walking and you'll reach the second bar, which has an exposed roof, dance floor, and smoke machines. If neither of those do it for you, there's also an awning overlooking the entire club where you can sit back and heap scorn on the plebeians below. Expect beers in the 75 NOK range (selection includes

Brooklyn Lager, Pilsner, and Carlsberg) and mixed drinks or shots around 110 NOK.

i *Oslo S. Walk down Karl Johans Gate. Gudruns is on the left. Must be 20+. Cover 100 NOK. Beer 80 NOK. Mixed drinks 110 NOK. Open F-Sa 11pm-3am.*

JOHN'S BAR

Universitetsgata 26   ☎400 07 078 www.johnsbar.no

If you're craving cheap drinks and Top 10 hits from the '80s, John's Bar is the place for you. Located one block over from Oslo's main road, the bar is packed on weekends by a motley crew of tourists, students, and bewildered onlookers. Try to get there on the earlier side, as it fills up quickly, and know that if you go, you will dance and, more likely than not, you will have drinks spilled on you.

i *Oslo S. Walk down Karl Johans gate. Turn right onto Universitetsgata. The bar is on the right. Must be 20+. Beer 80 NOK. Mixed drinks 100 NOK. Open Th-Su 10pm-3am.*

BAR FLY

Stortingsgata 12   ☎224 14 011 www.barfly.no

Any bar that names itself after Bukowski's autobiography has got some big shoes to fill—but Bar Fly does just that, and it does it in style. The dimly lit interior, surrounded by wall-to-wall mahogany, allows for several dozen people to sit comfortably in booths and stools. A shot of Jack Daniels fetches 78 NOK, which may not sound like a bargain, but it is significantly cheaper than the same shot at Dr. Jekyll's around the corner (116 NOK) or mixed drinks at nearby Lawo Terrasse (100-180 NOK). The crowd is often in its late 20s and older, but the laid-back atmosphere and central location make this an ideal stopover for anyone trying to get a taste of Oslo nightlife.

i *National Theater. Walk down Stortingsgata. The bar is on the right. Beers 90 NOK. Cocktails 75-180 NOK. Open M-Th 7pm-3am, F-Sa 6pm-3am, Su 9pm-3am.*

FYRHUSET

Maridalsveien 19   www.fyrhusetkuba.no

As the name might suggest, this bar looks like a fire house with a red brick exterior (the name actually means "lighthouse," but we're going to stick with our first impression). It has a standard selection of beers in the 80-95 NOK range—Ringnes on tap, a few IPAs and some foreign imports—but what really sets the place apart is its atmosphere. Play shuffleboard with burly Norsemen upstairs or challenge your table to a competitive game of Jenga on the ground level. The location on the edge of Kuba park and near a graphic design school makes Fyrhuset an excellent place for meeting locals and testing how much game you've got.

i *Take bus 54 to Telthusbakken. Walk into the park directly south and you'll see the bar. Beers 78-90 NOK. Open daily 3pm-midnight.*

CROWBAR

Torggata 32   ☎47 213 86 757

Despite the aggressive-sounding name, this place has nothing to do with armed robbery or segregation; it's a hip microbrewery in Grünerløkka just a few feet down the road from Café Sara. We would describe the environment as somewhere between a frat party and a Viking mead hall: On weekends it's packed wall to wall, and the scent of grilled meat and other partygoers fills the room with a musk and moisture that are hard to describe. The selection of beers is enormous, and the staff is very helpful with recommendations, but the real reason to come is the kebabs: part pork, part diet guilt, they're indescribably good after a couple brews and a game of ping pong upstairs.

i *Take bus 54 to Jakob Kirke. Turn left onto Hausmanns gate. Turn right onto Torggata. The bar is on the right. Beers 72-90 NOK. Tasting samplers of 6 beers 250 NOK. Open F-Sa 8pm-3:30am.*

INGENSTEDS
Brenneriveien 9   ☎950 96 829 www.ingensteds.no

This place is a hipster's wet dream. To get there, you walk through an alleyway plastered with colorful street art and enter into a large open space with tables, a dance floor, and enough paintings and sculptures to make up for that day you skipped the National Gallery. The outdoor portion overlooks a river and is shaded by trees, while the upstairs gives you a spot to kick back and contemplate what the fat baby in that Victorian-style painting is thinking about. The place is often rented out for artistic events like book launches or poetry readings, but on weekends it is always open to the public after 11pm.

i *Turn left onto Brenneriveien. Turn right onto Maridalsveien. The bar is on the right. Beers 72-82 NOK. Cocktails and mixed drinks 90-100 NOK. Open F-Sa 8pm-3:30pm.*

ESSENTIALS
Practicalities
Tourist Offices
Oslo Visitor Center (Østbanehallen to the right of Oslo S's main entrance. Jernbanetorget 1 ☎815 30 555 www.visitoslo.com. Open daily 9am-6pm.) Services include booking the Oslo Pass, city bike rentals, free brochures ("The Oslo Guide"), and currency exchange.

Tours
Several tours are available in Oslo.

- **BÅTSERVICE:** Fjord Sightseeing (☎233 56 890) leaves from Rådhusbrygge port 3, directly in front of City Hall in Aker Brygge. This guided tour takes you around the islands of the Oslofjord, the Opera House, and a number of interesting architectural sites along the harbor. Longer tours, starting in the evening and offering complimentary shrimp snacks, leave from the same area. 270 NOK. Earliest tours start at 10:30am, latest at 4:30pm. Tours last 2 hrs.

- **VIKING BIKING TOURS:** Viking Biking Tours (☎412 66 496 vikingbikingoslo.com/tours) are tours conducted in English that take you around the major sights of Oslo, from Aker Brygge to Vigeland to Karl Johans and beyond. Smaller groups can select customized tours in various European languages as well. All tours leave from the shop, located at Nedre Slottsgate 4 (Oslo S is nearest station). 250 NOK. Bike rental 125-200 NOK. Leave at 1pm daily. Tours last 3hr.

Money
If you want to exchange hard currency rather than withdraw from an ATM, Oslo Airport Gardermoen has two DNB exchange offices (one in arrivals and one in departures) that take a 2.5% commision on the cash you trade in. Generally, most commercial banks exchange at a ratio of of 1NOK to 12 cents, meaning they're skimming off roughly 7% of your cash.

If you still want to trade in your cash, know that banks in Oslo will often add a transaction fee (roughly 50 NOK or $6.30) on top of whatever percentage they take from the money you exchange. Forex Bank (with locations in the Oslo S airport express terminal and on Karl Johans Gate) does not do this and is a particularly good option for those exchanging small amounts. (☎221 72 265, website (in English): www.visitoslo.com/en/product/?TLp=181207. Open M-F 7am-11pm, Sa 9am-6pm, Su 10am-5pm.)

You can pay for almost everything in Norway with debit or credit cards, but most chain stores like 7-11 and Deli de Luca (located all around the Karl Johans/Oslo S area) will have an ATM. Do note you will likely be charged an extra fee for withdrawing cash abroad. ATMs and currency exchange are also available at Oslo Airport Gardermoen.

norway (side tab)

Luggage Storage

You can hire out a 24hr. locker at Oslo Sentralstasjon for 40-80 NOK depending on luggage size. The station is closed daily 1:10-4:30am, so plan accordingly.

Most (if not all) hostels offer free luggage storage during the day. Do this at your own discretion, however, as all guests have access to the luggage rooms.

GLBT Services

Health Centre for LGBT Youth (Mailundveien 23 ☎481 13 013 lhbt@bga.oslo.kommune.no. Open Wednesdays 4-7pm.) Walk-in health center for LGBT youth (13-30) offering information, medical care, and professionals to speak to about emotional or mental health issues.

Laundromats

Laundromat Café (Underhaugsveien 2 ☎213 83 629 www.laundromat.no. 30 NOK for wash, 40 NOK for 30min dry. Machines only take 10 NOK pieces and you must bring your own detergent. Open M-F 7am-1am, Sa-Su 10am-1am.) Going to a laundromat is about as fun as passing a kidney stone: it's smelly, it's boring, and only the most curious among us get a sexual thrill out of it. Laundromat Café, however, seeks to tear down that wall of boredom by turning laundry into a full-fledged dining activity: as you wait for your clothes to dry, you can order pizza and ribs off their menu, or simply kick back with tequila and craft beer until the world becomes as dizzy as the washing cycle.

Internet

Wi-Fi is available widely throughout Oslo, with places such as the Opera House, Mathallen Food Court, art museums, and most train stations offering free connectivity. All Oslo hostels listed here have free Wi-Fi, and some (such as Anker Hostel) do not require a password or username to log in.

Post Office

Oslo Sentralstasjon Postkontor (Jernbanetorget 1 inside Oslo S. Open M-F 9am-6pm, Sa 9am-3pm, closed Sundays.)

Emergency

Emergency Numbers

- **POLICE:** ☎112
- **FIRE:** ☎110
- **AMBULANCE:** ☎113
- **CONFIDENTIAL HELPLINES:** Mental Health Helpline (confidential): ☎810 30 030. The Social and Ambulatory First Aid Service (confidential, free suicide/abuse/sexual assault hotline): ☎234 87 090.

Medical Services

All of the following hospitals accept walk-ins from foreigners and speak English. Be sure to bring identification and relevant health insurance documentation for public hospitals.

- **OSLO EMERGENCY WARD:** (Storgata 40 ☎229 32 293. 24hr.) This is the recommended location for serious or life-threatening emergencies such as fractures, cuts, assault, etc.
- **OSLO AKUTTEN EMERGENCY WARD:** (Rosenkrantzgate 9 ☎220 08 160. Open M-W 8am-7pm, Th 8am-5pm, F 8am-4pm, Sa 9am-3pm, closed Sundays.) Private emergency ward that allows walk-ins. Specialist appointments can also be booked in advance by phone or email. Cost of evaluation by specialist (ENT, gynecologist, dermatologist, etc.) is 790 NOK, payable by card.

- **WALK-IN CLINIC:** Aker Brygge (Filipstad Brygge 1 ☎930 18 668 Open M-F 8am-8pm, Sa-Su 10am-6pm.) Walk-ins and scheduled appointments in a private hospital.

- **24HR. PHARMACIES:** Generally, you'll find an Apotek on every other block in Oslo. However, only two are open 24hr.: the Jernbanetorget Apotek directly opposite of Oslo S and Apotek 1 Emergency Room at Storgata 30, right next to the Oslo Emergency Ward.

Getting There

By Plane

Oslo Airport, Gardermoen (Oslo Lufthavn in Norwegian), is Norway's largest airport with roughly 23 million visitors a year. Located 47 km north of Oslo proper, it is the incoming destination for the majority of international flights into the country and operates 24hr per day. The cheapest way to get from the airport to Oslo is to take the Flytoget train directly from the airport. It leaves every 20 minutes and takes roughly 20 minutes to get to Oslo S (other stops include Lillehammer and Nationaltheatret). The cost of a one-way ticket to Oslo S is 180 NOK for adults and 90 NOK for students, seniors, and children. Tickets are available for purchase at the airport and at Oslo.

Flybussen offers cheap and convenient buses to and from the airport. Tickets can be bought (by card) on the bus or booked online. Adult tickets between the Oslo bus terminal (directly behind Oslo S) and the airport are 175 NOK; student and senior tickets are 100 NOK. (http://www.flybussen.no/en/Oslo/document/3448. Same service available for airport-downtown transportation in other Norwegian cities.)

Taxis from Oslo Airport can be booked and quoted at the Taxi Information Desk. Most taxi companies will have a fixed price to and from the airport. Oslo Taxi, for example, charges between 590-610 NOK before 5pm and 720 NOK after, while metered taxis will generally charge between 10-12 NOK per kilometer and may add on an extra fee for not booking in advance. To book a cab, call ☎232 32 323 or contact the taxi companies themselves. Our advice, though, is to stick to the bus or the train unless you have a lot of people and/or a lot of luggage.

By Train

NSB (Norwegian State Railways) is Norway's main rail company and runs 15 different lines that criss-cross the country, making it a convenient choice if you're travelling to Flåm, the Arctic Circle, or practically anywhere else. National trains leave directly from the main departures hall of Oslo Sentralstasjon, better known as Oslo S. (www.nsb.no/en/our-destinations/stations/oslo-s. Luggage storage available. Open M-F 6:30am-11:15pm, Sa-Su 10am-6pm. Waiting room open daily 3:45am-1:30am). For NSB tickets, schedules and more, visit www.nsb.no, or call ☎815 00 888 (press 9 for information in English). Eurail passes can be used except on the NSB Flytoget train that travels to and from the airport.

Buses

Most buses coming from the airport or elsewhere in Norway and Europe will arrive at the Oslo Bus Terminal, at Schweigaards gate 10, directly behind Oslo S and connected to it. (Storage lockers available, including some that are accessible 24hr. per day. ☎47 23 00 24 00 akt.as. Waiting room open 24hr. Ticket counter open M-F 7am-11pm, Sa-Su 8am-10pm.)

Getting Around

Public Transportation

Oslo is serviced by an extensive network of buses, trams, ferries and underground trains. To use public transport, you need to buy an NSB Card for a prepaid amount of time. (Single ticket 30 NOK; 24hr. 90 NOK; 7-day pass 240 NOK; 30-day pass 680 NOK. Prices cut in half for children, students, and seniors.) These can be purchased at Oslo S, most 7-11 stores, and a number of different public transportation stops.

Note: People will rarely check to see if your card is valid, but the fine for getting caught on transportation without one is between 950-1150 NOK. So buy a ticket. If you do not have a ticket, you can purchase a one-time ticket on board or on your phone, but the price goes up by about 20 NOK.

For those looking to pack a lot of traveling into a little amount of time, a good economic choice is to buy the Oslo Pass (24hr. 320 NOK; 48hr. 470 NOK; 72hr. 590 NOK). The pass allows you free use of public transportation in zones 1 and 2 of Oslo as well as free entrance to a number of museums and parking in municipal parks. It can be bought in Oslo S, the Oslo Visitor Center, and most hotels and hostels. For a full list of benefits, see www.visitoslo.com/en/activities-and-attractions/oslo-pass.

Taxis

Taxis are available in Oslo, but the cost and availability of public transportation make them a secondary option at best. Try Oslo Taxi (☎223 88 090). Prices increase over the course of the night and depend on whether you are hailing on the street or have pre-booked. For cars with four passengers or less, the minimum fare will be in the 109-170 NOK range and increase at a rate of around 8 NOK per minute.

Uber is also available in Oslo, with a base price of 65 NOK, a minimum fare of 100 NOK, and a cost of 5 NOK per minute. Surge pricing rates apply.

bergen

Bergen feels like Oslo's younger brother who quit the rat race years ago and decided to hike, fish, and sell organic glitter instead. Does organic glitter exist? We're not sure, but it's almost certainly available here if it does.

Though we may sound like a broken record, there really is something for everyone here. Bergen mixes the charm of a small town—with colorful wood houses and quaint mom-and-pop stores—with the bigger brands and buildings you'll find in any European metropolis. Surrounding everything are the Seven Mountains, which are not the newest craft beer out of Brooklyn but rather the tree-lined peaks covering the entire city. Visitors may also recognize the port as being the inspiration for the setting of *Frozen*, and while we can't promise you magic snowmen or sheltered princesses, we can promise you the freshest and tastiest fish you've ever had.

Backpackers and budget travelers will be relieved to know that Bergen is not as expensive as Oslo, though you should still be prepared to spend $80-100 a day if you want to live comfortably (and leave aside some money for a fjord tour). There is a huge student population here and an even better food scene, so don't be afraid to spend a few extra nights as you explore this town.

SIGHTS

FISH MARKET

Bergen Harbor

Ever seen *Free Willy? The Little Mermaid? Finding Nemo?* At Bergen's Fish Market, you can finally discover what the favorite protagonists from all these movies taste like—and do it cheaply, too! Walking past the various stands, you'll come across everything from salmon to herring to massive crabs in vaguely sexual positions. Many of the vendors actually give away free samples. Our thrifty researcher-writer munched on whale, salmon, cod, caviar, and reindeer salami in one visit. It may feel like a touristy place, but you can't beat the scenery: it's in a harbor that looks exactly like the one from *Frozen*. Take your prejudice and just let it go when you visit.

i Entrance free. Prices at stands vary. Open daily 7am-8pm.

norway

MARKEN GJESTEHUS $

Kong Oscars gate 45 ☎553 14 404 www.marken-gjestehus.com

Bergen is a small place, and Marken is one of your best options while you stay here: It offers shared rooms for cheap with amenities like a kitchen, ensuite lockes, and sockets by the beds. Individually, these may not seem important, but after a long a day of traveling you might just be on your knees thanking the Good Lord Cthulhu that you don't have to shell out extra cash to keep your stuff safe. The location in the middle of downtown is a huge plus, and the common room has a chilled-out atmosphere that makes it easy to meet other travellers. Just be sure to book in advance—the rooms sell out quickly.

i *Dorms 250-320 NOK. Singles 575 NOK. Doubles 870 NOK. Reception May-Sept 9am-11pm; Oct-Apr 9:30am-4:30pm.*

BERGEN YMCA HOSTEL $

Nedre Korskirkeallmenningen 4 ☎556 06 055 www.bergenhostel.com

YMCA might have the most "hostel-ian" (hostile?) feeling of any place in Bergen, and that's both a godsend and a curse. On the one hand, it's very easy to meet people here: the TV lounge and dining room are always full, the rooms have ensuite bathrooms, and the hostel is five minutes away from the city's main attractions. On the other hand, though, the dim lighting, broken computers, and cramped kitchen give it a somewhat rough feel. It's a good place to go if you're on a budget and want good location, but know that you're not going to be pampered.

i *Dorms 195 NOK. Singles 600 NOK. Doubles 850 NOK. Reception June-Aug 7am-midnight; Sept-Oct 8am-9pm; Nov-Mar 8am-3:30pm; Apr-May 8am-9pm.*

LEPROSY MUSEUM

Kong Oscars gate 59 ☎481 62 678 www.bymuseet.no

"I've got a hot date at the Leprosy Museum tonight!" said no one ever. There's a good reason for that: the museum, fascinating as it is, is seriously depressing. It tells the story of leprosy in Norway and is located on the site of a former leper hospital that operated for 500 years. Walking through the cramped rooms, you're exposed to the miserable conditions the lepers lived in, and the history of how we learned to beat the disease (spoiler alert: it involved a liberal interpretation of "patients' rights"). If you're interested in the history of medicine and have some extra time in Bergen, it's definitely worth a visit.

i *70 NOK, students 35 NOK. Open daily 11am-4pm.*

HAAKON'S HALL (BERGENHUS FORTRESS)

Bergenhus Festning ☎555 46 387 www.bymuseet.no

Can you imagine any better place to be than a Viking mead hall (that is, if you weren't a woman, peasant, priest, pig, or prisoner)? We can't, so we suggest you head to Haakon's Hall and tour a joint that even Beowulf would've considered "hip." Unfortunately, much of the original building was destroyed by fire, neglect, and Nazis—basically everything besides Charlie Sheen—so what you're actually walking through is a recreation. Nonetheless, the architecture is astounding and, as an extra perk, your ticket gets you a free coffee and tea at the cafe. Now how's that for a taste of Valhalla?

i *At the end of Bryggen road. 70 NOK, students 35 NOK. Open daily 6:30am-11pm.*

KODE 2: KUNSTMUSEUM

Rasmus Meyers allé 3   ☎555 68 000 www.kodebergen.no

Even if you can't tell the difference between a porcupine and a painting, this museum has some serious mojo. When you buy your ticket and go upstairs, you have a choice of two exhibits: Monuments and Contemporary. The former is a collection of 3D pieces showcasing various themes (giant yellow blankets that represent…mustard?). The latter is more free-form, with exhibits ranging from an arts-and-crafts room to a film of a woman describing all the creative ways she's trying to kill herself. If it all seems too meta for you, the museum also has an authentically "artsy" cafe and bookshop where you can try to forget all of the thinly veiled genitals you just saw.

i 100 NOK, students 50 NOK. Open daily 11am-5pm.

ULRIKEN CABLE CAR

Ulriken 1   ☎536 43 643 www.ulriken643.no

Yes, this is listed in every tourist brochure, and yes, we're supposed to be the ones on the front lines of finding you cool off-the-beaten-path stuff to do, but give us a break! This one is mainstream but totally worth it. The cable car offers breathtaking views of all of Bergen and is a good compromise for those who can't make a full hike. The ride up—though it may trigger vertigo—is the most fun you'll ever have getting high (we think). Tickets can be booked from the Bergen Tourist Office, and buses to the cable car leave regularly from there.

i One-way tickets 95 NOK. Return tickets 155 NOK. Bus and cable car 245 NOK. Open daily 9am-9pm.

FOOD

TREKRONEREN $

Kong Oscars Gate 1

Much like a frat party before 8pm, this place is a total sausage fest. They've got lamb, frankfurter, bratwurst, and about 10 other kinds of delectably tubed meats—all smothered in nutmeg, chili, and garlic. Our personal favorite has to be the reindeer sausage, which comes with mustard, ketchup, fried onions, and juniper berry jam... because why not. The small portion (55 NOK) is enough to keep you full for a good couple of hours. It doesn't get cheaper or tastier than this.

i Directly off of Fish Market. 150g sausage 55 NOK. 250g sausage 85 NOK. It's a pop-up stand so hours vary, but generally open in the morning until late.

HORN OF AFRICA $$

Strandgaten 212   ☎954 25 250

Horn of Africa encourages eaters to stick it to The Western Man by asking a fundamental question about modern society: why can't we eat with our hands? In here, there is no judgment or exclusion, only the piping hot sauces of the chili beef Tibbs, the buttery smoothness of the chicken wat, and the satisfaction of knowing you don't have to use a fork. For the uninitiated, Ethiopian food often includes scooping up spiced meats and veggies from a shared tray using a sour, spongy bread called injera—it's delicious, it's filling, and it's what Patrick Henry had in mind when he said "Give me liberty or give me death."

i Entrees 160 NOK. Beers 60-70 NOK. Open Tu-Th 3-10pm, F-Sa 3-11pm, Su 3-10pm, closed Mondays.

GODT BROD $

Vestre Torggaten 2   ☎555 63 310 www.godtbrod.no

This is not the newest rapper on a 2 Chainz tour but rather a cozy cafe with two locations in downtown Bergen. While most people use "cozy" liberally—employing it to describe $1200-a-month New York basements in order to justify their crumbling acting careers—we actually mean it here; Godt Brod is the kind of place where you feel comfortable wearing a tacky Christmas sweater as you waste away an hour over coffee and scones. The prices are reasonable: pastries and coffee are in the 30-40 NOK range, with some a little higher. And the mozzarella and herb spelt-bread sandwiches are surprisingly good for a chain store.

i Coffee 30-40 NOK. Pastries 30-40 NOK. Sandwiches 80 NOK. Open M-F 7am-6pm, Sa 8am-5pm, Su 9am-5pm.

NABOEN $

Sigurds Gate 4   ☎559 00 290 www.grannen.no/naboen2

Though the entrance level at Naboen's is a full-blown restaurant, you want to head straight downstairs when you enter the place. The pub in the cellar—perhaps Bergen's best-kept secret—has what may be the best meatballs east of the Mississippi (west of the Mississippi). Does Mississippi have meatballs?). For 136 NOK, you get you an enormous plate of meat, cranberries, cauliflower and gravy so juicy it gives Gushers a run for their money. Sampled with a Lucky Jack beer (our recommendation; 78 NOK), this might be the closest humankind ever gets to achieving orgasm in gastrointestinal form.

i Entrees 90-160 NOK. Beer 90 NOK. Open M-Th 4pm-1am, F-Sa 4pm-2am, Su 4pm-1am.

PINGVINEN $$

Vaskerelven 14   ☎556 04 646 www.pingvinen.no

As you might have noticed in your travels, Norway has a lot of ethnic food—kebab, noodles, sushi, etc.—but not a lot in the "Norwegian" department. Pingvinen is where that trend ends. This place has all the low-brow subtlety of a pub with food that could easily qualify for a four-star restaurant: meatballs, smoked herring, lamb stew, even horse meat all artfully concocted in a culinary celebration of the motherland. The space is small enough that you may need to wait for a table, but the staff seems particularly attentive to tourists and newcomers.

i Entrees 150-200 NOK. Open daily 11am-3am.

NIGHTLIFE

DICKENS KONTORET

Nygaardsgaten 2   ☎474 52 544 www.dickensbergen.no

Dickens is classy as shit. Wood paneling, a dimly lit interior, drink menu so decadent it may have come from a boozy pharaoh's tomb. This is the kind of place where you sip whiskey and talk about philosophy. So as you debate Lichtenstein's addendum to the Hamburger morality theorem—or, you know, whatever—consider the tangy burn of a Nikka from the barrel (98 NOK) or a cigar blend cognac (139 NOK). You can't go wrong with the menu here, though this place is probably best for dates or a quick drink to start the night before you move on to Bergen's cheaper, wilder locales.

i Drinks 100-150 NOK. Open M-Th 4pm-12:30am, F-Sa 4pm-2am, Su 4pm-12:30am.

KAOS

Nygaardsgaten 2   ☎452 60 706 www.kaos-bergen.no

Don't be that red squiggly line in a Word doc and try to grab a sharpie and write "Chaos" on the door of this student-run bar. No one likes a Grammar Nazi, and it's not likely to get you laid. What might get you laid (out) is the insanely cheap alcohol here: beers on tap go for 59 NOK, and shots of anything are 49 NOK. That's as cheap as the budget for *Leprechaun: Back 2 tha Hood* (look it up; it's a real thing), and every student in Bergen seems to know it. The place is often packed out the door, but squeeze into a booth in the cellar or upstairs area, and it's impossible not to make friends.

i Beers 59 NOK. Shots 49 NOK. Open M-F 3pm-3:30am, Sa 1pm-3:30am, Su 5pm-3:30am.

GARAGE

Christies gate 14   ☎553 21 980 www.garage.no

Garage is like Kaos's rougher, older brother from the wrong side of the tracks. Though it has a distinct heavy metal vibe, the clientele on any given night includes students, musicians, and a few hopelessly out-of-place Germans in Hawaiian shirts. The bar has a larger selection than Kaos does, though beers are about the same price (64 NOK on tap; slightly higher for bottled and imported) and shots are in the 70-90 NOK range (e.g., Jack Daniels 86 NOK). If you're craving a peek at Norway's (in)famous metal scene, Garage also hosts shows every night. The beer, sweat, and fun from this place will have you smelling like Ozzy Osbourne for the next week.

i Beers 64 NOK. Shots 70-90 NOK. Open M-F 3pm-3:30am, Sa 1pm-3:30am, Su 5pm-3:30am.

ESSENTIALS

Practicalities

- **TOURIST OFFICE:** Bergen Tourist Information Center offers services like souvenirs, tour booking, free Wi-Fi, and currency exchange. (Strandkaien 3 ☎555 52 000 www.visitbergen.com. Open June-Aug daily 8:30am-10pm; Sept daily 9am-8pm; Oct-Apr M-Sa 9am-4pm; May daily 9am-8pm.)

- **TOURS:** Best booked from the Bergen Tourist Information center. Help desk and representatives are available to help book fjord tours, daily excursions, trips to the Ulriken Cable Car, and tours of Bergen itself.

- **CURRENCY EXCHANGE:** If you're not using an ATM, the Bergen Tourist Information Center offers currency exchange at rates more or less the same as what you'll find at banks and the airport.

- **ATMS:** You can pay for almost everything in Norway with debit or credit cards, but the Bergen train station and most chain stores like 7-11 and Deli de Luca (located all around the Fish Market area) will have an ATM (in Norwegian: Minibank). You will likely be charged an extra fee for withdrawing cash abroad. ATMs and currency exchange are also available at Bergen Airport.

- **LUGGAGE STORAGE:** Luggage storage is available at both the Bergen train station and the bus station (directly next to each other) for 20 NOK per locker (with slightly higher prices for bigger lockers).

- **INTERNET:** Wi-Fi is available widely throughout Bergen, with hostels, hospitals, the tourist center and many of the bars and restaurants in the area near Dickens Kontoret offering free connectivity (often with a password). Internet is also available at the Bergen Public Library. (Strømgt 6. Open M-Th 10am-8pm, F 10am-5pm, Sa 10am-4pm, Su noon-4pm.)

- **POST OFFICE:** Bergen Sentrum postkontor is inside the Xhibition shopping center. (Småstrandgaten 3 Open M-F 9am-6pm, Sa 10am-3pm, closed Sundays.)

Emergency Numbers

- **POLICE:** ☎112

- **FIRE:** ☎110

- **AMBULANCE:** ☎113

- **CRISIS HOTLINES:** Kirkens SOS i Bjorgvin suicide hotline. (Offices also available at Kalfarveien 79 ☎815 33 300 www.kirkens-sos.no. Open M-Tu 8am-3pm, Th 8am-11pm, F-Su 8am-3am, closed Wednesdays.)

- **LATE-NIGHT PHARMACIES:** Duty Pharmacy (Apoteket Nordstjernen) is located inside the Bergen bus station. (☎552 18 384. Open M-Sa 8am-11pm, Su 2pm-11pm.)

- **HOSPITALS:** Helse Bergen. (Haukelandsveien 22. For emergencies, call ☎113; for minor injuries, call ☎555 68 760. Open 24hr.) Bergen Legevakt. (Vestre Strømkaien 19 ☎555 68 700 Open 24hr.)

Getting There

By Plane

Bergen Airport (Bergen Lufthavn) is Bergen's main airport, located about 12 miles away from the city's main attractions. It operates a number of international flights, particularly between cities in the UK, Sweden, Germany, and other European capitals.

The easiest way from the airport to Bergen is the Flybussen (www.flybussen.no; 90 NOK, students 70 NOK). The buses stop at a number of places throughout Bergen, with the most popular being the Bergen bus station, every 15 minutes (trip lasts around 25 minutes).

Cab rates change depending on time of day and number of passengers, but there is a taxi desk at the airport where you can find contact information and price quotes. For example, a taxi from the Fish Market to airport with Bergentaxi, midday on a weekday, comes out to a little less than 500 NOK.

Trains

NSB railways operates all of the trains coming into and out of Bergen (the average price of a ticket from Oslo to Bergen, one of the most scenic rail trips in Europe, is around 699 NOK, students 634 NOK. The route takes around six-and-a-half hours). All trains drop off at Bergen train station (Strømgt 4. Luggage storage, cab stand, ATMs, and cafes on site. Waiting room open daily 6am-12:10am. Ticket booths and services open M-F 6:45am-7:15am, Sat-Sun 7:30am-4pm.)

By Bus

most buses between Bergen and other Norwegian cities are run through Bussekspress and cost about as much as the train—550-700 NOK for a one way ticket from Oslo, 12 hours in total. All buses drop off at the Bergen bus station (Stromgaten 8).

Getting Around

Public Transportation

The town of Bergen is incredibly compact, and all of the main sights are within walking distance. Taking public transportation is often less effective because of the wait times and dropoff locations.

Bergen's public transportation is called Skyss and includes all of the buses and trams in the Hordaland region (the municipality in which Bergen is located). Much like in Oslo, tickets can be bought for 24hr. (90 NOK), 7-day (235 NOK), or longer periods and are available for purchase at every transportation stop. If you find yourself without a pass, you can also buy one directly on the bus or tram, though the cost will be higher.

Much like the Oslo Pass, the Bergen Card gives you free access to public transportation and discounts at a number of museums, restaurants, and parking spaces. It's a smart purchase if you're trying to pack a lot into a short amount of time, but if you're in Bergen mainly for hiking or low-intensity sightseeing, it might not be worth it. The card can be purchased at the Tourist Information Center at the following prices: 24hr. 200 NOK; 48hr. 260 NOK; 72hr. 320 NOK.

For 999 NOK, the Fjord Card grants unlimited 5-day access to express boats leaving from Strandkai Terminal (next to the tourist center). If you're planning on seeing a lot of fjords or exploring Bergen's offshore islands, this is a good investment.

fjord tours

A trip to Norway without seeing the fjords is like a night in Vegas, without the hookers and blackjack: it's certainly possible, but you can't really say you've had an authentic experience without them. Bergen proudly calls itself, "The Gateway to the Fjords" (new *Game of Thrones* title?) and a quick boat ride from here will send you past some of Europe's most dramatic scenery. Bergen is small enough to cover in a day or two, so we recommend you book one of these tours during your stay. Shorter trips, such as the **Skjerjehamn cruise** (465 NOK, students 365 NOK. 4hr.) will take you by boat through the mountainous coastline to offshore islands that are quaint, idyllic, and a dozen more great Instagram adjectives. Longer trips like the **Hardangerfjord cruise** (750 NOK, students 425 NOK) last 12 hours or more and often involve multi-step trips by bus and boat through terrain straight out of *The Lord of the Rings*. All tours can be booked at the Bergen Tourist Center the day before the trip; you can find a full listing of tours in the information pamphlets there. Once you try it, you'll be surprised how fun and a*fjord*able the whole experience is. Stop cringing—it was cute.

Taxis

One cab company is Bergen Taxi (☎559 97 050 www.bergentaxi.no). Prices vary dramatically depending on the time, day of the week, and number of passengers. For a sample, Friday nights for a cab with four people or less will start at 54 NOK if hailed on the street, and then go up by 9.30 NOK per minute, with a minimum fare of 136 NOK. For a full table of prices and times, see the website.

norway essentials

VISAS

Norway is not a member of the EU, but it is a member of the Schengen area. Citizens of Australia, Canada, New Zealand, the US, and many other non-EU countries do not need a visa for stays of up to 90 days. However, if you plan to spend time in other Schengen countries, note that the 90-day period of time you are allowed to visit without a visa applies cumulatively to all Schengen countries.

MONEY

Norway uses the Norwegian krone (NOK or kr.) as its currency.

Tipping is not usually expected in Norway. In restaurants, it is common to round up the bill to the nearest 10 or 100 NOK, or 6-10% of the bill if you have received exceptional service, but this is not required. Taxi drivers also do not expect tips, but if you wish to tip, round up the bill.

ATMs in Norway are common and convenient. They are often located in airports, train stations and major pedestrian areas. The two major international money networks are MasterCard/Maestro/Cirrus and Visa/PLUS. To find out what out-of-network or international fees you may be subject to by using ATMs, call your bank.

ALCOHOL

The minimum age to purchase alcohol in Norway is 18 for drinks below 22% ABV and 20 for drinks above 22% ABV. Selling alcohol to or buying alcohol for minors under 18 is illegal. Bars, clubs, and discos may have different age restrictions based on what they serve, but are usually either 18 or 20. Remember to drink responsibly and to never drink and drive. The legal blood alcohol content (BAC) for driving in Norway is under 0.02%, significantly lower than the US limit of 0.08%.

POLAND

Poland is a sprawling country where history has cast a long shadow. Plains that stretch from the Tatras Mountains in the south to the Baltic Sea in the north have seen foreign invaders time and time again. Meanwhile, the contrast between western and eastern cities is a remnant of Poland's subjection to competing empires. Ravaged during WWII, and later, viciously suppressed by the USSR, Poland is finally self-governed, and the change is marked. Today's Poland is a haven for budget travelers, where the rich cultural treasures of medieval Krakow and bustling Warsaw are complemented by wide Baltic beaches, rugged Tatras peaks, and tranquil Mazury lakes.

greatest hits

- **HERE BE DRAGONS:** Be king or queen for a day and visit the **Wawel Castle** (p. 603) in Kraków. Just don't wake up the infamous Wawel Dragon.

- **COFFEE AND KAFKA:** Bookworms and coffee addicts come together at this coffee shop with a library and book exchange (p. 597).

- **AUSCHWITZ:** A visit to this well-known concentration camp is a sobering, poignant experience (p. 600).

teçza

"A provocation." "Offensive." Are these describing *Let's Go* reviews? No—these are actually quotes from politician Stanislaw Pieta regarding Teçza, a rainbow sculpture that stands at the center of Plac Zbawiciela, otherwise known as Savior Square. The sculpture could itself use a savior, seeing as it has been attacked numerous times by those firmly opposed to the LGBTQ+ community. The work of Julita Wojcik, Wojcik insists that the sculpture isn't actually related to the LGBTQ+ movement at all—but that doesn't deter the haters. And it doesn't deter the lovers either. In protest of the arson the sculpture has repeatedly faced, LGBTQ+ advocates have taken it upon themselves to kiss in front of the sculpture. The rainbow has been rebuilt over and over, perhaps accidentally a symbol of hope for activists.

warsaw

The capital of Poland, Warsaw has lived through German and Soviet occupation, and counts the Holocaust and communism in its history. These experiences, combined with modernization, bring Warsaw to its current form: remnants of the Jewish ghetto, the Palace of Culture and Science, skyscrapers, parks, and the cobbled streets of Stare Miasto all meet. The city is complex, multi-dimensional, and cannot be reduced to a single word. Warsaw honors its history with sites like the Jewish Historical Institute, while welcoming the present with its towering skyscrapers. The rumble of cars borders the respite of parks, giving the air of New York smashed with Paris and Prague, topped off with Varsovian flair. The city was burned down during World War II and has since been rebuilt, giving it a mosaic feel of old and new. Warsaw is split by the Vistula River and counts mermaids as its symbol.

SIGHTS

ROYAL CASTLE

plac Zamkowy 4   ☎223 555 170 www.zamek-krolewski.pl

Originally built in the 14th century, the Royal Castle was produced by Italian architects, for Polish King Sigmund III, who descended from the royal Swedish Vasa family. Like a college brochure, this castle is the spitting image of diversity and pulls it off remarkably well. During World War II, the castle was completely destroyed by the Germans; the version that stands today is a reconstruction of the original. As of now, the castle counts the King's Apartment, Deputies' Chamber, and Royal Library as part of its tour and also has a permanent exhibit in the basement about the reconstruction process of the castle. Europe's first constitution, while signed at the Presidential Palace, was written up here. The Castle and Old Town have since been granted UNESCO World Heritage Site status.

i M1: Ratusz Arsenał. From the Metro station, get on the 26 tram toward Wiatraczna to Stare Miasto, where you can take the crosswalk to reach the Royal Castle. Castle tour 23 zł, reduced 15 zł. Entrance free on Sundays. Open M-W 10am-6pm, Th 10am-8pm, F-Sa 10am-6pm, Su 11am-6pm. For more detailed prices and hours for individual exhibitions, please check the website for the most up-to-date information.

TOMB OF THE UNKNOWN SOLDIER (GROB NIEZNANEGO ZOLNIERZA)

plac Pilsudskiego

A monument to Polish soldiers who died for their country, the Tomb of the Unknown Soldier holds the remains of a soldier who died in battle. As with any of the other tombs of unknowns found worldwide, the emphasis is not on the individual, but on what the individual represents. The soldier buried is a symbol of the sacrifice so many Poles made in defense of their country, and it is with that in mind that Warsaw honors this soldier fiercely. Found on plac Pilsudski, the monument is small but somber and poignant. The tomb lays at the center, flanked by guards and burning flames. The monument is not without its own story of turmoil—it has faced destruction, and its significance has transformed over time. As it stands today, however, the tomb is a beautifully-executed memorial to heroes past.

i M1/M2: Świętokrzyska. From the Metro stop, ride the N44 tram toward Zajezdnia Żoliborz for 3 stops to Hotel Bristol. From here, turn left onto Generała Michała Tokarzewskiego-Karaszewicza and then take the crosswalk.

PRESIDENTIAL PALACE (PALAC PREZYDENCKI)
Krakowskie Przedmieście 48/50 ☎226 951 070 www.prezydent.pl

The name says it all—the Presidential Palace in Warsaw is the official seat of the President of Poland. Recognizable by the huge white building and the guards standing outside, the aesthetic of this place is "stay out." What do you mean the President doesn't want to see us? What do you mean you need an invitation? We came out to have a good time, and honestly, we're feeling so attacked right now. The palace dates back to the 1600s and has seen some serious history play out. Stanisław II August Poniatowski was coronated here, an affair that cost over 2,000,000 zł, and a statue of his brother, Józef Poniatowski, stands out front. Chopin once performed at the Presidential Palace, and Europe's first constitution was signed here. You won't get to see the site up close, but a selfie with the stone lions out front is almost the same thing, right? Swap a politician for a stone-cold carnivore, and who could even tell the difference?

i M2: Nowy Świat – Uniwersytet. From the station, turn left onto Nowy Świat St. Continue onto Krakowskie Przedmieście. The palace is on the right.

PALACE OF CULTURE AND SCIENCE
plac Defilad 1 ☎226 567 600 www.pkin.pl

Built between 1952 and 1955, the enormous structure was a "gift from the Soviet people," offered by Stalin himself to the Poles, and its construction still prompts passionately divided public reaction. Regardless of opinion, this 42-story building looms over everything and there's no ignoring it at all. More than a palace though, the structure is a bit of a mini-village, with its own post office, shopping mall, a cinema with eight screens, four theaters, two museums, and an entire college spanned across two floors. Despite its size, the palace offers little to see, though it does have a stellar observation deck. With a panoramic view of the entire city, including the Vistula River, the deck is a prime date location, guaranteed to bring you plenty of class.

i M1: Centrum. From the station, walk onto plac Defilad. The palace is right ahead. Palace requires guided tour for admission.Tours for individuals available through CREATours (entrance on Marszałkowska). Admission 30 zł. Open M 10:30am-5:30pm, Tu-Th 10:30am-1:30pm, F-Su 10:30am-5:30pm.

JEWISH HISTORICAL INSTITUTE
Tłomackie 3/5 ☎228 279 221 www.jhi.pl

The Jewish Historical Institute of Warsaw stands as the only establishment in Poland that dedicates its collection entirely to the culture of Jews in Warsaw. Including exhibits of paintings, memoirs, and World War II testimonies from Jewish survivors of the Holocaust, the museum brings to life the vivid reality that Polish Jews faced in their everyday lives during the war. A key highlight of the museum is the Warsaw Ghetto exhibit, with photos and film footage from the ghetto itself, painting a troubling but accurate picture of the Jews' suffering. Many of the relevant Warsaw Ghetto sights, like boundary markers, still stand

poland

OKI DOKI HOSTEL $$

plac Dąbrowskiego 3 ☎228 280 122 www.okidoki.pl

Hostel life can get ugly. Indulge in a touch of beauty with Oki Doki's rooms, each with a separate theme and decorated by a Warsaw artist. A snoring hostelmate or a snoring hostelmate *and* art? Oki Doki is recognized as a member of Europe's Famous Hostels, a group that only selected one hostel in Warsaw. The hostel is about a 9-minute walk from the Palace of Culture and Science and offers 24hr. reception for whatever ungodly hour you return. There isn't a real need to go out late though. The hostel has its own bar, bringing fun even closer to you than it was before. As morning comes, hit up their 15 zł breakfast to refuel before hitting up sights.

i M1/M2: Świętokrzyska. From the station, take the stairs and turn left onto Świętokrzyska. Down two blocks, turn left onto Szkolna, and then right onto plac Dąbrowskiego, where the hostel is on your right. Dorms 67-72 zł. Check-in 3pm. Check-out 11am. Reception 24hr.

PATCHWORK HOSTEL $

Chmielna 5 ☎222 583 959 www.patchworkhostel.pl

As colorful as a quilt indeed, Patchwork Hostel finds itself in a very unique and lively part of town. One might even liken it to—a patchwork? The location is prime, though; close to the Palace of Culture and Science and to numerous stores, Patchwork keeps exercise to a minimum, enjoyment to a max. In a city as spread out as Warsaw, this is a real blessing. The new hostel on the block, the facilities are in great condition, and like any newbie, the staff is eager to please because if the staff is upbeat, so is the hostel.

i M2: Nowy Świat – Uniwersytet. From the station walk out and turn right onto owy Świat St. Walk about three blocks and turn right onto Chmielna, where the hostel will be on your left. Dorms 60-70 zł. Check-in 3pm. Check-out 11am. Reception 24hr.

MISH MASH HOSTEL $

Nowogrodzka 42 ☎512 951 446 www.mishmashhostel.pl

An artsy ambience greets you from the second you step in: gray patterned wallpaper and art reminiscent of Banksy. The rooms of Mish Mash are simple and minimalist, but they don't skimp on what's important: TV. You'll find one in each room, as well as in the common room. (We know how easy it is to slip into a soap opera obsession.) Mish Mash also offers a common kitchen and comfortable rooms. Mish Mash can be found in the Sródmiescie district, a little over 20 minutes away from Łazienki Park, and a nine minute walk from the Palace of Culture and Science.

i M1: Centrum. From the station, take the stairs and then turn right onto Marszałkowska. At the next block, turn right onto Nowogrodzka, where the hostel will be on the right. Dorms 50-80 zł. Check-in 1pm. Check-out 11am. Reception 7am-midnight.

today, and are certainly worth a visit. For those pressed for time, we suggest walking down Grzybowska street and seeing the ghetto boundary marker at Grzybowska 45, walking down the street to a remaining portion of the Ghetto Wall at Waliców 11, and visiting the Nożyk synagogue and Prozna.

i M1: Ratusz Arsenał. From the station, turn right onto aleja Solidarności/DW629, and then make a right onto Tłomackie. 10 zł, students 5 zł. Open M-F 10am-6pm, Su 10am-6pm, closed Saturdays.

FOOD

SAM $$
Lipowa 7a   ☎600 806 084

We all know a Sam. We all love a Sam. We love SAM. A restaurant, cafe, and bakery, SAM is the food trifecta, and it does each label justice. A relaxed and naturally lit open space, SAM is a breath of fresh air—particularly if you go for the outdoor seating. On the inside, a long table stands in the center with small ones to the side. Large windows let light flood in, ideal for the Vitamin D-deprived. The restaurant has your usual—ham and cheese sandwiches, omelets—but splits from the crowd with its vegan and vegetarian options and offerings like Thai rice, lime and chili ice cream, and saffron ice cream. Don't let the casually American name throw you. A meal at SAM can very much be an international experience.

i M2: Centrum Nauki Kopernik. From the station, walk down Wybrzeże Kościuszkowskie. Turn left onto Lipowa. The restaurant is on the left. Salads 24-36 zł. Vegetarian and vegan meals 16-36 zł. Meat dishes 7-38 zł. Open M-F 8am-9:30pm, Sa-Su 9am-9:30pm.

KAWIARNIA KAFKA $
Obożna 3   ☎228 260 822

On the edge of a park, Kawiarnia Kafka's layout invites customers to float in and out of the space, lounging on the grass, at the outside tables, or at the inside ones. Antlers decorate one wall, books another, but despite the name, Kawiarnia Kafka is anything but pretentious. The cafe boasts a book collection and book exchange, meaning patrons can get their fill of coffee, food, and words all in one stop. Buying a book is, much like us, cheap and easy—books are sold by weight, but reading in the cafe is our favorite: free. Kafka stands near the University of Warsaw; the cafe's extensive menu and 10% student discount draw the young intellectuals in. When Tinder inevitably disappoints, consider that you could probably do worse than the crowd here.

i M2: Nowy Świat – Uniwersytet. From the station, turn left onto Nowy Świat. At the next corner, turn right onto Mikołaja Kopernika and then take another right onto Obożna. The cafe is on your right. Salads 17-25 zł. Kanapki 9-14 zł. Coffee drinks 6-14 zł. Open M-F 9am-10pm, Sa-Su 10am-10pm.

PAŃSTWOMIASTO $
Generała Władysława Andersa 29   ☎224 009 464

High ceilings and neutral toned decoration punctuated with colorful art grant Państwomiasto the air of a Manhattan loft. (Like what we expect Taylor Swift's apartment looks like—she's got a blank space baby, but the rest of us don't have any space at all.) Państwomiasto, on the other hand, has large windows that let light flood in, and a wide floor space with scattered wooden tables. The cafe leads the pack by offering food options past sandwiches and salads. Protein and complex carbs join the menu, which features gems like tagliatelle with duck, and nachos.

i M1: Dworzec Gdański. From the station, walk onto Generała Władysława Andersa. Follow this road for 10min. Państwomiasto is on your right. Snacks 9-22 zł. Pasta dishes 25-27 zł. Salads 22-26 zł. Cocktails 15-22 zł. Open daily 9am-midnight. Kitchen closes at 10pm Su-Th, 11pm F-Sa.

COFFEE KARMA $
Mokotowska 17   ☎228 758 709

Wooden tables, window benches, and colorful cushions fill the inside of Coffee Karma, a cafe found on plac Zbawiciela, a hipster home. The cafe has a clear view of the controversial rainbow structure that stands at the center of the square. Coffee Karma has a mix of seating, making it a good place to work, meet a date, or soak up some sun outdoors. Put another way, it's a good place to go, whether you're trying to get the A or the D. Karma's numerous outlets and food options mean it's easy to spend a day here. On the other side of the roundabout, Plan B comes to life as Coffee Karma closes.

i M1: Politechnika. From the station, turn left onto Ludwika Waryńskiego, heading toward Polna. Turn left onto Jaworzyńska. Turn left at the end of the road onto Mokotowska where the cafe is on your left. Kanapki 13-21 zł. Salads 23-29 zł. Coffee drinks 6.50-15 zł. Open M-F 7:30am-11pm, Sa 9:30am-11pm, Su 10am-11pm.

CHARLOTTE $
aleja Wyzwolenia 18 ☎226 284 459

Also on plac Zbawiciela, Charlotte is a taste of France just a few borders away. Casually Parisian—oxymoron?—the bistro sells items like pastries, *croquees monsieur*, and *croques madame*. If you think there's a better way to start the day than with a croissant…that's blasphemy. Charlotte is all class, and it's the best place in the square to enjoy a glass of wine. Recommended for breakfast or a brunch date, the space is somewhat small but bustling, and it's very popular. For those of us dedicated to the pursuit of carbs, the bakery sells fresh products to take home. Bread for now, bread for later. We about that life.

i M1: Politechnika. From the station, turn left onto Ludwika Waryńskiego, heading toward Polna, and turn right into Nowowiejska. The cafe is across the square. Salads 8-18 zł. Breakfast 8-25 zł. Hot beverages 2-9 zł. Open M-Th 7am-midnight, F 7am-1am, Sa 9am-1am, Su 9am-midnight.

NIGHTLIFE

PARDON TO TU
plac Grzybowski 12/16 ☎513 191 641

Pardon To Tu, a popular nightlife spot, celebrates words. A record store, bookstore, pub, and music joint, Pardon To Tu is effortlessly hip, hold the "ster." Undoubtedly, this is a hipster hangout, but it swaps all of the tropes of hipsterdom for a genuine love for artistic expression. Pardon To Tu indulges in a contemporary and sleek look. One wall of the interior is covered in names of bands; the others hold assorted records and books for sale. In warm weather, the outside seating is the ideal place for a slow-paced, happy day. At night, the place hosts concerts for music aficionados who love to sip beer and say, "Right on."

i M1/M2: Świętokrzyska. From the station, turn left onto Bagno. Turn left onto plac Grzybowski. The bar is on your left. Nonalcoholic drinks 4-18 zł. Beer 6-12 zł. Cover for shows varies, usually between 20-80 zł. Often there is a student discount. Open daily 10am-late.

PLAN B
aleja Wyzwolenia 18 ☎503 116 154

The name drips innuendo. Plan B pretty much invented plac Zbawiciela, the beloved youth hub of Warsaw. The pub occupies the upper level of a space decorated with graffiti, and is credited with giving the square its cool reputation. Graffiti and slouchy couches contribute to the pub's "too cool to try" air. But it's still definitely hot—Plan B hosts plenty of events, fills up regularly, and can be easily spotted by the crowd lounging outside the doors.

i M1: Politechnika. From the station, turn left onto Ludwika Waryńskiego, heading toward Polna. Turn right onto Nowowiejska. The pub is across the square. Beer 7-15 zł. Wine 10 zł. Cocktails 13-27 zł. Snacks 10-12 zł. Open daily noon-3am.

BAR STUDIO
plac Defilad 1 ☎603 300 835

The Palace of Culture and Science, home to Bar Studio, inspires mixed emotions in Varsovians. The extensive structure is, to many, a reminder of Soviet domination and communist days. Others hold more positive perceptions, seeing it as an architectural gem that defines the city. At the heart of this controversial place, Bar Studio takes up residence in the Studio Theatre. A restaurant with

a cafe atmosphere and a bar at night, Bar Studio is easily an all-day affair. The outdoor seating offers a view of the rest of the palace while the inside seating is a comfortable and sleek place to get work done. As your day turns from coffee to vodka (or vodka to more vodka?), Bar Studio transitions into a bar. Bar Studio hosts regular events in their large space, and caters to the nightlife crowd. A historical building, there's hardly a better place to indulge in beats and drinks in an authentic Varsovian experience.

i M1: Centrum. From the station, the bar is right out on the courtyard of the Palace of Culture and Science. Cocktails 15-25 zł. Beer 4-15 zł. Entrance to events 5-10 zł. Open 9am-late.

ESSENTIALS
Practicalities

- **TOURIST OFFICES:** Palace of Culture and Science (plac Defilad 1 Open daily May-Sept 8am-8pm; Oct-Apr 8am-6pm.). Old Town (Rynek Starego Miasta 19/21/21a Open daily May-Sept 9am-8pm; Oct-Apr 9am-6pm.).

- **BANKS/ATMS:** ATMs are readily found throughout the city at most banks as well as by the arrival terminal at the airport. Shopping malls that have ATM machines are also commonly found around the city.

- **INTERNET:** Warsaw has free public Wi-Fi available in Old Town, in areas such as the Powiśle district and Krakowskie Przedmieście. Free Wi-Fi is also available at Starbucks, Costa Coffee, Coffee Heaven, KFC, McDonald's, and most hostels and hotels. There are also internet cafes available throughout the city: Arena Internet Cafe (plac Konstytucji 5 Open 24hr.) and A2 Cafe (plac Konstytucji 5 Open 24hr.)
- **POST OFFICE:** FUP Warszawa 1 (aleja Jana Pawła II 82 ☎223 132 388 Open M-Sa 8am-8pm, Su 10am-4pm.)

Emergency

- **EMERGENCY NUMBER:** ☎112
- **EMERGENCY NUMBER FOR FOREIGNERS:** ☎608 599 999 or ☎222 787 777 Available June 1-Sept 30, daily 8am-10pm.
- **POLICE:** ☎997
- **CITY GUARD:** ☎986
- **FIRE:** ☎998
- **HOSPITAL:** Szpital Orłowskiego: Strona główna (ulica Czerniakowska 231 ☎226 283 011). Szpital Kliniczny im. Księżnej Anny Mazowieckiej (Karowa 2 ☎225 966 100). Samodzielny Publiczny Centralny Szpital Kliniczny (Stefana Banacha 1A ☎225 991 000).
- **24HR.PHARMACIES:** Apteka Franciszkańska (Fanciszkańska 14 ☎226 353 525 Open 24hr.). Apteka 24h PZF Cefarm (ulica Gagarina 6 ☎228 413 783 Open 24hr.).

poland

Getting There

From the airport, you can take the SKM S2 train to the city center. Tickets for the train can be purchased at the Passenger Information Point in the Arrivals hall, from ticket machines placed at bus stops and next to the train station entrance, from ticket machines in SKM trains and on some buses, or from bus drivers.

You can also use buses. Bus 175 runs daily 4:30am-11pm and will take you to the city center. Bus 188 runs daily 4:45am-11:20pm and will take you through the city center and to the Praga district.

Getting Around

All public transportation tickets can be purchased at newspaper kiosks or ticket machines in the Metro stations. The price for a ticket for one trip is 4.40 zł. Tickets for one day (15 zł) or one weekend (24 zł) can also be purchased.

Ubers are readily available in Warsaw. You can also use cabs throughout the city, in which fares will start at 8 zł and cost 3 zł per kilometer during the day. Taxis can be called through the following companies: Glob Cab Taxi (☎666 009 668 www.globcabtaxi.pl) and VIP Taxi Warsaw (☎791 550 525 www.viptaxiwarsaw.pl).

auschwitz

Auschwitz-Birkenau is located about an hour and a half outside Kraków by public transportation. The concentration camp is found in the city of Oświęcim, 50 kilometers west of Kraków. What is colloquially known as "Auschwitz" is divided into three parts: Auschwitz I, Auschwitz II-Birkenau, and Auschwitz III. The last part is not open for tours, and a shuttle bus runs regularly between Auschwitz I and II. If you take a bus from Kraków, the bus will drop you off in front of the Auschwitz-Birkenau Memorial and Museum.

SIGHTS

Perhaps the best known of the concentration camps, Auschwitz-Birkenau was the largest of the Nazi concentration camps and understandably is taken by many as representative of one of the greatest tragedies in human history. A short distance from Kraków, the grounds offer visitors a sobering, poignant experience. The site witnessed some terrible crimes and as a result demands certain standards of respect. Certain blocks forbid camera usage out of respect for their specific exhibits, flash is forbidden indoors, and visitors are asked to remain silent inside of the gas chambers. While not forbidden, it is in poor taste to take selfies and questionable to chat loudly or pose for pictures with the blocks, crematoria, and ruins of warehouses. A visit to the concentration camp, or any concentration camp, is a deeply emotional lesson on humanity's capacity for both evil and compassion. Interspersed in the narrative of suffering, there remain many uplifting stories of courage and selflessness among the prisoners. To get as much out of the experience as possible, stay focused on the tour, and the gravity of what you are witnessing and, above all, prioritize respect for the area and its victims with your behavior. Guided tours are available and should be reserved online.

The Auschwitz-Birkenau Memorial and Museum tour covers Auschwitz I and Auschwitz II-Birkenau. Each site takes at least 90 minutes to fully visit, and a more thorough visit could easily take longer. Auschwitz III is not open for visitation. The tour includes exhibits of collections of prisoners' possessions, pictures of prisoners, a display of prison attire, cans of Zyklon B used in gas chambers, information on Josef Mengele's sadistic experiments, a visit to barracks and crematoriums, and a visit to a memorial enacted in Birkenau, among other elements. The tour begins at Auschwitz I and continues on at Auschwitz II-Birkenau with a shuttle bus taking visitors between the sites.

Three different tours exist. General tours last about 3½ hr. and visit both camps. One-day study tours last about 6 hr. and include the Central Sauna, a visit to different crematoria, and extra exhibits. While admission to the grounds is free, the tours are not.

i Admission free. General tour 40 zł, reduced 30 zł. 6 hr. study tour 65 zł, reduced admission 30 zł. Museum open daily Apr-May 8am-6pm; June-Aug 8am-7pm; Sept 8am-5pm; Oct 8am-4pm; Nov 8am-3pm; Dec 8am-2pm; Jan 8am-3pm; Feb 8am-4pm; Mar 8am-5pm.

ESSENTIALS
Emergency

- **EMERGENCY NUMBER:** ☎112

- **LOCAL POLICE:** ☎338 475 200

- **TOURIST INFORMATION:** Oświęcim Tourist Center. (12 St. Leszczyńskiej str. ☎33 843 00 91 www.it.oswiecim.pl Open May-Sept 8am-6pm; Oct 8am-5pm; Nov-Mar 8am-4pm; Apr 8am-5pm.) Auschwitz Jewish Center Tourist Information Point. (Pl. Ks. J. Skarbka 5, 32-600 Oświęcim. ☎338 447 002 www.ajcf.pl. Open Apr-Sept M-F 10am-6pm, Su 10am-6pm, closed Saturdays; Oct-Mar M-F 10am-5pm, S 10am-5pm, closed Saturdays.)

Getting There

There are many organized tours to Auschwitz, such as those run through SeeKrakow or Cracow Tours, and booking a tour through such agencies can save you the trouble of having to find transportation. However, it is also not difficult to make your way to Auschwitz independently. Buses leave regularly from Kraków main station, also called Kraków Główny railway station, or Dworzec Główny, and will drop you off in front of the Auschwitz-Birkenau State Museum. The station is conveniently located in the northeast side of Old Town, right by the Main Market Sq. and is within easy walking distance of most accommodations. You can purchase tickets online at www.lajkonikbus.pl by entering the departure station as Kraków and the destination as Oświęcim. This would reserve a seat for you, but, in a rush, tickets can be bought at the ticket offices in the bus station or on board the bus as well. The earliest bus leaves from Kraków at 5:30am, and the last bus leaves Auschwitz at 7:30pm; each way costs 13zł. Oświęcim and Kraków are on either ends of the bus route, and the trip will take 1hr. 25min. each way.

kraków

By our best unscientific estimates, Kraków is at least half fowl—but that's no foul. The Krakovians adore their pigeon friends, and some will even go as far as to let the birds rest on top of them. The touristy areas, Wawel Hill and Main Market Square in particular, are covered in the creatures, but the locals pay little attention to their fluttering. As legend has it, the animals are former knights, loyal to a prince past and transformed into avian form by the hand of a witch. There's much more to the city than its wildlife, however. Formerly the capital of Poland, the city is rife with historical buildings and noteworthy architecture, all wrapped up in legends and lore. The Wawel Castle on Wawel Hill, for example, served as the seat of Polish royalty for centuries—and the hill is said to have been the home of a dragon who demanded the sacrifice of young maidens. In Kraków you'll also find sights like the Main Market Square, St. Mary's Basilica, and Schindler's Factory. At a short distance from the city stands the Wieliczka Salt Mine, which hosts over a million tourists a year. The former concentration camp Auschwitz-Birkenau is also easily accessed from

Kraków, though you don't have to leave the city to better understand Jewish history and culture. The Jewish Quarter of Kraków is well developed and culturally rich, an homage to the past influences of Jewish culture on the city, and an insight into contemporary Jewish culture. Much of the city feels medieval and historical, but places like the Museum of Contemporary Art in Kraków will jolt you back into this century.

SIGHTS

WAWEL CASTLE

Wawel 5 ☎124 225 155 www.wawel.krakow.pl

For centuries, Poland's royalty resided atop a hill in Kraków, calling home the medieval Wawel Castle. (It definitely sounds better in Polish—more of a V sound.) The site the Castle occupies, Wawel Hill, is itself remarkably old, settled in the Paleolithic Age. The hill carries its own lore, including that of the Wawel Dragon. Said to live in a cave in the hill, the dragon terrorized the town, demanding the regular sacrifice of young girls. Coronations have been held in Wawel Cathedral since that of Władysław the Short. Several generations of Polish rulers took residence in Wawel Castle until it was occupied by the Austrians. Once again in Polish possession, the Wawel Castle is a large complex with several exhibitions operating as a museum. Among them: the Wawel Cathedral, the State Rooms, the Royal Private Apartments, the Crown Treasury and Armory, Leonardo da Vinci's *Lady with an Ermine*, Oriental Art, Lost Wawel, the Dragon's Den, Sandomierska Tower, and Wawel Architecture and Gardens. The last three are seasonal exhibits.

i From Main Market Square, walk onto Grodzka and continue onto droga Do Zamku. The castle is on your right. State Rooms 18 zł. Royal Private Apartments 25 zł. Crown Treasure and Armory 18 zł. State Rooms and Royal Private Apartments open Tu-F 9:30am-5pm, Sa-Su 10am-5pm, closed Mondays. Crown Treasure and Armory open M 9:30am-1pm, Tu-F 9:30am-5pm, Sa-Su 10am-5pm. For more detailed prices and hours for individual exhibitions, please check the website for the most up-to-date information.

MUSEUM OF CONTEMPORARY ART IN KRAKÓW

Lipowa 4 ☎122 634 000

A cafe, shop, and, of course, contemporary art exhibit, the MOCAK is one of the finest ways to spend an afternoon in Kraków. Highlighting the works of present-day artists, both Polish and foreign, the building itself, glass and concrete, is as interesting as the art it presents. The museum is quite new, having opened in 2010, and emphasizes Polish contemporary art that provokes social commentary. Within its walls, there's intellectual stimulation for the artistically inclined, whimsy for the artistically-disinclined. Have you seen art nowadays? Weird is good, and it's better than spending a day looking at portraits of constipated royalty. Six wives? Looking like that, Henry? Now that's just weird.

i From Main Market Square, walk onto Sienna, and continue onto Starowiślna. Continue onto most Powstańców Śląskich. Turn right onto Lipowa. The museum is on the right. 10 zł, students 5 zł. Free on Tuesdays. Open Tu-Su 11am-7pm, closed Mondays.

WIELICZKA SALT MINE

Daniłowicza 10, Wieliczka ☎122 787 302 www.wieliczka-saltmine.com

Attracting over a million tourists a year, the Wieliczka Salt Mine is undoubtedly popular. Once fully operational, the mine was built in the 13th century and produced table salt back when the industry was lucrative. Now it serves as a source of national pride as one of the 12 UNESCO-listed sites in Poland. The mine is a beautiful collaboration between man and nature, proof that sometimes beauty isn't skin deep, but actually 135m under the ground. Among the works exhibited you'll find a salt rendition of *The Last Supper*, plus altars and statues. The mine is also home to the Chapel of St Kinga, a majestic structure with a salt chandelier. The shortest guided route through the mine is about 2½hr. long, and they all include a lot of walking. It seems like a lot of effort, but considering this is as interesting as salt is probably going to get, it is well worth your time.

i *The salt mine is accessible from Kraków by public bus 304, which can be boarded from the Jubilat station by the supermarket. Get off 8 stops later at Wieliczka Kościół. From here it is a 10-minute walk to the mines. 79 zł, students 64 zł. Open daily Apr-Oct 7:30am-7:30pm; Nov-Mar 8am-5pm.*

MAIN MARKET SQUARE & CLOTH HALL
Rynek Główny 1-3   ☎124 335 400

Originally designed in 1257, Main Market Square has been the centerpiece of Kraków's Old Town since medieval times, functioning as a central meeting place for Krakovians and pigeons. The pigeons aren't that special but appear special due to their seemingly infinite quantity. At the center of the square is Cloth Hall, built in the 14th century and one of the oldest shopping malls in the world. It wasn't exactly a great place for the cool kids to hang out around after school, but convenient for traveling merchants from foreign countries to trade goods. Since then, Cloth Hall has become less for traveling merchants, more for traveling tourists, with a multitude of stalls lining the inside walls, presenting prime souvenir opportunities. Overlooking the square is St. Mary's Basilica. Its colorful interior is even more impressive than its height. One of the largest medieval squares in Europe, Main Market Square is definitely a must-see.

i *St. Mary's Basilica 10 zł, students 5 zł. Cloth Hall open Tu-Su 10am-6pm, closed Mondays. St. Mary's Basilica open M-Sa 11:30am-6pm, Su 2-6pm.*

SCHINDLER'S FACTORY
Lipowa 4   ☎122 571 017 www.mhk.pl/branches/oskar-schindlers-factory

In the small district of Podgórze, where the Jewish Ghetto was once centered during World War II, stands Schindler's Factory, which reopened in 2010 as a modern museum devoted to showcasing Kraków's daily struggles with war and its atrocities during the Nazi occupation. While currently an interactive museum, the factory was once home to an enamel factory run by Oskar Schindler, who hired Jewish employees from the ghetto, at first to reduce costs of production, but later on to prevent their persecution at great personal cost and risk. By the end of the war, Schindler had saved the lives of about 1200 Jewish workers at his factory. The museum has dedicated a portion of its space to features on Oskar Schindler's life and legacy but otherwise holds its main focus on the history of World War II and its influences on Kraków. The permanent exhibit called "Kraków under Nazi Occupation 1939-1945" features several multimedia installations with photos, recordings, and historical documents. Inside the museum is also a screening room for lectures, movies, and meetings. Kraków is otherwise a vibrant city, but Schindler's Factory serves as a somber reminder of Poland's more troubling history.

i *From Main Market Square, walk onto Sienna and continue onto Starowiślna. Continue onto Most Powstańców Śląskich. Turn right onto Lipowa, where the factory is on the right. 21 zł, students 16 zł. Free on Mondays. Open Apr-Oct M 10am-4pm, Tu-Su 9am-8pm, first Monday of the month 10am-2pm; Nov-Mar 10am-2pm, Tu-Su 10am-6pm.*

FOOD

ALCHEMIA $$
Estery 5   ☎124 212 200 en.alchemia.com.pl

Part pub, part restaurant, part music venue, Alchemia dabbles in everything, and it's got the Midas touch. The music festival Kraków Jazz Autumn, organized by Alchemia in conjunction with other groups, has received great praise, including the title of "Event of the Year 2012" by Jazzarium. The pub and restaurant, located off of bustling plac Nowy in trendy Kazimierz, is one of the most popular in the

CRACOW HOSTEL $

Rynek Główny 18   ☎124 291 106 www.cracowhostel.com

Sitting smack in the middle of Main Market Square, Cracow Hostel boasts a great location, surrounded by the life and hype of Cloth Hall by day and clubs, pubs, and bars by night. In addition to typical hostel amenities—including laundry service, towels, and locks—Cracow also has a cozy shared living room featuring high ceilings and a winding staircase leading up to well-lit rooms and dorms. The hostel takes up residence in a building hailing from the 14th century, making a stay here basically like a history lesson. With its direct view of Cloth Hall and abundant sunlight in the rooms, Cracow Hostel presents the perfect selfie opportunity for those looking to change their social media pictures. After all, if a backpacker backpacks but the internet doesn't see it, did he really go backpacking?

i From Main Market Square, the hostel is at the southeast corner of the square, by the Church of St. Wojciech. Dorms 43-60 zł. Check-in 1pm. Check-out 11am. Reception 24hr.

GREG & TOM BEER HOUSE HOSTEL $$

Floriańska 43   ☎124 212 864 beerhouse.gregtomhostel.com

Weekly live music events and daily pub crawls give this hostel its bubbly atmosphere. Located 5min. away from Main Market Square, Greg and Tom's Beer Hostel stands on a busy street with plenty of bars and clubs around to check out. Don't feel like going out? Worry not, for the hostel is also equipped with its own pub, providing plenty of opportunities for people to meet, talk, and drop their guards and, if willing, their pants too. With a young, vibrant atmosphere, Greg and Tom's provides plugs by every bed, reliable Wi-Fi, and, to top it off, good food from its restaurant, proving to be a great option for anyone with respectable priorities.

i From Main Market Square, find plac Mariacki and walk toward it. Walk onto Floriańska. The hostel is on the right about three blocks down. Dorms 57-70 zł. Breakfast included. Check-in 2pm. Check-out 10am. Reception 24hr.

MOSQUITO HOSTEL $$

rynek Kleparski 4   ☎124 301 461 www.mosquitohostel.com

Despite what its name suggests, this hostel actually does not suck—blood, or anything else—at all. Located just off Main Market Square, Mosquito is the cool mom of hostels. With daily events ranging from shisha evenings to Polish shot tastings and homemade cookie nights, Mosquito will responsibly introduce you to the wonders and blunders of Mad Dogs (trademark Polish shots) while also filling you with baked love. The hostel won't do your taxes or help you move into college, but it'll support you non-stop with a nearby supermarket, a Polish restaurant, and an ATM all open 24hr., making sure even your jetlagged sleep schedules are accommodated. All that in addition to 24hr. reception adds up to a great deal, and Mosquito is sure to take care of most of your needs.

i From Main Market Square, walk down Szczepańska. Turn right onto Basztowa and then turn left onto rynek Kleparski. The hostel is on the right. Dorms 65-80 zł. Laundry free. Check-in 1pm. Check-out 11am. Reception 24hr.

kraków

józefa street

Bright colors of galleries juxtaposed against the walls of peeling paint give this street its uniquely artistic atmosphere. Nestled in the Kazimierz district, the street is home to the High Synagogue, which stands as a reminder of the Jewish history that the street was borne out of. Once the center of Jewish life in Kraków, Kazimierz became one of the most dangerous districts of the city during the Communist Era. But since then, the district, and with it, Józefa Street has been revived by a newfound air of youthful hipsters and artists. The art galleries that line the street show that while the street may not be young and fresh, the talent certainly is. The works, ranging from traditional to contemporary works and cups shaped like heads, will make you question the definition of art. Is this art? Don't let it get to you; definitions are too mainstream anyway. The street is home to a slew of old and new shops, boutiques as well as cafes, bars, and plenty of opportunities to update your Snapchat story. With its vibrant atmosphere, Józefa has become a great hub for tourists and artists alike, and a must-stop place for anyone with that unique friend you never know what to buy for. What do you mean you didn't like your 'I Love Kraków' mug?

square, and deservedly so. In recent years, Alchemia has become increasingly well known and fields a steady stream of patrons every night. Medieval meets quirky, the pub decor feels old but not outdated. Candles illuminate the space, optimal for those of us who look better in dim light anyway. On the other hand, the kitchen part of the establishment, Alchemia od Kuchni, is sleek, modern, and well lit. While vodka shots are best taken in the dark, Alchemia understands that food deserves to be experienced with all five senses.

i From Market Square, walk down Sienna toward Stolarska. Continue onto Starowiślna. Turn right onto Dietla. Turn left onto Świętego Sebastiana, and continue onto Brzozowa, and then Jakuba. Make a right onto Warszauera. Alchemia is on the left. Street food 15-19 zł. Burgers 22-25 zł. Entrees 22-36 zł. Draught beer 6-11 zł. Cider 11-13 zł. Restaurant open M-Th 9am-11pm, F-Sa 8am-midnight, Su 8am-11pm. Club open M 10am-4am, Tu-Su 9am-4am.

PASJO CAFÉ
$
Wielopole 7 ☎782 101 201

A cozy Kraków cafe, Pasjo meets the highest standard we hold: the kind of place we'd want to see in the morning. Layered coffee sacks decorate the bar at the entrance; tables and armchairs fill the rest of the space. The overall ambiance is calming and pleasant, and Pasjo is one of the best places in the city for relaxing, indulgent cup of coffee. Their breakfast options are fresh and filling—we suggest opting for one of the simpler options like bread, butter, and scrambled eggs. However you like your eggs, Pasjo will come through.

i From Main Market Square, head down on Sienna toward Stolarska. Continue onto Wielopole. The cafe is on the right. Coffee drinks 6 -15 zł. Egg breakfasts 9-16 zł. Burgers 17-28 zł. Open M-Th 8am-8pm, F 8am-10pm, Sa 9am-10pm, Su 9am-8pm.

CHEDER CAFÉ
$
Józefa 36 ☎124 311 517

Hebrew for "room," Cheder is indeed that and more. Solidly in the Jewish Quarter of the city, the cafe occupies a former prayer house and bases its menu and decor off the culture. Armchairs, bookshelves, and a large carpet seating area compose the main fixtures of the place, accented with Jewish elements like the image of a menorah. Mint tea and hummus grace the menu as universal favorites—in layman's terms: Good. Put in mouth. The cafe prides itself as a Jewish meeting point and cultural hub, hosting various educational events on topics such as the Hebrew alphabet. Regardless of whether you're Jewish, the cafe is worth a visit. Wi-Fi and good coffee? Universal.

i From Main Market Square, walk down Sienna, then continue onto Starowiślna. Turn right onto Dietla. Walk down a block, and then turn left onto Świętego Sebastiana, continuing onto Brzozowa and then Jakuba. About two blocks down, turn right onto Józefa, where Cheder is on the left. Coffee drinks 8-12 zł. Teas 5-12 zł. Pitas 13 zł. Open daily 10am-10pm.

MOABURGER $

Mikołajska 3   ☎124 212 144

Thought by some to be the best burger joint in the city, it's definitely somewhere at the top of the list. Its meat comes on the most satisfying six inches (of bun) you've ever had and dips into unique flavors like mint yogurt and beetroot. Next to the Main Market Square, Moaburger is a Stare Miasto gem, close to many popular sights. The restaurant is slightly more upscale and quirky than your run-of-the-mill diner, but at the end of the day, it gives the people what they want: meat on bread. A New Zealand joint, Moaburger is the second-best thing to come from the land of the kiwis—Lorde is lord(e)—and a strong contender for the best-burger-in-Kraków debate that inexplicably rages on.

i From Main Market Square, walk onto Sienna toward Stolarska until turning left onto Mały Rynek. Beef burgers 17-27 zł. Vegetarian burgers 16-18 zł. Chicken burgers 17-22 zł. Open M-Sa 11am-11pm, Su noon-9pm.

NIGHTLIFE

MIEJSCE

Estery 1   ☎783 096 016

Sharing a name and owners with a retro furniture store, this Kazimierz bar draws significant influence from its sibling establishment. Quirky and colorful pieces fill the place, a clean break from the dark, mysterious style of neighboring Alchemia. On the first day, God said "Let there be light," and only Miejsce listened. Another flavor of hipster in the Kazimierz 50 shades, Miejsce is a calm and comfortable place to grab a drink.

i From Main Market Square, walk down Sienna toward Stolarska. Continue onto Starowiślna. Turn right onto Dietla. Turn left onto Świętego Sebastiana, and continue onto Brzozowa, and then Jakuba. Make a right onto Miodowa, and left onto Estery. The bar is on the right. Alcoholic drinks 12-21 zł. Tea 6-8 zł. Wine 9 zł. Open M-Th 10am-midnight, F-Sa 10am-5am, Su 10am-midnight.

KLUB PIĘKNY PIES

Bożego Ciała 9

Since it bears a name that translates to "Beautiful Dog," we are inclined to like this place. After all, we love all things dog—pugs, pomeranians, hot dogs, doggy style. Hip posters adorn the walls, red, black, and grey, of Klub Piękny Pies. Another Jewish Quarter bar and club, Piękny Pies is a magnet for the creative Kraków crowd. The club changes location like Taylor Swift changes boyfriends. (That is, sensibly and with thoughtful deliberation to move on to better things.) At home now in the Kazimierz area, Piękny Pies remains as popular as it was elsewhere. The venue leans toward rock and indie music, often bringing in live artists as well. Fiercely loved, the place keeps full and chatty late into the night.

i From Main Market Square, walk on Sienna toward Stolarska and continue onto Starowiślna. Turn right onto Dietla and walk for about three blocks until turning left onto Bożego Ciała. Piekny Pies is on your right. Cover for events varies. Cocktails 11-30 zł. Wine 7 zł. Prosecco 4 zł. Open daily 4pm-late.

the tale of the krakow dragon

There's nothing like a story of rags to riches, and this one starts with a dragon so it's got to be good. Legend has it that there once was a dragon that lived under Wawel Hill in Krakow, and every now and then it terrorized the village. In exchange for defeating the dragon, the King offered the throne after his death, and of course, because he could, his daughter's hand in marriage as well. One day, a young shoemaker named Krak challenged the dragon by placing a sulphur-soaked sheep in front of the dragon's lair, which it promptly gobbled up. The dragon was next seen roaring in pain and drinking half the Vistula River, after which is exploded and died. But how? Well, Young Krak would have been happy to tell you that sulphur is in fact flammable, and the dragon essentially died from its own flames. Because science. The moral of the story is, of course, that it does indeed pay to be a nerd, and sometimes payment comes in the form of royalty and a city named after you. Stay in school, kids.

ESZEWERIA
Józefa 9   ☎122 920 458

If your grandma opened a pub. (The cooler one, though.) Considering its dark and antique-y vibe, it's mildly surprising prune juice isn't on the menu. Brooding and soulful, Eszeweria is the place to work on your Tumblr poetry. (Bet it's going great, Frost.) Old couches and lamps define Eszeweria, making for a dimly lit, romantic aesthetic. Enjoy your drink inside or outside in the garden seating. The place keeps full but not boisterous; time rambles on here in the tranquil space. In the Kazimierz district, it's easy to wander from pub to pub, and this is certainly one worth trying.

i From Main Market Square walk on Sienna toward Stolarska and continue onto Starowiślna. Turn right onto Dietla. Turn left onto Bożego Ciała, and then left onto Józefa. Eszeweria is on the right. Beer 6-11 zł. Wine 8-40 zł. Coffee 6-9 zł. Open daily noon-late. Garden open noon-10pm.

ESSENTIALS
Practicalities

- **TOURIST INFORMATION CENTERS:** InfoKrakow is the official city information network run by Kraków. There are 5 tourist centers run in Old Town, as well as a hotline (☎124 320 060 Open daily 9am-5pm) available to call. They are Cloth Hall (Sukiennice) Tourist Center (Rynku Glowny Open daily 9am-7pm), Wyspianski Pavillon (Pawilon Wyspianskiego) Tourist Center (2 plac Wszystkich Swietych Square, at Grodzka, open daily 9am-5pm). Tourist Information Center (2 Sw. Jana Open daily 9am-7pm). Tourist Information Center (Szpitalna 25 Open daily May-Oct 9am-7pm; Nov-Apr 9am-5pm). Tourist Service Centre (Powisle 11 Open daily 9am-7pm).

- **BANKS/ATMS:** ATMs can be found all around the city outside or inside banks that are readily available in the shopping centers, on campuses, or public spaces in the city, especially in central Old Town.

- **INTERNET:** Internet access is not difficult to find within the city. At the airport, free Wi-Fi is available for an hour, and most cafes and restaurants will have free Wi-Fi available. Public libraries (buildings that end with "Biblioteka Publiczna") will also have free Wi-Fi available, but otherwise there are also internet cafes around the city that offer fast Wi-Fi at a small price such as Planet Internet Cafe (Rynek Główny 24 Open daily 10am-10pm) or Internet Cafe Hetmańska (Bracka 4 Open 24hr.).

- **POST OFFICE:** Most Kraków shopping malls will have a post office. The main office is on the edge of Old Town, just outside Planty Park. (Westerplatte 20 ☎124 210 348 Open M-F 7:30am-8:30pm, Sa 8am-2pm)

Emergency

- **EMERGENCY NUMBER:** ☎112
- **POLICE:** ☎997
- **AMBULANCE:** ☎999
- **FIRE:** ☎998
- **HOSPITALS:** The following are 24hr. hospitals with emergency wards that are obliged to help anyone who turns up regardless of nationality or health insurance. University Hospital of Krakow (Mikołaja Kopernika 36 ☎124 247 000). The Hospital of the Ministry of Internal Affairs (ul. Kronikarza Galla 25 ☎126 151 734)
- **PHARMACIES:** Magiczna Pharmacy. (ulica Ćwiklińskiej 10 ☎126 581 001 Open 24hr.)

Getting There

It is easy to use public transportation to get from the airport to the city center. There are a total of three bus lines that run: the 292 bus runs during the day and comes every 20 minutes; the 208 bus also runs during the day and comes every hour; and the 902 bus runs during the night between 11pm and 4am every hour. The tickets cost 4 zł and can be purchased at the RELAY shop in Terminal 1, at the vending machine at the bus stop, or from the driver. The journey from the airport to the Kraków Głowny station, called "Dworzec Glowny Wschod," takes about 40 minutes.

Taxis are also available at the airport through Kraków Airport Taxi, Kraków airport's official taxi service. The taxi ride from the airport to the city center costs about 75 zł, and reservations can be made online: www.krktaxi.pl/en/order_a_taxi_online.

Getting Around

Public Transportation

There is no subway in Kraków, but there is a system of trams and buses that connect districts in Kraków with Old Town. A one-way ticket for both trams and buses is 3.80 zł, and a two-way ticket is 7.20 zł. You can also purchase tickets for 20 minutes (2.80 zł), 40 minutes (3.80 zł), 1hr. (5 zł), or 90 minutes (6 zł) as well. Tickets can be purchased in blue ticketing machines by several bus and tram stops, or you can purchase a 1hr. ticket from the driver. Once boarding the tram or bus, be sure to insert your tickets into the yellow validating machines to start using the ticket. Once it's been validated, the ticket no longer needs to be validated again unless it is for a round-trip journey.

There is no public transportation that runs within Old Town, but it is very walkable and the town can be crossed by foot in about 20 minutes.

Taxis

Taxis are readily available at a relatively small price in Kraków, and fares should not go over 120 zł within city boundaries. Maximum rates within the main urban zone are 2.80 zł per kilometer during daytime on weekdays, and taxi ranks can be found around the city in streets such as ul. Rzeźnicza, ul. Retoryka, and ul. Bernardyńska.

kraków

poland essentials

VISAS

Poland is a member of the EU, and also a member of the Schengen area. Citizens of Australia, Canada, New Zealand, the US, and many other non-EU countries do not need a visa for stays of up to 90 days. However, if you plan to spend time in other Schengen countries, note that the 90-day period of time you are allowed to visit without a visa applies cumulatively to all Schengen countries.

MONEY

Despite being a member of the EU, Poland is not in the Eurozone and uses the Polish złoty (PLN or zł.) as its currency.

In restaurants, it is customary to tip 10% of the bill, or 15% if the service was exceptional. Be careful with saying "Thank you" or "Dziękuję" to the waiter when he comes to pick up the bill, since it usually means you don't want any change back. For taxis, tipping is not expected, but you may round up the bill or tip around 10% for good service.

ATMs in Poland are common and convenient. They are often located in airports, train stations and major pedestrian areas. The two major international money networks are MasterCard/Maestro/Cirrus and Visa/PLUS. To find out what out-of-network or international fees you may be subject to by using ATMs, call your bank.

ALCOHOL

The minimum age to purchase alcohol in Poland is 18, though technically there is no minimum age to drink alcohol (woo!). Remember to drink responsibly and to never drink and drive. The legal blood alcohol content (BAC) for driving in Poland is under 0.02%, significantly lower than the US limit of 0.08%.

PORTUGAL

Portugal draws hordes of backpackers by fusing its timeless inland towns and majestic castles with industrialized cities like Lisbon, whose graffiti-covered walls separate bustling bars from posh fado restaurants. The original backpackers, Portuguese patriarchs like Vasco da Gama, pioneered the exploration of Asia, Africa, and South America, and the country continues to foster such discovery within its borders, with wine regions like the Douro Valley, immaculate forests and mountains in its wild northern region, and 2000km of coastline for tourists to traverse and travel.

greatest hits

- **BAIRRO ALTO NIGHTLIFE.** Don't fear crowd-induced pit stains in this neighborhood—everyone drinks on the sidewalks (p. 616).

- **TAKE A TIME OUT.** **Time-Out Market** (p. 614) in Lisbon is that place where all the best chefs in Lisbon decided to cook their favorite dishes under one roof every single day. You're probably going to want to check it out.

- **LIFE'S A BEACH:** The **Praia Dona Ana** (p. 626) in Lagos is one of the most photographed shorelines in Portugal.

PORTUGAL

ATLANTIC OCEAN

Vila Nova de Cerveira
Valença do Minho
Caminha
Minho
Viana do Castelo
MINHO
Parque Nacional da Peneda-Gerês
Serra-Do Gerês
Caldas de Gerês
Lima
Parque Natural de Montesinho
Bragança
Cávado
Barcelos
Braga
Guimarães
Costa Verde
Tâmega
TRÁS-OS-MONTES
Mirandela
Miranda do Douro
Amarante
Vila Real
Parque Natural do Alvão
DOURO LITORAL
Serra Do Marão
Parque Natural do Douro Internacional
DOURO ALTO
Porto
Espinho
Douro
Ovar
Aveiro
Viseu
BEIRA ALTA
BEIRA LITORAL
Luso
Buçaco
Mondego
Guarda
Manteigas
Serra Da Estrêla
Sabugal
Coimbra
Parque Natural da Serra da Estrêla
Sortelha
Figueira da Foz
Conímbriga
Zêzere
Serra Da Gardunha
Monsanto
BEIRA BAIXA
Leiria
Batalha
Castelo Branco
Nazaré
São Martinho do Porto
Fátima
Alcobaça
Tomar
Ilhas Berlengas
Caldas da Rainha
Serra De Aire
Cabo Carvoeiro
Peniche
Óbidos
Tejo
Castelo de Vide
Marvão
ESTREMADURA
RIBATEJO
Santarém
Crato
Portalegre
Serra De São Mamede
SPAIN
Ericeira
Vila Franca de Xira
Mafra
Sintra
Queluz
ALTO ALENTEJO
Estremoz
Elvas
Cascais
Lisboa
Estoril
Parque Natural de Arrábida
Setúbal
Évora Monte
Troia Peninsula
Évora
Cabo Espichel
Sesimbra
Alcácer do Sal
Baía de Setúbal
Costa Azul
Santiago do Cacém
Sines
Beja
Guadiana
BAIXO ALENTEJO
Mira
Mértola
Costa Dourada
Lagos
Silves
ALGARVE
Portimão
Albufeira
Tavira
Cabo de São Vicente
Sagres
Faro
Olhão
Vila Real de Santo António
Golfo de Cádiz

0   50 kilometers
0   50 miles

lisbon

Portugal's capital is a mosaic, comprised of different neighborhoods that all come together to form the cohesive metropolis that is Lisbon. Each district has its own indelible character, from the graffiti-covered party that is Bairro Alto to chic Chiado and on to touristy Baixa and the crumbling tiles of Alfama—cross a single street or descend one steep staircase and you're someplace new. As is typical in Europe, the classic-to-the-point-of-cliché juxtaposition of ancient and modern holds here. But the true joy of Lisbon comes in peeling back the different layers of "old" that simultaneously exist. Pre-WWI tram cars run through the streets past buildings reconstructed after the earthquake of 1755. These are mixed in with remnants of the Renaissance, the Moorish invasion, and the Iron Age. Together, all of these layers form Lisbon, a city as full of surprises as it is of history. To experience its character to the fullest, get lost here. Let your nose lead you to *sardinhas assadas;* stumble through an alleyway to find an architectural marvel; talk to the locals at the hole-in-the-wall and take their advice. We promise you won't regret it.

SIGHTS

☒ TORRE DE BELÉM

Torre de Belém   ☎21 362 00 34

Portugal's most famous tower has risen out of the water (except at low tide, when it's connected to the shore by a narrow, sandy isthmus) from the banks of the Tejo for nearly 500 years, gracing visitors' memories and souvenir stores' postcards since its completion in 1519. Be prepared to relive childhood games (no, not The Floor is Lava) as you pretend to fire cannons on two different levels. Then head downstairs and check out the prison cells and ammunition area (hopefully this doesn't also remind you of your childhood). It's worth going up all the way to the top to see breathtaking panoramic views of Belém and the Tejo. There is also a rhinoceros carving in homage to the real rhino the king tried to bring back for the pope, because nothing garners favor from the pope like a large, horned animal.

i From Mosteiro dos Jerónimos, take the unmarked underground walkway in front of the monastery (from entrance, head toward the river; it's a small stairway) to other side of road and tracks and walk west along the river (to the right as you face the water) about 15min. Alternatively, walk in the same direction on the monastery's side of the road and take the pedestrian walkway over the road at the tower. €5, over 65 €2.50, students and under 14 free. Su before 2pm free for all. Combined ticket with Mosteiro dos Jerónimos €10. Open May-Sept Tu-Su 10am-6:30pm, Oct-Apr Tu-Su 10am-5:30pm. Last entry 30min. before close.

☒ MOSTEIRO DOS JERÓNIMOS

Pr. do Império   ☎21 362 00 34   www.mosteirojeronimos.pt

The Hieronymite Monastery was established in 1502 to honor Vasco da Gama's expedition to India. We're guessing the explorer's spirit is pleased with this ornate tribute. The Manueline building has the detail of its Gothic predecessors and the sweeping elegance of the oncoming Renaissance. In the 1980s, the monastery was granted World Heritage Site status by UNESCO and remains in pristine condition, both inside and out. The church contains tombs (both symbolic and actual) of Portuguese kings and bishops. Symbolic tombs (cenotaphs) include areas of tribute to Vasco da Gama and Luís de Camões, Portugal's most celebrated poet. Entrance to the cloister is not cheap (€7), but free Su before 2pm), but it's worth it to see one of Lisbon's most beautiful spaces, which somehow retains its charm despite being filled with hordes of tourists. Those on a shoestring budget can see the chapel for free, but the cloister is the real sight here.

i Tram #15E or bus #28, 714, 727, 729, 743, 749, 751 to Mosteiro dos Jerónimos. Free. Cloister and museum €7, over 65 €3.50, under 14 free; Su before 2pm free. Combined ticket with Torre de Belém €10. Monastery open Oct-Aug T-Su 10am-5:30pm, May-Sep T-Su 10am-6:30pm (last entry 30 minutes before close. Church open Oct-Aug T-Sa 10am-5pm, Su 2-5pm, May-Sep T-Su 10am-6pm. Free on Sunday after 10pm.

▨ CASTELO DE SÃO JORGE

Castelo de São Jorge ☎21 880 06 20 www.castelosaojorge.pt

Built by the Moors in the 11th century on the highest point in Lisbon, this hilltop fortress was captured by Dom Afonso Henriques, Portugal's first king, in 1147. With one of the best views in Lisbon, the castle also acts as a one-stop shop for the entire historical Lisbon experience. Walk along the ramparts, see live images of Lisbon fed from an ancient periscope, feel like Indiana Jones at archaeological ruins dating from the Iron Age to the Renaissance (whip optional), and gawk at the seemingly random, yet stunningly beautiful, peacocks that strut about. At night, "Lisboa Who Are You?," a show exclusively comprised of images and Portuguese music, tells the story of Lisbon from beginning to end (€15).

i Bus #737, or trams #12E and 28E; follow signs to Castelo €8.50, students and seniors €5, under 10 free. Open daily Mar-Oct 9am-9pm, Nov-Feb 9am-6pm. Last entry 30min. before close. Tours of the dig sites from 10:30am-7:30pm daily every hour to hour and a half. Max 20 people per visit.

MUSEU CALOUSTE GULBENKIAN

Av. de Berna, 45A ☎21 782 30 00 www.museu.gulbenkian.pt

Want an art history survey course for under €5? This museum has a large and eclectic collection of works from the ancient Mesopotamians and Egyptians to the Impressionists and beyond. The collection belonged to native Armenian and oil tycoon Calouste Gulbenkian, who came to Portugal on vacation in 1942 and never left. When he died, he gave his massive art collection to the state, which, like any good state, decided to charge people to look at it. The building itself is hideous, but the treasures inside are not—in particular the illuminated manuscripts from the Middle East to France seem to have been dunked in molten gold, and the dark, quiet room with a garden view is a lovely place to unwind.

i M: São Sebastião, or buses #96, 205, 716, 726, 746, 756. Exit M: São Sebastião at Av. António Augusto de Aguiar (north exit) and go straight uphill along the avenue until you reach the massive Pr. Espanha, then turn right. It is NOT the building that looks like a castle in the park to the right; keep going along the avenue. €4, students under 25 and seniors €2, under 12 free. Temporary exhibits €3-5. Open Tu-Su 10am-6pm.

FOOD

▨ TIME OUT MARKET (MERCADO DO RIBEIRA) $$$

Av. 24 de Julho 49 ☎213 46 11 99 http://www.timeout.com/market/

Time Out Market: that place where all the best chefs in Lisbon decided to cook their favorite dishes under one roof every single day. Time Out invites the best restaurants of Lisbon to a huge food hall where cheeky blurbs explain each one in Portuguese and English, a market after our own heart. Tables get super crowded, so make some friends or designate someone to sit lonely and hungry while everyone races around the stalls for some delicious specialty dishes. Options include sushi, burgers, tartar, seafood, and more. Some of the country's most famous chefs have their own stalls, so bask in the glow of gourmet food at half the price. Getting a full gourmet meal can add up, but it'll be the most delicious arithmetic you've ever done.

i Next to the Mercado do Ribeira. Entrees €8-12, drinks €2-4. Open M-Wed 10am-midnight, Th-Sa 10am-2am, Su 10am-midnight.

Lisbon's hostels are legendary in quality; for only a slightly higher price than the rest of the peninsula, you can get near hotel level amenities with a busy social life based exclusively on friends you just made 10 seconds ago. In fact, six of the top ten medium hostels worldwide are in Lisbon according to Hostelworld.

◪ GOODMORNING HOSTEL $$

Praça dos Restauradores, n. 65, 2nd fl.　　☎213 42 11 28 goodmorninghostel.com

Enter through an innocuous souvenir shop, go straight through the door in the back and you're in backpacker Narnia. "Good morning! Here's unlimited Belgian waffles with nutella and oregano crusted grilled cheese for breakfast. Would you like to go to Sintra with our private local tour or maybe on a beach excursion? Make sure you charge your phone (the outlet is safely in your locker with provided key) before unlimited free sangria night. Here are all the recommendations you will ever need, anything else we can do?" Yes. This is pretty much every day at Goodmorning Hostel. They even keep a whole floor available for those that want to extend their reservation (because nearly everyone does).

i M: Rossio. Right inside the tourist shop on the southwest end of the square. 4, 6, 8 and 10 person dorms €23-30. Private double €75. €5 key deposit. Reception 24hr.

◪ TRAVELLER'S HOUSE $$

R. Augusta　　☎021 011 59 22

On the central street of the Baixa downtown, Traveller's House looks like you've accidentally stumbled into a tasteful Manhattan duplex. Before you say "I'm sorry, wrong building" and back out slowly, stay for their unique and cheap events like the night-time boozy street art tour and fado excursion to the best place in the city. Breakfast is literally served to you (a choice of crepes and nutella, granola and yogurt or eggs and bacon) in the wood-floor and carpeted dining room. Actually-wood floors, marble, and plush carpets abound throughout the huge dorms, en-suite privates and living room, so use this as interior design inspiration for when you make enough money to move back to Lisbon for good. Plus, the staff will pretty much plan out your whole trip if you let them.

i M: Baixa-Chiado 4 and 6 bed dorm low season €14-20, high season €20-30. Double private low season €50, high season €60-70. Reception 24hr. Free towel.

HOME HOSTEL $$

R. de São Nicolau 13 2nd fl.　　☎218 885 312 www.homelisbonhostel.com

We wish our homes were more like Home Hostel, a mid-size apartment in Baixa with common spaces that resemble a 19th century wealthy bachelor pad just with free iPads and gaming systems. This Home comes with its own Mama, who serves up traditional Portuguese cuisine plus unlimited drinks every night for an additional price. Soft and cushy bunks come complete with plenty of outlets and reading lamps, though lengthy hallways mean the walk to the bathroom could feel endless. Arrive after 11am and a free shot of ginja awaits; if you ask for it before 11am, they might make an exception (but will also be a bit concerned).

i M: Baixa-Chiado. Walk right down R. Nova do Almada until a left on R. de São Nicolau. Walk until just after the intersection with R. dos Douradores, the large Home sign on your right. 4,6,8 person dorm low season €14-18, high season €24-30. Reception 24hr.

▩ POIS, CAFE $$

R. de São João da Praça, 93   ☎21 886 24 97 www.poiscafe.com

This Austrian-run cafe is quite comfortable, with couches, book-lined walls, and even a toy corner. Don't worry if it looks crowded inside; tables are shared. Almost everything on the menu has something inventive in it (e.g. apple and pesto on a veggie sandwich), although some more traditional options are available. Don't skip out on the custom lemonades, even though the coffee is almost as good.

i Tram #28E to Sé. From plaza in front of cathedral, walk to the right of cathedral; the cafe is on the right. Lunch menu €5. Baked goods €2-7. Open Tu-Su 11am-8pm.

PENTA CAFÉ $

R. do Ouro 115-117   ☎912 593 776

In the often overpriced Baixa district, Penta is a humble breath of fresh air. The simple surroundings don't look like much and the stock photos don't do the cheesy goodness justice, but Penta serves up the best tostas (panini-style sandwiches) in Lisbon. Even better they're cheaply priced by length and ingredients, so go crazy with all the toppings you desire and get anything from five centimeters upwards. If you're looking for adventure (basically, every ingredient packed onto the deliciously crunchy bread), we recommend the "Action" tosta. Wash your meter long sandwich down with a piece of meter long cake and huge smoothies (also in infinite combinations, though this time not ordered by length).

i M: Baixa-Chiado. From the Baixa exit, go one block down R. da Vitória and a left on R. do Ouro. Immediately on your left. Loaded tosta €25/meter. M-F 7:30am-8pm.

RESTAURANTE CABAÇAS $$

R. das Gáveas 8   ☎21 346 34 43 https://www.facebook.com/cabacasrestaurante/

One day God visited Lisbon and said, "Let there be three flank steaks cooked on a hot stone for €9," and it was good. Cabaças provides all the high quality raw meat, the stone provides the heat, and you provide the labor (mostly flipping the meat and flipping out at how good it is). The only explanation the menu needs is what kind of meat do you want in absurd quantities and whether you want it fatty or lean, then you're off to carnivorous heaven. Located right between Camoes square in Chiado and the nightlife in Bairro Alto, it's always a popular spot for a filling dinner before crawling through the bars next door.

i M: Baixa Chiado. Take the Chiado exit onto the square. Take R. das Gáveas, on your right. Meat entrees €8-12. Cash only. Open Th-F noon-3pm, 7pm-midnight, Sa-Su 7pm-1am

NIGHTLIFE

Go to Bairro Alto for steep streets lined with tons of cheap bars. This area was made for bar-hopping down towards the river where you can find "Pink Street," a stretch of larger bars with the sidewalk actually rose-colored. In Cais do Sodre by the river larger clubs blast music late at night and later in the summer, outdoor patios open up. Lisbon is a European capital, so dressing nice at larger clubs can be necessary, but the constant uphill ensures that heels will never be expected. Bars are popular from around 11:30pm-2am and clubs don't get going til 3ish, but don't worry about losing your buzz since it's typical (and absolutely legal) to take drinks out onto the street.

▩ LUX

Av. do Infante Dom Henrique   ☎21 882 08 90 www.luxfragil.com

This club is known far and wide as one of the best clubs in Western Europe; Lisboans abroad will tell you that if you visit one discoteca in Lisbon, it has to be this one. The enormous riverside complex has three stories of debauchery, though you'll leave with a few more of your own Chill on the calm rooftop

sintra

When in Lisbon, go to Sintra. Seriously, this idyllic fairytale town is only a 40-minute train ride away and is packed with palaces, castles and mansions—well worth one of your precious days in Portugal. The major attraction is the Pena Palace, a huge summer residence for Portuguese royals built in multiple styles. The patchwork palace is surrounded by a beautiful national park with multiple paths. It's easy to get lost and find some beautiful forgotten water feature or a small village or two. Other noble houses and castles abound. If you insist on limiting yourself to a day, the Moorish castle and slightly eerie mansion Quinta da Regaleira are must-sees.

The town itself is overrun with tourists, but still worth it for a visit to the famous bakery A Piriquita. There you can buy "travesseiros" or "pillows" which, if slept on, would ooze egg and almond cream from their huge pastry shells. Sintra town also specializes in serving the traditional cherry liquor ginja in a cup made entirely of dark chocolate. Pure magic.

with amazing views, start to get schwasty at a slightly more intense bar on the floor below that, then descend into the maelstrom on the lowest level to find a raging disco, howling and shrieking with electronic music. Drinks are pricey (cocktails €8-12) and everything is cutting edge. "We cannot escape from each other" is written all around the main bar, giving creepy single guys a great segue into awful pickup lines. The bouncers tend to be very selective, so just act cool and try to get on their good side by being polite and speaking Portuguese. Dress well—only wear jeans or sneakers if the jeans are super-skinny and the sneakers are canvas high-tops, since the stylin' hipster look tends to play well.

i M: Santa Apolónia, bus #28, 34, 706, 712, 735, 759, 781, 782, 794. Just east of Santa Apolónia train station, on the side of the tracks closest to the river. Cover usually €12. Open Tu-Sa midnight-6am.

◪ ASSOCIAÇÃO LOUCOS & SONHADORES BAR

R. da Rosa 261 ☎962 580 500

A few minutes away from the craziness of the Bairro Alto scene, you'll find a different kind of crazy. The Crazies' and Dreamers' Association sits quietly in a nondescript building, with only a small, mysterious yet welcoming wooden sign on the door. Once inside, you will be glad that this gem is a well-kept secret. Dimly lit, this smoky bar is filled with clutter, paintings, books and the occasional gramophone. The chatter of friends and the smooth sounds of jazz somehow allow it to be simultaneously gritty, sophisticated, and sincere. Beer is cheap, unlimited popcorn flows, and shareable snacks are low-priced and delicious.

i M: Restauradores. Cross the square and take a left onto C.. da Gloria in the northwest corner, then take a right on R. São Pedro de Alcantara. Take a left onto R. Luisa Todi, which becomes Tv. do Conde do Soure. At the intersection with R. da Rosa. Large beer €3, shared plates €3.5-6. Open M-Th 8pm-2am, F-Sa 7pm-3am.

PARK ROOFTOP BAR

Park Calçada do Combro 58 ☎215 914 011

Set atop an elevated parking lot in Bairro Alto, Park fully takes advantage of its 180-degree views of the city with plenty of comfortable wooden furniture scattered around a garden terrace. Considering the sophisticated look and well-made cocktails, the prices should be sky-high, but drinks and food are well-priced all day long. The dance-floor, partially indoors, rotates nightly through live performances and excellent DJs until closing time, much too early for the preference of the young crowd.

i Tram 28E. From Praça Luis de Camões, take R. do Loreto until it turns into Calçada do Combro. On your right, take the stairs all the way to the top of the parking lot. Cocktails €5-7. Open T-Sa 12:30pm-2am, Su 12:30pm-8pm.

BAR ACHÉ COHIBA

Bar R. do Norte 121 ☎213 43 12 10 www.achecohiba.com

Ache Cohiba is a little Havana planted right in the middle of Bairro Alto, complete with the best mojitos and dancers in town. Don't know how to salsa? No problem. The regulars have made it their mission to teach every new kid in town how to dance like a Portuguese Cuban (that is, really well). Come for daily 6-11pm happy hour for super cheap drinks, and, like everywhere else in the neighborhood, enjoy the party that spills out into the streets late at night. This one just has a whole lot more Latin flair.

i M: Baixa-Chiado (Chiado exit). From Praça Luís de Camões, take R. do Norte four blocks up, on your right. Cocktails €5-7. Open M-Th 6pm-2am, F-Sa 6pm-4am, Su 6pm-2am.

K URBAN BEACH CLUB

Av. Brasília ☎21 393 2930 https://www.facebook.com/Urban.Beach.K

K Urban Beach is its own sleek white and chrome peninsula jutting out onto the riverfront. With twinkling lights, glowing lanterns, and beautiful people everywhere, Urban Beach whispers that you too could become one of Lisbon's elite for a night. Check out the seemingly infinite number of bars like islands in a sea of, well, the ocean. The space is a warehouse of sound with multiple dancefloors spinning different genres. Plenty of decorative swimming pools that you probably shouldn't swim in and decorative women hanging out in the numerous VIP sections. Dress well (and be a woman) and you might even get the cover reduced. Make sure to keep the card they hand you at the entrance. You'll have to use it to pay the cover and exit, but you can also use that credit for the surprisingly well-priced drinks. The huge bouncers get very upset if cards are "lost."

i Buses 201, 706, 714, 727, 728, 732, 760 or 774. From Cais do Sodre station, walk west along the waterfront until it turns into Av. Brasilia. Large white building on the left. Cover €10-20 depending on dress and gender, cocktails €5. Open T-Sa 8pm-6am, Su 8pm-midnight.

ESSENTIALS
Practicalities

- **TOURIST OFFICE:** Main Tourist Office. (Pr. Restauradores, 1250 ☎21 347 56 60 www.visitlisboa.com. M: Restauradores, or bus #36, 44, 91, 709, 711, 732, 745, or 759. On west side of Pr. Restauradores, in Palacio da Foz. Open daily 9am-8pm.) The Welcome Center is the city's main tourist office where you can buy tickets for sightseeing buses and the Lisboa Card, which includes transportation and discounted admission to most sights for a flat fee. (R. Arsenal, 15 21 031 28 10) The airport branch is located near the terminal exit. (☎21 845 06 60 Open daily 7am-midnight.) There are also information kiosks in Santa Apolonia, Belem, and on R. Augusta in Baixa.

- **INTERNET:** Biblioteca Municipal Camões has free internet access. (Lg. Calhariz, 17 ☎21 342 21 57 www.blx.cm-lisboa.pt. M: Baixa-Chiado, tram 28E, or bus #58 or 100. From Pr. Lu.s de Cam.es, follow R. Loreto for 4 blocks. Open Jul 16-Sept 15 M-F 11am-6pm; Sept 16-Jul 15 Tu-F 10:30am-6pm.)

- **POST OFFICE:** Correios main office is on Pr. Restauradores. (Pr. Restauradores, 58 ☎21 323 89 71 www.ctt.pt M: Restauradores. Bus #336, 44, 91, 709, 711, 732, 745, or 759. Open M-F 8am-10pm, Sa-Su 9am-6pm.

Emergency

- **POLICE:** Tourism Police Station provides police service for foreigners. (Pr. Restauradores, 1250 }21 342 16 24. M: Restauradores. Bus #36, 44, 91, 709, 711, 732, 745, or 759. On west side of Pr. Restauradores, in Pal.cio da Foz next to the tourist office.)

- **PHARMACY:** Most pharmacies post a schedule of pharmacies open late at night or just look for a lighted, green cross.

- **HOSPITAL/MEDICAL SERVICES:** Lisbon's main hospital is Hospital de São José. (R. Jos. Ant. nio Serrano }21 884 10 00. M: Martim Moniz. Bus #34, 708, or 760. Open 24hr.) Hospital de São Luis is in Bairro Alto. (R. Luz Soriano, 182. M: Baixa-Chiado. From Pr. Lu.s de Cam.es, follow R. Loreto 4 blocks, then turn right onto R. Luz Soriano. Open daily 9am-8pm.)

Getting There
By Plane

All flights land at Aeroporto de Lisboa (LIS; ☎21 841 35 00), near the northern edge of the city. The cheapest way to get to town from the airport is by bus. To get to the bus stop, walk out of the terminal, turn right, and cross the street to the bus stop, marked by yellow metal posts with arrival times of incoming buses. Buses #44 and 745 (€1.75.

15-20min., daily every 25min., 6am-12:15am) run to Pr. Restauradores, where they stop in front of the tourist office. The express AeroBus #1 runs to the same locations (€3.50. 15min., daily every 20min., 7am-11pm) and is a much faster option during rush hours. A taxi downtown costs €10-15, but fares are billed by time, not distance, so watch out for drivers trying to take a longer route.

By Train

Those traveling in and out of Lisbon by train are regularly confused, as there are multiple major train stations in Lisbon, all serving different destinations. The express and inexpensive Alfa Pendular line runs between Braga, Porto, Coimbra, and Lisbon. Regional trains are slow and can be crowded; buses are slightly more expensive but faster and more comfortable. Urbanos trains run from Lisbon to Sintra and to Cascais, with stops along the way, and are very cheap and reliable. Contact Comboios de Portugal for more information (☎80 820 82 08 www.cp.pt). If you want to head south, go to the Entrecampos station. Estação Cais do Sodré is right at the river, a 5min. walk west from Baixa or a quick metro ride to the end of the green line. Estação Rossio is the gorgeous neo-Manueline building between Rossio and Pr. Restauradores and services almost all Lisbon suburbs, with lines ending in Sintra, Cascais, Azambuja, and Sado. Estação Santa Apolónia is one of the main international and inter-city train stations in Lisbon, running trains to the north and east. It is located on the river to the east of Baixa; to get there, take the blue metro line to the end of the line. Trains run between Santa Apolonia and: Aveiro (€26. 2.hr., 16 per day 6am-9:30pm); Braga (€32.50. 3.hr., 4 per day 7am-7pm); Coimbra (€22.50. 2hr., 20 per day 6am-10pm); and Porto (€24-30. 3hr., 16 per day 6am-11pm). Estação Oriente runs southbound trains. The station is near the Parque das Na..es, up the river to the east of the center; take the red metro line to the end of the line. Trains run between Oriente and Faro (€21-22. 3.-4hr., 5 per day 8am-8pm) with connections to other destinations in the Algarve.

By Bus

Lisbon's bus station Sete Rios (☎70 722 33 44 www.rede-expressos.pt) can be accessed by the metro station Jardim Zoologico. Check the Rede Expressos website or get the easy to use mobile app for buses running between Lisbon and Braga (€21. 4-5hr., 14-16 per day 7am-12:15am); Coimbra (€14.50. 2hr., 24-30 per day 7am-12:15am); Lagos (€20. 5hr., 14-16 per day 7:30am-1am); and Porto (€20. 3hr30min, 18-22 per day 7am-12:15am).

Getting Around

Carris (☎21 361 30 00 www.carris.pt) is Lisbon's extensive, efficient, and relatively inexpensive transportation system and is the easiest way to get around the city, which is covered by an elaborate grid of subways, buses, trams, and elevadores (funiculars, useful for getting up the steep hills). We recommend you first purchase a Viva Viagem card for €0.50 at any metro kiosk. Load up the card with the 'zapping' option which allows you to use the money for any type of transportation; if you purchase single-trips the card will only be valid for that particular type of transportation. With the Viva Viagem card bus, metro and tram trips cost €1.25. Prices climb without the card, particularly for the tram and funiculars (€2.85 and €3.60-€5).

If you're using a lot of public transportation, the easiest and most cost-effective option is the unlimited 24hr. bilhete combinado (€6), which can be used on any Carris transport. This means you don't have to go into a metro station to recharge your card before getting on a bus or tram. You can buy the bilhete combinado in any metro station, and you can fill it with up to seven days of unlimited travel.

By Bus

Carris buses (€1.80, €1.25 with Viva Viagem card) go to just about any place in the city, including areas not served by the metro.

By Metro

The metro (€1.25 with Viva Viagem card) has four lines that cross the center of Lisbon and go to the major train stations. Metro stations are marked with a red "M" logo. Trains run daily 6:30am-1am.

By Tram

Trams (€2.85, €1.25 with Viva Viagem card) are used by tourists and locals alike to get around. Many vehicles predate WWI. Lines 28E and 15E are particular popular for sightseeing, so be careful of crowding. Line 28E runs through Graça, Alfama, Baixa, Chiado, and Bairro Alto; line 15E goes from the Pr. Comercio to Belem, passing the clubs of Santos and Alcantara.

By Taxi

You can hail a taxi in Lisbon on streets in the center of town. Train stations and main plazas are good places to find a cab. Bouncers will be happy to call you a cab after dark. Rádio Táxis de Lisboa (☎21 811 90 00) and Teletáxis (☎21 811 11 00) are the main companies.

porto

Okay, let's clear it up once and for all. It's Porto in Portuguese and Oporto in English, ever since the English accidentally added the O (meaning "the") to the name. Now that we've got that settled, enjoy exploring this famous city on a slope. Home to some of the most beautiful condemned buildings you'll ever see, Porto has all the charm of Portugal wrapped into a port city and university town. Porto residents are hugely proud of their city—with a nickname like Ciudad de Invicta (City of Victory), hometown pride is a must. Check out one of the most beautiful bookstores in the world, Livraria Lello, and, for the slightly less literary, investigate their claim to having the most beautiful McDonalds (we'll let you decide). Do a classy port wine tasting in the storehouses across the river and learn that port isn't actually made, grown or stored in Porto. Keep an eye out for several inspirations for the Harry Potter books; JK Rowling spent some time here while writing. (It's not surprising when you see university students in black capes walking past the griffin-decorated fountain.)

SIGHTS

You can discover part of Porto's incredible character by simply wandering the streets and taking in the striking architecture. But that's not to say that there aren't specific sights to be seen. Most sights can be found near the twisting streets of Ribeira, alongside the river, or near the São Bento train station.

If you're in Porto, at least one visit to a winery is mandatory. They're either free or very cheap (under €5), and tours usually run about 30-40min. Most of the tasting occurs across the Douro in **Vila Nova de Gaia** and its 17 massive **port** lodges, and the best way to get to this port authority is to walk across the bottom level of the Ponte de Dom Luís from Ribeira.

IGREJA E TORRE DOS CLÉRIGOS

R. de São Filipe Nery   ☎22 200 17 29

The Torre dos Clérigos is one of Porto's most recognizable landmarks and Portugal's tallest tower, rising over the city and dwarfing everything around it. The church inside is also actually distinguishable from the millions of other European churches, since it is shaped like an oval, making it an intriguing novelty. The view from the top is spectacular but requires the strength to climb the 225 dizzying spiral steps (you may wonder as you climb why *they* didn't pay *you*

port in porto

You can see all these sights, but we know you came here to get wasted on dessert wine at 10am. Port wine, as you'll soon learn from every corner store, is a sweet wine variant drunk as an aperitif or with dessert and comes in at a heavyweight 20-23% alcohol content due to the alcohol added early in the fermentation process (2-3 days in). It's actually produced in the nearby Duoro wine valley (the first officially designated wine region in the world—take that Champagne!) and all the cellars are across the river from Porto in Vila Nova de Gaia, which has a completely different administration than Porto. So basically nothing about Port is actually from Porto, except the name and all the fame. Doing a tasting is a must—tours and tastings can be had anywhere from €4 and up. Since Gaia is also located on a steep hill down to the river, the cellars higher up are definitely more work, but worth the effort. (Closer to the river = easier access = more touristy.) Work for that sweet sweet port and stumble down tipsy and more sophisticated afterwards.

the €2 entrance fee) or a harness and pickaxe to go up the outside. (*Let's Go* strongly discourages climbing up the outside.)

i M: São Bento. Or bus ZH, 22, 202, 303, 500, 501, 507, 601, or 602. From M: São Bento, head straight up R. Clérigos. Free. Tower €2. Church open M-Sa 8:45am-12:30pm and 3:30-7pm, Su 10am-1pm and 9:30-10:30pm. Tower open daily Apr-July 9:30am-1pm and 2:30-7pm; Aug 9:30am-7pm; Sept-Oct 9:30am-1pm and 2:30-7pm; Nov-Mar 10am-noon and 2-5pm. Last entry 30min. before close.

IGREJA DE SÃO FRANCISCO
R. do Infante Dom Henrique   ☎22 206 21 00

This is a special treat for those passionate about gilded wood, although it is also perfectly enjoyable for people who just like pretty things. The gilded wood is beautiful, and this church has a ton of it, almost literally—there was at one time about 1000lb. of gold decorating the chapel's walls and altar, all donated by wealthy residents of Porto, who no doubt did it only out of the good of their own hearts—not because they wanted to buy their way into eternal paradise or anything. But let their deep-seated guilt become your traveling pleasure as you marvel at the workmanship inside the church. The museum next door has a collection of fairly generic religious artwork and a mass burial ground in the basement.

i M: São Bento. Or bus ZH or ZM. From M: São Bento, follow R. Mouzinho da Silveira downhill to Pr. Infante Dom Henrique, then turn right along the street at the far side. €3, students and seniors €2.50. Open daily June 9am-7pm; July-Aug 9am-8pm; Sept-Oct 9am-7pm; Feb-May 9am-6pm.

FOOD

⚑ PORTA'O LADO $
R. Campo dos Martires de Patria 51   www.portaolado.com

Next to a stretch of bars frequented by university students, Porta'o take Porto's meat and bread culture to another level. Just like its grittier neighbors, you can find classic bifanas and pregos (pork and steak sandwiches), but also a wider range of contemporary interpretations of petiscos or Portuguese tapas. Try the "gift of alheira," bacon-wrapped traditional chicken sausage that we'd be pretty happy to receive for a birthday or two. Snack on a finger food francesinha if you're having commitment issues with the impossible endeavour that is finishing the full size version. Great vegetarian options and a view of the Torre dos Clerigos from the terrace make Porta'o a favorite in the old city.

i M: Aliados, buses 305, 507, 601, 601, 705. Tram 18 and 22. From the northern side of Torre dos Clerigos cut directly through the other side of the park. It will be on your right. Petiscos €2-3.5, sandwiches €3.5-5.5.

CASA CONGA $
Rua do Bonjardim 314-8 ☎222 000 113 conga.pt

Famous for their bifana sandwiches, Conga brings something to the table that can be hard to find in Portugal—spice! Their housemade spicy sauce, chewy and tender pork, and crispy bread means that nearly everyone here orders their sandwiches in rounds. Round 1, I'll just try it; Round 2, maybe another; Round 3, screw it, I'll have four more with extra sauce. As a local institution, almost everything is "Conga" branded: the "Conga" francesinha, the "Conga" cod, the "Conga" restroom. After having undergone a 2012 renovation, the space is more modern than the old-school menu would suggest, but also means more space and less wait time for more dripping delicious sandwiches. Copious napkins necessary.

i M: Aliados. From Aliados, take R. Guillerme Costa Carvalho out of the square (on the right when facing the city hall). Next right on R. do Bonjardim, on the left. Bifana €2-4. Open T-W 9am-midnight, Th-Sa 9am-2am, Su 11am-midnight.

get a room!

porto

PORTO WINE HOSTEL $$
R. Campo dos Mártires da Pátria ☎22 201 3167 http://www.winehostel.pt/

This small hostel comes as advertised: Everything is about Porto's signature wines. Corks and wine crates as decoration, storehouse tours booked through the front desk, and in-house tastings (five wines for €5) all add more port wine to your daily life than you thought possible. Relax in the common room overlooking the square for the Happy (Five) Hours from 7pm-midnight. Sip a huge caipiporto (caipirinha cocktail made approximately 1000x better with port) for only €2.5 before heading out to the University nightlife district right around the corner.

i Bus 601 and 602. Tram 18 and 20. From the northern side of Torre dos Clerigos cut directly northeast through to the other side of the Praça da Cordoaria. It will be on your right. Dorms for 4,6, 8 €14-20. Private double €60-80. Breakfast (unlimited crepes) €3. Reception 24hr. Book ahead in summer

TATTVA DESIGN HOSTEL $
R. do Cativo 26 ☎22 094 4622 http://tattvadesignhostel.com/

Tattva tops the long list of Porto hostels with the revolutionary concept of super comfortable living spaces. Personal fans, reading lamps attached to each bed, and super-soft mattresses make this a possibly-better-than-home sleeping experience. We guess the "design" part comes in with the colorful fully wrap-around privacy curtains? Breakfast includes unlimited make your own pancakes (if you can rouse yourself before 10:30am). The hostel is large enough to sustain its own unique free tours and activities like daily Portuguese lessons. It's also five minutes from the nightlife district and steps away from the cathedral, so you don't even need to sort out your priorities.

i M: São Bento. From São Bento, take R. do Loureiro east. Follow until left on R. de Cimo de Vila until it becomes R. do Cautivo. On your right. Dorms high season €20-25, low season €16-20. Private double high season €60-70, low season €50-55.

NIGHTLIFE

ESPAÇO 77 CAFÉ/BAR

Trav. Cedofeita 22 ☎223 21 88 93

Espaço is a glowing beacon of drunk food and mini beers in the center of the university nightlife district. Known as the spot where most nights start or end (or sometimes both), they pride themselves on serving the most "minis" in the country—a 20cl Sagres (€0.5) is sold every 22 seconds! This cornucopia of cheap alcohol and meat/bread combinations makes for a young and energetic crowd, both gathering inside the brightly lit bar for a game of foosball and a stuffed pastry or spilling out onto the streets in classic Porto style. Revel in the lack of open container laws and take your drinks to go.

i M: Aliados. Go north on Av. dos Aliados until a left on R. do Dr. Ricardo Jorge. Continue onto R. da Conceição until it turns into Trav. Cedofeita. On your left. Mini beer €0.5, pizza €2.5. Open M-Sa 6pm-4am.

PLANO B CLUB

Rua Cândido dos Reis 30

In the middle of the Galeria de Paris nightlife district, Plano B corners the market on an elegant atmosphere that doesn't feel snobby or exclusive. Chandeliers, high ceilings, and a grand piano signal sophisticated class, but the dress code is relatively casual and drink prices stay low all night long. The cavernous basement area features two separate dance floors playing anything from electronic and Afro-Latin beats to top 40. Whether lounging upstairs on comfortable armchairs or raging downstairs amidst glittering mirrors and plaster statuettes, Plano B is pretty much Plan A for Porto nights.

i M: Aliados/São Bento. From Praça da Liberdade, head east on R. dos Clerigos, continuing onto R. das Carmelitas. Right on R. Cândido dos Reis, on your right. Cover/drink credit €5-10. Mixed drink €5, beer €2.5. Open Th-Sa 10pm-6am.

ESSENTIALS

Practicalities

- **TOURIST OFFICES:** The largest and most central office in town is located on the western side of the City Council (R. Clube dos Fenianos 25, ☎223 393 472. Open Nov-April 9am-7pm, May-Oct 9am-8pm, Aug 9am-9pm). The other major office is located next to the Cathedral (Calçada D. Pedro Pitões - Torre Medieval 15. Open Nov-April 9am-7pm, May-Oct 9am-8pm). There are also tourist information points at Campanhã train station (Open June 1st to August 31st 9:30am-6:30pm) and Praça da Ribeira (Open April-Oct 10am-7pm). These are the only government run tourist offices in town, though you will find many others whose main purpose is to sell private tours. Just make sure you are aware of this should you go in for information. An online chat service is available year round 7 hours a day on the government website, www.visitporto.travel.

- **WIFI:** There is free city wifi in many spots throughout the city including Av. dos Aliados, Casa da Música, and the Praça da Ribeira.

- **LUGGAGE STORAGE:** The airport and train stations all have luggage storage services. The airport service is located on floor 3 at the public departures area (Ppen 5am-11pm, up to 10kg €2.30/24hr, 10-30kg €3.48/24hr, over 30kg €6.93/24hr). The train stations Campanha (Open 4:45am-1:45am) and S. Bento (Open M-F 4:40am-12:50am, Sa-Su 5:40am-12:50am) offer a maximum 24hr use locker with a minimum payment of €1-2 for the first hour at time of storage and the rest paid upon retrieval (€0.50-3.50 per hour depending on size of locker and length of time).

- **POST OFFICES:** The main post office is the Município Post Office at R. Dr. António Luis Gomes (☎223 400 202 http://www.ctt.pt).

Emergency

- **EMERGENCY NUMBER:** ☎112.

- **POLICE:** Tourism Police: ☎222 081 833. The tourist police station, dealing with thefts and other tourist specific incidents, is located next to the main tourist office at Rua Clube dos Fenianos 25 (☎222 081 833, Open 8am-midnight). Officers are trained in English, Spanish, French, Italian, German and Serbo-Croatian. The most centrally located station for the local police, Polícia de Segurança Pública, Rua de Augusto Rosa (☎222 006 821).

- **PHARMACIES:** Most pharmacies are open M-F 9am-7pm and Saturday 9am-1pm, but each pharmacy takes its turn as the 24 hour location in the area. Schedules for this rotation are displayed prominently at all pharmacies.

- **HOSPITAL:** The closest public hospital to the city center is the Hospital Do Carmo at Praça de Carlos Alberto, 32 (☎222 078 400). The second largest public hospital in the country is Hospital Geral de S. João at Alameda Prof. Hernâni Monteiro (☎225 512 100 http://www.hsjoao.min-saude.pt)

Getting There

By Plane

Francisco Sa Carneiro Airport or Aeroporto do Porto (☎229 432 400) is located six miles outside town and serves in-country destinations (Faro, Lisbon, Madeira, Azores) as well as major European cities through budget airlines like Ryanair, TAP and Easyjet. There is a metro station serving the airport through the purple E line (Trindade or Bolhao to reach the city center. There is also an AeroBus that will drop you on the Praça de Liberdade. Taxis can be caught outside and a ride to the center should cost €20-30.

By Train

The train stations are São Bento (Saint Benedict) station, and the Campanhã station.

By Bus

International buses to Spain and France depart from the bus interface at Casa de Música metro stop. The Rede Espressos terminal from Lisbon and other in country destinations is at R. de Alexandre Herculano 366.

Getting Around

By Public Transportation

Porto has both a metro and bus system. The metro has 6 lines connecting the center of the city with its surroundings. One time tickets can be bought from the machines in the metro stations and from the central tourism office. An Andante pass (€0.50) can be purchased at shops marked with the Andante sign and in the Sao Bento train station.You can buy one day (€7) or three day (€15) Andante Tour tickets for unlimited travel on both the bus and metro though it's unlikely you'll need to use it this much since Porto is very walkable.

   Single bus journeys cost €1.80 in cash only if purchased on board. You can also use your Andante card for the bus (€1.20 every additional journey). Once you validate your card on the sensors it is functional for one hour. Each bus station has a detailed timetable and itinerary for the line that stops there.

By Taxi

Taxis are easy to find around the city. There are dedicated taxi stands at the airport, train station and Av. Aliados. You can also call Raditaxis at ☎225 073 900.

lagos

Tourists flock to Lagos like the flocks of annoying seagulls that have made it their mission to deprive you of sleep. But the crowds are worth it when you get down to the famous beaches strung along the cliff-lined coast. Some are reachable down rickety wooden stairs, some only by kayak, but all are worth a morning spent sunbathing and trying to catch the right angles to make that bikini body magically appear. Clear water, pure sand, and a carefree lifestyle make it a haven for backpackers, so the nightlife has evolved accordingly with plenty of dive-y bars and crowded late night streets. In the famous southwestern Algarve region, Lagos offers huge seafood dishes like the ubiquitous "cataplana" (mixed seafood), perfect for sharing or minimizing the need to spend money on more than one meal. While Atlantic water may always be pretty freaking cold, Lagos nights are hot hot hot.

SIGHTS

🏖 PRAIA DONA ANA

The most iconic beach of the Algarve, Dona Ana has been photographed and selfie-stick'd millions of times. Recent construction in 2015 extended the beach, which some believe reduced its beauty, but now it means more space to sprawl out and enjoy the sun. Snorkel in the unbelievably clear water or snack at the restaurant at the foot of the surrounding cliffs. Really, seize the moment; this is one of the most beautiful places in the world. Or embrace the basic and do a photoshoot in the coves and rock formations. Parasols and sun-chairs for rent €10.

i From the city center, follow Avenida dos Descobrimentos south, turn left at the fire station and then follow the road in the direction of the Iber Lagos hotel. Free. 24/7.

PONTA DE PIEDADE

This gorgeous lookout bypasses all the well-visited beaches of Lagos and goes straight to the point. You can view all the coves and hidden beaches of either side of the peninsula as you scramble over rocks and brush to reach the perfect picnic spot. The most beautiful place to check out the summer sunset after spending the day at the beach.

i Take Est. da Ponta de Piedade out of town, leads all the way to the point. Free. 24/7.

how to pick a beach

Possibly the toughest decision you'll face during your time in Lagos: Which beach? It's not life or death, but here are some features that might help you decide.

- **FAME.** Praia Dona Ana is the most famous and photographed of the nearby spots, and while it's been altered by extensions added in 2015, it still maintains the Most Picturesque award. Go for the Instagrams and stay for sunbathing.

- **DIFFICULTY LEVEL.** If you're willing to start your relaxation with some effort, Praia do Camilho is the one. 200 stairs all the way down and one of the farthest from town.

- **SOCIABILITY.** Stretching 4km right next to town, Praia Meia is where you can encounter a huge cross section of Lagos: surfers, families, Australian, locals, backpackers, and Australians.

- **EXCLUSIVITY.** Praia do Barranco can only be approached by kayak, thus making it one of the quietest. Silence and beach sand are golden.

FOOD

⚑ THE GARDEN BAR AND GRILL $$

Rua Lançarote de Freitas 27 ☎913 187 142 https://www.facebook.com/thegardenlagos

A paradise within paradise, The Garden is a beautiful open-air barbecue serving up easy to share appetizers like cod cakes and egg rolls and well-priced grill plates. It basically looks like someone took their cool vintage living room and moved it outside, adding a huge iron grill and 90 guests. The South African owners bring a little of their hometown to Lagos; this means delicious "bunnies," loaves of bread hollowed out and filled with mild curry, for that post-beach carbo load. The daily fish special is served whole—skin, eyes and all—with salad, wine and potatoes for just €9.90. Shirts are optional based on that tattooed Irishman in the corner.

i Look for the giant purple magnolia tree next to the mural of two snails kissing on Rua Lançarote. Entrees €7-12. Open M-Su 1pm-1am. Reservations necessary during high season after 6pm.

A FORJA $$$

Tanning on the beach can take a lot of energy, so you deserve an all in one meal that can restore it. In the evenings at A Forja, there'll be a line out the door, and let's be real, possibly during lunch as well. But it's worth either booking ahead or more realistically awkwardly posing at the outdoor stoop ready to race inside as soon as a table opens up. That's because they make some of the best seafood in a town overrun with it and they make it BIG. Prices are a bit high, but it's hard to put a value on a dish of perfectly cooked salmon steaks that could tide you over til the tide changes. Ideally dishes are to be shared, but you could eat solitary hangover breakfasts for nearly three days on those veal leftovers (€16 plus 30 cents for a takeout box).

i Fish entrees €7-9, meat entrees €7-22. Open M-F noon-3pm and 6:30-10pm, closed Sa. Open Su noon-3pm and 6:30-10pm. Reservation recommended.

OLIVE HOSTEL $$
R. da Oliveira 67 ☎915 296 129

The Olive is a homey maze of apartments far enough from the center of town to get some sleep and close enough for easy beach access. Claudia and her husband treat guests like their somewhat unruly and independent children, serving drinks and baking homemade pasteis that you can buy on the honor system. With daily yoga classes (€5) on the roof, jazz music playing in the stony courtyard, and candles sprinkled throughout the house at night (fun obstacle course for drunk people!), the Olive feels like home if you grew up in a loving though slightly disorganized commune.

i High season dorm €25-30, low season €15-17. High season private double €60, low season €40. Cash only. Towel included. Reception 24hr.

RISING COCK PARTY HOSTEL $$
Travessa do Forno 14 ☎968 75 87 85 http://www.risingcock.com/

The self-designated party hostel of the area, Rising Cock revels in its well-deserved hedonistic reputation. Nightly bar crawls and daily booze cruises keep guests drinking 24/7, but Rising also prides itself on being a family hostel. Mama cooks unlimited crepes and her famous hangover lemon tea for everyone who can manage to get up before 11am. It even advertises its "ecock friendly" practices (because even saving the environment needs innuendo). This is definitely not the place to get a good night's sleep; more the place to have a good night then a day's sleep.

i High season dorm €30-37, low season €10-16. Reception 24hr.

NIGHTLIFE

🎵 INSIDE OUT BAR
Rua Cândido dos Reis 19 https://www.facebook.com/InsideoutFace/

Inside Out is one of the most consistently energetic bars in Lagos. It's hard not to be when your drink specialty is a fishbowl full of vodka, juice and triple sec. Rope a few fellow travelers into sharing one and you'll have enough fuel to dance along to the live DJs every night.

i Fishbowl €30. Cocktails €5-7. Open M-Su 8pm-4am. Cash only.

BON VIVANT BAR/CLUB
R. 25 Abril 105 ☎282 761 019 www.facebook.com/BonVivant.Lagos/

Even if you choose not to go, Bon Vivant has been a pretty unmissable fixture in the center of Lagos since the 80s. Towering above the rest at three floors (this isn't really a skyscraper town), it's possible to see the whole town as you sip your mixed drink and mix with a more mature local crowd. Grab a caipirinha at each floor as you descend to the dancefloor at the bottom for Top 40 and Latin favorites.

i Beer €2, cocktails €5-6. Cash only. M-Su 2pm-4am.

JOE'S GARAGE BAR
R. 1 de Maio ☎967 333 959 http://www.joesgarage.eu.com/

Grunge and car names aplenty in this aggressively macho bar. The aesthetic could be best described as "grease and Jager," with shot combos that will start the night as explosively as the light show. From the outside, Joe's looks like a dive bar, and inside it looks like a dive bar (with more blacklight than you might

portugal

expect). Several bars surrounded the multi-level dance-floor, so rev your engines and get ready for more car puns.

i Shots €2.50-4.50. Cash only. Open daily 10pm-2am.

ESSENTIALS
Practicalities

- **TOURIST OFFICE:** The only tourism office in town is the Posto de Turismo de Lagos on the main square Praça Gil Eanes. (Right next to the aesthetically challenged statue of Dom Sebastião. ☎282 763 031. Open daily 9:30am-5:30pm.)

- **POST OFFICES:** The main post office is on Rua. Dr. Francisco Sá Cerneiro 46 (☎707 262 626, Open M-Su 8:30am-6pm).

- **ATMS:** There are plenty of ATMS in and near Praça Gil Eanes. Most places only accept cash (including hostels), so these will be useful.

- **PHARMACIES:** There are no permanent 24 hour pharmacies in town, but each pharmacy has a schedule on the door listing that day's hours.

Emergency

- **EMERGENCY NUMBERS:** Make sure to dial 00351 from a foreign cell phone for all Algarve phone numbers. Local police: ☎282 762 930. District hospital: ☎282 770 790. Private hospital São Gonçalo de Lagos: ☎282 760 181.

- **POLICE:** There is a small police post open in the summer next to the tourist office on the Praça Gil Eanes, but for more serious issues contact the main office at ☎282 762 930 (Largo Convento Nossa Senhora da Glória).

- **HOSPITAL:** The most accessible public hospital to the city center is the Hospital de Lagos or Centro Hospitalar do Barlavento Algarvio (Rua Castelo dos Governadores, ☎282 770 100). The larger private district hospital is the Hospital São Gonçalo de Lagos (Avenida D. Sebastião, ☎800 224 424).

Getting There
By Plane

In order to fly into Lagos, you must go through the Faro airport, 90 km away. To get into town, you can take a train (€7.30), bus (€5.90), or taxi (€87-112).

By Train and Bus

The bus station is located a 10 minute walk from the center of town and serves locations around the Algarve as well as buses to Sevilla and Lisbon (R. Mercado de Levante 9. Buses to Lisbon leave nearly every hour of the day during high season (May-September).

The train station (Estrada de São Roque) is a 15 minute walk from the center (just across the river from the bus station) and has connections mostly to local Algarve destinations including Faro and Portimão. Ticket office open daily 5:45-9:30am, 10-3:30am, and 4-8:10pm. Schedules are online at www.cp.pt.

Getting Around
Public Transportation

Walking is likely the fastest and definitely cheapest option for most destinations within the historic center, given the narrow streets. However there are several public bus lines that run between the beaches and nearby towns. Check http://aonda.pt/ for schedules and routes.

- **LAGOS TAXI COOPERATIVE:** ☎282 763 587
- **RADIO TAXI:** ☎266 73 57 35

evora

The Alentejo region makes up ⅓ of the area of the entire country, and yet somehow Évora, the walled capital on a hill, often gets forgotten. In a region producing 80% of the world's cork and famed for its livestock and agriculture, Évora adds seemingly infinite layers of cultural and artistic value. Baroque churches and Roman ruins abound and the tiled cloister of the university awaits the hordes of students that descend during the school year. Get some green wine, sheep cheese and the local specialty sopa de caçao (dogfish soup) and enjoy the bucolic medieval town up close and in person.

SIGHTS

CAPELA DO OSSOS CHURCH

☎266 704 521

"Nós ossos que aqui estamos pelos vossos esperamos" (We bones that here are, for yours await) is the welcoming inscription you see upon arrival to the bone chapel. And pretty fitting, given that you're about to enter an 18.7 x 11 meter room with walls entirely decorated with tastefully placed bones. Inside the 16th century Igreja São Sebastiao, a Franciscan monk decided that his brothers needed a greater reminder of the brevity of life, so he orchestrated the construction with about 5000 skeletons from nearby churches. Now you too can meditate on your own fleeting presence on Earth! The arched floral ceiling, added in 1810, provides an interesting contrast with the two corpses (one a child) hanging from ropes. The prettiest and most mildly terrifying memento mori we've found yet.

i Inside the Igreja São Francisco. General €3, students and seniors €2. Open daily 9am-6pm.

UNIVERSIDAD DE ÉVORA

Largo dos Colegiais 2 (entrance on R. do Cardeal Rei)   ☎266 777 000

This university, the second-oldest in Portugal after Coimbra, was founded in 1537 but won't stand for being second best. Shut down in different forms from 1759 to 1973, now the University is of central importance to the town. The most visited area of the complex is the cloister of the Colegio Espirito Santo, where each classroom is elaborately decorated with profane themes. Gorgeous 18th-century blue and white azulejo covers each wall according to the subject matter that was taught in each particular room. Some classes we might take today (geography, physics, etc.) but we can bet you didn't have a metaphysical philosophy or rhetoric class in your standard curriculum. And your professor probably didn't lecture from a pulpit set into the wall. Fun details abound, like the depiction of America with alligators pulling carriages (more or less accurate, right?).

i Cloisters door is on R. do Cardeal Rei. Tickets €3, under 12 free. Open T-F 9am-6pm, Sa 10am-6pm.

FOOD

Alentejo is a region known for its gastronomy and wine, and Évora takes full advantage of its tourist population by charging higher prices for typical meals that you might be able to get in the rest of the region for a few euros and a smile. Still, paying a little bit more can get you the price fix meal of your dreams, full of cod, lamb and

portugal

get a room!

EVORA TERRACE HOSTEL $

Praça do Giraldo 83   ☎963 67 70 52 http://www.evoraterracehostel.com/

This hostel is the most centrally located you can get without crashing on a bench in the Praça do Giraldo. With a rooftop terrace overlooking the red-roofed town on all sides, it earns its name and then some. Bathrooms are large and clean with the best water pressure on this side of Alentejo. While reception times can be irregular, breakfast is self-serve fruit, cereal, coffee and toast from 8:30-11am and can be easily enjoyed in a common room so cute it makes the woven blankets seem much more comfortable than they really are. So grab a cheap beer from reception, scrawl your bucket list on the common room chalkboard and head upstairs to enjoy the sunset.

i In Praça do Giraldo, if you're facing the church, on the left center. Dorms female or mixed €15, private double €35. Key deposit €5. No laundry facilities or air conditioning. Reception 9am-10pm.

OLD ÉVORA HOSTEL $

Rua Serpa Pinto 68   ☎934 734 493 http://oldevorahostel.blogspot.com/

Old Evora, equidistant between the bus station and the central square, provides spacious, comfortable and, somewhat ironically, sparkling new accommodations. The common area has a huge circular dining table, perfect to meet fellow travelers while enjoying the free toast, and the common room with pretty stenciled decals provides space to skim from the large book exchange shelf (though you may be limited to 1980s travel guides and German translations). Fully equipped kitchen perfect for avoiding overspending on the high-priced restaurants in the area. Its location on a main thoroughfare means traffic noise can intrude, but it's not a big problem for the typically short one to two day trips through the city.

i 4, 6, 8 bed dorms, €14-16. Cash only. Reception 9am-9pm.

evora

black pork. Budget travel warning: like fancier places in Lisbon, waiters will serve small plates at the beginning of the meal like olives and bread. Nothing is free! If you don't want it, just politely ask them to take it away and reduce the temptation to nibble.

🍴 **PÁTEO** $$$

R. de Outubro Beco da Espinhosa   ☎919 549 745 www.pateoevora.com

If you've always wanted to eat in a beautiful yet informative garden, páteo is your place. Set amid passion-fruit trees and a hoard of young servers from the nearby University, Pateo has historical panels about Évora all around as the former location of a tourist office. But the wishing well and garden terrace make it feel more magical than bureaucratic if the black pork with mushroom risotto (€14) hasn't already done that.

i Take R. 5 de Outubro north from Praça do Giraldo and take the third left onto the small alleyway of Beco da Espinhosa. Appetizers €4-8, entrees €14-20. Open daily 11:30am-1am.

CHAO DAS COVAS CAFÉ $$

Largo Chao das Covas   ☎266 706 294

This tiny, friendly café is tucked into the Roman aqueduct and our hearts. The vaulted ceiling and decorative photos remind you that you're in Évora (in case you forgot), while the chalkboard menu covers all the basics of Alentejano "petiscos" (tapas). Even the humble migas (breadcrumbs mixed with pork and

At the confluence of three rivers, Évora has always been a logical center of culture and trade. And that extends all the way back to 5500 BC when a bunch of Neolithic bros decided to create a megalithic enclosure right outside the current city. For reference, that's 2000 years before Stonehenge. Rediscovered in 1964, now 1500 megalithic sites are known to exist in the nearby Alentejo areas including huge funerary monuments like the Dolmen of Zambujeiro. While it may be difficult to get out there on your own, a small company run by a local archeologist, Ebora Megalithica (http://eboramegalithica.com/) runs excellent morning and afternoon tours for €25. Mário will explain the significance of the huge stones dropped seemingly out of nowhere and inscribed with confusing symbols.

served with an orange slice) gets treated with loving care and dished out in huge portions. The staff will be happy (almost too happy?) to explain the whole menu and give recommendations, whether those are through rapid fire Portuguese or hand gestures. Go for dinner or just coffee and follow that up with delicious desserts on the terrace underneath the stone arches.

i Petiscos €4.50-9. Open T-Sa 11am-3pm and 6pm-12:30am, Su 11am-3pm. Cash only.

NIGHTLIFE

☒ CAFÉ ESTRELA D'OURO CAFÉ/BAR
L. de São Vicente 59

You could stay in this arched medieval café from 9am until the unofficial closing well after 2am and observe the entire life of the city come and go. Serving up pastries, salads and coffee throughout the day and turning into a forever-open hotspot at night, Café Estrela will never disappoint you even during those quiet summers with no university students around (though once school's in session, it'll be even busier). Grab a chair and a beer, and look up at the collection of odd sculptures and puzzlingly large number of Mona Lisa copies perched on the towering alcoves. You might even catch one actually smiling.

i From Praça do Giraldo, take R. da República until a slight left onto R. Miguel Bombarda. On your left at the first intersection. Beer €1, cocktails €5-7. Open M-Su 9am-2am.

PRAXIS CLUB
R. de Valdevinos 21   ☎266 70 81 77 https://www.facebook.com/PraxisEvora

Hey, it's the only game in town (and it's not even that crooked). Praxis is where every night ends in Évora, and both its drink specials and the occasional major DJ passing through make it a worthwhile spot. Friday Ladies Night offers up two for three deals, and its location in the center of the Old Town means you can stumble out after a long night of dancing straight into the twisting medieval streets.

i From Praça do Giraldo, go up R. 5 de Outobro and turn right R. de Valdevinos. On your left. Cover €5. Open T-Sa 11pm-6am.

portugal

ESSENTIALS
Practicalities

- **TOURIST OFFICE:** The tourist office (Praça do Giraldo 73, ☎266 777 071) is open in the high season from April-October M-Su 9am-7pm and the low season from November to March M-F 9am-6pm and Sa-Su 10am-2pm, 3pm-6pm. They offer information about the city as well as the entire region of Alentejo and speak Spanish, French, German, Portuguese and English.

- **POST OFFICES:** The Posto de Correios de Evora is on Rua Olivença (☎266 745 480. Open T-F 8:30am-6:30pm, http://www.ctt.pt).

Emergency

- **EMERGENCY NUMBERS:** ☎112

- **LOCAL POLICE:** ☎266 76 04 50

- **HOSPITAL:** Hospital do Espírito Santo (Lg. Senhor Jesus da Pobreza, ☎266 74 01 00) is located near city wall at the intersection with R. Dr. Augusto Eduardo Nunes.

- **PHARMACIES:** Check the doors of pharmacies for each night's "farmacia de serviço" which will be open 24hrs for that period or go online at http://www.farmaciasdeservico.net/localidade/evora/evora.

- **POLICE:** Main local police station - R. Francisco Soares Lusitano, ☎266 76 04 50 www.psp.pt.

Getting There
By Train and Bus

Traveling by train and bus to Lisbon (the major nearby hub) is comparable in price and length of journey; the main difference is the frequency of service. The bus runs nearly hourly to Lisbon Sete Rios. The bus station Terminal Rodoviario (Av. São Sebastião, ☎266 76 94 10) is a five minute walk west from the city center. Check online at http://www.rede-expressos.pt for schedules. The train runs to Lisbon's Oriente station four times per day on weekdays and three on weekends, only at commuter hours (so nothing during the daytime). The train station is a 20 minute walk south from the center on R. da Estaçao.

Gettin Around
By Taxi

Call ☎266 73 47 34.

portugal essentials

MONEY
Tipping and Bargaining

Native Portuguese rarely tip more than their spare change, even at expensive restaurants. However, if you make it clear that you're a tourist, they might expect you to tip more. Don't feel obligated to tip; the servers' pay is almost never based on tips. No one will refuse your money, but you're a poor student so don't play the fool.

Bargaining is common and necessary in open-air and street markets. Haggling is also most effective when buying several items or in bulk. However, do not barter in malls or established shops.

Taxes

Portugal has a 13% **value added tax** (*imposto sobre* or *valor acrescentado*; IVA) on all meals and accommodations. The prices listed in *Let's Go* include IVA unless otherwise mentioned. Retail goods bear a much higher 23% IVA, although the listed prices generally include this tax. Non-EU citizens who have stayed in the EU fewer than 180 days can claim back the tax paid on purchases at the airport. Ask the shop where you have made the purchase to supply you with a tax return form, but stores will only provide them for purchases of more than €50-100. **Taxes,** presently 23%, are included in all prices in Portugal. Request a refund form, an *Insenção de IVA*, and present it to customs upon departure.

SAFETY AND HEALTH

Local Laws and Police

You should feel comfortable approaching the police in Portugal, although few officers speak English. The **Polícia de Segurança Pública** is the police force in all major cities and towns. The **Guarda Nacional Republicana** polices more rural areas, while the **Brigada de Trânsito** is the traffic police, who sport red armbands. All three branches wear light blue uniforms.

Drugs and Alcohol

Recreational drugs are illegal in Portugal, and police take these laws seriously. However, recreational drug use has been decriminalized, so instead of jail time and fines, perpetrators face community service and government-imposed therapy. The legal minimum drinking age is 18. Portugal has one of the highest road mortality rates in Europe. Do not drive while intoxicated, and be cautious on the road.

SLOVENIA

The first and most prosperous of Yugoslavia's breakaway republics, tiny Slovenia revels in republicanism, peace, and independence. With a historically westward gazy, Slovenia's liberal politics and high GDP helped it gain early entry into the European Union. Fortunately, modernization has not adversely affected the tiny country's natural beauty and diversity: it is still possible to go skiing, explore Slovenia's stunning caves, bathe under the Mediterranean sun, and catch an opera—all in a single day.

greatest hits

- **HAPPILY EVER AFTER:** Whether you're looking to swim along the beaches or hike up some mountain trails, **Lake Bled** (p. 642) will be the perfect fairy tale setting for your next Instagram post.

- **BRINGING SAX-Y BACK:** Like jazz? Great, head to **Sax Pub** (p. 640) in Ljubljana. Don't like jazz? Have a liter of rosé for €10. Then you'll love jazz.

- **BIG SAUSAGE SURPRISE: Klobasarna** (p. 638) in Ljubljana is a tiny joint that specializes in delicious, cheap sausages. Try the half sausage which only goes for €3.50.

ljubljana

Budapest is the new Prague. Bratislava is the new Budapest. Zagreb is the new Bratislava. Or maybe Prague is back in again? Keeping track of what's hot in Central Europe can be tricky. And that means it's easy to lose sight of Ljubljana—wait, how do you pronounce that? Is that in Slovenia or Slovakia?

Confusing spelling aside, Ljubljana is a charming city that should be a destination for anyone visiting Central Europe. Though the nightlife never rises to a fever pitch, the restaurants, classy bars, and stunning sights make it an attractive place for anyone looking for a more low-key vacation—or maybe you just need a scenic place to recover after raging in Prague. Check out the parks, the museums, the castle—or just sit alongside the meandering river with a can of Laško.

SIGHTS

PARK TIVOLI

Main entrance at Cankarjeva Cesta

Don't have time for a day trip during your stay in Ljubljana? No need to fret—Park Tivoli, the largest of Ljubljana's many parks, is a perfectly acceptable substitute for frolicking in the Slovenian countryside. Though it features some gorgeously landscaped gardens, a manmade pond, and a stately castle, Park Tivoli can also feel startlingly rural. Dubious? Just take a hike up Šišenski Hill, which divides the park from Ljubljana's zoo (worth a visit if you want to see horses that aren't on your dinner plate). If you're not really the nature type, pay a visit to Tivoli Castle, which regularly hosts art exhibits and also houses a cafe. If you're looking to exercise, the park has tennis, volleyball, and basketball courts, as well as soccer fields and a swimming pool.

i Admission free.

NATIONAL MUSEUM / NATURAL HISTORY MUSEUM

Prešernova 20   ☎01 241 09 40 www.nms.si

It's not quite two museums for the price of one—the two institutions have separate admission prices—but you'll get to check out two of Slovenia's most famous museums without a lot of walking. The National Museum takes up all of the first floor, some of the second, and a bit of space outside; the Natural History Museum gets the rest of the second floor. This makes sense, since the history of Slovenia is slightly more important than that of the development of life on planet earth. You'll see such artifacts as the remains of a 10th century woman from Bled, Roman ruins from Ljubljana, and also an Egyptian mummy that doesn't really have that much to do with Slovenia. Upstairs at the Natural History Museum, a gigantic woolly mammoth skeleton holds sway over somewhat less impressive skeletons. The dioramas may be more dramatic than you're used to—one shows a big cat with a bird stuck in its mouth—but that just helps to liven things up.

i National Museum €6, students €4. Natural History Museum €4, students €3. Combined ticket €8.50, students €6. Open M-W 10am-6pm, Th 10am-8pm, F-Su 10am-6pm.

MODERNA GALERIJA LJUBLJANA

Cankarjeva 15   ☎01 241 68 34

Odds are you've never heard of any of the artists in this museum. Zoran Musič? Misread Begi? Jakob Savinšek? Maybe you spotted Laibach in your goth cousin's industrial rock collection. But even if you know nothing about modern art in Slovenia, the Moderna Galerija still holds great appeal. Be warned, however, that this museum does not exactly give off good vibes—for proof of that, just see Savinšek's series of agonized sculptures with names like "Malice," "Nightmare," and "Falsehood." But if you can take a little moodiness, then walking through these galleries will give you an alternate history of modern art. As the decades pass by, the art gets louder and more aggressive—TV screens and jarring noises abound. If you're pooped from a walk in Tivoli Park, we recommend you start at this end—it's sure to wake you up.

i €5, students €2.50. Free on the first Sunday of every month. Open Tu-Su 10am-6pm.

LJUBLJANA CASTLE AND MUSEUM OF PUPPETRY

Grajska planota 1   www.ljubljanskigrad.si

Yes, this is the building on Ljubljana's coat of arms, and no, there's no dragon crouching on top (though there are numerous dragon toys for sale in the gift shop). Ljubljana Castle, originally built in the 11th century and rebuilt several times since then, has served as a military outpost, an arsenal, a penitentiary, and a WWI prisoner of war camp. Today, it's a fascinating look into Slovenian history, as well as the absolute best spot from which to view the city—the castle's tower offers 360° views of Ljubljana and its surroundings. Elsewhere, you can check out old prison cells, take a virtual tour of the castle in its heyday, or grab a bite to eat at the castle's restaurant. Also housed in the castle is the Museum of Puppetry, which is just as disturbing as you might expect. (Did you know that the first Slovenian puppet show proper was named "Dead Man in a Red Coat"?) Given the lengthy, winding walk necessary to get up to the castle—there's no straight path up the hill—it's worth buying a ticket on the funicular, the inclined railway that makes getting up and down a breeze.

i €7.50, students €5.20. Open daily, though hours vary by season. Check online for a more complete schedule. June-September castle open 9am-11pm, museum open from 9am-9pm.

SLOVENIAN ETHNOGRAPHIC MUSEUM

Metelkova 2   ☎01 300 87 00 www.etno-muzej.si

Spend a couple of days in Ljubljana, and you'll start to wonder. You'll see people eating deer medallions and horse burgers, reading Slavoj Žižek, talking about their bachelor parties where they locked a friend in a dog cage and made him drink tequila, and you'll start to think—what is this country? No better place to find that out than at the Ethnographic Museum, which, in its exploration of the world's culture, also penetrates deep into Slovenian identity. They've got everything from traditional country garb to Slovenian pressings of Tom Jones records, and while not all the wall text is in English, the artifacts can often speak for

Ljubljana

themselves. Special attention is paid to the mundane; this is, after all, a museum that mounted a special exhibition about doors in Slovenia, complete with walls full of different keys, doorknobs, and knockers.

i €4.50, students €2.50. Open Tu-Sa 10am-6pm.

FOOD

PIZZERIA FOCULUS $

Gregorčičeva ulica 3   ☎01 251 56 43. www.foculus.si

Scared of trying—gasp—Central European cuisine? First off, you shouldn't be. But if you're a picky eater or you're traveling with one, know that Slovenia, being close to Italy, is also home to some great pizza. One of the finest joints in town is the vaguely Roman-themed Pizzeria Foculus, located on the charming Gregorčičeva ulica. The staff proudly proclaims that theirs is the best in Slovenia, and they're certainly in the running: the thin-crust pizza is delicious with a variety of options for vegetarians and meat-lovers alike (ham, salami, pepperoni—pile it on!). The highlight may be the pizza bufala, topped with cherry tomatoes and chunks of mozzarella. If you're with a friend or are just absurdly hungry, go for the large size; otherwise, the so-called "small" is more than enough.

i Small pizzas €7-9. Large pizzas €8-10. Salads €6-8. Open daily 11am-12am.

PIVNICA UNION $

Celovška Cesta 22   ☎01 471 73 35 www.pivnica-union.si

Here's the easiest way to explain Pivnica Union: imagine Budweiser opened a brewpub where you could get their classic lager, specially hopped and unfiltered versions of their flagship brew, and various one-offs made by expert brewers. Imagine they served food, and it was both really cheap and really good. So far, Budweiser has done nothing of the sort, but Pivovarna Union, Ljubljana's second largest brewery (it's affiliated with the largest, Pivovarna Laško) certainly has. Beer enthusiasts will enjoy the special brews, but the real attraction is the constantly changing daily special. You're not likely to find a better deal than the most basic option, which gives you a full meal for only €6: roast chicken, pork, baked trout, and veal shank have all appeared on the rotating menu. And yes, you can get Laško and Union everywhere in Ljubljana, but won't it taste best where it's made?

i Daily specials €6-12. Beer €2-4. Open M-Th 11am-12am, F-Sa 11am-1am, Su 12pm-5pm.

KLOBASARNA $

Ciril-Metodov Trg 15   ☎51 605 017 www.klobasarna.si

Ljubljana has tons of restaurants serving Slovenian delicacies, but most of them will set you back at least €15 or €20. For a more economical but still delicious take on Slovenian cuisine, check out Klobasarna, a tiny joint that specializes in big sausages. Ok, yes, sausages, double entendres, very funny. We can stop giggling now. The 1/2 sausage only goes for €3.50, and it comes with a big bun as well as generous helpings of mustard and horseradish. Before you know it, you'll be full and no one will want to talk to you until you eat an entire pack of Altoids. If you're still hungry for more, grab some štrukel, or rolled pastries—€1.50 for 1 or €4 for 3. Perfect for a quick bite before you make the long trek up to Ljubljana Castle.

i Sausage €3.50. Pastries €1.50-4. Open M-Sa 10am-11pm, Su 10am-3pm.

NAMASTE $

Breg 8   ☎01 425 01 5 www.restavracija-namaste.si

You wouldn't necessarily expect Slovenia to have great Indian food, but it makes sense if you think about it: both cuisines do heavily feature both meat and potatoes. If that doesn't convince you, then a visit to Namaste, a North Indian restaurant located on the North bank of the Ljubljanica, will surely change your

HOSTEL AVA
$

Trubarjeva Cesta 5   ☎01 425 50 06 www.hostel-ava.si

Obsessed with Ljubljana's contemporary art scene? Then stay in this unique hostel, which is affiliated with Ljubljana's Academy of Visual Art. Couldn't care less about art but want a hostel with big rooms, clean showers, and a great location? Then you should also stay at Hostel AVA. Located on the very hip Trubarjeva Cesta—look out for vegan restaurants and smoke shops—Hostel AVA offers large suites at cheap prices. Even if you're in an 8- or 12-bed dorm, you're sure to have your own space. Though it feels more like a real hostel than some of Ljubljana's more apartment-like setups (hall bathrooms, big rooms pack with showers—you get the idea), it's still plenty comfortable.

i From the bus or train station, walk west on Trg Osvobodilne fronte, then take a right onto Resljeva Cesta. Take a left at Trubarjeva Cesta; the hostel is on your right. Dorms €13-15. Reception open Jul-Sept 8am-midnight; Oct-June 9am-1pm.

HOSTEL CELICA
$$

Metelkova 8.   ☎01 230 97 00 www.hostelcelica.com

Obsessed with Ljubljana's contemporary art scene, but want something a little more structured than art school? Then why not stay in Hostel Celica, which for over a hundred years was used as a prison? It sounds like a hostel that would be perfect for, well, Hostel, but Hostel Celica is actually one of the most distinctive and exciting places to stay in all of Ljubljana. Located in the vibrant Metelkova City, Hostel Celica has the usual amenities (Wi-Fi, clean bathrooms, towels), but it also boasts eclectic room design and unique history. This is probably the only hostel dorm that you'll ever be tempted to Instagram for good reasons. However, that history comes at a cost—Hostel Celica charges a good three or four euros more than other hostels in the area. But hey, at least they don't charge bail when you want to leave.

i Walk west from the bus or train station, then take a right onto Metelkova. Dorms €18-22. Private rooms €24-30. Breakfast €3. Reception 24hr.

ANA HOSTEL
$

Komenskega ulica 10   ☎01 292 7997 www.ana-hostel.com

Located midway between the train station and the Ljubljanica, Ana Hostel offers convenience as well as quiet—it's hard to get some sleep when there are rows of bars just feet from your room. Here, there's a decidedly classier vibe, part of which comes from the old townhouse it's housed in. The high-ceilinged rooms are filled with light as well as furniture: bookshelves and bedside tables abound. Some of the three-bedded rooms even have kitchens attached. Even the hall bathrooms look swanky—although you still have to share them. Common spaces include a courtyard out back—yeah, this is the good life.

i From the bus or train station, walk west on Trg Osvobodilne fronte, then take a right onto Resljeva Cesta. Take a left at Komenskega ulica; the hostel is on your left. Dorms €17. Privates €40. Reception 24hr.

ljubljana

mind. Though Namaste, like many of Ljubljana's restaurants, offers outdoor seating, its stylishly yellow interior is just as inviting. Though there are tons of tables, carefully arranged screens allow for privacy no matter where you're sitting. With a wide selection of chicken, lamb, and fish dishes, Namaste will easily satisfy your cravings for meat that's not spiced with horseradish or mustard. Vegetarians need not worry—there are copious veggie plates as well, something that's not always guaranteed in Ljubljana.

i Starters €5-7. Entrees €10-14. Open M-Sa 11am-12am, Su 11am-10pm.

REPUBLICA PASTA $

Slovenska Cesta 51 ☎40 151 705.

Slovenia has been inhabited since history began, and since then it's been ruled by a variety of different cultures: Austria-Hungary, Italy, Germany, Serbia, etc. Today, Slovenia is independent, but one of the ways it manifests its history is through its varied cuisine. Case in point: this tiny takeout joint on Slovenska Cesta. If you're down with pasta, then this is one of your best bets for quick, cheap, and delicious food in Ljubljana. Choose from a variety of toppings and sauces (beef with tomatoes, smoked salmon, and pesto are some of the highlights), then pick from one of their various pastas—which, incidentally, are also available for purchase if you want to bring them home (well, to your hostel) and cook them yourself.

i Small pasta €4. Large €5. Open M-F 10am-8pm.

NIGHTLIFE

SIR WILLIAM'S PUB

Tavcarjeva ulica 8a ☎sirwilliamspub-eng.webs.com

Step inside Sir William's, and you might think you've been transported to a posh English pub. But though they have a powerful selection from the British Isles (everything from good old Guinness to double IPAs from the Scottish beer punks at BrewDog), Sir Williams is as devoted to Slovenian craft beer as they come. Human Fish beers are always on tap, and offerings from Reservoir Dogs, Pelicon, Maister Brewery, and Pivovarna Mali Grad can be easily found to. Sir William's bills itself as a "House of Beer," and it deserves that mantle. Most other bars in the city stick to Union and Laško, two macro lagers owned by the same conglomerate (is there any difference? Well, some Slovenians have this motto: drink Laško, piss Union), so to explore some new lands and beers, come here .

i Beers from €2.50-7 (although only rare bottles will reach the upper part of that range). Open M-F 8am-1am, Sa 10am-1am, Su 5pm-12am.

SAX PUB

Eipprova 7 ☎05 180 44 50

In case you thought the word "sax" meant something different in Slovenian ("I dunno, maybe it means "good times" or "everybody, drink now!"), the drawing of an instrument on the menu will set you straight. Sax Pub is all about jazz. Well, kind of. They have jazz performances on a semi regular basis. Pictures of jazz legends hang on the wall. But even if you think Duke Ellington defeated Napoleon at Waterloo (it's the duke of Wellington, dude), you're still sure to enjoy this graffiti-covered bar. Like wine? Sax Pub is a place where you can get a liter of rosé for €10. Like weird spirits? Sax Pub distills their own—a shot of any of them goes for €2. If it's sunny (day drinking on vacation is no capital crime, after all), then Sax Pub's four massive umbrellas will protect you from the heat. If it's night, a charming set of vintage lightbulbs will bathe you in a yellow glow. The cigarettes of fellow patrons will also provide some light. Inside, you've got what looks like a normal, homey Slovenian country bar, albeit one overrun by jazz hounds. Chill out and listen to the music while enjoying your drink—it's sure to be a good night at Sax Pub.

i Shots €2. 1 L of wine €10. Open daily 10am-1am.

slovenia

TOZD

Gallusovo nabrežje 27   ☎04 06 99 453

The sleekly minimal signage signals upscale cocktail joint. The military green seat cushions, complete with the name TOZD in industrial lettering, screams boot camp. And the beakers they serve water in say "high school science fair." Confused yet? To put it bluntly, Tozd is a bit schizophrenic. But every element, no matter how disconnected it may seem, is geared towards ensuring your enjoyment. Of all the bars and cafes littered along the Ljubljanica, Tozd, located near Stari Trg is absolutely the finest. If it's alcohol you're looking for, they've got one of the strongest selections in Ljubljana. When it comes to beer, choose from Slovenian craft brewers Human Fish (on tap!), Reservoir Dogs, and Pelican, Austrian brewers Bevog, or Serbian brewers Kabinet. But don't worry—they've also got Lasko, Union, and the other Slovenian macros.

i Beers €3-4.50. Open daily 8:30 am-1am.

VINOTEKA MOVIA

Mestni trg 4   ☎01 425 54 48 www.movia.si/en/ljubljana-wine-bar-shop

You're looking to learn about Slovenian wine. But where to begin? Where can you really get the expert opinion? Why not start with a bar run by a family that's owned a winery since the 1820s? Vinoteka Movia, with its selection of wines crafted by the Movia estate, is a perfect place to spend a low key evening (what else would you expect from a bar partially located in City Hall?). Occasionally music from the neighboring bar will bleed into your conversation, but usually there'll be nothing but olives to distract you from your glass of white or red.

i Glasses of wine €2-6. Tastings €14-16. Open M-Sa 12pm-12am.

BIKOFE

Zidovska steza 2   ☎05 016 88 04

Bikofe is located extremely close to the University of Ljubljana, and the low-key vibe inside makes it seem like this hipster hangout is the world's coolest dorm room. That doesn't mean you'll be greeted with solo cups and blaring dubstep— expect some craft cocktails and downtempo techno instead. Carefully selected beers and wines are also available; if you're not looking to imbibe, they've got homemade iced tea for €2.50. Inside, you'll find older couples, young men in drag, groups of girls smoking cigarettes, dudes by themselves drinking beer and staring into the distance. It's eclectic, just like the many colored bar stools, mirrors, birdcages, and paintings that decorate its interior. Bikofe also has a fairly large deck with comfortable chairs; it's not uncommon to see the staff outside too, hanging on the stoop.

i Beers €2-3.50. Open M-F 8am-1am, Sa-Su 10am-1am.

ESSENTIALS

Practicalities

- **MONEY:** ATMs are everywhere—just look for the Bankomat sign. If you need to exchange money, there is a bureau of exchange in the train station, Železniška postaja, located on Masarykova Cesta.

- **TOURIST INFO CENTER:** Adamič-Lundrovo nabrežje 2 (☎01 306 12 15)

- **POST OFFICE:** Slovenska cesta 32. (Open M-F 8am-7pm, Sa 8am-12pm.)

Emergency

- **POLICE:** ☎113

- **MEDICAL EMERGENCY OR FIRE:** ☎112

ljubljana

- **HOSPITAL:** University Medical Centre Ljubljana, Zaloška 2 ☎01 522 50 50.
- **PHARMACIES:** Ljubljana Central Pharmacy (Prešernov trg 5 ☎01 230 61 00. M-F 7:30-7:30pm, Sa 8-3pm. Closed Sunday.) Lekarna pri Polikliniki (Prisojna ulica 7 ☎01 230 62 30. Open 24hr.)

Getting Around

The city center is highly walkable. If you need to use a bus, buy an Urbana Card for €2 euro at a tourist information center. Single rides cost €1.20.

bled

Just over an hour away from Ljubljana, Bled is a great choice for a day trip, but that doesn't mean you'll be bored out of your mind if you stay longer than that. There's tons to do here, from paddleboarding to touring a glacial gorge. Slovenia is Europe's third-most forested country, and places like Bled are where you get to appreciate those rural qualities. Just sit back, enjoy the lake, and try not to become so carefree that you decide to start gambling at Casino Bled.

SIGHTS

LAKE BLED

Unless you have a weird and twisted obsession with Bled Cream Cake, there is one reason and one reason only that you're visiting Bled: the lake. Whether you're looking to swim or to enact your fantasies of living in a fairy tale (just look at that island with the church on it!), Lake Bled will satisfy you.

Though walking along its perimeter will only take about an hour and a half, there are a variety of ways to approach Lake Bled. The best views can be had from Bled Castle and Osojnica, an observation point on top of one of the neighboring mountains. Needless to say, it's easier to get up to Bled Castle; though the trek uphill to Osojnica is punishing, you'll also be far more prepared to jump in the water once you get back down.

Along the lake, there are several designated swimming areas (elsewhere, boats will be docking, or the water is too shallow). One of these areas requires payment, but they also have water slides; if you're bummed there's no Six Flags Slovenia, maybe this spot is for you. If you don't want to swim, rent a boat or a paddle board—the hourly rates are reasonable, and some hostels will even give you a discount.

i Free. Open 24hr.

FOOD

GRILL BABJI ZOB $
Cesta svobode 8   ☎838 10584 grillbabjizob.si

This inviting joint (located just steps from the bus station and boasting a view of Lake Bled that's only slightly impeded by trees; hey, you can't win 'em all!) boasts that they have the best burger in town. Technically speaking, what they serve is not a burger but strips of meat accompanied by onions and chewy bread. But let's not quibble about semantics; it's still tasty, and as long as you don't go in expecting a quarter pounder with cheese you're in good hands. Why come all the way to Slovenia to get burgers anyway? In any case, the meat strips (now we see why they refer to them as burgers) are cheap—5 pieces cost just under €5, and probably kind of healthy. Onions are good for you!

i Burgers €5. Open daily 9:30am-11pm.

get a room!

BLED HOSTEL $

Grajska cesta 17   ☎04 250 57 45 www.bledec.si

Located just meters from the bus station, Bled Hostel is perfect if you're only in Bled a short while—you can dump your things in one of their lockers and be at the lake in minutes. But due to their comfortable beds, large kitchen and common area, and happening bar, you'd be just as happy if you stayed at Bled Hostel for a bit longer. The pub downstairs is often packed with locals, so be prepared to meet Slovenian friends as well as backpackers.

i Walk uphill from the bus station; the hostel will be on your left. Dorms €18-20. Reception 24hr.

HOSTEL BLEDEC $

Grajska cesta 17   ☎04 250 57 45 www.bledec.si

Though it's a bit farther away than Bled Hostel, nothing is really that far away in Bled—besides, you'll be slightly closer to Vintgar Gorge if you want to visit that! This is a clean, decently sized hostel; look for lots of fellow backpackers.

i Walk uphill from the bus station; the hostel will be on your left. Dorms €16. Reception 24hr.

PIZZERIA RUSTIKA $

Riklijeva cesta 13   ☎04 5768 900 www.pizzeria-rustika.si

The crowded street (ok, crowded for Bled, a town with a population of 6,000) that Pizzeria Rustika is located on? Not exactly rustic. The wooden interiors, complete with fuzzy photos of cows? That's more like it. Same goes for the wooden deck on the second floor. As is often the case in Slovenia, the so-called "small" pizzas are more than satisfactory—that's especially true here, as the crust is slightly thicker than you'll find elsewhere. If you don't think you're up to such a big meal, then just opt for one of their salads—just as tasty.

i Small pizza €6-8. Larger €7-10. Open daily 12pm-11pm.

NIGHTLIFE

PUB BLED

Svobode 19a   ☎04 574 26 22

No, not Club Med—Pub Bled! Ok, our apologies. Let's start over. Pub Bled's got a fairly refined, old school look—wood panelling, old photographs, located just above a fine dining restaurant. But make no mistake—this is a joint where people go to get wild. You see those TVs above the bar? One's for sports, and one shows a slideshow of all the different cocktails they have. Frustrated with bars that give you small cocktails? Get 3 liters of select cocktails (cuba libres and mojitos, among others) for €35. And yes, they've got Laško and Union—this is Slovenia, after all.

i Beers €2-3. Cocktails €5-7. Open M-Th 9am-1am, F-Sa 9am-3am, Su 9am-1am.

ESSENTIALS

Practicalities

- **MONEY:** There are two ATMs in the town center—one located in the Hotel Park complex by Svobode Cesta, and one in the shopping complex by Ljubljanska Cesta.

- **INTERNET CAFÉ:** Apropos Cocktail Bar has free Wi-Fi and a computer. Ljubljanska 4 ☎04 574 40 44. Open daily from 8am-12am.

- **POST OFFICE:** Ljubljanska 10 ☎04 578 09 00. Open M-F 8am-7pm, Sa from 8am-12pm.

Emergency

- **HOSPITAL:** Zdravstveni Dom Ble (☎04 575 40 00)

- **POLICE:** ☎113

- **MEDICAL EMERGENCIES, FIRE:** ☎112

- **PHARMACIES:** Bled Pharmacy, Ljubljanska 4.

Getting There

Buses leave from Ljubljana to Bled every hour. The journey takes a little over an hour and tickets cost €6.30. Tickets can be purchased at the bus station.

Getting Around

Bled is a small town and has no public transportation. Call Bled Taxi if you need a ride: ☎04 171 07 47.

slovenia essentials

VISAS

Slovenia is a member of the EU, and also a member of the Schengen area. Citizens of Australia, Canada, New Zealand, the US, and many other non-EU countries do not need a visa for stays of up to 90 days. However, if you plan to spend time in other Schengen countries, note that the 90-day period of time you are allowed to visit without a visa applies cumulatively to all Schengen countries.

MONEY

Slovenia uses the Euro (EUR, €) as its currency.

Tipping is not expected in Slovenia. In restaurants, it is common to round up the bill to the nearest euro, but this is not required. Taxi drivers also do not expect tips, but if you wish to tip, round up the bill.

ATMs in Slovenia are common and convenient. They are often located in airports, train stations and major pedestrian areas. The two major international money networks are MasterCard/Maestro/Cirrus and Visa/PLUS. To find out what out-of-network or international fees you may be subject to by using ATMs, call your bank.

ALCOHOL

The minimum age to purchase alcohol in Slovenia is 18, though technically there is no minimum age to drink alcohol. Remember to drink responsibly and to never drink and drive. The legal blood alcohol content (BAC) for driving in Slovenia is 0% for drivers with less than three years of experience, and 0.05% for everyone else, significantly lower than the US limit of 0.08%.

slovenia

SPAIN

Spain is a single, unified nation—but you wouldn't know it from traveling there. Each region's culture is as distinct from that of the rest as another country's. Just as the landscape varies from sun-soaked olive orchards in Andalucía to rainy and verdant hills in Galicia to windswept plains along the Camino de Santiago to Europe's best beaches all along the Mediterranean coast, so, too, do the languages and cuisines and attitudes change. And, of course, the fierce identities of Spain's unique cities can hardly be ignored. Quirky Barcelona, bureaucratic Madrid, sunny and southern Sevilla, and up-and-coming Bilbao will all claim to be the country's best; decide for yourself whether you prefer Madrid's stuffy museums to Barcelona's beaches, or tour Andalucía to figure out which city has the best mosque-turned-cathedral.

Where are you going? Make sure you have the right language, cuisine, and culture going in (don't try to order a pintxo in Granada or a pa amb tomàquet in Santiago), and enjoy the best Spain has to offer.

greatest hits

- **PICASSO, SHMICASSO.** See his works at the **Reina Sofía** in Madrid (p. 649) and the **Museu Picasso** in Barcelona.

- **GAGA FOR GAUDI.** With soaring, forest-inspired columns and incredible natural lighting, the **Sagrada Familia** (p. 678) is meant to be viewed on a kind of spiritual mushrooms.

- **SLOW BUT STEADY.** We won't lie: you will see a lot of cathedrals while in Spain. But the **Catedral Primada** (p. 735), which took nearly 300 years to constuct, is particularly impressive.

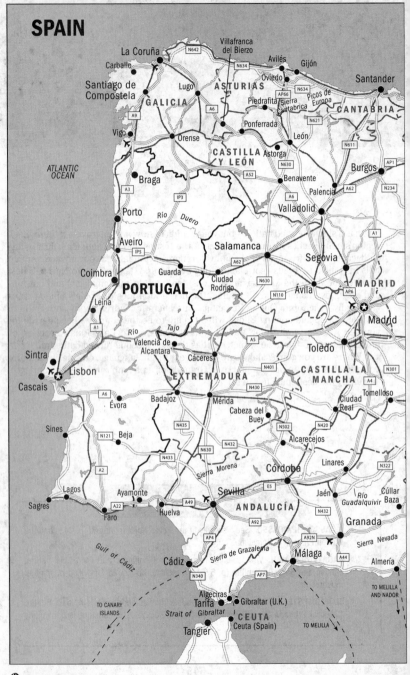

SPAIN

La Coruña
Carballo
Santiago de Compostela
GALICIA
Vigo
Orense
Lugo
A6
A9

Villafranca del Bierzo
ASTURIAS
Avilés
Oviedo
Gijón
Piedrafita
Sierra Cantabrica
Picos de Europa
Ponferrada
León
Astorga
CASTILLA Y LEÓN
Benavente
Santander
CANTABRIA
Burgos

ATLANTIC OCEAN

Braga
Porto
Río Duero
Aveiro
Coimbra
Guarda
Salamanca
Ciudad Rodrigo
Segovia
Ávila
MADRID
Madrid
Valladolid
Palencia

PORTUGAL

Leiria
Río Tajo
Valencia de Alcantara
Cáceres
EXTREMADURA
Toledo
CASTILLA-LA MANCHA
Tomelloso
Ciudad Real

Sintra
Lisbon
Cascais
Évora
Badajoz
Mérida
Cabeza del Buey
Alcarecejos

Sines
Beja
Sierra Morena
Córdoba
Linares
Jaén
Cúllar Baza

Lagos
Sagres
Faro
Ayamonte
Huelva
Sevilla
ANDALUCÍA
Río Guadalquivir
Granada
Sierra Nevada
Almería

Cádiz
Sierra de Grazalema
Málaga

Gulf of Cádiz

TO CANARY ISLANDS

Algeciras
Tarifa
Gibraltar (U.K.)
Strait of Gibraltar
CEUTA
Ceuta (Spain)
Tangier

TO MELILLA AND NADOR

TO MELILLA

spain

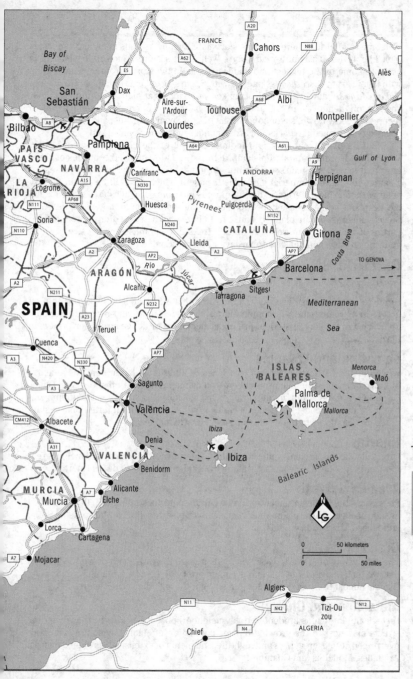

spain

madrid

Welcome to Madrid, where the days starts late, the nights ends later, and the locals look like Javier Bardem. Sound good? Well, there's more. Much more. Madrid is home to some of the biggest and baddest sights in the world, from museums filled with iconic art to *discotheques* packed with Spain's most beautiful. From Goya's *The Naked Maya* by day to the (almost) naked *madrileños* at night, Madrid insists that you stay on the move—in only the most laid-back style, of course. When it's time to recuperate, slow down, savor some of the best in Spanish cuisine, and lounge in one of the city's immaculate parks or gardens under the warm Spanish sun.

Madrid's plazas, gardens, and monuments tell of the city's rich history. After Philip II made it the capital of his empire in 1561, Madrid enjoyed centuries of being on top. It served as Spain's artistic hub during the Golden Age, becoming a seat of wealth, culture, and imperial glory, the legacy of which can still be felt in literary neighborhoods like Huertas, in the sumptuous interiors of royal estates like the Palacio Real, and in the badass collections of the museums along the Avenida del Arte. So get some rest on the plane, because from here on out, it's all dinners at midnight, parties at three in the morning, marathon treks through museums the size of small countries by day, and chasing down Javier at high noon.

ORIENTATION

El Centro

Home to administrative centers and important historical sites, El Centro is thin on non-touristy dining and accommodation options, but more and more are popping up every day. Check out student pricing at the Opera or dodge street performers in Plaza Mayor.

La Latina and Lavapiés

La Latina and Lavapiés represent two faces of Madrid. La Latina remains a center of down-home madrileño culture where you can tapas-hop with the locals on Calles Cava Baja and Cava Alta. In immigrant-heavy Lavapiés, trendy cafes are popping up like caffeinated weeds, but Calle Lavapiés is still stacked with international restaurants. It's also home to the weekly must-see Rastro market.

Huertas

Originally the intellectual center of Madrid, Huertas now has an abundance of great food and drink options, especially along the student-friendly C. de las Huertas.

Avenida del Arte

Possessing the highest concentration of culture per block in Madrid, this tree-lined avenue hosts the three major Madrid museums: Museo del Prado, Museo Reina Sofía, and Museo Thyssen-Bornemisza.

Gran Vía

The "Broadway of Madrid," Gran Vía tends toward the garish and overpriced chains that we tend to avoid, but it remains a main artery of the city, running from Plaza de España almost to Plaza de Cibeles and straight through the entire Centro.

Malasaña and Chueca

Historically known as student and gay neighborhoods, respectively, these winding streets play host to the growing hipster population of Madrid, which means more overpriced coffee, great bars and nightlife, and plenty of extensively groomed beards. Argüelles, Moncloa, and Chamberí

Outside the original city walls, these university areas have none of the twisting and turning streets and historic landmarks of the center, but cheap food and lesser-known museums like the Museo del Traje make them a chill place to hang out.

Salamanca, Retiro, and Ibiza

These neighborhoods north of El Centro are more posh residential areas, but they still have a lot of culinary life if you know where to look. Salamanca has the excellent Museo Sorolla and all the shops you might need to purchase your next designer purse. Retiro and Ibiza have great local restaurants and beautiful parks (along with plenty of small puppies and cute Spanish children).

SIGHTS

▧ MUSEO DEL PRADO

Paseo del Prado   ☎902 10 70 77 www.museodelprado.es

This sprawling palatial museum is the ultimate paean to Spanish art and high culture. Located along the Paseo del Prado, the museum's bricks and ionic columns are home to a collection of around 20,000 works of art (and one more now that you're here, dear reader). But don't worry, not all of them are on display at once! The Prado's ornate building was originally designed in 1785 to house the National History cabinet, but at the request of King Ferdinand VII and Maria Isabel de Braganza it was converted into a national museum of painting and sculptures in 1819. Today, the collection showcases some of the best-known pieces of the Western canon, including Hieronymous Bosch's The Garden of Earthly Delights (ground fl., room 56) and Rubens's The Three Graces (1st fl., room 29). Also impressive is the Prado's wide repertoire of Francisco Goya's paintings (ground fl., rooms 64-67). The museum owns more than 140 of his works including his famed "pinturas negras," or black paintings, found chillingly painted onto the walls of his villa. (As you look at Saturn Devouring One of His Sons, imagine that as a tasteful piece of decor!) Another Goya staple, The Third of May 1808, somberly depicts the aftermath of the Dos de Mayo uprising.

Navigate the overwhelmingly huge collection using the handy pamphlet of 50 masterpieces, or maybe start a race to find them all (just don't literally run afoul of the non-English-speaking guards). Or group your visit by the Old Masters themselves; this is the place to see Diego Velázquez's best works, including the famous Las Meninas (1st fl., room 12). The museum itself can be somewhat difficult to navigate (its main entrance is on floor zero, whose salas, or galleries, number 45-75; there's also a separate building housing the museum's special temporary exhibitions), but follow this booklet and you should find your way around the museum's 100-plus galleries without too much trouble. Saturday is the museum's busiest day, and museum officials recommend visiting between 1-3pm when most locals are eating lunch. If there's a popular exhibition going on, it's best to book ahead on the website; during the summer they tend to sell out the day of.

i Metro: Banco de España or Atocha. From Atocha, walk north up Paseo del Prado; the museum is on the right, just past the gardens. €16, students and under 18 free. Open M-Sa 10am-8pm, Su and holidays 10am-7pm.

▧ MUSEO NACIONAL CENTRO DE ARTE REINA SOFÍA

Pl. Emperador Carlos V or Santa Isabel, 52   ☎917 74 10 00 www.museoreinsofia.com

Housed in the southernmost leg of the Golden Triangle of Art, the Reina Sofía houses 20,000 pieces from the past 100 years. An artistic representation of the 20th-century Spanish experience spanning from the republic to dictatorship, some of the Reina's less than comprehensible contemporary art can still tell an important story. Get used to being confused, though: Salvador Dalí's *The Grand*

madrid

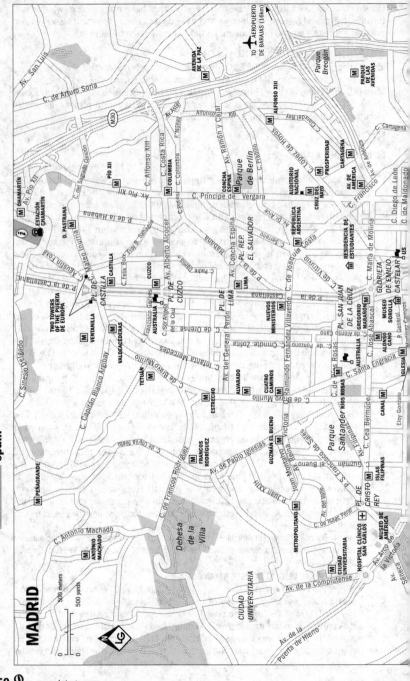

MADRID

spain

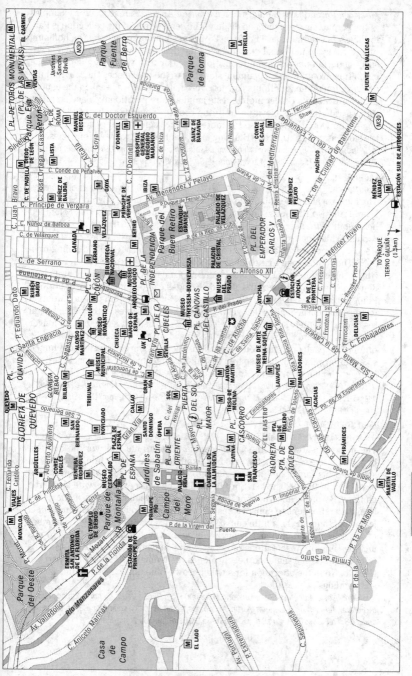

madrid

Masturbator and Luis Buñuel's film *Un Chien Andalou* are just some examples of the perplexing surrealism on display. The centerpiece of the collection is Pablo Picasso's Guernica, an 11½ ft. by 25½ ft. masterwork depicting the bombing of a key Basque industrial center during the Spanish Civil War. The guards are strict about no photos in the room, so take your time with every detail of the exhibition, from Picasso's planning sketches to the final piece. The labyrinthine organization of the four floors can get overwhelming; take a break in the central courtyard where a Calder mobile rests amid a more traditional palace architecture, or ride the glass elevator up to the roof for amazing views of Pl. Atocha and—who would have guessed?—more abstract contemporary sculpture. Use the side entrance to the New Building on C. Santa Isabel to avoid long lines.

i Metro: Atocha. €8, temporary exhibitions €4, students, under 18, and seniors free. Free M-F 7-9pm, Su 1:30-2:15pm. Open M 10am-9pm, W-Sa 10am-9pm, Su 10am-2:15pm.

PALACIO REAL
C. de Baillén   ☎914 54 87 00 www.patrimonionacional.es

The huge royal palace, inhabited by Spanish kings from the reign of King Philip V until Alfonso III, looks suitably intimidating from the outside. This columned behemoth is the largest palace in Western Europe at 135,000 sq. ft. and 3,418 rooms. While the exterior might seem plain, the interior is more ornate, with Rococo, Neoclassical, and Baroque finery alongside huge Catholic ceiling frescoes. The rooms open to the public showcase the opulence of Spanish royal life (think antechambers for their antechambers) and important works by Francisco de Goya, Diego Velázquez, and Juan de Flandes can be found throughout. King Philip V built the palace in 1734 on the site of a ninth- or 10th-century Moorish fortress that burned down that year. The building still serves as the official royal residence, but there's no use trying to catch a royal suitor, since they no longer actually live there. The space is primarily used for the occasional official celebration, EU pact, or abdication/coronation. The lines can get long in the summer, so either buy ahead or be prepared to wait for up to an hour. Backpacks are not allowed, though they can be stored in a locker with a deposit.

i Metro: Opera. Walk west down C. de Arrieta; Palacio Real is at the end of the road. €11, students, ages 5-16, and seniors €6. Free M-Th in summer 6pm-8pm; in winter 4-6pm. Open daily Oct-Mar 10am-6pm; Apr-Sept 10am-8pm.

MUSEO SOROLLA
C. General Martin de Campos, 47   ☎913 10 15 84 http://museosorolla.mcu.es

The museum showcases the artist Joaquín Sorolla's life and work in his own beautiful home. An intensely personal exhibition that delves into the relationship with his family and his art, parts of the space are set up as they would have been in the 1920s when Sorolla lived in the house with his wife and three children. Sorolla is known for his Impressionistic style that focuses on the use of luminous reflections to enhance beachscapes and portraiture. You'll almost feel jealous of (and maybe a little embarrassed for) his kids after seeing the number of paintings depicting them glowingly—even the vine border in the dining rooms includes mini representations of his wife and daughters. The house itself is as full of light as his fantastic beach scenes, including the famous El Baño del Caballo. Go in the afternoon for smaller crowds and take a siesta in the garden surroundings.

i Metro: Iglesia, Rubén Darío, or Gregorio Marañón. From Rubén Darío, go north 2 blocks on C. de Fortuny, turn left on C. General Martín de Campos, and it will be on your right. €3, students and under 18. Free Sa 2-8pm, Su all day. Open Tu-Sa 9:30am-8pm, Su 10am-3pm.

U HOSTELS $
C. Sagasta, 22 ☎914 45 03 00 http://en.uhostels.com

U Hostels bills itself as Madrid's "first luxury hostel," and regardless of whether that's true, it definitely has style. The common space, complete with dining tables and a bar, looks like an upscale cafe, and its movie theater—it has a movie theater!—is open for Netflix-viewing (chilling not advised) and sports-game freaking-out. Pool outings in the summer and free drinking games every night get the party going cheaply, and there are plenty of bars and clubs right out the door in Malasaña or just stops away from the two super-convenient metro stations. The prices can range high for Madrid on weekends, but that's the price we pay for "luxury."

i From Alonso Martínez, exit at C. Sagasta and go west until U Hostels on your left. Dorms €15-27; singles €32; doubles €64. Dinner €10. Reception 24hr.

THE HAT $$
C. Imperial, 9 ☎917 72 85 72 www.thehatmadrid.com

This hostel is basically a boutique hotel—plus bunk beds and minus obscene prices. We assume it's "The Hat" as in "top hat and monocle," given the custom-built wooden bunk beds, sparkling-clean bathrooms, and super-knowledgeable reception staff. The rooftop bar is one of the best and cheapest terrazas in the city, with a garden and a greenhouse-style indoor restaurant. We recommend grabbing a €3 doble overlooking the nearby Pl. Mayor even if you're not one of the fancy-pants staying here. The Hat is definitely one to book ahead, as the private rooms go fast in the summer.

i Metro: Sol or Tirso de Molina. From Tirso de Molina, take C. de la Colegiata north. Turn right on C. de Toledo, then turn right onto C. Imperial before Pl. Mayor. Look for the hats on the right. Breakfast €2.50. 8-bed dorms M-F €20, Sa-Su €27; 6-bed €23/31. Doubles M-F €65-70, Sa-Su €80-90. Reception 24hr.

HOSTAL LAS MURALLAS $$
C. Fuencarral, 23, 4th fl. www.hostalmurallas.com

Innocuously tucked right onto the busy shopping street C. Fuencarral, Las Murallas's single-room prices cannot be beat. Perfectly positioned for northern nightlife and southern touring sites, the guesthouse is run by an adorable elderly couple (be prepared for them to speak no English whatsoever, but they are very willing to awkwardly gesture), so reception hours can be irregular. Every room comes with a TV and a quiet comfortable stay, which cannot be overestimated in this city that barely sleeps.

i Metro: Gran Vía. Walk north on C. Fuencarral. It's in the apartment building on the left. Singles with shared bath €20-22; doubles with ensuite bath €38-42.

MAD4YOU $$
Costanilla de San Vicente, 4 ☎915 21 75 49 www.mad4you.com

Mad4You is standard hostel fare, with a great location and calmer atmosphere than some of the other cookie-cutter youth hostels in the area. The reasonable prices and reasonable common rooms are so very reasonable that you could reasonably stay there. Greatest hits include free sangria nights and particularly well-priced doubles for the area.

i From Noviciados metro, go north on C. de San Bernardo. Turn right on C. de San Vicente Ferrer, then left onto Costanilla de San Vicente. Towels €2. Laundry €6. Dorms €20-24; singles €36; doubles €52. Kitchen open 8am-midnight. Reception 24hr.

madrid

MUSEO THYSSEN-BORNEMISZA

Paseo del Prado, 8 ☎913 69 01 51 www.museothyssen.org

It's easy to forget about Thyssen-Bornemisza when hopping between the jugger-nauts that are the Reina Sofía and Prado. But that's good news for you—the lines for this world-class museum are short and sweet, while the collection spans the length of seven centuries. The museum is housed in the 19th-century Palacio de Villahermosa and contains the donated collection of the late Baron Henrich Thyssen-Bornemisza. Today, it is the world's most extensive private showcase, with items ranging from 14th-century Flemish altarpieces to an impressive col-lection of German Expressionist canvases from the early 20th century. Wander through the extension housing the Baroness Carmen's personal collection and marvel at how she acquired an actual Van Gogh in the 1980s. Their soft spot for expensive art is tourists' gain—whereas the Prado and Reina Sofía have exhibits focusing on very particular Spanish art, there's a more diverse selection here, including the likes of Edward Hopper and a few famous French Impressionists.

i From the Prado, walk north up the Paseo del Prado. The museum is at the corner of Carrera de San Jeronimo and Paseo del Prado. €12, students and seniors €6. Free on M. Open M noon-4pm, Tu-Su 10am-7pm.

PARQUE DEL BUEN RETIRO

Every large city needs a pedestrian-friendly park to diversify its otherwise concrete- and statue-ridden landscape. Madrid, though an unusually green city already, is no exception. Buen Retiro Park, a 350-acre plot of grass, trees, and walking trails, sits tranquilly between C. Alfonso XII and Av. de Menéndez Pelayo. The park, commissioned by the Count Duke of Olivares in the 1630s, is nearly 400 years old and saw the blossoming of Hapsburg court life, mock naval battles in its grand pond, and even Italian operas performed on its grounds.

While lush, meandering gardens and grassy lawns dotted with trees consti-tute the majority of the park, there are other attractions, like a large monument to Alfonso XII, the historic Casita del Pescador, and el Angel Caído, which some claim to be the only statue of the devil in existence (we're skeptical). The huge park has sections of bustling activity around the Palacio de Cristal, where the Reina Sofía puts on occasionally confusing contemporary art exhibitions, and around the central pond, but it also provides areas of escape and quiet from the bustling city.

Pack a picnic lunch and walk underneath the vine-covered Rosadela in the park's main garden or go boating on the majestic lake in front of Alfonso XII's monument. Even go for a short stroll through the park or join hundreds of other runners on a warm, breezy day. Also check out Madrid's literary festival, also located on Paseo de Carruajes, which runs from late May to mid-June each year, or the more permanent used bookstalls on C. de Claudio de Moyano along the southern edge of the park.

i Metro: Retiro. Or, from Atocha metro, pass the roundabout north onto C. de Alfonso XII, and the park will be on the right. Free. Open daily Apr-Sept 6am-midnight; Oct-Mar 6am-10pm. Row-boats for hire daily in summer 10am-8:30pm; in winter 10am-5:30pm. Rowboats M-F €5.80, Sa-Su €7.50.

PLAZA MAYOR

Pl. Mayor is the plaza of all plazas, the center of El Centro. Stand by the statue of Philip II and soak in the colorful facades, overpriced restaurants, and inexplica-bly costumed street performers. Because of its historic significance as the main market, bullfighting ring, coronation spot, and Inquisition execution central, the plaza can be a bit swamped by Segwaying tour guides and posed flamenco photos. Still, the cultural and tourism center in the former bakery la Casa de la Panidería and the super convenient location make Pl. Mayor a great place to

madrid's secret forest

Who knew!? To the west of the city, the Casa de Campo sits in all its expansive fairy-tale glory. Popular with local families, it's a great way to get away from all the tapas and cobblestones and find yourself in nature for a day or two (though nights not so recommended). You can metro to specific locations or take the 10min. Teleférico (cable car) from the Paseo Rosales to a trailhead and lookout point over the whole park. The Parque de Atracciones (metro: Batan) has a few water rides, roller coasters, and "Nickelodeonland" for a €24 entrance fee (check online for advance booking discounts), but purchasing rides individually makes for a cheaper and more customizable experience. Madrid's only Zoo Aquarium (metro: Casa de Campo) is also yours for the day for €23. To cap off your lengthy wanderings, take a refreshing dip in the popular lago (metro: Lago). Hitch a ride on the cable car back up to the Parque del Oeste, where it's only a short walk to the Templo de Debod to watch the sun set. Everything the light touches is now your kingdom.

start your tour of Madrid. The city's other central plaza, Puerta del Sol, is just down C. Mayor, where the touristy false statues and shifty magicians further stretch their domain. If you're hungry, head to the historic San Botín restaurant or the 24hr. churros of Chocolatería San Ginés. However, avoid the restaurants set right on the plaza as they tend to have higher prices. Instead, check out the nearby Mercado de San Miguel for multiple tapas stands, or hightail it to the Las Huertas bar area for more local options.

i Metro: Sol or Opera. From Sol, walk 2min. down C. Mayor toward Palacio Real. Pl Mayor is on the left.

CATEDRAL DE LA ALMUDENA

☎915 59 28 74 www.catedraldelaalmudena.es

Catedral de la Almudena is not your standard ancient venerated Gothic cathedral. In fact, it's not ancient at all, despite what you would expect from a fancy city like Madrid. The church took a while (read: 300 years) to get used to the idea of Phillip II moving the capital away from Toledo, so construction didn't begin until 1879. A little thing called the Spanish Civil War got in the way of construction, so the current structure was finished in 1993, and some paintings were still being added as late as 2004. Basically, this church is a millennial. This relative youth means the stained-glass and ceiling paintings have styles ranging from Impressionism to pop art. It's the rebellious child of Spanish cathedrals and worth checking out for these unique Modernist touches and its convenient location next to the Palacio Real.

i Right next to the Palacio Real. Free. Open daily 9am-8:30pm.

MUSEO NACIONAL DEL ROMANTICISMO

C. San Mateo, 13

☎914 48 10 45

It turns out Romanticism isn't what we were hoping it was (no gorgeous Spaniard was waiting to sweep us off our feet), but this small museum still has plenty of atmosphere. Focusing on the 19th-century Romantic period during the reign of Isabella II, the exhibit goes through historical and familial trends in the lives of the well-to-do. Your watchword here: 19th-century wealthy aristocrats are people too, my friend. Artifacts include period furniture, costumbrismo paintings, and, possibly most exciting, King Fernando VII's toilet (looks pretty comfy, though trying it out is not recommended). The free informational booklet covers the lifestyles of the bougie in both English and Spanish. If wandering

madrid

through stylish representative rooms isn't your style, then the cafe downstairs has reasonably priced drinks and snacks in a beautiful and romantic courtyard garden. That's more like it.

i From Tribunal metro station, go south on C. de Fuencarral, then turn left onto C. San Mateo. The museum is on the left at the intersection with Travesía San Mateo. €3, students €1.50. Free Sa after 2pm. Open May-Oct Tu-Sa 9:30am-8:30pm, Su 10am-3pm; Nov-Apr Tu-Sa 9:30am-6:30pm, Su 10am-3pm.

MUSEO NAVAL
Paseo del Prado, 5   ☎915 23 85 16 www.fundacionmuseonaval.com

Ever heard of the unbeatable Spanish Armada? Spoiler alert: it was beaten. You can learn all about the rise and fall of Spanish naval power at the Museo Naval, an overlooked member of the Paseo del Prado museum club. The museum is stuffed (and sometimes a bit stuffy) with detailed models of famous Spanish ships and artifacts related to trade and colonialism from the Catholic monarchs until the fall of the Spanish empire. The main attraction is the map of Juan de la Cosa from 1500, the earliest known map of the Americas. Note the image of St. Christopher completely covering where Central America should be and just let that colonialism sink in. There are plenty of guns, ships, and swords to go around, as well as an actual moon rock given to a Spanish naval officer from the United States—a nice touch for homesick Americans and moon aliens.

i From Banco de España metro station, follow C. de Alcalá east to Pl. de Cibeles. Cross to the other side of the plaza and follow Paseo del Prado south until you see the museum on your left. Free, but suggested donation €3. Open Tu-Su Sept-July 10am-7pm; Aug 10am-3pm.

FOOD

The Spanish tend to patronize their neighborhood bar more than anything else, and they demand quality food, so if you're in a less touristy area look for the local spot that has families and couples spilling out onto the street. They're guaranteed to have classic tapas and raciones along with some cheaper copas.

🔲 RESTAURANTE BADILA $$$
C. San Pedro Mártir, 6   ☎914 29 76 51

Arrive at this small restaurant right next to Tirso de Molina at precisely 2pm and you might notice a few other locals ready to sprint inside for their favorite menú del día. And madrileños don't sprint, so we know this must be some damn good menu. Badila does not disappoint (unlike those signs that promise the best Tex-Mex you've ever had—don't believe it!). The all-white interior evokes more beachside cafe than European villain's lair, and the super-rustic, delicious dishes (about seven options for both the first and second course) reinforce the good intentions. Meatballs become a religious experience, pasta is thick with chunky garlic, and absolutely everything from the bread to the smiling waiter seems homemade just for you.

i From Tirso de Molina metro stop, take C. San Pedro Mártir south until the corner with C. Cabeza. Weekday lunch menú del día €14. Open M-Th 2-4:30pm, F-Sa 2-4:30pm and 9pm-midnight, Su 2-4:30pm.

EL CAPRICHO EXTREMEÑO $
C. de Carlos Arniches, 30   ☎913 65 58 41

This is the place to go after a morning of treasure hunting at the Rastro market on the weekend. All products and the family that owns it come from Extremadura, a somewhat neglected region to the east of Madrid. But it's definitely well appreciated here; the line for the tostas (essentially an open-faced sandwich) piles out the door, but after 16 years they have it down to a science; your order should only take 5-15min. depending on the number of aggressive facedowns with abuelas. The 20 different tostas range from butter and jam to ham to eels

tapas: a primer

Take a look at the menu of any bar in Madrid and you'll see a confusing number of categories with variable pricing. Effectively (and cheaply) tapas-ing can even depend on the generosity of the server and charisma of the purchaser (*wink*), but here are tips to understanding how to extract as much bread and ham from this country as possible:

- **TAPAS:** Traditionally small portions served for free alongside a drink. When you're chilling in a standing-room-only local bar, you can place the small dishes on top of your cup—hence the name. (In Spanish, tapear means "to cover.") Nowadays in Madrid, stingy or touristy locales are less likely to offer free tapas, but if you politely ask for something to nibble, they'll likely bring over olives or a few sardines. Hit up a few of those or go to the famous Bar El Tigre for large greasy bites alongside your beer. You're set for a free meal!

- **PINCHOS/PINTXOS:** These are tapa-like foods on top of bread and generally a little more substantial than the free items. You can order these in bulk to share with friends, but if you go on an ordering spree, don't count on the waiter losing count; the name comes from the toothpicks served in each to keep track of consumption.

- **RACIONES:** Larger shareable plates that have a higher price tag, particularly for the famous jamón ibérico. Expect to shell out for high-quality ingredients, but as long as you have a few Spanish friends with whom to share the cost (and explain how to properly eat a tiny fish whole), they're a great deal.

and everything in between. The goat cheese with raspberry jam made by monks from Extremadura should be declared sacred; at least we hope it washes away Saturday-night sins.

i From Puerto de Toledo metro stop, walk along Ronda de Toledo until Pl. del Mundo Nuevo. On the left side of the square, find C. de Carlos Arniches. It's 100m up on your left. Tostas €2-3. Open Sa-Su 11am-3:30pm.

CHOCOLATERÍA SAN GINÉS $
Pasadizo San Ginés, 5   ☎913 65 65 46 http://chocolateriasangines.com

After a night out in El Centro, food options can seem thin, but then San Ginés glows from its own personal alley like a classy tiled green and white beacon. Waiters staff indoor and outdoor tables at this 24hr. haven for the tired, the hungry, and the masses yearning to eat deep-fried dough and gooey chocolate. Most go straight for the traditional churro, but the thicker porras are chewier and more substantial snacks for the drunk and sober alike.

i From Sol metro, take C. Arenal west. Turn left at Teatro Joy Eslava onto Pasadizo San Ginés. 6 churros €4. 2 porras €4. Open 24hr.

MALACATÍN $$
C. de la Ruda, 5   ☎913 65 52 41 www.malacatin.com

Serving up meat-heavy Madrid essentials, Malacatín has been a La Latina institution since 1895. From the dark wooden benches to the faded bullfighting posters and medals covering the walls, this places screams old Madrid louder than even the pot-bellied mustachioed waiters can. Its cocido (a pot of chickpea stew served up with four different types of pork) is considered a legendary best in Madrid. It even has its own confused naming mythology based on a local beggar who used to sing "malacatín tin tin" so many times that they just gave up and named the restaurant after him. The large cocido is on the expensive side

madrid

(€20), and there's a strict no-sharing policy, so get the degustación size (€5)—the size of your face rather than your torso and still enough for a filling meal.

i From La Latina metro, walk south on C. de Toledo. Turn left onto C. de la Ruda. It's on the end of the street on your right. Entrees €9-15. Open Th-F 11am-6pm and 8pm-midnight, Sa 11am-6pm.

EL JARDÍN SECRETO $$
C. Conde Duque, 2 ☎915 41 80 23 http://eljardinsecretomadrid.com

The creators of El Jardín Secreto ("The Secret Garden") bill themselves as "creators of dreams." Hey, it may be a bit presumptuous, but they definitely make every effort to turn this corner restaurant into a dreamscape. Foliage everywhere, bizarre light fixtures, action figures scaling a mini waterfall, and teddy bears in cages—it's like fairy-tale tea in the garden on acid. This sensation extends to the food and drink selection, a huge range of beverages, snacks, and entrees ranging from coffee to complicated cocktails. The menu presents the creatively described desserts first for good reason—doughnuts are "out of this universe" and the brownie sundaes are "orgasms." An English menu is available by request in a charming handwritten scrawl.

i Metro: Pl. de España or Ventura Rodríguez. From Ventura Rodríguez, take C. de San Bernardino until the corner with C. Conde Duque on the left. Entrees €8-13. Drinks €4-10. Open M-Th 5:30pm-12:30am, F-Sa 6:30pm-2:30am, Su 5:30pm-12:30am.

CASA LABRA $
C. Tetuan, 12 ☎915 31 00 87 www.casalabra.es

When you wander around Puerta de Sol, it seems like the chains offering American-style hamburgers never end. Into this soulless void steps Casa Labra to the rescue. Offering genuinely delicious and well-priced croquettes for over 150 years, Labra has never succumbed to bad quality because of the nearby tourist horde. Warm and creamy cod croquettes (croquetas de bacalao) are the specialty; if you ask for any other kind, they'll look at you like you're one croqueta short of a ración. The dining room has a surcharge of €0.10 per tapa, but most eat their famous tajada de bacalao (a huge chunk of fish and chips, minus the chips) out at the standing tables perfectly placed for El Centro people watching.

i Metro: Sol. Take C. Preciados north until the first left, C. Tetuan. It's in the nook on the left. Croquettes €1. Sandwiches €4-7. Open daily 9:30am-3:30pm and 5:30-11pm.

EL PEJCAITO $
C. Mayor, 44 ☎666 55 74 93 www.elpejcaito.com

The calamari sandwich is a staple of the madrileño diet—carbs plus meat plus let's add some more carbs in there. While El Brillante in Pl. Atocha proudly claims its own as the best one in the land, Let's Go is a fan of this more modest

ham it up

Compared to some of the larger regions in Spain, it may seem like Madrid doesn't have as much hometown pride. Not so! Madrid does have its own unique culinary delights: the famous yet sometimes overlooked *cocido*. It's a dish so traditional you might suddenly find yourself standing in the middle of a corrida del toros with elaborate facial hair. Or, less fantastically, you'll end up eating a delicious pot full of chickpea stew imbued with the flavors of no less (and sometimes more) than four types of meat. Savor chorizo, ham, black pudding, and bacon slow-cooked with a few vegetables thrown in for show. Each institution will vary it slightly, and everyone's abuela does it better than everyone else's. So this is how the *madrileños* get their energy for those late nights...

and much cheaper alternative. El Pejcaito (said as quickly as possible to disguise the impossibility of pronouncing it correctly) is a small fast-food joint that serves up heavenly and incredibly fresh bocadillos de calamares. You can easily see how the sausage (or rather the golden and crispy squid) is made, as it's doused in flour and fried to order along with a selection of different homemade sauces all wrapped up in an airy baguette. Take it to go and chew on some hometown Madrid goodness right next door in the iconic Pl. Mayor.

i Metro: Sol. Take C. Mayor all the way past Pl. Mayor; it'll be on your right. Calamari sandwich €2.50. Sandwich, fries, and a drink €5.50. Open daily 11am-10pm.

ZHUO YULONG $

Pl. de España ☎915 48 21 03

What's cooler than eating a cheap, filling, and delicious lunch in Pl. de España? Eating it under the plaza in a hidden spot known only to a select few—and by that we mean most of the locals in search of good value Chinese. Right at the western end of Gran Vía, down a set of innocuous parking garage stairs and a slightly less innocuous hallway, is Zhuo Yulong, where €3 can get you a plate of noodles and a seat in the crowded favorite. Given Madrid's relatively inadequate Chinese offerings, Zhuo does a great job of quickly serving up large plates on a generous schedule unheard of in siesta-accustomed Madrid. Mealtimes can get busy, though, so either grab a seat at the bar next to those cases of tongue and liver (authenticity!) or get it to go and emerge back into the world above.

i From Santo Domingo metro, go north on Gran Vía. Once you hit Pl. de España, look for the stairs to the parking garage along the border with C. de la Princesa. Entrees €3-7. Cash only. Open daily 10am-1am.

LA BICICLETA CAFÉ $

Pl. de San Ildefonso, 9 www.labicicletacafe.com

If you are an attractive person who likes to bike or a regular person who likes being around attractive people who like to bike, La Bicicleta has you covered. In the middle of the oh-so-trendy Malasaña neighborhood, Bicicleta takes the hipster cafe in its own direction with bike-focused decor as well as manuals and tools to fix them. This gimmick with charm comes with some great homemade sandwiches and a wide selection of drinks. The pierced and tattooed staffers have a workspace-oriented approach, meaning after you order something they'll never kick you out even if you charge every single electronic you own at the cafe's numerous and convenient outlets. It even has boxes to lock laptops in if you have to duck out for a second—we assume to fix your fixed-gear vintage roadster.

i From Tribunal metro, take C. de la Palma to the first left on C. Corredera Alta de San Pablo. Follow it until Pl. de San Ildefonso, and it'll be on the corner on the right. Sandwiches €7-10. Drinks €2-6. Open M-W 10am-1am, Th 10am-2am, F-Sa 11am-2:30am, Su 11am-midnight.

EL PEZ GORDO $$

C. del Pez, 6 ☎915 22 32 08

A local favorite, El Pez Gordo is a classic neighborhood tapas bar that stands out on a street packed with every new trendy thing (not another artisanal burger place!). It survives with a huge local clientele who come back for good prices and large raciones, including the great and slightly more unusual escabeche de pavo (marinated turkey; €8.50). Even in the midst of Malasaña and Chueca, El Pez keeps it deliciously relaxed.

i From Noviciados metro stop, go south on C. de San Bernardo, turn left on C. del Pez, and go almost to the end. It's on your left. Tapas €2-2.50. Raciones €5-12. Open daily 7:30pm-2am.

LATERAL $$

Pl. Santa Ana, 12   ☎914 20 15 82 www.lateral.com

People in here are hip AF, and you'll wish you had spruced up your T-shirt and shorts so you wouldn't decrease the cool factor of the white leather chairs and marble countertops. Still, your attire won't stop you from enjoying Lateral's raspberry mango foam (€4) or avocado-smoked salmon tartare (€5). Small modern tapas play nice with twists on traditional dishes like oxtail and blood sausage. The crowd on weekends can verge on Prado-like, so just visit its station dedicated to crafting five varieties of house mojitos (€7) as you wait and settle into the "Lateral experience."

i On the southwest corner of Pl. Santa Ana. Tapas €3-8. Cocktails €7. Open M-W noon-midnight, Th-Sa noon-1am, Su noon-midnight.

CAN PUNYETES $$

C. de San Agustín, 9   ☎914 29 94 83

So you're craving a huge piece of grilled meat. First: calm down—you're in Spain and you'll get it eventually. Second: go to Can Punyetes for Catalan-style carne a la brasa. Order straight from the carne section of the menu for reasonably priced and huge portions of steak and pork that seriously taste like they came from an animal (in the best possible sense). You can hear the barbecue sizzle from the kitchen as you take in the machismo of the old-style taberna. The name Can Punyetes is a slightly vulgar phrase in Catalan—so macho—and the Wi-Fi password is still about 15 characters long—so traditional.

i Metro: Antón Martín. From exit Magdalena, go north on C. del León, turn right onto C. de Cervantes, and turn left onto C. San Agustín. Grilled meat €6-12. Dessert €4-6. Open M-W 1-5pm and 8pm-midnight, F-Sa 1-5pm and 8pm-1am, Su 1-5pm.

NIGHTLIFE

TEATRO KAPITAL

C. de Atocha, 125   ☎914 20 29 06 www.grupo-kapital.com

Still the last word in seven-story Madrid superclubs, Kapital maintains a classy yet sweaty, touristy yet local, and never-endingly energetic all-night experience. Pretend you're in a different club on every floor, though the advertised music somehow all ends up sounding like a top 40 remix of some kind. The main floor features house and electronic music and writhing, scantily clad dancers on the stage, with each successive floor overlooking the masses from successive balconies. Go to the "Music Studio" for some beginning-of-the-night karaoke embarrassment, take on the Mojito and Cuba Libre level for cocktails and Latin-inspired beats, and brave "The Kissing Room" for…we're not completely sure what. Attire tends toward dressy, and leaving time tends toward sunrise.

i From Atocha metro, go 1 block down C. Atocha. It's the huge superclub on your right. Bring ID. Cover €15-20; includes 2 drinks. Shots €5. Drinks €12. Open Th-Sa midnight-6am.

CAFE BERLIN

C. Costanilla de los Ángeles, 20   www.berlincafe.es

After recently moving locations, the "Nuevo Club Berlin" still has a super loyal clientele and a really chill local vibe. In an underground space close to some major tourist sites without being touristy, Cafe Berlin has intimate concerts and, starting at 1am, converts into a club with a different theme every night. Funk, blues, jazz, and electronic are all options on the Cafe Berlin musical menu, so check online for something that piques your interest. The Wednesday flamenco jam nights are a particularly good deal at €7-8. It's definitely worth enduring the cognitive dissonance of being in a space attempting to be an East Berlin jazz club while playing Spanish music to an international audience.

i From Opera metro, take C. de los Caños del Peral until it merges with C. Costanilla de los Ángeles. It'll be on your right 50m up. Tickets €6-12. Cover F-Su €10; includes free drink. Check website for discounts. Concerts 8pm-midnight. Club open 1-5:30am.

INDEPENDANCE CLUB

C. del Doctor Cortezo, 1   http://independanceclub.com

So it's a Monday night and you're like, "Oh well, guess I'll head back to the hostel and cry salty tears of sadness." Stop right there: you're in Spain, which means there's definitely a party on a Monday. Get up (or wait until an appropriately madrileño time like 2 or 3am) and go to the Independance Club for "Fuckin' Monday," its weekly student night. It also has a salsa class every Monday at 10pm, so you'll arrive with the skills to charm all the madrileñas (€5; includes class and drink). Weekend events and prices vary, but its central location near many of the hostels makes it a great stop on a club hop. Sign up on its Facebook page ahead of time for free entry and other deals.

i From Tirso de Molina metro, head north on C. del Doctor Cortezo. It's on your right before the intersection. Fuckin' Monday cover €8; includes free drink. Shots €3. Club open 11:30pm-6am; opens earlier for select events.

TUPPERWARE

C. Corredera Alta de San Pablo, 26   ☎625 52 35 61 www.tupperwareclub.com

Idiosyncratically named and even more quirkily decorated, Tupperware is Malasaña's permanent alternative fixture for cheap drinks and good vibes. Empty vintage TVs with mildly creepy dolls living in them cover the back of the bar, and a collection of '60/'70s pop-culture icons make appearances in the mural around the first floor. Drink along with Mr. Spock while appropriately indie music and the chatter of Madrid's young but somehow nostalgic patrons plays in the background. Try to get there before midnight for discounted drinks, but then brace yourself for the onslaught of the club's busiest hour, midnight-1am.

i Metro: Tribunal. Head west on C. de la Palma, turn right on Corredera Alta, and keep your eyes out to your right. Beer €3.50. Shots €3. Cheaper before midnight. Open Tu-Th 8pm-3am, F-Sa 8pm-3:30am, Su 8pm-3am.

VÍA LACTEA

C. Velarde, 18   ☎914 46 75 81 www.lavialactea.net

This is a Spanish temple dedicated to rock, grunge, and everything '70s counterculture. Vía Lactea was founded in the early years of La Movida Madrileña, a youth-propelled revolution of art, music, fashion, and literature where famous artists like director Pedro Almodóvar would gather to listen to international music and fight the man (literally, when the man was Franco). Today, it's an eclectic mix of students and people who definitely were students at some point, possibly in the '70s. Every night, locals and tourists gather here to shoot pool, hang out under the warm neon glow, and attend the odd reading or local film premiere. No cover charge means you get a free visit to the Milky Way, unlike those suckers who pay Elon Musk $60 million to visit outer space for 10min.

i Metro: Tribunal. Walk north up C. Fuencarral and make a left onto C. Velarde. Beer €3.50. Cocktails €7.50. Open July-Aug M-Th 9pm-3am, F-Sa 9pm-3:30am, Su 9pm-3am; Sept-June M-Th 8pm-3am, F-Sa 8pm-3:30am, Su 8pm-3am.

VACACIONES COCKTAIL BAR

C. Espíritu Santos   ☎911 70 40 15 www.vacacionesbar.com

The only thing that might be missing from your landlocked Madrid stay is the beach, so Vacaciones brings the beach to the city—along with copious amounts of alcohol. Tropical colors, fun and friendly servers, and a fruity cocktail menu round out the staycation. There's a selection of incredible homemade cakes and a choice of Indian, Arabic, and traditional nachos. (Hey, curiosity killed the cat, not the taste bud.) Sit on the spacious terraza in Pl. Juan Pujol and pity the hipsters as you sip a gigantic supermargarita (€21). Technically it's supposed to be shared among three people, but we're not judging.

i From Tribunal metro, take C. de la Palma, then turn left onto C. de San Andrés. Once you get to Pl. Juan Pujol, it will be on the far-left corner of the square. Cocktails €6-9. Open M-Th 10am-1am, F-Sa 10am-2am, Su 10am-1am.

JOY ESLAVA

C. Arenal, 11   ☎913 66 37 33 www.joy-eslava.com

The gilded doors of Joy Eslava enclose an equally glittering population of Madrid's most beautiful. Going strong since the theater was turned into a club in 1981, the old-style glamor of the club's building corresponds with its escalating prices and exclusive approach. Only two blocks from Sol, you'll find a fair share of tourists and students mixed in with scantily clad models. Joy rotates music nightly, with events every week like Million Dollar Tuesdays or Clandestine Fridays. Dress like the madrileños: predominantly black and slightly upscale attire encouraged. After you're done dancing the night away under a perpetual New Year's shower of balloons and confetti, the famous 24hr. churro spot Chocolatería San Ginés is only steps away for a drunk bite.

i Metro: Opera or Sol. From Sol, leave the square by C. Arenal; the club will be on your left. Student night Th. Cover €12-18. Cocktails €12. Open M-Th 11:55pm-5:30am, F-Sa 11:55pm-6am, Su 11:55pm-5:30am.

spain

SPACE MONKEY CLUB

C. de Campoamor, 3   ☎654 51 14 57 www.spacemonkeyclub.com

Space Monkey is a student paradise of free-flowing alcohol. A basement with a dive-bar vibe but a club atmosphere, the Monkey is plastered with alternative rock posters from the mid-2000s and is filled with equally plastered international and local youths. With group-sized drinks like the "Porrón" (750mL of Tequila Sunrise) or "La Jirafa" (a gigantic long-necked beer), getting wasted is an epic spectacle. Themed events range from "hippie" body paint to Grease summer nights. Space Monkey is good for a relatively early (by Madrid standards) night of fun, plenty lubricated by alcohol. Pitch in with hostel buddies for a €6 pitcher of beer on Thursdays or go all the way for the literally flaming "Rocket" to get ready for a night (or early morning) out in the Malasaña nightclubs.

i From Alonso Martínez metro station, go south to Pl. Santa Barbara. Turn left onto C. Santa Teresa and right onto C. de Campoamor. The club is on your right. No cover. Beer before 1am €3. Shots €2. 750mL of Tequila Sunrise €18. Open Th-Sa 11pm-3:30am.

THUNDERCAT

C. de Campoamor, 11   ☎654 51 14 57 www.thundercatclub.com

Sometimes the Spanish want to feel like stone-cold, hardcore rockers. Don't we all? Thundercat is the place to get your head-bang on, with nearly three live acts per night covering hardcore rock classics. Since patrons tend to be at least 25 and there are nearly no tourists, blending in can be a struggle, but it's ultimately worth it for some quality music and authentic underground Madrid. Drinks are pricey, so hit up a few of the nearby bars on C. de la Palma before heading over for a late night.

i Metro: Alonso Martínez. Take C. de Genova to C. de Campoamor and turn right. Thundercat will be on your right. Cover free-€10 depending on concert or event. Drinks €9-10. Open F-Sa 10pm-6am.

BARCO

C. del Barco, 34   ☎915 31 77 54 www.barcobar.com

With a jam-packed program of nightly concerts, late-night DJ sets, and weekly jam sessions, this small venue covers a wide spread of musical terrain. BarCo has made a name for itself as a stalwart venue for local acts, with most bands drawing heavily on funk, soul, rock, and jazz. While the concert schedule is continually changing, the nightly DJ sets are given to a handful of veteran European DJs who have been spinning in Madrid for years. The Big Band features on Tuesdays and the Sunday-night jam sessions have loyal fans among the locals and bring in some of the city's best musicians. Though it makes a play for a New Orleans atmosphere, it's Spanish through and through (or so say the accents of the performers).

i Metro: Tribunal. Head 3 blocks south on C. de Fuencarral. Take a right onto C. Corredera Baja de San Pablo, walk 2 blocks, and take a left (south) onto C. del Barco. The bar is on the right. Cover €5-10. Beer €5. Cocktails €5. Cash only. Open M-Th 10pm-5:30am, F-Sa 10pm-6am, Su 10pm-5:30am.

GYMAGE TERRACE

C. de la Luna, 2   ☎915 32 09 74

Gymage is "2 hip 4 u," as the kids would say. Billed as Madrid's "first urban re-sort," it has a line out the door on weekends, so either come early or be prepared. It's located on top of a gym, so you can feel slightly physically inferior as you ascend through levels of Madrid's buffest physiques—and then feel extremely physically inferior as you take your seat at the bar next to Madrid's most gorgeous figures. The terrace sits right alongside the church of San Martín de Tours; the anticipation of the church bell ringing from 5 ft. away keeps partiers on their toes. Cocktails are huge and multicolored but also reek of price-gouging (the price you pay for a view among the urban elite). If you're feeling adventurous, ask for the Gymage Surprise (€7); the barstaff makes each one to order based on the customer's preferences, so you may end up with a mysterious glass of candy and liquor, perfect for pre-gaming nearby Chueca clubs.

i Metro: Callao. Cross Gran Vía and go to the right. Take a left on C. Concepción Arenal, and it will be across the square. Cocktails €7-11. Entrees €7-15. Open M-Th noon-1:30am, F-Sa noon-2:30am, Su noon-1:30am.

ESSENTIALS
Practicalities

- **TOURIST OFFICES:** The Centro del Turismo Plaza Mayor has tons of information and pamphlets on sights, activities, and orientation, though it tends to use an online database for its food and accommodation recommendations. (Pl. Mayor, 27. ☎914 54 44 10 www.esmadrid.com. From Sol metro stop, take C. Mayor west, then turn left on C. Felipe III the Pl. Mayor. The office will be on your right, on the north side of the plaza. Wheelchair-accessible. English spoken. Free Wi-Fi. Open daily 9:30am-9:30pm.) There are other offices throughout the city, marked by bright yellow "i" signs. Hours vary slightly by location, so check online. Also worth checking out is the Guía del Ocio (www.guiadelocio.com), which is online or €1 at newsstands and convenience stores and has good up-to-date monthly information.

- **TOURS:** A lot of area hostels host their own free or well-priced tours (tapas, bar crawls, historical, etc). Free historical tours meet daily at 10am, 11am, and 2pm in front of the tourist information office at Pl. Mayor (www.neweuropetours.eu).

- **LUGGAGE STORAGE:** You can store your bags in the tropical garden of the Atocha railway station. (Pl. Emperador Carlos V, 28. ☎902 32 03 20. Small bags €3.20 per day, medium €3.60 per day, large €4.78 per day. Open M-F 5:30am-10:20pm, Sa 6:15am-10:20pm, Su 6:30am-10:20pm.) The bus station Estación del Sur will also store your bags. (€1.25 per day. Open M-F 6:30am-11:30pm, Sa 6:30am-3pm.)

- **INTERNET:** Wi-Fi is available for free at all the tourism offices and public libraries as well as many restaurants (generally with purchase).

- **POST OFFICES:** Stamps are available at post offices or tobacco shops. The main post office is at Pl. de Cibeles. (Paseo de Prado, 1. ☎915 23 06 94 or ☎902 19 71 97. www.correos.es Open M-F 8:30am-8:30pm, Sa 8:30am-1pm.)

- **POSTAL CODE:** 28008

Emergency

- **EMERGENCY NUMBER:** General emergencies ☎112. Local police and ambulance ☎092. National police ☎091.

- **POLICE:** Call the tourist hotline Servicio de Atención al Turista Extranjera, or SATE (☎902 10 21 12), for English speakers and help with contacting embassies, reporting crimes, and canceling credit cards. Both the headquarters of the local national police chapter and the physical location of SATE are located at the Comisaría Centro. (C. Leganitos, 19. ☎915 48 77 98. Metro: Pl. de España or Callao. Open daily 9am-midnight.)

- **LATE-NIGHT PHARMACIES:** Call ☎089 for listings of 24hr. Pharmacies.

- **MEDICAL SERVICES:** Call ☎112 for medical emergencies. Non-emergency service for English speakers at Unidad Medica Angloamericana. (C. del Conde de Aranda, 1, 1st fl. ☎914 35 18 23. Open M-F 9am-8pm, Sa 10am-1pm.)

Getting There

The main airport is Aeropuerto Adolfo Suárez Madrid-Barajas, commonly just called Barajas (Av. de la Hispanidad. ☎902 40 47 04 www.aeropuertomadrid-barajas.com.) The easiest way to get into the center of the city is the metro from Barajas station (€4.50-5; 12-20min. walk from the terminals). Take Line 8 toward Nuevo Ministerios, transfer to Line 10 toward Puerta del Sur, get off at Tribunal (3 stops), transfer to Line 1 toward Valdecarros, and get off at Sol. The journey should take 45-60min. By bus, Línea 200 leaves from the national terminal (T2) and runs to the Av. de América metro stop in the city center (every 10-20min. 5am-11:30pm). Taxis (set price €30; 30min.) are readily available outside the airport.

Trains from northern Europe and France arrive on the north side of the city at Chamartín station. (C. Augustín de Foxa. ☎913 00 69 69.) Trains to and from Portugal and the south of Spain service Atocha station. (Pl. Emperador Carlos V. ☎902 32 03 20.)

The largest national bus company is ALSA (☎902 42 22 42 www.alsa.es), but there are many bus line options to all major locations throughout Spain. Most will go through Estación del Sur. (C. Méndez Álvaro. ☎914 68 42 00 www.estacionautobusesmadrid. com.) Inquire at the station or by phone for the latest schedules.

Getting Around

Madrid's metro system is the best, cheapest, and easiest way to get around the city. Used by tourists and locals alike, the metro is clean and runs fairly frequently. Electronic signs indicate the wait time on the platforms. A one-way ticket fare in Zone A is €1.50-2 (prices will rise farther away from the center). Abonos mensuales (monthly passes) are €54.60, and abonos turísticos (tourist passes) for one, two, three, four, or seven days cost €8.40-35.40, but if you'll be staying in the center most of the time, the best deal is the 10-ticket book (€12.20). Machines in the stations take credit, debit, and cash. Transit maps are available in the stations and also online at www.metromadrid.es. Trains run daily 6am-1:30am.

Registered Madrid taxis are black or white and have red bands and small insignias of a bear and madroño tree (the symbols of Madrid). You can hail them on the street or at a taxi stand. If you call to reserve, there's an extra charge of €5. During the day, a ride will cost you a base of €2.40 plus €1.05 per kilometer. At night (9pm-7am), the base fare is €2.90, and each kilometer will cost you €1.20. Taxis from the airport to the center have a flat rate of €30. One reputable company is Radio Taxi Gremial (☎914 47 51 80).

Though not a particularly recommended way to get around Madrid, certain places (Casa del Campo, Parque del Retiro) offer a nice opportunity for biking. Trixi rents bikes for up to one week. (C. de los Jardines, 12. ☎915 23 15 47 www.trixi. com. 1st hr. €4, increasing up to €50 for 1 week. Helmets €2.50. Requires a deposit of €50 and a photocopy of your passport or they keep your passport as collateral for the duration of the rental. Open M-F 10am-2pm and 4-8pm, Sa-Su 10am-8pm.) The city also has an electric bike-share system, called BiciMad, with stations placed around the city center. The stations offer cards for one-, three-, and five-day access to rentals. During the ticket validity period, €150 must be on your card and will be locked as collateral. (www.bicimad.com. 1st hr. €2, €4 per subsequent hr.)

Blafer Motos rents mopeds for €20-50 per day, including insurance, a helmet, and a lock, though you must remain within the city of Madrid. You must be at least 25 years old and have a license for motorcycles. (C. Clara del Rey. ☎914 13 00 47 www. blafermotos.com. 80km included; €0.40 per additional km. Open M-F 8am-8pm, Sa 10am-1:30pm.)

madrid

barcelona

Barcelona, a favorite travel destination for millions worldwide, is the second largest city in Spain and the capital city of Catalonia. The city is bustling and loud, and the first thing it will tell you is to get lost. Not in the "you don't belong here" sense, but because you can walk around aimlessly, with literally no idea where you are, and still have a good time. Around every corner there will be an alluring alleyway of stores, a museum of interest or beautiful building, or a tapas bar with a seat calling your name, and you genuinely need no directions to have a remarkable trip. This loudness also comes in a multitude of languages, and if you have come with the intention of practicing your Spanish, you'll need to make it known to the locals because they will talk to you in English if they are aware that you speak it. This is because Barcelona is an inherently social place. In many restaurants, there are more outdoor seats than indoor seats, because being integrated with the community is part of what makes the city so unique. With a thriving nightlife in front of a gorgeous beach, historical remnants of some of the world's most significant artists, and one of the best public transit systems of any global city, Barcelona has more than enough attractions to entertain travelers: young, old, single, or grouped.

ORIENTATION

Though a large and complex city, Barcelona's *barris* (neighborhoods) are fairly well-defined. The **Ciutat Vella** (old city) is the city's heart, comprised of **El Raval** (west of Las Ramblas), **Barri Gòtic** (between **Las Ramblas** and Via Laietana), **El Born** (between Via Laietana and Parc de la Ciutadella), and **La Barceloneta** (the peninsula south of El Born). Farther down the coast (to the left as you look at a map with the sea at the bottom) from the *Ciutat Vella* is the park-mountain **Montjuïc** and the small neighborhood of **Poble Sec** between Montjuïc and Avinguda Paral·lel. Farther inland from the *Ciutat Vella* is the large, central, rigidly gridded zone of **l'Eixample,** and still farther away from the sea is **Gràcia.** The **Plaça de Catalunya** is one of the city's most central points, located where Las Ramblas meets the Passeig de Gràcia; it is essentially the meeting point of El Raval, Barri Gòtic, and l'Eixample.

Barri Gòtic and Las Ramblas

You will get lost in Barri Gòtic. Knowing this, the best way to properly orient yourself in the confusing neighborhood, where streets still follow their medieval routes, is to take a day to learn your way around. **Las Ramblas** provides the western boundary of the neighborhood, stretching from the waterfront to **Plaça de Catalunya. Via Laietana** marks the eastern border, running nearly parallel to Las Ramblas. The primary east-west artery running between Las Ramblas and V. Laietana is known as **Carrer de Ferran** between Las Ramblas and the central **Plaça de Sant Jaume** and as **Carrer de Jaume I** between Pl. Sant Jaume and V. Laietana. Of the many plazas hiding in the Barri Gòtic, **Plaça Reial** (take the tiny C. de Colom off Las Ramblas) and Plaça de Sant Jaume are the grandest. The neighborhood is better known, though, for its more cramped spaces, like the narrow alleys covered with arches or miniature *placetas* in the shadows of parish churches. The **L3** and **L4** metro lines serve this neighborhood, with M:**Drassanes**, M:**Liceu,** and M:**Catalunya** along Las Ramblas (L3) and M:**Jaume I** at the intersection of C. Jaume I and V. Laietana.

El Born

El Born, which makes up the eastern third of the **Ciutat Vella,**is celebrated for being slightly less touristy than the Barri Gòtic and slightly less prostitute-y than El Raval. The neighborhood is renowned for its confusing medieval streets, whose ancient bends hide fashionable boutiques and restaurants both traditional and modern.

get a room!

You can find accommodations in any of the neighborhoods that *Let's Go* lists, and they will all have their pros and cons. For more recommendations visit, **www.letsgo.com.**

▨ HOSTAL MALDÀ $

C. Pi, 5   ☎933 17 30 02 www.hostalmalda.jimdo.com

Hostal Maldà provides a dirt-cheap home away from home, complete with kitschy clocks, ceramics, confusing knickknacks, and a kick-ass manager who could probably be your grandmother. She ensures that the multiple door keys, specific doorman procedures, and 24hr. reception will keep you and your valuables safe.

i *M:Liceu. Begin walking away from Las Ramblas in front of the house with the **dragon** and take an immediate left onto C. Casañas. Stay on this road as it passes in front of the church and through the Pl. del Pi. Enter the Galerias Maldà (interior shopping mall) and follow the signs to the hostel. Singles €15, with shower €20; doubles €30; triples €45; quads €60. Cash only. Reception 24hr.*

▨ SANT JORDI: SAGRADA FAMÍLIA $$

C. Freser, 5   ☎934 46 05 17 www.santjordihostels.com/apt-sagrada-familia/

From the fun staff to the hostel's apartment-style setup (and even a communal guitar in the main lobby), this place knows how to cater to the backpacking crowd. With rooms for one, two, or four people, you can pick your privacy without the isolation of a *pensión*. If closer quarters are more your style, they also have air-conditioned eight-, 10-, and 12-person dorms in the next building, whose common areas include Seussian wall niches and a small half-pipe on the terrace.

i *M:Sant Pau/Dos de Maig. Walk downhill on C. Dos de Maig toward C. Còrsega. Turn left onto C. Rosselló and stay left as the road splits to C. Freser. 4-bed dorms €16-28; 4-bed hostel rooms €16-28; 6-, 8-, 10-, and 12-bed hostel dorms €16-35 (triples are scarce); singles €18-40; doubles €30-45. Reception 24hr. Quiet hours after 10pm.*

▨ ALBERGUE-RESIDENCIA LA CIUTAT $

C. ca l'Alegre de Dalt, 66   ☎932 13 03 00 www.laciutat.com

This hostel crams 180 beds into a quiet location that's still close to some popular pubs and bars. Relax between the large lobby decorated with some funky cartoon wall art or the common room. The dorms are simple and brightly painted. Consider asking for a discount rate that skips breakfast to save you a few bucks.

i *M:Joanic. Walk along C. l'Escorial for 5-10min., passing through the plaza. Take a right onto C. Marti before the Clinic and take the 1st left onto C. ca l'Alegre de Dalt. 1- to 10-bed dorms €17-20; singles €35-50; doubles €52-60. 1st night deposit required for online booking. Visitors allowed only from 10am-11pm. Reception 24hr.*

▨ HELLO BCN HOSTEL $$

C. Lafont, 8-10   ☎934 42 83 92 www.hellobcnhostel.com

Finally, a place where exercise junkies can pump some iron while on vacation. This hostel boasts a gym, a large, spacious common room where dozens of college kids congregate on nightly basis, and late-night excursions. There are several opportunities to go on daytrips, from tanning on Barceloneta's beaches to trekking at the towering Mt. Monserrat.

i *M:Paral·lel. Follow C. Nou de la Rambla up into Poble Sec past Apolo Theater and turn left onto C. Vilà i Vilà, then right onto C. Lafont. Dorms €13-30; doubles €90-100; triples €110-120; quads €100-130. Reception 24hr.*

barcelona

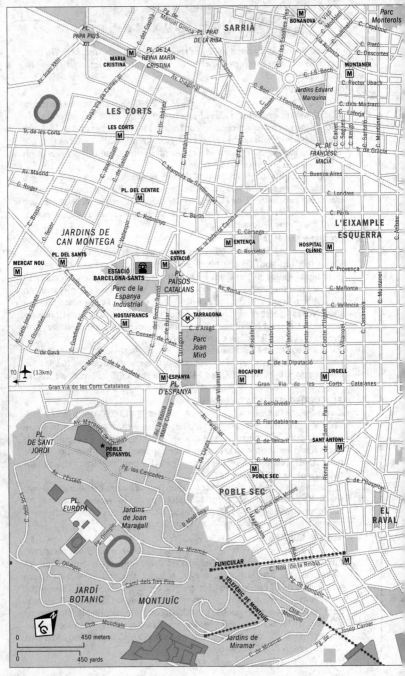

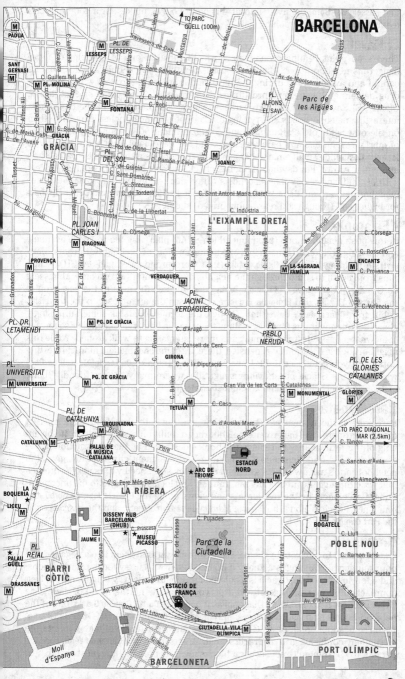

BARCELONA

PÀDUA

PL. DE LESSEPS

SANT GERVASI

C. Guillem Tell

PL. MOLINA

FONTANA

C. Sant Salvador

C. Camèlies

Av. de Montserrat

Av. de Montserrat

TO PARC GÜELL (100m)

Travessera de Dalt

C. de Martí

PL. ALFONS EL SAVI

Parc de les Aïgües

C. de l'Or

C. Providència

C. Rabi

GRÀCIA

C. Sant Marc

C. Montseny

C. Perla

C. Sant Lluís

GRÀCIA

C. de Maria Cubí

C. Ros de Olano

C. Terol

PL. DEL SOL

Tr. de Gràcia

C. Sant Domènec

C. Strasusa

C. de Tordera

C. Sant Antoni Maria Claret

C. Bonavista

C. de la Llibertat

C. Indústria

L'EIXAMPLE DRETA

PL. JOAN CARLES I

DIAGONAL

C. Còrsega

C. Còrsega

C. Còrsega

Av. del Geldi

PROVENÇA

ENCANTS

C. Rosselló

C. Provença

VERDAGUER

LA SAGRADA FAMÍLIA

C. Mallorca

PL. JACINT VERDAGUER

Av. Diagonal

PL. DR. LETAMENDI

PG. DE GRÀCIA

C. d'Aragó

PL. PABLO NERUDA

GIRONA

C. Consell de Cent

C. de la Diputació

PL. UNIVERSITAT

UNIVERSITAT

PG. DE GRÀCIA

PL. DE LES GLÒRIES CATALANES

TETUÁN

Gran Via de les Corts Catalanes

MONUMENTAL

GLÒRIES

PL. DE CATALUNYA

URQUINAONA

C. Casp

TO PARC DIAGONAL MAR (2.5km)

C. d'Ausiàs Marc

CATALUNYA

C. Fontanella

Ronda de Sant Pere

C. Tànger

PALAU DE LA MÚSICA CATALANA

C. Ribes

C. Sancho d'Àvila

C. S. Pere Més Alt

ESTACIÓ NORD

C. dels Almogàvers

C. S. Pere Més Baix

ARC DE TRIOMF

MARINA

LA BOQUERIA

LA RIBERA

BOGATELL

LICEU

DISSENY HUB BARCELONA (DHUB)

C. Lluîl

MUSEU PICASSO

C. Pujades

POBLE NOU

JAUME I

C. Ramon Turró

PL. REIAL

Parc de la Ciutadella

C. del Doctor Trueta

PALAU GÜELL

BARRI GÒTIC

DRASSANES

ESTACIÓ DE FRANÇA

Av. d'Icària

Pg. de Colom

Ronda del Litoral

CIUTADELLA-VILA OLÍMPICA

PORT OLÍMPIC

Moll d'Espanya

BARCELONETA

barcelona

The **Passeig del Born,** the lively hub of this quirky *barri*, makes for a good bar- and restaurant-lined starting point.

El Raval

There's no point beating around the bush: El Raval is one of Barcelona's more dangerous neighborhoods. But this doesn't mean that you should avoid it. Just be careful and aware—even during the day—and be prepared to deal with persistent drug dealers and aggressive prostitutes. In particular, avoid **Carrer de Sant Ramon.** Clearly, El Raval does not lack character, and it is actually one of the city's most interesting neighborhoods. Everything tends to be significantly less expensive than on the other side of Las Ramblas, and a large student population supports a bevy of quirky restaurants and bars. Areas around the **Rambla del Raval** and the **Carrer de Joaquim Costa** hide small, unique bars and late-night cafes frequented by Barcelona's alternative crowd. For daytime shopping, check out **Riera Baixa,** a street lined entirely with secondhand shops that also hosts a flea market on Saturdays, or the ritzier neighborhood around **Carrer del Doctor Dou, Carrer del Pintor Fortuny,** and **Carrer Elisabets** for higher-end (though still reasonably priced) shops.

L'Eixample

In this posh neighborhood (pronounced leh-SHAM-plah), big blocks, wide avenues, and dazzling architecture mean lots of walking and lots of exciting storefronts. *Modernista* buildings line **Passeig de Gràcia** (first word pronounced pah-SAYCH), which runs from north to south through the neighborhood's center (M:Diagonal, M:Passeig de Gràcia, M:Catalunya). **L'Eixample Dreta** encompasses the area to the east around the **Sagrada Família,** and **Eixample Esquerra** comprises the area closer to the **University,** uphill from **Plaça de la Universitat.** Though the former contains some surprisingly cheap accommodations for those willing to make the hike, the Eixample Esquerra is somewhat more pedestrian-friendly and more interesting to walk around. While this neighborhood is notoriously expensive, there are some cheaper and more interesting options as you get closer to Pl. Universitat. The stretch of **Carrer del Consell de Cent** west of Pg. de Gràcia boasts vibrant nightlife, where many "hetero-friendly" bars, clubs, and hotels give it the nickname **Gaixample.**

Barceloneta

Barceloneta, the triangular peninsula that juts out into the Mediterranean, is a former mariners' and fishermen's neighborhood, built on a sandbank at the beginning of the 18th century to replace the homes destroyed by the construction of the *ciutadella*. The grid plan, a consequence of Enlightenment city planning, gives the neighborhood's narrow streets a distinct character, seasoned by the salty sea breezes that whip through the urban canyons. Tourists and locals are drawn to the unconventional Barceloneta by the restaurants and views along the **Passeig Joan de Borbó,** the renowned beaches along the **Passeig Marítim de la Barceloneta,** and the *discotecas* at the **Port Olímpic.**

Gràcia

Gràcia is hard to navigate by metro. While this may at first seem like a negative, the poor municipal planning is actually a bonus. Filled with artsy locals, quirky shops, and a few lost travelers, Gràcia is a quieter, more out-of-the-way neighborhood, best approached by foot. M:**Diagonal** will drop you off at the northern end of the Pg. de Gràcia; follow it across Avda. Diagonal as it becomes **Carrer Gran de Gràcia,** one of the neighborhood's main thoroughfares. M:**Fontana** lies farther up on C. Gran de Gràcia. If you're heading uphill on C. Grande Gràcia, any right turn will take you into the charmingly confusing grid of Gràcia's small streets, of which **Carrer de Verdi,** running parallel to C. Gran de Gràcia several blocks away, is probably the most scenic. For bustling *plaças* both day and night, your best bets are **Plaça de la Vila de Gràcia** (more commonly known as Pl. Rius i Taulet), **Plaça del Sol,** and **Plaça de la Revolució de Setembre de 1868,** off of C. de Ros de Olano.

Montjuïc and Poble Sec

Montjuïc, the mountain just down the coast from the old center of Barcelona, is one of the city's chief cultural centers. Its slopes are home to **public parks,** some of the city's best museums, theaters that host everything from classical music to pop, and a kick-ass **castle** on its peak. Montjuïc (old Catalan for "mountain of the Jews," possibly for the Jewish cemetery once located here) also has some of the most incredible views of the city. Many approach the mountain from the **Plaça de Espanya,** passing between the two towers to ascend toward the museums and other sights; others take the funicular from M:Paral·lel.

The small neighborhood of Poble **Sec** (Catalan for "dry village") lies at the foot of Montjuïc, between the mountain and **Avinguda del Paral·lel.** Tree-lined, sloping streets characterize the largely residential neighborhood, with the **Plaça del Sortidor** as its heart and the pedestrian-friendly, restaurant-lined **Carrer de Blai** as its commercial artery.

SIGHTS

Sights in Barcelona run the gamut from cathedrals to casas to museums and more. Here's a brief overview of what each neighborhood has to offer. El Gòtic is Barcelona's most tourist-ridden neighborhood; despite the crowds of foreigners, however, the Gothic Quarter is filled with alley after alley of medieval charm. Beginning along the sea and cutting straight through to Pl. de Catalunya, Las Ramblas is Barcelona's world-famous tree-lined pedestrian thoroughfare that attracts thousands of visitors daily. El Born is a sight in itself, with ancient streets surrounded by sloping buildings or crumbling arches suddenly opening onto secluded *placetes.* El Raval has its own beauties, from the medieval Hospital de la Santa Creu i Sant Pau to the present-day artwork housed in the modern buildings of MACBA and CCCB. L'Eixample's sights are mostly composed of marvelous examples of modernista architecture; the Sagrada Família, in particular, is a must-see. Barceloneta is filled with Catalan pride, from the red-and-yellow flags hanging on apartment balconies to the museum devoted to Catalonia and its history. Gràcia contains the epic mountain/modernista retreat, Parc Güell, as well as a few independent examples of this historic Barcelonan style. Finally,Montjuïc—you know, that big hill with the castle on it that you can see from just about anywhere in Barcelona—is home to some phenomenal museums, a model Spanish village, and, of course, that castle.

Barri Gòtic and Las Ramblas

Beginning along the famous seaside, tree-lined pedestrian thoroughfare that attracts thousands of visitors daily, the walkway demarcated as La Rambla funnels thousands of tourists every year through its course. Marked by shady trees, cafes galore, tourist traps, and a multifarious array of street performers, gorgeous edifices, animal vendors, and extremely adroit pickpockets, the five distinct promenades seamlessly mesh to create the most lively and exciting pedestrian bustle in Barcelona (and perhaps in all of Europe). The *ramblas,* in order from Pl. de Catalunya to the Columbus Monument are: **La Rambla des Canaletes, La Rambla dels Estudis, La Rambla de Sant Josep, La Rambla dels Caputxins,** and **La Rambla de Santa Mònica.**

▨ MUSEU D'HISTORIA DE LA CIUTAT

Pl. del Rei   ☎932 56 21 00 www.museuhistoria.bcn.es

If you thought the winding streets of the Barri Gòtic were old school, check out the Museu d'Història de la Ciutat's Roman ruins, hidden 20m underneath Pl. del Rei. Beneath the medieval plaza lies the excavation site of the long-gone predecessor of Barcelona: the Roman city of Barcino. Raised walkways allow passage through the site of the ruins beneath the plaza; regardless, watch your step, as some parts can be dark and uneven. You'll probably catch sight of huge ceramic wine flasks dotting the intricate ancient mosaics—surefire proof of Barcelona's revelrous ancestry. The second part of the museum features the (comparatively) newer Palacio **Real Major**, a 14th-century palace for Catalan-Aragonese monarchs. Inside the palace, the glorious and impressively empty **Saló de Tinell** (Throne Room) is the iconic seat where Ferdinand and Isabella welcomed Columbus after his journey to the New World. The **Capilla de Santa Àgata** uses its rotating exhibits to delve into the intricacies of the modern Catalonian's way of life.

i M:Jaume I. Free multilingual audio tours. Museum and exhibition €7, students and ages 16-25 €5, under 16 free. Open Apr-Oct Tu-Sa 10am-7pm, Su 10am-8pm; Nov-Mar Tu-Sa 10am-5pm, Su 10am-8pm.

🏛 AJUNTAMENT DE BARCELONA (CITY HALL)

Pl. de Sant Jaume, enter on C. Font de Sant Miquel   ☎934 02 70 00 www.bcn.es

The stolid, 18th-century Neoclassical façade facing the Pl. de Sant Jaume hides a more interesting, 15th-century one, located at the old entrance to the left of the building (where the tourist office is on C. Ciutat). You can only get into the City Hall building on Sundays or if you get voted in, but once you're inside, it's marvelous. The lower level of this bureaucratic palace is home to many pieces of sculpture from modern Catalan masters, while the upper level showcases elaborate architecture, vivid stained glass, and lavish rooms like the *Saló de Cent*, from which the *Consell de Cent* (Council of One Hundred) ruled the city from 1372-1714.

i M:Jaume I. Follow C. de Jaume I to Pl. de Sant Jaume; City Hall is on the left. Tourist info available at entrance. To enter, take alley to the left of City Hall and take a right onto C. Font de Sant Miquel. Free. Open Su 10am-1:30pm. Tours every 30min. in Spanish or Catalan.

CATEDRAL DE BARCELONA

Pl. de la Seu   ☎933 15 15 54 www.catedralbcn.org

Located in the Gothic Quarter, the Cathedral of Santa Eulalia, or the Barcelona Cathedral, is a masterpiece architecturally and the seat of the archbishop of Barcelona. This beautiful gothic cathedral has 500 year old stained glass windows, a gorgeous garden, rooftop access by elevator, many naves and side rooms, and even roaming ducks. It is free to enter and there are no lines, but if you wish to tour the roof or see areas not free to the public such as the museum, the tour costs €6. It's not Sagrada Familia, but it's definitely worth a visit, even if only for an hour. You can get excellent views of the city from the top of the tour, and the inside of the church has spectacular sculptures and paintings. The atmosphere of the cathedral is peaceful and reverant. The sheer size and magnitude will have you in a state of wanderlust, and every window, chamber, and cloister makes for a great photo opportunity. Make sure to dress conservatively and respect those in prayer, and drink from the water fountain which is supposed to be good luck. It's open for mass some mornings, so if you're interested, make sure to check out the hours beforehand online. Otherwise, the cathedral is available for any and all to enter as they please during the hours that it's open.

i M:Jaume I. From the metro, turn left onto V. Laietana, then left onto Av. de la Catedral. Catedral free. Museu €3. Elevator to terrace €3. Inquire about guided visit to museum, choir, rooftop terraces, and towers, as hours vary. Catedral open M-Sa 8am-12:45pm and 5:15-7:30pm, Su 8am-1:45pm and 5:15-7:30pm. Entry with donation M-Sa 1pm-5pm, Su 2pm-5pm.

PALAU DE LA GENERALITAT

Pl. de Sant Jaume   ☎934 02 46 00 www.gencat.cat/generalitat/eng

Facing the Pl. de Sant Jaume and the Ajuntament, the Palau dela Generalitat is a big player in the plaza's popularity with protesters and petitioners. The 17th-century exterior conceals a Gothic structure that was obtained by the Catalan government in 1400. Although the majority of visitors will be stuck admiring its wonderfully authoritative feel from the exterior, with a bit of magic (i.e., good timing and advance planning), it's possible to see the interior. There, visitors will find a Gothic gallery, an orange tree courtyard, St. George's Chapel, a bridge to the house of the President of the Generalitat, many historic sculptures and paintings, and the **Palau's carillon,** a 4898kg instrument consisting of 49 bells that is played on holidays and during special events.

i *M:Jaume I. Take C. de Jaume I after exiting the station. Once in Pl. de Sant Jaume; Palau is on the right. Free. Make reservations online at least 2 weeks in advance. Open to the public on Apr 23, Sept 11, and Sept 24, and on the 2nd and 4th Su of each month from 10am-1:30pm.*

GRAN TEATRE DEL LICEU

Las Ramblas, 51-59   ☎934 85 99 00 www.liceubarcelona.cat

Though La Rambla itself is one of Europe's grandest stages (tourists being the main performers), the highbrow Liceu is known for its operatic and classical presentations. The Baroque interior of the auditorium will leave you gawking at the fact that it only dates to 1999. It was reconstructed following a 1995 fire, and you can't say they don't make 'em like they used to. A 20min. tour provides a glimpse of the ornate *Sala de Espejos* (Room of Mirrors), where Apollo and the Muses look down with their divine gazes and judge theater patrons during intermission. If you're lucky, you may just catch a glimpse of authentic Spanish ardor in the form of a director yelling furiously during a rehearsal. For a more in-depth tour that won't leave you spending half of your time looking at the stackable chairs in the foyer or being told about benefactors (always a pleasure, Plácido Domingo), arrange a behind-the-scenes tour with the box office or attend a performance in person (highly recommended—just check out schedules online first).

i *M:Liceu. Discounted tickets available. Tours start every 20min. Box office open M-F 1:30pm-8pm.*

PLAÇA DE L'ÀNGEL

Corner of Via Laietana and C. de la Princesa

The square immediately surrounding the M:Jaume I metro stop may now seem like nothing but a place to catch the train or grab a pastry and a lame tourist T-shirt, but the days of Roman Barcino saw this spot as the main gate allowing passage into the city. To revel in some of this seemingly absent history, simply walk parallel to **Via Laietana,** the ever-bustling street forming one side of the square's border. For a more contemporary piece of history (though it still dates from the triple digits CE), look no further than the statue of an angel pointing to her toe. This sculpture commemorates the event for which the plaza was named—according to legend, the caravan carrying the remains of St. Eulàlia from the church of Santa Maria del Mar stopped here; suddenly, the urn containing remains became too heavy to carry, and when the caravan members set them down, an angel appeared and pointed to her own toe, alerting the carriers that one of the procession's officials had stolen St. Eulàlia's pedal digit. With a shame equivalent to being published with a thumbs down symbol in a *Let's Go* travel guide, the church member returned the toe to its brethren and the remains miraculously reverted to their original weight.

i *M:Jaume I. Free.*

barcelona

COLUMBUS MONUMENT

Portal de la Pau   ☎933 02 52 24

The *Mirador de Colom* at the coastal tip of La Rambla offers a phenomenal view of the city and an absolutely killer sunrise/sunset just a smidge farther down the coastline (sometimes also called the extra *Rambla del Mar*). This area features a 60m statue, constructed in the 1880s for Barcelona's World's Fair in order to commemorate Christopher Columbus meeting King Ferd and Queen Izzy in Barcelona upon his return from America. Though some say the 7.2m statue at the top of the tower points west to the Americas, it actually points east (fail, right?), supposedly to his hometown of Genoa. Reliefs around the base of the column depict the journey, as do bronze lions that are guaranteed to be mounted by tourists at any given moment. Just don't try to mount them if you're stumbling back home up Las Ramblas at dawn, especially if you don't have a buddy's camera documenting the whole incident.

i M:Drassanes. Entrance located in base facing water €4, seniors and children €3. Open daily May-Oct 9am-7:30pm; Nov-Apr 9am-6:30pm.

El Born

This part of the *ciutat vella* (ancient city) is a sight in itself, with ancient streets surrounded by sloping buildings and crumbling arches suddenly opening onto secluded *placetes*. In addition to the joys of just walking through the neighborhood, there are certain sights you just can't miss.

▨ PALAU DE LA MÚSICA CATALANA

C. Palau de la Música, 4-6   ☎902 44 28 82   www.palaumusica.org

Home to both Barcelona's Orfeó Choir and the Catalan musical spirit, the Palau is Barcelona's most spectacular music venue (it became a UNESCO World Heritage Site in 1997). Lluís Domènech i Montaner, contemporary of Gaudí and architect of the **Hospital de Sant Pau, Casa Fuster,** and the Castell **dels Tres Dragons,** crafted this awe-inspiring *modernista* masterpiece from humble materials such as brick, ceramic, stone, iron, and glass in just a short three years. True to the *Art Nou* movement's principles, the building (1905-08) is covered inside and out with organic motifs. The breathtaking inverted dome of the stained glass ceiling and the tall stained glass windows make the luminous interior shimmer. Columns pose as abstract trees, while intricate ceramic flowers decorate the ceiling. In fact, the concert hall's designer packed the floral motif in just about every nook and cranny of the theater—see for yourself, it's rather eye-opening. Behind the stage, angelic muses emerge from the walls, which are part flat ceramic tiles, part stone sculpture. Above and around the stage, angels interact with trees, the riding Valkyries, and musicians such as Wagner and Beethoven. Back in commission after a 30-year hiatus, the Palau's glorious 3772-pipe organ stands front and center in the upper portion of the hall. Below it hangs the coat of arms of Catalunya in all its splendor, comprised of the cross of St. George (patron saint of Spain) along with four stripes. The Palau offers reduced-admission concerts regularly, which is a nice break from the typical €17 price tag. After touring, you'll officially be able to declare how artsy and Euro-knowledgeable you are.

i M:Jaume I. On Via Laietana, walk toward the cathedral for about 5min., then take a right onto C. Sant Pere Mas Alt. Palau de la Música Catalana is on the left. Schedule of events and ticketing info on website. Guided tours €17, students €11, under 10 free. 55min. tours daily 10am-3:30pm, in English every hr. and Catalan and Spanish every 30min. Guided tour schedules vary by season. Aug tours daily 9am-6pm, Easter week 10am-6pm. Box office open daily 9:30am-3:30pm; Jul and Aug 9am-8pm.

🖼 MUSEU PICASSO

C. de Montcada, 15-23   ☎932 19 63 10 www.museupicasso.bcn.cat/en

The Picasso Museum has free admission to all students, but is a very popular tourist destination that usually has long lines and limited capacity. Regardless, it's worth waiting for because it is truly a treasure trove of art. Upon entering, there are a series of rooms that start from Picasso's earlier years and lead into his critical success. The museum has informational signs written in Catalan, Spanish, and English that introduce each series of paintings, and each series typically features one defining work of that time. In the rooms that capture his formative years, you can see the original First Communion and Science and Charity paintings, as well as sketches he made for them and a history of their context. As the chronology progresses, the museum takes you through his different periods as an artists and explains the people and places that influenced him. More interesting however, may be the smaller paintings that were donated by his family which receive little to no attention beyond the museum. Many of these, such as "At the Sick Woman's Side" are beautiful masterpieces that fail to show up even through extensive internet searches. After viewing many of his famous works, the tour leads you to a section of art from the man who founded the museum (a friend and influence of Picasso's). After, you'll be sent to a gift shop where you can buy books, posters, and prints of many of the works in store. If you want something but can't take it around Barcelona with you, they also have a delivery service which might be of interest. The gift shop connects with the bottom of the museum, where you can either return to view more paintings, head to a limited time exhibition if they have it, or make your way out to explore the city.

i M:Jaume I. Walk down C. de la Princesa and turn right onto Carrer de Montcada. Admission €11; ages 16-24 and over 65 €6; under 16, teachers, PinkCard cardholders, and ICOM members free. Audio tour €3. Accepts Mastercard and Visa. 1st Su of each month free, other Su free after 3pm. Open Tu-Su 10am-8pm. Last entry 30min. before close.

PARC DE LA CIUTADELLA

Between Pg. de Picasso, C. Pujades, and C. Wellington

The Parc de la Ciutdella is a open park in the Ribera district near the city port. It's free to access and open throughout the day. Historically, it started as a fortress and was later turned into a park in 1869. It has beautiful gardens, a large lake, enormous sculptures from the 19th and 20th centuries, the Barcelona Zoo and Zoological Museum, a geology museum, several aesthetically appealing buildings, and the enormous Arc de Triomf. Between the Arc and the Parc are usually tons of street performers trying to earn cash quickly for their dances, bubble blowing, or musical talents. The parc has many attractions, but it's also a great place to relax or jog when it's not in peak hours. Because there's so much to do, it can often be exceptionally crowded and if you're trying to unwind then it may cause you more trouble than good. If you're coming to see the attractions, you can visit the zoo, rent out a boat on the lake for half an hour, or have a picnic and people watch. The parc is rated exceptionally well online, and often regarded as an attraction that cannot be missed. However, despite it's beauty it is just a park, and should not be considered over other great sites like the Sagrada Familia.

i M:Arc de Triomf. Walk through the arch and down the boulevard to enter the park. Free Wi-Fi available at the Geological Museum, Parliament building, and Zoological Museum. Park free. Museum €4.10-7, Su 3-8pm free. Zoo €17. Park open daily 10am-dusk. Natural History Museum open Tu-F 10am-7pm, Sa-Su 10am-8pm. Zoo open daily May 16-Sept 15 10am-7pm; Sept 16-Oct 29 10am-6pm; Oct 30-Mar 26 10am-5pm; Mar 27-May 15 10am-6pm.

barcelona

CHURCH OF SANTA MARIA DEL MAR

C. Canvis Vells, 1   ☎933 10 23 90 933 10 23 90

El Born is dominated by this church's stoic presence, but it's nearly impossible to get a good glimpse from the outside. Nearby streets allow remotely satisfactory views of the exterior from the Fossar de les Moreres at the end of Pg. del Born. The Pl. de Santa Maria, located at the west entrance of the church, holds the best outside views of the church's impressive rose window (which dates to 1459) and the intricate relief and sculptural work of the main entrance. The best view of the stained glass, of course, is from inside on a sunny day. Constructed between 1329 and 1383, this church exemplifies the Catalan Gothic style—tough on the outside, light and airy on the inside. The inside is spacious and open, with tall, slim, octagonal pillars lining the main nave and no constructed boundaries between the nave and the altar. Despite the beautiful architecture, the interior has limited decoration (apart from the stained glass, of course) due to a fire that gutted the church in 1936 during the Spanish Civil War. Be sure to check the secret, miracle-holding treasure room of eternal light in the back—okay, it's just the chapel, but it goes largely unvisited and grants a close-up of some amazing artistry and friezes of God near the ceiling.

i M:Jaume I. Walk down Carrer del'Argenteria to enter the plaça. Santa Maria del Mar is on the right. Free. Open M-Sa 9am-1:30pm and 5:30-8:30pm, Su 10am-1:30pm and 5:30-8:30pm.

ARC DE TRIOMF

Between Pg. de Lluís Companys and Pg. de Sant Joan

For a proper greeting from the city of Barcelona, be sure to get off the metro at the **Arc de Triomf Station. At** first glance, you'll notice that this is most definitely not Paris's Arc de Triomphe (this one is actually reachable and not swimming in an ocean of tourists); the slight differences between the two encapsulate why Paris is Paris and Barcelona is awesome. Where else can you find such a relatively unoccupied attraction? People don't really come to Spain to see this, so it's pretty much as private as a massive, open historic site can be. Situated at the beginning of a wide, cinematic-like boulevard leading to the **Parc de la Ciutadella,** the arch not only frames the palm tree- and *modernista*-building-lined road and its incredible terminus but also literally embraces visitors with a sculptural frieze by Josep Reynés inscribed with the phrase *"Barcelona rep les nacions,"* or "Barcelona welcomes the nations." This declaration was made along with the arch's construction for the 1888 Universal Exhibition, when it served as the main entrance to the fair grounds in the Parc. Today, the arch serves as little more than a historical artifact, but it's worth a look if you're in the area. The triumphant bricks-on-bricks of the arch was designed by Josep Jilaseca i Cassanovas in the Moorish revival style. Its exterior is decked out with sculptures of 12 women representing fame and a relief by Josep Lllimona that depicts the award ceremony. Much the opposite of gargoyles atop the structure are several white angel sculptures and eight massive. The whole thing graces the surrounding area with its architectural superiority.

i M:Arc de Triomf. Free.

El Raval

▩ PALAU GÜELL

C. Nou de la Rambla, 3-5   ☎934 72 57 75 www.palauguell.cat

Commissioned by Eusebi Güell, the wealthy industrialist of Parc Güell fame, Güell Palace has stood tall since its 1888 completion as the master creation of none other than Antoni Gaudí. Being the only project that Gaudí himself directed until its debut, Palau Güell represents one of the artist's early works. Its roots in the Islamic-Hispanic architectural tradition are visible in the Moorish arched windows that have been elongated and smoothed out with a typical Gaudí twist. Be sure to look up in the Saló Central to see another example of this: tiny holes in the conical ceiling allow in rays of light, reminiscent of a combination of God's light piercing clouds and a nicely constructed Indian harem. You'll probably have someone snicker at you as you stare with your mouth agape at the ceiling's rainbow, typically Gaudían ceramic-tiled chimney, and impressive geometric conglomerations dotting the inside.

i M:Liceu. Walk toward the water on Las Ramblas and take a right onto C. Nou de la Rambla. Rooftop closed when raining. Group reservations need 48hr. advance call €12, reduced €8. Free 1st Su of month. Audio tour included in admission. Open Apr-Oct Tu-Su 10am-8pm; Nov-Mar Tu-Su 10am-5:30pm. Last entry 1hr. before close.

🏛 MUSEU D'ART CONTEMPORANI DE BARCELONA (MACBA)

Pl.Àngels, 1 ☎934 12 08 10 www.macba.cat

Bursting out of the narrow streets and into its own spacious plaza, American architect Richard Meier's bright white edifice has sought to bring artistic enlightenment to the masses. The stark, simple interior displays an impressive collection of contemporary art, with particular emphasis on Spanish and Catalan artists, including a world-renowned collection of the interwar avant-garde and a selection of works by Miró and Tàpies. Found very near the CCCB, the Universitat, and a host of other sights around El Raval, MACBA is a must-see attraction for travelers, locals, and students alike. Be sure to check the website, as events, exhibitions, and even small concerts may occur within a week's notice. The museum completely transforms during Barcelona's Sónar music festival every year, converting into the Sónar Complex stage.

i M:Universitat. Walk down C. Pelai, take the 1st right, and turn left onto C. Tallers. Take a right onto C. Valldonzella and a left onto C. Montalegre. Admission includes English-language tour. Entrance to all exhibit €9; children under 14, Tarjeta Rosa, over 65, the unemployed, teachers, members of the AAVC, and ICOM members free. Open M-F 11am-7:30pm, Sa 10am-9pm, Su and holidays 10am-7pm. Library open M-Th 10am-7pm. Last entry 30min. before close.

CENTRE DE CULTURA CONTEMPORÀNIA DE BARCELONA (CCCB)

C. Montalegre, 5 ☎933 06 41 00 www.cccb.org

The Centre de Cultura Contemporània de Barcelona boasts everything from art exhibits of old African sculptures to Shakespearean theater to Roman literature to open-air beer expos—the best potpourri of culture you'll ever see. Three exhibition galleries host large and involved temporary exhibits that vary in quality and quantity by month. Two lecture halls, an auditorium, and a bookstore fill out the architecturally wonderful (and award winning!) complex comprised of several upright glass and mirror structures. Paired with the thought-provoking collections of the nearby MACBA, the CCCB offers everything to help one become the epitome of a cultured character.

i M:Universitat. Walk down C. Pelai, take the 1st right, and then turn left onto C. Tallers. Turn right onto C. Valldonzella and left onto C. Montalegre. General admission €6; seniors, under 25, large families, group visits, and single-parent households €4; 2 or more exhibitions €8/6. Exhibits open daily 11am-8pm. CCCB Archives open Tu-F 3-8pm, Sa-Su 11am-8pm. Guided tours in Spanish Sa 11:30am. Last entry 30min. before close.

L'ANTIC HOSPITAL DE LA SANTA CREU I SANT PAU

C. l'Hospital, 54-56

Now the site of the Institue d'Estudis Catalans, the Escola Massana, and the 1.5 million volume Bibilioteca de Catalunya, l'Antic Hospital de la Santa Creu i Sant Peu (or the Old Hospital of the Holy Cross and St. Paul) is a 15th-century Gothic building located in the middle of El Raval. Although it no longer functions as the neighborhood hospital, the interior courtyard, complete with an orangery and romantic perching spots, will nicely pad your collection of Facebook pictures.

barcelona

The operating theater has a rotating marble dissection table for the non-squeamish, and the archives hold records of the admittance of famous Catalan architect Antoni Gaudí to the hospital before his death in 1926. At that time, the hospital was used to treat the poor, and Gaudí was mistaken for a homeless man and brought to the premises after a tram struck him. Try to stop by the Gothic chapel art museum, La Capella, as well—it hosts multiple monthly exhibitions.

i M:Liceu. Walk down C. l'Hospital. Free Wi-Fi in courtyard. Biblioteca (932 02 07 97 www. bnc.cat). La Capella(932 42 71 71 www.bcn.cat/lacapella). Open M-F 9am-8pm, Sa 9am-2pm. Biblioteca open M-F 9am-8pm, Sa 9am-2pm. La Capella open Tu-Sa noon-2pm and 4-8pm, Su 11am-2pm.

L'Eixample

▨ CASA BATLLÓ

Pg. de Gràcia, 43   ☎934 88 06 66 www.casabatllo.es

Built sometime between 1875 and 1877, the Casa Batlló was originally designed for a middle class family in the luxurious center l'Eixample. Take a peek at yet another of Gaudí's creations in all its visceral, organo-skeletal design sprinkled with the ever-present hints of Nouveau Art. From the spinal-column stairwell that holds together the scaly building's interior to the undulating **dragon's** back curve of the ceramic rooftop to the skull-like balconies on the facade, the Casa Batlló will have you wondering what kinds of drugs Gaudí was on and where one might go about acquiring them if they lead to such remarkable renovations (it was originally built by Emilio Salas Cortés). Much of the inside is lined with *trancadís*, or scatters of broken tile that lend to gorgeous color transitions and contrasts. The building has hardly a right angle inside or out; every surface— stone, wood, glass, anything—is soft and molten. This architectural wonderland was once an apartment complex for the fantastically rich and is now the busiest of the three *modernista* marvels in the **Manzana de la Discòrdia** on Pg. de Gràcia. A free audio tour lets you navigate the dream-like space at your own pace, so be sure to spend some time with the doors of wood and stained glass, the soft scaled pattern of the softly bowed walls, and the swirly light fixture that pulls at the entire ceiling, rippling into its center. Gaudí's design ranges from the incredibly rational to the seemingly insane, including a blue light well that passes from deep navy at the top to sky blue below in order to distribute light more evenly. Be sure to visit the rooftop where you can get a great view of Barcelona below.

i M:Passeig de Gràcia. Walk away from Pl. Catalunya on Pg. de Gràcia; Casa Batlló is on the left. Tickets available at box office or through TelEntrada. Admission includes audio tour. €20.35, students and BCN cardholders €16.30. Open daily 9am-9pm. Last entry 40min. before close.

▨ SAGRADA FAMÍLIA

C. Mallorca, 401   ☎935 13 20 60 www.sagradafamilia.cat

If there is one building that stands out in all of Catalonia, it's la Sagrada Familia. Featured in every panoramic shot of the city, it's the Eiffel Tower or Statue of Liberty of Barcleona. It was Gaudi's lifelong project that he died working on (he was tragically struck by a tram and confused for a bum because of how he dressed). Since his death, construction has stopped and resumed for years, and will continue to do so until the projected completion date around 2030. However, the cranes and construction crew have become part of the scene thanks to their mere presence for so long. In recent years, the inside of La Sagrada Familia became open to the public to tour for a fee, and the church holds masses on a weekly basis inside. The view from the inside is as absolutely breathtaking as the view from the outside. The extremely tall ceilings are all adorned with incredibly intricate carvings and statues, and elaborately designed stained glass windows that let in and reflect the sun's light all throughout the basilica. Two sets of

spain

enormous doors on each side permit people to come and leave, and whenever a tourist steps in for the first time, they are temporarily paralyzed in wanderlust (and then they reach for their cameras). On the back end of the basilica is a wall with the Lord's Prayer written in hundreds of different languages, and on the opposite ends are televisions showing documentaries on the history and construction of the building, which lead to a private prayer area. Near the entrance doors are elevators which allow access to the top of the towers. Tickets for this cost extra, but are absolutely worth it because the towers are incredibly high above the city, and you can get an excellent view of the city, ocean, and horizon in the distance. Additionally, you can look down from the towers and see the rest of the construction from a different angle, as well as the hundreds of people that are touring around below you. Visiting La Sagrada Família is imperative for any body traveling to Barcelona. If you only have a few hours in the city, almost all of your time should be spent inside the basilica and above on the towers. The rest should be spent getting to and from there.

i M:Sagrada Família. Towers closed during rain. Basilica €13.50, with audio tour €21.50; students €11.50; under 10 free. Elevator €4.50. Combined ticket with Casa-Museu Gaudí (in Parc Güell) €17. Online ticketing strongly recommended. Open Apr-Sept daily 9am-8pm; Oct-Mar 9am-6pm; Dec 25-Jan 6 9am-2pm. Visitors must leave by 30min. past ticket office closing. Last elevator to the tower Nativity Lift 15min. before close. Passion Lift 30min. before close. Guided tours in English May-Jun M-F 11am, noon, and 1pm; Jul-Aug M 5pm; Sept-Oct M-F 11am, noon, and 1pm; Nov-Apr M-F 11am, 1, and 3pm.

CASA MILÀ (LA PEDRERA)

Pg. de Gràcia, 92 C. Provença, 261-265   ☎902 202 138 http://www.lapedrera.com/en/visitor-information

La Pedrera still functions as a home for the rich, famous, and patient—the waitlist for an apartment is over three decades long—as well as the offices of the Caixa Catalunya bank. Many portions of the building are open to the public, including an apartment decorated with period furniture (contemporary to the house, not designed by Gaudí) and the main floor. The attic, a space known as **Espai Gaudí**, boasts a mini-museum to the man himself, including helpful exhibits explaining the science behind his beloved caternary arches and what exactly it means for the architect to be "inspired by natural structures." It is complete with all his jargonistic models and Einsteinian mathematical formulas working behind the scenes to create his living oeuvres. Up top, a rooftop terrace gives light to what many a critic has called the perfect European Kodak moment, whether it be with the desert-like sculptural outcroppings part of the building or of the panorama overlooking Barcelona to the Sagrada Família. During the summer, the terrace lights up with jazz performances on Friday and Saturday nights in a series known as *Nits d'Estiu a La Pedrera*.

i M:Diagonal. Walk down Pg. de Gràcia away from Avda. Diagonal; La Pedrera is on the right. Purchase tickets to Nits d'Estiu a La Pedrera online via TelEntrada at www.telentrada.com. €16.50, students and seniors €14.85, under 6 free. Audio tour €4. Nits d'Estiu a La Pedrera €30; includes access to Espai Gaudí. 10 language options available for tours. Open daily Mar-Oct 9am-8pm; Nov-Feb 9am-6:30pm. Last entry 30min. before close. Concerts mid-Jun-late-Aug, some F and Sa 8:30pm.

CASA AMATLLER

Pg. de Gràcia, 41   ☎932 160 175 www.amatller.org

Finally another whimsical place that can rival some of Pg. de Gracia's other creations. Casa Amatller stands as the counterpart to Gaudí's neighboring acid-trip Casa Batlló, and it was the first in the trio of buildings now known as **Manzana de la Discòrdia.** In 1898, chocolate industrialist Antoni Amatller became the rich hipster of his time by veering form the Gaudí-dominated expert

barcelona

architectural sweets and instead commissioned **Josep Puig i Cadafalch** to build his palatial home along Pg. de Gràcia, and out popped a mix of Catalan, Neo-Gothic, Islamic, and even Dutch architectural motifs all expertly overlapping on a strict gridline. A carving of Sant Jordi battling that pesky dragon appears over the front door, accompanied by four divinely artsy figures engaged in painting, sculpting, and architecture. Also at the foot of the principal entrance is a tile on the ground marking 0km of the **European Route de Modernisme.** The start of this invisible path is Barcelona's age-old endeavor to spread the *moderniste* movement throughout Spain as well as the rest of Europe. The building's entrance is free to see—note the ornate lamps and amazing stained-glass ceiling in the stairwell, created by the same artist that did the ceiling of the Palau de la Música Catalana. The rest of the building is even more spectacular and is well worth the €10 tour.

i M:Passeig de Gràcia. Walk away from Pl. Catalunya on Pg. de Gràcia; Casa Amatller is a couple of blocks up on the left. Reservation by phone or email required for tour. Tours €10. Kid workshops €6 daily 10am-8pm. Guided tours M-F 10, 11am, noon, 1, 3, 4, 5, and 6pm.

HOSPITAL DE LA SANTA CREU I SANT PAU
C. Sant Antoni Maria Claret, 167   ☎933 177 652; guided visits 902 076 621

Considered one of the most important pieces of *modernista* public architecture, this hospital's practice challenges the meaning of "neouveau." Dating back to 1401 when six smaller hospitals merged, the Hospital de la Santa Creu i Sant Pau is the newer embodiment of the medical practice formerly housed in the **Antic Hospital de la Santa Creu** in El Raval. Wealthy benefactor Pau Gil bequested funds for the building with strict instructions, including the name appendage. Construction then began in 1902 under the direction of Lluís Domènech i Montaner (designer of the godly **Palau de Musica Catalana** in El Born), who in Gaudían fashion, died before its completion. His son saw the work to fruition, giving the hospital 48 large pavilions connected by underground tunnels and bedazzled with luxurious modern sculptures and paintings. Although the hospital ceased to function as a hospital in 2009, it has been named a UNESCO World Heritage Sight and ironically now welcomes even more visitors than it did as a hospital. Much of the complex is currently closed for renovation, but the little bits open around back are neat spots for a few selfies and snapchats (or 15).

i 8, over 65, and unemployed €5. Modernisme Route 50% discount. Bus Turístic 20% discount. Barcelona City Tour 20% discount. Tours in English M-Su 10, 11am, noon, and 1pm. Tours in French M-Su 10:30am. Tours in Spanish M-Su 11:30am. Tours in Catalan M-Su 12:30pm. Follow the information boards for updated information.

FUNDACIÓ ANTONI TÀPIES
C. Aragó, 255   ☎934 87 03 15 www.fundaciotapies.org

Housed in a building by *modernista* architect Lluís Domènech i Montaner, the Fundació Antoni Tàpies is unmissable thanks to the giant mess ball of wire and steel atop the low brick roofline. Made by the museum's namesake, Antoni Tàpies, it's actually a sculpture entitled *Núvol i Cadira* (Cloud and Chair; 1990) that supposedly shows a chair jutting out of a large cloud. Once inside, the lowest and highest levels are dedicated to temporary exhibitions on modern and contemporary artists and themes—recent shows have included work by Eva Hesse and Steve McQueen—while the middle floors hold Tàpies' own work. Start upstairs and work your way down, watching the descent from surrealist-symbolist beauty into a misshapen chaos of not so well-seeming forms.

i M:Passeig de Gràcia. Walk uphill on Pg. de Gràcia and turn left onto C. Aragó. €7; reduced entrance €5.60. Articket free. Open Tu-Su 10am-7pm. Closed Dec 25, Jan 1, and Jan 6. Last entry 15min. before closing. Museum shop open Tu-F 10am-7pm, Sa-Su 10am-2:30pm and 3:30-7pm. Library open Tu-F 10am-2pm and 4-7pm. Admission to library by appointment.

spain

FUNDACIÓ FRANCISCO GODIA

C. Diputació, 250   ☎932 72 31 80   www.fundacionfgodia.org

The next time you start making NASCAR the butt of a redneck joke, consider the Fundació Francisco Godia. Though Godia was a successful businessman by trade, his two true loves are the focus of this museum: art collecting and Formula One racing. The museum reflects these disparate interests—a front room filled with racing trophies and riding goggles amongst other racing paraphernalia. A man of exquisite taste and great artistic sensitivity, Francisco Godia gathered together an exceptional collection of paintings, medieval sculptures, and ceramics. Some of his favorite works are on display at the Francisco Godia Foundation, including many of his favorite 20th-century artifacts. Due to Godia's broad collecting interests, the permanent collection features everything from stunning 12th- and 13th-century wooden sculptures to medieval paintings to modern works by Santiago Rusiñol, Joaquím Mir, and Gutiérrez Solana. In fact, the foundation continues to acquire contemporary pieces, and temporary exhibits attempt to fit somewhere into the framework of the diverse collection.

i M:Passeig de Gràcia. Walk away from Pl. Catalunya on Pg. de Gràcia and take the 1st left onto C. Diputació. Guided tours in Spanish and Catalan free Sa-Su at noon. €6.50, students €3.50. Temporary exhibits €5-10. Open M-Sa 10am-8pm, Su 10am-3pm.

Gràcia

Some of the most defining features of Gràcia's cityscape are the cafe-lined **plaças** that seem to appear out of nowhere around every corner. The **Plaça de la Vila de Gràcia** (also known as Plaça de Rius i Taulet) is one of the largest and most beautiful, with a massive 19th-century clock tower (M:Fontana; take a left down C. Gran de Gràcia, then a left onto C. Sant Domènec). With your back to the powder-blue municipal building, head up the street running along the right side of the plaza, and in a few blocks you'll get to the **Plaça del Sol,** the neighborhood's most lively square, especially at night. Two blocks east of that (follow C. Ramon i Cajal) is the **Plaça de la Revolució de Setembre de 1868,** a long, open square with the word "Revolució" engraved in the pavement. Head up C. Verdifrom Pl. Revolució de Setembre 1868 and take a left at the third intersection, which will bring you to the shady **Plaça del Diamant,** while a right will bring you to the true gem that is the **Plaça de la Virreina.**

▨ PARC GÜELL

Main entrance on C. Clot

Park Guell is a garden, park, and housing complex that's located on the hill of El Carmel in the Gracia district. It was designed by Gaudi in the early 1900s as summer homes for really wealthy families in Barcelona, and now it's open for tourism as a UNESCO World Heritage Site. The tour used to be completely free, until recent years when the city added an €8 fee for entrance. The park outside the architectural site is still free, however. Getting to the park requires a long walk uphill, and you can get within 20 minutes of the site by taking the metro. The garden features several important Gaudi creations.

The first thing you'll see is the main terrace, which overlooks the park and has mosaic work along the benches along the perimeter. This offers the most complete view of Barcelona and the bay, where you can see other famous buildings like Sagrada Familia. You can walk down underneath it and see the unique dome shaped roofing. This eventually leads to the multicolored mosaic salamander known as "el drac" at the main enterence. You can take pictures with the salamander, but there's always a security guard watching it after it was vandalized in February 2007. After, you can continue down the stairs until the Gaudi House Museum, which shows several original works. Nearby is a restaurant and gift shop that are next to the street exit. Tickets are only for certain times, and make sure you arrive early because you're only supposed to stay in the park for a limited amount of time.

i M:Lesseps. Walk uphill on Travessera Dalt and take a left to ride escalators. Or M:Vallcarca. Walk down Avda. República Argentina and take a right onto C. Agramunt, which becomes the partially be-escalatored Baixada Glòria. Bus #24 from Pl. Catalunya stops just downhill from the park. Free. Guardhouse €2, students €1.50. Free Su after 3pm and 1st Su of each month. Ca-sa-Museu Gaudí €5.50, students €4.50. Park open daily May-Aug 10am-9pm; Sept 10am-8pm; Oct 10am-7pm; Nov-Feb 10am-6pm; Mar 10am-7pm; Apr 10am-8pm. Guardhouse open daily Apr-Oct 10am-8pm; Nov-Mar 10am-4pm. Casa-Museu Gaudí open daily Apr-Sept 10am-8pm; Oct-Mar 10am-6pm.

Montjuïc and Poble Sec

▨ FUNDACIÓ MIRÓ

Parc de Montjuïc ☎934 43 94 70 www.fundaciomiro-bcn.org

It's time to visit Fundació Miró. From the outside in, the museum serves as both a shrine to and a celebration of the life and work of Joan Miró, one of Catalonia and Spain's most beloved contemporary artists. The bright white angles and curves of the Lego-esque building were designed by Josep Lluís Sert, a close friend of Joan Miró.Since it first opened, the museum has expanded beyond Miró's original collection to include pieces inspired by the artist. A collection of over 14,000 works now fills the open galleries, which have views of the grassy exterior and adjacent **Sculpture Park.** The collection includes whimsical sculptures, epic paintings, and gargantuan *sobreteixims* (paintings on tapestry) by Miró, as well as works by Calder, Duchamp, Oldenburg, and Léger. Have fun gazing at Calder's politically charged **mercury fountain,** which was exhibited alongside Picasso's *Guernica* at the 1937 World's Fair in Paris. Like much of Barcelona, the foundation refuses to be stuck in its past—although an impressive relic of a previous era, Fundació Miró continues to support contemporary art. Temporary exhibitions have recently featured names such as Olafur Eliasson, Pipllotti Rist, and Kiki Smith, while the more experimental **Espai 13** houses exhibits by emerging artists selected by freelance curators. Overwhelmed? You should be. This is one of the few times we recommend paying for the audio tour (€4).

i M:Paral·lel. From the metro, take the funicular to the museum. €11, students €6, under 14 free. Temporary exhibits €4, students €3. Espai 13 €2.50. Sculpture garden free. Open Jul-Sept Tu-W 10am-8pm, Th 10am-9:30pm, F-Sa 10am-8pm, Su 10am-2:30pm; Oct-Jun Tu-W 10am-7pm, Th 10am-9:30pm, F-Sa 10am-7pm, Su 10am-2:30pm. Last entry 30min. before close.

MUSEU NACIONAL D'ART DE CATALUNYA (MNAC)

Palau Nacional, Parc de Montjuïc ☎936 22 03 76 www.mnac.cat

This majestic building perched atop Montjuïc isn't quite as royal as it first appears. Designed by Enric Català and Pedro Cendoya for the 1929 International Exhibition, the Palau Nacional has housed the Museu Nacional d'art de Catalunya (MNAC) since 1934. The sculpture-framed view over Barcelona from outside the museum can't be beat,and more treasures await on the inside.

Upon entrance, you'll be dumped into the gargantuan, colonnaded **Oval Hall,** which, though empty, gets your jaw appropriately loose to prepare for its drop in the galleries. The wing to the right houses a collection of Catalan Gothic art, complete with paintings on wood panels and sculptures that Pier 1 would kill to replicate. To the left in the main hall is the museum's impressive collection of Catalan Romanesque art and frescoes, removed from their original settings in the 1920s and installed in the museum—a move that was probably for the best, considering the number of churches devastated in the civil war just a decade later. More modern attractions grace the upstairs, with modern art to the left and drawings, prints, and posters to the far right.

spain

For those intoxicated by the quirky architecture of the city, Catalan *modernisme* and *noucentisme* works dot the galleries, from Gaudí-designed furniture to Picasso's Cubist *Woman in Fur Hat and Collar*. The collection, which spans the 19th and early 20th century, includes an impressive selection from the under-appreciated Joaquim Mir and a couple of large, fascinating works by the more renowned José Gutiérrez Solana. If art isn't your thing, check out the currency collection—though beauty may be in the eye of the beholder, this 140,000-piece brief in the history of Catalan coins will have hardly any detractors.

i M:Espanya. Walk through the towers and ride the escalators to the top; the museum is the palace-like structure. Permanent exhibit €12, students €6, under 16 and over 65 free. Annual subscription (permanent and temporary exhibits) €18. Combined ticket with Poble Espanyol €15. Articket €30. Audio tour €3.10. 1st Su of each month free. Open Tu-Sa 10am-7pm, Su 10am-2:30pm. Last entry 30min. before close.

POBLE ESPANYOL
Av. Francesc Ferrer i Guàrdia, 13   ☎935 08 63 00 www.poble-espanyol.com

One of the few original relics from the 1929 International Exhibition that still dots the mountain, the Poble Espanyol originally aimed to present a unified Spanish village. Inspired by *modernista* celebrity Josep Puig i Cadafalch, the four architects and artists in charge of its design visited over 1600 villages and towns throughout the country to find models to copy in constructing the village's 117 full-scale buildings, streets, and squares. Though intended simply as a temporary arts pavilion, the outdoor architectural museum was so popular that it was kept open as a shrine (or challenge) to the ideal of a united Spain that never was. It's perfect for those traveling only to Barcelona who want to get some idea of what the rest of the country looks like—the "Barri Andaluz" feels like a Sevilla street, with whitewashed walls and arches. Nowadays, artists' workshops peddle goods along the winding roads, spectacles take place during the day, and parties rage at night.

i M:Espanya. Walk through the towers, ride the escalators, and take a right €11, students €7.40, at night €6.50 (valid after 8pm); combined visit with National Art Museum of Catalonia €18. Audio tour €3. Open M 9am-8pm, Tu-Th 9am-midnight, F 9am-3am, Sa 9am-4am, Su 9am-midnight. Last entry 1hr. before close. Workshops and shops open daily in summer 10am-8pm; in fall 10am-7pm; in winter 10am-6pm; in spring 10am-7pm.

BARCELONA PAVILION
Av. Francesc Ferrer i Guàrdia, 7   ☎934 23 40 16 www.miesbcn.com

Though the original Barcelona Pavilion was dismantled when the International Exhibition ended in 1930, this faithful 1986 reconstruction recreates the original feel perfectly. **Ludwig Mies van der Rohe's** iconic 1929 structure of glass, steel, and marble reminds us that "less is more." The open interior is populated solely by the famous Barcelona chair and a reflecting pool with a bronze reproduction of Georg Kolbe's *Alba*. This pavilion—simple, tranquil, sleek—changed modern architecture, modern design, and the way we look at both, whether we realize it or not.

i M:Espanya. Walk through the towers and take the escalators up Montjuïc. Barcelona Pavilion is on the 1st landing to the right; follow the signs. €5, students €2.60, under 16 free. Free 30min. guide service Sa 10am, English 11am, Spanish noon. Catalan Bus Turístic, Barcelona Card, Barcelona City Tour reduction 20%. Cash only at front entrance. Open daily 10am-8pm.

CASTLE OF MONTJUÏC
Carretera Montjuïc, 66   ☎932 56 44 45 www.bcn.cat/castelldemontjuic

Built in 1640 during the revolt against Philip IV, this former fort and castle has been involved in its fair share of both Catalan and Spanish struggles. The fortress first saw action in 1641 against Castilian forces and continued its function as a

barcelona

military post until 1960, when it was ceded to the city and refurbished as a military museum by Franco (incidentally, this is the only place in Catalunya where one can find a statue of the narcissist). Despite being handed to the city, the fort was controlled by the army until 2007, when its direction was finally handed to the Barcelona City Council. The inside walkways offer mazes, incredible views of the harbor and city, as well as a moat-turned-beautifully-manicured-garden for those that make the hike (or shell out for the rather expensive, €11 cable car ride to the top). Once there, try to mount those massive steel juggernauts!

i M:Espanya. Montjuïc telefèric on Avda. Miramar. Free. Open daily Apr 1-Sept 30 9am-9pm; Oct 1-Mar 31 9am-7pm.

FOOD

Given the cosmopolitan character of Barcelona, you can find just about any food you crave in this city. The cheapest options are chain supermarkets (Dia, Caprabo, and Spar, to name a few) and local groceries that tend to run a few cents cheaper still; in terms of prepared food, kebab restaurants are some of the cheapest and most plentiful. Local Catalan cuisine is varied and includes food from land and sea: some of the most traditional dishes are *botifarra amb mongetes* (Catalan pork sausage with beans), *esqueixada* (cod with tomato and onion), *llonganissa* (a kind of salami), and *coques* (somewhere between a pizza and an open-faced sandwich; singular *coca*). The simplest and most prevalent dish is *pa amb tomàquet* (bread smeared with tomato, garlic, olive oil, salt, and pepper). Note also that the Catalan for "salad" is *amanida;* this bears no relation to the word in English or Spanish, which confuses some travelers poring over a menu in search of *ensalada.*

Barri Gòtic and Las Ramblas

LA BOQUERIA (MERCAT DE SANT JOSEP)
Las Ramblas, 89

If you're looking for ruby red tomatoes, leeks the size of a well-fed child's arm, or maybe just some nuts and a zumo smoothie, the Boqueria has you covered in the most beautiful way—quite literally. Just look for the stained-glass archway facing Las Ramblas that marks the entrance of this expansive tented open market. Though each neighborhood in Barcelona has its own *mercat*, the Mercat de Sant Josep is not only the biggest and most impressive in the city, it's the largest market in all of Spain. If filling your stomach from the glowing rows of perfectly arranged, perfectly ripened produce doesn't satisfy your gut, restaurants surrounding the market and dotting La Rambla offer meals made from produce directly from the nearby vendors.

i M:Liceu. Walk on Las Ramblas toward Pl. de Catalunya and take a left onto Pl. de Sant Josep. Open M-Sa 8am-8pm, though certain vendors stay open later.

ATTIC $$$$
Las Ramblas, 120   ☎933 02 48 66 www.angrup.com

After a long day along Las Ramblas, Attic provides a soothing world away from the performers, pickpockets, and fanny-packing crowds. Attic has no dress code, but you should really consider changing out of that pit-stained T-shirt and cargo shorts. With over 10 menus of varied price tags to choose from, Attic provides its customers with everything from €29.95 *Ocells* and *Flors* menus to the hefty €65 *Festa* menu. Perch yourself on the rooftop terrace floor overlooking Las Ramblas at dinner for a truly memorable experience.

i M:Liceu. On Las Ramblas, toward Pl. Catalonia. Appetizer €4.50-12. Meat entrees €8-14. Fish €10-13. Open M-Th 1-4:30pm and 7-11:30pm, F-Sa 1-4:30pm and 7pm-12:30am, Su 1-4:30pm and 7-11:30pm.

ESCRIBÀ $

Las Ramblas, 83 ☎933 01 60 27 www.escriba.es

Grab a coffee and feast your eyes on any of the colorful and sugary oeuvres patiently awaiting passage to some lucky customer's mouth. With beckoning tarts, croissants, cakes, and rings made of caramel, Escribà tempts even the most devout sugar-avoiders from all four corners of its beautiful *modernista*-style store. If you're not in the mood for sweets or a mug of their killer raspberry hot chocolate, try a savory dish, such as the croissant with blue cheese, caramelized apple, and walnuts (€4.50) or the "bikini" bread mold with ham and brie (€4).

i M:Liceu. Walk toward Pl. Catalonia. Escribà is on the left. Sandwiches €3.50. Menú €5.90. Sweets €3-5. Open M-Th 1-4pm and 8-11pm, F-Su 1-5pm and 8-11:30pm.

L'ANTIC BOCOI DEL GÒTIC $$$

Baixada de Viladecols, 3 ☎933 10 50 67 www.bocoi.net

Enter the lair of L'Antic Bocoi del Gòtic, where walls of stone and exposed brick surround patrons with cave-like intimacy. The restaurant specializes in Catalan cuisine, with fresh, seasonal ingredients, and prides itself on bringing new ideas to traditional food. The amicable staff recommends the selection of cheeses and their own take on the *coques de recapte*, a regional dish made of a thin dough with fresh produce and thickly layered meats (€8.50-9).

i M:Jaume I. Follow C. Jaume I toward Pl. Sant Jaume, then turn left onto C. Dagueria, which becomes C. dels Lledó, then Baixada de Viladecols. Reservations recommended. Appetizers €7-10. Entrees €10-21. Open M-Sa 7:30pm-midnight.

CAFÉ VIENA $

Las Ramblas, 115 ☎933 17 14 92 www.viena.es

This cafe has earned much renown for a fulsome 2006 *New York Times* article whose author raved for several paragraphs about Viena's *flauta ibèric* (Iberian ham sandwich; €6.60), calling it "the best sandwich I've ever had." The sandwich's secret, which the article's author almost figured out but couldn't quite discern, is that the *flauta* comes on *pa amb tomàquet*, the staple of the Catalan kitchen that involves smearing tomato on bread before seasoning it with salt, pepper, olive oil, and garlic. And it is a damn good sandwich, the sort that melts in your mouth with each bite. Munch away while the piano echoes its tunes from the veranda at this grandiose establishment.

i M:Catalunya. Follow Las Ramblas toward the sea. Sandwiches €2.40-9.30 (most under €4). Coffee €1.30-2.40. Open M-Th 8am-11:30pm, F-Sa 8am-12:30am, Su 8am-11:30pm.

LA CLANDESTINA $

Baixada de Viladecols, 2bis ☎933 19 05 33

This is a hidden—dare we say, clandestine?—tea house with the most relaxed atmosphere in all the Barri Gòtic. With an interior of clutter and many-colored walls, this establishment will envelop you in its thick air, fragrant with freshly brewed tea and hookah. The cavernous *teteria* makes for a great place to take a short (or long, if you're feeling real Spanish) reprieve from the frenetic pace of the Gothic Quarter. Everyone from the neighborhood book club to young'uns in their 20s will meet you here.

i M:Jaume I. Follow C. Jaume I toward Pl. Sant Jaume, then turn left onto C. Dagueria, which becomes C. dels Lledó, then Baixada de Viladecols. Free Wi-Fi. Sandwiches €4.20-4.40. Tea €2.50-6; pots €10-15. Juices €2.80-3.60. Cash only. Open M-Th 9am-10pm, F 9am-midnight, Sa 10am-midnight, Su 11am-10pm.

VEGETALIA $$

C. dels Escudellers, 54 ☎933 17 33 31 www.restaurantesvegetalia.com

Vegetalia delivers delicious, organic, natural, and environmentally conscious food at reasonable prices. Relax at the bar and chat with the easygoing staff about the ironic history of the Pl. de George Orwell or experience the square for

barcelona

yourself after ordering at the walk-up window. Try the popular bowl of nachos (€5.50) and wash it down a glass of fresh-squeezed lemonade (€2.20).

i M:Liceu. Walk down Las Ramblas toward the sea and take a left onto C. dels Escudellers. Organic store in the rear. Free Wi-Fi. Appetizer €5.50-12. Entrees €4-8.80. Desserts €2.50-4.50. Open daily 11am-11:30pm.

El Born

▨ EL XAMPANYET $$
C. de Montcada, 22 ☎933 19 70 03

Since its founding in 1929, El Xampanyet is as authentic as it gets, with sheepskin wine bags, an overwhelming selection of *cava*, and old locals spilling out the door and onto the street. Four generations of family ownership has lead to the museum of casks, blackened bottles, and kitschy bottle openers displayed against hand-painted ceramic tiles and topped by large, century-old barrels filled with vintage beer. We recommend that you try the cask-fresh *cerveza* (€3.50) or the house wine *xampanyet* (€2), and pad your stomach with some of the delicious tapas.

i M:Jaume I. Walk down C. de la Princesa and take a right onto C. de Montcada, toward the Museu Picasso. Xampanyet is on the right before the Placeta Montcada. Tapa €1-13. Beer €3.50. Wine and cava from €2. Open daily noon-3:30pm and 7-11pm.

▨ PETRA $$
C. dels Sombrerers, 13 ☎933 19 99 99

With dark wood, stained glass, Art Nouveau prints, menus pasted onto wine bottles, and chandeliers made of silverware, Petra's eccentric decor will have you expecting any meal to give your wallet liposuction. Luckily, the lively bohemian feel is matched by bohemian prices. Pasta dishes like the rich gnocchi with mushrooms and hazelnut oil (€5.20) and entrees such as the duck with lentils (€7.90) are easy on the wallet, as is the midday *menú* of a main course (varies daily), salad, and wine for €6.60—a true steal and a local favorite.

i M:Jaume I. Walk down C. de la Princesa and take a right onto C. del Pou de la Cadena. Take an immediate left onto C. de la Barra de Ferro and a right onto C. dels Banys Vells. Petra is located where C. dels Banys Vells ends at C. dels Sombrerers. Menú €6.50. Appetizers €5-7. Entrees €8. Open Tu-Sa 1:30-4pm and 9-11:30pm, Su 1:30pm-4pm.

▨ LA BÁSCULA $$
C. dels Flassaders, 30 ☎933 19 98 66

This working cooperative serves vegetarian sandwiches, *empanadas*, salads, and more—the menu changes daily. Doors laid flat serve as communal tables, and a mixture of art, environmentally-friendly sodas, and protest flyers set this restaurant apart. Though robed in the same antique exterior as more expensive places, Báscula provides a more reasonably priced alternative to the upscale eateries. Hours and seating availability may change as the restaurant fights for its right to serve in-house, but takeout is available no matter the outcome. Try the daily special (€8-10) or one of their recommended plates, like the vegetable curry couscous with coconut milk (€8.50).

i M:Jaume I. Walk down Carrer de la Princesa and take a right onto Carrer dels Flassaders. Entrees and salad €7-9. Sandwiches and soups €4-5. Piadinas €6. Cash only. Open W-Sa 1pm-11pm, Su 1-8pm.

▨ LA PARADETA $$$
C. Comercial, 7 ☎932 68 19 39 www.laparadeta.com

For the highest quality seafood, this hybrid fish market/restaurant is where Barcelona goes. The line often stretches down the ever-under-construction Carrer Comercial, but it's worth the wait to pick out a fresh fish to be cooked to your liking. When they call your number, head up and grab your meal, then sit back down and dig in. The authentic seaworthy feel of this establishment is worth of an ahoy or two, so drop by if you're feeling fresh (fish, that is).

i M:Jaume I. Follow Carrer Princesa all the way to Carrer del Comerç, then turn right, then left at Carrer Fusina (just before the market). Turn right onto Carrer Comercial. Market prices fluctuate. Open Tu-Su 1pm-4pm and 8pm-11:30pm.

El Raval

CAN LLUÍS
$$$

C. Cera, 49 ☎934 41 11 87

Can Lluís? Yes he can! This crowded restaurant has been an El Raval staple since its founding in the 1920s, when this neighborhood was Barcelona's Chinatown. Don't be intimidated by the fact that everyone already knows each other or that you'll almost certainly be spoken to in traditional Catalan. Just remember: *"Què vols?"* ("What do you want?") is your cue to order. Respond with an order of tiny faba beans with cuttlefish (definitely worth the €13.90) for an appetizer and the Monkfish Rounds with Spanish ham (€18.90) for your main dish.

i M:Sant Antoni. Follow Ronda Sant Antoni toward Mercat de Sant Antoni, bear left onto Ronda Sant Pau, and then head left onto C. Cera. Appetizers €7.40-16. Entrees €7.90-27. Desserts €3.20-5.50. Open M-Sa 1:30-4pm and 8:30-11:30pm.

SOHO
$

C. Ramelleres, 26

A welcome recent addition to the neighborhood, Soho might be confused for an average eatery given it's lack of flashy interior design. No matter—try the €2 Moroccan tea or the cheap and simple meat and vegetarian options (€2). The whole place feels very impromptu, with menu items written by hand and plenty of exposed plywood, but at prices this low, you can't really complain. There are smaller, more intimate rooms which are perfect for test-driving a hookah (€10) from the set available on the counter at the entrance.

i M:Universitat. Walk down C. Tallers and take a right onto C. Ramelleres. Pita and drink €3.50. Cash only. Open M-Sa 1-10pm.

JUICY JONES
$$

C. l'Hospital, 74 ☎934 43 90 82 www.juicyjones.com

Very similar to the kindred Juicy Jones down in the Barri Gotic, this place will give you some great Indian *thali dahl* and curry options as well as an ever present assortment of zumos and smoothies. The liquid landscape of the menu offers one kickin' Banana GoGo smoothie you would be a fool not to try (cacao, banana, soy milk, cane sugar, ice, and coconut shavings (€3.95). If you've ever wondered what M.C. Escher's art would have looked like if he used more color and took more shrooms, the interior will satisfy your curiosity.

i M:Liceu. Walk down C. l'Hospital. Juicy Jones is on the right at the corner of C. l'Hospital and C. En Roig, before Rambla del Raval. Tapas €2-4. Sandwiches €3-5. Daily thali plate €6. Menú €8.50. Open daily 1-11:30pm.

NARIN
$

C. Tallers, 80 ☎933 01 90 04

Sitting discreetly among the shops and cafes of C. Tallers, Narin is hiding the best baklava (€1) in Barcelona as well as equally scrumptious falafel, shawarma, kebabs, and pita bread combinations. You have to try the chicken and falafel pita, the perfect snack for a hot afternoon. Luckily, beers come cold and cheap (€1.80) for those looking to brave the bar. A tiled dining room provides a reprieve from the buzz of the electric shawarma shaver.

i M:Universitat. Walk down C. Tallers. Pita €2.50-4. Durums €3.50-6.50. Main dishes €6-8. Open M-Sa 1pm-midnight, Su 6pm-midnight.

barcelona

L'Eixample

⬛ LA RITA $$

C. Aragó, 279 ☎934 87 23 76 http://www.grupandilana.com/es/restaurantes/
la-rita-restaurantm

La Rita serves traditional Catalan dishes with a twist; the duck with apples, raspberry *coulis*, and mango chutney—you will surely find—go great with just about everything. Though the price is dirt-cheap given the quality and quantity of food off the pricey C. Aragó, the interior is anything but—expect an upscale but relaxed ambience that will make you appreciate the dressy casual clothes you brought instead of the traveler's reusable T-shirt. Try an order of the exquisitely steamed black sausage croquettes with apple sauce (€3.95) or the veal meatballs with cuttlefish (€8.55).

i M:Passeig de Gràcia. Walk up Pg. de Gràcia away from Pl. Catalunya and turn right onto C. Aragó. Appetizers €4.70-8.80. Entrees €7-12. Menu (two main courses and dessert) €19. Open daily 1-3:45pm and 8:30-11:30pm.

⬛ OMEÍA $$

C. Aragó, 211 ☎934 52 31 79 www.omeia.es

When you're tired of cheap shawarma stands, stop into Omeía for some authentic Middle Eastern fare. Devour an order of their lamb tagines with prunes and almonds (€13) or fill up with one of the traditional Jordanian dishes (€11-13). Pick something you haven't got a chance of pronouncing correctly and hope for the best! And remember that you can't ever go wrong by ordering yogurt with honey (€2.50).

i M:Universitat. Walk up C. Aribau to the left of the University building and turn right onto C. Aragó. Appetizers €6-7. Salads €6-6.50. Entrees €7.50-18. Traditional specialties €11-13. Lunch menú €7.50. Coffee €1.10. Wine €1.80-2. Open daily 12:30pm-4:30pm and 8pm-midnight.

Barceloneta

⬛ BOMBETA $$

C. de la Maquinista, 3 ☎933 19 94 45

A hardy, good old-fashioned tapas bar is personified in this local, nearly ocean-front establishment. Take heed of the warning scrawled above the bar,"*No hablamos inglés, pero hacemos unas bombas cojonudas*"—or, "We don't speak English, but we make ballsy *bombas*." The TV-aggrandized persona of the typical rough 'n' tough Spaniard finds its incarnation in the bar staff. Ask any question, and they will respond with rough Catalan accents and a trusty smile while doggedly assembling your order. Treat yourself to the house *pièce de résistance* known as *bombas* (scrumptious fried potato balls reminiscent of light garlic and onion scents stuffed with perfectly-seasoned, spicy ground beef and topped with an exquisite house sauce; €3.90 for 2).

i M:Barceloneta. Walk down Pg. Juan de Borbó (toward the beach) and take a left onto C. Maquinista. Appetizers €3-9.50. Entrees €5-18. Cash only. Open daily M-Tu 11am-midnight, Th-Su 11am-midnight.

⬛ SOMORROSTRO $$$

C. Sant Carles, 11 ☎932 25 00 10 www.restaurantesomorrostro.com

This extraordinary restaurant assembles a new menu every day based on selections from the catch of the day that the young chefs, Jordi Limón and Andrés Gaspar, have selected. Somorrostro is not cheap—its rotating menu of seafood dishes, *paella*, curries, and other dishes runs about €13-20 per entree—but the nighttime *menú* (€15-17) of the chefs' gastronomical experiments is the real treat. Try to beat the lunch and dinner rush by showing up more near the start of each serving session. The *Mostaca Synera* (€5.40) is the perfect starting drink and can be enjoyed as one wistfully gazes at and interprets the old black-and-white French photographs spanning the back wall.

i M:Barceloneta. Walk down Plà del Palau over Ronda Litoral, following the harbor. After crossing Litoral, take the 5th left onto C. Sant Carles. Free Wi-Fi. Appetizers €6-14. Entrees €13-20. Weekday lunch buffet €13 per kg. Dinner menu €15-17. Wine €3-6. Open M-Sa 8-11:30pm, Su 2-4pm and 8-11:30pm.

L'ARRÒS $$$

Pg. Joan de Borbó, 12 ☎932 21 26 46 www.larros.es

At first glance, L'Arròs ("Rice") appears to be a typical tourist trap, complete with a striped, blue and white canopy beckoning weary travelers into the pleasant shade. Although it may be found along Barceloneta's main beach drag, don't let the uninspired decor and multilingual menu of this *arrocería* fool you. What the restaurant lacks in atmosphere, it wholeheartedly makes up for with its Spanish *paella*, which Barcelona natives claim is some of the best in town. Top if off with soothing Tahiti vanilla ice cream (€5.90) or Syrian Rose Cake with custard, raspberries, and mango sauce (€7.20). Even more reason to smile is the special-diet-friendly menu, which offers mindful options for those lactose/gluten/nut-allergy intolerant.

i M:Barceloneta. Walk on Plà del Palau over Ronda Litoral and follow Pg. Joan de Borbó. Appetizers €8.75-19.50. Entrees €8.60-18.50. Open daily noon-11:30pm.

BAR BITÁCORA $

C. Balboa, 1 ☎933 19 11 10

During the summer months, the seemingly quaint, relaxed aura of this establishment's main room peers into a vibrantly painted, terrace-like back room crammed full of young people who flock from the beach like pigeons for a crunchy chunk of bread. The 10% surcharge to sit amid the Rubik's-cube assortment of colors in the courtyard terrace will give you a more memorable experience. Your respite from the heat and bustle of Barceloneta will be made much more enjoyable by the groovy atmosphere of the terrace room. A cheap but filling daily *menú* (entree with salad and *patatas bravas*, bread, a drink, and dessert; €5) offers travelers a nice cash-saving option; however, should the heat make you super adventurous, you can order a tangy house *Mojito* or *Caipirinha* (€5 each) and an order of refreshing and not too heavy *fresas con nata* (strawberries and cream; €3). Kick back with friends and listen to the varied music from all places international echoing throughout the bar's sound system.

i M:Barceloneta. Walk down Pg. Joan de Borbó (toward the beach) and take the 1st left after Ronda del Litoral onto Carrer Balboa. Tapas €2.50-8. Sangria €3. Menú del día €5-7. Open M-W 10am-midnight, Th-F 10am-2am, Sa noon-2am, Su noon-5pm.

Gràcia

🌿 UN LUGAR DE GRÀCIA $$

C. Providència, 88 ☎932 19 32 89

Un Lugar de Gràcia has the best-priced and most ample lunch special in the neighborhood by far: any two dishes from the midday *menú*—no distinction between first and second courses, so the very hungry may essentially order two main courses at no extra cost—bread, water or wine, and pudding/dessert for €11.20. The food may be a bit generic, with your typical assortment of pastas, meats, some fish options, and of course tapas; however, they come in great quantity for a steal of a price. For an ultra hearty meal, try the *bife ancho a la parilla de origen argentino*—that's grilled Argentinian flank steak.

i M:Joanic. From the metro, follow C. Escorial uphill and take a left onto C. Providència. Entrees €6-11. Open M-Th noon-4pm, F-Sa noon-4pm and 8-11pm. Also open for F.C. Barcelona matches.

SAMSARA $$

C. Terol, 6   ☎932 85 36 88

Samsara has a long regular menu with some of the best tapas in the neighborhood as well as about a half dozen *"novetats,"* which are daily tapas specials with international twists on customary Catalonian dishes. This restaurant also offers comfy cushions for its local and foreign customers; low rising communal tables and even lower cushioned ottomans will help you make new, hungry friends.

i M:Fontana. Head downhill on C. Gran de Gràcia, then turn left onto C. Ros de Olano, which becomes C. Terol. Tapas €1-7.50. Beer €2.20. Wine €3.30-3.50. Open M-W 8:30am-1:30am, Th 8:30pm-3am, F 8:30am-3pm, Su 7:30pm-1am.

LA NENA $

C. Ramón y Cajal, 36   ☎932 85 14 76

Welcome to grandma's house! But this was the cool grandma who used to feed you tons of sweets and spoil you as a kid. La Nena has an extensive menu of gourmet hot chocolate, crepes, *bocadillo* sandwiches, and quiches at unbeatable prices. Watch out, you party people—there's a hilarious banner displaying grandma's "no alcohol served here" declaration. This is a great place to slow down and have a *choco brasil* (hot chocolate with a ball of coffee ice cream inside; €4).

i M:Fontana. Follow C. d'Astúries away from C. Gran de Gràcia and take a right onto C. Torrent de l'Olla. Walk a few blocks and take a left onto C. Ramón y Cajal. Sandwiches €2.50-6. Quiches €6. Pastries €1.20-4. Cash only. May call to reserve. Open daily 9am-10pm.

GAVINA $$

C. Ros de Olano, 17   ☎934 15 74 50

Gavina is Gràcia's most heavenly pizzeria. The gigantic hand coming out of the wall, or the parade of angels encircling the chandelier, are bound to make you feel super holy (and hopefully hungry). You'll probably forget about the rather bulky pope figurine watching the tables near the door once you try the strawberry cheesecake tart (€4.50). The big draw, though, is neither the impressive kitsch nor desserts but is instead the gigantic, delicious pizzas (€6.50-14). Try the namesake Gavina (potatoes, ham, onion, and mushrooms; €12) or the pizza of the day—but be sure to bring friends or an otherworldly appetite.

i M:Fontana. From the metro, walk downhill on C. Gran de Gràcia and take a left onto C. Ros de Olano. Pizza €6.50-14. Midday menú W-F €10, includes pizza, dessert, and a drink. Chupitos €2. Open M 1pm-4am and 8pm-1am, Tu 7pm-1am, W-Th 1pm-4am and 8pm-1am.

Montjuïc and Poble Sec

spain

The neighborhood of **Poble Sec** hides a number of good, inexpensive restaurants and bars—perfect for those who don't feel like breaking the bank to eat at a museum cafe up on Montjuïc, or for those looking to explore a lovely neighborhood a bit off the beaten track.

QUIMET I QUIMET $$

C. Poeta Cabanyes, 25   ☎934 42 31 42

With five generations and 100-plus years of service under its belt, Quimet i Quimet knows what's up. If you're lucky enough to visit this place when it isn't super busy, take a moment to be mesmerized by the massive liquor bottle display lining the establishment's walls. Try the salmon, yogurt, and truffle honey or the bleu cheese with baked red pepper sandwich.

i M:Paral·lel. Follow Av. Paral·lel away from the water, past the small plaça on the left, then head left up C. Poeta Cabanyes. Tapas €2.50-3.25. Beer €5.75 per bottle. Open M-F noon-4pm and 7-10:30pm, Sa and holidays noon-4pm. Closed Aug.

NIGHTLIFE
Barri Gòtic and Las Ramblas

▓ BARCELONA PIPA CLUB

Pl. Reial, 3   ☎933 02 47 32 www.bpipaclub.com

With pipes from six continents, smoking paraphernalia decorated by Dalí, and an "ethnological museum dedicated to the smoking accessory," the only pipe-related article missing from this club—albeit somewhat appropriately—is René Magritte's *Ceci n'est pas une pipe* ("This is not a pipe."). Despite its cryptic lack of signage and the furtive ambiance of a secret society, the low-lit, amber-colored bar, pool room, and music lounge has a surprisingly high amount of visitors. Take a few puffs as you listen to the retro blues and ragtime tunes.

i M:Liceu. Walk on Las Ramblas toward the water and turn left onto C. Colom to enter Pl. Reial. Pipa Club is an unmarked door to the right of Glaciar Bar. To enter, ring the bottom bell. Rotating selection of tobacco available for sale. Special smoking events. Jazz jam session Su 8:30pm. Beer €4-5. Wine €4-5. Cocktails €7.50-9. Cash only. Open daily 11pm-3am.

▓ HARLEM JAZZ CLUB

C. Comtessa de Sobradiel, 8   ☎933 10 07 55 www.harlemjazzclub.es

With live performances nightly and a drink often included in the cover (check the schedule), this is a budget-conscious music lover's paradise. This sophisticated jazz house posts performance schedules on the door, letting you choose whether you'll drop in to hear lovesick English crooning or a saucier Latin flavor. Acts range from funk and soul to Latin jazz, and the crowd is just as varied.

i M:Liceu. Walk toward the water on Las Ramblas and take a left onto C. Ferran, a right onto C. Avinyó, and a left onto C. Comtessa de Sobradiel. Live music usually begins at 10 or 11pm. Calendar of events available online or at the door. Cover €5-6; sometimes includes 1 drink. Beer €3.80. Cocktails €7.80. Cash only. Open M 8pm-1am, Tu 8pm-12:30am, W-Th 8pm-1am, F-Sa 8pm-5am, Su 6pm-1am.

▓ SINCOPA

C. Avinyò, 35

At night, this music-themed bar—rumored to have once been owned by none other than Manu Chao—plays host to as many nationalities and performers as it has currencies and secondhand instruments on its walls. Of Barri Gòtic's bars, Sincopa undoubtedly sports some of the most colorful decor and clientele. One night, the crowd might be on a chemically-induced "vacation" and chilling to *Dark Side of the Moon;* the next, everyone will be salsa dancing.

i M:Liceu. Walk on Las Ramblas toward the water and take a left onto C. Ferran and a right onto C. d' Avinyò. Beer €2-4. Cocktails €7. Juices €2.50. Cash only. Open M-Th 6pm-2:30am, F-Sa 6pm-3am, Su 6pm-2:30am.

MANCHESTER

C. Milans, 5   ☎627 73 30 81 www.manchesterbar.com

The names of the drinks posted on the front door—Joy Division, The Cure, Arcade Fire, and many, many more—set a rockin' mood. After passing the spinning turntable at the entrance, you'll see intimate, perfectly dimmed red seating, and gleefully gabbing young people. The happy hour, with €1 Estrella Damms, will have you singing along to "Friday I'm in Love" before the evening's up.

i M:Liceu. Walk toward the water on Las Ramblas and head left onto C. Ferran, right onto C. d'Avinyó, and left onto C. Milans, before C. Ample. Manchester is at the bend in the street. Beer €2-4. Shots from €2.50. Cocktails €6. Cash only. Open M-Th 7pm-2:30am, F-Sa 7pm-3:30am, Su 7pm-2:30am. Happy hour daily 7-10pm.

barcelona

LAS CUEVAS DEL SORTE

C. Gignàs, 2   ☎932 95 40 15

The eponymous caves, with miniature stalactites on the ceiling, are filled with alcohol, partygoers, and a subtle earthy scent. Exquisite mosaics crop up in the most unexpected places, including the bathrooms. Seriously, though, it'll be the most aesthetically pleasing potty break you ever take. Downstairs, small tables and another bar surround a disco-balled dance floor, where revelers party on with cocktail in happy hand.

i M:Liceu. Walk toward the water on Las Ramblas and head left onto C. Ferran, right onto C. d'Avinyó, and left onto C. Gignàs. Cocktails €5-7. Open M 7pm-2am, W-Su 7pm-2am

El Born

🔲 EL CASO BORN

C. de Sant Antoni dels Sombrerers, 7   ☎932 69 11 39

This is a quieter alternative for those too cool to bother with the packed houses and inflated prices of nearby Pg. del Born. Cheap drinks tempt travelers, while relaxed seating, a chill crowd, and a drinks menu with cocktails named for the Bourne movies (the name is a pun on *El Caso Bourne,* the Spanish title of *The Bourne Identity*) provide ample reason to start the night here.

i M:Jaume I. Walk down C. de la Princesa and take a right onto C. de Montcada. Upon entering Pg. del Born, take a right onto C. dels Sombrerers and then take a right again onto the 1st street on your the, C. de Sant Antoni dels Sombrerers. Cava €1.80. Beer €2. Cocktails €5-7. Open Tu-Th 8pm-2am, F-Sa 8pm-3am.

🔲 LA LUNA

C. Abaixadors, 10   ☎932 95 55 13   www.lalunabcn.com

Another of Barcelona's most beautiful bars, La Luna sits under timeless vaulted brick arches, with dim lighting and mirrors behind the bar making it seem even larger. Comfortable lounge seating in front makes for a good place to camp out and take in the bar's beauty. The tropical mojito (with coconut rum for €7) and the *mojito de fresa* (€7.30), which replaces the lime with strawberries, are both quite popular. Leather upholstery exudes class, so do your best not to show up in basketball shorts and flip-flops.

i Open M-W 6pm-1:30am, Th-F 6pm-2:30am, Sa 1pm-2:30am, Su 1pm-1:30am.

LA FIANNA

C. Manressa, 4   ☎933 15 18 10   www.lafianna.com

A glass partition divides the restaurant and bar, but be prepared to push your way through on weekend nights no matter where you choose to wine or dine. Unlike at other places in the area, finding a seat at the bar is a distinct possibility; getting a spot on one of the comfy couches is another story altogether. Patience pays off with large mojitos (€7) made with special bitters as you gaze upon the Euro-rockin' interior design, super chic furniture, and just the right amount of dim lighting.

i M:Jaume I. Walk down Via Laietana and take a left onto C. Manresa. The restaurant is on the right after passing C. de la Nau. All cocktails €4.50 M-Th 6-9pm. Discounted tapas M-Th 7pm-12:30am, F-Sa 7pm-11:30pm, Su 7pm-12:30am. Tapas €2-4.80. Beer €2.50-3.40. Shots €4. Cocktails €6-7. Open daily 6pm-midnight.

EL BORN

Pg. del Born, 26   ☎933 19 53 33

Shed the themes and pretense and stop at El Born for a straight-up bar—no more, no less. Marble tables and green decor provide a simple, no games interior that nonetheless attracts burly jocks, retired dads, and everyone in between attempting who come here to watch the Champions League finals or the French Open (really, whatever's big in Euro sports at the time of your visit). With cheap beer (€2-2.50) and ambient music, it's no wonder this place is always full. Usual patrons are more of the male variety, so ladies should bear that in mind. Some filling options include the *empandas* (€2) or a *sandwich de Milanesa* (€2.90).

i M:Jaume I. Walk down C. de la Princesa and take a right onto C. de Montcada. Follow until you hit Pg. del Born and take a left. Free Wi-Fi. Beer €2-2.50. Mixed drinks €6. Open Tu-Su 10am-2:30am.

EL COPETÍN
Pg. del Born, 19   ☎607 20 21 76

This dance floor just won't quit: Latin beats blare all night long, attracting a laid-back, fun-loving crowd that knows how to move like Shakira. A narrow, tightly packed bar up front provides little reprieve for those who need a drink, as the waitstaff will probably be too busy shakin' anyway to tend to your every beck and call. Most people who come here come prepared to dance.

i M:Jaume I. Walk down C. de la Princesa and take a right onto C. de Montcada. Follow to Pg. del Born. Mixed drink €7. Open M-Th 6pm-2:30am, F-Sa 6pm-3am, Su 6pm-2:30am.

BERIMBAU
Pg. del Born, 17   ☎646 00 55 40

This *copas* bar, reportedly the oldest Brazilian bar in Spain (founded 1978), offers a range of drinks you won't easily find this side of the Atlantic. Try the *guaraná* with whiskey (€8), an orange and banana juice with vodka (€9.50), or the tried and true (and damn good) caipirinha (€8). Samba and Brazilian electronic music fill the room with a *brasileiro* feel as the wicker furniture and stifling heat complete the scene.

i M:Jaume I. Walk down C. de la Princesa and take a right onto C. de Montcada. Follow to Pg. del Born, then turn left. Beer €2.50-3. Cocktails €7-10. Open daily 6pm-2:30am.

CACTUS BAR
Pg. del Born, 30   ☎933 10 63 54 www.cactusbar.cat

Cactus Bar is renowned along Pg. del Born for its big, tasty, and potent mojitos (€8). If you can get a bartender's attention over the clamor, you generally don't need to specify which drink you want; just use your fingers to indicate how many mojitos it'll be. The constant stream—or devastating flood—of customers means the bartenders work as a team, creating a mojito assembly line that churns out over a dozen of the minty beverages at a time. Get your drink in a plastic cup to go instead of the weighty tall glasses and enjoy it on the (slightly) less crowded Pg. del Born right out front. If mainstream doesn't float your boat, try the house gin and tonic—it'll definitely wake you up (€7.50).

i M:Jaume I. Walk down C. de la Princesa and take a right onto C. de Montcada. Continue until you hit Pg. del Born, then take a left. DJs M and W. Beer €3. Cocktails €8. Breakfast €3.50-4.50. Sandwiches €2.50-3.70. Tapas €1.80-6.50. Open M-Sa noon-2am, Su noon-midnight.

El Raval

🏛 MARSELLA BAR
C. Sant Pau, 65   ☎934 42 72 63

Enter this amber-colored establishment lined with antique mirrors, cabinets, old advertisements, and ancient liquor bottles that have likely been there since the *modernisme* art form was first invented. The easygoing crowd is loyal to Marsella even after a few absinthes (€5). It may be a bit crowded in here, but it'll be well worth your glass of greenish glow (really, everyone orders one) below the ridiculously ornate chandeliers. Maybe you can even catch a glimpse of some long-past customers' phantoms, like Hemingway, Gaudí, or Picasso.

i M:Liceu. Follow C. Sant Pau from Las Ramblas. Beer €3. Mixed drinks €5-6.50. Cash only. Open M-Th 11pm-2am, F-Sa 11pm-3am.

MOOG

C. Arc del Teatre, 3   ☎933 19 17 89   www.masimas.com/moog

Buried in the heart of Old Chinatown and long changed since its days of flamenco bohemia, Moog still stands as one of Europe's most important dance
clubs, renowned for its electronic music. This club has featured several big
name DJs like Robert X, John Acquaviva, and many from the Berlin label
Tresor-all. Come inside to experience musical flavors favored by everyone
from electronica aficionados to lost souls just trying to find a place to dance
and shed some Spanish cuisine-induced pounds the fun way.

i *M:Drassanes. Walk away from the water on Las Ramblas and turn left onto C. Arc del Teatre.
Discount flyers often available on Las Ramblas. Cover €10. Open daily midnight-5am.*

BAR BIG BANG

MUSIC CLUB C. Botella, 7   www.bigbangbcn.com

Sitting in the Ciutat Vella for over 20 years now, Big Bang features everything
from jazz to blues to funky swing. Stand up and vaudeville-esque theater are
other acts that the crowd can drink to. Out front, customers are serenaded by
big band favorites—both local and national—from the stereo and projector
screen that have entertained patrons for years.

i *M:Sant Antoni. Walk down C. Sant Antoni Abad and take a right onto C. Botella. Free Wi-Fi.
Schedule of performances and special events on website. Shot €3. Beer €3-4. Open Tu-Th 10pm-
2:30am, Su 10pm-2:30am.*

BETTY FORD'S

C. Joaquin Costa, 56   ☎933 04 13 68

This ain't your dad's antique Ford, honey. During the earlier hours of the
evening, this bar and restaurant stuffs local students with its relatively cheap
and famously delicious burgers (€6.50). Happy hour (6-9pm) provides cheap
drinks, and later in the night, the place gets packed with a young, noisy crowd
that will actually overflow onto the street, so get here early!

i *M:Universitat. Walk down Ronda de Sant Antoni and take a slight left onto C. Joaquin Costa.
Burger €6.50. Shakes €3.50. Mixed drinks €5-6; happy hour drinks €4. Cash only. Open M 6pm-
1:30am, Tu-Th 11am-1:30am, F-Sa 11am-2:30am. Happy hour M-Sa 6-9pm.*

LLETRAFERIT

C. Joaquin Costa, 43   ☎933 17 81 30

A chillax oasis away from the hectic nightlife of C. Joaquin Costa, Lletraferit
(Catalan for "bookworm") offers some respite in the form of cute, colorful
drinks and a little bit of literature to accompany your liquid journey. Grab a
cocktail (€6-8.50) and settle into a comfy leather armchair or head around to
the back, where a cozy library and bookstore awaits you.

i *M:Universitat. Walk down Ronda de Sant Antoni and take a slight left onto C. Joaquin Costa.
Cocktails €5-8.50. Cash only. Open M-Th 4pm-2:30am, F-Sa 5pm-3am.*

VALHALLA CLUB DE ROCK

C. Tallers, 68

Words to our metalhead *Let's Go* readers: get ready to bust out your screamo
skills, air guitars, and '80s rock-on hand gestures. Step through the front
entrance, and you'll see what is a concert hall some nights and an industrial
nightclub on others. It's a haven for those who may gotten tired of the techno
at Moog or the eccentricity of Sant Pau 68. Free entry on non-show nights
means you can use the cash you save to try the entire selection of *chupitos del
rock*, specialty shots named after rock bands from Elvis to Whitesnake (€1).
It'll make you holla for Valhalla.

i *M:Universitat. Walk down C. Tallers. Search for Valhalla Club de Rock on Facebook to find a
calendar of concerts and special events. Shot €1-2. Beer €1.50-5. Mixed drinks €6-7. Cash only.
Open daily 6:30pm-2:30am.*

spain

L'Eixample

🏶 LES GENTS QUE J'AIME

C. València, 286 bis   ☎932 15 68 79

Start with a little red velvet. Then add in some sultry jazz and an environment redolent of gin and *modernisme*, and you'll be transported back some 100 years to a *fin-de-siècle* fiesta. Black-and-white photographs, cool R&B, and vintage chandeliers set the mood for you to partake in sinful pleasures. Not sure where to head for the rest of the night? Cozy up next to the palm reader or have your tarot cards read to avoid making the decision yourself.

i M:Diagonal. Head downhill on Pg. de Gràcia and turn left onto C. València. Les Gents Que J'aime is downstairs, just past Campechano. Palm reading €25-35) and tarot €20-30) M-Sa. Beer €4.50. Wine €5-10. Cocktails €5-10. Open M-Th 6pm-2:30am, F-Sa 7pm-3am, Su 6pm-2:30am.

🏶 LA FIRA

C. Provença, 171   ☎933 23 72 71

Decorated entirely with pieces from the old Apolo Amusement Park in Barcelona and featuring a slightly Latin vibe, this club is like that creepy carnival from *Scooby Doo*, but with a bar instead of a g-g-g-ghooooost. Check out the upgraded Scooby Snax (mojitos €10) as you jam out to top 40 and Latin tracks along with happy club goers.

i M:Hospital Clínic. Walk away from the engineering school along C. Rossello and take a right onto C. Villarroel. Take the 1st left onto C. Provença; La Fira is a few blocks down. Often hosts shows or parties, sometimes with entrance fee or 1 drink min. Cover sometimes €10, includes 1 drink. Beer €5. Cocktails €10. Open F-Sa 11pm-5am.

LUZ DE GAS

C. Muntaner, 246   ☎932 09 77 11 www.luzdegas.com

This is one of the most renowned clubs in the city, and with good reason. Imagine that George Clooney bought out the casino he and his crew robbed in *Ocean's 11* and then recruited hot, classy Spaniards to run it. That's Luz de Gas. Red velvet walls, gilded mirrors, and sparkling chandeliers will have you wondering how you possibly got past the bouncer, while the massive, purple-lit dance floor surrounded by multi-colored bars will remind you what you're here for. Big name jazz, blues, and soul performers occasionally take the stage during the evening hours, but after 1am, it turns into your typical *discoteca*. Ritzy youths dance to deafening pop in the lower area, while the upstairs lounge provides a much-needed break for both your feet and ears.

i M:Diagonal. Take a left onto Avda. Diagonal and a right onto C. Muntaner. For show listings and times, check the Guía del Ocio or the club's website. Cover €18, includes 1 drink. Beer €7. Cocktails €10. Open Th-Sa 11:30pm-5am.

ANTILLA

C. Aragó, 141   ☎934 51 45 64 www.antillasalsa.com

Be careful when entering—this Latin bar and dance club is so full of energy that dancers often turn into Shakira and J. Lo when getting down. You can do it, too, by attending salsa lessons from 10-11pm on Wednesdays at the Escuela de Baile Antilla. Enjoy it all between the palm trees painted on the walls and the Cuban *maracas*, bongos, and cowbells littering the sandy bar.

i M:Urgell. Walk along Gran Vìa de les Corts Catalanes and take a right up C. Comte d'Urgell. Walk 3 blocks and take a left onto C. Aragó. Cover €10, includes 1 drink. Beer €5-10. Cocktails €5-12. Open W 9pm-2am, Th 11pm-5am, F-Sa 11pm-6am, Su 7pm-1am.

ESPIT CHUPITOS (ARIBAU)

C. Aribau, 77

Shots, shots, shots—you know the rest. You can get your inner circus freak on here, as many shots involve spectacular sparks of pyromaniacal proportions.

Try the Harry Potter, which might literally light up the night. For a good laugh, order the Monica Lewinsky for somebody else and thank us later. Crowd in with everyone who loves to test this location's 45 person max. capacity or grab your drinks and go.

i M:Universitat. Walk up C. Aribau to the left of the university building; Espit Chupitos is 4 blocks uphill. Shot €2-4. Cocktails €8.50. Open M-Th 10:30pm-2:30am, F-Sa 10:30pm-3am.

Barceloneta

ABSENTA

Carrer de Sant Carles, 36   ☎932 21 36 38 www.kukcomidas.com/absenta.html

Not for the easily spooked, Absenta is like an episode of *The Twilight Zone* if you were inside the TV looking out while also experiencing a touch of the absinthe-induced hallucination this establishment is so famous for. This local hangout spot is the original Spanish speakeasy. With funky light fixtures and vintage proscriptions against the consumption of the vivid green liquor scolding you from above the bar, you will naughtily sip away at the eponymous absinthe (shot for €4, glass for €7). If the overhanging, life-size pirate fairy statue with a glass of absinthe in one hand does not grab your attention, perhaps the static TV sets with flickering art will. If you're in the mood to munch while lounging at any one of the several tables shy of the bar's entrance, try a house panini with ham or *empanadas de carne* (classic meat turnovers). Maybe the country-style blues playing overhead will let you muster up the courage to order the head mixologist's special 50-60% alcohol house-brew of absinthe.

i M:Barceloneta. Walk down Pg. Joan de Borbó toward the beach and take a left onto C. Sant Carles. Beer €2.30. Mixed drinks €7. Open M 11am-3am, Tu 6pm-3am, W-Sa 11am-3am, Su 11am-2am.

¿KÉ?

Carrer del Baluard, 54   ☎932 24 15 88

This small bar attracts internationals and provides a calm alternative to the crowded beaches and throbbing basses of the *platja* (not to mention ridiculously comfy bar stools). A Spanish sign that reads "Barcelona's most well-known secret" entitles you to be part of the in-crowd should you make it to this establishment. Frequented by celebrities, artists, and production crews for movies, this bar speaks for itself in all its vivacious, colorful splendor. The clementine-colored chandeliers shed only enough light to see bottles of all hues stacked on the wall or the barrage of dangly trinkets poised throughout the locale. Shelves doubling as upside-down tables, fruit decals along the bar, and a playful group of semi-creepy faces peering down from overhead will have you wondering "*¿Ké?*" as well. Sip on an infusion drink (€1.50), sangria (€5), a cocktail (€6), or a cheap beer (€2.50) as you jeer at the running slideshow of past bar events displayed on the main parlor TV screen.

i M:Barceloneta. Walk down Pg. Joan de Borbó toward the sea and take a left onto Carrer Sant Carles. Take a left onto Carrer del Baluart once you enter the plaça. Free Wi-Fi. Open M-Th 11am-2:30am, F 11am-3am, Sa noon-3am.

CATWALK

C. Ramón Trias Fargas, 2-4   ☎932 24 07 40 www.clubcatwalk.net

One of Barcelona's most famous clubs, Catwalk has two packed floors of *discoteca*. *Downstairs*, bikini-clad dancers gyrate to house and techno in neon-lit cages while a well-dressed crowd floods the dance floor. Upstairs, club-goers attempt to dance to American hip hop and pop in very close quarters. Dress well if you want to get in—really well if you want to try to get in without paying the cover (this mostly applies to the ladies). Don't bother trying to get the attention of a bartender at the first bar upon entering; there are about six others, and they're all less busy. Don't come before midnight or you'll find yourself awkwardly standing around semi-old people with those one or two guys on the dance floor who are always going a bit too ham.

i *M:Ciutadella/Vila Olímpica. No T-shirts, ripped jeans, or sneakers permitted. Events listed on website. Cover €15-20, includes 1 drink. Beer €7. Mixed drinks €12. Open Th midnight-5am, F-Sa midnight-6am, Su midnight-5am.*

OPIUM MAR

Pg. Marítim de la Barceloneta, 34 ☎902 26 74 86 www.opiummar.com

Slick restaurant by day and even slicker club by night, this lavish indoor and outdoor party spot is a favorite in the Barça nightlife scene. Renowned guest DJs spin every Wednesday, but the resident DJs every other night of the week keep the dance floor sweaty and packed, while six bars make sure the party maintains a base level of schwasty. Dress classy and be prepared to encounter the super rich, super sloppy, and super foreign internationals.

i *M:Ciutadella/Vila Olímpica. Events are listed on the website. Cover €20, includes 1 drink. Restaurant open daily 1pm-1am. Club open M-Th midnight-5am, F-Sa 1-6am, Su midnight-5am.*

Gràcia

🏮 EL RAÏM 1886

C. Progrès, 48 www.raimbcn.com

A few steps through the cluttered entrance reveals a calm buzz of chatting patrons who come here to unwind after a long week of work. This time capsule of an establishment is a mix of a Catalan bodega and '50s Cuban bar. Established in 1886, it is now a shrine to Cuban music and memorabilia that attracts down-to-earth locals with rum drinks like the incredible mojitos (€6).

i *M:Fontana. Walk downhill on C. Gran de Gràcia and make a left onto C. Ros de Olano. Walk for about 4 blocks and take a right onto C. Torrent de l'Olla. Take the 4th left onto Siracusa; El Raïm is on the corner at the intersection with C. Progrès. Wine €2. Beer €2.30-3. Shots €2-3.50. Mixed drinks €5.50-7. Open daily 8pm-2:30am.*

🏮 VINILO

C. Matilde, 2 ☎626 46 7 59

Join the locals on the comfy couches while you enjoy simple tapas and whatever is being played from the back monitor, whether it be movies, concerts, or F.C. Barcelona matches. Ponder at what would possess the interior designers to place such a big gramophone next to the bar and then marvel at the local works of art.

i *M:Fontana. Head downhill on C. Gran de Gràcia, turn left onto Travassera Gràcia, and take the 2nd right onto C. Matilde. Beer €2.50-3.50. Mixed drinks €6.50-7. Open in summer M-Th 8pm-3am, F-Sa 8pm-3:30am, Su 8pm-3am; in winter M-Th 8pm-2am, F-Sa 8pm-3am, Su 8pm-2am.*

🏮 EL CHATELET

C. Torrijos, 54 ☎932 84 95 90

El Chatelet features happens to dish out some of the biggest glasses of liquor *Let's Go* has ever seen. A cozy street corner setting with an adjacent room makes this a rather spacious environment that is nevertheless always crowded with chatty patrons. Big windows give you front row people watching seats that look onto C. Torrijos and C. Perla. Try the *sexopata* panini, composed of avocado, mayo, and that iconic Iberian ham.

i *M:Fontana. Head downhill on C. Gran de Gràcia and turn left onto C. Montseny. Follow it as it turns into C. Perla and turn right onto C. Torrijos. Beer €2-4. Mojitos €3.50, weekends €5.50. Mixed drinks €6. Panini €3.50-4.50. Open M-Th 6pm-2:30am, F-Sa 6pm-3am, Su 6pm-2:30am.*

barcelona

ASTROLABI

C. Martínez de la Rosa, 14

You will actually have fun cramming into this 38-person joint, as the live music this place features daily (starting around 9pm) is excellent. The neat, trinket-filled interior is a cozy scene in which to mingle with the happy patrons who frequent this place. Try the crowd pleasing *Great Estrella Galicia* (€2.80) as you merrily sing along with the mix of locals and internationals.

i M:Diagonal. Take a left onto Pg. de Gràcia, cross Avda. Diagonal, and turn right onto C. Bonavista before Pg. de Gràcia. C. Gran de Gràcia. Take a left onto C. Martínez de la Rosa. See Facebook group for special events. Beer €2.50-2.80. Wine from €2. Mixed drinks €6. Cash only. Open M-F 8pm-2:30am, Sa-Su 8pm-3am. Live music daily 10pm.

LA CERVERSERA ARTESANA

C. Sant Agustí, 14   ☎932 37 95 94 www.lacervesera.net

We must admit, it's pretty neat to drink in the only pub in Barcelona that brews its own beer on site. With a huge variety of brews—dark, amber, honey, spiced, chocolate, peppermint, fruit-flavored, and more—there's literally something for any beer-lover. Kick back with friends as F.C. takes on the world from any of the flat screen TVs in this never-too-crowded spot.

i M:Diagonal. Head uphill on Pg. de Gràcia and take a right onto C. Corsega, at the roundabout where Pg. de Gràcia meets Avda. Diagonal. C. Sant Agustí is the 3rd left. Beers €3.15-4.95. Open M-Th 5pm-2am, F 5pm-3am, Sa 6pm-3am, Su 5pm-2am.

OTTO ZUTZ

C. Lincoln, 15   ☎932 38 07 22 www.ottozutz.com

Like a multilayered rum cake, this place has three levels of boogie throughout its interior. The levels host DJs of varying musical genres, blasted for all of C. Lincoln to feel until dawn. As you might expect, a crowd of young people jostles around this club at all hours of the night, and as a result, it tends to get pretty hot during the summer months.

i M:Fontana. Walk along Rambla de Prat and take a left as it dead ends into Via Augusta. Take the 1st right onto C. Laforja and the 1st right again onto C. Lincoln. Cover €10-15; includes 1 drink. Beer €6. Mixed drinks €6-12. Open M midnight-6am, W-Sa midnight-6am.

THE SUTTON CLUB

C. Tuset, 13   ☎934 14 42 17 www.thesuttonclub.com

Don't even think about showing up in your black gym shorts, Converse sneakers, or light-wash jeans—wear as fine of threads as a traveler can manage. Make your z's sound extra Catalonian when talking to the bouncers, and don't make any sudden movements at the door. Once you're in, though, all bets are off: four bars provide mass quantities of alcohol to a dance floor that gets sloppier as the night goes on. Check online for concerts or special events.

i M:Diagonal. Turn left onto Avda. Diagonal, walk about 4 blocks, and turn right onto C. Tuset. Cover €12-18; includes 1 drink. Beer €7. Mixed drinks €10-15. Open M-Th 11:30pm-5am.

KGB

C. ca l'Alegre de Dalt, 55   ☎932 10 59 06

In Soviet Russia, the club hits you! But seriously folks, you'll be stunned by the varying music genres here, ranging from dubsteb and reggae all the way to top 40. It's small, but the overcrowding is what makes this place awesome. Entrance is free with a flyer; otherwise you'll have to pay €10-15 to join this Party.

i M:Joanic. Walk along C. Pi i Maragall and take the 1st left. Cover with 1 drink €10-12, with 2 drinks until 3am €12-16, free with flyer. Beer €4. Mixed drinks €7-10. Cash only. Check online for concert listings. Open Th 1am-5am, F-Sa 1am-6am.

spain

CAFÉ DEL SOL

Pl. Sol, 16   ☎932 37 14 48

One of the many tapas bars lining the Pl. del Sol, the Cafe del Sol offers cheap and delicious eats. Tune into the English pop rock sheltered by some subtle, dimmed lighting that makes for a fun soiree. Try the house recommended pumpkin ravioli and funghi sauce or the runny eggs with straw potatoes.

i M:Fontana. Walk downhill on C. Gran de Gràcia, turn left onto C. Ros de Olano, and right onto C. Virtut. Beer €2.80. Mixed drinks €6-7. Tapas €3.50-8.50. Entrees €4-8. Open daily 11pm-3am.

Montjuïc and Poble Sec

▓ BARCELONA ROUGE CAFÉ

C. Poeta Cabanyes, 21   ☎934 42 49 85

Just imagine walking into the newest chamber of the Playboy Mansion in all its lusty red glow. Throw in neat albums for sale and a kicking Moscow Mule (vodka, pickle, ginger, lime, and ginger ale), and you have Rouge. With a nice arrangement of leather chairs and a parade of vintage decor (like a shoddy copy of Jan van Eyck's *The Arnolfini Wedding*), this bar creates a sexy environment where a crowd of hip and friendly customers will party with you. If nothing else, you must try the signature Barcelona Rouge, comprised of vodka, berry liquor, lime juice, and shaved ice (€6.50).

i M:Paral·lel. With Montjuïc to your left, walk along Avda. Paral·lel. Take a left onto C. Poeta Cabanyes. Rouge Café is on the left, before Mambo Tango Youth Hostel. Free Wi-Fi. Beer €1.50-3. Cocktails €5-7. Open Th-Sa 9pm-3am.

▓ MAUMAU

C. Fontrodona, 35   ☎934 41 80 15 www.maumaunderground.com

The epicenter of Barcelona's underground, Mau Mau is best known for its online guide to art, film, and other hip happenings around the city (quick tip for the pro partier), but this is very much worth the hike up C. Fontrodona. The mega loft graciously doles out upwards of 20 gins and dozens and dozens of mixed drinks with all sorts of funky names, from Dark and Stormy (€8) to the proletarian Moscow Mule (€8). At a place where only the suavest go to socialize in a cool, open space, there isn't even a cover charge to keep you out.

i M:Paral·lel. Facing Montjuïc, walk right along Av. Paral·lel and take a left onto C. Fontrodona. Follow the street as it zig-zags; Mau Mau is just a few blocks down. 1-year membership (includes discounts at Mau Mau and at various clubs, bars, and cultural destinations around the city) €12. No cover for visitors. Beer €2-3. Mixed drinks from €6-11. Cocktails €6-8. Open Th-Sa and festivals 9pm-3am. Other days of the week for special events (see website for details).

LA TERRRAZZA

Avda. Marquès de Comillas, 13   ☎687 96 98 25 www.laterrrazza.com

One of the most popular clubs in Barcelona, La Terrrazza lights up the Poble Espanyol after the artisans and sunburned tourists call it a day. The open-air dance floor floods with many colored lights and humans as soon as the sun goes down. Try any of the mixed drinks (€8-12), all made quicker than you can twerk.

i M:Espanya. Head through the Venetian towers and ride the escalators. Follow the signs to Poble Espanyol. Free bus from Pl. Catalunya to club every 20min. 12:20am-3:20am; free bus from Terrrazza to Pl. Catalunya nonstop 5:30am-6:45am. Cover €18, with flyer €15; includes 1 drink. Beer €5-10. Open F-Sa 12:30am-6am.

TINTA ROJA

C. Creu dels Molers, 17   ☎934 43 32 43 www.tintaroja.net

Resulting from an inventive and artsy couple who have perfected a mix of eccentric and authentic, this establishment was been named after the 1941 tango, "Tinta Roja." Out front, you can sample any of their fine alcoholic beverages

barcelona

that use Argentinian *legui* as the main mixing agent. Inside the buzzing grotto, you can observe many of the head manager's impressive artistic. Ten paces away is where his wife gives dance lessons on Wednesdays at 8:30pm. See how well you can bust out some Spanish groove while a tad under the influence.

i M:Poble Sec. With Montjuïc to the right, walk along Avda. Paral·lel. Take a right onto C. Creu dels Molers; Tinta Roja is on the left. Tango classes W 8:30-10pm, dance from 10pm-1am. Wine €2.70-3.90. Beer €2.50-5.50. Argentine liqueurs €6.60-7.50. Mixed drinks €7.50. Open W 8:30am-midnight, Th 8:30pm-2am, F-Sa8:30pm-3am. Hours may change to accommodate special events.

Tibidabo

Tibidabo—the mountain that rises behind Barcelona—is easily reached by a combination of FGC and tram during the day, but a seriously long uphill hike once trams stop running at 10pm. A cab from Pl. Lesseps to Pl. Doctor Andreu is about €8; from Pl. Catalunya, it's about €13. Once you figure out a safe way to get home, head here for a night of incredible views that seem to twinkle more with every drink.

MIRABLAU

Pl. Doctor Andreu, S/N   ☎934 18 56 67 www.mirablaubcn.com

With easily the best view in Tibidabo—and arguably the best in Barcelona—Mirablau is a favorite with posh internationals and the younger crowd, so dress well. It also happens to be near the mountain's peak, so we only recommend walking up here if you prefer to sip your cocktails while drenched in sweat. The glimmering lights of the metropolis and the bar's quivering candles create a dreamlike aura that earns Mirablau a *Let's Go* thumbpick. If the club is more your style, head downstairs where pretty young things spill out onto the terrace to catch their breath from the crowded dance floor.

i L7 to FGC: Avinguda de Tibidabo. Take the Tramvia Blau up Avda. Tibidabo to Pl. Doctor Andreu. Th-Sa credit card min €4.70. Drinks discounted M-Sa before 11pm, Su before 6pm. Beer and wine €1.80-6. Cocktails €7-9.50. 11am-5:30am. Open M-Th 11am-4:30am, F-Sa 11am-5:30am

MERBEYÉ

Pl. Doctor Andreu, 2   ☎934 17 92 79 www.merbeye.net

Merbeyé provides a dim, romantic atmosphere on an outdoor terrace along the cliff. With the lights in the lounge so low that seeing your companion may be a problem, Merbeyé is the perfect place to bring an unattractive date. Smooth jazz serenades throughout, and with just one Merbeyé cocktail (cava, cherry brandy, and Cointreau (€9-10), you'll be buzzed real quick.

i L7 to FGC: Avinguda de Tibidabo. Takethe Tramvía Blau up Avda. Tibidabo to Pl. Doctor Andreu. Beer €2.50-4. Cocktails €9-10. Food €2-7.60. 11am-2am. Open Th 5pm-2am, F-Sa 11am-3am.

ARTS AND CULTURE

Music and Dance

For comprehensive guides to large events and information on cultural activities, contact the **Guía del Ocio** (www.guiadelociobcn.com) or the **Institut de Cultura de Barcelona (ICUB).** (Palau de la Virreina, La Rambla, ☎99933 16 10 00 www.bcn.cat/cultura. Open daily 10am-8pm.) Should you be super wary and wish to make good use of Spain's awful Wi-Fi services (and test your Catalan skills), check out **www.butxaca. com,** a comprehensive bimonthly calendar with film, music, theater, and art listings, or **www.maumaunderground.com,** which lists local music news, reviews, and events. The website **www.infoconcerts.cat/ca** (available in English) provides even more concert listings. For tickets, check out **ServiCaixa** (☎902 33 22 11 www.servicaixa.com. Located at any branch of the Caixa Catalonia bank. Open M-F 8am-2:30pm), **TelEntrada** (☎902 10 12 12 www.telentrada.com), or **Ticketmaster** (www.ticketmaster.es).

Although a music destination year-round, Barcelona especially perks up during the summer with an influx of touring bands and music festivals. The biggest and baddest of these is the three-day electronic music festival **Sónar** (www.sonar.es), which takes place in mid-June. Sónar attracts internationally renowned DJs, electronica fans, and partiers from all over the world. From mid-June to the end of July, the **Grec** summer festival (http://grec.bcn.cat) hosts international music, theater, and dance at multiple venues throughout the city, while the indie-centric **Primavera Sound** (www.primaverasound.com) at the end of May is also a regional must-see. *Mondo Sonoro* (www.mondosonoro.com) has more information and lists musical happenings across the Spanish-speaking world.

RAZZMATAZZ

C. Pamplona, 88 and Almogàvers, 122 ☎933 20 82 00 www.salarazzmatazz.com

This massive labyrinth of a converted warehouse hosts popular acts, from reggae to electropop and indie to metal. The massive nightclub complex spans multiple stories in two buildings connected by industrial stairwells and a rooftop walkway. The big room thumps with remixes of current and past top 40 hits, while the smaller rooms upstairs provide more intimate dance spaces. The open-air top floor could be mistaken for a low flying cloud due to the all the smokers bro-ing out here. If there isn't a concert going on, you can still find a young crowd doing the twist (read: grindage) to a DJ onstage.

i M:Bogatell. Walk down C. Pere IV away from the plaza and take the 1st slight left onto C. Pamplona. Razzmatazz is on the right. Tickets available online through website, TelEntrada, or Ticketmaster. Ticket €10-25.

SALA APOLO

C. Nou de la Rambla, 113 ☎934 41 40 01 www.sala-apolo.com

Looking to party but lamenting the fact that it's Monday? Sulk no more—for a number of years, Sala Apolo has been drawing locals to start the week off right with Nasty Mondays, featuring a mix of rock, pop, indie, garage, '80s, typical electro, and a special electronica dubbed "fidget house." In fact, the night is so popular that it has spawned Crappy Tuesdays (indie and electropop). Stop by later in the week when just about anybody and everybody is around, and check the website to see which of the latest indie groups may be rolling through. If you pop in on the right Sunday evening, you may even get to partake in Churros con Chocolate night, which is exactly what it sounds like, plus some dancing.

i Open daily midnight-6am, earlier for concerts and events; check website for event schedule.

Festivals

Barcelona loves to party. Although *Let's Go* fully supports the city's festive agenda, we still need to include some nitty-gritty things like accommodations and, you know, food, so we can't possibly list all of the fun annual events. For a full list of what's going on during your visit, stop by the tourist information office. As a teaser, here are a few of the biggest, most student-relevant shindigs.

FESTA DE SANT JORDI

Las Ramblas

A more intelligent, civil alternative to Valentine's Day, this festival celebrates both St. George (the **dragon**-slayer and patron saint of Barcelona) and commemorates the deaths of Shakespeare and Cervantes. On this day, Barcelona gathers along Las Ramblas in search of flowers and books to give to lovers.

Apr 23.

FESTA DE SANT JOAN

The beachfront

These days light a special fire in every pyromaniac's heart as **fireworks,** bonfires, and torches light the city and waterfront in celebration of the coming of summer.

Night of Jun 23-Jun 24.

barcelona

BARCELONA PRIDE

Parade ends in Avda. Maria Cristina, behind Pl.Espanya

This week is the biggest GLBT celebration in the Mediterranean, and Catalunya is no exception. Multiple venues throughout the region take active part in the festival, which culminates with a parade through "Geixample" and a festival.

Last week of Jun.

FESTA MAJOR

Pl. Rius i Taulet (Pl. Vila de Gràcia)

Festa Major is a community festival in Gràcia during which artsy intellectuals put on performances and fun events in preparation for the Assumption of the Virgin. Expect parades, concerts, floats, arts and crafts, live music, dancing, and, of course, parties.

End of Aug.

LA DIADA

C. Fossar de les Moreres

Catalunya's national holiday celebrates the end of the Siege of Barcelona in 1714 as well as the reclaiming of national—whoops, we mean regional—identity after the death of Franco. Parties are thrown, flags are waved, and Estrella Damm is imbibed—lots of Estrella Damm.

Sept 11.

FESTA MERCÈ

Pl. Sant Jaume

This massive outpouring of joy for one of Barcelona's patron saints (Our Lady of Mercy) is the city's main annual celebration. More than 600 free performances take place in multiple venues. There is also a **castellers** competition in the Pl. Sant Jaume; competitors attempt to build *castells* (literally "castles," but in this case human towers) several humans high, which small children clad in helmets and courage then attempt to climb.

Weeks before and after Sept 24.

Fútbol

Although Barcelona technically has two *fútbol* teams, **Fútbol Club Barcelona (FCB)** and the **Real Club Deportiu Espanyol de Barcelona (RCD),** you can easily go weeks in the city without hearing mention of the latter. It's impossible to miss the former, though, and with good reason. Besides being a really incredible athletic team, FCB lives up to its motto as "more than a club."

During the years of Francisco Franco, FCB was forced to change its name and crest in order to avoid nationalistic references to Catalunya and thereafter became a rallying point for oppressed Catalan separatists. The original name and crest were reinstated after Franco's fall in 1974, and the team retained its symbolic importance; it's still seen as a sign of democracy, Catalan identity, and regional pride.

This passion is not merely patriotic or altruistic, though—FCB has been one of the best teams in the world in recent years. In 2009, they were the first team to win six out of six major competitions in a single year; in 2010, they won Spain's Super Cup trophy; in 2010 and in 2011, FCB took Spain's La Liga trophy; and in 2011, they beat Manchester United to win the UEFA Champion's League, cementing their status as the best club in the world. Their world-class training facilities (a legacy of the 1992 Olympics) supply many World Cup competitors each year, leaving some Barcelonans annoyed that Catalunya is not permitted to compete as its own nation, much like England, Wales, and Scotland do in the United Kingdom. In fact, Spain's 2010 World Cup victory disappointed much of the Catalonian populous and many die-hard FCB fanatics.

Because FCB fervor is so pervasive, you don't need to head to their stadium, the Camp Nou, to join in the festivities—almost every bar off the tourist track boasts a screen dedicated to their games. Kick back with a brew and be sure not to root for the competition.

ESSENTIALS

Practicalities

- **TOURIST OFFICES: Plaça de Catalunya** is the main office, offering free maps and brochures, last-minute booking service for accommodations, currency exchange, and box office. (Pl. de Catalunya, 17S. ☎93 285 38 34 www.barcelonaturisme.com. M: Catalunya, underground, across from El Corte Inglès. Look for the pillars with the letter "i" on top. Open daily 8:30am-8:30pm.) **Plaça de Sant Jaume.** (C. Ciutat, 2. ☎93 270 24 29. M: Jaume I. Follow C. Jaume I to Pl. Sant Jaume. Located in the Ajuntament building on the left. Open M-F 8:30am-8:30pm, Sa 9am-7pm, Su and holidays 9am-2pm.) **Oficina de Turisme de Barcelona** (Palau Robert, Pg. de Gràcia, 107. ☎93 238 80 91, toll-free in Catalunya ☎012 www.gencat.es/probert. M: Diagonal. Open M-Sa 10am-7pm, Su 10am-2:30pm.) **Institut de Cultura de Barcelona (ICUB)** (Palau de la Virreina, Las Ramblas, 99. ☎93 316 10 00 www.bcn.cat/cultura. M: Liceu. Open daily 10am-8pm.) **Estació Barcelona-Sants.** (Pl. Països Catalans. ☎90 224 02 02. M: Sants-Estació. Open Jun 24-Sept 24 daily 8am-8pm; Sept 25-Jun 23 M-F 8am-8pm, Sa-Su 8am-2pm.)

- **LUGGAGE STORAGE: Estació Barcelona-Sants.** (M: Sants-Estació. Lockers €3-4.50 per day. Open daily 5:30am-11pm.) **Estació Nord.** (M: Arc de Triomf. Max 90 days. Lockers €3.50-5 per day.) **El Prat Airport.** (€3.80-4.90 per day.)

- **GLBT RESOURCES: GLBT tourist guide,** available at the Pl. de Catalunya tourist office, includes a section on GLBT bars, clubs, publications, and more. **GayBarcelona** (www.gaybarcelona.net) and **Infogai** (www.colectiugai.org) have up-to-date info. **Barcelona Pride** (www.pridebarcelona.org/en) has annual activities during the last week of June. **Antinous** specializes in gay and lesbian books and films. (C. Josep Anselm Clavé, 6. ☎93 301 90 70 www.antinouslibros.com. M: Drassanes. Open M-F 10:30am-2pm and 5-8:30pm, Sa noon-2pm and 5-8:30pm.)

- **INTERNET ACCESS:** The **Barcelona City Government** (www.bcn.es) offers free Wi-Fi at over 500 locations, including museums, parks, and beaches. **Easy Internet Café** has decent rates and around 300 terminals. (Las Ramblas, 31 ☎93 301 75 07. M: Liceu. €2.10 per hr., min. €2; day unlimited pass €7, week €15, month €30. Open daily 8am-2:30am.) **Easy Internet Café.** (Ronda Universitat, 35. €2 per hr.; day pass €3, week €7, month €15. Open daily 8am-2:30am.) **Navegaweb.** (Las Ramblas, 88-94. ☎93 318 90 26 nevegabarcelona@terra.es. M: Liceu. Calls to US €0.20 per min. Internet €2 per hr. Open M-Th 9am-midnight, F 9am-1am, Sa 9am-2am, Su 9am-midnight.) **BCNet (Internet Gallery Café).** (C. Barra de Ferro, 3 ☎93 268 15 07 www.bornet-bcn.com. M: Jaume I. €1 per 15min., €3 per hr., 10hr. ticket €20. Open M-F 10am-11pm, Sa-Su noon-11pm.

- **POST OFFICE:** Pl. Antonio López. ☎93 486 83 02 www.correos.es. M: Jaume I or M: Barceloneta. Open M-F 8:30am-9:30pm, Sa 8:30am-2pm.

- **POSTAL CODE:** 08001.

Emergency

- **EMERGENCY NUMBERS:** ☎112. **Ambulance:** ☎061.

- **POLICE: Local police:** ☎092. **Mossos d'Esquadra (regional police):** ☎088. **National police:** ☎091. **Tourist police:** Las Ramblas, 43 ☎93 256 24 30. M: Liceu. Open 24hr.

barcelona

- **LATE-NIGHT PHARMACY:** Rotates. Check any pharmacy window for the nearest on duty or call **Informació de Farmàcies de Guàrdia** (☎010 or ☎93 481 00 60 www.farmaciesdeguardia. com).

- **MEDICAL SERVICES: Hospital Clínic i Provincial.** (C. Villarroel, 170. ☎93 227 54 00. M: Hospital Clínic. Main entrance at C. Roselló and C. Casanova.) **Hospital de la Santa Creu i Sant Pau.** (☎93 291 90 00; emergency ☎91 91 91. M: Guinardó-Hospital de Sant Pau.) **Hospital del Mar.** (Pg. Marítim, 25-29. ☎93 248 30 00. M: Ciutadella-Vila Olímpica.)

Getting There

By Plane

There are two possible airports you may use to reach Barcelona. The first, **Aeroport del Prat de Llobregat** (BCN; Terminal 1 ☎93 478 47 04, Terminal 2 ☎93 478 05 65), is located slightly closer to the city, though both necessitate bus rides. To get to Pl. Catalunya from the airport, take the **Aérobus** in front of terminals 1 or 2. (☎92 415 60 20 www.aerobusbcn.com. €5.30, round-trip ticket valid for 9 days €9.15. 35-40min.; every 5-20min. to Pl. Catalunya daily 6am-1am; to airport 5:30am-12:10am.) To get to the airport, the **A1** bus goes to Terminal 1 and the **A2** goes to Terminal 2. For early morning flights, the NitBus **N17** runs from Pl. Catalunya to all terminals. (€1.45. From Pl. Catalunya every 20min. daily 11pm-5am, from airport every 20min. 9:50pm-4:40am.) The **RENFE Rodalies** train is cheaper and usually a bit faster than the Aérobus if you're arriving at Terminal 2. (☎90 224 34 02 www.renfe.es. €1.45, free with T10 transfer from Metro. 20-25min. to Estació Sants, 25-30min. to Pg. de Gràcia; every 30min., from airport 5:40am-11:38pm, from Estació Sants to airport 5:10am-11:09pm.) To reach the train from Terminal 2, take the pedestrian overpass in front of the airport (with your back to the entrance, it's to the left). For those arriving at Terminal 1, there's a shuttle bus outside the terminal that goes to the train station.

The **Aeroport de Girona-Costa Brava** (GRO; ☎90 240 47 04 www.barcelona-girona-airport.com) is located just outside of Girona, a city about 85km to Barcelona's northeast. However, **Ryanair** flights arrive at this airport, so it may be your best bet for getting to Barcelona on the cheap. The **Barcelona Bus** goes from the airport in Girona to Estació d'Autobusos Barcelona Nord. (☎90 236 15 50 www.barcelonabus. com. Buses from the airport to Barcelona Nord are timed to match flight arrivals. Buses from Barcelona Nord arrive at Girona Airport approximately 3hr. before flight departures. €12, round-trip €21. 1hr. 10min.)

By Train

Depending on the destination, trains can be an economical choice. **Estació Barcelona-Sants** (Pl. Països Catalans. M: Sants-Estació) serves most domestic and international traffic, while **Estació de França** (Av. Marqués de l'Argentera. M: Barceloneta) serves regional destinations and a few international locations. Note that trains often stop before the main stations; check the schedule. **RENFE** (reservations and info ☎90 224 02 02; international ☎90 224 34 02 www.renfe.es) runs to Bilbao (€65); Madrid (€118); Sevilla (€143); Valencia (€40-45); and many other destinations in Spain. Trains also travel to Milan (€135 via Girona, Figueres, Perpignan, and Turin); Montpellier (€60); Paris (€146); and Zurich (€136.) via Geneva and Bern. There's a 20% discount on roundtrip tickets, and domestic trains usually have discounts for reservations made more than two weeks in advance. Call or check website for schedules.

By Bus

Buses are often considerably cheaper than the train. The city's main bus terminal is **Estació d'Autobusos Barcelona Nord.** (☎90 226 06 06 www.barcelonanord.com. M: Arc de Triomf or #54 bus.) Buses also depart from **Estació Barcelona-Sants** and the airport. **Sarfa** (ticket office at Ronda Sant Pere, 21 ☎90 230 20 25 www.sarfa.es) is the primary line for regional buses in Catalunya, but **Eurolines** (☎93 265 07 88 www.

spain

eurolines.es) also goes to Paris, France (€80) via Lyon and offers a 10% discount to travelers under 26 or over 60. **Alsa** (☎90 242 22 42 www.alsa.es) is Spain's main bus line. Buses go to Bilbao (€43); Madrid (€29-34); Sevilla (€79-90); Valencia (€26-31); and many other Spanish cities.

By Ferry

Ferries to the Balearic Islands (Ibiza, Mallorca, and Minorca) leave daily from the port of Barcelona at **Terminal Drassanes** (☎93 324 89 80) and **Terminal Ferry de Barcelona** (☎93 295 91 82. M: Drassanes). The most popular ferries are run by **Trasmediterránea** (☎90 245 46 45 www.trasmediterrana.es) in Terminal Drassanes. They go to Ibiza (€90 9hr. 30min.) and Mallorca. (€83. 8hr.)

Getting Around

By Metro

The most convenient mode of transportation in Barcelona is the **Metro.** The Metro is actually comprised of three main companies: **Transports Metropolitans de Barcelona** (TMB ☎93 318 70 74 www.tmb.cat), whose logo is an M in a red diamond; **Ferrocarrils de la Generalitat de Catalunya** (FGC ☎93 205 15 15 www.fgc.cat), whose logo is an orange square; and **Tramvia de Barcelona** (Tram ☎90 070 11 81 www.trambcn.com), whose logo is a green square with a white T. The TMB lines are likely the ones you will use most. Thankfully, all three companies are united, along with the bus system and Rodalies train system, under the **Autoritat del Transport Metropolità** (www.atm.cat), which means that you only need one card for all forms of transport, and that you get free transfers. Most Metro lines are identified with an L (L1, L2, etc.), though some FGC lines begin with S, and all Tram lines begin with T. (1 day €6.20, 10 rides €8.25, 50 rides €33.50, 1 month €51. Trains run M-Th 5am-midnight, F 5am-2am, Sa 24hr., Su 5am-midnight.)

By Bus

For journeys to more remote places, the bus may be an important complement to the metro. The **NitBus** is the most important: it runs ▌all night long after the Metro closes. Look for bus lines that begin with an N. Barcelona's tourist office also offers a **tourist bus** (http://bcnshop.barcelonaturisme.com. 1 day €23, 2 days €30) that hits major sights and allows riders to hop on and off. Depending on how much you plan to use the route (and how much you fear being spotted on a red double-decker labeled "Tourist Bus"), a pass may be a worthwhile investment.

By Bike, Motorcycle, And Scooter

Motocicletas (scooters, and less frequently motorcycles—*motos* for short) are a common sight in Barcelona, and **bicycles** are also becoming more popular. Many institutions rent *motos*, but you need a valid driver's license recognized in Spain (depends on the company, but this sometimes means an international driver's license as well as a license from your home country) in order to rent one. Many places also offer bike rental. If you will be staying in the city for an extended period, it is possible to buy a bike secondhand (try **www.loquo.com**) or register for **Bicing** (☎90 231 55 31 www. bicing.cat), the municipal red and white bikes located throughout the city.

By Taxi

When other cheaper and more exciting options fail, call **Radio Taxi** (☎93 225 00 00). Taxis generally cruise at all hours; when the green light is on, the cab is free.

barcelona

ibiza

You've read about it. You've seen it in the Wanted's music video for "Glad you Came." You can only dream about the party capital of the world, Ibiza, but somehow you're here and somehow you need to figure it all out, fast—before your money's gone and your massive hangover's a little too massive for comfort.

In order to fully experience Ibiza Town, the island's biggest nightlife hub, you'll need to bake in the sun all day, party on a few booze cruises, and, at 3am, hit the clubs just as everything's getting exciting. Expect little sleep and lots of debauchery (you don't know what goes on in the place until you've actually arrived). Look out for free entrance passes on the beach (since a €60 entrance fee will do a little more than break your bank) and bustling bars perfect for a pregame.

But Ibiza Town isn't just party central. During the daytime, when you're not lounging on one of the city's many crystalline beaches, check out the city center, where amidst a labyrinth of narrow, cobbled roads and beautiful white and blue cottages you'll find a Renaissance-era castle, cathedral, and some incredible ocean views.

It's a city with many faces, but one thing's assured: you're in for a good time.

SIGHTS

CASTLE OF IBIZA

www.ibiza-spotlight.com

It's safe to say that when most young people visit Ibiza, touring castles isn't the first thing on their mind. But if you aren't too hung over from partying or sunburned from hours spent lying on the beach, hiking up to the city's historic center is well worth your time. Located in Eivissa, this ancient, fortified city within a city retains traces of Muslim civilization, though the building standing today hails from the 16th century. A gaunt cathedral designed in Gothic style occupies the highest point of Dalt Via. Construction for Ibiza's cathedral began in the 13th century, and rumor has it that it was built over a mosque. Today, it maintains a trapezoidal bell tower and a polygonal apse with five chapels. Although it's precariously perched on a steep hill above the Mediterranean Sea, the cathedral isn't going anywhere any time soon. It's brusque and concrete, strengthened by large buttresses.

Close to the cathedral are a number of museums, including the Puget museum, which is located in a palace that belonged to the noble Palou de Comasema family and dates back to the 15th century. Also make sure to stop by the Archaeological Museum of Ibiza and Formentera, whose collection includes various odds and ends, like coins, from the Prehistoric age all the way to the Islamic medieval times.

Perhaps the best thing about the "castle" of Dalt Via is the views that it offers. Walk along the fortified walls of this old city and gaze out into the turquoise Mediterranean—a view you're likely not to forget any time soon, no matter how much partying you've done on the island. You can see almost everything from the port to Bossa Beach. The sunbathers. The booze cruises. If you keep wrapping around the castle, you'll also happen upon some cannons (models, of course) that were used to defend the city against invasion.

FOOD

If you're coming to Ibiza to party all night long, your wallet—and your stomach—will be feeling pretty empty. Food in the city can be expensive, especially the closer you get to the water, but don't let that keep you from eating! (Because trust us, in order to survive financially on the island, people sometimes forgo eating for clubbing.)

HOSTEL GIRAMUNDO $$

Carrer de Ramon Muntaner, 55   ☎971 30 76 40 www.hostalgiramundoibiza.com

Cheap is a word rarely used in Ibiza. So as far as cheap accommodations go—forget it. You might as well try hiding out in Pacha's bathrooms for the night.

Kidding, of course. But if you're hoping to save a buck or two, you're best off staying at Hostal Giramundo, an open air, party crazy, young adult (not "youth") hostel located steps away from the beach (which one?). While the hostel doesn't offer too many social activities and events like some in other cities (but let's be honest, located in this city, pub crawls are not necessary), Giramundo does offer its guests an awesome desayuno of cafe con leche, zumo de naranja (orange juice), and a delicious croissant. But it's not just about the food—the hostel has a full bar, its own restaurant downstairs (which, as you'll find, will be significantly cheaper than anything else along the beach), outdoor patios, and a third-floor terrace great for pre-gaming for the island's famous clubs.

Its staff is very knowledgeable about Ibiza Town and can give you advice about how to get into the clubs for a discounted price (walking along the beach midday isn't a bad idea). The building is colorful, fun, and inviting—but with an open and bright layout come a few drawbacks. Naturally, the place is pretty sandy (it is steps away from the beach, after all). Wi-Fi, though free and available in the common rooms, is spotty at best. Sometimes, it will take an hour to connect to the Internet, if not more. Prepare yourself. Additionally, there is only one shower on each floor. Decision time. Forgo showering for a few days and instead bathe in the ridiculously salty Mediterranean, or battle it out among fellow hostellers. Win-win?

i *Mixed and female-only rooms €22-33. Privates € 44-55. Reception 24hr. Check out by 11am.*

BIORGANIC $

Av. Espana, 11   ☎971 39 36 21 www.biorganicibiza.com

If you're looking for cheap, quick, and healthy good eats for picnics on the beach, try Biorganic, a small cornerstone on Avanida Espana, Eivissa's main road. With all the great perks of a farmer's market, like local produce and lots of carrots, and prices that won't break your bank, this store is the perfect place to load up for a few days. You can cook yourself a meal with garbanzo beans (€2.67) or egg noodles (€2.99) or buy a premade meal like paella (€4.89). Food here is guaranteed to be fresh, bright, and delicious. Fresh fruit and vegetables—finally, you've found some! No scurvy for you in Ibiza—produce is stored in wooden crates near the front of the market, while dried goods like organic chips and beans are stored near the back. Mineral water (a must have) is also available cheap; as are juices, yogurts, and other cool summertime treats.

Biorganic also has a smoothie bar near the front of its store, just after the check out line. Mix and match your favorite fruits and vegetables for a refreshing drink that will fuel you for another day on the beach and under the sun. The store is located in the heart of Ibiza Town, just a quick walk from the beach, and as its name entails, you're guaranteed fresh produce whenever you want it (as long as you visit between the hours of 9am-10pm). Gluten free food is offered, too!

i *€1-10 for anything you could possibly desire. Open daily 9am-10pm.*

ibiza

CAN FLOW $$

Carrer des Passadis, 8   ☎653 77 24 44   www.biorganicibiza.com

Are you one of those people who likes eating cute bites of fancy-looking food? And you want to be vegan/gluten free/raw/whatever other weird diet you can think of? Ibiza Town has just the place for you! Can Flow (why the name, we don't know) has healthy, green tapas-sized meals for anyone and everyone, meat-eaters and plant-eaters alike. With bite-sized food comes bite-sized prices too—especially for Ibiza. Prices for meals range from €6-25. Try salmon tartar, veggie burgers, chicken burgers (anything burgers, really), and lots of fish. The plates themselves are so artistically done you may be afraid to eat. But then eat, because the food is fresh, filling, and of course, delicious.

Can Flow's food is organic and self-described "ecological" too, so your body will thank you after all that… partying during the night. And to add to the great food, you'll get a casual, laid back atmosphere too. Almost like you're eating your mom's best cuisine, all dolled up on a shining white platter, except in Ibiza, where you'll probably do things at which your mom would cringe. A lot.

i Tapas €6. Racions €8-15. Open daily 11am-1:30am.

MAR A VILA $$

Av. Ignasi Wallis, 16   ☎971 31 47 78   www.facebook.com/maravilaibiza

Ah, tapas. The only type of food you can afford in Ibiza Town. Kidding (but are we?). If you're going to do tapas, might as well do them right. Head over to Mar a Vila, a chic and beautifully decorated restaurant located in the heart of the city's center. Get your fill of five-star bites, like calamari, anchovy toast, mussels, and even chocolate. Tapas are modern, creative, and come in surprising combinations—peppers stuffed with goat cheese? Pickled mussels? The restaurant's name does have "mar" in it, after all. They're bound to have pretty darn good seafood.

For an inexpensive price, you and your friends can dine at the bar, at a table, or in the secret garden-esque, beautiful courtyard, which is decorated white and modestly with hanging plants and simple chairs and tables. It's refreshing to eat in a budget restaurant that tries hard not to look the best, but actually serve the best food to its guests. Food here is prepared and served artistically—plates are definitely worth a few Instagram posts. We only wish we could sneak back into the kitchen to watch the chefs work their magic.

Since you'll probably only chow down on a few plates of tapas, you may have room for some dessert. If not, make room. Lick your fingers after sampling some rich chocolate truffles, strawberry ice cream, or red wine compote. In fact, come back another time—just for dessert. Your taste buds will forever thank you.

i Tapas €3-8.75. Fish €12. Rice €10. Dessert €6. Open M-F 8:30am-midnight, Sa 11am-4:30pm and 7pm-midnight.

NIGHTLIFE

AMNESIA

Ctra. Ibiza a San Antonio, Km 5   ☎971 19 80 41   www.amnesia.es

It's tough to recommend just one club in Ibiza when the entire island is basically known for one thing and one thing only: partying. But one club everyone seems to rave about is Amnesia (warning: not actually located in Ibiza Town! Sorry folks, it's over in San Antonio instead). Known for its local, Spanish vibe and crazy ice cannon machine (more on that later), this place is worth remembering. Or not. You know you're in for a good time when you visit a club called Amnesia.

It's one of Ibiza's originals, founded in the 1970s, and most the famous, though perhaps overshadowed in recent pop culture by other giants like Privilege or Pacha. (Though it HAS won a number of "Best Global Club" awards in

spain

recent history.) The club was originally founded to accommodate hippies who wanted to "expand their minds" in the mysterious, bohemian island of Ibiza. Nowadays an eclectic mix of people visit the club, but that wanderlust, free-for-all ambience remains. Although the club is no longer open air (sad, we know), it still has two major rooms—a main dance floor and a terrace, the latter of which is only covered by a glass ceiling that you probably won't even notice at all when partying hard (you may notice it if you're still standing at daybreak, since sunlight floods the place). The club, currently run by Cream, invites a great mix of DJs to man the club—house music, techno, trance. Like all clubs on the island, Amnesia is "good" on certain day(s)—those days being Sundays and Mondays. Mondays are Cocoon nights (Sven Väth's big party) and can cost from €40-55. Amnesia is also known for hosting its famous foam party nights on Sundays (hygienic… we think not). Non-Monday/Sunday nights at the club are relatively inexpensive (for Ibiza!), costing around €25-40 depending on the profile of the DJ.

A night at Amnesia is one you'll never forget! Well…

i €25-40, €40-55 on M and Su. Generally open midnight-6am.

ESSENTIALS
Getting There
Ibiza is an island. That means no cars, trains, or buses will ever be able to reach Ibiza (unless man makes some sort of underwater bus, but that'll probably take a while). You have three options: airplane, ferry, swim. Let's just count that last one out. Major Spanish airports have direct flights to Ibiza, from cities like Madrid, Barcelona, Valencia, and Sevilla. Vueling, Ryanair, and Iberia are going to be your best bets for airlines. Round-trip prices (unless you're planning on staying there a while) can range—a lot. Ryanair will always be the cheapest (€90 round trip), but the cost can get as expensive as €400. Ryanair veterans know, cheap comes at a price. Not your greatest airline (first come first serve seating), but once you get to Ibiza you'll be thanking yourself for saving on plane tickets early on. Flights from Valencia, the closest airport, last around 45min.

Getting Around
Welcome to the land of horrible buses. Well, they're fine; really, they just don't run that often or late. Line 10 runs from the airport into Ibiza Town, and back. Other lines cross the island. Check http://ibizabus.com/ibiza/lineas for a comprehensive list of bus schedules and stop locations. The island itself is pretty small, but not small enough to cross by foot in a timely manner (believe us, we've tried). Check out the taxi service as well at www.turismoibiza.com/taxi. Rates start at €3.25 and cost anywhere from €0.98-1.65 per km.

córdoba

Córdoba may seem like a city with its best days behind it; how do you top being capital of the Moorish empire for 300 years running? But this city, known for its boiling heat, a huge mosque-cathedral, and a specific variety of tomato soup (not necessarily in that order), has much more hidden in its shady flowering courtyards. Try salmorejo cordobés, basically gazpacho on creamy delicious steroids (disclaimer: no steroids used in the actual making of this dish). In a vain attempt to escape the midday summer heat, crash its sweet patios with owners who may or may not let you in based on your charming personality. The cordobeses are hardy and friendly hard-drinkers (try their favorite, a "50" with half wine, half soda) used to escaping the heat and the tourists. The main square, Pl. de las Tendillas, offers a ton of cheap nearby bars along with the casual ruins of a Roman temple. And of course there's the famous Mezquita de Córdoba, which does double duty as the local cathedral and a must-see blend of cultures and time periods.

SIGHTS

◪ LA MEZQUITA-CATEDRAL DE CÓRDOBA

C. Cardenal Herrero, 1

This is what most people come to Córdoba for—a magnificent reminder of Andalusia's past life as an Islamic stronghold and its more recent present as an overwhelmingly Catholic one. You've heard about it (why else are you in Córdoba?), so definitely make the pilgrimage. The mesmerizing forest of arches and columns seems to go on forever—which makes sense because, at 23,000 sq. m, it's the third-largest mosque in the world. It was originally built in 786 and expanded several times under the caliphate to its current gigantic proportions. Spend an hour or two exploring the space, and in addition to some nice inner peace, you'll find an ancient basilica floor and glass cases with artifacts recovered from the period. As you wander through the columns, some appropriated from old Roman constructions, you'll also suddenly stumble onto a full-size Catholic cathedral. Surprise! After the Christian reconquest in 1236, the Catholics began using the building as their own place of worship, and four centuries later they decided to plop a towering Gothic cathedral into the very center of the space. In the 1600s, they took the minaret and replaced it with a bell tower on the north side, and presto! It's a "cathedral." Enjoy the contrast between the bright white and dark red and contemplate peace on Earth; if these architectural styles can mingle so well, why can't we?

In addition to the interior, which requires an €8 entrance fee, the exterior courtyard, called the Patio de los Naranjos, is free to wander around. The oranges are unfortunately not edible, but the fountains where worshippers came to wash are a peaceful way to end a day of touring. The mosque itself is also free every day 8:30-9:30am, but this means you might be interrupted in your reverie by a stern Spanish guard kicking you out precisely at 9:30.

i At the center of the historic district. €8, ages 10-14 and disabled €4, under 10 free. Open Mar-Oct M-Sa 10am-7pm, Su 8:30-11:30am and 3-7pm; Nov-Feb M-Sa 10am-6pm, Su 8:30-11:30am and 3-6pm.

spain

patios

One of the best ways to escape the heat of the Córdoban summer is hidden behind the walls of the whitewashed buildings—patios. These interior courtyards are basically residents' way of saying "Nyah nyah, we don't need air-conditioning and you do," as well as a center of private life of the home. But these hideaways aren't always inaccessible; La Asociación de Amigos de los Patios Cordobeses (C. de San Basilio, 50) offers a free visit to a typical patio with artisanal shops and more information. The San Basilio neighborhood in particular is famous for its beautiful courtyards. In the second week of May, the gardens are in full bloom, and these sometimes stingy owners open their hearts and their patios to the world as part of the annual Festival de los Patios.

SILICA
DE SAN PEDRO

córdoba

CÓRDOBA BED AND BE $

C. Cruz Conde, 22 ☎661 42 07 33 www.bedandbe.com

Bed and Be is located slightly north of the main city center, just close enough to the train station and local bar streets and just far enough from the tourist traps surrounding the Mezquita. Ceilings are high, windows are huge, and bunks are spacious, which does mean steeper stairs; however, the airy dining room, common room, kitchen, and rooftop deck spaces make the climb worth it. The comfort is in the details. Nightly tapas get-togethers are organized by the genuinely buddy-buddy staff, the free map has tons of local recommendations, and the complimentary towel comes with a piece of candy and a smile. Routers on every floor make it the fastest Wi-Fi you'll find in Andalucia. (Skype calls to your mom might actually be possible now. Just don't tell her that.) Fun fact: the apartment building that houses the hostel was designed by the same guy who helped restore the famous Mezquita (though it looked rather unremarkable to us).

i From Pl. de las Tendillas, walk north up C. Cruz Conde; the hostel is on your right. Dorms €17-20; private doubles €38. Bike rental €6 per 3hr., €10 per day with €50 deposit. Reception 24hr.

MAY FLOWERS $$

C. Enmedio, 16 ☎957 29 03 47 www.mayflowershostel.es

Walking into May Flowers, you might worry that you've stepped into a high-priced boutique hotel with its extremely well-kept common facilities and fancy logo. No, it's just a somewhat high-priced boutique hostel. Located in the untouristed San Basilio neighborhood, May Flowers takes its slightly sappy name to heart with a beautiful floral patio and rooms named after flowers. The free breakfast is definitely the best around, with different pastries every day alongside orange juice, coffee, tea, and assorted cereal. To top it all off, there's a bathroom in every room.

i From the Alcazar, walk along C. Caballerizas Reales away from the Mezquita. Continue onto C. Enmedio until number 16 on your right. 48hr. cancellation policy. Dorms €15-35; doubles €60-80. Reception 9am-10:30pm.

spain

ALCÁZAR DE LOS REYES CRISTIANOS

Pl. Campo Santo de los Mártires ☎957 42 01 51

One of the original residences of the one and only Ferdinand and Isabella, Alcázar often gets overlooked as second-best to neighboring Sevilla (even Game of Thrones passed on it as a filming location). True, the nearly empty interior is not much to Skype home about, but the three historic towers offer a panoramic view of the city as well as a reminder of Córdoba's shady past as a center for the Inquisition. The Catholic monarchs used the castle as a base for the final campaign against the Moors in the south, the location of one of the first Inquisition tribunals, and eventually its headquarters, turning even the baths into torture chambers. (Yeah, not so relaxing.) The northeastern Tower of the Homage even has a small additional tower (inaccessible to the public) where executions were carried out and the Tower of the Inquisition housed the archives of the inquisitors. If you get tired of reliving the Spanish Inquisition, spend the majority of your visit in the gardens recreated in beautiful Moorish style. The symmetrical hedges and pools in the Avenue of the Kings accompany statues of the rulers involved in the construction of the fortress. If you look closely in the fountains you might see the inscription "De plantano cordubensi," an inscription commemorating a visit by Julius Caesar to Córdoba. So make like Julius and stroll through the gardens, monarch of all you survey.

i €4.50, under 15 free. Open June 16-Sept 15 Tu-Sa 8:30am-3pm, Su 8:30am-2:30pm; Sept 16-June 15 Tu-F 8:30am-8:45pm, Sa 8:30am-4:30pm, Su 8:30am-2:30pm. Last entry 30min before close.

FOOD

Food is generally cheap in Córdoba, and there are plenty of Andalusian specialties to try out—salmorejo (thicker, better gazpacho), mazamorra (almond gazpacho), berenjenas con miel (eggplant "fries" in dark honey), and rabo del toro (oxtail—yeah, we know, but it's fall-off-the-bone delicious). The area around the mosque is packed with slightly overpriced, under-quality places that all look the same—venture farther north and east to go where the locals go. Pl. Vizconde de Miranda and Pl. de las Tendillas are great places for small, absurdly cheap tapas bars. Down by the river and Pl. del Potro, there are more modern international places (you can even get actual salads!). May through June is snail season; if you find one of the stands around town, you win a glass of snails (payment still required, sadly). Note: the salty broth must be chugged afterward in order to blend in appropriately.

🦑 LA TRANQUERA $$
C. Cardenal González, 53   ☎957 78 75 69

Along the riverside street leading to the Mezquita, you can find Argentina. Or is it Spain? Or is it… Spargentina? This Frankenstein establishment has delicious portions of excellent steak and other traditional Argentine options with Córdoban spins on them—for example, putting the local rabo de toro (slow-cooked oxtail) into an empanada and basically creating the perfect marriage of fried and meat. The dining space is draped with posters and memorabilia of famous Argentine and Andalusian stage actors, but it's also relatively small, so get your empanadas to go and stroll along the river toward the Roman bridge.

i From the Mezquita, walk along C. Cardenal González for 100m. It will be on your right. Entrees €6-10. Empanadas €3-4. Open daily 1-4:30pm and 8:30pm-12:30am.

LA BICICLETA $$
C. Cardenal González, 1   ☎666 54 46 90

If you're starting to think your body has somehow become 99% pork and olive oil, La Bicicleta is the place to take it for vitamin-infused boot camp. The bar is weighed down with a glorious cornucopia of fruits and veggies that the employees will craft into infinite permutations of smoothies. Its huge tostas (large pieces of toasted bread with toppings) can satisfy the needs of pretty much any variety of hangry. La Bicicleta's clientele consists of the kind of hipsters that you didn't even know Córdoba had. Located right between the zone of the Mezquita and the more local riverside bars, La Bicicleta is a flowering oasis in a sea of tourist kitsch.

i From Puente de Miraflores, walk north on Pl. Cruz del Rastro. Take a left onto C. Cardenal González, immediately to your left. Cash only. Tostas €4-5. Open July-Aug M-F 7pm-1am, Sa-Su 2pm-1am; Sept-June daily 10am-1am.

GARUM 2.1 $$$
C. San Fernando, 120-122   ☎957 48 76 73 www.facebook.com/Garum2.1

When someplace calls itself a "bistronomic tapas bar," you might want to walk quickly in the opposite direction while saying a dozen rosaries as protection against pretension, but Garum 2.1 turns out enough excellent food at moderate prices to make us change our minds. With dishes like a potsticker-style pastilla, Garum does traditional tapas with a twist (dessert as dinner, anyone? try the oxtail churro). It does have classic Córdoban cuisine too; this is the place to try

córdoba

rabo de toro done right, though some Andalusian grandmothers might disown us for saying so. Be careful; the staff's high-end professionalism may dazzle you into forgetting the shameless extra charge for bread.

i From Puente de Miraflores, walk north on Pl. Cruz del Rastro. As soon as it turns into C. San Fernando, it will be on the corner on your left. Tapas €3.50-6.50. Raciones €7-11.50. Open M-Th noon-midnight, F-Sa noon-2am, Su noon-midnight.

NIGHTLIFE

SOJO RIBERA

Pl. Cruz del Rastro   ☎667 42 50 08 www.gruposojo.es

The highest-end nightlife that Córdoba can offer comes in the form of this rooftop lounge, confusingly named Sojo in a bid for NYC sophistication. And it doesn't hit far off the mark: slightly overpriced cocktails, bright neon lights, and comfy lounge furniture complete the feeling of being on the deck of a moderately nice cruise ship. That's helped by the view directly over the river and straight to the iconic Roman bridge. Go for some flavored hookah to share with friends and bask in the bougie atmosphere.

i Across Paseo de la Ribera from Puente de Miraflores. Beer €3. Cocktails €7. Hookah €10-15. Open M-W 8am-3am, Th 8am-3am, F 8am-4am, Sa-Su 2pm-4am.

JAZZ CAFE

C. Rodríguez Marín   ☎957 48 14 73

Jazz Cafe brings in Córdoba's alternative music scene. Granted, this is a town where alternative means jazz and classic rock, but the venue reliably draws a devoted crowd of local 20- and 30-somethings. Tuesdays and Thursdays are popular open-mic nights, with a decent indecent group gathering starting around 11pm. Drink specials abound, but get your snacks at the nearby tapas places with rock-bottom prices. Enjoy stumbling out in the early morning with a direct view of the illuminated Roman temple—you can't even party without painfully banging your shin into something historic.

i From the Templo Romano intersection, go down C. Rodríguez Marín; it's on your right. Beer €2-3. Cocktails €5. Open daily 8:30pm-4am.

CAFE BAR AUTOMÁTICO

C. Alfaros, 4   ☎625 12 95 22 www.facebook.com/automaticobar/

Automático takes you back to a vintage '60s/'70s disco but doesn't hit you over the head with the time machine. Comfortable lounge chairs in the front make for a classy hangout space while you sip the specialty summer cocktail. Late on the weekends local DJs vamp up the space in back from an empty vinyl floor with a lonely disco ball to a full-on club atmosphere. Check its Facebook page for special events, poetry readings, and live music.

i From the Templo Romano intersection, go north on C. Capitulares until it merges into C. Alfaros. It's 50m up on your right. Cocktails €6-7. Open M-W 8pm-2am, Th 8pm-3am, F-Sa 8pm-4am, Su 8pm-2am.

ESSENTIALS

Practicalities

- **TOURIST OFFICES:** There is a tourist information office at the RENFE train station. (☎902 20 17 74 Open daily 9am-2pm and 4:30-7pm.) Another is centrally located in Plaza de las Tendillas. (☎902 20 17 74 Open daily 9am-2pm and 5-7:30pm.) The Centro de Recepción de Visitantes next to the Puerta del Puente by the Mezquita also has information about the Andalusian region. (Plaza del Triunfo. ☎902 20 17 74 www.turismodecordoba.org Open M-F 9am-7:30pm, Sa-Su 9:30am-3pm.)

- **TOURS:** There are multiple free tours that can give you a comprehensive sense of the city in 2-3hr.; ask your hostel or at the tourist offices for options.
- **POST OFFICES:** The main post office is at C. José Cruz Conde, 15. (☎957 49 63 42. Open M-F 8:30am-8:30pm, Sa 9:30am-1pm.)

Emergency

- **EMERGENCY NUMBERS:** ☎092.
- **POLICE:** ☎957 29 07 60.
- **HOSPITALS:** The closest hospital is Hospital Universitario Reina Sofia. (Av. Menéndez Pidal. ☎957 01 00 00.)

Getting There

The bus (Av. de la Libertad; ☎957 40 40 40 www.estacionautobusescordoba.es) and train (Av. de America; ☎902 32 03 20 www.renfe.es) stations are right next to each other to the north of the center. Bus and train lines go to nearby cities in the south as well as Madrid. Bus 3 (€1.20; tickets available from the driver) leaves from the stations and goes through town to the riverfront near the Mezquita.

Getting Around

Walking is likely the fastest and definitely cheapest option for most destinations within the historic center, given the narrow streets and limited bus access. Buses are the best option for destinations outside the center. Buy tickets on board for €1.20. Lines and information can be found at www.aucorsa.es. The best places to get taxis are at the stands at Pl. de las Tendillas and by the Mezquita. (☎957 76 44 44. During the day €1.50 base fare, €0.58 per km, €3.88 min. At night €1.86/0.70/4.82.)

sevilla

In Sevilla, the capital city of Andalusia both politically and culturally, things start early and end late, somehow with plenty of time for eating and sleeping in between. Walking through the winding sunny streets, you can find as many historical eras as there are levels of the famous Giralda tower. The central cathedral has numerous claims to fame, including a well-known resident who may or may not have discovered the New World (it's complicated). Visit the Real Alcázar's Moorish courtyards, explore the Pl. de España's commemorative murals, and see a bullfight at the 18th-century ring. Across the river in the Triana neighborhood, look (or rather listen) for spontaneous flamenco music, with its copious snapping, clapping, and stomping, plus bonus stylish outfits. Stumble upon the old tobacco factory and the university (surprise, they're actually the same building!). You might even find your favorite bar tucked amid the winding streets, so sit back with an ice cold caña and enjoy the warm summer sun before staying out til 7am in true Sevillan style.

SIGHTS

▩ CATEDRAL/GIRALDA

Av. de la Constitución ☎954 21 49 71 www.facebook.com/maravilaibiza

What's so special about Sevilla's cathedral? A few things. First, it's the third-largest church in the world by volume and the largest Gothic cathedral in the world. Second, its interior has the largest nave of any cathedral in Spain (42m high). And third, it's the burial site of everyone's favorite explorer Christopher Columbus. (OK, well at least you've heard of him.) Located in the heart of the city center, the mammoth cathedral was constructed starting in 1402 and finished in a timely 104 years. The locals who decided to build this new cathedral are reported to have said, "Let us build a church so beautiful and so grand that those who see it finished will think we are mad." Maybe they were a bit mad after all. The cathedral has four facades, 15 doors, 80 chapels, 11,520 sq. m in total floor

get a room!

HOSTEL ONE CENTRO
$$
C. Angostillo, 6 ☎954 22 16 15

This hostel takes you slightly away from the typical cathedral area and into the real local nightlife, only steps away from Alameda de Hércules. Nightly dinners made by the resident chef are delicious and free-ish (you really should tip the staff). The intensely social atmosphere is balanced with an attention to comfort, including well-enforced quiet hours in the soaring courtyard common area. Instead of getting shushed there late at night, go on the casual bar crawl (no upfront price, just come along for the ride), which takes everyone to the knowledgeable staff's favorite spots around the city—including the occasional speakeasy (but you have to promise you won't tell). Escape the heat with air-conditioning and a small pool on the roof.

i Dorms €20-30; singles €50-60; doubles €60-75. Reception 8am-10pm.

LA FLAMENKA
$$
Av. Reyes Católicos, 11, 2nd fl. ☎954 10 40 18 laflamenkahostel.com

La Flamenka's decor comes in several shades of pink; it's a bit like if a young cat lady suddenly made the switch to flamingos. Somehow this all adds up to an incredibly charming if slightly overbearing aesthetic with tons of details that make the hostel one of the nicest in Sevilla. Common spaces and beds are comfortable (despite alarming shades of, again, pink), and it has every type of toiletry you may have forgotten in addition to actual vanities in the female-only rooms. It may finally be possible to look more like a human being than a backpacker on this trip! Best of all, it has not one, but two decks with a small self-serve bar. These are so large that you could actually lose yourself looking at the sunset views; just remember to leave a trail of sangria to find your way back.

i From Puente de Isabel II, walk north on Reyes Católicos; the hostel will be on your right. Dorms €19-21; private rooms €35-50. Reception 8am-10pm. 2-night min. stay.

TRIANA BACKPACKERS
$
C. Rodrigo de Triana, 69 ☎95 445 99 60 www.trianahostel.com

On the "wrong side of the river" (which just means away from the the tourist hordes, so maybe it's the right side), lies Triana, a neighborhood known for its local nightlife and as the gypsy birthplace of flamenco. Three blocks in is Triana Backpackers, adopting the tiled style of its locale with flair and comfort. The beautiful marbled courtyard lobby has enough plants to make you feel like you've stepped into a city garden. The rooftop, along with hammocks and a hot tub, puts travelers close enough to the cathedral and other sights so they can scoff at the people who didn't know enough to enjoy the real Sevilla. The rooms themselves are comfortable, but pretty hostel-standard (metal bunks, slightly over-crowded); rooms and lockers are on the small side, and you must supply your own lock.

i Take the metro to Pl. de Cuba. Breakfast included 7-11am. Dorms €15-18; doubles €38-40. Bike rental €5. Bar crawl €10. Reception 24hr.

space, and the world's largest altarpiece. Like many Catholic cathedrals of the time, the cathedral was built on the site of a 12th-century Moorish structure, the Almohad Mosque. Although the cathedral is built in the Gothic style, it still retains a few traces of Moorish influence from the mosque, like the court in which visitors enter (the Patio de los Naranjos) and the then-minaret, now-bell tower Giralda. But where are Columbus's remains? We know that's all you care about. His tomb is located just off the entrance to the cathedral, on the south side at the Puerta de San Cristóbal. No, this isn't where he was originally buried, which was in Valladolid, Spain, where he died. In 1795, he split for the Havana Cathedral in Cuba, which Columbus had first encountered in his voyage of 1492. Upheaval from the 1902 Cuban revolution led Spain to transfer his remains to Sevilla, their resting place today. Visit for the history, the architecture, or Columbus. You're bound to learn a thing or two.

i €9, students and seniors €6. Audio tour €3. Open M 11am-3:30pm, Tu-Sa 11am-5pm, Su 2:30pm-6pm.

REAL ALCÁZAR DE SEVILLA

Patio de Banderas   ☎954 50 23 24 www.alcazarsevilla.org

If you've been traveling around in Spain for a while, you've probably seen your fair share of castles, cathedrals, etc. Maybe you're a little tired of them by now. Sure, they're beautiful, grand, and historical, but you can't help but feel that they all look a little bit the same. If this sounds like you, take a trip to the Alcázar of Sevilla, a former Moorish palace overrun by the Spanish Catholics that still retains that old-fashioned Islamic feel. Because its upper rooms are still used by the Spanish royal family to receive important visitors, the Alcázar is one of the oldest palaces still in use worldwide. Enter the 11th-century palace and get lost in its maze of large gardens and ceramic rooms. There is little to no furniture in the palace's interior—instead, find breathtaking, colorful tile work dappled with shells and Hand of Fatima motifs as well as arabesques. Walk through a few rooms in the palace and out into its many courtyards, like the Mannerist Garden of Troy, and find sleepy trees, bright bougainvillea branches, and plenty of self-important peacocks. Game of Thrones fanboys might recognize the Grutesco Gallery as the Water Gardens of Dorne, but then again, Game of Thrones fanboys probably planned their whole trip to Spain around this one destination. What's incredible about the Alcázar is that, from the outside, it's a very unassuming—if not drab—building. Only visitors who pay the entry fee can discover for themselves the true meaning of the phrase "don't judge a book by its cover." If you're an art history buff, you'll drool over the mixture of styles, from Mudéjar Renaissance to Baroque. Have we convinced you yet? This place is one of the most stunning in Spain, if not in the entire world. Yes, praise humanity for its architectural feats.

i €9.50, students €2. Open daily Apr-Sept 9:30am-7pm; Oct-Mar 9:30am-5pm.

PLAZA DE TOROS DE LA REAL MAESTRANZA DE CABALLERÍA DE SEVILLA BULLRING

Paseo de Cristóbal Colón, 12   ☎954 210 315, ticket office 672 366 815
                                                  www.realmaestranza.com

That's quite a mouthful. If something's got a name this long (and the word real, which means "royal," in it), you know it's worth a visit. Such is the case with Sevilla's famed bullring, allegedly the second-oldest in the world (after Ronda's) and with the capacity to seat 13,000. Its construction began in 1771 but wasn't actually completed until more than 100 years later, in 1881. Why is this bullring different than others? As the geometrically keen may notice, Sevilla's bullring is not in fact shaped like a circle. Instead, it takes the shape of an oval. Additionally, there is one prized gate in which the matador may exit, but only if he has gained the three "trophies" of his bullfight—two ears and the tail of the bull that

sevilla

he fights. Only when the matador completes this task does he have permission to exit through the ring's most important gate, which in Sevilla is called Puerta del Principe (Prince's Gate). The Sevillan salida a hombros occurs in the gate directly under the balcony where the royal family is intended to sit—hence the gate's name. (Does the royal family ever travel south of Madrid to watch a bullfight at Sevilla? Good question. Not really.) In addition to the bullring, visitors can view a museum showcasing the bullring's history, including some of its celebrity bullfighters like Juan Belmonte, Joselito El Gallo, and their very spectacular costumes (silver, gold, silk). Should you desire to see a live bullfight, Sevilla's season runs from Easter Sunday to October 12 and includes around 20-25 fights in total. Prices for the fights vary, with the most expensive tickets costing upward of €100. Substantially cheaper tickets can be bought for seats across the stadium.

i €7, students and seniors €4, ages 7-11 €3. Open daily 9:30am-7pm, bullfighting days 9:30am-3pm.

METROPOL PARASOL/"LAS SETAS"

Why would a building be called "the mushrooms"? It becomes all too clear when you see the gigantic structure built on Pl. de la Encarnación. The six twisting and turning wooden platforms have a texture that, at a distance, resembles a Belgian waffle (never design buildings when you're hungry, kids). The building's huge cost and construction overruns made the project highly controversial; it now claims to be the largest wooden structure in the world (which makes it a little better now, right?). The 28.5m high behemoth hosts a museum of Roman and Moorish ruins in the basement, a local market and restaurants on the first floor, a city skate park and plaza on its roof, and over 250m of winding passageways at the very top. The tickets to the viewing platforms are €3, which seems a bit steep until you get to enjoy the included free tapa and drink (tinto de verano, wine, beer, or water) with the best view of the city at sunset. Get a mushroom tapa for some extra inception with your relaxing evening.

i Viewing platform plus tapa and drink €3. Antiquarium €2.10. Viewing platform open M-Th 10am-10:30pm, F-Sa 10am-11pm, Su 10am-10:30pm. Antiquarium open Tu-Sa 10am-8:30pm, Su 10am-2:30pm.

FOOD

Food in Sevilla can be fantastically cheap and delicious; it can also be targeted toward tourists and somewhat overpriced the closer you get to major sights like the Giralda. Nearly every restaurant charges for bread; if you don't want it, politely say "No pan, gracias," as they'll usually place it on the table without asking. The ubiquitous terraza (outdoor seating) is always a bit more expensive (€0.10-0.50 per dish), but at more authentic places there's no air-conditioning or heating so it may be worth it. Sevillanos adhere to the traditional Spanish meal schedule even more intensely than most; dinner won't start until well after sunset when it's cooled down enough that human habitation is once again possible (after 10pm or so).

🏛 BAR ESLAVA $$
C. Eslava, 3-5   ☎954 91 54 82 www.espacioeslava.com

Sevilla is a town with high standards for food in general, but Eslava blows other tapas bars out of the water (just kidding, there's not enough water in this city for that) with a combination of creativity and quality ingredients. Its costillas a la miel (ribs with honey) are a must. The specialty huevo sobre bizcocho (cured egg over cake; €3) isn't easily shareable, but that just makes it easier to keep the unusually incredible caramel/runny-yolk combo to yourself. There'll be plenty of crowds, but an army of fast-moving and charming waiters keep everything

top places for a sevilla sugar rush

1. LA HELAMEDA. Stop mid-bar crawl to get one of these deliciously sweet cones. Unexpectedly in the middle of the Alameda nightlife area is a miraculous oasis of traditional Spanish gelato; this isn't your standard Italian gelato transplant. The vainilla mantecado is better than any vanilla you've ever tasted. La Helameda is open late enough for both local kids and drunk tourists. (Alameda de Hércules, 68. Open M-Th 6pm-1:30am, F-Sa 1pm-2am, Su 1pm-1:30am.)

2. LA FIORENTINA. The most popular ice cream place in town, and for good reason. Creative flavors like chocolate with chili and blueberry and the mysterious "crema de sevilla." The walls are plastered with newspaper articles proclaiming La Fiorentina queen of Sevillan ice cream, and who are we to disagree? Well, we often do, but this time we'll let it slide. (C. Zaragoza, 16. Open M-Th 1pm-midnight, F-Sa 1pm-1:30am, Su 1pm-midnight.)

3. BAR EL COMERCIO. The best place in town for the classic churro and chocolate breakfast. The cup of chocolate is generous, the churros are freshly fried, and the waiters are extremely friendly and surly in equal measure. Maybe they could use a dose of their own sweetness? (C. Lineros, 9.)

4. LA CAMPANA. La Campana is an institution that firmly endorses butter in a country dripping with olive oil, and we are definitely on board. Pastries, homemade candy, and more pale next to its signature pan de molde (€1.10), basically a super-rich brioche that might not need the half a stick of butter served with it. La Campana has been around so long that it has its own fancy seal on the napkins. A must-see destination on Semana Santa. (Sierpes, 1-3. Open daily 8am-midnight.)

running smoothly. Go for a lunch or early dinner which, remember, is around 9pm Seville time; the inevitable wait to go later is still worth it, though.

i *From Alameda de Hércules, head east on C. Conde de Barajas, then turn right on C. Teodosio. Turn right onto C. Alcoy, and it'll be on your right. Tapas €3-3.5. Glasses of wine €2.40-3. Open Tu-Sa 1:30-4pm and 9-11:30pm, Su 1:30-4pm.*

BODEGA SANTA CRUZ LAS COLUMNAS $

C. Rodrigo Caro, 1   ☎954 21 86 18 www.facebook.com/BodegaSantaCruzSevilla

Just a well-thrown stone away from the cathedral, Bodega Santa Cruz's thin room and corner terraza is always packed with what looks like burly sevillanos intently watching their soccer, though they may just be so big they cover up everything else. Even with its central location, it remains a local favorite for ice-cold beer and loudly shouting at the bartenders. Bills are literally chalked up on the bar, so, yes, they are definitely keeping track of all the succulent €2 pringás (pork sandwiches) you've been downing. We recommend the solomollo al whiskey with a beer so you can have both alcohol in your food and your drink—the sign of a quality establishment. On fútbol game nights you'll find some good-natured havoc; for slightly fewer drunken Sevillans, stop in for a cheap breakfast.

i *From the Giralda, walk down C. Mateos Gago, then turn right on C. Rodrigo Caro. It's on the corner on your left. Montaditos (small sandwiches) €2-2.50. Tapas €2. Raciones €10. Open M-Th 8am-midnight, F-Sa 8am-12:30am, Su 8:30am-midnight.*

BODEGUITA ROMERO $$

C. Harinas, 10   ☎954 21 41 78 https://bodeguita-romero.com

With the best pringá in town, Bodeguita Romero could just rest on its savory bacon, blood sausage, and pork laurels, but instead it delivers some of the best traditional Sevillan dishes out there. Through a curtain of ham hocks, the

From the name, you might assume that la Feria del Abril is a "fair" that takes place in "April." You would be almost correct. This annual blowout stretches from late April to early May and consists of over 1,000 casetas, or tents, set up in the southwestern neighborhood of Los Remedios. Over five days, there are afternoon parades in carriages and on horseback and daily bullfights, so everyone can assert how their Spanish Spanish-ness is really Spanish. The casetas are all privately owned and operated, so either befriend a Sevillan or throw your own rager in the street with plenty of beer stalls and other available beverages.

mustachioed waiters prep tapas portions so huge they will make you worry you actually ordered a larger size and frantically attempt to correct the imaginary miscommunication. The famous pringá (€2.50) is so much more than the simple pork paste of its competitors; basically it's the best parts of a pig between two slices. Everyone leaves happy—except maybe the pigs.

i *From the entrance to the Pl. de Toros, head away from the river on C. Montaditos. Round the corner to the right on C. Arfe and turn left on Puerta del Arenal until it turns into C. Harinas. Credit card min. €12. Tapas €2-3. Raciones €6-15. Open Tu-Th 9am-5pm and 8pm-midnight, F-Sa noon-5pm and 8pm-midnight, Su noon-5pm.*

MERCADO LONJA DE BARRANCAS $$

C. Arjona   ☎954 22 04 95 www.mercadolonjadelbarranco.com

This market has tapas optimized to perfection, with each small stall in the newly renovated space offering a particular dish. Ever wanted to try wasabi salmorejo or truffle croquettes? Neither did we, but after gazing at the mouthwatering displays, everyone's game for an adventurous taste. The huge glass and iron building is right on the waterfront, so you can stay inside and enjoy views of all the food you're about to consume and then go out onto the terrace for a look across the river into the Triana neighborhood. Explore stalls dedicated to rice, octopus, sushi, and more in an heavily air-conditioned dream while looking outside at the beautiful water. It's almost like it's not summer in Sevilla.

i *On the riverfront next to Puente de Triana. Tapas €3-8. Open M-Th 10am-midnight, F-Sa 10am-2am, Su 10am-midnight.*

NIGHTLIFE

The city is great for nightlife and early-morning-life too, but where do you go? Check out Alameda de Hércules, a huge bar-lined plaza near the center of the city, or Los Remedios. During the summer, most locals head to the river or to nearby terraces, so walk in that direction and you're sure to find something to do.

FUN CLUB

C. Alameda de Hércules   ☎636 66 90 23 www.facebook.com/SalaFUNCLUB/

The only major dance club along the Alameda de Hércules, this late-night spot acts like a magnet for indignant and energetic sevillanos fleeing the closing bars in search of FUN on a weekend. Don't come before 2am or you might as well be listening to "Dancing with Myself" on repeat. Music genre varies by night, but Fun Club prides itself on an alternative roster, serving up electronic and classic rock on a weekly basis. The chrome-accented dance floor is always packed by the end of the night. Check Facebook for numerous free entry nights.

i *Cover €4. Cocktails €6-8. Open Th-Sa 9:30pm-6am.*

spain

LOS 100 COCKTELITOS

Amor de Dios, 64 ☎954 90 22 34

This bar serves—yep, you guessed it—100 different kinds of cocktails. But unlike the name would suggest, these cocktails are anything but "-ito" (small and cute). Use the perpetual two-for-€9 special to get a full liter of glorious cocktail creation for just €4.50. The interior is as bizarrely neon as some of the more unusual cocktails. Sit on the white lounge chairs or take it to go along the huge Alameda plaza alongside hundreds of weekend sevillanos doing the exact same thing.

i Southern end of Alameda de Hércules. Small beer €0.70. 1L cocktails €4.50. Open M-W 6pm-2am, Th-Sa 6pm-3:30am, Su 6pm-2am.

BAR RUKO N' ROLL

C. Perez Galdos, 28

Creative spelling aside, this is a great place to start and possibly finish your night, depending on the number of its 12 different signature absinthe shots you choose to consume. The semi-hardcore rock atmosphere is reinforced by large murals of near-naked women and somewhat un-enforced by the TV playing top 40 music videos. It's a central spot for the nightlife neighborhood of Alfalfa and a favorite of Erasmus students. It's very easy to hop to other bars and back here as you make lifelong friends with the huge tattooed bartenders expertly doling out shots. Try the Flama de Juri; after you master the complicated ritual of drinking, waiting, drinking, inhaling, and avoiding getting burned by actual fire, you'll feel like a true regular.

i From Pl. de la Alfalfa, go north up C. Perez Galdos. It's on your right. Shots €1.50. Cocktails €6. Credit card min. $10. Open M-Th 10pm-3am, F-Sa 10pm-4am, Su 10pm-3am.

ESSENTIALS
Practicalities

- **TOURIST OFFICES:** The city's main tourist office is located at Pl. del Triunfo, the square in front of the Alcázar. (☎902 07 63 36 www.turismosevilla.org. Open M-F 9am-7:30pm, Sa-Su 9:30am-7:30-pm.) Smaller offices are located in Pl. San Francisco (☎954 59 52 88) and in the Santa Justa train station (☎954 53 76 26). Their staff speaks a number of languages, including English and French. There you can also pick up the monthly calendar of events in Sevilla and the rest of the region, El Giraldillo, for festivals and other seasonal items.

- **LUGGAGE STORAGE:** There is storage available at the bus station, Pl. de Armas. (☎954 90 80 40. €3 per 24hr. Open daily 5am-1:30am.) The train station, Estación Santa Justa, also has storage space. (Open daily 6am-12:30am.)

- **POST OFFICES:** The main post office is just across from Archivo de Indias. (Av. de la Constitución, 32. ☎954 22 47 60. Open M-F 8:30am-8:30pm, Sa 9:30am-1pm.)

Emergency

- **EMERGENCY NUMBERS:** General emergencies ☎112. Ambulance ☎061. Local police ☎092. National police ☎091.

- **POLICE:** Call the tourist hotline of Servicio de Atención al Turista Extranjera, or SATE (☎954 28 95 64), for English speakers for help with contacting embassies, reporting crimes, and canceling credit cards. Its physical location is right at the exit of the Real Alcázar, in the Patio de Banderas. (Open daily 9am-2pm.)

- **PHARMACIES:** Most pharmacies follow the typical siesta schedule, opening at regular business hours, taking a break in the mid-afternoon, and re-opening until close. If you need to visit one between 2-5pm or after about 8-8:30pm, know that each neighborhood has a rotating

sevilla

system of farmacias de guardia. Each pharmacy location at one point or another in each neighborhood of the city takes on the responsibility of being the all-night or all-day pharmacy. Check out the dates and times of these openings on the window of every pharmacy or in a local newspaper.

- **HOSPITALS:** Hospital Universitario Virgen del Rocio. (Manuel Siurot. ☎955 01 20 00.) Hospital Universitario Virgen de Macarena. (Av. Doctor Fedriani, 3. ☎955 00 80 00.)

Getting There

The San Pablo airport is the region's main airport and connects with airports throughout Spain and Europe. It's located 6 mi. outside the main city, so you'll need to take a bus or taxi into Sevilla. The airport is relatively small (it only has one terminal) and serves low-cost carriers like Vueling and Ryanair. Taxis outside the main terminal can take you to the city center for a fixed price of around €22-25, and the trip lasts around 15min. Alternatively, the airport offers a bus service, Especial Aeropuerto, that runs to and from the airport, stopping at the two bus stations and the train station along the way (€4, round-trip €6).

Sevilla has one train station, Sevilla Santa Justa. The national rail company RENFE (☎902 32 03 20 www.renfe.es) runs high-speed long-distance and short-distance trains to cities like Granada, Málaga, Córdoba, Cádiz, and Madrid. From Santa Justa, travelers can take buses that connect with the city center and the city's two bus stations. (Av. de Kansas City. 954 53 76 26. Ticket office open daily 8am-10pm.)

Sevilla has two bus stations, la Estación de Autobuses Pl. de Armas and the station at Prado de San Sebastián. Pl. de Armas primarily serves cities outside of the Andalucia region and Portugal (Av. Crito de la Expiración, 2. ☎954 90 80 40 or ☎955 03 86 65.) San Sebastián primarily serves the Andalucia region, with destinations like Ronda, Tarifa, Granada, and Córdoba. (☎955 47 92 90.) Local buses to and from the city center also connect with these stations.

Getting Around

Sevilla is a fairly well-connected city with an integrated metro, bus, and tram system. Currently, the metro has one line with 22 stops and runs 11 mi. through the city and its metropolitan area. It starts at Ciudad Expo and ends at Olivar Quinto. Alternatively, you can use the city tram (MetroCentro), which runs through the city center. The tram leaves from Pl. Nueva and follows Av. de la Constitución past the cathedral, stopping at the Archivo de Indias and then at San Fernando (Puerta Jerez). It terminates at the Prado de San Sebastián. Fares cost €1.20.

Sevilla's buses (www.tussam.es) are the heart and soul of its public-transit system. The buses cover all neighborhoods in the city and run from around 6am to 11:30pm, with night buses leaving from Prado de San Sebastián between midnight-2am. The city has "circular" buses (C3 and C4) that circle around the city center, while C5 follows a smaller route inside the center. Fares are €1.20. For travelers who are staying a day or three and traveling to different areas of the city, consider buying a one-day card (€8) or three-day card (€10) for unlimited travel. If you're staying for even longer, consider getting a Tarjeta Multiviaje, a card for which you pay a refundable €1.50 deposit. You then can pay €6 for 10 journeys without transfer (using more than one line) or €7 for 10 journeys with transfer. You can recharge at kiosks or estancos (tobacco sellers).

Sevilla recently installed over 140km of dedicated bike trails (though some may only be indicated with small metal knobs on the road and are easily overlooked). The city's bike-share system, Sevici, offers 250 stations with a minimum one-week rental card. (☎900 90 07 22 www.sevici.es. Short-term membership €13.33; 1st 30min. free, next 30min. €1, €2 per hour after that.) Reputable taxi companies include Radiotaxi

granada

Granada was one of the last Muslim strongholds in Spain, so it feels a little different from other nearby cities. Not like "you have a new mom" different, but more like "discovering a new ice cream flavor/sex position" different—good different. From the historic Albayzín neighborhood to the caves overlooking the city to the Alhambra, Granada isn't short on beautiful vistas and historic architecture. It's also known for its restaurants, which will give you free tapas as long as you're drinking. So it's pretty, calm, AND gives you an excuse to keep drinking alcohol? Perfect.

SIGHTS

▨ ALHAMBRA

C. Real de la Alhambra   ☎958 02 79 71 www.alhambradegranada.org

Sometimes things are popular for no reason (see: planking). The Alhambra is not one of those things. Established as a palace for the Nasrid dynasty in the 13th century but used as a fortress long before, this huge castle/palace/tourist breeding ground is a UNESCO World Heritage site and one of Spain's most popular tourist attractions. Its name means "the red one," and the huge crowd of tourists who turn out to see it means you need to book tickets way in advance—that, or show up at 6am and cross your fingers really tightly. Tickets can be bought online, at the Corral de Carbon, or at any La Caixa Bank ATM in Granada. Plan on spending at least 3hr. wandering the more than 142,000 sq. m of gardens, Islamic architecture, fortifications, fountains, ruins, and a couple little tourist shops that

el albayzín quarter

Don't be fooled into thinking that the Alhambra is all there is to Granada. Perhaps the most delightful, hold-hands-with-that-special-someone part of the city is the Albayzín neighborhood —the old Moorish quarter, a UNESCO World Heritage site. All-white painted houses line the narrow streets. Flowers spill out over the carmens—the open houses hidden by thick walls. Even the streetlights are quaint, for crying out loud. It's here you go to hear a flamenco show at El Tabanco or to drink a beer or coffee at 11:30am at Cafe Cuatro Gatos.

The best views of the Alhambra are on the wall next to Mirador San Nicolas. The surrounding area has countless restaurants and even the Barberia Albaicín – an amazing haircut place for the fellas out there. While you're in the neighborhood, take a hike up to the caves overlooking the city on Sacromonte. Up there, the sunset over Granada hits the Alhambra at the perfect angle, and the barking of the cave-dwelling dogs sounds like a John Williams soundtrack. It's an experience like no other.

There are about 28 water wells throughout the Albayzín, which at one point, believe it or not, had turtles swimming around in them. Because what makes you want to drink water more than having it smell and taste like turtles? They were actually used as a self-cleaning system, because they ate the bugs in the water, and as a poison detection system, because they died. Still, is drinking turtle water a fate better than death? Residents of the Albayzín seemed to think so.

granada

get a room!

MAKUTO GUESTHOUSE $
Calle Tiña, 18   ☎958 80 58 76

Many hostels claim to be a home away from home, but Makuto brings it to a whole new level. Situated on a quiet Albayzín street, this hostel offers hammocks, a treehouse, and a bamboo bar that constantly plays reggae. It's a solo traveler's paradise, as all the friendly guests who come through love to sit around in the open-center outdoor seating area and make friends. You can even play the gut-string guitar in the TV room. Just remember that everything except the bedrooms and the one communal bathroom closes at midnight, so if you want to hang out in a large group you'll have to take the party elsewhere. They'll give you a buzzer key to let yourself in after hours, though.

i Head up to Pl. San Gregorio from C. Elvira, continue past El Tabanco, then take a left, a right up the stairs, a left, and a right onto C. Tiña. Free Wi-Fi. Basic breakfast included; eggs and toast €2. Lockers available. Kitchen and laundry facilities. Free nightly walking tour around El Albayzín. 8-bed dorms €19; 4-bed (co-ed) and 5-bed (female-only) €23. Beer €1. Sangria glasses €1.50; pitchers €5. Dinner €6-8. Reception 8am-midnight.

OASIS BACKPACKERS HOSTEL $
Placeta del Correo Viejo, 3   ☎958 21 58 48

Sit back and relax, because in Oasis you're in good hands. Or, we guess, at an oasis. Really missed an opportunity with that one. Anyway, enjoy the sights off the rooftop terrace, cook in the kitchen, drink at the bar, and sleep in the beds. Besides doing actions in places, you ask, what does this hostel do for me? Oh, baby. How about comfy beds on classy wooden bunks? How about a tiled bar with €1 beers and €1.50 sangria that fills up every night? How about balconies overlooking the Albayzín quarter? How about the best location of any hostel in Granada? So go on your walking tour, take your tapas tour, and enjoy this lush piece of nature in the middle of a desert. What's that called again?

i Take the 1st left off the Moroccan street that runs perpendicular to C. Elvira right by Pl. Nueva. Breakfast not included. Laundry facilities and a kitchen. Free small safe. Elevator. Tapas tours, walking tours around El Albayzin, Spanish classes offered. Female-only dorms available. 10-bed dorms €18; 8-bed €20; 6-bed €22. Reception 24hr.

sell overpriced ice cream. Don't be the goof that goes to Granada without seeing the Alhambra. That's like going to Paris and not beating up a mime.

i Reachable via several tourist buses departing from Pl. Nueva; it's also about a 20min. walk from the center of the city. €15.40. Open Tu-Sa 9am-6:30pm, Su 9am-3:30pm. Get there early.

CATEDRAL DE GRANADA
C. Gran Vía de Colón, 5   ☎958 22 29 59

When the Catholics drove the Muslim Nasrid dynasty out of Granada in 1492, their first order of business was to build this huge cathedral: a moving, architecturally impressive, religiously significant middle finger to the Muslims they had kicked out. (Better a huge cathedral than just keying their car or hooking up with their best friend, we guess.) With intricate, soaring spires, white marble columns, and more gold trim than a rich girl's iPhone case, this cathedral is a must-see. Sometimes there will even be live music in the plaza right out front, which is a godsend for those of us without much church organ music on our iPods.

i Right on the main street. It's unmissable. €2. Open M-Sa 10:45am-6:45pm, Su 4-6:45pm.

spain

FOOD

BAR LOS DIAMANTES $

C. Navas, 26   ☎958 22 70 70

Did someone say seafood tapas bar? No? Well, they should. Los Diamantes is delicious, with cheap, refreshing drinks and a free "tapas choice of the day." Not only does this liberate you from having to peruse a menu and make a choice about which tasty thing you want, it ensures that the tapas you do end up getting are even more delicious. It's a Granada staple to get a free tapa with your drink, and few places do it better than Los Diamantes. The secret is out, though, and it gets busy during peak lunchtime (2-4pm).

i *Right off Pl. del Carmen. Drinks €1.50-4. Seafood dishes €6-12. Open daily 12:30pm-midnight.*

LA RIVIERA $

C. Cetti Meriem, 7   ☎958 22 79 69

For each €2 beer or other drink you get here, you'll be given a choice of tapias off a menu. It's unclear if the free food justifies the drinking here or if the drinking makes it necessary to have so much food. Either way, La Riviera has a dark pub atmosphere with a TV in the corner perpetually playing that day's soccer game. Considering the small size, it's also surprisingly easy to hit up with groups. Either sit outside or inside and let the waiter choose your free tapas for you. He knows much better than you do, and you can focus on drinking.

i *Right off C. Elvira, right next to Pl. Nueva. Beer €2. Other drinks €2-5. Limit 3 types of free tapas per group. Extra tapas €1.50. Open daily noon-1am.*

NIGHTLIFE

EL TABANCO FLAMENCO SHOW

Cuesta de San Gregorio, 24

Granada's nightlife is more toned down than its neighbors Málaga and Valencia, so why not take a night off from puking in handbags to get a little bit of culture? For some, flamenco can be too rhythmically complex to enjoy, but the singer and guitar player's pure passion as they work off each other is undeniably breathtaking. El Tabanco is little more than a one-room Albayzín house, but that kind of personal connection to the performers and other audience members makes the show much better than it would be in a huge auditorium. It's a mostly local crowd, since it's hard to find and hard to figure out when it's open and when it isn't, but it's worth it. They even give you a free plate of jamón ibérico and cheese with your drinks. Forget that dance-floor romance—this is the old-fashioned stuff.

i *Head straight up the main Moroccan stall street from C. Elvira, then turn right into the center of the Albayzín neighborhood. Tickets €7. Wine €1.50. Sangria (really just tinto de verano) €2. Shows F-Su 10pm, but it's best to stop by during the day to check the signs because it changes all the time.*

CHAPLIN'S BAR

C. Elvira

Situated on a side alley off C. Elvira, Chaplin's has, inexplicably, a loop of Charlie Chaplin films playing on a small flatscreen in a corner. It's also got everything else: cheap drinks, a pool table (€2 to play), a foosball table, and a long bar. You can make requests of the Spotify account open on the computer behind the bar—the friendly bartenders are more than open to it. Just don't make the mistake of heading here early (before 1am or so) or you'll find yourself all alone with just the Tramp to keep you company.

i *Go down C. Elvira from Pl. Nueva. Turn right down the alley just before C. Azacayas. Beer €2. Free shot with beer if you can find the promoter somewhere up C. Elvira. Open M-Th 10pm-3am, F-Sa 10pm-4am, Su 10pm-3am.*

granada

HANNIGAN AND SONS

Calle Cetti Meriem, 1   ☎958 22 48 26

Even if you're not Irish, this bar will be Irish enough for the both of ye. Sure, it's no hoity-toity Spanish wine bar, but sometimes an old-fashioned pint and soccer game is just what you need. Hannigan and Sons, packed with almost exclusively travelers and expats, has affordable drinks, cozy booths, and a great atmosphere, especially if you can get to it during an Irish national team game. There's even a table in the back to play beer pong. Really, this bar is about two things and two things only: drinking and shenanigans.

i Right down the street from La Riviera. Quiz night on M. Beer €2. Cocktails (be warned, they're pretty strong) €5. Open M-Th 4pm-3am, F 4pm-4am, Sa 1pm-4am, Su 1pm-3am.

ESSENTIALS

Practicalities

- **TOURIST OFFICES:** There are over 25 tourist offices in the greater Granada area. The primary offices are in **Citty Hall** (el Ayuntamiento) in Pl. el Carmen (☎95 824 82 80 www.granadatur. com), at the airport (☎95 824 52 69 iturismo.aeropuerto@dipgra.es), and in the **Alhambra** (Av. Generalife ☎95 854 40 02 www.andalucia.org).

- **TOURS:** The tourist bust line for Granada runs English-language tours that stop at 10 major sights. (www.citysightseeing-spain.com/html/es/tour. €10. 1¼hr., every 15min.) You can also join the free walking tour, run by **Oasis Granada**, which departs from the fountain in Pl. Nueva. (€3-5 tip recommended. Daily 11am.)

- **CURRENCY EXCHANGE: Interchange** is a money-exchange office that provides services for all major credit cards, including American Express. (C. Reyes Católicos, 31 ☎95 822 46 44. Open M-Sa 9am-10pm, Su 11am-3pm and 4-9pm.)

- **INTERNET: Biblioteca de Andalucía** has 8 computers that you can use for free for up to 1hr. (C. Profesor Sáinz Cantero, 6 ☎95 857 56 50 www.juntadeandalucia.es/cultura/ba. Open M-F 9am-2pm.) **Idolos and Fans** has photocopying, fax, scanning, Wi-Fi, and even a PlayStation 3. (Camino de Ronda, 80 ☎95 826 57 25. €1.80 per hr., €9 per 6hr., €12 per 10hr. Open daily 10am-midnight.)

- **POST OFFICE: Puerta Real.** (Intersection of C. Reyes Católicos and Acera del Darro ☎95 822 11 38. Open M-F 8:30am-8:30pm, Sa 9:30am-2pm.)

- **POSTAL CODE:** 18005.

Emergency!

- **EMERGENCY NUMBERS: Municipal police:** ☎092. **National police:** ☎091.

- **LATE-NIGHT PHARMACIES:** You'll find a few 24hr. pharmacies around the intersection of C. Reyes Católicos and Acera del Darro, including **Farmácia Martín Valverde** (C. Reyes Católicos, 5 ☎95 826 26 64).

- **HOSPITALS/MEDICAL SERVICES: Hospital Universitario Vírgen de las Nieves.** (Av. de las Fuerzas Armadas, 2 ☎95 802 00 00.) **Hospital San Juan de Dios.** (C. San Juan de Dios ☎95 802 29 04.) For an **ambulance,** contact a local emergency team (☎95 828 20 00).

Getting There

BY PLANE

Aeropuerto Federico García Lorca (GRX; ☎95 824 52 69) is located about 15km outside the city in Chauchina. The airport has daily flights to and from Barcelona, Madrid, Mallorca, and Sevilla as well as weekly flights to and from Paris' Orly and Rome's

Fiumicino airports. Air Europa, Iberia, Spanair, Ryanair, and Vueling Airlines all fly through Granada and offer connecting flights to and from cities across Europe.

A taxi will take you to the city center (€25) or directly to the Alhambra (€28). Call **Radio Taxi** in advance at ☎60 605 29 25 or wait in line at the airport. The bus company **Autocares José González** offers a direct service between the airport and the city center. (☎95 839 01 64 www.autocaresjosegonzalez.com. €3. Every hr. 5:20am-8pm.)

BY TRAIN

The main **train station** (☎95 827 12 72) is at Av. de los Andaluces. **RENFE** trains (www. renfe.es) run to and from Barcelona (€63. 11½hr.; daily 8am and 9:30pm), Madrid (€70. 4½hr.; daily 9:05am and 6:05pm), Sevilla (€24. 3hr., 4 per day 8am-9pm), and many other smaller cities. To get from the station to the city center, you can take a short taxi (€5. 5min.) or bus #3, 6, 9, or 11 (€1.20), which will take you to C. Gran Vía de Colón in the city center.

BY BUS

The bus station is at Carretera de Jaén (☎95 818 50 10). **Alsa** buses (www.alsa.es) run within Andalucía (☎95 818 54 80) and connect to the Madrid (☎95 818 54 80) and Valencia-Barcelona (☎90 242 22 42) lines. Buses run to and from Cádiz (€31. 5hr., 4 per day 9am-9pm), Madrid (€17. 5hr., 15 per day 1am-11:30pm.), Málaga (€10. 1½hr., 15 per day 7am-9:30pm), Sevilla (€20. 3hr., 10 per day 8am-11pm), and many other destinations. **Autocares Bonal** (☎95 846 50 22) also runs a direct route to and from **Sierra Nevada** ski resorts in winter. (25min.; M-F 3 per day, Sa-Su 4 per day.) City buses #3 and 33 on **Transportes Rober** run regular services between the station and the city center.

Getting Around

Transportes Rober runs almost 40 bus lines around the city as well as smaller direct buses to the Alhambra, the Albaicín, and the Sacromonte. (☎90 071 09 00 www. transportesrober.com. €1.20; 7 rides €5.) The **tourist lines** are #30, 31, 32, and 34. The **circular lines** (#11, 21, and 23) make full loops around the city. Rober also runs a special Feria line (€1.40). When most lines stop running at 11:30pm, the **Búho lines** pick up the slack. (#111 and 121. €1.30. Daily midnight-5:15am.)

málaga

Málaga is the height of living. Part beach town, part sprawling outdoor shopping mall, part historic old village, it's commonly known as a destination for bachelor parties, middle-aged women on shopping voyages, and students looking to get down. For somewhere that is so classy and laid-back during the day, it's surprisingly banging at night—great clubs and bars will top off an evening of tapas. Just don't get too sunburned out on the beach, or else grinding up against that attractive Spaniard is going to be a hell of a lot more painful. So pack your sunscreen, look up some facts about the artwork of Málaga native Pablo Picasso, and hop in. The water's cold, the nightlife is hot, and the rooms are, well, room temperature. Just right.

SIGHTS

LA ALCAZABA

C. Alcazabilla, 2 ☎952 22 72 30

Ever played a level in a video game where you get hopelessly lost and every door seems to lead to a dead end? La Alcazaba is built exactly like that. The 11th-century Hammudid fortress has old ramparts you can walk on and pretend you're a guard on patrol, minus all the diseases they probably had. It also has expertly manicured gardens and what were probably once some pretty nice pools and fountains before green gunk got all over them. The glass display cases in the side rooms contain shards and fragments of old jars and stuff, which is cool if you're into that sort of thing.

i €2.20, students €0.60. Combined ticket with Castillo de Gibralforo €3.55. Free Su after 2pm. Open daily in summer 9am-8pm; in winter 9am-6pm. Last entry 30min. before close.

CASTILLO DE GIBRALFORO

Camino Gibralforo, 11   ☎952 22 72 30

Still got something left in the tank after La Alcazaba? Head even farther up the huge huge hill to Castillo de Gibralfaro, Málaga's second Moorish castle! The Castillo de Gibralforo has, hands down, the best views of Málaga, but of course the tradeoff is that's because it's so high up. Still, it's worth it; there are way worse places to collapse from exhaustion. So pack some serious walking shoes for the breathtaking (literally) uphill walks and plan for a day of wandering the Moors.

i €2.20, students €0.60. Combined ticket with La Alcazaba €3.55. Free Su after 2pm. Open daily in summer 9am-8pm; in winter 9am-6pm. Last entry 30min. before close.

MUSEO PICASSO MÁLAGA

Palacio de Buenavista, C. San Agustín, 8   ☎952 12 76 00 www.museopicassomalaga.org

Picasso's hometown is Málaga, so there's no better place to see how he reps the East Coast (of Spain) than the Picasso Museum here. With hallways upon hallways of sculpture and paintings from Picasso's long and illustrious career, the museum is apt to lose and confuse you. Why is that woman's face coming out of her stomach? Art, my friend. Art. Luckily, the museum provides a free audio tour that holds your hand throughout the exhibits. Come for the cubist boobs, stay for the quaint cafe where parrots swoop down and drink from the fountain. Then, when you're all done, buy yourself a Picasso umbrella at the gift shop, because, otherwise, did you really go?

i Every sign in Málaga points to it, so you should have no trouble finding it. €10, students €5. Open daily July-Aug 10am-8pm; Sept-Oct 10am-7pm; Nov-Feb 10am-6pm; Mar-June 10am-7pm.

CATEDRAL/MUSEO CATOLICO

C. Molina Lario, 9

Shh! This cavernous testament to Spain's intense Catholicism is as lovely as it is impossible to be quiet in. Like the rest of Málaga, it has incredibly squeaky floors (that we have incredibly squeaky shoes) and boatloads of curious tourists. There is a designated shusher who walks around shushing people every few minutes or so. Speak not, lest ye be shushed as well. The church was constructed between 1528 and 1782 and now has artwork and exhibits from Málaga and beyond. Whatever religion you are, sit down and feel dwarfed by the Baroque style, then pray that you will someday have the wisdom to know what Baroque style is.

i It's the big church spire. You can't miss it. €5, students €3. Open M-F 10am-6pm, Sa 10am-5pm, Su 2-6pm. Closed on holidays.

MUSEO UNICAJA DE ARTES Y COSTUMBRES POPULARES

C. Manuel José García Caparrós

Sometimes you've just gotta relax and wander around a museum that has an authentic birthing chair from the 1800s that looks like a leather toilet. When you do, this is the place to do it. With several floors dedicated to life in Spain in the 19th century, it's a good starting point to understanding the ethnographic history of the country. It's cheap and worth an hour or so, but it's by no means big enough to be a whole-day activity—just a nice respite from all that shopping and beachgoing.

i Take C. Especeria away from Pl. de la Constitución, then take a left on C. Camas. It'll be up on your right, in the small square. €5. Open M-F 10am-5pm, Sa 10am-2pm. Closed holidays.

LIGHTS OUT HOSTEL $
C. Torregorda, 3 ☎951 25 35 25 www.lightsouthostel.com

A great, social hostel that offers solo travelers and groups an intensely communal experience, Lights Out Hostel is a near-perfectly balanced place to stay in Málaga. It's a 7-8min. walk from Pl. de la Constitución, right next to the Mercado Central. Bar crawls, communal dinner (€5-6), and €1 beers at the rooftop bar make it very easy for people visiting Málaga alone to, well, not have to do it alone. Every night 8-9pm is happy hour at the bar, and the sangria is free after 9pm. Each floor has single bathrooms as well as communal bathrooms with modern showers. Small word of warning: Mosquitoes can be a problem in the rooms at night. For a €1.50 deposit, the hostel will give you mosquito spray. We strongly recommend using it. Overall, though, this is a very small con to what is a really fantastic hostel, full of really friendly people. Accordingly, it sells out quick; it's best to book in advance.

i Take a right off Alameda Principal, then it's on a side street. Or turn right down the street from the Mercado Central Atarazanas. Free Wi-Fi. Breakfast included. Linens and towels included. 6-bed dorms €22. Reception 24hr.

FEEL HOSTELS CITY CENTER $
C. Concejal Agustín Moreno ☎952 21 82 68

An eclectic art style and brightly painted hallways seem a fitting metaphor for the kind of fun atmosphere Feel Hostels tries to promote: a bunch of people, in this weird beach city with high-end shopping, hanging out and having fun. The hostel organizes pub crawls and outings and is so insanely well located that you don't even have to worry about getting lost as you stumble back home after a long night at the surrounding clubs and bars. The bright, roomy dorm rooms are well-kept and comfortable, though you'll be drawn outside them to the lovely open-center architecture. Smell the food from the cozy restaurant next door, and grab some free sangria on the roof deck. Feels good, right?

i From the back left street of Pl. de la Constitución, take a right. The hostel should be up on your left, a little back from the street under the sign. Free Wi-Fi. Breakfast included. Nightly dinner €5. Free tea and coffee in the kitchen. Computer lab. Individual lights and outlets in each dorm bed. Dorms €22; private doubles €57.

FOOD

LAS MERCHANAS $$
C. Mosquera, 5 ☎654 74 42 57

God bless restaurants like these. This Christian-themed restaurant off a side street in central Málaga has everything—affordable but delicious food, copious cups of alcohol, a relaxed vibe, and a bizarre assortment of hyper-religious decals on the walls. Luckily, this seems to only be a design choice and not a reflection of the fun that can be had at Las Merchanas. So kick back, drink some cerveza, have fun with your friends, and don't do too much sinning. That's valuable time that could be spent on the €4 tapas.

i It's on a side street off C. Nosquera as you walk toward C. Comedias. Flamenquín con patatas (fried ham and cheese) €5.50. Calamares €4-6. Beer €2. Glasses of wine €1.50-2; bottles €12.

málaga

RECYCLO BIKE CAFE $

C. Marqués Villafiel, 4 ☎951 35 37 16

Can you say "10% discount if you bring your bike"? Hopefully you can, because it's a pretty simple sentence. This hipster haven is bike-themed and an absolute tour de France when it comes to alcohol and food. The €5 salads are amazing, a welcome change from the endless sausage and bread that Spanish people have somehow developed the intestinal fortitude to deal with. Sure, the health benefits of the salads might be offset by the €6 burgers—or the fact that you're downing cañas like they're going out of style—but maybe it'll encourage you to bike more and burn off those sweet sweet calories.

i Right in the same plaza as the Museo Unicaja de Artes y Costumbres Populares. Beer €1.20-2.40. Sangria €3.50. Cocktails €5-6. Salads €5-6. Burgers €6. Open M-Th 9am-midnight, F-Sa 9am-2am, Su 9am-midnight.

PEPA Y PEPE $$

C. Caldereria, 9 ☎615 65 69 84

The glory of seafood tapas is on full display here at this classic Málaga budget restaurant full of just as many locals as tourists, all stuffing their pudgy little faces. The waiters will toss cork after cork onto the ledge above the bar—a perfect omen for all the drinking you can do—and the owner's kids hanging around the counter are probably also a metaphor for something. Either way, this place is delicious and central, and it's as good a place as any to start that nightly pub crawl. Always good to have food in your stomach for that kind of thing. Beware: it gets crowded quickly because of its proximity to the main square.

i 2min. from Pl. de la Constitución. Cañas €2. Shrimp €5. Open daily 12:30-4:30pm and 7:30pm-12:30am.

NIGHTLIFE

SALA GOLD

C. de Luis de Velázquez, 5 ☎670 09 87 49 www.facebook.com/salagold/events

This nightclub is gold, Jerry, GOLD! Located in the middle of Málaga's sprawling club and bar district, this cavernous club has seemingly infinite bar counters, a big dance floor with TVs that play the music video of the song blasting from the speakers, and alcohol. (That last one probably goes without saying.) Still, you're better off getting drunk somewhere cheaper and coming here afterward. It's a slightly dressier place and doesn't get busy until far after 3am. It's worth the cover for the mix of Latin house music and danceable top 40 songs, but if you come before 3 looking for a hopping dance floor, you're going to be disappointed.

i Take C. Granada off Pl. de la Constitución, then take a left on C. Angel. Sala Gold will be right at the end of the street. 18+. Occasional themed parties. Cover €10. Cocktails €6. Open M-Th 10pm-6am, F-Sa 10pm-7am, Su 10pm-6am.

THEATRO CLUB

Calle Lazcano, 5 ☎670 09 87 49

Flaming champagne bottles, throbbing beats, and blasts of air to startle you into having a good time, oh my! Theatro Club is simply the bomb. If it seems like the huge crystal chandelier is going to come down because of the throbbing music, you know it's a good night. It probably won't, but, if it does, there are worse places to die than on this vintage-modern decorated dance floor. Just dodge the couples making out, the photographer wandering around looking for hot people to post on Facebook, and have a good time. Theatro has a varied schedule that sometimes includes live musical acts earlier in the night. And, unlike Sala Gold, the dance floor gets dancier earlier.

i Up the street and take a left from Sala Gold. Cover €10. Cocktails €5-7. Open M 10pm-6am, Tu 9pm-6am, W 7pm-6am, Th 9pm-6am, F-Sa 4pm-7am, Su 4:30pm-6am.

spain

MINIBAR

Pl. del Marques del Vado del Maestre   ☎695 16 35 74

For a chiller atmosphere than the clubs allow and stronger gin and tonics than have ever been poured in history, come to this bar. Not for the bar itself, but for the square outside—at night it becomes a buzzing open-air crowd of locals and tourists, all enjoying the warm night air of Málaga. While "mini" might refer to the size of the bar itself, the drinks are €5 and as strong as possible without becoming a health hazard. There aren't a ton of tables out in the square to put your drink down on, so you might as well drink it quick.

i *Right up the street from Sala Gold. On the far left of the square with the crowd. Cocktails €5.*

ESSENTIALS
Practicalities

- **TOURIST OFFICES:** Málaga is covered with tourist offices. The **municipal tourist office** has offices and kiosks throughout the city as well as an excellent website (www.malagaturismo. com) with PDF copies of all the pamphlets at the tourist offices. The main office in the Pl. Marina might not be the closest to your hotel, but it provides the most extensive services, including registration for city Wi-Fi and audioguides for self-guided tours (Pl. Marina, 11 ☎95 192 60 20. At the intersection of Alameda Principal and C. Marqués de Larios. Open Mar-Sept daily 9am-8pm, Oct-Feb daily 9am-6pm). Other locations include the **Centro de Recepción de Visitantes Ben Gabirol** (C. Granada, 70 ☎95 221 33 29. Open daily 10am-2pm and 3-6pm) and **branches** near the Alcazaba (Pl. Aduana. Open daily 9am-2pm and 3-6pm), across the river near the post office (Av. Andalucía, 1. Open daily 10am-2pm), at the Playa de Malagueta (Paseo Marítimo de Pablo Ruiz Picasso, 1. Across from the western end of the beach, near the intersection with C. Fernando Camino. Open June-Sept 10am-2pm and 3-7pm), at the Playa de Pedregalejo (C. Bolivia, 260. Across from the center of the beach, near the intersection with Paseo de las Acacias. Open June-Sept 10am-2pm and 3-7pm), and at Terminal 3 of the airport. (Open M-F 9:30am-2pm and 2:30-6pm, Sa-Su 10am-2pm.) The **regional tourist office** provides information about the city of Málaga as well as Sevilla, Córdoba, Granada, Cádiz, and the other provincial capitals of Andalucía. (Pasaje de Chinitas, 4 ☎95 130 89 11. From Pl. Constitución, proceed along C. Marqués de Larios and take the 1st left. Open M-F 9am-7:30pm, Sa-Su and holidays 9:30am-3pm.)

- **TOURS:** The municipal tourist office organizes **Málaga with 5 Senses,** a guided walking tour of the city that comments on the exteriors of the city's major sights. (☎66 239 79 61 guias-demalaga@yahoo.es. Departs from next to the main municipal tourist office in the Pl. Marina. Bilingual tours in Spanish and English; call ahead for French, German, or Italian. Min. group of 5. €5. 1½hr., M-Sa and holidays 11:30am.) Free audioguides and pamphlets are available at the Pl. Marina tourist office for eight different **themed self-guided tours**, such as Traditional Málaga, Religious Málaga, Picasso's Málaga, and Contemporary Málaga. (Available in Spanish, English, French, German, Italian, Japanese, Chinese, Arabic, and Russian. Credit card informa-tion and photocopy of passport required as deposit for audioguide. Pl. Marina tourist office open Mar-Sept daily 9am-8pm, Oct-Feb 9am-6pm.) **Málaga Bike Tours** offers a tour around the city that includes a drink. (C. Trinidad Grund, 4 ☎60 697 85 13 www.malagabiketours.eu. Departs from next to the main municipal tourist office at Pl. Marina. Tours in English. Bicycles and helmets included. Reservations recommended at least 24hr. in advance. €24. 4hr.; daily 10am, though other start times can be arranged in advance.) **bike2málaga** offers rickshaw tours of the city of varying lengths that leave from in front of the cathedral. (€10-30, depending on route. 20min.-1¾hr., available 10am-8pm.)

- **CURRENCY EXCHANGE: Banco Santander** (C. Marqués de Larios, 9 ☎95 221 37 97 www. bancosantander.es. Open M-F 8:30am-2:30pm) exchanges major foreign currencies, as do several of the banks along C. Marqués de Larios, especially near Alameda Principal. Outside of regular bank hours, head across the river to El Corte Inglés and go to the Customer Service

(Servicio de Atención al Cliente) desk on the 1st floor. (Av. Andalucía, 4-6 ☎952 07 65 00 www.elcorteingles.es. Follow Alameda Principal across the river. Open daily 10am-10pm.)

- **LUGGAGE STORAGE:** Lockers are available in both the bus station (€3.20 per day. Open daily 6:30am-midnight) and the train station. (Luggage goes through security screening. €3-5 per day, depending on size. Open daily 7am-11pm.)

- **INTERNET ACCESS:** Free public Wi-Fi is available at Pl. Marina and along C. Marqués de Larios, but first you have to sign up for an account at the main branch of the municipal tourist office. Free Wi-Fi and computers with 1hr. of free internet access are also available at the **Biblioteca Provincial Cánovas del Castillo,** northwest of the Pl. Merced (C. Ollerías, 34 ☎95 213 39 36 From Pl. Merced, proceed against traffic on C. Álamos, which curves to the left to become C. Carretería, then take the 4th right onto C. Ollerías. Ask at the information desk for a Wi-Fi password, valid for 24hr. Open July-Sept 15 M-F 9am-2pm, Sept 16-June M-F 9:30am-8pm. Closed Semana Santa.) For Wi-Fi and computers with internet access outside of library hours, try **TelSat.** (C. Gómez Pallete, 7 ☎95 222 77 84. From Pl. Merced, with your back to the traffic, take the 3rd left onto C. Gómez Pallete. Internet access €1 per hr. Open daily 10am-1:20am.)

- **POST OFFICE:** The main post office is just across the river from the centro histórico. (Av. Andalucía, 1 ☎95 236 43 80 www.correos.es. Follow Alameda Principal across the river; it's on the left. Open M-F 8:30am-8:30pm, Sa 9:30am-2pm.)

- **POSTAL CODE:** 29002.

Emergency

- **EMERGENCY NUMBER:** ☎112.

- **AMBULANCE AND EMERGENCY HEALTHCARE:** ☎061. Red Cross: ☎95 222 22 22.

- **INFORMATION:** ☎010.

- **FIRE:** ☎080.

- **POLICE: Local Police** (Av. Rosaleda, 19 ☎092 or ☎95 212 65 52 www.policiademalaga. com. From Alameda Principal, walk to the river, turn right, and walk 12min.) **National Police** (C. Ramos Marín, 4 ☎091 or ☎95 204 62 00 www.policia.es. From Pl. Merced, with your back to traffic, take the 2nd left onto C. San Juan de Letrán, then turn right at the end of the street.)

- **HOSPITAL: Hospital Regional Universitario Carlos Haya de Málaga** (Av. Carlos de Haya ☎95 129 00 00 www.carloshaya.net. Bus #8, 21, or 23 from Alameda Principal.)

- **PHARMACY:** There is a 24hr. pharmacy on Alameda Principal, near Pl. Marina. (Alameda Principal, 2 ☎95 221 28 58.)

Getting There

BY BUS

Buses from destinations across Spain arrive at the **Estación de Autobuses de Málaga.** (Paseo de los Tilos ☎95 235 00 61 www.estabus.emtsam.es. Bus #4 goes from the station to Alameda Principal.) **Daibus** (☎91 652 00 11 www.daibus.es) provides service from Madrid. (€24-25. 6-7¼hr. July-Aug 12 per day 7:30am-midnight; Sept-June M-Th 8 per day 7:30am-midnight, F 10 per day 7:30am-midnight, Sa 8 per day 7:30am-midnight, Su 10 per day 7:30am-midnight.) **Alsina,** a subsidiary of ALSA (☎90 242 22 42 www.alsa.es) runs buses from other cities in Andalucía, including Córdoba (€14. 2½-3hr., 4 per day 8:30am-5pm), Granada (€11-13. 1½-2hr.; M-Th 16 per day 7am-9:30pm, F 17 per day 7am-10pm, Sa 16 per day 7am-9:30pm, Su 16 per day 7am-10pm), and Sevilla (€17-22. 2½-4hr.; 6 per day 7am-8:30pm). **ALSA** also provides service from Barcelona. (€83. 16-17hr., 5 per day 7am-6:20pm.)

spain

BY TRAIN

Trains to Málaga run to the **Estación de Málaga-Maria Zambrano,** across the street from the bus station. (C. Explanada de la Estación ☎90 224 02 02 www.adif.es. .Bus #1, 3, 9, or 10 goes from the station to Alameda Principal. Open daily 5am-12:45am.) **RENFE** runs trains from: Barcelona (€58-70. 5½-12hr.; 3 per day 8:30am-3:50pm); Córdoba (€19-46. 45min.-2½hr.; M-Th 17 per day 7:40am-11:29pm, F 18 per day 7:40am-11:29pm, Sa 14 per day 10:10am-8:40pm, Su 15 per day 10:10am-11:29pm); Madrid (€36-88. 2¼-2¾hr.; M-Th 11 per day 7:35am-9:35pm, F 13 per day 7:35am-9:35pm, Sa 9 per day 7:39am-8:35pm, Su 11 per day 9:35am-9:35pm); Sevilla (€23-44. 2-2½hr.; M-Th 11 per day 6:50am-8:05pm, F 12 per day 6:50am-8:05pm, Sa 9 per day 7:40am-8:05pm, Su 10 per day 7:40am-8:05pm); Valencia (€61-107. 4-8¾hr.; M-F 3 per day 8:15am-4:10pm, Sa 2 per day 8:15am and 11:58am, Su 2 per day at 11:58am and 4:10pm).

To get to the *centro histórico* and its many accommodations from the train station, exit the train station onto C. Héroes de Sostoa (on the other side of the station from the bus station), turn right, take the 1st left onto C. Góngora, and take the 1st right onto C. Ayala; from the bus stop, take bus #1, 3, 9, or 10 to Alameda Principal.

BY PLANE

The **Aeropuerto de Málaga-Costa del Sol,** located 5mi. outside the city, is the second-biggest airport in Andalucía. (AGP; Av. Comandante García Morato ☎90 240 47 04 www. aeropuertodemalaga-costadelsol.com.) It receives domestic and international flights from across Europe from a variety of airlines, including budget carriers **easyJet** (www. easyjet.com), **Ryanair** (www.ryanair.com), and **Vueling Airlines** (☎80 700 17 17 inside Spain, ☎93 151 81 58 outside Spain www.vueling.com.) There are several ways to get between the airport and the *centro histórico.* The cheapest option, bus #19, runs between the airport and the Pl. General Torrijos, at the end of Paseo del Parque farthest from Pl. Marina, in both directions (€1.20. From airport to *centro* every hr. 8:03am-10pm; from *centro* to airport every hr. 7:35am-9:30pm). Bus A Express (bus #75), an express airport shuttle, cuts the journey to 15min. but is more expensive. (€2. From airport to *centro* every 30min. 7am-midnight; from *centro* to airport every 30min. 6:25am-11:30pm.) RENFE Cercanías train C-1 runs between the airport and the Málaga Centro-Alameda station. (€1.60. 12min.; from airport to *centro* every 20min. 5:42am-10:42pm; from the *centro* to airport every 20min. 6:20am-11:20pm.) A taxi from the airport to *centro* costs €25-30.

Getting Around

The *centro histórico*'s narrow streets are best navigated on **foot.** In fact, walking can get you pretty much anywhere you need to go in Málaga; even the trip from the bus and train stations to Pl. Merced is only a 20min. walk. Empresa Municipal de Transportes (☎90 252 72 00 www.emtmalaga.es) operates the city's bus lines, practically all of which stop along Alameda Principal. The most useful of these are bus #11 and 34, which run to the streets parallel to the Playa de la Malagueta and the Playa de Pedregalejo, and bus #36 (really more like van #36), which squeezes through the small streets of the old quarter; a limited number of late-night lines provide service throughout the night.

Bicycles are available for rent from **Málaga Bike Tours** (C. Trinidad Grund, 4 ☎60 697 85 13 www.malagabiketours.eu. Just off Pl. Marina; C. Trinidad Grund runs parallel to Alameda Principal. €5 per 4hr., €10 for 24hr., €26 for 3 days, €50 for 7 days. Open daily 10am-2pm and 4-8pm) and **Málaga Custom Bikes.** (C. Álamos, 42 ☎63 441 38 70 www.malagacustombikes.com. From Pl. Merced, with your back to the plaza, turn right onto C. Álamos. Credit card information and photocopy of passport required as deposit. Standard bikes €5 per half day, €10 per day; tandem bikes €15/25. Open daily 10am-2pm and 4-8pm.)

If you need a **taxi**, call **Unitaxi** (☎95 200 00 00 or ☎95 233 33 33 www.unitaxi.es) or **Taxi-Unión** (☎95 204 08 04 or ☎95 204 00 90 www.taxi-union.es).

pamplona

Pamplona: where Spaniards go to stab bulls and street sanitation workers go to stab themselves. San Fermín is one of the biggest festivals in Spain, attracting people from all over the world, including a surprising number of actual Spaniards. It all centers on el encierro: the actual running of the bulls, where a herd (flock? gaggle? murder? murder's probably the most appropriate, considering 15 people have died in the festival's history) of bulls runs along a fenced-in course while people in white with red handkerchiefs try to outrun them. It's a bloodthirsty spectacle, but when in Spain, do as the Romans did and take immense pleasure in seeing people and animals get hurt.

The festivities kick off at noon on July 6 with a crowded party in the main square. Revelers pour sangria on each other, people in balconies pour water and wine on those below, and everyone does a lot of shouting. For the rest of the day people wander the small town, following roving street bands and amassing plastic bottles of Don Simon, the sangria of choice.

As night falls, the partying only rises. A stunning fireworks display splashes across the sky starting at 11:30 every night. That's some serious stamina, with no refractory period. The best place to watch them is Vuelta del Castillo Park, right in front of the bus station. Some genius decided to sell ultra-high-powered green laser pointers, so any cloud of smoke left behind by the fireworks is immediately dotted with dancing green lights. It would be cool if it weren't so potentially blinding.

The clubbing and drinking and littering and peeing behind dumpsters continues until the next morning, when, at 8am, cannon sound to signal that the bulls have been released. People run through the streets, sometimes bailing out over the railings, sometimes getting trampled, and sometimes getting lifted by the bull's horns, gored, and thrown by the wayside. Make no mistake: el encierro is dangerous, not just some fun tourist activity. Ask anyone from Pamplona, and they'll tell you not to do it unless you're both prepared and athletic. If you've been drinking the entire night before, you're neither.

To get a good seat for el encierro, there are two options: arrive at 6am or earlier to stake out an uncomfortable seat for 2hr. on the wooden wall put up along the course or pay exorbitant amounts of money for a balcony. Both have their merits: it's a once in a lifetime sight, so it's worth paying for, but you'll probably be in the city early anyway from partying the night before. Do whatever fits your schedule best, but don't pay more than €50 for a balcony. It's not worth it for 2min. of action.

But what about eating and sleeping? No amount of drinking can make up for these basic necessities. You can get cheap food all over the city, as restaurants roll out bare-bones San Fermín menus that often feature €5 sandwiches. You might not want to stop drinking, you should probably hit pause and eat. You'll thank us around 3am when you see people vomiting in the streets.

Where to sleep? Unless you've booked months and months in advance, hostels are out of the question. Airbnb is reliable but pricy. There are campgrounds that offer tents and organized activities, which are worth it for solo travelers. For the best, albeit dirtiest, bang for your buck, you're fine sleeping with the hordes of other travelers in a park somewhere. Try not to think of all the people who have probably peed right where you're sleeping. We realize us saying that probably didn't help. Never mind. Think of kittens.

Popularized in the English-speaking world by Ernest Hemingway's The Sun Also Rises in 1926, Pamplona is still packed with references to the American author: notably, in hostels (Hemingway Hostel) and bars (Hemingway Bar & Grill). Hemingway loved bull runs and bullfights, and came to San Fermín many times. He never ran, though, so don't think you need to run to prove that you're as manly as Papa.

The Festival of San Fermín is the biggest, coolest, most overwhelming, grossest, craziest, most bloodthirsty, once-in-a-lifetime-est party there is. It's the kind of experience that you truly can't get elsewhere, and as long as you keep drinking water and shower afterwards, you'll make it through in one piece.

toledo

Welcome to Toledo, the world's oldest proponent for coexistence. In this ancient city perched atop a massive hill and surrounded by its very own moat (actually the Tagus River, but we can pretend), wander down any street and you're likely to find a Star of David, Arabic script, and a cross, all within a few yards of each other. This is a city of cathedrals, synagogues, and mosques, of Moorish architecture and cross-shaped transepts. Before the Spanish conquered Toledo in 1085, Muslim Moors ruled the land. The city itself dates back to the Bronze Age (for those of you not in the know, around 600 BC) and was under Roman rule. While visiting, make sure to check out the ancient Roman ruins and city walls—thousand-year remnants of a time long since passed.

Today, you'll find yourself at the heart of Spain's Catholic pulse. Spain's greatest cathedral (or so we think) is located just blocks away from Toledo's central Plaza, Zocodover, and churches with sky-high, panoramic views cover the city. While this sleepy, medieval town is known for its sharp souvenirs (check the sign at the train station that warns you about pointy objects crossing customs), take a hike across the hills and find the city's hidden nooks, from ancient Roman military fortifications to fishing spots on the river. While the town may seem touristy at first, it's exploration, creativity, and a bit of marzapan that will make your trip anything but ordinary—or, for that matter, 21st-century.

SIGHTS

Beyond the locations listed here, there are a collection of different religious sights that are definitely worth a visit, though each only warrants a short look. If you'd like to visit, there's a wristband (pulsera turística) that can maximize your ability to see really old beautiful religious stuff for €9. La Iglesia Santo Tomé has El Greco's masterpiece The Burial of Count Orgaz in its own separate room, so you know it must be special (it is!). Other such sights include the Moorish-style Sinogoga de Santa María la Blanca, Iglesia del Salvador, Mesquita del Cristo de la Luz, Iglesia de los Jesuitas (get a great view of the city from its double towers), and el Monasterio de San Juan de los Reyes with its cloisters made for deep philosophical introspection (or a nap). The bracelet is valid as long as it's intact on your wrist (it's also water-resistant, so please still shower!).

🏛 CATEDRAL PRIMADA

C. Cardenal Cisneros, 1   ☎925 22 22 41 www.catedralprimada.es

If you only see one thing in Toledo, go to the cathedral. But isn't it "just another cathedral"? Well, yes, but let's just say the 267 years it took to build definitely paid off. At 146 ft., it's easily visible among Toledo's hills, and the interior features both French Gothic and Baroque stylings. Try in vain to capture the twisting sculpture of the El Transparente altarpiece or get that perfect shot of the 700-year-old stained-glass window. The museum collection also contains a

ALBERGUE LOS PASCUALES $

Cuesta de Pascuales, 8   ☎925 28 24 22

This albergue is exactly what an overnight traveler to Toledo needs: it's comfortable, close to all the major sights, and incredibly well priced. Tucked into its own little winding street but still only a staircase away from the Alcázar, Albergue Los Pascuales combines local Toledo with its tourist-hub alter ego. After Madrid sticker shock, feel thrifty and smart with free Wi-Fi, free breakfast (just tea, instant coffee, and pastries, but still), storage with built-in locks, and linens, all for a standard low price. The proprietors are helpful and so nice they'll even spend 30min. tutoring you on the tricky front-door lock (side note: there's a tricky front-door lock).

i From Pl. Zocodover, walk straight down Cuesta Carlos V. Turn to the right and go down a small set of stairs; it's straight ahead. Breakfast included. Towel rental €1. Dorms €14.30. Reception 8:30am-8:30pm.

OASIS BACKPACKER'S HOSTEL TOLEDO $

C. de las Cadenas, 5   ☎925 22 76 50

Oasis doesn't slack despite being one of the only traditional hostel options in town. Part of a nationwide brand, it has everything you might need for rent/sale (spontaneous neck pillow? check). Beds and bathrooms are clean and comfy, though be careful if you're on the bottom bunk, as the top is lower than most. The real gem is the rooftop with patio seating and views that span the entire town and beyond. Go to the free breakfast of toast, butter, jam, coffee, and tea in the morning to find some friends who might be down for supermarket sangria at night. The kitchen is just a microwave and a hot plate, but the seating and air-conditioned views of the next-door bell tower might inspire culinary creativity.

i From Pl. Zocodover, go down C. de Comercio and take the 1st right onto C. Nueva. Turn left at the end, and it will be on your right. Breakfast included. Dorms €15-20; private doubles €50-60. Reception 9am-11:30pm but on call 24hr.

spain

surprising who's who of religious painters; its incredible collection of significant art includes works by Titian, Rafael, Goya, Caravaggio, and, most significantly, hometown boy El Greco's The Disrobing of Christ.

Though a bit pricy at €8, the included audio tour lasts about 1hr. and should be used as much as possible (particularly for the descriptions of the murals in the cloister for bonus lives of saints). Religious services at 9am, 10:30am, and 5:30pm may limit access to some parts of the building, but tourists are welcome to participate in the latter two liturgies. If you want just a peek inside, there's an entrance for worshippers on the opposite side from the main entrance; being quiet and respectful can pay off in a limited view of the interior.

i €8, with tower access €11. Open M-Sa 10am-6:30pm, Su 2-6:30pm.

MIRADOR DEL VALLE

Ctra. Cirvuncalación

Take advantage of those crazy Toledan hills by disobeying your instinct and walking up them. It's leg day in Spain, but for a good cause; the best lookout point to see the whole valley is directly between the two historic bridges—Puente de Alcántara and Puente de San Martín. Pick your uphill poison and walk across either one, then head toward the other. The 190m long Alcántara is the more picturesque (get that Instagram shot), and pieces of it have stood for more than 2,000 years, fulfilling Roman Emperor Trajan's inscription that "I have built a bridge that will last forever." The hike takes you alongside a road, so you could also take a taxi (€6) or the hop-on hop-off bus (but where's the fun and dirt-cheapness in that?). The whole loop takes about 90min.; bring plenty of water and a will of steel.

i Halfway point between Alcantara Bridge and San Martín Bridge on the opposite side of the river from the city. Free. Open 24hr.

MUSEO DEL EJÉRCITO/ALCÁZAR DE TOLEDO
C. Unión ☎925 23 88 00 www.museo.ejercito.es

You can't miss the huge alcázar (castle) rising above the entire city from right beside the main plaza. And you think you might know what's inside already—boring stones, boring carvings, and boring dead kings. Wrong! Coming off a 2010 reconstruction, the gigantic castle is home to both the public library and a collection of various museums that take you through the entire military history of Spain, both chronologically and thematically (flags, uniforms, weaponry, etc). The towering front atrium houses ruins dating from the Bronze Age (around 1200 BCE) all the way through the Romans, Visigoths, Moors, and Catholics. After three fires and two sieges, not much of the original fortress of Alfonso X exists, but the recreated chapel, patio, and terraces offer an unbeatable view of the entire town. The walkthrough of Spain's history offers the evolution of Spanish military style, hilarious film reenactments of important conflicts, and the fact that Spain once invaded Vietnam in the 19th century (who knew?).

i €5, with audio tour €8, EU students and under 18 free. Free for everyone on Su. Open M-Tu 10am-5pm, Th-Su 10am-5pm.

FOOD

🏛 EL RESTAURANTE CRISTAL DE LA LUZ $$
C. El Cristo de la Luz, 13 ☎622 54 12 97

Representing one of the three religions of Toledo's past, Cristal de la Luz is located right across from the remains of the mosque of the same name. While we assume the mosque came first, you wouldn't know it from the feet-thick walls, stone stairs, traditional terrace, or real-article ruins of the Roman city gate right under the main dining room. The Syrian owners are happy to give a brief tour along with delicious plates of falafel and cucumber cream (€4) and large salads (€6). The dining room is a mix of traditional and whimsical—sketches and photos give it the feel of unattainably authentic dorm decor. Also, the kitchen is open throughout the day—it's a perfect remedy for the siesta blues.

i Across the street from the Cristo de la Luz Mosque. Dishes €3-7. Menú del día €10. Open M-Th 12:30pm-midnight, F-Su 12:30pm-2am.

LIZARRAN $
C. de Toledo, 3 ☎925 25 71 84 www.lizarran.es

Yes, you can find Lizarran in 15 countries, but don't overlook this budget tapas option just because it's "too mainstream." Located right next to Pl. Zocodover, Lizarran is a bar/restaurant/watering hole where budget-traveler dreams come true. It's super international-user-friendly—unlike quite a few Spanish bars (ahem)—so the staff will be happy to explain how it works. But if you want to walk in like an expert, here's the rundown: The bar offers buffet-style tapas from €1.40-1.90. You serve yourself and, at the end of the feeding frenzy, the server will count up the toothpicks from each of your sizeable open-faced portions ranging from curry chicken to salmon and cream cheese (€1.90). They're not your typical Toledan tapas, but they're not at typical Toledan prices either.

i Pintxos €1.40-1.90. Raciones €6.90. Beer €1.50. Open daily 10:30am-midnight.

RESTAURANTE PALACIOS
C. Alfonso X El Sabio, 5   **$**

☎925 21 59 72

If all the €12 average menús del día are getting you down, Restaurante Palacios has the perfect remedy. Go to Palacios and get an appetizer, entree, drink, bread, and dessert all for €7. Its location in the university neighborhood means the cooks are familiar with the plight of the starving student. Sure, it's not five-star cuisine, but it offers tasty traditional Toledan stews and meats alongside tourist crowd-pleasers, all right next to some of the major sites (which means less hill-climbing for you!). The walls are covered with photos. "Celebrities?" you might think. Nope, just visitors so in love with the place that they send in memorial photos; we can only aspire to such greatness. In traditional surroundings with super-quick turnover time, Palacios is the place for a filling midday munch.

i *From Iglesia de Los Jesuitas, walk 100m north on C. Alfonso X El Sabio. It's on your left. Menú del día €7. Open daily noon-11pm.*

NIGHTLIFE

DRAGOS
C. Sillerías, 11   ☎92 5 67 22 23

By day this innocuous corner bar serves up delicious homemade menús del día (€12); by night, Dragos becomes the savior of Toledo's lagging nightlife and a crossroads of international students and Toledan youth. While the town isn't known for its vibrant club scene (it might have peaked in the 14th century), Dragos provides a flow of cheap alcohol along with plenty of space on the street or upstairs to make some friends and get wasted with said friends. The owner Jesús makes sure everyone is having a good time with a huge smile and some unexpectedly delicious (and deliciously cheap) shots.

i *1 block down C. Sillería from Pl. Zocodover. Huge cups of wine €2. Cocktails €3-6. Shots €1-2. Open daily 8:30am-6pm and 9pm-3am.*

LA NUIT CASCO HISTÓRICO AND LA NUIT TERRAZA
Plaza Corral de la Campana/El Recinto Ferial de la Peraleda   ☎699 71 95 49

One of the few genuine-article clubs in Toledo, La Nuit in the Casco Histórico shows up the fancy Madrid equivalents with free entry and relatively cheap drink prices. If you get lucky, you might see the Toledo soccer team—and really anyone in town with some measure of cool. Locals tend to dress their best for a night out; though you don't need to match their prom-dress-and-heels style, try to upgrade those sneakers and shorts a bit. An additional option for summer weekends: a 7min. drive outside the city center, hundreds of people gather in the Peraleda parking lots in the Spanish equivalent of a tailgate, with a post-pregame sport of heading to an ambiguously Asian-decorated open-air club. The party starts at 2am and goes late; getting a drink can be as difficult as climbing those Toledan hills, so make some Spanish friends quickly and enjoy a long night of reggaeton and Latin electronic.

i *Shots €1-1.50. Casco Histórico location open in summer W 11pm-6am, Th-Sa midnight-6am; in winter W-Th 11pm-4am, F-Sa 11pm-6am. Terraza location open in summer F-Sa 11pm-6am.*

ESSENTIALS

Practicalities

- **TOURIST OFFICES:** The most centrally located office is right on the main square, Pl. Zocodover, in the columned walkway area and marked with an "i." (Pl. Zocodover, 6. ☎92 526 76 70.) It can get overwhelmed easily, however. The other regional office is at the Puerta de Bisagra (Puerto de Merchán. ☎925 21 10 05.) There's also a municipal office at the train station. (Paseo de la Rosa. ☎925 23 91 21. Open daily 9:30am-3pm.) Take advantage of the maps at these locations and at your hostel; Toledo can be difficult to navigate, and the illustrations of major landmarks can be more helpful than Google Maps.

- **ATMS:** There are a large number of ATMs in the streets surrounding Pl. Zocodover.
- **POST OFFICES:** The main post office is at C. de la Plata, 1. (☎92 528 44 37. Open M-F 8:30am-8:30pm, Sa 9:30am-1pm.)

Emergency

- **EMERGENCY NUMBERS:** General emergencies ☎112. Local police ☎092. National police ☎091.
- **POLICE:** Call ☎925 28 85 00 for non-emergency local police inquiries. Call ☎925 33 05 00 for non-emergency national police inquiries.
- **HOSPITALS:** The closest hospital is Hospital Virgen de la Salud. (Av. de Barber, 30. ☎925 26 92 00.)

Getting There

The beautiful Moorish-style train station is at Paseo de la Rosa and is almost a tourist attraction in itself. (☎902 43 23 43. Open M-F 6am-10:30pm, Sa-Su 8am-10:30pm.) Trains arrive and depart from Toledo for Madrid nearly once every hour from the Estación del AVE starting after 6:30am on weekdays. Check the train schedule at www.renfe.com for changes in the late afternoon and on weekends. Buses 5 and 6 access the AVE train station from Pl. Zocodover (€1.40).

Buses to and from Madrid leave every 30min. from the Estación del Buses. (Av. Castilla La Mancha. ☎925 33 04 40.) Public buses 5 and 12 go to and from the bus station and Pl. Zocodover (€1.40), or you can walk and take the escalators up to the center (15-20min.). Taxis are €4.50.

Getting Around

Walking is the fastest option for most destinations within the center, given the narrow streets and limited bus access. The best places to get taxis are at the stands at Pl. Zocodover, Puerta de Bisagra, and the bus and train stations. Otherwise you can call Radiotaxi (☎925 25 50 50 or ☎925 22 70 70) or Servitaxi (☎925 66 50 60).

valencia

Valencia is a town that's as intensely proud of its history as it is proud of its present. Situated near the Turia River and on the coast of the Mediterranean Sea, its beaches are warm and its parks are warmer—unless you're in the shade. The former riverbed, now the Jardines del Turia (Turia Gardens), runs down the middle of the city, a lovely biking and reading spot. Valencia also has the biggest aquarium in Europe, the Oceanogràfic, which, even though it might cost an arm and a leg, is worth a see. And then of course there are the beaches: even though it's further north than Malaga, Valencia's soft sand and cool water are the envy of all. So pack some flip-flops for the beach and some Crocs for the clubs (show those cats your dominance). Valencia awaits.

SIGHTS

▨ CATEDRAL DE VALENCIA
Pl. de l'Almoina

According to this church, they have the Holy Grail. Yeah, that Holy Grail. The one from Monty Python. Unfortunately, they haven't let anyone test it to see if that's true. And there are about a dozen churches throughout the world that

get a room!

RED NEST $
C. de la Pau, 36   ☎963 42 71 68

A gem of a hostel: comfortable, modern, and with a kickass social scene to boot. Full of an eclectic mix of people (due in part to its popularity), Red Nest has something for everyone. Its graffiti-emblazoned stairway takes you up to a bar that blares Spanish party music all afternoon and into the night. Its rooms have reliable (praise the lord) air-conditioning as well as comfortable beds. The nightly pub crawl, heading either to the beach clubs or the city clubs, is a pretty good bang for your buck. If you feel like staying in, though, there's an in-house bar (beer €2; cocktails €4). The front desk offers tours and classes, and you can entertain yourself on the roof deck, in the computer room, or in the kitchen. Central and cheap, this is a must-stay during your time in Valencia.

i At the opposite end of Pl. de la Reina, take a left and follow the street down several blocks. Red Nest will be on your right. Free Wi-Fi. Lockers available. Linens included. Towels included. Female-only rooms available. Guests over 35 must stay in private rooms. 12-bed dorms €16; 6-bed €17; 4-bed €20. Key deposit €1. Reception 24hr.

HOME BACKPACKERS HOSTEL $
Pl. de Vicent Iborra   ☎963 91 37 97

"Honey! I'm Home (Backpackers Hostel)!" [sitcom laughter] A good option slightly more off the beaten path, Home Backpackers Hostel has sparse accommodations and a deceptively big upstairs bar/game room. The large communal bathrooms on each floor are well maintained, and, though the rooms don't have air-conditioning, they do have fans and a nice Valencian night breeze coming through the window (perfect for drying your underwear). The upstairs kitchen gets lively and social around lunchtime and dinnertime, and if you're there around 7pm you just might get some free sangria. Wi-Fi is free but nosy; when it asks you to connect your Facebook account to the Wi-Fi, just select "no social account" and put in a valid but old email address. When you're ready to be more social, the front desk offers tours, classes, and a nightly pub crawl.

i Head away from the Jardines del Turia on C. Guillem de Castro, then take a left onto C. del Pintor Zareña. It'll be all the way at the end, on the left. Locker deposit €2. Linens included. Credit cards theoretically accepted, but machine sometimes broken. "Superior" 12-bed dorms €16.50; "superior" 10-bed €17; 8-bed €15; 6-bed €18. Reception 24hr., but when it's really late (or really early) you've gotta ring the bell.

PURPLE NEST $
Pl. de Tetuán, 5   ☎963 53 25 61

Maybe we're cheating by including two Nest hostels, but the truth is, if you're looking for cheap, comfortable, and central hostels with plenty of amenities, these take the cake. Purple Nest is the newer and less central of the two but provides the same experience—the same tours and pub crawl, the same outdoor terrace and indoor bar—only, well, purpler. If forced to pick between Red Nest and Purple, pick Red, just because it's the original, and, as we learned from the remake of Planet of the Apes, the original is usually better. Red Nest fills up faster, though, so this might be an easier call for last-minute bookers.

i Right off Pont del Real from the Jardines del Turia. Free Wi-Fi. Lockers available. Linens included. A/C. Reception 24hr.; just ring the bell or bang on the glass door.

spain

claim to have the Holy Grail. But this might be the real one—as we know, Jesus spent a ton of time in Valencia because of its awesome nightlife. Valenciavalencia.com, a truly unimpeachable source, says that to doubt this as the location of the Holy Grail is an "uninformed reaction." Well, color us uninformed. If you want something more authentic, head up the tower on the Pl. de la Reina side for some of the best views of Valencia.

i Also accessible from the top of Pl. de la Reina. €6, tower only €2. Open daily 8am-8pm.

PLAYA MALVARROSA

Cool people come to Valencia to hit the beach, and don't you want to do what the cool people are doing? Like your friends who jump off a bridge in your mother's tired hypothetical, you're going to want to follow the crowd. And we do mean crowd—this beach is an ocean of umbrellas, sunbathers, paddleball players, and swimmers. In short, it's a beach. Do you really need our 57 years of wisdom on this one? Don't walk on sand barefoot. It gets hot. Now close the book and go enjoy the shore. There are good places to eat and party along the beach that make it worth the walk up and down.

i Several buses, like the 32 and 34, go to the seaside from the center of the city. Public toilets and showers available.

JARDINES DEL TURIA/CIUDAD DE LAS ARTES Y CIENCIAS

Ever seen a river and thought, "Wow, I wish that river weren't here?" Well, apparently the government of Spain decided that, after the Turia River devastatingly flooded Valencia in 1957, its flooding days were permanently over and diverted it. Its former location is now a lovely, modern park that spans the length of the city. There are fountains, ponds, sports parks, jungle gyms, forested areas, and more. At the top of the park is the Valencia Zoo. At the end is the City of Arts and Sciences, where you can go to the biggest aquarium in Europe, the Oceanogràfic, the Science Museum, or the Hemisfèric, the IMAX theater. Unfortunately, they're expensive and not especially worth the admission fee (except perhaps the aquarium, which is—of course—also the most expensive). It's worth renting a bike around Torres de Serranos (€5 or so) and biking up and down the park.

i The Jardines del Turia is the big green park through the top of the old city. The City of Arts and Sciences is at the end near the water. Hemisfèric €8.80. Science Museum €8. Oceanogràfic €28.50. Combined admission €37. Student discounts available. Jardines del Turia open 24hr., but best explored during the daytime. Science Museum open in summer daily 10am-9pm; in fall and spring daily 10am-7pm; in winter M-Th 10am-6pm, F-Su 10am-7pm. Oceanogràfic open daily in high season 10am-1am; in mid-season 10am-8pm; in low season 10am-6pm.

FOOD

◾ MERCAT CENTRAL $
Pl. de la Ciutat de Bruges ☎963 82 91 00

As much as it is a sight as it is a food option, the Mercat Central is an expansive open market in what looks like a modernist train station designed in 1914. It has stalls selling all kinds of food—fruits and vegetables, meats and cheeses, breads and pastries, and seafood. Because the food is so fresh and the market is less than air-conditioned, the market opens and closes early. Those looking for the best seafood would do well to arrive early, or you'll only be left with the seafood the locals didn't want and a smell like a dirty aquarium. Mercat Central is a good option if you've been blowing your money on too many paellas and menús del día, because you can get a hearty meal to cook back at your hostel or apartment for less than €8, including €0.55 for a loaf of just-cooked bread, €0.20 for an apple, and €3 for some really fancy jamón ibérico.

As the name might suggest, this bad boy is centrally located, so there's no excuse not to go eat here once, twice, or a dozen times. Try not to get too mesmerized by the hanging ham legs or the full squids on the stalls. If you look at them too long, you'll turn into a squid yourself. There's not a huge amount of English spoken, but lots of pointing and gesturing will usually get the job done. Just don't do what so many tourists do here and shout, "PEPPER! PEPPER—THAT PEPPER!" The stall worker's problem is not that you're speaking too quietly. Her problem is that you didn't learn the language before coming.

i Open M-Sa 7am-3pm.

TABERNA EL OLIVO $$

C. del Pintor Fillol, 1   ☎963 91 70 87

This delicious restaurant is called "the Olive Tavern" because at night they drag barrels, wooden tables, and chairs out under the olive tree in the square out front. The cool Valencia night breeze and atmosphere is matched only by the food: platters of assorted meats and cheeses complement must-try Valencian tomato dishes (€7) served on wooden plates. Throw in a great selection of beers and wines, and then, predictably, a plate of olives for each table. Newton may have discovered gravity sitting under an apple tree, but dinner under an olive tree is much tastier.

i Head straight down C. del Pare d'Orfens from C. de la Blanqueria, which runs along the Jardines del Turia. It's to the right of the main gate. Drinks €2-5. Tapas €6.50-8.50. Open daily noon-1am.

CERVEZERIA 100 MONTADITOS $

Pl. de la Reina   ☎963 91 92 27

This fast-food chain has over 350 stores in Spain and even more worldwide, but it's worth a mention because it's cheap and tasty, and that's what we do here at Let's Go. On Wednesdays, 100 Montaditos has €1 bocadito (tiny sandwich) night, and people turn out by the droves. There are a couple locations around Valencia, and they're always worth it, if only to grab a beer and get it in a hilarious little paper Coca-Cola cup to go. The sandwiches aren't big, so get three or four to try them all. Even the salads are surprisingly good for a fast-food chain.

i On the right, near McDonald's, when you're looking toward the cathedral. There are many locations around Valencia, though. Bocaditos €1.50-2, W €1. Drinks €2-4. Other menu items €1-5. Open M-F 9:30am-midnight.

TINTO FINO ULTRAMARINO $$$

C. de la Corretgeria, 38   ☎963 15 45 99 www.tintofinoultramarino.com

We hope you're not one of those people who says, "I'm just not ready for a relationship right now," because this is one of those restaurants where you just have to fall in love. Tinto Fino Ultramarino may be on the pricier side, but its dishes are surprisingly filling and its €12 bottles of local Valencian wine taste like they should be twice the price. Make sure to call ahead for a reservation, because it gets busy around prime romantic dinnertime. It also has a cool sliding wall that opens onto the bathroom, so what's not to fall in love with?

i Off the upper left side of Pl. de la Reina. Just follow that road, then take a left at the fork. Tapas €4.50-9.50; full plates €11.50. Glasses of wine €2.50-3; bottles €12. Open daily 1:30-4pm and 7pm-midnight.

NIGHTLIFE

▩ MYA CLUB

Av. Autopista Saler, 5   ☎695 67 68 67

Down near the architecturally stunning City of Arts and Sciences, Mya Club is the rare nightclub that looks like something you would stop by if you were going on an architecture tour of the city. The outside seems to be a good indication of what's going on inside, with four different club rooms downstairs, each playing different kinds of music. The upstairs open-air area is pink and palm-filled and a great place to gasp for air before diving back into one of the hardest-partying

For being in a country that's not doing super hot economically, Valencia sure likes to burn money. Not literal money: they just enjoy spending a ton on wood and sculptures and effigies and then burn those. From March 15 to March 19 every year, millions of tourists and locals swarm the city carousing and drinking, which, this close to fire, seems like a safety hazard.

Originating from the wooden boards carpenters would burn to celebrate the end of winter, this festival pays homage to San José. (If you were a saint, wouldn't you want people to pay tribute to you by burning stuff? We know we would.) The ninots, or wooden sculptures, are often built as satirical takes on well-known Spanish figures. They may be cruel, but they are also ash before too long, so people getting lampooned don't have to worry too much.

Every day at 8am during the festival, bands march through the street with fireworks, and at 2pm firecrackers are set off at Pl. del Ayuntamiento, in what is called La Mascleta, or the Concert of the Gunpowder. Neighborhoods compete for the best and loudest display—it's basically a pyrotechnic belching contest.

There's too much going on to describe it all here—music, dancing, costumes, drinking, partying, traditional culture, and good food. It's a uniquely Valencian festival that is a must-see for pyromaniacs and non-pyromaniacs alike.

---

clubs in Valencia. Don't expect it to get raucous until 3 at the earliest, and stay until 7. The joint is quite expensive, but that's to be expected; besides, clever partygoers find a club promoter or go on a hostel pub crawl to bypass the cover charge.

i *Down near the Ciudad de las Artes y Ciencias. It looks kind of like a big white ribcage. It'll be lit up pink and blaring music. Cover €10. Cocktails €11. Open way past your bedtime.*

FOX CONGO

C. dels Cavallers, 35 ☎617 70 74 22

Part club, part bar, Fox Congo is lit with bright neon colors and has a stage/ledge area on one side for those of you who like dancing and getting extra attention while doing it. The rest of the bar/club is dancy too, so bust out some moves and hold your drink tight. It's centrally located and is a good middle ground between the cheap bar where you drink a ton and the expensive club where you dance a ton. The DJ here has apparently taken it upon himself to get the biggest array of music possible and mash it into one frantic mix. We ain't complaining, though. The bar takes a while to get you your drinks, so plan ahead.

i *A straight shot from Pl. de la Virgen. Leave the square in the direction of the Palau de la Generalitat. No cover. Beers €5. Cocktails €5-8. Open daily 7pm-3:30am.*

UNIC DAILY GOODNESS

Pl. Sant Jaume, 1 ☎963 92 05 70 www.facebook.com/unicdailygoodness

This is another bar that keeps things dancy as all hell. Unic's big windows glint invitingly and pour red light out on the Northern Europeans smoking outdoors. There's a lounge area up top and a dance floor on the bottom. The bar likes to mix it up and has a different theme night every night, announced on its hyperactive Facebook page. The name reads like a combination kale/tofu smoothie bar, but it's instead just cocktails, beer, and dancing. Which are good for you too, just not in the same "healthy" way.

i *Keep heading away from Pl. de la Reina, past Fox Congo. It's a couple blocks up. Beer €4. Cocktails €5-7. Open daily 6pm-3:30am.*

ESSENTIALS
Practicalities

- **TOURIST OFFICES:** The **municipal tourist office** (www.turisvalencia.es) has several branches; the biggest is in the Pl. Reina (Pl. Reina, 19 ☎96 315 39 31. Facing the cathedral, on the right side of the plaza. Open M-Sa 9am-7pm, Su 10am-2pm), but there are also branches in the Pl. Ayuntamiento (☎96 352 49 08. Open M-Sa 9am-7pm, Su 10am-2pm), the beach (Paseo de Neptuno, 2 ☎96 355 58 99. Opposite the Hotel Neptuno. Open during Formula One (mid-June) M-F 10am-7pm, Sa-Su 10am-6pm; after Formula One to 1st week of Sept M-Sa 10am-5pm, Su 10am-2pm), at the Joaquín Sorolla train station (C. San Vicente, 171 ☎96 380 36 23. Free shuttle bus from Estación del Norte. Open M-F 9am-8pm, Sa-Su 10am-6pm), and on the arrivals floor at the airport (☎96 153 02 29. Open July-Sept M-F 8:30am-9:30pm, Sa-Su 9:30am-9:30pm; Nov-Feb M-F 8:30am-8:30pm, Sa 9:30am-5:30pm, Su 9:30am-2:30pm; Mar-Oct M-F 8:30am-8:30pm, Sa-Su 9:30am-5:30pm). All municipal tourist offices sell the **Valencia Tourist Card,** which entitles the bearer to free public transportation and discounts on tourist attractions (☎90 070 18 18 www.valenciatouristcard.com. Can also be purchased at 24hr. vending machine on arrivals floor of airport. 24hr. €15, 48hr. €20, 72hr. €25) and can help book accommodations, tours, and visits to popular attractions like the Ciutat de les Arts i les Ciències. The **regional tourist office** (C. Paz, 48 ☎96 398 64 22 www.comunitatvalenciana.com. From Pl. Reina, on the side opposite the cathedral while facing it, turn right onto C. Paz. Open M-F 9am-8pm, Sa 10am-8pm, Su 10am-2pm) has more limited services but provides information about the entire region of Valencia.

- **CURRENCY EXCHANGE: BBVA.** (Pl. Ayuntamiento, 9 ☎96 388 03 50 www.bbva.com. Diagonally across the Pl. Ayuntamiento from the Ayuntamiento. Open M-F 8:30am-2:15pm.)

- **LUGGAGE STORAGE:** Luggage storage is available at both the Estación del Norte and the Estación de Joaquín Sorolla train stations (24hr. €3-5, depending on size. Estación del Norte 8am-9pm, Estación de Joaquín Sorolla 9am-9pm) and at the bus station (☎96 346 62 66. 24hr. €3-4, depending on size. Open 24hr.).

- **INTERNET ACCESS:** Free Wi-Fi is available in public places denoted on the tourist office map with a Wi-Fi symbol, including the Jardines del Real and the Jardines del Turia near the Palau de la Música. Free Wi-Fi and free computers with internet access are also available at the **Biblioteca Pública de Valencia Central.** (C. Hospital, 13 ☎96 256 41 30 www.portales.gva.es/bpv. From Pl. Reina, walk away from cathedral on C. San Vicente Mártir, then turn right onto C. Garrigues, which will turn into C. Hospital. Open M-F 9am-2pm and 5-8:30pm.)

- **POST OFFICE:** Valencia's main post office is so beautiful it's worth checking out even if you're all set with stamps. (Pl. Ayuntamiento, 24 ☎96 351 23 70 www.correos.es. Across the plaza from the Ayuntamiento. Open M-F 8:30am-8:30pm, Sa 9:30am-2pm.)

- **POSTAL CODE:** 46002

Emergency

- **EMERGENCY NUMBERS:** ☎112

- **POLICE:** Municipal Police (Av. Cid, 37 ☎092. M: Av. del Cid.)

- **PHARMACY:** **Late-night pharmacies** rotate by night—check listings in local paper *Levante* (€1.10) or the *farmacias de guardia* schedule, posted outside any pharmacy around the Pl. Reina and Pl. Virgen.

- **HOSPITAL/MEDICAL SERVICES: Hospital General Universitari.** (Av. Tres Cruces, 2 ☎96 197 20 00. Bus #3.)

valencia

Getting There

By Bus

Buses arrive at the bus station across the riverbed. (Av. Menéndez Pidal, 13 ☎96 346 62 66. Bus #8 runs between the bus station and the Pl. Reina and the Pl. Ayuntamiento. Or, from Pl. Virgen, with cathedral behind you, turn left onto C. Caballeros and continue through Pl. Tossal as it becomes C. Quart, then turn right at the towers onto C. Guillem de Castro, cross the Puente de las Artes, and turn left onto Av. Menéndez Pidal.) **ALSA** (☎90 242 22 42 www.alsa.es) runs buses from: Alicante (€20. 2½-5½hr.; M-F 23 per day 6:30am-4:30am, Sa 22 per day 7am-4:30am, Su 23 per day 6:30am-4:30am); Barcelona (€27-33. 4-4½hr.; M-F 9 per day 7am-1am, Sa 22 per day 7am-4:30am, Su 23 per day 6:30am-4:30am); and Málaga (€55. 9½-11½hr.; 4 per day 8am-1am). **Auto-Res,** a subsidiary of Avanza Group (☎90 202 00 52 www.avanzabus. com) provides service from Madrid. (€28-35. 4-4½hr.; M-F 14 per day 7am-1am, Sa 13 per day 7am-1am, Su 13 per day 8am-1am.)

By Train

Valencia has two train stations: the beautiful **Estación del Norte,** which receives regular domestic trains (C. Xàtiva, 24 ☎90 243 23 43. At intersection of C. Marqués de Sotelo and C. Xàtiva. Ticket windows open daily 8:45am-10:10pm) and the **Estación de Joaquín Sorolla,** which receives high-speed and international trains. (C. San Vicente Mártir, 171 ☎90 243 23 43. Shuttle bus from Estación del Norte. Ticket windows open daily 7am-10pm.) Free shuttle buses run between the two stations. **RENFE** (☎90 232 03 20 www. renfe.es) runs trains to the Estación del Norte from: Alicante (€19-27. 2hr.; M-F 8 per day 7:21am-7:44pm, Sa 6 per day 7:21am-6:45pm, Su 7 per day 8:01am-7:44pm); Barcelona (€29-41. 3-5hr.; M-F 9 per day 8am-9:30am, Sa-Su 8 per day 8:30am-9:30pm); Granada (€51-53. 6¾-7½hr.; M at 8:55am and 10:15pm, Tu-W 10:15pm, Th at 8:55am and 10:15pm, F 10:15pm, Sa at 8:55am and 10:15pm, Su 10:15pm); and Madrid (€79. 7hr.; daily 7:30am). High-speed trains run to the Estación de Joaquín Sorolla from: Barcelona (€27-45. 3hr.; M-F 7 per day 7am-8:30am, Sa 6 per day 7am-6pm, Su 5 per day 10am-8:30pm); Madrid (€32-80. 1½-2hr.; M-F 17 per day 7:10am-9:10am, Sa 11 per day 8:40am-9:10pm, Su 14 per day 8:40am-9:10pm); and Sevilla (€42-104. 4½hr.; M-F 3 per day 8:45am-5:22pm, Sa 8:45 am, Su 3 per day 8:45am-5:22pm).

By Plane

Flights to the Valencia area land in the **Aeropuerto de Valencia,** also known locally as the Aeropuerto de Manises (VLC; ☎91 321 10 00 www.aena.es), 8km. from the city. Getting between the airport and the city center is fairly straightforward: city bus #150 runs between the airport and the bus station (€1.35. 45min.; to Valencia M-F every 15min. 5:25am-11:10pm, Sa every 20min. 5:20am-11:10pm, Su and holidays every 20min. 6:25am-11:10pm; to airport M-F every 15min. 5:45am-11:50pm, Sa every 20min. 5:20am-11:40pm, Su and holidays every 20min. 6:25am-11:45pm) and Metro lines #3 and 5 go between the airport and C. Xàtiva, near the train station. A taxi from the airport to the city center will a bit faster and a lot pricier.

By Ferry

Trasmediterránea offers ferry service to Valencia from Palma de Mallorca, Mahón, and Ibiza. (Muelle de Poniente ☎90 245 46 45 www.trasmediterranea.es. Bus #4 from Pl. Ayuntamiento or #1 or #2 from the bus station.) Reserve through a travel agency or accept the inconvenience—and risk of a "Sold Out" sign—of buying tickets at the port of departure.

spain

zaragoza

At first glance, it might seem like Zaragoza is a boring wasteland from which you should flee immediately. But after spending a couple days there, you'll see that there are some things to do in the city. You can go to Catedral-Basílica de Nuestra Señora del Pilar de Zaragoza, see the river, and... did we mention the cathedral? Is Zaragoza particularly special compared to the array of incredible cities there are to see in Spain? No. But do we want to offend the fine people of Zaragoza for saying their city's boring? Also no. (And the fine people of Zaragoza are legion: it's the fifth-biggest city in Spain, which makes you wonder—what are the other cities doing? Step up your game, people. If you're getting beaten by Zaragoza, you know something's wrong.) So strap in, we're going to Zaragoza. Or don't strap in. We're not going very fast, so you should be fine.

SIGHTS

🏛 CATEDRAL-BASÍLICA DE NUESTRA SEÑORA DEL PILAR DE ZARAGOZA

Pl. del Pilar ☎976 39 74 97

How and why was this cathedral built? Legend has it that St. James was preaching in Spain in the '40s (the 1040s) when the Virgin Mary appeared to him next to the Ebro River (that's right, she was a ghost—and could therefore go anywhere—and she chose Zaragoza of all places) and told him to build a cathedral in her honor. To sweeten the pot, she gave him a column of jasper and a small wooden statue of herself. (Apparently the Virgin Mary got pretty self-absorbed as a ghost.) Long story short, there's now a cathedral with a cool tower so you can look over Zaragoza, a little golden bowl you can bend and kiss (no tongue please), and even some bombs that were dropped on the cathedral in the 20th century. It's important that you remember to look at the bombs and kiss the bowl, not the other way around. Who knows if they're still live.

i It's the big cathedral in the big square. Just follow the sound of angels singing. Wear something appropriate. Free, but there are numerous donation boxes around the church. Open M-Sa 7am-8:30pm, Su 7am-9:30pm.

ALJAFERIA

C. de los Diputados ☎976 28 96 83

Medieval Muslims loved making fortresses in Spain almost as much as subsequent Christian royalty loved reconquering and repurposing them. Such is true for this castle, built at the end of the 11th century and now used as the regional parliament of Aragon. Walking around the Aljaferia is a romp through classic Spanish/Islamic architecture and offers an education about the past and present of Aragon. Less educationally, it's just a cool castle and a nice stroll for an hour or so. Plus, St. Elizabeth of Portugal was born here. With all the romantic architecture, she was probably conceived here too.

i From Pl. Europa, take C. de los Diputados as it curves around to the front of the castle. Free information booklets available in English, Spanish, German, French, and many other languages. €5, free on Su. Open daily 10am-2pm and 4:30-8:30pm.

FOOD

🍽 CAFE BOTANICO $

Santiago, 5 ☎976 29 60 48

They say you can't have your cake and eat it too. We say that's the only way to eat cake. If you don't have the cake, whose cake are you eating? Are you stealing cake? Let's Go urges our readers to only eat cake that you have. We also urge our readers to go to Cafe Botanico, a little coffee and cake shop decorated like a garden. It's small and charming, and its wide range of cakes, coffees, and even

ALBERGUE ZARAGOZA HOSTEL $

C. de los Predicadores, 70   ☎976 28 20 43

Like the one ugly guy stuck on a desert island with seven Victoria's Secret models, the Albergue Zaragoza Hostel starts to become attractive because it's really the only option. That's not to say it's bad—the bar downstairs is a cave-like 15th-century palace that has live music and shows many nights. It's a cool feature and helps add to the atmosphere of the place, although 15th-century Zaragoza was not known for its ingenious and beautiful palace design. The beds are comfortable, rooms are roomy, and the air-conditioning works well. The keycard lockers are huge enough to fit a small person if you and your tiny friend want to minimize costs, and the hostel also has a full kitchen with beer and coffee vending machines. That brings us to the showers. Ah, yes, the showers. Seemingly designed by a man afraid of long streams of water, the showers need to run their 8sec. water burst, then turn off fully, before being pushed again. This may not sound like a problem, but why not let the shower user keep up a steady stream of water by pushing the faucet while the previous burst is still going? Maybe we're dwelling too much on the showers, but you have a lot of time to think about the subpar engineering when you're standing in the cold for a moment every 8sec. Other than that, this hostel is totally groovy!

i *From the basilica, it's just about a straight shot along the river to the left. It's the street running parallel to Echegaray y Caballero. Free Wi-Fi. Breakfast included. Lockers available. Linens €3. Towels €1.50. 12-bed dorms €17; 10- and 8-bed €19; 6-bed €20; 4-bed dorms €21. Reception 24hr.*

beers makes it a must-go. If the sugar isn't your style, you can also get toast and jamón serrano. Just remember you can't eat your cake if someone else has it. We're not super sure about the laws in Spain, but we're pretty sure that's frowned upon.

i *Right behind Hotel Pilar Pl. Zaragoza off the main square. Coffee €1.50. Generous cake slices €2-4. Ham and bread €4-6. Open daily 9am-10pm.*

EL BROQUEL $$

C. Broqueleros, 3   ☎628 47 47 38

Out of the way and well-regarded by locals, El Broquel is a cool little place where the bartenders drink wine right alongside the patrons. With one long bar and some scant tables, you can pick the food options right from the glass shelves on the bar. There are croquetas, meat and cheese and bread tapas, and empanadas. There are also some more exotic meats, including crocodile, for those of you from Down Under who want a taste of home. As one would expect from a place where the employees drink too, the wine is even better than the food, and everyone is as friendly as it gets.

i *Follow Av. de César Augusto from Puente de Santiago, take a right on C. San Blas, then take your 1st left. El Broquel's on that small side street. Tapas €1.50-5. Beer and wine €2-6. Open M noon-4pm, Tu-Su noon-4pm and 8pm-midnight.*

spain

NIGHTLIFE

CANTERBURY SALAMERO
Av. de César Augusto, 30 ☎976 21 01 84

This bar is dark and loud, like cave sex with a banshee. To really make sure they're pleasing everyone, the bar plays one music video on the TVs behind the bar and a totally different song on the blaring speakers. This is great because sometimes you need to watch an Adele music video while listening to *autotune voice* Jayyy-sunnn De-ruuuuulllooo. The pints are good, and they even bring some peanuts to your table. Which is good, because peanuts are high in protein. Thanks, George Washington Carver. And thank you, Canterbury Salamero.

i Right off Pl. de Miguel Salamero, above the Casco Viejo. Beer €2. Pints €3.50. Cocktails €4-7. Peanuts free, so eat them to your heart's content.

UMALAS BAR
C. Jussepe Martínez, 7 ☎615 18 56 18

With a trendy lounge area and trendy cages hanging from the ceiling with trendy stuffed crabs in them, Umalas Bar is what happens when a good bar decides to spend all its decoration money on their ceiling. There are surfboards up there, along with a not-small number of colored balls. Besides the expansive bar, there are restrooms that are far nicer than any bar restrooms have any right to be. Seriously, like, go in for 45min. and just bask in their glory. In sum, hit up Umalas Bar for the drinks, the ceiling, and, most of all, the bowel-based comfort.

i Take C. de Alfonso I up from Pl. del Pilar, then take a left onto C. Jussepe Martínez. Pints €4. Gin and tonic €5. Open M-W 4pm-1:30am, Th-Sa 4pm-4:30am, Su 4-10pm.

ESSENTIALS

Practicalities

- **TOURIST OFFICES:** The main tourist office has maps, pamphlets, and booklets that are mostly in Spanish but sometimes in English. The staff can help you in either language. It's right across from the cathedral in Pl. del Pilar. (☎902 14 20 08 or ☎976 20 12 00 turismo@zaragoza.es Open daily 8am-8pm.)

- **LUGGAGE STORAGE:** Available at Zaragoza-Delicias train station.

- **POST OFFICES:** There's one on Paseo Independencia, right up from el Corte Inglés. (Paseo Independencia, 33. ☎976 23 68 68 Open M-F 8:30am-8:30pm, Sa 9:30am-1pm.)

Emergency

- **EMERGENCY NUMBERS:** General emergencies ☎112. Ambulance ☎061.

- **HOSPITALS:** Hospital Clínico Universitario Lozano Blesa. (Av. San Juan Bosco, 15. ☎976 76 57 00)

Getting There

Major international carriers serve Zaragoza Airport, 16km outside of Zaragoza. (Ctra. Aeropuerto. ☎976 71 23 00) Taxis are your best shot to get to and from the airport. Zaragoza-Delicias is a pretty expansive train station that is both a midway point for trains going through and a destination in and of itself. (C. Rioja, 33. ☎902 43 23 43. Open 24hr.) Trains arrive from Barcelona (€28) and Madrid (€26). From the station, bus 34 will bring you to the center of Zaragoza. Intercity buses arrive at Estación de Autobuses de Zaragoza. (Av. de Navarra, 80. ☎976 70 05 99. Open 24hr.) Buses go anywhere you might want to go, including Barcelona (€15) and Madrid (€17). Local buses 51, 129, and 142 get you from the bus station to the center of Zaragoza.

zaragoza

salamanca

Salamanca is called "La Dorada" or the "Golden City" because the stone used in practically all its buildings reflects the light of the sun. Strolling through illuminated streets, you casually pass by the nearly 800-year-old university where crowds frantically search for a lucky frog carving in the building's facade (Googling its location doesn't count toward the good karma). Salamanca is also Spain's capital of Spanish-language education, so international students abound, funding its profuse collection of dive bars and late night clubs. Wander along the river's picturesque Roman bridge or climb the twin towers of the Scala Coeli for an unforgettable view of the golden sprawl.

SIGHTS

CATEDRAL NUEVA Y VIEJA
Pl. de Anaya   ☎923 21 74 76 http://catedralsalamanca.org

Both Salamanca's Old Cathedral and New Cathedral are, in reality, pretty darn old—the 12th century and the 16th century, respectively. Enter the bi-cathedral complex at Puerta de Ramos, taking note of the two tombs on either side. Admission comes with a free audio tour, but it's really monotonous and way too detailed, so here are some highlights. The 17th-century capilla of Our Lady of Truth (#4) contains a statue of the Virgin Mary that is said to have nodded to resolve a dispute between a Jew and a Christian—not sure Mary was totally unbiased in that one. At #6, the crucified image of Jesus has real hair and a real loincloth (hopefully not pre-used). #18 is an 18th-century cupola replaced after the 1755 Lisbon earthquake reached all the way here to knock down the old one. Damn those Portuguese! On your way out, check the facade of the New Cathedral for images of an astronaut and a gargoyle eating ice cream.

i €4.75, students and seniors €4, children €3. Audio tour included. Free Su 5-7:15pm or bank holidays 5-7pm. Open daily 10am-7:15pm.

PLAZA MAYOR

Considered the most beautiful and classic central square in all of Spain (sucks to be one of those other Spanish plazas), Pl. Mayor has everything you might want from a major plaza—elaborately carved Baroque stone, bounteous overpriced cafes, and super lit facades (at night, literally). Finished in 1755, the square was originally ordered by Felipe V as a bullfighting ring. All roads lead to the plaza, so once you figure out whither each of its six exits go, you're practically as capable of navigating the center as a Salamanca native. Sure, the cafe con leche may be a little overpriced at the surrounding multi-colored tables, but it's worth it for the view of the plaza's approximately 247 balconies. Just make sure you pick the cafe with maximum shade for the day and watch the bulk of the city rush in, out, and through.

i All roads in central Salamanca pretty much lead to Pl. Mayor, so you'll find it eventually. Free. Open 24hr.

FOOD

📓 BAMBÚ $$
C. Prior, 4   ☎923 26 00 92 www.cafeteriabambu.com

Bambú combines modern decor with the beloved tradition of free tapas with every drink. And instead of a sad dish of olives begrudgingly slammed down on the table, Bambú takes its free tapas seriously. Buy a beer and you can choose from a huge array of tapas, from divine morcilla-and-goat-cheese hamburgers to grilled-to-order ribs. Get extra small plates for €1.40 each and you have yourself a huge meal for under €10. There's a fancier restaurant version next door, but

ERASMUS HOME $

C. Jesús, 18 ☎923 71 02 57 www.erasmushome.com

Owned by the same proprietors as the popular Erasmus Bar around the corner (yay discounts), Erasmus is one of the only genuine modern youth hostels in Salamanca. Staircases are collaged with good times from the bar that remind you that you, too, could have good times. Passive-aggressive stick-figure cartoons remind you that, while you could have good times, don't have too much of them in the rooms. Less than a 10min. walk from any major tourist destination in the city center, beds are comfy (if cramped), and the common room and mini-kitchen (minus stove and oven) skew the "Home" part more college-dorm than home-sweet.

i Face away from Casa de las Conchas and go down C. de Jesus. It's on your right. Dorms €15-20. Key deposit €5. Locker rental €1.50. Towel rental €1.50. Reception 24hr.

stick with the uber-popular bar section for the same delicious flavors and better back-and-forth with the expert bartenders.

i From Pl. Mayor, take the entrance with the Burger King. Halfway down the block, take the stairs down on your right. Beer €2. Tapas €1.40. Bar open daily 9am-12:30am. Restaurant open daily 12:30-4:30pm and 8pm-midnight.

MANDALA $$

C. de Serranos, 9-11 ☎923 12 33 42 mandalasalamanca.com

Possibly the best menú del día in Salamanca, both in price and quality. Also not entirely made of meat options (a rarity in Salamanca)—bread, a drink, dessert or cafe, plus nine options for a first course and 10 options for the second. And vegetarian choices galore! You can also cool down with one of the 45 milkshakes or 54 juice combos. So enjoy the first vegetable you've seen in days, with fusions of Mediterranean, Middle Eastern, and East Asian flavors that reflect the design choices of Moroccan wall carvings and Buddhas scattered everywhere.

i Next to Casa de las Conchas. Menú del día/noche €10.50/12.50. Smoothies and milkshakes €3.90-4.80. 20-cent price difference between bar and table. Open M-Th 8am-11pm, F-Sa 9am-1am, Su 9am-11pm.

NIGHTLIFE

CAMELOT

C. Bordadores, 3 ☎923 21 21 82 www.camelot.es

On the packed C. Bordadores, Camelot is a stalwart bar/club mixture, capitalizing on its unique surroundings inside an old convent with iron trappings and heraldry flags all around. And it lives up to its Knights of the Round Table legacy with live music events and plenty of alcohol (wait, we may be forgetting our Arthurian legends…). There are constant Erasmus gatherings for nearby university students, so the crowd skews younger and the drinks skew cheap. This is a great place for those moments when you just want to shamelessly dance to Beyoncé on a stage jutting out from a medieval stone wall. When in Salamanca…

i Cocktails €4. Beer €2. Shots from €0.50. Open M-W 6pm-5am, Th 6pm-6am, F-Sa 6pm-7am, Su 6pm-5am.

GRAN CAFE MODERNO

C. Gran Vía, 75 ☎637 53 81 65 grancafemoderno.com

Salamanca loves its themed bars, and Gran Cafe Moderna is no exception (also check out the Marvel comics one next door for this trend taken to the extreme).

Salamanca

Walk through the Art Nouveau door and you'll think you've walked onto a 19th-century Parisian cobblestone street. Beer flows from taps under a mirrored storefront advertising "pure milk for children and patients." Set under the street lights, plenty of cafe-style rickety chairs are easily pushed to the side as the dancing gets going later in the evening. The patrons of bars along Gran Vía, just outside the medieval walls, are more local than those closer to Pl. Mayor. So communicate in a confusing mix of Spanish, French, and English as you sip and relax in the grand cafe.

i *Beer €2.50. Open daily 3:45pm-4:30am.*

ESSENTIALS

Practicalities

- **TOURIST OFFICES:** The largest and most central office in town is located at Pl. Mayor, 32. (☎923 21 83 42. Open in summer M-F 9am-2pm and 4:30-8pm, Sa 10am-8pm, Su 10am-2pm; in winter M-F 9am-2pm and 4-6:30pm, Sa 10am-6:30pm, Su 10am-2pm.)

- **POST OFFICES:** The central post office is at Gran Via, 25-29. (☎923 26 44 96.)

Emergency

- **EMERGENCY NUMBER:** ☎112.

- **POLICE:** The local police are headquartered at Ronda Sancti Spiritus, 8-12. (☎923 26 53 11 or 092.)

- **HOSPITALS:** The most central hospital is Hospital General de la Santísima Trinidad. (Paseo de las Carmelitas. ☎923 26 93 00.)

Getting There

By Train

The national railway (RENFE) train station (Ave. de la Estación) connects to Madrid Chamartín as well as other cities in the Castilla y León region (Valladolid, Burgos, León). Check www.renfe.es or call ☎902 24 02 02 for schedules. Bus 1 connects the station to Pl. Poeta Iglesias in the center.

By Bus

The bus station (Av. Filiberto Villalobos, 7; ☎923 22 60 79) is about a 15min. walk from Pl. Mayor down Av. Filiberto Villalobos and runs several buses per day directly to Madrid-Barajas Airport and Madrid's Estación de Autobuses Sur bus station. Check online at www.avanzabus.com or call ☎902 02 09 99 for the schedule.

Getting Around

Salamanca is an easily walkable city, though city buses are available for longer distance routes at €1.05-1.50 per ride. You can also find a taxi stand right outside Pl. Mayor, next to the Mercado Central, or call one at ☎923 188 518 or ☎923 249 751.

spain

spain essentials

MONEY

Tipping and Bargaining

Native Spaniards rarely tip more than their spare change, even at expensive restaurants. If you make it clear that you're a tourist—especially an American—they might expect you to tip more. Don't feel like you have to tip, as the servers' pay is almost never based on tips.

Bargaining is common and necessary in open-air and street markets. If you are buying a number of things, like produce, you can probably get a better deal if you haggle. Do not barter in malls or established shops.

Taxes

Spain has a 10% value added tax (IVA) on all means and accommodations. The prices listed in Let's Go include IVA unless otherwise mentioned. Retail goods bear a much higher 21% IVA, although the listed prices generally include this tax. Non-EU citizens who have stayed in the EU fewer than 180 days can claim back the tax paid on purchases at the airport. Ask the shop where you have made the purchase to supply you with a tax return form, but stores will only provide them for purchases of around €50-100. Due to the economic crises sweeping Europe, don't be surprised if Spain increases its VAT even more.

SAFETY AND HEALTH

Local Laws and Police

Travelers are not likely to break major laws unintentionally while visiting Spain. You can contact your embassy if arrested, although they often cannot do much to assist you beyond finding legal counsel. You should feel comfortable approaching the police, although few officers speak English. There are several types of police in Spain. The policía nacional wear blue or black uniforms and white shirts; they guard government buildings, protect dignitaries, and deal with criminal investigations (including theft). The policía local wear blue uniforms, deal more with local issues, and report to the mayor or town hall in each municipality. The guardia civil wear olive-green uniforms and are responsible for issues more relevant to travelers: customs, crowd control, and national security. Catalonia also has its own police force, the Mossos d'Esquadra. Officers generally wear blue and occasionally sport berets or other interesting headgear. This police force is often used for crowd control and deals with riots.

Drugs and Alcohol

Recreational drugs are illegal in Spain, and police take these laws seriously. The legal drinking age is 16 in Asturias and 18 elsewhere. In Asturias, however, it is still illegal for stores to sell alcohol to those under age 18. Spain has the highest road mortality rates in Europe, and one of the highest rates of drunk driving deaths in Europe. Recently, Spanish officials have started setting up checkpoints on roads to test drivers' blood alcohol levels. Do not drive while intoxicated and be cautious on the road.

Terrorism

Until very recently, Basque terrorism was a serious concern for all travelers in Spain. A militant wing of Basque separatists called the Euskadi Ta Askatasuna (ETA; Basque Homeland and Freedom) continued to have an active presence well into the 2000s, but has recently taken a more dormant stance. Historically, ETA's attacks have been politically targeted and were not considered random terrorist attacks that endanger regular civilians. In January 2011, ETA declared a "permanent and general cease-fire," and at this point, many of ETA's leaders have been arrested. The group has also announced a "definitive cessation of its armed activity."

LANGUAGE

There are four main languages spoken in Spain, along with a slew of less widely spoken ones. Here are the ones you're likely to come across.

Spanish/Castellano

Castilian or Spanish is the official language of Spain. Spain's Spanish is distinct from its Western Hemisphere counterparts in its hallmark lisp of the z and soft c and its use of the vosotros form (second-person plural).

Catalan/Valenciancatalà/Valencià

Along the Mediterranean coast from Alicante up to the French border, the main language spoken is Catalan, along with its close relative Valencian. Throughout the regions of Catalonia, Valencia, and the Balearic Islands, as well as parts of Aragon, this Romance language sounds to most ears like a combination of Spanish, Italian, and French. It's also the official language of the small principality of Andorra. Never imply that Catalan is a dialect of Spanish—this is untrue and will turn the entire nation of Andorra against you.

Basque/Euskara

Basque looks extraterrestrial—full of z's, x's, and k's—but the Basques don't care how pretty their language looks; they just care about preserving it. After decades of concerted efforts by Franco to wipe euskara out, it is still the official language of about 600,000 people, though you won't need to know a word of it to get by in País Vasco's main cities.

Galician/Galego

Somewhere between Spanish and Portuguese falls Galician, spoken in Galicia, in the northwest corner of the peninsula. As with Basque, you won't need your Spanish-Galician dictionary to get by, though it'll probably help with most menus.

Other Languages

In the British territory of Gibraltar, English is spoken, of course, though the locals also speak a creole known as Llanito. Languages you're less likely to come across in your travels include Asturian, spoken along parts of the northern coast; Leonese, in the area around Astorga; Extremaduran, in Extremadura; Aranese, in the valley around Vielha; Aragonese, in the mountains of Aragon north of Huesca; and Caló, spoken by the Romanior gypsy community across Spain.

spain

SWEDEN

With the design world cooing over bright, blocky Swedish furniture and college students donning designs from H&M, Scandinavia's largest nation has earned a reputation abroad for its chic style. At home, Sweden's struggle to balance a market economy with its generous social welfare system stems from it belief that all citizens should have access to education and healthcare. This neutral nation's zest for spending money on butter instead of guns has also shored up a strong sense of national unity, from reindeer herders in the Lappland forests to bankers in bustling Stockholm.

greatest hits

- **POSEIDON, LOOK AT ME NOW:** Take a cruise along the archipelago in Stockholm (p. 756) for a breathtaking tour through nature. Maybe you'll spot some Wildlings along the way.

- **A CHANCE OF MEATBALLS:** Hungry in Stockholm? Head to **Husmans Deli** (p. 759) for a huge portion of the classic dish: Swedish meatballs.

- **BE A SQUARE:** From afternoon coffee chats to protests, **Lilla Torg** (p. 766) is the perfect people-watching square in little Malmö.

stockholm

To put it simply, Stockholm is the real deal: a veritable Mordor-Death Star combo of everything that is young, hip, and Anglophone. You'll find artisanal hot dog stands next to Gatsby-themed speakeasies next to garlic bars and kebab-Vietnamese fusion. It's like Narnia in modern form, and you'll absolutely love it.

Stockholm is the best place for backpackers in Scandinavia (if not Europe). The sheer size and vibrancy of the city means that you have every kind of accommodation at your disposal from nature cabins to Betty-Boop themed free-pasta compounds. There is something for even the pickiest travellers here. The nightlife, like in any big

get a room!

CITY HOSTEL $$
Fleminggatan 19   ☎8 410 03 830 www.cityhostel.se

In Hollywood, hostels are often portrayed as the travelling equivalent of Animal House: the drinking is non-stop, the baby-making is on point, and some guy named Hans is playing the guitar. On your travels, though, you might have found most hostels to be full of more snoring men than hedonistic youth—until City Hostel. This place feels vibrant, fun and new. The rooms are spacious and come with their own lockers, while the community kitchen and bathrooms are both spotless and quite large. The hostel offers little treats like laundry service and their own guidebook to Stockholm (though you already have us!)—but most importantly, the clientele is almost entirely college students. With shared rooms at around 250 SEK a night, it's an excellent deal.

i *Singles 450 SEK. Doubles 600 SEK. Dorms 220-250 SEK. Reception 9am-6pm.*

CITY BACKPACKERS' HOSTEL $
Upplandsgatan 2a   ☎8 20 69 20 www.citybackpackers.org

The place looks like it was designed by Andy Warhol on a mescaline trip, and we mean that in the best way possible: an average walk down the hallway takes you past vintage skateboards, 50's TV sets, and posters featuring North Korea's national ski team. It's the kind of place that feels youthful and artistic without being cheesy, and its young clientele and cleverly-designed social spaces might make it the best hostelling experience you'll have in Sweden. Though the basic price of a room is the same as in other places around Stockholm, we recommend you shell out extra here for the breakfast: they have a full-time chef who serves a six-part meal with everything from sandwiches and yogurt to juice and fruit plates.

i *Singles 600 SEK. Doubles 890 SEK. Dorm 190-280 SEK. Reception 8am-midnight.*

SKANSTULLS $$
Ringvägen 135   ☎8 643 02 04 www.skanstulls.se

Skanstulls is the same price as other Stockholm hostels but with much nicer amenities. Book collection? You got it. Free pasta? Done. Actual wooden bunk-beds that don't feel like prison cots? Check, check, check. Its location in Södermalm means you are 10 minutes away from some of Europe's best-rated nightlife and restaurants, and the mass of people in the kitchen at dinnertime makes it incredibly easy to make friends.

i *Singles 500 SEK. Doubles 600 SEK. Dorms 220-250 SEK. Reception 9am-8pm.*

sweden

city, is diverse and affordable, while the food never disappoints: whether it's noodles or meatballs, burgers or buffets, Stockholm does it and it does it well.

Like the other Nordic countries, the standard of living is high here, and that means that prices are a bit above what you're used to. If you want to eat out twice a day, go to bars and museums, and stay at a nice hostel, it may be hard to spend less than 80 USD a day. Nonetheless, it always feels like money well spent here: whether you take quiet stroll in a park, visit a Viking exhibit, or grab beers on a boat heading around the archipelago, you will be amazed at how fun and diverse an experience in Stockholm can be.

SIGHTS

VASA MUSEUM (VASAMUSEET)
Universitetsgata 13   ☎8 519 54 800 www.vasamuseet.se

A wooden monument to King Gustav Adolf's small penis, the Vasa ship was commissioned in 1626 and was supposed to be the largest seagoing vessel of its day. Unfortunately, the guy whose job it was to say "Wait! You can't put 64 cannons on a boat like that. It'll sink!" was sick the day the Vasa took off, so in 1628, the entire Swedish government watched as their life savings sank beneath the waves of Stockholm's harbor. Thankfully, the ship has been dredged up from the seafloor and is on full display at the museum today. For just 100 SEK, you can relive all the hubris and ambition of 17th century Sweden while avoiding the scurvy and drowning that followed it.

i *130 SEK, students 100 SEK, free for under 18. Open daily 8:30am-6pm.*

NORDISKA MUSEUM (NORDISKA MUSEET)
Djurgårdsvägen 6-16   ☎8 519 54 600 www.nordiskamuseet.se

This museum covers all aspects of life in Sweden from holiday practices, to clothing, to the indigenous Sami minority and seeks to impress upon visitors the diversity of Nordic tradition. While some displays may be a tad excessive on the details (trust us, you don't need to know all seven kinds of biscuits Swedes ate in the 19th century) it's nonetheless one of the coolest museums you'll find in Stockholm.

i *100 SEK, free for under 18. Free Sept-May on Wednesdays 5pm-8pm. Open M-Tu 10am-5pm, W 10am-8pm, Th-Su 10am-5pm.*

ARMY MUSEUM
Riddargatan 13   ☎21 98 20 00 www.armemuseum.se

Guns! Tanks! Bombs! If any of these words gives you a brain-boner, the Army Museum should be your #1 stop in Stockholm. It traces the history of the Swedish military from the past to the present—covering everything from the 30 Years War to the Napoleonic Wars to World War II—and even has machine guns and uniforms you can play with. The exhibits are incredible and make this a perfect place for anyone with an interest in military history. Or Sweden. Or vaguely attractive mannequins in revealing poses.

i *80 SEK, students 50 SEK, free for under 19. Open June-Aug daily 10am-5pm; Sept-May Tu 11am-10pm, W-Su 11am-5pm.*

SPIRITS MUSEUM
Djurgårdsvägen 38   ☎8 121 31 310 www.spritmuseum.se

At the Spirits Museum, you can learn everything you never knew about Swedes' love-hate relationship with alcohol: how it brings together families, how it tears apart relationships, how it smells great when you mix in a lil' cinnamon or cardamom and oh my god this smelling room is getting me high on spice. The art exhibit at the entrance walks you through the last 30 years of advertising from Absolut Vodka, and we have to say that these posters are just as cool as anything you'll see in art museums. After that, you can walk through exhibits on the history of beer, fumble your way through a hangover simulation, and lie down in a movie theater that tries to immerse you in one man's boozy night out. And yes, you can book tastings if you call in advance.

i 100 SEK, students 90 SEK. Open M 10am-6pm, Tu 10am-8pm, W-Su 10am-6pm.

FOTOGRAFISKA

Stadsgårdshamnen 22 ☎8 509 00 500 www.fotografiska.eu

Like most modern art museums, this place seems bizarre to the uninitiated: the opening exhibit features a lot of boob and sideboob, but we're not sure what the deeper meaning is. Nonetheless, the photographs on display here are some of the most interesting you'll find in Europe, with exhibits from the world's leading nature photographers, fashion designers, and artists making a constant rotation in the galleries. For art-fans and confused tourists alike, it's an incredible place to spend the day—even if you're only pretending to understand that photo of a headless horse.

i 120 SEK, students 90 SEK. Open daily 9am-11pm.

SWEDISH HISTORY MUSEUM

Narvavägen 13-17 ☎8 519 55 600 www.historiska.se

This museum's main attraction is its Viking collection and damn is it impressive: rings, swords, graves, even runestones are all on display. If that weren't enough, you can participate in activities like mock archeology digs, archery practice, and sailing on a replica Viking boat because we are all Vikings on the inside. Additionally, there's an interactive exhibit on the prehistory of Sweden that walks you through the entire country's history up until today. This museum feels like it was built for adults with the attention span of a carrot and the wondrous curiosity of a child, and we love it!

i 100 SEK, students 80 SEK, free for under 18. Open June-Aug daily 10am-6pm, Sept-May Tu 11am-5pm, W 11am-8pm, Th-Su 11am-5pm, closed Mondays.

IKEA

Kungens kurva ☎77 570 05 00

Is IKEA "the" place to hang out in Stockholm? Probably not, unless you're a. over 80 or b. seriously convinced that Yin-Yang Tables are going to turn your life around. Nonetheless, a trip to Sweden without IKEA would be more sacrilegious than not eating a single baguette in France, so head over to this wonder emporium when you have the chance. Unfortunately, it's about 20min. outside of Stockholm by bus, but IKEA's free shuttle leaves from outside the central train station every hour. Once there, you'll be struck by how Ikéaic (?) everything is: the sofas are plush, the meatballs are succulent, and the shoppers are a healthy mix of tourists, Swedes and more tourists. Even if you're not looking to buy something, it's surprisingly fun to simply visit this altar of consumption and see what all the hubbub is about.

i Free shuttle buses leave every hour starting at 10am from Vasagatan 10 to Kungens kurva, ride takes about 20-30min. Open daily 10am-7pm.

GRÖNA LUND AMUSEMENT PARK

Lilla Allmänna Gänd 9 ☎8 587 50 100 www.gronalund.com

Do you need the threat of serious bodily harm to make you feel alive? Instead of joining a fight club, why not just come down to Gröna Lund and push the limits of what human beings define as fun? Whether it's The Eclipse (a giant 43mph "wave swinger" that only requires you be 4 feet tall) or the Fritt Fall Tilt (which drops you from a dizzying 250 feet in the sky), there's something for everyone here. Thankfully the park also has accommodations for the less crazy of us, like bumper cars and a "haunted house" (though we can only imagine shareholders screaming "pussy!" every time a customer gets on the carousel).

i 110 SEK. Hours vary, usually open 11am-10pm during the summer, but check calendar online for the most up-to-date opening and closing times.

ARCHIPELAGO

Strandvägen berth no 15 and 16 ☎8 519 54 800

www.stromma.se/en/stockholm/excursions/day-trips/archipelago-tour-with-guide

The archipelago is a breathtaking tour through nature. Over the course of three hours, you sit back and cruise through Game of Thrones-style scenery: dramatic inlets, lakes, forested islands—hell, we may have even seen a piece of the Wall and some Wildlings along the way. Some of the most interesting spots are Tegelön Island and the little rock outcroppings that shoot out of the sea before you reach Tynningö. Our recommendation: try and book a boat that goes to Vaxholm Island; the port and nature there feel more Nordic than Odin shopping at Ikea.

i 260 SEK. Tours leave M-F at 10:30am, noon, 1:30pm, and 3pm; Sa-Su at noon. Trip takes 2.5-3 hrs.

FOOD

HUSMANS DELI $

inside Östermalms Saluhall at Östermalmstorg ☎8 553 40 480 www.husmansdeli.se

Sweden without meatballs is like middle school without awkward outfits and photos: It might exist, but our sources tell us your experience is woefully inauthentic if you miss it. When it comes to these tiny bundles of animal flesh, we haven't yet found a place that tastes as good as Husman's Deli. For 95 SEK, you get a huge portion of meatballs, mashed potatoes, and juniper berry jam, all floating in enough succulent gravy to drown any sorrow. For the price and portions, this place is a must-go; even better, it's located in a complex with a dozen other shops selling fruit, cheese, and meatballs of their own.

i Entrees 80-120 SEK. Open M-Th 9:30am-6pm, F 9:30am-7pm, Sat 9:30am-4pm; closed Sundays.

top 5 apps to use in stockholm

1. SWEDISH BY NEMO: As Nelson Mandela said, "When you speak to a man in his mother tongue, you are speaking to his heart." We almost feel guilty writing that because we know you'll only use this app to get laid, but at least you'll be snatching hearts in a foreign language!

2. FOOD LOVERS STOCKHOLM: Crowd-sourced, impartial reviews of restaurants and wine bars throughout Stockholm. Can't shine a candle to StreetKak (below) but we suppose it has its plebian charm.

3. MUSEUMS IN STOCKHOLM: Easy and simple—an offline guide to Stockholm's most popular museums. Includes times, short descriptions, and a map

4. TRANSIT MAP STOCKHOLM: Though the train system here is nothing like New York's, it can still be tricky to navigate. With this offline map, you can search where the stations are and which trains service them. Easy, simple, super practical.

5. STREETKAK: Do you ever find a food cart that you simply can't find again? You no longer have to hit Craigslist's Missed Connections because now there's an app for that! With StreetKak, you can watch Stockholm's food carts move in real time and see what they're serving. If you're broke and looking for cheap eats, this may just be the best option next to selling plasma.

stockholm

CHUTNEY $

Katarina Bangata 19   ☎8 640 30 10 www.chutney.se/om-chutney

Located in Stockholm's trendy Södermalm neighborhood, this place has all the charm of a hippie Indian restaurant. For 98 SEK, you order from a preset menu that includes dishes with rice, stewed vegetables, and several kinds of chutney. That's good enough, but the real reason to go here is the portions: you can get seconds (even thirds) for free, and there are enormous plates of carrots, salad, breads, and sauces that you can use to spice up or enhance your dish. It's an excellent choice for the budget traveller.

i *Entrees 98 SEK. Open M-F 11am-10pm, Sa noon-10pm, Su noon-9pm.*

PONG THAI BUFFET $$

Drottninggatan 71 C   ☎8 20 45 63 pongasian.se/pong-buffe

Swedes are huge on Thai food, so if you're sick of meatballs and kebab, you can find Pad Thai on practically every corner here. At Pong Thai Buffét, you can scarf down as much food as you can take for only 168 SEK. That may sound like a lot, but remember that it's all-you-can-eat in one of world's most expensive cities, and the selection is huge: spring rolls, noodles, satay, orange chicken, chicken fingers, coconut beef, stir fry, lychees, mandarins, cream pudding… we're practically singing "My Favorite Things" as we write out the list.

i *All-you-can-eat buffet 168 SEK. Lunch buffet open M-F 10:30am-2pm. Dinner open M-Th 5pm-10pm, F 5pm-11pm, Sa noon-11pm, Su noon-10pm.*

FRICK & HAGBERG AB $

Food truck, address varies   ☎70 355 92 81 www.frickochhagberg.se

This food truck changes locations every day, but trust us: it's worth the trek. They're 100% organic and absolutely delicious; our order, the Original, came with gruyère cheese, onion, pickles, mayo, and meat that was flavorful and enlightening. With an average price of about 80 SEK, these burgers are both filling and affordable. And they even have veggie options! To find them, follow their FB page for weekly updates on locations.

i *Burgers 75-90 SEK. Double patties, add on 45 SEK. Open daily 11am-1pm and 5-7pm.*

KOH PHANGAN $$

Skånegatan 57   ☎8 642 50 40 www.kohphangan.se/sodermalm

In wintertime—when Swedes spend months on end fighting darkness and snow—we imagine this place is a cheery reminder of what non-Stalingrad weather looks like. In summer, though, tourists might find the tiki-torches, strobe lights, and beach-bar more like the venue for a tacky Sweet 16 than a genuine foodie destination. To its credit, though, Koh Phangan serves a mean Mai Tai and decent rosés (around 70 SEK a glass), while the chicken pad thai and complimentary fish sauce salad are also quite tasty. This place is a hit with locals and could be a genuinely fun place to start out the night—just be prepared to spend in the 200 SEK range if you want to feel full and satisfied.

i *Entrees 150 SEK. Open M-F 4pm-1am, Sa-Su noon-1am. Kitchen closes at midnight.*

URBAN DELI $$

Nytorget 4   ☎8 599 09 180

Urban Deli is part upscale grocery store, part restaurant-bar, and the food tastes like what Zeus would eat after a particularly long-night of nectar and nymph-boning. The Iberian ham plate (145 SEK) and Fiskgoyta (mussel/salmon fish pot; 205 SEK) are definitely recommended, while the chocolate almond pudding is likely the closest mankind will ever get to orgasm in culinary form. The drink menu is about twice as good as the food listing, and most beers go for around 80 SEK. It's certainly on the pricier end of things, but if you're going to treat yourself on a night out this is the place to do it.

i *Entrees 150 SEK. Open daily 8am-10pm.*

sweden

HURRY CURRY

$

Slöjdgatan 11   ☎8 23 30 80 www.hurrycurry.se

This Indian restaurant doesn't engage in the huge portions (or vegan tomfoolery) of Södermalm's Chutney, but the food is equally good. While the menu is admittedly limited, the butter chicken is a bargain at 90 SEK, and the vegetarian options (our personal favorite: vego vindaloo) are also pretty tasty. Like a one-night-stand, though, it's best to dip in and out rather than linger too long here; the place can get crowded and is much more suited to a quick meal than a drawn-out dinner.

i Entrees 100 SEK. Open M-Sa 11am-9pm, Su noon-5pm.

RAMEN KIMAMA

$

Birger Jarlsgatan 93   ☎8 15 55 39 www.kimamma.se/ramen

Some of best ramen in Stockholm and possibly Scandinavia. This place has all the classics—shoyu, shio, miso—each sprinkled with garlic, boiled egg, bamboo shoots, pork, and, of course, noodles. The broth is perfect, and the food itself had an incredible aroma. We went for the shoyu ramen with an Asahi beer and were not disappointed in the least. For those with less soupy inclinations, they also have standard fare like gyoza, yaki soba, kimchi, and more. The drinks are reasonably priced (50 SEK for beers, 90 SEK for wines) and most main dishes are around 115 SEK or more.

i Ramen 115 SEK. Alcoholic drinks 50-90 SEK. Open M-F 11:30am-2:30pm and 5pm-9:30pm; Sa 5pm-9:30pm, Su 5pm-9pm.

VIGARDA

$

Norrlandsgatan 13   ☎8 505 24 466 www.vigarda.se/mood

An excellent place for a quick, cheap burger in Stockholm's Östermalm neighborhood. Though it's a more upscale joint, the prices aren't bad by Stockholm standards: the bacon cheeseburger goes for 75 SEK, while the burger of the month (when we visited, "Thai spice" with coriander and chili) is 95 SEK (fries and salad included). In a true act of gluttony, our researcher threw in an extra 50 SEK to make his cheeseburger a double and did not regret it. Perhaps not as good a burger as Frick & Hagberg, but certainly worth a quick visit.

i Burgers 75-100 SEK. Open M-Tu 11am-9pm, W-Sa 11am-11pm, Su 11am-7pm.

JOHAN & NYSTRÖM COFFEE CONCEPT STORE

$

Swedenborgsgatan 7   ☎8 702 20 40 johanochnystrom.se

You'll see an Espresso House or Wayne's Coffee on every block in this city, but Johan & Nyström beats them all with its engaging staff, cheap pastries, and décor of a mini Scandinavian Williamsburg. The staff here told us it was the best coffee shop in Stockholm, and their cappuccinos and cardamom buns positively convinced us of that. This place is an absolute must-go coffee lovers, whether you're stepping in for a quick macchiato or preparing for a forlorn, day-long affair with your computer and a sandwich.

i Coffee 30-60 SEK. Pastries 30 SEK. Open M-F 7:30am-6pm, Sa 10am-4pm, Su 11am-4pm.

MUGGEN

$

Götgatan 24   ☎8 642 50 40 www.muggen.se

Do you want scones best described as "bitchin'"? Paninis and salads that won't break the bank, and coffee that's fresher than a new pair of Jordans? At Muggen, you can get all these and more in the heart of Södermalm, Stockholm's coolest neighborhood. Our personal rec: go for the House croque. With gouda, oregano and juicy ham, it's a delectably sinful sandwich that goes great with the cappuccinos and ironic neckbeards you'll see everywhere here.

i Coffee 30 SEK. Pastries 30 SEK. Sandwiches 115 SEK. Open M-F 8am-11pm, Sa-Su 8am-10pm.

stockholm

NIGHTLIFE

GARLIC AND SHOTS

Folkungagatan 8   ☎8 640 84 46 www.garlicandshots.co

As you may have guessed, Swedes really don't beat around the bush when it comes to names: this place is indeed a garlic-themed restaurant and bar. Though you may choke through nausea and bad breath as you make your way down the menu, the prices here are unbeatable: each of their 101 shots—with flavors such as garlic and bourbon, tequila and chili, and vodka and licorice—costs 50 SEK. For biohazard reasons, you may want to bring a pack of breath mints or at least a 48-hour abstinence pledge if you end up going, but the location in the hip Södermalm neighborhood makes this one of Let's Go's favorite bars in Stockholm.

i Shots 50 SEK. Open M-F 5pm-11pm, Sa-Su 5pm-11:30pm.

AIFUR

Västerlånggatan 68b   ☎8 20 10 55 www.aifur.se

Let's say your life flashes before your eyes. You've definitely had some accomplishments: that Little League game you won, that trip to London you took, that "girlfriend" you had in 6th grade. But all of those mean nothing if you haven't tried mead. Part honey, part wine, all deliciousness, it's an ancient beverage with more flavors than Paris Hilton has STDs. At Aifur, a Viking-themed cellar in Stockholm's Gamla Stan neighborhood, you can sample this holy nectar while surrounded by waiters dressed in medieval garb. The outfits and prices may make it seem like a bit of a tourist trap, but it's the kind of tourist trap Let's Go 100% embraces.

i Mead 80 SEK. Open M-Th 5pm-11pm, F-Sa 5pm-1am, closed Sundays.

CARMEN

Tjärhovsgatan 14   ☎8 641 24 12

One native informant cheerily referred to Carmen's clientele as "a melting pot," explaining: "you've got students and musicians, winos and drunks, grandparents and tattoo artists…basically everyone besides Batman!" And while the place is certainly no Bruce Wayne in hiding (it's a simple dive bar—what you see is what you get), the prices are great by Swedish standards. Beers (including imports like Brooklyn IPA) are in the 50-65 SEK, while mixed drinks clock in at around 100 SEK or more. It's a cheap spot to get your buzz on, though the size of the crowd and the 1am closing time mean that it's best to come here earlier in the night before moving on to bigger and better things.

i Beers 50-65 SEK. Mixed drinks 100 SEK. Open daily 4pm-1am.

EXIT BAR & LOUNGE

Götgatan 53   ☎8 644 77 77 www.exitloungebar.se

Though this bar's name is about as inspired as "Bathroom on the Left," we still like the place. The atmosphere here is quiet and subdued, with a slightly older clientele who look like extras from a James Bond film (or, given the number of requests for Old Fashioneds, perhaps Mad Men). It's much better for cocktails than beers, so be sure you order correctly: we highly recommend the Dark and Stormy and Lynchburg Lemonade. Exit is great for a quiet drink before moving on to rowdier locales; seeing as you're across the street from Södermalm's Medborgarplatsen station and surrounded by other cool bars and restaurants, the world is your oyster.

i Drinks 100 SEK. Open M-F 3pm-1am, Sa-Su 2pm-1am.

TIKI ROOM

Birkagatan 10   ☎8 33 15 55 www.mellowbar.com

Do you want to drink alcohol out of a carved Polynesian chest with 3 foot-long straws? Who are we kidding—you'd have to be the ultimate bougie bitch to think that wasn't cool. With the Tiki torches, calypso music, and a drink called "Missionary's Downfall," what more could you want from a kitschy bar? This place is pretty average price-wise (cocktails are in the 160 SEK), but the atmosphere can't be beat.

i Drinks 150 SEK. Open M-Th 4pm-midnight, F-Sa 4pm-1am, closed Sundays.

BERNS
Skånegatan 57   ☎8 642 50 40 www.berns.se

Every city has its massive, multi-story nightclub that you "have" to go to: New York has Studio 54, Prague has Karlovy Lázně, and Stockholm has Berns. We've been told Edith Piaf used to sing here; if that's the case, though, she probably did not write La Vie en Rose about this place. To start off, the cover charge is a bit high—200 SEK after 10pm— and the bouncers, in true Stockholm style, can be very dismissive and intimidating to non-locals. With its minimum age of 23, Berns is also clearly shooting for an older crowd, but still expect a 30+ minute wait if you're getting there late at night. If you really hate nightlife, our best recommendation is to come here early in the evening for a cocktail: you're paying mostly for the scenery anyway, so why not enjoy your G&T without a sweaty Swede getting his pheromones on you at 1 in the morning?

i Cover 200 SEK after 10pm on weekends. Mixed drinks 100 SEK. Hours in different clubs/floors vary, usually open 11pm-3am.

TWEED
Lilla Nygatan 5   ☎8 506 40 082 www.tweedbar.se

If Casablanca is your favorite film, rest assured that you'll always have Tweed. It's the kind of place where you sit back in a Chesterfield armchair and talk about beating the Gerries; a 40's-style lounge that transports you back to the classiest days of the empire over bourbons and a cuban cigar. If that weren't enough, they cook up some mean burgers to temper your boozy nostalgia, though in the 195-220 SEK range, it may be best to come here for after-dinner shenanigans. Tweed's main room is unfortunately closed for much of the summer but its rooftop bar, The Sanchez, remains open.

i Drinks 120 SEK. Open M-Th 5pm-midnight, F-Sa 5pm-1am, closed Sundays.

ESSENTIALS
Practicalities

- **TOURIST OFFICES:** Stockholm Visitor Center (Kulturhuset, Sergels Torg 5 ☎8 508 28 508. Open May-Sept M-F 9am-7 pm, Sa 9am-4pm and 6pm July-Aug, Su 10am-4pm.)

- **CURRENCY EXCHANGE:** Possible at Arlanda Airport and stores such as 24Money and Forex (the latter of which probably has the most competitive rates). The best bet may be simply to withdraw cash from an ATM, though: the exchange rates are not much different than what you'll get in stores.

- **ATMS:** You can pay for almost everything in Sweden with debit or credit cards, but the Central Train Station and most chain stores like 7-11 will have an ATM (Bankomat in Swedish). ATMs and currency exchange are also available at Stockholm Airport and are easy to locate along major pedestrian streets such as Drottninggatan and the T-Centralen metro stop.

- **LUGGAGE STORAGE:** You can hire lockers in public areas such as Cityterminalen, the bus station directly connected to Stockholm Central Station. Average costs are about 70 SEK for 24hrs in a medium-sized box, 90 SEK for a large box, and 120 SEK for an extra large box

- **LAUNDROMATS:** Most hostels offer laundry services either for free or at a low cost (City Backpackers: machines are free, soap is 50 SEK; City Hostel 30 SEK). Independent laundromats include Tvättomaten i Stockholm (Västmannagatan 61B ☎8 34 64 80. Open M-F

8:30am–6:30pm, Sa 9:30am–1pm, closed on Sundays.) This laundromat is often better for dry-cleaning needs—if you're just washing a sack of dirty clothing, it will cost at least 100 SEK.

- **INTERNET:** Wi-Fi is available widely throughout Stockholm, with hotspots in the Stockholm Visitor Center, Arlanda Airport, Central Station, and most hostels and hostels. Additionally, certain chain stores you'll see on every corner—such as Espresso House and Wayne's Coffee—also offer free connectivity. There's also an app called the Free Wi-Fi Map, which helps you identify places near to you and provides any necessary login information

- **POST OFFICE:** Centralposthuset (Vasagatan 28-34) in the center of Stockholm is a massive, century-old building designed by the Swedish architect Ferdinand Boberg.

Emergency

- **EMERGENCY NUMBER:** ☎112
- **POISON CONTROL:** ☎8 33 12 31, open 8am-5pm
- **24-HOUR EMERGENCY MEDICAL ADVICE:** ☎1177
- **SUICIDE HOTLINE:** ☎20 22 00 60, nationellahjalplinjen.se, open M-Th 5am-10pm.
- **RFSL STOCKHOLM (FOR COUNSELING ON LGBTQ-RELATED ISSUES):** ☎8 501 62 970, www.rfsl.se
- **LATE-NIGHT PHARMACIES:** 24-Hour Apoteket Pharmacy (CW Scheele, Klarabergsgatan 64, near T-Centralen ☎8 45 481 30.)
- **HOSPITALS:** Non-Swedish citizens need identification, insurance papers, and a photocopy of their passport when visiting a public hospital. As always, call the emergency services at 112 if you need an ambulance or other kinds of medical help. Generally, in-patient care is free but you (or your insurer) have to pay the costs of outpatient care. Stockholm South (Sjukhusbacken 10 ☎8 616 10 00. 24hr emergency room.)

Getting There

By Plane

Arlanda is Stockholm's main airport, located about 23 miles away from the city's center. It is the largest airport in Sweden and services the majority of domestic and international flights coming into Stockholm (though a smaller number of aircraft also land at Bromma Airport, to the northwest of the city). The easiest and quickest way to get from the airport to the heart of Stockholm is to take the Arlanda Express, a train running every 15min. between the airport and Central Station. For people under 25, the price of a one-way ticket is 150 SEK, while adults over the age of 25 must pay 280 SEK. The main advantage of taking the Express is that the trip takes only around 20 min. Tickets can be booked online (www.arlandaexpress.com) or at kiosks in the airport/train station. The earliest airport express train from the city center leaves at 4:35am.

By Bus

The Flygbussarna buses leave every 15min. from both Arlanda and City Terminalen (connected to Central Station) on a trip that takes roughly 35-40min. Tickets can be booked online (www.flygbussarna.se) and cost 99 SEK for adults and 89 SEK for students.

By Taxi

Taxis are much more expensive than buses and trains and, with wait times, will probably make your trip to the airport/city center longer than it needs to be. Nonetheless, you can book companies like Taxi Stockholm to pick you up for a fixed price: 520 SEK to the airport and 620 SEK from the airport.

Getting Around
Public Transportation

Stockholm does not do transportation on the honor system; you must swipe your card to access all trams, subways, and buses. Cards can be purchased at the stations and most major bus stops; note that you must pay an initial fee of 20 SEK to get the card itself, but then can fill it up indefinitely. Single-use ticket 36 SEK (students 20 SEK); 24-hour ticket 70 SEK; 7-day 300 SEK (students 180 SEK).

Stockholm Card: This card gives you free access to public transportation and discounts at a number of museums, restaurants, and parking spaces. The full list of attractions and prices are available on the official Stockholm tourist website (www.visitstockholm.com/en/Stockholmcard/), but sample prices are: 1 adult for 2 days 765 SEK; 1 adult for 3 days 895 SEK.

By Train

Stockholm Central Station (Centralplan 15, Main Hall open daily 5am-12:15am; rail lines open M-F 5am-1:15am, Sa-Su 5am-2:15am) is the main hub for local, national, and international trains coming into the city. Long distance buses such as Swebus also drop off here.

By Taxi

Taxi Stockholm (☎8 15 00 00, www.taxistockholm.se). Prices vary depending on the number of passengers, the time of day, and the length of the trip, but for a sample ride: a taxi ride on weekend nights with two people booked in advance starts at 45 SEK, goes up 9.5 SEK a minute in addition to 13.6 SEK per kilometer. Be wary of black taxis—individuals with a car offering to drive you places for cash. You'll often see them outside of crowded clubs and bars in Södermalm. They're illegal, unlicensed, and potentially dangerous. Uber is widely available in Stockholm, though their prices don't differ dramatically from standard cabs (especially during surge pricing).

malmö

Malmö straddles a number of identities. It's a medieval town with plenty of old architecture to show for it, but it also boasts stunning skyscrapers, beautiful parks, and a huge immigrant population that makes it one of Sweden's most diverse cities. It's a foodie's paradise, with many of its younger, vibrant neighborhoods offering everything from organic Middle Eastern to Mexican-Turkish fusion, and on the nightlife front you'll find your fair share of German beer houses and music clubs.

The cash-strapped traveller will be happy to know that Malmö is much cheaper than Stockholm. The city itself is a 30-minute train ride from Copenhagen and only 15 minutes from the Swedish town of Lund, so you're ideally placed to explore new shores. Just avoid plundering them when you land.

SIGHTS

SLOTTSPARKEN AND MALMÖ CASTLE
Fågelbacken   ☎20 34 45 00

Yes, it's called "Slottsparken." Haha. Grow up. Unfortunately, this place does not offer the liberal sexual dalliances that its name implies to English-speakers, but it's still a gorgeous place for a walk. The small reservoirs, surrounding boathouses, and the nearby Torso skyscraper give the impression that its planners watched Woody Allen's *Manhattan* and felt inspired. Head to the north and you'll approach its giant slott (stop giggling). You're going to see your fair share of castles in Scandinavia, but Malmö Castle is particularly impressive: it was

get a room!

MERCURE HOTEL $$
Stadiongatan 21   ☎40 672 85 70 www.mercure-hotel-malmo.com

Have you heard that Malmö is the Vegas of Sweden? No? Maybe because we just made that up. But if you theoretically wanted a luxurious bachelor party, a room here would be the place to do it. For the low price of just 550 SEK, you can book a sizable wood-paneled double with TV, Wi-Fi, and a King-Solomon-style breakfast buffet. Though this place is essentially a 4-star hotel going for 2-star prices, that trade-off comes at a cost: the hotel is located in a removed part of town whose nearest attractions are a shopping mall and apartment blocks. Thankfully, you're only 10 minutes away from downtown by public transport, so the revelry can continue into the city.

i Singles 500 SEK. Reception 24hr.

STF VANDRARHEM $
Rönngatan 1   ☎40 611 62 20 www.hihostels.com/hostels/malmo-city

Malmö does not have much of a hostelling culture, so this place is one of your only choices if you're looking to economize. The hostel has all the amenities a backpacker needs (kitchens, clean bathrooms, a central location, and helpful staff) and the prices are pretty standard for Scandinavia. It's not a party hostel nor a particularly exciting place to stay, but if you need a good, cheap bed to come home to at night, this hostel is a great choice.

i Doubles 850 SEK. Dorms 330 SEK. Hostelling International members get 50 SEK discount. Reception open Tu-Sa 8am-8pm, Su-M 8am-4pm.

built in the 15th century and served as one of the strongholds of Denmark. The castle today is composed of several museums, including the City Museum, where you can learn about the culture and history of Malmö; the Technology and Maritime Museum, where you can walk onto a submarine; and the Malmö Art Museum, which boasts a large collection of Swedish art and furniture.

i Park free. Castle 40 SEK. Park open 24hrs. Castle open daily 10am-5pm.

LILLA TORG
intersection of Larochegatan and Hjulhamnsgatan

If you've got a degree in people-watching, Lilla Torg is an excellent spot for you. Meaning "little square" in Swedish, it's where you'll find the native Malmö-ites eating, shopping, and drinking coffee every afternoon. Everything from casual afternoon chats to protests to counter-protests happen here. In a city that can sometimes feel small, sterilized, and underwhelming, Lilla Torg is a welcome dose of excitement and youth culture.

i Free. Open 24hrs.

RIBERSBORGS OPEN-AIR BATHHOUSE
Limhamnsvägen, Brygga 1   ☎46 26 03 66 www.ribersborgskallbadhus.se

The Ribersborgs Kallbadhus is the epitome of the sauna experience: whether you want to steam up, jump in the Baltic, or kick back with an espresso or two, this place is a definite must-go in Malmö. There are three bathhouses—one male, one female, one mixed—and we must say there's something oddly liberating about sizing up everybody's junk in a room full of naked strangers (be sure to man-spread because that is how you establish dominance.) Bring your own

sweden

lock and towel (you're not allowed to wear clothes inside) and enjoy your day of detoxing before the inevitable retoxing.

i *Sauna 55 SEK. Open May-Aug M-Tu 9am-8pm, W 9am-9pm, Th-F 9am-8pm; Sa-Su 9am–6pm; Sept-Apr M-Tu 10am-7pm, W 10am-8pm, Th-F 10am-7pm, Sa-Su 9am-4pm.*

FOOD

BAR BURRITO $
Fersensväg 14   ☎40 615 32 78 www.barburrito.se

Bar Burrito was easily Let's Go's best food experience in Malmö—this place makes its own dough and throws a big middle finger to the establishment by putting garlic sauce in the burritos (note to Chipotle: you're slacking). The food is fresh and affordable: a burrito with guac will put you back 69 SEK and the home-made lemonade is only 15 SEK. Eating here is as satisfying as watching Gandhi punch Hitler in the face—and we mean that in the best possible way.

i *Burrito or burrito bowl 69 SEK. Frozen yogurt 20-30 SEK. Lemonade 15 SEK. Open M-Th 11am-8pm, F 11am-9pm, Sa noon-9pm, Su noon-7pm.*

NORDIC STREETFOOD $$
Food truck, address varies   ☎706 20 20 94 facebook.com/nordicstreetfood

The food truck phenomenon has hit Sweden faster than reality hit Eddie Murphy's career after Pluto Nash, and Nordic Streetfood is a perfect example of that. For the last two years, the humble van has been serving up delicious, locally-sourced food with an interesting Swedish touch. Our recommendation: the pulled pork burger. With beets. And coleslaw. Or the chanterelle (mushroom) wrap. Everything here, as Shakespeare would say, is "on fleek."

i *Sandwiches and burgers 100 SEK. Check on their FB page (facebook.com/nordicstreetfood) for weekly schedules and locations.*

DONER KEBAB $
Sankt Johannesgatan 1E   ☎40 30 09 11

Do you want hunks of garlic beef wrapped in the oily goodness of a pancake-sized wrap? Basically, this is your place if you're in search of tasty, spiced meats. It's as healthy as bathing in gasoline, but no one goes to a Turkish fast food joint if they're trying to slim down. Our recommendation is to go for the durum doner (easily one of the tastiest we had in Malmö) though the shawarma is equally good.

i *Wraps 69 SEK. Open M-F 11am-8pm, Sa-Su 11am-7pm.*

SALTIMPORTEN CANTEEN $
Grimsbygatan 24   ☎70 651 84 26

This restaurant is like a cat. It refuses to work for your attention and only gives you the time of day when it feels like it…by which we mean this place is only open for two hours a day. And closed on weekends—it's like they're daring you to try and get in. If you do manage to make it between noon and 2pm though, you'll be blown away. The menu changes every day and only has a few items, but the food is always cooked to perfection: whether pork chops, prime rib, or chili with thyme and cauliflower, it's fresh, delicious, and at 85 SEK, it's pretty cheap. Though the riverside warehouse the restaurant is housed in looks a little sketch, don't shy away. We can't recommend this place enough!

i *Entreés 85-100 SEK. Open M-F noon-2pm.*

NIGHTLIFE

BIERHAUS
Drottninggatan 36   ☎40 23 60 01 www.bierhaus.se

Located right off of Malmö's main pedestrian street, this beer house feels ridiculously authentic. They've got every kind of beer imaginable at knockout prices:

malmö

though we're partial to the Berliner Kindl and Warsteiner Pilsner, practically everything here is tasty and Teutonic. Whatever you order, we highly recommend shelling out money for the currywurst—part sausage, part curry ketchup, it's the ultimate drunk food to set your night in the right direction.

i Beers 100 SEK. Open Tu-Th 4pm-1am.

BIERHAUS MALMÖ
Norra Parkgatan 2 ☎40 23 60 01 www.bierhaus.se

This is one of Malmö's biggest and best clubs. Even though our Scandinavia researcher would prefer getting cholera to going clubbing, even he had to admit this place was fun. The clientele is usually a mix of young professionals and a college-age crowd, and the space is big enough (between the patio, lounge room, bar, and music stage) to find your own groove. Start off at the bar to try one of the 20 beers on tap here. Then get ready to dance the night away. The music can range from house to hip hop to 80s rock. If all the music and bumping is getting you claustrophobic, step outside. You're in the heart of Malmö's coolest pub neighborhood, so you're sure to find something here that won't kill your vibe.

i Cover varies depending on performers. Beers 150 SEK. Open Tu-Sa 4pm-1am.

MALMÖ BRYGGHUS
Bergsgatan 33 ☎40 20 96 85

If your average beer intake include Keystone and Miller Lite, congrats on being a patriot. But we encourage you expand your horizons a bit by visiting the Brygghus, Malmö's only microbrewery. Though the giant metal vats give off a Breaking Bad vibe, the beer here is so high quality, it's clear they pour all of their time into making it. You can't go wrong with the tap selection—Pilsner, lagers and a few IPA's—but for the more adventurous, their monthly selection is where it's at. Even better, they offer tasting tours (at roughly 250 SEK) and a full food menu to battle the beer hangover you might have the next morning.

i Beer 30-150 SEK. Tasting tour 250 SEK. Bar snacks 100 SEK. Open M-Tu 5pm-11pm, W-Th 4pm-1am, F-Sa 4pm-3am, closed Sundays.

ESSENTIALS
Practicalities

- **TOURIST OFFICES:** Malmö Turistbyrå (Börshuset, Skeppsbron. ☎40 34 12 00. www.malmotown.com. Open M-F 9am-5pm, Sa-Su 10am-2pm.)

- **CURRENCY EXCHANGE:** Possible at Malmö Airport and stores such as Forex (which has three locations in Malmö, including in Central Station).

- **ATMS:** Swedbank and Nordea ATMs are located throughout Malmö (especially along crowded pedestrian streets such as Scheelevägen and the area directly adjacent to Slottsparken) and many give you an option of withdrawing in Swedish Kronor, Danish Kronor, or Euros.

- **LUGGAGE STORAGE:** If you're not storing your luggage at a hostel or hotel, you can rent out a small, medium or large lockers at Malmö Central Station (available for periods of 12 and 24 hours or longer; can use coins or card).

- **GLBT SERVICES:** Next to Stockholm, Malmö may be the most gay-friendly city in Sweden—you'll find plenty of gay bars in the area around Folkets Park (for a full list of clubs, bars and restaurants, consult the Malmö city website www.malmotown.com/en/article/gay-friendly-places/).

- **INTERNET:** Almost all cafes have free Wi-Fi (you'll find plenty of Swedish national chains, such as Espresso House, alongside independent coffee shops). You'll also get connectivity at the City Library (Kung Oscars väg 11) and major train stations such as Central Station and Triangeln.

- **POST OFFICE:** Posten Företagscenter (Krossverksgatan 7 ☎40 15 58 92. Open M-F 8am-6pm.)

Emergency

- **EMERGENCY NUMBER:** ☎112

- **LOCAL POLICE:** ☎77 114 14 00

- **POISON CONTROL:** ☎20 22 00 06

- **SWEDISH NATIONAL SUICIDE HOTLINE:** ☎31 711 24 00

- **RFSL MALMÖ:** ☎40 10 33 21, for questions related to the organization and LGBTQ-related issues. Phone available Tuesdays and Thursdays from 12pm to 4pm.

- **24 HOUR MEDICAL ADVICE:** ☎1177

- **LATE-NIGHT PHARMACIES:** Apoteket Gripen (Bergsgatan 48 ☎77 145 04 50. Open daily 8am-10pm.)

- **HOSPITALS:** For emergencies, always call ☎112 for an ambulance or ☎1177 for medical advice. If you are not a Swedish citizen, make sure to bring your passport and insurance information if you go to the doctor. Vårdcentralen Granen (Grangatan 11 ☎40 623 42 00. Best time for drop-ins is weekdays 10am-12pm and 1-3pm, but primary care and phone lines are open 8am-5pm on weekdays.)

Getting There

Malmö Airport (known previously as Sturup) is 17 miles away from the city center and services both Malmö and Lund. There are several daily flights between here and Stockholm, as well as other Scandinavian and continental European cities. The cheapest and quickest way to get from the airport to the city center is to take the shuttle bus, Flygbussarna, directly from the departures terminal. Tickets can be purchased online (www.flygbussarna.se/en/malmo) or at the airport at a price of 105 SEK for adults and 95 SEK for children. The bus takes 30-40 minutes to arrive at Malmö Central Station.

As elsewhere in Sweden, cabs to and from the airport are more expensive than public transportation. Cheaper rides from companies such as Taxi 23 (☎40 23 23 23) go for a flat rate of 359 SEK. Always confirm the fare with the driver before getting in the car.

Getting Around

Public Transportation

Jojo: To use public transportation, you must first purchase a Jojo card. The card costs 20 SEK (available at Malmö Central Station) and you can then add as many fares as you want onto it. Each ride costs 22 SEK, but you get a 20% discount (ie price of 17 SEK per ride) if you upload more than 200 SEK onto the card.

Malmö City Card: This card gives discounts at around 600 separate places, whether that be 50% off at public museums, 10% off taxi rides, or free dessert at restaurants. The card also provides 24 hours of free parking and can be purchased via an app or in person at the Tourist Information office. Full price offerings are available online, but the 1 day for 1 adult and 2 kids is 170 SEK, while 2 days is 200 SEK.

By Taxi

Taxis are not as expensive here as they are in Stockholm, though prices change depending on time of day and number of passengers. The following are prices for an average 10 km/15-minute trip (though there's an extra tax if you're traveling after

malmö

9 o'clock on weekends). RD Taxi (☎20 30 03 00): 241 SEK. Taxi Kurir (☎40 700 00): 245-261 SEK. Taxi Skåne (☎40 33 03 30): 263 SEK.

lund

College students make up about half of Lund's population. That young population means that there are cheap eats galore—everything from vegetarian and sushi to kebab and dumplings—and a very active nightlife. As it's such a small place, there isn't much of a backpacker's scene; in fact, Lund only has one hostel, though there are reasonably priced hotels and B&Bs as well.

That might seem a bit limiting for the young traveller, but you'll probably stay here only day or two in the first place; the town is roughly the size of a medium pizza, and you can see all the main sights in a single day. Nevertheless, Lund has plenty of hidden charm: whether its touring the Tolkien-esque cottages or finding bargains at the student thrift shops, there are plenty of ways to fall in love with this town. Do note, though, that while the medieval cathedral and botanical park are certainly beautiful places to walk through, in summer, the whole town tends to be as dead as Al Gore's presidential hopes. So if you're looking for wild college parties, try to come while school is still in session.

SIGHTS

LUND CATHEDRAL
Kyrkogatan 6   www.lundsdomkyrka.se

Every city has something to be proud of. Lund is no different with its massive medieval cathedral that is absolutely beautiful to look at. It has been here for close to 1000 years, and whatever botox the building uses is clearly working: the stonework is immaculate, the arches are perfectly preserved, and the pews inside have got more wood than most mornings. The cathedral is an imposing landmark, and, better yet, is five minutes away from all the parks, museums and restaurants you'll want to visit while on a trip to Lund. If you're lucky, you may even come during one of the free tours of the cathedral, which are offered daily during the summer.

i Free. Open M-F 8am-6pm, Sa 9:30am-5pm, Su 9:30am-6pm.

BOTANICAL GARDEN
Östra Vallgatan 20   ☎46 222 73 20 www.botaniskatradgarden.se

This garden, managed by Lund University, boasts over 7000 species of plants and some beautifully curated walking paths. The place is swarming with flowers, trees, blackbirds (who, like Poe's Raven, quoth "uh uh, nevermore!" when you try to pet them), and a number of greenhouses and tranquil ponds. Spend an afternoon walking through this historic garden—it has been around since the 1600s—and learning about our world's greener friends.

i Free. Open daily May-Sept 6am-9:30pm; Oct-Apr 6am-8pm.

LUND UNIVERSITY
University kids make up about half of the population in this town of 80,000, so it only makes sense you should drop by their alma mater. The campus covers a significant portion of Lund proper and includes everything from medieval towers to French-style style gardens and palatial ivy-lined libraries. The campus also hosts the Historiska Museum, the second-largest museum, in Sweden, as well as a number of beautiful tree-lined gardens. Look smart and see what your college years could've looked like without Netflix.

i Free.

sweden

get a room!

WINSTRUP HOSTEL $

Winstrupsgatan 3 ☎723 290 800 www.winstruphostel.se

You'd think that being the only hostel in town would make these guys drunk on power; that they, like some budget-travel version of Monsanto, would jack up prices and give substandard service because it's a monopoly. However, the accommodations here actually went above and beyond: all of the beds in the shared rooms have lamps, power outlets, and curtains that effectively turn them into mini-cubbies. You can actually stay here without ever interacting with the other people in your room, and the introvert in us loves that! Moreover, the place comes equipped with a full kitchen and offers 25% discounts at a cafe around the corner. It's comfortable and affordable and, along with love, that's all you need.

i Dorms 275 SEK. Linens 65 SEK. Laundry 50 SEK. Breakfast 69 SEK. Reception open 7am-11am and 3pm and 8pm.

CHECKINN B&B B&B $$

Hantverksgatan 6 ☎723 290 800 www.checkinn.se

CheckInn is run by the same people who own Winstrup, and clearly they're doing something right: the place is cute and cheap while still maintaining a hotel-level quality of service. The cheaper rooms go for around 600 SEK a night, but each usually has a bathroom, TV, air conditioner, and wooden floors (because only peasants decorate with shag carpet). It's a short walk away from the train station and might be the comfiest accommodation you'll find while here—if you're only staying a night or two, we highly recommend this place!

i Studio apartment 600-900 SEK. Doubles 800-1000 SEK. Breakfast included. Reception open 7am-11am and 3pm and 8pm.

RUNESTONE MOUND

on Lund University's campus, off Paradisgatan

These runes are a stone's throw away from Lund University's main buildings and are arranged in a curious pattern on a raised mound. We've heard tell that coming here at midnight and whispering "bloody murder" three times will summon the ghost of Ivar the Boneless, but thankfully that's not too much cause for concern. Probably a good guy to grab a beer with. The stones themselves are incredibly old and fascinating to look at. Most of them are eulogies to fallen warriors, with inscriptions like "here lies Björn, a fighter of wide renown," but others are much longer and more artistically written out. Though our Old Norse skills leave a lot to be desired, it's entirely possible the bigger inscriptions say something like "End of the World Sale: all axes half off at Leif's Wonder Emporium, December 31st, 999 A.D." (Note: this is actually not possible.)

FOOD

HUMMUS BAR $

Bangatan 8 ☎12 63 00

The entrance to this place has an illustrated guide on how to eat hummus with pita, but thankfully informs its customers that they won't judge if you use a fork. Thanks, Hummus Bar. You the real MVP. And we say that not only for your tolerance of our primitive ways, but also because of the wallet-friendly Middle Eastern goodness of all your dishes. Our recommendation: the falafel (65 SEK) comes wrapped in a blanket of tahini and hummus and also includes two small side salads.

i Wraps 65-85 SEK. Open M-F 11am-7pm, Sa noon-7pm; closed Sundays.

WOKERIAN $
Knut Den Stores Torg 2 ☎12 23 23

This popular student haunt fries up tasty dumplings and serves them fast. The restaurant is directly in sight of the train station and not far from the university, and with most dishes in the 70-90 SEK range, it's filling and affordable. They cook up a full menu of Chinese and Japanese dishes, so this is an ideal spot if you're looking to spoon noodles, kung pao chicken, or maki rolls into your eager mouth.

i Entrees 70-100 SEK. Open M-Sa 11am-9pm, Su noon-8pm.

LUND SALUHALLEN $$
Mårtenstorget 1

You'll find plenty of saluhallen throughout Scandinavia, and Lund's is pretty typical: there are about 15 restaurants, a couple delis, and, for those of you looking to spend half your paycheck on a shot of vodka, a Systembolaget liquor store. We're huge fans of Persian food and highly recommend Shiraz Restaurant (the chicken kebab, at 85 SEK, gave us a whole new perspective on life), though other spots like Thai Way and Wasabi Sushi are also tasty. Our best advice: get lost in here and let the food choose you.

i Prices vary. The delis are a bit more upscale, though both the Thai and Persian places are in the 85SEK range. Open M-W 10am-6pm, Th-F 10am-7pm, Sa 9:30am-3pm; closed Sundays.

CAFÉ & CREPERIE OSKAR $
Klostergatan 14C ☎72 329 08 00

Café Oskar is truly an excellent spot for breakfast and snacks. Whether you're looking to nibble on a crêpe or plow through a week's worth of sandwiches and coffee, the prices are affordable and the food is delectable. If you're a guest at Winstrup, CheckInn, or Hotel Oskar, you get a 25% discount here, and the breakfast buffet—with all the classic Scandinavian trappings like eggs, cured meats and marmalade—is excellent for both light eaters and food juggernauts.

i Coffee 25 SEK. Pastries 70 SEK. Open M-F 7am-5pm, Sa-Su 8am-5pm.

NIGHTLIFE

CAFÉ ARIMAN
Kungsgatan 2 ☎46 13 12 63 www.ariman.se

This place seems to be Lund's loud, leftwing answer to Starbucks. By day it's a cafe filled wall to wall with neckbeards and berets, but at night it becomes a club and bar that's a major hit with students. Unfortunately, the DJs take off during the summer, but it's still a good place for quick beers or a cocktail as you debate Liechtenstein's critique of the Hamburger Palpability Theorem or whatever intellectual people talk about.

i No cover. Drinks 70 SEK. Open M-Sa 11am-late (usually 3am on weekends), Su 3pm-11pm.

ESSENTIALS

Practicalities

- **TOURIST OFFICE:** Lunds Turistbyrå (Botulfsgatan 1A ☎46 35 50 40. www.visitlund.se. Open M-F 10m-6pm, Sa 10am-3pm, Su 11am-3pm.)

- **CURRENCY EXCHANGE:** There are two Forex locations in Lund: Bankgatan 8 and at Botulfsgatan 2.

- **ATMS:** There are a number of ATMs in the shopping area adjacent to Central Station. It's the first place you will see when you arrive at the train station

- **LUGGAGE STORAGE:** Lockers are available at Lund Central Station (payable by credit card or coins). Medium sized luggage costs 50 SEK per day. Larger lockers are available for 60 SEK a day.

- **INTERNET:** Wi-Fi is available at the central station, tourist center, public library (Lund Stadsbibliotek—Sankt Petri Kyrkogatan 6), and most cafes.

- **POST OFFICE:** Posten Företagscenter Lund City (Gasverksgatan 3A ☎10 436 10 35. Open M-F 8am-6pm.)

Emergency

- **EMERGENCY NUMBER:** ☎112

- **LOCAL POLICE:** ☎77 114 14 00

- **MEDICAL ADVICE:** ☎1177

- **SWEDISH NATIONAL SUICIDE HOTLINE:** ☎31 71 124 00

- **PHARMACIES:** Apotek Hjärtat (Mårtenstorget 12 ☎40 54 05 223 51. Open M-F 9am-8pm, Sa 9am-7pm, Su 10am-7pm.)

- **HOSPITALS:** For emergencies, always call ☎112 for an ambulance or ☎1177 for medical advice. If you are not a Swedish citizen, make sure to bring your passport and insurance information if you go to the doctor. Skane University Hospital in Lund (Getingevägen 4 ☎17 10 00.)

Getting There

Lund is serviced by Malmö Airport. The cheapest and quickest way to get from the airport to the city center is to take the shuttle bus, Flygbussarna directly from the departures terminal. Tickets can be purchased online (www.flygbussarna.se/en/malmo) or at the airport for 105 SEK. The airport flat rate for a cab from Taxi Skåne is 445 SEK, and other companies have similar prices

Getting Around

Public Transportation

Lund is tiny and there's little need to use public transportation here, but the town does have an extensive bus network which uses the Jojo card. The card costs 20 SEK and you then upload as many fares as you want onto it. Each ride costs 22 SEK, but you get a 20% discount (17 SEK per ride) if you upload more than 200 SEK onto the card.

Malmö City Card: This card gives discounts at around 600 separate places, whether that be 50% off at public museums, 10% off taxi rides, or free dessert and extra burgers at restaurants. The card also provides 24 hours of free parking and can be purchased via an app or in person at the Tourist Information office. Full price offerings are available online, but the 1 day for 1 adult and 2 kids is 170 SEK while 2 days is 200 SEK.

By Taxi

Taxi Lund 121212 (☎046 12 12 12.) Generally, weekend prices are 35 SEK as a base, 11.50 SEK per km and 5 SEK per minute, though the exact rates change depending on time of day and number of people.

lund

sweden essentials

VISAS

Sweden is a member of the EU, and also a member of the Schengen area. Citizens of Australia, Canada, New Zealand, the US, and many other non-EU countries do not need a visa for stays of up to 90 days. However, if you plan to spend time in other Schengen countries, note that the 90-day period of time you are allowed to visit without a visa applies cumulatively to all Schengen countries.

MONEY

Despite being a member of the EU, Sweden is not in the Eurozone and uses the Swedish krona (SEK or kr.) as its currency.

In restaurants, a gratuity or service charge is often included, in which case you don't have to tip. If no gratuity is added, tip your server 5-10%, or to round up the bill to the nearest 10. To tip a taxi driver, also just round up the bill.

ATMs in Sweden are common and convenient. They are often located in airports, train stations and major pedestrian areas. The two major international money networks are MasterCard/Maestro/Cirrus and Visa/PLUS. To find out what out-of-network or international fees you may be subject to by using ATMs, call your bank.

ALCOHOL

There is no minimum age in Sweden to purchase alcohol under 2.25% ABV in super-markets. The minimum age to purchase alcohol in restaurants and bars, or alcohol above 2.25% in supermarkets is 18. To purchase alcohol from a Systembolaget, you must be 20. Bars, clubs, and discos often have age restrictions higher than 18, and are usually either 20 or 23. Remember to drink responsibly and to never drink and drive. The legal blood alcohol content (BAC) for driving in Sweden is under 0.02%, significantly lower than the US limit of 0.08%.

SWITZERLAND

Switzerland is a dazzling array of crystal-clear lakes, lush greenery, quaint wooden churches, soaring mountain peaks, and of course, obscene amounts of gourmet chocolate. But as one of the most expensive destinations in Europe, Switzerland isn't the most popular choice for travelers on a budget. Fear not, frugal backpacker! We've compiled the top spots that won't make your wallet (totally) hate you. Whether you come during the winter to take advantage of its world-class skiing, or spend a balmy summer evening hiking its serene trails, Switzerland's beauty won't cease to amaze. Meander through the winding cobblestone lanes of Zurich; munch on freshly baked bread and cheese in Bern; and bike along the historic chapel bridge in Lucerne, all without breaking the bank.

greatest hits

- **TA-DA(DA)!** The birthplace of the Dada movement is **Cabaret Voltaire** (p. 778) in Zurich. Unsurprisingly, it continues to push the envelope and operate pretty off the beaten path.

- **CLIMB EVERY MOUNTAIN.** While you won't exactly be hiking the Swiss Alps (though they're in view in the distance), hiking up **Mt. Pilatus** (p. 783) is a worthwhile excursion on a trip to Lucerne.

zurich

In his novel Tender is the Night, F. Scott Fitzgerald describes life in Zurich as "a perpendicular starting off to a postcard heaven," with the idea that quintessential Swiss beauty—with its snow-capped Alps, meandering funiculars, and cuckoo clocks—surrounds the city, but doesn't pervade Zurich itself. We're inclined to agree with Scotty: though well within daytripping distance of natural beauties like Jungfrau, the Rhine Falls, and Germany's Black Forest, Zurich proper is more sleek and contemporary than charming and rustic. The largest city in Switzerland, Zurich is a financial and commercial metropolis, and home to the famously discreet Swiss banks that hold the fortunes of mafia godfathers and unscrupulous businessmen across the globe. Indeed, a staggeringly high percentage of the world's money flows through Zurich, and a high percentage of your own budget may shrink away in this pricey town. Yet wealth and modernity have their benefits: Zurich boasts excellent shopping, extensive art, and interesting nightlife.

SIGHTS

KUNSTHAUS

Heimplatz 1 ☎044 253 84 84 www.kunsthaus.ch

Zurich's premier "contemporary" art museum actually houses a collection spanning the 16th to 21st centuries. Artists featured in Kunsthaus' strategically lit interior include a gaggle of Swiss painters, Impressionists Degas and Cézanne, and Modernists Klee, Picasso, Warhol, and Ernst. Gaze to your heart's content at three expansive iterations of Monet's iconic water lilies, as well as Van Gogh's famous self-portrait. Allow at least 3hr. for a leisurely walk-through (more for the special exhibition), and be sure to snag a free audio guide before you begin. Lockers are available and, as in all Swiss museums, the toilets are clean and free.

i Kunsthaus tram stop. Tu 10am-6pm, W-Th 10am-8pm, F-Su 10am-6pm. Collections 15CHF (students 10CHF), exhibition 22CHF (students 17CHF), combined 25CHF (students 18CHF). Zurich-CARD holders receive student price.

GROSSMÜNSTER, FRAUMÜNSTER, AND ST. PETER CHURCHES

Grossmünsterplatz ☎044 252 59 49 www.grossmuenster.ch
Münsterhof 2 ☎044 211 41 00 www.fraumuenster.ch
St. Peterhofstatt ☎044 211 60 57 ww.st-peter-zh.ch

Three of Zurich's most distinctive landmarks, each a bastion of religious orthodoxy, are sufficiently unorthodox, and all are blessedly free of charge. The twin towers of Grossmünster, tiered like a peculiar wedding cake, dominate the skyline and, when climbed, afford sweeping views of the old town. Fraumunster, literally "women's abbey," was historically a convent. A squishy side entrance was used to police particularly voluminous hoop skirts in an effort to discourage decadence. St. Peter boasts the largest clockface in Europe, which befits the watch-making capital of the world. Unlike those of TAG Heuer or Omega, the timepiece on St. Peter gives the hour for free.

i Grossmünster: Helmhaus tram stop. Church open daily Mar-Oct 9am-6pm, Nov-Feb 10am-5pm; tower open M-Sa 10am-5pm, Su 1pm-5pm. Free (tower 4CHF, students/children 2CHF). Fraumünster: Helmhaus tram stop. Daily Apr-Oct 10am-6pm, Nov-Mar 10am-4pm. Free. St. Peter: Paradeplatz tram stop. M-F 8am-6pm, Sa 9am-4pm, Su 11am-4pm. Free.

FOOD

✇ PHO NA $

Josefstrasse 42 ☎043 833 05 23 http://phona.website

Besides your trusty supermarket chains, the best bet for cheap eats in Switzerland is ethnic food. Join the entire Vietnamese population of Zurich to marvel at

switzerland

get a room!

CITY BACKPACKER / HOTEL BIBER $$$
Niederdorfstrasse 5   ☎044 251 90 15 www.city-backpacker.ch
Give thanks for this hostel's prime location in the thick of the old city, just
a 10min. walk from the train station, but be prepared for a hike up three
flights of stairs to reach reception. If you care to continue on up, you'll
find that the rooftop terrace is a sunny and social space. The Äss-Bar
across the alley is another boon; grab a sandwich for lunch for 2-3CHF.
i Cross Bahnhofquai and enter old town, turn right onto Niederdorfstrasse (10min. walk).
Dorms 37CHF, singles 77CHF, doubles 118CHF. Wi-Fi, linens (3CHF), kitchen, lockers, key
card access, laundry for hire. Reception 8am-noon and 3-10pm.

YOUTH HOSTEL ZURICH $$$
Mutschellenstrasse 114   ☎043 399 78 00 www.youthhostel.ch/zurich
Zurich's official youth hostel is a 15min. bus ride from the city center,
which is unfortunately not covered by a short-distance ticket. As such,
each one-way ride will require a 4.30CHF ticket, or you can opt for a
day pass (8.60CHF) or use a ZurichCARD discount. Location aside,
this well-populated accommodation offers cozy bunks, clean showers,
speedy Wi-Fi, and a top-notch breakfast buffet.
i Take tram 7 to Morgental, then walk 5min., or take S-Bahn train 8 to Wollishofen, follow signs on Staubstrasse for 5min. Dorms from 52CHF, doubles from 116CHF. Wi-Fi (on
ground floor only), breakfast, linens, lockers. Limited parking available. Reception 24hr.,
check-in 3pm.

Pho Na's display of steaming curries (13.50CHF) and fragrant summer rolls
(7.50CHF). More elaborate dishes like the eponymous pho are pricier, but this
casual family operation on the corner of Josefstrasse has mercy on your hem-
orrhaging wallet; bahn mi, stuffed with mint and coriander, costs 13CHF—in
Switzerland, as sensational a steal as any bank heist.
i Walk along Museumstrasse, which turns into Zollstrasse, turn right onto Hafnerstrasse and left
onto Josefstrasse (15min. walk). Stir-fries and curries 9.90-13.50CHF, add 2CHF for side of rice or
noodles, bahn mi 13CHF, pho 19CHF. M-Sa 11am-10pm.

STERNEN-GRILL $
Theaterstrasse 22   ☎043 268 20 80 www.sternengrill.ch
Swiss cuisine is uncomfortably pricey for the budget traveler: at casual
restaurants, expect 25CHF for a pot of fondue or 40CHF for platters of zürcher
geschnetzeltes—a popular but phonetically impossible dish consisting of sliced
veal and hash browns. So don't pass up the opportunity to get an affordable
taste of Switzerland at Sternen-Grill, upstairs a restaurant and downstairs a
bustling take-away with seating available. Indulge in the sausage party—the
all-male staff whips out the traditional bratwurst (7.50CHF) and its variants, like
currywurst (8.50CHF). Complimentary hunks of bread and sharp mustard make
for a full meal.
i From Bürkliplatz, cross the Quailbrücke bridge and continue onto Rämistrasse, turn right onto
Bellevueplatz. Sausages 6.50-14CHF, beer 4.50-7CHF, wine 5.20-7CHF. No credit cards. Daily
10:30am-11:45pm.

INDIA STREET FOOD $
Langstrasse 213
If you tire of Switzerland's famously low crime rate and its rosy-cheeked affabil-
ity, have a wander through Zurich's red light district for a samosa or two at India

zurich

daytrip: rhine falls

If in search of Fitzgerald's "postcard perfection" and the famed natural beauty of Switzerland, take a daytrip to Europe's largest waterfall, a 40min. train ride away. Options for getting up close and personal with this literal force of nature are many—viewing platforms on either side of the falls provide dramatic vantage points of the flow from above. The roughly 45min. climb up costs 7.50CHF. Even better, boats and their intrepid operators conduct bumpy 20min. voyages within meters (and spraying distance) of the falls for 10CHF. Squint through the water spray at the perpetual rainbows shimmering above the mist. Apparently the bed of the Rhine is a graveyard of dropped iPhones and cameras, so keep hold of your devices as you snap photos.

Street Food. True to its name, this booth—crammed between a tacky gown shop and a "massage parlor"—demands you shovel down your lamb, chicken, or vegetable curry (10CHF) on the street, as there is zero seating available. Come with cash; thankfully, given the prices, you won't have to spend too much of it.

i Walk along Museumstrasse, which turns into Zollstrasse, turn right onto Neugasse, right onto Langstrasse (15min. walk). Samosas 3.50CHF, entrees 10-14.50CHF. No credit cards. M-Sa 11:30am-11:30pm.

VEGELATERIA $
Müllerstrasse 64   ☎044 558 70 35 https://vegelateria.ch

Vegan gelato might sound like the sadistic brainchild of health nuts and hippies, but the selection at Vegelateria, a.k.a. The Sacred, is sweetened with honey and apples and good enough for all of us. Inspired by the teachings of Indian guru Sri Chinmoy, this restaurant offers exclusively vegetarian and vegan cuisine. The owner is far more friendly than he looks, and he shares his philosophy of the fruit as he persuasively shuttles you from the gelato case to the impressive buffet, which includes dishes like enchiladas and Thai curry.

i From Stauffacher stop, head down Lutherstrasse, right onto St. Jakobstrasse, left on Müllerstrasse. Buffet 3.90CHF/kg (appx. 10-15CHF per meal), vegan pastries 3-4CHF, 1 scoop gelato 3.50CHF, 2 scoops 6CHF, 3 scoops 9CHF. M-Sa 11am-9pm.

NIGHTLIFE

CABARET VOLTAIRE
Spiegelgasse 1   ☎043 268 57 20 www.cabaretvoltaire.ch

Disgusted by WWI, Hugo Ball donned his construction-paper dunce cap and cape, chanted "blago bung blago bung," and that bizarre post-post modern and anti-art artform known as Dada was born in this deliciously quirky nightclub. The ground floor houses a bookstore and art gallery, as well as a restroom full of performers and their eccentric props (e.g. a vagina onesie). On the upper level, share a beer (3.50CHF) with hoary old poet types staring blankly into the ether and ask yourself, as does the black-and-white wall print, "to be da-da or not DaDa?" On certain nights (check the website), unintelligible but fascinating live performances ensue in the back room, which is ever permeated by the synthetic smell of the in-house fog machine.

i Cross Bahnhofquai and enter old town, turn right and follow Limmatquai south, left onto Marktgasse, right onto Münstergasse, left onto Spiegelgasse (15min. walk). Beer 3.50CHF, cocktails 7CHF. Wi-Fi available. M-Th 11am-midnight, F 11am-2am, Sa 10am-2am, Su noon-7pm.

switzerland

ROTE FABRIK

Seestrasse 395   ☎044 485 58 58 www.rotefabrik.ch

A relic of Zurich's once important textile industry, this fabric factory now serves as a youth mecca: a combined music venue, theater, cultural center, and bar. Check the website for event details, or show up anytime for the camp-like ambiance and cocktails (13-15CHF). The soundtrack includes the likes of Mumford & Sons as well as the gentle sloshing of Lake Lucerne, just beyond the light of the colored incandescent bulbs hanging from the trees. Like elsewhere in gritty Zurich, graffiti reigns supreme, including this charming ditty: "I made Love with a tree/ Whilst High on LSD." Good times have been had at this place.

i *From Wollishofen tram stop, head down Seestrasse for 10min. Beer 4.50-7.50CHF, cocktails 13-15CHF, coffee/tea 4-5.50CHF. Credit cards accepted over 20CHF. Tu-Su 11am-midnight (later on concert nights).*

WINGS

Limmatquai 54   ☎043 268 40 55 http://wings-lounge.ch

This "airline bar and lounge" is intimately concerned with the magic of flight. Following the bankruptcy of Swissair in the 2001 aviation crisis, the newly unemployed pilots and flight attendants reinvented their careers and opened a bar. The walls are punctuated with mock airplane windows, the seats are of red leather, and the bar itself is a curvy white number reminiscent of the bulge of a wing. The drinks list is extensive and is as worldly as the international arrivals gate—try an "Airforce One" (16CHF) if you fancy white peach, or a "Sex on the WINGS" (16CHF) for notes of passion fruit. The final page of the menu reads, "Wings—let your soul fly." We will, Wings, we will.

i *Cross Bahnhofquai into old town, continue down Limmatquai for 10min., destination on left. M-Th 4pm-midnight, F noon-2am, Sa 2pm-2am. Wi-Fi available. Beer 4.80-9CHF, wine 7.50-8.50CHF, champagne 16CHF, cocktails 11.50-20CHF.*

ESSENTIALS

Practicalities

- **TOURIST OFFICE:** Zurich Tourist Service, located in the main train station. Book city tours, purchase ZurichCARD and tickets for public transport or museums, make hotel reservations, pick up free pamphlets and guides. ☎044 215 40 00, touristservice@zurich.com. M-Sa 8am-8:30pm, Su 8:30am-6:30pm.

- **MONEY:** ATMs available at banks (UBS is ubiquitous). Banking hours M-F 8:30am-4:30pm.

- **POST OFFICE:** Central post office is Sihlpost (Kasernenstrasse 97, ☎084 888 88 88. Sihlpost tram stop. M-F 6:30am-10:30pm, Sa 6:30am-8pm, Su 10am-10:30pm).

- **PUBLIC TOILETS:** At major tram stops, 1CHF (Apr-Oct 6:30am-9:45pm, Nov-Mar 6:30am-8:45pm).

- **WI-FI:** The first hour of Wi-Fi is free in the train station (and all Swiss train stations), but you'll need to register the first time with a phone number. The Zurich airport offers 90min. of free Wi-Fi, registration required. At the tourist office, you can also rent wireless modems with unlimited data, info at www.travelerswifi.com (40CHF for 3 days, 65CHF for 7, 130CHF for 15).

- **WATER:** Tap water is potable, and fountains around town are very drinkable.

Emergency

- **AMBULANCE:** ☎114.

- **POLICE:** ☎117.

zurich

- **HOSPITALS:** Universitätsspital (Rämistrasse 100, ☎044 255 11 11, ETH tram stop), Stadtspital Triemli (Birmensdorferstrasse 497, ☎044 466 11 11, Triemli tram stop), and Stadtspital Waid (Tièchestrasse 99, ☎044 366 20 55, Bucheggplatz tram stop) all open 24hr.

- **PHARMACIES:** On Su, the only shops permitted to open are in railway stops and petrol stations. Pharmacy in the main train station is open until midnight, otherwise shops in the railway station are open 9am-8pm. Some groceries open until 11pm—the large Coop supermarket next to the main railway station is open M-Sa 7am-10pm.

Getting Around

Zurich cradles Lake Zurich, with the old town and most attractions on the right bank of the river Limmat, while the left bank houses the modern city and Zurich HB (pronounced "haa-bay" and short for Hauptbahnhof, or main train station).

Public transport options (VBZ) are tram, bus, boat, and train. The three former options are used to get around the city and Lake Zurich, and run appx. 5am-1:30am. On F-Sa, the night network (Nachtnetze) kicks in from 1-5am and requires two tickets, a normal transport ticket and a night supplement ticket (5CHF, or 6 for 27CHF, discounts and ZurichCARD not applicable). Text "NZ" to ☎988 to purchase the supplement.

The confusing public transport network is divided into zones. Zurich city is zone 110, which includes the old city and most of the sites (excluding swimming spots, the popular mountain lookout Uetliberg, the airport, and the official youth hostel). Short-distance tickets (2.60CHF) are valid for 30min. in zones 110 (Zurich) and 120 (Winterthur), but usually for only 5-6 stops, so check the listing on the ticket machine at purchase. Day pass for zone 110 is 8.60CHF (river boat included), pass for 1hr. is 4.30CHF. Additional 2CHF per zone to travel through multiple zones. Buy tickets at blue machines located at every stop (most take credit cards or coins only, no bills). No need to validate on board, but keep your ticket; the fine for traveling without one starts at 90CHF. Travelers under 25 get a reduced price for multi-day passes, multiple-journey tickets, and group tickets; carry ID in case of inspection. For full list of prices, check www.stadt-zuerich.ch.

Save money with the ZurichCARD (24CHF for 24hr., 48CHF for 72hr.), which provides free access to public transport for zone 110 and to and from the airport, as well as discounts or free entrance to many museums and clubs, and free sides or desserts at participating restaurants with the purchase of an entree. Sold at most ticket machines and the tourist office in main train station, where you can pick up a pamphlet for complete list of benefits. Before using, validate once at a blue ticket machine or orange validator on one of the platforms.

Taxis are clean and safe but expensive (initial fee 6-8CHF, then 3.80-5CHF/km or 80CHF/hour). Taxis around the train station are especially exorbitant. Uber is cheaper.

Bicycle rentals are free, but require ID and 20CHF deposit. Stations just outside train station, near track 3 (M-F 8am-9:30pm) and 18 (M-F 9am-7:30pm), info at www.zuerirollt.ch.

lucerne

Lucerne, or Luzern to the German-speaking locals, is often relegated to the role of convenient rest stop, a less expensive bed for aspiring Alpinists whose real objects are mountains such as Pilatus, Rigi, and beyond. While high-altitude daytrips, particularly to the nearby Pilatus, are well worth the splurge, the city proper is replete with natural and rustic Germanic charms. Gabled wooden bridges (including the famous Kappellbrücke in the city center), earthy painted façades, and turreted medieval

Official Swiss youth hostels charge a daily membership fee (6CHF/night). For longer stays, consider buying an annual membership (33CHF for 18+, student rate 22CHF).

YOUTHHOSTEL LUZERNE $$$

Sedelstrasse 12   ☎041 420 88 00 www.youthhostel.ch

Enter to the shrill howls of a life-sized ceramic bull, painted with the Hostelling International logo and grazing on an artificial patch of grass. Alas, you'll quickly realize that the racket actually emanates from the many small humans playing at the statue's feet. Lucerne's official youth hostel attracts quite the young clientele, so expect to dodge children on the stairs and munch your breakfast among the families. Speaking of breakfast, the large spread and variety of fixins will make up for the noisy neighbors.

i From Lucerne Station, take bus 18 to Jugendherberge (12min.) or bus 19 to Gopplismoosweg (7min.), then it's a 5min. walk. Look for yellow Hostelling International signs. Reception 7am-midnight. Wi-Fi on ground floor and 1st floor only; breakfast, dinner for purchase; includes linens, city guides, lockers, refrigerator. Dorms 43CHF (20 person) or 49CHF (4-6 person); singles from 91CHF. Check-in 3pm, check-out 10am.

walls of your childhood fairy tales await you in Lucerne. A bit heavier on tourists than your average Swiss town, due to its strategic location, the city even offers the odd international ugly to play the part of ogre.

SIGHTS

LÖWENDENKMAL (LION MONUMENT)
Denkmalstrasse 4

An oversized statue of a dying lion might not seem like much of an attraction, but trust us (and the swarms of photobombing tourists): the Lion Monument is well worth a visit. Chiseled into sheer marble rock face, the dying lion, draped atop broken shields and spears, honors the Swiss soldiers who fell during the French Revolution. The size of the sculpture, as well as the decidedly humanoid anguish on the lion's face, make for an arresting sight, and what Mark Twain dubbed "the most mournful and moving piece of stone in the world." The pond below the monument is uncharacteristically murky, adding to the poetic melancholy. Don't miss it.

i From Löwenplatz bus stop, follow Löwenplatz, left onto Denkmalstrasse, right to stay on Denkmalstrasse (4min. walk). Free.

KAPELLBRÜCKE (CHAPEL BRIDGE)
The most iconic of Lucerne's attractions, this oddly angled bridge spanning the Reuss River immediately catches the eye upon exiting the train station—for both its beauty and its crowds. Kapellbrücke is the oldest covered wooden bridge still standing in Europe (hey, on a continent this history, can we blame them if the superlatives are a stretch?). The aesthetic is charmingly medieval, with flower boxes hanging off the sides, stubby wooden shingles, and triangular paintings on the gables created to support Catholicism during the Counter Reformation. The looming Wasserturm, or water tower, was a dungeon back in the day, and is unfortunately not accessible to the public. You can, however, visit the tacky

lucerne

souvenir shop halfway along the bridge, after wading through the swarm of ambling tourists.

i *From train station, walk toward the bank of the river. You can't miss it.*

MUSEGGMAUER (MUSEGG WALL)

Schirmertorweg   www.museggmauer.ch

The ancient city walls and battlements look straight out of Monty Python and the Holy Grail— that's how quintessentially medieval the Museggmauer is. The protective walls date back to the 14th century and are punctuated by nine towers. During the summer, a portion is open to the public free of charge. Once inside, you'll appreciate the physical fitness of bygone generations as you trudge up the impossibly high wooden stairs. The ramparts afford decent views of the city, but hoof it to the top of the airless bell tower for the best vantage point.

i *From Brüggligasse bus stop, sharp left onto Museggstrasse, left onto Schirmertorweg (10min. walk). M-Su 9am-7pm. Free.*

FOOD

☒ TANDOORI $$

Löwengraben 4   ☎041 410 63 03 www.tandoori.ch

Don't let the peeling samosa decals out front deter you—the massive silver trays of spicy Indian curries and stewed vegetables, each priced at a mere 10CHF, will send you into a sweaty, satisfied food coma. The dim interior is tiled with glossy wall mosaics that glitter in the glare of a mounted TV screen, broadcasting provocative Bollywood music videos on loop. After you finish, your bulging paunch will feel decidedly flabby in comparison to the chiseled midriffs doing the body wave on screen. The curried meats are halal, and vegetarian options are available.

i *Head north on the bridge away from the train station, left onto Rathausquai, right to stay on Rathausquai, left onto Furrengasse, right onto Eisengasse, left onto Weggisgasse, right onto Löwengraben (4min. walk). Entrees 10CHF, naan 5CHF. No credit cards. Public restroom available. M-Sa 11:30am-9:30pm.*

MASHIDA $$

Rössligasse 2   ☎41 412 30 00 http://mashida.ch

This posh Korean-Japanese fusion restaurant thankfully has a tiny takeout offshoot, called "The Cup & Cook," that serves East Asian food-court classics such as udon (13CHF) and chicken teriyaki (15CHF). The prim matron in a spotless white apron inquires if you can handle your ramen spicy. Heh, bring it, Switzerland. Enjoy the updated K-pop soundtrack as you wash down your meal with a bottle of Asian iced tea (3.50CHF).

i *Head north away from the train station, left onto Rathausquai, right to stay on Rathasquai, left onto Furrengasse, right onto Eisengasse, left onto Weggisgasse, which turns into Rössligasse (5min. walk). Entrees 10-18CHF. M-F 11:30am-7:30pm, Sa 11:30am-4pm.*

NIGHTLIFE

Many bars close during summer months—check websites for schedules. Most don't take credit cards.

☒ MADELEINE

Baselstrasse 15   ☎076 326 75 76 http://lamadeleine.ch

This former porn cinema has not lost its lust-er; squint to read the extensive drinks menu by the coquettish flicker of candlelight and red-tinted lamps. When you've thrown back a tumbler of liquid courage (10-18CHF), join the dirty dancing on one of two dance floors. If you fancy a more solitary setting as you plan your advances, the second floor is obligingly dim and the seats are comfy.

Madeleine obligingly offers to fulfill all your nighttime fantasies, and nowadays does so legally.

i *From Kasernenplatz stop, head down Route 2 toward Kasernenplatz, sharp right onto Kasernen-platz (2min.). No credit cards. Cocktails 10-18CHF, beer 5-8CHF, on W, add 1CHF for the DJ. W 9pm-1:30am, Th 9pm-2:30am, F-Sa 9pm-4am.*

METZGERHALLE

Baselstrasse 1   http://metzgerhalleluzern.ch/

Despite the meat cleaver logo, rest assured that this rustic tavern is not actually a slaughterhouse, as the literal meaning of its name might suggest. Formerly a punk-alternative headquarters, this quintessential Swiss pub has since been overrun with brunch-loving hipsters. In addition to serving Mediterranean food, Metzgerhalle offers cheap drinks (4-9CHF) and occasional live concerts in the bucolic beer garden out back. Check the website for scheduled performances.

i *Two minutes from Kasernenplatz bus stop. Beer 4-7.30CHF, wine 5.50-7CHF, cocktails 6.50-9CHF, coffee 3.90-5.50CHF. No credit cards. Wi-Fi available. Tu-F 4pm-1:30am, Sa 5pm-1:30am, Su 2:30-11:30pm.*

ESSENTIALS

Practicalities

- **TOURIST OFFICE:** Zentralstrasse 5, at the main train station. (☎041 227 17 17 www.luzern.com. M-F 8:30am-7pm, Sa 9am-7pm, Su 9am-5pm.)

- **MONEY:** ATMs found outside and around banks. Closest to station are UBS and Credit Suisse, both just across the bridge and on the left. Use CHF to avoid poor exchange rates.

- **WI-FI:** Wi-Fi, a.k.a. WLAN, is free in the train station and around the city center for one hour; look for network Luzern.wlan and register with a phone number. Many cafes, bars, and restaurants offer free Wi-Fi.

- **WATER:** Tap water and spigots around town are potable.

- **CONVENIENCE STORES:** Pharmacies are called apotheke. Benu is located in the underground shopping area of train station (☎041 220 13 13. M-Sa 7:30am-9pm, Su 10am-8pm).

mt. pilatus

Lucerne is nestled in the physical and mythological shadow of Mount Pilatus; locals imaginatively house all manner of legendary figures in the shrouded peak, from the ghost of Pontius Pilate to a friendly dragon. If skies are clear, and your budget allows, Mount Pilatus demands conquering. The most popular route is as follows: Take the boat that departs just in front of the train station across the lake to Alpnachstaad, photographing the clusters of lakeside cottages along the way, at which point you'll ascend to the summit (Pilatus Kulm) via the world's steepest cogwheel train. Hike around at the top and admire the snow-capped Alps in the distance, before riding either the cable car or the gondola down to Kriens, from which a bus will take you back to Lucerne. Roundtrip tickets (106CHF) are available at the blue booth in front of the train station. The summit is also accessible via a strenuous, full-day hiking trail (free!). If at all possible, spring for the ticket; Lucerne and Pilatus offer rare easy access to the renowned Alps, and the combination of boat, funicular, and cable car ensure every moment is spent in scenic bliss. Double your fun and purchase a combined ticket to ascend Mount Titlis the next day for just 53CHF more. Purchase online or at Lucerne train station.

lucerne

- **PUBLIC TOILETS:** In train station. (2CHF, 1.50CHF for urinal).

- **POST OFFICE:** Poststelle Universität. (Frohburgstrasse 3. M-F 9am-8pm, Sa 9am-4pm, Su 1:30pm-5:30pm.)

Emergency

- **AMBULANCE:** ☎114.

- **POLICE:** ☎117.

- **HOSPITALS:** Hospital Kantonsspital Luzern. (Spitalstrasse 31 ☎041 205 11 11 www.luks.ch. 24hr. emergency walk-in service. Buses 18 and 19 from station, Kantonsspital stop.)Permanence Medical Centre. (Bahnhofplatz ☎041 211 14 44 www.permanence-luzern.ch. Walk-in medical center located in main train station, underground. M-Th 7am-11pm and nonstop from F 7am to Su 11pm.)

- **POLICE STATIONS:** Station Hirschengraben. (☎041 248 86 66 M-F 9am-noon and 1:30pm-5pm.)

Getting Around

By Bus

The old city is very much walkable—the distance from the historic city wall to the train station and Kapellbrüke area is less than 1km. Buses connect to the outer areas, including the youth hostel, though most areas are still accessible on foot. Travel within the city limits is included a zone 10 ticket. Day pass for zone 10 is 8CHF, single ticket for 1hr. 4CHF, short distance tickets valid for up to six stops for 30min. are 2.50CHF.   Public transport runs roughly 5am-12:30am; night buses (called nachtstern) run F and Sa nights—must get special tickets from bus driver (7-10 CHF).

By Train

The state-run SBB train company is exorbitantly priced, so make the effort to purchase SuperSaver tickets—these are up to 50% off popular routes at off-peak times. Select the SuperSaver option at http://sbb.ch. You can reserve seats on specific trains for extra, but don't—the trains are hardly ever full. If you're traveling around Switzerland a lot, you might consider getting a half-fare card for one month for 120CHF (applies to all public transport) or the Swiss Travel Pass (210-440CHF depending on duration), which gives free access to public transport (often including funiculars and boats) and free entrance to museums. Or consider the Tell Pass, if you're visiting the Alps as well as central Switzerland—includes travel on all trains, buses, boats, and aerial cable ways (including Pilatus, Rigi, and Titlis) for 2 (170CHF), 3 (200CHF), 4 (220CHF), 5 (230CHF), or 10 (280CHF) days. Fine for boarding train without ticket is 90CHF.

By Boat

Tickets for boat rides on the vast Lake Lucerne range 3-45CHF, depending on duration. Get tickets at the blue stand at Schwanenplatz, across from the train station.

By Bike

Bicycle rentals available from Nextbike at 2CHF/hour and 20CHF/day. Download the app, or check website (www.nextbike.ch), or call (041 508 08 00) to locate one of 60 stations around town and pay with a credit card. You'll receive a code to unlock your bike.

By Taxi

Taxis are expensive (initial 6CHF, then 3.80CHF/km up to 20CHF, thereafter 3.50CHF/km). RF Taxi and McTaxi are a bit cheaper. Taxi stands at train station, Schwanenplatz, and behind Hotel National.

switzerland

bern

The most popular caveat offered to backpackers in Switzerland is the country's wallet- and soul-sucking prices. That aside, know that the country's capital is a capital place! Stroll along the spotless cobblestone alleys of the old town, populated with street performers, giant chessboards, and quirky fountains spouting drinking water and topped with colorful statuettes (our personal favorite is the Kindlifresserbrunnen, or "Fountain of the Eater of Little Children"). If you have a bit more time, Bern's central location makes it an ideal home base for daytrips to Interlaken, the Reichenbach Falls, and must-see Alps destinations such as Jungfrau and Grindelwald.

SIGHTS

GURTEN

Park im Grünen   ☎031 970 33 33 http://gurtenpark.ch

You know the ending of The Sound of Music? When the von Trapps, having graced the Salzburg Festival stage with their dulcet tones after escaping the attendant Nazis, enter Switzerland to the soaring orchestral reprise of "Climb Every Mountain"? This scene was not shot on Bern's local mountain, but it might as well have been; the Gurten has all the requisite rolling, cow-strewn hills and rustic footpaths, and on clear days, you can spot the distant Alps as you whirl in giddy circles, roaring "The Hills are Alive." Julie Andrews daydreams aside, the summit—accessible by cable car or on foot—also features an extensive children's play area, an observation tower, and a miniature railway (for the young and young at heart).

i From the main train station, take tram 9 to Gurtenbahn. Hike 40min. to top, or take the cable car (every 10-30min, M-Sa 7am-11pm, Su 7am-8pm, free with transport card, otherwise 10.50CHF round trip).

ROSENGARTEN

Alter Aargauerstalden 31b

Rosengarten is Bern's contribution to the roster of elegant European parks that America can't quite imitate. Atop a hill across the river from the old town, the Rosengarten (literally "rose garden") offers charming views of the city's steeples and gabled roofs, nestled within the elbow of the Aare. Neat lawns and corridors of trees are lined with over 100 varieties of roses and almost as many canoodling couples.

i Cross Nydeggbrücke bridge heading away from train station, walk through roundabout and take third exit onto Alter Aargauerstalden. Turn left and continue up the slope (10min. walk). M-Su 9am-11:30pm. Free.

FOOD

Here's what you need to know: Toblerone was invented in Bern. By all means, consume it to your heart's content, because 1) it's delicious, and 2) it's among the more affordable sustenance options in Switzerland. Most casual restaurants demand 30-40CHF per dish, so if you do eat out, do so at lunch, and opt for the cheaper ethnic restaurants. Note that almost everything closes on Sundays, so plan accordingly—the groceries in the train station are open. Your cheapest bet will be dining at a grocery store, such as the omnipotent Coop or Migros chains, with the latter being slightly less expensive. But hey, at least you can still snag a bottle of vino for 3.50CHF around here. Here's a (cold) tip: tap water is potable, and it flows freely from fountains throughout city.

bern

ÄSS-BAR $$

Marktgasse 19 Kellerlokal ☎031 558 27 72 www.aess-bar.ch

2.50CHF sandwiches? Can it be? Hold tight and never let go, except on Sundays when everything in Bern, Äss-Bar included, shuts down. Inspired by the comically low prices, we're going to say Äss-Bar as many times as possible in this listing, so please chuckle accordingly. Working off a zero-waste concept, Äss-Bar doesn't actually bake any of its products; instead, Äss-Bar resells imperfect and day-old bread or pastries from nearby bakeries, which accounts for Äss-Bar's miraculously low prices. What does the umlauted ass in Äss-Bar actually mean? No clue. Never change, Äss-Bar, never change.

i From train station, walk down Neuengasse, turn right onto Waisenhauspl., then left onto Marktgasse. Sandwiches from 2.50-3CHF, toast 2CHF, croissants 1.50CHF, pastries 3CHF, coffee 3-4.50CHF, tea 3.50CHF, soft drinks 3.50CHF. No credit cards. M-F 9am-7pm, Sa 9am-5pm.

TONG FONG $$

Brunngasse 9a

Drop into Tong Fong and you're in for tasty and authentic takeout served by a sweet maître d' and her husband. At 9.50-12.50CHF a plate, this lineup of stir-fries and noodles are among the cheapest lunches in the city. The portions aren't enormous, but if you supplement with a few packs of Toblerone from the nearest grocery, you've got enough fuel for an afternoon on the town. Snag one of the two tables or pay an additional 2.80CHF for takeout.

i From Kindlifresserbrunnen, a.k.a. the Child-Eater fountain (it's pretty great), turn right onto Rathausgasse and left onto Brungasse; walk for 2min. Entrees 9.50CHF-12.50CHF. No credit cards. M-F 10:30am-3pm and 5pm-9pm.

KAPPA $

Rathausgasse 59 ☎031 318 33 13

Falafel has a reputation throughout Europe for low prices and odd hours, and, with 8CHF falafel and late closing times (by Swiss standards, anyway), Kappa fits the bill. This side-alley dive serves up takeout options from adjacent Greek restaurant Kappadokia, which demands standard Swiss sit-down prices. The two even share a kitchen, which would account for the layered creamy and spicy flavors in your wrap. Good thing the food is tasty, as the atmosphere leaves something to be desired. But hey, after all those supermarket sandwiches, we're not complaining.

i Walk down Marktgasse towards the river, turn left onto Kornhausplatz, right onto Rathausgasse. 8CHF falafel, 5CHF hot dogs. M-Sa 11am-2pm and 6pm-10pm.

get a room!

BERN BACKPACKERS HOTEL & HOSTEL GLOCKE $$$

Rathausgasse 75 ☎ 031 311 37 71 www.bernbackpackers.com

Also listed as Hotel Glocke Backpackers Bern, this standout establishment has an unbeatable location: snooze in the heart of the old town, a 10min. walk from the train station. Rooms are a steal and critter-free, unless you count the throngs of tourists. This acme of accommodations, presided over by savvy Swiss youths, is among the cheapest in the city.

i From the train station, walk down Spitalgasse and Marktgasse. At the Zytglogge (clock tower), turn left and walk toward the bridge for 50m; turn right into Rathausgasse (10min. walk). Included: Wi-Fi, linens, kitchen, city maps, city tours, TV, luggage storage, lockers. Singles 84CHF, dorms 39CHF. Tourist tax 5.30CHF per person per night. Reception 8am-noon and 3pm-10pm, check-in 3pm.

switzerland

river aare

If you have time for only one activity in Bern, then take an exhilaratingly chilly swim in the River Aare. The river (clean enough for swimming!) is unique for its unusually swift current that hurls swimmers downstream with abandon. The best place to take a dip is located along public pool Marzili, at Marzilistrasse 29, where you'll find changing rooms, lockers (2CHF with 20CHF deposit), and bright red ladders descending into the water. The object is to leap in toward the middle of the river (avoiding the rocky bank), experience the aquatic elation of an otter, and climb out via one of the ladders farther down. Punny signage asks, "Aare you safe?" But be warned: in rare cases, people have been known to disappear in the river, so be sure you're a skilled swimmer before attempting. It's best to enjoy the river when other locals are about, which is just about any warm day in Bern.

NIGHTLIFE

📰 CLUB BONSOIR

Aarbergergasse 33/35   http://bonsoir.ch

Even the German-speaking portion of Switzerland retains a French flair, as evidenced by the names of nightlife establishments in Bern. Club Bonsoir is no exception, but is culturally neutral, instead operating according to the universal customs of drunk, frisky young people. Prepare to wade through writhing hoards of the scantily clad in pursuit of the bar, where you'll be rewarded with absurdly cheap 4CHF shots. The slight gruginess lends this basement labyrinth a certain underground vibe, while theme nights such as "Trap Queen" keep things sufficiently basic.

i From station, turn left onto Genfergasse, then right onto Aarbergergasse. Entrance 10CHF. Liquor 10-15CHF, shots 4-6CHF, beer 4.50-9CHF, nonalcoholic drinks 4-6CHF. Hours vary; see website for events.

RETRO BAR

Genfergasse 10   ☎079 787 45 99

Think vinyl records, Chuck Norris, and original Gameboys. Retro Bar's slogan, "Good Drinks. Good Sounds. Good People." if uninspired, is accurate. The drinks are strong, if a bit mysterious—the hawt bartenders clad in black (à la John Travolta in Grease) don't keep a menu, so ask for a classic. The "sounds" ('70s and '80s pop—remember "YMCA"?) and people (casual youths and middle-aged women) jive surprisingly well together.

i From train station, turn left onto Genfergasse (2min. walk). Cocktails 14CHF. Hours vary. Find them on Facebook under Retro Bar Bern.

ESSENTIALS

- **TOURIST OFFICE:** In the shopping mall text to train station, Bahnhofpl. 10A. http://bern.com, 031 328 12 12, M-Sa 9am-7pm, Su 9am-6pm. Offers museum guides, city guides, maps, event brochures, and hostel reservations.

- **WI-FI:** The first hour is free in the train station (and all Swiss train stations), but you'll need to register the first time with a phone number. Or visit the McDonald's at Zeitglockenlaube 6.

- **SHOPPING:** Generally department stores in the city center are open M-W 9am-7pm, Th 9am-9pm, F 9am-8pm, Sa 9am-5pm. Other shops open M-W and F 9am-6:30pm, Th 9am-9pm, Sa 9am-4pm.

bern

- **MONEY:** For the land of banks, ATMs are a bit scarce, at least in the old part of the city. There's one at Zibelegässli 14 in the arcade, directly across from Mekong restaurant. Like most European ATMs, this one requires a chip in your card. Credit cards are widely accepted. 1 CHF = roughly 1 USD, so yay.
- **POST OFFICE:** PostParc. (Schanzenstrasse 4 ☎084 888 88 88. M-F 7:30am-9pm, Sa 8am-5pm, Su 4pm-9pm)

Emergency
- **AMBULANCE:** ☎144.
- **POLICE:** ☎117.
- **HOSPITALS:** Inselspital. (Freiburgstrasse. ☎031 632 21 11)
- **POLICE STATIONS:** City Police. (Waisenhausplatz 32. ☎031 634 41 11)
- **PUBLIC TOILETS:** Railway station (called McClean, 1.50CHF). Free restrooms at the public swimming pools.

Getting Around
The best way to appreciate Bern's old-world charm is on foot. The entire Old Town and most of the city's attractions are completely walkable. Bern's nightly tourist tax (5.30CHF per person) includes a Bern Ticket that gives you free public transportation within central city zones 100 or 101 and to or from airport. Single journey on metro/bus is 4CHF and daily pass is 12.40CHF.

Free bicycle and skateboard rentals are available at Bern Rollt bike rentals—present a valid ID and 20CHF deposit at one of the bike pick-ups around the city, and your vehicle is free for the first four hours and then 1CHF for each additional hour. There's one on Hirschgraben, open 9am-9:30pm.

switzerland essentials

VISAS
Switzerland is not a member of the EU, but it is a member of the Schengen Area. Citizens of Australia, Canada, New Zealand, the US, and many other non-EU countries do not need a visa for stays up to three months. However, if you plan to spend time in other Schengen countries, note that the 90-day period of time you are allowed to visit without a visa applies cumulatively to all Schengen countries.

MONEY
Switzerland uses the Swiss Franc (CHF) as its currency. Tips are typically included in hotel and restaurant bills. However, it is acceptable to tip 10-12% for services like luggage handling and waiting tables. Credit cards are widely accepted, though some small restaurants are cash only. ATMs are widely available.

ALCOHOL
The official legal drinking age in Switzerland is 16 for beer and wine, and 18 for hard spirits; these restrictions also apply to buying, consuming, and possessing alcohol. However, in Ticino (a southern canton), the legal drinking age is 18 across all alcohol. Additionally, many institutions no longer sell alcohol between the hours of 10pm-6amRemember to drink responsibly and to never drink in drive; this behavior could result in severe fines and potential imprisonment. The legal blood alcohol content (BAC) for driving in Switzerland is under 0.05%, lower than the US limit of 0.08%.

ESSENTIALS

You don't have to be a rocket scientist to plan a good trip. (It might help, but it's not required.) You do, however, need to be well prepared, and that's what we can do for you. Essentials is the chapter that gives you all the nitty-gritty you need to know for your trip: the hard information gleaned from 576 years of collective wisdom and several months of furious fact-checking. Planning your trip? Check. Where to find Wi-Fi? Check. The dirt on public transportation? Check. We've also thrown in communications info, safety tips, and a phrasebook, just for good measure.

greatest hits

- **WE ARE ONE.** Poli Sci majors may think of the EU as a bureaucratic nightmare, but it's awesome for you—the **Schengen Agreement** allows you to move between most European countries without going through customs. (p. 791)

- **WE ARE ONE, PART TWO.** Entire economies have been ruined by the euro, just so you don't have to change money when crossing borders. Take advantage. (p. 792)

- **ONE-EURO FLIGHTS.** Yes, it's true—budget airlines are a wonderful thing. We've compiled the continent's cheapest and most convenient. (p. 793)

- **WE AREN'T REALLY ONE.** As integrated as Europe becomes, they'll always speak some wildly different languages. Enter our handy dandy phrasebook. Can you say "Traveling is awesome"? Can you say it in Czech"? (p. 798)

planning your trip

DOCUMENTS AND FORMALITIES

We're going to fill you in on visas and work permits, but don't forget the most important one of all: your passport. **Remember to bring your passport!**

Visas

Those lucky enough to be EU citizens do not need a visa to globetrot throughout the continent. You citizens of Australia, Canada, New Zealand, the US, and various other non-EU countries do not need a visa for stays of up to 90 days, but this three-month period begins upon entry into any of the countries that belong to the EU's **freedom-of-movement zone.** Those staying longer than 90 days may apply for a longer-term visa; consult an embassy or consulate for more information.

Double-check entrance requirements at the nearest embassy or consulate for up-to-date information. US citizens can also consult http://travel.state.gov. Admittance to a country as a traveler does not include the right to work, which is authorized only by a **work permit.** You should check online for the process of obtaining a work permit in the country you are planning to work in.

entrance requirements

- **PASSPORT:** Required for citizens of Australia, Canada, New Zealand, and the US.

- **VISA:** Required for citizens of Australia, Canada, New Zealand, and the US only for stays longer than 90 days.

- **WORK PERMIT:** Required for all foreigners planning to work in the EU.

TIME DIFFERENCES

Most of Europe is on Central European Time, which is 1hr. ahead of Greenwich Mean Time (GMT) and observes Daylight Saving Time during the summer. This means that in summer it is 6hr. ahead of New York City, 9hr. ahead of Los Angeles, 1hr. ahead of the British Isles, 8hr. behind Sydney, and 10hr. behind New Zealand. (In winter, it's 10hr. to Sydney and 12hr. to New Zealand.) However, the UK, Ireland, and Portugal are on Western European Time (subtract 1hr. from Central European Time)—a.k.a. Greenwich Mean Time. In addition, Greece and some parts of Eastern Europe are on Eastern European Time (add 1hr. to Central European Time).

money

GETTING MONEY FROM HOME

Stuff happens. When stuff happens, you might need some money. When you need some money, the easiest and cheapest solution is to have someone back home make a deposit to your bank account. Otherwise, consider one of the following options.

essentials

money

Wiring Money

Arranging a **bank money transfer** means asking a bank back home to wire money to a bank wherever you are. This is the cheapest way to transfer cash, but it's also the slowest and most agonizing, usually taking several days or more. Note that some banks may only release your funds in local currency, potentially sticking you with a poor exchange rate; inquire about this in advance.

Money transfer services like **Western Union** are faster and more convenient than bank transfers—but also much pricier. Western Union has many locations worldwide. To find one, visit **www.westernunion.com** or call the appropriate number: in Australia ☎1800 173 833, in Canada ☎800-235-0000, in the UK ☎0808 234 9168, in the US ☎800-325-6000, or in France ☎08 00 90 01 91. Money transfer services are also available to American Express cardholders and at selected **Thomas Cook** offices.

US State Department (US Citizens Only)

In serious emergencies only, the US State Department will help your family or friends forward money within hours to the nearest consular office, which will then disburse it according to instructions for a US$30 fee. If you wish to use this service, you must contact the Overseas Citizens Services division of the US State Department. (☎+1 202-501-4444, from US 888-407-4747)

WITHDRAWING MONEY

ATMs are readily available in most major European destinations. To use a debit or credit card to withdraw money from a cash machine (ATM) in Europe, you must have a four-digit Personal Identification Number (PIN). If your PIN is longer than four digits, ask your bank whether you can just use the first four or whether you'll need a new one. Credit cards don't usually come with PINs, so if you intend to hit up ATMs in Europe with a credit card to get cash advances, call your credit card company before leaving to request one.

TIPPING

Europe is nowhere near homogenous when it comes to common tipping practices, but suffice it to say that no one tips quite as much as Americans. If you try to tip in a bar you'll be treated as the foreign freak you are; in fact, the only place you'll ever need to think about tipping is a restaurant. Even there, 10% will be considered generous, and no one will chase you down the street if you leave a big fat zero (thank decent minimum wage laws for that).

TAXES

Members of the EU have value added tax (VAT) of varying percentages. Non-European Economic Community visitors who are taking goods home may be refunded this tax for certain purchases. To claim a refund, fill out the form you are given at the shop and present it with the goods and receipts at customs upon departure.

essentials

the euro

Despite what many dollar-possessing Americans might want to hear, the official currency of 19 members of the European Union—Austria, Belgium, Cyprus, Estonia, Finland, France, Germany, Greece, Ireland, Italy, Latvia, Lithuania, Luxembourg, Malta, the Netherlands, Portugal, Slovakia, Slovenia, and Spain—is the euro. This makes travelling a dream as your change left over from one country can be put to good use in the next. Outside the eurozone, holdouts such as the UK, Denmark, and several eastern European countries still have their own currencies. For up-to-date info, check a currency converter (such as www.xe.com).

getting around

BY PLANE

Commercial Airlines

For small-scale travel on the continent, Let's Go suggests **budget airlines** (below) for budget travelers, but more traditional carriers have made efforts to keep up with the revolution. The **Star Alliance Europe Airpass** offers low economy-class fares for travel within Europe to 220 destinations in 45 countries. The pass is available to non-European passengers on Star Alliance (www.staralliance.com) carriers. The oneworld alliance (www.oneworld.com) also offers the **Visit Europe Pass** that allows flexibility in booking flights using its 10 major airlines.

BY TRAIN

Trains in Europe are generally comfortable, convenient, and reasonably swift. Some still offer old-fashioned compartments, which offer a great chance to meet fellow travelers. Make sure you are on the correct car, as trains sometimes split. Towns listed in parentheses on European train schedules require a train switch at the town listed immediately before the parentheses.

You can either buy a railpass, which for a high price allows you unlimited, flexible travel within a particular region for a given period of time, or buy individual

budget airlines

No-frills airlines make hopscotching around Europe by air remarkably affordable, as long as you avoid their rip-off fees. The following airlines will be useful not only for crisscrossing countries but also for those ever-popular weekend trips to nearby international destinations.

- **EASYJET:** Who knew London had so many airports? EasyJet did. (www.easyjet.com)
- **EUROWINGS:** German efficiency, Greek prices. (www.eurowings.com)
- **NORWEGIAN:** Despite the name, flies all over the place at reasonable fares (www.norwegian.com)
- **RYANAIR:** A budget traveler's dream, Ryanair goes most everywhere, especially in France and Italy. (www.ryanair.com)
- **PEGASUS:** For your inner Bellerophon. (www.flypgs.com)
- **TRANSAVIA:** What every Northern European dreams of: cheap flights to the Mediterranean. (www.transavia.com)
- **WIZZ AIR:** Short hops from Krakow to Paris. (www.wizzair.com)

point-to-point tickets as you go. Almost all countries give students or youths (under 26, usually) direct discounts on regular domestic rail tickets, and many also sell a student or youth card that provides 20-50% off all fares for up to a year. Tickets can be bought at stations (many have English-speaking staff), but most Western European countries offer big discounts to travelers booking online in advance, sometimes up to three months before travel.

rail resources

The sites below are useful for searching schedules and passes, but note it's best to shop around for the cheapest tickets, as search tools often inflate prices.

- **WWW.RAILEUROPE.COM:** Info on railpasses, point-to-point fares and schedules..
- **WWW.RAILSAVER.COM:** Uses your itinerary to calculate the best railpass for your trip.
- **WWW.ROME2RIO.COM:** Plan routes between destinations by rail, bus, ferry, and more.

BY BUS

Though European trains are extremely popular, in some cases buses prove a better option, particularly as you head farther east. There are numerous operators across the continent, but Eurolines is the largest company running international coach services. We get misty-eyed just thinking about their unlimited 15- and 30-day passes to 41 major European cities. (www.eurolines.com) For a high price but dreamy flexibility, Busabout offers numerous hop-on-hop-off bus circuits covering 29 of Europe's best bus hubs. (☎44 845 026 7576 www.busabout.com)

safety and health

In any type of crisis, the most important thing to do is **stay calm.** Your country's embassy abroad is usually your best resource in an emergency; registering with that embassy upon arrival in the country is a good idea. The government offices listed in the **Travel Advisories** feature below can provide information on the services they offer their citizens in case of emergencies abroad.

Whenever necessary, *Let's Go* lists specific concerns and local laws in the **Essentials** section of the relevant chapter. Basically, if you want to read about prostitution in Amsterdam, just flip back.

travel advisories

The following government offices provide travel information and advisories:

- **AUSTRALIA:** Department of Foreign Affairs and Trade. (☎61 2 6261 3305 www. smartraveller.gov.au)

- **CANADA:** Global Affairs Canada. Visit the website for the free booklet "Bon Voyage, But..." (☎1-800-267-8376 www.international.gc.ca)

- **NEW ZEALAND:** Ministry of Foreign Affairs and Trade. (☎64 4 439 8000 www. safetravel.govt.nz)

- **UK:** Foreign and Commonwealth Office. (☎44 20 7008 1500 www.fco.gov.uk)

- **US:** Department of State. (☎888-407-4747 from the US, ☎1-202-501-4444 elsewhere http://travel.state.gov)

PRE-DEPARTURE HEALTH

Matching a prescription to a foreign equivalent is not always easy, safe, or possible, so if you take **prescription drugs,** carry up-to-date prescriptions or a statement from your doctor stating the medications' trade names, manufacturers, chemical names, and dosages. Be sure to keep all medication with you in your carry-on luggage.

Immunizations and Precautions

Travelers over two years old should make sure that the following vaccines are up to date: MMR (for measles, mumps, and rubella); DTaP or Td (for diphtheria, tetanus, and pertussis); IPV (for polio); Hib (for *Haemophilus influenzae* B); and HepB (for Hepatitis B). For recommendations on immunizations and prophylaxis, check with a doctor and consult the **Centers for Disease Control and Prevention (CDC)** in the US (☎ 800-232-4636 www.cdc.gov/travel) or the equivalent in your home country.

keeping in touch

BY EMAIL AND INTERNET

Hello and welcome to the 21st century, where you're rarely more than a 5min. walk from the nearest Wi-Fi hot spot, even if sometimes you'll have to pay a few bucks or buy a drink for the privilege of using it.

Wireless hot spots make internet access possible in public and remote places. Unfortunately, they also pose security risks. Hot spots are public, open networks that use unencrypted, unsecured connections. They are susceptible to hacks and "packet sniffing"—the theft of passwords and other private information. To prevent problems, disable "ad hoc" mode, turn off file sharing and network discovery, encrypt your email, turn on your firewall, beware of phony networks, and watch for over-the-shoulder creeps.

Data roaming lets you use mobile data abroad, but it can be eye-wateringly pricey. If you refuse to latergram and hyperventilate at the idea of losing access to Google Maps, firstly reconsider your life, but secondly get an international travel plan with your carrier or consider getting a local phone.

BY TELEPHONE

If you have internet access, your best—i.e., cheapest, most convenient, and most tech-savvy—means of calling home are probably our good friends Skype (www. skype.com), FaceTime or whatever calling app you prefer.

For those still stuck in the 20th century, **prepaid phone cards** are a common and relatively inexpensive means of calling abroad. Each one comes with a Personal Identification Number (PIN) and a toll-free access number. You call the access number and then follow the directions for dialing your PIN. To purchase prepaid phone cards, check online for the best rates; www.callingcards.com is a good place to start. Online providers generally send your access number and PIN via email, with no actual "card" involved.

Another option is a **calling card,** linked to a major national telecommunications service in your home country. Calls are billed collect or to your account. Cards generally come with instructions for dialing both domestically and internationally. Placing a collect call through an international operator can be expensive but may be necessary in case of an emergency. You can frequently call collect without even possessing a company's calling card just by calling its access number and following the instructions.

international calls

To call Europe from home or to call home from Europe, dial:

1. THE INTERNATIONAL DIALING PREFIX. To call from Australia, dial ☎0011; Canada or the US, ☎011; Ireland, New Zealand, the UK, and most of Europe, ☎00.

2. THE COUNTRY CODE OF THE COUNTRY YOU WANT TO CALL. To call Australia, dial ☎61; Austria, ☎43; Belgium, ☎32; Canada, ☎1; Croatia, ☎385; Czech Republic, ☎420; Denmark, ☎45; France, ☎33; Germany, ☎49; Greece, ☎30; Hungary, ☎36; Ireland, ☎353; Italy, ☎39; the Netherlands, ☎31; Norway ☎47; New Zealand, ☎64; Poland ☎48; Portugal, ☎351; Slovenia ☎386; Spain, ☎34; Sweden ☎46; Switzerland ☎41; the UK, ☎44; the US, ☎1.

3. THE CITY/AREA CODE. *Let's Go* lists the city/area codes for cities and towns in Europe opposite the city or town name, next to a ☎, as well as in every phone number. If the first digit is a zero (e.g., ☎020 for Amsterdam), omit the zero when calling from abroad (e.g., dial ☎20 from Canada to reach Amsterdam).

4. THE LOCAL NUMBER.

Cellular Phones

The international standard for cell phones is **Global System for Mobile Communication (GSM).** To make and receive calls in Europe, you will need a GSM-compatible phone and a **SIM (Subscriber Identity Module) card,** a country-specific, thumbnail-size chip that gives you a local phone number and plugs you into the local network. Most modern SIM cards will work in any country, but charges for this can vary wildly, so check with your carrier and decide whether it may be cheaper to get a new SIM at your destination. Many European SIM cards are prepaid, and incoming calls are frequently free. You can buy additional cards or vouchers (usually available at convenience stores) to "top up" your phone. For more information on GSM phones, check out www.telestial.com. Companies like **Cellular Abroad** (www.cellularabroad.com) and **OneSimCard** (www.onesimcard.com) rent cell phones and SIM cards that work in a variety of destinations around the world.

BY SNAIL MAIL

Sending Mail Home from Europe

Airmail is the best way to send mail home from Europe. Write "airmail," *"par avion,"* or the equivalent in the local language on the front. For simple letters or postcards, airmail tends to be surprisingly cheap, but the price will go up sharply for weighty packages. Surface mail is by far the cheapest, slowest, and most antiquated way to send mail. It takes one to two months to cross the Atlantic—good for heavy items you won't need for a while, like souvenirs that you've acquired along the way.

Receiving Mail in Europe

There are several ways to arrange pickup of letters sent to you while you are abroad, even if you do not have an address of your own. Mail can be sent via **Poste Restante** (General Delivery). Address Poste Restante letters like so:

Napoleon BONAPARTE
Poste Restante
City, Country

The mail will go to a special desk in the city's central post office, unless you specify a local post office by street address or postal code. It's best to use the largest post office, since mail may be sent there regardless. Bring your passport (or other photo ID) for pickup; there may be a small fee. If the clerks insist that there is nothing for you, ask them to check under your first name as well. *Let's Go* lists post offices in the **Practicalities** section for each city we cover. It is usually safer and quicker, though more expensive, to send mail express or registered. If you don't want to deal with Poste Restante, consider asking your hostel or accommodation if you can have things mailed to you there. Of course, if you have your own mailing address or a reliable friend to receive mail for you, that will be the easiest solution.

climate

Europe is for lovers, historians, architects, beach bums, and…weather nerds? In fact, the smallest continent has quite the diverse climate. Southern Europe is known for the warm weather surrounding the Mediterranean Sea. This area has warm, wet winters and hot, dry summers. Northern and Eastern Europe areis marked by temperate forests, where cold Aarctic air in winter contrasts with hot warm summers and rain whenever God feels like mocking you. In between sits the exception: the mile-high Alps, where things are generally colder and wetter.

AVG. TEMP. (LOW/HIGH), PRECIP.	JANUARY			APRIL			JULY			OCTOBER		
	°C	°F	mm	°C	°F	mm	°C	°F	mm	°C	°F	mm
Amsterdam	-1/4	30/39	68	4/13	39/55	49	13/22	55/72	77	7/14	45/57	72
Athens	6/13	43/55	62	11/20	52/68	23	23/33	73/91	6	15/24	59/75	51
Barcelona	6/13	43/55	31	11/18	52/64	43	21/28	70/82	27	15/21	59/70	86
Berlin	-3/2	27/36	46	4/13	39/55	42	14/24	57/75	73	6/13	43/55	49
Brussels	-1/4	30/39	66	5/14	41/57	60	12/23	54/73	95	7/15	45/59	83
Budapest	-4/1	25/34	37	7/17	45/63	45	16/28	61/82	56	7/16	45/61	5
Dublin	1/8	34/46	67	4/13	39/55	45	11/20	52/68	70	6/14	43/57	70
Lisbon	8/14	46/57	111	12/20	54/68	54	17/27	63/81	3	14/22	57/72	62
London	2/6	36/43	54	6/13	43/55	37	14/22	57/72	57	8/14	46/57	57
Madrid	2/9	36/48	39	7/18	45/64	48	17/31	63/88	11	10/19	50/66	53
Marseille	2/10	36/50	43	8/18	46/64	42	17/29	63/84	11	10/20	50/68	76
Paris	1/6	34/43	56	6/16	43/61	42	15/25	59/77	59	8/16	46/61	50
Prague	-5/0	23/32	18	3/12	37/54	27	13/23	55/73	68	5/12	41/54	33
Rome	5/11	41/52	71	10/19	50/66	51	20/30	68/86	15	13/22	55/72	99
Venice	1/6	34/43	37	10/17	50/63	78	19/27	66/81	52	11/19	52/66	77
Vienna	-4/1	25/34	39	6/15	43/59	45	15/25	59/77	84	7/14	45/57	56

To convert from degrees Fahrenheit to degrees Celsius, subtract 32 and multiply by 5/9. To convert from Celsius to Fahrenheit, multiply by 9/5 and add 32. The mathematically challenged may use this handy chart:

°CELSIUS	-5	0	5	10	15	20	25	30	35	40
°FAHRENHEIT	23	32	41	50	59	68	77	86	95	104

measurements

Like the rest of the rational world, Europe uses the metric system. The basic unit of length is the meter (m), which is divided into 100 centimeters (cm) or 1000 millimeters (mm). One thousand meters make up one kilometer (km). Fluids are measured in liters (L), each divided into 1000 milliliters (mL). A liter of pure water weighs one kilogram (kg), the unit of mass that is divided into 1000 grams (g). One metric ton is 1000kg. Gallons in the US and those in Britain are not identical: one US gallon equals 0.83 Imperial gallons. Pub aficionados will note that an Imperial pint (20 oz.) is larger than its US counterpart (16 oz.).

MEASUREMENT CONVERSIONS	
1 inch (in.) = 25.4mm	1 millimeter (mm) = 0.039 in.
1 foot (ft.) = 0.305m	1 meter (m) = 3.28 ft.
1 yard (yd.) = 0.914m	1 meter (m) = 1.094 yd.
1 mile (mi.) = 1.609km	1 kilometer (km) = 0.621 mi.
1 ounce (oz.) = 28.35g	1 gram (g) = 0.035 oz.
1 pound (lb.) = 0.454kg	1 kilogram (kg) = 2.205 lb.
1 fluid ounce (fl. oz.) = 29.57mL	1 milliliter (mL) = 0.034 fl. oz.
1 gallon (gal.) = 3.785L	1 liter (L) = 0.264 gal.

phrasebook

ENGLISH	ITALIAN	FRENCH	SPANISH	PORTU-GUESE	DANISH	SWEDISH
Hello	Buongiorno	Bonjour	Hola	Olá	Hej	Hallå
Goodbye	Arrivederci	Au revoir	Adiós	Até logo	Farvel	Adjö
Yes	Sì	Oui	Si	Sim	Ja	Ja
No	No	Non	No	Não	Nej	Nej
Please	Per favore	S'il vous plaît	Por favor	Por favor	Må jeg bede	Snälla du
Thank you	Grazie	Merci	Gracias	Obrigado/a	Tak	Tack
You're welcome	Prego	De rien	De nada	De nada	Selv tak	Du är välkommen
Sorry!	Mi scusi!	Désolé!	¡Perdón!	Desculpe!	Undskyld	Förlåt!
My name is...	Mi chiamo...	Je m'appelle...	Me llamo...	O meu nome é...	Jeg hedder...	Mitt namn är...
How are you?	Come sta?	Comment êtes-vous?	¿Cómo estás?	Como você está?	Hvordan har De det?	Hur mår du?
I don't know.	Non lo so.	Je ne sais pas.	No sé.	Eu não sei.	Jeg kender ikke	Jag vet inte.
I don't understand.	Non capisco.	Je ne comprends pas.	No entiendo.	Não entendo.	Jeg forstår jeg ikke	Jag förstår inte.
Could you repeat that?	Potrebbe ripetere?	Répétez, s'il vous plaît?	¿Puede repetirlo?	Você pode repetir?	En gang til?	Kan du upprepa det?
Do you speak English?	Parla inglese?	Parlez-vous anglais?	¿Hablas español?	Fala inglês?	Taler du engelsk?	Pratar du engelska?
I don't speak ___.	Non parlo italiano.	Je ne parle pas français.	No hablo castellano.	Eu não falo português.	Jeg kan ikke tale dansk	Jag talar inte svenska.
Why?	Perché?	Pourquoi?	¿Por qué?	Porque?	Hvorfor	Varför...?
Where is...?	Dov'è...?	Où est?	¿Dónde está...?	Onde é...?	Hvor er...?	Var är...?
What time is it?	Che ore sono?	Quelle heure est-il?	¿Qué hora es?	Que horas são?	Hvad er klokken?	Vad är klockan?
How much does this cost?	Quanto costa?	Combien ça coûte?	¿Cuánto cuesta esto?	Quanto custa?	Hvad koster det?	Hur mycket kostar den här?
I am from the US.	Sono degli Stati Uniti.	Je suis des Etats-Unis.	Soy de los Estados Unidos.	Eu sou de os Estados Unidos.	Jeg er fra de USA.	Jag är från USA.
I have a visa/ID.	Ho un visto/carta d'identità.	J'ai un visa/identification.	Tengo una visa/identificación.	Eu tenho um visto/identificação.	Jeg har et visum/identifikation.	Jag har ett visum / ID.
I have nothing to declare.	Non ho nulla da dichiarare.	Je n'ai rien à déclarer.	No tengo nada para declarar.	Não tenho nada a declarar.	Jeg har intet at erklære.	Jag har inget att deklarera.
I will be here for less than three months.	Sarò qui per meno di trè mesi.	Je serai ici pour moins de trois mois.	Estaré aquí por menos de tres meses.	Eu estarei aqui há menos de três meses.	Jeg vil være her i mindre end tre måneder.	Jag kommer att vara här för mindre än tre månader.
One-way	Solo andata	Aller simple	Ida	Ida	En vej	En väg
Round-trip	Andata e ritorno	Aller-retour	Ida y vuelta	Ida e volta	Rundtur	Rundresa
Hotel/hostel	Albergo/ostello	Hôtel/auberge	Hotel/hostel	Hotel/albergue	Hotel/ vandrerhjem	Hotell / vandrarhem
I have a reservation.	Ho una prenotazione.	J'ai une réservation.	Tengo una reserva.	Tenho uma reserva.	Jeg har en reservation.	Jag har en reservation.
Single/double room	Camera singola/doppia	Chambre pour un/deux	Habitación simple/doble	Quarto individual/duplo	Enkeltværelse	Enkel / dubbel rum
I'd like...	Vorrei...	Je voudrais...	Me gustaría...	Gostaria...	Jeg vil gerne...	Jag skulle vilja...

ENGLISH	ITALIAN	FRENCH	SPANISH	PORTU-GUESE	DANISH	SWEDISH
Check, please!	Il conto, per favore!	L'addition, s'il vous plaît!	¡La cuenta, por favor!	A conta, por favor!	Må jeg bede om regningen!	Notan tack!
I feel sick.	Mi sento male.	Je me sens malade.	Me siento mal.	Eu me sinto doente.	Jeg føler mig syg.	Jag mår illa.
Get a doctor!	Telefoni un dottore!	Va chercher un médecin!	¡Llama un médico!	Chamar um doutor!	Ringe til en læge!	Få en läkare!
Hospital	Ospedale	Hôpital	Hospital	Hospital	Hospital	Sjukhus
I lost my passport/luggage.	Ho perso il mio passapor-to/i miei bagagli.	J'ai perdu mon passeport/baggage.	He perdido mi pasaporte/equipaje.	Eu perdi o meu passaporte/a minha baga-gem.	Jeg har mistet mit pas/min bagage.	Jag förlorade mitt pass / bagage.
Help!	Aiuto!	Au secours!	¡Socorro!	Socorro!	Hjælpe!	Hjälp!
Leave me alone!	Lasciami stare!/Mol-lami!	Laissez-moi tranquille!	¡Déjame en paz!	Deixe-me em paz!	Lad mig være i fred!	Lämna mig ifred!
Go away!	Vattene!	Allez-vous en!	¡Vete!	Vá embora!	Gå!	Gå bort!
Call the police!	Telefoni alla polizia!	Appelez les flics!	¡Llama la policia!	Chamar a polícia!	Ringede til politiet.	Ring polisen!

ENGLISH	GERMAN	DUTCH	CZECH	POLISH	HUNGAR-IAN	GREEK PRONUNCI-ATION
Hello	Hallo/Tag	Dag/Hallo	Dobrý den	Cześć	Szervusz	yah sahs
Goodbye	Auf Wie-dersehen/Tschüss	Tot ziens	Nashledanou	Do widzenia	Viszont-látásra	yah sahs
Yes	Ja	Ja	Ano	Tak	Igen	neh
No	Nein	Nee	Ne	Nie	Nem	oh-hee
Please	Bitte	Alstublieft	Prosím	Proszę	Kérem	pah-rah-kah-LO
Thank you	Danke	Dank u wel	Děkuji	Dziękuję Ci	Köszönöm	Ef-hah-ree-STO
You're wel-come	Bitte	Alstublieft	Prosím	Nie ma za co	Kérem	pah-rah-kah-LO
Sorry!	Es tut mir leid!	Sorry!	Promiňte!	Przepraszam!	Elnézést!	sig-NO-mee
My name is...	Ich bin...	Mijn naam is...	Mé jméno je...	Nazywam się...	A nevem...	meh LEH-neh
How are you?	Wie geht's (geht es Ihnen)?	Hoe gaat het?	Jak se máš?	Jak się masz?	Hogy vagy?	tee KAH-neh-teh
I don't know.	Ich weisse nicht/Keine Ahnung.	Ik weet het niet/Geen idee.	Nevím.	Nie wiem.	Nem tudom.	dthen KSER-o
I don't under-stand.	Ich verstehe nicht.	Ik begrijp het niet.	Nerozumím.	Nie rozumiem.	Nem értem.	dthen kah-tah-lah-VEH-no
Could you repeat that?	Können Sie wiederholen?	Kunt u dat herhalen?	Můžete opa-kovat, že?	Czy mógłbyś to powtórzyć?	Meg tudnád ismételni ezt?	bor-EE-teh na ep-an-a-LAH-vet-eh ahv-TO
Do you speak English?	Sprechen Sie Englisch?	Spreekt u Engels?	Mluví an-glicky?	Czy mówisz po angielsku?	Beszél angolul?	mee-LAH-teh sng-lee-KAH
I don't speak _____.	Ich kann kein Deutsch.	Ik spreek geen Neder-lands.	Nemluvím Česky.	Nie mówię po polsku.	Nem tudok (jól) mag-yarul.	dthen meel-AOH eh-lee-nee-KAH
Why?	Warum?	Waarom?	Proč?	Czemu?	Miért?	gee-ah-TEY
Where is...?	Wo ist...?	Waar is...?	Kde je...?	Gdzie jest...?	Hol van...?	poo EE-ne
What time is it?	Wie spät ist es?	Hoe laat is het?	Kolik je hodin?	Która godzina?	Hány óra van?	tee O-rah EE-neh

phrasebook

ENGLISH	GERMAN	DUTCH	CZECH	POLISH	HUNGAR-IAN	GREEK PRONUNCI-ATION
How much does this cost?	Wie viel (kostet das)?	Wat kost het?	Kolik to stojí?	Ile to kosztuje?	Mennyibe kerül?	PO-so kos-TI-dzeh ahv-TO
I am from the US.	Ich bin von Amerika.	Ik ben uit de VS.	Já jsem ze Spojených států.	Jestem z USA.	Én vagyok az Egyesült Államok.	EE-meh ap-OH tiss een-o-MEN-ess pol-ee-TEE-ess
I have a visa/ID.	Ich habe ein Visum/eine ID.	Ik heb een visum/ID.	Mám víza/ID.	Mam wizę / ID.	Van egy vízumot.	EH-oh mia theh-OH-ray-sey/tahf-TOH-tay-ta
I have nothing to declare.	Ich habe nichts zu verzollen.	Ik heb niets aan te geven.	Nemám nic k proclení.	Nie mam nic do oclenia.	Nekem van egy azo-nosítója.	Dthen EH-oh TEE-poh-teh na day-LO-so
I will be here for less than three months.	Ich reste hier für weniger als drei Monate.	Ik blijf hier minder dan drie maan-den.	I tady bude za méně než tři měsíce.	Będę tu przez okres krótszy niż trzy miesiące.	Én itt leszek kevesebb, mint három hónap.	Tha EE-meh eth-OH gee-ah lig-OH-teh-ro ap-OH treess MAY-ness
One-way	Einfache	Enkele reis	Jedním směrem	Jednokierun-kowa	Csak oda	mon-OH-drom-OSS
Round-trip	Hin und zurück	Rondreis	Zpáteční	Podróż w obie strony	Oda-vissza	met ep-eess-tro-FACE
Hotel/hostel	Hotel/Her-berge	Hotel/hostel	Hotel/uby-tovna	Hotel / Hostel	Hotel/szálló	kse-no-dtho-HEE-o/ksen-OH-na
I have a reser-vation.	Ich habe eine Reservierung.	Ik heb een reservering.	Mám rezer-vaci.	Mam rezer-wację.	Foglaltam asztalt.	EH-oh CAHN-ee KRA-tay-say
Single/double room	Einzelzimmer/ Doppelzimmer	Eenpersoon-skamer / Tweepersoon-skamer	Jednolůžkový/ dvoulůžkový pokoj	Pokój jed-noosobowy / dwuosobowy	Egyágyas / kétágyas szoba	mo-NO-klin-oh/DIE-klin-oh
I'd like...	Ich möchte...	Ik wil graag...	Prosím...	Chciałbym...	kérek...	THAH EE-the-lah
Check, please!	Die Rechnung, bitte!	Mag ik de rekening!	Paragon, prosím!	Sprawdź, proszę!	A számlát, kérem!	oh lo-ghah-ree-yah-SMOS, pah-rah-kah-LO
I feel sick.	Ich bin krank.	Ik ben ziek.	Je mi špatně.	Czuję się chory.	Rosszul érzem magam.	EE-meh AH-rose-tose
Get a doctor!	Hol einen Arzt!	Haal een dokter!	Najít lékaře!	Zawołać lekarza!	Orvost!	PAH-re-te HEN-ah yiah-TROH
Hospital	Krankenhaus	Ziekenhuis	Nemocnice	Szpital	Orvos	no-so-ko-MEE-o
I lost my passport/luggage.	Ich habe mein Reisepass/ Gepäck verloren.	Ik heb mijn paspoort/ba-gage verloren.	Ztratil jsem pas/ zavaza-dla.	Zgubiłem pasz-port / bagaż.	Elvesztettem az útlevelem / poggyász.	EH-ah-sa toh dthaya-vah-tee-ri-o/vah-LEE-tsah moo
Help!	Hilfe!	Help!	Pomoc!	Pomoc!	Segíts nekem!	vo-EE-thee-ah
Leave me alone!	Verloren gehen!	Laat me met rust!	Nech mě být!	Zostaw mnie w spokoju!	Hagyj békén!	a-FIS-te me EE-si-kho (m.)/ EE-si-khee (f.)
Go away!	Geh weg!	Ga weg!	Prosím odejděte!	Idź stąd!	Távozzék!	FOO-geh
Call the police!	Ruf die Polizei!	Bel de politie!	Zavolejte policii!	Wezwać policję!	Hívja a rendőrséget!	kah-LESS-ee teen ah-stih-noh-MIH-ah

INDEX

index

ACKNOWLEDGMENTS

ABDI THANKS: Shaun for being a great co-worker and friend; Michael for making this guide possible; Rameen and Kathryn for giving summer office hours life; Jim for being a great coach and mentor; Zeb, Hayley, Kenny, Noel, Will, Claire, Mike, Laura, Tiffanie, Emily, and Andy for being amazing Researcher Writers's; my brothers Josh, Louis, Reggie, IB, Nuha, and Rob for your constant support and guidance. To Mr. and Mrs. Melvoin for changing my life and always believing in me even when I didn't; To Hamza, Hanan, and Ekram for being the life of the Shemsu household and to mom and dad for being my biggest source of motivation and love in life. Thank you for everything you do for me and for all the sacrifices you have made to make my dreams come true.

SHAUN THANKS: The LG-pod squad: Abdi, for being the best Let's Go co-parent I could ask for. I'll always cherish that thing that happened that one time—and then they, so we, and it was so crazy, right? Rameen, for your boundless energy, and for providing me with the opportunity to be a renegade PAF. Kathryn, for being my faithful eye-rolling buddy, and sketching that portrait on a Post-It note. To Maharaja, Spotify group playlists, and the Ethiopian food outing that could have been. To Jim and Michael, for your endless patience, wisdom, and much-needed sass. And to my stellar team of RWs: Andy, for your bountiful humor and meager beard; Claire, for the almost-Spanish lessons and for being the most organized member of the office; Emily, for truly embodying the spirit of Sisters, and the dope PlacePass vids; Mike, for not getting beat up in Morocco and not beating up that guy in Spain; Laura, for being game for any challenge, and for your game-changing blogs; Noel, for almost sleeping in hostel kitchens and indirectly contributing to my K-Pop playlist; Tiffani, for wondrous marginalia and enduring sanitizer-pelting Irishmen; To Will, for your Instagram skillz, and for being my dad; Zeb, for submitting killer photos and killing a submitted chicken; and Hayley and Kenny, for island-hopping, canoe-surfing, bike-hiking, yoga-drinking, and paddle-pedalling your way into our hearts.

DIRECTOR OF PUBLISHING   Abdurezak Shemsu

EDITORIAL DIRECTOR   Shaun Gohel

PRESIDENT, HARVARD STUDENT AGENCIES   Stephen Xi

GENERAL MANAGER, HARVARD STUDENT AGENCIES   Jim McKellar

ABOUT LET'S GO

THE STUDENT TRAVEL GUIDE

Let's Go publishes the world's favorite student travel guides, written entirely by Harvard students. Armed with pens, notebooks, and a few changes of underwear stuffed into their backpacks, our student researchers go across continents, through time zones, and above expectations to seek out invaluable travel experiences for our readers. Because we are a completely student-run company, we have a unique perspective on how students travel, where they want to go, and what they're looking to do when they get there. If your dream is to grab a machete and forge through the jungles of Thailand, we can take you there. If you'd rather bask in the Riviera sun at a beachside cafe, we'll set you a table. In short, we write for readers who know that there's more to travel than tour buses. To keep up, visit our website, www.letsgo. com, where you can sign up to blog, post photos from your trips, and connect with the Let's Go community.

FIFTY SEVEN YEARS OF WISDOM

Let's Go has been on the road for 57 years and counting. We've grown a lot since publishing our first 20-page pamphlet to Europe in 1960, but over five decades and 75 titles later, our witty, candid guides are still researched and written entirely by students on shoestring budgets who know that train strikes, stolen luggage, food poisoning, and marriage proposals are all part of a day's work. Meanwhile, we're still bringing readers fresh new features, like color photos; a revamped, user-friendly layout for our listings; and greater emphasis on the experiences that make travel abroad a rite of passage for readers of all ages. And, of course, *Europe 2017* is still brimming with editorial honesty, a commitment to students, and our witty and irreverent style.

THE LET'S GO COMMUNITY

More than just a travel guide company, Let's Go is a community that reaches from our headquarters in Cambridge, MA, all across the globe. Our small staff of dedicated student editors, writers, and tech nerds comes together because of our shared passion for travel and our desire to help other travelers get the most out of their experience. We love it when our readers become part of the Let's Go community as well—when you travel, drop us a postcard (67 Mt. Auburn St., Cambridge, MA 02138, USA), send us an email (feedback@letsgo.com), or sign up on our website (www.letsgo.com) to tell us about your adventures and discoveries.

For more information, updated travel coverage, and news from our researcher team, visit us online at **www.letsgo.com**.

HELPING LET'S GO. If you want to share your discoveries, suggestions, or corrections, please drop us a line. We appreciate every piece of correspondence, whether a postcard, a 10-page email, or a coconut. Visit Let's Go at **www.letsgo.com** or send an email to:

feedback@letsgo.com, subject: "Let's Go Europe"

Address mail to:

Let's Go Europe, 67 Mount Auburn St., Cambridge, MA 02138, USA

In addition to the invaluable travel advice our readers share with us, many are kind enough to offer their services as researchers or editors. Unfortunately, our charter enables us to employ only currently enrolled Harvard students.

Maps © Let's Go and Avalon Travel

Distributed by Publishers Group West.
Printed in Canada by Friesens Corp.

ISBN-13: 978-1-61237-050-7
Fifty-seventh edition
10 9 8 7 6 5 4 3 2 1

Let's Go Europe is written by Let's Go Publications, 67 Mt. Auburn St., Cambridge, MA 02138, USA.

Let's Go and the LG logo are trademarks of Let's Go, Inc.

QUICK REFERENCE

YOUR GUIDE TO LET'S GO ICONS

| ☒ | Let's Go recommends | ☎ | Phone numbers | *i* | Other hard information |

EMERGENCY PHONE NUMBERS (POLICE)

Austria	☎133	Ireland	☎999
Belgium	☎101	Italy	☎113
Croatia	☎192	The Netherlands	☎911
Czech Republic	☎158	Norway	☎112
Denmark	☎114	Poland	☎997
France	☎17	Portugal	☎112
Germany	☎110	Slovenia	☎133
Great Britain	☎999	Spain	☎092
Greece	☎100	Sweden	☎112
Hungary	☎107	Switzerland	☎117

USEFUL PHRASES

ENGLISH	FRENCH	GERMAN	ITALIAN	SPANISH
Hello/Hi	Bonjour/Salut	Hallo/Tag	Ciao	Hola
Goodbye/Bye	Au revoir	Auf Wiedersehen/Tschüss	Arrivederci/Ciao	Adiós/Chau
Yes	Oui	Ja	Sì	Sí
No	Non	Nein	No	No
Excuse me!	Pardon!	Entschuldigen Sie!	Scusa!	¡Perdón!
Thank you	Merci	Danke	Grazie	Gracias
Go away!	Va t'en!	Geh weg!	Vattene via!	¡Vete!
Help!	Au secours!	Hilfe!	Aiuto!	¡Ayuda!
Call the police!	Appelez la police!	Ruf die Polizei!	Chiamare la polizia!	¡Llame a la policía!
Get a doctor!	Cherchez un médecin!	Hol einen Arzt!	Chiamare un medico!	¡Llame a un médico!
I don't understand	Je ne comprends pas	Ich verstehe nicht	Non capisco	No comprendo
Do you speak English?	Parlez-vous anglais?	Sprechen Sie Englisch?	Lei parla inglese?	¿Habla inglés?
Where is...?	Où est...?	Wo ist...?	Dov' è...?	¿Dónde está...?

TEMPERATURE CONVERSIONS

°CELSIUS	-5	0	5	10	15	20	25	30	35	40
°FAHRENHEIT	23	32	41	50	59	68	77	86	95	104

MEASUREMENT CONVERSIONS

1 inch (in.) = 25.4mm	1 millimeter (mm) = 0.039 in.
1 foot (ft.) = 0.305m	1 meter (m) = 3.28 ft.
1 mile (mi.) = 1.609km	1 kilometer (km) = 0.621 mi.
1 pound (lb.) = 0.454kg	1 kilogram (kg) = 2.205 lb.
1 gallon (gal.) = 3.785L	1 liter (L) = 0.264 gal.

31901060372655